# BLOOD MOON'S
# HOLLYWOOD REMEMBERED

## GLITZ, GLAMOUR, TRIUMPH, & TRAGEDY

### DARWIN PORTER
### WITH DANFORTH PRINCE

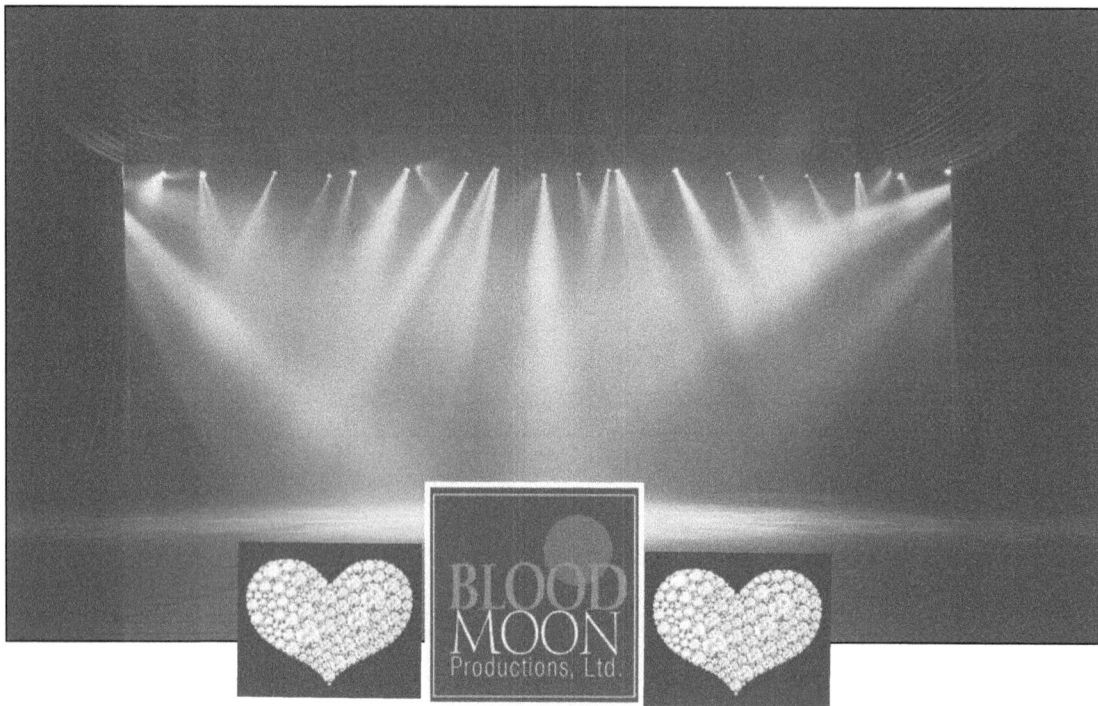

## WHAT IS BLOOD MOON PRODUCTIONS?

*"Blood Moon, in case you don't know, is a small publishing house on Staten Island that cranks out Hollywood gossip books, about two or three a year, usually of five-, six-, or 700-page length, chocked with stories and pictures about people who used to consume the imaginations of the American public, back when we actually had a public imagination. That is, when people were really interested in each other, rather than in Apple 'devices.' In other words, back when we had vices, not devices."*

*—The Huffington Post*

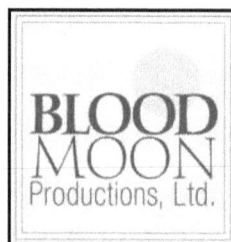

*Challenging the Status Quo's Beliefs about Celebrity & the Ironies of Fame*

# BLOOD MOON'S
# HOLLYWOOD REMEMBERED

### GLITZ, GLAMOUR, TRIUMPH, & TRAGEDY

How a small independent press captured the attention of the
tabloids, worldwide, during the decline of the entertainment industry's
golden age

## BY DARWIN PORTER
## WITH DANFORTH PRINCE

ISBN  978-1-936003-92-1

The galleys for this book were composed and laid out on Quark Express.
It was manufactured in the USA, and it's distributed worldwide through
Ingram, Amazon.com, and internet vendors everywhere.

# THIS BOOK IS DEDICATED TO
# ANITA FINLEY

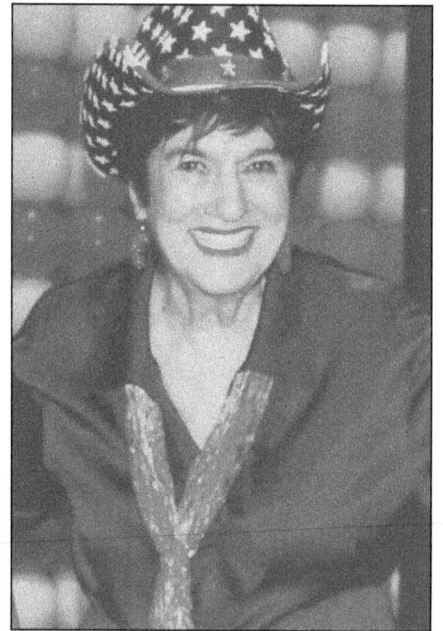

*Portraits of a Lady*
**Anita Finley**

# WOMEN WE LOVE

## How I Enrolled Zsa Zsa Gabor, Linda Lovelace, and Anita Finley into the same South Florida book tour

### By Danforth Prince

I met Anita during the "barely controlled" frenzy of a book tour I organized in South Florida during my double-barreled introduction there of some recently released biographies from Blood Moon. The tour, I decided, would "pair," in perhaps uncomfortable juxtaposition, references to the strong- willed protagonists of two books, each published by Blood Moon in 2013: *Those Glamorous Gabors, Bombshells from Budapest;* and *Inside Linda Lovelace's Deep Throat.*

Indeed, the association of Zsa Zsa with Ms. Lovelace was unexpected. But in the words of Gloria Vanderbilt (remember her?) "it seemed like a good idea at the time." And indeed, the association of the divas' names with my tour inspired some GREAT publicity slogans: *"Two Books, Two Birds, One Book Tour,"* and *"Danforth, Zsa Zsa, and Linda: Are they having a three-way? And is he man enough to handle them? "*

*(The correct answer, which I yelled out from a podium, midway through the tour, was **"Of course he is, dahlink!"**)*

Thus, I began "pumping" South Florida to determine who might want to watch me shake, rattle, roll and "Power Point" my way across the socially complicated landscapes of the Sunshine State.

QUESTION: Who wanted to showcase me during my chivalrous efforts to render Zsa Zsa and Linda glam again, this time post-mortem? **ANSWER:** EVERYBODY…**including Anita Finley.**

Thus, over the course of what evolved into an ten-day road trip, we (I mean, me with the ghosts of Zsa Zsa and Linda) maneuvered our ways through **libraries,** midafternoon Q & A's in the rec rooms of some **retirement homes; Cinema Paradiso's lecture hall** (packed with applauding fans who had adored "the Mad Hungarian Bombshells"); **Naomi Wilzig's** *(remember her?)* **Erotic Art Museum** on Miami Beach; **bookstores; radio stations; the Boca Raton Resort**; and one awesomely ostentatious party at an awesomely ostentatious private home associated with a benefactor of Cinema Paradiso. Years later, and "before I forget," I remember this book tour with its flurry of *brouhahas* as one of the high points of my career.

Why am I telling you all this? Because during its frenzy and occasional dysfunctions, I met the smart, charming, and wonderful **ANITA FINLEY.** And a while later, after my return to NYC, I introduced her and her since deceased then-husband, Bill, to **Darwin Porter** at a meal we choreographed within a restaurant in SoHo…… And the rest is history, as conveyed, I hope, within the pages of this book.

*Bravissima*, Anita, with thanks and good will. Thanks for the memories, thanks for the encouragement, thanks for being a mensch,* and thanks for being a supportive ally of Darwin Porter.

### X with respect and affection from Danforth Prince

*In his book, **The Joys of Yiddish**, author Leo Rosten defined **a mensch** is someone "of noble character" who displays "rectitude, dignity, and a sense of what's right." Mensch derives from the German word for "human being." In Yiddish, it translates as "a good person." Linguists agree that there is no specific feminine version of "mensch." In Anita's case, it should probably be phrased as "a lady who's also a mensch."*

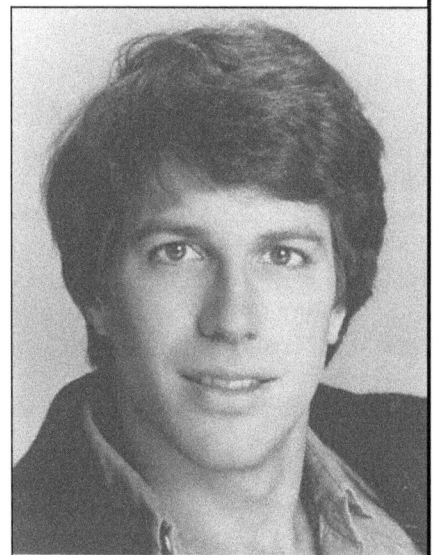

**Danforth Prince** went from stage actor to travel book author, noted biographer, and, ultimately, award-winning publisher.

# COULD IT BE LOVE?

## HOW, FOR MORE THAN TWENTY YEARS —THROUGH HER MAGAZINE, HER RADIO PROGRAM, AND ON YOUTUBE— ANITA FINLEY & DARWIN PORTER WOKE UP SOUTH FLORIDA

A Jazz Age comedy act at the *Folies Bergère* in Paris. But which is **Danforth**? Which is **Darwin**? And which is **Anita**?

### ANITA MET DARWIN AT THE RIGHT TIME— WHEN THE 21ST CENTURY WAS STILL IN DIAPERS.

She had established a popular magazine for senior citizens in South Florida, and shortly before she met Darwin, she had arranged a distribution deal with the *Miami Herald.*

Issued monthly, *Boomer Times* was filled with fascinating articles intended to help senior citizens lead happier, healthier, and better lives. Of particular interest were her overviews of current trends in BOOKS, and ENTERTAINMENT, a subject on which Darwin was well-versed and spoke and wrote about (some even said "obsessed" about) frequently.

But other than the humor, glitter, and flash that Darwin brought to it, *Boomer Times* for the most part focused on practical subjects of everyday merit, enriched with advice from experts.

Here are some sample headlines Anita's readers witnessed during its evolution:

HOW TO RESOLVE MARRIAGE CONFLICTS CAUSED BY RETIREMENT
TERM Vs. PERMANENT LIFE INSURANCE
THE PROMISE OF MEDICAL BREAKTHROUGH IS NOW!
HOW TO REVERSE BRAIN AGING
NEW BEGINNINGS FOR YOUR FINANCIAL WELL-BEING
DO YOU BANK ON SOCIAL SECURITY FOR YOUR RETIREMENT INCOME?

\*\*\*

When Anita began to publish columns by Darwin, he was the most widely read author of travel guides in the world. Since 1960, often in partnership with **Stanley Mills Haggart** (1910-1980), Darwin had written many dozens of travel guides to cities, regions, and countries of Europe, and to states or regions of the U.S. from California to New England. Depending on the assignment and its venue, he had been based, for practical and sometimes whimsical reasons, in venues as far-flung as New York, Los Angeles, London, Paris, and Rome.

\*\*\*

**BUT THE TIMES, THEY WERE A-CHANGING:** Intuitively, and perhaps with a sense of impending doom for "the way it was," Darwin realized early in the New Century that travel guides in the form we knew during our heydays would fade in both popularity and sales. Indeed, as the travel industry's *status quo* went "Gone With the Wind," he shifted his writing talents to biographies, mostly of Hollywood stars of the

**ASK ANITA, ASK DARWIN, ASK SALVADOR DALI**

**Is it futile to try to delay the passage of time? Their answer is YES!**

**Salvador Dali** was one of the great surrealist artists of the 20th Century. Showcased above is a theme that reappeared frequently in his work: **A melting clock**, aka, a "droopy watch". a metaphor for **the omnipresence of time** and its mastery over humans.

**Inter-Generational Hollywood archivists with a shared sense of historic destiny**

*Left to right*, Socialite to the stars **Maria Jane Haggart**; her son **Stanley Mills Haggart** (a Hollywood insider and "leg man" for Hedda Hopper); and film historian **Darwin Porter**, as photographed by Stanley Haggart in the 1960s.

Golden Age. He had multiple caches of research data at his disposal—mostly in the form of oral histories he'd been collecting, obsessively, since his early teens.

What did these stories have in common? Each shared a theme that focused on **The IRONIES OF FAME**! *Boomer Times* provided a venue for the publication of social truths that were too hot for release when they originally unfolded. From this monthly collaboration, A STAR WAS BORN: Her name is Anita Finley, to whom this book is dedicated.

# BAD THINGS HAPPENED IN THE GOOD OLD DAYS
## HOW DARWIN AND ANITA COLLECTIVELY REMEMBER HOLLYWOOD

**The Last of the Red-Hot Mamas**
and a mentor of Darwin Porter
when he was an adolescent
**Miss Sophie Tucker**

**During the so-called "Golden Age" of American film** (the 1930s, '40s, and '50s), movie studios like Warner Brothers, Fox, and MGM hired agents to suppress scandals generated about, or by, their stars.

Even a whiff of scandals, of course, could sabotage a career—especially for players in the entertainment industry. Although secrets proliferated (Hollywood was often compared to the Biblical allegories of Sodom and Gomorrah) could not be revealed. They might include someone getting "knocked up": **Clark Gable** impregnation **Loretta Young** during the filming of *Call of the Wild*, for example. Or perhaps the *"otherwise not-particularly-shocking by modern standards"* decision of **Randolph Scott** and **Cary Grant** to live together as lovers.

Darwin, blessed with talent, an enquiring mind, and boundless energy, was the right man in the right place at the right time. He had inherited an enormous cache of data (including interview notes) on what was going on behind the scenes in Hollywood during its Golden Age.

A lot of it derived from **Stanley Haggart**, his former writing partner, who had died in 1980. When he'd emerged in Hollywood in 1910, he remembered it as a friendly, rather eccentric small town with miles and miles of orange trees.

In small-town Hollywood, everybody got to know everybody else, and "stars" were readily accessible. The first movie star he met was **Charlie Chaplin**, who entered a crowded cafeteria and found that the only seat available was next to Haggart. Naturally, they talked.

Stanley's boyhood friend, actor **Philippe De Lacy**, was cast as **Greta Garbo**'s son in *Love* (1927). The introductions that followed sparked Haggart's life-long association with Garbo. From there, he went on to befriend **Gloria Swanson, John Gilbert, Marlene Dietrich, Gary Cooper, Joan Crawford, Bette Davis, Tallulah Bankhead, Joan Blondell, Norma Shearer, Ramon Novarro**, and dozens of others. His loquacious mother, **Maria Jane Haggart**, rented a house in Laurel Canyon next door to **Adela Rogers St. Johns**, then the best-known columnist in the entertainment industry, and indiscreet stories were swapped "over the garden gate." These gossipy "truths" were transferred by Maria to Stanley, who passed them on to Darwin.

In time, Stanley got to know **Spencer Tracy** and **Humphrey Bogart**. In his younger days in New York, Haggart had worked as a model at the same modeling agency (Powers) that had employed Betty Joan Perske (later **Lauren Bacall**).

Haggart, in the late 1930s, became a "Leg Man" for gossip columnist **Hedda Hopper**. Rigorously avoiding evening commitments, she ferociously safeguarded her preference for retiring every night at 10pm, entrusting Haggart (shoulder-to-shoulder with her son, **William Hopper**) the task of prowling the nightclubs of LA for stories. ( Hopper later played Paul Drake, a private investigator, on the hit TV series, *The Perry Mason Show*.)

**Haggart,** in his last will and testament, **bequeathed to Darwin** the dozens of boxes of data he'd accumulated since the days of silent films. A lot of that data included scandals that Hedda didn't dare—for legal reasons—to publish in her syndicated columns.

Through Haggart, Darwin was introduced to dozens of stars, many of whom had not worked since the end of silent pictures. Articulate and sometimes embittered, a horde of them were still alive in the 60s and 70s.

What about Darwin? On his own, the star-struck teenager began meeting stars as a pre-teen, during the era when his young, single, and charismatic mother, **Hazel**, fresh from the economically ravaged valleys of Appalachia, thrived as a personal assistant to **Sophie Tucker**, "The Queen of Miami Beach."

Thrilled by the roaring good times of "Boomtown Miami of the 40s," Young Darwin (then known as "Hink") would rush home from school to see who was calling on Miss Sophie. Not infrequently, it was **Judy Garland** or **Frank Sinatra**. On one occasion, he met **Ronald Reagan** who, at the time, was maintaining a secret affair with a rising starlet, **Marilyn Monroe**.

(For that particular press engagement, he'd invited **Doris Day**, but she was busy.) What was all the fuss about? Reagan, Day, and **Ginger Rogers** had co-starred in *Storm Warning* (1951), which was being showcased at the time for its premiere in Miami.

For three years, Haggart had been the "housekeeper" for **Randolph Scott and Cary Grant**. (Yes, there were rumors.) They introduced him to **Katharine Hepburn**. Haggart earned extra money when Scott got him work as an extra at RKO. There, **Ginger Rogers**, became his "gal pal," and the source of many indiscreet anecdotes. Through her, Haggart was designated as an extra on her hit movie, *Top Hat,* in which she danced with **Fred Astaire**. Earlier, he had been a "background prop," in formal evening wear, waltzing his way through scenes of **Erich Von Stroheim**'s *The Merry Widow* (1925), the silent version with **John Gilbert** and **Mae Murray**. Haggart, as the years evolved, emerged as an "Ali Baba's cave," a resource for the then-underpublicized indiscretions of early movie stars and the formidable writing powers of Darwin Porter.

With the dawn of the 21st Century, Darwin became convinced that those boxes of data, and those troves of anecdotes, researched haphazardly and at the time, randomly, by Haggart and himself, were too valuable to waste. Thus, as the travel guidebook industry waned, he began a series of celebrity biographies whose compilations continue to this day.

# BOUNTIFUL, BEAUTIFUL ANITA

**At least some of the revelations within each of Darwin's first three "Movie Star Biographies" were unveiled for the first time in Anita Finley's Boomer Times,** usually in advance of the splashier exposures of bigger, more mainstream broadsheets. Adding additional fuel to the publicity flares, she also invited Darwin onto her radio and YouTube shows for interviews of her own

For years, her friends and fans in South Florida awakened early to hear "the latest" from Anita questioning Darwin.

The first columns she published were part of his *"Hollywood Remembered"* series. This theme continued for many years until they were replaced with *"Media Buzz."* That newer "more inclusive" title expanded his potential focus, morphing it beyond Hollywood and into the world at large.

**DID YOU KNOW?** that in 2023, **Anita**, a gerontologist known for her formidable interpersonal skills, made **MARITAL NEWS** after a fast-paced late-in-life romance (and sudden marriage) to one of the most eligible bachelors in South Florida?

Born amid the rocks and conifers of Idaho, he's former **Naval Commander John Patrick Derr.** After his retirement from active dury in 1977, he worked for ten years as the Emergency Management Director of Charlotte County, Florida and organized charter sails from Florida to the British Virgin Islands. He's pictured *in the left photo, in 2024 (*post-nuptial), with **Anita** on the driveway of their home in Port Charlotte, FL. Above, right, he's taking care of active Naval duties in the 1960s.

In the wake of their wedding in 2023, dozens of Anita's fans nationwide said **"BRAVISSIMA!"** and sent heartfelt congratulations to each of them.

# WHY DID WE WRITE AND PRODUCE THIS BOOK?

We did it "before memory fades" as a celebration of the Darwin/Anita collaboration, and as an "autobiography" of Blood Moon Productions. Listed below are examples of *Hollywood Remembered* that Darwin, through Anita, premiered to the world at large through **Boomer Times**. Many of them appear in this book in formats which we've amplified from their original presentations.

\*\*\*

SOME OF THE COLUMNS BY DARWIN PORTER WHICH MADE THEIR WAY INTO THE "CANON" OF
## HOLLYWOOD REMEMBERED
ORIGINALLY APPEARED, IN TRUNCATED FORMATS, WITHIN ANITA FINLEY'S *BOOMER TIMES*.
IMPROVED AND ENLARGED, THEY'VE BEEN RE-PUBLISHED WITHIN THE PAGES OF THIS BOOK. THEY INCLUDE:

**Burt Reynolds**: How a Nude Centerfold Seduced Hollywood
**Steve McQueen & Paul Newman** Were Lovers
**Liz Taylor**: Her Teenage Dalliance with **Ronald Reagan**
The XXX-Rated Life of **Peter O'Toole**
**Kirk Douglas**: A Century of Sexual Conquests
**Linda Lovelace** Deep-Throated **Frank Sinatra**
**Elvis Presley** Got Down and Dirty with **Marilyn Monroe**
**Michael Jackson** became infatuated with a young (very young) **Prince William**
**June Allyson** Slept with Two (Future) U.S. Presidents
**Marlon Brando**, the Master; **James Dean**, the Slave Boy
**Rock Hudson** on the Casting Couch
**Judy Garland's Gay Husbands**
Movie Stars Reveal "Their First Time"
**Vivien Leigh** Bedded Guys—and Girls
**Katharine Hepburn & Spencer Tracy**: Platonic Lovers in Public, LGBTQ "Buddies" in Private
Future First Lady **Nancy Davis** wanted **Clark Gable**, but Settled for **Reagan**
**Merv Griffin** Seduces **Tarzan**
Revenge Porn
**Bogie** May Have Slept with 1,000 Women

# Darwin's Celebrity Contributions to Anita's *Boomer Times*

The material we inserted into this book reflect the American obsession with fame Much of it focuses on scandals which were suppressed during Hollywood's Golden Age.

Darwin composed most of it when the "Fires of September" burned deep within his heart. Now, "Deep in December" and in a radically different era, it provides ironic insights—tempered by our own advancing ages—into the public and private histories of public figures who once captured our collective  imaginations.  Now, the nostalgia-soaked final days that remain for us, it's time to revive our collective memories; time to build a tender, self-forgiving overview of "the way we were."

Some of the people whose names appear within this book have morphed into immortality. Others have been forgotten, and others are facing their final curtain even as this is being written.

So—because it seems crucially important at this late stage in our lives—let's take a journey back to yesterday.

Although the columns we've encased within the pages of this celebrity-studded book were all published during the 21st Century, for the most part, they focus on Golden Age Hollywood and the glittering movie stars who made it sparkle. Like gods and goddesses from ancient mythology, they captured the imagination of the world. Players we love included Joan Crawford, Clark Gable, Marilyn Monroe, Elvis Presley…and beyond.

**But writing about them retrospectively requires clear thinking and a vivid sense of skepticism.**

During the Golden Age, most of the scandals and secrets of Hollywood stars were suppressed. Studios hired "fixers" to squelch bad (or unflattering) news,

They also employed publicity staffs to falsify facts, emphasize the glam, ignore the mundane, and to relentlessly churn out falsehoods and/or exaggerations.  If, early in her career struggles, a beautiful young starlet had configured herself, perhaps briefly, as a hooker in, let's say San Francisco, her revised profile emphasized that she'd been a Red Cross worker in Idaho…or something equivalently respectable.

When Darwin composed the first of his inaugural bios (subjects included Humphrey Bogart, Katharine Hepburn, and Marlon Brando), Anita was the first newsperson to discover his *oeuvre*. She asked him to write a monthly column for her publication, *Boomer Times and Senior Life*, and she invited him as a guest on her radio and zoom TV shows.

At the time, her magazine, *Boomer Times* was distributed within both Broward and Palm Beach Counties by *The Miami Herald* and other major outlets in South Florida.

To their  mutual delight, many of the "breaking news" revelations he included within his (early) columns were picked up, re-configured, and re-distributed by major-league media which included *The New York Times* and *The Daily Mail*.

Thanks in part to that publicity, fans of Darwin, over the years, have been saturated with *insider-ish* data about the private lives of, among others, **Marilyn Monroe, Michael Jackson, Rock Hudson, James Dean, Tennessee Williams, Zsa Zsa Gabor, Frank Sinatra, Lana Turner, Marlon Brando, Howard Hughes, Merv Griffin, and more recently, Debbie Reynolds, Carrie Fisher,** *Playboy's* **Hugh Hefner, Kirk Douglas, Judy Garland, Desi Arnaz, Lucille Ball**, and **both Henry and Jane Fonda.**

Four of Darwin's biographies focus on **John F. Kennedy, Bill and Hillary Clinton, and Ronald Reagan and his two wives, Jane Wyman and Nancy Davis.** His largest is *Jacqueline Kennedy Onassis, Her Tumultuous Life & Her Love Affairs.* Insights that appeared within all of them, in some form, have, over the years, appeared within various editions of *Boomer Times.*

# So Who is this Media-Savvy Hipster, Anita Finley?

With Hungarian ancestry, she was born in New York City, and grew up on Miami Beach. Later, at the University of Miami, she studied literature for two years. She earned a bachelor's degree in film, radio, and fine arts from Sam Houston State University. After graduation, she earned a Masters of Professional Services degree from Lynn University's Institute of Gerontology at Boca Raton, Florida.

Anita is a gerontologist, a modern-day Amazon, and a Renaissance woman capable of thriving wherever she happens to land. She is a woman of influence, shaping public opinion, and spreading wide her message of tolerance and love.

Her personal conviction is that it is never too late to learn or to try something new.

Her cheery optimistic voice, as broadcast throughout South Florida, gives hope, even in these troubled times.

As she states it, "I am very encouraged about life, even with some tragedies, but when one looks up at the sky in the morning, with the billowing clouds, shades of blue, the landscape becomes a painting. Many early mornings, when I am at the station for our early Saturday morning show, the view of the sunrise is magical. The hues of reds turning into other subtle colors are breathtaking. Nature in all its fantasy can start your day off with deep breaths of joy and appreciation. Open your blinds and look outside, up and down and all around you—and wish yourself a bright future."

The columns within this anthology first appeared, over the course of more than twenty years  in various editions of *Boomer Times.* Here, because perhaps you've forgotten some of the celebrities we've mentioned, they're interlaced with photographs which will bring them quickly to mind when you see their faces.

This illustrated collection of columns, often provocative, is brought to you by Blood Moon Productions, a publishing venture which is currently releasing more celebrity bios than any other media venue in America.

Our latest titles include *Hollywood Babylon with Detours to Gomorrah.* This is an enlarged and more shocking new edition of the scandal-soaked anthology that made Blood Moon famous.

Also recently published is a two-volume set devoted to the "Fabulous Fondas," Henry, Jane, and Peter. Volume One covers Henry from 1903 to 1960 and is entitled *He Did It His Way.*

Its companion volume, *Triple Exposure,* extolls the latter days of Henry along with Jane and Peter, mainly from 1961 to 1982.

Many critics have hailed them as the best biographies of their kind, loaded with information that's "definitely not for the timid, the prudish, or the faint of heart."

# And Who Is Darwin Porter?

**Darwin Porter** grew up in Miami, where he attended the University of Miami. Early in his career, he became a reporter and columnist for *The Miami Herald.* He later became bureau chief of the *Herald's* Key West office at the time of the Cuban Revolution.

Previously, he had interviewed Eleanor Roosevelt at the Fontainebleu Hotel in Miami Beach. In Key West, he took morning walks with Harry S Truman during his last visit to his former presidential vacation retreat.

Darwin's first movie star interviews in Key West were with Cary Grant, Tony Curtis, and Dina Merrill, the former owner of Mar-a-Lago. All of them were shooting *Operation Petticoat* (released in 1959) at the time.

Later, he relocated to New York City, where he became the youngest vice-president of an advertising agency on Madison Avenue.  His agency specialized in hiring movie stars to hawk their commercial products.

Later, and for decades to come, he was the chief writer of the **Frommer Travel Guides**, which introduced millions of readers to the charms of Europe and the little nations of the Caribbean Sea.

He operated from bases in Miami, Hollywood, New York, San Francisco, Rome, London, and Paris.

He quickly released that NOTHING LASTS FOREVER and that TIME, TECHNOLOGIES, AND TRENDS ARE FICKLE. Long before the inevitable twilight of the once-burgeoning travel guide industry, and alert that if he was to survive, he'd have to adapt, he began composing and releasing celebrity biographies.

Thanks to his role as the chief writer at Frommer, he was already a widely respected commentarian on trends in travel. And as a "down low and on the side" venture that coincided with his passion for trends in the entertainment industry, he often showed up on film sets in London or Los Angeles.  In Rome, during a break from duties associated with *Frommer's Italy* and *Frommer's Rome,* he visited Elizabeth Taylor and Richard Burton while they were falling in love on the set of *Cleopatra* (1963).

During the course of his on-site research in Europe for Frommer, he continued to visit movie sets, "following his private passions and private (but consuming) field of study—the Entertainment Industry.  That included, as a journalist,  following the trail of Peter O'Toole  in Spain during his filming of *Lawrence of Arabia* (1962).  And this, and all the while continuing to bash out hotel, restaurant, shopping, and museum reviews for various titles within the Frommer "universe," he continued plotting, scheming, and "obsessing" over how to record, in manuscript form, the fast-changing entertainment and celebrity scenes, too.

As the years went by, more and more biographies poured out of Darwin's now-antiquated Smith-Coronas. Some of his best sellers "re-defined' Elizabeth Taylor, Peter O'Toole, Frank Sinatra, Judy Garland, Liza Minnelli, Debbie Reynolds, Carrie

Fisher, Lucille Ball, Desi Arnaz, Steve McQueen, Paul Newman, Rock Hudson, Vivien Leigh, Laurence Olivier, Kirk Douglas, Burt Reynolds, Tennessee Williams, Zsa Zsa Gabor, Howard Hughes, and J. Edgar Hoover.

Once, while being interviewed on a San Francisco radio show, he was asked, "Who were the most dazzling movie stars he had met?"

Among the women he cited were Marilyn Monroe, Elizabeth Taylor, Ava Gardner, Bette Davis, Joan Crawford, Greta Garbo, Mae West, Vivien Leigh, and Gloria Swanson.

Among the men he named were Rock Hudson, Burt Reynolds, Cary Grant, William Holden, Marlon Brando, Paul Newman, Richard Burton, and Warren Beatty.

The vast repertoire of books he crafted including "wild cards." The biography he devoted to Michael Jackson, has helped define Darwin as what one critic called "The Walter Winchell of the 21st Century—with a dollop of Hedda Hopper."

**Three views of Darwin Porter**: *Left and right:* Yesterday, when he was young, and *center photo* from around 2010, being interviewed at home during a televised interview with documentarians from a Japanese television station.

# SUNRISE, SUNSET, WHERE HAVE ALL THE YEARS GONE?
## By Anita Finley, Publisher of Boomer Times

### Where do I begin?

*Senior Life*, the original name, was an early idea that turned into a living accumulation of messages, formulas, interviews, and new information and tactics that were put into print, packaged as a newspaper and delivered to a small group of seniors living in South Florida.

It was 1990, and seniors were about to explode across the U.S., and South Florida was a destination for many of these retirees. They were smart, upbeat, active and rarin' to go, wanting to know all about what was in store for them as they were aging. It was a powerful opportunity for entrepreneurs to offer senior services and products to satisfy their desires.

Growing up in Miami Beach, I found myself very curious and infatuated by the elder population living on South Beach, in small hotels on the beach, in tiny apartments sprinkled throughout the city and enjoying the beautiful weather and safe, carefree living. In fact, my grandmother lived in one of the first senior retirement hotels on Washington Avenue, the heart of what became known as "a ghetto of elders." She lived there until she died at 95. That left quite an impression on my psyche.

My dedication to helping champion the older folks, while I was living in Huntsville, Texas, I co-founded a senior citizens center, attained a Bachelor's Degree in Communications at Sam Houston State University, dedicating my resources to retired college professors. The more I interviewed them on my college radio show, the more I knew I wanted to specialize in this generation's needs and wants.

Fast forward ... although I found myself in the real estate business in Boca Raton in the 1980s, I developed and wrote a column in the Palm Beach Post for ten years, naming it **STARS (Seniors Taking Active Roles in Society)**. It was a Q and A column, featuring a senior each week, showing how productive that STAR was. I also hosted weekly radio shows, interviewing both seniors and owners of businesses and medical personnel who helped these seniors stay healthy, wealthy and wise.

When the College of Boca Raton (now Lynn University) offered a Gerontology Master's degree, I began my five year studies and completed it, giving me knowledge and credentials to make my dream come true. In 1992, I co-authored a book with my late husband Bill Finley, *Live To Be 100 Plus,* and made hundreds of speeches throughout South Florida, and appeared on national TV and radio explaining how this was the future of our society.

Looking back, it was destiny that I would along with my husband, Bill, start a newspaper to complete my passion of communicating to seniors and the up-coming baby boomers.

Senior Life then became *Senior Life & Boomer Times,* and we were a full-fledged company, producing a monthly newspaper, with smart and talented writers and health professionals and advertisers who were looking to gain the attention of seniors and baby boomers in South Florida. We had a stroke of luck when *The Miami Herald* found us and asked us to insert our newspaper monthly. We then graduated to a magazine format.

My business acumen was in full gear to keep our magazine growing and to add Seminars, Symposiums, and EXPOS. This required a talented staff who also felt the mission of assisting the senior and boomer population. For the 33 years of our successful organization, my appreciation for the executives and assorted production team is heartfelt. Again, I must applaud our fantastic writers, many from across the country, many famous in their own right.

In 1998, our hard work and creative ideas brought us an exciting opportunity to expand our multi-media company. dedicated to all the seniors and beamers in the U.S. We were on the verge of being inserted in all the major newspapers similar to our insertion success in *The Miami Herald.* We were about to receive $18M to insert our magazine similar to *Parade* and *USA Today* magazines. All was looking like we scored big but unfortunately, the 9/11 tragedy occurred and our investors bailed out! Those three years of planning caught us and we went back-wards! What a great disappointment!

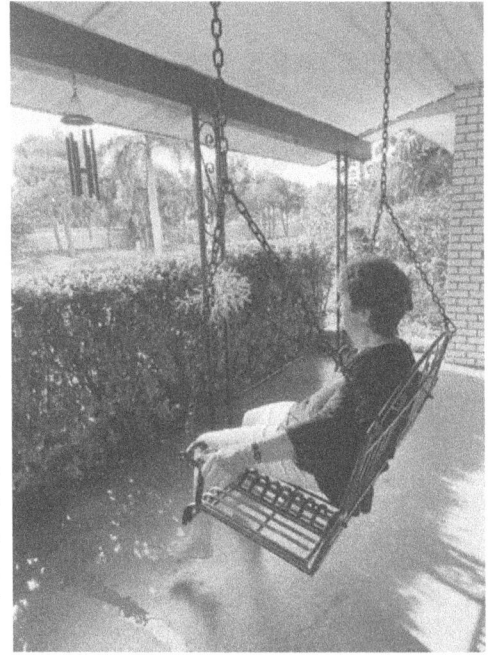

**Anita Finley**

At peace with the universe, at home, in a gar-den, in Port Charlotte, Florida,

*photo by John Derr*

As in our lives, change is always there. After my unbelievably talented husband in so many fields, passed in 2017, it was more difficult to operate Boomer Times (the shortened name), that created changes in the sales and organization-al structure. The question was not answered as to what I was going to do and it was COVID that ultimately caused our company (as well as many others) to see our sales and operation take a nose dive.

GOOD NEWS! The sun always comes out after the storm and I was introduced, through the Internet, to a 93-year-old smart, kind and youthful man who has changed my life for many reasons. We dated for one year, fell in love and he asked me to marry him on November 21, 2022. The next change is that he lives in Port Charlotte, on the west coast of Florida. His name is John P. Derr. He is a 26-year retired Navy commander, along with other executive successes, and he is a prize. You can Google him and see how this Annapolis graduate, originally from Idaho, has an incredible spirit and the body of a 75-year-old. His one condition for our marriage was that he wanted me to retire with him and not continue *Boomer Times.*

To all our advertisers over the years, and all the devoted readers; the past radio listeners, and our vibrant expo attendees and exhibitors, you are special and have been a superb group!

THANK YOU!
Anita.

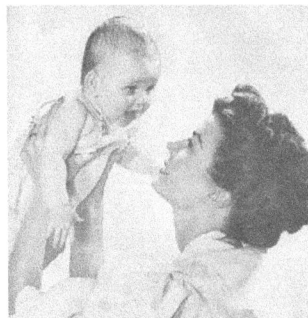

The Birth of the
Baby Boomers

# MORE STARS THAN IN HEAVEN ITSELF: HOLLYWOOD REMEMBERED.

## WHOSE "INSIDE DISH" WILL YOU ENCOUNTER WITHIN THIS ANTHOLOGY?

Marilyn Monroe
ELVIS PRESLEY
Princess Diana
Michael Jackson
John Lennon
Nikita Khruschchev
James E. Dougherty (first husband of MM)
Elizabeth Taylor
Frank Sinatra
Ryan O'Neal
Humphrey Bogart
Burt Reynolds
Laurence Olivier
Vivien Leigh
Peter O'Toole
Carrie Fisher
Debbie Reynolds
Judy Garland
Liza Minnelli
Tony Bennett
CYD CHARISSE
Howard Hughes
Arnold Schwarzenegger
Julia Roberts
Doris Day
Justin Bieber
Lucille Ball
Desi Arnaz
Rita Hayworth
Anthony Quinn
Kirk Douglas
Jane Russell
Patti Davis
Clark Gable and Vivien Leigh in Gone With the Wind
Margaret Mitchell
Groucho Marx
Jane Fonda
James Dean
Channing Tatum
Mickey Rooney
Franklin D. Roosevelt
Linda Lovelace
Carol Channing
Rock Hudson
Olivia de Havilland

JULIAN ASSANGE
Charlie Chaplin
Warren Beatty
Jennifer Jones
Lana Turner
Montgomery Clift
David Bowie
Marlon Brando
JOAN CRAWFORD
J. Edgar Hoover
Leonardo DiCaprio
Grace Kelly
Raymond Burr
Paul Newman
Vincent Sherman
June Allyson
Louis B. Mayer
Darryl F. Zanuck
Truman Capote
Gore Vidal
Tennessee Williams
Fabian
BILL COSBY
Robert Goulet
Carol Lawrence
Shelley Winters
William Randolph Hearst
"Baby Peggy"
Carla Laemmle
Ronald Reagan
Nancy Davis
Jane Wyman
ZSA ZSA GABOR
Liz Renay
HILLARY CLINTON
Greta Garbo
Gary Cooper
Jean Harlow
Sigmund Freud
Florence Nightingale
Marcel Proust
Lindsay Lohan
Paris Hilton
PETER ALLEN
Steve McQueen

# Contents

## PART THREE:  BLOOD MOON'S TRINITY OF TABLOID TRIUMPHS

## PART FOUR: IN THE ERA OF SELFIES AND SOCIAL MEDIA, EVERYONE IS A STAR

## PART FIVE:  YESTERDAY IS GONE AND MANY OF ITS PLAYERS ARE DEAD

# PREVIOUS WORKS BY DARWIN PORTER
# PRODUCED IN COLLABORATION WITH BLOOD MOON

## BIOGRAPHIES FROM BLOOD MOON'S
## MAGNOLIA HOUSE SERIES

*The Donald: How Did It Happen*
*The Gathering Storm*
*Henry Fonda, He Did It His Way,*
*(Volume One — 1905-1960 — of a Two-Part Biography)*
*The Fondas, Henry, Jane, & Peter*
*(Volume Two — 1962-1982 — of a Two-Part Biography)*
*Lucille Ball & Desi Arnaz: They Weren't Lucy & Ricky Ricardo*
*(Volume One — 1911-1960 — of a Two-Part Biography)*
*The Sad & Tragic Ending of Lucille Ball*
*(Volume Two — 1961-1989 — of a Two-Part Biography*
*Marilyn: Don't Even Dream About Tomorrow*
*(a 2021 revised version of the best-selling Marilyn at Rainbow's End: Sex, Lies, Murder, &*
*the Great Cover-Up (2012)*
*The Seductive Sapphic Exploits of Mercedes de Acosta*
*Hollywood's Greatest Lover*
*Jacqueline Kennedy Onassis, Her Tumultuous Life & Her Love Affairs*
*Judy Garland & Liza Minnelli, Too Many Damn Rainbows*
*Historic Magnolia House: Celebrity & The Ironies of Fame*
*Glamour, Glitz, & Gossip at Historic Magnolia House*

\*\*\*

## BIOGRAPHIES FROM BLOOD MOON
## NOT ASSOCIATED WITH ITS MAGNOLIA HOUSE SERIES

*Burt Reynolds, Put the Pedal to the Metal*
*Kirk Douglas, More Is Never Enough*
*Playboy's Hugh Hefner, Empire of Skin*
*Carrie Fisher & Debbie Reynolds,*
*Princess Leia & Unsinkable Tammy in Hell*
*Rock Hudson Erotic Fire*
*Lana Turner, Hearts & Diamonds Take All*
*Donald Trump, The Man Who Would Be King*
*James Dean, Tomorrow Never Comes*
*Bill and Hillary, So This Is That Thing Called Love*
*Peter O'Toole, Hellraiser, Sexual Outlaw, Irish Rebel*
*Love Triangle, Ronald Reagan, Jane Wyman, & Nancy Davis*
*Pink Triangle, The Feuds and Private Lives of Tennessee Williams, Gore Vidal,*
*Truman Capote, and Famous Members of their Entourages.*

*Those Glamorous Gabors, Bombshells from Budapest*
**Inside Linda Lovelace's Deep Throat,**
*Degradation, Porno Chic, and the Rise of Feminism*

**Elizabeth Taylor,** *There is Nothing Like a Dame*
**J. Edgar Hoover and Clyde Tolson**
*Investigating the Sexual Secrets of America's Most Famous Men and Women*
**Frank Sinatra,** *The Boudoir Singer. All the Gossip Unfit to Print*
**The Kennedys,** *All the Gossip Unfit to Print*
**The Secret Life of Humphrey Bogart** *(2003), and*
**Humphrey Bogart, The Making of a Legend** *(2010)*
**Howard Hughes,** *Hell's Angel*
**Steve McQueen,** *King of Cool, Tales of a Lurid Life*
**Paul Newman,** *The Man Behind the Baby Blues*
**Merv Griffin,** *A Life in the Closet*
**Brando Unzipped**
**Katharine the Great, Hepburn,** *Secrets of a Lifetime Revealed*
**Jacko, His Rise and Fall,** *The Social and Sexual History of Michael Jackson*
**Damn You, Scarlett O'Hara,**
*The Private Lives of Vivien Leigh and Laurence Olivier*

## FILM CRITICISM
**Blood Moon's 2005 Guide to the Glitter Awards**
**Blood Moon's 2006 Guide to Film**
**Blood Moon's 2007 Guide to Film,** *and*
**50 Years of Queer Cinema,** *500 of the Best GLBTQ Films Ever Made*

## NON-FICTION
*Hollywood Babylon, It's Back!* and *Hollywood Babylon Strikes Again!*

## NOVELS
*Blood Moon,*
*Hollywood's Silent Closet,*
*Rhinestone Country,*
*Razzle Dazzle*
*Midnight in Savannah*

## OTHER PUBLICATIONS BY DARWIN PORTER
## NOT DIRECTLY ASSOCIATED WITH BLOOD MOON

## NOVELS
**The Delinquent Heart**
**The Taste of Steak Tartare**
**Butterflies in Heat**
**Marika** *(a roman à clef based on the life of Marlene Dietrich)*
**Venus** *(a roman à clef based on the life of Anaïs Nin)*
**Sister Rose**

# TRAVEL GUIDES
## MANY EDITIONS AND MANY VARIATIONS OF *THE FROMMER GUIDES*, *THE AMERICAN EXPRESS GUIDES*, AND/OR *TWA GUIDES*, ET ALIA TO:

Andalusia, Andorra, Anguilla, Aruba, Atlanta, Austria, the Azores, The Bahamas, Barbados, the Bavarian Alps, Berlin, Bermuda, Bonaire and Curaçao, Boston, the British Virgin Islands, Budapest, Bulgaria, California, the Canary Islands, the Caribbean and its "Ports of Call," the Cayman Islands, Ceuta, the Channel Islands (UK), Charleston (SC), Corsica, Costa del Sol (Spain), Denmark, Dominica, the Dominican Republic, Edinburgh, England, Estonia, Europe, "Europe by Rail," the Faroe Islands, Finland, Florence, France, Frankfurt, the French Riviera, Geneva, Georgia (USA), Germany, Gibraltar, Glasgow, Granada (Spain), Great Britain, Greenland, Grenada (West Indies), Haiti, Hungary, Iceland, Ireland, Isle of Man, Italy, Jamaica, Key West & the Florida Keys, Las Vegas, Liechtenstein, Lisbon, London, Los Angeles, Madrid, Maine, Malta, Martinique & Guadeloupe, Massachusetts, Melilla, Morocco, Munich, New England, New Orleans, North Carolina, Norway, Paris, Poland, Portugal, Provence, Puerto Rico, Romania, Rome, Salzburg, San Diego, San Francisco, San Marino, Sardinia, Savannah, Scandinavia, Scotland, Seville, the Shetland Islands, Sicily, St. Martin & Sint Maarten, St. Vincent & the Grenadines, South Carolina, Spain, St. Kitts & Nevis, Sweden, Switzerland, the Turks & Caicos, the U.S.A., the U.S. Virgin Islands, Venice, Vienna and the Danube, Wales, and Zurich.

# BIOGRAPHIES

***From Diaghilev to Balanchine,*** *The Saga of Ballerina Tamara Geva*
***Greta Keller,*** *Germany's Other Lili Marleen*
***Sophie Tucker,*** *The Last of the Red Hot Mamas*
***Anne Bancroft,*** *Where Have You Gone, Mrs. Robinson?*
*(co-authored with Stanley Mills Haggart)*
***Veronica Lake,*** *The Peek-a-Boo Girl*
***Running Wild in Babylon,*** *Confessions of a Hollywood Press Agent*

# HISTORIES

***Thurlow Weed,*** *Whig Kingpin*
***Chester A. Arthur,*** *Gilded Age Coxcomb in the White House*
***Discover Old America,*** *What's Left of It*

# Biographies
# from Blood Moon Productions

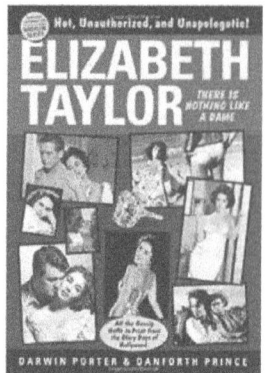

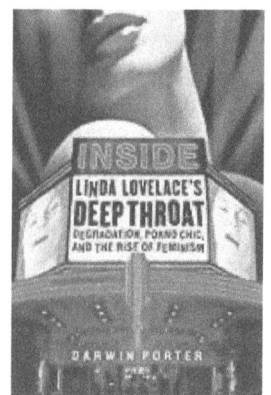

# More Biographies
# from Blood Moon Productions

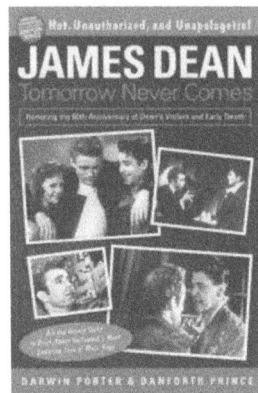

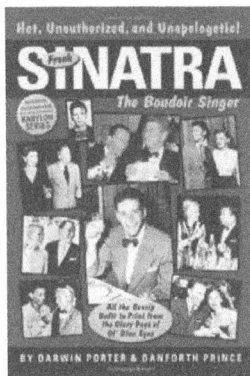

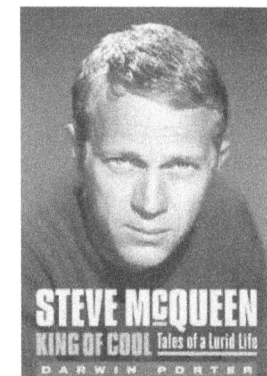

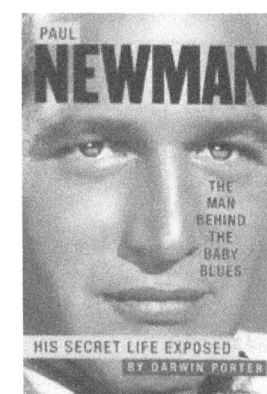

**Marilyn:**
*Don't Even Dream About Tomorrow*
Sex, Lies, Her Murder,
& the Great Cover-Up
*Darwin Porter*

**PLAYBOY'S**
HUGH HEFNER
*Empire of Skin*
Darwin Porter & Danforth Prince

**Rock Hudson Erotic Fire**
Darwin Porter & Danforth Prince

**Jacqueline Kennedy Onassis**
Her Tumultuous Life & Her Love Affairs
Darwin Porter & Danforth Prince

**DONALD TRUMP**
THE MAN WHO WOULD BE KING
DARWIN PORTER & DANFORTH PRINCE

Hot, Unauthorized, and Unapologetic!
**JAMES DEAN**
*Tomorrow Never Comes*
DARWIN PORTER & DANFORTH PRINCE

**BILL & HILLARY**
SO THIS IS THAT THING CALLED LOVE
DARWIN PORTER & DANFORTH PRINCE

**J. EDGAR HOOVER & CLYDE TOLSON**
INVESTIGATING THE SEXUAL SECRETS OF AMERICA'S MOST FAMOUS MEN AND WOMEN
DARWIN PORTER

Hot, Unauthorized, and Unapologetic!
**SINATRA**
The Boudoir Singer
BY DARWIN PORTER & DANFORTH PRINCE

**Humphrey Bogart**
Making Legend
by Darwin Porter

**HOWARD HUGHES Hell's Angel**
America's Notorious Bisexual Billionaire
By Darwin Porter

**STEVE McQUEEN KING OF COOL** Tales of a Lurid Life
DARWIN PORTER

**BRANDO Unzipped**
Bad Boy • Megastar • Sexual Outlaw
BY DARWIN PORTER

**MERV GRIFFIN**
A Life in the Closet
Darwin Porter

**Katharine The Great**
a lifetime of secrets... revealed by Darwin Porter

**PAUL NEWMAN**
THE MAN BEHIND THE BABY BLUES
HIS SECRET LIFE EXPOSED
BY DARWIN PORTER

Clark Gable
King of Hollywood

Volume One (1901-1938)
of a Three-Part Biography
Darwin Porter & Danforth Prince

Gone With the Wind
FRANKLY, MY DEAR, HE DID GIVE A DAMN

Volume Two (1938-1939)
of a Three-Part Biography of Clark Gable
Darwin Porter & Danforth Prince

Clark Gable
Where Love Has Gone

Volume Three (1940-1961)
of a Three-Part Biography
Darwin Porter & Danforth Prince

What's
NEW
What's
NEXT

# WHAT'S NEW AND WHAT'S NEXT FROM BLOOD MOON PRODUCTIONS?

He influenced America's definition of Manhood; he became a Mega-Celebrity before they invented the word; and despite intense rivalry with lesser actors, he was widely applauded as **THE KING OF HOLLYWOOD.**

He led a mind-bending life which Blood Moon has configured into THREE SPECTACULAR VOL-UMES, choreographed in ways never achieved, despite multiple hackneyed attempts from other publishing venues. He was THE KING. Volume One of this trilogy will be available in time for Christmas, 2024.

## HE'S CLARK GABLE

## LIKE HE'S NEVER BEEN SEEN BEFORE

At the peak of his career, flush with the success of his starring performance in history's most poignant film about the end of the Old South (*Gone With the Wind*), **Clark Gable** had become a symbol of American pride and power itself. His role as an icon was so pronounced that Adolph Hilter placed a bounty on his head and stated his intention of capturing him alive and dragging him, caged and in chains, as a trophy through the streets of Nazi Berlin.

**GABLE!** He's here, alive and thriving, the beneficiary of years of research from the creative team at Blood Moon. So complicated is his story that no single tome can contain all that's needed to say in this ULTIMATE look at CLARK, GLORIOUSLY GABLED, the focal point of a three-volume biography spearheaded by film historian **Darwin Porter.**

BLOOD
MOON
Productions, Ltd.

# PART ONE
# SUPERNOVAS

## MARILYN MONROE & ELVIS PRESLEY

# Marilyn & Elvis

## AMERICA'S ULTIMATE DREAM COUPLE

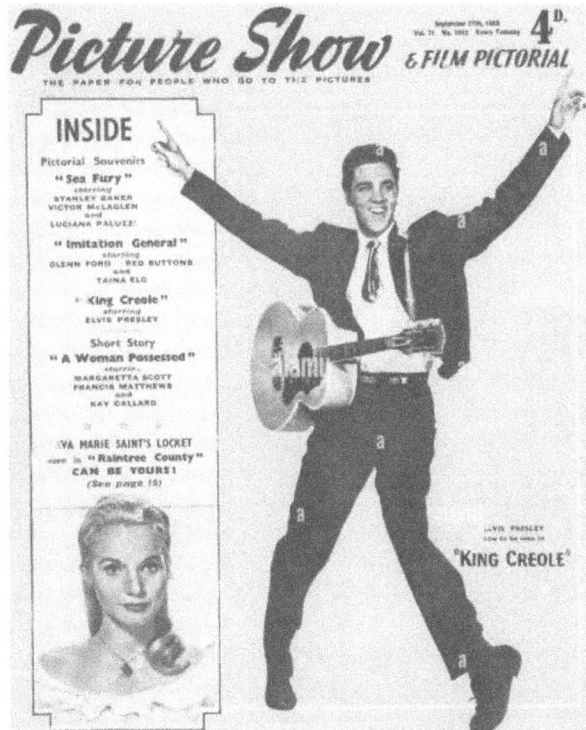

Take dozens of **Marilyn Monroe** and **Elvis Presley** biographies, and in most cases, you'll never find any cross-references indicating that either of them ever even met, much less got intimate. Yet because of recent media revelations, news of the Elvis/Marilyn affair has become public knowledge.

What isn't known, except to some longtime Hollywood insiders, is that the affair lasted longer and was more intense than had originally been known. Spilling the beans were Nick Adams, Elvis' closest pal, and Shelley Winters, former roommate of MM's and a life-long, rather gossippy *confidante*.

Although Shelley kept most of Marilyn's secrets during MM's lifetime, after the star's tragic death in 1962, Shelley became a virtual "talking head" about Marilyn's secret life and passions.

"It's true," Shelley said. "Marilyn and I fucked some of the same guys, but I never got around to Elvis. From what I hear, I didn't miss all that much. Give me Burt Lancaster or John Ireland any day."

# Love Me Tender

The text that follows first appeared in the November 2006 edition of Anita Finley's *Boomer Times*. We've amplified it here with different photographs.

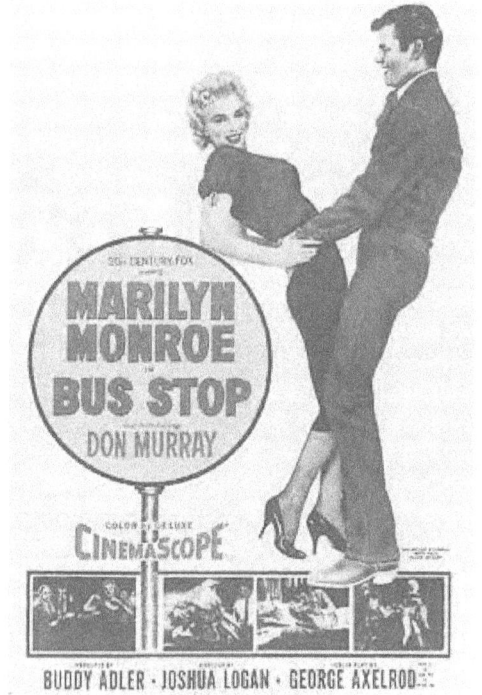

**Elvis and Marilyn** forever regretted that Col. Tom Parker, Elvis' manager, nixed the deal for them to co-star together in *Bus Stop* (1956). Even so, Marilyn's 24th film, made shortly after *The Seven Year Itch*, offered a vehicle for her greatest performance to date.

As Bosley Crowther noted in *The New York Times*, director Josh Logan got Marilyn to "do a great deal more than wiggle and pout and pop her big eyes and play the synthetic vamp in this film. He got her to be the beat-up B-girl of Mr. William Inge's play, even down to the Ozark accent and the look of pellagra about her skin. He got her to be the tinseled floozy, the semi-moronic-doll who is found in a Phoenix clip-joint by a cowboy of equally limited brains."

When The Colonel turned down the part for his money maker, the role intended for Elvis went instead to actor Don Murray, who was credible, but not brilliant, as the young and innocent cowboy, Bo Decker.

"Try as he could, Don Murray was no Elvis," said a disappointed Logan. "Marilyn and Elvis together would at least have had the power of the atomic bomb dropped on Hiroshima, maybe a nuclear blast that would have made them the screen team of the century."

**A poll taken in the summer of 2007** of presumably straight adults (ages 21 to 35) revealed the names of the two sex icons of the 20th century that these Americans would most like to bed. By overwhelming majorities, women went for Elvis Presley, the men predictably going for Marilyn Monroe.

There was always talk in Hollywood of pairing this dream couple in a film, especially the picture, *Bus Stop* (1956), one of Marilyn's most successful hits. But Col. Tom Parker, Elvis's greedy manager, always blocked such deals, insisting that Elvis keep turning out such quickie junk as *Blue Hawaii* (1961).

Nearly all biographers agree that Elvis and Marilyn met, but only briefly, in the mid-50s. Those books will have to be rewritten in the wake of revelations in October of 2006 by Byron Raphael, a retired William Morris agent who worked for Elvis. He spilled the beans on a salacious secret he'd been harboring for nearly half a century, revealing a "one-night stand" between Elvis and the blonde goddess in 1956.

Raphael claimed that he received a call one night from Elvis, requesting that Marilyn be brought to him at the Beverly Wilshire Hotel. The agent called Marilyn, doubting if she'd accept such a request. Even though she'd been recently married to playwright Arthur Miller, Marilyn took the bait and agreed to the secret rendezvous. At the time, she was also secretly dating a handsome young senator from Massachusetts, who would one day become the President of the United States. Actor Peter Lawford had set up that liaison.

"**Elvis** could deliver, I guess," Marilyn confessed to Shelley. "But he sure wanted to postpone penetration as long as possible. In my opinion, I think his ideal form of sex would be mutual masturbation. He sure likes to play with you down there. But he likes to use his fingers more than he likes to use the rod. One night, I was a bit drunk and jokingly kidded him, 'Spare the rod, spoil the fuck, Elvis.'"

"He didn't like that at all. In fact, he got up and put on his pants and told me to go home. But he called the next day and apologized."

Raphael reported that when Marilyn came into Elvis's suite, the famous pair started kissing even before saying a word to each other. Finally, Marilyn broke the silence, telling Elvis, "You're not bad for a guitar player." After only a few minutes on the living room sofa, according to Raphael, they got up and disappeared into the bedroom. He waited in the living room to take Marilyn home, but fell asleep, awakening hours later to find Marilyn and Elvis, both nude, emerging from the bedroom.

Not knowing when their sexual gymnastics would end, Raphael said he "bolted" from Elvis's suite. Five days later when he encountered Elvis, Raphael asked how it had gone with Marilyn. "She's a nice gal, but a little tall for me," Elvis said. She was also nearly a decade older than Elvis, but he was too much of a Southern gentleman to bring that up.

Raphael got the "historic" coming together of Elvis and Marilyn right. But there was much more to the story than what he knew.

One night in 1966, at an actor's hangout off Times Square in New York, Shelley Winters, Marilyn's roommate when she first hit Hollywood, revealed to actor John Ireland (star of the 1949 version of *All the King's Men*) and Darwin Porter a lot more about Marilyn and the King. She claimed that their one-night stand blossomed into an on-again, off-again affair that lasted for the rest of the 50s, interrupted only by Elvis singing the *G.I. Blues* when he was stationed in Germany with the U.S. Army.

A lifelong friend and confidant of Marilyn, Shelley said that Marilyn also told her that Elvis the lover

didn't match the allure of baseball legend Joe DiMaggio (Marilyn's former husband). She also claimed that Elvis "didn't have Joe's bat to hit home runs with."

When Shelley asked Marilyn why she continued to see Elvis over the years, MM said, "Other than me, he's the most famous person there is. How could I refuse? I don't think Albert Einstein would be a great lover either, but if he called me to his bed, I'd come running. After all, I think he invented the atomic bomb or something."

Porter also knew a young actor, Nick Adams, who arguably was Elvis's best all time male friend. Nick had appeared with James Dean in *Rebel Without a Cause* (1955), but is remembered today chiefly for his 1962 TV series, *The Rebel*. Nick died, allegedly from a drug overdose, in 1968. Many Hollywood insiders, including actor Forrest Tucker, insisted that he was murdered.

In 1964 when he was making *Hell Is for Heroes*, Nick Adams confirmed to Porter details about the Elvis/Marilyn tryst, telling much the same story that Shelley did.

"Elvis was never really *that* attracted to Marilyn," Nick claimed. "Not only was she an older woman, she wasn't really his type. He much preferred Ann-Margret."

"Then why did he keep seeing her?" Porter asked.

"It was an ego trip for him," Nick said. "At the time, she was the world's most beautiful and sexiest woman. And she probably found it thrilling to fuck with the man every other woman wanted. Hanging out together was a thrill for both of them. The sex was mere icing on the cake--not the cake itself."

After Elvis and Marilyn stopped dating, around 1960, and as a token of his gratitude, he bought her

Elvis read less than one percent of the fan mail he received, and **Marilyn** read even less. But the two of them liked to share some of their more outrageous letters with each other. Men throughout America sent Marilyn nudes of themselves, telling her in graphic detail just what they'd like to do with her in bed. And dozens of lesbians wrote, with similar requests.

Most of Elvis' mail – some ten thousand letters a week – came from young girls. Many of them wanted Elvis "to take my virginity," and most enclosed photos of themselves ready, willing, and eager to be deflowered. Some of them threatened suicide if Elvis didn't agree to meet them. The strangest letters came from distraught parents, who threatened to kill themselves if Elvis didn't "cool down his act."

"You're turning my girl evil!" was a typical comment among these parental letters.

"I don't see how I could be a threat to any parents' daughters. I'm just up there on that stage doing what comes naturally," Elvis said.

"Forget it," Marilyn told him. "You're doing fine. Just keep doing what you're doing. Speaking of doing what comes naturally, why don't you come over here and join me in bed and we'll let Mother Nature take her course?"

**Marilyn's** most memorable evening with **Elvis** – at least according to Shelley Winters – was when he danced "Jailhouse Rock" for her in the nude. "I giggled as I watched him flipping up and down. It was very funny and strangely erotic," Marilyn later confessed.

Sometimes Elvis didn't want sex at all with Marilyn, and told her, "I just want to cuddle." During some of these evenings, he would talk about his beloved mother, Gladys.

Marilyn confessed to Elvis that mental illness ran in her family and that her maternal great-grandfather, Tilford Hogan, hanged himself at the age of 82. Her maternal grandmother, Della, died in a mental asylum at the age of 51 – one year after Marilyn's birth. She also told Elvis that her grandmother tried to smother her before being shipped off to the mental ward. But it is unlikely that Marilyn could remember such an incident, since she would have been barely 13 months old. Elvis later confided to Nick Adams that "Marilyn fantasizes a lot about her past. Shit, man, she even told me that Clark Gable was her father."

a moon-shaped bed whose headboard was upholstered in "shocking pink" leather with scarlet-red sheets and accessories.

When a truck pulled up with the bed at Marilyn's bungalow, she refused to accept delivery. "Tell Mr. Elvis that I don't rock and I don't roll in a Valentine box," she told the deliverymen. "I would never sleep in a bed that would attract more attention than me. After all, I'm the star!"

## Marilyn died on August 5, 1962, and

**Elvis** was depressed about it for weeks. "I'm next," he told his cronies. "First Marilyn, then me. Me and her always talked a lot about it. We both knew we were going to die young. I don't know when my time is coming, but I know it's coming soon. I got a lot of people out there wanting to get me. My death will probably be faked to look like a suicide. But I bet they'll get me the way they got Marilyn."

Until the day he died, Elvis refused to believe that Marilyn's death was a suicide. "It was Robert Kennedy," he said. "That son of a bitch had Marilyn murdered. She knew too much. She was threatening to destroy the Kennedys, and she could have if she'd wanted to."

So incensed was he at Marilyn's death that Elvis hired two private detectives to prove that Robert Kennedy had flown to Los Angeles for "a final meeting" between Marilyn and himself. Allegedly, Marilyn had angrily told Peter Lawford, "I refuse to be treated like a piece of meat by either Bobby or Jack. I'm gonna make them pay for that." It was when Lawford informed Robert Kennedy of that threat that he allegedly flew to LA to deal with Marilyn.

Kennedy later claimed that at the time, he was at Gilroy, a ranch 300 miles northwest of Los Angeles. But Elvis said that his detectives discovered that the attorney general had secretly flown to Los Angeles only hours before Marilyn's untimely death.

According to Elvis, "By making that threat to that cocksucker Lawford, Marilyn sealed her doom."

## Elvis told Marilyn that the one thing he hated about

working in films was that he was always pursued by homosexuals. "I can't stand fags," he once told her. "And Hollywood's full of them. I'd run a hundred miles to get away from a fag."

"Now, now, Elvis," Marilyn cautioned, "We're both in show-business. A little tolerance is called for. Homosexuals are people too. God loves all his children."

Marilyn was well aware of Elvis' own involvement with Nick Adams. She knew Nick personally, and they shared many a conversation about Elvis.

In 1962, at the time of Marilyn's death, Elvis was filming *Fun in Acapulco*. In one scene, Elvis had to emerge from the sea being carried aloft by six men, in a sort of victory march. Elvis kept blowing the scene because he couldn't stop wiggling around. Finally he went to his Memphis Mafia and said, "Boys, there's a fag in that bunch. Every time they pick me up, one of them six guys grabs me by the balls."

During the next take, the assistant director, Mickey Moore, spotted the guy and fired him on the spot. "He just told this fag quietly that there were too many people in the scene," said Red West, one of Elvis' pals. "We, of course, near died laughing. Elvis wasn't as amused. He was very upset at being handled in a most intimate way by a fag."

## When Elvis confessed to Marilyn that he was always being pursued by homosexual gay men, she also claimed that she was often the object of desire from lesbian or bisexual women. She said that she had met the bisexual actress, **Marlene Dietrich** (above *right*), in New York on January 7, 1955.

.

She'd called a press conference to announce the formation of Marilyn Monroe Productions, Inc., with theatrical agent Milton Green. "I'm tired of sex roles," she told the press. "I want to do dramatic parts like *The Brothers Karamazov*."

"Do you want to play one of the brothers?" one of the reporters asked jokingly. Marilyn almost lost her temper. "No, I want to play Grushenka, the girl part."

After meeting Dietrich, Marilyn was invited to visit her apartment. "I stayed over," Marilyn confessed. "But lesbian sex is not my main thing. Although like most actresses in Hollywood, I have indulged. Marlene is very oral. She did her own thing down there, but I didn't reciprocate. In the morning, she made her famous scrambled eggs for me."

Elvis told her that he never objected to two lesbians getting it on. "In fact, I rather enjoy watching bitches going at each other."

## Marilyn sometimes confessed amusing tidbits about her life to Elvis. She claimed that at the Empire Theatre in London at a Royal Command Film Performance, she was introduced to **Queen Elizabeth II.**

"Let's face it, we're both Queens. She's the Queen of England and I'm the Queen of Hollywood. Before Her Majesty extended her hand to me, I caught her running her eyes up and down my figure and looking right at my breasts. Do you think she's a lesbian like Princess Margaret? Marlon Brando told me all about that one."

In the receiving line, Marilyn stood next to **Victor Mature** *(left of Marilyn)*. "He screwed the hell out of me," Marilyn claimed. "His dick's too big. He made me bleed. He wanted repeats. No way!"

# MARILYN & ELVIS

## Dead Stars of Yesterday
## Will "Live" Again

(From *Boomer Times'* Edition of February, 2017)

Elvis Presley and Marilyn Monroe always wanted to co-star in a movie, especially William Inge's *Bus Stop* (1956). Regrettably, Elvis' agent, Col. Tom Parker, objected, and consequently Marilyn shot the film with Don Murray as the lovesick rodeo cowboy instead.

However, within five years, it is highly likely that Marilyn and Elvis will finally get to team up and make a movie together, and Clark Gable and Vivien Leigh might bring back Rhett Butler and Scarlett O'Hara in a sequel to *Gone With the Wind*. And perhaps those ill-fated lovers of *Casablanca*, Humphrey Bogart and Ingrid Bergman, whose onscreen images parted from one another in 1942, will reunite in a sequel that brings them together at war's end in 1945.

"Impossible!" you say. "These stars have either been cremated or are in the ground!" But they (or at least their moving images) can live again as a new frontier of movie magic has already begun.

This new technology is best seen in *Rogue One: A Star Wars Story*, that 2016 space opera epic that has already grossed more than $1 billion. Peter Cushing, the English horror actor who died in 1994, is back on the screen again as General Moff Tarkin, one of Darth Vader's top officers.

Carrie Fisher died in December of 2016, but she reappears as a young Princess Leia in this latest release of the *Star Wars* franchise.

Although other attempts have been made to bring back the dead, *Rogue One* succeeds as no movie before. It's a product of technical wizards who have conquered one of the final visual effects frontier: The Human Face.

This miracle is possible as a result of "visual effects" (a term sometimes abbreviated by techies as "VFX"), a process where imagery is created and/or manipulated outside the live action shot. This technique involves the integration of live action footage and generated imagery to create an environment that looks realistic.

Cushing looks as he did in the first *Star Wars* in 1977. Critics found that his reappearance dazzles because it is seamless—not cheesy, pasted-in, or wooden—but a living, breathing, resurrected star. As one critic noted, "We always knew that movie stars were gods. Now they've become immortal, too."

In upcoming years, VFX wizards will be hell-bent on perfecting this technology, which already is stunning. The prospects are endless. James Dean and Audrey Hepburn interacting in a love story; Ava Gardner and John Wayne emoting together in a western.

Of course, the estates of these dead actors will have to approve, and they've proven themselves a greedy bunch. Many of today's heirs have never even met the stars generating millions for them. James Dean died with $3,000 in the bank and left no will, but his heirs are raking in millions by leasing his image for the manufacture of everything from T-shirts to coffee mugs.

VFX has already been employed when an actor died before completing his final scenes. Such was the case when the English actor, Oliver Reed, died in 1999 during the filming of *Gladiator* in Malta. His scenes had to be completed through the use of computer-generated imagery (CGI) and, in one instance, a studly-looking mannequin. A more advanced application of these techniques were used for the completion of the 2015 film, *Furious 7*, when actor Paul Walker died.

Technicians were able to shave 25 years off Brad Pitt's face for a brief sequence in *The Curious Case of Benjamin Button* (2008). It was the story of a man who ages in reverse, dying as an infant despite his chronological age of 84.

The possibilities associated with the upcoming decade are endless: Kirk Douglas, age 100 today, might play the son of his own son, Michael Douglas. What about Greta Garbo *("I want to be alone")* in a space adventure? Emma Stone dancing with Gene Kelly? Even Paul Newman teaming up for a bromance movie with Cary Grant?

The morality of bringing back the dead for mass entertainment has been questioned. A lot of Baby Boomers fear that their memories of these stars will be spoiled. *The Huffington Post* called it "a giant breech of respect for the dead." *The Guardian* admitted that although the technology works incredibly well, even now in its infancy, "It's still a digital indignity."

Many of today's actors don't like the technology or its associations. "It's hard enough getting an acting job today, with all the competition," complained an actress. "Now, I'll have to compete with Bette Davis and Joan Crawford."

There is, however, a brighter side. Off-screen lovers Tyrone Power and Lana Turner, at the height of their beauty and wrapped up in the intensity of their passion in the 1940s, wanted to co-star in a romance entitled *Forever*. Although their involvement in that wannabe deal fell apart during their heydays, it seems appropriate (and poignant) that the technology might be available to pull it off, post-mortem.

As they themselves might have defined it, it's an ethereal story about an eternal love longer than life and stronger than death.

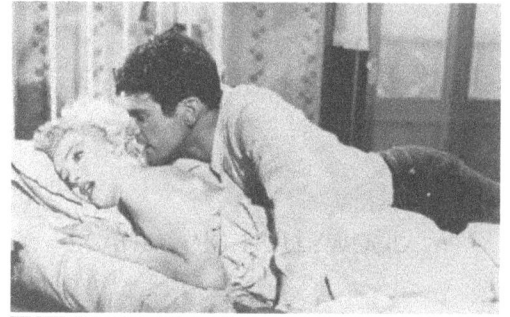

Shown above are **Marilyn Monroe** and **Don Murray,** horizontal and on a bed together, in a somewhat risqué publicity photo from **Bus Stop.**

But whereas censors in 1956 might have yelled "cut" at this point, one wonders about how whatever's happening might continue in computer-generated remakes and "reformattings" in more technically sophisticated years to come.

**Carrie Fisher** was alive when this replica of her image appeared in *Star Wars.*

But for animated sequences of her image in remakes and re-formattings of that blockbuster moneymaker, she won't necessarily have to be.

As a devoted friend and fan of **Joan Crawford,** Darwin Porter undertands the Insults and colossal indignities she suffered during her lifetime.

Post-mortem, a raft of new outrage remains to be inflicted upon her, digitally.

In 1947, this publicity photo was distributed to newspapers around the world as evidence of the enduring love between **Lana Turner** and **Tyrone Power.**

Perhaps with more sophisticated technologies, their celluloid lust saga might continue—at least electronically.

# Reflections on Post-Mortem Movie Stars
# CASHING IN FROM THE CRYPT

Financially speaking, certain famous entertainers are richer dead than alive. There is a good strategy for would-be immortals like Marilyn Monroe or James Dean: Live fast, die young, and leave your heirs the name and address of a tough licensing agent.

At the time of her suicide (or murder?), Monroe had been fired by 20th Century Fox. But in recent years her estate has generated $7 million in licensing fees as her image hawked everything from Levi's jeans to Nestlé after-dinner mints.

In death, Michael Jackson will be worth more than when he was alive and moon-walking. During his lifetime, he spent money like Louis XIV at the Court of Versailles. Flirting with bankruptcy, he purchased multi-million-dollar antiques and paid off little boys. Now that he's dead, his three kids in the years to come may inherit a vast fortune in royalties from their spendthrift dad.

For years, the estate of Elvis Presley was America's all-time money earner. From the grave, Elvis took in $42 million in 2009, $15 million of it generated by ticket sales to Graceland.

But, suddenly, "the king was toppled from his throne," the crown going to Kurt Cobain of the singing group, Nirvana. His heir, the controversial and drug-addled Courtney Love, took in an astonishing $50 million in 2008. Cobain committed suicide in 1994. The irony of this is that the singer hated commercials and advertising. His widow, Courtney, however, never met an ad agency she didn't like.

Just because you're dead doesn't mean you can't make a good living. Other members of the dear departed who are growing rich in a crypt include *Peanuts* creator Charles Schultz, former Beatle John Lennon, Jimi Hendrix, Bob Marley, Andy Warhol, author J.R.R. Tolkien, Frank Sinatra, Jerry Garcia, and James Dean.

A surprise on the list of celebrities growing rich from beyond the grave is Albert Einstein, who died in 1955 at the age of 76. Although he didn't really know how to make money during his lifetime, his estate developed the Midas touch after he died. His estate took in $20 million in 2008 alone. Corbis, the licensing giant, says its most requested image is Einstein's wild-haired visage. Disney pays an annual fortune to replicate images of the genius in its "Baby Einstein" line.

Sometimes, heirs didn't even know their benefactor. Such was the case with

Nineteenth-century grave robbers (ghouls) at a cemetery, perhaps near Baltimore, at the time (because of its many medical schools) the center of North America's grave-robbing cult.

In the U.S., there weren't many laws granting unclaimed bodies to medical schools. The act of donating a body to science was rare, and the supply of corpses to dissect was limited.

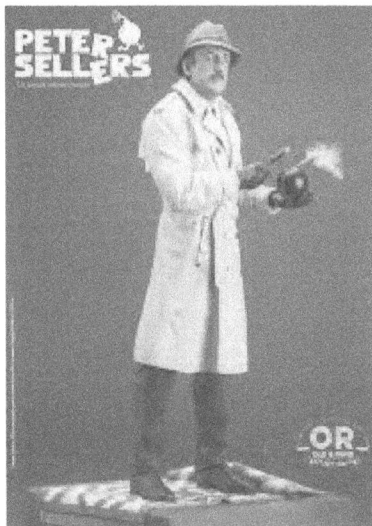

**FOR SALE**: Post-mortem effigies of **Peter Sellers**, whose bizarre estate settlement made news worldwide, especially in the U.K.

There are LOTS of ways to "worship" **Elvis**, and zillions of bizarre photos that illustrate the fiscal value of his post-mortem legacy.

Here, he's at the White House, bonding with then-president **Richard Nixon**. Who laughed last?

Casey Unger, a college student attending UCLA in California. She's hauling in millions from the estate of Peter Sellers, including residual rights from his records and films.

Shortly before he died, the star who played Inspector Clouseau in the original "Pink Panther" films was in the process of disinheriting his former wife, the minor British actress Lynne Frederick. But in 1980, he suffered a sudden heart attack and died before the legal papers could be drawn up and finalized.

Frederick inherited the estate over the protests of Sellers' three children, then rushed into a very short marriage to broadcaster David Frost. After divorcing him, she had another short marriage to California heart specialist Dr. Barry Unger, which ended in divorce but produced Casey Unger.

Addicted to cocaine and booze, the once beautiful Frederick, by then weighing 250 pounds, died in 1994, leaving the Sellers' fortune to her daughter with Unger. Casey had been born four years after Sellers died, and it is rumored that she's never seen any of her benefactor's movies.

Licensing laws are complicated and vary from state to state. California protects the images of its deceased citizens for 70 years, New York only if they are alive. The most generous state is Tennessee, the former abode of Elvis. In theory, the singer's heirs are granted protection for two centuries. Can you imagine some little Elvis 200 years from now hauling in the loot from "Hound Dog?"

Of course. not all celebrities generate money upon death. A spokesperson for CMG Worldwide, whose first client was the estate of Elvis, said that only "icons" are in demand. For most stars, no one wants them. But certain legends like Humphrey Bogart, who died in 1957, are venerated by future generations. The heirs of Bogie clean up by having him promote such stunts as touting Diet Coke, a drink unknown to him during his lifetime.

As technology progresses, the stars of the Golden Age may make comebacks in digitized images. For example, the film, *Sky Captain and the World of Tomorrow* (2004), featured digitized images of Lord Laurence Olivier.

"I don't think it'll ever happen" said an industry spokesman, "but 50 years from now you might see a young James Dean and a young Marlon Brando starring as cowboy lovers in a remake of *Brokeback Mountain*. Tomorrow's movie world holds infinite possibilities. Just because the platinum blonde, Jean Harlow, died in 1937 doesn't mean that she—or her image—won't be making movies in the next millennium."

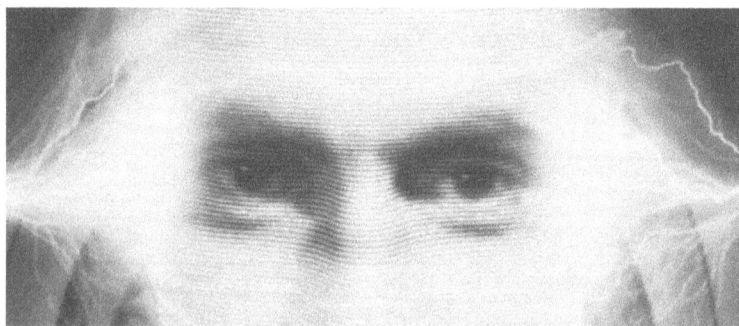

**Postmortem Michael**

**BOGART:** He suffered through a career in Hollywood, four difficult marriages, and cancer of the esophagus, but thanks to new technologies, **HE'S ALIVE** and hawking a non-alchoholic beverage! *(Who knew?)*

In this detail from a 1992 filmclip ad for Diet Coke, an effigy of **Humphrey Bogart** seems to have been culled directly from *Casablanca* (1942), but the beautiful woman on the right is **NOT Ingrid Bergman.** But thanks to the inter-generational magic of digitalization, the joint is jumpin' and EVERYBODY seems to be having a merry good time.

An effigy of **Dooley Wilson** (aka **"Sam"**) and live images from **Elton John** figured into the ad's narrative, too.

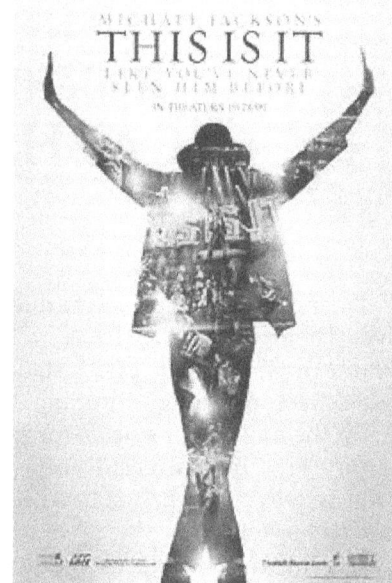

Who (post mortem) played a key symbolic role in the charming British sci-fi flick, *Sky Captain & the World of Tomorrow* (2004)? It's a digitalized replica of **LORD LAURENCE OLIVER**, gamely resurrected as **Dr. Todtenkopf.**

# FANS VOTE ON WHO THEY MOST WANT
# RESURRECTED FROM THE GRAVE

FROM *BOOMER TIMES* EDITION OF SEPTEMBER 2013

Today, it's easy to conduct a poll on just about anything. Take the bizarre, rather morbid poll just made by *60 Minutes* and the magazine *Vanity Fair*.

Poll respondents were asked, "Which dead celebrity would you want to bring back to life?"

Just so that Marilyn, Elvis, and JFK would not dominate the list, only celebrities who died between 1994 and today were included in the vote. Of the top seven, four were drug addicts.

Diana, the 36-year-old Princess of Wales, topped the list, garnering 35 percent of the vote. She died on August 31, 1997 in a car crash in a Paris tunnel, with carloads of paparazzi in hot pursuit.

First runner-up was Apple founder Steve Jobs (14 percent). The next four celebs on the list were drug addicts—Michael Jackson and Whitney Houston (tied at 11 percent each); actor Heath Ledger (9 percent); and grunge rocker Kurt Cobain (6 percent). The recently deceased star of *Sopranos*, James Gandolfini, landed at the bottom of the list at an unimpressive 3 percent.

Speculation about the death of Princess Di reached an alltime high this year. She's making headlines around the world, especially in Britain, where Scotland Yard reportedly has reopened an investigation into her untimely death.

After the car crash, she lived only a short time, dying in a hospital. But her boyfriend, Dodi Fayed, and the drunken driver of their Mercedes-Benz, Henri Paul, were pronounced dead at the scene. Di's bodyguard, Trevor Rees-Jones, survived, but had no memory of what happened.

Dodi's father, billionaire Mohamed al-Fayed, still claims that Di and his son were murdered. Most of the accounts point a finger at a former soldier, a member of an elite unit in the British military, along with two accomplices. The soldier is said to have flashed a light into the face of the driver, blinding him. Today, the soldier is said to be hiding out in Croatia on a forged passport. Obviously, if this is true, he was acting on orders from a higher authority. Speculation has even pointed to a member (or members) of the royal circle, but so far, no smoking gun has emerged.

The most serious accusations have been toward ruthless arms dealers who make millions selling weapons to terrorists and corrupt governments. Di's campaign against land mines, or so it is reported, made her a prime target.

Steve Jobs, the charismatic pioneer of the personal computer revolution, died on October 5, 2011, age 56, of complications from pancreatic cancer. He'd undergone a liver transplant in 2009.

Prior to its release, the movie *Jobs,* starring Ashton Kutcher, was envisioned as a hit, but failed at the box office. Critics claimed that the film did not navigate the passions, perfectionism, demons, desires, artistry, devilry, and obsessions of its subject. In a mock turtleneck and "mom jeans," Kutcher struggled valiantly in the role, but millions of Steve Jobs fans stayed away.

Detail from **Piero della Francesca**'s fresco, *The Resurrection,* c. 1463-65, from the Museo Civico, Sansepolcro, Italy

Once the most "watched' celebrities in the world: **Jack and Jackie Kennedy**.

Always headliners, dead or alive: **Diana & Dodi.**

**Steve Jobs** introducing the iPhone 4 in 2010

13

Since his death on June 25, 2005, Michael Jackson, age 50, never left the headlines. As he prepared for his comeback concert series, *This Is It,* the singer died of acute propofol intoxication after suffering cardiac arrest. The Los Angeles County Coroner ruled the death a homicide.

Jackson's personal physician, Conrad Murray, was convicted of involuntary manslaughter and was sentenced to four years in prison. He is scheduled for release this month (October, 2013).

Jackson continued to make headlines all summer, as his estate sued concert promoter AEG for billions, claiming that they failed to properly investigate the doctor and his record. AEG officials denied ever hiring him, maintaining it was Jackson himself who employed Murray.

Tied with Jackson by fans hoping for a "resurrection" was Whitney Houston, who died, age 48, on February 11, 2012. The most awarded singing star of all time, Houston was found unconscious and submerged in her bathtub at the Beverly Hilton Hotel. Before getting into the water, she'd consumed large amounts of cocaine.

An Australian, actor Heath Ledger, died in New York City, age 28, on January 22, 2008 from accidental intoxication from prescription drugs. He had just finished interpreting the role of "The Joker" in *The Dark Knight,* which became the biggest-grossing film of the year. Most of his millions went to his daughter, Matilda Rose Ledger, born to the actor's girlfriend, actress Michelle Williams, who had starred with him in the 2005 *Brokeback Mountain.*

Kurt Cobain, the lead singer of the American grunge band, *Nirvana,* was found dead at his home on April 8, 1994, apparently having committed suicide three days prior. A persistent drug addict, he may have shot himself with his own gun. But speculation continues to this day that he was murdered. His wife, singer Courtney Love, hired private detectives, but the issues associated with his death have never been resolved.

New Jersey born James Gandolfini scored a big hit as the troubled crime boss, Tony Soprano, on the TV series *The Sopranos.* In Rome, he was discovered on the bathroom floor of his hotel suite by his 13-year-old son, Michael. He was pronounced dead within 20 minutes of his arrival at a local hospital. Michael inherited the bulk of his father's $70 million estate.

\*\*\*

Groundbreaking co-star of *Brokeback Mountain,* **Heath Ledger**

The late "Grunge Rock" megastar **Kurt Cobain** and his publicity-addicted wife and heir to his enormous estate, **Courtney Love,** as they appeared in **Nick Broomfield's** devastating 1998 documentary.

**Whitney Houston**

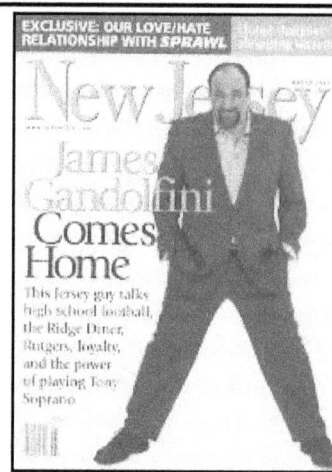

In 2021, two years after his death, a group of **Michael Jackson fans** compiled some of his unreleased soundtracks and marketed them as, GUESS WHAT? *RESURRECTION.*

Loosely linked to tracks that, had he lived, might have been part of his 11th studio album, and plagued with copyright problems, *Resurrection* remains one of the music industry's most hotly litigated celebrations of a dead artist's *oeuvre.*

Jersey's (and *The Sopranos)* Finest: **James Gandolfini**

14

# WHO PANTY-RAIDED MARILYN?

## A PARTIAL LIST OF HER LOVERS

Milton Berle
Marlon Brando
Yul Brynner
Yves Montand
Oleg Cassini
Paddy Cheyefsky
Harry B. Cohn
Tony Curtis
Rock Hudson
Sammy Davis Jr.
Blake Edwards
Alfred Einstein
Howard Hughes
George Jessel
John Houston
Anton LaVey
James Dean
Peter Lawford
Johnny Roselli
Joe DiMaggio Jr.
Shelley Winters
Joan Crawford
Barbara Stanwyck
Keith Andes
Darryl Zanuck
Walter Winchell
Johnny Hyde

Franchot Tone
Bugsy Siegel
Porfirio Rubirosa
Elia Kazan
Robert Mitchum
Glenn Ford
Guy Madison
Rory Calhoun
Ronald Reagan
Mickey Rooney
Clifford Odets
Frank Sinatra
Sam Spiegel
George Sanders
Mel Torme
Orson Welles
Nicholas Ray
Fred Karger
William Holden
Jose Bolanos
Joe Schenck
James Bacon
Damon Runyon
Natasha Lytess
Don Murray
Clark Gable

***

# THE MM "MURDER HOUSE" IS SOLD

### THIS FIRST APPEARED IN *BOOMER TIMES* IN AUGUST 2010

**Marilyn's "death house"** at 12305 Fifth Helena Drive in Brentwood.

A notorious parcel of Los Angeles real estate has gone on the block, with an asking price of $3,595,000. The hacienda-style *casa* sits in the Brentwood area of Los Angeles at 12305 Fifth Helena Drive. Arguably, no other house in Hollywood has been the subject of so many rumors and conspiracy theories.

The voluptuous and legendary Marilyn Monroe, age 36, was either murdered in this home on August 5, 1962, or else died from an alleged drug overdose. In recent years, the murder theory seems to have prevailed.

Late in 1961, Marilyn and her housekeeper, Eunice Murray, discovered this house at the tail end of an isolated cul-de-sac, shut off from the world. Marilyn fell in love with the property, and purchased it for $90,000 in March of 1962, less than six months prior to her death.

Strapped for cash, she took out a mortgage, making monthly payments of $320 a month. Built in 1929, the house had three bedrooms and a kidney-shaped pool out in the backyard, ideal for nude swims. This was the only house that Marilyn ever owned. Shortly after its purchase, she flew to Mexico to purchase art and furnishings for her new home.

Her sojourn in this house was brief. The probate of her estate didn't come to an end until the autumn of 1963. At that time, the Nuñez family purchased the property and its contents, including Marilyn's Hoover vacuum cleaner.

Apparently, they were unhappy with the house, which attracted too many ghoulish sightseers. After the Nuñez family left, ownership or occupancy of the property over the decades is murky, with contradictory reports as to just who was living there.

Actress Veronica Hamel (*Hill Street Blues, Lost*), and her husband Michael Irving moved in in 1972. They hired a contractor to replace the roof and remodel. While ripping off the roof, they discovered a sophisticated eavesdropping and telephone tapping system that blanketed every room in the house.

This technologically sophisticated apparatus was not commercially available at the time of Marilyn's death. Such equipment , however, was in use at the time by the F.B.I., suggesting that J. Edgar Hoover might have ordered the bugging.

One reason Hoover might have wanted to tape Marilyn involved the accumulation of blackmail evidence on her lovers, President John F. Kennedy and his brother, Robert Kennedy, the U.S. attorney general. Bobby wanted to fire Hoover, and those F.B.I. tapes could have been used by Hoover as blackmail to keep his job.

In the wake of Marilyn's death, virtually everyone linked to her last days, regardless of how remotely, lied about the circumstances of her death. Call it mass hysteria….or whatever.

Of course, some people had reason to lie—take Bobby Kennedy, for example. He claimed that he wasn't even in Los Angeles on the day Marilyn died, despite overwhelming evidence to the contrary.

Over a period of several years, housekeeper Eunice Murray gave three different versions of what happened that night. Evidence now suggests that each of her tall tales were just that. Right before her death on March 5, 1994, Murray admitted that she'd been part of a cover-up, but failed to name who had ordered and no doubt paid her to keep her mouth shut.

Whoever buys MM's house may also inherit an unlikely tenant. Many of the occupants of the house at Fifth Helena Drive have claimed that late at night, they've seen the ghost of Marilyn swimming in her backyard pool—nude, of course.

As of this writing, the house is occupied by Jasmine Chiswell, an Internet-famous Marilyn Monroe impersonator with more than 16 million followers on Tik Tok.

After a major-league bidding war, the house was sold to her for $2.7 million in February of 2019. Jasmine and her husband, Maverick McNeilly, are said to evoke Marilyn and JoeDiMaggio, her second husband, who lived with her in this house for less than a year before their messy divorce.

**BOOK NEWS for Immediate Release**

Blood Moon proudly announces the immediate availability of a revised new edition of its widely reviewed, award-winning classic about the murder of Marilyn Monroe.

As stated by its publisher, Danforth Prince, "This is an improved version of the most successful and notorious book we ever published. Intensely controversial, it's the personal statement of a devoted and deeply respected Marilyn expert whom the media defined after its publication as "The Master of Guilty Pleasures, the Proust of Pop Culture, and the Goethe of Gossip," Darwin Porter."

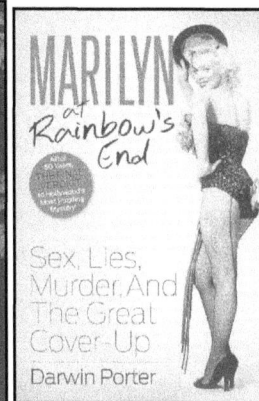

"We were awakened to the fact that original, first-edition copies of this "hysterically controversial" classic were selling as collectors' oddities for three or four times their original retail price. And despite the passage of time (the suppresion of evidence associated with her murder began almost 60 years ago), her associations with The Kennedys and the Mob are still hot and still shocking. Perhaps as a distraction from more recent scandals associated with Covid and election politics, we wanted new generations of classic movie fans to realize, perhaps for the first time, just how murky "the swamp" associated with her death really is."

WHERE TO GET IT, WHERE TO FIND IT: It's available NOW online through Amazon.com and other internet purveyors worldwide.

WHAT DID REVIEWERS SAY ABOUT THIS TITLE WHEN IT FIRST HIT THE TABLOIDS BACK IN 2012?
Some of their reviews appear on the second page of this press announcement.

## MARILYN: DON'T EVEN DREAM ABOUT TOMORROW
### SEX, LIES, HER MURDER, & THE GREAT COVER-UP

BY DARWIN PORTER
BIOGRAPHY/ENTERTAINMENT & PERFORMING ARTS
AVAILABLE EVERYWHERE, WORLDWIDE, NOW ON INTERNET SITES THAT INCLUDE AMAZON.COM AND INGRAM LIGHTNING SOURCE
SOFTCOVER, 474 PAGES, WITH ABOUT 100 PHOTOS. 6x9, $32.99    ISBN 978-1-936003-79.2
For more information, contact DanforthPrince@BloodMoonProductions.com

Or click on the "OUR BOOKS" tab of
BloodMoonProductions.com

# Here's What Critics and Media Reviewers Said About Blood Moon's Investigation of Marilyn Monroe's Murder

*"With scrupulous research, Darwin Porter pretty much sums up the underside of American entertainment, political and criminal activities during the mid-twentieth-century. He does not paint a pretty sight, but Porter does present, with scathing honesty, the Monroe death's lies and cover-ups, stopping just short of JFK and RFK. And for those who still believe that lone gunmen were responsible for the deaths of the Kennedy Brothers, is that the sound of sleigh bells on the roof?*

*"It's been said that he deals in muck because he can't libel the dead. Well, it's about time someone started telling the truth about the dead and being honest about just what happened to get us in the mess in which we're in. If libel is lying, then Porter is so completely innocent as to deserve an award.*

*"In all of his works he speaks only to the truth, and although he is a hard teacher and task master, he's one we ignore at our peril. To quote Gore Vidal, 'power is not a toy we give to someone for being good.' If we all don't begin to investigate where power and money really are in the here and now, we deserve what we get. Yes, Porter names names. The reader will come away from the book knowing just who killed Monroe. Porter rather brilliantly points to a number of motives but leaves it to the reader to surmise exactly what happened at the rainbow's end, just why Marilyn was killed. And, of course, why we should be careful of getting exactly what we want. It's a very long tumble from the top."*

**—Alan Petrucelli, Examiner.com**

\*\*\*

*"This is the best book about Marilyn Monroe ever published."*

**—David Hartnell, New Zealand's Resident Expert on Hollywood Lore,
Recipient, in 2012, of New Zealand's Order of Merit (MNZM) for services to the entertainment
industry as defined by Her Majesty, Queen Elizabeth II**

\*\*\*

*"I like to think that if Sinatra were still alive, he'd be taking a swing at both Darwin and Danforth for spilling so many juicy, juicy secrets! I love the Porter/Prince books. They are the biographies I dreamed about as a child."*
**—Paul Bellini, *FAB Magazine*, Toronto**

\*\*\*

*"With this sizzling book, Blood Moon scores again."*
**—Richard LaBonté, *Books to Watch Out For***

\*\*\*

*"Porter's book concludes with an account of Marilyn's death that would certainly have gotten the author a pair of cement over-shoes or a bullet in the head, had he published it 30 years ago. Marilyn played with some very, very dangerous people and in the end, she paid a high price for it—but what a ride she had!"*
**—Tobias Grace, Editor Emeritus, *Out in Jersey* Magazine**

# MARILYN MONROE
# *vs.* THE KENNEDYS

## SOME LIKE IT HOTTER

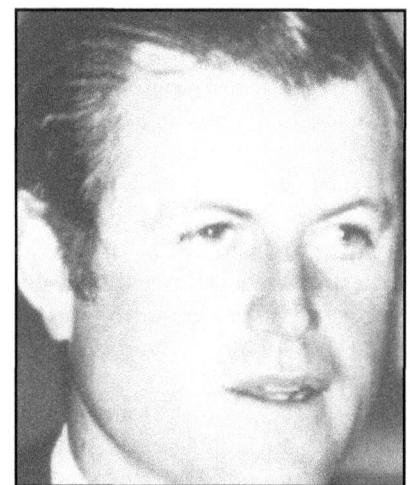

**Marilyn Monroe** made the rounds, going through all the Kennedy men, beginning with **Jack Kennedy** *(upper left)* in 1946. When she met Senator Kennedy years later at a Hollywood party, he didn't remember deflowering **Norma Jean Baker.** But, in fairness to the senator, in 1946 she didn't look like the woman who had turned herself into Marilyn Monroe. She was also accompanied by her husband, Joe DiMaggio. "Joe and Jack were like roosters when they came together," Marilyn later recalled.

Sometimes Sammy Davis Jr. served as "the black beard," escorting Marilyn to a party at the home of Peter Lawford, though she later disappeared with Jack. When **Joe Kennedy** *(lower left photo)* first seduced Marilyn, she was so little known she was referred to as "a minor starlet." When his son was running for president, Marilyn told Joe, "It would be nice to have a president who looks so young and good looking."

John Miner, an associate clinical professor at the University of Southern California Medical School, heard the tapes recorded for Marilyn's psychiatrist, Dr. Ralph Greenson. Miner later claimed, "Marilyn was very explicit about the sexual relationship she had with both **Jack and Robert**." It wasn't until 2010 that her relationship with **Teddy Kennedy** *(lower right)* was revealed in F.B.I. reports.

# THE SAD SAGA OF MM
# & THE KENNEDY MENFOLK

*"Happy Birthday…Mr. Pres…i…dent,*
*Happy Birthday…to you."*

—*Marilyn Monroe, onstage at Madison Square*
*Garden in New York City, May 19, 1962*

**The Kennedy brothers** *(left to right)* **Bobby, Teddy,** and **JFK**—often passed women around, including Marilyn Monroe. Many of these same women were also enjoyed by **Joe Kennedy** *(center inset photo).*

As president of the United States and attorney general, both Jack and Bobby were vulnerable to scandal, and each of them became duly alarmed when an out-of-control Marilyn threatened to destroy their political dynasty.

To remove her from the scene, both men urged her to remarry Joe DiMaggio. But Marilyn told the Kennedys that she could never do that. "As a husband he is too possessive. He is capable of physical violence."

Marilyn entertained fantasies of marrying either Jack or Bobby, but not Teddy. "He's just a plaything for me," she told Jeanne Carmen. "I call him my overgrown Teddy Bear." Joe feared scandal and was planning to buy Marilyn off. But before he could do so, he suffered a devastating stroke.

**According to dozens of biographies**, Marilyn Monroe met Senator John F. Kennedy at a party in 1954 at the home of agent and producer Charles Feldman. She was there with her husband, Joe DiMaggio.

"Don't we know each other?" Marilyn asked JFK in front of DiMaggio.

JFK said, "Surely not. If I ever met you before, you'd be unforgettable."

By then, DiMaggio was fuming. After he'd had a few drinks and had to go to Feldman's ground floor bathroom, Marilyn slipped JFK her private phone number. She whispered in his ear, "It was at Robert Stack's place." Suddenly he remembered her. "But you were so different then."

"Norma Jean Baker has become Marilyn Monroe."

Stack had guided a pre-war Jack Kennedy through a galaxy of Hollywood stars in 1940. When JFK returned from the Navy, Stack also arranged a number of introductions to young starlets. Stack had never liked Marilyn; his animosity began on their first date. He'd arrived to take her to a dinner party, and she kept him waiting one and a half hours while she decided what gown to wear from her meager selection. When they finally arrived at the party, the other guests had already eaten.

Ultimately, Stack remembered his sexual tryst with Marilyn as unsatisfactory, claiming "there was just no chemistry between us." But when Jack spotted her picture in a portfolio of photographs, he wanted to have a chance at her. Stack warned him about her shortcomings, but Jack was persistent, and eventually, an evening rendezvous was arranged between Jack and Marilyn.

That night in Stack's apartment, Jack seduced Marilyn for the first time. He apparently told no one, not even Stack, his reaction to the experience. Marilyn later claimed she gave him her phone number back then, but he never called. When he met up with her again, in 1954, he could hardly imagine that she'd be the biggest star in Hollywood.

Of course, even at that point, Jack had had sexual experiences with so many women, often for such brief periods, that he could hardly be expected to remember all of them, even Marilyn. In fairness, Marilyn in 1946 hardly resembled the Marilyn he encountered in 1954, during his stint as one of the senators from Massachusetts, at Feldman's party.

She tried to explain to him. "When you met me after the war, I wasn't Marilyn Monroe yet."

At Feldman's party, he told her that he'd call her as soon as he had a "little work done on my back—an old sports injury." That made him sound more athletic than he really was.

The day after her reunion with Jack, Marilyn informed her best friend, Jeanne Carmen, "That Jack Kennedy couldn't take his eyes off me." Before he returned to the East Coast and the hospital, he was eager to see Marilyn and impetuously telephoned her at the home she was sharing with then-husband, Joe DiMaggio.

The first time he called, DiMaggio picked up the phone. Hearing a man's voice he did not recognize, DiMaggio asked, "Who's this?"

"A friend," JFK said.

DiMaggio slammed down the phone.

After his return to the East, during Jack's post-surgical stint in the hospital, several visitors noted a pinup poster of Marilyn wearing tight-fitting blue shorts, with her legs spread apart. JFK had hung the poster upside down, thereby making it more suggestive.

Arthur James, who had known Marilyn during the early 1950s, was a witness to the blossoming of the Monroe/Kennedy affair. He told all to biographer Anthony Summers, author of *Goddess, The Secret Life of Marilyn Monroe*.

James associated the JFK/MM sexual liaison with the final months of her crumbling marriage to DiMaggio. According to James, their favorite watering hole was the raunchy Malibu Cottage; a battered bar and grill with fewer than a dozen stools, sawdust on the floor, and a handful of rentable bedrooms. "Kennedy wasn't known on the West Coast then, and he and Marilyn were very open. They also used rooms at the Holiday House Motel in Malibu." The two lovers were also seen coming and going from the Chateau Marmont on Sunset Boulevard.

Marilyn once told the columnist, James Bacon, with whom she'd had a brief fling, that "Jack won't indulge in foreplay because he's on the run all the time."

Henry Rosenfeld, MM's New York confidant, said Marilyn not only saw JFK at an apartment of a friend on 53rd Street near Third Avenue in New York, but also visited him at the Mayflower Hotel near the White House in Washington, DC. Rosenfeld was almost certain that she was never smuggled into the White House in disguise.

When Robert Kennedy was Attorney General in the 1960s, Marilyn and JFK used the bedroom above his office at the Justice Department for their sexual trysts. Often, when working late, Bobby himself slept there, too tired to drive back to his home in Virginia, Hickory Hill.

During the course of the MM/JFK affair, the lovers rendezvoused every time Jack flew to Los Angeles. The affair was usually conducted at the beachfront home of Patricia Kennedy and Peter Lawford.

"Pat knew all about what was going on," said Frank Sinatra. "She knows her brother wasn't a saint. Neither was Pat. I even made it with her when she was married to Peter." He told that to Joey Bishop, Judy Garland, and Sammy Davis Jr.

Peter Summers, a senior Kennedy aide, said that once, he had to locate Jack because of some sort of emergency, and he saw Marilyn and him emerging dripping wet from the shower together. "They didn't seem in the least embarrassed."

Dean Martin and "some floozie" [his words] had reported seeing Jack and Marilyn walking hand in hand on the beach in the early evening.

Jeanne Carmen told a red-hot story to the tabloid newspaper, the *Globe*, which

**MARILYN WEDS JOE DiMAGGIO**

When **Joe DiMaggio** married **Marilyn Monroe** in 1954, the headlines they generated were bigger than anything he ever inspired during his sports career.

Their marriage lasted only nine months. Tabloids at the time suggested that a fleshy publicity stunt for the promotion of *The Seven Year Itch* led to the dissolution of their marriage

Neither of them ever fully recovered. Neither did his fans.

Marilyn's emotionally desperate phone calls to **Bobby Kennedy** at **The Justice Department** *(depicted above)* and her equivalently indiscreet phone calls to **Jack** at **The White House** raised eyebrows and contributed to the brothers' conclusion that she was, for them, at least, "the most dangerous woman in America."

Since anyone could remember, the Kennedy patriarch, Papa Joe, had dabbled in show-biz financing, and cultivated sexual affairs with movie stars who had included both Gloria Swanson and the then-*ingénue* Marilyn Monroe.

But the family's links to Hollywood grew even stronger (some said more sinister) through the marriage of then 29-year-old **Patricia Kennedy** (left) to **Peter Lawford** *(center)*.

The photo above shows Patricia, sheathed in *couture* white satin, with her new Hollywood husband and his mother, the imperiously malevolent British socialite **Lady Lawford**, at NYC's Plaza Hotel on April 24, 1954. Lawford is credited for introducing (and pimping) Marilyn to the Kennedy brothers, especially Jack.

21

ran a four-part series called *True Confessions of a Hollywood Party Girl.*

In the series, Carmen recalled a wild pool party at Peter Lawford's house to celebrate JFK's nomination in 1960. Both Carmen and Marilyn were invited to the party.

Carmen claimed that after a swim, she retreated to a back bedroom within the Lawford home to take a shower. MM, she said, knocked on her door and told her that the Democratic presidential nominee wanted a three-way.

At first Carmen turned down the offer, telling MM, "I don't do that."

But Monroe pleaded with her, claiming "We can think of it as doing something for our country." Finally she told Carmen that she'd have to reject JFK herself, up close and personal. Accordingly, Carmen went into another of the house's bedrooms, finding Jack in his underwear.

A master seducer, he began to massage her shoulders. He whispered that MM and herself should think of themselves "as pioneers on The New Frontier of the 1960s."

Carmen admitted that finally she gave in—"overwhelmed by Jack's extraordinary charms, good looks, and a buzz from the alcohol I'd consumed at Peter's party."

As she looked up after JFK had tongue kissed her, she saw Marilyn dropping her towel and moving toward the bed.

\*\*\*

After Marilyn's divorce from DiMaggio early in 1955, she took a small apartment in New York. Once installed in Manhattan, she had a rendezvous with JFK in his duplex penthouse suite at the swanky Hotel Carlyle.

Her friend, Henry Rosenfeld, said that Marilyn was as excited as a teenager to be having an affair with the handsome senator. "He told me he's going to become President of the United States one day," Marilyn said, breathlessly.

After a session with JFK at the Carlyle, Marilyn confided to columnist Earl Wilson, "I think I made his back feel better—but don't print that."

Before leaving that night, she said, "Earl, you're a dear. Take a good look at me. You're looking at the future First Lady of the United States."

"But what about Jackie?" Wilson asked.

"He'll divorce that old bag," she said. "I heard it from Jack himself that she won't do all of the things I'll do. She's too much of a lady, I guess."

Because of his bad back, JFK liked to have sex with a woman on top of him. Lem Billings told biographer Lawrence J. Quirk that "Jack had claimed that Marilyn gave great head—hers was a true labor of love."

Marilyn confided to her friend, Helen Ferguson, that Joe DiMaggio didn't think of me "as another notch on his belt like Jack Kennedy. But he is a square—strictly missionary position, macho Italian athlete." The star confessed to Ferguson that fellatio was her favorite sexual position. But she claimed that "Joe didn't like to be fellated." She admitted, however, that JFK "loved me to do that to him."

Launched into an affair with Marilyn, then the hottest thing on celluloid, Jack placed a call to his father, Joseph P. Kennedy, in Palm Beach to tell him the latest news.

Joe had constantly bragged to his son that he had "bagged" Marilyn around 1950. He claimed he'd seduced her one night at the Chateau Marmont, and that

Showgirl and pinup queen, **Jeanne Carmen**, appears *above left* with **Elvis Presley** as a "squaw' maiden" at a Halloween party in LA in 1957, and *above right* in a publicity photo for *Portland Expose* (1957) She was also Marilyn's best friend and confidante during her involvements with the Kennedys.

Carmen recalled the night she drove with Marilyn to meet JFK:

Marilyn was gushing over the presidential candidate. "I just know he's going to be the next president," Marilyn told Carmen. "Wouldn't it be funny if we got married and I became the First Lady?"

Carmen warned MM that Jack was already married. "So what?" Marilyn answered. "So was Arthur Miller. But that didn't stop me. If they want you bad enough, they'll do whatever it takes to get you."

In her first "breakout" role (1950) **Marilyn** cultivated the look that would attract the roving eye of the lusty Kennedy patriarch, **Joseph**. His son, John, had seduced the blonde goddess when she was known as Norma Jeane.

later she'd accepted an off-the-record weekend invitation to go with him to Palm Springs, where they stayed in a private villa.

Marilyn was desperately looking for a father figure, and after a weekend with Joe Sr. she referred to him as "Daddy."

"You didn't get to her first," Jack told his father, according to Jack's closest friend, Lem Billings. "I got to her first. While I was staying with Robert Stack, she was one of the girls I fucked." Joe reportedly was furious, because he often played a one-upmanship game with his son as to which of the Kennedys could seduce a woman first. Seductions that followed were graphically referred to as "sloppy seconds."

Director John Huston had introduced Joe to Marilyn on the set of *The Asphalt Jungle* (1950), a film in which the budding starlet had a minor role.

Huston later capitalized off his friendship with Joe Kennedy. In Richard Condon's *Winter Kills*, a thinly disguised story about the Kennedy assassination, Huston played the role of the patriarch, who is the villain who orders his son's assassination.

Photo *above, left*, shows **Joseph Kennedy Sr.** flanked by his wife and some of his children in London in 1938 after his appointment by FDR as Ambassador to the Court of St. James's. Although it ended disastrously (he was recalled for what seemed like attempts to appease the Nazis), it was, at the time, one of the resounding social triumphs of the Kenneday clan's pre-presidential history.

About a decade before, Kennedy, *pere,* had maintained a romantic and business dalliance with **Gloria Swanson** *(right photo)*, one of the most imperious divas of filmdon's silent era. Years after it ended, Swanson maintained to anyone who would listen that her business arrangements with Kennedy marked the beginnings of her financial ruin.

Jeff Bridges played Nick Kegan, a Bobby Kennedy-like character, brother of an assassinated U.S. President. John Huston, cast as "Pa Kegan," admitted to co-star Anthony Perkins that he based his characterization on Joe Kennedy himself—"a friend from yesterday, but not that much of a friend."

The part was originally offered to Frank Sinatra, but he rejected it because he didn't want to appear in any film that libeled the Kennedy family, even though his own relationships with many of them had been strained.

Huston also directed Marilyn in her last picture, *The Misfits* (1961), in which she co-starred with her childhood idol, Clark Gable, and her emotionally disturbed friend, Montgomery Clift. The director prophesized that within two years, "Marilyn, bless her, will be either stark bonkers or else at Forest Lawn."

Several people have suggested that during his pursuit of Marilyn, Jack was, in essence, following in the footsteps of his father. Joe Sr. had conquered Gloria Swanson when she was the reigning screen vamp of the silent screen, although she was about to lose her crown at the time. In contrast, Jack pursued Marilyn at the time when she was the most talked about movie star in the world.

In 1938, when Jack was twenty-one years old, he had entered the hospital to be circumcised because of a tight foreskin. Lem was away but writing letters to him. Jack later chastised him for taking undue interest in his circumcision. Years later, Lem told Quirk that "When you're circumcised at a much later age like that, you think of it as a kind of castration, a threat to manhood, so you have to keep on proving 'it' is okay by any means possible."

"Jack kept proving that 'it' was okay with Marilyn time and time again," Lem claimed.

When JFK became president, Marilyn was thrilled, telling Jeanne Carmen that he was going to divorce Jackie and marry her.

Here's young **JFK** with one of his best friends, **Lem Billings**, a prep school chum who discreetly self-defined as a homosexual. He evolved into a politically savvy and ferociously loyal enabler during JFK's rise to the presidency.

It was Lem who shuffled JFK through crisis after crises, de-fusing many of his sexual indiscretions with women who included Marilyn Monroe.

"That would be political suicide," Carmen cautioned her. "Surely by now, you know a line when you hear one."

"You're awful," Marilyn said. "I know Jack. He's sincere. He'll carry through on his promise."

Carmen told her friends, "Marilyn is heading for heartbreak. The president will dump her one day sooner or later. I heard he does that with all his women."

Marilyn told her sometimes lover Peter Lawford, "The next time I see the president I want to be wearing my

Somalian leopard coat. That way, he will think of me as a predatory animal."

According to reports, Peter Lawford used to dress Marilyn up like an ugly secretary with a stringy black wig and slip her into the Carlyle for a sexual tryst upstairs in JFK's suite. Once, the blonde bombshell was even slipped aboard Air Force One wearing this dowdy disguise.

Marilyn was given Jack's private phone number in the White House, but he warned her that if Jackie answered, she was to hang up because her voice was too well known.

When Jayne Mansfield learned that Marilyn had replaced her as one of Jack's mistresses, she sneered, "Marilyn is just a dumb broad. One of Jack's fucks handed down by me when I was finished with him."

Joe desperately wanted Jack to run for a presidential second term in 1964, and he viewed Marilyn as a "walking time bomb." He feared if news about her having sex with Jack was revealed, it would destroy his son's political career.

Joe called Marilyn and offered a huge financial statement; some sources place it as much as a million dollars. "The price of silence," he told Jack. Marilyn, or so it is said, agreed to make the deal.

But as negotiations lingered into the Christmas season of 1961, and before the deal was consummated, Joe suffered a stroke. He was left sitting in a wheelchair, helpless, mute, and drooling. Marilyn would soon go to her own death, with very little money left in her checking account and her mortgage not yet paid off.

JFK, as noted in numerous biographies, was fond of having himself photographed naked with various beautiful women, sometimes pictured during fornication with him or else when one of these women was fellating him.

It was rumored that Peter Lawford was called in to photograph some of these vignettes in Santa Monica. During one of her reunions with Shelley Winters, her former roommate, in the late 1940s. Marilyn confided that Peter had taken nude pictures of President Kennedy and herself within a large bathtub at Peter's house. She also claimed that after one of the photo shoots, Peter joined JFK and herself in bed for a three-way. "Peter has quite a gay streak in him and welcomed the chance to get at Jack," Marilyn claimed to Carmen. "Just for a thrill, Jack allowed himself to be serviced. All of us had a gay old time, especially the president. He didn't do much for us that night. But both Peter and I serviced him."

The existence of the notorious photograph of Marilyn performing fellatio on JFK while lounging in that large marble bathtub was first exposed in C. David Heymann's *A Woman Named Jackie*. The whereabouts of that photograph is not known today; it may have been destroyed, but then again…

Fashion photographer **Milton Greene** (1922-1985) worked his magic on Marilyn, becoming her Svengali. Marilyn was told that Milton was a warm and sensitive guy, but, if crossed, his enemies claimed he would become a killer. "Nobody takes me seriously as an actress," MM told Green.

"I do," he said, reassuring her. "Hang in with me and I'll see to it that you become more acclaimed than Garbo. You are the hottest talent in Hollywood, far better than the dumb blonde parts they give you. Fox is only paying you $1,500 a week. You should be getting a million dollars per picture. What about launching Marilyn Monroe Productions?"

Considered by many as Marilyn's "definitive photographer," Greene stands before one of his "until then unpublished" photos at New York's Brenner Gallery in April of 1978. When asked why he never displayed the photograph before he replied, "I just didn't feel like it".

\*\*\*

Bobby, or so it is believed, met Marilyn in early February of 1962 during a trip to Los Angeles at the home of his sister, Patricia Kennedy Lawford, and her actor husband, Peter.

Another blonde beauty, Kim Novak, was also present. Bobby already knew "Hollywood's lavender blonde" (there had been rumors).

When Peter had asked RFK what star he most wanted to meet in Hollywood, his first choice had been MM.

In a letter to Arthur Miller's teenage son, MM praised Bobby's sense of humor and also claimed, "He's not a bad dancer either."

Peter later warned Bobby, "When Ethel's in the room, you shouldn't hold Marilyn so close when you dance with her. Her bosom was pressing into your chest, not to mention something else."

Joan Braden, a family friend of the Lawfords, recalled Marilyn's arrival at their home in Santa Monica. The blonde star was dressed in black lace, wearing no brassière. Throughout the night, Bobby devoted all his attention to her, finishing off a bottle of champagne with her. She even taught him how to do the twist. Right in front of Pat and Peter, Marilyn asked Bobby, "As Attorney General, have you ever arrested a woman in bed?"

"No, but I've done other things to them," he said.

After that night, Bobby made frequent trips to Los Angeles, promoting his book on organized crime, *The Enemy Within,* which he wanted developed as a film project.

Bobby's sister, Jean Kennedy Smith, wrote from Palm Beach, "Dear Bobby, I hear you and Marilyn Monroe are the new, hot item among Hollywood gossips."

After he finished a fourteen-country goodwill tour with Ethel, Bobby immediately called Marilyn for a rendezvous. Their affair was about to begin. At the time, Marilyn was also sending handwritten love poems to JFK at the White House.

One of Marilyn's closest friends, Carmen, who lived nearby, remembered opening the door to Marilyn's house to discover Bobby Kennedy on the doorstep. When she heard who it was, Marilyn came rushing out of the bathroom. "She jumped into his arms," Carmen said, "and they started kissing madly. We had a glass of wine together before Marilyn reminded me that I had important business to take care of."

After that, Marilyn logged many calls to Bobby at the Justice Department. "She called him almost daily during that summer of 1962, her last on Earth," claimed Ed Guthman, a Kennedy press aide. Then he added a tantalizing note, one that hasn't yet been fully documented within the Kennedy scandals. "Judy Garland placed almost as many calls to Bobby as Marilyn. What was going on between Dorothy and Bobby? I never found out."

"When Bobby wasn't on the West Coast, they talked for hours on the phone," claimed Hazel Washington, Marilyn's maid at the time. "I think they invented phone sex. Marilyn actually made love to Bobby on the phone. I heard everything."

"Jack was the first to sample the honeypot," Marilyn told Carmen. "Bobby had his turn. I wasn't in love with Jack, but I fell in love with Bobby."

Carmen also claimed that she went with Marilyn and Bobby to a nude beach near the present Pepperdine University north of Santa Monica. Marilyn, according to the report, wore a black wig, and Bobby had on sunglasses and a fake beard. Each of them went unrecognized. "Could you imagine what a sensation it would have been if a nude Marilyn Monroe and a nude Attorney General had been snapped on the beach by some photographer?" Carmen asked.

Bobby bragged about bedding Marilyn to Kennedy aide David Powers. Powers at first didn't believe him, calling him "the biggest bullshitter in the world." He later claimed, "Bobby wouldn't have the balls to play like that in the big league."

But Bobby claimed it was true. "Not only have I had Marilyn's pussy but I think she's in love with me."

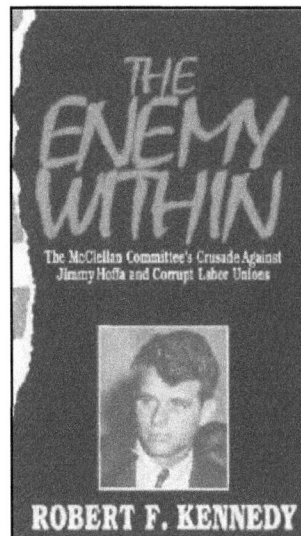

**ROBERT F. KENNEDY**

The political and interpersonal conflicts between Marilyn and the Kennedys were all becoming "too much." As Marilyn's affair with the Kennedys— **Bobby (The Attorney General) in particular**— became more passionate, his high-profile pursuit of organized crime became more intense.

Here's the cover of the best-selling and vaguely autobiographical book he developed and released in 1960. *The Enemy Within*, was a near-apocalyptic warning about the pervasive effects of organized crime, especially as it affected corruption and graft within organized labor, including the Teamsters.

Only a handful of her friends ever really understood the motivation of **Marilyn Monroe**'s marriage to the brilliant but emotionally withdrawn playwright **Arthur Miller.**

Some of them, including Darwin Porter's partner, Stanley Mills Haggart (one of Miller's confidants and friends) have suggested that he was a stepping stone to her candidacy for brainier and better movie roles. Regardless, the marriage (1956-1961) of "the beauty and the beast" seemed doomed by emotional apathy and misunderstandings from the very beginning.

Here's a photo from their June 1956 wedding in Westchester County, north of New York City.

Marilyn told her friend, Jeanne Carmen, "I'm still married to Arthur but he makes me unhappy. My marriage to him has only months to go."

Her friend, Henry Rosenfeld, said, "Marilyn lived in her own dream world. Her fantasy was to marry Jack Kennedy after his divorce from Jackie. She contemplated calling Jackie and urging her to divorce her husband."

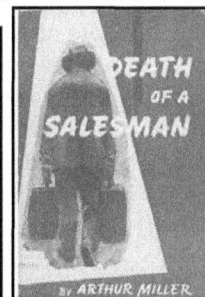

**DEATH OF A SALESMAN**

Arthur Miller's two-act tragedy about the dark side of the American Dream is sometimes reviewed as one of the best plays of the 20th Century.

***

Nearly every person in America has heard about President Kennedy's affair with Marilyn, and at least a million have heard about her affair with Bobby. But only a few thousands know that she also had an affair with Teddy.

That revelation came to light in 2010, thanks to disclosures within formerly confidential files from the F.B.I. In June of 2010, in the wake of Teddy Kennedy's death from cancer in August of 2009, the bureau released some 2,352 pages of formerly secret documents.

According to the files, there were several orgies staged at JFK's suite at the Carlyle. At least three included Marilyn Monroe as "guest of honor." Rat packers Frank Sinatra, Sammy Davis Jr., Peter Lawford, and even Patricia Kennedy attended at least one of the orgies.

The F.B.I. named Mrs. Jacqueline Hammond as a source of much of this information. Hammond was the divorced wife of a former ambassador to Spain.

Marilyn's eight-month affair with Teddy, which began at an orgy within the Carlyle attended by all three of the Kennedy brothers, extended until right before her murder.

Jack's younger brother, Teddy, had been very competitive about Judith Campbell Exner when she was the mistress of the president. He pursued her, and one night, he openly propositioned her in Las Vegas. But she turned him down, finding him "childishly temperamental."

After that orgy at the Carlyle, Teddy pursued Marilyn. One night in New York, she agreed to let him come to her apartment, where he found candlelight, roses, champagne, and Marilyn in a see-through nightgown.

"Teddy was all too eager," said Peter Lawford when he learned about their coupling. "The night Teddy met Marilyn at the Carlyle, he had to wait his turn, taking sloppy thirds after Jack and Bobby had finished with her. But I was glad to hear that Teddy got to have Marilyn all by himself for a night and didn't have to wait in line."

Teddy's seduction of Marilyn, although known by many Kennedy aides, never surfaced in any public way during the star's lifetime.

The F.B.I. documents were so explosive that Teddy's widow, Victoria, fought to have them squelched forever. She was ultimately defeated by a law court which upheld the Freedom of Information Act.

Teddy told Senator George Smathers, "I'm now screwing the woman whose poster Jack used to jack-off to when he was in the hospital, Marilyn Monroe Herself. She told me I make better love than either of my two brothers." Unknown to Teddy, she'd also told Bobby that he was a "far better lover than Jack."

Author Christopher Anderson claims, "Teddy, like the rest of his family, was engaged in an almost frantic pursuit of power, money, and sex."

In a particularly bizarre revelation, Carmen remembered drinking wine one late afternoon with Marilyn in her living room. The star was dressed in a stunning gown, but wouldn't tell her friend where she was going. "I have a date tonight."

The doorbell rang and Marilyn hurried to the bathroom to check her make-up. "Be a doll, Jeanne, and get the door," she called out. Carmen was stunned to open the door to discover both John and Robert Kennedy, with two men standing behind them, presumably Secret Service agents. She ushered them into the living room. JFK claimed "We don't have much time."

"Marilyn rushed out of the bathroom and gave each of them what looked like a prolonged tongue kiss," Carmen claimed. "Neither the President nor the Attorney General seemed embarrassed. Of course, Bobby and I had been intimate, so I didn't expect him to turn red faced. I guess Jack Kennedy, considering his lifestyle, was beyond mere embarrassment at that point in his life."

She claimed that the brothers didn't stay long, and that both of them left very soon afterwards, with Marilyn in the car's back seat. She apparently never confided to Carmen any of the details about where she was taken that night. Charles (Chuck) Spalding later revealed that JFK had

In 1991, decades after the assassinations of his brothers, JFK and RFK, an older and wiser **Teddy Kennedy** appears above with his second wife, diplomat/attorney **Victoria Reggie**, during one of his re-election campaigns. She is credited with stabilizing his private live and revitalizing his polical career after the MM debacle and among, others, the Chappaquidick scandal.

Charismatic, ferociously loyal, and widely "appraised" as "one of the best things that ever happened" to the Massachusetts senator, she lobbied, unsuccessfully, for the suppression of the FBI files describing the links between Marilyn Monroe and the Kennedys.

In 2022, after Teddy's death in 2009, President Joe Biden appointed her as U.S. Ambassador to Austria, in recognition of her hard work and her many contributions to key Democratic party causes.

told him that Marilyn was taken to the private villa of a friend of his in Bel Air. Teddy Kennedy arrived later. "Marilyn got to sample not only Jack's charms but Teddy's and Bobby's that night. Of course, as president, JFK was first in line." At least that is what Spalding claimed that JFK had revealed to him.

If this testimony is true, it means that Marilyn and the Kennedy brothers were repeating the theme of their orgy at the Carlyle Hotel in New York, details of which were revealed in those F.B.I. files.

Rumors still persist that Marilyn checked into Southern California's Cedars of Lebanon Hospital under an assumed name to have President Kennedy's child aborted. Others insist that it was Bobby's child. It has never been explained how Marilyn persuaded a doctor to perform an illegal abortion within a major U.S. hospital, when other movie stars were crossing the border into Mexico.

Never revealing the identity of the father, Marilyn claimed she had had a miscarriage. She told that to her publicist, Rupert Allen; her hairdresser Agnes Flanagan, and to a Laguna Beach realtor, Arthur James. She was considering at the time buying a house in Laguna Beach.

Marilyn's gynecologist, Dr. Leon ("Red") Korhn, denied any abortion stories, although he did say that Marilyn had become pregnant three times, losing each fetus in a miscarriage because of the massive amounts of drugs and liquor she shared with the unborn.

Considering the timing, chances are that if any of the Kennedy brothers had been the father, it would be Bobby and not JFK. Marilyn made a crude joke to Carmen about "Bobby Baby-maker's big dick."

When Jackie learned the details of JFK's affair with Marilyn, she threatened to divorce him, which would have cost him the 1964 election, had he been alive to run for office.

According to Senator Smathers, the president told Jackie, "Look, it really is over. It was nothing anyway."

Jack told Smathers that his affair hadn't been worth it. "Jackie more or less gives me free rein around here, and I don't want to fuck this up. Let's face it; Marilyn's day has peaked in Hollywood. For these 36-year-old glamour gals, it's all downhill from there. I can live without Marilyn. In fact, she's become a god damn nuisance calling up all day. It's time for an *adios*."

Then-Florida senator **George Smathers** *(left figure)* shares a laugh with **Leroy Collins** *(center)*, then the governor of Florida, and **JFK** during a moment of "lawmakers levity."

As president of the student body and editor of the student paper at the University of Miami during Smathers' administrative heyday, author **Darwin Porter** was deeply entrenched within Smather's political and personal orbit during the peak years of "Gorgeous George's" skirt-chasing heyday.

Some of the anecdotes that Smathers confided to Darwin, long ago and far away, are contained within the pages of his books.

There would be one more grand event incorporating the lives of Marilyn, Bobby, and JFK. It would eventually capture the imagination of the world and become part of the JFK/MM legend.

When Jackie learned that Marilyn had been invited to his birthday celebration, she said, "Screw Jack" and left the room. Then she packed to leave town, heading for Virginia.

On May 19, 1962 Marilyn ran away from the set of her film, *Something's Got to Give* (1962), to sing for the president in New York City at a fund-raising birthday party at Madison Square Garden. Peter Lawford was the Master of Ceremonies.

After Marilyn missed her first cue, Peter introduced her as "the late Marilyn Monroe," a word usage which would prove eerily prophetic.

She dazzled the world that night in her tight, glittering, almost transparent $12,000 Jean-Louis dress of "skin and beads." The flesh-colored dress had to be sewn on her. She didn't wear underwear, of course.

The president stared in fascination at Marilyn. "What an ass! Gene. What an ass!" That was JFK's comment to his writer Gene Schoor, who sat in the presidential box with him.

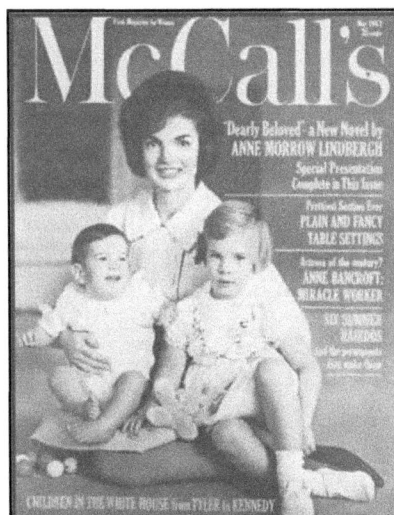

The political implications of a sexual dalliance between The Kennedys and MM couldn't have been more incendiary. The cover of *McCall's* edition of May, 1962 focused on **Jacqueline Kennedy** and the presence of "Children in the White House."

When JFK came onto stage, he joked with the audience, "Now I can retire from politics after having 'Happy Birthday' sung to me in such a sweet, wholesome way."

After her appearance before the entire world, Marilyn retreated to her dressing room where she had to be cut out of her designer dress. After a bath, she headed for a party given by Arthur Krim, the theater magnate, president of United Artists.

Statesman/politico Adlai Stevenson was there. He later claimed, "I never got to dance with her. Bobby Kennedy put up strong defenses around her. He was dodging around her like a moth around the flame."

Dorothy Kilgallen reported in her column that Bobby danced with Marilyn five times. What she didn't report was that Ethel, in a far corner of the room, stood glaring at them with a bubbling fury about to spill over.

Before dawn of the next day, Marilyn was slipped into the Carlyle where she later told Peter, "I had sex in one bedroom with Jack, then I came to the other bedroom and took care of Bobby." This was the last time the president, as far as it is known, ever saw Marilyn again. Bobby still lay in her future, his exact role the subject of ferocious debate today.

JFK was seen leaving the Carlyle at around 6am the following morning. It would be the last time he ever saw the blonde goddess. Bobby left at ten o'clock that morning.

May 19, 1962: Dress by **Jean-Louis**, birthday ballad by **Marilynf Monroe**, and humor by **JFK**. NYC temperatures that evening outside Madison Square Garden exceeded 99 degrees, and network coverage was unforgiving and nationwide.

It was arguably the most visible and talked-about event in the stadium's political history. Marilyn would be dead within three months; **JFK** within 18.

In a stern chastisement of her son, Rose Kennedy urged Bobby to drop Marilyn "and spare your family another disgrace."

Although the lid had been kept on them for years, by 1963, stories about JFK and Marilyn were about to break wide open in the press. JFK told Senator Smathers, "It's all become too public. I can't see her any more."

JFK even sent William Haddad, a former New York Post reporter working at the time for the Peace Corps, to the top editors at *Time* and *Newsweek*, cautioning them not to print news about his alleged affair with Marilyn. "It simply isn't true," Haddad claimed.

Peter Lawford later claimed that "Marilyn couldn't get it through her head that the party was over. I kept telling her that she didn't know Bobby and Jack like I did. When they're through with a woman, they're toast. She really knew that, but somehow couldn't bring herself to admit it. She wrote constant letters to Jack at the White House, begging him to take her back. At one point, she was so bitter she told me that Jack made love like a thirteen-year-old boy. When she wouldn't let up, Jack sent Bobby out here to cool her down."

Like Jack, Bobby believed that his romance with Marilyn was becoming high profile, and he, too, retreated from her. He also claimed that she was consistently reckless because of her high consumption of alcohol and drugs. "Bobby is moving on from me the way Jack did," Marilyn told Peter. "The Kennedy brothers…they treat women like that. They use you, then they dispose of you like so much rubbish."

She also confided to Jeanne Carmen that she exempted Teddy from that charge. "He truly loves me, and wants to be with me anytime I'm willing. I let him do it because he loves it so much, but I'm not in love with Teddy. What I really want is for Jack and Bobby to make love to me at the same time. At the Carlyle one night, they both made love to me but not in the same bed at the same time."

In California, Bobby delivered the news to Marilyn in person. She was not to see Jack or him again. Nor was she to place any more calls to the White House or the Justice Department.

In hysterics, she began to scream after hearing this ultimatum from Bobby himself. He tried to comfort her. When a man went to comfort Marilyn, that meant only one thing, sex. At least for a moment, he was overcome by her seductive charms.

But by the following morning, a clearer head would emerge on Bobby. Holding onto power, both for himself and his brother, was far more important to Bobby than bedding an aging sex symbol.

Marilyn refused to obey Bobby's ultimatum and continued to call both Jack and Bobby in Washington.

"Jack was the first to refuse my calls to the White House," Marilyn told Jeanne Carmen. "And now Bobby won't speak to me at the Justice Department either. But Teddy is in touch with me. He still loves me and we're going to get together soon. I don't love Teddy, but I'm in love with the idea that one of the Kennedy brothers still worships me, unlike those older meanies."

"I've already sent word to both Jack and Bobby that I'm going to call a press conference and reveal everything about our relationships," Marilyn said. "But because of Teddy I will probably not do that. Peter Lawford is dead set against it too."

"Monroe could not accept that her affair with Bobby was over," said author Lucy Freeman, who interviewed Monroe's psychiatrist on several occasions. "Bobby's rejection reawakened her father's complete abandonment of her. Because of her father's early desertion, she created the sex goddess, the one that no man could possibly abandon."

RFK called Peter Lawford. The two men had never liked each other. The Attorney General ordered Peter to "cut Marilyn off from all contact with the First Family—see to that." Then he abruptly hung up the phone, offending Peter.

Not only had JFK and RFK abandoned her, but on June 2, 1962, her studio fired her. Fox press agents were instructed to launch a negative publicity blitz, defining their former star as mentally ill.

Bobby would be forced to make one final visit to Marilyn's home in an effort to contain her and keep her from going public about her affairs with the Kennedy men. Of course, as the world knows, Marilyn never activated that threat. She was found dead on August 5, 1962, before she could make good on her promise.

Langdon Marvin, a Kennedy aide, remembered being called to RFK's Hickory Hill estate in Virginia during January of 1964. There his boss handed him a dozen or so letters, ordering him to "get rid of them—burn them."

Marvin did as he was told, and shredded each of the letters. Later he learned from RFK they were "love missives" to both JFK and RFK from Marilyn herself. "I should have saved them. If genuine, they would be worth a fortune if sold today to collectors."

Director George Cukor later said, "Marilyn was not a lady who would have taken aging well. Her forties would have been a horror for her. She didn't have the integrity of a true actress—she would not have welcomed the richness of character interpretations, as a true actress would have. She was a star trading on certain gimmicks, and in her heart she knew that."

# WHO MURDERED MARILYN MONROE?

On the day she died, author and journalist Darwin Porter began gathering evidence, focusing on tantalizing details about her mysterious demise.

Over the decades, at least 650 "people of interest" were interviewed. There was a massive cover-up, and an extraordinary number of people seemed to have been included in its deceit.

The results, released in 2012 during the 50th anniversary of Marilyn's death (and re-released in 2020) have connected the dots and resolved a half-century of speculation.

Two different editions of the same book: both by **Darwin Porter**, both with the most stunning overview of **Marilyn's murder** ever published.

# MARILYN, THE CIA, & RUMORS OF A PLOT TO KILL JFK

Jose Bolanos, the Mexican screenwriter, is sometimes known as "the last lover of Marilyn Monroe." He later claimed that Marilyn and he planned to get married, although it appears that she was also promising a re-marriage to the Yankee slugger, Joe DiMaggio.

Bolanos was one of the last people to talk to Marilyn on the night of her death on August 4, 1962. In contrast to Peter Lawford's report about her voice being slurred, Bolanos claimed that she was exuberant and making plans for the future.

What has tantalized reporters for years is one of Bolanos' statements: "Marilyn told me something that, if true, would rock the world." At the time, he chose not to reveal what that awesome secret was.

In October of 1963, Bolanos was working in Mexico on a commercial for the New York City-based television production company, TV Graphics, which was shooting a beach scene near Puerto Vallarta.

Also near Puerto Vallarta, Richard Burton and Ava Gardner were filming the movie version of Tennessee Williams' play, *The Night of the Iguana*. Elizabeth Taylor had flown to Puerto Vallarta to stay with Burton during the filming.

Tennessee arrived unannounced on the scene with his lover *du jour*. He met Bolanos on the beach and invited him as the guest of honor at a Mexican dinner he was hosting for a few select friends. Williams had read about Bolanos in accounts of Marilyn's death the previous year, and was most intrigued.

It evolved into a drunken night of revelry, and Tennessee exercised his talent for zeroing in on his subject. "And exactly what did our dear friend Marilyn tell you that was so shocking?"

Before he answered, Bolanos had to fill in some background, explaining that Marilyn had developed a friendship with Fred Vanderbilt Field, an avowed Communist and the leading American expatriate in Mexico City. Bolanos said that he'd introduced Marilyn not only to Field, but also to E. Howard Hunt, who, as he claimed, "has CIA connections."

"I talked to Marilyn on the phone right before she died," Bolanos said. "She'd received this terribly disturbing call from Field in Mexico City. According to him, he'd just learned that Hunt, who was my friend, was plotting the assassination of President Kennedy."

Tennessee said that it was his understanding that a sitting U.S. President gets death threats every day. "I get death threats for suggesting homosexuality in my plays."

None of the guests at the party that night paid much attention to the comment, and no one tried to reach the Associated Press on the phone. Perhaps no one at the time knew who E. Howard Hunt was.

But with the passage of time, it appears that Field was definitely onto a plot to assassinate the President.

E. Howard Hunt died on January 23, 2007. His own son, Saint John Hunt, said that his father, on his deathbed, asserted that he was involved in dialogues about assassinating JFK.

As ironic as it seemed, Marilyn may have known of that. Hunt's son reported that his father admitted his involvement in plotting to kill JFK at least a year before he was shot in Dallas. The alleged co-conspirators even had a code name. Their operation was called, "The Big Event."

Although Marilyn learned of the President's danger, she remained unaware of her own impending doom. Forces were already heading for her new home in Brentwood on that hot summer night in August of 1962.

MARILYN'S VERY PUBLIC AFFAIR WITH A LEFTIST

Radical Mexican screenwriter **Jose Bolanos** emoting with **Marilyn Monroe** in 1962 at the Golden Globe Awards.

Mexico-based left-leaning heir to part of the Vanderbilt fortune, a friend of Marilyn, testifying before HUAC in the early 1950s: **Fred Vanderbilt Field.**

Shortly before his death in 2007, CIA spymaster **E. Howard Hunt** confessed, to his son, **Saint James Hunt**, his role in the Watergate burglary and his murky association with CIA operatives plotting to kill JFK. Its publisher marketed it as a personal account of a dysfunctional family caught up in two of the biggest political scandals of the 20th century. Peripherally, Marilyn was part of the narrative

Debauched movie stars in a tequila-soaked Mexican hideaway in a highly suggestive film adaptation of a decadent play: Here's **Ava Gardner** with **Richard Burton** in the movie version of Tennessee Williams' *The Night of the Iguana.*

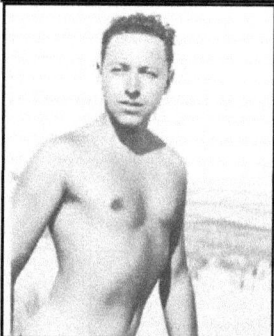

America's greatest playwright, **Tennessee Williams,** undressed and on a Provincetown beach in the late 1940s.

# ANOTHER YEAR, ANOTHER PRESIDENT

## MM's Fling with Ronald Reagan

**During World War II, Captain Ronald Reagan** was stationed in California, handling PR for the Army. In that capacity, Captain Reagan ordered his staff photographer, Private David Conover, to go to a local factory to take pictures of women on the homefront who were turning out aircraft, munitions, and parachutes. These morale-boosting photos of pretty girls contributing to the war effort were for publication in *Yank* magazine. .

One of the girls he photographed that day was named **Norma Jeane**. She could hardly know at the time that she'd eventually have an affair with Private Conover's commanding officer – or that the officer would become, long after her own death, the President of the United States. Conover later claimed that the eyes of Norma Jeane "held something that touched and intrigued me. She should be a movie star."

After lunch, he requested that she change into a red sweater, and he took more pictures of her in which her breasts were more prominent. When Conover came into the office of his boss (Reagan) a week later, he noticed that he'd pinned up that picture of Norma Jeane. Reagan said, "This young lady, not Lana Turner, should be called **The Sweater Girl**."

# REAGAN'S TOUGH CHOICE
## FOR A TROPHY WIFE AND
## POLITICAL PARTNER

### WHO WOULD MAKE THE BEST FIRST LADY?
### DORIS? NANCY? PATRICIA?

# BUT NOT MARILYN!

**Ronald Reagan, of course,** was the only Hollywood actor and (except for Donald Trump) the only divorced man to ever become President. But Reagan's road to the White House had a few romantic potholes.

As early as 1950, he was dreaming the impossible dream of one day becoming President of the United States, even though he'd recently divorced actress Jane Wyman. He dated a lot of starlets, mostly one-night stands, but had settled on two women he particularly liked, Doris Day and Nancy Davis.

He was the president of the Screen Actors Guild but had loftier ambitions in politics because his screen career had stalled. Actor/dancer George Murphy, who'd been Guild president from 1944 to '46, was his role model. Murphy also wanted to go into politics and would indeed become a U.S. Senator from California (1965-71).

Reagan turned to Murphy not only for political advice but for affairs of the heart. "If you want to be president one day, you've got to have a suitable First Lady," Murphy told him. "Nancy is too mousy with no personality. Doris is nothing but personality. She can sing, too. Even if you bore your audience with one of your long-winded speeches, they'll stick around to hear Doris sing 'Sentimental Journey.'"

At this same time yet another starlet was about to enter Reagan's life. In 1948 Marilyn Monroe had met Fred Karger, a musician, who was also working as a vocal coach at Columbia. Almost within days she'd fallen in love with him, even though he was bitter about women. "No female is capable of genuine love," he told her. At the time, he'd just been dumped by Rita Hayworth. In spite of what he said, Marilyn wanted to marry him. But he did not think she would make a proper stepmother for his young daughter from an earlier marriage. Marilyn was bitterly disappointed.

Had Ronald Reagan pursued his first "first choice" for a second marriage after his divorce from Jane Wyman, **Doris Day** *(above)* might conceivably have become First Lady of the United States. Both Day and Reagan had been cast in the film, *Storm Warning* (1951) about the KKK. It also starred Ginger Rogers. Although Rogers was famous for her dancing and Day for her singing, neither star was called upon to do either. Both instead were cast in dramatic parts.

Reagan dated Day, who said that "two things about Ronnie impressed me. How much he liked to dance and how much he liked to talk. There was a little place on La Cienega where he used to take me. It had a tiny dance floor. When he didn't dance with me, he talked to me. Not talk, really. Not real conversation. It was rather talking at you, sort of long discourses on subjects that interested him. I remember telling him he should be touring the country making speeches. I turned out to be a prophet. He was very good at it. He believed everything he said, or at least he made you think he believed."

Unknown to Day, Reagan was also dating Patricia Neal who was still in love with Gary Cooper. "From what I heard, Gary's a tough act to follow, " Reagan said.

Could he have been referring to Coop's legendary endowment? At this time, starlet Nancy Davis was dating Reagan, but not going steady with him.

Unknown to Marilyn at the time, another woman had also fallen for Karger. At the peak of her star power in Hollywood, Jane Wyman, the ex-Mrs. Ronald Reagan, also wanted to marry Karger. He ended up proposing to Jane. Marilyn was furious and wanted to get even.

In one of those coincidences that often occur in life, a drunken Marilyn encountered Jane in the women's room of Chasen's Restaurant in Los Angeles. In an altercation, Marilyn lunged for Jane, accidentally ripping her wig off. Jane was wearing a wig that night to conceal a scalp irritation. When novelist Jacqueline Susann heard of that catfight, it inspired the most dramatic scene in her *Valley of the Dolls*, one of the best-selling novels of all time.

Marilyn couldn't have Karger, but she went after Jane's "discard," hoping that would make her rival jealous even though she'd divorced him. Marilyn called Reagan, ostensibly to discuss problems with her membership in the Guild. This led to a dinner date and a subsequent affair.

Later when Reagan had business in Miami Beach, he invited Marilyn to fly down to join him. He bought her a ticket on a separate plane. He even insisted on booking her a suite in a different hotel from his own on Miami Beach, stashing her secretly at the Helen Mar.

Why the secrecy? Reagan was between marriages and could date whomever he chose. But he did not want Doris or Nancy to know he was seeing yet another starlet. The only time Reagan and Marilyn were seen together in public was during their secret "date" in a dimly lit Miami Beach night club that starred Sophie Tucker. As a fading star, Reagan attracted no attention, and Marilyn was yet to become a household word.

Flying back to the West Coast again on a different plane from Marilyn, Reagan had a final dinner date with the star, telling her "it's over between us." She burst into tears. He also broke up with Doris, who married Marty Melcher in 1951. During the course of that marriage, his profligate spending nearly drove Doris into bankruptcy.

Ignoring Murphy's advice, Reagan went on to marry Nancy on March 4, 1952. He was 41; she was 30. "We had a kid in the oven," he told Murphy. Their daughter, Patti, was born that October 21.

Wyman married Karger in 1952, but divorced him in 1954. She remarried him in 1961 but walked out on him in 1965, divorcing him again. She never remarried.

After reigning as "the queen of TV" on the soap opera, *Falcon Crest*, while Reagan presided over the Free World in the 80s, she went into seclusion, suffering from arthritis and diabetes.

Her last public appearance was in 2004 at Reagan's funeral. Concealed behind sunglasses, she was hidden in the background, and most of the much-younger paparazzi and journalists didn't recognize her. Jane had wanted to attend to pay her respects but privately told friends, "This is Nancy's time to shine—not mine."

She died at the age of 90 on September 10, 2007, at her home near Palm Springs. Her adopted son, Michael Reagan, issued a statement in which he said, "Hollywood has lost the classiest lady to ever grace the silver screen."

When **Nancy Davis** *(above)* latched onto **Ronald Reagan**, she held tightly and was determined not to let go. Unlike Jane Wyman, Nancy pretended to be "vitally interested" in Reagan's political views, listening to him talk for hours. She used every feminine wile to attract his attention, and later told her old friend, Spencer Tracy, "I am wholeheartedly in love." But Reagan wasn't ready to commit. At first, he saw other women while dating Nancy on and off.

At the time, Nancy's career was in serious jeopardy. Her starring roles in *The Next Voice You Hear* (1950) with James Whitmore bombed at the box office, as did *Night into Morning* (1951), a maudlin melodrama she made with Ray Milland (who, by the way, was still in mourning after having been dumped by Grace Kelly).

On September 7, 1951, Nancy received bad news from MGM. After her series of box office failures, her three-year contract would not be renewed.

**Ronnie and Nancy** *(photo, right)* at their wedding in 1952. She'd finally won her long sought-after prize. They are flanked by **Ardis Marshall** *(left of Reagan)* and **William Holden** *(right of Nancy)*.

At the time, Mr. and Mrs. Holden were Reagan's best friends. Known on the screen as Brenda Marshall, Holden's wife had appeared opposite Errol Flynn in *Sea Hawk*, opposite Alan Ladd in *Whispering Smith*, and opposite Joel McCrea in *Espionage Agent*. Holden became a role model for Reagan, who copied his style on screen all the way down to the way he lit a cigarette. He began dressing like Holden and even adopted the actor's cynical raised eyebrow.

**Nancy never achieved her goal**, which was to become as famous as another actress named Davis – Bette, that is. After appearing in some duds, Nancy was cast in *Talk About a Stranger* (1952), with song-and-dance man and Reagan's friend, George Murphy. Neither Murphy nor the movie-going audiences were impressed with Davis' acting. Nonetheless, determined to make a career, she signed on for yet another project. *Donovani's Brain*, starring Lew Ayres, was possibly her best film. The irony of Davis starring with Lew Ayres was certainly amusing: Ayres had been the lover of Jane Wyman during Wyman's marriage to Reagan.

In 1957, the producers of *Hellcats of the Navy* came up with what they believed to be an inspired idea – casting the husband-and-wife team of **Ronnie and Nancy** in the same picture. Ironically, it sent Nancy's Hollywood career into a tailspin. The only other film that followed was the aptly titled *Crash Landing* in 1958.

**Ronald Reagan's** film career was also winding down. When Nancy announced her retirement from the screen in '58, people paid little attention. F. Scott Fitzgerald once wrote that there are no second acts in American lives. Both Reagans proved him wrong.

With her husband facing an uncertain film future, Nancy Reagan decided she couldn't afford a maid and did her own cooking and housekeeping. As a means of maintaining an aura of glamour, she sometimes wore high heels while doing the daily chores. This *(below, right)* is how Reagan found **Nancy** when he returned from shooting his last film for Warner Brothers in 1952.

In that film, entitled *The Winning Team*, Reagan portrayed Grover Cleveland Alexander, one of baseball's immortals. Doris Day was cast as his wife, but received top billing. At that point, her romance with Reagan had already cooled. Reagan departed from the Warner Brothers lot on January 28, 1952, after fifteen years of involvement. There was no fanfare. "Not even a gold watch from Jack Warner," he told Nancy when he got home. "I thought an *adios* from Jack might be possible. I only got silence. I asked for my final paycheck. They told me, 'It's in the mail.'"

As he pulled his car out of the studio lot that day, he noticed an attendant removing his "permanent" nameplate. Although facing an uncertain future, Nancy and Ronald were married on March 4, 1952.

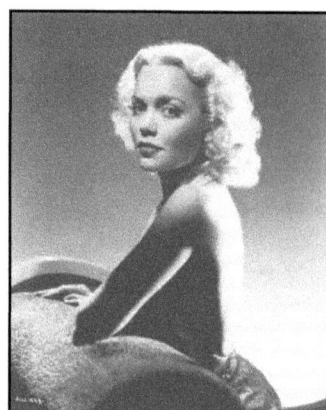

**SAILOR, CAN YOU SPARE A DIME?** Fans of **Jane Wyman** *(four photos above)*, who knew her only from her TV role in *Falcon Crest*, may never have known that a younger, brassier, sexier Wyman ever existed. She trained as a dancer in her younger days, but ended up as a radio singer. Taking the last name of her first husband, whom she'd divorced in her teens, "Jane Wyman" went through the Warner Brothers casting mill and came out a B-rated chorus girl, a dumb blonde backup in a "Torchy Blane" mystery (she played a hat check girl). In *Brother Rat* (1938), she played a blonde chasing cadet Reagan. She caught him in real life and married him in 1940.

"Jane was a fly-away girl," said Glenda Farrell. "Very blonde – too blonde, in fact. She was a party girl. Word at Warners was that she was available, if you know what I mean."

"I just had to go dancing and dining at the Troc or the Grove or some nightspot every night to be happy," Wyman said. She was seen in a booth kissing John Payne one night, and flirting with attorney Greg Bautzer another. (Bautzer's sole aim seemed to be to screw every major female star in Hollywood. He was most visibly successful with Lana Turner and Joan Crawford.) Wyman even fell for Bing Crosby when they co-starred in *Here Comes the Groom* (1951).

**Jane Wyman** (the ex-Mrs. Ronald Reagan) and **Rock Hudson** made two successful movies together, both of which were soapy: *Magnificent Obsession* in 1954 and *All That Heaven Allows* in 1955. During the filming of both pictures, Wyman had a fling with the handsome actor, eventually learning that he was a homosexual. Wyman wasn't as savvy as Hudson, and found it "a bit incomprehensible that Rock can make love to a woman so successfully even though he's gay." Despite her eight-year real-life role as Mrs. Ronald Reagan, "the talker" had never explained the finer points of homosexuality to his first wife. Previously, Hudson had even made love to an aging Joan Crawford, who'd praised the size of his equipment.

*Magnificent Obsession* was the granddaddy of all tearjerkers: A handsome, reckless playboy accidentally blinds a woman and then falls in love with her. Searching for spiritual meaning in his life, he returns to medical school, becomes a doctor, and cures her blindness. Director Douglas Sirk later said, "Rock rode into stardom on the skirttails of Jane Wyman."

Because of the success of *Magnificent Obsession,* the studio cast Wyman and Hudson together in *All That Heaven Allows,* with filming beginning in January of 1955. It was another older woman/younger man-themed film, and was almost guaranteed to thrill middle-aged women across the country, most of whom were completely unaware that Hudson was a closeted gay.

By the middle of the shoot, Wyman had lost all interest in Hudson, having learned too much about his private life from well-meaning friends. Even so, the public drew parallels between *All That Heaven Allows* and the star's personal life. She caused a scandal when the public learned that at the age of 38, she'd become engaged to a dashingly handsome 26-year-old, Travis Kleefeld. Public opinion turned against the marriage, and Wyman dropped Kleefeld, not wanting to further alienate her fans.

Evelyn Keyes convinced **Fred Karger** *(with* **Wyman** *in photo, left)* a musician at Columbia, to put together a band to play at a party hosted by the John Hustons. Escorted by Reagan, to whom she was married at the time, Wyman was introduced to Karger that night. Little knowing that she would eventually marry him--not once, but twice--she eloped with him in November of 1952 after the termination of her marriage to Reagan. By doing so, she seriously pissed off gossip maven Louella Parsons, who had wanted the scoop.

The public was eager for details about Wyman's "mystery man." Reading the papers, Marilyn Monroe said, "I could tell them plenty about Fred Karger, more than they'd be able to print. And I'll get even with that bitch Wyman if it's the last thing I ever do."

Upon hearing of his marriage to Wyman, Rita Hayworth told friends, "Jane is welcome to him! Frankly, I don't know why Marilyn is so crazy about the guy." Previously, Karger had been involved in Hayworth films which included *The Loves of Carmen* and *Affair in Trinidad.*

Even though Wyman's second marriage to Karger lasted longer than the first, it wasn't successful. This was despite the fact that her career was winding down and she had more time to devote to him.

In March of 1965 he charged her with "desertion." She counter-charged, citing "grievous mental cruelty," and that he had "an uncontrollable temper."

**Marilyn Monroe** *(three photos, above)* had two objectives when she pursued Ronald Reagan: She told best pal, Shelley Winters, that she thought Reagan was cute, but more important than his good looks was her personal vendetta against Jane Wyman. A few months earlier, Wyman had taken Fred Karger, a musician, away from Marilyn. In Marilyn's view, sleeping with Jane's former husband was a suitable revenge.

Marilyn later recalled details of her affair with Reagan to Winters. "He was the only man I know who took a shower and brushed his teeth before and after sex. He was very clean. Not terribly passionate, though. It was sort of automatic, and he went directly to the spot. No preliminaries. He did feel my breasts but didn't go in for all that armpit licking and toe sucking that some guys like. No wonder Arrow shirts used him as a model. Reagan is straight as an arrow. He told me that he was shopping around for a wife, but she'd have to be suitable as a president's wife. I was disqualified because he said I was a showgirl and had posed for nude pictures. For some reason, my background disqualifies me for everything except to play a dumb blonde on the screen."

**Anyone who visits the Ronald Reagan Presidential Library,** in the Simi Valley of California, might never know that Jane Wyman even existed, since it contains few, if any, references to her role in his life. Yet during the 1940s, she was married to Reagan for eight years. She was a far bigger star than her husband ever was, having won an Oscar for her portrayal of a deaf mute in *Johnny Belinda* (1948). As George Murphy put it, "When Ronnie lost Jane, a really big star, he married down. Nancy Davis never made it. She couldn't even be called a Grade B star. How about going down the alphabet a bit? She never had any charisma on the screen ... or off, as far as I'm concerned."

By 1941, the differences between **Reagan and Wyman** *(photo left)* had become painfully apparent. As he became more political (she hated politics), she became more and more withdrawn, devoting nearly all her time to the advancement of her film career. The tension brewing between them exploded one night at a Hollywood party given by William Holden. "So you don't think I'm spending enough time at home?" she shouted. "One day I'm going to win an Oscar. That's something that will never happen to you."

After **Rita Hayworth** *(right)* dumped musician Fred Karger, he fell into the arms of Marilyn Monroe. Hayworth later said, "Fred got off on the legends about me – not me. He particularly liked the fact that GIs pasted a pinup photo of me on the first atomic bomb dropped on Hiroshima. *Talk about incendiary.*"

During her affair with the musician, Hayworth maintained no particular loyalty or fidelity to him. She enjoyed on-again, off-again affairs with Kirk Douglas, Glenn Ford, Howard Hughes, Peter Lawford, Victor Mature, Tony Martin, David Niven, Tyrone Power, and James Stewart.

"She liked to go to bed with movie stars," said her second husband, Orson Welles. "But then, so did I."

**As his marriage to Wyman deteriorated, Reagan** spent more and more time socializing with MGM star, **George Murphy**, pictured above left *(alone)* and above center with **Judy Garland i**n *Little Nelly Kelly* (1940).

**Dick Powell** *(above, right)* also became part of that circle. Both he and Murphy were ardent Republicans who greatly influenced Reagan's political direction. Although firmly entrenched as the (Democratic) President of the Screen Actors Guild, Reagan would eventually switch his allegiance from the Democrats to the Republicans.

Preoccupied with her own career, Wyman resented Reagan's attempt to expound on everything. One evening while Reagan was debating with Dick Powell about politics, Wyman leaned over to Powell's wife, June Allyson, and said, "Don't ask Ronnie what time it is because he will tell you how a watch is made."

Murphy entered politics before Reagan, running successfully for the seat of a California senator. He urged Reagan to enter politics by running for the governor of California. "From that position, you can parlay your fame into the presidency, but only if you run on the Republican ticket."

**Nearly broke, and with bills accumulating, Ronald Reagan**, centerpiece of the two photos immediately above, accepted a two-week vaudeville gig in Las Vegas which began on February 15, 1954. Best pal George Murphy had once told him that Las Vegas was a land of "has-beens, almost-rans, and never quites." Even so, Murphy agreed to help Reagan privately with his dance routines.

The future president was booked to appear with **The Continentals** *(above, left)*, a dimestore version of the zany Marx Brothers. Other than horsing around, using a guttural German accent, and acting drunk, Reagan played straight man to the slapstick comics and told bad Irish jokes that got him booed.

At one point he appeared in an apron advertising Pabst Blue Ribbon Beer with the German phrase – *Vos vils du haben?* – incorrectly written. As part of the same act, Reagan also appeared with **The Adorabelles** *(above, right)*, gorgeous showgirls clad in Carmen Miranda-inspired Brazilian costumes and plumed headdresses that towered more than two and a half feet high.

With Nancy sitting out front every night cheering him on, Reagan attracted only modest business. After his opening night, a local critic asked the question, "Is Las Vegas going to become a retreat for fading Hollywood stars?" At the wheel driving back to Los Angeles, Reagan told Nancy, "I'll never sink that low again." Fortunately, an offer was pending at General Electric which eventually designated Reagan as host of the syndicated TV series, *The General Electric Theater*, launching him on what would eventually become the road to the White House.

**Marlon Brando**, seen here with **Grace Kelly**

**Milton Berle**

**Spencer Tracy**

**Yul Brynner**

**Alfred Drake**

**Peter Lawford**

**Frank Sinatra**

**Robert Walker**

**Clark Gable**, seen here with **Vivien Leigh**

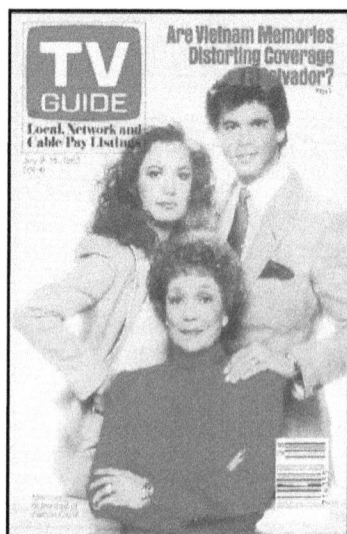

As Angela Channing, empress of *Falcon Crest*, **Jane Wyman** became the highest-paid actress on television in the 1980s. The hit series made its debut one year after Ronald Reagan was inaugurated as U.S. president, with Nancy, not Jane, as his First Lady. Industry insiders pointed out that "there were dozens of aging actresses in the Hollywood Hills who would be ideal for the part." (Bette Davis? Anne Baxter? Eleanor Parker?) But the studio wanted to take advantage of Wyman's unique status as the president's ex-wife. At the White House, Reagan was said to have been a faithful fan of the series, even though Nancy left the room whenever it was aired.

Wyman was in the California wine country filming an episode when she received word that Reagan had been shot by a would-be assassin, after he'd been president for only two months and nine days. She retreated to her dressing room and didn't emerge until the following morning, when she announced abruptly, "It's back to business, fellows! The nation goes on, and so does *Falcon Crest!*"

Portrayed *(left)* on a cover of *TV Guide* with some key cast members of *Falcon Crest*, Wyman received massive publicity because of the series, but consistently refused to talk to reporters about the nation's new president.

38

# Trivia Quiz—Did You Know?

## WHATEVER DID JANE WYMAN HAVE TO DO WITH *VALLEY OF THE DOLLS*, AND WHY WAS SHE SO ANGRY WITH ITS AUTHOR, JACQUELINE SUSANN?

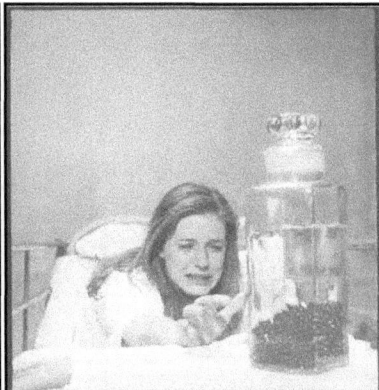

**Judy Garland knew a thing or two about pill addiction**, but when she was fired from the original cast of **Valley of the Dolls,** the role of the aging star, Helen Lawson, went to **Susan Hayward**. In one of the most dramatic confrontations within that film, **Patty Duke** (seen above caving in to her character's substance abuse issues) grabbed Hayward's wig, ripped it off her head and then flushed it down a toilet. By the end of the scene, Lawson, as played by Hayward, was revealed as a grotesque, wrinkled, has-been, way beyond her prime.

The hair-pulling battle between Duke and Hayward has entered camp movie history as one of its grander episodes. Jane Wyman saw *Valley of the Dolls* and was furious, knowing that its author, **Jacqueline Susann,** had ripped off an episode from her own life--i.e., her confrontation many years previously with Marilyn Monroe over Fred Karger in a Los Angeles restaurant. Several decades after that episode, at a party, when Susann came up to Wyman to greet her, Wyman tossed her drink in Susann's face and stormed out of the room.

Susann, incidentally, lived a life that paralleled many of her best-selling novels, a life filled with tragedy and triumph. Her most successful novel, and one of the most successful novels of all time, was *Valley of the Dolls,* whose theme involved pill addiction and sexual betrayal in Hollywood. Naturally, bidding for its movie rights was intense. Some critics suggested that the role of Helen Lawson was based on the life of Judy Garland, who was a personal friend of Susann's. Actually, however, it was based on the life of another faded musical star, Ethel Merman, with whom Susann had once suffered through an abortive lesbian love affair. Susann, who died in 1974, never forgave Merman, and "got her revenge" by depicting the star as a dumpy, semi-psychotic, over-the-hill monster.

Among other ironies, the film also starred the ill-fated **Sharon Tate,** who met a grisly death two years after the 1967 release of the film at the hands of the lunatic Charles Manson clan.

# THE RAPE OF MARILYN MONROE

**According to Shelley Winters,** MM's former roommate and longtime friend, "Marilyn Monroe was the biggest liar who ever set foot in Hollywood. Don't get me wrong. I loved the gal dearly. But the biographers of Marilyn's early life each bought into her fantasy."

Shelley continued: "**Marilyn confused her real life as Norma Jeane with the movie script of Norma Jeane that she kept rewriting in her head**. I remember a story she told me about childhood rape. Over the years she told me three different versions of the same story, forgetting what she'd said previously. In time, I think Marilyn could no longer distinguish between what was real and what wasn't. To her, the movie script of Norma Jeane became more real than the actual events. Marilyn became the star of a Greek tragedy that was her life. The only thing that Marilyn was ever completely honest about was the inevitability of the casting couch. In her early days, she spent far more time on that couch than she did in front of a camera. But as for the rest of it, it's too late now--no one will ever know the complete truth."

Marilyn's former lover, Ted Jordan, understood her contradictions better than most. He wrote that she was "the extremely vulnerable child-woman incapable of hurting a fly, who was also a hardheaded bitch consumed by ambition; the innocent *ingenue* moving through life in a kind of daze was also petty, vindictive, and cruel, a woman consumed by a need to be loved who was also manipulative and uncaring."

# Goodbye Norma Jeane,
# Hello Marilyn Monroe

The world took little note in 2005 of the passing of a man known throughout his life as "Mr. Marilyn Monroe."

A retired Los Angeles detective, James E. Dougherty, lived for decades in the shadow of sixteen-year old Norma Jeane Baker, whom he married on June 19, 1942, before going off to sea as a merchant marine. Death came to him at the age of 84 in San Rafael, California, where he'd be suffering from leukemia.

Throughout most of his life, Dougherty refused to talk about his life with Marilyn. Gordon Howard, the California tycoon, arranged for reporter Darwin Porter to meet Dougherty several times over a period of three weeks in Los Angeles in 1968.

In Porter's words: "I felt that Gordon, a generous person, had paid Dougherty for granting me that privilege, but I don't know that for a fact. The soft-spoken, unassuming, and rather kind detective, who still maintained a slight trace of his former good looks, had nothing in common with Marilyn's later two husbands: Baseball great Joe DiMaggio and playwright Arthur Miller. At first, Dougherty wanted to talk only about his hobby (special weapons), but I eventually steered him onto the subject of Marilyn. Dougherty insisted that I refer to her as Norma Jeane, saying, 'I don't know any Marilyn Monroe.' Dougherty admitted that he'd married 'a very damaged woman, unloved for most of her life.' But he was quick to dispel some rumors about Marilyn's early life. The one I found most intriguing was the claim he made about Marilyn's virginity—or lack thereof," Porter said.

"Norma Jeane came to our marriage bed a virgin," Dougherty claimed. "She and I had never had sex before. Her delicate threshold had never been crossed before. She cried out in pain, and I was aware and sensitive to her." *Those were his exact words.* After losing her virginity to her new husband on her wedding night, Norma Jeane "just fell crazily in love with sex," Dougherty claimed. "I was one lucky man!"

But what of all those other stories, as detailed in countless biographies, about Marilyn's abuse and rape in foster homes?

"Pure fantasy on Norma Jeane's part," Dougherty insisted. "She made up those stories to win the public's sympathy when she was revealed as the model who'd posed for that nude

One of **Norma Jeane's** few family-friendly poses was shot with her breasts carefully concealed and with this fluffy white lamb in 1946. Usually her photographs were much sexier, but this photographer decided he wanted her looking "farm girl wholesome."

When he saw the photograph, her modeling agent told her, "There's no way, gal, with a face like that, that you're going to look wholesome. From now on, we're sending you out on different jobs."

After making a voyage around the world, Dougherty arrived home and waited three hours for his wife to return. She claimed she had run overtime on a modeling assignment. Actually, she was detained giving the photographer a blow-job.

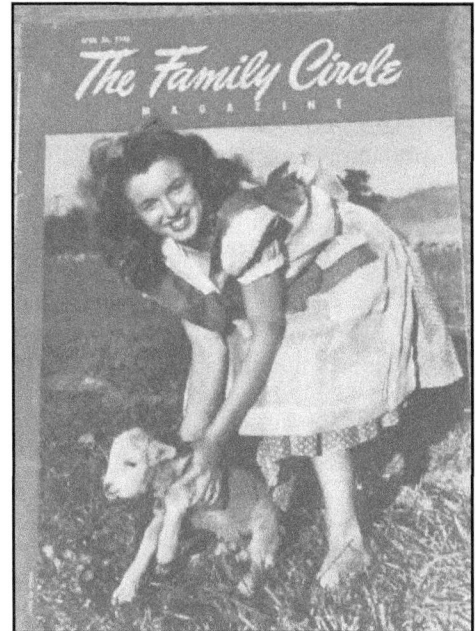

**In an interview later in life, James Dougherty** (*seen here in uniform with* **Norma Jeane,** *aka* **Marilyn,** *wearing a corsage*) revealed, "I should have known who Norma Jeane was when I married her. It's funny how I kidded myself into thinking her innocent like I wanted her to be."

"The clue came the first night I took her dancing. With her eyes shut extra tight, she pressed her body as tight as she could against me. Naturally, I got a hard-on. The third night when I took her dancing, she pressed so hard against me that I almost came. I was shocked when she took that delicate paw of hers and felt my hard-on. Oh, my God, I almost ruined my pants on the spot. When the music stopped, I had to stand on the dance floor until my erection came down."

calendar hanging in every men's toilet in every garage in America. She got the sympathy vote. Her ploy worked. Her career was saved."

Once he was launched into the subject, Dougherty had a lot to say about Marilyn, enough to fill a book. "I'm a skeptical reporter," Porter said, "but 'the first husband' talked so convincingly and provided so many clinical details about his wedding night with Norma Jeane that I believed his account. He did provide one unsettling detail about his honeymoon. 'Unknown to me at the time, Dougherty claimed, 'Norma Jeane had trench mouth.'"

If the detective's story rings true, and there is no reason to believe otherwise, only one man as far as it's known—ever raped Marilyn Monroe.

His name was Jumpin' Joe DiMaggio, and it happened one night in Los Angeles.

The debut of **Norma Jeane's** modeling career marked the beginning of the end of her marriage to James Dougherty. To be fair, the relationship had been rocky from the beginning.

The photographer who shot her photo for the cover *(above)* of *Diary Secrets* later said, "she had a 35-inch bust at the age of nineteen – and knew how to project those tits to the last centimeter." Marilyn disagreed with this appraisal, and in 1954 said her epitaph should read: **HERE LIES MARILYN MONROE – 38-23-36.**

After her appearance on the cover of *Diary Secrets,* modeling jobs began to pour in, especially after word spread that Norma Jeane had a surprise waiting at the end of every shoot. She truly lived up to the promise on the cover of *Diary Secrets*: **I PLAYED KISS AND RUN.**

In her late teens, Norma Jeane still kept her hair color dirty blonde. But she noticed it became lighter in the summer sun of California. She liked that look and decided to go blonde all the way and all year round. She later told Shelley Winters that "all the way" meant dying "down there," too.

**Marilyn Monroe** and James Dougherty had very different impressions about Monroe's teenage sexuality. When Marilyn married Dougherty in 1952, she claimed, "There were no thoughts of sex in my head." Dougherty concurred, stating "She began our married life knowing nothing, absolutely zero, about sex. My mother had cautioned me to go easy on Norma Jeane, knowing I was to be the first to pierce her hymen. I went gentle with her, crossing a delicate threshold that had never been crossed before. Not ever! It didn't hurt her at all. She took to it like a pig to shit and couldn't get enough of me. She wanted it all the time. God, I was one tired man."

Nearly a decade later, Marilyn had a different story: "Marriage just added to my lack of interest in sex. Jim enjoyed himself. I did not. He didn't even seem to know that he wasn't satisfying me."

Over the next several years, Norma Jeane would come to know men with far greater endowments than Jim's.

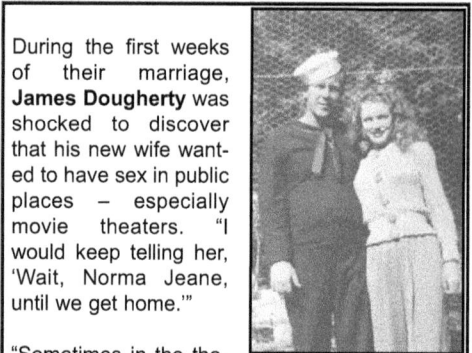

The marriage of **Norma Jeane Baker** and **James Dougherty** on June 19, 1942 was doomed from the start. She was just three weeks past her sixteenth birthday. He wanted a faithful and dutiful housewife who would be waiting for him when he returned home from work. He also wanted a woman to cook his dinner, wash his underwear, and succumb to his sexual demands. Finally, he'd wanted a virgin, thinking he was getting one when he married her.

He had no way of knowing that the sixteen year old he'd wed would one day become the sex goddess of the century -- a *femme fatale* whose sexual conquests would include two American presidents, Joan Crawford, and Barbara Stanwyck.

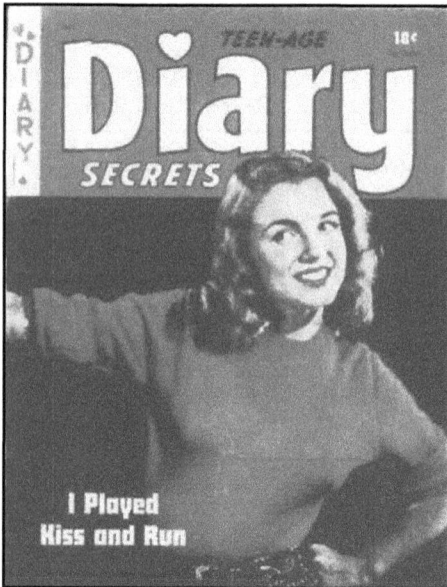

During the first weeks of their marriage, **James Dougherty** was shocked to discover that his new wife wanted to have sex in public places – especially movie theaters. "I would keep telling her, 'Wait, Norma Jeane, until we get home.'"

"Sometimes in the theater, she'd get down on her knees on the dirty floor and unbutton my pants and blow me. She also liked to get fucked in dangerous places where a policeman was likely to discover us. She preferred side streets or even back roads in San Fernando Valley."

"One night some hunters found us and shined a flashlight into our car. I quickly concealed myself but Norma Jeane let the four guys get a free look. When I drove her home, I told her I didn't want to have sex in public places anymore."

"Why not?" she said. "We're married, aren't we? It's not like we're doing anything illegal."

**"Marriage Without Kisses!"** The headline on this edition of *Personal Romances* might have described Norma Jeane's deteriorating relationship with her first husband, James Dougherty. When he came home on leave, she was no longer passionate. She seemed distant and removed from him, and only submitted to sex. He later told friends, "It was like fucking a zombie."

Norma Jeane had moved out of her home with Dougherty's parents—"I needed more freedom." What she actually needed was privacy in order to bring home tricks to help launch her modeling career. James was furious when he found out she'd quit her job for modeling – he feared that she couldn't count on getting modeling jobs all the time.

Placing her hand on her hip, Norma Jeane challenged Dougherty, "Do I look like a factory girl?" With that, she stormed out of the house and didn't return until three o'clock the following morning. She refused to tell him where she'd been. When he threatened physical violence, she claimed, "I was out with the girls."

After posing for this cover, **Norma Jeane** sent a letter to Dougherty informing him that she was no longer "your Norma Jeane – **from this day on, I am Marilyn Monroe!!!"** (The three exclamation points were her own.) "One photographer told me today that I should go to Hollywood and replace Betty Grable who's getting a little long in the tooth." That photographer turned out to be a prophet.

Although the magazine was called *True Experiences*, the story it ran about Marilyn's Cinderella-like childhood was completely false. The only true confession it contained was that she was, "A lonely girl with a dream – *who awakened to that dream come true.*"

The full actualization of that dream, however, would be a long time coming, if, in fact, it ever came at all. Even at the time of her death, Marilyn still remained that "lonely girl" looking for a love she would never find, except for perhaps "a few good days with Joe DiMaggio."

**In need of money to pay the rent, Marilyn** posed nude for photographer Tom Kelly in 1949 when she was 21 years old. He eventually sold the pictures for $200 to Western Lithograph Company, who subsequently reproduced a calendar series three years later. The tantalizing nudes of Marilyn were hanging in garage and barbershop walls throughout America until some hawkeyed fan did some research – the face on the calendar belonged to Marilyn Monroe, the new blonde goddess at 20th Century Fox.

In the early 1950s, such a display of nudity could have easily destroyed the career of a young actress. Exposure in the press, however, had the opposite effect for Marilyn. If anybody in America had not heard of her already, the massive media coverage it generated soon remedied that. Marilyn truly became a household word. A legend was born.

But at first the executives at Fox considered not releasing *Clash By Night*. Marilyn had starred in the movie with bisexual actress, Barbara Stanwyck, with whom she'd had a brief affair.

Marilyn, far ahead of the Fox executives, sensed that the country and its mores had changed – no doubt due to the upheaval brought about by World War II. The nude calendar, bestseller of all time, is still a hot seller today. Over the decades it has generated revenues in the millions. Marilyn received fifty dollars. One of the nude calendar shots was purchased for $500 by Hugh Hefner, and it was featured in the first edition of his startling new magazine, *Playboy*. On its cover, Marilyn appeared fully clothed.

An original of this first edition is now a valued collectors' item. In 2007, Playboy printed 20,000 replica copies and sold them for $25 each. Many collectors who purchased these copies have been fooled into thinking they own an original.

**This tantalizing effigy of "Marilyn Monroe"** on the cover of a 1979 edition of *Playboy* is not the real thing. Chicago model Cheryle Larsen replicated the blonde bombshell of the fifties. Playboy's executive art director, Tom Staebler, gave Larsen the hairstyle, beauty mark, and glossy red lips. Larsen did the rest, parting those succulent lips in her best come-hither style.

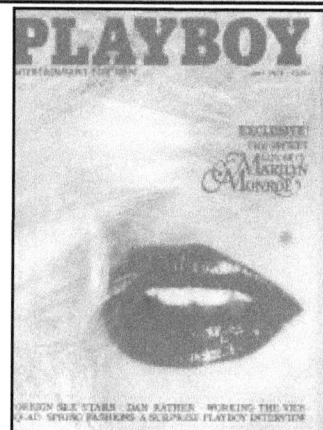

The magazine itself contained an exposé of ***"The Private Life of Marilyn Monroe,"*** a memoir as revealed by Lena Pepitone, her personal maid and seamstress. In 1957, Pepitone rang the bell of Marilyn's New York apartment where Marilyn was waiting, nude, to interview her as a job applicant.

"She was anything but what I had expected. Her blonde hair, which appeared unwashed, was a mess. Without makeup, she was pale and tired-looking. Her celebrated figure seemed more overweight than voluptuous. I was astonished by the way she smelled. She needed a bath. Badly. Still, she was pretty."

Hired for the job, Pepitone noted that Marilyn spent an unusually long time in the bathroom. "One day, thinking Marilyn was out, I went into the bathroom to straighten up, and I found her perched on the toilet, legs up, performing an elaborate ceremony with a bottle of some chemical and two toothbrushes. She was bleaching her pubic hair blonde. She shrieked with embarrassment. Both Marilyn and I were beet red with embarrassment. Then she started laughing uncontrollably. 'Now you know my secret!' she told me. 'You know, it has to match my hair.' I had always assumed Marilyn was a natural blonde all over. Now I knew better. 'With all my white dresses and all, it just wouldn't look nice to be dark down there. You could see through, you know,' she said."

**The marriage of "The Last Hero," Joe DiMaggio, with Marilyn Monroe** became a glamorous tabloid fiesta and ended in heartbreak and grief. The last hero, as we now know, wasn't a hero at all, and Marilyn was hardly a romantic heroine. When a blind date was arranged between Marilyn and DiMaggio, she claimed, "I've heard that name. He's that Italian actor, isn't he? Don't tell him, but I've seen none of his pictures."

"Marilyn, he's the greatest baseball star in America," said business agent David March.

"Okay, big guy," she said, "If you know so much about sports, tell me the difference between baseball and football."

Almost before their honeymoon began, the tension in the marriage began to surface. Always zealously guarding his privacy, DiMaggio was horrified at how she immediately went into her "Marilyn Monroe act" every time she saw a photographer. "She's a total exhibitionist," DiMaggio told his pal, Frank Sinatra. "Publicity is to Marilyn what fresh meat is to a tyrannosaur."

Even though she claimed to enjoy sex with DiMaggio, she admitted to Shelley Winters, "I can't have a climax with him. That's something no man can seem to give me. Maybe one day I'll meet the man who can – Porfirio Rubirosa with that rubber hose of his went at me all night, and he was mighty determined – but even he didn't succeed. The only climax I get is the one I give myself."

Despite of her ongoing lack of fulfillment, the sexual attraction between Marilyn and DiMaggio was a powerful link. Within two weeks, she'd nicknamed him "Slugger."

44

**Despite their public displays of affection**, the clashing egos of **DiMaggio and Marilyn** – called "Mr. and Mrs. America" – appeared as a match made in heaven. In reality, it was nine months of hell. Marilyn wasn't the first movie star DiMaggio had fucked. His pal, Frank Sinatra, had arranged liaisons with lots of other stars, including Marlene Dietrich. After their brief fling, DiMaggio complained to Sinatra about Dietrich's bad breath.

During his marriage to Marilyn, DiMaggio was insanely jealous, as his wife continued her affairs with other men. One night he arrived home and found Sinatra leaving Marilyn's room in only his underwear.

Sinatra and DiMaggio were both first generation Americans, the two most famous Italians in the world. Although they'd been pals for years, their friendship was severely strained that night, as Sinatra quickly dressed and left the apartment. DiMaggio later told his cronies, "I gave Marilyn the beating of her life that night. I even threatened to ruin her face for life, and I was so mad I almost did it. As for Frankie boy, I'm not going to banish him from my life forever. We've been too close for that. I'm still going to speak to him, maybe even hang out with him from time to time. But it will never be the same between us. I'll get even. The first thing I'm going to do is call up Ava Gardner and go over and fuck her. She's nothing but a whore anyway. Just like that blonde I married."

In spite of his secret fury with Sinatra, DiMaggio continued to see his old friend from time to time. His deep-seated resentment became obvious when he refused to invite Sinatra to Marilyn's funeral, despite Sinatra's pointed requests to pay his final respects.

In what could be viewed as a fortuitous prediction of her young death, Marilyn had always stated that she wanted Sinatra's music to be played at her funeral. Instead, DiMaggio ordered that Judy Garland's "Over the Rainbow" be played. Days after the funeral, DiMaggio told friends, "Sinatra, and the others, including those God damn low-life bastards, the Kennedys, killed Marilyn. That faggot, Peter Lawford, also had a hand in it. If one of those Kennedys had showed up for Marilyn's funeral, I would have taken a baseball bat and bashed in their faces. All of those sons of bitches killed Marilyn."

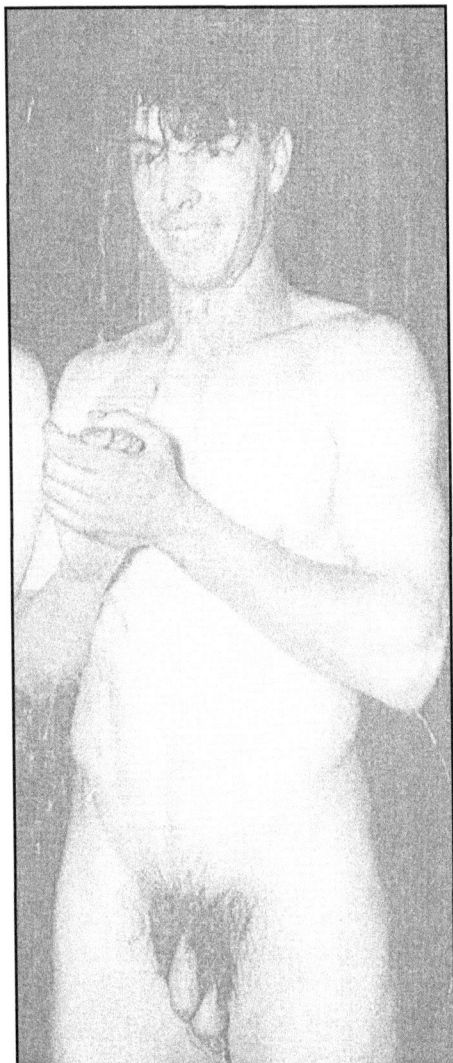

**"He's a grower, not a show-er,"** Marilyn told Shelley Winters when describing her lover/husband **Joe DiMaggio**. His uncut penis didn't initially impress some of the showgirls he seduced, but from most reports it usually rose to the occasion and was quite impressive when fully extended.

After his divorce from Marilyn, DiMaggio's reputation as The Great Lover spread. "There was something to that reputation," said author Richard Ben Cramer, "because in those years, more than ever, women just fell all over him. That was partly about Marilyn, too. Every female of a certain age in America had wondered what it would be like to be Marilyn Monroe. (A lot of 'em were willing to try it for a night.) But it was something about Joe, too – because he was so publicly, famously hurt … it gave him a softer edge, a vulnerability, that drew women in, like bears to honey – a lot of volunteers to fix his broken heart."

Behind Joe's back, Marilyn hired the famous lawyer, Jerry Giesler, to begin the divorce proceedings. The usual charge of mental cruelty was cited, along with a "conflict of careers." Considering the latent hostility DiMaggio felt for Sinatra, it was ironic that he chose to spend the night his divorce was finalized, along with Marilyn, in the singer's apartment in LA.

The divorce became final on October 17, 1954. DiMaggio and Marilyn had been married for 286 days. No longer married to her "Slugger," the divorce having gone through only hours before, Marilyn, also in a surprise move, chose to spend the first night of her newly found freedom with her (suddenly former) husband. Joe was no longer in a position to demand conjugal rights, as he had so many times in the past. She later said she just wanted to "be alone with Joe and cuddle with him." He had other plans.

Humiliated by the divorce, he wanted to re-establish his dominance over her. When she refused to have sex with him, he ripped her dress from her body. As was her habit, she wore no underwear. He knocked her down on the carpeted floor of Sinatra's living room and held her firmly. He proceeded to rape her as violently as he'd ever seduced any woman. At one point, she later confessed, she no longer resisted him but began to sob uncontrollably. That seemed to excite him all the more. He became even more brutal. He continued trying to kiss her but she turned her head away. Nevertheless, he forced her lips to meet his. Instead of kissing her, he bit her lip until it bled.

After raping her, he stormed out of the apartment but later reconciled with her. They continued to have sex until her death. She forgave him for his brutal actions. "Only that night, only when he was raping me," she told Peter Lawford, "did I truly understand just how much he loved me."

# MARILYN, JOE, & ME

## A Distant, Dubious Relative of the DiMaggios "Tells It Like It Wasn't"

**The December 2005 issue of *Playboy* carried the promise of "new evidence" into the mysterious death** of Marilyn Monroe. Hugh Hefner's magazine assured readers they would get to read "Her Last Words Uncensored." The so-called revelations were excerpted from one of the most controversial books every written about the star. Entitled *Marilyn, Joe & Me*, it was penned by June DiMaggio who asserted that she was the daughter of Louise and Tom DiMaggio, brother of the baseball icon.

Even her blood link to the DiMaggio family came into question as bloggers cited that June's mother was merely a second wife to Joe's brother, Tom. Although the book is reported to be the first from the usually silent DiMaggio family, researcher Lebh Shomea claimed that "June is not a DiMaggio and she was born June M. Elpine on June 11, 1923 to Rosetta Louise Rovegno and Albert U. Elpine. The assertion is made that her mother married Tom DiMaggio sometime in the 1940s when June was an adult and not living at home. June is not Joe DiMaggio's niece," Shomea claimed.

A minor actress, June states that she was a confidante of Marilyn for eleven years, as have so many other "close friends." Bloggers charged that the book was "another sad, pathetic attempt to make money off a dead legend."

The obvious errors were there, and they were big. Gloria Swanson played an actress named Norma Desmond in *Sunset Blvd.*, not "Desdemona," a character from Shakespeare's *Othello*. Marlon Brando did not star in *The Rose Tattoo*, Burt Lancaster did. The 1952 MM film with Richard Widmark was *Don't Bother to Knock*, not *Don't Bother Knocking*. The book even contains such embarrassing assertions as "Cabina (sic) Wright was a syndicated Hollywood gossip columnist, the Luella (sic) Parsons of her time." Of course, it was Cobina Wright and Louella Parsons.

Jill A. Adams, an MM historian for more than 30 years, called June's book "a complete hoax." Adams cited a Long Beach *Queen Mary* exhibit to which June was connected. The "artifacts" on display were said to have been in the possession of Marilyn herself, although the exhibit was not authenticated. For example, one questionable display was a Clairol hair curling set complete with blonde hair still attached. Since Clairol manufactured that set in 1972 and Marilyn died in 1962, the chances seem slim that she actually used it to curl her hair.

Assertions are made that June cooked a homemade pizza which Marilyn ate shortly before her death. Coroners, however, found Marilyn's stomach empty of food. Even though the (alleged murder) house was tightly sealed by the police, June also claimed that in the early hours of the morning after Marilyn's death, she drove over to the dead star's house and used a pass key she'd been given to open the back door. Her claim is that there was no one in the house at the time. She alleges that from the house she retrieved a teddy bear – Marilyn called it "Barbie Bear" – that she'd given Marilyn, along with her pizza pan. How June managed not to be seen by all the reporters and photographers, along with the idle curious assembled outside Marilyn's house, is not explained.

In the most controversial claim within June's memoir, she writes, "Marilyn had been talking with her on the phone, Mother told me, when intruders entered Marilyn's room. In her terror, Marilyn dropped the phone, but the killers never hung it up. Mother told me that she had heard it all – the voices in the room, the struggle, the silence. All accounts that I know of state that when Marilyn was found, her phone was still off the hook."

June alleges that her mother "knew who killed Marilyn but that knowledge absolutely terrified her, and to protect us, she said that she would never reveal the details of what she knew."

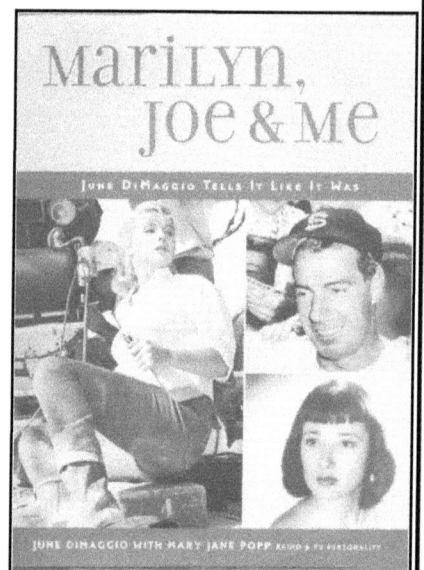

46

# COVER-UP EXPOSED
# MARILYN WAS MURDERED!
## Bombshell NEW evidence!

---

## COVER-UP EXPOSED!
# MARILYN WAS MURDERED!

By Rick Haydan

SCREEN siren Marilyn Monroe died at the hands of five Mafia hit men just before the brokenhearted star planned to hold a press conference that would have shattered the lives of the Kennedy clan and Mob boss Sam Giancana.

That's just one of the shocking claims in a blockbuster new biography of Monroe, who passed away just over 50 years ago on August 5, 1962.

"A lot of people had a lot to lose if Marilyn spoke out," says the book's author, acclaimed investigative journalist Darwin Porter. "Her close friend, actress Jeanne Carmen, told me Marilyn thought she was too big to touch."

The book — Marilyn At Rainbow's End: Sex, Lies, Murder And The Great Cover-Up (Blood Moon) — makes the definitive case against the men he blames for Monroe's murder, especially Bobby Kennedy, says Porter.

And the tell-all tome totally debunks the official story that the 36-year-old Monroe died alone in her Hollywood home after taking an overdose of barbiturates.

The Some Like It Hot star was bitter over being used and dumped by the Kennedy brothers, Porter says, but she had plenty to live for, including new screen deals, an offer for a Vegas show and two marriage proposals — one from her ex-husband Joe DiMaggio.

"I went to see Marilyn's surviving friends," Porter says. "Many were dying and had nothing to lose by finally telling the truth."

If Monroe had lived, she could have revealed her affairs with John F. Kennedy, Robert F. Kennedy and even a fling with Ted Kennedy, says Porter. And she could have disclosed JFK's ties to Giancana, including the men's shared mistress Judith Campbell Exner. And she might have revealed how Giancana's Mob helped her get her first movie contract and how she paid them back by bedding powerful men they wanted to blackmail, says Porter.

Bobby Kennedy and his actor brother-in-law Peter Lawford visited Monroe hours before her death, he says. And the journalist believes Bobby had a lot to do with Monroe's murder.

"Of course Bobby didn't do it," says the author. "He was a very smart man."

Monroe was set up by a Mob boyfriend who left her door unlocked for the five hit men, says Porter. The killers surpri[sed the] star and knocked her o[ut with] a chloroform-soaked rag [then] they stripped her nake[d and] administered an overd[ose of] barbiturates.

"Sam Giancana had [a mo]tive to kill her — she was [threat]ening to blow the lid [on his] operations," says Porte[r. "But] it also begs the questio[n: did] someone pay him to [kill] Marilyn? And if someo[ne did] pay him, the only perso[n I can] think of is a Kennedy."

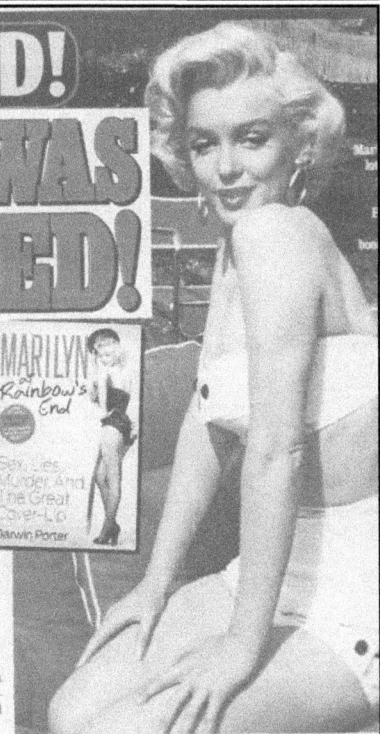

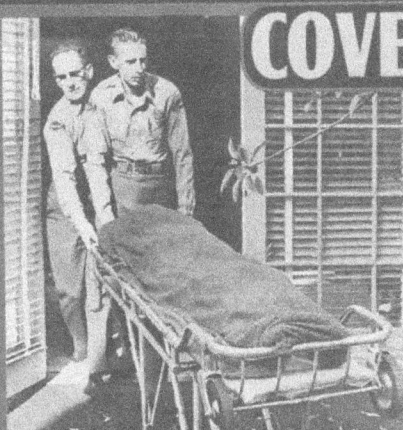

### Bombshell new evidence blows up suicide theory

Mobster Sam Giancana

MARILYN at Rainbow's End

Sex, Lies, Murder And The Great Cover-Up
Darwin Porter

Medics remove Marilyn's body (above) hours after she met with RFK (left, with JFK)

The room where Marilyn's body was found near prescription pills (inset)

# ELVIS, JFK, AND TEMPEST STORM

## SHARED TASTES, AND A TEMPEST FOR
## THE QUEEN OF BURLESQUE

**America's fabled stripper, Tempest Storm,** was a friend of Marilyn Monroe. Tempest's springboard to stardom was her "Million Dollar Treasure Chest." The women became friends and shared their memories of bedding both John F. Kennedy and **Elvis Presley**.

Tempest said she developed large breasts while still in seventh grade, and "all the boys made fun of me." Like Marilyn, she was introduced to sex early in life at the age of twelve. "The sheriff's son grabbed me and threw me in a car when I was coming out of an ice cream parlor. They dragged me into the hills where they took turns raping me, five of them."

Elvis had to climb an eight-foot fence to get at Tempest, and according to her, "he tore his pants pretty badly." JFK seduced her in the comfort of his apartment. Tempest said, "All he had to do was take off his pants and drop his underwear. As far as Jack is concerned, I believed then, and I believe now, that when a man strays, there's something wrong at home, something he's not getting."

# "THE GEORGIA PEACH"

## FAMOUS FOR HER
## 44DD-25-35 FIGURE

*"A woman's greatest weapon is a man's imagination"*
—Burlesque Queen Anne Corio

Tempest Storm, so far as it is known, is the only known woman, except for Marilyn Monroe, who shared the bed of both JFK and Elvis. Reporters always asked her the same question: Which of these men was better in the haystack? Allegedly, the stripper said, "Both were quick on the trigger, but Jack had more stamina."

The American stripper, Tempest Storm, was born Annie Blanche Banks in Eastman, Georgia, on February 29, 1928. Her career in burlesque spanned half a century, one of the longest runs of all burlesque artists.

Like Blaze Starr (her rival), she became famous for her naturally red hair and her measurements (44DD-25-35). In the late 1950s, her breasts (she called them her "moneymakers") were insured by Lloyds of London for one million dollars. She was married four times, one time to Herb Jeffries, Duke Ellington's singer "and the first black singing cowboy."

In 1987 she shocked America by publishing *Tempest Storm: The Lady Is a Vamp*, in which she detailed her affairs with both JFK and Elvis.

She first met the young senator from Massachusetts in 1955 when she was performing at the Casino Royale, a cabaret-style strip club in Washington. After her show, one of JFK's aides came backstage to arrange a meeting, but the stripper wasn't interested. At the time she thought most senators were pot-bellied and bald. She asked the aide if Senator Kennedy were married, and he told her that he was "but it didn't matter."

She asserted that a wedding ring meant "married" to her, and she wasn't going out with Senator Kennedy. Even though she turned down the offer to date him, she took a quick peek at him from behind the cur-

**In her memoirs, Tempest claimed** that when JFK was angry, "He was even more handsome and appealing than when he was happy and flashing that famous smile. However he was, he melted me like butter over an open flame."

"That youthful side of him came through one evening after we'd finished dinner and his driver was taking us for a leisurely ride through Washington. We were passing a little park, down near the Potomac River. Suddenly he told the driver to stop. He said, 'I'll race you to the river.' I fell along the way, and he collapsed beside me, kissing me long and passionately. Then he picked me up and carried me to the car. He told his driver to take us to the Mayflower Hotel where I had a suite."

This must be the only time ever recorded that JFK's back was in working order.

tain, and was stunned by his good looks.

Not one to take no for an answer, Senator Kennedy and his pals appeared the following night to see her show a second time. The same aide appeared again backstage after her show with the same request.

This time, Tempest relented, joining JFK at his table, where she found him not only handsome, but charming and witty. They made a date for the following night when she had off from the club.

She wasn't overwhelmed by him on the first date, claiming she'd dated far more famous men in Washington than him. Even when he told her that one day he'd become President of the United States, she was very skeptical, ranking that in the category of every actor who announced in advance that one day he would win an Oscar.

Although it got off to a slow start, their relationship heated up, and he saw her every night he could during her extended engagement, even if their unions had to be scheduled at two o'clock in the morning. Their affair became "stormy" at

times, especially when she was habitually late, like another of his mistresses, Marilyn Monroe. He demanded punctuality.

As he made love to her and indulged in pillow talk, she found him a contradiction—"both a little boy who wouldn't grow up and at times one of the most mature men" she'd ever bedded.

In a suite at Washington, D.C.'s Mayflower Hotel one night after making love, he confided in her that he was not happily married, "Jackie is very cold to me," he claimed.

"In my memory, Jack Kennedy's sex drive lives up to the legend that has developed around it since his death," Tempest wrote. "The man just never wore out."

Their affair went from being a "Tempest" to a slight breeze blowing across the Potomac, but it became one of his most memorable affairs. "I'd rather be screwing Tempest Storm than a dozen Marilyn Monroes," he told Senator George Smathers. "She's got better hygiene than Marilyn and doesn't let a man leave her bed until he's completely satisfied on all levels. And those tits can't be beat. She's amazing, and they're real, too."

Exit Senator Kennedy, enter Elvis Presley.

In 1957 in Las Vegas, Elvis developed a taste for strippers. At the time, Tempest was reaching the height of her fame, and Elvis went to see her perform as part of the Minsky's Follies Revue at the Dunes Hotel. Colonel Tom Parker, an expert on such matters, told Elvis that Tempest was the "real deal" when it came to burlesque.

Elvis got a seat down front and was immediately turned on when Tempest came out, her hair a flaming red, her bosom bursting out like spring. The Georgia sharecropper's daughter had Elvis murmuring under his breath, "Rock, Baby, Rock" as she heated up the room.

The next day, he telephoned her at her hotel, but she wasn't immediately turned on, admitting "at that time I could have my pick of celebrities, and Elvis

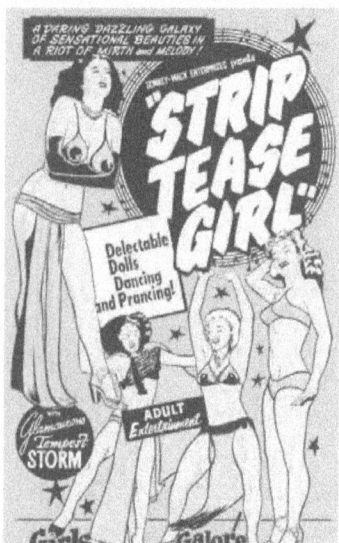

In 1951 when Jerry Lewis and Dean Martin were appearing in Vegas, they claimed that **Tempest** "has the two best props in show business."

There's no record of her having seduced Martin, but she did bed one of his fellow Rat Packers, Sammy Davis Jr.

**ELVIS & TEMPEST ARE DATING!** headlined a paper in Las Vegas.

In gold lamé, the stripper, **Tempest Storm**, was photographed with the pop star who was still a Hound Dog then and not "The King." Her right breast is seen practically stabbing him in the chest.

"We haven't done bad," she told him. "I went from a sharecropper's daughter to become the Queen of Burlesque, and you were a truck driver. Now all the gals in Vegas are trying to find out what's in your underwear. I hope it's not a disappointment."

When asked to appraise Tempest, Elvis later said, "I found her titillating."

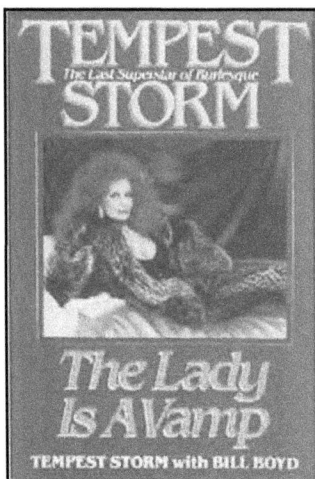

TEMPEST STORM
*The Last Superstar of Burlesque*

*The Lady Is A Vamp*

TEMPEST STORM with BILL BOYD

In 1987, long after the publicity associated with her show-biz heyday had faded and died, **Tempest Storm** released a memoir.

It was marketed as the story of "a Georgia sharecropper's daughter who achieved fortune as a star of burlesque who is sure to draw attention for the list of men with whom she claims to have had affairs. They include John F. Kennedy, Mickey Rooney, Sammy Davis Jr., Nat King Cole, Elvis Presley, Vic Damone and Engelbert Humperdinck. With the aid of *Macon* (Georgia) *Telegraph and News* columnist **Bill Boyd**, she tells of her wretched childhood, gang-rape at age 14, her stepfather's attempt at incest, running away from home in her early teens, failed marriages, serious mistakes as a mother and the death of her last lover. "Those who enjoy peeping into the bedrooms of the famous will have a field day," Boyd said.

wasn't that big a star at the time."

At first she didn't go out with him, but did agree to meet him at the Dunes Hotel. She wore a gold lamé, snugly fitting outfit and wanted to get some shots with him that she could use for publicity.

When he came face to face with Tempest, he licked every finger on her right hand.

"C'mon, Elvis," she said, "keep that up and I'll need a towel. What dime store clerk in Memphis taught you that trick?"

Obviously Elvis found Tempest's hand as "finger lickin' good" as Tennessee fried chicken. Throughout their encounter, he took note of her prominent breasts.

When a photographer arrived for their photo session, she instructed Elvis to think "naughty thoughts like we just got out of bed together."

In her steamy memoirs, *The Lady Is a Vamp*, the stripper claimed she and Elvis became almost inseparable after that posing session—"dining together, dancing together, laughing together. I enjoyed the feeling of power that came from having the idol of millions idolize me."

After the night he first seduced her, he claimed he was "as horny as a billy goat in a pepper patch."

After news of Elvis' affair with Tempest became widely gossiped about, Colonel Parker was furious. "If you keep hanging around that stripper woman, those screaming teenagers are going to quit screaming. And when they stop screaming, they'll stop buying your records, and then where the hell are you going to be? Back in Memphis driving a goddamn truck."

Even though she was genuinely attracted to Elvis, calling him the "most famous and desired man in the world," Tempest knew that their nights together were numbered. The colonel would see to that—"and that bastard called the shots for Elvis."

In the future, other singers lay in her boudoir, including Vic Damone and Frank Sinatra. "In some ways," Tempest told a girlfriend, "Vic and Frankie aren't as big as Elvis, but in other departments they are *so much bigger*."

Other celebrity lovers included Mickey Rooney and Engelbert Humperdinck.

She could be reassuring to her boyfriends, as when Engelbert doubted his prowess as a lover, and once jokingly asking her if she thought he needed a transplant. She told him he had the right equipment but had to learn how to use it.

On November 10, 2010, the former Queen of Burlesque returned to the stage to shake her stuff and show her boobs. The queen's "flame hair," for which she was once famous, may have come from a bottle during recent years, but reviewers have nonetheless noted that her breasts are not altogether fallen.

She overcame personal adversity in her life, plus a changing entertainment scene, to remain "a force in show business," as she refers to herself. Even at her age, she claims she's still looking forward to forming "new relationships" to add to the notches on her belt.

She feels the great names of burlesque will endure, including Gypsy Rose Lee and Sally Rand, and "I'm proud that mine will be added to that list of enduring legends."

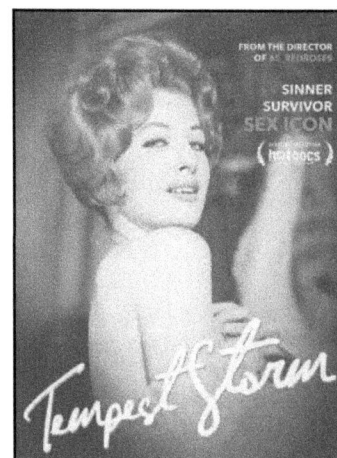

FROM THE DIRECTOR OF *SI BRIDGES*

SINNER
SURVIVOR
SEX ICON
( *RICHOCS* )

In 2016, five years before her death at the age of 93 in 2021, Director **Nimisha Mukerji** crafted a documentary on the life of **Tempest Storm**, celebrating her role as a tasteful player in an industry that has only begun to be understood by the ME, TOO movement.

In it, the sadder and wiser Georgia Peach who prompted its insights into the Age of Sputnik delivered several poignant insights into the Then vs. Now aspects of the "skin and coochi-coochi game."

# ELVIS PRESLEY'S *LOVE ME TENDER*

### The Confederate-Themed Hollywood Musical the Studio Marketed as

## "MR. ROCK 'N' ROLL IN THE MOVIE HE WAS BORN TO PLAY"

**Elvis Presley made his film debut** in this musical Western set during the Civil War. He was hired by 20<sup>th</sup> Century Fox to play the third lead, his publicity credits listed beneath both of his other co-stars, Richard Egan and Debra Paget. Robert D. Webb was assigned to direct.

Between 1945 and 1968, Webb had directed sixteen movies and won a "Best Assistant Director" Oscar for his contributions to *In Old Chicago* (1938). It was the last time the "Best Assistant Director" category was offered.

According to Webb, "I feared Elvis would strut in and try to take over, but he followed my directions and was a real good boy from the Old South. Before Elvis signed on, I had offered the role to Robert Wagner and later to Jeffrey Hunter. Both of them turned me down, claiming that the part was too small."

Before *Love Me Tender* (1956), Webb had directed Paget in *White Feather* (1955), a Western with Robert Wagner. He'd also helmed Egan in the historical adventure film, *Seven Cities of Gold* (1955).

Elvis, with his "good buddy," actor Nick Adams, arrived on the set of *Love Me Tender* before the film was fully cast. He met with both Webb and the film's producer David Weisbart, trying to persuade them to cast Adams in the role of Ray Reno, second-youngest of the Reno brothers.

"They really pissed me off in refusing to give the role to Nick," Elvis said.

Three days later, they introduced Elvis to James Drury, saying that Drury had been cast as Ray. "Who in the fuck was this Drury guy?" Elvis asked. "Never heard of him."

Originally titled *The Reno Brothers*, the film was retitled *Love Me Tender* right before its premiere. Advance sales of Elvis' recording of that song, as a single, had surpassed one-million copies. It would pass into movie history as the only film for which Elvis took third billing.

A talented and far more experienced cast than Elvis had already been assembled. Egan had been cast as Vance Reno, the oldest of the Reno brothers. Clark Gable had died in 1960 and Egan—temporarily, at least—had been approved as a possible occupant of the throne left vacant by the late King of Hollywood. Of course, that never happened.

During World War II, Egan had served in the U.S. Army. His mil-

Although both **Richard Egan** *(left)* and **Debra Paget** *(center)* were listed as its stars, with a then-relatively unknown **Elvis** *(right)* configured as a distant third, *Love Me Tender* (1956) established him as the country's most appealing celebrity renegade.

As part of its pre-release press and PR, writer Leonard Bennett in the August 1956 edition of *Cabaret* magazine wrote, in an article entitled *Who the Hell is Elvis Presley*, "The hottest singer in country today is King of Rock 'n' Roll rythms who has been called the closest thing to a "male strip teaser," but he is still an unknown to many adult squares not aware of newest teenage craze."

itary duties involved teaching recruits "How to kill a Jap with a knife." He served a year in the Philippines and was discharged with the rank of captain. Right before working with Elvis, he had co-starred in *The Revolt of Mamie Stover* (1956) alongside busty Jane Russell, who had dyed her hair red for her interpretation of the dance hall queen "Flaming Mamie." *[Russell had previously shot to fame in Howard Hughes'* The Outlaw *(1943).]*

After the release of *Love Me Tender*, Egan was voted the 13th biggest star in America. He told the press, "I owe all this success to 'The Pelvis.'"

Debra Paget portrayed the woman who marries Clint (Elvis), the youngest of the Reno brothers. As the potboiler gets hotter, it's revealed that she is still in love with Vance (Egan), who had been erroneously reported as dead from wartime injuries after a Union assault.

Paget, a native of Denver, Colorado, had just completed her greatest role in Cecil B. De Mille's epic, *The Ten Commandments* (1956). Her mother had been a burlesque queen. Paget would later imitate "Dear Old Mom" when she performed a *risqué* "snake dance" in a scene from *The Indian Tomb* (1959).

The other two Reno brothers were cast with William Campbell as Brett and James Drury as Ray.

The mother of this brood is character actress Mildred Dunnock as Martha. Born at the turn of the 20th Century, she had been Oscar-nominated for *Death of a Salesman* in 1951.

In minor roles were Neville Brand, Robert Middleton, Bruce Bennett, and Dick *Sargent [later the husband of Elizabeth Montgomery in the final three seasons (1969-1972) of* Bewitched]; uncredited as a Confederate soldier.

Although hardly remembered today, Paget worked with such stars as James Stewart, Jeff Chandler, Robert Wagner, Jeffrey Hunter, and Dale Robertson. She also appeared on the *Lux Radio Theater*, as did such stars as Burt Lancaster and Tyrone Power.

Throughout his screen career, Elvis became known for seducing many of his leading ladies, most of whom were minor actresses. Although tabloids learned about (and publicized) most of his A-list romances, Elvis' liaisons with these lesser stars will never be known. After working with him, many of them faded into obscurity.

During one of his first attempts to seduce one of his leading ladies, Elvis struck out. "He came on to me like gangbusters," Paget revealed. "He seemed to think that I would swoon and surrender to his outstretched arms. After all, a few million teenage girls were begging for his love-making. I preferred to be wooed by a man with smoother manners, with a lot more romance in his soul. Elvis struck me like the kind of guy who tells a girl, 'Drop your panties, babe. I ain't got all day.'"

*Love Me Tender* marked the only time Elvis played a historical figure, in this case within the context of the North American War Between the States. In the screenplay by Robert Buckner, he was cast as Clint Reno, the younger brother who stays at home to take care of his mother as his older brothers go to war, fighting for the Confederate cause.

As time goes by, the family learns that Vance (Egan) has been killed on the battlefield. Before he left, Vance had been in love with Cathy (Paget).

After four years, despite rumors of his death, Vance and his other brothers return home. Vance learns that Cathy is now married to Clint (Elvis). However, Cathy still loves Vance.

The plot is about to start churning, leading to a dramatic climax involving Clint's (Elvis') death.

Elvis objected violently to that "death scene ending." His position was softened, however, when his ghostly

**BEEF AND CHEESECAKE IN THE AGE OF SPUTNIK**
**(aka, There Was Life After Elvis for his Co-stars)**

*Left:* **Richard Egan** in a Speedo, *Right:* **Debra Paget** snake-dancing in *The Indian Tomb.*

Actor **Nick Adams** *(left)* is pictured here with **Elvis Presley.** He later wrote a book about their relationship called *The Rebel and the King.*

"I lived and traveled with Elvis from Hollywood to Memphis, from Houston to New York."

He later confessed to friends, "The greatest moment s of my life was when we escaped all his fans and hangers-on and stripped down and retreated to bed. At long last, I had him to myself, and we could share our secret desires as we whispered to each other."

image appears in the final minute singing "Love Me Tender."

On the set, Elvis bonded with William Campbell, who was cast as Brett, the second-oldest of the Reno brothers.

Little did Elvis know at the time that Campbell would achieve spectacular notoriety through his ex-wife, Judith Campbell (aka Judith Campbell Exner) , to whom he was married from 1952 to 1958.

*[Judith Campbell Exner catapulted herself into the celebrity Hall of Fame when she was called before a Congressional committee in 1975 to testify about her role as the mistress of (and message-carrier) for and between U.S. President John F. Kennedy and Mafia kingpin Sam Giancana—head of the Chicago mob—and Johnny Roselli. She had been introduced to JFK by Frank Sinatra, who met her during one of his gigs in Las Vegas.*

*Later, in 1988 and again, in multiple interviews with major-league journalists, she "doubled down" and reinforced her historic role as a go-between, crisscrossing the country carrying clandestine communications between JFK and members of the mob, especially as it concerned alleged CIA-backed plots to assassinate Cuba's leader, Fidel Castro.*

*All of this, however, was far removed from Elvis' association, on the set of Love Me Tender with William Campbell, Judith Exner's ex-husband.]*

According to Robert Web, the film's director, "Bill (Campbell) had to go to San Diego for three days on business. He was not needed on the set. To my surprise, Judith showed up on the first day and returned for the next two days. It was none of my business, but she was seen entering Elvis' dressing room. Her arrival was timed for when I did not need Elvis on the set. I figured that what Bill didn't know wouldn't hurt him."

Decades later, If Elvis had desired, he could have bragged that he seduced Exner before John F. Kennedy did, even before gangster Sam Giancana and Johnny Roselli seduced her too.

Bruce Bennett (once known as Herman Brix) had bonded with Elvis, too. As a boy, Elvis had seen his on-screen interpretations of Tarzan. A former Olympic athlete in the late 1920s, he had a film career that spanned forty years.

In 1931, MGM decided to bring an Edgar Rice Burroughs' Tarzan adventure to the screen. Bennett had a sculpted physique. He could also act. He was selected for that role. However, right before filming, he was completing a football-themed movie, *The Touchdown* (1931). He fell on the field and broke his shoulder. MGM then cast swimming champion Johnny Weissmuller as Tarzan—and the rest is film history.

However, by 1935, Bennett (still being billed as Herman Brix) appeared in the The New Adventures of Tarzan. *[Its plot involved Tarzan's migration from Africa to Guatemala, in search of Mayan artifacts and an idol containing priceless jewels and the key to a powerful explosive that could win wars for anyone who controlled them.]*

Bennett became a familiar face in the movies of the 1940s, including *Mildred Pierce* (1945) starring Joan Crawford in her Oscar-winning performance, and in *Dark Passage* (1947) with Humphrey Bogart and Lauren Bacall.

He was still in athletic shape at the age of 96 when he was photographed skydiving from an altitude of 10,000 feet near Lake Tahoe. He outlived all the cast of *Love Me Tender,* dying at the age of 100 on May 19, 2006.

Here, actor **William Campbell** appears with **Elvis** as one of his brothers in *Love Me Tender*.

Campbell went on to a respectable career as a B-list actor with unspectacular news coverage EXCEPT for scandals associated with his ex-wife, **Judith Campbell Exner.**

As described in the tabloid coverage that dogged her, she became the focal point of an issue which, as defined by the U.S. Justice Department, "involved a serious threat to national security."

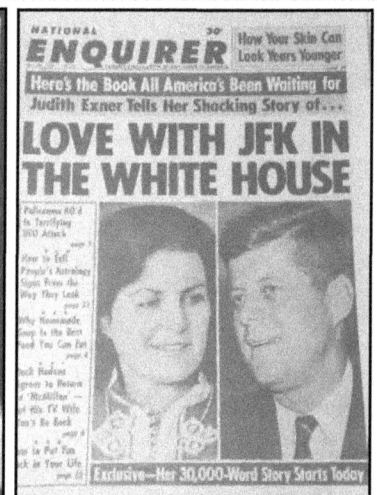

Years after **William Campbell**'s divorce in 1958 from **Judith Campbell Exner**, she became the self-admitted mistress of both **JFK** and the Chicago-based mobster, **Sam Giancana**. The front pages of both *The Star* and the *National Enquirer*—each dated shortly after her forced testimony before Congress in December of 1975—spread her notoriety to heights never dreamed of (or achieved by) her former husband.

As Exner herself said in her defense, "I was 26 and I was in love. Was I supposed to have more judgment than the President of the United States?"

*Love Me Hard, Love Me Tender, Love Me in Peacetime, Love Me in War*

At the opening of *Love Me Tender,* the trio of Reno brothers, as Confederate cavalrymen, attack a Union train carrying a Federal payroll slightly more than $12,000. The brothers didn't know that Robert E. Lee had surrendered the day before. America's Civil War was over.

After reviewing their circumstances, the men who fought for the South decide to keep the money. As it turns out, that was one big mistake, leading to a fatal shootout in which Elvis' character is killed.

Some critics pointed out that $12,000 was a lot of money in 1865. But to lead to such violence and such an uproar, the scriptwriters should probably have raised the amount to $50,000.

On a comical note, during the robbery, Egan, as a Confederate officer, orders the Union soldiers to strip down to their "long johns."

The Southerners then donned the discarded blue uniforms, thereby disguising themselves as Union soldiers. One critic snidely noted that the underwear of the Union soldiers looked like it had just emerged from a modern-day washing machine's rinse cycle. After having worn it constantly in the field for six months—as was the custom of the day—their undergarments would probably not have looked so Spic-and-Span pearly white.

*Love Me Tender* established Elvis as a bankable movie star. Made for $1.2 million, the film took in $5 million at the box office. Today, it can still be seen through streaming video services on your TV.

After its release in 1956, Elvis told a reporter from *Variety,* "When I was a teenager, I briefly worked as an usher in a movie house. My screen idols were James Dean, Marlon Brando, and Tony Curtis. Now I'm a screen idol myself."

Hal B. Wallis, Elvis' boss, pondered which script to present to Elvis for his next picture. Amazingly, for a brief moment he considered steering him into upcoming movies with Jerry Lewis. *[Lewis had broken from his long-term partnership with Dean Martin.]* Fortunately, that idea was almost hysterically nixed by Col. Tom Parker.

Although all of Elvis' films received both praise and attacks, no one ever assaulted him more ferociously (some said "vindictively") than what a reviewer of *Love Me Tender* published within *Time* magazine:

*"Is it a sausage? It's certainly smooth and damp-looking, but who ever heard of a 172-pound sausage six feet tall? It is a Walt Disney goldfish? It has the same sort of big, soft, beautiful eyes and long, curly lashes. But who ever heard of a goldfish with sideburns? Is it a corpse? The face just hangs there, limp and white with its little drop-set mouth, rather like Lord Byron in the wax museum. Suddenly, he launches into a wild belly dance as a peculiar sound emerges. A rusty foghorn? Or merely the noise produced by a cricket by the violent stridulation of his legs. Words occasionally can be made out like raisins in cornmeal mush."*

## Please Don't Call Me Tarzan

Foreword by Danton Burroughs

By Mike Chapman

*The life story of*
*Herman Brix/Bruce Bennett*

This "end of life overview" of a long and complicated Hollywood career describes **Bruce Bennett** (*aka* **Herman Brix**) and his saga as the screen's eighth Tarzan...and more. It endorses Brix as the ultimate "Ape Man," and details the scope and eclecticism of his subsequent film career too.

It was released five years before the actor's death in 2006.

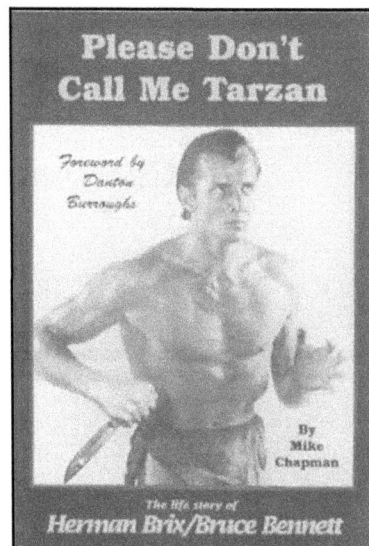

**Elvis**: White heat and Southern charm in *Love Me Tender*

Here's a view from above Manhattan's Paramount Theater during the 1956 premiere of *Love Me Tender.* That's a plastic effigy of Elvis poised above the marquis, with an emphasis on his guitar and his status as America's fastest-emerging pop icon. With its release in the North, at least, there were very few references to his portrayal in the film as an unrepentant Confederate accomplice in a train robbery.

# ELVIS' MEMPHIS MAFIA

### GUARDING HIM, INDULGING HIM, PIMPING FOR HIM, AND
#### (BY ONE MEMBER'S ACCOUNT)

### "THREE-WAYING IT" WITH HIM AND THEIR WIVES

The origin of the Memphis Mafia actually began when Elvis attended high school. The future megastar styled his hair and sideburns in ways that weren't cool back then in the Deep South. A crew of badass bullies decided to do something about it, and one of them found a pair of scissors.

After lunch, they followed him to the men's room, where they assaulted him, holding him down to begin their role as his barber, with the intention of "cleaning him up" with a G.I. haircut.

Red West, a burly football player who was known as a "badass," entered the men's toilet and, in Elvis' words, gave each of the bullies a bloody nose, sending them rushing out the door.

Elvis rarely forgot a favor. That afternoon marked the beginning of the first member inducted into the Memphis Mafia, which would soon be enlarged with the recruitment of Elvis' cousin, Sonny West.

Years later, Sonny claimed, "Elvis' twin died in childbirth, so I more or less became the brother he never had."

Another member was Joe Esposito, who met Elvis in 1958 when they were stationed at a U.S. Army Base in Friedberg, West Germany. [Known at the time as "Ray Barracks," the operation there was closed in 2007 and returned to the German government.] It was the beginning of a friendship that would last until the final months before Elvis died.

Esposito became one of the best authorities on the life of his former boss. He released books on the singer and served as one of the principal consultants for the 1981 documentary released by Warner Brothers, This Is Elvis. [Grossing $2 million in the U.S. and Canada, it re-enacted key episodes in Elvis' life when he was 11, 18, 35, and 42, and replicated commentaries from friends and members of his family, as mouthed by paid actors.]

Among others, Charlie Hodge also joined the coven followed by Alan Fortas, Marty Lacker, "Chief" Ray Sitton, Jerry Schilling, Mike Keaton, Dave Hebler, Lamar Fife, Richard Davis, and Sam Thompson.

Of them all, Esposito stood out, serving as Elvis' chief road manager and personal aide for seventeen years. Lacker served for several years as Presley's personal aide, too. He and Esposito were each best men at Elvis' wedding to Priscilla. Scotty Moore and Bill Black drove Elvis around.

"Almost from the beginning, no one loved Elvis as much as Sonny West," claimed Lee Majors. "He was devoted to the King of Rock 'n' Roll."

Billy Smith was a charter member of the gang, and he was still with Elvis in 1976. "Elvis was a rough-and-ready hillybilly cat who knew how to swivel provocatively, putting the girls in the audience in white heat." Smith would share his memories of Elvis in a book he co-authored with Lamar Fike and Marty Lacker.

It was Lacker who addressed the gay rumors swirling around Elvis. "You could see why gay men were attracted to Elvis. His cousin Gene Smith was looking at Elvis one day and said, in that funny way he talks, 'Elvis,

**Elvis** with members of his entourage

**Elvis,** overweight, heaving, and straining in 1977, three months before his death. He was also ingesting, daily, astonishing amouns of amphetimines and barbiturates.

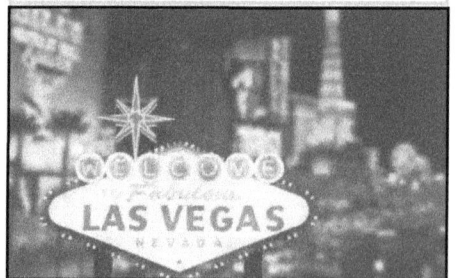

Drowned by the excesses of the "let it rip" resort he helped to create, **Elvis** became a casualty of "too much is not enough" in **Vegas.**

you know I ain't no god damn queer, but you're the prettiest thing I've ever seen."

Other "good ol' Southern boys" were recruited into the club, too.

Vernon Presley, Elvis' father, disliked them and didn't want them around, but Elvis was the boss, since he was the only one bringing in any money.

*\*\*\**

"In Memphis, Elvis loved going to the picture show," Red West said. "He rented the theater after midnight, where a special screening was set up just for Elvis and the boys. He even rented Libertyland Park for the gang. His favorite ride was the Zippin' Pippin, a roller coaster."

"On a more serious level, we handled death threats that came in for Elvis," Sonny said. "His concerts often irked guys who witnessed their gals screaming over the sexual allure of Elvis."

**Liberace,** a consummate performer and stage presence, is seen here playfully rehearsing with **Elvis.** It was that brilliantly flamboyant "fag" who fancied up Elvis' onstage dress code.

Sonny also claimed, "When Elvis didn't arrange a date with a young gal himself, he had us do it for him. When we spotted a hot piece of ass, we would go up to the bitch and ask, 'Would you like to meet Elvis Presley?' I don't recall that we were ever turned down."

The name "Memphis Mafia" was assigned to the gang in Las Vegas when they were seen arriving and leaving various venues in big black limousines, wearing black mohair suits and dark sunglasses.

Lamar Fike handled the stage lighting at Elvis concerts. Esposito collected the money before handing it over to Col. Tom Parker, "where the greedy bastard took more than his share."

As it happened, Red West was also a songwriter, and Elvis recorded two of his numbers, "Separate Ways" and "If Everyday Was Like Christmas."

Esposito said, "We took pills to stay up until dawn. Who knows who Elvis might be entertaining next? Marlene Dietrich, Fats Domino, Della Reese. We went to a late show in Vegas every night. The fag of fags, Liberace, became infatuated with Elvis. That queen got Elvis to abandon his more casual outfits in favor of those outlandish things he wore in the 1970s."

Ostentatiously obvious, and in constant proximity to the megastar, "The Memphis Mafia became better known in Vegas than Frank Sinatra's Rat Pack," claimed Sonny West.

**Frank Sinatra,** who detested **Elvis Presley,** nonetheless staged a "Welcome Home Elvis" musical TV show on Miami Beach on March 12, 1960. "The Pelvis" was back home after serving in the U.S. Army. Ol' Blue Eyes wanted the ratings, and he got them as millions of Americans sat by their TV sets. A highlight of the show occurred when the two singers switched songs—Elvis sang "Witchcraft" and Frank sang "Love Me Tender."

They joined Elvis riding bumper cars in the Las Vegas Valley and riding horses with him in the wilds of California. Otherwise, they spent a lot of time just "hanging out" with him at Graceland. Red West and Sonny West sometimes appeared uncredited in minor appearances in Elvis' roster of films.

The Colonel resented the gifts that fans or wannabe friends bestowed on Elvis. His motto was that any benefits acquired by his client should be equally divided with him.

Peter Guralnick, a specialist in the history of early rock 'n' roll, claimed that in Las Vegas, Elvis often included members of his gang when he entertained other celebrities. As such, they were with Elvis when he welcomed Sammy Davis Jr.—even though most of them had grown up in rural Mississippi, where blacks and whites rarely mixed socially.

Sinatra had his reasons for hating Elvis, who had knocked him off the charts and made off with his mistress, Juliet Prowse. Not only that, but he was dating Sinatra's daughter, Nancy.

As entrenched insiders, members resented actor Nick Adams when he came to Graceland for a prolonged stay there with Elvis. "Elvis actually slept with that fag in his bedroom," Red West claimed. "I could imagine what was going on. No, I didn't want to know."

A video of this historic onstage encounter has been remastered and released on a "Memphis Recording" label.

Elvis sometimes paid members of "the gang" salaries that ranged from $300 to $500 a week, offering most of them an occasional bonus plus a gift of a car and even a house. Although individual members came and went, many stuck around from the 1950s until 1977 when Vernon Presley fired them a month before Elvis' death. Elvis, as the leader of the pack, made it clear, "I'm the boss and what I say goes."

After the death of his son, Vernon admitted, "The happiest day of my life was when Elvis told me to fire that rotgut crowd of spongers, the so-called Memphis Mafia. Each of them was just a shithead, seeing how much they could get out of Elvis. After my son's divorce from Priscilla, his financial condition headed south. The easy money came and went, with Col. Parker taking the lion's share. He was a real bastard and a crook."

After they were fired, Red and Sonny West, along with Dave Hebler, released an "as told to" book by Steve Dunleavy (who had many links to Rupert Murdoch), entitled *Elvis: What Happened?* It was touted as "the dark other side of the brightest star in the world…Three of Elvis' closest companions tell a shocking bizarre story."

To attract a wide readership, the publisher, Ballantine Books, summarized the revelations when the paperback was issued.

The book depicted Elvis as "brooding, violent, and obsessed with death. It revealed that one night, he invited Mafia members for a 3AM tour of a mortuary to look over the corpses and talk about embalming.

He also plotted killing "the man who stole Priscilla from me."

"He was strung out and sexually driven," Sonny West alleged.

The book was published on August 1, 1977, two weeks prior to Elvis' death. Eventually, it sold three million copies. One of them was found on his nightstand. Some insiders claim that Elvis was horrified and infuriated, and that he'd been betrayed.

One of its more shocking revelations involved Elvis' penchant for sleeping with a Mafia member and his wife. *[The French sometimes define something like this as a* ménage à trois. *Memphis Mafia members referred to it as a "three-way."]*

Sonny West, in particular, objected to the tone of many competing books about Elvis, accusing their writers of something akin to "class distinctions."

"The writers *[of those books]* made us out to be white trash. Just because you're poor doesn't mean you're white trash. That son of a bitch, Albert Goldman in 1981 wrote a book about Elvis. His revelations made me sick. Just because you come from a family of sharecroppers with a hint of incest doesn't mean you're trash."

After Elvis' death, confronted with fury and condemnation from many of Elvis' diehard fans for what he'd authorized within *Elvis: What Happened?*, Sonny told a reporter, "We thought that if Elvis read the truth about what had been written about him by people who knew him well, he would look and reflect on where all his heavy drug-taking was leading him. He might think he had to get it together and change his life, since he was heading for an early grave if he didn't give up drugs. They were ruining his life. If he quit binge-eating and looking like a fat pig, and went into rehabilitation and emerged drug free, he might go on for another twenty years."

As told to and through the writer and journalist Alanna Nash, Billy Smith, Marty Lacker, and Lamar Fike also came out with a thick book, *Elvis and the Memphis Mafia* in 2005.

In *Entertainment Weekly*, Greg Sandow wrote: "The book is utterly human and utterly real. We've heard the myths., Now we know the truth. For anyone who cares about Elvis, the book is a dream come true."

Another reviewer claimed, "If Elvis were still around, he wouldn't call it a dream, but a nightmare."

The book is filled with running commentaries, none of them flattering, from three former members of the Elvis Mafia. One such revelation centered on Lamar Fife's comment about Elvis and Frank Sinatra when they appeared on television together after Elvis' return from West Germany following his military service there in the U.S. Army.

"Elvis didn't like doing the show. He didn't like Sinatra back then. Sinatra had made a lot of derogatory remarks about Elvis when he was starting out in 1956. He claimed that "The music of Elvis is deplorable, a rancid-smelling aphrodisiac….the most brutal, ugly, degenerate, various form of expression it has been my displeasure to hear."

***

There are many sad ironies associated with the Memphis Mafia—their fawning sycophancy, and ultimately, their collusion against the megastar who organized and nurtured them. Latter-day readers might conclude that the "takeaway" is a warning to other celebrities: When somebody asks, *"Who Loves Ya, Baby?"*…BEWARE!

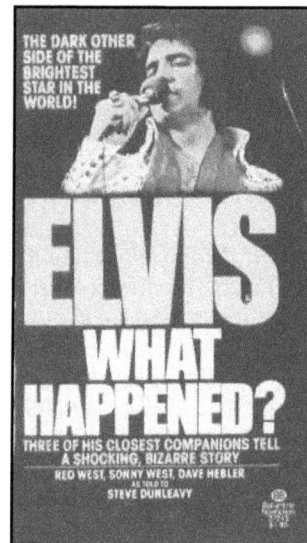

**Three of Elvis' body-guards**—each of whom had tasted the pleasures and felt the pain of everyday life with the most fabulous star in showbiz history—collaborated in this *exposé* of "the dark other side of the brightest star in the world."

Elvis died a few weeks after reading it.

**"Iconhood is a strange business.** Who could have predicted that Elvis, fat and long past crooning when he died sitting on a toilet, would take up permanent residence in the imaginations of fans not yet born?"

**—Daphne Merkin** in *The New Yorker*, May 31, 1998.

# ELVIS
## & THE RICHEST WOMAN IN THE WORLD

**Elvis Presley** was an unlikely conquest for **Doris Duke**, the steel-gloved tobacco-industry heiress. Although she had an affair with the less well-endowed, more homosexually inclined Cary Grant, she preferred men like her second husband, the heavy-hung Porfirio Rubirosa, the Dominican playboy-diplomat.

Her lovers included actor **Brian Aherne**, who claimed "Doris had the most beautiful legs in the world." She often wrapped those legs around his neck. Others of her lovers included **Errol Flynn, David Niven, Aristotle Onassis, Gilbert Roland, George Sanders, General George C. Patton, and lots of Hawaiian beach boys**. She told Truman Capote that she had a sexual preference for "dark meat."

**An  Odd Couple** is a concept that refers to more, much more, than merely a hit TV comedy series with fussbudget Tony Randall and lovable slob Jack Klugman.  The phrase more often refers to  bizarre couplings in unexpected combinations.

Everybody's heard of the affair between President Kennedy and Marilyn Monroe.  Less well-known is the brief sexual encounter between tobacco heiress, Doris Duke, the world's richest woman, and Elvis Presley.

In 1967, having just healed from "history's finest plastic surgery," Duke flew to Las Vegas to see Elvis "in the flesh," so to speak.

Still slender and attractive, she was a ripe 55, Elvis only 32.

He'd been born into poverty, she with a silver spoon in her mouth—or a least a cigarette.

Yet they shared some common ground, as both of them belonged to the Self-Realization Fellowship in Los Angeles. Each of them had the same fashionable guru, and both of them adored black soul music.

At one time, Duke had even taken dancing lessons from "Bojangles" Robinson and singing lessons from Aretha Franklin's father. Her favorite singer, however, was Elvis, upon whom she'd developed a lingering crush, almost a fixation.

For dinner in her Vegas hotel suite, Duke invited not just The King, but the gossipy and rather effeminate Truman Capote. At dinner, she served Capote lobster and caviar, but for Elvis, she offered fried bacon and melted cheese sandwiches with thick chocolate milkshakes.

Years later, Capote revealed the subject of this strange trio's conversation. "Toilet paper." She urged Elvis to install paperless toilets at Graceland, as she had recently done at her estates. "Otherwise, the servants will use so much toilet paper that you'll go to a pauper's grave," she warned Elvis.

Capote claimed that at some point, way after midnight, Elvis disappeared with Duke into her bedroom, leaving the author alone to finish off the vintage champagne.

A year later, at a dinner party at Duke's palatial estate in New Jersey, Capote asked her how it had gone with Elvis. She frowned before admitting that she'd proposed marriage to him. "I found him very, very sexy. But he turned me down." Then she sighed. "American men have no talent for marrying rich women."

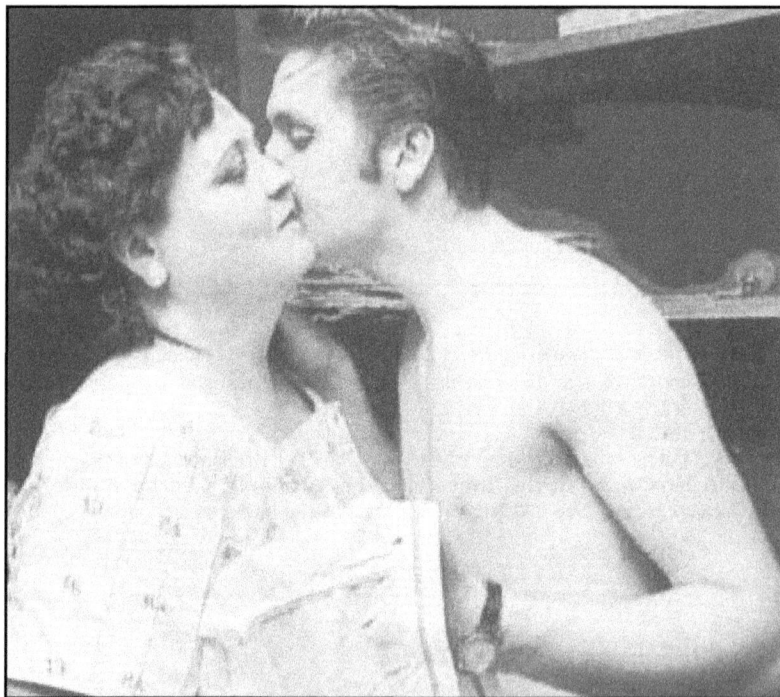

The relationship between **Gladys Presley** and her son, **Elvis**, was defined as "incestuous, if not physically, then spiritually" by Elvis' stepmother.

Gladys was horrified when she heard Elvis was receiving letters from the tobacco heiress. In 1957 she warned her son "never to contact that awful woman again."

"Don't worry mama," Elvis said, "We'll never hook up. I was told that the bitch likes her toes sucked, and white boys don't do that."

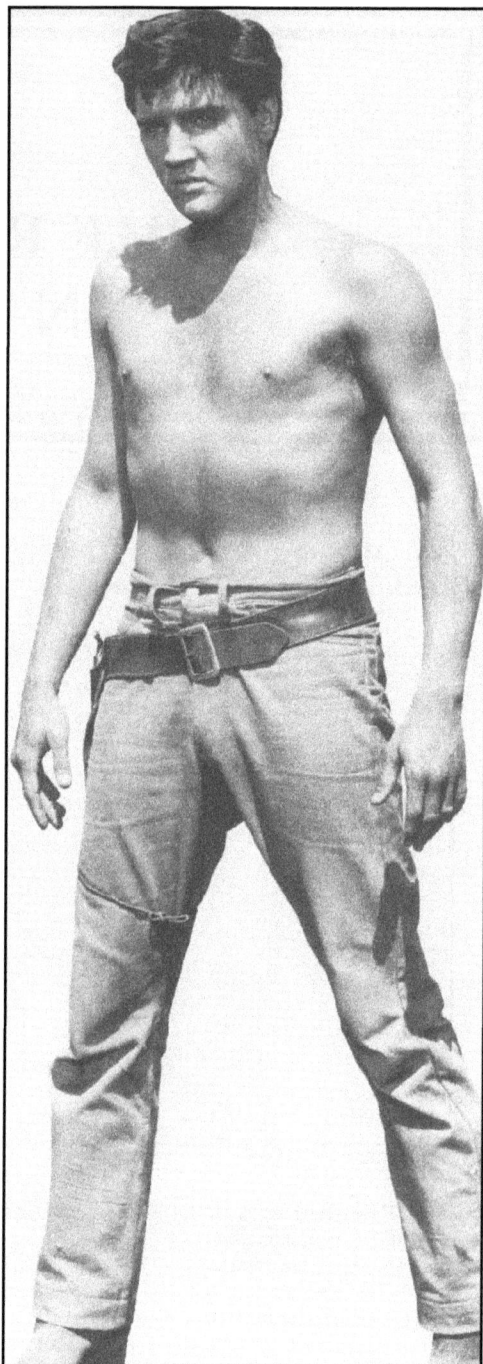

**Doris Duke** developed a fixation on **Elvis Presley** after seeing him go shirtless in the movie, *Flaming Star* (1960). She was said to have seen all of his movies, some films more than once. Jokingly, she summarized all the plots of the Elvis films to Truman Capote: "A Southern boy beats up a guy and then sings to him."

Duke even sat through such mindless crap as the ditsy *Tickle Me*, and claimed that her favorite song of Elvis' was from *Paradise – Hawaiian Style*.

She even predicted that "Queenie Waheenee's Papayan Surprise" would become "immortal Elvis."

Known both for both out-of-control spending and penny-pinching, **Doris Duke** inherited $50 million in 1925 when she was 12.

The debutante who broke all the rules became a star in endless legal battles and a renowned collector of Islamic and Buddhist art.

An accomplished musician and jazz pianist, she also had a brief, inconclusive affair with Elvis Presley.

When **Elvis** and **Truman Capote** dined together at Duke's estate in Hawaii, Capote later reported on the only serious conversation they ever had. Capote complimented Elvis for having the courage to be an "ass-kicking rocker willing to take on all the bullies at school who mocked you for your Tony Curtis hair-do and punk look, even your blue suede shoes. In many ways—as a straight, of course—you behaved like a young gay male who dresses in drag walking down the meanest street in town, knowing that your very appearance will get the shit beat out of you."

Elvis was quick to respond. "I'm not a guy to be pushed around. I was in pursuit of a dream, and I was never willing to let anybody come between me and my dream."

"So how do you respond to critics who say your act is a male burlesque show?" Capote asked.

"I move my pelvis with the same gyrations I use in the fuck," Elvis claimed.

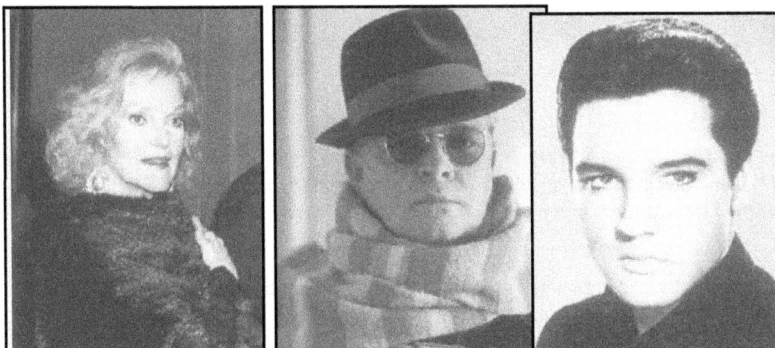

For some reason, **Doris Duke** kept extending invitations to both **Elvis** and **Truman Capote** at the same time. Privately, Elvis told Duke that Capote was a "faggot," but Capote's satirical wit and razor sharp parodies of the rich and famous soon had Elvis in stitches. Capote, known for stretching the truth, told Elvis that, "Jacqueline Kennedy – my closest friend – has a secret crush on you. I can arrange for you to have a rendezvous with her to fuck her."

Elvis said he'd be eager to accomplish that mission, but Capote, of course, never followed through with his promise. After some time at Duke's palatial and aptly named Shangri-la in Hawaii, Elvis left while Capote stayed behind for a dinner Duke had planned with Greta Garbo.

Duke later said of that evening, "Garbo is the most boring woman in the world."

**Doris Duke** was not alone in sampling the wares of **Porfirio Rubirosa** (1909-1963), who had once been married to the sluttish Flor de Oro Trujillo, daughter of The Dominican Republic's dictator, Rafael Trujillo, an autocrat who was nicknamed "The Goat" because of his sexual excesses.

Duke took Rubirosa as her second husband, but had to share his sexual favors with, among others, Joan Crawford, Evita Peron, Ava Gardner, Veronica Lake, Jayne Mansfield, and Marilyn Monroe. He even seduced Patricia Kennedy Lawford, the U.S. president's sister. When John F. Kennedy heard about that, he bluntly asked her, 'Is it as big as they say?" His sister refused to answer, but her husband, Peter Lawford, claimed he had the exact measurements: "Eleven inches long and thick as a beer can. That guy can balance a chair with a telephone book on it on the tip of his erection."

**Duke** (above) is photographed on her wedding day in 1947. Having been coerced a few moments before the ceremony into signing a prenuptial agreement, Rubirosa smoked a cigarette during the delivery of his wedding vows and later fainted in her arms.

**Rubi,** Doris's husband, a man with a talent for marrying rich women, appears in the photo (below) with Doris's rival, the almost-as-rich-as-Doris **Barbara Hutton**.

After his divorce from Duke, the Latino fortune hunter would marry the Woolworth heiress in 1953.

# WHEN ELVIS WENT UP TO SEE HER

## THE KING OF ROCK 'N' ROLL MEETS MAE WEST

**The love affair of the century** was NOT launched on the night **Elvis Presley** came to call upon **Mae West.** Mae would have been willing if Elvis hadn't bolted. He might even have gone along with it had he not suspected that Mae was a female impersonator. After all, he didn't always go for 14-year-old girls, and he'd been known to seduce older women before, including Doris Duke.

"Let's face it," Mae declared to Elvis. "There are only two great sex symbols left in the world today--yours truly and the man I'm looking at right now in those tight pants. I wish I'd been born in a different era, when men wore tight pants and not those baggy trousers they used to wear. After all, a gal should know what she's getting. Don't you agree?"

Elvis didn't think the question required an answer.

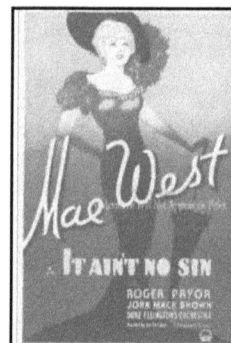

# ELVIS AND THE QUEEN OF CAMP

**The film, if it had ever been made,** would have become *the* jawdropping camp classic of the 20<sup>th</sup> century.

Elvis harbored a dream of appearing opposite, not Marilyn Monroe or even Jayne Mansfield, but Mae West, who at the time was 72 years old.

He didn't care that her last film, *The Heat's On*, had bombed shortly after its release in 1943. Watching the Oscar ceremonies in 1958, Elvis had been fascinated when West, with Rock Hudson, generated wild applause with a hilarious duet, "Baby It's Cold Outside."

In 1964 when Elvis was evaluating the script for *Roustabout*, he decided that the role of the fairground owner, Maggie Morgan, would be ideal for the ageless sex goddess. He demanded that his producer, Hal Wallis, offer her a contract, and announced that he intended to sing three separate duets onscreen with her.

The next day Wallis told Elvis that West would agree to the role only after a private audition with him "to check on our mutual chemistries." Elvis called West, and she invited him to "come up and see me sometime like tonight at eight."

Aware of her reputation for seducing young men, he invited his sidekick, Nick Adams, to join him.

West greeted "the boys," as she called them, in a long, white, rhinestone-studded gown that evoked her 1934 film, *Belle of the Nineties*.

West and Elvis were sympathetic souls, and genuinely seemed to like each other. She regaled the men with indiscreet stories of her decades in show business. When she excused herself to "powder my nose," Elvis whispered to Adams that he'd heard rumors that West was a drag queen. "Now that I've met her in person, I'm sure of it."

Had he wanted to, Elvis that night could have learned first hand if West were a man or a woman. After three hours of additional dialogue, he excused himself, claiming he had another appointment. Actually, he had a late-night date with Ann-Margret.

In urging him to stay, West claimed that she liked to "audition" her leading men before signing a contract. "I want to know if they swing my way." Seeing doubt on Elvis's face, she assured him, "I have the body of a 26-year-old gal."

In spite of the offer, he politely excused himself and headed for the door with Adams trailing. The next morning Wallis told Elvis that West had liked him and would sign the contract. But before the deal could be finalized, Elvis's manager, Col. Tom Parker, intervened. He threatened to shut down production on the picture if West were signed. The savvy old showman knew that she'd rewrite the script, zapping it with her famous *double-entendre* one-liners.

**Mae West** was impressed that Elvis was called **"Elvis the Pelvis."** In her one and only meeting with The King, she claimed that the hip action of the pelvis was almost as important as the sex act itself. She also revealed that a "sexercise" of her pelvis was a work-out she performed every morning to prepare herself for the action to follow that evening.

"You've got to keep the pelvis muscles really firm," she told Elvis, "Completely toned. Pelvis exercise also tones the leg muscles and thigh muscles as well. Even the stomach muscles. In sexual activity, you've got to use not just your pelvis, but your thighs and your stomach."

At the age of 72, she demonstrated her technique. Lying on her stomach upon the thickly carpeted floor of her living room, she extended her arms into what she called a "T Position." She proceeded to demonstrate her pelvis exercise, the rules of which she later defined within her infamous book, *Mae West on Sex, Health & ESP*. She had three rules: "Take a deep breath and lift your legs as high as you can but keep them straight. Hold that position for the count of five. Maybe even ten on a good day. Now exhale slowly and bring your legs to the floor. Now take it easy for a minute or so to get your breath. Repeat that same exercise five times. You'd be surprised how good the sex act will feel later if all your muscles, including the pelvis, are in tiptop shape."

She admitted that Elvis shaking his pelvis onstage would achieve the same effect as her sexercise. "With all that pelvis action, I bet you're a treat for the gals."

"*Roustabout* would be a Mae West picture with Elvis as her stooge," Col. Parker shouted at Wallis.

Elvis was bitterly disappointed when he learned that West was out, the role going to Barbara Stanwyck instead. The former speakeasy dancer from Brooklyn was the biggest female star Elvis had ever appeared with. She was available only because she, along with Joan Crawford, had been fired from the latest Bette Davis movie, *Hush...Hush, Sweet Charlotte*.

Elvis and Stanwyck hated each other on sight. On the second day of the shoot, Stanwyck overheard Elvis telling some of his Memphis Mafia boys that she was "the most closeted dyke in Hollywood."

She never spoke to him again except when delivering her lines in front of the camera. When the picture wrapped, Stanwyck told Wallis, "As an actor, Mr. Presley is pathetic. *He has no star quality*." Then she stormed off the sound stage.

\*\*\*

**Mae West became** the all-time gay icon among movie divas and was for decades the single most impersonated actress by drag queens. One of her first plays, *The Drag*, became notorious for dealing with the then-taboo subject of homosexuality. When the show opened in New York, there were fears it would cause a riot.

For a woman born in 1893, she was rather tolerant of the gays she encountered in vaudeville, and later the movies. Yet even at their best, many of her views on homosexuality were Victorian. She referred to gays as "The Third Sex" and claimed that "the homosexual act" was really a form of masturbation, "bringing temporary relief but no real satisfaction." She also felt that a "bitchy homosexual can be worse than a bitchy woman." (EDITOR'S NOTE: PERHAPS SHE WAS RIGHT.)

In contrast to her tolerance for gay men, Mae had a disdain for lesbians. She once recalled her meeting with Marlene Dietrich, whom she claimed had "made a bigger name through her publicity than her talent."

"I've always washed my own hair when I was shooting a picture," Mae wrote. "I'd get to the studio very early to do it the way I liked. One day I was standing at the sink rinsing my hair when the door opened. I turned off the water and felt a towel being placed on my head, then hands moving it around as they dried my hair. I still didn't know who the hands belonged to, and when I turned around, I was surprised to see Marlene Dietrich staring at me, wearing nothing but a flimsy robe."

"'You are very beautiful,' I told her. 'I've always been an admirer of yours.'"

"At that point, Dietrich's robe opened, and she stared at me waiting for me to catch the pass she was throwing. Never at a loss for words, I found the right ones: 'You'd better button up dearie. You're gonna catch cold.'"

According to Miss West, Miss Dietrich left and never returned,

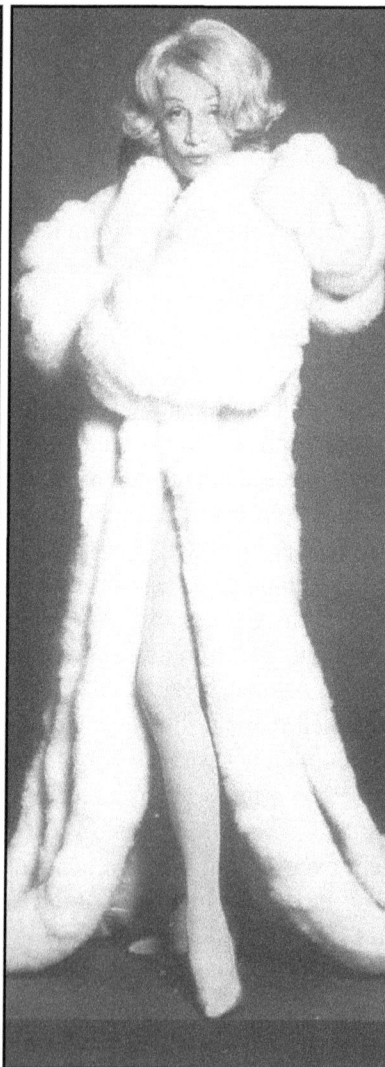

**Nick Adams**, at the time, Elvis' best pal, attended the historic meeting between the King of Rock 'n' Roll and the aging Queen of Sex, Miss **Mae West**. Unlike Elvis, who did not succumb to Mae's vintage charms, Adams was the eternal star fucker.

"Age or sex didn't matter to Nick," said one of his best pals, Forrest Tucker. "All he demanded of the fuckee was that he/she/it be a star. And there was no doubt that Mae West stood for stardom."

During his meeting with Mae, Elvis got up and requested to "go to the little boy's room." It was then that Nick moved in on Mae. "Little boys like Elvis are fine, but, as you know, sometimes a lady such as yourself needs a big boy," Nick said. "Accent on big."

Size-queen Mae got the point and accepted the phone number offered. She made Nick wait three weeks before calling him. She phoned and he visited, and he hadn't exaggerated his male charms.

But when Mae called again for a repeat performance, Nick was unavailable. He later told Rock Hudson, "I woke up to reality. At this point in her career, Mae West couldn't do anything for her own career – much less mine. Now John Wayne, that's a guy who can get parts for me. In the future, you're gonna see me hanging out with the Duke." And so it came to be.

64

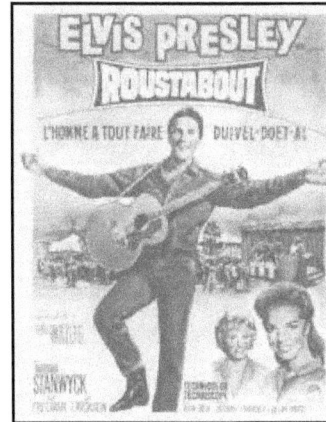

**Barbara Stanwyck** was a great actress, as these pictures with **Elvis** in the 1964 film, *Roustabout,* indicate. Although personally, she detested Elvis, her on-screen chemistry and sense of professionalism made it appear that she adored him.

Elvis made a mistake on the first day of the shoot by suggesting to Stanwyck that he was going to learn a lot from her and be as devoted to her as he was to his own mother, Gladys. "I know I can learn a lot about acting from you. I'm sure you'll be like a mother to me and get me through this damn picture."

"I'm nobody's mother," Stanwyck shot back. "And certainly no mother to Elvis Presley."

Actually, Stanwyck did have an adopted son, Dion, an arrangement finalized during her marriage to her first husband Frank Fay. But throughout his life, she virtually ignored Dion, sending him away to boarding schools or to live with relatives.

Perhaps as a means of getting back at her, Dion exposed details about her marriage to Robert Taylor in the pages of *Confidential*. The headline blared, *DOES MY MOTHER, BARBARA STANWYCK, HATE ME?* The article was published in 1959, around the time Dion was arrested for selling pornographic materials.

**Colonel Tom Parker,** Elvis' control freak, money-grubbing manager, nixed the deal to star Elvis with Mae West in *Roustabout,* preferring Barbara Stanwyck instead. Stanwyck later admitted that she was shocked when Hal Wallis called and asked her to appear with Elvis.

"The idea of working with Mr. Presley intrigued me, because that would bring me into a younger audience than I'm accustomed to. And I thought it would be rather fun."

How wrong she was. To the press she said, "Elvis was a wonderful person to work with. His manners are impeccable, he is on time, he knows his lines, he asks for nothing outside of what any other actor or actress wants."

Privately she denounced him to Joan Crawford as, "A shithead, a selfish, uneducated oaf, surrounded by Southern redneck retards, and no doubt a closeted homosexual like my dear cock-sucking former husband, Bob Taylor."

**Stanwyck** had first seen **Elvis** on *The Ed Sullivan Show,* which she watched faithfully every week. In the photo (left), Col. **Tom Parker** *(left figure)*, **Elvis** *(center)*, and **Sullivan** *(right)* face a tense moment behind the scenes.

Sullivan had just told the colonel and Elvis that the rock 'n' roll star was to be photographed or filmed only from the waist up. His gyrations, according to Sullivan, were deemed obscene for young TV audiences. Elvis voiced strong objections to this, but Parker calmed him down. After Sullivan had left, Parker told Elvis, "We'll just take the fucker's money and run to the bank with it."

**Marilyn Monroe**

**1926-1962**

**REST IN PEACE**

**Elvis Presley**

**1935-1977**

**REST IN PEACE**

# PART TWO

## MOVIE STARS

# THERE IS NOTHING LIKE A DAME

## "BRUNETTES ARE BETTER, and BRUNETTES HAVE MORE FUN,"

says Danforth Prince, President of Blood Moon Productions, about the release, this week, of his company's hot new biography of Hollywood's ultimate goddess, **Elizabeth Taylor.** Continue reading for information about what readers should expect from a woman defined by her enemies as:

*AN UBER-DIVA, THE SERPENT OF THE NILE,*
*AND THE MEGA-CELEBRITY WHO REDEFINED HEDONISM AND POP CULTURE IN AMERICA.*

**NEWS FROM BLOOD MOON:** AVAILABLE IN OCTOBER
The most comprehensive overview of scandals associated with

# ELIZABETH TAYLOR

ever published, with detailed descriptions of dozens of incidents that the *Über*-goddess would NEVER have tolerated during her lifetime.

**For IMMEDIATE RELEASE** Blood Moon proudly announces an October release of **Darwin Porter's** startling new overview of the life of America's most famous brunette movie star, **Elizabeth Taylor.**

Porter is the author of dozens of other critically approved *exposés*. According to Porter, "Thanks to the completion of the Taylor project, I will have written definitive and revisionistic statements about most of the leading film stars of America's 'Golden Age.'"

The release of this book will follow (and complement) the publication, last April, of Porter's seminal and award-winning biography, *Marilyn at Rainbow's End*, a widely publicized biography of America's OTHER most famous female movie star, **Marilyn Monroe.**

According to Danforth Prince, President of Blood Moon, "Miss Taylor, by her own admission, developed a woman's body when she still had the mind of a child. More than all but a handful of other stars, she operated very effectively in that bizarre milieu known as the Entertainment Industry. This book showcases her experiences with other high-profile celebrities (Ronald Reagan, Errol Flynn, John F. and Jackie Kennedy, Peter Lawford and dozens of others) in ways never outlined in any other book. Her life was one of staggering excess—too many men, too much money, too much jewelry, too much scandal."

## WHAT A DAME!

For more than 60 years, Elizabeth Taylor dazzled generations of movie-goers with her glamour, her devotion to charity, her astute business sense, and her all-consuming passion for life. She was the last of the great stars of Golden Age Hollywood, coming to a sad end in 2011 at the age of 79.

Shortly before she died, appearing on the Larry King show, she insisted that her biographers had revealed "only half of my story. I can't tell the other half in any memoir, because I'd get sued."

Throughout her long and complicated life, Miss Taylor consistently generated hysteria among her fans. Within this much-anticipated release from Blood Moon, hundreds of Ms. Taylor's personal secrets are relayed with brutal honesty and in rich, juicy detail, with a new revelation on every page.

Her scandals are exposed, and a lot more, in a saga that's both sympathetic and shocking. *There is Nothing Like a Dame* contains enough irony, drama, and detail to fascinate anyone who's ever been intrigued with the lore and legend of the 20th century's most notorious *femme fatale.*

*"I'm called a scarlet woman. That's wrong. I'm positively purple."*

—Elizabeth Taylor

*"Before they wither, Elizabeth Taylor's breasts will topple empires."*

—Richard Burton

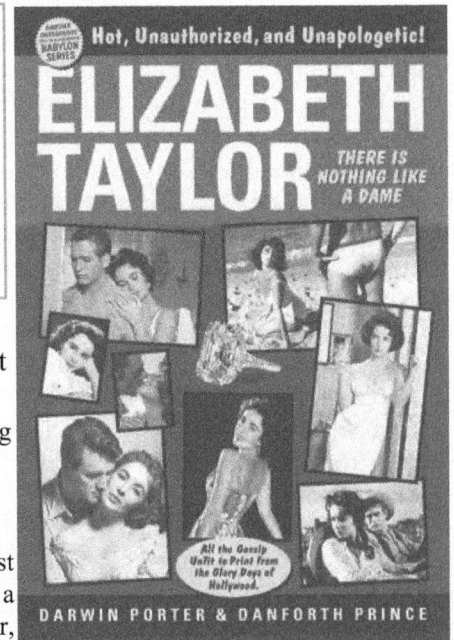

# Saying Goodbye to a Hollywood Legend
# DAME ELIZABETH TAYLOR
## (1932-2011)

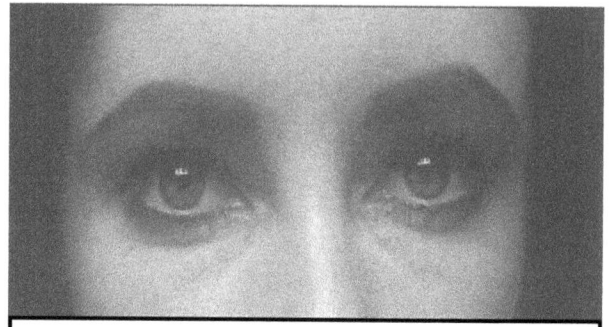

Because "legend" is an often misused word, it should be reserved for only a chosen few, Elizabeth herself being among them. *[She hated the name "Liz."]* A beauty for the ages, who touched generations with her glamour and passion for life, she was the last of the great stars of a once-golden age. She died on March 23, 2011, at age 79.

From London, as an adolescent pre-teen, "The Little Refugee" fled to California "when Hitler started dropping those damn bombs." She won our hearts in the *Lassie* films and in *National Velvet* (1944), in which she played a jockey. The statement she made then summed up her life: "I'd be thrown from my pony and would climb back up, and off I'd go again—the faster the better."

**Elizabeth Taylor** was known throughout America for "fabulous tits and ass", multiple marriages, her penchant for scandal, and a jewelry collection that was the envy of gem collectors worldwide.

Yet it was her eyes—soulful and violet with long, long lashes—that many of her fans found mesmerizing.

Most of us grew up with Elizabeth. We followed her through each of her eight marriages (twice to Richard Burton), and through countless love affairs. We went in and out of hospitals with her; read about her scandals; were fascinated by her emperor's trove of emeralds and diamonds, and in time, applauded her for raising much-needed funds for "The Black Death" of AIDS that overtook the world in the 1980s.

Having read many of her biographies, her fans thought they knew all about her, as she was one of the most widely publicized figures of the 20th Century. But on *The Larry King Show,* she admitted that those authors who tried to chronicle her life each had failed miserably. "They didn't even know the half of it," she later disclosed. "Me? Write a tell-all memoir? NEVER. Too many people would sue for libel."

Although she became a beloved figure, she was reviled when she snapped crooner Eddie Fisher from the arms of "America's Sweetheart," Debbie Reynolds. Their feud raged for years until they dined together aboard *The Queen Elizabeth* during one of its transatlantic crossings. During their shipboard encounter, both of them admitted that "Eddie wasn't worth all the bother."

When Elizabeth fell in love with Richard Burton on the set of *Cleopatra* in Rome in the early 60s, she was denounced in headlines around the world, even by the Vatican. As for Burton, although he never liked her "short dumpy legs," she said, "I get an orgasm just listening to that voice of his."

Howard Hughes pursued her, offering jewelry and $1 million in cash, but she rejected him. In anger, he said, "Every man should have the opportunity of sleeping with Elizabeth Taylor—and at the rate she's going, every man will."

Her third husband, showman/producer Mike Todd, who died in an airplane crash, was the second love of her life, after Burton.

"Lemme tell ya," he said. "Any minute that this little dame spends out of bed is totally wasted."

Her eighth and final marriage—to truck-driving Larry Fortensky, whom she met in rehab— was doomed from the start. Michael Jackson staged the couple's *[some said "elaborately dysfunctional"]* wedding, when the justice of the peace asked for the names of her former husbands, Elizabeth snapped, "What is this, a memory test?"

Contrary to what some people believed, Elizabeth's life was not an open book. She committed everything to her secret binaries, which may or may not get published one day. Already, revelations are being leaked to the press—her steamy encounter with Marilyn Monroe; her long-enduring trysts with President Kennedy and her catfight with Jackie; the rape of her then-husband Eddie Fisher by a jealous Richard Burton, who did it with the intention of showing the ambivalent singer who was "the man;" Burton's discovery of his wife's affair with Sammy Davis Jr.; the child of Frank Sinatra's that she aborted; the pursuit of her by Prince Rainier, who would have preferred marriage to her instead of to Grace Kelly—and the revelations go on and on.

This great-grandmother to four has at last been laid to rest, but her memory may linger for generations. A battle for her billion-dollar (plus) estate raged after her death.

As for her epitaph, Dame Elizabeth could have written it herself: "MGM taught me how to be a star, and I have never really known how to be anything else."

Here's pre-teen **Elizabeth Taylor** with her older brother, **Howard,** a politicized "non-conformist' who—like her—became a prominent activist in liberal causes. Both were born in the UK to cultured, arts-oriented parents.who emigrated to Los Angeles before the outbreak of World War II

Their socially ambitious mother's extra-curricular affair with a well-positioned diplomat (a friend of the family) led to widespread speculation about Elizabeth's paternity.

# WHAT DAME ELIZABETH KEPT HIDDEN

*"I dig sex and I've had my share of handsome hunks."*

When the syndicated columnist Liz Smith heard that there was a posthumous book about to be published on Elizabeth Taylor in the wake of her death in 2011, she cynically asserted, "Oh, *puh-LEEZE,* I challenge him (the author) to find another scandalous revelation we haven't heard already."

In a biography I released in 2012, *Elizabeth Taylor, There is Nothing Like a Dame,* I have met that challenge—*and how!*—even though it took me only 50 years to do so.

Dame Elizabeth herself has suggested in many interviews, including one with Larry King, that her previous biographers had recorded only the tip of the iceberg, never what really lurked beneath the waters. What was hidden from the public's view from the surface could have sunk the *Titanic.*

"Marilyn Monroe and I sometimes seduced the same men. All of them told me I was a better lay and had better hygiene," Elizabeth claimed.

Over the years, every friend or enemy of Elizabeth I talked to, from Mary Astor to Tallulah Bankhead, had stories, and strong points of view, both good and bad, to relay about her. No one contributed more than her two closest friends, actor Roddy McDowall and her longtime personal secretary, Dick Hanley, both friends of mine. In fairness to them, neither man knew I was planning to write a book about the star they both worshipped, although each was acutely aware of her dark side.

Elizabeth and her affair with and subsequent marriage to Richard Burton dominated the media of the 1960s, when she was a meal ticket for the *paparazzi.* Elizabeth's acquisitions of husbands led to her denunciation on the floor of the U.S. Senate. Bags of hate mail arrived daily at MGM. She bravely carried on, collecting lovers, furs, diamonds, art, and mansions. *The New York Times* asserted that she represented the apogee of vulgarity. She replied, "Vulgar? Would you have me any other way, darling?"

She certainly had her share of handsome hunks. To name only a few: Errol Flynn, Tyrone Power, Robert Taylor [*at 16, she portrayed that then-38-year-old actor's wife in* Conspirator], Victor Mature, Prince Rainier, Peter Lawford, Frank Sinatra [*whose child she aborted*], Elvis Presley [*he wanted to co-star with her but never got the chance*], Bobby Kennedy, John Derek, Robert Wagner, Paul Newman, Rock Hudson [*yes, he also slept with women*], Prince Aly Khan, and even the Swedish boxing champion, Ingemar Johansson.

Ironically, the news that propelled this book into the national spotlight involved her sexual flings with two future U.S. Presidents: John F. Kennedy [*as part of a three-way with Robert Stack*], and Ronald Reagan.

The indiscretion with Reagan occurred as part of her lobbying campaign to win the role of the female lead in *That Hagen Girl,* a sappy flop, released in 1947. The role eventually went, to Elizabeth's fury, to her arch-rival and nemesis at the time, Shirley Temple. Ironically, that film's spectacular failure at the box office helped to sabotage Temple's career as a post-adolescent movie star. Not realizing at the time what a disaster the film would be, Elizabeth extracted a cruel revenge: She engaged in a torrid affair with actor John Agar—"Little Miss Lollipop's" errant husband at the time.

Elizabeth later claimed that she developed a powerful crush on John F. Kennedy in England, in 1939, just prior to the outbreak of World War II. She was seven, he was twenty-two, and their families were linked to each other socially. Elizabeth and JFK spent an afternoon horseback riding. When it was over, she said, "One day, I'll become either your wife or your girlfriend."

Elizabeth was martially pre-empted by Jackie, of course, but nonetheless managed to temporarily captivate JFK after his discharge from the U.S. Navy. "I got him long before Jackie ever got her claws into him," she boasted to her friends.

Dame Elizabeth, always a sultry *femme fatale* who later evolved into an AIDS activist, was always gay friendly, even after she discovered that four of her husbands were bisexuals: Nicky Hilton, Michael Wilding, Eddie Fisher, and Richard Burton. One day, when she returned home to discover Burton in bed with Peter Lawford, she blithely called out, "Carry on, boys, while I fix myself a drink."

This newest release from Blood Moon Productions contains detailed accounts from friends, fans, and enemies about episodes in Dame Elizabeth's life which, otherwise have gone unreported, until now: The booze, the brawls, the world-class fame, the bitter breakups, the betrayals, those diamonds, and her underlying passions.

Elizabeth Taylor blazed like a comet through the 20th century, entertaining us both on and off the screen. No other woman represented the glitz and glamour of Imperial Hollywood than its pre-eminent brunette, La Liz.

Dame Elizabeth, responding to a gauntlet thrown down by Marilyn Monroe, once said, "Blondes might have more fun, but brunettes are more dangerous. I proved that when I starred in *Cleopatra.*"

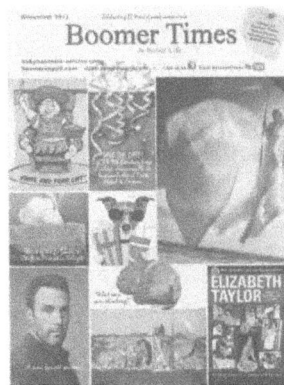

**Anita Finley's Boomer Times** was the first publication to pick up on Blood Moon's then-new spin on the scandal-drenched life of America's Atomic Brunette. Here's the text of the scoop it printed in its edition of November 2012.

**Elizabeth Taylor** in *Cleopatra* (1962) as "the Serpent of the Nile"

# From the AVN Media Network

*AVN Media Network is a publishing, digital media and event management company for the adult entertainment industry. The text that follows derives from their review of a component within Blood Moon's biography of Elizabeth Taylor, **There is Nothing Like a Dame**, by Darwin Porter and Danforth Prince*

# How Will the Faithful Spin Ronald Reagan as a Child Molester?

By AVN Staff Oct 11th, 2012

**HOLLYWOOD, Calif.**—American exceptionalism really comes into play with our unique ability to positively spin the lives (and loves) of the people we place on pedestals. Over the past twenty years or so, few have been so exalted as President Ronald Reagan, who is now often referred to as one of the country's greatest leaders. Hindsight, it seems, is not always 20/20, but whatever the motivation for re-making Reagan into a president worthy of adulation and emulation, it will be interesting to see what the faithful do with the revelation in a recent book that he bedded Elizabeth Taylor when she was only 15 years old.

No matter where you are from in this country, what social set you belong to, what privilege or status you invoke, when a 36-year-old sleeps with a 15-year-old, it's usually considered a crime... unless the two are married or getting married, and that was certainly not the case with Reagan and Taylor. In fact, *Elizabeth Taylor: There is Nothing Like a Dame,* an unauthorized bio penned by **Darwin Porter and Danforth Prince,** makes clear that the assignation was meant to be what it ended up being: a night to remember.

But it also claims that the great movie star, whose world-class beauty was manifest at a young age, was the aggressor when it came to getting down to business. Reagan may have inappropriately invited the teen over to his place for an intimate dinner, but she apparently took it from there.

According to the *London Daily Express,* "[Taylor] told a close pal, 'Reagan was treating me like a grown woman, and that thrilled me. We sat on his sofa and I could tell he wanted to get it on but he seemed reluctant to make the first move. I became the aggressor. After a heavy make-out session on the sofa, we went into the bedroom.'"

What happened in the bedroom is not spelled out, but the clear implication is that they weren't playing chess. However, the book also alleges that Taylor lost her virginity to Peter Lawford when she was 17, so there appears to be some inconsistencies about who popped that famous cherry, and when.

Still, this is Reagan we're talking about, and the 1940s, when the prevailing code of conduct said you get married if you're going to fool around. We're not naïve

For a brief moment, Jack Warner pondered over casting Ronald Reagan and Elizabeth Taylor in *That Hagen Girl* (1947). The plot called for a young girl to become involved with a middle-aged man.

In part because Warners would have had to borrow Elizabeth from MGM, the part was eventually awarded to **Shirley Temple**. Temple appears with **Ronald Reagan** in this press and publicity picture in advance of the film's release.

*That Hagen Girl* morphed into a cringe-worthy failure for both the actors and the studio. EVERYONE noted the subliminal sexuality that radiated off the screen. Reagan himself later evaluated it as his "most embarassing show-biz moment."

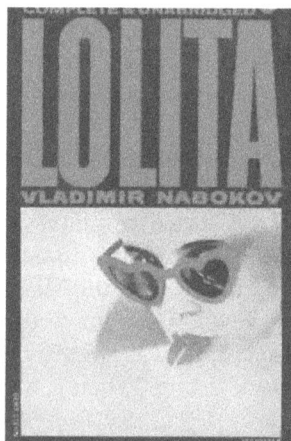

In 1962, Stanley Kubrick adapted the controversial novel, **Lolita**, into a movie. James Mason falls in love with his sullen but sultry teenaged stepdaughter, played by **Sue Lyon**.

After Elizabeth Taylor saw it, she said that she wished it had been released in the late 1940s, when she could have played the nymphette "instead of all that syrupy fare like *Life With Father.*"

**JAILBAIT:** Underaged **Elizabeth Taylor**, shown here in a cheesecake shot, admitted that she was "ready, willing, and able" to have an affair." When it became clear that she was being considered as the screen counterpart for Ronald Reagan in *That Hagen Girl*, she and the future president were rumored to have indulged in dinner and some heavy petting, perhaps not "going all the way.".

enough to think plenty of people were not doing the dirty outside the bounds of matrimony, but still... this is *Reagan* we're talking about, *the* major conservative politician of the last half of the 20th century, and a man literally revered by every single Republican holding any office in the land. Even if that's an exaggeration, is there one Republican holding any office who would dare speak ill of Reagan publicly? **Case closed.**

So the question remains: how the hell are they going to spin the fact that their patron saint came on to a 15-year-old, and that he took her "into the bedroom?" It's not close to the same as Dubya being a drunk until he was 40. Hard to spin this as a lack of maturity when the guy was 36. No, child molestation is not the sort of crime that can be easily explained away as being the fault of the teen. That, after all, is the lame excuse Humbert Humbert made in *Lolita!*

Maybe they'll say he was still under the spell of lecherous Hollywood and hadn't yet developed into the wise and traditional conservative that lore would have him be. Or maybe they'll simply dismiss it the way they dismiss every such fall from grace perpetrated by a political hypocrite who violates the very principles they demand of others.

Reagan is long dead, of course, and his stunning political legacy shows no sign of slowing, but only growing, as many Democrats also hold him up as the sort of conservative who would not succeed in today's hyper-partisan environment. That may or may not be true, but it certainly supports the idea that nothing short of the disclosure that Reagan sold military secrets to the Chinese could tarnish his reputation, even one that has him seducing a 15-year-old girl whose apparent fascination with him was based on the fact that he was treating her like a grown woman!   (***Editor's note:*** *To be clear, who took young Elizabeth's virginity? It was Peter Lawford. Her session with Reagan might be classified as "heavy petting."*)

Elizabeth **Taylor** played her "young and virginal" *schtick* for as long and as hard as any actress of that era possibly could have.

In the upper photo, she appears in a small role with her **Jane Powell**, the featured star in *A Date for Judy*.

In the lower photo, she's kissed by one of her "real life" fuck buddies, **Peter Lawford** in *Julia Misbehaves (1948)*

And then suddenly, she was a ravishingly beautiful bride, and America seemed to collectively swoon!

**Elizabeth Taylor's** engagement to hotel heir **Nicky Hilton** neatly coincided with the release of MGM's blockbusting ode to the values of the uptight 50s, *Father of the Bride*. Their respective chronologies unleashed armies of fans, who followed her virtually everywhere.

Hilton, although good at first impressions, emerged as an alcoholic, a heroin addict, and a compulsive gambler who was also *schtupping* his glamourous stepmother, **Zsa Zsa Gabor.**

Ironically, in the months before her "real life" wedding—depicted above on the left—Elizabeth, through MGM, had already spent months "prepping" her fans with news about her appearance with Spencer Tracy in *Father of the Bride (right photo, above)*.

Hearts fluttered nationwide for both events. Neither was anything like what the public imagined at the time.

And then, **La Liz** began playing a whore, and her fans remained absolutely numb and awed by her abrupt transformation.

In the *upper photo*, she appears with her then-husband (#4; **Eddie Fisher**) as a prostitute in *BUtterfield 8.*

In the *lower photo*, in an awkward "proprietary" move from **Richard Burton** (husband no. 5 and 6, shown *standing on the left*), **Elizabeth** sits in the lap of **Eddie Fisher** during that marriage's death knells.

# Liz Taylor Dead? Never!

## SHE LIVES ON IN DARWIN PORTER'S BRILLIANT NEW BOOK

### BY ALAN PETRUCELLI

**Arts Reviewer Alan Petrucelli** appears here with **Suzanne Somers.**

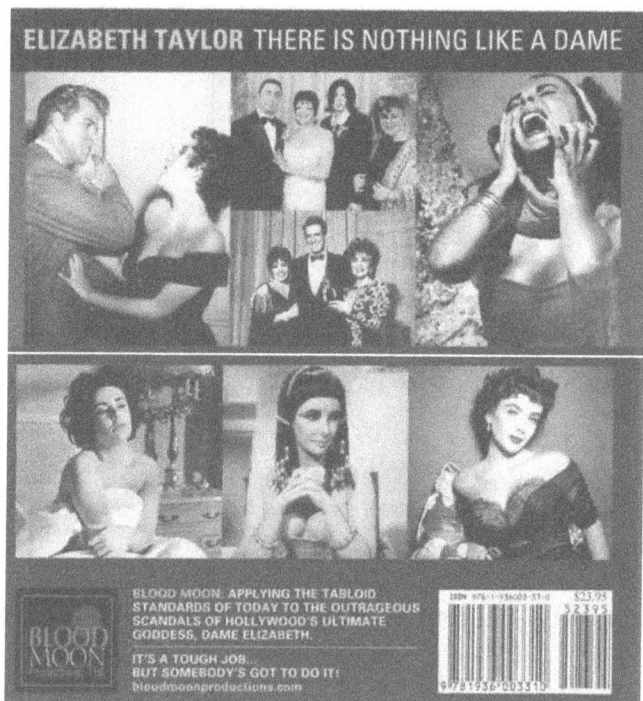

ELIZABETH TAYLOR THERE IS NOTHING LIKE A DAME

BLOOD MOON: APPLYING THE TABLOID STANDARDS OF TODAY TO THE OUTRAGEOUS SCANDALS OF HOLLYWOOD'S ULTIMATE GODDESS, DAME ELIZABETH.

IT'S A TOUGH JOB... BUT SOMEBODY'S GOT TO DO IT! bloodmoonproductions.com

**Darwin Porter has done it again**, not that we ever doubted that he'd do it again and again and again. But this time, he's chosen as his canvas someone considerably larger and more enveloping. Now, in this day of 30-second sound bites and 24- hour news cycles, it's difficult to recall those thrilling days of yesteryear when a movie star's passion could easily eclipse the Cuban Missile Crisis.

**Elizabeth Taylor spans the 20th century like a bawdy queen surveying her subjects**. And Porter's new work, *Elizabeth Taylor: There Is Nothing like a Dame* (Blood Moon Productions, $23.95), tells this dame's life with all the laughter, heartbreak, illness, wealth, animosity, love, arguably more laughter, heartbreak, illness, wealth, animosity and love than any other man or woman in the last century.

Taylor made her film debut at 10 in the 1942 *There's One Born Every Minute*, co-starring with Carl "Alfalfa" Switzer and her last film, *These Old Broads*, with Joan Collins, Shirley MacLaine and in 2001, a decade before she died. She loved everyone she married (and she married a lot); in-between and during the marriages, she had legions of lovers, from presidents to farm hands. She had a lot of love to give, and loved to give it.

As Porter richly and explicitly describes her life, the rank hypocrisy of the age where, as her salary zoomed ever higher, her popularity swung like a pendulum. She nearly dies during a tracheotomy, we love her; she breaks up the patently constructed Eddie Fisher-Debbie Reynolds faux romance, we hate her; she wins an Oscar and we love her; she steals the one great love of her life, from his family and wife of 13 years . . . you get the idea. So did she: Taylor understood manipulation of image better than anyone else.

Each page brings more information about old Hollywood, the mark of Porter's genius. There probably can be a debate as to if this is truth or gossip, but never has a fact stated by Porter been questioned and found to be untrue. And, like any good historian, Porter peppers his prose with unknown factoids that lubricate the style along. Among other small pieces of new info here is *über*-sissy Franklin Pangborn's longtime companion. Yes, he was a movie actor for 40 years, and no, we're not going to spill the beans.

Comparisons of Porter's work to Kenneth Anger's *Hollywood Babylon* are no longer issues. Anger's speed-fueled Palm Springs weekend, barfing up all the gossip, true and false, he'd heard in a 10-year failed Hollywood career, is the basis of his major work. Anger's films are not for the masses. Porter, on the other hand, remains consistently on point, scrupulously researched and always a joy to read. His works now fill a small shelf that future historians of the 20th century will find invaluable.

**Taylor was the greatest star of them all, and Darwin Porter is the only man who could capture her.**

***

Alan W. Petrucelli has always been fascinated by dead celebrities. His first professional byline article was the 1980 obituary of David Janssen that he wrote for *Photoplay*. Since then, Alan has traveled the world, looking for the rich, (in)famous and dead, leaving prayers and, in the Jewish parts of town, stones.

In his latest book, *Morbid Curiosity: The Disturbing Demises of the Rich and Infamous,* he unearths the most disturbing, unexpected, occasionally humorous and often outright appalling details of the final moments of the rich and powerful. His writings have appeared in *The New York Times, People, Us Weekly, Family Circle, Ladies' Home Journal, Cape Cod Times, The Desert Sun, Prevention, USA Weekend, New York Daily News, Pittsburgh Post-Gazette,* and *Working Mother.* He hosted *The Entertainment Report* on the CBS Radio Network.

"...THE GIRL WHO HAD EVERYTHING"

**Latino Love**

Foreplay with
**Fernando Lama**

Blood Moon Announces the Release of
Darwin Porter's HOT new biography of Elizabeth Taylor

# THERE IS NOTHING LIKE A DAME

## TIPS AND TITILLATIONS FOR WHAT LIES WITHIN

**Shirley Temple** with her husband, **John Agar.**

**Mary Astor**

Reviewer Philip Cortland wrote: "In his latest book, this tome devoted to Elizabeth Taylor, celebrity biographer Darwin Porter faced a daunting challenge: To tell us some hot stuff about La Liz that we have not already heard."

In Darwin Porter's latest celebrity book, *Elizabeth Taylor, There is Nothing Like a Dame,* he meets that challenge—with gusto!

Dame Elizabeth herself has suggested in many interviews, including one with Larry King, that her previous biographers have only recorded the tip of the iceberg, not what lay beneath the waters. "My marriages didn't work out. My second husband was the English actor, MIchael Wilding. We started out as husband and wife, and became brother and sister."

It took decades for our author to compile the stories in this book, but he has created a behind-the-scenes portrait of an Elizabeth we never knew.

Over the years, every friend or enemy of Elizabeth he talked to, from Mary Astor to Tallulah Bankhead, had a story about her, good or bad. We have not particularly done her a disservice by giving a warts-and-all portrait. She herself said that she couldn't write her own memoirs, because in her words, "too many people would sue me."

**June Allyson**

**Lex Barker**

Well, most of those men, except for George Hamilton and Robert Wagner, have gone to some great celebrity graveyard and therefore can't file that libel suit.

The author was especially grateful to two important sources, without whom he would probably never have written the book. They included Roddy McDowall, her friend since their filming of *Lassie Come Home* in 1943, and Dick Hanley. Dick had been secretary to Louis B. Bayer for 13 years. After Mayer fired him, he became a personal assistant to Elizabeth's third husband. When Mike Todd died in a plane crash over New Mexico, Dick became Elizabeth's handler and personal secretary. He knew virtually everything going on in her life.

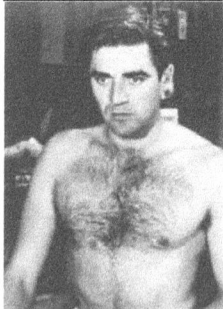

In fairness to both Roddy and Dick, the stories they told were never intended for publication. But their memories of Elizabeth and all facets of her life were too revealing not to be valuable to those who adore her and want to know what was really going on in her life.

From the very beginning of Dame Elizabeth's life, even her birth was shrouded in mystery and controversy.

Weighing 8 ½ pounds, Baby Elizabeth was born in London on February 27, 1932. There is no doubt that her mother was the B-list Broadway actress, Sara Taylor. There is considerable doubt who her father was. It is commonly assumed that he was an art dealer, Francis Taylor. But it could well have been Victor Cazalet, a conservative Member of Parliament, who was one of the members of a *ménage à trois* with Sara and Francis at the time of Elizabeth's birth. Victor and Francis were lovers, and Victor eventually became the lover of Sara as well. After Elizabeth's birth, Sara told Victor and Francis, as the three of them were gathered beside her bed, "the three of us have a healthy baby daughter."

Victor, a close friend of Sir Winston Churchill, supported the Taylor family and let them live in luxury on his estate. He showered presents on young Elizabeth and presented her with her first pony, a gift that perhaps prepared her for her first really prominent role in the 1944 classic, *National Velvet*.

Elizabeth later admitted that her first serious crush was on a twenty-two year old John F. Kennedy, the son of Joseph P. Kennedy, who in the late 1930s was the American ambassador to the Court of Saint James's in London.

Elizabeth was only seven years old when she spent a day in the country with the future U.S. president. She warned him that when she grew up, Jack would either become her boyfriend or husband. As time progressed, he would evolve into the former, not the latter, much to the chagrin of Jaqueline Kennedy.

With the onset of World War II, the Taylors fled to Beverly Hills, where Elizabeth wanted to become Hollywood's next Shirley Temple. Thousands of hopefuls also wanted to assume that role, but Elizabeth actually did.

Growing up in Hollywood in the 1940s, Elizabeth admitted that her body developed faster than her mind. By sixteen, she was already appearing opposite Robert Taylor in *Conspirator,* playing his young wife. But her interest in boys began long before her affair with Robert Taylor, who was married at the time to the bisexual actress Barbara Stanwyck.

Elizabeth met her first boyfriend at school. He was six years older than she was,

the handsome and charismatic Derek Harris, who later evolved into actor John Derek. He later became famous for his marriages to a series of stunning beauties. It was Derek who introduced Elizabeth to the facts of life, long before she was a legal age. From here, she evolved into a teenaged Lolita, "boy crazy" by her own admission, and coveted by increasing numbers of mature players in Hollywood.

As she relayed to Dick Hanley, Roddy McDowall, and her fellow MGM star, Judy Garland, it was actually the actor Peter Lawford, also British born, who had initially taken her virginity during a weekend retreat at San Simeon, the estate of press baron William Randolph Hearst. At around this time, she appeared with Peter in such films as the 1949 *Little Women.*

Movie magazines claimed that when Elizabeth married hotel heir Nicky Hilton, she went to her bridal bed a virgin. That was not completely true.

She'd had a number of affairs before that, including with actor John Agar, the dashingly handsome husband of her arch rival Shirley Temple, who, like Elizabeth, was desperate to transfer their success as childhood stars into adult roles. For a time, both of these young women, each an already deeply entrenched diva, also competed for John Derek.

Elizabeth's most bizarre fling was with the much older Ronald Reagan, when she wanted to star with him in *That Hagen Girl,* the role eventually going to Shirley Temple. Many people have discounted Elizabeth's assertion that Ronald Reagan seduced her while she was still a teenager. Apparently, he didn't go "all the way."

However, the 2011 publication of Piper Laurie's memoirs convinced many readers that Reagan wasn't above seducing teenaged girls. Piper played Reagan's teenage daughter in *Louisa* (1950), and during the filming, Piper has asserted that Reagan took more than a fatherly interest in her. Her memoir, *Learning To Live Out Loud,* contains the full account.

Ironically, Elizabeth later became friends with the Reagans, Ronald and Nancy, when they lived in the White House during the period she was married to the Republican Senator, John Warner, whose main accomplishment involved keeping known homosexuals out of the U.S. military. Of course, gay-friendly Elizabeth disagreed violently with her husband's rigid opposition to gays.

Just prior to her marriage to Nicky Hilton, Elizabeth had a tumultuous affair with her screen hero, the swashbuckling Tasmanian, Errol Flynn. Robin Hood's fondness for under-aged girls had already been widely exposed in court cases during his trials for statutory rape.

Elizabeth also attracted the sexual attention of the legendary Joan Crawford, but she managed to avoid Crawford's entrapments, devices which had already bagged such young starlets as Marilyn Monroe.

Almost from the first month of her marriage to Nicky Hilton, Elizabeth discovered he was not only a womanizer, but that he was sleeping with men as well. For a brief time, the handsome screen idol, Tyrone Power became Nicky's lover. He was one of four bisexuals that Dame Elizabeth married, the others being Michael Wilding, Eddie Fisher, and Richard Burton.

**Jean Harlow** modeling a dress by Adrian

**Doris Duke** with **Porfirio Rubirosa**

**Elizabeth Taylor** in *A Place in the Sun*

**Jeanne Carmen**

**Clark Gable**

Starlet **Nancy Davis** aka **Nancy Reagan**

**Zsa Zsa Gabor**

**Judy Garland**

**Errol Flynn**

**Stewart Granger** & **Jean Simmons**

**Tyrone Power** & **Lana Turner**

Marlon Brando

Rock Hudson, seen here with Taylor in Giant.

Farley Granger

Libby Holman

Hedda Hopper

Greer Garson

James Dean, seen here with Taylor in Giant.

Debbie Reynolds, seen here *on the right* with Taylor and Eddie Fisher

Conrad Hilton

Young JFK

After her divorce from Nicky, Elizabeth had to compete with the sultry but aging *femme fatale,* Marlene Dietrich, for the affection of her second husband, Michael Wilding. Not only that, Elizabeth was also up against another screen swashbuckler, British actor Stewart Granger, whose affair with her husband had been launched during World War II.

Elizabeth had two sons with Wilding. She later told Roddy McDowall, "He prefers Stewart Granger as a bed partner more than me."

Because she was so often married, many of Elizabeth's love affairs were never covered in the sappy movie magazines of the time. She secretly dated—well, actually more than dated—such actors as Robert Stack, Farley Granger, and Steve Cochran. And in her words, she fell "head over high heels" for the singer, Vic Damone.

An affair with one of the true loves of her life, Montgomery Clift, was never fulfilled because he was, in his own words, "almost 100% homosexual." However, they produced a powerful on-screen chemistry together in 1951's *A Place in the Sun,* one of her truly memorable films.

Mired in alcohol and drugs, Monty was a mess, but he brought out the nurturing side of Elizabeth. She helped him get through life and got roles for him when studios wouldn't otherwise have hired him. Together, they went on to film *Raintree County* and *Suddenly, Last Summer*.

Both Monty and Elizabeth were intrigued with Frank Sinatra. As a friend, Sinatra had bonded with Monty when they co-starred in *From Here to Eternity.* Of course, it was Elizabeth who eventually got Ol' Blue Eyes, but when she became pregnant, he demanded that she abort their child.

One of Elizabeth's strangest romantic interludes was with the gangster, Johnny Stompanato, who had previously had an affair with one of her closest friends, Janet Leigh. When Janet dropped him, Elizabeth took up with him. Johnny secretly taped a film of them having sex together, for eventual use as an instrument of blackmail against her. When Elizabeth discovered this, she was horrified, of course, but with a certain wry humor, she jokingly referred to it as "My first porno flick."

Perhaps fortunately for Elizabeth, and unfortunately for the sake of that film, which was never made public, Stompanato was stabbed to death at the home of another of his lovers, Lana Turner. You be the judge: He was either murdered by Lana herself, as was rumored, or by her teenaged daughter, Cheryl Crane.

Ronald Reagan once declared that whenever he made a movie, he developed a case of "leading-lady-it is," his affairs with his female co-stars lasting only for the duration of the shoot.

Not really satisfied with her marriage to Michael Wilding, Elizabeth for a while developed "leading man-itis," engaging in a series of affairs, beginning with Stanley Donen, her director in *Love Is Better Than Ever.*

Later, during the filming of *The Girl Who Had Everything,* she became involved with both Fernando Lamas, Lana Turner's temperamental lover, and the tragic Gig Young, who later killed both himself and his young wife at the time in their New York City apartment in 1978.

**Howard Hughes**

**Vivien Leigh**

In *Rhapsody,* Elizabeth fell for Shelley Winters' husband, Vittorio Gassman, who later dumped her.

And when Elizabeth replaced Vivien Leigh as the female lead in *Elephant Walk,* after Leigh's very visible and widely publicized nervous breakdown, she also lured away Vivien's boyfriend, Peter Finch, at least temporarily.

When Elizabeth filmed her classic, *Giant,* in 1956, she managed to seduce the otherwise gay actors, James Dean and Rock Hudson, at least after they stopped sleeping with each other.

**Marilyn Monroe**

During the making of *Raintree County,* Elizabeth got no loving from Monty Clift, so she turned instead, albeit briefly, to the rugged and usually rather crude Lee Marvin.

**Elsa Maxwell**

And during the filming of *Cat on a Hot Tin Roof,* her third husband, Mike Todd, died tragically in an airplane crash over New Mexico. She turned to comfort from her co-star, Paul Newman, and indeed, in the aftermath, his blue eyes met her violet eyes up close and personally.

Eddie Fisher was Mike Todd's best friend, and he also offered her more than comfort after Todd's death. And although Fisher's marriage was all but over when he divorced Debbie Reynolds so that he could marry Elizabeth, that perceived betrayal (of Debbie) caused outrage across America.

**MGM chief Louis B. Mayer** with a very young, Lassie-era **Elizabeth Taylor.**

Elizabeth later admitted that after a few months, she become very bored with Eddie. Before that, her closest friends, including Dick Hanley and Roddy McDowall, claimed that Fisher, Todd, and Elizabeth operated as a *ménage à trois.*

**Ann Miller**

The book goes on to describe her romance with Richard Burton during the filming, in Rome, of the ill-fated *Cleopatra,* a paparazzi-choked brawl that fed on the notoriety of the biggest love story of the 20<sup>th</sup> Century. For our coverage in this new book, we supply details about what was really going on behind the *Dolce Vita* scenes during the filming of this epic—revelations that the ravenous international press didn't pick up on at the time. Those included the bisexual Burton's original affair with Roddy McDowall, during the run of Camelot on Broadway, and of Burton's "rape" of Eddie Fisher at the Villa Pappa in Rome, where Elizabeth lived with Fisher.

**Roddy McDowall** with MGM film superstar, **Lassie.**

**Terry Moore**

Our book also covers Dame Elizabeth's saga through the making of the film classic, *Who's Afraid of Virginia Woolf?* for which Elizabeth won an Oscar and for which Burton didn't.

The real story behind Elizabeth's first marriage to Richard Burton is explored, often in lurid and graphic detail. Their so-called "marriage of the century" was definitely not one of the traditionally defined unions that conservative Congressmen always seem to be talking about.

**Aristotle Onassis,** with his first wife, **Tina Livanos.**

**Tyrone Power**

As the tough Welshman told her, "I love you. Love is one thing, sex is another. Don't expect me to be faithful."

It's all here, Blood Moon's newest release—the illicit sex, the booze, the brawls, the scandals, the gossip, the incredible fame, the bitter separations, the jewelry, the betrayals, and the undying passion.

**Robert Stack**

**Grace Kelly**

**Mae West**

It's certainly an inside track on the gossip and tempests associated with America's most famous brunette movie star. Even more, it's an insight into legend, passion, and iconography during "the American Century," with a cast of hundreds of glitterati from the worlds of entertainment and politics:

They include cameo roles played in Elizabeth Taylor's life by Marilyn Monroe, Princess Grace, Clark Gable, the Duke and Duchess of Windsor, Marlon Brando, Judy Garland, Noël Coward, Ava Gardner, Tony Curtis, Tennessee Williams, Rex Harrison, Peter O'Toole, Aristotle Onassis, Jackie Kennedy, Robert (love on the Beach) Kennedy, John Huston, Audrey Hepburn, and Greta Garbo herself.

\*\*\*

**Lana Turner** with **Johnny Stompanato**

Harry S Truman's wife, First Lady **Bess Truman**

## ELIZABETH TAYLOR, THERE IS NOTHING LIKE A DAME
### by Darwin Porter

©2012 Blood Moon Productions, Ltd. All Rights Reserved
ISBN 978-1-936003-31-0
Softcover, 624 pages, with photos, 6"x 9"
Available Everywhere Now

Elizabeth Taylor once said, "If I ever had a few stiff drinks and sat down with a writer to record my love affairs, Hollywood wives would be calling their divorce lawyers."

In response to that challenge, Blood Moon presents history's most comprehensive compilation of the unpublished—until now—secrets of Dame Elizabeth. With photos, this meaty and startling newest installment of Blood Moon's Babylon series offers a juicy feast of till-now untold tales about the 20th century's most headline-generating actress, relayed with empathy and brutal candor.

Formerly a bureau chief and entertainment columnist for *The Miami Herald,* **Darwin Porter** is one of the world's leading celebrity biographers, the winner of almost 30 literary awards and author of critically acclaimed overviews of such other stars as Marilyn Monroe, Marlon Brando, the Kennedys, J. Edgar Hoover, Lana Turner, Katharine Hepburn, Judy Garland, Lucille Ball, Frank Sinatra, and Vivien Leigh/Laurence Olivier. Over the course of many decades of meeting and talking with celebrities, and several encounters with "the violet-eyed goddess" herself, he accumulated a vast trove of stories and information about one of his favorite brunettes, Elizabeth Taylor. **All of them are included within this ode to a great Dame and a fabulous movie star.**

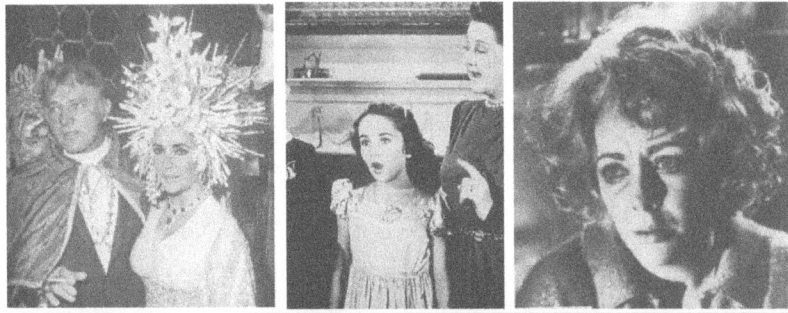

We knew her as Hollywood's most mercurial woman, **DAME ELIZABETH**, the central figure in a whirlpool of world-class scandals that have never before been compiled into one definitive exposé.

**ALL OF THAT CHANGED WITH THE PUBLICATION OF THIS BOOK!**
It's all here. sympathetic but shocking—a richly detailed roster of revelations and insights into **LA LIZ** and her ongoing role within America's Entertainment Industry during the peak of its muscle and power.

"I was married to Richard Burton twice. Was he faithful to me? Why not ask Claire Bloom, Zsa Zsa Gabor, Ava Gardner, Tammy Grimes, Jean Simmons, Susan Strasberg, Lana Turner, Racquel Welch...and the beat goes on."

—ELIZABETH TAYLOR

# CONTENTS

**Bombshell book reveals:**
# LIZ's SHOCKING SECRETS!
- Her **AFFAIR** with Reagan
- Chilling **SUICIDE** attempt
- She **HATED** Shirley Temple

*Hot, Unauthorized, and Unapologetic!*

**ELIZABETH TAYLOR** *THERE IS NOTHING LIKE A DAME*

DARWIN PORTER & DANFORTH PRINCE

## GLOBE

NEW PHOTOS INSIDE

# LIZ TAYLOR UNMASKED!

**NEW BOOK CLAIMS SEX SIREN:**
- ✓ **Seduced Ronald Reagan**
- ✓ **Had threesome with JFK and Robert Stack**
- ✓ **Tried to blackmail Sinatra into marriage**
- ✓ **Slashed her wrists after losing movie deal**

Taylor with Peter Lawford in 1948

Ronald Reagan and Liz were lovers, the authors say

ELIZABETH TAYLOR's most scandalous secrets are laid bare in a blockbuster new book that reveals her shocking affairs with a Hollywood Who's Who of leading men, her chilling suicide attempt, and why she hated Shirley to be "so much better than that goody-goody, curly haired, chubby-cheeked lollipop sucker." Her plan was to NOT be a Miss Goody Two Shoes, the book reveals.

At age 11, Liz auditioned for National Velvet and "ripped open her white blouse and flashed her bosom" to producer Pandro Berman. She'd been applying "fast grow" rubbing

---

The Globe, Excerpt from their front page cover story of October 22, 2012,

## Elizabeth Taylor, There Is Nothing Like a Dame

# LANA TURNER
## America's Ultimate Movie Star

Sultry Lana Turner (1920-1995), with her scarlet-painted lips, her stenciled eyebrows, and her shimmery blonde halo of hair, was the ultimate movie star. Mervyn LeRoy, her director, once said, "If the movies had not existed, we would have had to invent them just to showcase Lana Turner."

In her first major-league movie role, *They Won't Forget* (1937), a 16-year-old Lana sauntered provocatively down a street, playing a murder victim. She wore a tight sweater and no bra, bouncing along all the way. Upon the release of the movie, she became an overnight sensation, forever known as "The Sweater Girl." The platinum blonde, Jean Harlow, had died that same year, and America needed another blonde goddess. Lana filled the bill.

Opposite such box office stars as Robert Taylor and Clark Gable, Lana blazed across the screens of World War II, immortalizing herself in film classics by 1946 when she stunned audiences with her appearance in *The Postman Always Rings Twice*. As one G.I. put it, "Watching Lana made me realize what I'd been fighting the Nazis for—what a gal to come home to."

Once again pictures of this star and her astonishing ice blonde beauty will be gracing the cultural pages of America's newspapers and magazines. Her daughter, Cheryl Crane, is publishing a book, *Lana: The Memories, The Myths, The Movies*. It's a loving portrait from a daughter, not a scandalous attack of the *Mommie Dearest* sort penned by the ungrateful daughters of Joan Crawford and Bette Davis.

Cheryl doesn't ignore her mother's legendary love affairs. One chapter, called "Lanamours," is devoted to a parade of the handsomest

After Betty Grable, but before there was Marilyn, America's penchant for popcorn blondes focused on **LANA TURNER**, *aka* **"the ultimate movie star,"** and for sailors and marines, "the girl we hope to find in every port."

As depicted above, sixteen-year-old Lana, suggestively outfitted in a French beret and a tight sweater (and without a brassiere), appeared only for a minute or two during the opening scenes of *They Won't Forget*. But based in part on the catcalls that roared out from movie audiences, this otherwise mediocre movie sealed Lana's destiny as a fast-emerging Love Goddess for the generation that went on to win World War II

From humble origins in Idaho, **Lana Turner** evolved into the lust object and sex goddess for the soldiers, marines, and sailors who hoped she was the girl they would (or could) come home to.

In the *upper photo*, she's replicated in the nihilistic *film noir* that every horny Hollywood fan adored, *The Postman Always Rings Twice*.

Ironies abound In the *lower photo*: In it, an "almost new to Hollywood" neophyte emerges with her name in neon for other teenaged girls to admire—and emulate—throughout America.

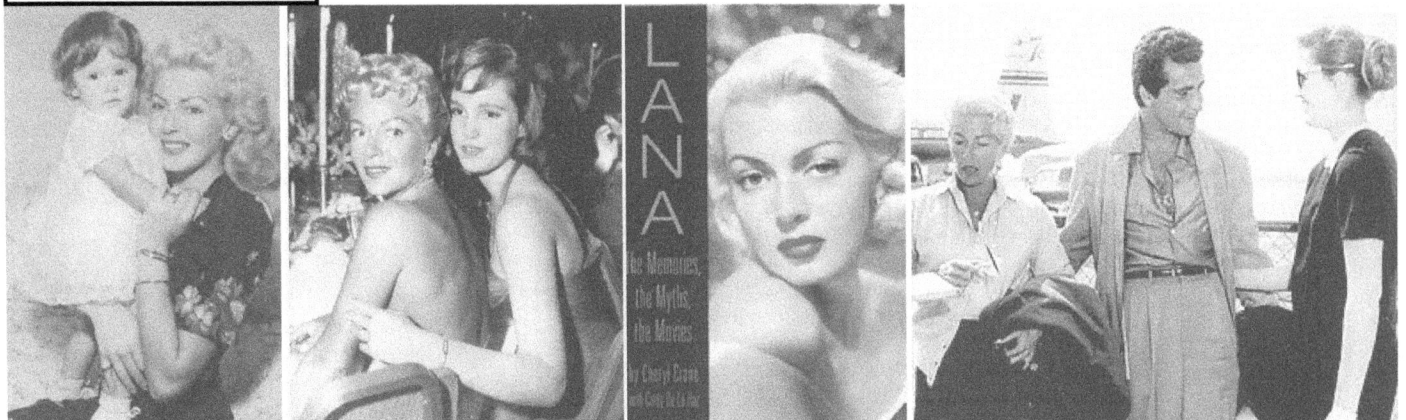

The closest that Lana's career ever came to crashing and burning occurred in the aftermath of the death, by stabbing, of Lana's mob-linked man friend, Johnny Stompanato, within her bedroom. Although the belief persists that the knife was wielded by Lana, the courts declared, after statements from Lana's then-teenaged daughter, Cheryl, and a lot of coaching from the family's lawyers, that it was Cheryl who had perpetrated the crime.

The photos, *left to right*, above, show **Lana** as a proud new mother; **Lana and Cheryl** a dozen or so years later; **the cover of Cheryl's book tribute to the glamour and beauty of her mother**, and (*far right photo*) **Lana** after disembarking from an airplane with (**center figure**) her abusive mob-linked boyfriend, **Johnny Stompanato** shortly before his death by stabbing. **Cheryl Crane** herself stands at the far right.

hunks ever to hit Hollywood. This chapter alone takes up 61 pages. Lana's most scandalous marriage was to Lex (Tarzan) Barker, who ended up repeatedly raping Cheryl. In this new book, Cheryl also writes about her coming out as a lesbian.

Cheryl still maintains that it was she—not her mother—who fatally stabbed Lana's gangster lover, Johnny Stompanato in 1958. Cheryl took the blame but insider Hollywood has long suspected that it was Lana herself who killed Stompanato. Frank Sinatra, who rushed to the murder house before the police arrived, told Peter Lawford that Lana did it.

Lana's lover, Howard Hughes, also believed that the star herself had killed the low-rent gangster. In the *tsunami* of tabloid coverage that followed, Hughes hired bodyguards to protect Lana from the wrath of gangster Mickey Cohen, based on Cohen's threats to destroy Lana's beauty by throwing acid in her face, revenge for having killed his friend Stompanato.

My own take on the murder will appear in the upcoming DVD release of *The Rains of Ranchipur,* a film Lana made in 1955 with Richard Burton. As a "voiceover' for the digitalized re-release of this movie by 20th Century Fox, I provided the commentary.

One night at the Star on the Roof Club at the Beverly Hilton Hotel, Lana told me, "Penis size was not all that important to me. I went from average size—Clark Gable, Robert Taylor, Kirk Douglas—to the gigantic: Lex Barker, Frank Sinatra, Victor Mature."

She also made another startling admission. "Everybody writes about President Kennedy and Marilyn Monroe. What they don't know is that I had a longer and more intense love affair with Jack than Marilyn did. **I was his original blonde bombshell."**

the Rains of Ranchipur
CINEMASCOPE
LANA TURNER · RICHARD BURTON · FRED MacMURRAY · JOAN CAULFIELD · MICHAEL RENNIE

Floodwaters were on the verge of destroying Ranchipur (India) when **Lana Turner**, portraying a British-American horse breeder (Lady Esquith) and inprobably clad in white, falls madly in love with a "noble savage," (**Richard Burton**), wearing dark makeup and a scarlet tunic that symbolized the passion of his emotions. Photos, *left to right*, show three views of Lana with or without Richard Burton.

Here's how MGM publicized the "subliminally sexual' context of this "**We'll Always Love Lana"** disaster movie: *Bursting the floodgates of emotion, shattering all barriers of race and time, The Rains of Ranchipur sweeps everything before it with torrential power."*

Recognizing Darwin Porter's gift for both historical reportage and satire, an affiliate of MGM hired him for voice-over commentary for the film's re-release.

As **Darwin Porter** (*right photo, snapped in 1968)* knew, Lana Turner was a "1940's celluloid sex goddess who survived."

*Left photo, above:* Prim, dignified, mysterious, and respectable, **Lana** appears here as a tragedy-soaked and wrongly accused defendant (the charge was murder) in the tear-jerking *Portrait of Madam X* (1966).

*Right photo above* shows Lana as a well-preserved matron in the low-budget hippy-psychedelic cult film *The Big Cube* (1969), a few years before Darwin Porter conducted a "confessional" interview with her over drinks at an an upscale bar in Beverly Hills she frequented regularly.

Based on LOTS of witnesses, during the course of her Hollywood career, Lana got "down and dirty" with a LOT of guys, including more than a few of the terrified soldiers, sailors, and marines headed out to the battlefields of World War II.

The most famous of her partners included **JFK** (depicted in left photo during a White House press conference in 1963). and **Lex Barker**, the most handsome and charming of Hollywood's many Tarzans.

Lana eventually married him, a tabloid-pumped union (1953-1957) that lasted for four stormy years. Barker appears on the *near right* as the focal point of *Tarzan and the She-Devil* (1953). On the *far right*, as romantics everywhere swooned, he dances with Lana. Hollywood wits made endless reference to the high-drama "camp factor" that seemed to dominate their ill-fated marriage.

EDGAR RICE BURROUGHS
TARZAN II SHE-DEVIL
LEX BARKER
JOYCE MacKENZIE

# LUSCIOUS LANA TURNER
## CELLULOID LOVE GODDESS OF THE '40S

## HEARTS & DIAMONDS TAKE ALL

### DARWIN PORTER'S AWARD-WINNING AND "RELENTLESSLY INDISCREET" NEW BIOGRAPHY REVEALS EVERYTHING YOU'VE EVER WANTED TO KNOW ABOUT "THE SWEATER GIRL"

On Valentine's Day, 2017, in recognition of the 20th anniversary of her death, Blood Moon released a biography loaded with information that members of the movie-going public never knew. Tragic, myth-shattering, and uncensored, it focuses on "The Ultimate Movie Star," MISS LANA TURNER, the blonde cult goddess of the 1940s and beyond.

After Betty Grable, but before there was Marilyn, America's penchant for popcorn blondes focused on LANA, the movie star who had it all: Looks to die for, money to burn, the romantic adulation of the world, and lovers who included the world's most desirable men.

In her 1937 film, *They Won't Forget,* a 16-year-old Lana, without wearing a brassiere, walked down the street with her boobs bouncing. Censors protested, but when it was shown, America cheered and nicknamed her "The Sweater Girl."

From there, Lana competed with Betty Grable and Rita Hayworth as the preeminent pinup girl ("so many men, so little time") of World War II. Horny GIs referred to her as "the Girl We'd Like to Find in Every Port."

From the start, her private life was marked with scandal: She aborted Mickey Rooney's baby; seduced a young John F. Kennedy; and fell for Frank Sinatra, who later caught her in bed with another love goddess, Ava Gardner.

In 1942, after a nationwide campaign promoting the sale of War Bonds, Carole Lombard frantically boarded a small plane headed back to Hollywood, suffering a fiery death when it crashed within 13 minutes of takeoff. The risk she took during that thunderstorm was motivated, it was said, by her obsession with rescuing her husband, Clark Gable, from the amorous clutches of Lana Turner.

Tyrone Power—tall, dark, and photogenic—eventually evolved into the greatest love of her life until the Aviator, Howard Hughes, arguably the most psychotic billionaire in the history of Hollywood, flew in to seduce both of them.

Lana (aka *"The Ziegfeld Girl")* didn't hear *The Postman Always Rings*

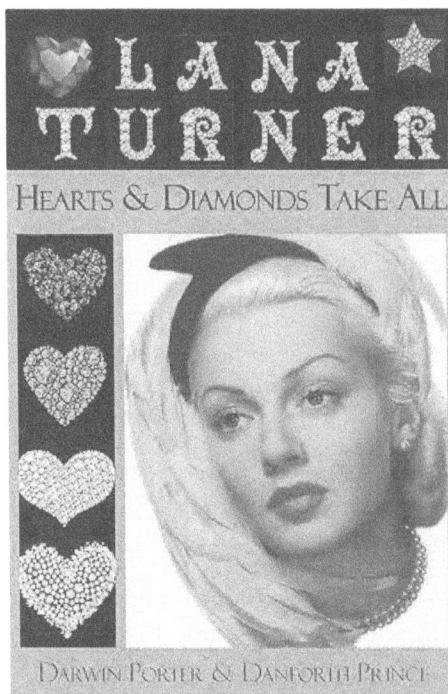

Depicted above are two of the most hyped and desirable women of the mid-20th century, **Ava Gardner** *(left)* and **Lana Turner.** Each was (or had been) sexually and emotionally involved with some of the same men, including Frank Sinatra.

Yes, there were lesbian allegations and accusations—especially from Frank, who caught them in bed together one night at his home in Palm Springs.

Read all about it in *Hearts & Diamonds Take All.*

Its author, Darwin Porter, has been fascinated by everything assciated with Ms. Turner since he was an adolescent, in the years after the outbreak of World War II, sneaking away from home and finding solace in movie theaters screening such hits as the fascinating and brilliant ode to self-destruction in Hollywood, *The Bad and the Beautiful* (1952).

**Winner of a BEST BIOGRAPHY** award from the San Francisco Book Festival, it's the most insightful and provocative biography of the social phenomenon known as **LANA TURNER** ever published.

Almost everyone in North America and Europe knew the story of **Carole Lombard's** *(left figure in photo above)* "to the grave" love for **Clark Gable**.

**DID YOU KNOW?** that the motivation for Lombard's hard-fisted lobbying to board an (unsafe) flight in a small plane (which later crashed and killed her) was based on her perception that LUSCIOUS LANA was working her seductive magic on Gable and that Lombard was afraid he'd succumb?

At the time, Gable and Lana were co-starring in *Somewhere I'll Find You* at MGM.

*Twice* because she was in bed with John Garfield. Later, in search of love, she spent a *Weekend at the Waldorf* before moving to *Green Dolphin Street* and later to the notorious *Peyton Place*. Later, she found it during an experiment with an *Imitation of Life*.

Gable took her to a *Honky Tonk* and vowed, "Somewhere I'll Find You," before their *Homecoming* reunion. With Ray Milland, she found *A Life of Her Own* before dancing to *The Merry Widow* waltz with sexy Fernando Lamas.

Many notoriously hot men—some of them her film making co-stars—lay in her future: Richard Burton, Sean Connery, and Errol "in like Flynn." Samson (Victor Mature) was said to be "Lana's Biggest Thrill." Lana rescued Peter Lawford from Elizabeth Taylor; Ricky Ricardo from Lucy; and, when not singing *amore* with Dean Martin, Kirk Douglas learned that she was *Bad and Beautiful* both on and off the screen.

"The bombshell" once said, "I wanted one husband and seven babies, but I got the reverse—seven husbands and an only child!" She married *Tarzan* (Lex Barker) after his designation as "The Sexiest Man in the World," but the union ended when she caught him seducing her teenaged daughter.

Opinions about Lana were as varied as her changing looks. "She was amoral," said MGM's CEO, Louis B. Mayer. Robert Taylor commented: "She was the type of woman a guy would risk five years in jail for rape." Gloria Swanson sniffed, "She wasn't even an actress ... only a trollop."

And then there was that embarrassing murder: Did Lana fatally stab her gangster lover, Johnny Stompanato, known for his links to the Mob? Or was the heinous act committed by her daughter, a traumatized teenager who, after time in reform school, officially outed herself as a lesbian?

How did these whirlwinds of scandal affect the gal who had it all? According to Lana, "I'd like to think that in some small way, I've helped to preserve the glamour and beauty and mystery of the movie industry."

Never before has there been, until now, a definitive, uncensored, and comprehensive biography of "the Ultimate Movie Star," **LANA TURNER**.

***

LANA TURNER · KIRK DOUGLAS
WALTER PIDGEON · DICK POWELL
**The Bad And The Beautiful**

The *photo above* derives from page four of the program passed out in a Sydney (Australia) theater on the occasion of **Craig Russell's "Down Under" tour of 1980.**

It shows the world's then most-famous female impersonator, **Craig Russell**, a frequent long-ago guest at Darwin Porter's **Magnolia House** in Staten Island. According to Darwin, "Craig was charming, funny, self-destructive, and 'beyond the pale' of any other drag artist I ever met."

Whereas Craig brilliantly imitated, on stage to crowds who roared their approval, Bette Davis, Carol Channing, Tallulah Bankhead, and Mae West, he never "tackled" Lana Turner, simply because, as he phrased it, *"her blend of prim allegiance to the manners of the bourgeoisie and raw sexuality was too subtle to satirize."*

In the *upper photo*, **Craig** impersonates **Tallulah**; in the *lower photo*, he's doing **Mae**.

During World War II, **Lana Turner** rivaled Rita Hayworth and Betty Grable as pinup girls beloved by American G.I.s. In the aftermath of the fighting, her popularity zoomed as she made some of her greatest films. Through it all, she retained her image as "The glamourous but sexually accessible girl next door."

*On the left*, in October of 1946, **Lana** appeared in very *haute couture* on the cover of *Photoplay*.

*On the right*, decades later, in 1976, cast as an aging matriarch in *Bittersweet Love* (1976), she seemed to cling more desperately than ever to her expensive accessories.

Nobody (YES, NOBODY) played love scenes like **Lana Turner**, who often seduced her leading men.

In the illustrations above, she appears with **Kirk Douglas** in the fascinating and "over the top" ode to Hollywood publicity, fame, and failure, *The Bad and the Beautiful* (1952).

In it, Lana plays an ego-bruised, substance-addicted star on the rebound; Kirk Douglas is her effective (but loathed and despised) show-biz Svengali.

# BLOOD MOON ANNOUNCES THE RETURN OF

# LANA TURNER

## A LOVE STORY IN SEARCH OF A HAPPY ENDING

*Imitation of Life* (1959), starring **LUSCIOUS LANA:** It was senti-mental, it was sappy, and it was Hol-lywood's second attempt to adapt a bestselling novel about race, class, and gender to the screen.

But its intentions were noble, and it allowed their respective fans to drink deeply from then-novel Hollywood debuts of, among others, **Sandra Dee, Juanita Moore,** and **Mahalia Jackson.**

Also, it nurtured the roots of what evolved into small-screen themes for daytime soaps that included *Peyton Place*

And if you love Lana, like we do, it's worth a sodden, late-night screening, especially for views of the then-most-handsome actor in Hollywood, **John Gavin,** later, Ronald Reagan's des-ignation U.S. Ambassador to Mexico.

Long before Marilyn Monroe dazzled the world, there was another "popcorn blonde" who became a legend. She was the ravishingly beautiful Lana Turner, the last of the great screen goddesses of Hollywood's Golden Age before America bought TV sets.

She was at first called "The Sweater Girl," and then "The Ultimate Movie Star." She electrified America in *They Won't Forget* (1937) when, at the age of sixteen, provocatively clad in a tight sweater with no brassiere, she walked down the street on the way to her rape and murder on screen. Stores across America immediately reported a rush on sweaters.

In only four years, she evolved from a scullery maid in San Francisco into "The Queen of MGM," and a famous pinup girl of World War II. U.S. Airmen named their war planes after her; sailors voted her "the most desirable woman in the world"; and her pinup picture was carried by marines onto the sands of Iwo Jima and during the death march through Bataan, usually as a soldier's reminder of "what we're fighting for."

From the launch of her controversial career, her life was marred by scandal—in fact, it was often interpreted as an enduring soap opera. Mickey Rooney was among the first to succumb to her charms. Later, she opted to abort his baby.

Deserting Rooney, she took up with a young contract player who had also been signed by Warners. Handsome and charming, his name was Ronald Reagan. In what President Donald Trump would define as "locker room talk," Reagan asked his close friend, William Holden, "In what cathouse did she learn those tricks?"

Within months after her arrival in Hollywood, Gary Cooper, James Stewart, and Spencer Tracy warmed her bed. So did Robert Taylor, her co-star in *Johnny Eager* (1941); and Clark Gable, with whom she'd make four movies.

Howard Hughes flew in to propose marriage to Lana, but never carried through with it. Based on hookups she established while entertaining G.I.s at the Hollywood Canteen in World War II, according to her first husband, bandleader Artie Shaw, Lana "dated" 150 servicemen. Shaw later married her best friend, Ava Gardner. Lana also seduced Frank Sinatra before he married Ava.

At war's end, a young naval lieutenant, John F. Kennedy, fresh from a survival in the Pacific, arrived in Hollywood and announced his first goal. He said to his buddy and room-mate, actor Robert Stack, "I want to seduce Lana Turner—get her for me."

Her affair with the future president continued on and off for years to come.

"The love of my life," as Lana herself claimed, was the bisexual actor and matinee idol, Tyrone Power. To her bitter disappointment, he later ditched her for a minor starlet, Linda Christian, and an ongoing affair with Rock Hudson.

Her fourth husband was screen Tarzan Lex Barker, once voted "The Sexiest Man in the World." It was even suggested that Lex's male beauty inspired thoughts of religious de-votion, with some fans asserting that he was Adam, "the first man created by God." That marriage ended abruptly after she caught him raping her teenage daughter, Cheryl Crane.

Lana had her critics: Louis B. Mayer called her "amoral," and the silent screen vamp, Gloria Swanson, defining her as "not an actress ... only a trollop."

And then there was the notoriously murky murder of her lover, Johnny Stompanato, henchman to mobster Mickey Cohen. The official version was that Lana's lesbian daughter, Cheryl, stabbed him, but years later, Lana admitted to close friends that she'd done it, let-ting her daughter take the blame because she'd get off easy.

**Luscious Lana,** looking well-dressed, well-bred, quizzical and confused as her matriarchal belief patterns are "shot out of the water' in this still shot from *Imitation of Life* (1959).

87

An inveterate smoker, Lana died of cancer in 1995. Among her final words were, "I like to think that in some small way I preserved the glamour and beauty of the movie industry. There are those who say I put the Tinsel in Tinseltown."

For the first time in any comprehensive way, my co-author, Danforth Prince, and I have brought the celluloid life of Queen Bee Lana Turner to life again in *Hearts & Diamonds Take All*. We still like to think of Lana carelessly slipping a mink coat around her delectable shoulders, rushing off into the night for a rendezvous with one of her secret lovers—perhaps Robert Wagner or Robert Mitchum or Robert Stack or Robert Hutton or MGM producer Robert Evans. Or maybe she'll stay at home with her sixth husband, Robert Eaton.

The legend of Lana Turner lives on today and she's become a cult goddess to thousands still drawn to the stardust memories of yesterday when love was new and, to many Baby Boomers, all sunsets were iridescent. For decades, as presented to millions, Lana Turner was the eternal love story in search of a happy ending.

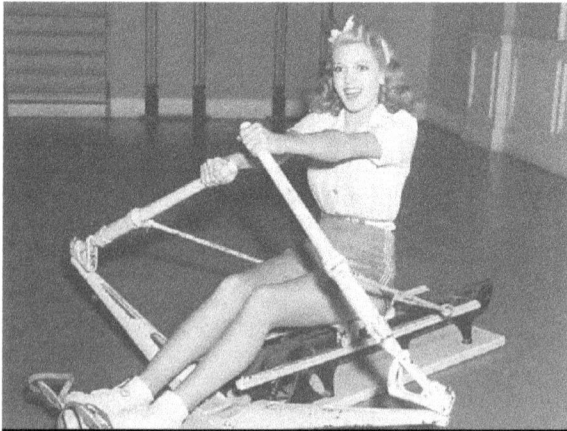

Through publicity shots like this, MGM "proved" that their newest starlette was, indeed, just a hometown slice of Americana. Cynics quipped that this gym shot did nothing more than strenthen **Lana's** back muscles and improve the shape of her breasts.

## GETTING BIBLICAL WITH LUSCIOUS LANA

In this publicity shot for *The Prodigal (*1955), **Lana** bravely emulates—in an era soaked with censorship issues and squeamish sexuality—a fertility goddess for the love cult of Astarte.

A big-budget costume drama from MGM, it ends with the adventure-seeking hero (Edward Purdom) returning as a penitent to his tribe.

It doesn't end as happily for Lana. After dozens of costume changes and gamely presiding over cultish-looking rites that never come near an "adults only" rating, she throws herself off a ledge and into the flames of Hell.

According to Darwin Porter, "It's easy to mock and satirize this 'way over the top' age-of-Sputnik' morality tale, but for fans of Lana Turner, it's an essential part of her repertoire. She was terrific!—and gamely collaborative to cast and crew throughout its filming. "

Two views of one of the world's then-most-famous bandleaders, **Artie Shaw**, with (*upper photo*) a scantily clad and intensely photogenic newcomer, **Lana Turner.** In *Dancing Co-Ed* (1939). she had been assigned the title role.

Self-defined as a "very difficult man," Shaw sustained marriages to eight women during the course of his long and emotionally complicated life. His marriage to Lana began and ended in 1940.

*Lower photo* shows Artie with **Ava Gardner** in an "unhappy together" night on the town. His marriage to Ava was a bit more long-lived: From 1945 to 1946.

Ruefully, Ava and Lana later agreed that Artie seemed to experience "buyers remorse" a few moments after each of their respective weddings.

## CELEBRATING LANA!!
### How Hollywood's Love Goddess of the 1940s
### Helped Thousands of American G.I.s Win World War II

World War II was new and it permeated the media. American twenty-and-thirty-somethings had volunteered for military service in droves, but they were frightened and they were confused. A few of them are depicted above (*right-hand photo*), risking annihilation on the beaches of Normandy in 1944.

The military worked frantically to supply motivation and direction, and Hollywood helped. One sure-fire morale builder involved a shared appreciation for LUSCIOUS LANA TURNER, *photo, above left.*

Inadvertently, her contribution to the war effort involved (perhaps sexist) references that every G.I. cheerfully understood. And bawdy references to Lana (even if they were off-color) were frequent and invariably good for morale.

Overheard aboard a troop transport ship on its way to a shattered Europe: *"GUESS WHAT!! I KNOW A GUY WHO KNEW A GUY WHO F...CKED LANA TURNER!"* **Do You?**

Although born a brunette, **Lana** evolved into one of the most famously blonde celebrities in the world, widely emulated by other women in the U.S. and abroad.

Both **Eva Braun** (*left photo*), the mistress and last-minute wife of Adolf Hitler; and **Eva Peron** (*far-right photo),* co-dictator, with her husband, of Argentina, were widely rumored to have "copied" her hairdressing, makeup, and fashion statements.

Could part of Lana's appeal derived from her screen and real-life associations with men who included (*two center photos*) **Clark Gable**?

## Lana Was Famously Known as a Blonde—Until She Wasn't

Until the final sad and tragic years of her decline, **Lana Turner** generated multi-million dollar profits for MGM. During her heyday, she was so famous that every modification of her "look" was publicized (and emulated) worldwide.

Born in Wallace, Idaho, to working-class parents, **Lana** relocated to California. In 1936, at the age of 15, she was discovered by a talent scout at the Top Hat malt shop in Hollywood. **Photo #1 shows Lana, aged 15.**

**Photo #2** shows **Lana** in hip boots, modeling fishing gear in a "barely legal" photoshoot at around aged 16.

**Photo #3** Publicity photo of **17-year-old (brunette)** Lana under the stewardship, pre-MGM, of film producer Mervyn LeRoy.

**Photo #4**. Lana in a small part as an Oriental princess, cast with Gary Cooper in *The Adventures of Marco Polo* (1938), one of the most elaborate and costly of Samuel Goldwyn's productions.

**Photo #5 Lana** with an **unidentified serviceman** in 1941. Like thousands of others, he might have been on the verge of being shipped off to his possible death or dismemberment in Europe or the Pacific. With America at war, Lana's sometime frenzied appeal among members of the armed forces cannot be overemphasized. In the photo, each seems (understandably) charmed by the other. Gallantly—accompanied by gossip that spread like wildfire among the troops—Lana offered whatever comfort she could to many of them.

**Photo #6**. **Lana** with **Clark Gable** in *Betrayed* (1954), an espionage war thriller set in the Nazi-occupied Netherlands. Is she a double agent?

**Photo #7:** Gorgeous and underaged, Lana is uncomfortably perched, poolside, on a handrail.

**Photo #8:** Young Lana, looking more sophisticated than she probably felt at the time; and

**Photo #9:** In this publicity shot, "Juvenile Stars of Tomorrow" include (*left to right)*, **Judy Garland, Bonita Granville, Jackie Cooper, Lana Turner,** and **Robert Stack.**

In this, one of the most famous publicity shots in the history of Golden-Age Hollywood, a deceitful **Lana** appears as an accessory to murder in *The Postman Always Rings Twice* (1946)

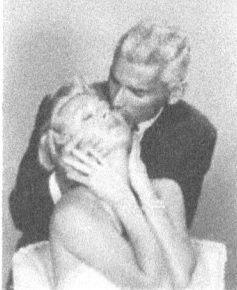

Some of her fans assess this as the most beautiful image of **Lana Turner** ever taken. We agree.

Perky and wholesome, **Lana** didn't always camp it up as a vamp.

In the *upper photo*, she appears as the kind of postwar "factory gal" any G.I. might introduce to his mother.

The film (*The Lady Takes a Flyer; 1958*) was the kind of convoluted, rather silly romance that only Lana could (believably) handle. Her two-timing husband (*lower photo*) is **Jeff Chandler.**

The demented visionary, billionaire **Howard Hughes** (*left photo*) demonstrated better than anyone else the aftermath of what happens when insane amounts of money are "unleashed' in Hollywood. In the process, he changed the worlds of aviation and entertainment forever. He's remembered today for lessons about what money can buy—and what it can't.

Notoriously secretive and camera-shy, he's seen above *(right photo)* dancing with Lana Turner.

And then there was the blockbuster hit, *Peyton Place*, based on a best-selling novel about repressed sensuality in a small, uptight New England village.

It marked Lana's reluctant but very convincing segué into what her detractors called "her matronly period." No one did it more glamourously than Lana. Here, she's seen counseling her onscreen daughter, as portrayed by **Sandra Dee.**

As everyone knows, *every gal in show-biz has gotta have a good lawyer.*

**Luscious Lana** appears above with **Greg Bautzer,** the notoriously promiscuous movie colony's "super-lawyer" of Hollywood's Golden Age.

"How," everyone asked, "did she manage to remain alluring but prim, gorgeous but straight-laced, all at the same time?

Here's **Lana** playing nice with **Bob Hope**, each of them slogging through a coyly suggestive but cornpone plot. One headline read, "LANA TURNER TO PLAY STRAIGHT MAN TO BOB HOPE."

During her moments of greatest triumph, and during moments of her deepest grief, **Lana** tended to wear white.

*Left photo*: Lana, ostentatiously clad in ermine, greats crowds of adoring fans in 1941. *Right photo*: Mortified and as cameras clicked, Lana exits from a hospital with her wrists bandaged in the aftermath of a suicide attempt. Pictures of her in this outfit appeared on frontpages of newspapers across the country.

After years as the Queen of MGM, **Lana** accepted roles in some low-rent stinkers..

One of them was *The Big Cube* (1968). Released during the peak of America's LSD craze, the plot calls for her to be assaulted by her greedy stepdaughter and her hippie boyfriend. After forcing her to ingest LSD as part of a bid to have her declared insane, **Lana** (*right photo*) shares a primal scream.

**Lana** made several attempts to dump **Johnny Stompanato** because of his increasing violence toward her. At one point, he threatened to shoot her. But in public, they concealed what was going on behind the scenes.

A week after the death of Johnny Stompanato, **Lana** was grilled on the witness stand. Some members of the press claimed that she gave "the greatest Oscar-worthy performance of her career."

Mary Astor — June Allyson — Fred Astaire

Lucille Ball — Jack Benny — George Cukor

Marion Davies — Sammy Davis, Jr. — Yvonne De Carlo

Police records revealed that during the early 1960s, long before he met Lana, **Stompanato** had been arrested eight times, based on suspicion of robbery to vagrancy.

**Cheryl Crane** *(right)* is depicted entering the courtroom with her parents, **Lana Turner** and **Stephen Crane**. Her fate was to be decided by a judge.

Anita Ekburg — Errol Flynn — Zsa Zsa Gabor

Ava Gardner — Cary Grant — Merv Griffin

Rock Hudson — Alan Ladd — Janet Leigh

When **Barbara Stanwyck** saw this publicity photo of herself with a pair of scissors, she said, "That's what I'd like to do to Lana Turner for fucking Robert Taylor during the filming of *Johnny Eager.*"

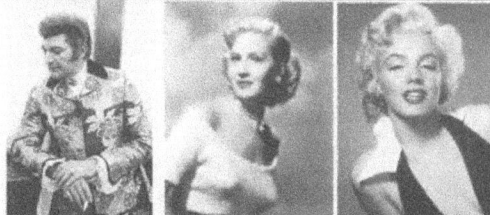

Liberace — Marilyn Maxwell — Marilyn Monroe

Barbara Payton — Cole Porter — George Raft

Spencer Tracy — Clifton Webb — Lovely Lana Turner

LANA

# BLOOD MOON
### Productions, Ltd.

LANA

**AT LAST!** Hollywood's Most Comprehensive Overview of
## "The World's Most Desirable Woman"

Luscious Lana, Celluloid Venus, was *The Bad & the Beautiful*, the last great Love Goddess of the Silver Screen. Her life of unbridled passion and scandal, including murder, was a real-life soap opera loaded with romance, betrayals, spotlights, *paparazzi*, and drama.

Here, published for the first time, is the inside story of how she evolved into the ULTIMATE MOVIE STAR and an Enduring Legend for the generation that helped make America Great.

# THE WORLDWIDE PHENOMENON KNOWN AS

# LINDA LOVELACE

The notorious **Linda Lovelace** was America's first Queen of Porn, presiding over a fast-developing multi-billion-dollar film industry during the decadent 1970s. Her movie, *Deep Throat*, redefined the nation's views on obscenity and was credited with changing America's sexual attitudes more than anything since the 1948 Kinsey Report. But at decade's end, Linda, in a complete about-face, emerged as one of the more compelling voices of the feminist movement, denouncing the degradations of her cinematic past.

In 2013, Blood Moon produced and published history's first empathetic and politically "engaged" overview of her life.

Decades after her death, **Linda Lovelace** remains a potent symbol of her era's free-spirited optimism and its sordid underbelly.

In 2013, Blood Moon documented her bizarre and tragic life with a biography, which later won a literary award *(runner-up to Best biography of the Year)* from the **Los Angeles Book Festival.**

Her style was crude. But as a witness to subcultures and lifestyles imagined and whispered about by millions of consumers, yet directly experienced by only a few, her saga has merit and dignity.

Therefore, because of what her story tells us about the bizarre social and sexual dramas of the greatest nation on earth, we dedicated this book to **LINDA LOVELACE**

**LINDA BOREMAN LOVELACE MARCHIANO**
(1949-2002)

**GONE BUT NOT FORGOTTEN REST IN PEACE**

According to Danforth Prince, Blood Moon's president, "Whereas this is not a pornographic book, it is a book about pornography. It's a no-holds-barred overview of contemporary sex-industry reality, with cultural implications and historical references that go way beyond its immediate subject, Linda Lovelace and the pornographic media in which she starred. Compiling it required a firsthand witness with the talent and experience of celebrity scandal-monger **Darwin Porter** to bring Ms. Lovelace (tastefully) alive as a sociological commentary whose implications extend to the core values of America itself."

## WHAT IS IT?

"Blood Moon envisions this project as a hot, commercially successful paperback divided into three distinct sections," its publisher continued. "We urge bookbuyers and critics to extend their vision and judgments beyond *Part One,* which, in deference to the subject matter, is necessarily *piquant* and sexually graphic. And we loudly maintain that the revelations and insights of *Parts Two* and *Three* might immediately thrust this book into the glare of major media attention."

Blood Moon's choice of January 2013, as the publication date for this book will coincide with the upcoming release of a major A-list movie (*Lovelace*) starring **Amanda Seyfried, Peter Sarsgaard,** and **James Franco.**

Blood Moon (and Darwin Porter) are not unfamiliar with the scandals of America's Entertainment Industry and their implications. Their other recent releases have included critically acclaimed overview of the Kennedys, Frank Sinatra, Marlon Brando, Merv Griffin, Katharine Hepburn, and many of the less-acclaimed but always gossipworthy stars of Hollywood's so-called Golden Age, as exposed in three titles of Blood Moon's BABYLON series.

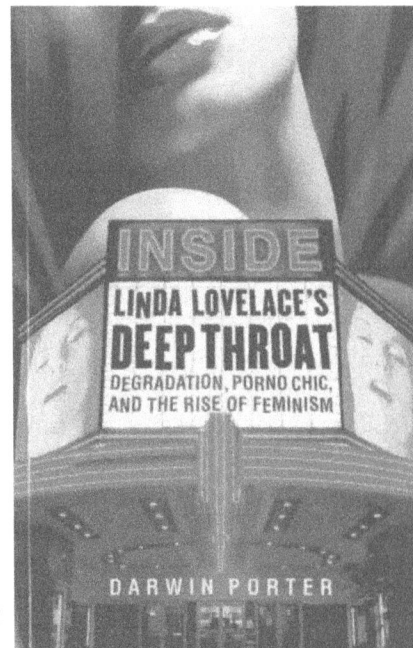

\*\*\*

93

## INSIDE LINDA LOVELACE'S DEEP THROAT IS DIVIDED INTO THREE PARTS

In the 1970s, Linda Lovelace, so to speak, opened her throat to the world. She became the reigning sex goddess of the decade after the release of Deep Throat, the most successful sex film in history. In her own words, "I had learned to do things with my mouth and vagina that few women anywhere can ever hope to achieve."

## PART ONE  (Degradation)

Part One traces her origins as a Catholic school girl, mockingly identified by her male contemporaries as 'Miss Holy Holy" through her journey into the most degrading aspects of prostitution. It describes how she fell into bondage under the influence, often at gunpoint, of her pimp (Chuck Traynor), her involvement in bestiality films, and how she coped with his oft-expressed advertising of her sexual skills as "There is no human desire that Linda Lovelace can't satisfy."

Part One is, by necessity. the most graphic section of this book

## PART TWO (Celebrity and Porno Chic)

The bulk of this book, Part Two, deals with the filming of and public reaction to *Deep Throat*, the highest-grossing sex film of all time. The film made Linda Lovelace the most infamous porn star who ever lived. It remains a controversial topic about which no one is indifferent.

After its release in 1972, it surged into the public mainstream, ushering in the pre-AIDS era of "porno chic," a defining milestone in the cultural history of America. Into movie theaters paraded personalities who included Barbara Walters, Truman Capote, and Norman Mailer, who later arranged to sample Linda's specialty up close and personal. Linda Lovelace became the decade's love goddess, the focus of T-shirts, coffee mugs, even condoms. "Linda Lovelace for President" badges were distributed as a form of political protest against the Richard Nixon regime, and the title of the movie in which she had starred was adopted by the mainstream media as the name of an (otherwise anonymous) key source in the downfall of the U.S. president.

Part Two explores how *Deep Throat* was confronted with more legal challenges than any film since the 1915 release of D.W. Griffin's *The Birth of a Nation*. After its release, it was banned in 27 American states. A court in Memphis ordered jail terms for some of its (Mafia-connected, Mafia-financed) producers. By cooperating as a state's witness, Linda avoided jail time.

Part Two continues, in graphic detail, with descriptions of Linda's sexual contacts with some of the biggest celebrities in America. Al Goldstein, the infamous publisher of *Screw* magazine, once asked Linda in an interview which actor in Hollywood presented her with her "biggest problem." Her answer was never printed, but in Part Two, Blood Moon "sizes up" the matter. As her fame grew,

*Deep Throat,* the largest-grossing porno film of all time, inspired both Frank Sinatra and Sammy Davis Jr. to seduce its female star, **Linda Lovelace.** Here she is, seen with a "doctor," **Harry Reems**, who discovers that she has a misplaced clitoris. It is not tucked behind the lips of her vagina, but lodged several inches down her throat.

Shortly after its release, **Sammy Davis Jr**. did more than any other celebrity to popularize this XXX-rated flick in California, even renting a theater for a private screening for his friends. They included **Frank Sinatra** and **Spiro Agnew,** the disgraced vice president under **Richard Nixon.** "If he'd been in town, I would have invited Nixon, too," Sammy said. "He has to get off too."

In 1972, *Deep Throat* opened on the same day in about three hundred theaters across America. Many liberal newspapers ran reviews of it, never having promoted a porno flick before. *Deep Throat*, a 59-minute film with graphic scenes of oral copulation, got millions of dollars worth of free advertising.

**Chuck Traynor**, Linda's husband, began getting calls from movie stars who wanted to sleep with Linda. **Sammy Davis Jr.** was the first big star to call.

It was released for public consumption in the era before DVDs and streaming videos, during the final last gasps of the public's willingness to physically buy a ticket for access to a movie theater.

Celebrities saw it in droves. One of them was **Jacqueline Kennedy Onassis**—who was escorted to a matinee screening by author **Gore Vidal** Almost instantly, America was ruptured with protests and calls for moral decency.

it became a stylish rite of passage for male celebrities to sample the sexual skills of Linda Lovelace. This book, based on dialogues with Linda and with witnesses to the phenomena, names the dates she arranged, through an expanded network of appointment secretaries, with famous celebrities.

## PART THREE  (The Price of Fame and the Rise of Feminism)

**Part Three** describes and analyzes what Linda meant when, in the 1980s and as influenced by such feminists as Gloria Steinem, she declared that "Linda Lovelace is dead!  A new, more independent and courageous woman is born." She appeared on stages across the nation, declaring "The dirty movie business is, in fact, a dirty business," and emerged as a spokesperson for Women Against Pornography, even testifying before a U.S. Senate subcommittee.

Desperate for money, she accepted her final "sex-for-hire" booking with a celebrity, the aging Johnny Weissmuller, known to millions of fans as the most durable of the movie industry's many versions of Tarzan. The Austria-born former Olympic athlete was selling swimming pools at the time. Linda recalled her encounter with the former "Lord of the Apes" as a "Me, Tarzan-you, Jane" kind of *schtick*.

Her newly discovered voice met with hostile fire from the ever-expanding porn industry, as performer after performer denounced her claims, beginning with Eric Everett, her original onscreen sex partner in her early 8mm loops. "She wasn't particularly attractive, nor could she act. She merely claimed that she was forced to do disgusting things. To me, she looked like a girl enjoying her work."

Eric Edwards, who starred with Linda in several of her loops, claimed that "she was a sexual super freak who had no boundaries and was a pathological liar."

Dozens of other industry professionals agreed with Evans and Everett, condemning Linda for her anti obscenity stands.

Linda fought back, portraying herself "as the typical rape victim who gets raped all over again in the court of public opinion when she decides to finally tell the truth."

Linda now found herself in the position of having added yet another new expression, "The Linda syndrome" to the English language, describing women who abandon pornography and repudiate their previous career by condemning the industry.

In the 1970s, Linda married Larry Marchiano, a TV cable installer who later established a drywall installation business. With him, she had two children. Marriage and motherhood brought her some stability and happiness, although she never escaped the curse of being Linda Lovelace. She was both hounded and sought after wherever she went, suffering a gang rape from university athletes in Colorado.  Faced with financial difficulties, excess drinking, and spousal violence, her marriage to Marchiano collapsed in 1996.

Her health deteriorated rapidly during her 40s. Plagued with poverty, she ended up scrubbing floors in office buildings, even though the infamous film she had helped propel to notoriety was still making millions around the world.

\*\*\*

With the release of the low-budget *Deep Throat*, **A STAR WAS BORN**...Albeit not a particularly conventional one.

95

# HOW DID MEDIA HIPSTERS DEFINE

# LINDA LOVELACE

### A Sex-Crazed Nymphomanic?
### Or a Victim of Tragic Abuse?

"**Deep Throat,** strange as it may seem, changed America's sexual attitudes more than anything since the first Kinsey Report in 1948. It altered the lives of everyone associated with it. It super-charged the feminist movement. It gave the Mafia its most lucrative business since Prohibition. And it changed the nation's views on obscenity forever."

**—Journalist Joe Bob Briggs**

"Somebody told me that the two best-known names of 1973 were Henry Kissinger and Linda Lovelace. We each made notable breakthroughs: The distinguished Mr. Kissinger helped open the doors to Red China and Russia. I opened my throat for all the world to enjoy…I've learned to do things with my mouth and my vagina that few women anywhere can ever hope to achieve."

**—Linda Lovelace**

"Norman Mailer and I had a competitive relationship. Frankly, he wanted to be Hemingway but never made it. He always had to top one of my stories. One night at a party in Brooklyn, he told me that he came home, woke up his wife, and bragged to her that he had just fucked a black drag queen. He also told me that one night he hired Linda Lovelace, who brought him to three climaxes without removing his penis from her throat. Oh, that Norman."

**—Author Gore Vidal**

"My initiation into prostitution was a gang rape by five men, arranged by Chuck Traynor. It was the turning point in my life. He threatened to shoot me with the pistol if I didn't go through with it. I had never experienced anal sex before, and it ripped me apart. They treated me like an inflatable plastic doll, picking me up and moving me here and there. They spread my legs this way and that, shoving their things at me and into me. They were playing musical chairs with parts of my body. I had never been so frightened, disgraced, and humiliated in my life. I felt like garbage."

**—Linda Lovelace**

"The biggest status symbol this year is to have your cock sucked by Linda Lovelace. You guys had better book a date with her, or else you'll no longer be the Kings of Cool."

**—Sammy Davis, Jr., to fellow Rat Packers**
at the Sands Hotel in Las Vegas in February 1973

"Sammy Davis Jr. was subject to bouts of debauchery and dissipation that nearly wrecked his life and threatened to compromise his career. For instance, he spent periods of his life hanging out with the denizens of the hard-core porn industry and with practitioners of Satanism. He even suggested marriage to Linda Lovelace when she was at the height of her career, cruising Hollywood and Las Vegas as a sex toy for the very rich and famous."

**—Gerald Early**, from The Sammy Davis Jr. Reader

"I have met stars who were my idols when I was little—Elvis Presley, Warren Beatty, Hugh Hefner, Elizabeth Taylor, Ann-Margret, and Frank Sinatra—and I've been keeping a diary."

**—Linda Lovelace**

"I went to see Deep Throat at a movie theater on Duval Street in Key West. I don't know what all the excitement is about. I can swallow bigger cocks than that."

—**Truman Capote** to Tennessee Williams

"Steve McQueen's seduction of Linda Boreman marked a turning point in her life. Upon the sensational release of Deep Throat, she became the reigning Queen of Porn. Not only that, she became the "party favor" [her words] to movie stars, sports figures, one U.S. senator, and one vice president of the United States. In all, she estimated that she performed fellatio on more than fifty household names who range from Frank Sinatra to Joe DiMaggio, from Elvis Presley to Desi Arnaz, from Marlon Brando to Johnny Carson."

—**Columnist James Bacon** at a stag roast
for Ed McMahon in Palm Springs, 1978

"The reason I attended a showing of Deep Throat in Los Angeles was because I suspected that Desi had had a fling with her. Frankly, I wanted to see the girl's technique. I didn't want Desi to have to go outside the house for what he could get at home. After I saw the movie, I knew I could never top her. You see, I have this gag reflex."

—**Lucille Ball** to Ethel Merman

"I was the Queen of Porn and John C. Holmes was the King of Porn and known for his 13½ inch penis. A private film collector offered me $5,000 on a bet, claiming that he knew for sure I couldn't swallow the whole thing. He paid Holmes $1,000 and I won the $5,000. Yes, indeed, I did it! Down to the last inch. That was a private film. Porn collectors should try to find a copy of "Exotic French Fantasies" if they want to see John and me together."

—**Linda Lovelace**

"There is a disconnect between the freedom of expression that Deep Throat promised and what actually transpired. Now we have total liberation of sexual things, but we also have the Patriot Act. We never made the connection between sexual speech and political speech. Sex today has nothing to do with revolution anymore. It's about capitalism and protecting little profit centers."

—**Novelist Erica Jong**

"I was in Toronto recently, and the city is like being in middle America. And you've got very hot, young 18- to 20-year old girls with tongue studs, and they are simply publicly advertising that they are interested in and capable of giving you really good oral sex if you're interested. And that's not even designed to be shocking. We owe it all to Linda Lovelace."

—**Brian Grazer,** producer of Apollo 13 and How the Grinch Stole Christmas

"Linda Lovelace has the air of fresh carnality, the air of thoroughly debauched innocence, the sense of a woman exploring the limits of sexual expression and feeling. Linda Lovelace is the girl next door grown up into a shameless woman."

—**Kenneth Turan and Stephen F. Zito** in their book, Sinema

"Linda kept staying at my house, and I was having sex with the three or four other girls living with me. We had a giant waterbed, and Linda just sort of became one of the girls on the giant waterbed. She now says that the orgies went on there were actually setups for hooker deals, and that she hated that. She said I'd beat her up if she didn't do it, but that was bullshit. Everybody just got stoned and partied."

—**Chuck Traynor** in The Other Hollywood

"Giving more head, she became frantic—her tongue and lips were everywhere. Then I felt the muscles in the back of her throat opening up. Her head lowered over me. Suddenly, I could feel my cock go right into her throat. I couldn't believe she ate the whole thing. My cock and balls and half my pubic bush were all engulfed in that cavernous, Deep Throat of hers."

—**Harry Reems,** co-star of Deep Throat

97

"Throughout most of the 1970s, I was used as a sex toy in New York, Las Vegas, Palm Springs, and Hollywood. I was treated like a cheap whore. Once I'd satisfied a client, I was shown the door. Dozens of celebrities—mostly men, but also Katharine Hepburn—wanted to date me. For the most part, they requested only one thing. My specialty."

—**Linda Lovelace** in a speech before feminists in Denver, 1984

"Imagine: A major adult star like Linda Lovelace in a bestiality movie. It was very graphic. Linda is indeed having sex with the dog in nearly every position one can imagine in a porn flick. Bestiality is illegal in most states now, so one must take care to view it. It was made in a time when things were more liberal."

—**Csmineatlast's** online review of *Dogfucker*

"In a memoir, I wrote about a famous movie star and his son who did all sorts of perverted things together, with me, at the same time.. My publisher wouldn't let me reveal their names. But I can tell you who they were. Paul Newman and his son, Scott. Okay, Newman does a lot for charity, and I give him credit for that, but he's not so squeaky clean. He can get down and dirty. I've gone to bed with enough Hollywood stars to know that their image is one thing, reality the other."

—**Linda Lovelace**

"All of us do that kind of stuff—but not all of us want to be on camera."

—**Shirley MacLaine,** after viewing *Deep Throat*

"If you're having a male sexual experience, after you have your orgasm, your next impulse is not to bend down and look over and watch someone's scrotum pounding against someone's shaved beaver or whatever."

—**Jack Nicholson** during an interview with *Screw* magazine regarding his viewing of *Deep Throat*

"By the time I got around to sampling the specialty of Linda Lovelace, her throat was too loose. I turned the bitch over and fucked her in the ass. She was real tight."

—**Gangster Mickey Cohen**, to Liz Renay

"Linda Lovelace said she was forced into sex. Like hell she was. I spent a weekend with her in a hotel in Las Vegas, and she couldn't get enough of me. She wore me out, and I'm what is known as a sex maniac."

—Actor **Forrest Tucker** to John Wayne at a health club in Los Angeles

"My husband, Chuck Traynor, beat me physically. I literally became a prisoner. I was not allowed out of his sight, not even to use the bathroom, where he watched me through a hole in the door. He slept on top of me at night; he listened to my phone calls with a .45 automatic eight pointed at me."

—**Linda Lovelace**

"This is the woman who never took responsibility for her own choices, but instead blamed everything that happened to her in her life on porn."

—Adult film actress **Gloria Leonard**

"Teddy Kennedy rented Linda Lovelace's Deep Throat for one night. She was taken to this house in Los Angeles. I think it may have been the home of Jack Nicholson. I heard about it, but I didn't personally arrange it. Sammy Davis did the honors."

—**Chuck Traynor**

*"Does Dick Nixon look like a man who has ever gone down on a woman? If he had, or if he could, I bet the country would be different."*

**—Linda Lovelace**

*"In her book,* Ordeal, *Linda left out a number of incidents involving Hugh Hefner and his Playboy Mansion in Los Angeles, even though they were newsworthy incidents of sex and celebrities."*

**—Gloria Steinem**

*[Note: We at Blood Moon do not share Linda's restraint. Her heavily censored testimony is published for the first time in this book]*

*"Good riddance to trash. She was a good cocksucker. She was a piece of shit. Her book,* Ordeal, *was a lying piece of crap. She was a hooker, a scumbag, a lying trollop. I'm glad Chuck Traynor taught her to suck cock. I dropped several ejaculations down her throat. I want to do a final load, so that when she goes to hell, my sperm will go with her."*

**—Al Goldstein**, in his epitaph to Linda Lovelace in 2002

*"It was really hard and kind of terrifying playing Linda Lovelace. The director gave me some liberties, but I had to play someone who existed in history, someone who had quite an established reputation for something very extreme. I don't have to say what that specialty is, since millions of people saw her do it."*

**—Amanda Seyfried,** star of the biopic *Lovelace*

*"The movie,* Lovelace, *stars Amanda Seyfried as Linda Lovelace. It also stars Hollywood favorite James Franco as a young Hugh Hefner, who also seduced Lovelace. Sarah Jessica Parker plays the feminist Gloria Steinem. Demi Moore had to drop out of the role during her split with Ashton Kutchner and his cheating heart. Lindsay Lohan was to play Lovelace, but was fired after her repeated bouts in court."*

**Advance Publicity associated with Lovelace (the movie)**

# STRANGERS IN THE NIGHT
## LINDA'S CONVOLUTED RELATIONSHIP WITH
## FRANK SINATRA AND THE RAT PACK

*"Frank Sinatra was almost handsome and wore neatly tailored clothes that he'd take off for the right woman. What he lacked in muscles he made up in staying power. He was also well hung. Frank should have been the star of Deep Throat instead of Harry Reems. He found I had many talents, and he was anxious to try them all. When he plunged in, he didn't want to pull out again. Of course, he also sampled my Deep Throat. Not only that, he ended the night by a blast up my rear. He was some kind of man."*

**—Linda Lovelace, the era's most famous porn star, on Frank Sinatra**

Sammy Davis Jr. not only flirted with Satanism, he was also a devotee of XXX-rated porn flicks, especially those depicting acts of sadomasochism. Of all the Hollywood stars, he was said to have amassed the largest collection of what used to be called "blue movies," and that was in a day when they were not openly sold in stores or exhibited on cable TV.

In the days before videos, Sammy spent a huge part of his budget for his bootleg film collections, many of which were stolen from private collections. His favorite was a secret tape of Errol Flynn seducing a fourteen-year-old boy and a fifteen-year-old girl at the same time.

Sammy not only collected porn, he often appeared in it. He purchased some of the best video equipment of his day and had a cameraman film orgies of both men and women fornicating at his home. In addition to straight sex, he encouraged some of his friends to indulge in woman-on-woman action or male-on-male lovemaking.

When *Deep Throat* starring Linda Lovelace opened at the sleazy Pussycat Cinema in Los Angeles, Sammy attended the midnight showing and sat through four screenings.

It had caused a scandal when it had first opened in New York in June of 1972 at the same time the Watergate burglars had broken into the offices of the Democratic National Committee. In fact, the informant who provided the secrets to bring down the Richard Nixon administration during the Watergate scandal was called *"Deep Throat"* by reporters Carl Bernstein and Bob Woodward.

Culture vultures later claimed that the release of *Deep Throat* changed America's sexual attitudes more than anything since the Kinsey Report in 1948.

It also gave the Mafia its most lucrative business since Prohibition and altered the nation's laws on obscenity forever. The film continues to make money to this day. So far, during its decades-long run, it has grossed more than $600 million, perhaps a lot more, making it the most financially successful porno film of all time. Men and women across America who had never attended a porno showing before went to see *Deep Throat* for reasons never fully explained.

Sammy had read that Ed McMahon, the sidekick of Johnny Carson on The Tonight Show, had attended the showing of *Deep Throat* at the World Theater in New York and had invited his celebrity friends.

After attending the Los Angeles showing, Sammy got an idea. In fact, he later credited himself with inventing "porn chic." He decided to rent the entire Pussycat Cinema for an evening and invite some of the biggest names in Hollywood.

For his screening, Sammy, of course, invited Frank and recommended that he bring "a hard-to-get-chick. After watching Linda in action, she'll get so hot you'll have her before the night is over."

Sammy later claimed he was absolutely shocked when Frank turned up with his "date" for the evening. It turned out to be Spiro Agnew, the former Vice President of the United States, who had been forced to resign in disgrace for accepting a bribe.

In the audience that night were Milton and Ruth Berle, Warren Beatty, Mr. and Mrs. Dick Martin, even Lucille Ball and Gary Morton, her husband. Among other A-list guests were Truman Capote, Rat Packer Shirley MacLaine, and Nora Ephron.

At the end of the showing of *Deep Throat*, Sammy had made a special point of inserting a porn "loop" called The Masked Bandit: He Steals Pussy. In it, two beautiful girls were completely naked and exposed to the camera, but the lone male star, who looked very young and skinny, had his face covered by a mask throughout the entire loop. Although he had a small frame, the boy in the film, who looked under twenty years old, boasted a prodigious endowment. Unknown to the audience, the actor was a very young Frank Sinatra.

Since his friends weren't likely to recognize Frank's younger self, especially through the mask, Sammy wanted to have the projectionist run the clip as a prank on Frank. They were always pulling practical jokes on each other.

Previously, at the Sands in Las Vegas, Frank heard that an elderly man had died from a heart attack within one of the bedrooms. Frank asked the manager to have the corpse delivered secretly and very late at night to Sammy's suite when he was asleep.

The next morning around 10am, Sammy walked into the living room of his suite to discover a nude dead man sitting upright on his sofa. "I shit bananas," Sammy later told Frank. "Wait till I get even with you."

Sammy's revenge included a screening of The Masked Bandit at the Pussycat Cinema in front of dozens of Frank's friends.

"After the showing, Agnew and Frank filed out of the Pussycat. All of the guests thanked Sammy for his hospitality—

except one and that was Frank himself.

Later that night Sammy told his wife, Altovise, "Ol' Blue Eyes looked at me. No polar night ever had such a chill. I think I've really fucked up big time. Obviously, Frankie didn't appreciate my little joke on him."

"It wasn't so little," Altovise told her husband.

In Sammy Davis' discussions with Peter Lawford during his organizing the rental of the Pussycat Cinema, he admitted that he'd watched the Lovelace/Reems scenes from *Deep Throat* "a hundred times—and that is no exaggeration."

But Sammy wasn't satisfied by just watching scenes from *Deep Throat*. He personally wanted to sample the special oral talents of Linda Lovelace. Through an agent, Sammy arranged an off-the-record weekend with Linda and her porn-industry husband, Chuck Traynor, at Frank's villa in Palm Springs. Frank was not given any details about who would be on the guest list when he turned his property over to Sammy.

At first, Sammy had the agent ask a crucial question: "Do Chuck and Linda fuck with niggers?" When he learned that they had no racial prejudices, he asked the next question. "Do they believe in wife swapping?" He was told that Traynor and Linda frequently performed with multiple partners and were willing to play at orgies. For a price, of course.

First, Sammy had to get the approval of his wife, an African American entertainer, Altovise Davis, whom he'd married in 1970. Reared in Brooklyn, she was both an actress and a chorus-line dancer. The Rev. Jesse Jackson had officiated at their marriage ceremony.

Far more conservative than Sammy, Altovise did not want to join in wife swapping or any other sexual games. But as a means of holding on to Sammy, she became an unwilling participant. "But my heart was never in it," she once confided to Peter Lawford and Frank.

At Frank's villa in Palm Springs, Traynor arrived with Linda. Like Sammy, Traynor wore beads and Linda was provocatively attired in hot pants. Traynor, a well-built ex-Marine, had brought along some short porno "loops" in which he, not Linda, was the featured star. As the night unfolded, Traynor showed the loops to Sammy, who was impressed, and Altovise, who was not. Even so, Sammy's wife ended up as Traynor's sexual partner for the night, and Sammy retreated to the master bedroom to experience firsthand Linda's famous and widely publicized talents.

Over pillow talk, Linda confessed to Sammy that Traynor had kept the $1,200 she'd made for performing in *Deep Throat*. She also claimed that he beat her and at gunpoint made her endure rape from various men he brought to their apartment. Since Sammy was fascinated by S&M, he seemed turned on listening to Linda's trauma.

Later, in Las Vegas, Sammy relayed details of his encounters with Traynor and Linda to Frank. Frank himself wanted to try out Linda, and asked Sammy to have her flown into Las Vegas and delivered to his suite. Frank gave his permission for Traynor to accompany her to Vegas, but he didn't want him in his suite. "I want Linda to arrive by herself. I generally don't like to seduce women in front of their husbands." There was a smirk on his face that followed, when he looked at his friend. "Unlike you, Sammy boy."

Linda never described her encounters with Frank in any of her biographies and provided only a "vanilla account" of her experiences with Sammy himself, since both Frank and Sammy were still alive when she was wrote autobiographies which included both *Meet Linda Lovelace* and *Ordeal*.

In fact, Linda was discreet in not offering Sammy a particularly detailed overview when Sammy called her a week after her encounter in Frank's suite in Las Vegas.

Like a voyeur, Sammy wanted a blow-by-blow description of what went on between Frank and herself. "Unlike you, Sammy, he seems to prefer normal sex—you know, with the man on top, regular fucking preceded by a deep-throat blow job. I did my duty and was paid for it—and that's that."

In the months to come, Linda broke from Traynor and inaugurated plans which eventually culminated in their divorce.

She made several attempts to get in touch with Frank, wanting to become his mistress, but he never returned her calls. She scribbled a message for him and asked the receptionist at the Sands in Las Vegas to deliver it to his suite.

"I'm still waiting by the phone, Frankie," she wrote. "Just give me a call at any time, day or night, and I'll come running."

The message, if it were ever delivered, was never answered

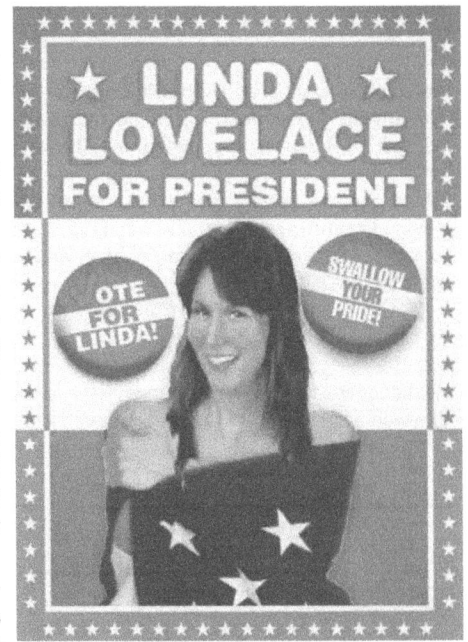

**Linda Lovelace,** the Fellatio Queen of America, was touted by fans as a candidate for President of the United States. Her competition included **Gerald Ford**, who had become president after **Richard Nixon** had been forced out of office during the Watergate scandal. An informant (nicknamed "Deep Throat") from within the White House had exposed the ex-president's nefarious deeds.

Linda's competition also included a peanut farmer from George, **Jimmy Carter.** "No man, not even Jimmy, wants to be compared to a peanut," she told campaign audiences in Los Angeles.

According to Linda, "If **Spiro Agnew**--who I deep throated one night--was not such a crook and had become president, I might have become to him what Marilyn Monroe was to JFK."

***

More pimp than husband, **Chuck Traynor** is depicted here with his then-wife **Linda Lovelace.** Later, he married (and promoted) America's OTHER most famous porn queen, **Marilyn Chambers**.

A former model for print ads for **Ivory Snow**, the beautiful and wholesome-looking **Chambers** later made worldwide headlines when her former association with that family-friendly product was exposed in tabloid coverage worldwide.

According to Traynor, "I don't think Linda was a prostitute before I met her, and she really wasn't one after I met her either,. But she was not the little inexperienced farm girl from northern New York like she'd have you believe. She was a kind of hot-to-trot, sleep-around kid."

the all-American girl

MARILYN CHAMBERS

Behind the Green Door
adults only

**Marilyn Chambers** was America's "Other Queen of Porn." The photo shows her promoted for an XXX film that, like *Deep Throat,* also broke previous records for notoriety and sales.

When she met Chuch Traynor (whom she later married), she told him she wanted to do only one or two erotic films, then move on.

"I really wanted to go on stage in Vegas. I wanted to be the next Ann-Margret."

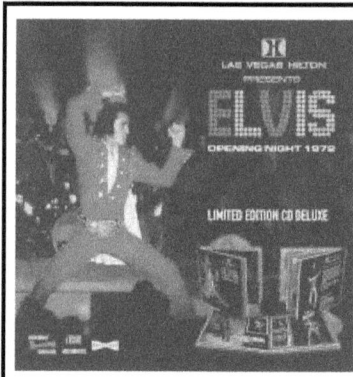

LAS VEGAS HILTON
PRESENTS
ELVIS
OPENING NIGHT 1972
LIMITED EDITION CD DELUXE

When she was in Las Vegas, Linda attended a performance of **Elvis Presley.**

"He was fat. It wasn't the guy that was hanging on my wall when I was a kid. I felt sorry for him. I went backstage, and he invited me up to his hotel suite. Once I got there, he showed me karate moves, not much else. I don't think he could get it up anymore."

INSIDE LINDA LOVELACE
BY LINDA LOVELACE
STAR OF DEEP THROAT

...Linda is the new sex goddess of the 70s!"
—Hugh Hefner, Playboy
The Intimate Diary of Linda Lovelace

ORDEAL
LINDA LOVELACE
WITH MIKE McGRADY

Since Linda Lovelace didn't make any money off *Deep Throat*—her husband, Chuck Traynor, confiscated the $1,200 she was paid—she became a virtual publishing cottage industry, turning out book after book relating her experiences.

The first and most successful was **Meet Linda Lovelace**. It begins with the claim, *"Somebody told me that the two best-known names of 1973 were Henry Kissinger and Linda Lovelace."* In the book, she shared the secrets of her *Deep Throat* techniques, claiming that after months of practice on many different men of all shapes and sizes, she became "one of the supreme cocksuckers of all time."

"Everyone wants to be the best in some field of endeavor, and since I'm not exactly material for a Nobel Prize in literature, I do what I can with what I have," Linda said.   She invited her readers to get inside her throat. Some hookers used to have trouble deep-throating Frank Sinatra, but Linda, with all her experience, claimed that once Frank's penis passed her throat muscles, "length became no problem."

Let's face it," Richard Nixon told Henry Kissinger. "We can't rely on Sinatra's support. He's really a Democrat. He's only hanging in with Spiro Agnew and me because he hates the Kennedys for kicking him out of the White House. I saw a poll. Black Americans hate me, but I know how to solve that. I'm going to invite Sammy Davis to visit me in the Oval Office. I hear he's wildly popular with the Negroid vote. I'm appointing him to the National Advisory Council on Economic Opportunity."

When Sammy arrived at the White House on July 1, 1971, Nixon was waiting with a photographer. They made small talk for a few minutes. Within the hour, a White House photo of Sammy with Nixon was going out over the wires.

Later, Sammy said, "Now I'm bigger at the White House than Frank. Tell him I'm now summoned by presidents for my advice."

Later, Nixon said to Kissinger, "I'm going to mention that Davis boy at a press conference. Is it appropriate to call him—what is it they say?—a soul brother?"

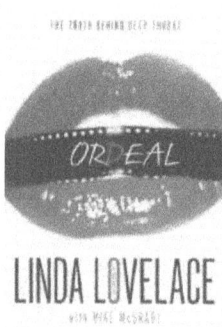

Linda Lovelace

During her controversial heyday, efforts to market **Linda** and the "gift" she was famous for became frenzied and ferocious, provoking censorship crackdowns and screams of outrage nationwide.

Investors proposed franchise deals of everything from **"Linda's Melt-in-Your-Mouth chocolates'** to her endorsement of "other fetishes," none of which ever really took off.  Posted above is one of pieces of marketing with which she was associated.

Ironically, many of the endeavors to "monetize" her were eventually sabotaged by Linda herself.

# FRANK SINATRA
## THE BOUDOIR SINGER

**Hot, Unauthorized, and Unapologetic!**

SINATRA
*The Boudoir Singer*

BY DARWIN PORTER & DANFORTH PRINCE

Everything you ever wanted to know about **Sinatra—and more.**

**Miss Sophie Tucker**—the Last of the Red-Hot Mammas and, when his own mother worked for her, a surrogate mother to then-adolescent **Darwin Porter**

**Frank Sinatra** and **Ava Gardner** at their wedding. Paparazzi clamored to get inside to see it, despite the elaborate measures they'd taken to keep its location secret.

*"Every time I sing a song, I'm actually making love on stage. Call me 'The Boudoir Singer,'" or so claimed Frank Sinatra. The crooner's career spanned more than half a century, earning him millions of fans. His boudoir conquests involved some of the most stunning women of the 20th-century. But exactly, who was this mercurial, enigmatic man? Darwin Porter, America's leading chronicler of Golden Age Hollywood, turns over more than a few boulders in Sinatra's secret garden, especially for those, who thought they'd heard it all. For the compilation of this compendium of show-biz scandal, Darwin Porter, former bureau chief and entertainment columnist for The Miami Herald, drew upon a treasure trove of celebrity contacts he accumulated over the decades.*

## "I WROTE IT MY WAY"

### The Boudoir Singer
### by Darwin Porter

After she was widowed during World War II, my beautiful mother moved to Miami Beach, where she became the most ardent fan of Frank Sinatra, who was called "The Voice" by screaming bobbysoxers. She collected each of his records and played them endlessly, never tiring of hearing the same songs.

In time, she became the personal secretary and wardrobe mistress of Sophie Tucker, "The Last of the Red Hot Mammas," and "The Queen of Miami Beach." Booked into Miami for a singing engagement, Frank came to call on Miss Sophie.

At long last, my mother came face to face with her idol, and something clicked between them. I interrupted their *tête-à-tête* to ask for an autograph. Frank reached into his pocket and removed a ten-dollar bill. "Get lost, kid," he said.

That very night, I began compiling Frank Sinatra stories. As the years faded into decades, my files burgeoned. My travel-writing career took me everywhere, where I constantly encountered Frank-in New York, Atlantic City, in Las Vegas and Reno, in Palm Springs and Beverly Hills, in Hollywood, in La Romana (The Dominican Republic), in Rome, and in Madrid, where I spotted him dining at La Bola with his estranged wife,

FRANKIE GOES HOLLYWOOD
Bobby-sox brigades

**Upper photo:** Bobbysoxers (a baffling phenomenon that reached its peak in 1943) strut their stuff while waiting for FABULOUS FRANKiE to appear. Rumors said that Sinatra's manager sometimes paid them to scream—with or without sexual hysteria—whenever he appeared.

**Middle and lower photos**: Although the fans who stalked Elvis, the Beatles, and Tom Jones did it more blatantly and with more sexual aggression, **Frank Sinatra** is credited with setting a style for celebrity lunacies that followed.

*In the lower photo*, snapped in 1943 in Pasadena, that's Frankie in the center—the one who's generating the screams

Ava Gardner. The dinner ended in disaster when she dumped her platter of paella into his lap.

It seemed that everybody I met in show business had a tall tale to tell about Frankie, especially Peter Lawford, who became my friend. Of course, famous people such as Tony Curtis or Lucille Ball had the most revelations. But so did bartenders, room service waiters, and Las Vegas showgirls. A portrait emerged of a man who had a Dr. Jekyll and Mr. Hyde personality. As his mentor, band leader Tommy Dorsey recalled, "He's the most fascinating man in the world, but don't stick your hand in the cage."

His lovers gave mixed reviews. In Tangier (Morocco), Marlene Dietrich claimed, "*Mais oui* ... the Mercedes-Benz of men!" Bogie's widow, Lauren Bacall, differed. "A complete shit!" In London, Ava Gardner said, "Our problems were never in bed. Our fights began on the way to the bidet." Marilyn Monroe proclaimed, "He was no DiMaggio."

From Grace Kelly to Natalie Wood, Frank loved his women, occasionally coming home to one of his four wives. Dean Martin, his fellow Rat Packer, said, "When he dies, they're giving his zipper to the Smithsonian." Elizabeth Taylor detested him after he forced her to abort their love child and refused to marry her.

When I heard that director Martin Scorsese was going to make a biopic of Ol' Blue Eyes, possibly starring Leonardo DiCaprio as Frank, I decided at long last to gather up my tales and tattle them in a book I released in 2011, *Frank Sinatra, The Boudoir Singer*. Actually, he gave me the title. He said, "Every time I sing a song I make love. I'm a boudoir singer."

Since time had, indeed, moved on, I dared write about a lot of stuff that would have been unprintable in the 50s and 60s. As a quick preview, I wrote about his two "unknown" daughters born out of wedlock; the porno movie he made in 1934 when he was alone and starving in New York City; the women he almost married--Marilyn Monroe, Dame Elizabeth herself, and Grace Kelly.

His romances with such black divas as Billie Holiday and Lena Home are documented, as is his "rape" of Zsa Zsa Gabor, and his torrid affair with porno queen Linda Lovelace, star of *Deep Throat*. "Every day brought something new to do," he sang. Maybe it involved fighting Elvis Presley for the charms of dancer Juliet Prowse, or perhaps being temporarily inducted into the Church of Satan by Sammy Davis Jr.

Pleasure shifted to debauchery; mood swings turned violent, joy often led to pain, triumphs to tragedy. There's no doubt about it, he did it "My Way." He turned down editor Jackie Onassis who wanted to work with him on his memoirs. "I've done too many things in my life I'm not proud of," he told her.

Despite the scandals and revelations, my picture-filled book, co-authored with Danforth Prince, is actually a tribute to the most charismatic entertainer of the 20th century.

What would Frank do if he were still around to read *The Boudoir Singer*? First, he'd make a phone call to some of the boys. "Go get him!" he'd order. Then he'd probably burst into a song called, "That's Life."

\*\*\*

The text *(but not the photos or their captions)* that follows is

# From the November 19, 2022 edition of THE MAIL ONLINE,

Their review, by **Dalya Alberge**, of Darwin Porter's *Frank Sinatra, The Boudoir Singer* appears immediately below.

Struggling to get his singing career started, a homeless and hungry Frank Sinatra was persuaded to appear in a porn film, according to a new biography.

He was paid $100 for his contribution to a 1934 movie called *The Masked Bandit* at the age of 19 - and spent the rest of his life hoping it would stay a secret.

The claim is made by Darwin Porter, who has been researching his biography, Frank Sinatra, The Boudoir Singer, for decades.

He says he was told about the film by British actor Peter Lawford, one of the five members of the Rat Pack—Sinatra's gang of movie pals from the 1960s which also included Dean Martin and Sammy Davis Jr. Lawford revealed that Davis— a collector of porn films at a time when they were not sold openly—had a copy of *The Masked Bandit*.

In 1972, he played a prank on Ol' Blue Eyes at a party of celebrity friends, inserting footage of it into a reel of the notorious porn film *Deep Throat*, which he screened for the guests.

Because Sinatra was masked, nobody at the private screening except Lawford, Davis, and Sinatra knew who the skinny teenager frolicking with two naked actresses was.

The Rat Pack often played pranks on each other but Sinatra wasn't amused.

He masked his anger to keep the secret and, says Porter, was going to "cut Sammy Davis Jnr off for life, but then realized Davis might reveal his secret."

Davis later agreed to destroy his copy of *The Masked Bandit*.

Referring to Sinatra's involvement with the Mafia, Porter added: "Years later, a segment of *The Masked Bandit* was considered for insertion in a film about stars such as Joan Crawford, who had appeared in porn before they became famous. When Frank heard about this, he called his friends in the mob. *The Bandit* loop never resurfaced."

Porter, who has published books on other Hollywood figures, adds: "A lot of stars do a porno loop when they are struggling. So many have this little dark period."

Sinatra's career took off in the next decade, and was revived in 1954 when he won an Oscar for his performance in *From Here to Eternity*.

\*\*\*

FRANK SINATRA  DEAN MARTIN  SAMMY DAVIS JR.  PETER LAWFORD

**THE RAT PACK**
THE EARLY YEARS

Desperate and broke when he was 19, **Frank Sinatra** got paid $100 to star in a porn film, *The Masked Bandit*.

Decades later, in a drunken and probably spontaneous stab at "ribbing" him, fellow members of the infamous **Rat Pack** acquired a copy and screened it at a hipster Hollywood Party.

Ol' Blue Eyes was furious and later,—when someone attempted to distribute it to a larger audience—he called the mob.

THE *REAL* HOLLYWOOD, THE FORBIDDEN SCENES THE CENSORS SLASHED,
INCLUDING
**PRIVATE Erotic Films of the Stars!**

HOLLYWOOD
BLUE

A Blue Lite Presentation
Written by
Mike Lite & David Seller
Photographed by
Howard Ziehm
Edited by
Mike Lite
Produced by
Bill Osco
& Howard Ziehm

IN COLOR
Showtime  12:00  2:00  4:00
            6:00  8:00 10:00
EKOS
Special Midnight Show on Saturdays
7165 BEVERLY BLVD.
One Block West of La Brea
935-3909
EXCLUSIVE ENGAGEMENT

***On the Left,* Hollywood Blue** was a low-budget porn film released in 1970 to "art cinemas" in big cities like L.A., San Francisco, and New York. Erotic clips derived from indiscreet, "down-on-their-luck" decisions of stars who included **Betty Grable, Hedy Lamarr, Sophia Loren, Jayne Mansfield, Ronald Reagan, Mamie Van Doren, Mae West, Fay Wray,** and even (*Call the Police! Jailbait Alert!*) **Shirley Temple.**

Critics noted that soft-core "gauzy" shots were interspersed with clips that were more hard core. Ironically, except for some frenzied "legal or not' phone calls, Frank Sinatra's then-anonymous 1934 appearance in THE MASKED BANDIT might have been spliced into *Hollywood Blue's* final cut.

# FRANK SINATRA, THE BOUDOIR SINGER
## As Marketed by the National Book Network

This book reveals exactly what Sinatra meant when he sang he did it "My Way."

*"Every time I sing a song, I'm actually making love on stage. Call me 'The Boudoir Singer.'"*
**—Frank Sinatra**

**Marilyn Monroe**

Frank Sinatra's career spanned more than half a century, earning him millions of fans. His influence on popular music in the 20th century was unsurpassed. But exactly what was this mercurial, enigmatic man really up to?

You would think that there were no stones left unturned in one of the most heavily exposed lives of any entertainer. But Darwin Porter, America's leading celebrity chronicler of Golden Age Hollywood, manages to turn over more than a few boulders in Sinatra's secret garden. After all, Sinatra lived in an era when "inconvenient truths" were conveniently (and systematically) buried.

**Lee Radziwill**, as she appeared in *Agnelli* (2017).

The "Stranger in the Night" international icon had it all—fame, untold riches, stunningly beautiful women, the world for a playground. "That's Life" was lived not in the sun, but in shadows. Pleasure became debauchery, moodswings turned violent, joy brought pain, triumphs tragedy. Within the pages of this book, one of the most controversial, elusive figures of the 20th Century emerges as "The Man Behind the Myth."

For *The Boudoir Singer*, Porter drew upon a treasure trove of celebrity contacts over the decades and the so-called "little people" *[room service waiters, bartenders, Las Vegas call girls, etc.]* who surrounded Sinatra throughout his life.

Co-authored with Danforth Prince, *Frank Sinatra, The Boudoir Singer*, the latest in Blood Moon's Babylon Series, answers many mysterious questions that have puzzled the public for decades.

**Charles, Prince of Wales** (aka King Charles III)

The text is illustrated with hundreds of photographs, many being published in book form for the first time. Sinatra's life is revealed not just in his music, but in words and pictures, many of them embarrassingly candid.

\*\*\*

Within his biographies of Golden Age Hollywood, celebrity writer Darwin Porter includes the darkest secrets that never made the tabloids. As an aspiring teenage journalist, he first met Sinatra in 1955 in the home of the earthy vaudeville star Sophie Tucker, "Queen of Miami Beach." At the time, Darwin's mother was employed as Miss Tucker's "Girl Friday."

**Shirley Temple**

"Ever since Ol' Blue Eyes disappeared into the night with my beautiful mum, I've been on Sinatra's trail," said Porter. Over the decades, he's interviewed at least two thousand eyewitnesses to Sinatra's life, including such actresses as **Judy Garland** (in Los Angeles), **Marlene Dietrich** (in Tangier), and **Ava Gardner** (in London). Bandleaders, singers like **Merv Griffin**, Las Vegas showgirls, room service waiters, the madam of a bordello in Havana, more actresses, and women in all occupations of life each had something to reveal about the crooner. When Porter's revelations about the Chairman of the Board were published for the first time, many of his fans could never look at their idol in quite the same way again.

A lot of "insiders" had a lot to say about
**FABULOUS FRANKIE AND HIS SEX LIFE**

They included (*left to right*) **Judy Garland, Marlene Dietrich,** and **Ava Gardner** (*depicted here adjusting Sinatra's tie*).

They also included and singer/talk show host **Merv Griffin.** a closeted enigma about whom Darwin Porter devoted an "all to himself" biography 2009.

106

# OPINIONS ABOUT SINATRA
## WERE AS VARIED AS BLACK AND WHITE.

**Marilyn Monroe, Marlene Dietrich, Lauren Bacall:** "He was no Joe DiMaggio in bed," said Marilyn Monroe. "Mais oui, the Mercedes-Benz of men!" sang out Marlene Dietrich. "A complete shit," claimed Lauren Bacall when he dumped her at the altar.

**Tommy Dorsey:** "He's a fascinating bird of prey, and don't stick your hand in the cage," was the opinion of bandleader Tommy Dorsey.

**Ava Gardner:** "Our problems were never in bed," said Ava Gardner, his greatest love. "We were always great in bed-10 pounds of Frank, 110 pounds of cock."

**Prince Charles**: "I was not impressed with the creeps and Mafia types he kept around him," said Prince Charles.

**Dean Martin:** 'When Sinatra dies, they're donating his zipper to the Smithsonian," predicted Dean Martin. "You name 'em, he's had 'em--Lana Turner, Gloria Vanderbilt, Natalie Wood, Lee Remick, Lee Radziwill, Janet Leigh, Kim Novak, Shirley MacLaine, Judy Garland, Zsa Zsa Gabor, Angie Dickinson, Jacqueline Bisset. I'm leaving out 2,000 other women."

There are even some other stars that Dean Martin didn't know about: **June Allyson, Ingrid Bergman, Joan Crawford, Bettie Page, Betty Grable, Veronica Lake, Susan Hayward, Hedy Lamarr, Linda Lovelace** (of *Deep Throat* fame), and **Miss Mae West** herself. "Only **Shirley Temple** ever eluded me," Sinatra bragged.

***

SINATRA
The Boudoir Singer

Hot, Unauthorized, and Unapologetic!

BY DARWIN PORTER & DANFORTH PRINCE

When a teenaged **Mia Farrow** arrived at the Rancho Mirage villa of **Frank Sinatra** to begin their affair, she was mildly perturbed that the house was filled with photographs of **Ava Gardner** looking her loveliest. Although Frank and Ava had long ago divorced, he seemed to be living in the past. The place was a bit like a memorial to her.

On their second night together, he talked about his singing, claiming he learned a lot about phrasing and the technique of "sneaking breaths from Tommy."

Who's Tommy?" she asked her startled middle-aged boyfriend. He patiently revealed that Tommy was actually **Tommy Dorsey**, one of the great band leaders of America in the late 1930s and early 40s. "I was his boy singer."

"I never knew you sang with a band," she said.

"I also made movies in the 1940s," he told her.

"You did?" she said. "I'm amazed. I thought *From Here to Eternity* was your first picture."

"Kid, you've got a lot to learn." He lit a cigarette and headed out to the pool, perhaps wondering what a fifty-year-old man had in common with a nineteen-year-old.

"The sex is good," he later told **Dean Martin**. "I guess that's reason enough to keep her around. She's a very sweet girl, a little mixed up, perhaps. She's up on **Elvis** and **the Beatles**, but she's never heard **Bing Crosby** sing or seen one of his movies."

### SINATRA WAS A STAR IN OTHER MOVIES, TOO!

Here **Frank Sinatra** appears as a hot-to-trot sailor with a two-day shore leave, with **Gene Kelly** *(left)* in *Anchors Aweigh* (1945)

**Barbara Marx**, former showgirl, and **Frank Sinatra** get affectionate on their wedding day in 1976. He had two pronouncements to make:

"Barbara is no ordinary broad," he told his honored guest, **Ronald Reagan**, four years before he became president of the United States. "Barbara will be the last Mrs. Frank Sinatra."

He also told Reagan. "It's time for me to settle down, but on my terms only. Of course, even a man of my advanced age will stray from time to time."

Frank told another of his honored guests, the disgraced ex-Vice President **Spiro Agnew,** something more shocking:

**"My mother, Dolly**, does not approve of the marriage. I sent my attorney to tell her the bad news. I was too afraid. I also made one final call to **Ava Gardner** begging her to take me back. She told me, 'I'm not the marrying kind.'"

In London, Ava complained to her longtime companion, **Reenie Jordan**, "Frankie finally tied the knot with his gal."

"But that god damn wedding fucked up my plans to have a vacation in Palm Springs," she continued. "I need one...real bad. I've got this hangover from hell that won't go away."

# PORTER'S DISCOVERIES REVEAL

## *THAT THERE IS STILL MUCH TO TELL ABOUT OL' BLUE EYES*

### HERE IS JUST A SAMPLING OF WHAT AWAITS THE READER
### WHO OPENS THE PADLOCKED DOOR TO SINATRA'S CLOSET

NEWS: His secret affairs with two First Ladies occupying the White House. These trysts were conducted when John F. Kennedy or Ronald Reagan were out of town.

NEWS: The night a drunken Sinatra almost ordered the "execution" of Elvis Presley.

NEWS: His little-known affair with Elizabeth Taylor and their agreement to abort their child
A discovery by Sinatra that led to his booting of Sammy Davis Jr. and Peter Lawford from The Rat Pack.

NEWS: His 11th hour negotiations to prevent the marriage of Grace Kelly to Prince Rainier of Monaco. Sinatra wanted her to marry him instead.

NEWS His long, tortuous affair with Judy Garland-"We kept each other from committing suicide," he said.

NEWS: The sultry brunette, Judith Campbell, that Sinatra shared with both JFK and mob boss Sam Giancana.

NEWS: The role of Sinatra as White House pimp, delivering a string of Hollywood goddesses to the bedside of president.

NEWS: How Sinatra planned to marry Marilyn Monroe but called it off at the last minute. Even so, he prevented her from presiding over a press conference that could have destroyed the Kennedy political dynasty. He also investigated the murder of Monroe and concluded who did it.

NEWS: What really happened that night Sinatra arrived unexpectedly at his Palm Springs compound and discovered Lana Turner and Ava Gardner. What made him kick both of these glamour girls out into the night?

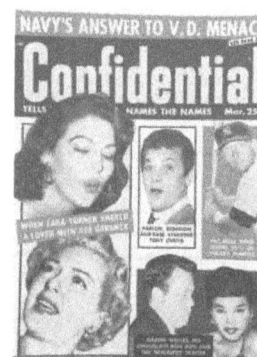

This undated photo shows **Sinatra** with **Nancy Davis Reagan,** who's dancing in the arms of "the man of my dreams."

On another occasion, on July 5, 1981, at the White House, during a celebration of her 60th birthday, she once again danced with Sinatra. But then-President Reagan put a stop to that. He tapped on Sinatra's shoulder to cut in. The First Lady's face barely concealed her anger.

**A U.S. PRESIDENT, A MOB BOSS, AND THE BRUNETTE COURIER THEY SHARED:**

**SINATRA, AS A "FIXER" KNEW IT ALL**

This "Triptych" of secrecy" shows *(left to right),* **JFK,** Mafia Moll **Judith Exner,** and crime boss **Sam Giancana.**

This 1957 edition of **Confidential** magazine hinted "ever so gently' at the lesbian links of Frank's wife, **Ava Gardner,** with one of World War II's most luscious pin-up girls, **Lana Turner.**

**Darwin Porter's** *The Boudoir Singer* tells even more.

# TOM CRUISE

*from the October 2022 Edition of Boomer Times*

From the New York islands to Hollywood Boulevard, the talk is of a "homeless" boy finding shelter under the roof of the moribund United Artists. Tom Cruise, the couch-jumping action hero of the *Mission Impossible* series, along with business partner Paula Wagner, has been given the daunting challenge of trying to breathe life into the MGM-controlled United Artists.

Cruise has some big shoes to fill. The actor, a shorty himself, is following in the footsteps of another shorty, Charlie Chaplin, who, along with Mary Pickford, director D.W. Griffith, and Douglas Fairbanks Sr., founded United Artists 87 years ago. The dream of those legendary stars of the silent screen turned into a nightmare. Pickford and Chaplin raged and shouted at each other so much they became enemies for life. "The Little Tramp" called "America's Sweetheart" an "iron butterfly." She shot back that he was "a dirty little man."

Over the decades and under new management, United Artists did pull itself out of a grave with such hits as *Rocky, The Pink Panther,* and the James Bond "007" series. But MGM shuttered most of UA's operations when it was sold to a consortium of investors in 2004. The *über* star *Cruise* landed at UA because he got too "bizarro" for Paramount.

After 14 years and billions of dollars in profits, Cruise was booted off the Paramount lot by 84-year-old mogul Sumner Redstone, head of Viacom/Paramount. Redstone claimed that Cruise's off-screen behavior was "not acceptable" to Paramount and that the former *Top Gun* star had cost Paramount $150 million in lost revenues on *Mission: Impossible III*. A poll of the movie-going public in 2006 seemed to back up Redstone. Of those polled, more than half claimed they now had an unfavorable view of Cruise. Some headlines were kinder than others—*Mission: Terminated*, as an example. Others were blatant: *"Cuckoo" Cruise Fired!*

A "crazy-in-love" Cruise not only jumped up and down on Oprah Winfrey's sofa to proclaim his love for Katie Holmes, but he attacked psychiatry and specifically Brooke Shields for taking prescription drugs to treat postpartum depression.

Many of those polled found that his public displays of affection with Holmes were designed to cover up the damage caused by worldwide headlined allegations of homosexuality. Cruise has gone from a pure box office phenomenon to a pop culture punchline. Even when Cruise, Holmes, and their baby daughter, Suri, appeared in a family portrait on the cover of *Vanity Fair*, one mocking headline asked: *Who's the Father? Surely Not Daddy Weirdest?*

Behind the scenes, Redstone also objected to Cruise making himself the poster boy for the cult religion of Scientology. Before becoming the Number One Box Office Star in the World, the handsome, boyish actor had toyed with the idea of becoming a Catholic priest. But his dyslexia made it difficult for him to read the Bible.

As to the larger question of whether Cruise can rescue UA, the battle lines of opinion are forming on both the left and right. A Hollywood insider told me that "the ballyhooed deal with MGM/UA is just a ruse. Cruise is being used as a stalking showhorse. What those boys at MGM want to do is sell United Artists, and they hope the Scientology-tainted Tom Boy will drive up the price. MGM wants to make its package look really pretty

**TOP GUN:** Here's **Tom Cruise** graphically demonstrating his pleasure—perhaps at himself as Hollywood's replacement of Clark Gable as "King of Box-Office Hollywood."

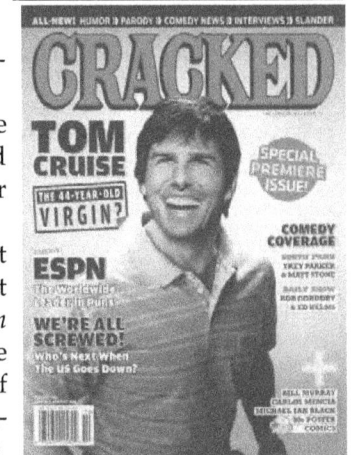

**Tom Cruise's** devotion at the time to his ex-wife Katie Holmes got icky when he allegedly told GQ magazine that he wanted to eat the placenta of their upcoming baby, later named Suri. Perhaps he was joking. Remarks like that moved him onto the cover of *Cracked*.

Viacom chief **Sumner Redstone** *(above)* not only fired Tom Cruise but denounced him. "He was embarrassing the studio. And he was costing us a lot of money."

Urged on by his wife, Paula, who had long ago soured on Cruise, Redstone gave Cruise the boot, refusing to renew Paramount's megabucks deal with Cruise's production company.

"Paula, like women everywhere, has come to hate Cruise," Redstone claimed.

Admiration for, and ridicule of **Tom Cruise** have flooded the movie-going consciousness in equal measure.

At least some of the ridicule, however, has softened as recognition of his status as a superstar has become more obvious—and as blatant examples of his personal eccentricities lessened.

DOMINATION WRESTLING 3

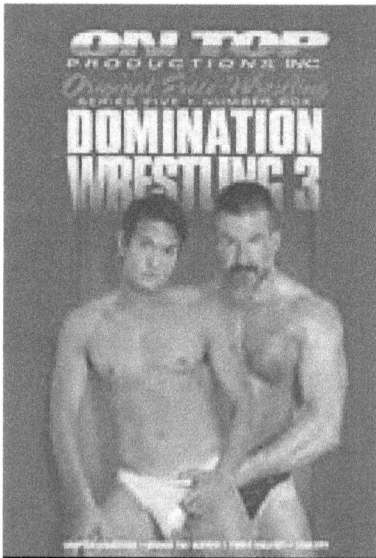

Then there were the gay rumors, some of them, at least, sparked by Tom Cruise's lawsuit, filed in Los Angeles Superior Court, against a male porn star.

It claimed that the erotic wrestler, **Chad Slater (aka Kyle Bradford** (*the left figure in the photo above*) "concocted and spread the completely false story that he had a continuing homosexual affair with Tom Cruise, and that this affair was discovered by Mr. Cruise's wife, leading to their divorce."

When pressed, that wife at the time, Nicole Kidman, dismissed it: "I personally don't believe in doing huge lawsuits about that stuff. Tom does. That's what he wants to do. That's what he's going to do. You do not tell Tom what to do. That's it. Simple. He is a force to be reckoned with."

before they dump it on the market again for investors. In spite of his age, Cruise still looks pretty." It's true that MGM, early in 2006, tried to dump UA but investors "laughed" at the $400 million asking price.

MGM needs to put up seed money to launch UA films, but Cruise will need to raise millions in hedge funds to produce movies. Faced with a fading market for DVDs, private equity companies are balking at dumping millions into films. This year alone, private investors have lost billions in backing films. *Poseidon* this past spring sank like the *Titanic*. The public stayed away in droves from such duds as *Lady in the Water* and the animated *The Ant Bully*, both released in the summer of 2006.

Under his new deal, Cruise and partner Wagner are committed to make four films a year, but Cruise himself is not obligated to star in any of them.

An executive of MGM in New York spoke off the record. "What the studio is doing is panning for fool's gold. Or, rather, real gold put up by fools. MGM wants to lure private investors to fund Cruise's next projects. But even dummies will soon learn how dangerous it is to invest in movies. You have a better chance of making money if you buy a lotto ticket."

Cruise's cheerleading squad, especially from within his Scientology camp, are loudly predicting that his movies will continue to make billions at the box office, leaving Summer Redstone crying in his beer. One thing, however, is certain: All Hollywood, especially investors, will look at Cruise's every move in the months ahead.

In 1983 the actor captivated American audiences when he danced in his jockey shorts in *Risky Business*. His new venture might be called *Risky Business— The Sequel*.

In this still shot from the infamous dance scene in *Risky Business*, the code language was that dance equated with sex.

As one critic said, "**Tom Cruise**'s ecstatic sole gyrations are the best covert wank-off in movie history. And, of course, he's damn cute. Even when he became more overt, it was about 'natural sex,' not the sordid, icky stuff."

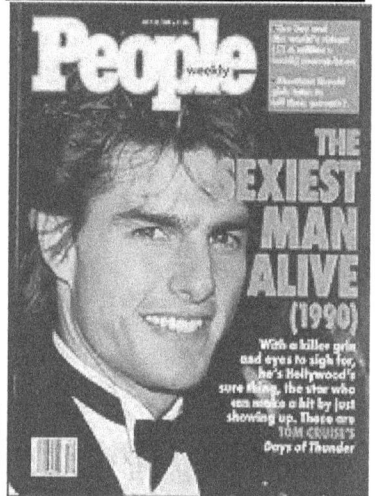

People weekly — THE SEXIEST MAN ALIVE (1990)

Is it or was it true? Enquiring minds everywhere began asking...

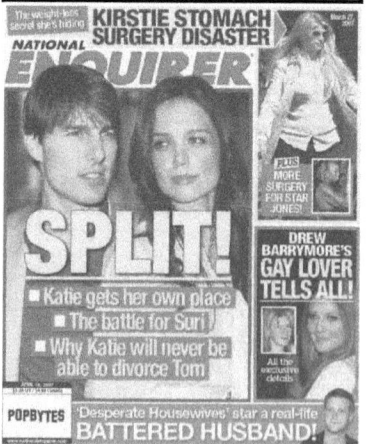

NATIONAL ENQUIRER — KIRSTIE STOMACH SURGERY DISASTER — SPLIT! ■ Katie gets her own place ■ The battle for Suri ■ Why Katie will never be able to divorce Tom — DREW BARRYMORE'S GAY LOVER TELLS ALL! — 'Desperate Housewives' star a real-life BATTERED HUSBAND!

His divorces were widely publicized, too. Depicted above is the *Enquirer's* cover ballyhooing **Tom's** embarrassing divorce from **Katie Holmes**.

Widely (some said "hysterically") promoted romances and/or marriages of **Tom Cruise** with *(left to right)* **Mimi Rogers, Nicole Kidman,** and **Penelope Cruz.**

# CRUISING
# THE LAST MOVIE STAR

**THE LAST MOVIE STAR**

The sometimes silly antics of Tom Cruise's past are dead and gone. Almost forgotten, they belong to yesterday. In the summer of 2022, he turned 60. But instead of fading into the Hollywood Hills, like so many other movie stars of yesterday, he's still around, still a commanding presence and moneymaker.

As we write this, and to the surprise of many, Cruise morphed into a box office champion. Entertainment industry moguls had successfully banked on their belief that he can continue to lure adults back into movie houses (or at least streaming services) across America.

A brash 24-year-old at the time, Cruise was a lot younger when he played Lt. Peter ("Maverick") Mitchell in *Top Gun* more than three decades ago. Since then, despite the odds, Cruise has entered the realm of Hollywood Royalty where he has remained, despite his occasional stinkers.

He has outlasted his competitors, doing much better than Johnny Depp, Brad Pitt, or Leonardo DiCaprio. Of course, Cruise had some duds like the 2017 reboot of *The Mummy*. But roles like the homicide investigator Jack Reacher and his incarnation of secret agent Ethan Hunt in *Mission Impossible* did well, and even generated some new fans.

His forty-four films have earned some four and a half billion dollars in the U.S. and Canada alone. Their success has allowed him to maneuver his way into some of the sweetest deals of any actor in Hollywood. Now, he usually receives a percentage of the box office gross that each of them generates.

The latest *Top Gun* cost Paramount $175 million to make, but sales have shot beyond the $1 billion mark. Originally scheduled for release in 2020, it was delayed because of the pandemic. Basing its bet in part on nostalgia, Paramount succeeded in luring some of the same adults who originally screened the original *Top Gun* 36 years ago.

Writing in *The New York Times*, Nicole Sperling said, "Audiences have remained loyal to Cruise through his offscreen controversies—his connection to Scientology, the infamous couch-jumping scene on the *Oprah* show, his failed marriages, including to the actress Katie Holmes. He has remained focused on making movies and then promoting them to as many people as possible—often through very controlled public appearances, where he is unlikely to face any uncomfortable questions about his private life that could embarrass him or turn off moviegoers."

During the Golden Age of Hollywood, Clark Gable reigned as King at the box office. His fans were so loyal they went to see any movie he made, good or bad. But in the New Age of Hollywood, the choice of movies and emerging actors clamoring for attention is bewildering.

"The studio-created movie star is dead and gone," claimed Wyck Godfrey, former Paramount executive in charge of production. " Gone forever is the heyday of Clark Gable, Errol Flynn, Gary Cooper, and John Wayne. When Cruise started out, 'Ah-nold' and 'Rocky' Stallone were big deals. Today, they are not even known to a new generation, who have streaming cellphones and the internet."

As Cruise begins that long climb to the age of 70, the question remains, "How long can he last?" Cast as his superior in *Top Gun: Maverick*, an "also-aging" Ed Harris tells the

Before becoming the Number One Box Office Star in the world, a handsome, boyish **Tom Cruise** toyed with the idea of signing on as a Catholic priest.

Decades later, after rivers of hype that promoted everything from Cruise as a closeted gay to one of the genuine heterosexual studs of the century, his status as a mass market action-adventure movie hero has led to ticket sales surpassing those of the previous "King of Hollywood," **Clark Gable** (*photo right*).

*Photos above and right:* Playing it predictably bad for sales which morphed into numbers that were predictably good: **Tom Cruise.**

His fast-aging peers and competitors have retreated, for the moment at least, into positions less prominent. *Left to right, above,* **Brad Pitt, George Clooney,** and **Johnny Depp.**

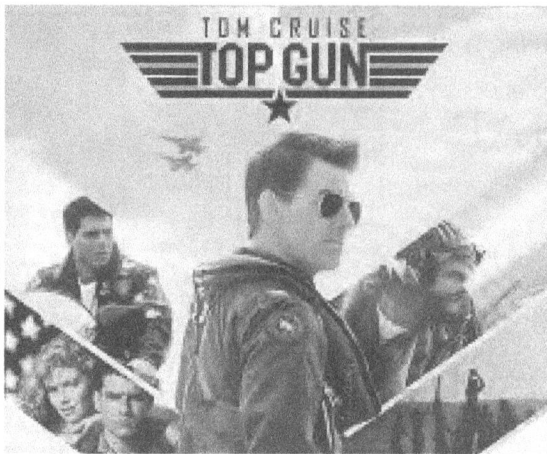

now mature and seasoned character portrayed by Cruise, "The end is inevitable. Your kind is headed for extinction."

Cruise fires back at Harris: "Maybe so, sir. But not today."

As summed up by critic Calum Marsh: "Tom Cruise has all the qualities you want in a movie star and none of the qualities you expect in a human being. As a screen presence, his is singular: As a person he is inscrutable. It's his inscrutability that has allowed him to achieve superstardom, one that exists almost entirely in the movies, uncontaminated by mundane concerns. Cruise the star burns brighter than his contemporaries, and far brighter than any who have come up since, in part because he continues to throw more and more of himself into his work and give less and less of himself anywhere else. Who is he? You have to look to the movies to find out."

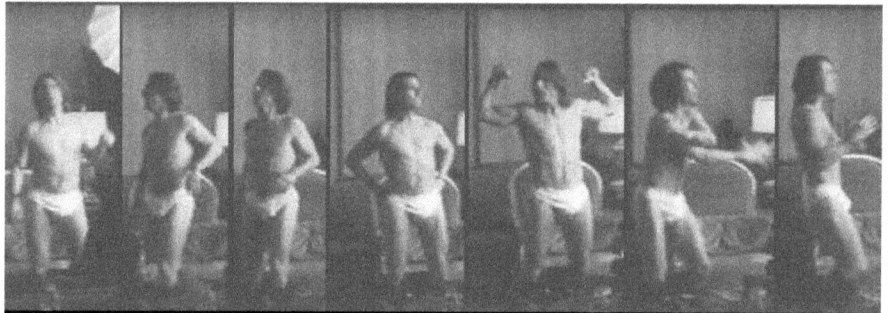

No, these stills from one of **Tom Cruise**'s dance sequence aren't the REALLY famous ones from his breakthrough film, *Risky Business* (1983).

They come from an equivalently clad scene in *Magnolia* (1999). It was an epic mosaic of several inter-related characters from the San Fernando Valley, each searching for happiness, forgiveness, and meaning. Although disappointing at the box office, it did earn Cruise a nomination for an Oscar as best supporting actor. He lost.

Appearing on the **Oprah Winfrey** show *(photo above)* in 2005, **Tom Cruise** was just plain batty over his relationship with Katie Holmes, jumping up and down on her couch, while televised, to prove it. Claiming that his love for Holmes is "beyond cool...I can't be laid-back, and I want to celebrate it."

His likeness to a televised jack-in-the-box made him the butt of jokes across the country. Later, Cruise appeared on Jay Leno's televised couch, pumping his arms and mocking his previous appearance on Oprah.

In June of 2005, **Matt Lauer** and **Tom Cruise** practically came to blows on *The Today Show*. The TV talk show host asked Cruise about his criticism of Brooke Shields, who had acknowledged the joint role of medication and psychotherapy during her battle with postpartum depression.

"You don't know the history of psychiatry," Cruise ranted. "I do. There's no such thing as chemical imbalance. You don't even—you're glib, Matt. You don't even know what Ratalin is. You should be a bit more responsible in knowing what it is because you communicate to people."

# PETER O'TOOLE

## Hellraiser, Sexual Outlaw, & Irish Rebel

### An Unprecedented New Look at the 20th Century's Most Outrageous Actor

**Born to a vagabond bookie working the U.K's racetracks**, Peter O'Toole became "the most notorious sailor in Her Majesty's Royal Navy" and then worked as a street vendor, a paparazzo, a newsman, and a steeplejack before drifting into the London theatre.

After his spectacular success in David Lean's four-hour epic, *Lawrence of Arabia*, he announced, "I've arrived! Ignore me at your peril!" He then went on to be nominated for seven Oscars before emerging as the Crown Prince of the British Theatre.

An orgiastic hellraiser, he starred in week-long binges and sex orgies of near Biblical proportions, bedding everyone from Elizabeth Taylor to Princess Margaret, who relentlessly pursued him. Mercurial acting talent on the screen was combined with a lethal off-screen life that "would have landed most blokes in jail" (his words).

In 2015, Blood Moon released the world's most comprehensive exposé of the eccentric, hell-raising actor.

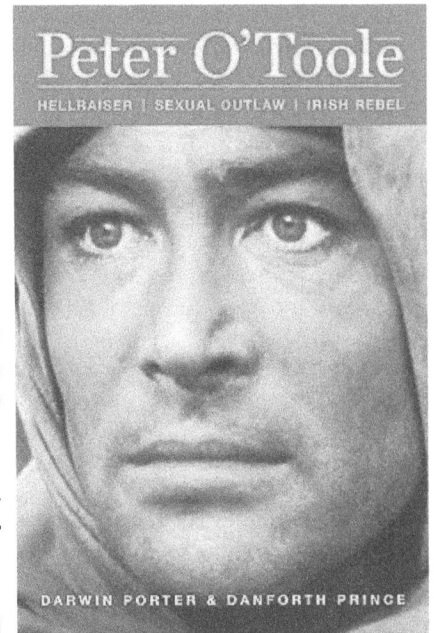

**Peter O'Toole**
HELLRAISER | SEXUAL OUTLAW | IRISH REBEL
DARWIN PORTER & DANFORTH PRINCE

**Blood Moon's exposé of PETER O'TOOLE**--one of the Baddest of the Bad Boys of fhe London stage and later, of Hollywood, received a *tsunami* of favorable reviews and news coverage after its release in 2015.

The pages that follow replicate just a few of them.

NEW YORK JOURNAL OF BOOKS

### Here's how it was reviewed by Vinton McCabe in the NEW YORK JOURNAL OF BOOKS.

*Something decidedly odd is going on at Blood Moon Productions,* whose Babylon Series has recently released its latest Hollywood biography: *Peter O'Toole: Hellraiser, Sexual Outlaw, Irish Rebel*.

Where, in the past, the subjects of these "tabloid biographies" (written in chapters that resemble nothing so much as photocopies of *The Enquirer* and *The Weekly World News)* have been written about in a manner that some readers might consider salacious (Nancy Reagan, in her youth, is alleged to have been particularly skilled at treating her gentlemen callers to oral sex, Zsa Zsa Gabor is said to have had sexual congress with both John F. Kennedy *and* Richard Nixon) the latest celebrity to be put under the microscope—the aforementioned Peter O'Toole—is treated with something alarmingly akin to respect.

Which might, under other circumstances, be considered a good thing.

But consider the subtitle: *Hellraiser, Sexual Outlaw, Irish Rebel*.

Understandably, the suggestion that Peter O'Toole had a fling with England's Princess Margaret Rose on the island of Mustique might, in some (royal) households, be enough to grant him the title of "sexual outlaw," but after all the allegations of sexual misconduct and/or experimentation ascribed to various Reagans, Kennedys, and Gabors, to say nothing of writers along the line of Gore Vidal, Tennessee Williams, and Truman Capote, and a string of Hollywood all-stars from Barbara Stanwyck to Marlene Dietrich to that ultimate hellraiser (and a sexual outlaw who knew what being a sexual outlaw was all about), Errol Flynn, the stuff that O'Toole is said to have attempted leaves him several notches down on the outlaw scale from his dear friend Richard Burton, and many, many slots below the ultimate outlaw, Mr. Flynn.

What Peter O'Toole mostly appears to be is very consistent actually, especially where his goals, self- congratulatory comments, and rude behavior are concerned.

In all these, he started out pretty early in life.

For instance, on his 18th birthday, he called his best friend to tell him that he had decided to give up his job at a local newspaper and run away to London:

"I decided that I don't want to be a journalist," he said, "I don't want to write about the affairs of other people. I want journalists writing about my affairs. I think I want to be a famous actor . . . I've decided to storm the formidable walls of London Town . . . I'm heading south to conquer. Get out of my way [Sir Laurence] Olivier, or else I'll knock you down and walk over your tired old body to claim my right in the spotlight."

In this brief quote, O'Toole reveals two of the major themes of his life: ambition and the need for attention/fame.

What he proposed next to his friend on the day of his 18th birthday, August 2, 1950, illustrates another lingering theme:

"In the meantime, let's get pissed. Booze is the most outrageous of drugs. That's why it's my preferred choice."

Getting pissed and staying pissed seem to have been intertwined goals for O'Toole that placed second only to heterosexual intercourse on his ongoing bucket list. Acting, it seems, came in third.

When it came to sexuality, O'Toole insisted that he was decidedly straight and reportedly turned down Laurence Olivier, John Geilgud, Noel Coward, and Alan Bates, among many other interested suitors. This is despite the fact that many found his enraptured dance when first fitted with Arab robes in *Lawrence of Arabia* as a sign of fey tendencies. And the fact that his role as a "babe magnet" in *Casino Royale*—a role that had been cast with Warren Beatty, who quit the film, allowing O'Toole to take it over—was met with reviews that sighed with their regret that Beatty had been replaced. O'Toole, the reviewers insisted, made for a poor on-screen lothario. And the fact as well that the nuns in the Catholic school he attended as a child gave him the nickname "Bubbles."

And then there's this: while discussing the experience in Catholic school, O'Toole reportedly commented, "Nuns aren't that smart. Imagine denying yourself cock all your life. If I were a heterosexual woman, I would take on at least six men a night from early morning to midnight."

*Hmmm.*

Still, Peter O'Toole got around. He made a wager with a friend that he could bed British actress Diana Dors, as well as Anita Ekberg and Jayne Mans-

Princess Margaret Rose, Countess of Snowden. Well intentioned, but often blocked from expressing her true feelings, this tragic "younger sister of the Queen:" was looking for love and perhaps a handsome prince.

Here's **Peter O'Toole**, cast as the Prince of Denmark in the National Theatre's 1963 production of *Hamlet*. Was he, for a time, the best Shakespearan actor in the English-speaking world? Regardless of who did it best, Margaret Rose, for a while, at least, selected him as her friend and playmate.

Here's **Peter O'Toole** in *Caligula* (1972) as the syphilus-ridden and very dangerous psychotic, Tiberius, Emperor of Rome. Still viewed as an authentic (and pornographic) overview of ancient Rome, it was described at the time as "the most debauched movie ever made."

Here's **Peter O'Toole** with **Audrey Hepburn** in that stylish romp about art forgeries and *haute couture*, **How to Steal a Million** (1966).

field and won the bet. And reportedly had an affair with the then-Mrs. Richard Burton, Elizabeth Taylor, while the three of them, the Burtons and O'Toole, were filming an adaptation of Dylan Thomas's *Under Milk Wood*.

*[While cheating on his wife Sian Phillips often enough to ultimately send her into the arms of another man, O'Toole did at least once rather famously state, in a spirit of fairness, that, "She's a free woman. Just because she's married doesn't mean she has to be a servant to her man. There's a wedding ring on her finger, not in her nose."]*

The Peter O'Toole who emerges from these pages is less a hellraiser than a braggart, less a sexual outlaw than a womanizer who proved to be a poor husband and a worse father, and less an Irish rebel than a pugnacious drunkard. He is, as presented in these pages, something of a bore.

But there is also Peter O'Toole the artist. Peter O'Toole the actor, who attained an iconic status early on with *Lawrence of Arabia*, who more than held his own on-screen against Katharine Hepburn in *A Lion in Winter*, and who returned after a period of flops and attempts to put his drinking behind him with *The Stuntman* and *My Favorite Year* and who acknowledged both his old age and his personal failures with a late-life minor masterpiece with *Venus*.

Where the gossip in this biography is played down compared to others written by the same authors, it is in the study of the man and the specifics of his movies that it succeeds.

And the biography produced seems less entertainingly outrageous than the others produced by the House of the Blood Moon, more centered as a traditional Hollywood bio, giving the reader some rather good anecdotes about the making of this full film catalogue. And, indeed, the chapters dedicated to the making of *Lawrence of Arabia*, from the details of the nose job that O'Toole was required to endure in order to secure the role to a lively recreation of O'Toole's bromance with Omar Shariff, form the beating heart of the book and are very satisfying indeed.

Even better—and equal to any salacious details that the authors have given us in any of their other, more outrageous, biographies—is any section of the book in which the Burtons appear. Tales of drunken binges, threesomes, banquets with food flown in from around the world, and battles, bruises, and screeched oaths bring the book to vibrant life and raise the question as to why the authors have not until now turned their attention to the most famous, oversized couple in world history: Liz and Dick?

If ever there were to be a perfect blending of authors and subjects, it would be Richard Burton and Elizabeth Taylor and Darwin Porter and Danforth Prince.

That would surely be the stuff of which bestsellers and Lifetime mini-series are made.

Here's **Peter O'Toole**, in bed with **Elizabeth Taylor** in a money-losing production of Dylan Thomas' *Under Milkwood* (1972). They're each portraying a resident of the fictional Welsh village of Llareggub.

Did they do it alone, or was Richard Burton also involved in the scene?.

*Vinton McCabe is a critic-at-large, whose running commentary of pop culture began more than 20 years ago in the pages of the Advocate Newspapers of CT and MA, continued on the pages of New England Monthly, and blared out of radios tuned to WGCH in Greenwich, and other Connecticut stations. He is the author of the novel* **Death in Venice, California.**

No one could portray an eccentric, arrogant, outraged, and aristocratic Brit like **Peter O'Toole.** *On the left*, he's shooting up an oasis in *Lawrence of Arabia* (1962).

*On the right*, he's satirizing the "mad as a hatter" British aristocracy in *The Ruling Class* (1972). A commercial failure at the time, it was described by O'Toole as "a comedy with tragic relief." It's now a cult classic.

Darwin Porter's biography reveals the drama-within-the-dramas associated with the celebrated Anglo-French genius **Jeanne Moreau. O'Toole** is pictured in the *left photo* as a hapless (and English) foreign diplomat trying to avoid being enrolled as the sex slave of the sex-crazed Russian Empress in *Great Catherine* (1968)..

*The middle photo* shows the world's then-most famous transsexual, **April Ashley,** as she appeared during the peak of their affair; and

*The right-hand photo* shows **O'Toole** as Henry II, emoting with his drinking buddy and frenemy, **Richard Burton** as **Thomas Becket** during their filming of the Oscar-winning historical drama, *Becket* (1964). Becket, a principled Saxon commoner who was later designated as the **Archbishop of Canterbury**, arranges debaucheries for the king when he isn't busy running Henry's court.

# PETER O'TOOLE

## "I'VE DONE EVERYTHING POSSIBLE"
### by Darwin Porter

Insouciant, offensive, brilliant, and brash, actor Peter O'Toole once said, "God put me on this earth to raise hell—and I did just that."

His week-long drug and drinking binges, coupled with sex orgies, reached near Biblical proportions. It was said that he matched Don Juan's legendary total of 1,033 seductions.

Hailed by some critics as the greatest actor of the 20th century—move over Olivier and Gielgud—he was nominated for eight Oscars as Best Actor of the Year, but lost every time, although he did win an Oscar for Lifetime Achievement in 2003.

This charismatic man lives again in the pages of my latest biography, *Peter O'Toole—Hellraiser, Sexual Outlaw, & Irish Rebel,* written with co-author Danforth Prince.

Growing up in industrial Leeds in England, the son of a crooked Irish bookmaker, O'Toole claimed, "I was part of the criminal class, not the working class." Discovering sex as a very young teenager, he later proclaimed, "There is nothing on earth as good as a man and a woman."

He mesmerized the world by appearing in white flowing robes in *Lawrence of Arabia* (1962), hailed as one of the greatest films of all time. Marlon Brando had turned down the role of T. E. Lawrence, the Imperialistic Brit who helped to unify the Arabs of the Saudi Peninsula in a successful campaign to overthrow the Turkish Ottoman Empire.

Flirtatiously, playwright Noël Coward told O'Toole, "If you were any prettier, you'd be called "Florence of Arabia."

O'Toole went on from there to make some 90 other films—some of them memorable, others so horrible that studios didn't want to release them. As one reviewer said, "O'Toole would overact; he would be ridiculous, but he was never dull and was often riveting. He battled alcoholism and came to look and behave like his own ghost near the end of his life. We are unlikely to see the likes of him again."

In 1958, he married the brilliant Welsh actress Siân Phillips, a turbulent liaison that would last until 1979, when she divorced him to marry a younger actor. He proclaimed, "The happiest married men I know have a wife to come home to—not to come home *with.*"

His bosom buddy, a rival on the screen and in the boudoir, was Richard Burton. O'Toole had seduced Elizabeth Taylor before Burton met her. Originally, she had wanted O'Toole to co-star with her as Marc Antony in *Cleopatra* (1963).

In addition to Taylor, O'Toole's affairs included some of the world's most beautiful women, ranging from Vivien Leigh to Ava Gardner to Audrey Hepburn. He even went aristocratic at times, conquering the Duchess of Alba and Sarah Churchill (Sir Winston's daughter). But often, his conquest was some "wench" he met in a pub during one of his legendary drinking forays.

"I was a disreputable rake," he confessed. No affair was more notable than Her Royal Highness, Princess Margaret, the "Black Sheep" of the House of Windsor. He later told Burton, "I found her insatiable."

In spite of a cycle of dissipation he pursued on a virtually epic scale, he outlived most of his friends, dying in 2013 at the age of 81.

In his final years, he said, "the only exercise I get these days is walking behind the coffins of my friends, those who actually exercised."

He was a headline maker. When he starred as *Hamlet* (1963), in London, he called it "the worst play ever written." His controversial performance as *Macbeth* (1980) was hailed as the world's most atrocious. "The Bard is turning over in his tomb," wrote one reviewer, who likened his performance to that of "monstrous Bette Davis in *What Ever Happened to Baby Jane?*"

His own comment: "I was as popular as a pork sausage in a synagogue."

Reporters always found him good copy. One from London's *Daily Mail* asked him how he wanted to be remembered.

"For making the world's best French toast."

He also was asked what was his greatest thrill.

He answered, "To go out pubbing one night in London and to wake up in Mexico."

\*\*\*

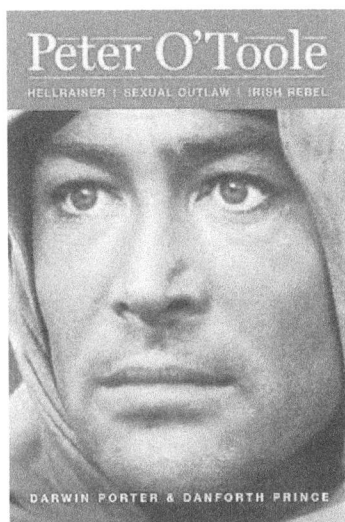

## PETER O'TOOLE—Hellraiser, Sexual Outlaw, Irish Rebel,
by Darwin Porter and Danforth Prince.
An Unprecedented New Look at the 20th Century's
Most Talented (& Most Outrageous) Actor

Trade Paperback, 6"x9", 623 pages. ISBN 978-1-936003-45-7
Available everywhere in June, 2015, in bookstores everywhere and online.
**Blood Moon: Entertainment About How America Interprets Its Celebrities.**

www.BloodMoonProductions.com

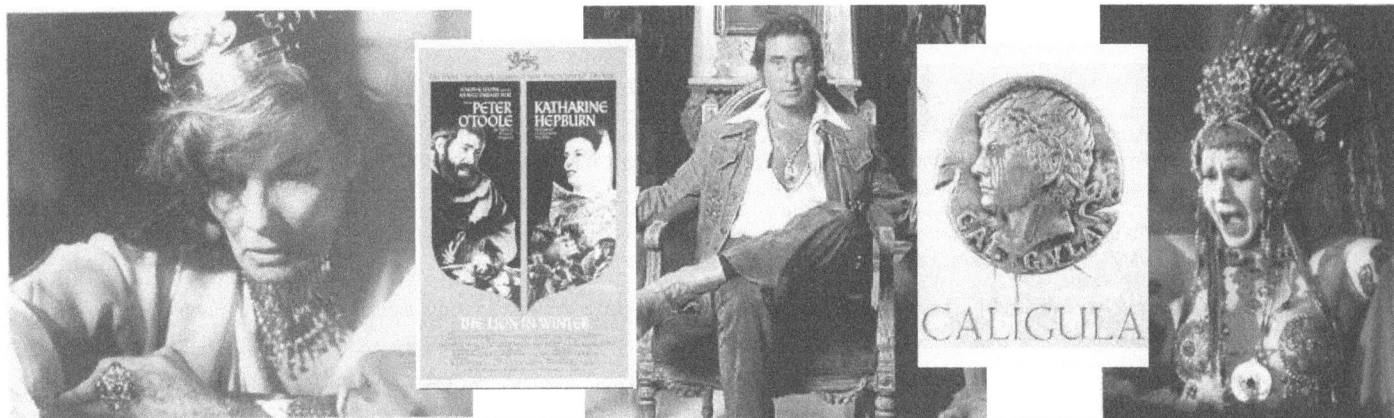

Peter O'Toole's life and times intersected, sometimes intimately, with some of the most watched celebrities of his era: *Left Photo:* His co-star, **Katharine Hepburn,** as Eleanor of Aquitaine, "the most famous woman of the Middle Ages," as she appeared in Peter O'Toole's homage to a dysfunctional Imperial family, *A Lion in Winter* (1968).

*Middle photo:* Lifestyle guru and founder/President of *Penthouse*, **Bob Guccione,** from around the time he financed a film whose costs almost instantly spun out of control, *Caligula* (1979). It showcased **O'Toole** in his portayal of Tiberius, an insane, syphilitic tyrant.

*Right photo:* The distinguished British actress, **Helen Mirren,** shown here as Caesonia, "the most promiscuous woman in Rome." Mirren, of course, went on to portray other, more restrained historic figures, including Queen Elizabeth II.

# FILMS *in Review*

**BLOOD MOON** Productions, Ltd.

**Peter O'Toole**
HELLRAISER | SEXUAL OUTLAW | IRISH REBEL

DARWIN PORTER & DANFORTH PRINCE

**PETER O'TOOLE:** Audiences loved him in *Lawrence of Arabia*. Later, he reigned as both a film star and "babe magnet" hounded, worldwide, by the tabloids, adulated in both London and Hollywood.

And now, the film historians at FILMS IN REVIEW have weighed in with their opinion of his recent biography from Blood Moon Productions. Here's the review, lifted verbatim from the much-anticipated CHRISTMAS COLUMN, 2015, as authored by film producer and cinema historian Roy Frumkes, whose biography appears below:

## *PETER O'TOOLE – HELLRAISER, SEXUAL OUTLAW, IRISH REBEL*
BloodMoonProductions.com. Writers: Darwin Porter & Danforth Prince. 620+ pages. Book Smell: subtle.

It has to be a reflection of modern technological advances, it can't be anything else: all the Blood Moon books, most of them several hundred pages in length, are written by the same two people – Porter & Prince. I mean, how is that possible? Each book should have taken two years. Well, it must be something to do with the ease of writing with WORD, combined with the extraordinarily easy access to information on the internet. I've never seen a more thorough use of these modern breakthroughs than here.

And while the book has the feeling, at times, of collage, it's never any less than fun, and it's infinitely more substantial than a mere gossip tome. I mean, I loved Kenneth Anger's Hollywood Babylon books (I had the pleasure of putting him up at my apt for a few days once, and that was fun, too), but they (and this, at first glance) are nothing more than gossip. However in their cumulative, lurid glow, like Weejee's LA photos, the O'Toole bio becomes something more than what is on the surface – much, more, certainly than what Anger gave us. O'TOOLE takes itself a level more seriously than gossip, and its text is informative, both about the British stage and the American screen.

In terms of glorious gossip, however, wait till you get (just as an example) to page 126. O'Toole is invited by Jules Buck, his friend and business partner, to join him for drinks with two other friends, who turn out to be Ava Gardner (they meet in her suite at the Savoy Hotel in London) and Burt Lancaster, neither of whom O'Toole had previously met, and both of whom had acted together in Robert Siodmak's THE KILLERS. Their unexpurgated stories that evening are absolute jaw-droppers. Lancaster's bi-sexuality and Gardner's sexual appetites are tossed away like everyday, casual knowledge. Their fast-flowing repartee and awareness of each other's sexual adventures pile on, paragraph after paragraph, story after story, and it's heady stuff. Add in some bizarre here-say out of nowhere about Evita Peron, and it's a kinetic, wonderfully written chapter. And there are plenty more to follow.

I mentioned this book to FIR's quirky film critic, Victoria Alexander, and after reading it she ordered the one on Elizabeth Taylor and said it was just as good. Blood Moon has found a winning formula.

*For access to the orginal text of this review, click on:   http://69.195.124.61/~filmsinr/2015/12/20/christmas-column-2015/*

**Roy Frumkes**, *the author of this review, followed his childhood dreams of filmmaking, and has been producing, writing and/or directing motion pictures for thirty years. Roy was a member until 2013 of the National Board of Review of Motion Pictures since he got out of college in 1966. He wrote for FIR for thirty years before purchasing the magazine from the NBR in '96 with co-owner Joe Anderson. Prior to that Roy was Managing Editor of the home theater magazine The Perfect Vision. From 1985 to 1994 Roy co-produced and co-directed the annual D.W.Griffith Awards Ceremony, working with the likes of Paul Newman, Bette Davis, William Hurt, Steven Spielberg, Kirk And Michael Douglas, Sidney Poitier, Jodie Foster and Sean Connery.*

*Currently, Roy teaches film history and screenwriting at The School of Visual Arts, which he considers the finest film school on the East Coast*

**For More about this book, click on KNEWS, Southern California's News and Talk Radio**, which discusses the role of Peter O'Toole as the stage and screen's most enigmatic Hellraiser. Bill Feingold interviews Danforth Prince about an actor whose first and last names EACH had phallic implications https://youtu.be/t3oU356dhPI

**DAILY NEWS**

MEDIA GROUP

**Food Trade News** | **Food World** | **FINANCIAL EXPRESS** Read to Lead | **DAILY NEWS**

# Peter O'Toole Affair: Did 'Lawrence Of Arabia' Get It On With Queen Elizabeth's Sister Princess Margaret?

By Victoria Guerra in *FOOD WORLD* Magazine
May 26, 2015 11:13 AM EDT

Known as one of the best film actors of all time after breathtaking performances like the title role in "Lawrence of Arabia" and even voicing critic Ego in the Pixar favorite "Ratatouille," the famous "bad boy" genius actor has a new biography under way - and it talks about a supposed Peter O'Toole affair with **Princess Margaret.**

Classic Hollywood glamour won't ever die even if most of its biggest stars have already passed away, and rumors about some of the time's biggest performers still continue well into the 21st century, decades after their prime - including Peter O'Toole's affair with a royal.

Besides the new revelation of Peter O'Toole's affair, other "gossip" that has continued to live long after stars' primes include new information about the death of "West Side Story" legendary actress **Natalie Wood** in the 80s, **Sophia Loren** discussing her infamous picture with J**ayne Mansfield, Rock Hudson**'s ex boyfriend speaking out publicly for the first time after and even the recent discovery that there was a tunnel connecting **Kirk Douglas'** home to **the Playboy Mansion.**

According to *Financial Express*, a new biography about the "*Becket*" actor has revealed Peter O'-Toole's affair with **Princess Margaret**, the younger sister of **Queen Elizabeth of England** - when he was married to Welsh actress **Siân Phillips** and the royal was ending her marriage to **Lord Snowdon**.

The *New York Daily News* reports that the Peter O'Toole affair claims first came out in a new biography of the actor called "*Peter O'Toole: Hellraiser, Sexual Outlaw, Irish Rebel*," written by authors **Darwin Porter** and **Danforth Prince.**

*The Mirror* reports that the book claims that the iconic actor and the royal allegedly enjoyed a secret holiday in the Caribbean and a similar one in a private villa in Morocco in the 1970s after having met years previously at a screening of O'Toole's film "*Lord Jim*."

The biography claiming Peter O'Toole affair with the princess will come out next month.

**—FOOD WORLD NEWS**

# Daily Mail

IN REFERENCE TO BLOOD MOON'S BIOGRAPHY OF PETER O'TOOLE, THE LARGEST-CIRCULATION BROADSHEET IN THE WORLD, THE DAILY MAIL, PUBLISHED THIS (THE TEXT ON THE PAGES THAT FOLLOW) IN THEIR EDITION OF MAY 22, 2015

***

### Peter O'Toole was the Hellraiser who told Burton: 'I've slept with Liz and she says I'm better in bed than you."

**Peter O'Toole was famed for wild boozing.
But a new book claims his biggest thirst was for women
Biography reveals infamous womanizing of Peter O'Toole,**

## ONE OF LAST GREAT HELLRAISERS OF THE BRITISH STAGE

**Book claims he had affairs with Elizabeth Taylor, Audrey Hepburn, Vivien Leigh, Diana Dors - even Princess Margaret. One night he tested his friendship with Richard Burton by claiming Taylor - his wife - thought he was better in bed**

By Tom Leonard in New York for the DAILY MAIL
PUBLISHED: 19:32 EDT, 22 May 2015 | UPDATED: 00:44 EDT, 23 May 2015

A frail, sad, and in-decline **Pete O'Toole** in one of his last movies,, *The Decline of an Empire*. He died before its release in 2014

**April Ashley** was one of the world's most beautiful models and had already had **Elvis Presley** propose marriage to her when she met the actor Peter O' Toole.

He and **Omar Sharif** were filming the 1962 epic *Lawrence Of Arabia* and the young O'Toole swept Ashley away when they met at a party thrown by Spanish leader General Franco's daughter near Seville in southern Spain.

As she later lay in bed with O'Toole, she whispered in his ear: 'I was born a boy.' As Miss Ashley, a former merchant seaman and the first British person to undergo sex-change surgery, later recalled: "Peter was too far gone at that point to worry about what sex I had been born."

According to a new book, legendary actor Peter O'Toole had affairs with numerous stars including **Elizabeth Taylor**, pictured with O'Toole and her husband **Richard Burton**

It's an astonishing tale but, as the last of the great hellraisers of British stage and screen, it's easy to accept such outrageous stories about Peter O'Toole. He was a star who revelled in his notoriety and debauched reputation.

The white-suited dandy with the cigarette holder and the piercing blue eyes once threw a New Year's Eve party at his Hampstead home, saying the house rule was: "Fornication, madness, murder, drunkenness, shouting, shrieking, leaping, polite conversation and the breaking of bones; such jollities constitute acceptable behaviour."

A more complicated personality than his fellow thespian dissolutes, **Richard Burton, Richard Harris and Oliver Reed,** the unrepentant, hard-drinking troublemaker was also a self-described romantic who claimed to know all 154 of Shakespeare's sonnets.

"All the larks I got up to as a young actor were never reported, thank God," he said a few years before his death aged 81 in 2013. 'If anyone had dared to talk about my sex life in my prime, I'd have said very simply: "Remove your eye from the keyhole."

**The last of the great hellraisers of British stage and screen, Peter O'Toole** was a star who revelled in his notoriety and debauched reputation

Now a rip-roaring new biography has put its eye to that keyhole and spied a star whose sexual high-jinks were almost as dissipated as his alcoholic ones.

According to **Peter O'Toole: Hellraiser, Sexual Outlaw, Irish Rebel**, outside his stormy 20-year marriage to Welsh actress **Sian Phillips,** he had affairs with **Elizabeth Taylor, Audrey Hepburn, Vivien Leigh, Diana Dors** — even **Princess Margaret.** The book's American authors, **Darwin Porter** and **Danforth Prince,** have a track record of dredging up old stories and gossip about stars who were spared such public scrutiny when they were alive.

Born and raised in poverty in rural Ireland and later in a rough suburb of Leeds, O'Toole was obsessed with his own sexual gratification and lost his virginity to a prostitute when he was 13. He always liked to insist he was not working class but 'criminal class'.

His drinking was legendary. Once, playing Shylock in his mid-20s in an early RSC production of *The Merchant of Venice*, O'Toole came on stage to deliver a crucial speech and was so intoxicated he started spouting lines from *King Lear.*

Fellow RSC members at Stratford-on-Avon once watched him down a bottle of whisky in one go and at an aftershow party he sat on stage with a pedal bin on either side — one filled with beer and the other with brandy, alternately scooping a two-pint mug into each.

Even if his drunken rowdiness frequently landed him in a police cell, his fine looks and tall, lean frame meant he was always a hit with the ladies. They also gave him a good start in acting.

As a student at RADA, he said he was so outnumbered by women that he didn't do any work the first year and "just fucked myself stupid."

He could be charming when he wanted but in private it was often a different story. He married the elegant **Sian Phillips** in 1959 after they fell in love while playing a brother and sister in an RSC play.

Life with him could be exhilarating — he once came to pick her up in a yellow sports car, told her to get her passport and headed off for Rome. O'Toole, the world's most terrifying driver, then took a wrong turn and they ended up in Yugoslavia.

"After one year of marriage," he said, "For me life is either a wedding or a wake."

Disapproving of his wife's clothes one day, O'Toole hurled her entire wardrobe out of a window, and she spent the next few days having to wear his clothes

His impulsiveness could also be maddening. Disapproving of his wife's clothes one day, O'Toole hurled her entire wardrobe out of a window and she spent the next few days having to wear his clothes.

On another occasion, he bought her a Morris Minor but borrowed it for a trip to Bristol. That night, police rang her to say a sozzled O'Toole was in the cells after wrecking her vehicle by driving it into a squad car.

Phillips managed to stick out the marriage for two tempestuous decades, giving him two daughters before having an affair. O'Toole, discovering she had finally rebelled from her life of drudgery, kicked her out of their Hampstead house.

In her biography, she described how, when she wasn't raising her family on her own while her husband was filming, she had to endure this "abominable' binge-drinking, crockery-hurling tyrant" whom she never dared challenge.

According to the new book, O'Toole had quite a nerve in throwing her out for having an affair because he had enjoyed a string of them. Predictably, they were invariably with women who shared his penchant for hard living and drinking. "I'm good at picking fast women and slow horses," he once said.

When O'Toole co-starred with **Ursula Andress** in *What's New, Pussycat* in 1965, news of a rumored affair made the tabloids.

**April Ashley** was one of the world's most beautiful models and had already had **Elvis Presley** propose marriage to her when she met the actor **Peter O' Toole**. As she later lay in bed with O'Toole, she whispered in his ear: "I was born a boy."

**Richard Burton** was for many years O'Toole's favourite drinking buddy until, said O'Toole, their carousing came to an abrupt end when his friend married Elizabeth Taylor. The book claims that O'Toole and Taylor *(pictured in bed on set of the film Under Milk Wood)* started an affair when she was married to the American singer **Eddie Fisher**

Could there have been another reason? The book's authors think so, claiming O'Toole and Taylor started an affair when she was married to the American singer Eddie Fisher and staying in a suite at the Dorchester in London.

The actress, it is claimed, had been impressed with O'Toole's Shakespeare stage performances and wanted him to play Mark Antony alongside her *Cleopatra* in the 1963 epic of the same name. Of course, the part eventually went to Richard Burton and his affair with Taylor started there on the set.

It is alleged that O'Toole continued to see Taylor romantically for years. Then, he "severely tested" the friendship with Burton one night when both were very drunk and O'Toole reportedly confided to Burton: "She tells me I'm much better in the sack, at least more reliable, than you are." **Vivien Leigh** and **Laurence Olivier,** another famous acting couple, were also friends of O'Toole. It's claimed O'Toole long envied actor **Peter Finch**'s affair with the beautiful Leigh after she split up from Olivier.

He got his own chance near the end of her short life when he watched her perform in a Noël Coward play and took her to dinner. After agreeing that actors should never marry, Leigh invited him back to share her "lonely bed."

O'Toole later confided to a friend he had to make love in a room festooned with nine photographs of Olivier, but "still managed to rise to the occasion."

The list of sexual conquests didn't stop there. As well as his liaison with transsexual **April Ashley**, it is claimed that O'Toole ended up, after another Andalusian society party, naked in bed with **Sarah Churchill,** the hard-drinking actress daughter of **Sir Winston Churchill**. The actor reportedly told friends he couldn't remember if anything had happened between them.

O'Toole and **Princess Margaret** were good friends, the Princess once surprising his colleagues when she dropped in on a rehearsal of O'Toole's notoriously awful 1980 production of *Macbeth.*

O'Toole spent more than two years making *Lawrence Of Arabia*, the film that turned him into an international star. As his wife stayed at home bringing up their first child on her own, he recalled carousing in the "fleshpots" of Beirut during filming, enjoying bathtubs filled with champagne, and once gambling away nine months' wages in one night. Again, his drinking was out of control.

According to **Alec Guinness,** a local dignitary invited the film's stars to a party only for O'Toole to get in a row with their host and hurl a glass of champagne in his face. "O'Toole could have been killed — shot or strangled," Guinness told a friend. "And I'm beginning to think it's a pity he wasn't."

On another occasion, O'Toole was out boozing with his friend **Peter Finch** one night when a pub refused to serve them as it was after closing time. O'Toole's solution was to buy the pub, writing out a cheque on the spot.

Next morning, having sobered up, he rushed back to the pub. Fortunately, the landlord hadn't yet cashed it. The actors became friends with the landlord and even went to his funeral. But they got drunk first and, having become noisily emotional at the graveside, realised to their horror they were attending the wrong service. Alcohol permeates nearly every story of O'Toole's exploits. He was sipping champagne when, in 1964, **Diana Dors**, Britain's answer to Marilyn Monroe, allegedly seduced him as she sat wearing a diaphanous black *négligée* in the sitting room of her London flat.

Two weeks later, she invited him to one of her infamous orgies and he apparently went, though primarily to speak to her guest of honour, an American movie star named **Bruce Cabot**, about Hollywood.

**Jayne Mansfield,** equally blonde and busty but American, was also in O'Toole's sights in his glory years of the Sixties, it is claimed. Their night of passion came after three bottles of pink champagne in her suite at The Dorchester. He is said to have visited her home in Los Angeles where they swam in her heart-shaped pool.

The new book claims he had a fling with **Audrey Hepburn** before they started filming in Paris, with O'-Toole visiting her suite at the Ritz three nights in a row and telling a friend: "She seems too good to be true." Drama ensued when, during filming, she confided she was pregnant. Either he or her husband, actor **Mel Ferrer**, could be the father. She subsequently miscarried, it is claimed. Whether the affair ever happened, O'Toole later described Hepburn publicly as "delightful but troubled."

And what of **Princess Margaret**?

A tryst with O'Toole sounds far-fetched but the actor **David Niven** is widely believed to have had an affair with her and perhaps also **Peter Sellers**, so it is not impossible.

Certainly they were good friends. The Princess once surprised his colleagues when she dropped in on a rehearsal of O'Toole's notoriously awful 1980 production of *Macbeth*. (O'Toole was at the time in a relationship with the play's First Witch, alias **Trudie Styler**, the future wife of rock star **Sting**.) It is claimed the actor's friendship with Margaret started after they met at the 1965 Royal Command performance of the film *Lord Jim*.

O'Toole was invited to a string of parties at Kensington Palace where she would reportedly complain to him about her worsening relationship with husband **Lord Snowdon**. On one occasion, in the Seventies, O'Toole flew to Morocco to join her at the famous **Villa Taylor in Marrakesh,** where **Churchill** and **Roosevelt** had stayed during the 1943 Casablanca Conference.

The villa's owner said she gave **Princess Margaret** Churchill's old suite complete with a vast bath. O'Toole occupied an adjoining suite with connecting doors. The new book also claims O'Toole later joined Princess Margaret on her Caribbean island getaway, Mustique, but their relationship petered out in 1975.

Did any woman ever turn him down? **Katharine Hepburn,** who is widely believed to have been a lesbian, proved impervious, but that's not to say he didn't try to get close to her.

He starred with her in *The Lion In Winter*. Shooting a scene on a lake, Hepburn was out in a boat so O'-Toole paddled out to talk to her, only to trap his finger between their vessels.

The tip of his finger was severed and with no doctors around, O'Toole carried it back to shore, dipped it into a glass of brandy to preserve it and later put it back on, wrapped in a poultice. Only when he took the bandages off did he discover he'd drunkenly put it back the wrong way round.

O'Toole said he was often asked if Lawrence of Arabia was homosexual. Indeed, the same question was frequently asked about him. His response? "I think I've established my straight certificate by seducing a scad of *(female)* movie stars and a bevy of barmaids."

O'Toole claims he never indulged in homosexuality but had plenty of offers. One such, says the book, came early in his acting career from **Cary Grant**. Visiting his hometown of Bristol while O'Toole was working there, the Hollywood star reportedly made a "subtle" pass after inviting O'Toole for dinner at his hotel.

Perhaps O'Toole never became notorious for his womanizing because the world was so distracted by his Olympian drinking, which he largely gave up in 1975 after stomach cancer almost killed him. Some insist he was always simply too inebriated to be much success as a Don Juan, but that may be a little naïve.

As a teenager, O'Toole scribbled in his notebook: "I will not be a common man. I will stir the smooth sands of monotony." Even if we may never know the full sordid details, nobody can deny he didn't succeed.

*Peter O'Toole: Hellraiser, Sexual Outlaw, Irish Rebel* by **Darwin Porter** and **Danforth Prince** is published by **Blood Moon** in June.

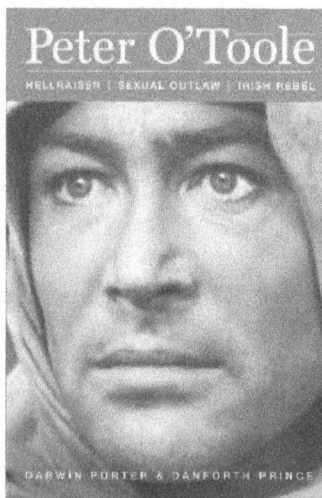

**BOOK REVIEW NEWS**

# Peter O'Toole:

**They loved him in London,
They adored him in Hollywood,**

**and now, they've reviewed him critically in
THE MIDWEST BOOK REVIEW:**

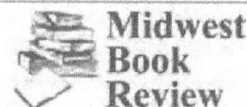

Midwest
Book
Review

BLOOD MOON Productions, Ltd.

**FOR IMMEDIATE RELEASE:** Blood Moon's seminal biography of Peter O'Toole, the Anglo-Irish superstar described by some critics as the best actor of the 20th Century, has been critically reviewed by Diane Donovan, Senior Reviewer at the highly prestigious *Midwest Book Review*. Her text is replicated below:

*Peter O'Toole: Hellraiser, Sexual Outlaw, Irish Rebel*
*Darwin Porter & Danforth Prince*
*Blood Moon Productions*
*ISBN 9781936003457  Softcover, 6"x9", 632 pps with photos  $26.95    www.bloodmoonproductions.com*

"One might expect that *Peter O'Toole: Hellraiser, Sexual Outlaw, Irish Rebel* would hold the usual biographical survey of the actor's life and times; but in fact it's a story that offers something far greater: an analysis of O'Toole's life and career that features a new look at the actor's passion, controversies, and determination to 'raise hell'.

"Lest readers think this will be a rehash of prior biographies, it should be mentioned that *Peter O'Toole: Hellraiser, Sexual Outlaw, Irish Rebel* represents decades of research by writers who define their efforts as being steeped in media and celebrity stories - and therefore replete with the high tension, drama, and eye-popping gossip and grit of Hollywood's most outrageous moments and characters.

"So don't anticipate a casual coverage: it's an account of a hellraising, outrageous personality and is itself steeped in the culture it investigates, cultivating lively language, newly-revealed shocking truths, and passionate descriptions to capture the life and times of a film star who, according to Peter O'Toole, "...became the toast of international society. The decadent part, those who live just to fornicate on the Costa del Sol.  It's the new gathering place for panty sniffers, child molesters, drunkards, prostitutes, pimps, gigolos, pillheads, and poon stalkers. I adore it. It seems that all the big names want to go to bed with me. A lucky few actually manage to accomplish that splendid feat."

"Outrageous? You bet. It's not for the morally faint - and that promises that *Peter O'Toole: Hellraiser, Sexual Outlaw, Irish Rebel* will be a frequent flyer out of library collections and film reference holdings alike."

MORE ABOUT THIS BOOK, AS FORMATTED ON YOUTUBE:
**KNEWS, Southern California's News and Talk Radio**, discusses the role of Peter O'Toole as the stage and screen's most enigmatic Hellraiser. Bill Feingold interviews Danforth Prince about an actor whose first and last names EACH had phallic implications https://youtu.be/t3oU356dhPI

*Peter O'Toole, Hellraiser, Sexual Outlaw, Irish Rebel,* a **Videotaped Description:** https://www.youtube.com/watch?v=k5f4dIbXTLk

In June of 2015, Blood Moon's biography of *Peter O'Toole* was designated by **The New York Book Festival** as Runner Up to Best Biography of The Year.

Depicted above is Blood Moon's President, **Danforth Prince**, with **Rebecca Li-Huang**, whose poignant memoir of her emigration to the U.S. from China (*Green Apple, Red Book*) was also designated as winner of a prestigious literary award.

124

# REVEALED! BOOZER O'TOOLE'S HOLLYWOOD HAREM

MOVIE icon Peter O'Toole flew under the radar as a ladies man, but the Lawrence of Arabia hunk bedded a slew of screen beauties including Audrey Hepburn and Elizabeth Taylor.

His steamy romp with Liz got him in trouble with his longtime drinking buddy, Richard Burton, his co-star in 1964's Becket.

During a night of guzzling, O'Toole told Burton he'd also been with Liz, adding, "She tells me I'm much better in the sack, at least more reliable than you are."

His boast "shattered" the friendship of the two stars, according to a new tell-all due out June 15, Peter O'Toole: Hellraiser, Sexual Outlaw, Irish Rebel.

Authors Darwin Porter and Danforth Prince write that Liz met and had a fling with O'Toole after

**PETER LOST PAL BURTON AFTER BEDDING LIZ**

New book dishes on O'Toole

Peter bedded Burton's babe Liz. Below, he also romped with Audrey Hepburn

seeing him on stage. She wanted him to play Mark Anthony in her 1963 Cleopatra flick.

The part eventually went to Richard Burton and his affair with Taylor started there on the set.

But the authors reveal that "O'Toole continued to see Taylor romantically for years." The hell-raiser's conquests also included Britain's Princess Margaret, Vivien Leigh, actress Diana Dors and Jayne Mansfield.

But the notorious boozer kept a special place in his heart for Audrey Hepburn, his leading lady in the 1966 flick How to Steal a Million.

They had a fling before filming started in Paris. Weeks later, Hepburn told him she was pregnant and didn't know if he or her hubby, Mel Ferrer, was the father, say the authors, adding she later miscarried the baby.

The book says O'Toole described the beauty as "delightful, but troubled" and "too good to be true."

# OMAR SHARIF RAVAGED BY DEMENTIA

SCREEN hunk Omar Sharif starred in some of Hollywood's biggest flicks, but now the Alzheimer's-stricken actor can't remember them – or what happened yesterday!

The Egyptian-born star of Funny Girl, Doctor Zhivago and Lawrence of Arabia still knows he's a famous actor, but he recently stared at a photo of him with then-wife Hamama and infant son

Omar (left) and Peter O'Toole in Lawrence of Arabia

Tarek and asked: "Who's this?"

Sharif, 83, also confuses fans with people he once knew. "Often,

he thinks it's someone he knew from before and whose name he has forgotten," says Tarek, 58. "Most of the time it's a fan."

Tarek says the illness makes Sharif, who mainly lives in hotels, "insecure." Because of his poor memory, he often refuses to leave his room. Ironically, he was once one of the Top 10 bridge players in the world, relying on his memory to win tournaments.

BLOOD MOON

125

**Diana Dors**

**Elizabeth Taylor**

**Jayne Mansfield**

**Ursula Andress**

**Princess Margaret**

**Sarah Churchill(**
(daughter of Sir Winston)

**April Ashley**

**Vivien Leigh**

**Audrey Hepburn**

# HOW KIRK DOUGLAS
## Navigated Hollywood's Suicide-Soaked Boulevards of Broken Dreams

*EDITOR'S NOTE: On February 5, 2020, at the age of 103, Kirk Douglas died at his home in Beverly Hills. He was buried in the same plot as his son, Eric. On April 29, 2021, his wife, Anne, died at the age of 102 and was buried next to him and their son.*

\*\*\*

For the first time, I found inspiration in researching the life of a movie star. Kirk Douglas's amazing story is one of struggles, tragedy, and triumph. He has regained his youth, vitality, and ability to teach some primal lessons in my latest Hollywood biography, *More is Never Enough*. At the age of 102, he is the last surviving male star of Golden Age Hollywood. And unlike celebrities who died at the peak of their strength and beauty, his personal growth during his physically diminished final decades is unique in the history of show-biz.

A stroke in 1996 caused him to lose his speech, and very briefly, he contemplated shooting himself, but instead, learned to speak again with the daily help of a speech therapist.

And despite his impairments, he continued to make films, sometimes cast as a stroke victim, throughout the early years of the 21st Century. His career lasted longer than anyone else's in Hollywood. As a leading film actor, it began in 1946 opposite Barbara Stanwyck. His last screen appearance was in the poignantly titled 2009 film, *Kirk Douglas: Before I Forget*.

Around 1910, his Yiddish-speaking parents had fled from Russia, where Jews were being killed by the Czars only to encounter anti-Semitism in the New World. But Kirk overcame it, changing his name from Issur Danielovitch to Kirk Douglas. "People thought I was Scottish."

As a star in Hollywood, he was known as a "horndog," romancing love goddesses who included Ava Gardner and Lana Turner. His second marriage to Anne Buydens clicked, and, although they were confined to wheelchairs during the later years of their lives, they remained married until the end.

As a star, and in a strange coincidence that happened again and again, he worked with numerous directors and actors, who committed suicide when their dreams of fame and wealth and glory did not come true. Instead of reinventing themselves, they chose death instead.

As a tragic example, Kirk had a two-year affair with Irene Wrightsman, the Palm Beach socialite and daughter of Charles B. Wrightsman, the famous benefactor of New York City's Metropolitan Museum. She committed suicide. So did her younger sister, Charlene. So did their mother.

As the decades rolled on, Kirk attended endless funerals for the children of his famous colleagues. Many had killed themselves before they were 30 as part of what some insiders interpreted almost as an epidemic of Hollywood suicides.

Kirk himself had four sons, two from each of his marriages. Based on the many self-inflicted deaths he became aware of, it was painfully clear to him that being the offspring of rich and fabled stars had many pitfalls.

Kirk asked himself in some of the books he wrote, "Could the pain of all those doomed kids have been alleviated if they'd had some spiritual guidance—not just material things? Could that have enabled them to endure and conquer their suffering instead of choosing death? I could have done a lot more to help my own sons. Believe me, the list is long."

Golden Age Movie Star **Kirk Douglas** led a life that was absolutely fascinating.

Here, he appears cheerful and victorious, moments before being beaten to a pulp, in *The Champion* (1949), a gritty *film noir* about tough guys, tenacity, and corruption.

Marked by relentless ambition and staggering talent, **Kirk Douglas** was one of the 20th Century's best examples of **MORE IS NEVER ENOUGH.**

Here, he appears during the peak of his romance with **Irene Wrightsman**, daughter of Charles Wrightsman, the owner of Standard Oil of Kansas and donor of the Wrightsman Collection to NYC's Metropolitan Museum. She later committed suicide.

Read all about it and others of Kirk Douglas's romancees in Blood Moon's overview of the Hollywood star who defined himself, with irony, as "The Rag-Pickers Son."

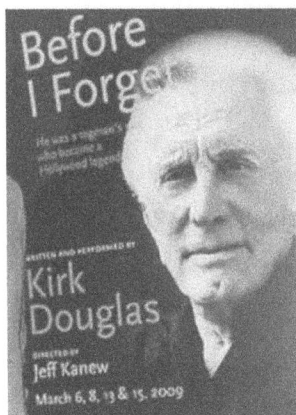

Here's the cover of Kirk Douglas' timely autobiography.

Its title, *Before I Forget*, is aimed at Boomers who remember, but are afraid that they (or their descendants) might soon forget both them and their staggering accomplishments

In the writings he completed during the final years of his life, Kirk Douglas raised horrifying questions about the high incidence of suicide among the children of major-league movie stars, and noted the comforts he tried to offer to their (famous and) deeply grieving parents.

*Left to right*, above, are celebrities who suffered through the suicides of one or more of their children: **Louis Jourdan, Marlon Brando, Carol Burnett, Charles Boyer, Carroll O'Connor, Bing Crosby,** and **Paul Newman.**

Perhaps with a sense of horror, he even compiled a list of the funerals he'd attended, with notes about the comfort he'd tried to offer to stars mourning their lost sons and daughters.

Here are some examples of suicides that influenced Kirk and for whom he grieved:

Drug overdoses killed the offspring of Mary Tyler Moore, Louis Jourdan, Carol Burnett, Ray Milland, and Paul Newman.

Kirk's friend and co-star, Carroll O'Connor (*aka* Archie Bunker), lost his son Hugh to a self-inflicted gunshot wound.

In a triple, interconnected tragedy, Charles Boyer's 21-year-old son, Michael, killed himself. Then, Boyer's wife, Pat, died shortly after that from cancer. A few days after burying them, Boyer himself committed suicide two days before his 79th birthday.

Jonathan Peck, son of Gregory Peck, shot himself, leaving no note. Bryan Englund, son of actress Cloris Leachman and producer George Englund, was found dead of an overdose in a Manhattan YMCA.

Peter, the son of Kirk's close friend and producer, Ray Stark, jumped to his death from a 14th-floor apartment in Manhattan. Jennifer Jones' daughter chose the same method, plunging from the roof of a 20th-floor hotel in Los Angeles.

Bing Crosby lost two of his seven children to suicide. His youngest son, Lindsay, shot himself when his lawyer told him that his inheritance had "evaporated." Then, his brother Dennis, deeply distraught by his own recent divorce and his alcoholism, also committed suicide.

Marlon Brando's daughter, Cheyenne, hung herself in Tahiti. Her death came four years after her half-brother, Christian, murdered her Tahitian lover, Dag Drollet.

"After all those funerals, it became my turn at bat," Kirk said. "A phone call came in from New York. A maid found my son Eric dead from an overdose. I'd sent him to 21 rehabs, but nothing worked for my boy. The world we live in makes it difficult for all children, not just the kids of stars."

"I turned to the Torah to learn how the great patriarchs raised their kids. It seems they had their problems, too. Take King David—great monarch, lousy father. Solomon was the greatest king of the Jewish people. But his son, Rehoboam, was a fool, arrogant and greedy. He told his people, 'I will flog you with scorpions.'"

**Kirk Douglas** seemed naturally gifted at playing what he liked to call "tough sons of bitches," and flawed men who were, one way or another, gaming the system.

Here he appears as Colonel Dax, in Stanley Kubrick's ***Paths of Glory*** (1957), a bloody epic set in the trenches of World War I. His cynicism about military commanders and their egos eventually blots out whatever pride he took in his heroic conduct.

**Kirk Douglas** appears above in 1959 as the centerpiece of four sons, all of them males blessed (or burdened) with his legacy.

Clockwise from upper left, **Michael** (later an Oscar-winning actor); **Joel** (later a film producer); **Peter**, and (*lower left*) **Eric.**

**REST IN PEACE**

Depicted on the left is **Eric Douglas**, adult son of Kirk Douglas and his second wife, Anne Buydens,

Eric was found dead of a drug overdose in his Manhattan apartment at age 46 in July of 2004. Friends and allies suggested that in later life, he physically resembled his father more closely than any of his siblings.

His father, Kirk, grieved openly, citing his son's death as the (horrible) catalyst for his later authorship of books, aimed at young adults, citing heroes of the Old Testament as a source of inspiration and strength.

# KIRK DOUGLAS
## A CENTURY OF CONQUESTS

**Happy Birthday, Kirk!** Here he appears—in marked contrast to a publicity photo that illustrates his youthful glory— in a photo-op celebrating his status as a centenarian.

At last, a decades-long question can be answered. Which big movie star from Hollywood's Golden Age would (physically) survive all others? Certainly not Clark Gable, Gary Cooper, Tyrone Power, Errol Flynn, or Robert Taylor. These matinee idols died relatively young.

**The answer is Kirk Douglas,** the first anti-hero superstar of the postwar era. The owner of the screen's most celebrated cleft chin was born Issue Danielovitch on December 6, 1918, in Amsterdam, New York. Survivor of a serious stroke, he lived to celebrate his 100th birthday in December of 2016, and was met with such headlines as "LEGENDARY HOLLYWOOD HORNDOG TURNS 100."

*[The longest-lived Golden Age female star was Luise Rainer, who died in London at the age of 104. She was the first actress to win two consecutive Oscars, each of them back to back—The Great Ziegfeld (1936) and The Good Earth ('37).]*

Douglas immortalized himself in film after film, but had a rough go of it: He was beaten up in *The Champion* ('49); stabbed in the stomach in *Ace in the Hole* ('51); lost a finger in *The Big Sky* ('52); rolled in barbed wire in *Man Without a Star* ('55); cut off his ear as Vincent van Gogh in *Lust for Life* ('56), had his eye put out in *The Vikings* ('58), was crucified in *Spartacus* ('60), and was whipped by his servant in *The Way West* ('67).

Throughout his career, when he was on talk shows hawking his latest film, interviewers wanted him to reveal the secrets of his love life. Talk show host Dick Cavett didn't want to talk about *A Gunfight* ('71). Instead, he wanted the dish on his leading ladies. "What about Faye Dunaway in *The Arrangement* ('69), or Kim Novak in *Strangers When We Meet* ('60)?" he asked.

Douglas was furious.

But by the time he turned 71, his tongue had loosened during the composition of his autobiography, *The Ragman's Son.* He had been married twice, once to actress Diana Dill, with whom he became the father of the future mega-star, Michael Douglas. After their divorce, he married Anne Buydens, a film publicist.

At fourteen, he lost his virginity to his English teacher. His first movie star seduction was on a rooftop in Greenwich Village with a sultry teenage blonde model, Betty Bacall. Later, she went to Hollywood, changed her name to Lauren, and married Bogie. Although for years, each of them denied her "deflowering," near the end of her life, she said, "Of course he did. Don't be a fool!"

The other Hollywood candidate for the "they'll live forever" award is **Luise Rainer.**

She is credited with what is known as the "Oscarjinx." After carrying home the gold twice, her career drifted into oblivion. She was married to the acclaimed playwright Clifford Odets from 1937-1940.

Death came to the once celebrated actress on. December 30, 2014, at the age of 104.

\*\*\*

In a nutshell, here are some tantalizing insights into how Douglas bedded the screen goddesses of yesterday:

**Joan Crawford:** "She was the aggressor, ripping off her dress in the foyer, too eager to go upstairs. I was nearly overcome with the fumes of her bad breath."

**Rita Hayworth:** "I went to bed with my fantasy of *Gilda* (her most famous film '46). I woke up to find a sweet, unsophisticated girl whose likeness had been stamped on the first atomic bomb dropped on Hiroshima."

**Evelyn Keyes:** "Scarlett O'Hara's Younger Sister wrote in a memoir that I was parlor-sized."

**Marlene Dietrich:** "She preferred fellatio and had sex without preference for gender."

**Marilyn Monroe:** "She kept me waiting for two hours. I practically had to put things on ice, I was so eager."

**Marilyn Maxwell:** "She was no lady, telling me she preferred Frank Sinatra."

**Rita Hayworth** appears above as *Gilda,* (1946). the film that immortalized her.

**Mae West** claimed, "I auditioned Kirk Douglas for my bodybuilder show, but rejected him. I wanted to see more in the bread basket."

**Ann Sothern**: "She played my wife in *A Letter to Three Wives* ('49). We rehearsed our husband-and-wife scenes in my bed."

**Ava Gardner:** "She turned to me when Sinatra kicked her out of his house."

**Patricia Neal:** "She cried during the whole thing, claiming she was cheating on the man she loved—the much-married Gary Cooper."

**Gene Tierney:** "She was a good kisser once you got beyond the overbite."

**Lana Turner:** "She was my co-star in her most memorable movie: *The Bad and the Beautiful* ('53). She told me I was twice as good as Ronnie Reagan and ten times better than Senator John F. Kennedy."

**Pier Angeli:** "She wanted to marry me when not in the beds of James Dean or the singer, Vic Damone. (He actually married her.)"

Kirk Douglas' most bizarre seduction occurred one summer when he worked as a bellboy at a resort in New York State. It was owned by a vicious anti-Semite woman who didn't know he was Jewish. "Before I left that summer, she seduced me. At the point of her glorious (sexual) climax, I screamed in her ear, 'I'm a Jew!'"

*\*\*\**

# BOOK NEWS for Immediate Release

Blood Moon Productions proudly announces the availability of history's most comprehensive biography of Kirk Douglas, as penned by one of the film industry's most respected, prolific, and controversial authors, Darwin Porter.

According to a spokesperson for Blood Moon, "Of the many male stars of Golden Age Hollywood, Kirk Douglas became the final survivor, the last icon of a fabled, optimistic era that the world will never see again. When he celebrated his birthday in 2016, headlines noted—LEGENDARY HOLLYWOOD HORNDOG TURNS 100. He was both a charismatic actor and a man of uncommon force and vigor. His volcanic energy is reflected both in his films and through his many sexual conquests. Our newest book places him squarely in the center of the seismic changes roaring through America during his reign as one of its most visible representatives at home and abroad."

Douglas was the son of Russian-Jewish immigrants, his father a collector and seller of rags. After service in the Navy during World War II, he moved to Hollywood, oozing masculinity and charm. Conquering Tinseltown and bedding its leading ladies, he became the personification of the American dream, moving from obscurity and (literally) rags to riches and major-league fame.

Critics have hailed Douglas as "the first anti-hero of the post-war era.. His film, *Spartacus* (1960) remains his most enduring film legacy." In it, as a rebellious slave, he leads a crusade against the forces of the Roman empire, for which he is later captured and put on a cross like Jesus Christ.

A restored version released in 1991 can be seen on your television set. Never before had Douglas worked with such a talented cast: Laurence Olivier, Charles Laughton, Tony Curtis, Peter Ustinov, and John Gavin.

All of this is brought out, with photos and stories you've probably never heard before, in this remarkable testimonial to the last hero of Hollywood's swashbuckling Golden Age, an inspiring testimonial to the values and core beliefs of an America that's *Gone With the Wind*, yet lovingly remembered as a time when it, in many ways, was truly great.

*KIRK DOUGLAS*
*MORE IS NEVER ENOUGH*

BY DARWIN PORTER AND DANFORTH PRINCE

BIOGRAPHY/ENTERTAINMENT & PERFORMING ARTS
AVAILABLE EVERYWHERE NOW
SOFTCOVER, 680 PAGES, WITH 200 PHOTOS. 6x9.

ISBN 978-1-936003-61-7

# MICHAEL DOUGLAS'
## (SELF-ADMITTED)
## ADDICTION TO CUNNILINGUS

## DISEASE ALERT: "SEXUAL THRILLS MADE ME ILL"

In June, Michael Douglas sent shock waves across the country by making a jaw-dropping confession that he contracted throat cancer not from smoking or drinking—but from oral sex. He admitted to an addiction to cunnilingus in an interview with the British newspaper, *The Guardian*.

Later, the Oscar-winning actor's PR people went into spin control, claiming he didn't actually say that. But the editors at *The Guardian* had taped his interview and stood by their story.

In 2012, 68-year-old Michael was informed by his doctors that he had a walnut-sized tumor at the base of his tongue. He entered into extensive treatments and claims today that he is free of the disease.

In his confession, he did not name the sexual partner who gave him the disease. Of course, the first suspect was his 43-year-old bride, Welsh actress Catherine Zeta-Jones, whom he married in 2000. There have been no reports that she has the disease, although some newspapers suggested that she might be a "Typhoid Mary."

If it isn't Zeta-Jones, then who is the culprit? If it were an unnamed sexual partner, it could be very costly for Michael. When he married, he signed a most unusual agreement, known today in Hollywood as a "love contract."

Their pre-nup stipulates that she is to receive $2.8 million per year of marriage if they divorce. In addition to that, she is to get $5 million as a bonus if he is caught cheating. In 1992, he was reportedly treated for sex addiction.

He once said, "Growing up with Dad was like growing up with the Kennedys. We were taught that women were just there to be used."

Born in 1916, screen legend Kirk Douglas, Michael's father, was one of the few remaining male stars from Hollywood's Golden Age. He led a promiscuous life, bedding such actresses as Marlene Dietrich, Linda Darnell, Rita Hayworth, Evelyn Keyes (Scarlett O'Hara's younger sister), Gene Tierney (when not occupied by JFK), Patricia Neal (when not busy with Gary Cooper), Ann Sothern, Lana Turner (when not busy with everybody), and even Safia Tarzi, the princess of Afghanistan. He dropped Joan Crawford because she had bad breath. Taryn Power, the beautiful daughter of matinee idol Tyrone Power, was also romantically linked to Michael.

Michael also admitted that he has been under undue stress since his son, Cameron, 34, was convicted in 2010 for selling methamphetamines and for heroin possession. He was sentenced to four years' imprisonment, but was given another 4½ years when it

**Michael Douglas** appears above as Gordon Gecko, the visionary and numbers-playing genius in *Wall Street* (1987), a role for which he won an Oscar.

Michael Douglas is the son of one of Classic Hollywood's hardest-driving, most relentlessly ambitious veterans of the armed services during World War II, **Kirk Douglas**

Kirk entitled his autobiography *The Rag Picker's Son*, a reference to his family;s origins in a Shtetl of Ukraine,where his father drove a junk cart.

**Michael Douglas** and **Catherine Zeta-Jones:** Lovers and spouses with a complicated pre-nup and, in his case, a complicated (but self-admitted) sexual style.

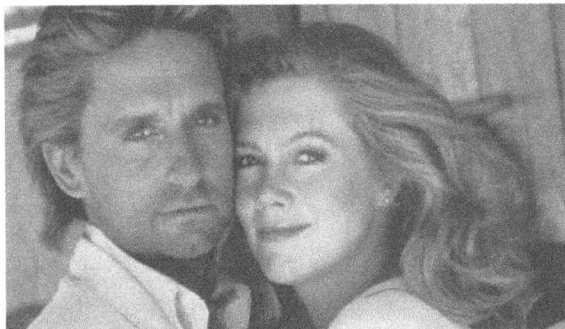

Michael got screen-teamed with beautiful **Kathleen Turner** and went on to make other romantic adventure yarns with her, including *Romancing the Stone*, a still from which appears above.

**Taryn Power**, born in 1953, is the daughter of Tyrone Power and Linda Christian.

**Michael Douglas** with **Brenda Vaccaro,** co-stars of *Summertree* (1971).

**ONLY IN HOLLYWOOD** *Cameron Douglas after a prison stint and rehab. Insets show the position of portrait tatoos of (left side) his father, Michael Douglas, and (right side) his grandfather, Kirk Douglas.*

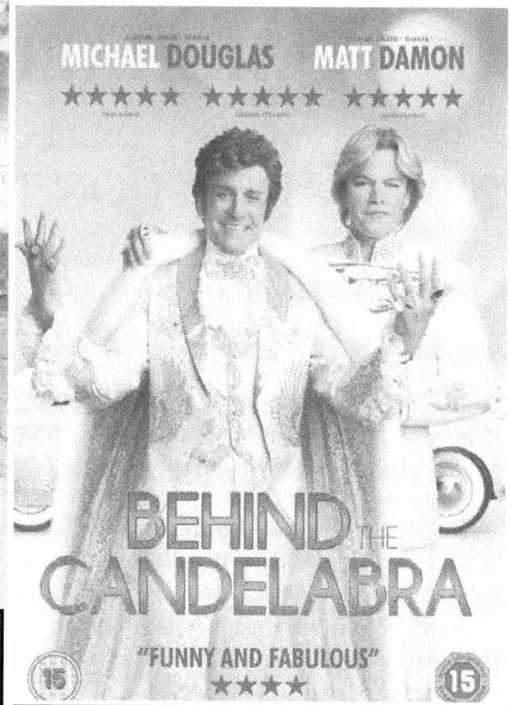

was discovered that he broke prison rules by arranging to get drugs during his confinement.

In the wake of his confession, Michael has divided the nation. Is he a hero or villain because of his revelation?

The harshest criticism came from *New York Post* columnist Andrea Peyser, who wrote: "Catherine Zeta-Jones, who bravely went public with her diagnosis of bipolar disorder, is likely humiliated, devastated, and hunting for a divorce lawyer to unbind her from this delusional crackpot."

In scientific quarters, Michael was applauded for "unzipping his lip" and bringing awareness of the growing menace of HPV (human papillomavirus). Older patients used to get this form of throat cancer from excessive drinking and smoking. Today, more than 60 percent of oral cancers are linked to sexual acts, predominantly passed from women to men during oral sex.

Officials at the Oral Cancer Foundation have endorsed Michael's comments and have used him as a spokesman and star in their public service announcements. According to the foundation, one type of HPV (known as HPV16) is linked to oral sex. Cervical cancer is the primary concern for women, and doctors cite HPV as the main culprit.

*The Journal of Clinical Oncology* claims that the rate of HPV associated with head, neck, and throat cancer skyrocketed by an amazing 225 percent since 1988. There are more than 100 different types of HPV, and experts say that nearly every sexually active person in America will be exposed to at least one type of the virus during his or her lifetime.

In addition to his sexual confession, Michael recently attracted a record-breaking three million viewers to HBO. They watched him portray the flamboyant entertainer, Liberace, in the movie, *Behind the Candelabra*. Although he never admitted it, Liberace died of AIDS in 1987.

Matt Damon played Liberace's lover, Scott Thorson, in the film. Reportedly, Thorson is battling advanced anal cancer today, and is also facing sentencing this month (July) before a judge in Reno for using stolen credit cards.

"Women I've never laid eyes on claimed they've slept with me," Michael Douglas told the press. More or less on record are actress Brenda Vaccaro, his co-star in *Summertree* (1971), as well as Sherri Lansing, a production executive, and actress Taryn Power.

"Mike is full of charm and humor, but don't ever cross him," claimed Kathleen Turner, his co-star in *War of the Roses* (1989).

In 1987, Mike did more than seduce women. He won the Best Actor Oscar for *Wall Street* (1987).

\*\*\*

Perhaps his credentials as a bona-fide heterosexual with an addiction to cunnilingus allowed **Michael Douglas** (*above left*) to camp it up as Liberace in *Behind the Candelabra.*

His co-star, **Matt Damon** (*right*), portrayed as the flamboyant musician's enabler, driver, lover, and legal antagonist, **Scott Thorson,** contributed to the flamboyantly brilliant portrayal of the recently deceased showman.

**DID YOU KNOW?** Blood Moon's blockbusting, sexually indiscreet biography, by Porter and Prince, of Michael Douglas' horny, swashbuckling and groundbreaking father, **KIRK DOUGLAS**, was released in 2019.

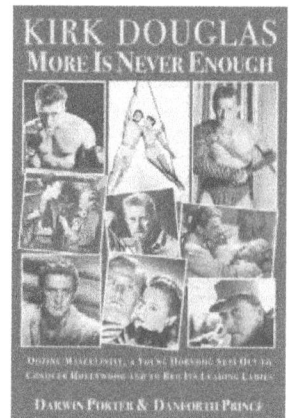

# R.I.P.
# GRACE KELLY

More than a quarter of a century has passed since the death of the regal, white-gloved Grace Kelly, Princess of Monaco. Following a car crash in the hills of the French Riviera, her life ended on September 14, 1982.

But she is hardly forgotten. In the last 18 months, five books have been published about her life. Louis Vuitton, Prada, and Calvin Klein are featuring Grace-inspired fashions, highlighting her glacial glamour.

All of her films, including her Academy Award winning *The Country Girl*, have been released on DVD. Many destinations, such as New York and Monte Carlo, have launched special exhibitions devoted to her life and style.

In spite of the mountains of material written about the late Princess, mystery and rampant speculation remain surrounding the final two days of her life. I was in Nice, researching *Frommer's France*, when I heard the news of Grace's accident. I drove to Monaco that morning. During my stay there, I was able to speak to several eyewitnesses who were privy to information about Grace's final hours on earth. Here is what I believe happened:

The Royal family had spent a troubled weekend filled with tension at their retreat, a farm estate, Roc Agel, high in the hills above Monaco. Their hideaway was actually on French soil. Grace awoke that sunny morning in Provence feeling bloated and fat, far too matronly at the age of fifty-two. She'd been drinking heavily, but planned to go on a rigid rejuvenation scheme to prepare for her comeback in movies.

She wanted to return to the screen starring in Gore Vidal's *A Search for the King*, a novel the author had written in 1950 when he was about twenty-five. The book told the fabled story of the 12th-century English king, Richard the Lion-Hearted, who was kidnapped by the Austrians.

Stricken with migraines that morning, Grace had fought all weekend with her rebellious, iron-willed, 17-year-old daughter, Stephanie. With 15 stitches in her head, the result of a waterskiing accident in Antigua, Stephanie had returned to France. Once back home, she announced to her parents that she was going to move in with Paul Belmondo, the son of the famous French actor Jean Paul Belmondo. Not only that, but she planned to become a race car driver.

Both Grace and Prince Rainier, of course, bitterly opposed both moves. That morning at 8:15, Prince Rainier had said good-bye to Grace and headed for Monaco. Grace loaded down the backseat of her 11-year-old brown Rover 3500 with so many dresses that there was room for only two in the car. She demanded that Stephanie drive back to the palace with her so she could continue to press her case against her daughter's latest career move.

Grace's chauffeur, Christian Silvestri, knowing that her Majesty was "the worst driver in Monaco," tried to dissuade her from

All-American **Grace Kelly**, shown here in an MGM publicity photo

**Grace Kelly** (aka *Her Serene Highness, Princess of Monaco*,) tying the knot with the **Prince of Monaco**. He was royal and rich; she was beautiful and a Hollywood star. Both were Catholic. What could possibly go wrong?

The hairpin turn on Monaco's Corniche that killed **Princess Grace**, some said during a motorized argument with **Stéphanie**. On September 13, 1982, Grace lost control of her 1972 Rover PS 3500 and drove off the steep, winding road, crashing into someone's garden, many feet below. Her daughter had tried, but failed, to regain control of the wheel.

taking the wheel. He volunteered to drive Grace and Stephanie to the palace and come back later for the dresses. She turned him down and set out at 9:45 along the steep, narrow, two-lane *Moyenne Corniche* with its hairpin bends. Her cranky daughter was in the passenger's seat beside her.

A French truck driver, Yves Raimondo, was behind Grace's car as she headed down the mountain. He was unaware of the identity of the occupants of the Rover in front of him. About two hundred yards before the most dangerous curve along the Corniche, he reported that he saw the vehicle ahead zigzagging dangerously, the Rover even sideswiping the mountain on the left. He blew his horn, and the Rover straightened out to face the dangerous curve that lay ahead.

Then a strange thing happened. Raimondo claimed the driver did not step on the brakes, but the accelerator. The car speeded ahead and plunged 150 feet over the mountain side, coming to a stop on its roof in a French garden.

Apparently, Grace had suffered a seizure. In her attempt to control the fast-moving vehicle, she'd stepped on the wrong pedal. The impact of the crash had thrown her into the back seat. She'd always refused to wear a safety belt because the contraption made her feel claustrophobic.

Badly injured, Stephanie escaped on the driver's side to summon help from a French farm woman for her mother, who was unconscious and trapped in the rear of the Rover, which might explode at any minute. Within only half an hour, an ambulance arrived at the ironically named Princess Grace Hospital, carrying Grace's unconscious body.

Grace had once told her best friend, Gwen Robyns, that "one day someone is going to die on that awful curve in the road. I can just feel it." Her prediction was about to come true.

At the hospital Grace's doctors worked frantically to revive her, fearing major internal trauma. Precious time was wasted because the hospital did not have a CAT scan. She was transferred to the office of a private doctor shortly before midnight on the day of the crash. There it was determined that her injuries were so serious that she was dying. She was taken back to the hospital.

A member of the palace staff issued a *communiqué* of total lies, claiming Grace was in satisfactory condition. In the hospital room next to Grace, Stephanie had sustained a fracture of the vertebra. The injury was so serious that she could have been paralyzed from her neck down for the rest of her life. Already rumors were spreading that Stephanie had actually been the driver of the car.

Prince Rainier was told that even if Grace lived, she'd spend the rest of her life "as a vegetable." Locked in an embrace with his children, a sobbing Prince Rainer made the most painful decision of his life, and Princess Caroline and Prince Albert agreed with him. Rainier ordered that Grace be taken off life support. "Let my wife die," he told doctors before heading to Stephanie's hospital room. When he told her the sad news, her blood-curdling scream could be heard throughout the hospital. Prince Rainier, Caroline, and Albert filed into Grace's room, and each kissed her farewell. Death came at 10:35 on the night of September 14.

Even before Grace was entombed, lurid tabloid headlines dominated world

**SERENE, SEDATE, AND (ON THE SURFACE) UNCONTROVERSIAL**

Her Royal Family, late 1960s. *Left to right,* **Caroline, Rainier III, Grace, Stéphanie,** and **Albert.**

Royal daughter **Stéphanie,** the Grimaldi's crankiest "wild child" and (at least during her formative years) perennial rebel, poses (resentfully, some said,) for this very formal portrait.

BING CROSBY    GRACE KELLY    FRANK SINATRA

*High Society*

CELESTE HOLM · JOHN LUND
LOUIS CALHERN · SIDNEY BLACKMER
*and* LOUIS ARMSTRONG *and his band*

COLE PORTER

**HIGH SOCIETY: Grace** was born into it, demonstrated it during her teen years with "white glove" manners, replicated it in films *(see above),* and later, as Her Serene Highness, Princess of Monaco, lived it.

The poster above promotes one of the most talked-about films of the Sputnik era. Her affairs with both **Bing Crosby** and **Frank Sinatra,** her co-stars, was consistently hinted at in the tabloids.

news. Her promiscuous lifestyle was fodder for the press, including details of her many affairs with movie stars such as Clark Gable, Gary Cooper, Bing Crosby, David Niven, William Holden, Ray Milland, Frank Sinatra, James Stewart, and Spencer Tracy, as well as designer Oleg Cassini, Ismailian playboy Prince Aly Khan, and the Shah of Iran. Readers eagerly devoured details of her previously unknown affair with President John F. Kennedy.

The "fairytale romance" that had led to Grace's wedding to Rainier in 1956 was brutally debunked. Stories highlighted several affairs she'd had with young men during her tenure as Princess of Monaco. Not only that, but Prince Rainier's many off-the-record trysts with young women were revealed, including the identity of a mistress he kept in Paris.

A macabre coterie of hairdressers, makeup artists, and morticians attempted to prepare her face for an open-coffin funeral. Grace's body lay in state in the Palatine Chapel of the Royal Palace, as thousands filed past to view her body. Covering her head was a hideous blonde wig that even Mae West would have rejected. Her face was so heavily made up to conceal injuries that Albert claimed, "My Mummy looks like a streetwalker."

The day Grace was buried, the lights of glittering Monaco went off, as mourning descended over the little principality. "Without our Princess, the sparkle is gone from our Kingdom." said one Monégasque, a shopkeeper.

Famous for her vulnerability and beauty, **Grace** became adept at playing a princess long before she was formally crowned by the Monegasques.

Above, she appears with one of her lovers, **Ray Milland**, in the mid-Fifties thriller, *Dial M for Murder*

Fashion columnists sometimes ridiculed some of **Grace Kelly's** fashion statements, which occasionally seemed a bit frumpy, especially when compared to those of the intensely tailored Jacqueline Kennedy. Here, she appears at table with **David Niven** in something "diaphanous."

**Grace Kelly** with "**Badda Badda Bing Crosby.**"

According to author Gore Vidal, "She almost always laid her leading man."

During her "salad days," Rainier III of Monaco's Grimaldi clan was not the only royal scion Grace was rumored to have been intimate with. There were brief interludes with **Mohammed Reza Pahlavi** (*aka* the **Shah of Iran**, *left*) and **Prince Aly Khan**, *above*), each a fabulously wealthy heir to a Middle Eastern fortune.

In marked contrast to the "Races at Ascot" style of Prince Aly Khan, another of Grace's lovers (**Gary Cooper**, depicted above) seemed to look best when he was "wide and open and Home on the Range."

Grace Kelly as a reluctant newlywed with Gary Cooper in what critics often define as "the greatest Western-themed psychological drama ever made," *High Noon.* According to Cooper, "She was a cold dish until you got her pants down. Then she'd explode."

Grace (looking fabulous) with William Holden (looking fabulous) in the mid 1950s, shortly before the starting bell of her gig as a Monegasque princess.

*"Heavy lies the head that wears the crown."*

—William Shakespeare

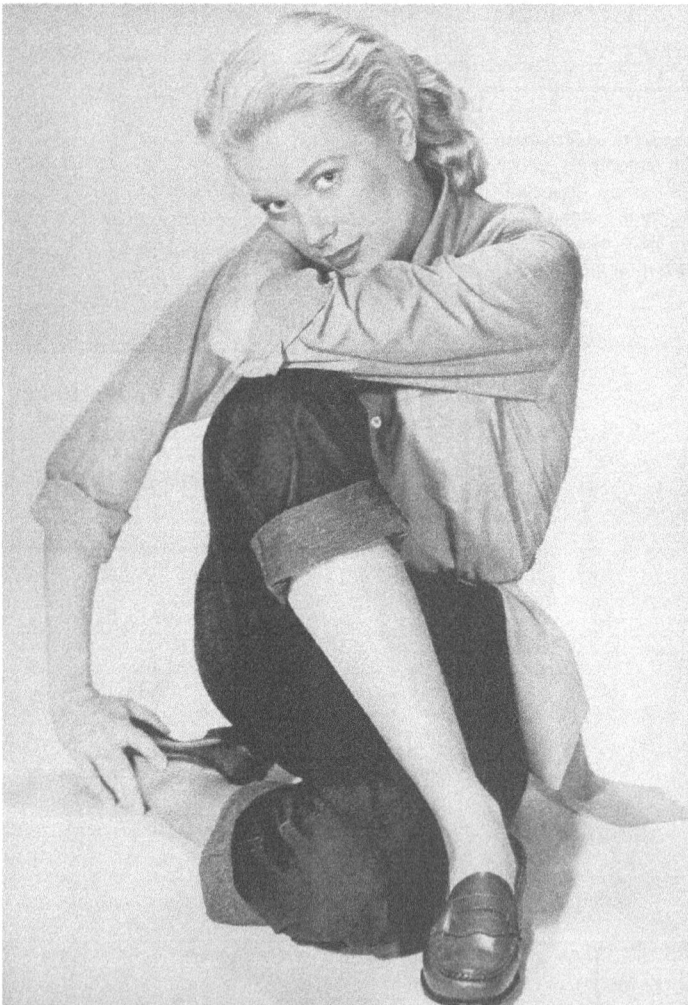

The photo layout Grace (coyly) crafted for *Modern Screen* in 1954... and which ALMOST EVERYONE in France gossipped about cruelly after her marriage to Rainier and her "elevation" to Princess.

*The Country Girl,* holding her Oscar, gets on onstage kiss from Brando, also holding his Oscar for his performance in *On the Waterfront* (1954). Later that night, she gave him another "reward."

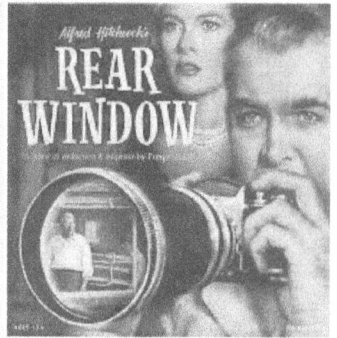

Grace Kelly and James Stewart became lovers off screen. "According to my count, she was my 251th seduction."

And then there was that embarassing fling with JFK and ALL those resentments it generated with Jacqueline.

The President said, "I'm not finished with a dame until I've had her three ways."

Oscar time for Grace Kelly, who holds the coveted Best Actress Oscar for her performance in *The Country Girl,* co-starring Bing Crosby and William Holden.

An immediate outcry arose, as loyal fans of Judy Garland claimed that the Oscar should have gone to her for *A Star Is Born.*

# THE UNHAPPY BUT VASTLY PROFITABLE LIVES OF LUCILLE BALL & DESI ARNAZ

*"They Weren't Lucy and Ricky Ricardo"*

### ANNOUNCING VOLUMES ONE (1911-1960) AND TWO (1961-1989)
### OF A TWO-PART BIOGRAPHY BY DARWIN PORTER

**The most famous woman in the history of TV** wasn't exactly what she appeared to be on *I Love Lucy* with her husband, Desi Arnaz. Gritty, feisty, abrasive, intelligent, and edgy, Lucille Ball ("Love!" she said. "I was always falling in love!") lived through the heady years of 1930s show business as a chorus girl. But her wild run-away years as a starlet have been kept largely concealed from her adoring public. Here--with its triumphs, frustrations, and tragedies--is the ultimate close-up of this extraordinary redhead.

According to Blood Moon's president, **Danforth Prince**, "The lives of this brilliant but tormented couple and the decades they survived was too convoluted for just one volume. So with the understanding that Volume One, covering the period from 1911 to 1960, hit the street on Mother's Day, (May 9, 2021)... Volume Two —1961 to their respective deaths in 1986 (Desi) and 1989 (Lucy)—was released about a year later."

"These books represent **A CELEBRATION OF THE AMERICAN CENTURY** and the pop culture it generated in the aftermath of World War II. We present them to the reading (and TV-watching) public as an act of "I Love Lucy" and the most detailed and comprehensive biography of these two great American movie stars ever published.

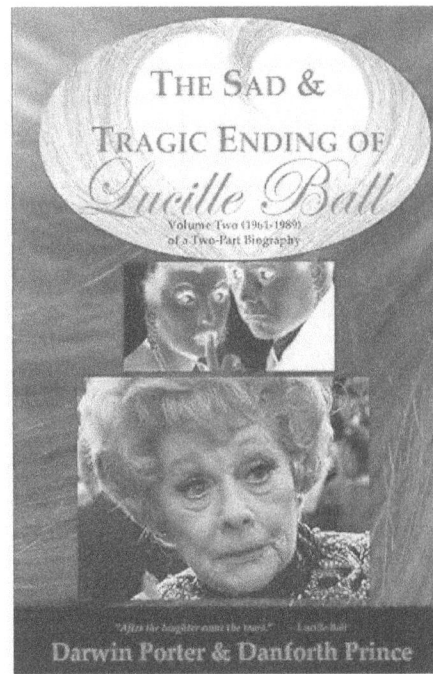

**They're here!** A wham-slamming two-part biography of America's favorite redhead, a sitcom veteran who survived careers as a showgirl, a B-list movie star, the early days of television, and over the span of many decades, the fickle attention span of Baby Boomers. **HERE'S LUCY** and the era in which she thrived, **by Darwin Porter.**

137

Blackglama

**In 1955, a survey revealed that Lucille Ball was the most recognizable face on Planet Earth.**

With her husband, Desi Arnaz, a bandleader and émigré from Cuba, they had launched TV's most successful sitcom, *I Love Lucy*, at the tail end of the Golden Age of Hollywood.

Even today, somewhere in the world, the series is still being shown on a 24-hour cycle. The original black-and-white celluloid is being colorized for new generations, and Nicole Kidman is set to star as Lucille in an upcoming feature film.

Millions of fans believe that Lucille and Desi played themselves as Ricky and Lucy Ricardo, their fictional characters on TV. As this book reveals, that isn't exactly true.

Both were savvy business executives. Lucille, for example, morphed herself from a $50-a-week RKO extra into a multi-millionaire. Along with Desi, she bought RKO, the major-league movie and TV production studio formerly owned by the spectacularly unstable aviator and oil-industry mogul, Howard Hughes.

Despite their enormous success, many aspects of their personal lives were tragic. As Desi himself once said, "We had our daughter, we had our son, we had a fabulous career, and we were in love. Then the shit hit the fan."

For such a well-publicized couple, their complete story has never been told, especially their early years. This has radically changed with the publication of Blood Moon's latest biography, *Lucille Ball & Desi Arnaz: They Weren't Lucy & Ricky Ricardo*. I co-authored it with Danforth Prince.

Their stormy and struggling early days live again. Growing up in western New York State, Lucille was known as "The Jamestown Hussy." At sixteen, she launched an affair with Johnny DaVita, a dangerous but sexy local hoodlum.

She later pursued a career as a model in Manhattan, posing topless between stints as a fashion plate for *haute couture*. By 1933, she'd drifted to Hollywood as a scantily clad "Goldwyn Girl." In her first picture, she portrayed a nude Roman sex slave, her vital zones concealed only with the tresses of her long blonde wig.

Before **Lucille Ball's** perky sitcom character became a hit with American audiences in the early days of television, her movie *persona* was that of a sexy, exhibitionistic showgirl—"the kind of fast-talking broad your mother wouldn't like."

She appears above as a gum-chewing street-walker named "Bubbles" at a dance audition in *Dance Girl Dance (1940)*.

In 1968, **the Great Lakes Mink Association (aka Black-glama)** launched a new ad campaign to sell more mink. Dozens of glamourous celebrities signed on, many photographed by Richard Avedon. For a while, at least, many received a furpiece of their choice, and the satisfaction of knowing that they were "instantly recognizable," even when their names weren't spelled out, to millions of consumers.

In 1979, **Lucille Ball**, with a team of stylists, pulled herself together and joined their ranks.

Since then, thanks partly to the "instant recognizability' quotient of the "Lucy We Love," Blackglama's campaign has been cited as one of the most successful ever launched.

Thanks to animal rights activists, who lobbied furiously against it, it's also been cited as the end of an era.

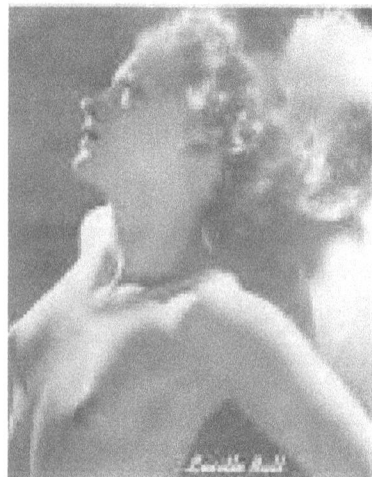

Before she was Lucy, **Miss Ball** paid for acting lessons and the rent with gigs as a nude model *(left photo)*; as an "artfully topless" chained-up slave in the pre-Code talkie, *Roman Scandals* (1933); and *(right photo)* as a sometimes blonde, sometimes brunette, and eventually redheaded "Goldwyn Girl," in scantily clad revues onstage.

From there, she worked her way up the Hollywood ladder, rung by rung. Her mentor, Lela (mother of Ginger) Rogers, advised Lucille that the quickest way to stardom was on the casting couch. In addition to producers and directors, she sometimes seduced movie stars, notably Henry Fonda, Peter Lawford, William Holden, Victor Mature, and Robert Mitchum.

Her many affairs were fewer than those of her future husband, Desi Arnaz, a copious philanderer, even during his two decades of marriage to Lucille.

After a revolution in his native Cuba, he and his father arrived penniless in Miami. Desi got a low-end job cleaning out bird cages, but in time, he re-invented himself as a musician, eventually rounding up a band of his own. He became famous for introducing a giddy, inhibition-reducing version of the Conga to millions of *norteamericanos.*

In Manhattan, Desi became the city's latest Latin lover, eventually seducing Ann Miller, Ginger Rogers, Lana Turner, Gene Tierney, Betty Grable, and (according to legend) each of the young women employed at Polly Adler's bordello, the most notorious in America.

Owned by "Lucy & Desi," **Desilu,** until 1962 was the second-largest independent television production company in America. Parts of it had previously been associated with RKO Pictures, one of Lucy's early employers. After Lucy divorced Desi, she ran the studio for years, becoming the most successful female executive in Hollywood.

Desi once said, "Marriage is okay, but adultery is more fun. Just ask Lucille."

Their saga is not described just through their affairs. As "the King and Queen of Television" they launched the *I Love Lucy*" series, which made them millionaires. Eventually, they bought RKO and launched Desilu Productions.

Lucie Arnaz, their daughter, reflected on the marriage of her parents: "They had one of those historic marriages like Napoléon and Josephine or Richard Burton and Elizabeth Taylor—destined to be troubled but also destined for them to never find anyone else so passionate or so fabulous."

As authors, we opted to divide their amazing story into two Volumes, the first of which will be released this month through, along other vendors, Amazon.com.

*Volume Two* (1961-1989), a post-divorce, post *I Love Lucy* saga, gets released sometime in September.
It describes each of their second marriages, and how each, with varying degrees of success, struggled to replicate the smashing success of their earlier gigs.

Yes, both volumes are permeated with self-doubt, anguish, and tragedy, yet each reflects an overview of "The American Century" and its go-go 50s that few other sagas can replicate.

In 2001, the U.S. Postal Service evaluated the key role Lucille Ball played in our lives and issued a 34-cent stamp emblazoned with her likeness.

*Left to right:* **Young Desi Arnaz** primping his image as his era's then-most-popular Latino dance master; a press photo from one of the most popular daytime TV comedy schticks ("**The Chocolate Factory**"; an episode of *I Love Lucy*) ever filmed; and a "part true, part fiction" love photo of **Ricky and Lucy Ricardo** at home.

# HOW LUCILLE BALL
## (AND/OR THE CHARACTER WE KNEW AS LUCY)

## SURVIVED PRE-CODE SHOW BIZ, THE AGE OF SPUTNIK, A CAREER IN EARLY TELEVISION, MOTHERHOOD, THE SEXUAL REVOLUTION, THE BREAKUP OF HER MARRIAGE, THE VIETNAM WAR, AND "REINVENTING HERSELF" AS A NOSTALGIA-SOAKED SPOKESPERSON FOR "HOLLYWOOD & THE WAY WE WERE."

From 1951 through 1956, *I Love Lucy* was the most-watched show in television. Its launch was as rocky as the marriage of the real-life show-biz pros who crafted it.

After their divorce in 1960, Lucille Ball appraised Desi Arnaz, her former husband: "He's like Jekyll and Hyde. He drinks and gambles, he's awash in broads and booze, and that gay actor, Cesar Romero, is his devoted slave. Love?" she asked. "I was always falling in love with the wrong man. Including Desi."

Arnaz summed up his marriage to Lucille: "We were anything but Lucy and Ricky Ricardo. They had nothing to do with us. We dreamed of success, fame, and fortune. And guess what? It all led to hell."

Their early struggles were epic. As a girl, Lucy at times was literally chained to her backyard in Jamestown, New York. As a teenager, she broke away and earned a reputation as "The Jamestown Hussy," riding around with Johnny DaVita, a local hoodlum.

Later, she broke into show business, hustling "sugar daddies" and stage-door Johnnies who gave her money and gifts. When she was desperate, she worked as a nude model.

In the 1930s, she migrated to Hollywood and made films for RKO. Offscreen, its executives used her as a gussied-up hooker to "entertain" exhibitors and clients from out of town.

*Left photo:* **Lucille,** ready for prime time in 1957, showing off her children, **Desi Arnaz Jr.**, and **Lucie Arnaz**. Relying heavily on the fame and connections of their battling parents, each of them would morph—less successfully than either their mother or father—into tepid but traumatic show-biz careers of their own.

*Center photo*: **Lucille Ball** and her ex-husband and ongoing business partner **Desi Arnaz**, ruefully joked that they were the only struggling actors who "bucked the trend" of studio oppression by actually buying the outfit (RKO, whose name they changed to Desilu) that had oppressed them. The implications for the TV industry were staggering...and left scars on each of them that never went away

*Right photo*: WHO KNEW? That the usually staid U.S. Postal Service would celebrate Lucy's comedic career with (Gasp!) a postage stamp in her honor. With every "page" of 20 stamps was included a photo of LUCILLE doing one of her *schticks*.

Desi, however, was born to wealth and privilege in Cuba. At the age of twelve, as an incentive to helping him lose his virginity, he was escorted to a local bordello by his father.

Having lost most of their assets in the Cuban Revolution, his family fled. In Miami, Desi got a job as a janitor cleaning out canary cages. Later, in Manhattan, he accepted whatever gigs he could get. He became the "kept boy" of the gay composer Lorenz Hart, sustaining an affair with superstar Ginger Rogers on the side. That included the task of escorting her into Canada for an abortion. He was eventually hired by bandleader Xavier Cugat to "beat hell out of those Afro-Cuban drums." After drifting to Hollywood, he spotted Lucille on a sound stage "dressed like a two-dollar whore who had been badly beaten by her pimp."

[That was, indeed, the character she developed for her role in *Dance Girl Dance* (1940). During its filming, she "more or less politely" resisted the lesbian advances of her director, Dorothy Arzner.]

Desi succeeded where Dorothy Arzner failed, marrying Lucille that same year. Characterized by violent fights and long separations, their stormy marriage staggered along for two traumatic decades.

Desi's obsession with sex became legendary. He seduced every prostitute in Polly Adler's infamous NYC whorehouse. In Hollywood, Lana Turner and Betty Grable came and went from his life, along with countless showgirls and hometown gals attending his on-the-road band shows.

Meanwhile, Lucille waited for his return, occupying her nights with the son (Elliott Roosevelt) of the U.S. president; actor/mobster George ("Black Snake") Raft; and George Sanders, Zsa Zsa Gabor's suicidal husband. Coming and going from her boudoir were—among many others—William Holden, Milton Berle, Henry Fonda, Orson Welles, and Robert Mitchum.

By the early 1950s, the careers of both Lucille and Desi had run out of gas. TV executives objected to his Cuban accent. But *I Love Lucy* was launched nevertheless and shot up in the ratings, morphing into the most successful sitcom in TV history.

"With gold arriving in wheelbarrows" (Desi's words), Lucille and Desi bought RKO Studios and launched Desilu Productions. It became the second-largest motion picture and television studio in the world.

These two volumes are a first-of-their-kind biography of TV's wackiest and most eccentric couple. They're generously stuffed with ironic facts and blunt assessments from their frenemies. As a paired set, they radically lampoon some of the premises of the American Dream.

# PART 2 of 2
# THE SAD AND TRAGIC ENDING OF LUCILLE BALL

Volume Two (1961-1989) of a Two-Part Biography by Darwin Porter

It's been said by many, including the novelist, F. Scott Fitzgerald, that there are no "Second Acts" in American lives.

That's wrong. Ronald Reagan and Lucille Ball are good examples of American celebrities who each succeeded at crafting influential "Second Acts," components of which were massively and consistently broadcast to the world at large.

As an obsessive fan of the history of Hollywood, I have never had to subdivide any of the biographies I've written into two separate volumes. That changed when I tangled with the long-enduring saga of Lucille Ball, who in the mid-1950s rose to the top of the Gallup Poll as the most famous woman on earth.

First came Volume One, *Lucille Ball & Desi Arnaz: They Weren't Lucy and Ricky* Ricardo. It was released (and widely publicized) about five months ago.

Now, media "guns" are already aimed at the upcoming release, in early December, of **Volume Two**. Consumers have good reasons to anticipate this with gusto: To my astonishment, the limited number of previous Lucille Ball biographies have each virtually ignored the last thirty years of her life. They imply that her life ended in 1960 after her divorce from Desi Arnaz. One noted biographer summed up her three (emotional and fraught) final decades in five abbreviated pages.

In vivid contrast, we maintain that Lucille, an artist and renowned businesswoman, deserves more.She gets it in the 500+ pages (with photos) of this biography's Volume Two: *The Sad and Tragic Ending of Lucille Ball.*

141

The plot of **Too Many Girls** (1940) was frothy, frilly, predictable, and filled with manically flirtatious scenes where everybody danced the conga. But it goes down in Hollywood history as the set where **Lucille Ball and Desi Arnaz** rehearsed their dance steps and fell in love. Later, Lucy adopted its title as the reason her marriage failed.

Years after any possibility of a reconciliation was cold and dead in its grave, she ruefully self-analysed with this: **"My divorce from Desi was the worst mistake of my life. Neither of us has ever been the same since, mentally or physically."**

## AFTER DESI, WHAT REALLY HAPPENED TO LUCILLE BALL?

A new life began for her. One aspect involved Gary Morton, a "Borscht-Belt" stand-up comedian with a gift for diplomacy and the tactful handling of divas.

She also reinforced her status as a reliable television "staple" with at least two ongoing (albeit derivative) series, *The Lucy Show, Here's Lucy,* and as a last hurrah, the ill-fated *Life With Lucy.*

In reference to her second marriage, she confessed, "Now I wear the pants." Multiple witnesses assert that from her (separate) bedroom adjoining Morton's, whenever she clanged a bell on her nightstand, he'd come running.

My Volume Two also examines the final years of a fast-collapsing Desi Arnaz, who, "post-Lucy," gambled away his millions and destroyed his health with late nights, liquor, and endless Havana cigars.

Volume Two is also the first to explore the drug addiction (and recuperation) of Lucille's son, Desi Jr., and the show-biz struggles (and occasional resentments) of both of her children, including Lucie Arnaz.

The book also contrasts Lucille's "vintage mystique" with the emerging careers of other (younger) stars who admired and perhaps resented her, too. They included Carol Burnett, Mary Tyler Moore, Tom Selleck, Arnold Schwarzenegger, Cher, and about forty others.

It's also filled with details about Lucille's behind-the-scenes banter with MGM's and Warner Brothers' and Fox's "dragons of yesteryear," once-celebrated stars dragged, by Lucille, back into the limelight through a formulaic and sometimes repetitive roster of "TV Specials" that celebrated a fast-dying way of American life.

Warning: Lucille was famous for more of a "potty mouth" than either Frank Sinatra or Elizabeth Taylor. Her comments, often scathing, were sometimes (how do I say this delicately?) *"piquant."*

Extra-marital, post-Desi indiscretions? Let's just say that our favorite redhead liked her men big and strong—"No pretty boys for me."

Her most frequent co-star in the final decade of her life was the nostalgic "for the way things used to be in Hollywood," Bob Hope. A reporter asked Lucille to reveal something "we didn't already know about ol' Ski Nose."

She answered in a way that surprised almost everyone: "Spiro Agnew, the disgraced Vice President of Richard Nixon, writes a lot of Bob's jokes, although many of them are too dirty to ever get televised."

In one format or another, the very durable Lucille Ball appeared on television every year of the last thirty years of her life, making her last appearance (alongside an even more durable show-biz warhorse, Bob Hope) at the Academy Awards on March 29, 1989. She died about a month later of heart failure. Tributes poured in from around the world.

Her legend, obviously, continues to thrive, stronger, perhaps, than ever.

This month, Director Aaron Sorkin will release a feature film about a "micro moment" in Ball and Arnaz's life, *Being the Ricardos*, starring Nicole Kidman as Lucy and the Spain-born actor Javier Bardem as Desi. TCM will be broadcasting tributes to her, too, and episodes of *I Love Lucy* are being colorized for new generations of fans. Blood Moon Productions will release, as noted above, Volume Two of our two-part biography, the most comprehensive ever published. From the grave, Lucille might, with irony and humor, refer to these media *brouhahas* as "My Comeback."

Actually, she has never gone away. Her telecasts have been broadcast somewhere, in some country, every day since the 1950s. And in some regions of the world, little girls are, to an increasing degree, being named "Lucy."

Her reign continues. Me? **I LOVE LUCY.**

Lucille crafted a new life for herself after her divorce from Desi. His name was **Gary Morton,** a stand-up comedian with a knack for handling high-maintenance divas.

Decades after their heyday in the 70s, it's hard to imagine the attention that tabloids poured onto anything to to with "Liz and Dick" (i.e., **Elizabeth Taylor** and **Richard Burton**).

Here, they appear with Lucille Ball on the cover of *TV Guide*. It referenced an episode of *Here's Lucy* that revolved around Elizabeth's then-most recent acquisition...another oversized, overwrought diamond.

Horrifed by what she considered a collapse of American standards during the swinging Sixties, **Lucille** became increasingly linked to televised celebrations of "America The Way It Was."

One of the over-the-hill icons she cultivated was **John Wayne.** Here, they appear together in one of her "on the verge of running out of gas" sitcoms, whose ratings sputtered along for years until, frankly, they ran out of steam.

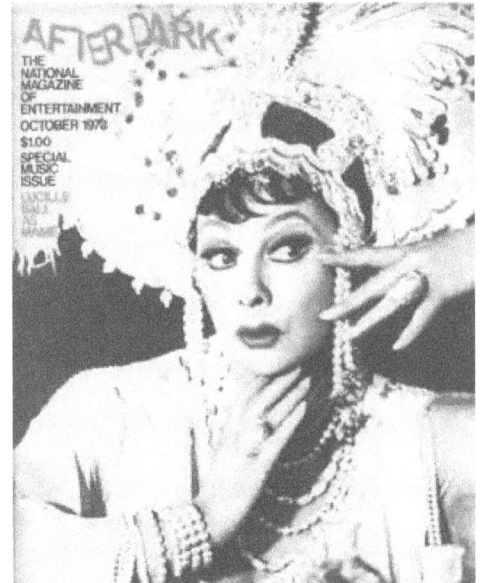

For **Lucille**, the prospect of reprising Rosalind Russell's portrayal of *Auntie Mame* in an updated film version was absolutely terrifying. But despite her frail health and not-robust singing voice, she bravely shouldered the role anyway.

Here's how she appeared on the cover of the then-flourishing arts magazine, *After Dark*.

Her frenemies quipped that as **Lucille** got older, she smoked more and more cigarettes and took longer and longer to pull herself together every morning to replicate her red-headed glory. Here's one of the last photos taken of her in public. **Gary Morton**, on her right, is partially hidden.

The subject was "Motherhood," and when it was announced as a theme for an episode of one of their sitcoms, Lucy and Desi imported their respective mothers for an "all in the family" photo. **Lucille Ball with her mother, De-De Ball Hunt**, widow of a telephone line repairman for Bell Telephone, appear on the left. **Desi** with his once-wealthy mother **Dolores de Acha**, wife of the deposed governor of Santiago, Cuba, appear together on the right. The cultural presuppositions of everyone involved were complicated, and everyone had a LOT to say.

*Photo left* derives from MGM's 1943 musical fantasy, *DuBarry Was a Lady*.

**Here's Lucy** as an imperial French courtesan with **Red Skelton** as a dime store version of Louis XV.

*An oversexed bandleader arrives in Manhattan.*
*In Hollywood, a young seductress proclaims, "Love! I'm always falling in love!"*

# WE LOVE LUCY, TOO!

Franchot Tone    George Sanders    Victor Mature    George Raft    Peter Lawford

William Holden    John Hodiak    Henry Fonda    James Craig    Robert Mitchum

**BLOOD MOON
PRODUCTIONS**
ENTERTAINMENT ABOUT
HOW AMERICA
INTERPRETS ITS
LEGENDS AND MYTHS

GETTING A GRIP ON THE
LUCY WE LOVED WAS A
BLOODY, CONFUSING, &
CONTROVERSIAL JOB, BUT
SOMEBODY HAD TO DO IT.

ISBN 978-1-936003-71-6

BloodMoonProductions.com

# WARREN BEATTY

## AMERICA'S 20ᵀᴴ-CENTURY CASANOVA?

A Hollywood story presently making the rounds—perhaps it's apocryphal—has a child saying, "Daddy, didn't you used to be Warren Beatty?"

Born in 1937, Beatty is still around and still married to Annette Bening, whom he met when she was cast in his 1991 *Bugsy*. The screenwriter James Toback recalled Beatty's reaction. "He let out a growl. A primordial yelp of love, lust, and desire, a sound that one would expect a starving man to make at the prospect of finally being able to devour a huge and delicious meal." This roaming Lothario seems to have settled, since then, into domestic bliss.

In the past few weeks, Beatty's life has been scrutinized under a microscope as never before, with reviews in the nation's leading newspapers. Three biographers have released books on the charismatic star, documenting his many love affairs: *The Sexiest Man Alive* by Ellis Amburn; *Star* by Peter Biskind, and *A Private Man* by Suzanne Finstad.

Of these writers, Biskind estimates that Beatty has had at least 12,775 women, excluding daytime quickies, drive-bys, gropings, and stolen kisses. This is an amazing record for a clean-cut, All-America football player from Virginia, who didn't lose his virginity till he was 20. He certainly made up since then for lost time.

Beatty today is hailed as the "Founder of the New Hollywood," and even his detractors have to credit some of his achievements, such as the groundbreaking classic *Bonnie and Clyde*. Originally, his sister, Shirley MacLaine, was set to star as Bonnie. "I would love to have done a kissing scene with my brother to see what the fuss is all about. Today, I keep my daughter as far away from Warren as possible."

Classics aside, he has also made some of Hollywood's worst flops, notably *Ishtar*, costarring Dustin Hoffman. Beatty's appearance in the ill-fated film *Town & Country* virtually ended his movie career. In the wake of its release, *Variety* referred to it as "Hollywood's biggest modern-day flop." Ironically, in the reviews of his life, Beatty's film career seems to play second fiddle to his role as an international Don Juan.

"Sex was his hobby," MacLaine said. The best-selling novelist, Jackie Collins, claimed, "Warren would proposition a chair if it looked at him sideways." Her sister Joan, one of Beatty's early lovers, found him too much man for her. "Three, four, five times a day, once a record-breaking seven, was not that unusual for him. And he was able to accept phone calls at the same time."

"I'm just a very normal guy," Beatty once said. *Yeah, right!* How many everyday guys do you know who have made love to Jacqueline Kennedy Onassis; her socialite sister Lee Radziwell; and Christina Onassis, the shipping heiress and daughter of Aristotle Onassis, Jackie's second husband?

Jackie had long been attracted to Beatty. According to her friend Truman Capote, she had this thing for actors, and had had affairs with both William Holden and Marlon Brando. At the debut of her affair with Beatty, she'd warned him to be discreet. "I don't want us ending as fodder for the tabloids." As might have been predicted in liaisons among the very famous, one night at a social gathering, she approached him from behind and overheard him bragging to male friends about his conquest of her. She dropped him that very night and refused to take his calls, the next day and forever.

Beatty also struck out with Jackie's first husband, JFK himself. Jackie had wanted Beatty to portray her husband in the biographical World War II drama, *PT-109*. JFK preferred the acting skills and persona of Cliff Robertson but gave in to his wife's wishes. He invited Beatty to the White House "to soak up the atmosphere." But Beatty wired back: "No, I much prefer you come to Hollywood and soak up the atmosphere here." When the White House received that (admittedly impertinent) telegram, Beatty suddenly found himself off the picture.

His list of conquests reads like a *Who's Who* in Hollywood—Barbra Streisand, Elizabeth Taylor, Natalie Wood, Candace Bergen, Cher, Brigitte Bardot, Vanessa Redgrave, Mary Tyler

*A 20th Century American Casanova?*

**Warren Beatty** gets frisky with **Annette Bening** (whom he later married) in *Bugsy* (1991).

Do women like him because he's more fun? Here, **Warren Beatty** appears on a murderous rampage with **Faye Dunaway** in *Bonnie and Clyde* (1967), a film critics then defined as "a biographical neo-noir crime film, and one of the first examples of "The New Hollywood."

In *PT-109*, a publicity photo for which is displayed above, **Cliff Robertson** portrayed an "attentive to his duties" young JFK. Beatty turned down the role.

Moore, et al.

Madonna, whom he cast opposite him in *Dick Tracy*, was one of his most widely publicized affairs. "She had no inhibitions," he recalled. The Material Girl really abused him, dragging him night after night to gay discos and calling him a wimp.

Jane Fonda thought Beatty was gay after their first meeting. She learned later that he wasn't. He had high praise for her in the boudoir. "She has this ability to virtually unhinge her jaw like a python that swallows prey much larger than itself."

Beatty seduced Julie Christie shortly after she was nominated for an Oscar for her lead role in *Darling*. Another of his lovers, the French *gamine*, Leslie Caron, claimed, "Warren always falls in love with girls who have won or been nominated for an Academy Award. Diane Keaton, for example."

In spite of his star-studded list of seductions, he was an equal opportunist. A fan wrote that her husband wouldn't have intercourse with her any more after breast cancer forced her to have a mastectomy. "Fly to Hollywood; I'll send a ticket," he wired her. "Tell your husband I'll do the job for him." He was a man of his word.

It might be easy to write Beatty off at this point in his career. He has millions of dollars in investments, a good wife, a loving family, and devoted friends. He could easily retire. But he's not completely given up on films, however. He still wants to play Howard Hughes, even though Leonardo DiCaprio and director Martin Scorsese beat him to the goal post with their *The Aviator*. Beatty is considering playing Hughes in his declining, demented years, portraying the period when he became the world's most famous (and enigmatic) recluse.

Close friends also claim that Beatty is still interested in politics. He considered, at least for a brief period, running for governor of California against Arnold Schwarzenegger. Beatty was instrumental in the ill-fated 1984 and 1988 presidential campaigns of Gary Hart. It was said that Beatty and Hart each wanted to be the other.

"What he really wants is to become president of the United States," said a close friend who doesn't want to be named. "To those who say he's too long in the tooth, I point out Ronald Reagan, another actor. Annette Bening is a great actress and could play the role of First lady better than Nancy, who was only a minor movie star."

In spite of the revelations within those fat biographies presently being digested and reviewed, Beatty will have the final word: "Whatever you have read or heard about me, through books or gossip, forget it. I am nothing like *that* Warren Beatty. I am nothing like what you've read."

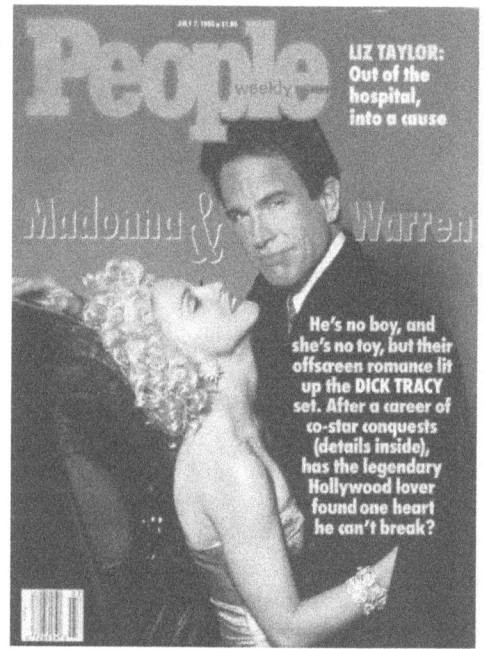

*DICK TRACY* (1990) It sold a lot of magazines and generated a lot of press, but the onscreen mating of **Warren** with **Madonna** was not a particularly comfortable fit.

**Leslie Caron** (as *Gigi* in 1958) and **Diane Keaton** *(right)*

**OTHER LADIES WHOSE HISTORIES COINCIDED INTIMATELY WITH WARREN'S**

**Jane Fonda** *(left)* in 1963; **Julie Christie** *(center photo)* in 1966; and the **Bouvier sisters** (**Jacqueline Kennedy** and **Lee Radziwill**) in the 60s.

# IF JOAN CRAWFORD

HAD REMAINED ALIVE AND LITIGIOUS,
NO ONE WOULD HAVE WRITTEN, OR READ, OR REVIEWED, OR QUOTED

# *MOMMIE DEAREST*

*As I make the rounds* promoting various Hollywood biographies I write, the most frequently asked question is: "Why do you write only about dead people?" A fair question. Here's the answer: Writing about the dead is better for your bank account. The dead can't sue for libel; the law protects a person's reputation only when he or she is alive. Once dead, the right to privacy ends. Joan Crawford's adopted daughter, Christina, would never have written that vindictive and scurrilous rag, *Mommie Dearest,* if Crawford were alive.

To show how dangerous it is writing about the living, take the recent case of Hollywood producer Jon Peters. He announced that he'd accepted a $700,000 advance to write his memoirs, *Studio Head,* for HarperCollins.

Once the most famous hairdresser in Hollywood, he made millions of dollars cutting women's hair. One day, wearing skintight jeans and no underwear, he showed up on the doorstep of Barbra Streisand, carrying a scissors, a comb, and a brush.

It was love at first sight. This former street tough with a seventh grade education soon moved in with Barbra as a career advancement. In no time at all, he put away those scissors and became a producer, beginning with her film, *A Star Is Born* (1976). He brags that he became "a Hollywood legend for seduction as much as production," bagging not only Streisand, but Salma Hayek, Catherine Zeta-Jones, Pamela Anderson, and Kim Basinger, plus a pre-*Basic Instinct* Sharon Stone. "Not even I could turn Sharon into the superstar she expected to be fast enough," Peters said.

To gain his advance from a publisher, Peters had to submit a proposal for his autobiography. No sooner had he done that, than a spy at HarperCollins leaked the details of that proposal to various parties who had shared Peters' notorious past. A firestorm raged in Hollywood.

Within weeks, both Peters and HarperCollins were threatened with massive litigation. So much so, Peters had to withdraw his book proposal, returning the $700,000. His autobiography might more aptly have been entitled *The Man Who Knew Too Much.*

"Someone let the cat out of the bag even before the cat was in the bag," Peters said. "That cat became a wild jungle tiger on the loose. So before this becomes the story of *The Tiger That Ate Hollywood,* I'm pulling back and cooling it."

When trouble comes in Hollywood, it is often compounded. Currently, Peters is also being sued by Brian Quintana, his co-producer on the film, *Superman: Man of Steel.* In his suit, Quintana charges that he was "sexually roughed up by Peters" and constantly harassed for sexual favors. The relationship between the two former friends is currently more radioactive than Kryptonite.

That in a nutshell is why I choose not to write books about Tom Cruise, Brad Pitt, Arnold Schwarzenegger, Sylvester Stallone, or others among the living. A star like Cruise retains powerful lawyers. As the actor himself said, "I've sued before and I'll sue again."

If I write a book on Cruise, I'll lock it in bank vault with instructions to my heirs," publish it forty years from this date, or whenever." Cruise might live to be 115, and then no one will remember who he was, much less care what he did in his lifetime.

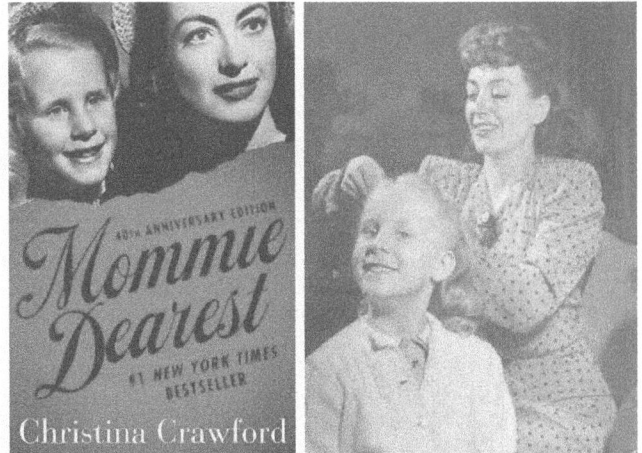

**MOMMIE DEAREST:** This scurrilous, mean-spirited, emotionally destructive book was written by **Christina Crawford** to trash the reputation of **Joan Crawford**, who had adopted her.

It looks like a fun-loving mother and daughter (**Christina** and **Joan Crawford**) enjoying themselves.

The daughter got even with her mother for what might be called "damage to her ego' and for leaving her out of her will.

Many of Joan's friends challenged the accuracy of the book, defining it as a hatchet job. They included Bob Hope, Cesar Romero, Van Johnson, Katharine Hepburn, Barbara Stanwyck, Sydney Guilaroff, Ann Blyth, and Myrna Loy.

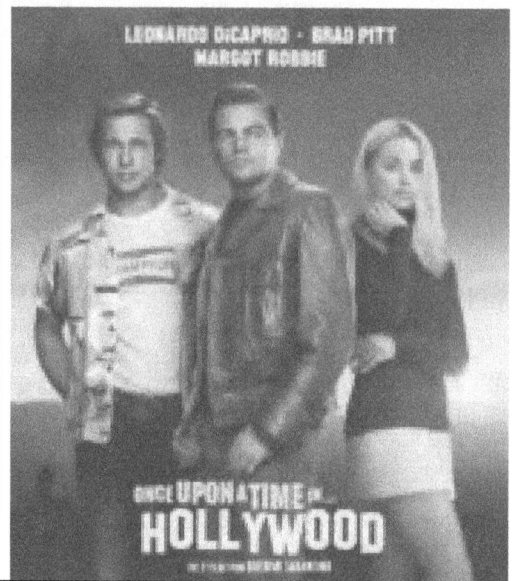

(*Left to right*) **Brad Pitt, Leonardo DiCaprio,** and **Margot Robbie** star in Quentin Tarantino's quirky *Once Upon a Time in Hollywood* (2019).

Set in 1969 Los Angeles, the film follows a fading actor (DiCaprio) and his stunt double (Pit) as they navigate the rapidly changing film industry, with the looming threat of the Sharon Tate murders hanging overhead.

In part because of his vast wealth, **Tom Cruise** is considered the "Mother Lode" for gratuitous lawsuits. Beware, because Mother can (and does) bite back, legally speaking.

Porn performer Kyle Bradford (aka "Chad Slater") was sued by Cruise after he publicly alleged that they had had an affair. Cruise won a mega judgment of $10 million against him—money which, of course, Bradford (aka Slater) did not have.

**Arnold Schwarzenegger** was the world famous Austrian bodybuilder who became the governor of California. His personal life was marred with accusations of drug use and sexual misconduct.

In May of 2011, Maria Shriver, niece of JFK, ended their 25-year relationship. It was revealed that he had fathered a son more that fourteen years earlier with their household's maid.

**John Travolta** has been pestered with rumors that he is gay. He always denied them.

However, in 2017, a sexual assault case was filed against him by the male co-pilot, Doug Gotterba, of one of his planes. Gotterba alleged that he had had a six-year affair with his boss before leaving voluntarily in 1987.

After **Sylvester Stallone** became an overnight film star In *Rocky*, rumors surfaced that earlier in his life, he'd co-starred, nude, in a porn flick. Released in February of 1970, it was originally named *The Party at Kitty and Stud's*, with Stallone cast as Stud. Two days of work brought the actor $200.

After the success of *Rocky*, the porn movie was retitled *The Italian Stallion*. Some of Stallone's detractors rushed to informally rename it as *The Italian Pony.*

**Jon Peters.** His "tell-all" book about damsels in Hollywood (*left to right*, **Zeta-Jones, Streisand, Hayek, Stone,** and many others) was litigated into oblivion, even before publication.

# RYAN O'NEAL

## HOLLYWOOD'S WORST FATHER

LOVE**STORY**
LOVE MEANS NEVER HAVING TO SAY YOU'RE SORRY

Three views of **Tatum O'Neal**: *Upper photo*, with her father, **Ryan O'Neal** in *Paper Moon; middle photo*: after receiving her Best Actress Oscar in 1974; and, *lower photo*, articulate, adult, and in recovery.

Anyone who walks out the door is likely to be caught on camera. Unsuspecting people are sometimes photographed while sitting on the "throne" in a public toilet. Privacy is something you remember nostalgically like that pinup picture of Betty Grable in WWII. This is not the dawning of the "Age of Aquarius" as promised in the musical *Hair*, but the age of the TV reality show. Who needs script-writers any more? More and more celebrities, including Sarah Ferguson and even Bristol Palin, are allowing or going to allow the camera to intrude upon their private lives.

The most glaring example of a celebrity TV reality show, so far, stars Hollywood has-been Ryan O'Neal—nicknamed "Father from Hell"—and his drug-addicted daughter, Tatum, who once had the promise of movie stardom when she starred with dear old dad in *Paper Moon* in 1973, for which she won an Oscar.

Their reality series, *Ryan and Tatum: The O'Neals*, is airing on Oprah Winfrey's new cable channel, OWN. Personal embarrassment seems not to be a problem for this dynamic duo.

Ryan provocatively admits, "I'm a hopeless father. Just look around at my kids. They're either in jail or should be."

In addition to Tatum, Ryan with different women had three sons, Patrick, Redmond, and Griffin.

Although he never married her, Ryan and actress Farrah Fawcett for a time were the most publicized lovers in Hollywood. Farrah captured the imagination of America when she appeared as the star of *Charlie's Angels*, a crime-busting TV series, in 1976. Her tousled blonde hair, called "The Farrah 'Do," was widely adopted by women across America. "My success could only be due to the fact I didn't wear a bra," she said at the time. Her poster became an international best-seller, and her cover-girl face graced hundreds of magazines and tabloids.

As could have been predicted, their love affair was doomed to failure, as Ryan continued his philandering ways with the likes of Joan Collins, Melanie Griffith, Mia Farrow, Bianca Jagger, Liza Minnelli, Linda Ronstadt, Diana Ross, Barbra Streisand—and the beat goes on.

### A LOVE STORY THAT WASN'T

Two views of **Ali MacGraw** with **Ryan O'Neal,** both associated with the most successful and famous movie of 1970. Willdy successful on college campuses in a year when the nation was in chaos, it was received with snickers, tear-jerking sobs, seven Oscar nominations, and box-office receipts of $130 million worldwide, rescuing Paramount Pictures (and its CEO, Robert Evans, MacGraw's husband at the time) from financial disaster.

Critics poked fun at its dewy-eyed , hippy-era plot about "*Love Means Never Having to Say You're Sorry*," but, in the words of Kurt Vonnegut, "Criticizing Love Story was like criticizing a chocolate éclair."

It launched Ryan O'Neal on the road to fame and an often tragic public life.

Ryan's union with Farrah did produce a son, Redmond O'Neal, who as a teenager was arrested on several occasions for possession of drugs. He's been in and out of jails and rehabilitation centers.

Another of Ryan's sons, Griffin, like his sister, Tatum, also had a serious drug problem. In 1983, Ryan knocked out his son's front teeth, and in 2007, he fired gunshots at Griffin while whacking his son's pregnant wife in the head with a fireplace poker.

In a boating accident in 1986, Griffin killed Gian-Carlo Coppola, the son of the famous director Francis Ford Coppola. Ironically, at the time, Ryan was starring in a movie the father was directing. Coppola immediately fired Ryan from the set of *Gardens of Stone*.

Tatum maintained that she was more or less "left on the curb" when Ryan ran off with Farrah. She was also neglected by her mother, Joanna Moore. In her autobiography, Tatum claimed that she was molested by her father's best friend  and was physically and emotionally abused by Ryan himself. She also detailed her own heroin addiction. Ryan denounced her, claiming, "It is a sad day when malicious lies are told in order to become a best-seller."

In 1986, Tatum married the temperamental tennis champion, John McEnroe, the former number one professional player in the United States. Because of Tatum's drug abuse, he was awarded custody of their three children upon their divorce in 1994.

Ryan came back into Farrah's life in 2009 when she was dying of cancer. Her struggle against the disease was recorded in her reality show, which was aired by NBC. This *cinema verité* film was the first time an American celebrity ever allowed herself to be filmed dying.

Redmond attacked his father for coming back into his mother's life. "Ryan is nothing more than a gold-digger," Redmond charged. "He came back to Farrah when she was dying just to get in her will. It was so disgustingly transparent as soon as he found out she was terminal. I consider him a vulture presiding over a carcass."

Redmond won the day. Ryan was cut out of her will, and Redmond was awarded her $6 million estate.

Both Tatum and Ryan showed up at Farrah's funeral. They hadn't seen each other in two decades. It was reported that Ryan, not recognizing his own daughter, came on to Tatum and tried to pick her up.

At the Oscar ceremonies in March of 2010, the Academy of Motion Picture Arts and Sciences excluded mention of Farrah in its "In Memorium" montage, highlighting the recent deaths of such stars as Bea Arthur and Ed McMahon. The unexplained exclusion of a star of Farrah's magnitude was denounced by many members of the academy, including the outspoken Jane Fonda.

Farrah is hardly resting in peace. Lawsuits are still swirling over the NBC documentary of her life. The oncoming drama has all the makings of its own TV reality show, with threats of violence, a death bed transfer of legal rights, and warring lawsuits and counter-lawsuits.

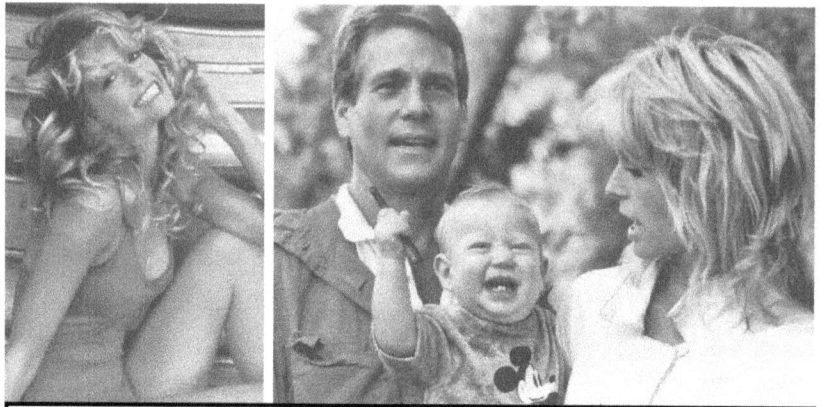

***

*Left photo:* **Farrah Fawcett**, posing as one of *Charlie's Angels* for the poster that evolved into one of the best-selling graphics (twelve million copies) in history.

*Right photo:* **Ryan O'Neal** with his domestic partner **Farrah Fawcett** (they never married) and their infant son, **Redmond**, as they appeared in 1986.

Tatum's hard-driving, high-maintenance husband, tennis champion **John McEnroe**, appears here in a press photo from 2015.

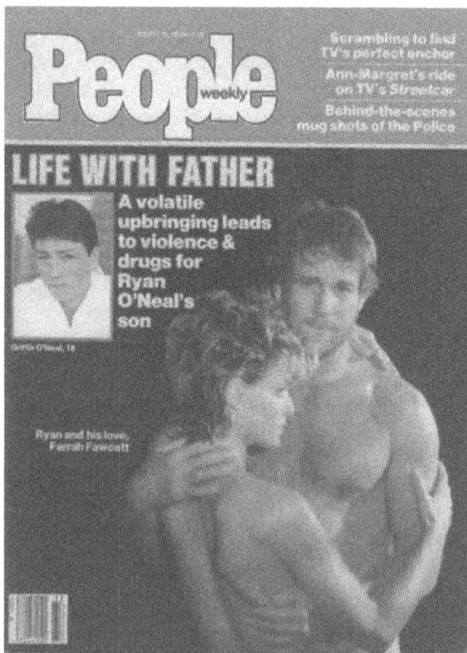

**HOLLYWOOD DYSFUNCTION**: Two views of **Griffin O'Neal**. His relationship with his abusive father was not only not a love story...its violence and horror was widely reviewed in tabloids across the nation.

150

# FARRAH FAWCETT

## THE MOST SOUGHT-AFTER BLONDE IN THE HISTORY OF TELEVISION

Farrah Leni Fawcett was born on the morning of February 2, 1947 in Corpus Christi, Texas. As she grew up, she started winning beauty contests even in her freshman year. In both high school and college, she was voted "most beautiful." She also received that honor in her sophomore, junior, and senior years.

Her photos reached Hollywood agents, and Farrah was summoned to Tinseltown, where she and her blonde hair-do became a sensation. In time, she would win four Primetime Emmy nominations and six Golden Globe nods.

In terms of popularity, her starring role in the hit TV series, *Charlie's Angels*, became a global success. It led to a cottage industry of peripheral products that included both posters and fashion dolls.

Women all over the world tried to imitate her hair-do. At one time, back when movie magazines were popular, she appeared on the cover of eighteen periodicals in just one month.

In the late 1960s, she began to date actor Lee Majors. Born Harvey Lee Yeary in 1939 in Michigan, he later starred in the hit TV series, *The Big Valley* (1965-1969), where Farrah first saw him and told her friends, "He's the sexiest man on television." For the role of Heath Barkley, he beat out 400 actors including Burt Reynolds. His co-star on *The Big Valley* was the formidable Barbara Stanwyck.

He was offered the role of Joe Buck in *Midnight Cowboy* (1969), later voted Best Picture of the Year. However because he had already committed himself to another seasonal series of *The Big Valley*, he had to relinquish the role of the male hustler to Jon Voight, who got an Oscar nod for his performance.

During this period, the tabloids hailed Majors as "the blonde Elvis Presley" because of his resemblance to the singing sensation.

By the time Farrah entered his life, he'd already had one unsuccessful marriage (1961-64) to Kathy Robinson. Apparently, the Fawcett-Majors union was based on love at first sight. They began dating during the late 1960s and were married from 1973-1982.

But by 1979, long before their divorce, she fell in love with another "gorgeous hunk" (her words), Ryan O'Neal.

Their love affair was troubled from the beginning. As she confessed to *TV Guide*, "Sometimes Ryan broke my heart. But he, more than any other person, gives me confidence in myself. I love him. As a lover, I'd call him a dream fantasy come true."

The couple never married, and there were frequent periods of violence, as later revealed by Tatum O'Neal. They gave birth to a son, Redmond James Fawcett O'Neal.

Fawcett (*center*), alongside fellow beauties **Kate Jackson** (*right*) and **Jaclyn Smith** (*left*), starred as a gun-toting law enforcer in the TV series *Charlie's Angels*.

Conceived and produced by the then-hottest name in TV, Aaron Spelling, it premiered to astonishingly high ratings. Critics were less enthusiastic, but the television-watching public loved it, and the three women became overnight sensations—the most beautiful crime-busting trio on TV

For most of his adult life, Redmond struggled with drug addiction, which led to an arrest in 2008 at his Malibu home. He was put on probation but resorted to drugs again.

This led to his probation being revoked, after which he was sentenced to three years in the California Department of Corrections and Rehabilitation.

In 2018, he hit the tabloids again when he was arrested and charged with attempted murder, robbery, assault, and drug possession after he allegedly tried to rob a convenience store in Santa Monica.

Months later, he gave an interview to a reporter from the *Los Angeles Times:* "I blame my troubles on two people, Farrah Fawcett and Ryan O'Neal."

**Ryan O'Neal** (*left*) with his son, **Redmond,** during a cringeworthy reunion.

The biological son of O'Neal with Fawcett, Redmond was named after Redmond Lyndon, the swashbuckling 18th-century adventurer that O'Neal, *père*, had portrayed in the rollicking Restoration-era saga, *Barry Lyndon* (1975)

# THE UNHAPPY FINAL YEARS OF RYAN O'NEAL

On February 8, 2023, television and news media announced the death of Ryan O'Neal at the age of 82. His son, Patrick O'Neal, revealed his death to the press, without giving the cause or the place. During the previous few months, the actor who had enchanted the world in *Love Story* with Ali MacGraw, was reported to be suffering from "health problems."

The star and former boxer was known for "having the face of a good guy and a gift of mixing wit and innocence. *The New Yori Times* headlined him as "The Master of Meet-Cute."

In an obituary, Ronald Bergan encapsulated the essence of O'Neal. "With his blonde good looks and blue eyes, he was often cast as a callow, boy-next-door type in 1970s films that made him internationally famous. Back then, his clean-cut, on-screen image offered few clues about the notoriety of his private life. But his troubled relationship with three of his children, Tatum, Griffin, and Redmond, his drug-taking, and tempestuous relationship with Farrah Fawcett, would come to overshadow his long, fluctuating acting career."

Other than *Love Story*, O'Neal's second most popular film was *Paper Moon* (1973), in which he co-starred with his daughter Tatum. At the age of 10, she became the youngest actress to win an Oscar.

Another huge success for O'Neal was *Barry Lyndon* (1975), a historical drama based on an 1844 novel by Thackeray that was directed by Stanley Kubrick. It recounts the philandering exploits of an 18th Century Anglo-Irish rogue and gold digger who eventually marries a wealthy widow.

At the 48th Academy Awards presentation, *Barry Lyndon* was nominated for Best Picture. It also won four Oscars, including Best Cinematography.

O'Neal was born on April 20, 1941, in Los Angeles, just months before America went to war. Of Irish and English descent, he was the son of Charles O'Neal, known as "Blackie," a novelist and Hollywood screenwriter.

Ryan O'Neal married his first wife in 1963, and the couple produced two children, Tatum and Griffin. "I got married at 21, and I was not a real mature 21," O'Neal later claimed.

His second marriage was to Leigh Taylor-Young (1967-1974), with whom he had a son, Patrick. He had fallen in love with her when they co-starred in the hit daytime-TV series, *Peyton Place* (1964-1969).

His longest relationship was with Farrah Fawcett, from 1979-1997, and after a separation, again from 2001-2009. The couple never married, but had a son, Redmond, who was named after O'Neal's character in *Barry Lyndon*.

O'Neal was diagnosed with chronic Myelgenous leukemia in 2001. He was frequently seen at the bedside of Fawcett as she battled cancer before her death in 2009.

In April of 2012, O'Neal battled prostate cancer.

He told *People* magazine, "For Farrah and me, it was *Love Story* acted out in real life. I just don't know how to play this one. I won't know this world without her. Cancer is an insidious enemy."

Before the music stopped and the lights went out: A late-in-life publicity photo of **Ryan O'Neal.**

*Barry Lyndon* (1975) was **Stanley Kubrick**'s Restoration costume drama that had everyone going *ga-ga* over the Irish-American (**Ryan O'Neal**) who played the Anglo-Irish rogue.

In the *left photo*, **Kubrick and crew** pose with **O'Neal**, who's clad in 18th-century finery and ready for his closeup. Lavishly costumed, the film received seven Oscar nominations, including Best Picture. It won four Oscars, including Best Cinematorgraphy

*RIGHT PHOTO*: **O'Neal** appears as himself on a California beach in a widely reproduced photo that helped to entrench him as a heartthrob among young women and gay men.

# HOW DARWIN PORTER
## (THROUGH BLOOD MOON PRODUCTIONS)
# BROUGHT BABYLON
## (IN THREE VOLUMES)
# BACK TO HOLLYWOOD

# HOLLYWOOD REMEMBERED

### By Danforth Prince

When **Kenneth Anger**'s tame and tepid duet of Babylons were published in Paris in the early 1960s, they raised censorship hackles across America

Today, they seem mild and rather quaint—tepid **oooh-la-las** and a litany of twice-told tales of Tinseltown already known to millions of movie fans. They contain such revelations as "Elizabeth Taylor got fat," and "J. Edgar Hoover investigated Jean Seberg."

Beginning in 2008, **Darwin Porter** matched and surpassed the Kenneth Anger legend by doing him, "one, two, and three" better.

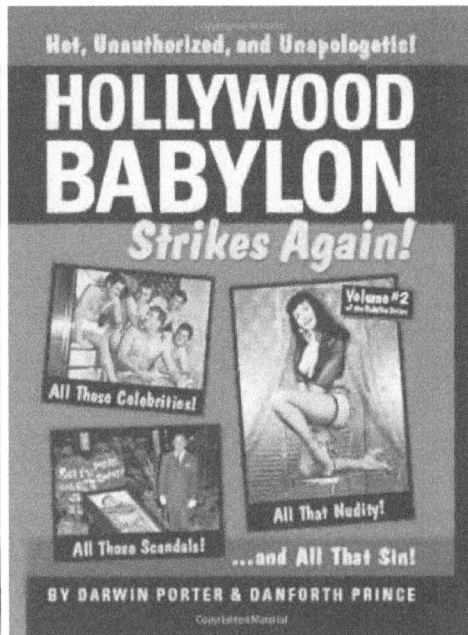

## No Longer New, but Still Pertinent, Unauthorized, and Hot

*Babylon* has been used as a metaphor for sin and depravity since Biblical times, and its association with the film community is by now familiar to manyAmericans. The first edition of **_Hollywood Babylon_**, penned in the 1960s, by avant-garde filmmaker Kenneth Anger, was rejected by virtually every US publisher who saw it as too libelous to print. Consequently, it was first released in Paris, with its eventual U.S. release delayed until 1975.

It became a grass-roots, scandal-tinged success, with Elizabeth Taylor depicted as a grotesque, jewel-draped slob on one of its covers, and then-shocking revelations about Hollywood which by today's standards look almost demure.

Ironically, its title became more famous than any individual revelation contained within its covers. Who today, thanks to that book, doesn't associate *Babylon* with *La-La land* and the film community's ongoing addiction to depravity and excess? Post-millennium, rumblings within the publishing world hinted at the need for an update that reflected changing standards, changing times, and a changing cast of actors. Ulysses himself would have found such an Odyssey daunting.

Veteran *spinmeister* Darwin Porter responded with **_Hollywood Babylon—It's Back_**. But be warned: his newest title is anything but coy and demure. The publisher, Blood Moon, describes it as "an overview of exhibitionism, sexuality, and sin as filtered through 85 years of Hollywood scandal."

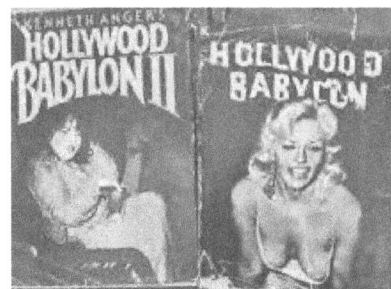

**_Hollywood Babylon—It's Back_**, and its saucy sequel, **_Hollywood Babylon Strikes Again_**, by Darwin Porter and Danforth Prince through Blood Moon Productions. Each is a hardcover with at least 400 pages and about a thousand *risqué* pictures. Each volume is unique, unprecedented, and available online from Amazon.com and at fine bookstores everywhere.

153

In distinct contrast to 21st-century tabloids which focus on the oft-repeated antics of bimbos, nymphets, and looney-toons who are younger than my grandchildren (and usually a lot less interesting), Porter steps back for a historian's overview of the embarrassments of life in the entertainment-industry's fast lane. It's akin to a roll in the hay with a library-friendly chronicler of pop culture who's surprisingly brainy. "Lurid," (once a naughty word) in this case approaches something of an art form.

My favorite part? Paris (what's her name?) Hilton and the way-overexposed Britney Spears are barely mentioned, thank god, but scandalous allusions to Ava Gardner, Bette Davis, mobster Mickey Cohen, Barbara Hutton, Elvis, Mae West, Nancy Reagan, and MM are rife. There's stuff about Rock Hudson, Guy Madison, Sal Mineo, and *Johnny Yuma, the Rebel* (Nick Adams—remember him?) that will curl your hair. Cary Grant plays a role as a doting father to his adopted son through Babs Hutton, Doris Duke as a jazz-baby nympho gets her turn, Weissmuller and the Tarzan Yell take on new meanings, and there's stuff about Judy Garland and her almost-last rites that will probably make the movie history books. The shenanigans of modern-day bad boys aren't ignored, either. I'll never think of *The Terminator,* Ewan McGregor, or *Cruise Control* in the same way ever again.

Writer James Elroy once defined L.A. as "a smog-shrouded netherworld orbiting under a dark star, blinded by the glare of scandal-rag flashbulbs." This book picks up where that quote ended. The theatrics it examines were, till now, so far underground that no journalist who wanted to live would have dared, at the time they occurred, to publicize them. All of that changed with the release of this book.

This is the most hip and least reverent movie book in the history of publishing, but despite the litany of sins it examines, it nonetheless conveys Porter's deep affection for films, and the power they exerted on the fabric of the American experience. Bring a sense of humor and an open mind, and prepare to be WOWed by what's inside. It gives new meaning to the Good, the Bad, and the Fabulous.

Immediately below is how Blood Moon defines its authors' love affair with the somewhat soiled inner sanctums of the entertainment industry:

To those who love her, Hollywood was and is a gossipy, mendacious (Big Daddy's word) and whorish place that remains captivating despite the passage of time. In this, the reinterpretation of ***Hollywood Babylon***, it's depicted at its sleaziest, most venal, and most deliciously unseemly.

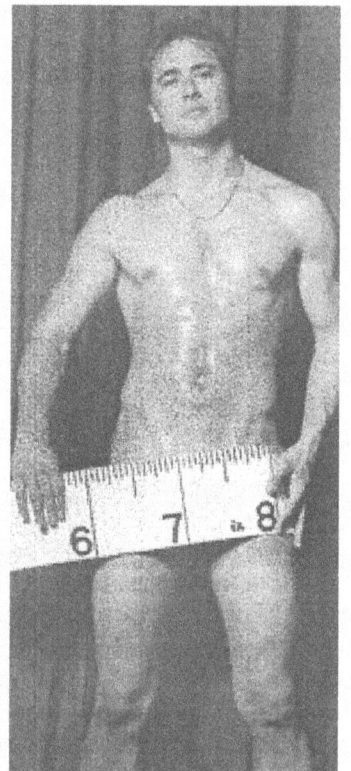

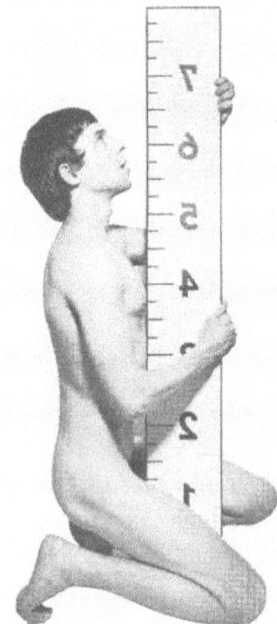

## Well-Hung Hollywood & Penile Pertinence

*Ask Lana! Ask Ava! Ask Monty! Ask George! Ask Clara!*

## To Succeed in Woody-town, It Sometimes Takes More Than Just Talent

THEN, IN TIME FOR THE HOLIDAYS, 2021, BLOOD MOON SUPPLEMENTED VOLUMES ONE AND TWO OF THEIR BABYLON SERIES WITH THIS: THE ULTIMATE YULETIDE COFFEE TABLE BOOK:

HOT, SHOW-BIZZY, UNAUTHORIZED, UNAPOLOGETIC, AND NEWSWORTHY FROM BLOOD MOON PRODUCTIONS: **A NEW AND EXPANDED EDITION OF THE SCANDALOUS ANTHOLOGY** THAT MADE US FAMOUS WHEN ITS (SMALLER, THINNER) PREDECESSOR FIRST APPEARED IN 2008. THIS TIME, WE'RE CALLING IT:

# *HOLLYWOOD BABYLON*
# *WITH DETOURS TO GOMORRAH*

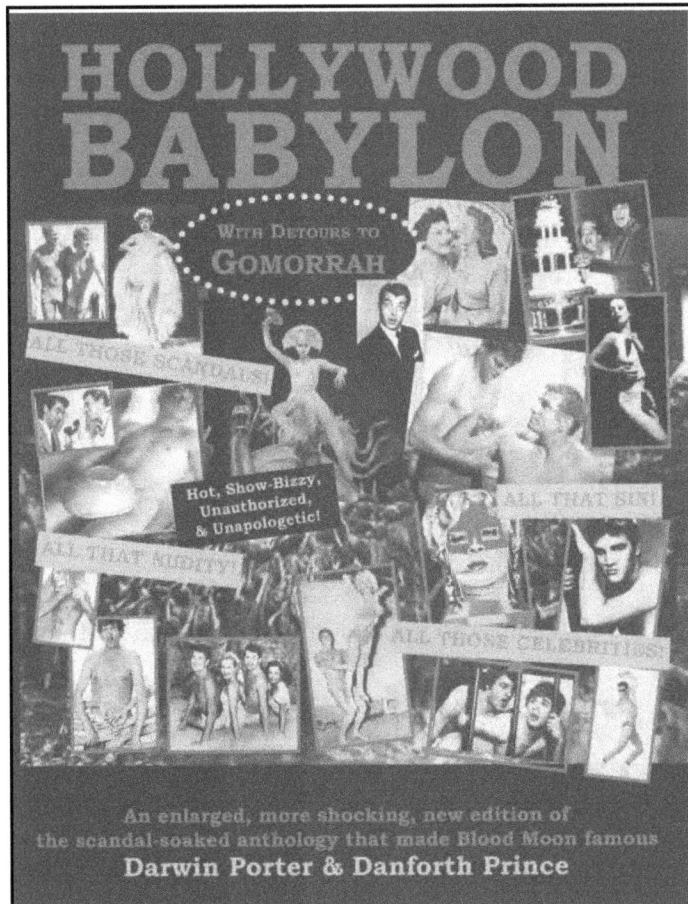

HOLLYWOOD BABYLON

WITH DETOURS TO GOMORRAH

ALL THOSE SCANDALS!

Hot, Show-Bizzy, Unauthorized, & Unapologetic!

ALL THAT SIN!

ALL THAT NUDITY!

ALL THOSE CELEBRITIES!

An enlarged, more shocking, new edition of the scandal-soaked anthology that made Blood Moon famous
**Darwin Porter & Danforth Prince**

ALL THE SCANDAL PREVIOUSLY UNFIT TO PRINT

ANOTHER DARING COMPILATION OF UNMENTIONABLES FROM THE PEAK YEARS OF AMERICA'S ENTERTAINMENT INDUSTRY

LURID BUT AMUSING IMPROPRIETIES FROM HOLLYWOOD'S GOLDEN AGE AND BEYOND

HOT, UNAUTHORIZED, UNAPOLOGETIC, AND SHAMELESS
*"Dishing with abandon, the authors spare no one—especially not the dead."*
—Rush & Molloy, *The NY Daily News*

BLOOD MOON: APPLYING THE TABLOID STANDARDS OF TODAY TO THE SCANDALS OF HOLLYWOOD'S GOLDEN AGE.

IT'S A TOUGH JOB, BUT SOMEBODY'S GOT TO DO IT!
www.BloodMoonProductions.com

ISBN 978-1-936003-88-4
56000

Dishing with abandon, the authors spare no one--especially not the dead. Marilyn Monroe had an affair with Ronald Reagan. Marilyn also had a tryst with Joan Crawford but refused to make it an ongoing liaison. James Dean showed a disconcerting interest in a 12-year old boy in the early 1950s. Lucille Ball launched herself into show business as a hooker, and her husband Desi Arnaz had a fling with Cesar Romero. Cary Grant had an incestuous relationship with his stepson, Lance Reventlow. And this, by the way, is only the tip of the iceberg."

**Rush & Molloy, *The NY Daily News***

# MAKING AMERICA GREAT AGAIN

## FOR IMMEDIATE RELEASE, FROM BLOOD MOON PRODUCTIONS

# *Hollywood Babylon, with Detours to Gomorrah*

**In the tradition of GREAT AMERICAN GOSSIP**, Blood Moon offers this COMPELLING ANTHOLOGY OF GOSSIP to anyone who ever had any nagging questions about Show-biz indiscretion, mendacity, and excess.

**WHAT IS IT?**   According to Blood Moon's President, Danforth Prince, "It's the best feature-length compendium of Hollywood gossip ever compiled, lavishly illustrated, and loaded with examples of the PR hurricanes generated by the false gods of fame, physical beauty, lust, greed, narcissism, and exhibitionism. This book might not be everybody's fantasy about what they really wanna crawl into bed with, but as a publishing phenomenon, it's the very best of its genre."

**HOW HAS IT BEEN REVIEWED SINCE ITS FIRST EDITION?**
**ANSWER**: With spectacular praise and enthusiasm from publications that include the NY DAILY NEWS, London's EXPRESS, a passel of entertainment-industry publications "Down Under," and show-biz blogsites around the world.

**HOW BIG IS IT AND HOW MUCH DOES IT COST?**
**ANSWER**:  This anthology was conceived and designed as a softcover **COLLECTOR'S ITEM** for placement on COFFEE TABLES in living rooms that need a little nudge. It has a BIG footprint—something akin to an 8 1/2 x 11" news magazine—and the central image of its front cover is Fritz Lang's 1920s 'perhaps demented' image of THE WHORE OF BABYLON. Debauched and persuasive, she hovers over a passel of spectacularly famous, partially undressed celebrities culled from a century of show-biz mania.  In this case, you can acquire her "favors" for $60.

Danforth Prince continued: "We're marketing this as the most lewdly sophisticated 'coffee table book' of the holiday season. It's a one-of-a-kind 'conversation stopper' or (depending on your point of view) 'conversation starter.'  This is a 'hipster to hipster' gift you'd give to an embittered survivor who's already deeply familiar with the casting couch.   It's the best accumulation of tabloid trauma ever published....a drunken sorority party's first prize; a 'I'm ready for another martini' cocktail *klatsch's* most embarassing panty raid."

"We've doubled its content from its previous edition," Prince continued, "by adding the 'concentrated cream' from ripsnorting OTHER biographies within Blood Moon's (very extensive) backlist.  This anthology is what happens when Classic Hollywood gets down and low with the literary *avant-garde* of the Fabulous 50s, the Free Love Sixties; the Sexy Seventies, and the big-haired teledrama-driven Eighties."

"WHO'S NEW?** There's More about Ronald Reagan and Nancy than you might wanna know, and a cross-section of ONCE AGAIN IN THE NEWS stars you might, if not for this book, have forgotten."

**IT'S BACK.! IT'S BABYLON!** And it's available everywhere, now, through **Amazon.com, Barnes & Noble.com** and other online booksellers worldwide.

## HOLLYWOOD BABYLON with DETOURS TO GOMORRAH
**By Darwin Porter and Danforth Prince      www.BloodMoonProductions.com**
**488 pages, 8 1/2" x 11" softcover.  ISBN 978-1-936003-88-4**

## A ONE-OF-A-KIND COLLECTOR'S ITEM AND COFFEE TABLE SHOWPIECE.

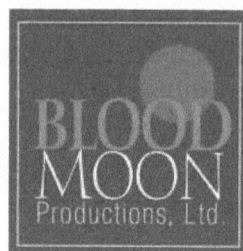

156

# MICKEY ROONEY

## THE RUNT WHO SEDUCED HOLLYWOOD

"I was a 14-year-old boy for 30 years," says Mickey Rooney, "The Runt," who stands tall at 5 feet, 3 inches. Born in 1920 at the time Warren Harding was elected president, the trouper is still going strong at 90, his most recent engagement at the Regency Hotel in New York. He appears with his wife, the singer, Jan Rooney, whom he married in 1978.

Jan is Mickey's eighth wife. "I finally got it right," he said. The first wife was the sultry beauty Ava Gardner, whom he married for a brief time in 1942. That marriage seemed doomed from the beginning. On her honeymoon night, she told him, "if you ever knock me up, you son of a bitch, I'll kill you."

In between love affairs with every beauty from Lana Turner to Betty Grable, Mickey had seven other wives. "I'm the only man who had a marriage license made out TO WHOM IT MAY CONCERN. He got stuck with a lot of alimony payments. "Paying alimony is like pumping gas into another man's car," he said. "Always get married early in the morning," Rooney claimed. "That way, if it doesn't work out, you haven't wasted a day."

Mickey didn't divorce each of his wives, notably Carolyn Mitchell (voted "the prettiest gal in Phoenix"). His wife's lover shot her in the head be-

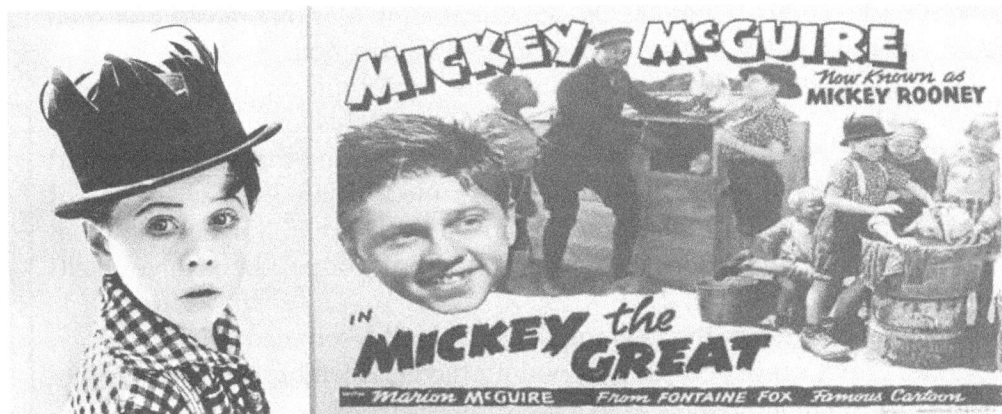

**Mickey Rooney** began his career as a child actor, a silent-screen star known at the time as **Mickey McGuire**, a name that inspired the name Walt Disney later affixed to his cartoon character of Mickey Mouse.

McGuire (aka Rooney) grew up fast, evolving into a sex-savvy prodigy who was almost frighteningly precocious, in ways that might be interpreted today as "manic."

Even as an early teen, **Rooney** was often maneuvered into roles that focused on his fast-growing image as a male who was good with (or at least obsessively intrigued with) females.

In the *left photo*, above, as Andy Hardy, he's winsomely embraced by **Judy Garland.** In the *right photo*, he's depicted with **Ava Gardner** after their widely publicized wedding in 1942. Although each of them would move briskly on to other marriages (in Mickey's case, eight), it was a widely publicized "first" for each of them.

**Rooney** became known for being extravagantly well-connected (*as shown in the left photo* with **Clark Gable**), and with MGM head, **Louis B. Mayer** (*right photo*) during a 1939 press and PR photoshoot at Mayer's Santa Monica Beach house. Who's in the center. cutting the cake? It's DOROTHY (**Judy Garland**), the 'impossibly famous' recent star of *The Wizard of Oz.*

fore committing suicide himself.

Born to vaudeville parents, Mickey made his first stage appearance in 1922 before he was two. As an infant, he actually slept backstage in a steamer trunk.

He went on to lodge 88 years in show business, presumably a world's record. He's the only living screen actor who starred in silents—billed as Mickey McGuire in those days. Allegedly, Walt Disney named the cartoon character of Mickey Mouse after him.

At his peak, Mickey outgrossed James Cagney, Spencer Tracy, and Clark Gable at the box office. Laurence Olivier, Cary Grant, Marlon Brando, and even Fred Astaire hailed Mickey as the best actor in Hollywood.

During the 30s and 40s, Mickey played the prototypical movie teenager in the Andy Hardy series, often opposite Judy Garland, his longtime pal.

Mickey's boss, MGM honcho Louis B. Mayer, learned that his 16-year-old super star was having an affair with 36-year-old Norma Shearer, widow of MGM *Wunderkind* Irving Thalberg. "You're Andy Hardy," Mayer shouted at him. "You're the United States! You're the Stars and Stripes! Behave yourself! You're a symbol!"

At the time, Shearer, the reigning queen at MGM, seduced young Mickey, he was already experienced in the boudoir, having been broken in at the age of ten by a girl named "Ann," aged 11.

Mickey reached his sexual apogee in the 1940s at an orgy, when he "serviced" 16 Japanese women.

Although he made more than $600 million for the film studios, Mickey ended up bankrupt and drug addicted. Then, as he claims, an angel appeared to him in a coffee shop and turned his life around.

After meeting Jan, he settled down and has even become a born again Christian.

He admits that his biggest career mistake involved turning down the role of Archie Bunker in the hit TV series *All in the Family* in 1971. Mickey has made 361 movies, the latest being *Night Club,* co-starring Ernest Borgnine. "Borgnine is a jerk," Mickey claims.

In my last interview with Mickey, I asked him if he ever planned to retire. He's already lost his singing voice and dance steps, but none of his charm.

"My motto," he said, "is don't retire—INSPIRE!"

"And how can you do that?" I asked.

"Just remember one thing," he said. "Failure is the thing you pass on the way to success."

Heading out the door, he had some parting words. "You must remember this. I was the number one star in the world. Hear me? THE WORLD!"

**MICK ROONEY'S WIFE NO. 5 SLAIN**

*Find Jealous Lover a Suicide*

Estranged Wife and Actor Were to Reconcile

**All of His (Eight) Marriages Didn't End in Divorce**

During the course of their marriage, one of them, **Carolyn Mitchell** (aka **Barbara-Ann Thomason**), was murdered by her boyfriend-at-the-time (Milos Milosec, a Yugoslav-born stand-in for Alain Delon) who committed suicide (on top of her) a few minutes after shooting her in the head.

Mitchell, an aficionado of bodybuilding and weight-lifting, appears *above left* in 1954 after being crowned "Miss Muscle Beach." In preparation for her win, she went on a month-long "starvation diet," during which she ate one meal every three days, thereby fast-losing, it was alleged, eight pounds.

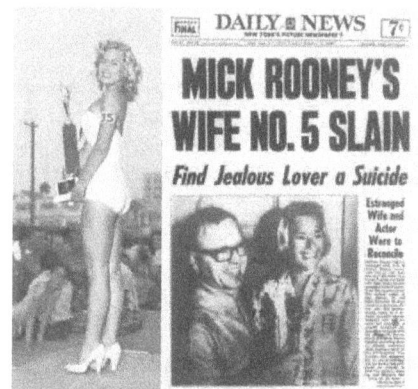

**CABARET**SCENES

YOUR NIGHTCLUB GUIDE SEPTEMBER 2010 $4.50 USA

Jan & Mickey Rooney

54 Cabaret Reviews

Gary Marshall

Cabaret Hotline Online 20th Anniversary Gala

Peter Leavy

**Making News Again, This Time on the Cabaret Circuit**

**Mickey Rooney** with his eighth and final wife and stage partner, **Jan Rooney.**

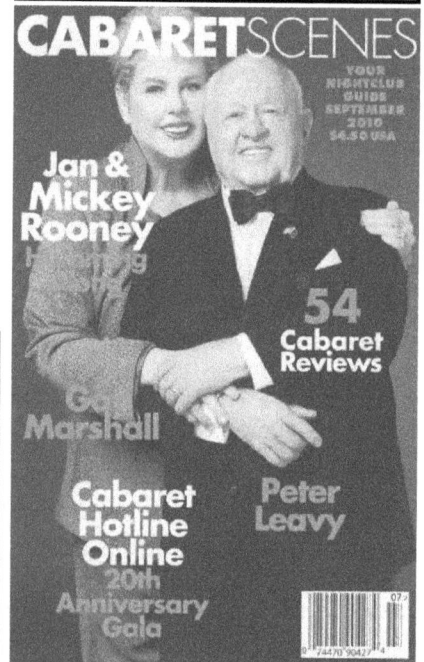

**Others of Mickey Rooney's Inamorata:**

**Lana Turner** *(left)***,** and (as she appeared in 1926), **Norma Shearer**

# JANE RUSSELL

## Even Christians Have Bosoms

The world took little notice of the passing of the sultry, busty brunette, actress Jane Russell, who died of respiratory failure in March of 2011 at her home in Santa Monica. She was 89.

Boys or young men growing up in the late 1940s and early 50s often had a picture of Jane taped to their locker room door. It depicted her in a cleavage-revealing blouse falling off one shoulder as she rested in a haystack holding a gun. The scene was from the most notorious A-list film of the 1940s, Howard Hughes' controversial *The Outlaw*, shot in 1941. Jane was cast as a sagebrush vixen, Rio McDonald, playing opposite an equally sexy Jack Buetel as Billy the Kid. The film provoked one of America's greatest censorship battles, with Hughes eventually emerging triumphant.

Tons of newsprint centered on a specially engineered bra that Hughes had designed for his 38D leading lady. But Jane later claimed she tossed it in the wastepaper basket and wore her own support.

Tame by today's standards, *The Outlaw* played for nine weeks in San Francisco in 1943, Hughes advertising it as "Two good reasons to go see this film." Then he put it in mothballs until a 1947 New York opening. It wasn't until 1950 that Florida residents got to see it.

For most of her life, Jane was under contract to Hughes. Her most memorable film was the 1953 *Gentlemen Prefer Blondes*, in which she co-starred with Marilyn Monroe. The blonde bombshell just seemed to ooze femininity whereas Jane came off as brusquely butch.

Although a great success, the movie marked Jane's decline. Her haystack picture came down from those locker walls to be replaced by MM's nude calendar. Even though Jane's career fizzled, she came back into the public spotlight in the 70s and 80s when she was the TV spokeswoman for Playtex bras, hawking them for "full-figured gals like me."

After a botched abortion in 1942 before she married her high school sweetheart, U.C.L.A. football player Bob Waterfield, Jane could never have any more children. She became an outspoken opponent of abortion and an advocate of adoption, founding the World Adoption International Fund in the 1950s.

After nearly a quarter of a century of married life with Waterfield, she divorced him when she caught him "playing around." In 1968 she married actor Robert Barrett, who died three months later of a heart attack. In 1974, she wed a retired Air Force Lieutenant, John Calvin Peoples. Before his death in 1999, she became an alcoholic for several years before rehabilitation.

Robert Mitchum, Jane's sleepy-eyed, sardonic co-star in *His Kind of Woman* and *Macao*, once said, "Minnesota-born Ernestine Jane Geraldine Russell showed the world what a gal with a pair of knockers could do."

Although Jane slept with some of her leading men, notably Mitchum and Victor Mature, she later claimed "my longest running affair was with a living doll." By that, she meant God.

Unlike most Hollywood sex symbols such as Lana Turner, Jane spent most of her life as a devout Christian. "I'm a teetotal, mean-spirited, right wing, narrow-minded, conservative Christian bigot, but not a racist," she said. "Bigotry just means I don't have an open mind."

Even though Jane and MM are gone, we suspect that some two-hundred years from now they will still be appearing in their classic duet, thrilling future audiences with their "Two Little Girls from Little Rock."

As one WWII veteran remembered, "Jane was not the girl next door. She was

Although as time went by, **Jane Russell** *(right photo*, above) developed an extensive fan base of her own, her beginnings in Hollywood derived from the "favored status" she (and her breasts) enjoyed with the demented billionaire and aviator, **Howard Hughes** *(left photo above).*

"Jack Buetel, my co-sar in *The Outlaw*, dropped trou for Hughes, but I continued to resist him."

Howard Hughes spent obsessive hours arranging details associated with the brassiere of an "artfully unclad' **Jane Russell** for photoshoots promoting **The Outlaw**, his ode to Billy the Kid and the Wild West.

**Jane Russell,** early in her marriage to her high school sweetheart, football hero **Bob Waterfield.**

lust, desire, and everything good boys weren't supposed to dream about."

In summation of her life, Russell claimed that she always knew "if I could just hold tough a little longer, I'd find myself around one more dark corner, see one more spot of light and have one more drop of pure joy in this journey called life."

Self-admitted sex fiend and "bad boy" **Robert Mitchum,** with the by-then-well-established film star, **Jane Russell,** in *His Kind of Woman*.

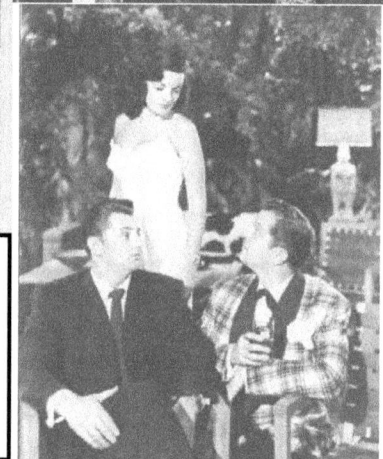

**MATURE PASSION in LAS VEGAS**

Three views of **Jane Russell** with **Victor Mature** in *The Las Vegas Story.* The photo in the *lower right* also includes **Vincent Price.**

**Russell:** As glam as the era got

Two views of **Jane Russell** in *Gentlemen Prefer Blondes* (1953)

*Upper photo:* **Jane** admires a gymnast; *Lower photo:* **Jane,** with **Marilyn Monroe,** lament their (improbable) status as "gold diggers without dates."

**MM** (left) and **Jane Russell** displaying radically different seductive styles in this "Blonde vs. Brunette" dance number, "Just Two Little Girls from Little Rock" in *Gentlemen Prefer Blondes* (1953).

**IRONIES, HUMILIATIONS, SHOW BIZ, AND THE MARCH OF TIME**

Curvy, full-figured **Jane Russell,** perhaps remembering her previous gig as a muse for Howard Hughes, tele-promoting a product from Playtex marketed as a "Living Bra."

160

# LESBIANS, EARLY HOLLYWOOD, & THE GOLDEN AGE OF AMERICAN THEATER

Darwin Porter's new biography of
**MERCEDES DE ACOSTA**
addresses the female version of
THE LOVE THAT DARES NOT SPEAK ITS NAME
as it applied to the early days of American show-biz

A self-defined "seductress of beautiful women" and the by-product of an immense fortune, lesbian activist **Mercedes de Acosta** (born in 1892) was descended from Spain's Dukes of Alba and a beneficiary of the best education and best social skills that her parents' Gilded Age fortune could buy. From her perch within the aristocracy of the Belle Epoque, and continuing as an arts-industry "swinger" until her death in 1968, she became notorious for seducing—and then "outing "--at least a dozen women who fast-evolved into the most widely publicized and romantically "unattainable" celebrities in the world. Her heyday coincided with the sexually permissive "Pre-Code" free-for-all of the Silent Screen and Hollywood's early talkies.

Her lovers included the self-enchanted silent screen mogul, **Nazimova**; the "live fast and die young" tragedienne **Jeanne Eagels**; the blue-blooded aristocrat of the Jazz Age's Broadway stage (**Katharine Cornell**); the most famous film goddess of the 30s and early 40s (**Greta Garbo**), and at least a dozen others. Within the deeply entrenched, phobically closeted lesbian circles of the first half of the American century, Mercedes became quirkily famous as "Hollywood's Greatest Lover."

One of her paramours, the German-born bisexual **Marlene Dietrich**, put Mercedes' promiscuous indiscretions into context: "During Germany's Weimar Republic (1919-1933), in places like Berlin, Paris, London, and in the dives and cabarets of Hollywood and New York, promiscuity was rampant and without any particular preference for any specific gender."

In 1960, Mercedes published a "watered down" memoir (*Here Lies the Heart*) that instantly became notorious. In it, she "outed" many of her same-sex partners. A few years later—aged, crippled, blind in one eye, and desperately in need of money—she sold, for publication, some of the love letters addressed to her decades ago from, among others, **Greta Garbo**. Near the end of her life, within his home, **Magnolia House in Staten Island**, she was frank, unvarnished, and unapologetic during extensive interviews with the film historian, Darwin Porter.

The fruits of those interviews, and that friendship, are now revealed, posthumously, within the pages of this book. We at Blood Moon present it as a testimonial to a flamboyant, never-to-be-repeated combination of lesbian love and same-sex yearning during the Golden Age of early Hollywood & the American theater.   No other book has ever interconnected so many dots. No one, until now, ever had the courage.

A self-admitted lesbian in an age when it wasn't fashionable, **Mercedes De Acosta** forged links to some of the most of the creative geniuses of her era. Her knack for celebrating Sapphic love made her one of the most controversial socialites of her era.

Adored by the female cognoscenti of the U.S. and Europe, she "sealed her social doom' (her words) after she "outed: many of her former confidants (including Greta Garbo) in a notorious memoir (*Here Lies the Heart*) published in 1960.

Near the end of her tumultuous and tragic life, she granted interviews to Darwin Porter with the full understanding that he'd one day publish a memorial to her life and times.

Some of those revelations and "confessions," along with insights into the "haute celebrities' of her heyday, appear in the pages that follow.

**Magnolia House,** a landmarked 19th-Century home in Staten Island, has been described as "A *grande dame* with a knack for nurturing creative eccentrics."

It was here that Darwin's interviews with his illustrious friend, **Mercedes de Acosta,** unfolded.

MERCEDES DE ACOSTA WAS THE ENABLER, INSPIRATION, MUSE, MENTOR, AND SEDUCTRESS
OF SOME OF THE WORLD'S GREATEST ACTRESSES.

## As Reviewed by Diane Donovan

### The Seductive Sapphic Exploits of Mercedes de Acosta, Hollywood's Greatest Lover

**contains all the draw of a gossip piece paired with the** seductive lure of sexual exploits among the rich and famous. It reviews the life of **Mercedes de Acosta**, a celebrity whose passions rivaled the most notorious lovers in early 20th century history. It's also a preview of the empowerment of women in an era when America and Europe produced legions of cultural giants, many of them women, rising in every manifestation of the arts, especially theater, filmmaking, and literature.

**Mercedes,** a Spanish beauty confessed stories about these world-romping exploits to film historian **Darwin Porter** in the last years of her life, but this biography explores the stories behind these confessions, using firsthand accounts to explore circumstances before and after these affairs.

For those not in the know about Mercedes de Acosta, she was a lesbian activist born in 1893, descended from Spanish aristocracy to a life of wealth and privilege. She became notorious for seducing socialites. Her lovers included some of the biggest names in Hollywood, from silent film actresses to the new 'talkie' stars.

More than just a survey of her sexual exploits, Porter and Prince embrace the extent of Hollywood's politics and social scene, from actors and actresses to producers, filmmakers, and Darwin's own relationship with Mercedes.

Black and white photos and illustrations abound, as do sidebars of Hollywood news events, giving the biography the drama and feel of real life events. It moves through how Mercedes's role as a translator and 'tour guide' introduced others to the world of "Old Spain" pre-war to her involvement in New York stage productions and the personal lives of actresses who flocked to her Manhattan townhouse.

While readers might anticipate the spotlight will always shine on Mercedes, much background information is included about many other famous figures who operated during that time, from American stage and film actress (and former Ziegfeld Girl) Jeanne Eagels to the ravishing part time lesbian lover Natacha Rambova, who entered Mercedes' life steeped in the allure and mystery of Old Russia. **Also reviewed in rich detail is the saga of Mercedes' decade-long affair with Greta Garbo** (later exposed in her memoirs, published in 1960), her (shorter) liaison with **Marlene Dietrich**, her interchanges with **Gertrude Stein**, and lengthy insights into such then-stellar stage and film luminaries as **Katharine Cornell, Tallulah Bankhead,** and **Nazimova.**

The events, personalities, politics, and social milieu are fully explored with a sassy and lively inspection that takes Mercedes de Acosta's exploits and elevates them into a rich social and cinematic commentary on Hollywood's relationships and evolving sexual female figures.

Any reader interested in more than a staid survey of Hollywood history—one which delves into the interrelationships and sexual exploits of its major participants—will find *The Seductive Sapphic Exploits of Mercedes de Acosta: Hollywood's Greatest Lover* much more than a singular production. It holds the power to attract a wide audience; especially those who relish the high drama and social commentary of gossip, **the struggle for self-expression,** and eye-popping truths.

**Diane Donovan,**
Senior Reviewer for
*California Bookwatch* and
the *Midwest Book Review*

Midwest Book Review

Publicity photo of **Mercedes de Acosta**, as it appeared in *Here Lies the Heart,* the memoir that enraged many of her previous A-list lovers. Published in 1960, it opened with this epitaph:

*"When I was young, the Spanish painter,* **Ignacio Zuloago,** *said to me, "All great people function with the heart." He placed his hand over my physical heart and continued, "Here lies the heart. Always remember to think with it, to feel with it, and above all, to judge with it."*

*"Many years later, when I was in India in 1938, the great Sage,* **Ramana Maharshi,** *placed his hand on my right breast and said, "Here lies the Heart—the Dynamic, Spiritual Heart. Learn to find The Self in it."*

*"The Enlightened One raised the artist's counsel to a higher level. Both, at just the right moment, showed me The Way."*

162

Seattle GAY NEWS

Seattle GAY NEWS

**Mercedes De Acosta**
at the beach in 1910

**Maggie Bloodstone**
Contributing Writer to the
*Seattle Gay News*

# Some of the best reads of 2020

by Maggie Bloodstone
*SGN* Contributing Writer

WWW.GOFUNDME.COM/F/SEATTLE-GAY-NEWS-NEEDS-YOUR-SUPPORT-NOW · VISIT SGN.ORG

▽ **Books**

*Mercedes De Acosta:*
*Hollywood's Greatest Lover.*
*Glamor, Glitz, and Gossip*
*at Historic Magnolia House*
by Darwin Porter
and Danforth Prince,
Blood Moon Productions

Image courtesy of Blood Moon

*"Here lies the heart."*

Blood Moon Productions has, for the past decade and a half, given the world a raft of unauthorized bios of the uber-famous of Hollywood, American politics, and pop culture, all with great admiration for their subjects' art and accomplishments, while not shying away from their more ignominious and often plainly degenerate proclivities. Darwin Porter knew many of these icons and raconteurs personally, and they had some stories to tell, believe you me. One such acquaintance was Mercedes De Acosta, who Porter met in her twilight years and was immediately fascinated by, not only for the stories she had to tell about quite literally anyone who was anyone in the first trimester of the 20th century, but for the sheer force of her personality and rapturous approach to life. She had just written her 1960 memoirs, *Here Lies The Heart*, and in physical decline, but willing to share her often-beyond-belief experiences with the young writer. This is something of a departure from the usual Blood Moon offerings, as De Acosta is relatively obscure compared to the likes of Brando, Marilyn, Bogie, the Clintons, and the Kennedys, et. al., but this detailed and heavily illustrated tale is every bit as un-put-downable as any of Porter and Prince's other works.

Women never seem to rate the appellation of "great lover" as their male counterparts often (and sometimes undeservedly) do, since we are seldom seen as being active participants as opposed to passive receptacles for male passion. Or, just plain "whores." But no other title suits Mercedes De Acosta, whose sapphic dance card includes names like Gertrude Stein and Alice B Toklas, Tallulah Bankhead, Katharine Cornell, Isadora Duncan, both of Valentino's wives, and most notably, Greta Garbo and Marlene Dietrich. De Acosta certainly deserved to have her name be synonymous with unabashed, joyful and prolific sensual abandon like Casanova and Don Juan, and in a world where female sexuality is not defined by the male gaze, she certainly would be. She was admittedly a bit of a groupie when it came to the artists of the Belle Epoque and the Roaring Twenties, but she definitely had taste. And keep in mind, this was when the famous were famous for actually *doing* something (sorry, Facebook/YouTube/Tik Tok "superstars"). She was the original Six Degrees Of Separation, mingling with and inspiring everyone from Pavlova to Enrico Caruso to Puccini to Barrymore to Marie of Romania to the aforementioned legends of film and letters. Mercedes was herself a poet, playwright, and screenwriter, though never as

well known as many of her vast circle of friends and lovers, but her life could certainly be considered a work of art at its purest and most outrageous. Someone please make a biopic or documentary about this woman now.

I had the distinct pleasure of staying at Magnolia House on Staten Island in 2010, on my first trip to NYC, at the behest of Danforth Prince and Darwin Porter, and I do not exaggerate when I say I was enchanted the minute I walked through the door. Built in the mid-1800s and packed to the rafters with every book ever printed on movies and its stars, this is the ideal home for the notorious Blood Moon Productions and a must-stay air B&B for film, art, and pop culture buffs. It should be as well known as the Chelsea Hotel right across the bay, for the number of famous and infamous guests and residents, and Glamor, Glitz, and Gossip is certainly the ultimate if-these-walls-could-talk collection of show biz histories too outrageous not to be real. It's a packed digest of Blood Moon's previous dishy and irresistible bios, and the perfect intro to the work of the obvious heir to Hollywood Babylon's salacious legacy. (FYI: Next up from Blood Moon, *Too Many Damn Rainbows*, the story of mother and daughter legends, Judy and Liza.)

**Mercedes de Acosta**
at the peak of her beauty

*From Garbo to Dietrich, from Eleanora Duse to Isadora Duncan, from Eva Le Gallienne to Tallulah Bankhead to Katharine Cornell—even to Valentino's two wives—star seducer Mercedes de Acosta was the Perfect Sapphic Lover."*

— Alice B. Toklas

FROM "GO" MAGAZINE'S EDITION OF APRIL 9, 2021

# 'The L Word' In The Golden Age

## Meet Mercedes de Acosta,
### Hollywood's Most Romantic Lesbian

### by Margaret Hetherman

**Margaret Hetherman,**
Reviewer for *GO Magazine*

*Modern lovers pining for the one who got away, take heart:*
*Even Hollywood's greatest lesbian romantic was dealt an unrequited hand.*

Born in 1893 in New York City to wealthy Spanish immigrants, **Mercedes de Acosta** was a poet, playwright, screenwriter, novelist and socialite. She traveled in circles that included **the Vanderbilts, Rodin, Debussy, Sarah Bernhardt** and a host of cultural icons who charmed the world in a gracious age. But Mercedes is most remembered as lover to some of the most intriguing female artistes of her day—glamorous pioneers of stage and screen, such as **Greta Garbo, Marlene Dietrich** and more.

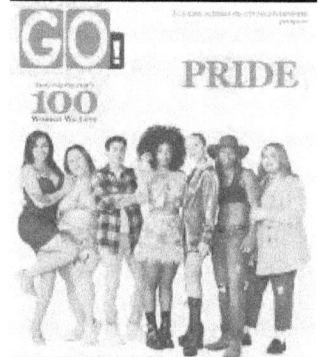

**Go Magazine's PRIDE**
edition of 2023

To tour her life is to traverse the Gilded Age, through the Golden Age of Hollywood and beyond. GO's guide: celebrity biographer **Darwin Porter**, 83, who accompanied many divas of yesteryear to *soirées* and personally knew Mercedes. They first met at a dinner in 1961 at the home of **Maria Voigt**, jewelry designer for Tiffany's. He had been talking about his recent trip to Spain, when Mercedes walked in and declared, "The last time I went to Spain, I drove down there with **Gertrude Stein** and **Alice B. Toklas**! From that moment, I don't know why she liked me, but I adored her!"

Darwin told GO. that he and partner in crimes of the pen and heart, **Danforth Prince**, 67, recently published ***The Seductive Sapphic Exploits of Mercedes de Acosta: Hollywood's Greatest Lover.*** It is a delicious account o f Mercedes' bold pursuits.

So put on your corsets and embroidered lace—or trousers if you prefer—for a look back to the unabashedly authentic life of **Mercedes de Acosta** (herself, partial to the tricorn hat, highwayman cape and pointed buckled shoes).

**Tallulah Bankhead**

### ROMANCING THE SOUL
ON DANCERS, MERCEDES WROTE, "*I AM ATTRACTED TO THEM BY SOME PECULIAR THING THEY EMANATE, A SHADOW OF SOME WINGED ESSENCE WHICH CLINGS TO THEIR SPIRIT.*"

Mercedes met **Isadora Duncan**, "The Mother of Modern Dance," in 1917 at Amagansett in New York: "*I caught my first sight of Isadora standing in the sun, and at once I felt the dunes, the reeds, the beach, the sea—all of these—in some strange way mingled with her and she was part of them.*" In her memoir, *Here Lies the Heart*, Mercedes described a long involvement with the free spirited revolutionary, writing that it was that first impression that allowed her to be always tolerant: "*Tolerant of her violence, her recklessness, of all her wild and uncontrolled love affairs. understood all these passions in her as I could say I understood thunder, or a hurricane ...*"

Mercedes' deep connection to her lovers transcended physical space; it was at times spiritual, even psychic, by her account. The allure? "*She could look a little bit into your soul,*" Darwin told GO.

**Sarah Bernhardt**

"The mother of Modern Dance,"
**Isadora Duncan**

## "I NEVER TALK LIKE THIS.
## I DON'T KNOW WHAT MADE ME OPEN MY HEART TO YOU."

Mercedes' memoir documents how Isadora told her about the tragic death of her children in a car crash. Tears poured down Isadora's face and Mercedes was compelled to ask her to dance for her. *"Without a word she led me across the sand, back through a cornfield and into an empty old barn."* The dancer appeared entirely carried out of herself. Mercedes wrote, *"I moved toward her, and it seemed as if I walked on a beam of light."*

They spent time together mostly in France. After a long separation, during which Mercedes embarked on her writing career —and other romances—the two reconnected in 1925. Mercedes found Isadora broke, in a seedy hotel in Paris. She urged the dancer to write her autobiography. But before Isadora could see its success, fate turned grave, when her long red scarf, blowing in the wind, got tangled in the wheel of an open Bugatti car, snapping her neck.

During those years, Mercedes also enjoyed a five-year affair with **Eva Le Gallienne**, a British-born actress, director, and producer. They had theater in common, as well as intimacies with the Russian born Art Nouveau actress, **Nazimova**.

**Greta Garbo,** snapped by Mercedes de Acosta during a weekend alone with her in the Sierra Nevada.

Once, during a visit to Darwin's home, Mercedes told him: *"If you write my life story one day—and I suspect you might—you'll need a chapter devoted to my love affair with Eva Le Gallienne. We were madly in love, our affair lasting for five tumultuous, argumentative, jealous years. Yes, we 'strayed' and fell into the arms of other lovers, but we always returned to each other for comfort, solace, understanding, and a grand and fiery passion."*

A mutual friend had introduced the women at the Ritz Hotel in 1921. Eva wanted to meet Mercedes, aware of their mutual admiration for Italian actress **Eleanora Duse** (reportedly also a paramour of Mercedes'). They "feverishly" compared notes over lunch. Meanwhile, Mercedes was engaged to painter **Abram Poole** in what would be a marriage of lavender convenience (and little coital action). Mercedes returned from her honeymoon in Europe and watched Eva act for the first time in "Liliom" on Broadway. Her memoir illuminates what happened next: *"When all the visitors had gone and she had taken off her make-up, I went home with her to her flat"*

*Sidebar:* While Mercedes was on her honeymoon with Poole, Eva attended a party, and danced with a drunken **John Barrymore**. When she refused his advances, he took her hand to his pants, Darwin reports. *"He told me to feel it, and he said he despised the rumors going around Broadway that he stuffed his crotch with a sock whenever he came on stage in green tights."*

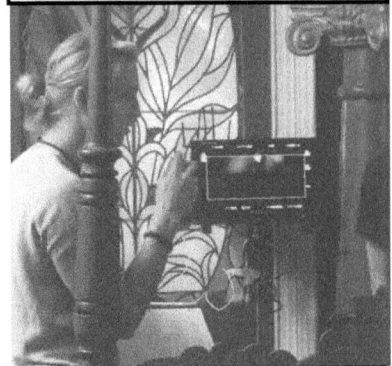

During their conversations, **Mercedes de Acosta** relayed her belief in the powers ot stained glass "to filter and display the essence of God."

After her death, Darwin commissioned the design and installation of a stained glass window as a memorial to their time together.

In the photo, above, it appears as a backdrop for a film crew who rented Magnolia House in 2021.

Suspecting that one day he might "pass on for posterity" some of the indiscretions she revealed, De Acosta cautioned **Darwin Porter**, "Don't be vulgar, dear, and promise me that you won't publish anything while my friends are still alive."

He honored her request by waiting until 2020 to release these astonishing insights into the underground lesbian contexts of the stage, screen, and publishing scenes during the first half of "The American Century."

The photo on the right is of **Darwin Porter**, as snapped in 1968 by Stanley Haggart.

They dated, attended *avant-garde* parties on East 19th Street, and in Paris watched **Mata Hari** "dance in the nude at a private party for a coven of American lesbian expatriates," Darwin/Danforth write. Mercedes wrote of her time in France with Eva, finding a fisherman's house in which they hoped to be boarders. After they knocked on the door, a widow answered. *"She installed us in a loft at the top of the house and got out her linen wedding sheets."*

But it was not **Eva Le Gallienne** who would prove to be the love of Mercedes' life. "I got the feeling that Eva was of mixed emotions about Mercedes," Darwin told GO. "It was almost like the love affair that could have been, but never became—because Eva had moved on to women that she found more compatible. And I think also, that she didn't want to hear about Garbo all the time."

Mercedes fell in love with **Greta Garbo** alone in a dark cinema, watching *The Torrent* (MGM 1926). *"I did not know then,"* she wrote, *"...that there is a secret area of the soul which, when kept pure, can act as a magnet and draw to itself a desire."*

Her wish was realized when they met at the home of Austrian actress/screenwriter **Salka Viertel.** The doorbell rang. **Greta Garbo** walked in. *"Her feet were bare and, like her hands, slender and sensitive."* When Garbo left, Salka told Mercedes *"Greta liked you very much."*

Two days later they had breakfast with Salka who was expecting a producer to swing by later on business. So Salka offered the women the run of a place while she was house-sitting. From the window they saw the blue Pacific, and played records on the phonograph, doing the tango to *"Schone Gigolo."* Greta invited her back to her place for lunch, but Mercedes had afternoon plans—plans interrupted when a butler announced, "Mia de Costa you are wanted on the telephone." It was Greta. "Now make for your car, and come to my house," Greta laughed.

Mercedes rushed to find the star waiting in her driveway in a Chinese dressing robe. They spent the evening together, but not the night; Garbo was in a production of *Susan Lenox* and as Darwin, tells it, had to face "[Clark] Gable's bad breath tomorrow morning."

When the film wrapped, Greta invited her again. They entered the living room, but Greta caught her thought. "I never use this room. I live in my bedroom," she said, and they went upstairs.

Greta soon announced she would rejuvenate "utterly alone" in a cabin in the Sierra Nevadas. Sad. But two nights later, Greta phoned. She was 300 miles away with her chauffeur, on her way back through the hot Mojave Desert to fetch Mercedes for a six-week stay, during which they sunbathed nude. As Mercedes recalled, "In the Sierra Nevadas she used to climb ahead of me, and with her hair blown back, her face turned to the wind and sun, she would leap from rock to rock on her bare Hellenic feet. I would see her above me, her face and body outlined against the sky, looking like some radiant, elemental, glorious god and goddess melted into one."

Modern lovers pining for the one who got away, take heart: Even Hollywood's greatest lesbian romantic was dealt an unrequited hand. Greta did things her way. *"Mercedes desperately wanted that to be a great love affair, and it was open door, closed door, open door, closed door,"* Darwin told GO.

They remained friends for 30 years, until 1960, when financially destitute and ill with a brain tumor, Mercedes published her tell-all autobiography, ***Here Lies the Heart.*** It alienated many friends and former lovers who felt "outed" and betrayed. Garbo never forgave her; she had written Mercedes 181 letters, cards, and telegrams. Mercedes sold her papers to the Rosenbach Museum in Philadelphia.

**Natacha Rambova**
Valentino's 2nd Wife

Friend of the family:
**Alfonso XIII,**
King of Spain

**Marlene Dietrich** *(right)*
with **Edith Piaf**

**Nazimova**
"Queen of MGM"

**Marlene Dietrich**—who swamped Mercedes' house beyond capacity with roses—was an outlier. She liked the book. Her lipstick-stained scarf, a gift to Mercedes, is housed today in the Rosenbach collection.

During her life, Mercedes produced three volumes of poetry, two novels, and plays. Still, commercial success eluded her. MGM hired her but shelved her screenplays. Sadly, we will never see the scene she wrote with Greta Garbo escaping from a window dressed as a man. We do, however, have Mercedes to thank for introducing her to pants.

How to honor a life like the one pursued by Mercedes de Acosta? Pursue passion without restraint. Know that some things *"hold forever tightly, and some things are never to be more than dreamed."* And should you find yourself in a theater with someone who makes your palms sweat—maybe she has short dark hair, deep set eyes and scarlet lips—for the love of all things fiery and fine, take her hand in yours.

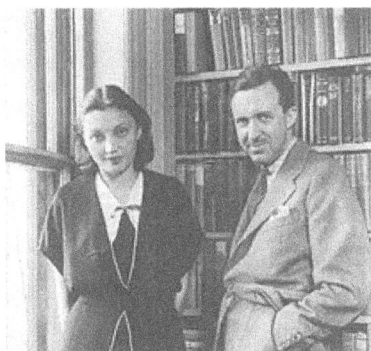

Bisexuals in a Lavender Marriage that became the Toast of Broadway: Here's a "soaked-in-domestic bliss" view of the celebrated **Katharine Cornell** (participant in a fling with Mercedes) with her husband and manager **Guthrie McClintic.**

To denizens of the theater world at the time, McClintic and Cornell were almost messianic...a faraway dream for then-destitute Broadway hopefuls like the later superstar, Kirk Douglas.

THE SEDUCTIVE SAPPHIC EXPLOITS OF

MERCEDES DE ACOSTA

Hollywood's Greatest Lover

*"From Garbo to Dietrich, from Eleonora Duse to Isadora Duncan, from Eva Le Gallienne to Tallulah Bankhead to Katharine Cornell—even to Valentino's two wives—star seducer Mercedes de Acosta was the Perfect Sapphic Lover."*
—Alice B. Toklas

ANOTHER UNORTHODOX OVERVIEW OF CELEBRITY AND FAME FROM

DARWIN PORTER & DANFORTH PRINCE

Ferocious *Grande Dame* of the American Theater, & scion of a dynasty: **Ethel Barrymore.** Winston Churchill wanted to marry her. She said "no."

Portrait of **Rita de Acosta Lydig** (Mercedes' rich and beautiful sister), circa 1911, by society portraitist **Giovanni Boldini**

Italian stage superstar **Eleonore Duse**

Both of **Rudolph Valentino's** wives were lesbians, Here, he appears with his first, **Jean Acker**

Art Connoisseur and Zeitgeist Star **Gertrude Stein**

The tragic, fatally outspoken sweetheart of the silent screen, **Jeanne Eagels**

**If you assumed that the greatest lovers are men,** some of the most famous actresses of the early- and mid-20ᵗʰ-Century might emphatically disagree.

To film historian Darwin Porter, in the final years of her life, the notorious Spanish beauty MERCEDES DE ACOSTA (1892-1968) confessed indiscreet truths about her romantic exploits in New York, London, Paris, and Hollywood. Her targets were women, each of them celebrated in the theater, filmmaking, and literary scenes.

This book focuses on the "stories behind the story" of some of the women who evolved into America's most admired stage and early screen goddesses. Here, culled from firsthand accounts, is an unvarnished, unapologetic glimpse at what happened AFTER the vamps and sirens of the first half of the 20th Century walked down the red carpet of show-biz fame and in rare cases, fortune.

SALVAGING THE SECRETS OF THE GRAND DIVAS OF THE EARLY FILM INDUSTRY: IT'S A TOUGH JOB, BUT SOMEBODY HAS TO DO IT!

BloodMoonProductions.com

ISBN 978-1-936003-75-4

9 781936 003754

Eccentric, ideosyncratic, brilliant, and odd, and at the center of the Lost Generation's artistic cross-currents stood **Alice B. Toklas** *(left)* and **Gertrude Stein** as they appeared in 1928

According to Mercedes, "The first time I met Stein, and spent some time with her, she stood up after three hours and told me it was time to go, our talk to be resumed tomorrow," Mercedes said. "In departing, Miss Stein found herself intensely kissed on her succulent mouth."

As a translator, facilitator, bedmate, and "tour guide" for Stein and Toklas during their long sojourn in Spain, **Mercedes de Acosta** wore many hats, making herself useful. allowing herself to be "worshipped," and soaking up the last vestiges of "Old Spain" before it disappeared into the jaws of its Civil War.

Drawing on her language skills and the rigors of her Cuban/Iberian roots, she became well versed in the severe and fascinating aesthetics of Spain.

In reference to the interpersonal dynamics of her tour, she confided to Darwin Porter, "Gertrude was the alpha male of our *ménage*."

*On the left.* one of Mercedes's sexual flings, **Nazimova,** appears with her conveniently homosexual, conveniently British, and conveniently respectable husband, **Charles Bryant,** who absolutely never outshone or eclipsed her onstage or on the screen.

*On the right,* in this scene from the allegorical and ultra-artsy silent film she directed, starred in, and produced (*Salome*; 1922, based on a play by the British homosexual, Oscar Wilde) she appears on the verge of enslaving and sacrificing a satyr.

Although the paparazzi salivated at any opportunity to capture Greta Garbo at unguarded private moments, as they did in the photo above, the sight of **Greta Garbo** *(right figure in photo above)* with her lover, **Mercedes de Acosta** *(left)* sauntering along Hollywood Boulevard was by then an everyday occurrence to jaded Los Angelenos.

Decades after their passion had died, the details that Mercedes recorded (and later published) about their romantic trysts shocked "ordinary mortals" and absolutely horrified Garbo, who furiously denounced and rejected Mercedes after their publication in 1960.

Although Mercedes' memoir had revealed indiscretions about many other bisexual women in Hollywood, too, they focused more extensively on Garbo than on anyone else. Garbo's reaction, according to sources at the time, was "litiginous and volcanic."

In 1931, MGM released a potboiling tearjerker (*Inspiration*), which had been adapted from a French novel by Alphonse Daudet entitled *Sappho*.

The "Eugénie Hat" that Adrian designed for its star, **Greta Garbo** *(photo above)* became a sensation across America.

It was named in honor of the French Empress **Eugénie de Montijo**, the wife of Napoléon III, who had popularized it in the 1850s.

Garbo's endorsement of the style led to a nationwide milliner's revival that continued until the beginning of World War II.

His release of *The Seductive Sapphic Exploits of Mercedes de Acosta* was not **Darwin Porter's** first immersion into the murky snake pit of **Lesbian Literary Chic**.

In 1982, Darwin released *Venus*, a novel suggested by the life of the feminist literary icon, **Anaïs Nin.** For decades, he'd been captivated by stories of her years in Paris in the 1920s, moving within the inner circles of **Henry Miller, Gertrude Stein**, and **Alice B. Toklas**.

Darwin agreed with the assessment of author **Erica Jong**: "Anaïs left so many trails of clues about her several lives that she could have confounded Sherlock Holmes himself."

Feminists and literary scholars from academia and pop culture flocked to meet her at Darwin's home (*Magnolia House*) to learn more about her scandal-soaked and very competitive life and travails.

Darwin Porter's frenemy and inspiration for *Venus*, **Anaïs Nin**, depicted above, asked him, "Would you like to read my pornography? I wrote it when I was young, in Paris and was paid two dollars a page."

Mercedes de Acosta had a lesbian romance with **Marlene Dietrich**, too.

Here's Dietrich with **Ernest Hemingway**. Soaked with literary prizes and stories about his wartime adventures in Europe, he affectionately referred to her as "The Kraut."

**Mercedes**' passion for conversation and her ongoing immersion in the *avant-garde* continued long after the fires of her sexual appetites diminished.

Here, late in life, she appears as a frumpy but deeply well-informed member of the *cognoscenti*, capable of sustaining long intellectual and artistic dialogues about whatever was new and in vogue among "The Smart Set" of her era.

Perhaps it was her early immersion into "polite society" as a child... but in any event, she became widely respected as a booster and catalyst to the creative output of dozens of news-making writers, musicians, philosophers, and painters.

Some of the greatest names in the world of dance, of letters, and of the theater gravitated to her, in some cases, forming life-long friendships.

As revealed to Darwin Porter about her fascination with the dance world, **Mercedes** said, "During the years I followed the Ballets Russes, I met the most incredible people—and not just **Picasso**. In addition to my friend, **Igor Stravinsky, Diaghilev** commissioned such composers as **Claude Debussy** and **Sergei Prokofiev;** artists such as **Vasily Kandinsky, Henri Matisse,** and **Alexandre Benois**; and costume designers such as **Coco Chanel** and **Léon Bakst**."

"I got to see the great **Anna Pavlova** dance," Mercedes claimed. "But to me, **Tamara Karasavina** was just as good. She became my lover."

The photo above shows **Tamara Karasavina,** the Russian-born British ballerina (with whom Mercedes sustained an affair) with Vasily Nijinski in Diaghilev's *Le Spectre de la Rose* (1911).

Born in 1889, the French poet, novelist, and playwright **Jean Cocteau** was already a legend among the "*ultra avant-garde*" when he met Mercedes de Acosta.

Spectacularly flamboyant, and for a period, friends with both **Marcel Proust** and **André Gide**, he was an "*enfant terrible*," horrifying the entrenched bourgeoisie of the French-speaking world.

Although a homosexual, the long-time lover of the French actor, Jean Marais, he had lost his virginity to the legendary music hall entertainer, **Mistinguett.**

Novelist **Edith Wharton** described Cocteau as a man "to whom every great line of poetry was a sunrise, every sunset the foundation of the Heavenly City."

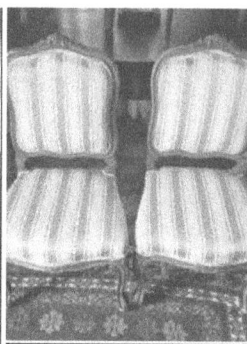

**Artifacts from the Lost Generation are now at Magnolia House**

Two of a set of four 18th-century Louis XIV chairs, formerly part of *enfant terrible* Jean Cocteau's home at Milly-la-Forêt, an hour's drive south of Paris, are now owned by Darwin Porter.

Sold by Cocteau in the 1930s to the American artist and socialite **Woody Parrish-Martin** (who was sustaining an affair with Cocteau at the time), they were later bequeathed to **Stanley Mills Haggart**, a long-time associate of **Darwin Porter.** They now "reside" with the authors of this book at Magnolia House in Staten Island.

**Katharine Cornell** (a spectacularly famous *grande dame* defined by Mercedes de Acosta as one of her "*inamoratas*") appears here as the Countess in the stage adaptation of Edith Wharton's **The Age of Innocence**.

Gladys Malvern, who wrote about the theater, said, "Flappers with their flimsy, knee-length skirts crowded into New York's Empire Theatre to see Katharine Cornell in trains, bustles, and velvets."

BLOOD MOON Productions, Ltd.

*The far left and far right photos above show* **Jeanne Eagels** (1890-1929), an adored star of the silent screen. A fragile American beauty of charm, humor, and grace, her most successful roles portrayed her as a "fallen woman," usually an unrepentant (but deeply wounded) prostitute. She was the first in a long lineup of subsequent actresses to portray the empathetic hooker, Sadie Thompson, based on a short story by W,. Somerset Maugham.

A bisexual, Eagels died young and tragically in 1929. *The Boston Post* summed up her legacy like this: "The thing that made Miss Eagels great, that perhaps made her the greatest emotional actress of her day, was her eventual ruin."

**Mercedes de Acosta**, with an almost unlimited understanding of the sense of isolation shared by many lesbians (then and now) sustained and comforted her during the substance abuse, poverty, and emotional instability of her final months.

Here are two views of **Oona Munson**, the actress who played Belle Watling—the manager of Rhett Butler's favorite whorehouse—in *Gone With the Wind (1939)*.

Even same-sex affairs with women who included **Marlene Dietrich, Nazimova, Mercedes de Acosta**, and the **Countess Dorothy di Frasso** (mistress of **Gary Cooper**) didn't save her from crippling depressions and a suicide (in 1955) derived from an overdose of barbiturates.

170

**"BUT WHAT?" HER FANS MIGHT BE ASKING, "ABOUT MARLENE DIETRICH?
IN THE AFTERMATH OF THIS OVERVIEW OF MERCEDES DE ACOSTA,
ISN'T THERE MORE, MUCH MORE, THAT THE TEAM FROM BLOOD MOON
MIGHT WANT TO CONVEY?**

The answer, with vigor, is *JAHWOHL, OUI, SI, and YES!*

**DID YOU KNOW** that in the late 1970s, Darwin Porter crafted a NOVEL based on Marlene Dietrich's complicated life? And DID YOU KNOW that when it was released it generated almost as much outrage as the star herself?
Here's the story:

**As a devoted, decades-long fan** of Marlene Dietrich, the senior co-author of this book, Darwin Porter penned, in 1977, a *roman-à-cléf* based on her extraordinary life.

It was quickly designated as *Book of the Month* in the Netherlands and became "required reading" for many of the aging actresses within the orbit of **Lucille Lortel**, the "Queen of Off-Broadway" in whose circle Darwin at the time was regularly and frequently involved.

One member of that clique who devoured its contents, and who had it on her bedside table at the moment of her death, was ballerina **Tamara Geva**, the ex-wife of **George Balanchine**. She described its startling opening scenes (a lesbian encounter of an aging "Marlene" with a neophyte wannabe) as "a brilliant parable for the story of my life"

Arbor House, its publisher, marketed it with the following slogans: "A fabled superstar from the glamorous era of **Garbo and Dietrich**, *Marika* was a fascinating mixture of elusive sensuality and bold innocence. Soaring from the depths of poverty to the brilliant decadence of Berlin and the sweet temptations of Hollywood, she is haunted by the looming betrayal of her own secret past."

How did the REAL Marlene Dietrich "self-define and introduce herself" during her first encounter with Darwin at a show-biz cocktail party in Paris in the 1970s?

*"Helloooooooo. My name is Marlene Dietrich, and I am a cabaret entertainer."*

DARWIN PORTER

MARIKA

A novel about one of the                 world's most shocking women

Philanthropist, Feminist, Humanitarian, & Union Organizer **Anne Tracy Morgan**

Photographer/Anthropologist **Gertrude Kasebier**

Gilded age socialite **Rita Stokes Lydig**

Novelist, philanthropist, & francophile, **Edith Wharton**

*Grandes Dames,* arbiters of taste, and Broadway investors **Elizabeth** ("Bessie') **Marbury** with **Elsie de Wolfe** ("Lady Mendl")

Supernova stage and film star **John Barrymore** ("The Profile') with his third wife, **Dolores Costello,** previously his co-star in *The Sea Beast,* Warners' highest-grossing film of 1926, an adaptation of Herman Melville's *Moby DIck* .

Anglo-Russian prima ballerina **Tamara Karsavina**

**Libby Holman** with **Clifton Webb** *(left)* and **Fred Allen** *(right)*

*Chanteuse* and intellectual **Yvonne George**

British comedienne **Beatrice ("Bea') Lilly**

Über-diva & stage actress **Eleanore Duse**

French cabaret entertainer and model for Toulouse-Lautrec, **Yvette Guilbert**

Mystical & Magical: **GARBO**

# MICHAEL JACKSON

### HE'S "BAD." HE'S "DANGEROUS."

### HE'S "INVINCIBLE." HE'S A "THRILLER," AND

# HE'S BACK

Before he turned white—and still had a nose; before scandalous kiddie sex charges and weird marriages; before money woes and widely televised humiliations; Michael Jackson was the world's most dazzling show biz legend.

OK, so he's Wacko. Frank Sinatra hated him; Elvis Presley would probably have shot him, but the Gloved One profoundly changed the face of pop music, selling more than 45 million copies of *Thriller*, the mega-hit album of all time.

THE MAN IN THE MOONWALK. Remember the time? The madness? The music? That dance?

In this exposé by acclaimed celebrity biographer Darwin Porter, Blood Moon presents the first-ever complete saga of an incredible American life: the good times, the very bad times, the desperate attempt to stay on top, and the international aftermath of "those lawsuits" when everything, including Neverland, came crashing down.

Even his loudest detractors admit that they love his music. He changed the entertainment industry forever. This candid bio from the author of *Brando Unzipped* and *Hollywood Babylon—IT'S BACK* takes you behind closed doors to explore the star-studded, bizarre world of America's most maligned superstar.

**Michael Jackson** at the peak of his "*Thriller*" fame in the 1980s was probably the most famous person on earth. Undeniably, thanks to his reign as the King of Pop, he was the world's biggest superstar. He was also the most famous African-American entertainer in the history of show business.

But after the turn of the millennium, the front pages of such tabloids as *The New York Post* were screaming **PETER PAN OR PERVERT?** How could Michael Jackson's career and personal life have gone so wrong?

To answer that, you have to look at Michael's roots in the grimy industrial city of Gary, Indiana, "murder capital of the U.S." Here, on the scorching night of August 29, 1958, Michael Jackson entered the world.

| | | | | | |
|---|---|---|---|---|---|
| **MJ** with **Naomi Campbell** | **MJ** with **Elizabeth Taylor** at **Liza Minnelli's** wedding | **MJ** with **Hugh Hefner** | **MJ** with **Jackie-O** | **MJ** with **Jane Fonda** | **MJ** with POTUS **Bill Clinton** |

*"When Michael Jackson sings, it is with the voice of angels, and when his feet move, you can see God dancing."*
—**Sir Bob Geldorf**

*"I grew up in a fishbowl. I will not allow that to happen to my children"*
—**Michael Jackson**

*"He is one of the last living innocents who is in complete control of his life. I've never seen anybody like Michael. He's an emotional child star. He's in full control. Sometimes he appears to be wavering on the fringes of the twilight, but there is a great conscious forethought behind everything he does. He's very smart about his career and the choices he makes. I think he is definitely a man of two personalities."*
—**Steven Spielberg**

*"If it weren't for my desire to help the children of the world, I'd throw in the towel and kill myself."*
—**Michael Jackson**

*"Whether he's 90 years old and moonwalking at one mph, the world will be right there to watch."*
—**Soul crooner Pharrell**

# THE MAN BEHIND THE MASK

## JACKO, HIS RISE AND FALL
### THE SOCIAL AND SEXUAL HISTORY OF MICHAEL JACKSON

*From celebrity biographer Darwin Porter, this is the most honest and journalistically important biography of Michael Jackson ever published, with a roster of literary reviews that outnumber and outclass any equivalent bio on the market. After its original release in 2007, it was widely reviewed as the most thorough and comprehensive biography of the superstar published anytime during the previous fifteen years—and a LOT had happened to him since then.*

*Following the superstar's death at the age of 50 in June of 2009, Porter edited and amplified his already controversial texts to include startling new information about The Gloved One, adding a final chapter and a post-mortem epilogue reflecting the mysterious circumstances surrounding Jackson's death and an analysis of its aftermath.*

\*\*\*

### From *Boomer Times'* review of April 2007

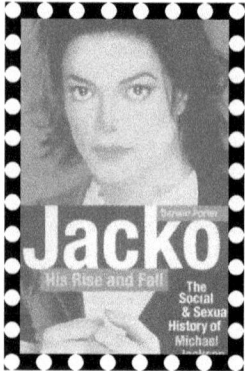

Just when we thought we knew everything there was to know about Michael Jackson, along comes Darwin Porter's *Jacko, His Rise and Fall*. Early reviews have claimed that it presents a revelation about this enigmatic personality on every page. Jacko, of course, is the most famous entertainer of the past quarter-century, with fans who range in age from 8 to 80+.

Amazingly for a star of his magnitude, no comprehensive biography that includes developments in the singer's life during the late 1990s and post-millennium has ever been published. All of that changed with the release this month by Blood Moon Productions of Darwin Porter's newest book.

Meticulously researched over several tumultuous decades, Porter reveals the secrets that Jackson wanted to hide from the world. What would Jacko do with the bones of Marilyn Monroe had he been able to buy them? Did he marry the real Lisa Marie Presley or an imposter? Why did he want to marry Elizabeth Taylor? Why did Jacqueline Onassis—the long-suffering editor of his autobiography, Moonwalk—cut off all communications between the megastar and her son, JFK Jr.? Did Jacko really have an "affair" with Princess Di, as he claimed, and did he try to convert Prince William into one of his "special friends?" What would Jacko's best male friend, Marlon Brando, have done if Jackson had indeed been convicted of those child molestation charges? And

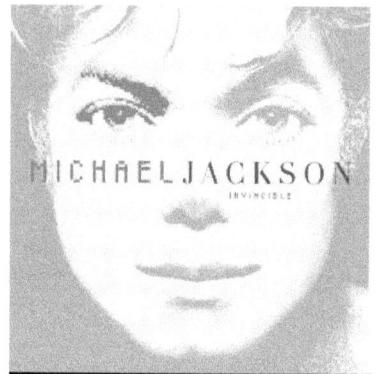

During the 1980s, at the peak of his career, **Michael Jackson** became the most famous man on the planet, a sex symbol known for wearing fetish gear and grabbing his crotch onstage, and galvanizing millions of fans worldwide.

Post-millennium, he became an object of ridicule and scorn. Hounded by both the press and by the courts, he morphed into a defendant in as many as 50 new lawsuits a year.

Darwin Porter's book examines the meanderings of his decline. A reviewer from *The Daily Mail* said, "It's the story of a pop-culture icon who wandered into a treacherous Garden of Eden and tasted its forbidden fruit."

Even his loudest detractors admitted that they loved his music, and that he changed the entertainment industry forever.

This candid, unauthorized biography takes you inside the bizarre world of the icon of American pop music—everything from his bizarre marriage to Lisa Marie Presley to his paying a woman to have his children.

During his lifetime and after his death, the number of feature magazine covers devoted to Michael Jackson was staggering.

The layout above shows only a few of the hundreds of times marketers associated his effigy with sales. An exception to the focus on Michael himself is **Playboy's** edition of March 1989 *(third magazine cover from left)*, where his sister, **LaToya**, was featured as a "celebrity centerfold."

what really went on between Jacko and "Dreamgirl," Diana Ross? And how far did Jacko go, and how many millions were paid, to squelch lawsuits from the parents of underaged boys?

Central to the book is the ultimate question, richly analyzed, with commentary from the most credible of Jackson's many associates: *Is The Gloved One really a pedophile*, "a monstrous freak who abuses young boys," or an innocent victim of his own wealth and fame?

Porter's biography is the story of a brown-skinned poor boy from the American Rust Belt who moonwalked his way to fame and fortune and became "white," with a radically re-sculpted nose, face, and public image. Using his formidable journalistic skills, in a fair and even-handed presentation that equips readers with information from a wide array of sources, Porter examines the twisting route of Jackson's decline. It's a sort of a pop-culture icon who wandered into a treacherous Garden of Eden and tasted its forbidden fruit.

It's also a saga about how, during the "Thriller" 1980s, Jackson became the most famous man on the planet, a symbol known for wearing fetish gear and grabbing his crotch onstage. Post-millennium, he became an object of ridicule and scorn, hounded by the press and by the courts, the victim of as many as 50 new lawsuits a year. It's a tale that could only have happened in America.

Michael Jackson, as interpreted by Darwin Porter, became Peter Pan, a child-man who invited to his beds boys far too young, although in some cases, far advanced in their sexual savvy. Jacko's obsession cost him dearly: After a "sleepover," young Jordie Chandler walked away with $25 million. In another case, cancer victim Gavin Arvizo, who also sued Jackson, lost his battle in court and got nothing.

In an unbiased journalistic style which Porter's fans have come to expect, this newest biography illuminates much more than just its principal subject: Sharing second billing is an octogenarian Katharine Hepburn, an aging Jane Fonda, the amazingly durable Dame Elizabeth, and a lengthy cast of other famous characters, many from the Golden Age of Hollywood. The list of *glitterati* interacting with Jackson, with provocative stories about each of them, include Fred Astaire, Gene Kelly, Liberace, Mae West, Madonna, Mick Jagger, Prince, Paul McCartney, Tatum O'Neal, Brooke Shields, James Brown, Sammy Davis Jr., Coretta Scott King, Quincy Jones, Johnnie Cochran, Gregory Peck, Charlton Heston, Michael Jordan, Frank Sinatra, Louis Farrakhan of the Nation of Islam, Mick Jagger, Shirley Temple, and Elvis Presley. (In Nevada, Jacko once came face to face with his future father-in-law.)

Jackson, it's said, wants the phrase, "Don't judge me" inscribed on his tombstone. But after racing through this hot and controversial new biography that lines up incidents like the details in a bizarre and intensely dramatic trial, readers can't help but feel like jurors on a hot seat themselves.

*"The world sees me as this monstrous freak who abuses little boys," Michael Jackson complained to his friend, Elizabeth Taylor.*

\*\*\*

## PR TEXTS FROM BLOOD MOON RE MICHAEL JACKSON

The most comprehensive biography of entertainment legend MICHAEL JACKSON has been written by noted Hollywood biographer Darwin Porter.

Its original edition brought rave reviews by publications which included the *London Observer* ("Porter's newest bio is dangerously addictive") and *Foreword Magazine*.

*Jacko, His Rise and Fall* traces the social and sexual history of The Gloved One. In this explosive tell-all, that sequin-covered glove comes off, and so does his mask. It traces the life and drama of the dethroned King of Pop. During its compilation, Porter sorted through mountains of information, both pro and con, associated with the man-boy whose attraction to underaged boys led to public derision and his near-ruin.

It's based on countless interviews and hundreds of unpublished testimonials accumulated over the course of nearly 30 years of observation. Porter reveals how Michael charmed America's A-list celebrities, and how many of them indulged and reacted to the masked man's often bizarre escapades. Among the hundreds of previously unpublished testimonials is that of Liberace's former boyfriend, who describes a dinner which the pianist gave for young Michael and his special guest, Mae West.

Porter's biography follows the meandering path of a then-poor, brown-skinned. and supremely talented boy as he moonwalked from a childhood in America's Rust Belt into fame and fortune, radically changing his appearance and his skin color along the way. It interconnects the dots that

**MJ** with **Diana and Charles,** Princess and Prince of Wales.

Diana's lover, filmproducer and heir to an Egyptian fortune, **Dodi Al-Fayed**

**Prince William**, heir to the British throne.

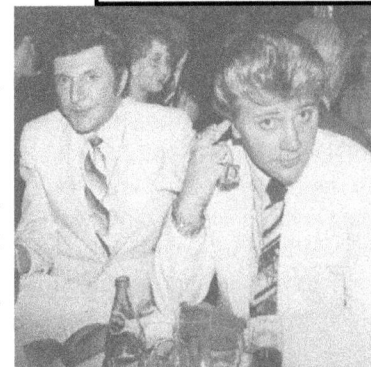
**Liberace** with his lover-turned-litigant, **Scott Thorson**

The Gloved One has tattooed onto the consciousness of his enemies, his fans, and those who are convinced that Jacko's rise and fall represents a sociological phenomenon that historians will discuss in years to come.

There's a revelation on every page, each laid out in a chronological progression like it's never been done before. bringing in commentary from friends and enemies alike. There are amplifications and layouts of episodes involving Michael's attempt to purchase the bones of Marilyn Monroe for display within a museum; the charges, filed in court, of Lisa Johansen, who claims that she's the real daughter of Elvis Presley and that Michael married an imposter; and that in spite of denials, Jacko did want to marry Elizabeth Taylor and adopt a brood of children, a situation that would have dwarfed headlines about the baby acquisitions of Brad Pitt, Angelina Jolie, and Madonna.

It's further revealed why Jackie Onassis, the long-suffering editor of Michael's so-called autobiography, *Moonwalk,·* abruptly cut off relations between the pop idol and her handsome, then very young son, JFK Jr., when shc discovered an "undue" interest.

Porter explodes the myth that Jacko had an "affair" with Princess Di, as he claimed to his wife, Lisa Marie Presley, during the course of their sham marriage. Instead, Porter alleges that Jacko's most compelling interest during his involvement with the royal family involved turning Prince William—a direct heir to the throne of England— into a "special friend."

Other revelations follow, including details about the stormy relationship between Jacko and his "Dream-girl," Diana Ross. Their friendship exploded when Miss Ross caught the very talented young Michael in her dress, imitating her voice and movements in front of a full-length dress mirror at her home in Los Angeles.

Tantalizingly, Porter also reveals details about the only known encounter between young Michael and his drugged and bloated future father-in-law, Elvis Presley, in Nevada.

Jacko's friendships with the *glitterati* of Golden Age Hollywood are described in spicy detail—Katharine Hepburn, Jane Fonda, Gregory Peck, Fred Astaire—even gun-*totin'* Charlton Heston. Not all of the superstars took to Michael: Frank Sinatra in Las Vegas once threw a bottle of liquor at a TV set when Jacko came on-screen.

Jacko's friendships, sometimes followed by feuds and jealous rages with other pop stars, are laid bare. including an episode where Mick Jagger and Rudolf Nureyev made Michael the "meat' in their sandwich on a dance floor. Porter explores how Jacko "doublecrossed" Paul McCartney by secretly buying the Beatles catalogue based on information which McCartney had provided, and how Madonna failed in her attempt to seduce Jacko. *[Madonna later referred to Jacko as "a drag queen from Outer Space."]*

With an index and about a hundred photographs, the book introduces us to the key players, all of them young boys, who came in and out of Michael's orbit, including Sean, the son of John Lennon and Yoko Ono. Like a child-man, Jackson as Peter Pan lured boys to his bed for sleepovers, a "nap" that in some cases lasted for months. Porter alleges that some of those boys, although technically minors at the time. were already far advanced in their sexual savvy and not altogether innocent victims, as is sometimes portrayed.

Even so, as a means of "firewalling" certain kinds of information from the media and from the courts, much of the money Jackson gathered during his "*Thriller*" period was paid out to the families of some of these boys.

"Boy Beautiful" Jordie Chandler became the Grand Lotto winner when he walked away with $25 million in a pre-trial out-of-court settlement. In marked contrast, cancer-victim Gavin Arvizo, whose case slogged its well-publicized way through a California courtroom, got nothing. At the time of this writing, he's working at a fast-food joint in Los Angeles.

Porter's intention involved presenting the world's first even-handed, journalistically unbiased biographical overview of an entertainer whose fame surpassed, in some places. that of the Pope and the US President. It's all here: Ironically, we believe that Michael Jackson has genuinely hated the way the world has, in many cases, judged him unfairly. It's even been said that the phrase that he wants written on his tombstone is 'DON'T JUDGE ME.' But the author, in this biography, has put the reader in a hot seat that's equivalent to that of a juror being confronted with the question, "Is The Gloved One really a pedophile—a monstrous freak who abuses young boys—or an innocent victim of his own infamy and his own once-vast fortune which he squandered like a terrorist raid on Fort Knox?"

*Left,* **Marilyn Monroe** arriving at Ciro's for an event celebrating Louella Parsons in 1953, and *(right photo)* an artist's rendition of her bones. Michael tried to buy them.

**Michael** and **Madonna** were frenemies until she tried (and failed) to seduce him. When he referred to her in public as "heifer," she shot back, "I'd rather be a cow than a drag queen from Outer Space."

**Michael Jackson** *(center)* with his parents, **Katharine** and **Joe**, a music promoter. A year after their marriage in 1949, they bought a very small, one-story house in Gary, Indiana. Cramped and nondescript, it had two bedrooms, a living room, a kitchen, and a small utility room. They eventually produced 10 children, one of whom died a few hours after birth. All of their sons slept in one of the bedrooms, Katharine and Joe in the other, and their daughters in the living room.

As alleged by Michael, Joe rehearsed them, abusively and brutally, for their early stage routines. Their musical fortunes "turned" in March of 1969, when their family ensemble, **The Jackson 5** arranged a record contract with Motown

Each with "big hair," here's **The Jackson 5** during their heyday in 1969. **Michael**, who joined the group when he was 5, morphed within a few years into a "bubblegum pop" star in his own right. In this publicity photo, he appears in the center.

# JACKSONMANIA SWEEPS THE NATION

The King is dead. The day-and-night blitzkrieg of TV coverage that followed Michael Jackson's death rivaled the assassination of John F. Kennedy.

**Liza Minnelli**

For those of you who still haven't got enough of the King of Pop, here are more startling revelations—presented in no particular order—that appeared in the August release of my biography.

Accused of child molestation later in his life, Michael as a young boy was also molested by some key figures in the record promotion industry. John Stoffer, of Detroit, admitted right before he died that the talented young boy was pimped to pedophiles in the business to promote the careers of the Jackson 5.

In Detroit it was also alleged that Papa Joe Jackson seriously considered having Michael castrated, in the tradition of the *castrati* of Italy in the 17th century, to maintain the high pitch of his voice. When word reached the streets, Michaels's most overzealous fans grabbed at his groin "to see if it's still there."

**Yoko Ono**

Next door neighbor Liberace introduced Michael to Mae West, who advised the young star to take two or three enemas a day for lasting beauty and youth—"but no drugs." Michael took only the first recommendation, obviously not the second.

After author Truman Capote introduced Michael to Jacqueline Kennedy, the budding star switched role models. Out, Diana Ross; in, Mrs. Kennedy. Capote later said, "Only in America can you be born a poor black ghetto boy and grow up to become a rich white woman."

Jackie promoted a friendship with Michael and edited his autobiography, *Moonwalker*, but cut off a budding relationship with her young son, "The Hunk," when she learned that Michael had developed a "fixation" on JFK Jr.

Young Michael's early role model (hair, makeup, and personal style) was **Diana Ross.**

Likewise, a savvy Princess Di refused all of Michael's invitations to Prince William to visit Neverland and spend the summer in a prolonged sleepover. She also returned countless gifts Michael sent to woo the future heir to the British throne.

Michael claimed to have had an affair with Princess Di, which appears laughable. However, he did have a prolonged affair with her beau, Dodi Al-Fayed, who was killed in that car crash with the Princess in Paris. The bisexual Middle Easterner movie producer, famous for collecting trophy women such as Barbra Streisand, promised he'd make Michael a movie star and would cast him as Peter Pan, the boy who never grew up.

**MJ** with **Sophia Loren**. They met at a party at the U.S. Embassy in Rome. Already-established show-biz pros found his "celebrity I.Q." irresistible.

Depicted above, **Michael Jackson's gold-plated casket** appears onstage at a televised public memorial for him at one of the top sports and entertainment stadiums in the world, the Staples Center in downtown Los Angeles. The date was September 3, 2009.

The grieving Jackson family fearing that his corpse would be dug up or damaged, went to great lengths to preserve it. His body--dressed in full stage costume that included a wig and white gloves--was buried in a gold coffin set in concrete. The venue was at the Holly Terrace Grand Mausoleum at Glendale Forest Lawn Memorial Park, five miles north of Hollywood. His brothers, Jermain, Tito, Randy, Jackie and Marlon, were among his pallbearers.

**Michael Jackson**, *center*, dressed in one of his stage costumes, stands with **President Ronald Reagan** and First Lady **Nancy Davis Reagan** on the South Lawn of the White House on May 14, 1984. Always quick to recognize the vote-getting merits of celebrities, the show-biz savvy Reagans had arranged a Presidential award for his contribution to their drunk driving awareness program.

**HE MARRIED HER!**
Here's **Lisa-Marie Presley,** celebrity daughter of Elvis and Priscilla. Their bizarre marriage (1994-1996) produced oceans of speculation, but no children, One can only wonder what Elvis would have thought.

**WHO KNEW?**
As the most famous male dancers of their respective eras, **Fred Astaire** and **MJ** found each other fascinating.

Michael famously tried to acquire the bones of the Elephant Man. What is known to a lesser extent is that he attempted to purchase the bones of Marilyn Monroe to display in a museum on Hollywood Boulevard. He also failed in two other acquisitions—one, to acquire the intestines of Elvis Presley (removed during an autopsy), and another to pay $1 million for the inflamed appendix removed from Pope John Paul II. Michael promised to donate the money to Catholic charities. The Pope said no.

Michael gave another million to Swiss scientists working on a potion to make people invisible. Yet another million went to Scottish scientists for their experiments in human cloning. Michael wanted both a male and a female version of himself cloned.

Finally, Michael proposed a May-December marriage—and strictly platonic—to Elizabeth Taylor. Such a union, he hoped, would lead to the adoption of 20 some children from various continents. Dame Elizabeth wisely turned down the offer.

Elvis Presley, onstage in Las Vegas, and *(right)*, **John Merrick**, the tragic "Elephant Man" of Victorian England.

The tabloids touted MJ's aberrant interest in acquiring the preserved body parts of each of them.

These statements were thoroughly investigated and appear to be true. But wild and wacko rumors about Michael are just beginning and, as in the case of Elvis, may last for 50 years or more. They began with La Toya's assertion to the tabloids that her brother was murdered.

# WHAT THE CRITICS SAID

"A new biography of Michael Jackson contains stories that are eyebrow-raising even for his weird life.::
—**The New York Daily News**

"In JACKO, Darwin Porter manages to provide the one thing that many journalists have failed to produce in their writings about the pop star:  A real person behind the headlines."
—**Foreward Magazine**

"I think the story of Michael Jackson reflects our times perfectly, and will be something historians in future centuries  (provided there's still a planet) will explore. He has been totally destroyed by success.  I did the promotion of the movie "The Wiz" in the 1970s and Michael was the tin man. Met him at the studio and found him to be normal, quiet, and very sweet. Not a prima donna at all. But this was before the first nose job and the skin-bleaching."
—**Virginia Hayes Montgomery,** *Pres, Montgomery Communications*

"I'd have thought that there wasn't one single gossipy rock yet to be overturned in the microscopically scrutinized life of Michael Jackson. But Darwin Porter's exhaustive but zippy hybrid of celebrity bio and solid reporting proves me quite wrong. It's all here: The abuse Jackson suffered as a boy from the fists of his father, rough early years on the "chitlin' circuit," his rocky relationship with Diana Ross and his quirky relationship with Liz Taylor, his sham marriages and his oddly conceived three children; unflagging rumors of his homosexuality; and his scandalous affection for generations of adolescent boys. Definitely a page-turner. But don't turn the pages too quickly: Almost every one holds a fascinating revelation."

—**Richard Labonte**
*Books to Watch Out For*

Sometimes, it looks like the world isn't quite big enough to support the myth of Wacko Jacko. Literature (if you can call it that) on America's weirdest and most talked-about superstar abounds, and increasingly so in the form of biography. Darwin Porter's Jacko: His Rise and Fall, which looks at Jackson 'from the inside out', claims to be the most comprehensive of the lot.

Porter takes the face off the Michael Jackson we think we know. "Michael is a normal kid, living in abnormal times," Porter says. "He may be the subject of corporeal punishment by his father and allegations of knife threats from his brother, Jermaine, and of accusations of homosexuality, bisexuality, and even asexuality by the media. But in Porter's account, he 'always got up to go to the Sunday meeting of the Jehovah's Witnesses,' experienced "history's worst case of acne" and refused Andy Warhol's request to film his face while being penetrated anally with the words: "No thanks. It's long past my bedtime." This is the story of the good boy turned rotten, or 'Peter Pan grows up.'

J.M. Barrie wouldn't be impressed. "Literature" it certainly isn't, but this biography is dangerously addictive."

**--Chloe Todd Fordham for London's *Observer*, April 29, 2007**

"Jackson's life is well-known for its eccentricity and tumult. Since his death, blogs and Web sites have been speculating about the most likely candidates to pen additional memoirs, as well as projected celebrity tributes... Darwin Porter's Jacko, His Rise and Fall provides over 500 pages of in-depth biography. Porter's account is widely held as one of the most comprehensive accounts of Jackson's life. As it came out in 2007, it stands as one of the most up-to-date. The public's appetite for Michael Jackson books is at an all-time high, so publishers and biographers are certainly striving to uncover the details of his life, which will emerge for years to come."
**—Examiner.com**

"This is the story of a brown-skinned boy with a big nose who moonwalked his way into "the world of white," eventually with a re-sculpted face and financial assets that the rest of the world seemingly felt free to pillage. Michael is Peter Pan, the child-man who invited to his bed boys who were too young, yet too far advanced in their savvy, not to react, sometimes with venom. Jordie Chandler walked away with $25 million after "sleeping over." Cancer-ridden Gavin Arvizo, who sued Michael and lost, got nothing."

**—The National Book Network**

You've heard scattered segments of The Michael Jackson saga, but never in a smooth chronological progression that bonded all the elements together, and managed, en route, to include many of the entertainment industry's most intriguing celebrities: Jackie-O, the Reagans, the Bushes, the Windsors, the aristocraciy of America's pop culture, and many of the movie stars of Hollywood's Golden Age. They all opened their doors and sometimes their arms to MICHAEL, the Gloved One, the Thriller.

From humble beginnings as a bubblegum star in Gary, Indiana, to his unenviable role as the most famous, and most maligned, celebrity in the world, this comprehensive biography reveals the good, the bad, and the ugly. It's the publishing industry's first comprehensive overview of a career that could only have happened in America. NO ONE, until now, has ever published a full journalistic overview of a superstar whose fame equals (and possibly exceeds) that of Elvis, Marilyn Monroe, the Queen of England, and the Pope. But here it is: MICHAEL, The Gloved One, the Thriller, the pop star whose antics—onstage and off—generated more ink, episodically, than any other living entertainer. Don't let this one pass you by! This spring, this biographical sizzler will generate controversy, and perhaps some empathy, for the much-maligned superstar.

## Blood Moon Productions:
## Salvaging the oral histories of Hollywood before they disappear forever.

This book was a finalist in Foreward Magazine's BOOK OF THE YEAR Awards,
and it generated an Honorable Mention from the Hollywood Book Festival the year it was published.

# THE MANY FACES OF MICHAEL JACKSON

## Rest in Peace, M.J.

1958-2009

NEWS FOR IMMEDIATE RELEASE OF A HOT CELEBRITY BIO, AVAILABLE IN MAY, WHOSE CONTENTS WILL BE UNIVERSALLY UNDERSTOOD BY THE ALIENATED ADOLESCENT THAT'S DORMANT BUT LURKING IN ALL OF US.

# JAMES DEAN
## Tomorrow Never Comes

Honoring the 60th Anniversary of Dean's Violent and Early Death

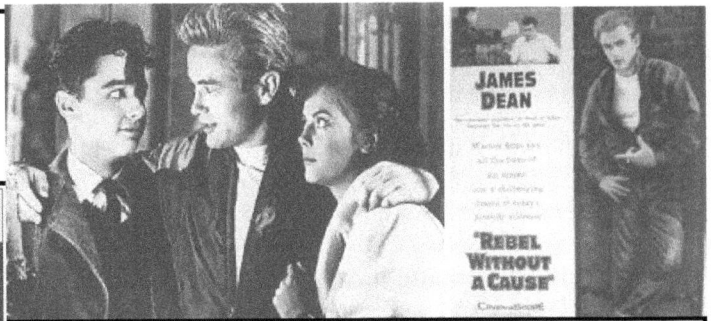

*Left to right, above,* **James Dean** *(center)* celebrates his character's bisexual trysts with *(left)* **Sal Mineo** and *(right)* **Natalie Wood** in *Rebel Without a Cause* (1955).

AFTER A FAST LIFE AND A VIOLENT EARLY DEATH, James Dean emerged from Hollywood in the 1950s as America's 2nd-most famous icon, with a "celebrity quotient" that's surpassed only by that of Marilyn Monroe.

In 2016, in commemoration of the 60th anniversary of his violent death, Blood Moon Productions released the most startling, unapologetic overview of James Dean ever published.

According to Blood Moon's president, Danforth Prince, "Until now, no one ever delivered a comprehensive, unapologetic overview of the brilliantly talented but emotionally disturbed farmhand from Indiana who maneuvered, manipulated, and seduced his way to the highest levels of media 'immortality.'

We're honored that its merits have already been recognized with a critical review from a respected book reviewer, two distinguished literary awards (see below for more information) and about a dozen news reports from mainstream newspapers and tabloids."

*East of Eden* (1955) was Hollywood's adaptation of John Steinbeck's allegory of the Cain and Abel story of the Old Testment. Central to its theme is the brothers' competition for the love and approval of their father.

In the publicity photo above, **James Dean** *(left)* unwittingly wins the heart of his brother's *fiancée* (**Julie Harris**, right) while clowning around with his stern and morally rigorous sibling *(center)* as portrayed by **Richard Davalos**.

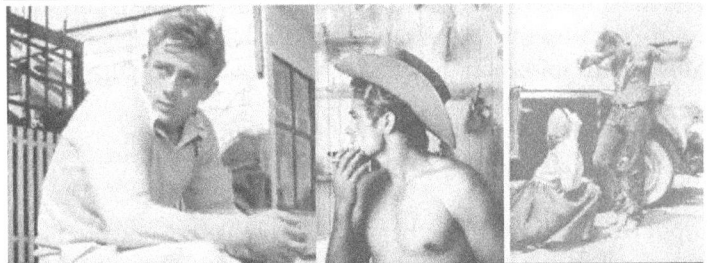

***

America's most enduring and legendary symbol of young rebellion, **James Dean** continues into the 21st Century to capture the imagination of the world. In recognition of his enduring appeal as Hollywood's most visible symbol of unrequited male rage, bars from California to Nigeria and Patagonia are named in his honor.

*Left photo*: In *East of Eden*: **James Dean** waiting forlornly to meet, for the first time, the mother who abandoned him
*Middle photo*: Dean as a Texas wildcatter before he strikes "black gold."
*Right photo*: Dean, with empathy, counsels Elizabeth Taylor, a frustrated but married woman, in *Giant*.

Dean, a strikingly handsome heartthrob, is a study in contrasts: Tough but tender; brutal at times but remarkably sensitive; a reckless hellraiser badass who could revert to a little boy in bed. From his climb from the dusty backroads of Indiana to the most formidable boudoirs of Hollywood, his saga is electrifying. He claimed that sexually, he didn t want to go through life with one hand tied behind his back. He corroborated his identity as a rampant bisexual through sexual interludes with **Marilyn Monroe, Rock Hudson, Elizabeth Taylor, Paul Newman, Natalie Wood, Shelley Winters, Marlon Brando, Steve**

McQueen, **Ursula Andress, Montgomery Clift, Pier Angeli, Tennessee Williams, Susan Strasberg,** and (are you sitting down?) both **Tallulah Bankhead** and (as a male prostitute) FBI director **J. Edgar Hoover.**

Woolworth heiress **Barbara Hutton** wanted to make him her toy boy. *Tomorrow Never Comes*, the newest in Blood Moon' s critically acclaimed Babylon Series, is the most penetrating look at James Dean to have emerged from the wreckage of his Porsche Spyder in 1955.

He flirted with Death until it caught him. Ironically, he said, "If a man can live after he dies, then maybe he s a great man." Before setting out on his last ride, he also said, "I feel life too intensely to bear living it."

CBS TV Producer
**Rodgers Brackett**

BEST BIOGRAPHY 2016 The Los Angeles Book Festival

**JAMES DEAN**
Tomorrow Never Comes

**BLOOD MOON** Productions, Ltd.

Honoring the 60th Anniversary of Dean's Violent and Early Death

Dean's early mentor & "enabler," **Alec Wilder**

# The enigmas surrounding one of Hollywood's best-known cults has at last

been decoded, thanks to the upcoming arrival, in early may (2016) of the first comprehensive biography of the rise to fame of hollywood icon, James Dean.

Written to commemorate the 60th anniversary of the violent death of a star who lived fast, died young, and became a legend, it's the recipient of the coveted **BEST BIOGRAPHY award from the 2016 LOS ANGELES BOOK FESTIVAL**, and the subject of widespread coverage in the tabloids just before its release.

**Walt Disney**

The most insightful and unvarnished book to have emerged from the wreckage that killed him, it was compiled after fifty years of input from James Dean's friends, lovers (male and female), and enemies. Much of the information within it has never been published before. new, uncensored, and unauthorized, it's the first comprehensive biography of the actor ever published, a groundbreaking, one-of-a-kind overview of the widely marketed yet widely misunderstood symbol of the inarticulated rage of america's rebellious youth.

Input from hundreds of other players revealed strong opinions, both good and bad, about the seductive but psychologically damaged powerhouse in their midst. Many of the revelations derived from specific first-hand sources whose voices have never been heard before.

FBI Director and sex client **J. Edgar Hoover**

**RODGERS BRACKETT,** a flamboyant but deeply closeted TV producer at CBS, Brackett first "discovered" James Dean, then a parking lot attendant and hustler turning tricks on the streets of Los Angeles. Falling desperately in love with him, Brackett paid his bills, introduced him to many of the entertainment industry's casting directors, and configured him as his live-in lover. Suffering through Dean's emotional aberrations and his perhaps bipolar mood swings, Brackett tolerated his "mercy fucks" and calculated infidelities with a constellation of other, often very famous, sex partners, all of which are documented. He also included insights into the young actor's murky explorations of the sexual undergrounds of New York City and L.A. Another

*Left photo:* Art director and set designer **Stanley Haggart,** friend and sometimes lover of Hollywood actor *(middle photo)* **William Hopper,** who portrayed private investigator Paul Drake on the TV series *Perry Mason.*

Hopper was the son of the much-feared gossip maven **Hedda Hopper** *(right photo)* . She employed Haggart as one of her "leg men." For years, he confirmed (and sometimes amplified) information associated with stories she eventually printed for nationwide distribution in her syndicated columns.

key source of information was:

**ALEC WILDER.** an influential and avant-garde composer of the early 50s, well-connected on Broadway and in hollywood, Wilder housed Dean during the early days of his migration to New York, introducing him to key players in the entertainment industry, including scriptwriters, television directors,singers such as **Peggy Lee**, and such playwrights as **Tennessee Williams** and **William Inge**. Many of them enticed Jimmy (or were enticed by him) onto their casting couches.

Another prominent source about Dean was **STANLEY HAGGART**, who was a "leg man" for **Hedda Hopper** and the lover of her son, **William Hopper**. Haggart was also an art director in the nascent days of early television, where Dean got his start. Haggart had first arrived in Hollywood in 1910. He knew seemingly everyone and by the time Dean entered the scene, Haggart had already befriended (and slept with) many stars. Haggart became a sort of advisor and counselor to Dean, providing a setting within his luxurious apartment in Manhattan or at his showcase home in Laurel Canyon, in Hollywood, for many of Dean's off-the-record trysts.

In addition to the testimonial of the three figures noted above, over the course of many decades, **Darwin Porter,** himself a long-time scholar of the celebrity scenes of NYC and LA, also drew upon never-before-published revelations from dozens of Dean's close friends and frenemies, **Montgomery Clift, Tennessee Williams, Geraldine Page, Eartha Kitt**, and at least a hundred others.

Revealed in this book for the first time are fact-driven overviews of Dean's friendships, feuds, and love affairs with his competitors...i.e. the other bad boys of Hollywood: **Marlon Brando, Steve McQueen, John Kerr, Monty Clift, Paul Newman, Rock Hudson, and Tony** ("Psycho") **Perkins**. Separate chapters are devoted to the backlot intrigues associated with the trio of movies that established James Dean as a Hollywood immortal: *East of Eden, Rebel Without a Cause*, and the saga indelibly associated with the oil industry of Texas, *Giant.*

This book also contains revelations about budding starlets Dean seduced, and a detailed behind-the-scenes look at his television and theater career, including his involvement in almost 40 teleplays (some of which are lost forever) in which he starred. In one of them (a Broadway production of André Gide's *The Immoralist*), he convincingly portrayed a male Arab prostitute and blackmailer. In another, *The Dark, Dark Hour*, he pointed a gun at a fading B-picture actor (**Ronald Reagan**) and threatened to blow out the brains of the character he was portraying.

James Dean long maintained, as richly described in this book, that he was sexually active—sometimes repeatedly—with some of the biggest names in Hollywood. Now, through the revelations in this book, we're aware of quite a legendary few: **Cole Porter, Tallulah Bankhead, Barbara Hutton, Judy Garland, Joan Crawford, Marilyn Monroe, Elizabeth Taylor, Grace Kelly**, and **Spencer Tracy**. Two unexpected but tantalizing outings include **J. Edgar Hoover** and the very closeted **Walt Disney**.

As Dean himself said, "Time spent on a casting couch is a lot easier that living on the hard, cold sidewalk, and I refuse to go through life with one hand tied behind my back."

America's then-most-celebrated playwright **Tennessee Williams**

Europe's then-most-sought-after photographer, **Cecil Beaton**

The ferociously ambitious TV star and gay/bisexual social climber, **Nick Adams,** portraying Johnny Yuma in ABC's TV series (1959-1961) *The Rebel*

*Two left-hand photos*: A theater marquee and a poster each identify **Giant**, the hit movie adapted from a novel by **Edna Ferber**. Her effigy is honored in a postage stamp celebrating her literary achievements. *Far right photo* is one of the most iconic photos aver associated with **James Dean.** In *Giant*, he plays an unlikely wildcatter who strikes it rich, and then self-destructs, during the unrestricted boom of Texas' early oil industry.

Woolworth heiress **Barbara Hutton** (left) with the **Duke of Buckingham** (in drag) at a costume party in the mid-1950s

Spectacularly handsome and spectacularly charming, the very promiscuous: **Rock Hudson** was James Dean's co-star in *Giant* (1956) and sometimes lover.

**"I Remember Mamma"**

In *East of Eden*, **James Dean** meets, for the first time, the mother who abandoned him, the "boss" of a local whorehouse, as brilliantly portrayed by **Jo Van Fleet**.

# JAMES DEAN

Beginning with his climb from the dusty backroads of Indiana to the most formidable *boudoirs* of Hollywood, the tortured saga of cult icon James Dean is electrifying. This new biography presents a penetrating and unapologetic look at show biz's most enduring icon of male rage—the most insightful and unvarnished to have emerged from the wreckage of the car crash that killed him.

Daily **Mail**
.com

News

Home | Showbiz | Femail | Royals | Sports | Health | Wellness | Science | Politics | Money | U.K. | Video | Travel | Puzzles

Shopping | Breaking News | Australia | Video | University Guide | China | Debate | Meghan Markle | Prince Harry | King Charles III | Weather | Most read | Login

## EXCLUSIVE: Marlon the master and James Dean his slave: Stars had 'secret master and slave S&M relationship' as Streetcar Named Desire star stubbed out cigarettes on his younger lover

- New book claims James Dean was in love with Marlon Brando and they become lovers - but it was a twisted S&M affair
- Brando was 'only in love with Brando' and would make Dean loiter outside his apartment in the desperate hope his idol would invite him in for sex
- When Dean first met Brando, in 1949, he told him he was 'his biggest fan' and the two kissed
- Dean showed Rogers Brackett, a Manhattan advertising executive who was his on-off boyfriend, how Brando stubbed out cigarettes oh him
- Book, called James Dean: Tomorrow Never Comes, also claims Dean had a gay threesome with Walt Disney and My Fair Lady director George Cukor

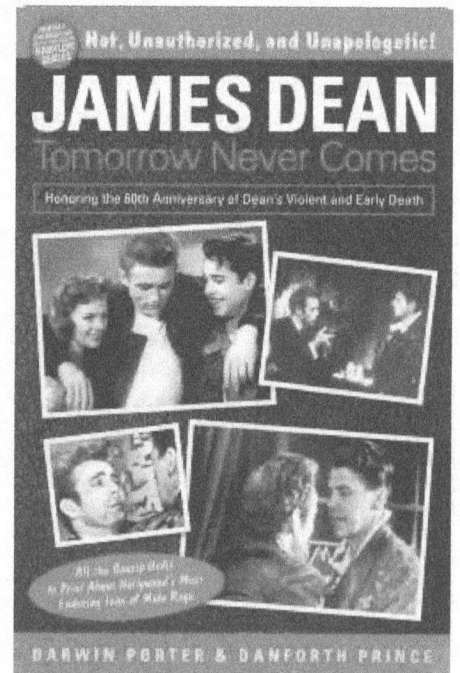

Hot, Unauthorized, and Unapologetic!

**JAMES DEAN**
Tomorrow Never Comes

Honoring the 60th Anniversary of Dean's Violent and Early Death

**DARWIN PORTER & DANFORTH PRINCE**

184

# JAMES DEAN
## Tomorrow Never Comes

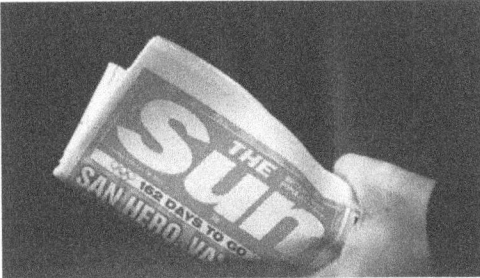

THE Sun

# THE TRUTH

THE Sun 100 122 DAYS TO GO SAN HERO, VA

---

Saturday, March 19, 2011 · The Sun 27

# ANYTHING GOES SEX LIFE OF A HOLLYWOOD LEGEND

By EMILY FAIRBAIRN

# S&M with Brando, threesomes with Garland, gay porn ...James Dean, the rebel without a care

THE DEAN MACHINE actor was 'insatiable'

KINKY Brando and Dean had a sadism and masochism sexual relationship

'I came to realise what a masochist Jimmy was'

ONE-OFF ... Jean Cromwell had breast slapped him.

STAR TURNS threesomes with Judy

SULTRY Brando wanted Marilyn off Dean

He stripped off. Spencer Tracy burst into tears

AMERICAN ACTOR
JAMES DEAN

Was Born on February 8, 1931
In The Seven Gables
Apartment House which
stood at this site

He starred in three
major Motion Pictures
*East of Eden*
*Rebel Without a Cause*
*Giant*

James Dean died on
September 30, 1955 at age
24 in a traffic accident
on a California Highway

He was laid to rest at Park
Cemetery in Fairmount,
Indiana, just 10 miles south
of this location

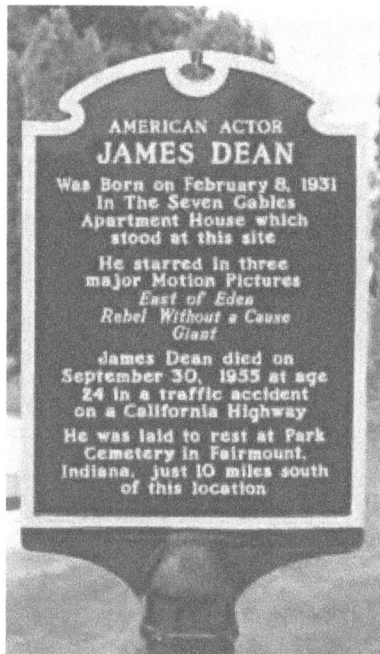

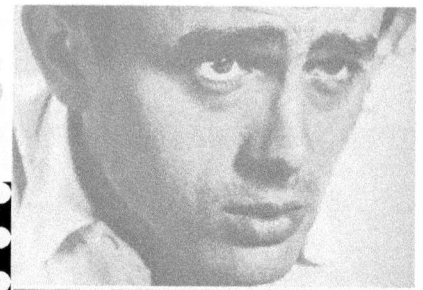

Rest in Peace
**James Dean**
(1931-1955)

**Fame is the most fickle of addictions**. She's capricious when, with her magic wand, she bestows her recognition on just a select few.

During their respective eras, many people achieve greatness and a kind of short-term recognition, but in the long course of history, most are forgotten. Only a handful emerge, generations later, to recapture the imagination of the world.

Cleopatra was not the greatest of the ancient pharaohs—her reign over Egypt was a disaster. But she immortalized herself through (highly politicized) affairs with both Julius Caesar and Marc Antony, then committed suicide with the poisonous bite of an asp as her empire crumbled around her. The drama, purported romance, and epic scope of her story prolonged the life of her legend.

*Moving forward to mid-20th Century Hollywood*: Despite the huge numbers of household names that emerged, only three of them became enduring pop culture icons: Elvis Presley, Marilyn Monroe, and James Dean.

Marilyn did not have a particularly distinguished career. Most of her early films are still unknown to the general public. But as a pop icon, she's remembered and in many cases, celebrated by each new generation. Her affairs with the Kennedy brothers, her controversial death, and perhaps her status as "the ultimate blonde" made her a legend.

Each of these three luminaries from "The American Century's" middle years—Elvis, Marilyn, and Jimmy Dean—had one element in common: Each of them died young and violently, and each is forever associated with the implicitly tragic motto "Live fast, die young."

Had she lived, Marilyn might have evolved into an aging, blowsy showgirl, desperately clinging to her elusive glory and fast-fading sexual charms. As her last director, George Cukor said, with pointed irony, "Marilyn was not meant for old age."

In contrast, as the youngest of the three (he died when he was 24), Jimmy might have gone on to make some of the greatest movies in Hollywood. At the time of his death, he could have had virtually any role he wanted in Hollywood. He was big, and growing bigger by the day.

Through Blood Moon Productions, in honor of the 60th anniversary of James Dean's death (September 30, 1955), I just released the most complete overview of his unfulfilled life ever told. During the fifty years I spent researching it, hundreds of witnesses, friends, "frenemies," and enemies, emerged with testimonials—many of them soaked with scandal—that have never been published before.

I was fortunate to have known and worked in television with many of the key figures of his life, each with a story to tell. During the course of its compilation (I actually began it back in 1970), I managed to obtain at least three prolonged "deathbed" confessions from mentors who loved and/or nurtured him, and who no longer had careers to protect. Some of the greatest stars, both male and female, seduced him; others detested him. Whereas Marlene Dietrich held him in contempt; Gary Cooper treated him like a son. As actress Geraldine Page told me, "No one ever knew the real James Dean because he only shared one small part of his life with each person, hugging the rest close to his breast."

Intense, handsome, vulnerable, and highly original, he mesmerized moviegoers and still does to this day. Each new generation reads into his legend their spin on what he symbolizes. Marlon Brando, to whom Jimmy was often compared, said, "Nothing fascinates the public as much as an unfinished life. All of us speculate what might have been in our own lives had we taken a different path."

*What the Critics Said about JAMES DEAN, TOMORROW NEVER COMES:*

## FROM THE MIDWEST BOOK REVIEW:

"*James Dean: Tomorrow Never Comes* arrives on the 60th anniversary of the violent death of a young star who became a legend, but if readers who are prior fans of other James Dean biographies expect this to be another rehash of information, they'd be happily mistaken.

"Much of its information has never been published before, because it offers new unauthorized details, uncensored information, and also includes powerful, in-depth analysis of a supporting cast of contemporaries. Insights from a closeted TV producer who first discovered James Dean, and others who interacted with him and often suffered from his mental swings and murky sexual explorations add to and expand the existing popular literature on this icon.

"From Dean's early TV career and his involvements with other actors and actresses to the truths about his sexual liaisons, the parade of women who marched into and out of his life, and his frustrations in the industry, *James Dean: Tomorrow Never Comes* makes for a vivid read especially recommended for prior fans of Dean's life and times.

"Be forewarned: this audience shouldn't expect a light coverage. The in-depth survey, with its amazingly large cast of contemporaries and characters, myths refuted and realities explored, and high-octane drama packs in over seven hundred pages of detail, which may look daunting, but which offer a rollicking good read.

"With so many facts and insights packing its pages, *James Dean: Tomorrow Never Comes* is a highly recommended book for any who would uncover more facets of the life and times of James Dean."

Senior Reviewer **Diane Donovan**
*The Midwest Book Review* and *California Bookwatch*

\*\*\*

## FROM THE WASHINGTON BLADE, Their edition of March 18, 2016

"Legendary Hollywood heartthrobs Marlon Brando and James Dean may have been more than fellow celebrities.
"LGBTQ Nation reports a new book,"*James Dean: Tomorrow Never Comes*," claims Brando and Dean had a sexual relationship that went far beyond vanilla trysts.
"Co-authors Danforth Prince and Darwin Porter interviewed Stanley Haggart who claims to have been a friend of Dean's at the time. Haggart says Brando and Dean would engage in slave and slave master sex play with Brando as the slave master and Dean as the slave.
"Haggart continued that Brando would force Dean to watch Brando have sex with strangers and make Dean wait outside Brando's apartment in the cold begging to be invited for an S&M session.
"'I got the impression that Jimmy was engaged in a cat-and-mouse affair with Brando, with Brando being the cat, of course," Haggart says. "Brando seemed to be toying with Jimmy for his own amusement. I think Brando was sadistically using Jimmy, who followed him around like a lovesick puppy with his tongue wagging."
"Brando opened up in his own 1976 biography that he wasn't afraid to admit he had same-sex experiences: 'Like a large number of men, I, too, have had homosexual experiences and I am not ashamed. I have never paid much attention to what people think about me,' Brando wrote.
"Rumors have swirled around Dean being bisexual or gay since his death in 1955."

"*The release of this book represents a milestone for Blood Moon. It's a tantalizing portrayal of the early days of television and of Hollywood in the 50s. We are especially proud of its senior co-author, Darwin Porter. His work has changed, permanently and forever, some of America's most deeply entrenched myths about fame, celebrity, and show-biz—and perhaps some of the core values of the American experience itself.*"

—Danforth Prince

# JIMMY STARS IN AN EXHIBITION
## AT A HOLLYWOOD PARTY HOSTED BY CECIL BEATON FOR BRITISH GAYS

Although largely devoid of details, the story of Jimmy's occasional performances at private sexual exhibitions has been documented in books before, including a mention in one edition of The Hollywood Babylon series. As he confessed to his roommate, William Bast, Jimmy performed in a sexual exhibition with **Roddy McDowall**, whom he'd met while filming *Hill Number One*. After their brief fling, Roddy suggested that "for a lark," they perform before some members of the cream of the crop of British expatriates, living in or else visiting Hollywood.

**Cecil Beaton**, the famous designer, photographer, and author, was staying in a mansion in Beverly Hills. He was throwing a party only for those "born and bred in Britain." It took some persuasion, but apparently, Roddy finally convinced Jimmy to perform a sex act with him in front of Beaton's mostly celebrated guests. **Cary Grant** was rumored to have attended the exhibition.

Beaton was an intimate friend of some of the most distinguished people on earth, including **Picasso, Jean Cocteau, Winston Churchill, Laurence Olivier**, and **André Gide**. He was known for his affair with **Greta Garbo**, and he also photographed members of the Royal family, including **Queen Elizabeth**.

Roddy and Jimmy arrived early at Beaton's rented manse. He was one of the most talkative men Jimmy had ever met. "Welcome to this *nouveau riche* home," Beaton said. "It's the ultimate statement in Hollywood vulgarity— that's why I love it so. When in Hollywood, why not wallow in vulgarity?" As the three men talked over drinks, whereas the British-born Roddy chatted amicably with Beaton, Jimmy had little to say. "I have seduced women but I infinitely prefer men,"

Beaton said. "I've gone from **Gary Cooper** to **Marlene Dietrich**. Women have their place. I love to dance with them, including the **Duchess of Windsor**. Cecil Beaton, depicted in the unattributed photo (probably a self-portrait) right, was the most arts-connected and avant-garde photographer in Europe. When he came to Hollywood on a "getting to know you" visit, he rented a house and threw some parties..... Jimmy was part of the entertainment. intimate parties, I've also danced and kissed the duke."

"I like to talk to women about plays, gowns, fashion," Beaton continued. "I'm particularly interested in their lovers—take **Porfirio Rubirosa**, for example. He has one of those enormous octaroon cocks."

"My time in Hollywood is made more endurable because I have my own octoroon cock upstairs," Beaton claimed. "He used to be a boxer. He's not the first black boxer who's made love to me. He is built to the point of monstrosity. God should put a limit on penile measurements. The penis can be just too gross in some instances." Before his guests arrived, Beaton took Jimmy and Roddy into a studio, where he asked them to strip so he could photograph each of them in the nude—"Only for my private collection, darlings, no one else will see them."

Details of that night became known only because author **Christopher Isherwood** attended, and later revealed what happened to such friends as **Tennessee Williams, Gore Vidal,** and ultimately, **Truman Capote**, who virtually broadcast it to everyone on his grapevine.

According to Isherwood, about thirty guests were shown into the master bedroom where Jimmy and Roddy were lying nude under a spotlight on a kingsize bed. Otherwise, the room was in darkness.

The bodies of both Roddy and Jimmy were met with sighs of approval. Slowly, the two young men began to make love to each other. A wild sixty-nine was followed by Jimmy sodomizing Roddy. After the voyeurs filed out, Jimmy and Roddy put back on their clothing and went downstairs to have drinks with their flirtatious voyeurs, some of whom tried to line up dates with them.

When Jimmy discussed the exhibition with Bast, his roommate wanted more details, but didn't get them. All that Jimmy told him was this: "I wanted the fucking limeys to see what an all-American boy, born and bred in the cornbelt of Indiana, looked like. I'm suntanned all over, as you know. That really turned them on. Those Brits don't get enough sunshine in their country. All of them have lilywhite bodies. When they get to Hollywood, they really go for suntanned boys."

He did add one final comment: "Roddy and I should have been paid."

**Roddy McDowall,** years after his co-starring role with Elizabeth Taylor as the child star of *Lassie Come Home* (1943), appears here in the late 1940s—all grown up and connected to every underground scene in Hollywood.

**Cecil Beaton,** depicted in the unatttributed photo *(probably a self-portrait)* above, was the most arts-connected and avant-garde photographer in Europe. When he came to Hollywood on a "getting to know you" visit, he rented a house and threw some parties.

**James Dean** was part of the entertainment.

Grand and gay literary chic: **Christopher Isherwood** attended a Los Angeles "exhibition" for British expatriates.

# Do You Remember THE FONDAS?

## We're talking about the Celebrated Golden Age Movie Star, Henry, and his Rebellious, News-Making Children, Jane and Peter

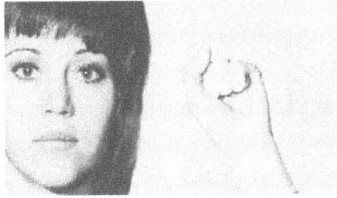

They were an acting dynasty that captivated the imagination of the American public for longer segments of the 20th Century than any other inter-generational family team in Hollywood.

Blood Moon Proudly announces the release of a two-volume biography that covers their saga in greater detail, and with more savvy and verve, than any other publishing project in history.

In September of 2022, in recognition of the 40th Anniversary of Henry Fonda's death, Blood Moon released Volume One of a two-part biography about one of the American Century's most celebrated Actors:

## HENRY FONDA: He Did It His Way

### by Darwin Porter and Danforth Prince

**What else?** Six months later, on Flag Day, 2023, in honor of a great American family (and a great American holiday), those same authors "unleashed" Volume Two

## THE FONDAS: Henry, Jane, & Peter  TRIPLE EXPOSURE

### Intertwined Sagas of Dysfunction, Tragedy, and Triumph

This two-volume set gives the most compelling and fascinating overview of the Fondas ever published.

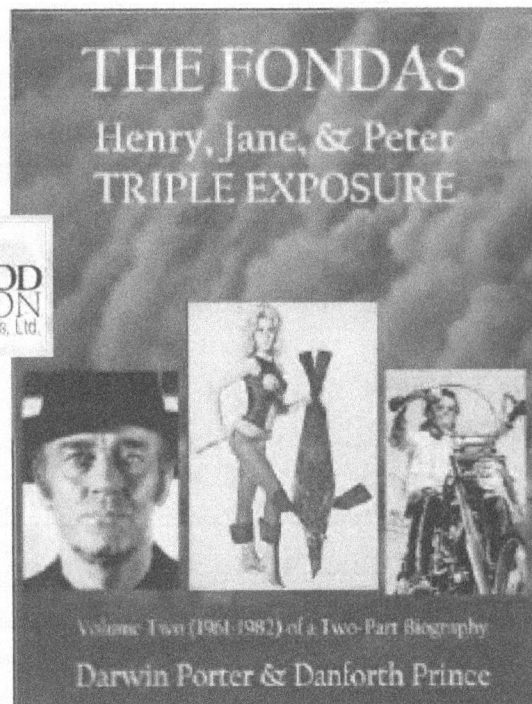

**Throughout his forty-five year career**, **Henry Fonda**—a stable, reassuring archetype of the American male—never gave a bad performance. immortalizing himself in such films as *Young Mr. Lincoln, The Grapes of Wrath,* and *Mister Roberts.* The torments of his introverted private life vied with his on-screen dilemmas. Personal dramas included five wives (two of whom committed suicide) and involvements in many of the seminal events (including active service in the Navy during World War II) of the 20th Century. His affairs starred such mega-divas as Lucille Ball, Joan Crawford, and Bette Davis, and with his second wife, Frances Seymour, he founded a Hollywood dynasty with movie star children, Jane and Peter.

This, **Volume One (1905-1960)** covers Henry's origins in Depression-era Nebraska, his rise to fame, his complicated dynamics with other celebrities,and his middle-aged years navigating his passion for acting with the business realities of Hollywood.

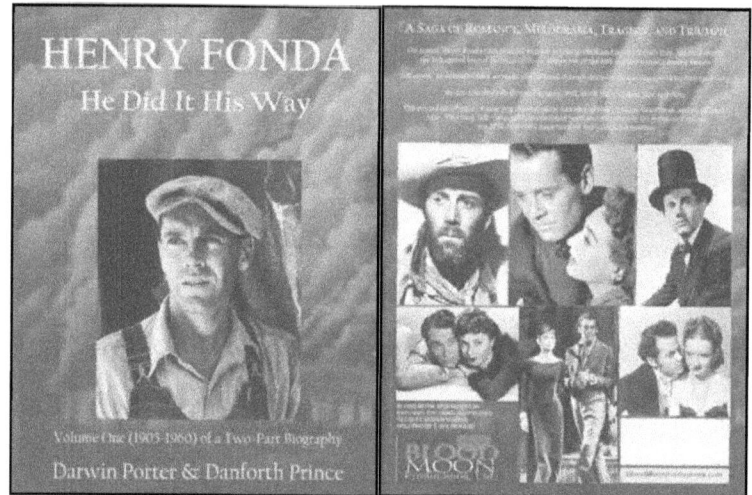

**HENRY FONDA: HE DID IT HIS WAY**
Volume One (1905-1960) of a Two-Part Biography
345 pages, with hundreds of photos
Available everywhere in September, 2022 through Ingram and Amazon.com,
ISBN 978-1-936003-84-6

**Volume Two (1961-1982)**, available in 2023, covers his complicated relationships with his famous and newsworthy daughter, Jane, and his (deceased) son, Peter.

Together, these books give the clearest, most detailed overview of this great American actor ever published.

## THE EARLY EVOLUTION OF THE AMERICAN ARCHETYPE KNOWN AS HENRY FONDA

The moody and frequently alienated patriarch of his clan, **Henry Fonda** evolved into the taciturn, integrity-soaked archetype of the American male.

*Here's a evolution of young* **Henry Fonda***:* **Photo #1** with **Jane Darwell** in *The Grapes of Wrath* (1940). **#2** as a bored (and somewhat boring) assistant to an inventor in *The Story of Alexander Graham Bell* (1939)*;* **#3** as an homesteader defending his family in *Drums Along the Mohawk* (1939); and **#4** with **Spring Byington** in *Way Down East.*

Throughout his forty-five year career, Henry Fonda,—a stable, reasuring archetype of the American male—never gave a bad performance. Personal tragedies included five wives (two of whom committed suicide) and affairs which starred such mega-divas as Lucille Ball, Joan Crawford, and Bette Davis.

This, **Volume Two (1961-1982)**, of Blood Moon's FONDA project, turns klieg lights on three emotionally intertwined mega-celebrities, two of them Oscar winners: The lanky and boyish American hero, **Henry**; his beautiful daughter, "the eternal rebel," **Jane**; and his son, **Peter,** a preppy-looking thrill-seeker indelibly linked to the "bad boy on a bike" narratives of the 60s.

It's the second, and final, installment of Blood Moon's coverage of the FABULOUS FONDAS, one of Hollywood's most talented but tormented families. It reflects the private agonies of a father, daughter, and son engulfed by the divisions of their respective generations and the ironies of the American Experience.

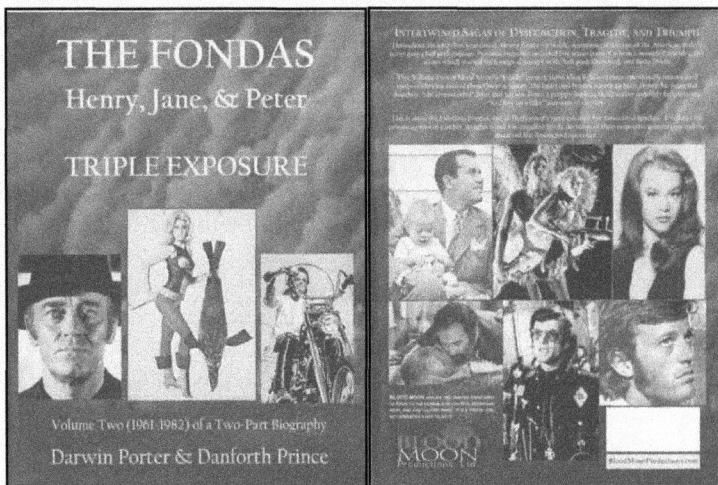

## The Early Evolution of Peter Fonda

In contrast to the daredevil, bike-riding, enraged hippy he eventually personified, **Peter Fonda** began his acting career in  bland "clean-cut preppie" roles.

But as the 20th Century roared forward, however, he morphed into a symbol of the revolutionary ferment of the 1960s.

*On the left,* he contributes, with **Sandra Dee**, to the squeaky-clean happy quotient of *Tammy and the Doctor* (1963). *On the right*, he's an uncomfortable draftee in the not-particularly-distinguished Broadway production of *Blood, Sweat, and Mr. Poole* (1961).

## The Early Evolution of Jane Fonda

Henry Fonda's firstborn, **Jane**—a freethinking child of Hollywood royalty—showed a curiosity and cosmopolitan flair that was otherwise rare among her peers.

Many of her early movies emphasized the easy, breezy, and kittenish aspects of her "easy on the eyes' physicality.

*Above left,* she tries to ensnare **Tony Perkins** in *The Tall Story;* (1960); *above, middle,* co-starring with **Robert Redford**, she's a "starved for affection" newlywed in *Barefoot in the Park' (1967)*. *In the right photo,* she "shows her best side (her words) in *Cat Ballou (1965)*.

HENRY FONDA
He Did It His Way

Volume One (1905-1960) of a Two-Part Biography
Darwin Porter & Danforth Prince

# NEW BOOK EXPOSES THE TROUBLED PRIVATE LIFE OF HENRY FONDA

By **Peter Sheridan**, posted September 21, 2022, as seen in: *The Daily Express, The Daily Mail, The Daily Mirror, The Sunday Mirror, The Mail on Sunday, The Daily Star (UK), The Sydney Morning Herald, Boing Boing, The Age, The Irish Mirror, and more.*

A shocking new biography exposes the troubled and tormented private world behind the actor's facade.

"Henry Fonda was very different offscreen from his public persona as the face of America," says **Darwin Porter**, co-author of a new two-part biography.

"He was a bad husband and bad father, self-absorbed, uncomfortable displaying emotion, not a very lovable man. And he was a womanizer, unfaithful through four of his five marriages.

On screen he represented traditional American values, but in his personal life strayed far from them."

Fonda careered through affairs with a series of Hollywood leading ladies including **Joan Crawford, Greta Garbo, Marlene Dietrich, Bette Davis, Tallulah Bankhead** and **Barbara Stanwyck**, the book reveals.

"I'm not going to let marriage stop me from having fun on the side," Fonda told friends.

He had a decades-long on-off affair with comedy star **Lucille Ball**, and Porter claims: "She was the love of his life. I think he regretted not marrying Lucille."

Though known as a family man, father to famous offspring **Jane and Peter Fonda**, in reality he ran from parental responsibilities.

"Henry Fonda is the first to admit he's a lousy husband and an absentee father," said his fourth wife, Italian baroness **Afdera Franchetti.**

Born in small-town Nebraska, printer's son Fonda was traumatized at the age of 14 by witnessing a lynching. Riddled with bullets, the mutilated body of the black victim was dragged through the streets.

"It was the most horrendous sight I'd ever seen," recalled Fonda, who became a lifelong human rights advocate.

After dropping out of university he found fame on Broadway, and in 1931 married beautiful actress **Margaret Sullavan**. But like many of Fonda's lovers, she found the handsome star a let down in bed. "You're 26 years old and still don't know how to make love to a woman," Sullavan raged at him.

Waspish movie legend **Bette Davis** was more scathing, describing her fling with Fonda as "the easiest 30 seconds I've ever spent with any man".

Within months of the marriage, Sullavan began having affairs, and soon abandoned her husband, divorcing in 1933. "She had mental issues, and Fonda didn't give her the love and support she needed," says Porter. When her fame faded, Sullavan became depressed. She died of what was ruled an accidental overdose in 1960.

Meanwhile, Fonda became roommates with rising star **Jimmy Stewart** in New York and then Los Angeles, forging a life-long friendship. "We shared everything from a single bed in a cramped apartment to much later some of the greatest stars in Hollywood, like **Greta Garbo**," recalled Fonda with boastful vulgarity.

Porter claims: "The only person Fonda ever really cared for was Jimmy Stewart."

But the next woman in his sights was wealthy widow **Frances Seymour Brokaw**, an American blue-blood blonde beauty. They wed in 1936 after a whirlwind romance, producing children Jane and Peter. Yet Jane, born in 1937, recalls her father as emotionally distant, confessing: "I was desperate for his attention."

This,Volume One (1905-1960) the first of a two-volume set, celebrates the cinematic subtleties of an actor who was said to never give a bad performance, and whose children evolved into mega-celebrities in their own right.

Henry's private life was about passion, a rise from poverty, suicides, artistic victories, heartbreak, and on occasion, love.

It reveals painful, unvarnished truths about a self-effacing actor who evolved into everyone's image of the quintessential American male during the "midpoint years" of the American Century.

Porter explains: "Fonda was not an emotional or present father. Sometimes he'd come home after a day's work and have a meal sent to his room rather than eat with his family. He felt competitive with his children, and was jealous when Jane won two Oscars before he got his own."

He finally got close to the acclaim he craved for the role of Tom Joad in the 1940 classic *The Grapes Of Wrath.* Nominated for an Academy Award, he lost out to his best friend Jimmy Stewart in *The Philadelphia Story.* Fonda lamented: "Never again will I have such a triumph… I feel like my one chance to ever win an Oscar has come and gone."

The book reveals intriguing Hollywood classics that might have been. **Olivia de Havilland** wanted Fonda to play Ashley Wilkes in *Gone With The Wind.* "The part was written for me," Fonda told friends, but producer **David Selznick** ruled against him, hiring **Leslie Howard** instead.

Fonda also turned down 1949's *The Sands of Iwo Jima* – one of John Wayne's best films – and 1952's *High Noon,* Gary Cooper's greatest Western. Fonda called it "the mistake of my life".

He even refused the lead part in *It's A Wonderful Life,* handing his friend Stewart the role of a lifetime. Though he starred in several Westerns, Fonda secretly hated them, because "horse riding leaves me with a sore a***".

A literary elitist, he starred in 1956 epic *War & Peace* but dismissed it as "the Reader's Digest version of the Tolstoy novel".

When America entered the Second World War, Fonda, then aged 37, enlisted in the US Navy seeking action, rejecting the chance to stay at home making patriotic movies.

He fought heroically in the Pacific, his ship surviving two kamikaze bombing attacks, but Jane offered an alternate theory for his enlistment: "I think he also wanted to escape life as a family man, at least for a period."

Fonda returned to Hollywood, but combat had changed him into even more of "a hardened, distant man." Porter's biography – *Henry Fonda, Volume One (1905-1960)* – claims. "His family got the worst of it. He had extreme difficulty expressing his emotions."

Meanwhile, wife **Frances** was slipping into mental illness, tormented by his barely hidden affairs. When Fonda asked for a divorce, she spun into depression. Removed to a mental hospital, she fatally cut her throat rather than endure the ignominy of their split.

Fonda had been cheating on Frances with 20-year-old **Susan Blanchard**, half his age, soon to become his third wife in 1950. They adopted a baby daughter, **Amy**, but Fonda still fled at the sight of a dirty nappy, confessing: "Fatherhood was never really my calling in life."

Susan felt abandoned. "After two months of our marriage I realized he was the wrong companion for me," she said. She endured six unhappy years before filing for divorce.

Fonda's brides only grew younger. He next wed Italian socialite **Afdera Franchetti,** 26 years his junior, in 1957, who squandered his fortune on lavish parties and jewels. Fonda was forced to star in TV series *The Deputy* to pay the bills. But their age gap proved a yawning chasm, and she filed for divorce in 1961.

Disillusioned with Hollywood, Fonda returned to Broadway in the early 1960s. "He wasn't getting the roles he wanted," says Porter. "And he despised the Method acting of **Marlon Brando** and **James Dean.**"

Back in New York, Fonda met his fifth wife, **Shirlee Mae Adams,** 27 years his junior. "Henry was an older man, but he was God-damned handsome," she said.

They wed in 1965, and against all odds stayed together until he died from heart disease in 1982, aged 77. "Shirlee saved me from the depths of my depression on many a night," said Fonda.

But Porter reveals: "He was not a happy man in his final years. Until he made *On Golden Pond* in 1981, finally winning his Oscar, he didn't like most of the films he was making in his later years, taking them only for the money. His final years were marked by illness, ageing ungracefully."

Fonda ultimately came to admit he was not the man moviegoers knew and loved. "I ain't Henry Fonda, that man on the screen or stage," he said. "Nobody could have that much integrity."

*Henry Fonda, Volume One (1905-1960)* **by Darwin Porter and Danforth Prince (Blood Moon Productions)**

En route to fame and fortune, **HENRY FONDA** sustained five —for the most part— miserably unhappy marriages

Girls with soft smooth skin have appeal!... says MARGARET SULLAVAN

**#1: Margaret Sullavan.** Vain, insecure, caustic, and blithely cruel, she inflicted psychic wounds that some observers defined as sadistic.

**#2 Frances Ford Seymour.** Unstable, and beneficiary of a very large trust fund, she committed suicide in a mental asylum after a devastatingly unhappy sojourn with her new husband in Hollywood. She was the mother of Jane and Peter.

**#3 Susan Blanchard.** More a friend to Jane (her contemporary) than to her perpetually distracted husband, Henry, it was intense and heavy—until it wasn't

**#4 Baroness Afdera Franchetti.** Petulant, pretentious, and outrageous, she was described as "a woman who doesn't get hangovers...she gives them."

Distantly linked to headliners in the recently deposed Fascist regime of Italy, she thrived within the postwar *Dolce Vita* and reveled in its links to Hollywood. She spent LOTS of her celebrity husband's money before the marriage faded into oblivion.

**#5 Shirlee Mae Adams.** Congenial and diplomatic, with good "people skills," this former flight attendant nurtured Henry through his final days and—as everyone agreed—his happiest marriage.

# Boomer Times
## & Senior Life

# JANE FONDA
## HOW BARBARELLA BECAME A GOLDEN GIRL

After an absence of 46 years, Jane Fonda has returned to Broadway. The two-time Oscar winner was last seen on The Great White Way in the 1963 drama, *Strange Interlude*.

The 1960s "sex kitten" of *Barbarella* and *Cat Ballou* had just turned 71 when she signed to appear on stage again in Moises Kaufman's *33 Variations*.

Her character in the play is a musicologist suffering from Lou Gehrig's disease. Every night on Broadway Jane is racing against time and mortality while trying to solve one last mystery. Why did the increasingly deaf Ludwig van Beethoven, also racing against the clock, spend his last precious months on earth writing 33 variations of a pedestrian waltz written by Anton Diabelli, the Viennese music publisher. Beethoven himself had derided the piece as "a cobbler's patch."

Regrettably, Kaufman's play is soggy, not a worthy comeback vehicle for such a great star as Jane Fonda, who immortalized herself in such roles as *They Shoot Horses, Don't They?* in 1969 and *Klute* in 1971. In *Klute* she played a prostitute. The night she won the Oscar for *Klute,* she told reporters, "Working in Hollywood does give one a certain expertise in the field of prostitution."

Reviews of Jane's performance in *33 Variations*, as a character confronting "the betrayal of my body," were impressive, but the play itself was panned. In a headline, *The New York Post* proclaimed, "It's Not Music to Our Ears."

Coming out of a long retirement, the daughter of Henry Fonda has aging on her mind these days. She admits to being shocked at looking at realistic, unadorned photos of herself. "I am old," she said. "I am matronly. I asked one of my co-stars, "How come bags under Vanessa Redgrave's eyes look noble and under mine they look like crap?"

In addition to playing an "expiring" character on Broadway, Jane has also signed with Random House to write a book on aging. Formerly she was the guru of feminine physical fitness in America, reigning as our aerobics queen.

Jane first confronted aging when she appeared in the 1981 *On Golden Pond*, arguably Hollywood's greatest film on the subject. This was the only movie she ever made with her father, Henry. *On Golden Pond* also starred Katharine Hepburn.

In 1982 Jane and her famous father became the first father-daughter couple ever to be Oscar nominated in the same year. She didn't win, but accepted the Oscar on behalf of her father, who was too ill to attend the presentations.

In 2005, also with Random House, Jane published her autobiography, *My Life So Far*. It was a worthy book, full of insight, but it was marred by scandalous headlines. The veteran screen goddess claimed that her late and former husband, Roger Vadim, who had directed her in *Barbarella,* had forced her to join in three-way orgies with other women. She called these sex sessions "cruel and misogynistic."

"It seems shocking that I did that, but I convinced myself that it was fine, even though

it was killing my heart," she wrote. She divorced Vadim in 1973.

In another book, *Prisoner of X,* Allan MacDonell, editor of *Hustler* magazine, claimed that Jane, with her third husband, media mogul **Ted Turner**, had appeared in a home movie, a porno flick with an unidentified brunette. Other editors have confirmed the existence of this racy videotape, whose exposure made unwelcome headlines for Jane around the world.

It was particularly embarrassing for her, as she'd become a Born Again Christian while living in her present home in Atlanta, Georgia. In 2001 Jane divorced her empire builder husband after a tumultuous decade-long marriage.

The existence of the smutty video was only a minor controversy. Jane is long accustomed to unwelcome headlines, often painting her as a monster, like the character she portrayed in her comeback film in 2005, *Monster in Law.*

She was born to privilege, growing up among Hollywood's elite. **Frances Seymour Brokaw,** her mother, named her "Lady Jane Seymour Fonda" on her birth on December 21, 1937. The lady part in her name was inspired by Lady Jane Seymour, one of the ill-fated wives of Henry VIII, to whom Jane is distantly related on her mother's side.

When Jane was 12 years old, her mother committed suicide. Jane grew up with her father, whom she claimed was cold and distant—"as chilly as an Arctic night." Escaping to Vasser, a women's college, in her late teens, she "went wild" in her own words, becoming a sort of sex addict.

She lost her virginity to an older man in 1955 and has been losing it ever since in the arms of everyone from **Warren Beatty** to assorted members of the Black Panthers during the 1960s.

Her first marriage was to **Tom Hayden**, an antiwar activist and politician. He led Jane into her most controversial role, that of a major and highly visible protester against the Vietnam War. For this, her reputation was forever tainted as "Hanoi Jane."

In a photograph that shocked America, Jane allowed herself to be seen sitting on an enemy aircraft gun in North Vietnam in the middle of the war. She later expressed her regret for her support of the Viet Cong. "It hurt many soldiers," she lamented. "It galvanized such hostility. It was the most horrible thing I could possibly have done. It was just thoughtless."

Despite her apology, the memory of Vietnam veterans is long. Every night on Broadway, Jane is confronted with dozens of protesters, who scream "traitor" as she enters the theater.

One vet, **Frank Careccia**, told the press, "When her day of reckoning comes, I trust that God has reserved a special place for her in the bowels of hell."

Faced with her protesters, Jane holds her head high and walks past them, having long ago moved away from her political positions of yesterday and her errant husbands, none of whom was a great candidate for marriage.

After I left the theater after watching Jane perform brilliantly in an unconvincing drama, I was struck by one sentiment she'd expressed on stage.

Like the character she plays in *33 Variations,* some of us in the years that remain will also have to face a body that will inexorably degenerate. But when there is so much living yet to do, so much to accomplish, an inevitable question might appear, as it did to Jane in the play. The question asked is, ***"How does one begin to let go?"***

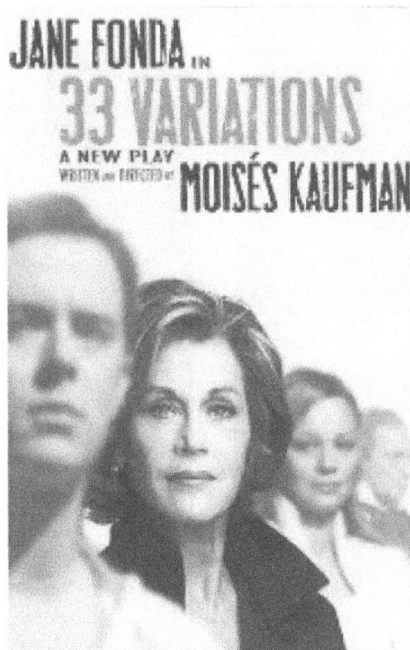

JANE FONDA in
33 VARIATIONS
A NEW PLAY
WRITTEN and DIRECTED by MOISÉS KAUFMAN

### *33 Variations*

as reviewed by Stephanie Zacharek in March of 2009:

In Moisés Kaufman's *33 Variations*, Jane Fonda plays an American musicologist—a Beethoven specialist—who decides to go ahead with a research trip to Bonn, Germany, even though she's just been diagnosed with ALS (Lou Gehrig's disease).

The action in *33 Variations* shifts not just between countries but also from century to century. Fonda meets the challenge like a warrior queen. She uses her trim, sturdy frame to suggest the myriad ways in which our bodies—one way or another, either through aging or ill health—can ultimately betray our minds.

What *33 Variations* suggests, ultimately, is that when ideas breathe at all, it's because human beings have given shape to them in the first place. We're their alphabet, their notation, and the form we give them can linger, miraculously, even after we're gone.

## Where Sex is Currency
### Jane Plays a very modern Damsel in Distress

Remember that *noir* survelance thriller, *Klute* (1971)? In it, Jane (convincingly) played a tough but vulnerable "hooker in trouble."

Targeted by a mad serial killer, she spills her guts only to her psychiatrist, and to a police detective, played by Donald Sutherland who morphs into her lover.

Feminism rocks, Jane wins the day. We, the audience, rooted for her wildly.

And then there was *On Golden Pond* (1981) Jane's chance to both memorialize her iconic father and to engage with him as an actor. Loaded behind the scenes with high anxiety on every level, it reached ambitiously and succeeded in ways that even made her Daddy proud.

Here, **Henry Fonda** (never noted for his emotional warmth) replicates the dysfunctional "old days" with the brilliantly irritable **Katharine Hepburn**...who was never particularly noted for her emotional warmth either. Ailing with Parkinson's Disease at the time, she soaked everything about the drama with a passion and direction it would not otherwise have had.

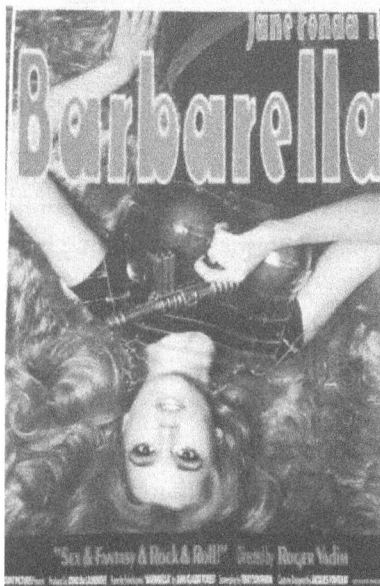

The experimental low-budget clunker, *Barbarella,* starring **Jane** as directed by her then-husband—the Franco-Russian eccentric, Roger Vadim—endeared her to the *nouvelle vague* of Europe. It was artsy, yes. But was it endearing or even interesting? Somehow, that never seemed important.

**Henry Fonda** *(left),* along with daughter **Jane** and **Peter,** look over a movie script that would have united the trio on screen. Jane would have been cast as his whorish daughter, with Peter "running wild."

Collectively, they rejected the script.

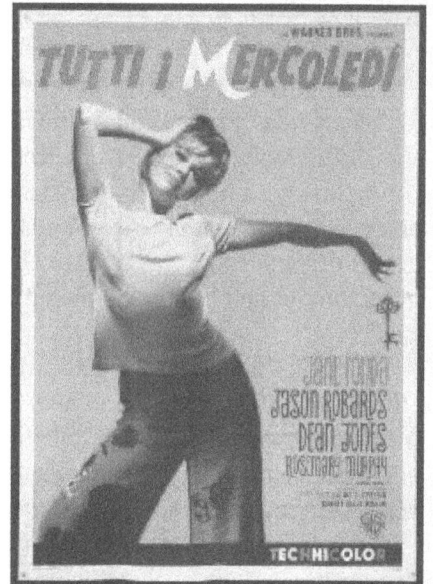

**Jane** with **Dean Jones** in the frothy, sexually suggestive romp, *Any Wednesday* (1966).

*Lower photo*: Press and PR for *Tutti i Mercoledi,* its Italian-language adaptation.

**Jane**, more than any other actress who preceded her, taught two or three generations of foreign men that American women are hot.

**Love, American Style**. Steeped in the allure and mores of France, thanks to her very *avant-garde* marriage to **Roger Vadim,** Jane "imported" some of the kittenish aspects of **Brigitte Bardot** to the U.S. Here she appears with **Robert Redford** in *Barefoot in the Park* (1967).

The newlyweds find themselves in a five-story walkup apartment, which is the comedy's running gag.

# CLIMBING THE LAVENDER LADDER

### Blood Moon's Newest Biography is a Disavowal of Mainstream Belief Patterns about Paul Newman: His Secret Life as a Bisexual

How a gaggle of lovers, friends, enemies, acquaintances, and admirers recall his tempestuous early decades—with LOTS of information about the sexual underground of Hollywood and Broadway from 1950 to around 1975.

### Darwin Porter Dares to State the Perhaps Gigantic News that Newman was a Promiscuous Bisexual During scattered episodes and eras of his career.

This is a pioneering and posthumous biography of Paul Newman, a charismatic icon of Tinseltown whose rule over the hearts of American moviegoers lasted for more than half a century. It's loaded with never-before-published revelations that look behind the innocent-looking baby blues that enthralled the movie-going public.

He became one of the most potent, desirable, and ambiguous sex symbols in America, a former sailor from Shaker Heights, Ohio, who parlayed his ambisexual charm and extraordinary good looks into one of the most successful careers in Hollywood.

Shortly after its release, this title won an honorable mention for biography from the NEW ENGLAND BOOK FESTIVAL.

His eyes were blue, his gait was macho, and his demeanor was cool, so cool. Here' are two views of film superstar **Paul Newman**.

In the upper photo, he plays a character inspired by Billy the Kid in *Left Handed Gun*. In the lower photo, he radiates masculine beauty and male cool in *Butch Cassidy and The Sundance Kid*.

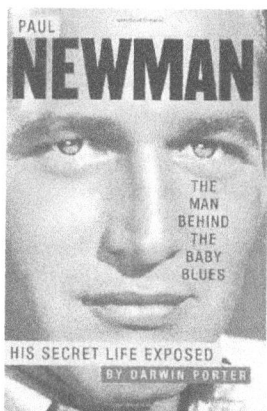

The public's awareness of the emotional links between Georgia-born **Joanne Woodward** *(left figure in each of the photos above)* and **Paul Newman** became as deeply entrenched as Katharine Hepburn's association with Spencer Tracy and Clark Gable's legendary obsession with Carole Lombard.

But on the down-low, Hollywood insiders (and a lot of the Broadway intelligentsia too) always took those marital "links" with hefty doses of salt. Rumors about each of their respective same-sex infidelities were widely bruited around and about. The most credible of the lot were carefully examined within Darwin Porter's widely reviewed biography

**In the opinion of many of his fans**, Paul Newman's emotional and sexual involvements with the women in his life (Monroe, Crawford, Taylor, Grace Kelly, Audrey Hepburn, and perhaps most importantly, Joanne Woodward) are more compelling than the equivalent relationships he shared with men.

But according to a hot new biography by Darwin Porter, the full story of what Newman did as a means to his end in Golden-Age Hollywood hasn't ever been fully revealed — until now. Published by Blood Moon, the book is *Paul Newman, The Man Behind the Baby Blues, His Secret Life Exposed.*

During a span of more than 50 years, insiders on Broadway and in Hollywood have spoken of Paul Newman's closeted life. Details about the megastar's bisexual history have been among the entertainment industry's worst-kept secrets.

For decades, the underground press has included Paul Newman on their list of bisexual or gay stars, a list that included Rock Hudson, Roddy McDowall, Richard Chamberlain, Farley Granger, Tab Hunter, Burt Lancaster, Marlon Brando, James Dean, Montgomery Clift, and countless others. "WAS PAUL NEWMAN GAY?" ran one headline. Yet another proclaimed: "DEEP INSIDE THE HOLLYWOOD CLOSET: RUMOR MILL IMPLICATES PAUL NEWMAN. "

Even during Newman's lifetime, Larry Quirk, the dean of Hollywood biographers, wrote about Paul Newman's "homosexual panic" and how he maneuvered his way "up the lavender ladder," a veiled reference to his casting couch interludes with playwrights Tennessee Williams (author of Newman's star vehicle, *Cat on a Hot Tin Roof)* and William Inge. (Newman's first starring role on Broadway was in Inge's *Picnic.)*

The secret life of Paul Newman reached the peak of its exposure and speculation during the 1970s, when Newman acquired the film rights to *The Front Runner,* a best-selling novel about a homosexual coach who falls desperately in love with his (male) star athlete.

In his role as the film's producer, Newman originally offered the role of the athlete to Robert Redford, who refused to play a gay character, fearing that it would harm his image at the box office. Consequently, Newman negotiated with Cal Culver, America's leading gay porn star of the 1970s, to play the role. Cal, a friend and confidant of Darwin Porter, later revealed to the gay press that he had had an affair with Newman. Additionally, Darwin's best

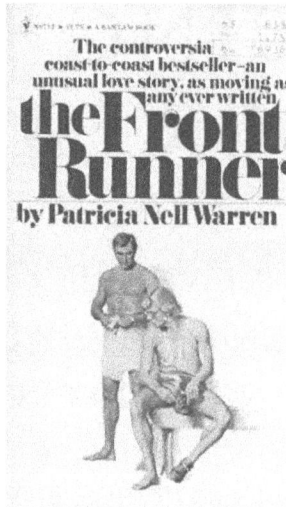

After its proven success as a bestselling gay-themed novel, **The Front Runner**, by Patricia Nell Warren entertained frantic bids from Hollywood producers who wanted to adapt it into a film. Before the project shriveled and died, Paul Newman was suggested for the (gay) coach and **Cal Culver** (aka **Casey Donovan**), then a widely acknowledged porn star with mainstream ambitions) lobbied strenuously for the role of the coach's love interest.

During the brouhahas that (briefly) raged, Culver insisted, publicly, that as part of the "audition" process, he and Newman had sustained a sexual affair.

Out, proud, and defiant, **Sal Mineo** *(right)* a vocal advocate for gay rights and aesthetics, also asserted, frequently, that he and **Paul Newman** had been, for a while, a "'ride 'em cowboy' item."

In the photo above, they're seen touring the hills around Jerusalem during their filming of Otto Preminger's *Exodus (1960)*

Beginning with *Butch Cassidy and the Sundance Kid* (upper photo) and ending with *The Sting* (lower photo)**, Robert Redford** and **Paul Newman** made a great screen team together.

It was Redford who broke free from their movie-making alliance, fearful that the growing interest in Newman's fluid sexuality might negatively affect his own commercial appeal as a bankable star.

friend, novelist James Leo Herlihy, had an affair with Newman when he was trying to persuade him to star as Joe Buck in the film version of his novel, *Midnight Cowboy.*

Many of Newman's personal friends, particularly those from the Actors Studio, spoke privately over the years about Newman's sexuality. They included actress Janice Rule (who later became a psychotherapist, with a respected practice in New York City), Rod Steiger, Geraldine Page, Eartha Kitt (who was introduced to Newman via her best friend, James Dean), and "Vampira," (aka Maila Nurmi), TV-land's first Goth,

198

Early in their respective careers, **Tony Perkins** admitted to an affair with Paul Newman when they were roommates at the Chateau Marmont in Hollywood.

Perkins appears above in a scene with **Jane Fonda**—who plays a horny coed—in her first full-length feature film, *Tall Story* (1960).

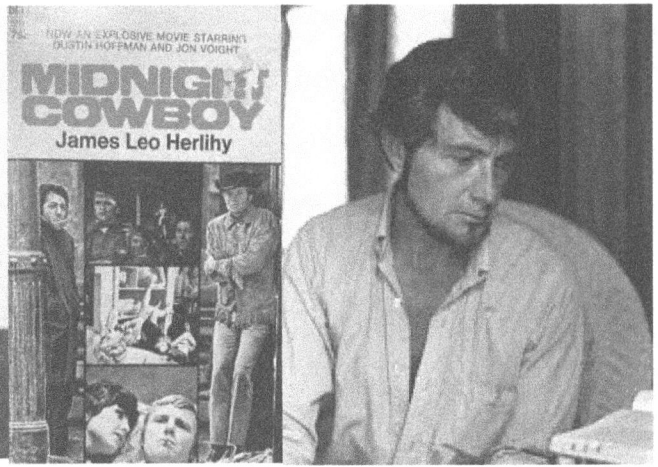

and a famous personality of the 1950s.

Tony Perkins, a friend of Herlihy's, privately admitted that he'd sustained a sexual affair with Newman when they both lived at the Chateau Marmont in Los Angeles in the 50s. The self-admittedly gay writer Gore Vidal spoke openly about his near-obsessional fixation on Newman during Newman's appearance in Gore's teleplay of *Billy the Kid*. And during one particularly complex point in their relationship, Paul Newman and his then "mistress," Joanne Woodward, shared a Malibu beach house with Vidal and his "husband," Howard Austen. Throughout that chapter of their lives, all four members of the *ménage* remained "artfully nonspecific" as to the direction of the emotional links going on within that beach house.

**James Leo Herlihy** *(photo, right)* author of the pop novel *Midnight Cowboy* and a then-resident (with Darwin Porter) in Key West, also tried to engage Paul Newman (left photo) into both his literary ambitions and his erotic dreams.

Confronted with meager sales of his then-shocking novel about a male hustler-cowboy on the make in NYC during the swinging sixtiies, Herlihy lobbied hard to "package" Newman, as Joe Buck, a role which later won an Oscar nomination for Jon Voight.

Herlihy's sales pitches to Newman ended up in a sexual affair with the object of his lust, Newman himself. News of their affair reverberated through the arts communithy of Key West. It was Newman who, according to gossip at the time, backed out of the deal, afraid as he was of its commercial consequences.

**Part of Marlon Brando's appeal** as a film star derived from how richly he exuded raw, macho sexuality from virtually every pore. Self-acknowledged as a bisexual, with an entrenched reputation as a very promiscuous sexual player, he had this to say about the public's perception of his rival (displayed here as he appeared in *Hud* (1963) **Paul Newman:**

*"Paul Newman had just as many on-location affairs as the rest of us, and he was just as bisexual as I was. But whereas I was always getting caught with my pants down, he managed to do it in the dark, with not a paparazzo in sight. He might have bedded Marilyn Monroe or Elizabeth Taylor the night before, but he always managed to show up for breakfast with Joanne Woodward, with those baby blues looking as innocent as a Botticelli angel. He never fooled me. It takes an alleycat to know another alleycat. Did I ever tell you what really happened between Newman and me? If that doesn't grab you, what about what went on between James Dean and Newman? Let me tell you about the so-called model husband if you want to look behind those famous peepers."*

**—Marlon Brando**

**Montgomery Clift,** shown here on a studio backlot with **Elizabeth Taylor** during the peak of their respective youth and beauty, was a famously closeted and notoriously promiscuous homosexual

His brother, Brooks Clift, a close personal friend of Darwin Porter when they both worked in TV advertising in New York City, often discussed his self-destructive brother's prolonged sexual affair with Paul Newman

**Paul Newman** with his first wife, the unlucky and unsuccessful actress, **Jackie Witte**. They lived together on the north shore of Staten Island, in a nondescript apartment a few blocks from Darwin Porter's home.

During the course of their otherwise nondescript marriage (which produced three children) Paul struggled, unrecognized, for small parts and "slept around" during the then relatively disease-free years before AIDS. Nearly everyone agrees that their marriage hit the rocks when Paul met Joanne Woodward.

199

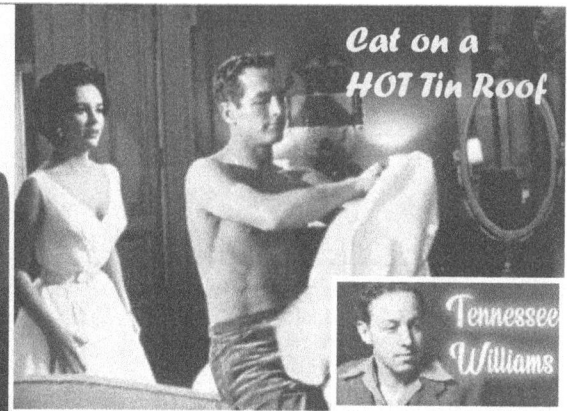

Cat on a HOT Tin Roof

*Tennessee Williams*

Young **Paul Newman**, clad in the style of white T-shirt that had helped make Marlon Brando famous, poses in front of a poster advertising the Broadway production of *Picnic*.

At least some of the credit for then-new-comer-to Broadway Newman's acquisition of the role derived from the very famous (gay) playwright **William Inge**, who had lobbied ferociously on his behalf.

Having begun her show-biz career as a dancer in a chorus lineup, **Janice Rule,** shown here with **James Stewart**, abandoned acting to become a licensed therapist to a clientele of other actors. Later in her life, she had a lot to say about the down-low lavender life of Paul Newman.

As the female lead in the screen adaptation of William Inge's Broadway play, *Picnic,* she learned a lot about the onstage dynamics of the play that had preceeded her film, and about Inge's convoluted relationship with one of the male stars **(Newman)**.

After Paul's collusion with William Inge in *Picnic*, another impossibly famous (gay) playwright set his eyes on Paul. Newman. It was the quixotic and temperamental **Tennessee Williams**, another close acquaintance of **Darwin Porter.**

It was Williams who "eased" Paul's transition into the role of Brick, a victim of "heterosexual terror" as laid out in Williams' script for *Cat on a Hot Tin Roof.* When it was adapted into a movie co-starring a sexually frustrated **Elizabeth Taylor**, shown above with her unco-operative husband **(Newman)** in a boudoir, Williams strenuously lobbied for the role to go to **Paul.**

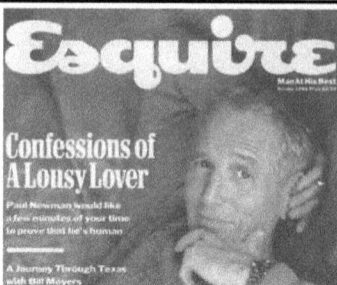

Depicted above, at the peak of their careers as a director and playwright, respectively, are **Elia Kazan** *(left)* and **William Inge.**

Each was fully aware of the sexual ambiguities of their hot new star, Paul Newman...In Inge's case, because of his ongoing sexual obsession for him.

In this grainy snapshot, author and scriptwriter **Gore Vidal** (left), as "supervised" by **Joanne Woodward**, faces **Paul Newman.**

The photo dates from the years they lived together as a "quartet of friends." The fourth member of their quandrangle was Howard Austen, Vidal's long-time companion, who isn't shown. Outsiders widely gossiped that the sexual links within their quartet often blurred to encompass Newman and the ferociously opinionated Vidal. Years later, Vidal maneuvered Newman into the screen personaification of his literary replica of *Billy the Kid.*

Confessions of A Lousy Lover

*Photo, left,* is a partial replica of the front cover of *Esquire's* edition of October, 1989.

**Lee Pfeiffer**, a reviewer for *Cinema Retro,* said, "Darwin Porter has opened a Pandora's Box of controversey simply because Newman himself was so uncontroversial. He rarely sought the public spotlight, stayed in an apparently idyllic marriage for decades, and gave countless millions to charity through his food product line...Thus, Porter is taking on an American icon—and a beloved one at that."

The child of immigrants from Finland, **Maila Nurmi** scored work as an actress during the early days of TV through her gig as **VAMPIRA**, the late-night horror host that no one could resist.

A close friend of James Dean, she attested, years later, to the sexual affair sustained by her "best male friend at the time (Dean) with **Paul Newman.**

Sal Mineo confessed to having sustained a sexual affair with Newman that began on the set of *Somebody Up There Likes Me.* That affair continued during the period they made *Exodus* together for Otto Preminger. Sal confessed his undying love for Paul to yet another author, Larry Quirk, who published this then-first-time news in a book released by Taylor Publishing Company. Later, an unauthorized feature story on Newman revealed that Jackie Witte (Newman's first wife) threatened to leave him when she learned about his affair with James Dean.

Brooks Clift revealed the details of an affair that his brother, Montgomery Clift, had had with Newman. And actor Frank McHugh, a close friend of Spencer Tracy and a member of the hard-drinking "Irish Mafia" of Hollywood, claimed that he accidentally walked in on Newman and the recently deceased actor Jack Lord, catching them together "in an embarrassing position." Newman, Lord, and McHugh were each at the time filming a teleplay together.

Sal Mineo

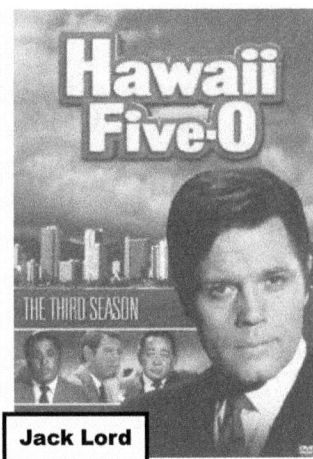
Jack Lord

For more on the startling details associated with the bisexual side of the actor of whom no one seemed to be able to get enough, and with the understanding that these revelations are based on long-standing oral histories, we hereby present Darwin Porter's newest biography.

Depicted above is **Brooks Clift**, Montgomery Clift's older brother. Brooks was a work associate and close friend of **Darwin Porter** over the course of many years, and the long-time companion of **Kim Stanley, a** powerhouse stage, television and film actress hailed during her heyday as "The Female Marlon Brando."

Brooks provided many insights to Darwin about his brother's complicated friendship with Paul Newman.

Over the course of many years, **Paul Newman** and **Joanne Woodward** evolved into respected and beloved survivors of many storms and many experimental film projects. Here, they appear in an ad for a not-particularly-compelling romanctic misadventure they crafted together in 1963.

As regards their first meeting back in the 50s, "I hated him on sight," Woodward later explained. "He was pretty and neat, like an Arrow collar ad. He looked like a snobby college boy in an unimpressive seersucker suit, the kind insurance salesmen wore in summer down in Georgia."

"Paul guickly got Joanne to change her mind about him," claimed director Josh Logan. "It wasn't a qustion of IF they'd start fucking, but when."

One of the most fecund sources for the information in this book was **Frank "the Horse" Merlo**, a neighbor and close friend of author **Darwin Porter** during Darwin's tenure as Key West Bureau Chief for *the Miami Herald*.

On the right is **Tennessee Williams**, Merlo's lover and long-time companion. When they broke up, Williams'—usually defined as the greatest play wright of the Twentieth Century—fell apart...for forever.

*"Most of Newman's same-sex experimentation occurred during his struggle to find a career niche, in the years before he 'calmed down' for a life of domestic bliss in Westport with Ms. Woodward, his family, his philanthropies, and his salad dressings. At the very least, this book documents material which would otherwise have been lost forever."*

—Danforth Prince

# PAUL NEWMAN

## THE MAN BEHIND THE BABY BLUES

The image above shows part of the front cover of **Boomer Times'** edition of September, 2009. It included a replica of the **Newman** biography's front cover.

The image below replicates the biography's back cover. Chapter Two (entitled "**CROTCH ACTING**") is devoted to Paul's meteoric rise as a sex symbol. What is Crotch Acting? Tennessee Williams defined it like this: "An actor like Newman, Brando, or Ralph Meeker comes onstage in tight pants jutting out their crotches."

The summer release of *Paul Newman: The Man Behind the Baby Blues* set off a firestorm in the supermarket tabloids and among bloggers.

After exposing the secret life of the man who for a time was the number one movie star of the world, I was massively attacked for spoiling a carefully manicured public image.

Since this is a divided country we live in, I have also received dozens of e-mails of praise from people linked with the late, great star. One woman from Los Angeles e-mailed me that her grandfather worked with Paul on all his MGM films. "My grandfather said he was one of the nicest people he had ever met, but just as sexually voracious as everyone else."

And so he was. Paul Newman was a great American and contributed some $250 million to charity through his food products, notably his spaghetti sauces. But he was not Mother Theresa. Red blood flowed through his veins.

"When he arrived in Hollywood, this beautiful man was pursued by dozens of starlets (or stars)," said his friend, Joan Collins. Another friend, Steve McQueen, said "Paul could not resist temptation forever. At some point he had to give in to it as I did."

Actually, Paul gave in to temptation early in his career. While married to the former actress, Jackie Witte, with whom he had three kids (a boy and two girls), he deserted her most of the time and shacked up with a blonde from Georgia, Joanne Woodward. They enjoyed a secret adulterous relationship until Paul finally divorced the long-suffering Jackie and made an honest woman out of Joanne.

As anyone who has a computer and knows how to *Google* can learn, Jackie threatened to divorce Paul as early as 1954, not just because of Joanne, but because of his torrid affair with James Dean. In the words of Tennessee Williams, "Paul was a dear boy but he liked to walk both sides of the waterfront."

Paul's sexual liaisons with A-list Hollywood stars became legendary among Hollywood gossips of the time, including his involvements with everybody from Judy Garland to Anthony Perkins (star of *Psycho*).

Long revealed as a roving Lothario in America's underground press, beginning back in the 50s, Paul rarely starred in front page scandals in major newspapers. There was an exception here or there. He was a virtual alcoholic since his college days, graduating from Kenyon College "magnum cum lager" as he put it. There must be 1,000 pictures of him

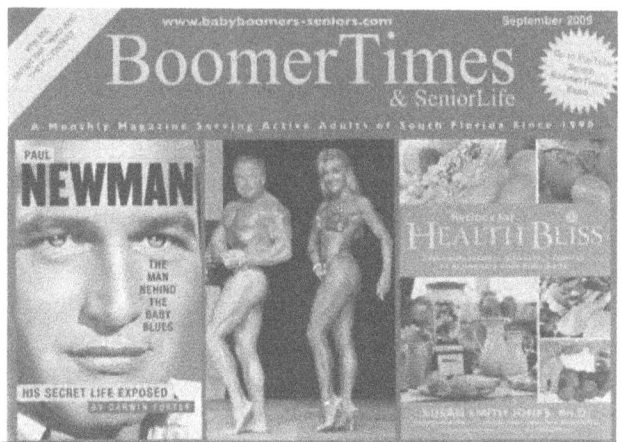

## THE ADVENTURES OF A YOUNG MAN ON BROADWAY AND IN HOLLYWOOD

"Paul Newman had just as many on-location affairs as the rest of us, and he was just as bisexual as I was. But whereas I was always getting caught with my pants down, he managed to do it in the dark with not a paparazzo in sight. He might have bedded Marilyn Monroe or Elizabeth Taylor the night before, but he always managed to show up for breakfast with Joanne Woodward, with those baby blues looking as innocent as a Botticelli angel. He never fooled me. It takes an alleycat to know another one. Did I ever tell you what really happened between Newman and me? If that doesn't grab you, what about what went on between James Dean and Newman? Let me tell you about this so-called model husband if you want to look behind those famous peepers."

—MARLON BRANDO

A GAGGLE OF LOVERS, FRIENDS, ENEMIES, ACQUAINTANCES, AND ADMIRERS RECALL NEWMAN'S TEMPESTUOUS EARLY DECADES.

*Right photo:* The sexually frustrated Maggie the Cat (**Elizabeth Taylor**) confronts Paul Newman in *Cat on a Hot Tin Roof*.

**If you want to find out what kind of salad dressing Newman and other stars of his era were really making out of their lives, this book is for you.**

with a beer in his hand, and he even made front pages when he was arrested in the mid-50s on Long Island for drunk driving.

Most of his affairs were conducted in secret. But Nancy (Buni) Bacon, a gossip writer for **Confidential** and a cheesecake model, put an end to that. Meeting him on the set of *Butch Cassidy and the Sundance Kid,* she launched a torrid affair with him that lasted for 18 months. Their boudoir secrets were revealed in her autobiography, *Stars in My Eyes ... Stars in My Bed.*

News of the affair hit the mainstream press, and the Newmans were forced to take out a $3,000 half-page ad in the Los Angeles Times, claiming that their marriage was still intact. Obviously there must have been tension behind the scenes. Even a forgiving wife like Joanne could take only so much.

The Newmans started giving interviews to prove they weren't divorcing. Their performances rivaled those of Hillary Clinton "standing by my man" when news of Bill's long affair with the bimbo, Gennifer Flowers, made world headlines.

For decades, the underground press has included Paul Newman on their list of gay or bisexual movie stars. The usual list includes Rock Hudson, Tab Hunter, Roddy McDowall, Richard Chamberlain, Farley Granger, Montgomery Clift, James Dean, Burt Lancaster, and countless others. WAS PAUL NEWMAN GAY? ran one headline.

It was Paul himself who wrote his own epitaph. "Whenever I do something good, right away, I've got to do something bad, so I know that I'm not going to pieces."

Most of his fans (they numbered in the millions, worldwide) thought that **Paul Newman**'s life was an ongoing series of cinematic and philanthropic successes---amiable, seamless, uncontroversial.

But things were far more complicated than moviegoers at the time ever thought.

Here, from the writer who unzipped **Marlon Brando** and brought **Babylon** back to Hollywood is the world's most revelatory, and most startling, postmortem overview of America's most iconic male sex symbol.

Kissing Richard Jaeckel both on and off the screen

"You can't help feeling sorry for guys like Newman. They have too much to lose if they make one false step. Look what *Confidential* did to Tab Hunter. Whenever Joanne Woodward came up, Newman became all macho. He was sad in many ways. Having to pretend to be what he wasn't. But most of us Hollywood hunks in the 1950s had to do that."

Matinée heartthrob Jeffrey Hunter

Jeffrey Hunter

Unlike earlier, more obsequious and breathlessly reverential biographies of **Paul Newman**, the information within this book is based on insider reports from his friends and enemies.

Paul Newman once won Hollywood's "Unzippered Award" for having never been sexually associated with anyone other than his wives. Author Darwin Porter punches holes in that bag of myths to reveal that when Newman was the pre-eminent male sex symbol of Hollywood, he enjoyed off-the-record sexual and emotional trysts with **Elizabeth Taylor, Marilyn Monroe, Judy Garland, Audrey Hepburn,** and **Grace Kelly,** plus sexual encounters with a coterie of "cougars" that embraced **Joan Crawford, Vivien Leigh, Susan Hayward, Ava Gardner,** and **Lana Turner.**

As has been rumored in underground Hollywood for years, Newman also led a busy closeted life as a bisexual. Darwin Porter's newest biography exposes the megastar's bisexual history and his complicated liaisons with, among many others, Marlon Brando, James Dean, Anthony Perkins, and Sal Mineo.

It also deals with touchy underground speculation about Newman and his relationships with co-stars **Tom Cruise** and **Robert Redford.** Falling like bombs from the pages of this book are revelations about the death of Paul's only son, **Scott Newman.**

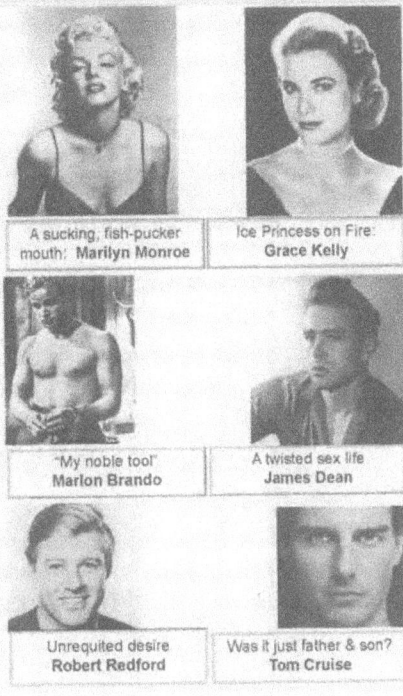

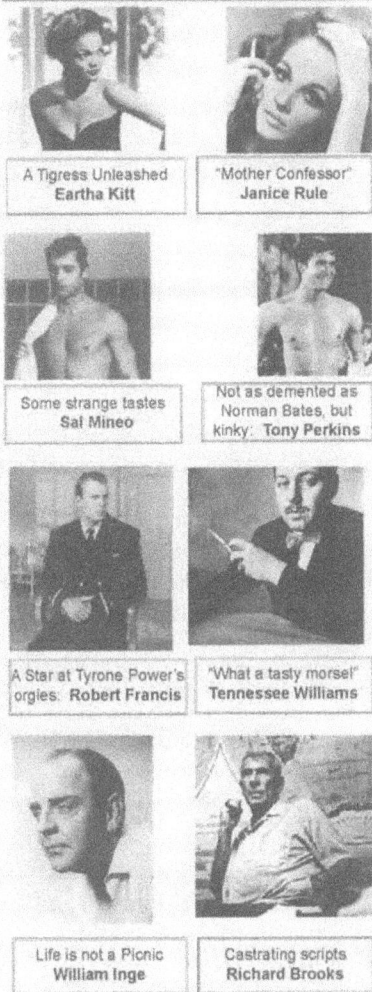

A sucking, fish-pucker mouth: **Marilyn Monroe**

Ice Princess on Fire: **Grace Kelly**

"My noble tool" **Marlon Brando**

A twisted sex life **James Dean**

Unrequited desire **Robert Redford**

Was it just father & son? **Tom Cruise**

For their important contributions to the information that's contained within this biography about PAUL NEWMAN, the author wishes to acknowledge the following sources:

A Tigress Unleashed **Eartha Kitt**

"Mother Confessor" **Janice Rule**

Some strange tastes **Sal Mineo**

Not as demented as Norman Bates, but kinky: **Tony Perkins**

A Star at Tyrone Power's orgies: **Robert Francis**

"What a tasty morsel" **Tennessee Williams**

Life is not a Picnic **William Inge**

Castrating scripts **Richard Brooks**

Learn what the ladies, during their unguarded, "off-the-record" moments, had to say about Paul.....

Elizabeth Taylor
"Meeting Temptation"

Joan Crawford
Auditioning the new kid on the block

Lana Turner
"You're my next husband."

Ava Gardner
A tragic loveliness

"Vampira"
Gay men have more fun

Vivien Leigh
"Don't call me Scarlett!"

Jacqueline Kennedy
The Longest Night

Janet Leigh
From JFK to Harper

Shelley Winters and then-husband Tony Franciosa.
Invitation to a three-way

# Paul Newman's SECRET AFFAIRS
### Jackie Kennedy | Natalie Wood | JAMES DEAN, too!

**BLOCKBUSTER BOOK:**

# GLOBE

## Heartthrob loved LADIES and MEN & BEDDED BOTH with abandon
— SHOCKING BOOK CHARGES

May 25, 2009
$3.59 US / $4.99 Canada

# PAUL NEWMAN'S SECRET SEXCAPADES!

**BLOOD MOON Productions, Ltd.**

BELOVED Paul Newman is being slammed in a shocking new book that outrageously claims the late movie star had sizzling affairs with many of Hollywood's most famous beauties – and hunks!

Author Darwin Porter says he's ripped the lid off the heartthrob's secret sex life in his upcoming biography, Paul Newman: The Man Behind the Baby Blues.

James Dean and even Jackie Kennedy (below) had a thing for Newman

introduced to Newman in 1959 by playwright Tennessee Williams and collected stories about the Cool Hand Luke star until the day he died.

In the 1950s, Newman, the handsome "new boy in town," bedded screen queens Grace Kelly, Judy Garland, Natalie Wood, Lana Turner, Rita Hayworth and Marilyn Monroe, says Porter.

And he's believed to have had a sizzling one-night stand with widowed Jackie Kennedy in early 1968, Porter writes.

JFK's widow had invited Newman to her New York apartment to try to get him to switch his support from Democratic presidential contender Eugene McCarthy to her brother-in-law Robert Kennedy. He arrived in the evening and "left her apartment at 8:30 in the morning," writes Porter.

Newman was also believed to have plunged into an affair with Elizabeth Taylor while filming the 1958 flick Cat on a Hot Tin Roof.

Paul and Joanne were married 50 years.

"She and Newman got very close," Porter claims. "It was shortly after her husband Mike Todd died.

"Newman became intimately involved in her private life, and actually helped her get through the filming.

"If they weren't actually having sex, they were very, very close to it."

Porter also says famed playwright Williams claimed to have pleasured Newman "one night when they flew down to San Juan and shared a hotel room."

Porter insists Dean and Newman also had a fling. He claims Mineo fell for him, too, when they filmed 1956's Somebody Up There Likes Me, and "pursued him for many years" before finally bedding him.

Porter tells GLOBE Newman's wild ways lasted through his seven-year marriage to Witte and into the early part of his union with Woodward, now 79. Newman had three children with each wife.

"Obviously, he cheated on his first wife," Porter says, adding that, despite tales of having a storybook marriage, he betrayed Woodward, too. He insists the star "definitely did have affairs into the Sixties."

But the Newman family friend blasted Porter's claims, calling them "disgusting allegations."

"Paul knew there were rumors out there about his sexuality," says the friend, "and to have to face them when he's not here to dispute them, is Joanne's worst nightmare."
— JIM NELSON

---

## EXCERPT #1

### PAUL NEWMAN
as defined by the ferociously ambitous diarist and cultural gadabout ANAIS NIN

"Newman is just as much of a narcissist as Gore Vidal, but he disguises it completely, and, like the most skilled of actors, puts up a mask to confuse the world. I suspect he will go far in an industry that is all about illusion. There is no self-awareness in this handsome young man at all. He is an obvious homosexual, but does not dare admit that to himself. He's a selfish rogue while pretending to be benevolent, supporting all the right causes. He has a facile charm but no depth. In spite of the hot sun out here, he already knows that California is a cold, harsh land. He does not want it to hurt him. So what will he do? What must he do? He will inflict emotional pain on others, therefore avoiding the pain of having the blows strike him first. I predict Newman will turn into a cardboard figure. There will be no reality to him. He can't be real. A tragedy, really. But, this is, after all, Lotusland."

204

# THE
# CASTING COUCH

*(Rock Hudson Rose to Stardom on That Couch)*

## YESTERDAY & TODAY

*From Boomer Times' Edition of December 2017*

**Rock Hudson** was one of the most desired and genuinely liked male stars of the 1950s. But it took more than qualities like that to get him parts. Some insiders said that he "perfected" the art of auditioning for, or swapping sexual favors for, movie roles from the relative comfort of a casting couch.

Hudson appears above as the young object of Jane Wyman's affection in *Magnificent Obsession* (1954).

Jane herself, by then a celebrated actress with a BEST ACTRESS award under her belt, was no stranger to the fine art of maneuvering around a casting couch, having already climbed the treacherous ladder of Hollywood success—in her case, a decade or two before Rock was even born.

The entertainment industry is evaluating Darwin Porter's latest biography, *Rock Hudson Erotic Fire,* for salacious information about how the casting couch operated during the dying days of Golden Age Hollywood. Its November release coincided with an avalanche of charges of sexual harassment currently being splashed across the tabloids, many of them dominating television's 24-hour news cycle.

Perhaps beginning with Bill Cosby and in time embroiling producer Harvey Weinstein, accusations against sexually harassing "gropers" have engulfed an astonishingly wide range of men, everyone from Dustin Hoffman to the Rev. Jesse Jackson; Alabama's senatorial candidate Roy Moore; even such unlikely malfeasants as the ex-Prez, George H.W. Bush, 93, who admitted, "I once liked to pat women's rears and was known as David Cop-a-Feel."

During Rock's heyday, the term "sexual harassment" didn't exist, entering the public lexicon as late as 1977. Many young men and women arrived in Hollywood during the post-war years, expecting to extend their sexual favors as the vehicle that would help them break into show-business. Rock Hudson, it's revealed, played the game very well, indeed.

After service in the Navy, in the Philippines, during World War II, Rock—handsome, strapping, charming, and hunky—arrived in Hollywood at around the same time as another hopeful, Marilyn Monroe.

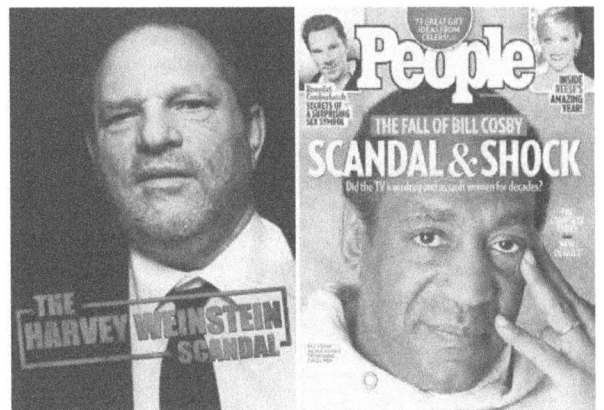

Hushed up as they were at the time, Rock Hudson's edgy promiscuity never reached the hurricane-force after-effects of abuse associated with Hollywood moguls **Harvey Weinstein** *(left)* and **Bill Cosby** *(right)*. Many of Hudson's defenders even define him as the victim, not the aggressor, in his "weaponization" of (what might we call it?) the "oldest profession in the world" tradition.

They met after she'd been been fired from Columbia, and appeared on the Universal lot (Rock's "home studio") looking for a job. He had ten dollars in his pocket, and she had nothing. Their affair began when he bought her breakfast. It was intense but brief. She advised that if they ever wanted to become movie stars, they each needed to spend lots of time as cooperative hopefuls on as many casting couches as possible.

Her advice played out well—not only for herself, but for him, too. The head of Universal, Ed Muhl, despite his status as a married man and the father of three, fell under Rock's spell. At three o'clock every afternoon, Rock was summoned into Muhl's office, and the door was firmly locked with them alone together in the room. Muhl's rising young star left about an hour later, and within months, he was awarded with a string of starring roles.

Men of various sexual persuasions were not alone in their emphasis on casting couches. Many powerful leading ladies of the day, including Joan Crawford, Marlene Dietrich, and Bette Davis, maneuvered sexual favors from whomever was awarded laurels as their leading men.

This brings us, of course, back to Rock Hudson: In a series of romantic encounters that hugely influenced his career, Oscar winner Jane Wyman (ex-wife of Ronald Reagan) developed a crush on him and insisted that he be cast as her leading man in the 1954 remake of *Magnificent Obsession.* *[An earlier version of this "four-hanky weeper" had been released in 1935.]* The picture helped morph

Dozens of Hollywood power brokers and millions of fans were turned on by **Rock's charm** and his sculpted physique.

Hudson into a superstar, leading to his Oscar-winning performance in Edna Ferber's sprawling saga of Texas, *Giant* (1956).

Rock spent many a night at Wyman's home during the making of *Magnificent Obsession*. Her affair with Rock ended abruptly when Rock, Wyman, and her husband, bandleader Fred Karger, flew to Manhattan to attend the premiere of the film.

To her horror, after returning unexpectedly to her suite at the Plaza, she found Karger in bed with Rock. Although she continued her professional relationship with Rock, she divorced her errant young husband shortly thereafter, remarrying him in 1961, and then divorcing him again in 1965. Rock, in contrast, emerged as the world's Number One box office attraction for an undisputed seven years in a row.

Since his widely publicized death from AIDS, most of the public erroneously assumes that Rock was gay when, in fact, he was a rampaging bisexual, especially during his younger days. He seduced obsessively, and without gender preference, everyone from Elizabeth Taylor

**Elizabeth Taylor** emotes with **Rock Hudson** in Edna Ferber's story about treachery, triumph and the oil industry in Texas: *Giant* (1956)

Casting Couch Maneuvers as an "assist" to being assigned a role? Ask any of the icons: They'd been doing it for decades before Rock Hudson even arrived on the scene.

Depicted above, *clockwise from upper left*, **Bette Davis, Joan Crawford,** and **Marlene Dietrich.**

In the dying days of Hollywood's Golden Age, Rock Hudson was the most celebrated phallic symbol and lust object in America. This book describes his rise and fall, and the Entertainment Industry that created him.

Rock didn't limit his sexual expressions to persons of just one gender: Included in his conquests were three Royal Princesses—even if their grip on real political power was more ceremonial than political. But as entertainers have often wryly commented, *"That's Show Biz, Darling!"*

They included, left to right, **Grace of Monaco, Soraya of Iran,** and **Margaret Rose of the UK.**

to James Dean, from Lana Turner to the inevitable Miss Crawford, even such bizarre couplings as Tallulah Bankhead and Liberace. He fathered a son, and became sought-after in some of the upper-tier society circuits of Europe, even enjoying sexual intimacies with three royal princesses: Margaret Rose of Kensington Palace; Princess Grace of Monaco; and Princess Soraya, the former queen of Iran.

Researched over a period of decades, *Erotic Fire* reveals details—for the first time—about the often tragic life of this astonishingly successful fallen idol. He was the first mega-celebrity stricken with AIDS, and became, in 1985, the first famous person to succumb to a black death that, in time, killed millions of men, women, and children, especially in the sub-Sahara.

On Rock's deathbed, he told Elizabeth Taylor, "If my dying calls world attention to this plague, and people will raise money to try to find a cure, then this will be my shining hour."

Beautiful Elizabeth took up the banner and became the chief fundraiser for AIDS. The rest is history.

BLOOD MOON APPLIES THE TABLOID STANDARDS OF TODAY TO THE IRONIES OF SEXUALITY IN HOLLYWOOD'S HEYDAY.

IT'S A TOUGH JOB, BUT SOMEBODY'S GOT TO DO IT!

BLOOD MOON Productions, Ltd.

BloodMoonProductions.com

$32.95

ISBN 978-1-936003-55-6

53295

9 781936 003556

\*\*\*

206

# ROCK HUDSON, EROTIC FIRE

## Soaked in Scandal, Unvarnished, & Uncensored,

Before There was Dwayne Johnson, there was THE ROCK (i.e., ROCK HUDSON)

This is about How We Described Him in Blood Moon's Newest Biography)

### By Danforth Prince

Greetings from Blood Moon. I'm Danforth Prince, its president, here to describe one of the hottest and most entertaining books we've ever released.

It's *Rock Hudson, Erotic Fire,* an apt title for a startlingly handsome, 6'4" hunk with charm, humor, and survival skills that served him well during his Hollywood ascent. For seven years, he reigned as the world's number one box office attraction. His breakthrough began with *Pillow Talk* (1959). An artfully campy romantic comedy about the battle of the sexes, he co-starred in it with Doris Day.

Our co-author, celebrity biographer Darwin Porter, spent decades, on and off, investigating revelations he laid out in *Erotic Fire.*

Until now, little was known about the private life of this superstar, one of the last big name movie legends who rose up during the dying years of Hollywood's Golden Age.

With a shock that some people who survived "the Age of AIDS' remember with horror, the world learned that Rock died of AIDS in 1985. He was the first famous person to succumb to the dreaded disease that would eventually kill millions worldwide.

That, however, was merely the tragic ending of Rock Hudson's story. The details of his incredible rise to fame and glory —never completely documented until now—began when he served in the Navy in the Philippines during the closing months of World War II. In his native Illinois, he fathered a son during one of his leaves from the Navy.

Storming Hollywood after the war, and determined to emerge as a major movie star, he became a truck driver. As he said at the time, "I don't care how many casting couches I have to sleep on."

*Erotic Fire* presents the uncensored, unvarnished, scandal-soaked saga of this incredible insight into the American experience. He enjoys a unique chapter in the history of Hollywood.

He had enemies, of course, but for the most part his friends, lovers, and co-workers adored him for his humor, charm, and good will. Many, too, were in awe of his male beauty.

The world has a misconception that Rock was gay: bisexual would be a more apt description of his sex life. Buttressing his reputation as an "omnisexual horndog," he seduced some of the world's most celebrated women, beginning in his early days with Judy Garland and Joan Crawford. In 1949, he met a struggling actress at Universal, Marilyn Monroe. They launched a torrid affair, even though she was also slipping around and spending some nights with Tony Curtis. After Marilyn

**HUNKY, HORNY, HOPPABLE HUDSON**: as he appeared (*left to right*) *in Taza, Son of Cochise;* (1954); during a contemplative moment with a cigarette; with **Doris Day** in *Pillow Talk (1959);* and as the subject of a 1950s-era tabloid feature engineered to make fans fall in love with him.

moved on, Curtis and Rock became lovers, though later, they were rivals.

As Rock's fame grew, many people considered him the most desirable male on the planet. Both men and women fell for him. That was true during his filming of *Giant* in 1955 with co-stars Elizabeth Taylor and James Dean, who took turns sharing Rock's bed. Dean and Rock became enemies, but Elizabeth morphed into his lifelong friend.

During the peak of his "Dolce Vita" years, Rock even managed to seduce a trio of princesses: Her Serene Highness Grace Kelly of Monaco, Princess Margaret Rose of the U.K., and Princess Soraya, the exiled (former) queen of Iran.

His horndog hormones prompted him to seduce other celebrities without gender preference: Marlon Brando, Monty Clift, George Peppard, Tony Perkins, Guy Madison, and Rory Calhoun, among others.

Rock also ended up in the beds of those fading matinee idols of the '30s and '40s: Robert Taylor, Errol Flynn, and Tyrone Power.

In a bizarre twist, one of Rock's most acclaimed co-stars, Jane Wyman, the ex-Mrs. Ronald Reagan, fell in love with him on the set of *Magnificent Obsession* (1954). But love turned to instant hatred when she returned to her hotel suite in Manhattan, finding Rock in bed with her handsome and "just-married' young husband, bandleader Fred Karger.

Rock had an amazing ability to seduce many (otherwise "straight") actors who appeared in his films. The list is long, but included such aggressive, virile, and good-looking studs as Scott Brady, Robert Stack, Jeff Chandler, Steve Cochran, Nick Adams, and Rod Taylor.

But not the famously prickly John Wayne, Rock's co-star in *The Undefeated* (1969). The Duke said, "What a waste of a face on a queer. You know what I could have done with that face?"

During his dying days, Elizabeth Taylor was Rock's frequent visitor. He told her, "This is my shining hour. At least I focused world attention on this plague, that could strike anybody—not just me."

Today, Rock Hudson's films draw fans from each new generation. He has morphed into the Golden Boy of a glamourous but "gone forever" age.

## HE LIVES AGAIN IN THE PAGES OF *EROTIC FIRE.*

We hope you'll enjoy it, the "no holds barred' life story of this amazing man, the defiant star of his own drama, the charming, handsome, funny, and endearing "lust object and phallic symbol' of the age that created him.

From his origins as a "home from the war" sailor in 1945 *(upper photo)*, to a position on the front cover of this 1955 edition of *Life*, **Everybody Loved Rock!**

The "Stud of Your Dreams" factory of talent scout **Henry Willson** *(left figure in photo above)* churned out camera-ready male charm with factory-like efficiency and precision.

Here's Henry Wilson with his "chomping at the bit" newcomer **Roy Fitzgerald (aka Rock Hudson),** around the time Wilson was prepping, priming, rehearsing, and coaching him for a celebrity upgrade.

"Hot, Bankable Pussies and Hot Bankable Studs" was a widely accepted guideline for Hollywood casting directors in the 1950s, and both **Yvonne de Carlo** *(left)* and **Rock Hudson** *(right)* did their best to live up to expectations. Posted above is a publicity photo from *Scarlet Angel* (1952).

**Its plot?** In 1865, Frank and Roxy meet in New Orleans in a disreputable saloon. After purloining a dead woman's baby and disguising herself as the scion of a wealthy family, Roxy (De Carlo) heads back East to meet them. Meanwhile, obsessed with her beauty, sea captain Frank (Rock) does his best not to screw things up.

# ROCK HUDSON'S ARRANGED MARRIAGE to
## THE LESBIAN BLACKMAILER & EXTORTIONIST

# PHYLLIS GATES

**I NEVER SUSPECTED HE WAS GAY**

Rock Hudson's only wife finally opens the book on their three-year marriage

Years after **Rock Hudson**'s widely publicized suffering and death from AIDS in 1985, his larcenous ex-wife, **Phyllis Gates**, enjoyed a short but cringe-worthy revival, thanks to misleading, self-promotional overviews in the tabloids like the one inserted above.

James Frey's so-called memoir, *A Million Little Pieces*, about drug addiction and alcoholism, is a national scandal and bestseller in spite of its infamy. Oprah Winfrey first promoted the book to millions of her fans, then turned on Frey, exposing him on TV as a fraud and a liar.

But fake memoirs are old hat to insider Hollywood. Bennett Cerf, publisher at Random House, once told Marlene Dietrich that in her memoirs she must have confused her own infamous life with the saintly days of Mother Teresa. Joan Crawford privately admitted that her self-serving 1962 *Portrait of Joan* "was only fodder for fans."

The world took little note this winter of the death of another fake memoirist, Phyllis Gates, who died of cancer at the age of 80 in Marina del Rey. On November 9, 1955, this beautiful "farm girl from Minnesota" married Rock Hudson, the most popular movie star in the world at the time. He died of AIDS at the age of 59 in 1985. Two years later, Gates wrote *My Husband, Rock Hudson*, portraying herself as an innocent victim who didn't know her husband was gay when she married him.

The innocent-faced Gates was a blackmailer and an extortionist, the memoir a lie. Her boss was Henry Willson, a notorious homosexual agent who ruled the male flesh market of 1950s Hollywood, creating "Rock Hudson" (actually Roy Fitzgerald) and numerous other pretty boy stars such as Tab Hunter and Rory Calhoun. Willson paid Gates $50,000 of Hudson's money to enter into this sham of a marriage before scandal-mongering *Confidential* magazine exposed the handsome macho star as a homosexual.

Before working as a secretary for Willson, Gates was known in lesbian circles of the 1950s. She'd been the "girl toy" of the cross-dressing heiress, Jo Carstairs, whose grandfather had left her mega-millions in petroleum dollars he'd earned with John D. Rockefeller.

After her divorce from Hudson in 1958, Gates became infuriated at the meager terms she'd agreed to, and wanted more money—millions, in fact. She threatened to blackmail her former mate, demanding 75 percent of his future earnings. She warned him that "25 percent of something is better than nothing." She could have destroyed Hudson's burgeoning career.

Willson to the rescue. He presented Hudson's lawyers with a five-inch file on the nefarious blackmailing schemes Gates had attempted with some of her more famous lesbian friends, an activity that brought her to the attention of the FBI. "It was a Mexican standoff," one of Hudson's lawyers once told me. "She had us, and we had her." Gates called off her blackmail threats, returning to a quiet life with her lesbian girlfriends—she called them "my sewing circle."

As many a Hollywood star painfully knows, not all blackmailers look like a white-suited Sidney Greenstreet in an old Bogie film. Some of them, as in the case of Phyllis Gates, looked like she could have reigned as queen of a 1950s senior prom.

Blackmailer and extortionist **Phyllis Gates**, a farm girl from Minnesota and wannabe actress, appears here with her fiance, **Rock Hudson**, and her employer, Hollywood kingmaker **Henry Willson** in this congratulatory "soon to be married" photo from 1955.

Reasons, at the time, were unknown to Rock's millions of ardent fans—but as the world learned within just a few years, it wasn't entirely for love.

**Movieland**

ROCK RATES HIS LOVE AND MARRIAGE

COULD YOU TRAP ONE OF THESE BACHELORS?

DICK EGAN
MARLON BRANDO
BOB WAGNER
TAB HUNTER
GEORGE NADER
JEFF HUNTER

*Exclusive*

GAIL RUSSELL TELLS HER TRUE UNTOLD STORY

A 1955 edition of *Life* magazine had pointedly asked, "Fans are urging 29-year-old **Rock Hudson** to either get married—or explain why not:"

This post-marital edition of *Movieland*, which ostentatiously included *Phyllis Gates* on its cover, too, reassured readers that "everything is fine."

Newlyweds **Phyllis Gates and Rock Hudson**: A celebration of "normalcy," as defined by the Eisenhower Era, the Age of Sputnik, and the moviegoing public.

# ROCK HUDSON: THE ESSENTIAL TRUTH

## (AKA EROTIC FIRE)

### AS REVIEWED BY VINTON MCCABE IN THE NEW YORK JOURNAL OF BOOKS

*Vinton Rafe McCabe is the past Arts Editor for* **the Advocate Newspapers** *of CT and MA and a former producer/host for* PBS *in New England. He worked as a restaurant critic and feature writer for* **New England Monthly,** *and a theater and book critic for the* **PBS** *series "Artsweek." Mr. McCabe's freelance work has appeared in such diverse publications as* **The New York Times,** *the* **Stamford Advocate,** *and* **Corpus Christi** *magazine. He is also the author of the novel* **Death in Venice, California.**

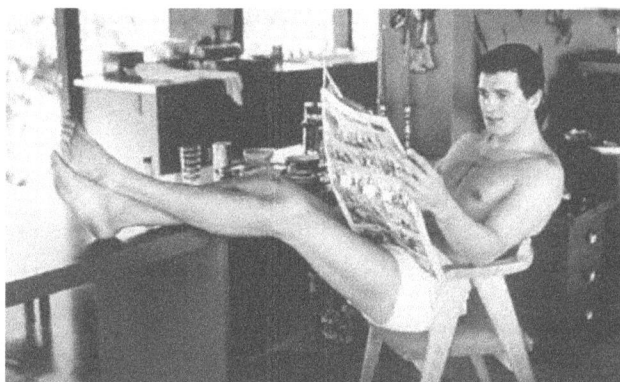

The film historian and actor Illeana Douglas first became aware of Hudson through the comedies he made with Doris Day:

"They always played on television on a Saturday afternoon," she said. "They seemed like the way life should be: Everybody's wearing fantastic clothing, everything working out in the end. The secret of **Rock Hudson**'s appeal was that he seemed to understand women better than their own husbands. He was good-looking, masculine, funny, charismatic and he could dance the cha-cha-cha. And he's never a brute. He's flirting with women but he's not pawing them."

**Although the reader** has more than once felt as if a given Hollywood biography produced by Blood Moon Productions ought to have opened with the familiar phrase "Once Upon a Time," he nonetheless has, over the years, developed a fondness for the folks of Blood Moon and for the books that they publish.

So have the folks at the Huffington Post, apparently. When writing about Blood Moon biographies, they say this:

*"Blood Moon, in case you don't know, is a small publishing house on Staten Island that cranks out Hollywood gossip books, about two or three a year, usually of the five-, six-, or 700-page length, chocked with stories and pictures about people who used to consume the imaginations of the American public, back when we actually had a public imagination."*

Or to be more succinct about it, as Blood Moon Productions says about itself: "Award-Winning Entertainment About How America Interprets Its Celebrities."

That word "interprets" is all-important. In the world of the Blood Moon Hollywood biography, time shifts about strangely. Important moments are visited and revisited more than once in the same brick-like volume. But in spite of the fact that the details of a given life may end up a bit out of whack, the important thing about these works is that the essential truth always outweighs (almost used the word "trumps," which used to be a perfectly good word) the true truth.

Therefore, in all their many Hollywood screeds, it may be said that the authors are writing about the same thing: stardom. And what it costs. And what benefits it brings.

To date, Blood Moon has issued volumes on such luminaries as Lana Turner, Elizabeth Taylor, Frank Sinatra, Peter O'Toole, James Dean, and Humphrey Bogart. They also published a pip of a volume on Zsa Zsa Gabor and her mother and sisters called The Glamorous Gabors, Bombshells from Budapest that remains to this day one of the finest examples of True Hollywood Stories available today.

Over the years, Blood Moon has also branched off into the area of politics, but only in the cases of those politicians who might rightly be considered stars, in volumes like *The Kennedys, All the Gossip Unfit to Print* and *Bill and Hillary, So This Is That Thing Called Love.* Jackie Kennedy got her own volume (*A Life Beyond Her Wildest Dreams*) and Ronald Reagan got a Hollywood/politics mash-up in *Love Triangle, Ronald Reagan, Jane Wyman, & Nancy Davis.*

At the top of the Blood Moon heap is another book that involved a step away from Hollywood, with *Pink Triangle, The Feuds and Private Lives of Tennessee Williams, Gore Vidal, Truman Capote, and Famous Member of their Entourages.* And believe me, that one had it all.

But I digress.

With their new book, Blood Moon returns to form with maybe the most Hollywood of all Hollywood stories, as well as perhaps the most culturally important of all the various stars lives.

## The book: *Rock Hudson Erotic Fire.*

The title gets explained on the very first page: "Almost from the moment he set foot in Tinseltown, young Rock set off an 'erotic fire' that blazed all the way to the Hollywood Hills."

And on the back jacket, Darwin Porter and Danforth Prince, the authors of *Erotic Fire* promise that: "In the dying days of Hollywood's Golden Age, Rock Hudson was the most celebrated phallic symbol and lust object in America. This book describes his rise and fall, and the Entertainment Industry that created him."

And they keep their promises, especially the part about the phallic symbol.

They also along the way, accomplish something more.

There is, for instance, a sort of a "ripped from the headlines" aspect to *Rock Hudson Erotic Fire* that the authors could not have foreseen.

In the post-Harvey-Weinstein world, Hudson's apparent willing, almost joyful complicity bewilders, especially in an oddly moving sequence in which Hudson and Marilyn Monroe exchange anecdotes concerning what each has had to do in order to attain and maintain the fame that was so important to each.

By the end of the brief conversation, it is apparent that Hudson was both better at and more willing to continue granting any or all sexual favors that he deemed necessary, or potentially pleasurable, which strikes the reader as rather a damning fact, given that the actor was at his sexual peak during a time in which it was required of him that he remain deeply and permanently closeted. And that the requirement that he held his sexuality secret was made of him by the very men who he continually "sucked up" to in order to continue in his guise as a macho leading man.

The fusion of this macho stance, this sexually charged gay man with his dumbed-down, shallow, and hollow presentation of a hetero "self" that he offered onscreen and on the red carpet (to the point of entering a false and loveless marriage for the sake of his career) brings a complexity to the character of Rock Hudson as presented on the page, and to the text itself, which transcends anything that any other Blood Moon Hollywood biography has had to offer.

Combine this with the freight train that we know is coming, the fact that Hudson will, after he has aged out of the Hollywood stud market, after he has left movies for television, contract AIDS, and still be so mired in his desire for a career long past the time that his need for fame or money could possibly be a motivating force that we will ultimately, in that notorious Dynasty episode, be willing to kill actress Linda Evans, although (A) he knew full well that he had contracted that then-deadly disease, and, (B) he could not be certain—no one could, in the mid '80s—that he was not able to spread the disease with a single kiss.

The Rock Hudson in these pages has been placed there somewhat tenderly.

And the man who strides in in the opening chapters, someone so tall and broad-shouldered that his first agent named him "Rock," becomes something bewildered and then frightened and then rather hopeless as he (A) watches the world pass him by in its search for "the next Rock Hudson," and then (B) notices daily from—what?—age 35 or 40, as his "erotic fire" fades to flickering coals, as Hudson, over the years, has to count on his money and his mansion more than this profoundly good looks and his apparently oversized male organ to bring in the men. And finally there's (C), when he begins to notice night sweats and rashes and the fact that he is losing weight.

There's a lot of freight here, a lot for the authors to dig into. It seems, in reading it, that Porter and Prince (sounds like a Broadway-musical-writing-duo in a Fred Astaire movie) decided that they would do the guy proud. And in presenting him as a confused, complex, vain, lecherous, fame-obsessed narcissist who is also a bit of a dim bulb, they do. And they manage to sustain the bio for their usual 700 pages without for a moment losing the reader's interest.

There is a question that needs answering. This is a Blood Moon Hollywood biography—is there sufficient sex in it?

Oh, my, yes.

The reader wonders how the man ever managed to make one movie, much less the myriad films that he turned out. Most of us would have had to have rested far more than he and acted far less.

No man was safe. As were few women. (Judy Garland, apparently, was one of his conquests, as were Tyrone Power, Anthony Perkins, Jane Wyman's husband, Fred Karger, Montgomery Clift, Jeff Chandler, Robert Taylor, Hugh O'Brian, and Tab Hunter. Only Errol Flynn—Hudson's equal with both men and women if gossip is to be believed—avoided being bedded by Rock, and then only because he was drunk, sad, and had a broken ankle.

Instead, they compared notes.

Like all the best True Hollywood Stories, Hudson's has high-highs (he was the number one Hollywood Star for seven years) and low-lows (his rotten childhood, his apparent inability to ever be able to share his true being nature or to have true intimacy in any relationship) with plenty of stardust and glitter tossed about in between.

Get past the many, many penises on parade in these pages and there is something stirring. Something that will surprise the reader and, by page 700, move him.

In short, *Rock Hudson Erotic Fire* is more than just erotic (although, truth to be told, Eros skips from page to page). It is serious and thoughtful enough that it could alternatively been called Rock Hudson, the Essential Truth. Although, as titles go, that one would never sell.

\*\*\*

Rock Hudson reigned in the late 1950s and early '60s as "Hollywood's greatest ambisexual swordsman," seducing icons who included Marilyn Monroe, Elizabeth Taylor, Tyrone Power, Joan Crawford, and Lauren Bacall, as well as hundreds of other lesser-known players willing to share some "Pillow Talk." Mamie Van Doren, one of Hollywood's bustiest, most provocative, and most promiscuous bombshells, asserted loudly that "the boulder that Rock's agent named him after was a big one."

Just released from the Navy, the muscled, 6'4" hunk, then known as Roy Fitzgerald, arrived in Hollywood with a clear understanding of what he wanted: "I don't want to be an actor…I want to be a movie star! And I don't give a damn how many casting couches I have to lie on!" To that end, between gigs as a truck driver, he donned very tight, faded jeans and seductively stationed himself near the entrances of such studios as Warners and Universal. Eventually, he was "discovered."

He was assigned roles in a string of B-pictures, playing handsome Apaches, easy-on-the-eyes sea captains, and drop-dead gorgeous "Ordinary Joes" whose charm moviegoers remembered way beyond the limited scale of his roles. Meanwhile, power players in Hollywood clamored for him up close and personal, too. According to Yvonne de Carlo, "Rock was predatory after midnight."

Stardom finally arrived based on a performance opposite Jane Wyman (she had divorced Ronald Reagan) in that tear-jerking melodrama, *Magnificent Obsession* (1954). Replicating her passion offscreen, she demanded (unsuccessfully) that he marry her.

Hudson had already been defined as "the sexiest man alive" when he was assigned the role of a Texas cattle rancher in *Giant* (1956). During its filming in the dusty hamlet of Marfa, Texas, he sustained affairs with both Elizabeth Taylor and James Dean.

Three eventful years later, his status as one of the most popular (and most consistently profitable) actors in Hollywood was reinforced, based on his co-starring performance opposite Doris Day in the spectacularly successful *Pillow Talk* (1959). Together, as a captivating duo, they went on to appear together in other "artfully campy" battles of the sexes.

Compiled as a memorial for the 30th anniversary of his death, *Rock Hudson Erotic Fire* is based on dozens of face-to-face interviews with Rock Hudson's friends, co-conspirators, and enemies. Researched over a period of a half century by Hollywood insider Darwin Porter, it reveals the secretive actor's complete, never-before-told story within a context of scandal-soaked and historic ironies, many of which have never been fully explored—until now.

Although maligned by the media because of the stigmas associated with his AIDS-related death, Rock showed inner courage and manly grace as he lay dying. "This is my shining hour," he told his closest friends, as the media rushed to "Out" him as a "celebrity bisexual" who'd been stricken by the then-stigmatizing scourge.

Today, beloved by hordes of cultish fans and film buffs around the world, Rock Hudson is the often misunderstood (until now) Golden Icon of a glamorous bygone era.

ROCK HUDSON–PRINCE CHARMING OF FILMS

NOVEMBER 17, 1925
OCTOBER 2, 1985

**DEAD OF AIDS** Film superstar Rock Hudson died of AIDS yesterday in Beverly Hills, Calif. He will be remembered by millions as the suave romantic superhero of the '50s and '60s as seen in 1965 studio portrait (above). **Stories begin on page 3; picture history in centerfold**

IN MEMORIAM
ROY FITZGERALD /
ROCK HUDSON
**REST IN PEACE**

Rock Hudson Erotic Fire

Darwin Porter & Danforth Prince
Another Outrageous Title in Blood Moon's Babylon Series

# JUDY & LIZA
## Too Many Damn Rainbows

*"You've got only one life to live, so make it a hell of a ride."* (Judy)

*"What good is sitting alone in your room?"* (Liza)

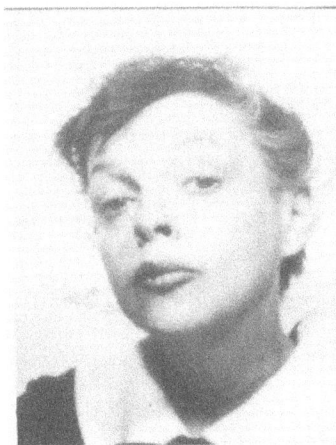

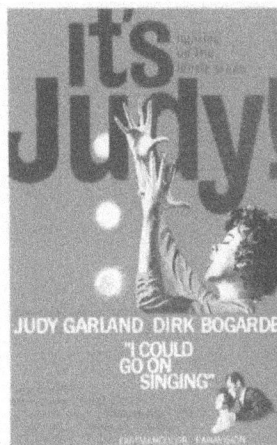

**For millions of fans,** Judy Garland will forever remain a relentlessly cheerful adolescent (Dorothy) skipping along a yellow brick road toward the other side of the rainbow. Liza followed her down that hallucinogenic path, searching for the childhood, the security, and the love that eluded her.

Ferociously loyal but fiercely competitive, they live, laugh, and weep again in the tear-soaked pages of this remarkable biography from the entertainment industry's most prolific archivists, Darwin Porter and Danforth Prince.

In *A Star Is Born* (1954), **Jack Carson** was cast as the press agent of Esther Blodgett (**Judy Garland**). He appears in front of a blown-up photo of the star he helped discover. His admiration for her is matched only by his contempt for the decadence and perceived egomania of her husband, Norman Maine, who was also his client.

During each of their joint appearances together, **Liza Minnelli** *(left)* and her mother, **Judy Garland**, never managed to conceal their competition with each other. Liza retained many ambivalent feelings, and was often awash in drugs. In 1965, when Liza won a Tony for Best Actress in a Musical, Judy went immidiately into a hospital with an "emotional upset."

In the 1960s, **Blackglama** came up with a novel idea to rescuscitate lagging sales of ranch-bred mink. The company hired legends such as **Judy Garland** to model (and hype) their furs. Judy's image (rivaled only by those of Marlene Dietrich and Joan Crawford) had the greatest impact. Andy Warhol adapted her ad into a series of colored silkscreens worth millions to collectors today.

Imitating her mother, **Liza Minnelli** also hustled Blackglama fashions. In a variance of her mother's pose, she added a lit cigarette. Two other models, author Lillian Hellman and Bette Davis, also posed for the "celebrity legends" campaign, also wearing mink and also holding lit cigarettes.

# Judy Garland

**Judy Garland**, an icon whose memory is permanently etched into the American psyche, continues to thrive as a cult goddess. Revered by thousands of die-hard fans, she's the most poignant example of both the manic and depressive (some say "schizophrenic") sides of the Hollywood myth.

With her oldest child, Liza Minnelli, she emerged as the greatest, most colorful, and most tragic entertainer in show biz history.

As a mother-daughter team, they live, laugh, and weep in the tear-soaked pages of this remarkable biography from the entertainment industry's most prolific archivists, Darwin Porter and Danforth Prince. Buttressed with eyewitness reports from friends, frenemies, and enemies, it's a compelling "post-modern" spin on their years together prior to Judy's death in 1969. As MGM's tap-dancing Ann Miller predicted, "It's unlikely that the world will ever see the likes of these two ever again."

According to Liza, "My mother—hailed as the world's greatest entertainer—lived eighty lives during her short time with us." With deference for Judy's status as a spectacularly talented and wounded genius, this book addresses, with love but without apology, most of them.

In Darwin Porter's latest oeuvre, their stories unfold through eyewitness accounts of the typhoons that engulfed them. They swing across glittery landscapes of euphoria and glory, detailing the betrayals and treachery which the duo encountered almost daily. There were depressions "as deep as the Mariana Trench," suicide attempts, and obsessive identifications on deep psychological levels with their respective roles. Fueled by klieg lights and rivers of negative publicity, there were also some jealous actress-to-actress rivalries which, as Judy declined and her *malaise* increased, sprouted like malevolent mushrooms on steroids.

Eventually, Liza roaringly emerged as a star in her own right. "I did it my way," Liza said. She survived the whirlwinds of her mother's drug addiction with a yen for choosing all the wrong men in patterns that weirdly evoked those of Judy herself.

The story of their years together includes tantalizing details about Judy's show-biz mania, her lovers and husbands, especially the acclaimed director, Vincente Minnelli, famous for his steerage of schmaltzy classics (*Meet Me in St. Louis, Gigi,* and *An American in Paris*). Before dumping him for a unfulfilling roster of "Men That Got Away," Judy complained that he spent more time in bed with Gene Kelly than he did with her.

For millions of fans, Judy will forever remain the cheerful adolescent (Dorothy) skipping along a yellow brick road toward the other side of the rainbow. Liza followed her down that hallucinogenic path, searching for the childhood, the security, and the love that eluded her.

Deep in her 70s, Liza is still with us, too, nursing memories of her former acclaim and her first visit as a little girl to her parents at MGM, the "Dream Factory," during the Golden Age of Hollywood.

\*\*\*

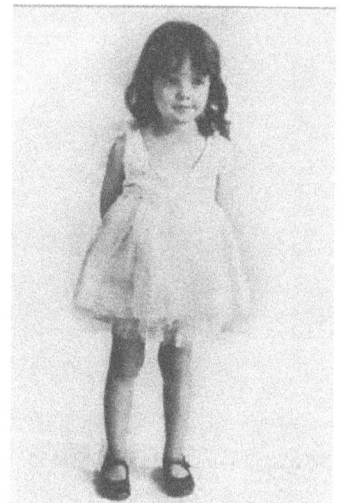

Born an unwanted child, **Baby Frances Gumm** later said, "The first three years of my life were the happiest I would ever know, the only tranquil period I ever had before my memory set in."

*Family Circle* reviewed **Judy Garland** (who appeared with Mickey Rooney in *Babes on Broadway* in 1941) as "back with a bang. The film is well done enough to make it a great musical. Highlights are the scenes of the two transported by imagination in imitation of famous stars."

In those frothy musicals of the 1940s, **Judy** was at the height of her physical allure, as shown on the cover of *Screenland*. But beginning in the late 1930s and throughout the rest of her life, Judy had weight problems and deep, unnerving anxieties.

# JUDY! LIZA! Too Many Damn Rainbows

The greatest mother-and-daughter saga in show biz-live again in the tear-soaked pages of my latest show biz biography, *Too Many Damn Rainbows,* co-authored with Danforth Prince for Blood Moon Productions.

The tragic ending of the last days of Judy was recently brought to the screen by Renee Zellweger in the film, *Judy,* which won her a Best Actress Oscar. The real Judy died young and nearly destitute at the age of 47 in a mews house in London, where she was living with her fifth husband, Mickey Deans.

The unique saga of the teenage girl who immortalized herself as Dorothy in *The Wizard of* Oz is evoked for today's audience. It's all here—the glamour and the glitz, the countless love affairs that included Frank Sinatra and John F. Kennedy; the drugs and the booze; the nightmares and the suicide attempts; and also the triumphs and glory.

One of Judy's biggest hits was the song, "The Man That Got Away." In her case, all of her lovers got away, as she plunged into five disastrous marriages and many aborted affairs.

Having been fired by MGM, she made a spectacular comeback in *A Star is Born* (1954), but her glory was short lived. We visit the concerts where an ovation could last thirty minutes, or end in disaster as she was pelted with objects thrown at her from the audience.

As MGM's tap-dancing Ann Miller predicted, "It is unlikely the world will ever see the likes of Judy and Liza ever again."

"My mother-hailed as the world's greatest entertainer-lived eighty lives during her short time with us," Liza said.

Lesser known is the sometimes jealous rivalry between these two stars, as Judy faded into the 1960s, and Liza began her slow emergence. She crawled out from behind Judy's shadow to become a star in her own right, especially in the film *Cabaret* (1992).

"I did it my way and on my own," Liza said. She had her own whirlwind of heartbreaks, battles, and a dizzy, fast-changing love life, choosing all the wrong men, as her mother had done. Each of them led roller coaster lives, Judy telling her daughter, "You've got only one life to live, so make it a hell of a ride."

For the first time, the secret life of the acclaimed director, Vincente Minnelli, is revealed. Liza's father (Judy's husband) was one of the creative forces behind *Meet Me in St. Louis* (1944), *An American in Paris* (1951), and *Gigi* (1958). Judy complained that her flamboyant, lipstick-wearing husband spent more time in bed with Gene Kelly than with her.

For millions of fans, Judy will forever be the innocent Dorothy dancing down the Yellow Brick Road in *The Wizard of* Oz (1939) to the other side of the rainbow. Liza followed her down that road, searching for both the childhood and the love that always eluded her.

Judy Garland survives today as a cult goddess, her movies still shown and her recordings heard (and sometimes memorized by fans) around the world.

Liza is still with us, nursing memories of her former acclaim and her first visit as a little girl when she went to visit her parents at MGM, the" dream factory" of the Golden Age of Hollywood. For many stars, none more so than Judy, Hollywood became the Boulevard of Broken Dreams.

This book reveals a pithy slice of it.

**Baby Liza** appears above in one of her first press and P.R. photos after her christening. With her are her "impossibly famous" show-biz parents, **Judy Garland** and director/producer **Vincente Minnelli**.

Years later, after oceans of child-rearing and substance abuse drama, **Liza** *(center)* and **Judy** *(right figure)* pose with Liza's newest husband, the self-admittedly gay and spectacularly flamboyant Australian entertainer, **Peter Allen**.

Despite many world-class triumphs of her own, **Liza** never fully escaped from the shadow of her widely-adored mother, **Judy Garland**. On the cover of *Time, (left photo)* she's acknowledged for her darkly brilliant portrayal of the scatterbrained and promiscuous cabaret entertainer, Sally Bowles, in Weimar-era Berlin.

*In the right-hand photo,* **Liza** sparkles onstage in a TV special with the expatriate Russian ballet star **Mikhail Baryshnikov**, then the greatest male hearthrob of the dance world.

## Judy Garland & Liza Minnelli, Too Many Damn Rainbows

—As reviewed by **Diane Donovan** *(photo, above, right)*,
Senior Editor, *The Midwest Book Review & California Bookwatch*

"At first glance, *Too Many Damn Rainbows* would seem an entertainment guide to the careers of Judy Garland and Liza Minnelli (which it also is), but actually, the book is so much more. It's a survey of their evolving relationship, of the rigors of mother-daughter acts in show business, and a gossip *exposé* tell-all in keeping with other Blood Moon productions that ladles previously unknown (or underpublicized) revelations with a wealth of black and white photos.

"Fans of Judy Garland and Liza Minnelli will appreciate that the extensive interviews with both friends and those who criticize them range from personal connections to professionals and peers who worked with them in the entertainment business.

"While the primary focus is on Judy Garland, the insights on their relationship, the psychology of Minnelli's journey in her famous mother's footsteps, and the fierce blend of competition and love that drove their relationship and dual successful careers create an in-depth survey that will especially delight those who like their gossip served hot.

"Many of the interviews are as passionate as the authors are about their subject. Here for the first time is a complete overview of Judy's troubled, scandal-soaked marriages to five men, three of whom were gay. Husbands were not her only problem: Her beaux were memorable and varied, many of them show-biz stars and in some cases, political lions in their own right. They included John F. Kennedy, bandleader Artie Shaw, *avant-garde* filmmaker Orson Welles, billionaire Prince Aly Khan, matinee idol Tyrone Power, Yul ("*The King and I*") Brynner, and James Mason, her co-star in *A Star Is Born*. Also prominent (and notorious since she was underaged at the time) was her teenaged dalliance with the much older actor, Spencer Tracy.

"Because so much information is included, it would have been too easy for *Too Many Damn Rainbows* to have become weighty and overloaded. The information is complimented (and the weighty feel of over 700 pages is countered) by the book's inviting structure and its obvious admiration of Judy Garland as the greatest entertainer in show-biz history. Sidebars of information, photos on nearly every page, and an attention to lively, controversial, appealing details makes this read a delight.

"Whether it's the lovers who got away or the reams of insights and anecdotes associated with Judy's bruising New York, Las Vegas, and European Tours, prior fans of either Judy Garland or Liza Minnelli are in for a real treat with *Too Many Damn Rainbows*. The only prerequisite to enjoyment is some basic familiarity with or interest in either or both women."

# MORE ABOUT JUDY

Shortly before its publication in 2020, the book review editor of a major newspaper requested answers, in writing, about this biography's contents. As part of this project's historical record, we've replicated both the editor's questions and the answers we provided.

Why? Because now, years later, we interpret them as a memorial to the deadline-driven frenzies of that period of our editorial pasts.

*****

### WHAT WAS JUDY'S CHILDHOOD LIKE AND WHAT SORT OF ROLE WOULD YOU SAY THAT IT PLAYED IN FUELING THE INSECURITY THAT WOULD PLAGUE HER THROUGHOUT HER LIFE?

Judy Garland carried the wounds of her childhood with her for the rest of her life. Her early days were filled with insecurity and anxiety attacks that never left her. She once said, "If you think being Judy Garland is rough, imagine what it was like growing up as Frances Gumm."

"With all the acclaim heaped on me by the world, I never transcended my childhood. It was brickbats thrown at me that I could never erase from my memory. One time when I was only eight years old, they threw cheese at me and a rotten tomato. One critic called me 'a pathetic ornament left over from the dying days of vaudeville.'"

Sent out to entertain onstage at the age of two, she was almost literally "Born in a Trunk," the youngest of three Gumms sisters born to two veteran vaudevillians her father Frank and her mother Ethel.

The little girl lost was exploited, becoming the breadwinner of a dysfunctional family. At the age of two, she made her first appearance on the stage in the new grand theater in Grand Rapids Minnesota, joining her two older sisters. Collectively billed as "the Gumm Sisters," it wasn't until July 17th, 1927, that she experienced her first solo billing at the Lancaster theater in Lancaster, California.

She adored her father but hated her devouring stage mother, later calling her "The true Wicked Witch of the West."

Time and time again, her father brought tragedy into her life, but her love for him remained steadfast. As manager of the local movie house in whatever town they lived in, he seduced a series of teenage boys. Whenever exposure came, he had to uproot his family and flee to another town, another theater, where the same thing happened time and time again. He could not control his sexual obsession with the underage boys he hired as ushers.

"Long before *The Wizard of Oz*, I took that Yellow Brick Road and wandered over the rainbow. But I never found what I was looking for. It was not that legendary pot of gold. I was looking for love, which I wanted more than anything in the world. I never found it. "

*****

### WHAT MOMENT OR PARTICULAR CIRCUMSTANCE MADE IT CLEAR THAT THERE WAS SOMETHING SPECIAL ABOUT JUDY THAT ALLOWED HER TO STAND OUT FROM HER SIBLINGS?

Frances Gumm learned to sing before she could talk. As veteran showbiz professionals, both Frank and Ethel soon realized that their two older daughters were only mediocre singers and dancers. As her mother predicted, it was only little Frances who demonstrated star quality.

Her first stage appearance was at the age of two, when she came out to sing "Jingle Bells" to an audience in Minnesota. Receiving thunderous applause, she sang it four more times until Frank came and took her off the stage. Her first solo billing was on July 17th, 1927 at the Lancaster Theater in Lancaster CA both parents realized that "A Star Is Born."

"All my life I'd heard warblers on stage, but never the sounds coming from a little girl like

**Frank & Ethel Gumm,** onstage, as vaudevillians

. **Baby Frances**

**The Gumm Sisters,** *left to right,* in 1925. **Baby Gum Drop** *(aka Baby Frances)* the star of the trio, is on the right.

Frances," Frank would say. "There was a certain magic to her strong, clear voice that could be heard in the balcony. It combined the pathos of an older woman with the sweet innocence of a little girl. She belted out a song with a high, throbbing sound, a sort of 'no holds barred' soprano. Her voice was heartbreaking, or at least a heart about to burst. Even more remarkable was the audience. They wanted to protect her."

*** 

**Judy Garland** with **Toto** in *The Wizard of Oz* (1939)

### IN COMPARISON TO OTHER STARLETS OF THE TIME, HOW HARD DID HER LOOKS WORK AGAINST HER? OBVIOUSLY THERE MUST HAVE BEEN SOMETHING IN THAT MGM ALWAYS SEEMED TO BE WANTING TO CHANGE HER LOOK.

More or less grown up at the age of 13, Judy had always been insecure about her looks. When she joined "the MGM family," Louis B. Mayer made her more insecure, calling her "my little hunchback."

In the late 1930s, he was promoting such *femme fatales* as Joan Crawford. Soon, he was signing up Lana Turner and Hedy Lamarr.

Judy didn't feel she could compete with those beauties, but in 1941 she was assigned to co-star with them in *Ziegfeld Girl*. It's grueling dance acts, long rehearsals, and internal politics turned her into a pill popping wreck. In it, she was memorable singing "I'm Always Chasing Rainbows."

Back when Judy first arrived at MGM, makeup guru Bill Craig was assigned to give her a new look. "She looked like a high school girl in skirt and sweater. No glitter. No sex appeal. Anything but a movie star. Of course, that would in time be perfectly suited to Dorothy in *The Wizard of Oz*. but I was told to give her some glamour. Mayer asked me, "How many roles do I have for a female Huck Finn?"

After Joan Crawford was introduced to Judy, she told her, "You'd be ideal for character roles."

**Louis B. Mayer** with **Judy Garland** in a publicity photo for *Easter Parade* (1948).

"Whereas Lana Turner was the girl you wanted to run away to Palm Springs with," said Busby Berkeley, her future director, "Judy was the kind of gal you could take home to Mom."

He also said, "at first we didn't know what to do with her. She was somewhat awkward and very ordinary. Her singing was good but on-screen appearance is everything. She stood just under five feet, ideal to play opposite a midget like Mickey Rooney. She had a big chest for 13 but a neck that just disappeared on screen. Her waist was very short, and her legs were too long."

When Judy sat through the final cut of *Pigskin Parade* (1936), she said, "I'm sure this will be my last film. I look like a fat, frightened pig with pigtails. Too pudgy."

***

**Hedy Lamarr,** a Ziegfeld Girl with Judy.

### WHAT WAS IT ABOUT HER COLLABORATIONS WITH MICKEY ROONEY THAT CONNECTED WITH THE AUDIENCE THE WAY THAT THEY DID?

It wasn't until her third film with Mickey Rooney, *Babes in Arms* (1939), that Judy scored a big hit. MGM racked up high box office grosses.

Those Andy Hardy films made money and made Rooney the highest grossing male box office star in America. Judy and Mickey became the wholesome boy or girl next door, hardly an accurate reflection of what was going on in their private lives.

"Judy and Mickey helped America get over its Depression Blues," said Louis B Mayer.

Critics hailed them as the perfect match, two sympathetic hearts falling in love for the first time. Mickey was confident and cocky, and Judy, in contrast, played it vulnerable. No heavy petting. More like an arm around the shoulder thing, a Big Brother. They played innocent, nostalgic Americans, the way they used to be.

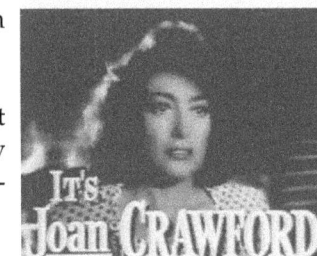

It's Joan CRAWFORD

By 1943, however, America was at war. Their last movie together was *Girl Crazy*.

Lewis Stone, cast as the father of Andy Hardy, said, "For a brief golden moment, America went to see kids like Judy and Mickey. It was all good fun. But times were changing. Sons, husbands, boyfriends were dying on the battlefields of Europe and in the islands of the Pacific. A new breed of stars rose up in the movies, and *femmes fatales*—pinup girls like Lana Turner, Rita Hayworth, and Betty Grable—began to dominate the screen."

*\*\*\**

## THE WIZARD OF OZ. FOR MGM IT SEEMS LIKE IT WAS JUST ANOTHER MOVIE THAT THEY WERE TURNING OUT, BUT HOW IMPORTANT WAS IT FOR JUDY AT THE TIME IT WAS BEING MADE, ITS RELEASE AND IN ITS AFTERMATH?

*The Wizard of Oz*, released in 1939, with Judy cast as Dorothy, marked a turning point in her career. It was the beginning of her later legend, as she danced along the Yellow Brick Road in Ruby Slippers which, decades later, would fetch big bucks at an auction. *The Wizard* became one of the biggest box office bonanzas of all time, seen before Judy's premature death in 1969 by a billion people worldwide.

Actually, Mayer didn't offer the lead to Judy at first, preferring Shirley Temple, the reigning box office champ over at Fox, but Darryl F. Zanuck refused to release "my goldmine."

Had Temple been cast, *The Wizard of Oz* might have been long forgotten, but Judy stamped it with a special poignancy that may live on deep into the 21st century. The critics agreed: Judy made the unreal real and the unbelievable believable.

From her throat emerged the haunting melancholy words of "Over the Rainbow," that she would sing forever, or at least until her final concert. Fans around the world demanded it. Almost no song ever written expressed such a bittersweet yearning, filled with hopes and dreams that all of us dare to dream. "America has its anthem," Judy said, "and I have mine."

*The Wizard of Oz* elevated Judy to stardom but it lost the Best Picture of the Year Oscar to *Gone With the Wind*.

Before making it, many executives at MGM expressed regret that they had released Deanna Durbin Universal. "We got stuck with Judy," lamented Meyer, who changed his mind after *The Wizard of Oz* was released.

The world reached out to take Dorothy, a lonely lovable orphan and her dog Toto to its heart. It did the same for Judy Garland, skyrocketing her on a career that led to her becoming one of the world's greatest entertainers. According to Judy, "I even made the state of Kansas famous around the world."

Today, *The Wizard of Oz* is being shown somewhere in the world at any given moment, enchanting each new generation.

*\*\*\**

## FOLLOWING THE WIZARD OF OZ, WHAT WAS THE REST OF JUDY'S TIME WITH MGM LIKE FOR HER? WHAT ARE THE STANDOUTS, AND WHAT ARE THE OPINIONS YOU MIGHT HAVE ABOUT EASTER PARADE AND MEET ME IN ST. LOUIS?

Judy followed *The Wizard of Oz* with one of the biggest hits so far in her career. Both *Oz* and *Babes in Arms* were released in 1939, the same year of MGM's biggest success, *Gone With the Wind*. She had most recently worked with Mickey Rooney in *Love Finds Andy Hardy* (1938), and he was enjoying a brief reign as Hollywood's box office champ. *Babes in Arms* reunited him with Judy.

It was in the months that followed that Judy began her long addiction to pills, swallowing them to keep her energy high before the camera, or else to put her to sleep during her tortured nights.

She never stopped making MGM movies and was rushed into *Andy Hardy Meets Debutante* (1940), another boisterous screen musical.

**Mickey Rooney** as Andy Hardy, with **Judy Garland**

**Lewis Stone** *(left)* with **Mickey Rooney** and **Fay Holden** *(right)* in *Love Finds Andy Hardy* (1939).

**Deanna Durbin** competing (on many levels) with **Judy Garland** in *Every Sunday*

Love goddess **Rita Hayworth**

In *Little Nelly Kelly* (also 1940), Judy was allowed to grow up, playing a double role with George Murphy in which she was cast as his young wife in Ireland who dies in childbirth. She is later depicted as Murphy's young daughter.

The picture made a profit, but was not a blockbuster favorite, as it was defined as "too sentimental."

Along came *Ziegfeld Girl* (1941) in which, to Judy's horror, she was cast opposite two of the most glamourous women in the world, Lana Turner and Hedy Lamarr. Judy held her own and didn't get entirely lost in this tribute to stage beauties.

Louis B. Mayer couldn't let Judy escape forever from those hit movies of the late 1930s, and he recast Rooney and Judy together in *Life Begins for Andy Hardy* (1941), but the series was growing stale.

Judy and Rooney followed that with a musical extravaganza, *Babes on Broadway* (1941). That film is only memorable in that Judy stole scenes from the greatest scene-stealer in the history of Hollywood.

*For Me and My Gal* (1942) was notable mainly for teaming Judy with an emerging newcomer, Gene Kelly, for the first time. Although American soldiers were being shipped abroad to fight the Nazis and Japanese, the background for Judy's movie was World War I. She gave a lift to those old ballads, "After You've Gone," and "Till We Meet Again."

In 1943, the film adaptation of Booth Tarkington's novel, *Presenting Lily Mars*, was originally conceived as a vehicle for Lana Turner. Mayer ordered Joe Pasternak to turn it into "a Judy Garland Musical,"

She was presented as a stage-struck small town girl, which led *The New York Times* to suggest that Metro should "let her grow up and stay that way."

Louis B. Mayer did not heed that advice and presented Rooney and Judy together in *Girl Crazy* (1943). *The New York Times* proclaimed that Judy has "outgrown her adolescence most gracefully."

Judy's breakthrough role came in the 1944 *Meet Me in St. Louis,* with Margaret O'Brien (playing her baby sister), Mary Astor, Tom Drake, and Marjorie Main. The director was Vincente Minnelli, slated to become her second husband.

Judy recalled her first day on the set. "He was wearing more lipstick than I had on. Working with him was a horror. He insisted on take after take until I finally pleased him. I deepened my intake of pills to stand up to this effeminate brute. Minnelli convinced me I had no talent, and he even complained to Mayer."

On the set, Judy was attracted to Tom Drake, "the boy next door."

One night, she managed to lure him into bed, but was disappointed when he could not perform. To her horror, she found he had already lain on Minnelli's "casting couch."

In spite of the off-screen intrigue, *Meet Me in St. Louis* established Judy as one of MGM's biggest stars. She received raves from across the country, and the picture was a major box office hit, one of her greatest.

According to Judy, "I hated going to work every day to face Minnelli in this stupidly sentimental story."

Obviously, the war-weary American public did not agree with her assessment.

Using her new star power, Judy demanded a dramatic role—and got one when she was cast in *The Clock* (1945), a World War II romance with a handsome young soldier played by Robert Walker.

Once again, she "defrosted" her relationship with Minnelli, her director, claiming, "He made me look beautiful on the screen, so I could forgive him for anything." She began seeing him for quiet dinners and confessed, "I was tootsie-woosing with him."

For sex, she turned to Walker, who was still in mourning for the loss of his wife, Jennifer Jones, to David O. Selznick.

Walker was recovering from his grief not just with Judy, but with Peter Lawford and starlet Nancy Davis (later Reagan), too.

Before the end of World War II, Judy emerged as one of the biggest box office attractions in America. She was awarded the lead in *The Harvey Girls* (1946), a lavish Technicolor drama set in the Old West. A fictional account of Fred Harvey's traveling waitresses, *The Harvey Girls*, became an explosive hit, *Variety* hailing Judy as the "All Time Box Office Champion."

In it, she warbled the hit song "On the Atchison, Topeka, and the Santa Fe."

She followed that with *Ziegfeld Follies of 1946.* In collaboration with an all-star cast (Astaire, Lucille Ball, Gene Kelly) Judy starred as a campy movie queen giving an interview.

**George Murphy, Judy Garland,** and **Gene Kelly** in *For Me and My Gal.*

**Gene Kelly**

**Margaret O'Brien**

**Tom Drake** with **Judy Garland** during the filming of *Meet Me in St. Louis*

**Robert Walker** kissing **Judy** in the "soldier's homecoming" tearjerker, *The Clock*

She followed immediately with *Till the Clouds Roll By* (1946), playing stage star Marilyn Miller with Robert Walker as Jerome Kern.

Then along came *The Pirate* (1948), directed by Minnelli and co-starring Gene Kelly This was the first picture in which Judy's bad health and drug addiction caught up with her, causing endless production delays.

Later, she lamented to tap-dancing Ann Miller, "Vincente spent more time in bed with Gene Kelly than he did with me." *The Pirate* became the only MGM film of Judy's that did not make money.

At this point in her floundering career, Judy needed a hit and found it when Alfred Freed cast her in *Easter Parade* (1948), co-starring Fred Astaire. She had been scheduled to make the picture with Gene Kelly, but he'd fallen and seriously injured his leg. MGM coaxed Astaire out of semi-retirement to make what became a huge box office hit. Judy loved working with him and thanked him for his help with her dance steps.

*Easter Parade* was her highest grossing film from her heyday in the 1940s. She was in desperate physical shape, having just been released from what she called "the nuthouse:" a reference to the Campanes Sanitorium, where she had threatened suicide.

Consistently, she showed up late on the set and caused endless production delays. By now, she was in constant conflict with Mayer and others at MGM.

Judy ended her greatest decade in films (the 1940s) by co-starring with the gay actor, Van Johnson, in the film, *In the Good Old Summertime* (1949). It marked the screen debut of Judy's 2 1/2 -year-old daughter, Liza Minnelli.

Because of the production delays Judy had caused, MGM had suspended her. They brought her back, however, to make this sentimental, lighthearted movie.

Meanwhile, her marriage to Minnelli was becoming unglued. She told Johnson, "Vince and I are better apart." This was a bitter time in Judy's life. Her friend, actress Joan Blondell, said, "She was furious at everybody, especially MGM, but also with her mother, whom she called 'The Wicked Witch of the West.' Minnelli, too, provoked rage in her. Clearly, she was on the verge of another total nervous breakdown."

Despite many dire warnings about Judy's physical and mental state, MGM went ahead and cast her as the sharpshooter cowgirl, Annie Oakley, in *Annie Get Your Gun* (1950). It had been a big hit on Broadway with Ethel Merman. Judy was ordered to lose weight and, to do so, she increased her intake of pills.

As she recalled, "I was in desperate shape. I spent my pre-dawn hours calling what few friends I had left. Between calls I was downing Nembutals and Seconals. Before I even showed up at MGM [*for the first day of its filming*], I had undergone six electric shock treatments."

Later, on the set of *Annie Get Your Gun*, according to director George Sidney, "Garland feuded with me, with [*the film's co-star*] Howard Keel, and with everybody else on the cast and crew. Her early scenes were horrible. She was clearly falling apart before our eyes. Mayer finally got the message and fired her, the role going to Betty Hutton, who did a terrific job."

Judy's swan song at Metro was *Summer Stock* (1950), co-starring with Gene Kelly. Although it made some money at the box office, it was not a runaway hit. Director Charles Walters said, "Judy was utterly difficult to work with and control, yet after much struggle she came out looking great on the screen. But, as was her custom, she caused endless delays. MGM was facing major fallout in box office receipts because of the rise of television. Tolerance for temperamental stars was coming to an end."

Eventually, Judy was cast in one final picture, *Royal Wedding* (1951), opposite her co-star, Fred Astaire. Its director, Stanley Donen, said, "From day to day, we never knew if Judy would show up or not. Finally, MGM executives could take her antics no more, and we notified her that she was

**Judy Garland** taming the Wild West (and **John Hodiak**) in *The Harvey Girls.*

**Judy** "enslaves" the men of the chorus in *Ziegfeld Follies of 1946.*

*Left photo,* **Judy Garland** as Annie Oakley before she was fired from the set of *Annie Get Your Gun* (1950). *Right photo:* **Betty Hutton,** her emotionally troubled, much-persecuted replacement.

**Judy Garland** on the cover of *Life*, their edition of Sept 13, 1954

*Left photo:* Judy with Fred Astaire in *Easter Parade* (1948). *Right photo:* Starlet, girl about town, and future First Lady **Nancy (Davis) Reagan**

fired." Her glory days at MGM had faded into history. In June, her dismissal from MGM generated nationwide headlines.

Those were followed by yet another headline: JUDY CUTS THROAT.

\*\*\*

## Do you have any comments on Judy's husbands? Also, in terms of Sid Luft, how important was *A Star is Born* to her and how devastating were cuts made by Warner Bros to the film and to her?

Nineteen-year-old Judy had reached a crucial crossroads in her young life when she met composer **David Rose**, who was thirty-one at the time. He was recovering from his disastrous marriage to Martha Raye, and she was trying to get over the heartbreak caused by bandleader Artie Shaw when he unexpectedly eloped to Las Vegas with Lana Turner.

United in their mutual unhappiness, Judy and David Rose were married in 1941. MGM was adamantly opposed to the marriage, based on the belief that it would damage her innocent image on the screen.

"He spent part of our marriage playing with his network of electric trains in our back yard," Judy said. "After dinner, instead of spending evenings with me, he put on his train engineer hat and ran the railroad by electric lights. He never came to bed until shortly before midnight."

As Judy freely admitted, she was not cut out to be a housewife and knew nothing about cooking, cleaning, and laundry. Her mother lived nearby and came to run the house for her, even cooking meals for Rose when Judy wasn't home, which was most of the time.

She had begun a torrid affair with the handsome, dashing actor, Tyrone Power, the biggest male star at 20th Century Fox. When he wasn't with Judy, he sustained affairs with men who included Errol Flynn and Noël Coward.

Within months, gossip maven Louella Parsons began reporting that there was trouble in the Rose/Garland marriage. Trouble really began when he made her pregnant. MGM warned her that her "girl next door" image would be sabotaged if she had a baby.

"Both David and my mother, Ethel, virtually forced me to abort my infant," Judy said. "I wanted the baby. I never forgave either of them."

Her drug dependencies and suicide attempts put a terrible strain on their marriage, and she complained to Mickey Rooney that "David can't satisfy me in bed. No wonder Martha Raye dumped him."

Marked by tension and long separations, the couple divorced in 1944. Rose later said, "Judy was the love of my life, and I never forgave myself for not rescuing her from her demons."

During her affair with Power, he also impregnated her, leading to yet another abortion.

\*\*\*

**Husband number two, Vincente Minnelli** (1945-1951), "was a lousy spouse but a brilliant director," Judy told Van Johnson. "I'm not sure why I married him., The only good thing that

223

**Judy Garland** announces her engagement to her first husband, **David Rose**.

(Sometimes) omniscient and all-powerful: **Louella Parsons**

**Lana Turner** and bandleader **Artie Shaw** after their wedding in 1940.

Operatic songbird **Kathryn Grayson** in *So This Is Love* (1953).

Newlyweds **Vincente Minnelli** with **Judy Garland**.

**Tyrone Power**, shown here with **Loretta Young**.

**Martha Raye** in *Taking a Chance on Love*.

came from that union was my daughter, Liza. It was not sex that brought us together, but his ability to make a big star out of me."

Through Minnelli's lens, the girl once known as "the ugly duckling" looked glamourous up there on the screen in glorious Technicolor.

"At home," Judy continued, "he sometimes provoked an argument with me so he could run off and spend the night with his lover, Lester."

She was referring to his longtime lover, Lester Gaba, who had a beautiful home in the Hollywood Hills. A hip Hollywood crowd often invited "Vince and Lester" to parties instead of Vince and Judy.

MGM's other singing star, Kathryn Grayson, said, "Vincente was so ugly I couldn't bear to look at him. Judy sure didn't marry him for his looks, and she'd already had that beautiful Tyrone Power. Some people thought Minnelli had the small head of a baby dinosaur, but he reminded me of a lizard, always pursing those painted lips. He was also very effeminate, a real queen."

"Let's face it, Vince is as gay as a May Day parade," Judy said to Gene Kelly. "I'm sure he's come on to you. He talks about you all the time. Lester is very jealous."

Kelly had no comment.

"On the nights he sleeps over, he gets up early to spend an hour at his makeup table," Judy said. "He doesn't need false eyelashes, but he always wears a covering base, eye shadow, and lots of Victory Red lipstick."

"But don't feel sorry for me," she said. "Joe Mankiewicz, the love of my life, keeps leaving me, but that's only temporary. I want to divorce Vince and marry Joe, but he won't leave his wife. He's the best sex I've ever had, and I've been around the block more than once."

Judy and Minnelli slugged along in their sham marriage until their divorce in 1951.

When she heard the news, her friend, June Allyson, remarked, "Minnelli was wrong for Judy, totally, totally wrong. How did she put up with him for so long? More to the point, why did she marry him in the first place? He didn't love Judy. He loved that Lester."

*\*\**

**Sid Luft,** a former boxer and test pilot, was the only true macho Judy ever married. When they were introduced in 1952 at Billy Reed's Little Club in Manhattan, she was immediately attracted to him. As Luft later boasted one night to Frank Sinatra, "I took her back to my hotel and we made it. For the rest of the night."

Soon she was telling Hedda Hopper, the gossip columnist, "A woman needs a man to protect her and to love her. And it looks as if I've found him at long last. Mr. Sid Luft, the producer and impresario. He's going to stage my comeback in the movies."

Born in 1915, Luft was seven years older than Judy "and not quite divorced." She was not quite divorced either, but each of them would be within a few months.

In addition to relaunching her film career, Luft and Judy became the parents of Lorna Luft and a son, Joey. Luft worked for months to obtain financing for a remake of the famous movie, *A Star is Born.* An earlier version had starred Janet Gaynor and Fredric March in 1937.

Except this time, Luft wanted a musical version. His producing company, Transcona, was behind it, and in time, he convinced Jack Warner to finance its costly production. "I'll make sure Judy shows up on time and camera ready," he assured Warner.

Luft set out to find a leading man who would agree to play a has-been. With that as his goal, he met with a series of male movie stars, each of whom rejected his offer. They comprised an impressive list of rejections: Gregory Peck, Stewart Granger, Laurence Olivier, Ray Milland, Glenn Ford, James Stewart, Tyrone Power, Richard Burton, Robert Taylor, and Cary Grant. Finally, James Mason took the bait. "Why not?" he asked. "It was a great part, and my film career at the time was stagnant."

Luft made a wise choice in approving the gay director, George Cukor, to helm *A Star Is Born*—and in Technicolor, no less. The lyrics of Moss Hart and the songs of Harold Arlen and Ira Gershwin would be showcased.

The film would be shot in CinemaScope with the hope of luring Americans away from their TV sets.

Judy almost didn't star in the movie. In Los Angeles, on November 21, 1952, she gave birth to her second daughter, Lorna Luft. Four days later, she tried to commit suicide by cutting her throat. Luft discovered her (unconscious) body in time summoned emergency help

**Joe Mankiewicz** *(right figure)* with an unidentified assistant in a 20th Century Fox publicity picture for *Cleopatra* (1963).

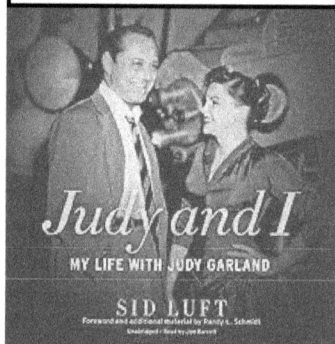
**Sid Luft** with **Judy Garland,** as they appear on the cover of his "too late, baby," tell-all memoir about their marriage

**Hedda Hopper,** Hollywood's "other" most influential (and terrifying) gossip columnist.

In this horrifying scene from *A Star Is Born* (1954), faded matinee idol Norman Maine, portrayed by **James Mason,** drunkenly but accidentally slugs Vicky Lester (portrayed by **Judy Garland**), his loyal superstar wife, during a televised awards ceremony onstage.

to stop the bleeding. She was rushed to the hospital, where she recovered. "I held Judy together during the shoot of *A Star Is Born,*" Luft claimed.

It would be a spectacular comeback for her. "Every day I told her she was making a Hollywood classic and her greatest film. *Oz* was cute but *Star* was great drama."

Throughout the shoot, Luft endured attacks from Jack Warner, who constantly complained of Judy's temper tantrums and her unreliable and unprofessional behavior in showing up late—or not at all— before the cameras.

` Luft also tangled with Cukor. A famous example of that was when Cukor wanted to ax Judy's rendition of "Born in a Trunk." Luft demanded that it be kept in, and it became one of Judy's alltime hit songs.

At its world premiere, *A Star is Born* received critical and popular acclaim, the likes of which Judy had never seen before. However, theater operators complained to Jack Warner that the film was too long, a situation that reduced the number of times it could be shown in one day. Consequently, Warner himself demanded that thirty minutes of footage be cut.

Judy was devastated to hear from Luft that, "Warner has butchered our *Star Is Born.*" Although she was outraged by "those brutal cuts," there was nothing she could do. Critics, too, joined in attacking the cuts, but Warner prevailed.

Adding to her grievances, Judy—in her greatest role—lost the Oscar, "My one and only chance"—to Grace Kelly for *The Country Girl* (1954). Groucho Marx sent Judy,--in the hospital at the time after giving birth to her son, Joey—a telegram: "Your loss of that Oscar was the biggest robbery since Brinks."

She won the Golden Globe Best Actress Award, and *Time* defined her performance as "Just about the greatest one-woman show in movie history."

After the release of the movie, Luft became the guiding force in launching Judy into another phase of her life: An around-the-world gaggle of concert tours.

Footnote: On July 19, 1983, twenty-nine years after its initial premiere, *A Star Is Born* was rebirthed for a second premiere. Those devastating cuts had been restored, and it was screened as it was originally intended. The Hollywood elite, including Judy's three children, attended and redefined it as a cinematic masterpiece.

At the screening's end, pandemonium broke out in the auditorium. Hysterical applause that went on and on. Although Judy had been dead for fourteen years, it was her greatest ovation.

Today, Judy's reissued version, the full-length *A Star Is Born,* is regarded as one of the great Hollywood classics, ranking up there with *Casablanca, Gone With the Wind,* and *Citizen Kane.*

***

Judy's tour promoter, **Mark Herron,** became her fourth husband. She married him aboard a freighter moored at the time in Hong Kong harbor. The ceremony—legally, at least—was a sham, since her divorce from Luft had not yet been granted, and in theory, at least, she could have faced charges of bigamy.

When her divorce was finally granted in May of 1965, she waited until the following November to repeat her (this time, legal) wedding ceremony to Herron. She was in ill health throughout most of their short marriage. Within six months, they had separated. She later claimed that the marriage was never consummated.

"I should have dedicated my song, 'By Myself,' to Mark," she said, ruefully.

"It was a marriage in name only," she claimed. "He married me only to further his career as an actor. He's taken advantage of stars—including both Charles Laughton and Tallulah Bankhead--before."

Herron asserted that he suffered verbal abuse during the course of their short marriage, and she claimed that he once beat her severely.

In latter-day analyses from many experts, Judy suffered from a bipolar condition even in the best of times. Her illness worsened during her marriage to Herron. After their separation and eventual divorce, he returned to his longtime lover and fellow actor, Henry Brandon. They continued to live together until Brandon's death twenty-five years later.

***

Seventy years after its release, gems from **Judy Garland's *A Star Is Born*** (1954) still flourish in the memory of her fans.

During her "concert tours' era, songs culled from its score became onstage hits rivaled only by that "Too Many Damn Rainbows" (her words) hit from *The Wizard of Oz*, "Over the Rainbow."

Oscar winner **Grace Kelly,** deliberately frumpy, with **William Holden** in *The Country Girl* (1954).

**Mark Herron** with **Judy Garland** at the Cocoanut Grove in 1965.

Judy married Mickey Deans, husband number five, in 1969, the year her divorce with Herron was finalized. He was thirty-four when the publicist, John Springer, one of the owners of Manhattan's then-popular disco, Arthur, gave him a bag of amphetamines with instructions to rush to Judy at her hotel suite.

She seemed grateful to get them, and enjoyed the company of this handsome young man, since she was lonely. She invited him to spend the night and returned the following night… and the nights thereafter.

"From the very beginning, I thought Mickey looked like Sid Luft's son," she said. "I talked him into finishing up his business and to fly with me to London, where I hoped to make another comeback. He agreed to go. I wanted to get out of Dodge because I owed the IRS $4 million."

In London, on March 15, 1969, they were married at the Chelsea Register Office. The press was waiting outside to photograph Judy and her new husband. In some photographs, she looked old and decrepit. Her years of drug addiction had caught up with her.

Together, the newlyweds moved into a dilapidated mews house on Cadogan Lane in Belgravia.

Almost immediately, Mickey began promote his new status as the husband, consort, and business manager of Judy Garland, which he believed would be very lucrative to him since he planned to manage all her money. When she faced the press, she told a reporter, "After four failures, I finally found the right husband."

For months, Deans worked the phones all day, every day, calling various booking agents, lawyers, and promoters. He wanted to book Judy into another series of concerts and also to persuade a producer to finance a documentary of her eventful and troubled life. He even tried to launch a series of Judy Garland Theatres across America.

The gay singer, Johnnie Ray, arrived on the scene, as he and Judy were planning a concert tour together in Scandinavia. When Judy was sleeping off her heavy ingestion of drugs, Ray and Deans had sex.

After dark, Deans often left the house they shared, heading for Piccadilly Circus. As he told a club owner, "A man can take Judy Garland for only a few hours every day."

She spent her final birthday, June 10, 1969, alone. Deans had forgotten about it, and was out cruising, wandering the streets of London, looking for "tricks."

Judy with Mickey Deans (husband #5). London, December 1968, four months before their wedding.

Judy Garland wasn't the only aging diva associated with younger men. Above, Tallulah Bankhead appears onstage in an experimental production of Tennessee Williams' *The Milk Train Doesn't Stop Here Anymore* (1964). Her out-of-his-depth co-star was Tab Hunter.

Tallulah, too, had been the victim, it was widely rumored, of the financial maneuverings of Judy's previous husband, Mark Herron. So had Charles Laughton (*photo below*)

***

### JUDY HAD DONE A RADIO VERSION OF A STAR IS BORN YEARS EARLIER. ANY THOUGHTS ON THAT?

"I've done dozens of radio shows in my day," Judy said. "Years before my 1954 film version of *A Star Is Born*, I starred in a radio adaptation based on its 1937 version. I'm a star on the rise, married to a drunken actor whose film career is fading."

Produced by Cecil B. De Mille, the one-hour drama starred Walter Pidgeon as the husband, with Adolphe Menjou in a supporting role.

Its premiere was on December 28, 1942. Many Americans had tuned in on their radios because they wanted to hear Judy sing, but then realized that she was about to introduce a serious drama.

"After the broadcast, I knew at once that I'd like to play this role in a film remake, but a musical version," Judy said. "But when I pitched the idea to Mayer, he looked horrified.

"Are you out of your mind?" he asked. "That's no role for Judy Garland. Perhaps Susan Hayward."

***

Here's British actress Elsa Lanchester with her gay and errant husband, Charles Laughton, on a promotional press and PR visit to Disneyland.

*Lower photos* show Lanchester as the *Bride of Frankenstein* (1935) and Laughton, in 1939 as *The Hunchback of Notre Dame*

### WHILE MANY SEEMED TO BE WRITING OFF HER FILM CAREER, SHE TURNED AROUND AND DID JUDGMENT AT NUREMBERG. WHAT DID THAT FILM "SAY" TO THE WORLD ABOUT JUDY?

At the dawn of the 1960s, when she was considered washed up in films, Judy startled her

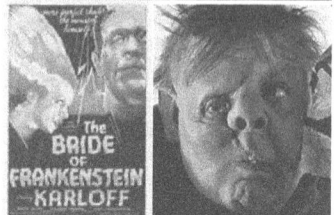

fans by accepting a minor role in Stanley Kramer's *Judgment at Nuremberg* (1961). It was a wise choice, leading to an Oscar nomination for Best Supporting Actress that year and also a nomination for a Golden Globe.

For $50,000, Kramer cast her as a dowdy, overweight German *hausfrau*, who, during the Nazi regime was thrown into prison for not participating in a plot to execute a Jewish man who was innocent of any crime.

In reference to her reduced circumstances, she uttered a *cliché* to the press: "There are no small parts, only small actors."

"I wanted to show the world that Judy Garland had not ended up in a crypt at Forest Lawn," she said. "The picture was a milestone in my career since I had been off the screen for six years. I got to work with an old friend like Spencer Tracy and to hang out with Marlene Dietrich."

"Stanley Kramer was a brilliant director, guiding me through my every move as Irene Hoffman Wallner."

After its premiere, Judy was pleased with the critical response, one reviewer writing, "Judy Garland is no longer Andy Hardy's girlfriend."

"*Judgment at Nuremberg* was notable in my life, as it led to a few more film roles," she said. "Before that, I had been viewed as a has-been who would never find work again, like James Mason, my husband in *A Star Is Born.*"

***

**The next stage of Judy's evolution involved her live concerts, including the one that resulted in her Carnegie Hall album. How transformative was this period of her life personally and professionally?**

After she was booted from MGM, Judy began her "concert years" that would take her from New York to London and all the way to Australia.

Her first major concert occurred in 1951 at The Palladium in London. Her last concert appearance was in Copenhagen in March of 1969.

In between those dates, she made at least a hundred personal appearances. They brought in much-needed money which was quickly spent. Most of her concerts were triumphs, each delivered to beloved fans. A few ended disastrously, to some degree because she was in bad shape because of her addiction to drugs.

Even when her singing voice was no longer assured, her most devoted fans, especially the gay ones, applauded her every move. She also reached out to wider audiences, although perhaps not being rewarded with the same fanatical devotion. Her concert years cemented "The Judy Garland Legend."

As an entertainer, she built up a rapport with her audience that was never replicated in the same way by any other singer except perhaps Elvis Presley. To relate to audiences, she used a self-deprecating humor, as if to say, "Sure I have flaws—don't we all?"

"She made the audience part of her act," said Frank Sinatra. "She put her vulnerability on open display."

Walter Winchell wrote, "Judy Garland has done the impossible—she has revived vaudeville."

Audiences virtually demanded that she replicate the most memorable songs from her films—especially "Over the Rainbow," requests for which were screamed loudly from many audiences.

Sometimes, onstage, she reverted to that little farm girl from Kansas, wistfully singing of a faraway land but concluding "There's no place like home."

According to Dean Martin, "She lamented the man who got away, and how someone else made her love him. All the old favorites included a ride on the trolley to Santa Fe. The last I saw her on a stage in Vegas wasn't a concert. It was a love fest."

Judy's greatest concert—indeed, one of the greatest in the history of music—occurred on a Sunday night as spring blanketed Manhattan.

The date was April 21, 1961 at Carnegie Hall where she appeared before sold-out crowds. She sang "When You're Smiling", "Swanee (aka Suwanee)", and "I Can't Give You Anything

**JUDGMENT AT NUREMBERG**

**Films and Filming**

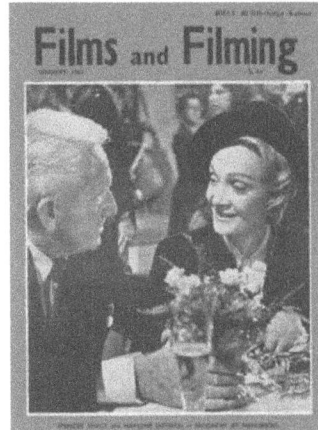

Although **Judy Garland** *(middle photo, above)* had only a small part in *Judgment at Nuremberg* (1961), It generated massive interest in an era when issues associated with the collapse of the Nazis was of compelling interest.

In the lower photo, the performances of both **Spencer Tracy** and **Marlene Dietrich** were analyzed endlessly...including by the editors of filmmaking journals like the one displayed above.

Stage and movie pro **Dean Martin** appears here onstage with bunny-inspired chorines.

227

But Love"—all the time-tested favorites.

The audience went wild. That concert at Carnegie Hall became known as "the greatest single night in show business history."

The two-record album that came out of that concert became certified gold, remaining on the *Billboard* chart for 95 weeks, including for thirteen weeks as Number One. At the Grammy Awards, Judy walked away with the prize for Best Female Vocalist of the Year and Best Album of the Year.

Concerts rescued her from the debris of her failed film career, and "kept me alive, believing in myself and my ability to entertain even on my darkest night."

"One of my suicide attempts might have worked were it not for the love I was getting from my audience—and not from one of those bastards I married."

***

**Judy,** basking in the adoration of fans during her Carnegie Hall gtriumph of 1961. Bing Crosby gave his review: "There wasn't a thing that gal couldn't do—except look after herself."

THROUGHOUT ALL THIS TIME, THERE SEEMED TO BE CONSTANT PERSONAL DE-CLINES, BUT SOMEHOW SHE'D RISE UP AGAIN. TO OTHERS I'VE DRAWN A COMPARI-SON, AS SILLY AS IT SEEMS, TO ROCKY BALBOA AND THE CHARACTER'S SPEECH THAT IT DOESN'T MATTER HOW HARD YOU GET HIT BY LIFE, IT'S ABOUT GETTING HIT AND GETTING UP AGAIN. SHE SEEMED TO EMBODY THAT.

*"If life knocks you down eight times, get up nine."* So said Judy Garland, commenting on her frequent falls from grace and her multiple "returns" to show business.

One commentator compared her to Rocky Balboa, the boxer that Sylvester Stallone portrayed in *Rocky* (1976).

He seemed to echo her earlier philosophy, "It's not how you get hit by life. It's about getting up again."

**Gloria Swanson** in a publicity photo for *Sunset Blvd.* (1950). Was she self-satirizing? Perhaps not...

"I estimate that I've made 185 comebacks," Judy said. "Surely that must be a world record. I was beginning to feel like Gloria Swanson in *Sunset Blvd.*"

In 1968, a year before she died, she made an appearance on *The Dick Cavett Show.* "I've done so many comebacks, I've been dubbed 'The Queen of Comebacks.' I'm getting tired of coming back. I really am. I can't even go into a restaurant and go to the powder room without making a comeback."

"One of the biggest hurdles I had to face came early in my film career. I had to cross the bridge from child star to adult performer. For most child stars, that ain't gonna happen. Take Shirley Temple, for instance."

"Mayer wanted me to be sexless on the screen at first, except for the time he was fondling my breasts, telling me I should sing from the heart. I knew where my heart was. He didn't have to show me with his probing fingers."

"Except for *The Wizard of Oz,* I resented most of the roles I was offered in the 1930s, fearing these bright-faced youngsters would represent the end of me as I was growing older every day."

"But after *The Wizard of Oz,* I came back and finally graduated to older parts."

"Call my transformation from child star to a grown-up singer my first big comeback."

Two views of **Judy**, each from around 1965, of an actress noted for her sense of hip and her powers of articulation. *On the left,* she's poised, forthright, and "in control." *On the right,* at a New York airport, minutes after a conflicted, press-badgered return from London, she's more rattled.

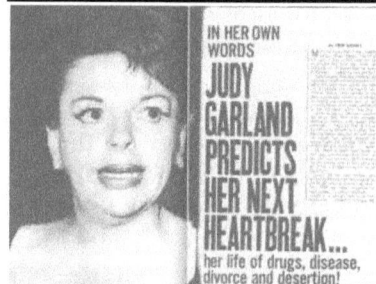

***

THE JUDY GARLAND SHOW. I'D LOVE TO GET YOUR ASSESSMENT OF THAT SHOW; WHAT IT OFFERED, WHETHER OR NOT IT WORKED, THE BATTLE WITH THE NETWORK, ETC.

IN HER OWN WORDS
JUDY GARLAND PREDICTS HER NEXT HEARTBREAK...
her life of drugs, disease, divorce and desertion!

The tabloids were usually cruel. Here's an embarrassing excerpt from *Movie Mirror Magazine.*

Judy had high hopes for an extended gig on network TV after a meeting with James Aubrey, Jr. Nicknamed "the Smiling Cobra," he was the President of CBS's Television Network.

She never expected to topple NBC's popular Sunday night western series, *Bonanza,* and she pleaded with Aubrey to give her another time slot—but he refused.

She bravely set forth, and her show premiered on September 29, 1963 and went off the air on March 19, 1964. *Bonanza* had already knocked *The Jack Benny Show* off the air, and although optimistically, Judy realized she could only expect to come in at second place, she never achieved that, either.

Her show had its highlights, as when Ethel Merman, Judy, and fellow "belter," Barbra Streisand, performed together one night, or when Judy sang a heart-rending "Battle Hymn of the Republic" in memory of the death of the recently assassinated President, John F. Kennedy.

Although Aubrey had criticized her tribute to the slain president *["In a few months, no one will remember or even give a damn about who Kennedy was"]* Judy had been Kennedy's friend. From time to time, he had telephoned her from the Oval Office just to get her to sing "Over the Rainbow" to him.

From the beginning of her TV show, Judy tangled with its producer, Norman Jewison, who objected to her "touchy-feely" style of relating to her audience.

Ordering her to remain more aloof, he wanted her to be more like Dinah Shore and had her filmed in activities that included hosting a Texas barbecue. "I want to take her glamorous image down a peg or two," he told his staff. "Make her more homelike and domestic."

He also made her the butt of tasteless, unfunny jokes, when she didn't fit in with the show's comic, Jerry Van Dyke.

She was, however, very much at home with her guest artists, many of them her friends—take Frank Sinatra, for instance, or Dean Martin, Lena Horne, June Allyson, Donald O'Connor, Mickey Rooney, Tony Bennett, or even Liza Minnelli. "Jewison preferred me to be the Betty Crocker of TV," she protested. Try as she might, she just could not get those ratings up.

As a lot of conflicts over her show swirled around her, she turned more and more to pills. She was often late for rehearsals.

Her conflicts with Aubrey increased, especially when he was quoted in the press as having said, "I do not dislike Judy Garland. I don't dislike her at all. I despise her."

She shot back, telling a reporter, "On Sunday night you'll catch me watching *Bonanza.*"

When *The Judy Garland Show* went off the air, it had the dubious distinction of being the costliest flop in television history.

The *Chicago Sun-Times* commented on her show's demise: "CBS hired Judy Garland, a big star, but then wouldn't let her be one."

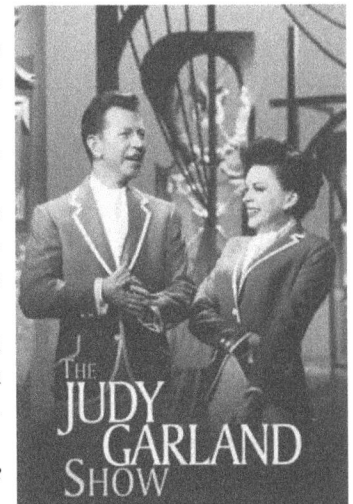

**Judy Garland,** shown here with **Donald O'Connor,** showed CBS that she could orchestrate an hour of weekly primetime TV in formats that —at their best—entertained and in many cases, delighted millions of viewers.

**Dean Martin, Judy Garland,** and **Frank Sinatra,** hoofing and hustling their ways together across prime-time TV.

\*\*\*

THAT FINAL STAGE OF HER LIFE IN LONDON. WHAT WAS THAT LIKE FOR HER? WHILE SHE ENJOYED PERSONAL SUCCESS, HER PRIVATE LIFE WAS SPIRALING TOWARDS THE END. GIVEN THE WAY HER LIFE WENT, DOES IT SEEM INEVITABLE THAT IT ENDED THE WAY THAT IT DID?

As her close friend, Mickey Rooney, said, "Judy—and I love her dearly—began committing suicide in 1940. It was a slow, lingering death, as she led a life of drug overdoses, broken love affairs, impossible husbands, bankruptcy, and heartbreak. I think she wanted to leave us by 1969 as she just couldn't take it anymore. I'm not suggesting suicide…instead, she took the slow road to death."

The end of her life found her living with Mickey Deans in a dismal, dilapidated mews house in the Belgravia district of London.

It seemed inevitable that she'd die young because of her morbid depressions, cavalcade of pills, and her penchant for self-destruction as shown by *all* those suicide attempts. Many of her close friends, whose numbers by now had dwindled to a precious few, feared her early death. When she arrived for her final sojourn in London, she looked skeletal.

As if predicting her own early demise, she spoke to Deans a few hours before she died: "There will be a new beginning for me, a new beginning for us." But there was no conviction in her voice.

At her last concert, the audience had demanded more. She confronted them and said. "There is no more."

During her final days, Deans kept inventing excuses to leave their flat, deciding that she was "too morbid to be around."

In one of her last calls to her gay friend, John Carlyle, to whom she had once proposed marriage, she said, "I've lost my audience. They were all I had left."

Her last time on American soil occurred on June 17, 1969, when her friend, Robert Jorgen whispered to Deans, "Take good care of Judy—she's dying."

Deans was asleep on June 22, 1969 when a call came in from Carlyle in Los Angeles. He was worried about Judy and wanted to speak to her again. Deans noticed that she was not in bed and headed for the bathroom to look for her.

Its door was locked. After pounding on it and hearing no response, he went out onto the roof and peered in through the window. Through its glass, he saw Judy hunched over and sitting on the toilet. After breaking in, he lifted her body from the stool. As he did, the last gasp of air exited from her lungs.

The songs which had emerged from those lungs had entertained millions from around the world.

The first bulletin coming out of London was replicated in New York and then around the world: JUDY GARLAND DEAD.

**ALL THESE YEARS LATER, THOUGH, DESPITE EVERYTHING, THERE IS STILL ENORMOUS PASSION FOR JUDY GARLAND. WHAT IS IT ABOUT HER THAT ALLOWS HER TO CONTINUE TO TOUCH PEOPLE ALL THESE YEARS LATER?**

At her funeral in New York, James Mason, Judy's co-star in *A Star Is Born*, told the assembled crowd, whose members included her three children, "Posterity doesn't remember entertainers."

How wrong he was.

The legend of Judy Garland—as has the legend of Marilyn Monroe— has grown and grown over many passing decades.

"To become a legend," said Bette Davis, "you have to die young."

Legions of Garland's fans have grown up since her death. The sound of her voice is vividly remembered by tens of thousands.

A sobbing Mickey Rooney said, "Judy said it all in song. Forget your troubles and just get happy. Get ready for the Judgment Day."

As the funeral hearse pulled away after her mother's funeral, Liza Minnelli was overheard saying, "Go, mama, go!"

All over the world, millions continue to watch *The Wizard of Oz*, even if they have never seen any other Judy Garland film. Year after year they take delight in watching Judy dance down the Yellow Brick Road to see what lies on the other side of the rainbow.

Long before her death, Judy predicted that flags would fly at half mast over the gay mecca of Fire Island when news of her death flashed across the nation.

And so they were.

More was to come. That night in Greenwich Village, police raided the gay bar, The Stonewall Inn, arresting its patrons for merely having assembled there. The patrons fought back. A new and more defiant aspect of Gay Liberation had begun.

Many of Judy's fans claimed that she set off the movement that swept across the nation.

"Judy Garland will never die in our hearts," said Jerry Sage, president of her fan club. "She touched our hearts as no one ever had. She will live on as long as children want to dream. They'll follow Dorothy to meet the Wizard."

Vincent Canby of *The New York Times* wrote: "The greatest shock at the death of Judy Garland is that there is no shock. People wondered how she had survived for so long."

FINIS

230

**DAILY NEWS**

**JUDY GARLAND DIES IN LONDON**

**Husband Finds Body in Home**

JUDY! JUDY! JUDY! - HER LIFE STORY BEGINS ON PAGE 3

**DAILY NEWS**

**JUDY WAS STAR IN FINAL ROLE**

**Hundreds Linger After Funeral**

The day Judy died, as legend has it, there was a tornado in Kansas.

**REST IN PEACE**
**JUDY GARLAND**

Born 1922 in Grand Rapids, Minnesota

Died 1969, Cadogan Lane, London, U.K.

# THE RISE OF "HAGSPLOITATION"

## AGING ACTRESSES DEFY CONVENTIONAL WISDOM ABOUT THEIR AGE

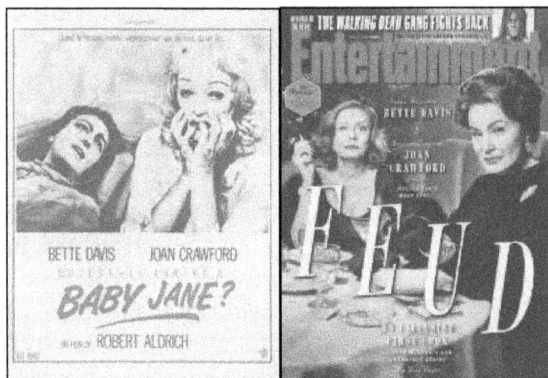

Left photo: **Joan Crawford** and **Bette Davis** revived their sagging careers in the horror flick **What Ever Happened to Baby Jane?** (1962).

Right photo shows a scene from **Feud** (2017), a TV series replicating the hatred between Davis (**Susan Sarandon**, left) and Crawford as played by **Jessica Lange.**

DIANE VON FURSTENBERG: "AGING IS OUT OF YOUR CONTROL. HOW YOU HANDLE IT THOUGH, IS IN YOUR HANDS."

GEORGE BERNARD SHAW: "YOU DON'T STOP LAUGHING WHEN YOU GROW OLD, YOU GROW OLD WHEN YOU STOP LAUGHING."

JULIANNE MOORE: "YOU CAN'T BE ANYWHERE EXCEPT WHERE YOU ARE."

**There was a time when older actresses** seemed to have "expiration dates" tattooed on their foreheads. To consumers seemingly obsessed with youth, few roles in the entertainment industry even existed for mature women.

But in the last few months, there has been an explosion of roles for "seasoned" women delivering strong, emotionally charged performances in dramas attracting millions of viewers. This audience is perhaps tired of stories about zombies, vampires, aliens, car chases, rap music, and various computer-generated versions of the Apocalypse.

Seen by the largest audience was the TV series, *Feud*, which chronicled the ferocious rivalry between Bette Davis and Joan Crawford during the filming of their mega-hit, *What Ever Happened to Baby Jane?* in 1962.

Jack Warner, never known for his delicacy, derisively called their casting "hagsploitation."

The series (broadcast as eight episodes FX TV) focused not only on the "gladiatorial combat" between these two battling divas, but on sexism, ageism, and misogyny in Hollywood.

Critics hailed the creatively wicked performances of Susan Sarandon (playing Davis) and of Jessica Lange (as Crawford) as examples of what really makes Hollywood great—the women.

Sarandon is known for her social and political activism and for memorable film performances that include *Thelma & Louise* (1981), for which she was nominated for an Oscar. A daughter of the Middle West, Lange was once billed as "the most dangerous and exciting actress in America," appearing in such movies as *Tootsie* (1982) opposite Dustin Hoffman in drag, and winning an Oscar as the forlorn, disorderly wife in *Blue Sky* (1994).

Born in 1947, Glenn Close has had a career spanning four decades, and is one of the most acclaimed of all Baby Boomer actresses, winning six Oscar nominations.

After a long absence from the screen, **Gloria Swanson**, in 1950, "came back" in her most memorable role, that of the fading screen diva **Norma Desmond.**

Actress **Glenn Close** told a reporter, "It took a pair of balls, so to speak, for me to take on the role of Norma Desmond on Broadway. I dreaded comparisons with Ms. Swanson."

Close's interpretation of the diva opened at the Belasco Theater on Broadway on March 9, 2017.

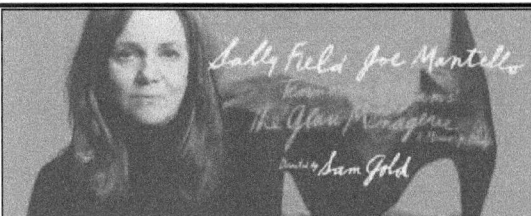

**Sally Field** also feared comparisons to Gertrude Lawrence when she dared play Amanda Winfield in a Broadway revival of Tennessee Williams' **The Glass Menagerie**.

"I just knew I could impersonate a fading Southern belle—and so I did."

She is currently making a triumphant return to Broadway in a revival of *Sunset Boulevard*. In it, she plays the fading silent screen vamp, Norma Desmond, in this Andrew Lloyd Webber musical based on the 1950 film, *Sunset Blvd.* (note the different spelling), which brought Gloria Swanson her one and only Oscar nomination.

All of the great lines from the movie are still here: "*I AM big. It's the pictures that got small.*"

Norma lives in a dream world of delusion, delivering a heart-rending number, "As If We Never Said Goodbye," a lament to her thousands of fans who deserted her decades ago.

Sally Field is also back on Broadway, after having a hard time finding suitable roles. This two-time Oscar winner for *Norma Rae* (1979) and *Places in My Heart* (1984) appears as Amanda in the evocative Tennessee Williams drama, *Glass Menagerie,* based on the playwright's own (spectacularly dysfunctional) family.

And, lest we forget, the outrageous, multi-talented Bette Midler returns to Broadway in a revival of *Hello, Dolly*, originally made famous by Carol Channing on Broadway and Barbra Streisand in the movie version.

The most exciting opening, an original musical, *War Paint,* has opened on Broadway starring two supremely talented Baby Boomers. "The Cosmetology Queens" are played by Patti LuPone as Helena Rubinstein and Christine Ebersole as Elizabeth Arden. Before they evolved as arbiters of fashion, only prostitutes and "loose women" painted their faces. Today, they're remembered as pioneering icons of female empowerment during an era when women were fighting for the right to vote. Fashion historians, take note: Never has Broadway seen such a monumental sweep of cross-generational finery, as the actresses' costumes span eras from the foxtrot to the frug.

Their show-stopping number that helps define these "take charge and devour" lionesses? It's entitled "What Man Has Half the Balls That I Have?"

Adroit at their rivalries, and adept at backstabbing and man-stealing, each of these mature female stars are at the peak of their dramatic power. Singing and performing with dagger-edged precision, both are in their 60s, appearing at a time when most big musical roles for women are limited to Momma Rose in *Gypsy*.

LuPone is a two-time Grammy Award winner and a two-time Tony winner as well, and is still remembered for her landmark portrayal of Eva Perón in the 1979 original production of the musical, *Evita*. The lady from Chicago, Ebersole, is also a Tony winner based on her performances in *42ⁿᵈ Street* and *Grey Gardens*.

Rubinstein once said of Arden: "With her packaging and my product, we could have ruled the world. Too bad we hated each other's guts."

The titanic queens of beauty battled with each other for half a century. By the 1950s, new challengers appeared on the horizon as Charles Revlon skyrocketed to fame and fortune with his nail polish, which the two *grandes dames* contemptuously dismissed as vulgar.

Although other challengers were on the way, the two *uber-fashionistas* carried on until their respective ends. That came for Rubinstein in 1965, when she died at the age of 92. Arden died eighteen months later at 89.

An era had passed, but not before these two dueling powerhouses changed the faces of women around the globe.

Channing did it first and best, followed by Streisand, who almost made it. Now it's **Bette Midler,** former Queen of the Continental Baths, having a blast at out-schmaltzing Dolly Levi in a 2017 revival of the musical that made Yonkers famous—and making us all laugh at the poignant *chutzpah* of the human heart.

**Jessica Tandy,** who took our breath away in unfunny Tennessee Williams dramas in the 50s, now playing a cranky but soft-hearted geriatric alongside **Morgan Freeman** in *Driving Miss Daisy* (1989).

Both have huge fan bases, and both are great as bitchfest dragons. Here are **Dolly Parton** and **Olympic Dukakis** in *Steel Magnolias* (1989).

**WHO KNEW** that they'd be brilliant as late-in-life friends and self satirists?

Here are **Joan Collins, Shirley MacLaine, Elizabeth Taylor,** and **Debbie Reynolds,** burying the hatchet and having a laugh in *These Old Broads* (2001).

All Dolled Up and Ready for Church:

**Patti LuPone** as Helena Rubinstein and **Christine Ebersole** as Elizabeth Arden in *War Paint* (2017).

For each, it was, a Swan Song:

**Lillian Gish** and **Bette Davis,** each a long-ago queen of the silver screen, in the gently nostalgic *The Whales of August* (1987).

## DEATH OF A DESERT SHEIK
# OMAR SHARIF

In one of the greatest moments in cinematic art, the Egyptian actor, Omar Sharif, appears at first as a tiny speck on the desert's far horizon. Slowly, a black-robed figure becomes visible until finally, the camera zooms in on the full figure of the desert warrior, Sherif-Ali, riding a camel.

His appearance was considered one of the most dramatic entrances in world cinema, and his camel ride also became a journey into international stardom, where he was hailed as the new Rudolf Valentino.

His co-star was another charismatic actor (Peter O'Toole), whose role as the desert warrior, T.E. Lawrence, plunged him into international stardom as well.

Although coming from completely different backgrounds, both of these handsome, charismatic actors became lifelong friends. Each man recognized in the other a sexual outlaw and hellraiser. When not due on the set of *Lawrence*, they escaped to the bordellos and gambling casinos of Beirut, where they sometimes squandered months of their salaries in a single night.

In addition to his high stakes gambling, Sharif was a racehorse owner and one of the world's greatest contract bridge players.

In July, 2015, after making some 100 movies (many for TV), the swashbuckling heartthrob that was Sharif died in a Cairo hospital. At the age of 83, he had a heart attack after suffering for years from Alzheimer's disease.

Originally, Sharif had been set to make his American film debut in *Joseph and His Brethren* (never filmed), co-starring, it was believed at the time, with Rita Hayworth. "I rank my one weekend with the Love Goddess as reason enough for me having been placed on this earth," he said.

While researching *Frommer's Paris* in the 1970s, I sought Sharif out and found him living alone in a small hotel on the Left Bank. He was an amusing, sophisticated man, with a somewhat jaded view of life.

Born into a Melkite Greek Catholic family from Lebanon, Sharif converted to Islam when he married Faten Hamama, the Egyptian actress who, as a child, was called Egypt's answer to Shirley Temple. She had never been kissed on screen until he took her in his arms in the 1954 Arabic-language film, *Struggle in the Valley* (1954). They fell in love and had a son, Tarek El-Sharif. The marriage ended in 1974, and he never remarried.

"I have entertained many girls only because I am searching for the right one and have never found her," Sharif said, as we enjoyed a bottle of wine (actually more than just a bottle). "No woman must ever contradict me. I can contradict a woman because I'm a man and because arrogance is the nature of man."

"I never set out to seduce some of the world's most celebrated beauties," he said. "They pursued me. I put sex, food, and wine in the same category, each to be enjoyed by a man after a hard day's work. What is this thing called love? You don't need love to have sex."

Born into a wealthy family of Syrian and Lebanese parents, **Omar Sharif** grew up speaking French as a boy. Later, he learned Arabic and in time, became the only international male star to rise out of Egypt. He was ideal when cast in darkly romantic roles.

**MUCH ADO ABOUT NOTHING**

Sharif's name was prominently hyped as the then "almost unknown' male lead in in a film, *Joseph and His Brethren*, that was never made. Had it been completed, his co-star would have been the sensual and lovely **Rita Hayworth**, *depicted above*.

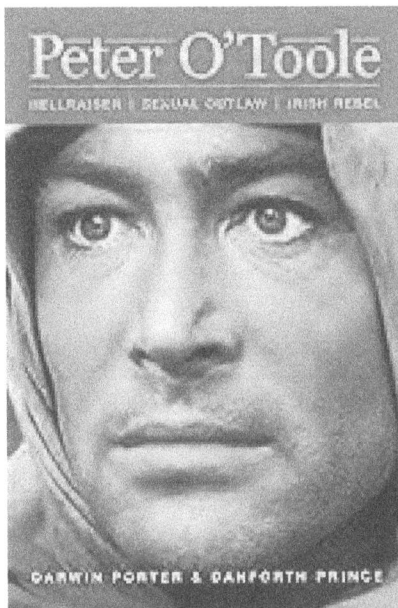
**Peter O'Toole**
HELLRAISER | SEXUAL OUTLAW | IRISH REBEL
DARWIN PORTER & DANFORTH PRINCE

Wanna know more, much more, about the often shocking **Omar Sharif**? Read about it here, in the pages of Darwin Porter's seminal biography of Sharif's co-star, bad boy and thrill-seeker, **Peter O'Toole**.

233

Sharif's conquests read like a *Who's Who* from the cinematic world. He remembered Ingrid Bergman, his co-star in *The Yellow Rolls-Royce* (1964). "My first Swedish beauty, but there were things she wouldn't do."

He had nothing but loving memories of Julie Christie, his co-star in *Dr. Zhivago* (1965). In that landmark classic, he played the brooding, sensitive Zhivago plunged into a doomed love affair with another man's wife. "For greater verisimilitude on screen, we had to rehearse love-making off the screen."

"My greatest challenge was co-starring with Ava Gardner and Catherine Deneuve in the 1968 film, *Mayerling*. Both Catherine and Ava were rivals for the title of the world's most beautiful animal. I was kept busy with those two. Love by dawn's early glow, by the noonday sun, with tea in the afternoon, love after dinner, followed by a midnight rendezvous with one or the other. Making love to Catherine or Ava was like embracing part of the universe."

"My most controversial affair was with Barbra Streisand when we made *Funny Girl* in '68, based on the life of Fanny Brice," he said. "She struck me as ugly at first. Then she cast her spell over me, and I fell madly in love with her. The feeling was mutual, but when word reached Egypt that I was making love to a Jewish girl, there were almost riots in the streets of Cairo. Barbra was a fund-raiser for Israel. Of course, *Funny Girl* was banned in Egypt."

"My one failure with a woman occurred when I was accosted in a Dallas hotel room by a woman armed with a gun. She broke into my room and forced me to strip naked, then demanded that I make love to her. I motioned to my flaccid penis and told her, 'Madam, at the moment, it is not possible.'"

"Perhaps my greatest thrill involved bedding the stunningly beautiful April Ashley, Britain's most famous transsexual."

"I'll even share my philosophy of life with you," he said. "Live every moment as if it were your last. Don't worry about what you've done in the past, fretting over all the hearts you've broken. Don't think about tomorrow, because it may never come. Think about what you're going to do tonight and the heart you'll break before the sun rises over Paris."

*Left photo:* Sharif's first (some said "breakthrough") wife was a leading figure in Egyptian cinema when she married him. Her name was **Faten Hamama.** Their marriage lasted from 1955-1974. In 1996, nine of the films she starred in were included in the top hundred films in the history of Egyptian cinema by the critics at Cairo's International Film Festival.

*Right photo:* **Omar Sharif** emotes with his then-wife ("the love of my life') **Faten Hamama** in *Land of Peace* (1957).

Left photo: **Sharif** with **Ingrid Bergman** in *The Yellow Rolls Royce;* and *right photo*, with **Julie Christie** in the Russian-based saga, *Dr. Zhivago.*

**POMP AND CIRCUMSTANCE AMONG THE HABSBURGS**: Two views of **Omar Sharif** in the historical drama *Mayerling (1968)*. *Left* with **Ava Gardner,** and *right* with **Catherine Deneuve.**

His onscreen romances (and off-screen friendship) with **Barbra Streisand** *(right)* led to his films being banned in Egypt and scads of negative publicity throughout the Middle East.

# SCARLETT & HEATHCLIFF

### (AKA VIVIAN LEIGH AND LAURENCE OLIVIER)

## TOGETHER ON THE ROAD TO HELL

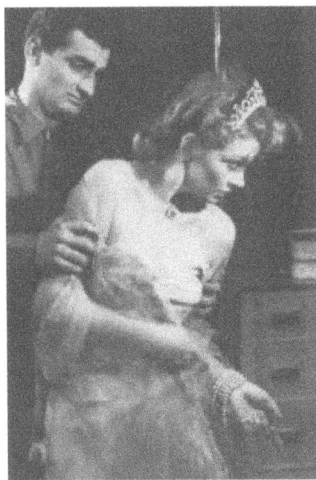

Bookbuyers took special notice this week at news that copies of Blood Moon's newest celebrity *exposé* had been delivered to the warehouses of both The National Book Network and Turnaround for distribution soon to bookstores in the US, Britain, Canada, and Australia.

According to Blood Moon's president and founder, Danforth Prince, "This is a unique, first-of-its-kind overview of the private lives of two of the 20th century's most revered actors, brimming with first-ever revelations about their sexual and emotional indiscretions and the ongoing frustrations that affected their stage and cinematic performances on both sides of the Atlantic.

Its authors by no means meant to simplify their artistic yearnings into a list of bulleted indiscretions, but for reasons of clarity, here are some of the talking points associated with the Romeo and Juliet of their era, the doomed Lord Nelson and Lady Hamilton, the tragic Hamlet and Ophelia, as revealed in this explosive double biography:

\*\*\*

Born to a middle-class clergyman, Olivier was sexually abused as a young boy, the victim of both an Anglican priest and his schoolmates.

Born into a privileged English colonial home in Calcutta, with frequent excursions to the romantic uplands of Darjeeling, Vivian Hartley (later, Vivien Leigh) was the beautiful daughter of wealthy parents who filled their home with servants. In the class-conscious world of the British Raj, Leigh—as a porcelain-skinned pre-teen—was molested by her mother's lover.

As an awkward and insecure young actor, Olivier slowly came to realize that he was a bisexual and set out to pursue both men and women in the promiscuous venues associated with RADA (the Royal Academy of Dramatic Arts) and the British Theatre. His assignations included some of the industry's most celebrated visionaries: Poet and playwright Siegfried Sassoon; the ingenue actress who evolved into Dame Peggy Ashcroft; "England's most beautiful man" (Ivor Novello), actress Angela Baddeley, and impresario/playwright Noel Coward, who proclaimed in musical verse that he was "Mad About the Boy."

Motivated by the hope of advancing his career, Olivier married Jill Esmond, a closeted lesbian and member of the West End's theatrical royalty. The marriage wasn't sexually consummated until years after their socially prominent wedding. When sexual intimacy finally occurred, it led to the birth of a son, Tar-

Here's **Vivien Leigh** writhing with anguish during her portrayal of Blanche DuBois on a London stage in a production of *A Streetcar Named Desire* directed by her husband, Laurence Olivier.

A critic noted, "Playgoers sat silently in rapt attention as she went through the uninhibited sexual gyrations of a nymphomaniac. Miss Leigh's lust," he continued, "rolls off the stage like a tropical storm cloud, causing vague stirrings in old codgers far past their prime."

"But it was the closing minutes of the play that would later be regarded with such deep significance– when the sex-mad heroine, unable to satisfy her craving for more and more lascivious adventures, suffers a complete mental breakdown."

In his autobiography, Marlon Brando—her co-star in *Streetcar*'s 1951 film adaptation— praised Jessica Tandy for her performance onstage with him in New York. But he also stated that Vivien Leigh ended up as the definitive Blanche. "She was Blanche."

Long before either of them wowed American and Australian audiences in films like *Wuthering Heights* and *Gone With the Wind*, **Laurence Olivier** and **Vivien Leigh** were the most famous and admired actors in the U.K. Their talent and their marital union were as assured in the public imagination as the Bank of England—and vitally important to maintaining England's morale during World War II.

*Upper photo:* "**Larry and Viv'** as archived in Britain's National Portrait Gallery. During their celebrated heydays, they were prized as part of the "National Patrimony," and widely adored.

*Middle photo:* Marketed as Britain's most celebrated acting team, they're shown here as co-stars in a 1951 London stage production of *Antony & Cleopatra*.

*Lower photo:* The excitement of their arrival is reflected in this photo from a train window at Paddington Station.

quin.

During her initial struggle for recognition as an actress, a "highly ornamental" Vivien Leigh met a dashing young barrister in Devon and married him, leading to the birth of a daughter. After that, while still married, she dated other men, often with advantages to her career.

In Hollywood, although Olivier was rejected by Greta Garbo, he found comfort in other arms, notably with the ultra-dashing scion of Old Hollywood, Douglas Fairbanks Jr. Olivier's wife, Jill Esmond, preferred the company of Fairbank's bisexual wife, Joan Crawford.

During rehearsals for his role in a homosexual drama on Broadway, *The Green Bay Tree*, Olivier was raped by theatrical producer Jed Harris, "the monster of the Great White Way," who had previously seduced Cary Grant.

Back in London, Olivier ended up on the casting couch of John Gielgud, with Leigh being (successfully) pursued by producer and cinematic mogul Alexander Korda. Later, as their respective affairs became more notorious in the West End, Olivier launched an affair with Greer Garson, as Leigh began a troubled relationship with John Buckmaster, the emotionally disturbed matinee idol and son of London's theatrical *grande dame*, Gladys Cooper.

Tormented by her bipolar disorders, Leigh often became the victim of sexual predators who included the lesbian actresses Jeanne de Casalis and Isabel Jeans.

When Korda cast Olivier and Leigh together as co-stars in *Fire Over England*, their torrid affair burst publicly into flames. And although they managed to keep some of the details of their respective marital infidelities from the British press, Leigh pursued Olivier to Capri, where she "crashed" what had originally been envisioned as a second honeymoon for Esmond.

When not specifically shacked up with Olivier, Leigh pursued sexual affairs with co-stars who included Rex Harrison and Robert Taylor. In Hollywood, after Olivier temporarily abandoned her for a sojourn on Broadway, the dashing British actor Stewart Granger opportunistically filled in for him during his absence.

In Hollywood, Olivier was discovered by the swashbuckling Tasmanian actor Errol Flynn. Olivier had already seduced Flynn's wife, the French-born vamp Lili Damita, when they'd co-starred in a film together.

During the filming of *Gone With the Wind,* Leigh sustained sexual flings with both Leslie Howard (the love interest of the character she so adroitly played, Scarlett O'Hara) and Ona Munson, who played the *châtelaine* of the local brothel.

In 1941, on the dawn of the Japanese attack on Pearl Harbor, Alexander Korda recruited both Olivier and Leigh as secret British agents to spy on a long list of power brokers and opinion makers in Hollywood. Persons of interest to the British government included heiress Barbara Hutton, anyone associated with the German film industry, and actors Victor McLaglen, Errol Flynn, Gary Cooper, and Cary Grant.

As Britain suffered from wartime bombings and deprivations, Olivier and Leigh abandoned the safety and prosperity of Hollywood and David Selznick's assurances that he'd transform them into superstars. Aware of their value as motivational figureheads for the British war effort, they sailed from New York to Lisbon aboard a ship loaded with Nazi agents and collaborators, rarely venturing

Flush with cash from a series of West End successes, Larry bought **Notley Abbey**, a medieval homestead within a reasonable drive from London, and immediately embarked on a ruinous series of historic renovations.

It evolved into a weekend respite for himself, for Vivien, and their hard-partying cohorts. Their houseparties became famously stylish, and famously debauched.

Increasingly unstable, and increasingly intolerant of her husband's bisexual philandering, Vivien was charming and wonderful with her guests—until she wasn't.

Keeping things stylish was Cecil Beaton. a frequent visitor to Notley Abbey. Deliberately ignoring the hurricane-force arguments on display between "Larry & Viv," he wrote, "The life they lead in the country is most suitable for Shakespearean actors. The whole atmosphere of the place is suitable for giving performances of *Twelfth Night, A Midsummer Night's Dream* and *Hamlet*."

**ACTORS WHO SLAVED FOR THEIR CRAFT**

**Larry** and **Viv** onstage as *Caesar and Cleopatra.*

**Larry** became England's answer to Hollywood's preference for breathtakingly handsome matinee idols.

*On the left*, he appears as **Henry V,** heroic and victorious against the enemies of England at Agincourt. *On the right*, he's **Oedipus Rex** (1946) on the London stage.

Newlywed **Douglas Fairbanks, Jr.** appears here with his then-wife, **Joan Crawford**. In the 1930s, rumors flourished about a shipboard romance between the menfolk of the "Stage Royals' of the U.K. and U.S., respectively. The alleged participants? **Larry and Doug.**

In London and Hollywood, **Danny Kaye** *(left)* and **Laurence Olivier** were known as "the Odd Couple."

"Of course, I knew that Larry and Danny were engaged in an affair," claimed Dame Peggy Ashcroft.. "So did their wives. So did London's theatrical circles. Why is America always the last to know?"

## DEEP HOLLYWOOD HUMILIATIONS

On the left is a press announcement about how **Dana Andrews, Vivien Leigh, and Peter Finch** were on the verge of a cinematic blockbuster.

*Right photo:* An ad for the film's eventual release as a mini-hit starring another brunette (**Elizabeth Taylor**), who replaced Vivien Leigh on location in Sri Lanka (then known as Ceylon) after Vivien's widely publicized nervous breakdown.

from their cabin for fear of being murdered. In Lisbon, they were given a diplomatic pouch for transport to England. Within that dossier, or so it was believed, was proof of the Nazi sympathies of both the Duke and Duchess of Windsor, and proof of Hitler's promise to the former King (Edward VIII) that he'd be restored to the British throne after the Nazis conquered England.

In the blistering heat of North Africa, while entertaining Allied troops, sometimes in full Scarlett O'Hara drag, Leigh was given a secret diplomatic pouch, as arranged by Eisenhower, with instructions to deliver it to King George VI in Tunisia. The dossier is believed to have contained the name of German officers willing to overthrow Hitler and sue for peace with the West in 1943—a kind of advance preview of the more dramatic (and ultimately disastrous) Operation Valkyrie a year later.

Prior to Vivien's role in counter-espionage in North Africa, back in Bath, England, Olivier delivered secret documents to his contact, the notorious Duke of Kent, fabled for his seduction of celebrities, both male and female, both in and out of wartime. Olivier launched a sexual affair with the Duke (who was the brother of the equally notorious Prince of Wales, *aka* King Edward VIII, *aka* the Duke of Windsor), which endured until the Duke of Kent's still-mysterious death in a suspicious airplane crash off the coast of wartime Scotland.

One of Olivier's longest-running affairs, this one with the American *schtickster* and comedian Danny Kaye, is documented for the first time. According to Dame Peggy Ashcroft, "He loved Danny as much as he loved Vivien, maybe more."

\*\*\*

With tact and understanding, Vivien Leigh's bipolar schizophrenia is explored in all its horrific detail. This emotional and mental condition prompted her to obsessively and indiscriminately encounter men on the sidewalks of London for spontaneous sexual encounters. Her trysts included episodes with men who ranged from taxi and lorry drivers to de-

Whereas **Larry** and **Viv** managed to hold things more or less under control on their home turf, their suppressed rage became glaringly obvious under the klieg lights of Hollywood.

Here they are, displaced and confused, adjusting to the 24-hour glare of southern California.

## OIL AND WATER: LARRY'S AMERICANIZED DISASTER

*Displayed above* is a press photo of **Marilyn Monroe** and **Sir Laurence Olivier.** It was widely distributed to publicize the fact that they would be making a film together, *The Sleeping Prince.* Before its release, its title was changed to *The Prince and the Showgirl.*

*Inset photo:* Larry bitterly (and frequently) resented Marilyn Monroe's sloppy rehearsals and inefficient scheduling. British Insiders tended to support him (not her) in the battles which raged during their joint film endeavor.

He had decades of brilliant stage and screen experience behind him, which he used to buttress his accusations.

*The lower photo* shows Larry Olivier, with passion, delivering a blood-soaked sililoquy from his celebrated 1955 film production of Shakespeare's *Richard III.*

For decades after that, thousands of viewers compared his portrayal of the doomed king as a reference to agonized Brits defending their "sceptered isle" from the Nazi menace.

livery men. On occasion, she was mistaken for a hooker from Soho, and from time to time, she was actually paid for her sexual services during the rare moments when she wasn't instantly recognized by her johns.

Olivier and Leigh often became enamored of the same men, sharing the bisexual favors of actors who included both Richard Burton and the "devastatingly handsome" Terence Morgan. The couple's most widely publicized on-going three-way was with the bisexual actor Peter Finch.

During the Hollywood filming of *A Streetcar Named Desire* with Marlon Brando, the Method actor went from bed to bed within the Olivier household, eventually retreating from both Olivier and Leigh as a means of salvaging his own emotional health.

Brando was not the only outside player within the orbit of the Olivier family's sexual dramas. Deep into middle age, Olivier launched an affair with young Jean Simmons on the set of *Hamlet*, while Leigh became momentarily infatuated with Warren Beatty on the set of Tennessee Williams' *The Roman Spring of Mrs. Stone.*

The divorce of Lord and the first Lady Olivier became infamous. And whereas Olivier escaped into the arms of Joan Plowright, whom he eventually married, Leigh lived with actor Jack Merivale, who witnessed firsthand her final mental and physical deterioration. She sustained a brief sexual fling with actor Peter Wyngarde, with whom she was appearing in the West End play, *Duel of Angels.* Wyngarde discovered her running nude one night in the gardens of central London's Eaton Square, where soonafter she encountered a policeman. "Go home," he told her. "There's no way in bloody hell I'm going to arrest Scarlett O'Hara for public nakedness."

## "THEY WERE THE DARLING OF THE GODS, NATIONAL HEROES, THE MOST BELOVED PUBLIC FIGURES IN ENGLAND"
### BY DARWIN PORTER

Vivien Leigh and Laurence Oliver were called "The Darling of the Gods." They become the most romantic couple of the theatrical world, the stuff of legend. But who were they, really, after the curtain went down on this doomed Romeo and Juliet, this Hamlet and Ophelia?

In my latest biography, *Damn You, Scarlett O'Hara*, I try to answer that question. The title was inspired by Vivien's own lament in never escaping from her "Pigeon-holing" role in *Gone With the Wind.*

Her husband, Laurence Olivier, electrified World War II audiences with his portrait of the tragically romantic Heathcliff in Emily Brontë's *Wuthering Heights.* Later, he returned to the screen with a Jean Harlow dye job to portray *Hamlet*, in another brooding role that garnered him an Oscar. As Scarlett, Vivien had already won her own Oscar.

\*\*\*

In an attempt to crack the code of their secret lives, I co-authored the book with the noted British biographer, Roy Moseley, an intimate friend of the Oliviers over many a year. He had lived with them through many of their triumphs and tragedies. With data collected over the decades, the book drew on oral histories, unpublished revelations, letters, and documents from both friends of foes of the Oliviers.

The white heat of their love affair began in 1936 when they starred in *Fire Over England*. Each of them was married to others, Larry to actress Jill Esmond (a lesbian) and Vivien to a barrister, Herbert Leigh Holman, for whom she no longer had any passion.

Vivien and Larry lived through a tumultuous and adulterous four years before their divorces were finalized in 1940. On the way to their wedding in Santa Barbara in 1940, they got into a fight, according to her maid of honor, Katharine Hepburn. The wedding was almost called off.

Their wedding night was a harbinger of countless conflicts to come over the next two decades. They had an open marriage, each launching affairs with other men and women. Yet, before the world, they tried valiantly to live up to the false image created for their fans.

Behind the scenes, a very different Lord and Lady Olivier emerged. She was mentally ill, suffering from a bipolar condition that caused her to occasionally lash out at both her husband and friends.

He became a notoriously promiscuous bisexual, launching affairs with screen beauties and fellow actors that included a long-running liaison with Danny Kaye. Sometimes, "Larry and Viv" carried on affairs with the same men, notably Richard Burton, Peter Finch, and Marlon Brando.

Finally, in 1960, Larry could take it no longer and filed for divorce, settling into a

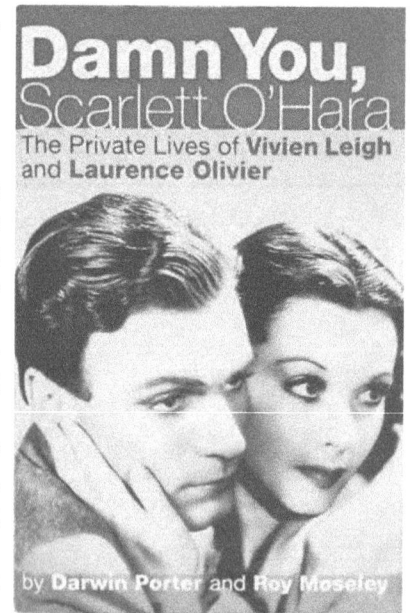

**Damn You,**
Scarlett O'Hara
The Private Lives of **Vivien Leigh** and **Laurence Olivier**

by **Darwin Porter** and **Roy Moseley**

**At last,** thanks to Blood Moon Productions, the curtain has risen on the secret private lives of **Laurence Olivier** and **Vivien Leigh**, the greatest man-and-wife acting team of all time.

As Larry said, "For an actor, performing onstage isn't enough. One must turn one's private life into an artistic performance. Vivien and I did just that."

238

marriage with actress Joan Plowright.

Vivien would never marry again but found comfort in the arms of actor Jack Marivale. Suffering from tuberculosis, Vivien met her death in 1967. Larry would go on to various other tragedies, triumphs, and illnesses before dying in 1989.

Their dear friend, Noel Coward, said, *"The gods gave them so much in the way of beauty and talent, but they paid such a wicked price for these gifts."*

\*\*\*

## LARRY, VIVIEN, AND *THAT HAMILTON WOMAN*

### WAS IT LOVE OR WAS IT PROPAGANDA?

No one could play it rich, historic, and *hoity-toity* like **Larry and Viv.**

Here, they appear in Alexander Korda's ode to Britain's naval prowess and its durability under stress.

At the time of its release, World War II was raging but the U.S. was still officially neutral.

Pearl Harbor hadn't yet been bombed; the Soviet Union was still officially allied with the Nazi Germany; and Poland, the Netherlands, Norway, France, Belgium, and Denmark were each already occupied by the armies of the Third Reich.

Times were, indeed, terrifying for the U.K.

In part because of the U.K's dire straits at the time of its release, *That Hamilton Woman* elevated its romantic leads, **Vivien Leigh** and **Laurence Olivier**, into national heroes.

*The lower photo* shows the interior of New York City's **Radio Music Hall** during the film's American debut in 1941. All 6,000 of its seats were sold out, and news about it roared through newspapers nationwide.

The fame, influence, and profitability of *Gone With the Wind* (1939)—that saga to a romanticized version of the Civil War South —cannot be over-emphasized.

**Vivien Leigh** and **Clark Gable** made it work. Although many other actors competed for their roles, no one today can imagine it without the dynamic they created onscreen.

Vivien, of course, remained "unrepentantly English" throughout her long and neurotic life. Yet each of her two Oscars were awarded for her portrayal of Southern belles. The first was for her performance as Scarlett O'Hara in *Gone With the Wind*. The other was for her interpretation of Blanche DuBois—a sexually hysterical damsel fleeing from her ruined plantation—in *A Streetcar Named Desire* (1951).

Here, *on the left and right* are posted commemorative portraits of **Emma, Lady Hamilton** and **Admiral Horatio Nelson**.

Marinated in romantic embellishments, **Emma** has been morphed into a Pre-Raphaelite beauty. A courtesan and former dance hall hostess, she had married Sir William Hamilton, Britain's ambassador to the Kingdom of Naples. Later, she became Admiral Nelson's mistress.

**Nelson**, fresh from the Napoleonic wars and lauded as "the hero who saved England from the French," is appropriately regal.

## NOBODY COULD "GET GORGEOUS" LIKE VIV

*Left photo:* **Vivien Leigh** as *Anna Karenina* (1948), wearing what was said to have been her most beautiful on-screen wardrobe. It was designed by Cecil Beaton. *Right photo:* In *The Mask of Virtue* (1935). producer Sidney Carroll went searching for "the most beautiful and talented actress to play the key role" in this romantically complicated 18th-Century costume drama. He found what he was searching for in **Vivien Leigh**.

Critics suggested she would become England's answer to Sarah Bernhardt. John Betjeman, one of Britain's poet laureates, defined her as "the essence of English girlhood."

In *Fire Over England* (1937), **Larry and Vivien** played young lovers in the politically treacherous Tudor court of Elizabeth I. Its producer, Alexander Korda, cast Flora Robson as the stern Queen Elizabeth I. Laurence Olivier played sea officer Michael Lingolby, and Vivien Leigh was cast as Cynthia, one of the queen's ladies-in-waiting.

Vivien told Korda, "At long last, I get to make love to Olivier, at least on the screen."

"I can't stand the c***," **Marlon Brando** told director Elia Kazan after three days of shooting *A Streetcar Named Desire* with his co-star, **Vivien Leigh**. "Miss Scarlett O'Hara, Miss Vivien Leigh. It's 'good morning, Mr. Brando.'" He imitated her, accenting *"Good afternoon, Mr. Brando."*

"She suffocates me with her politeness. I can't wait for the rape scene."

The first time he sat down to talk to her privately, he found a vulnerable character, not the "prissy English bitch" he'd envisioned. She reached out and gently touched his hand, as she spoke of the first time she'd read the Tennessee Williams' script. "I was touched by the haunting quality of Blanche," she said. " The play seemed to speak to the woman inside myself, who lives within my own heart. Blanche DuBois is the *animus* of my own being."

After that, and until the end of the eight-week shoot, Vivien and Marlon became almost inseparable.

**Vivien Leigh:** They said she was the most beautiful woman in England. Even today, thousands of fans on both sides of the Atlantic, heartily agree.

On July 8, 1967, the day news of her death blasted its way onto airwaves worldwide, every theater in London's West End extinguished their marquee lights for one hour in her honor.

A memorial service was held at St Martin-in-the-Fields and Leigh's cremated ashes were spread on the lake at her summer home, Tickerage Mill in East Sussex, England.

Many diehard fans continue their love affairs with her from afar. The co-authors of this book are two of them.

# REST IN PEACE
# VIVIEN LEIGH
### (1913-1967)

# OLIVIA DE HAVILLAND

## HOLLYWOOD LEGEND AND CENTENARIAN GOES TO COURT

*Editor's Note: This column was written and published when Ms. De Havilland was still alive.*

Born in Tokyo in 1916 to British parents, Hollywood legend Olivia de Havilland immortalized herself in the role of Melanie in that screen classic, *Gone With the Wind* (1939). She played opposite Clark Gable (portraying Rhett Butler) and Vivien Leigh (as Scarlett O'Hara). Today, she remains the only star who's still living from the legendary cast of that Civil War epic.

In June of 2017, two weeks before her 101st birthday, she was named Dame Commander of the Order of the British Empire, the oldest woman ever to receive that honor. Facing her 102nd birthday in July of this year, she is also the oldest living female star of Golden Age Hollywood.

Although deep in December of her life, "Dame Olivia" is in a fighting mood, filing a lawsuit against the FX Network and writer Ryan Murphy, citing "defamation and libel."

She took grave offense at her portrayal on the TV screen by Catherine Zeta-Jones, The Welsh actress portrayed her in *Feud: Bette and Joan.* The series depicted the decades-long rivalry between Bette Davis and Joan Crawford, who had co-starred in the horror flick, *What Ever Happened to Baby Jane?* (1962).

In her lawsuit, de Havilland maintains that the TV producers violated her right of privacy and publicity. In her suit, she charges that she was portrayed as a "vulgar hypocrite who peddles gossip to promote myself. I always had a reputation for honesty, integrity, and good manners. Dialogue assigned to me in the series was fiction, not words from my mouth."

Attorneys for FX maintain that if de Havilland's case prevails, it will pose a threat to any writer or producer who wants to create stories based on public figures. It has been a long tradition in movies or TV docudramas to invent dialogue on an "as remembered" basis.

In the courts, she faces an uphill battle, as judges have shown great leniency, citing the free speech clause in the First Amendment. Creators of stories dramatizing the lives of other Hollywood legends, including Clark Gable and Joan Crawford, have been allowed to "take liberties."

De Havilland never cooperated with a biographer, refusing to discuss any of her various relationships, most notably with the notoriously promiscuous swashbuckler, Errol Flynn, with whom she made a series of movies, the most famous being *The Adventures of Robin Hood* in 1938.

She has also refused to discuss her relationship with director John Huston. In my biography of Howard Hughes, *Hell's Angel,* I wrote that the billionaire aviator and film producer once proposed marriage to both sisters at the same time.

Like Crawford and Davis, Fontaine and de Havilland had a decades-long feud, the most famous sibling rivalry of the Golden Age. In 1941, Fontaine won the Best Actress Oscar for *Suspicion* opposite Cary Grant. She beat out her sister that year for her role in *Hold Back the Dawn.*

De Havilland bounced back from her defeat, winning an

**Olivia de Havilland**—a long time resident of Paris—appears in the photo above as the very imperial *grande dame* she had become, shortly before her death, in Paris, in July of 2020.

Press material promoting the FX teledrama wherein **Catharine Zeta-Jones** portrays Olivia de Havilland—much to the centenarian star's fury.

The screenplay which De Havilland sued over involved the bitter but always newsworthy feud between two equivalently ferocious divas, **Bette Davis** *(left)* and **Joan Crawford** *(right).*

241

Oscar for *To Each His Own* (1946) and another for *The Heiress* (1949).

The Associated Press quoted de Havilland as calling her sister "Dragon Lady." That was not my impression. In her later years, when Fontaine lived in New York City, I frequently escorted her to gala events and to restaurants and night clubs. She knew how to make an entrance, projecting serenity, poise, timeless beauty, and a kind of vulnerability that caused occupants of any room to turn their heads to gaze upon her. Many had fallen in love with her image based on roles she played in movies which included *The Constant Nymph* (1943) and *Jane Eyre* (1944).

Regardless of what happens in de Havilland's pending lawsuit, one thing is certain: Two groups, "The Greatest Generation," whose members won World War II, and who became the mothers and fathers of the Baby Boomers, will forever remember these two screen goddesses for their remarkable talent, their regal looks, and luminosity that lit up any screen.

With memories of their decades-long feud fading like the last rose of summer, they remain two historical figures of Golden Age Hollywood. Perhaps Fontaine summed up both of their tumultuous lives in the tile of her 1978 memoir, *No Bed of Roses.*

**EDITOR's NOTE**:  On March 26, 2018, an appellate court judge in California dismissed de Havilland's lawsuit against FX Networks over its series *Bette and Joan.* The judge ruled that the screen actress "does not have the legal right to control, dictate, approve, disapprove, or veto the creator's portrayal of actual people." She was ordered to pay the network's legal fees.

It was ruled that Catherine Zeta-Jones' portrayal of the Oscar-winning actress "was not highly offensive to a reasonable person as a matter of law."

As part of her complaint, de Havilland had argued that her portrayal "damned my professional reputation for integrity, honesty, generosity, self-sacrifice, and dignity."

She charged in court that the docudrama, without her permission, "seriously damaged my reputation by casting me in a false light as a hypocrite, selling gossip in order to promote myself at the Academy Awards, criticizing fellow actors, using vulgarity and cheap language. I take particular issue with Zeta-Jones referring to Joan Fontaine as 'my bitch sister.'"

***

De Havilland was born on July 1, 1916 in Tokyo. At the time of her death on July 26, 2020, at the age of 104, she was the oldest living and earliest survivor on the list of Academy Award winners. She was the last surviving superstar from *Gone With the Wind* (1939)..

She rose to prominence in adventure films such as *Captain Blood* (1935) with Errol Flynn. As mentioned, her breakthrough role came as Melanie in *Gone With the Wind* (1939). She was nominated for a Best Supporting Actress Oscar, but lost to Hattie McDaniel, who played a maid in *Gone With the Wind.* A native of Kansas, born in 1895, she became the first black actress to win an Oscar.

De Havilland's greatest roles included *Hold Back the Dawn* (1941), *To Each His Own* (1946), *The Snake Pit* (1948), and *The Heiress* (1949).

**SHADES OF GREATNESS PAST: Olivia de Havilland** *(left to right)*, with **Errol Flynn** in *The Adventures of Robin Hood (1938)* **, as** Melanie in *Gone With the Wind* (1939) and with **Montgomery Clift in** *The Heiress.* (1939).

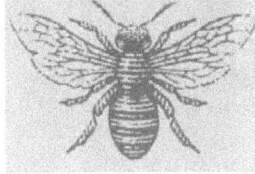

THE SUPPRESSION, AFTER ALMOST 90 YEARS SINCE ITS RLEASE IN 1939, OF

# *GONE WITH THE WIND*
## MILITANT CENSORS WANT TO BAN IT

Censorship, or "Cultural Revisions" of films, plays, TV shows, and books, is rearing its ugly head again.

In a robust democracy, censorship is rare. As a pervasive part of a culture, it belongs more to totalitarian regimes as evidenced by what can be seen—or not—in China and Russia today. In the past, Josef Goebbels, the Nazi propaganda minister, was adept at censorship, even book burning.

Since the birth of motion pictures, self-appointed American censors have aggressively tried to impose their values on their fellow citizens. In 1897, an early silent film provoked outrage by portraying a man passionately kissing his wife.

In 1907, Chicago became the first city in America to grant its chief of police the power to censor any film before it was released. That was followed with towns and cities across America appointing censorship boards.

Fearing Federal regulation, Hollywood in the 1930s imposed its own censorship board, stifling free expression until independent producers broke free in the 1960s.

Now, in 2020, new outcries of rage are being expressed as self-appointed "cultural commissars" want to decide what you can see or read.

The most notorious case calls for suppression of that enduring American classic from 1939, Margaret Mitchell's film adaptation of *Gone With the Wind.*

Seen by millions upon millions, it's the highest-grossing film of all time (adjusted for inflation). Starring Vivien Leigh

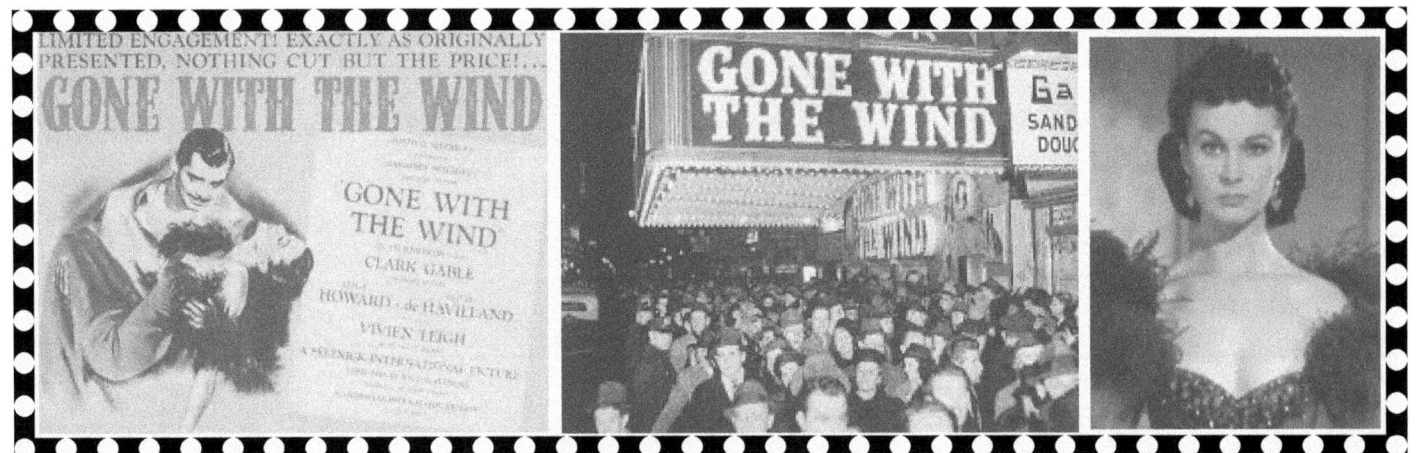

**Gone With the Wind**, while not glossing over the repulsive reality of slavery, acknowledged that it was just one part of a complex, if flawed, American civilization forever altered by war. When it premiered in Atlanta in 1939, the governor of Georgia declared a statewide holiday, and newsreels celebrated it as the most important film of the decade.

Whereas many aspects of re-screening it today still evoke the thrills audiences experienced in 1939, newly-articulated (and justifiable) resentments about slavery have tarnished the film, its context, and many points of view from the era that produced it.

as Scarlett O'Hara and Clark Gable as Rhett Butler, the movie is attacked for its "romantic" depiction of the Antebellum South and its tolerance (or endorsement) of slavery.

Actually, it's not much about slavery at all. It's the saga of Scarlett, born into a bucolic life on a plantation, who is plunged into surviving a war that ravishes her land and family. Later, she charts a new life for herself as an independent woman forced into the business world during Reconstruction. It's also the story of a woman torn between two lovers.

Hattie McDaniel was the first African American woman to win an Oscar for her memorable portrayal of Mammy. Some critics single her out as the smartest woman in the movie. She even bosses Scarlett around, holding her adolescent rebelliousness in check and continually prompting her to comport herself "like a lady." During her heyday, in reference to her role, McDaniel told a reporter, "I'd rather play a maid than be a maid."

In contrast, Butterfly McQueen told me that her role as the lazy, flighty slave, Prissy, "ruined my life. I had to play Prissy in film after film after that." She immortalized herself with one of the most iconic lines ever uttered onscreen: *"Miss Scarlett, I don't know nothin' 'bout birthin' babies."*

Early in the post-Covid censorship wars, HBO stopped its streaming distribution of *Gone With the Wind*, but later enabled it for streamings with a *caveat*: Jacqueline Stewart, an African American film historian and a host of Turner Classic Movies, will narrate a brief discussion, inserted as an introduction before each screening.

Spike Lee, the best known African American director, defended *Gone With the Wind* on the TV talk show, *The View.* He also inserted a sequence from that film into his movie, *BlacKkKlansman.*

"I think people should see this movie even though it's openly racist," Lee said.

More "radical," Lee screened *The Birth of a Nation,* considered by some as D.W. Griffth's masterpiece, to students in his film studies classes at New York University. Interpreted by many as the most racist film ever made, it depicts the KKK as a heroic force for the preservation of "American values" and the White Supremacist social order.

If these recent trends in American censorship prevail, virtually the entire output of films made during the first half of the 20th Century, including those with a theme of "John Wayne vs. The Indians" could be pulled from circulation.

But that won't happen without some artistic objections: Author Judith Miller wrote, "The impulse to self-censor, however powerful in such politically polarized times, is deadly to any vibrant culture. No matter how seemingly compelling its justification, it must be resisted."

It's no secret that the authors of this book are wildly enthusiastic fans, forever, of **Vivien Leigh**. Here she is, as Scarlett O'Hara, primped, cosseted, coquettish, and spoiled, reacting to "before the war" confusion as her party plans go awry.

Here's Scarlett (aka **Vivien**) "demurely enduring" the advances of the hottest, richest man in town, Rhett Butler (as portrayed by **Clark Gable**).

Seductive, charming, and devilish, he's a Confederate blockade runner who's proud of his skill at making a profit from the suffering South. Later, he repents.

The war, after wreaking horror on the still-intact (and now biracial) *ménage* at Tara, has chastened the arrogance of Miss Scarlett—but not dampened her ferocious resolve to regain her former grandeur.

As the female protagonists eye the tattered remnants of what used to be their "conquering heroes," it's obviious that seismic changes are on their way. *Left to right,* above, **Hattie McDaniel, Olivia de Havilland,** and **Vivien Leigh.**

**QUESTION: In the film, WHO WAS MAMMY?**
**Hint: The answer to each of the options listed below is YES.**

1) Was she a loyal, dignified, and eminently trusted family retainer?
2) Was she a substitute mother with a deep commitment to taming the manipulative beast in Miss Scarlett? Or
3) Was she an enslaved person making the best of a horrible lot.?

Her story is part of the emerging, and fascinating, discussions permeating post-millennial interpretations of *Gone With the Wind.*

# HOLLYWOOD CASTINGS

## & WHAT MIGHT HAVE BEEN

### MARGARET MITCHELL WANTED GROUCHO MARX

In the most absurd casting idea in the history of Hollywood, the wise-cracking comedian, Groucho Marx, pleaded. with David 0. Selznick, producer of *Gone With the Wind* (1939), to cast him as Rhett Butler. Believe it or not, the author, Margaret Mitchell, of the book on which the film was made, told the press in Atlanta that she felt that Groucho would be perfect as Rhett.

Selznick may have considered it for two seconds before showing Marx to the door. Instead, he toyed with casting Gary Cooper, Ronald Colman, Errol Flynn, Basil Rathbone, and Fredric March, but the public demanded Clark Gable.

Practically every actress in Hollywood, from Bette Davis and Paulette Goddard to Joan Crawford, even Lana Turner, wanted to play Scarlett O'Hara. At the last minute, a relatively unknown British actress, Vivien Leigh, graced the screen in her Oscar-winning portrayal.

Another great picture from 1939, *The Wizard of* Oz, might have had Shirley Temple cast as Dorothy, but Fox wouldn't release her. Louis B. Mayer reluctantly cast "my little hunchback," Judy Garland, as Dorothy. Deeply insecure, she walked down the yellow brick road into screen immortality.

The entire history of Hollywood would have to be rewritten if the original stars who were cast had actually completed their respective movies. *Casablanca* (1942) is hailed by some critics as the greatest film ever made. What would it have been like with Ronald Reagan and Ann Sheridan in the leading roles? Of course, it would be Humphrey Bogart and Ingrid Bergman remembering, "We'll always have Paris."

Cary Grant rejected Frank Capra's *It's a Wonderful Life* (1946), which means that every Christmas we get to watch James Stewart, fresh out of the U.S. Army, on our TV screens.

Three great actresses, each in their most memorable roles, competed for the Oscar in 1950: Bette Davis, Gloria Swanson, and Judy Holliday. Each of them almost lost their star parts.

Claudette Colbert signed for *All About Eve* as Margo Channing but couldn't perform after injuring her back. In her place, Bette Davis rushed into the role. Before that, studio chief Darryl F. Zanuck had considered Susan Hayward, Marlene Dietrich, and Katharine Hepburn.

The director of *Sunset Blvd.*, Billy Wilder, offered the role of Norma Desmond to Pola Negri, Mae West, and Mary Pickford before awarding it to Swanson. In it, she gave her greatest screen portrayal as the unhinged silent screen diva, Norma Desmond.

Montgomery Clift was originally tapped to play her gigolo, Joe Gillis, but rejected the role. In his place, the part went to William Holden.

Judy Holliday for her performance as the daffy blonde in *Born Yesterday* (1950) beat out Swanson and Davis for the Best

Since the suggestion derived directly from Margaret Mitchell, it BRIEFLY seemed like a good idea at the time: **Groucho Marx** in *lieu* of **Clark Gable** for Rhett? **Lana Turner** instead of **Vivien Leigh** as Scarlett?

*Upper photo* **The Wizard of Oz's** WINNER was **Judy Garland**, seen here being advised by **Billie Burke**, aka The Good Witch of the North.

*Lower photos*: **Margaret Hamilton,** as the Wicked Witch of the West, might have aimed her claws at **Shirley Temple**, who "almost" got the iconic role of Dorothy

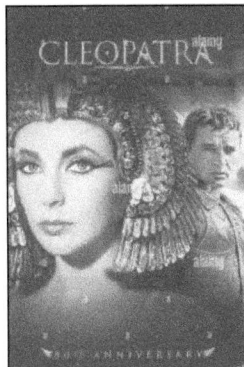

*Photo, left:* Everyone involved in 1963's WAY over budget production of **Cleopatra** never recovered from its fiscal and emotional horror.

During the peak of its dysfunction, its producers considered substituting **Joan Collins** for **Elizabeth Taylor** as the Queen of the Nile.

Collins appears *on the right* during her (unsuccessful) screen test for the role.

Actress Oscar. MGM had originally considered Lucille Ball, Barbara Stanwyck, and Rita Hayworth.

*From Here to Eternity* (1953) is hailed in some quarters as one of the best of all World War II dramas. But it might have had Robert Mitchum and Joan Crawford in bathing suits on the beach at Pearl Harbor playing one of the most torrid love scenes ever. Burt Lancaster and Deborah Kerr took the roles. They turned each other on, since they launched an off-screen affair, too.

Grace Kelly won the Best Actress Oscar in 1954 for *The Country Girl*, opposite Bing Crosby. She beat out Judy Garland in her second most memorable role in *A Star is Born*. For a very brief time, Greta Garbo considered making a comeback in *The Country Girl*.

In 1956, four veteran actors—William Holden, Clark Gable, Alan Ladd, and Gary Cooper--competed for the role of Bick Benedict in Edna Ferber's *Giant*. Instead, a relative newcomer, Rock Hudson, won the career-making role. Grace Kelly was to be his leading lady, but when she ran away with the Prince of Monaco, the choice role went to Elizabeth Taylor.

Frank Sinatra was originally tapped to play the lead in *Carousel* (1956), but the role went to Gordon MacCrae. That same year, although Dinah Shore and Marlon Brando were to star in *The King and I*, the lead roles went to Deborah Kerr and Yul Brynner instead.

Billy Wilder's *Some Like It Hot* (1959) is hailed as the greatest of all screen comedies. The original cast had Mitzi Gaynor cast opposite Sinatra and Bob Hope in drag. At the last minute it would be Tony Curtis and Jack Lemmon dressing up like female musicians.

As originally conceived, Joan Collins was set to star in *Cleopatra* (1963). Also up for the role were two examples of almost impossible miscasting: Marilyn Monroe and Audrey Hepburn. Of course, it would be Elizabeth Taylor, falling in love with her co-star Richard Burton, who would bring the ill-fated production to the screen.

In 1964, it was assumed that Julie Andrews would co-star in *My Fair Lady* in the wake of her triumph on Broadway. But Audrey Hepburn ended up as Eliza Doolittle instead. She was to have co-starred with Cary Grant, but the male lead went to Rex Harrison.

Doris Day turned down the memorable role of Mrs. Robinson in *The Graduate* (1967), the role eventually awarded to Anne Bancroft, whose character seduced Dustin Hoffman onscreen.

Two great pictures in 1972 might have had very different casts. *The Godfather* became Brando's most memorable role, but Burt Lancaster and Laurence Olivier were among the runnersup.

Henry Fonda and Charlton Heston were once set to co-star in *Deliverance* in the wilds of northeast Georgia. But at the last minute, the parts went to Jon Voight and Burt Reynolds in his most memorable role.

Talk about bizarre casting: Bette Midler, Barbra Streisand, and even Cher were considered to star in the 1976 remake of *King Kong*, the part ultimately won by Jessica Lange.

In modem times, Tom Cruise was set to star as Jack Dawson in that super box office bonanza, the ill-fated *Titanic* (1997). But Leonardo DiCaprio won the role instead.

We could go on and on with enough bizarre casting to fill a book, but at least you get the idea of what might have been.

Left: **Bogart** and **Bergman** immortalizing their thwarted wartime love affair in *Casablanca* (1942).

Right: Screen team **Ronald Reagan** with **Ann Sheridan** in *Juke Girl* (also 1942).

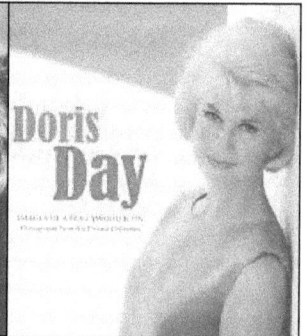

Left: **Anne Bancroft** was brilliant as a sexually frustrated on-the-prowl cougar in *The Graduate* (1967). Fans of *(right photo)* **Doris Day**, however, would have LOVED to see her cast "against type" in Bancroft's place. *Que Sera!*

Imagine Margot Channing (the egomaniacal diva in *All About Eve*) cast with someone NOT **Bette Davis**. *C'est impossible!* Yet for **Claudette Colbert** (pictured in the *right* photo with **Clark Gable** in *It Happened One Night*), it almost came true.

Photos left to right: **Gloria Swanson** as Norma Desmond consulting with **Cecil B. De Mille**; **Mae West,** considered at the time as appropriate for the tragic role of *Sunset Blvd.'s* crazed *Über-diva*; **William Holden**, as a tormented gigolo to **Swanson's** Norma Desmond; and **Montgomery Clift**, who rejected the role of Joe Gillis based on personal reasons associated with his then-mentor, Libby Holman.

# A SALUTE TO ZSA ZSA GABOR

Zsa Zsa Gabor, the last great courtesan of the 20th Century, passed into immortality on December 19, 2016, after a decade of health problems. In Bel Air, she suffered a fatal heart attack only weeks before she would have been 100 years old.

Many newspapers in Europe and America heralded her passing as "the end of glamor" that flourished in the mid-20th century. Indeed, she was the lustrous *femme fatale* of a bygone era, seducing some of the world's most famous men, including John F. Kennedy and Prince Philip.

Through her boudoir marched every man from movie stars (Richard Burton, Frank Sinatra, Sean Connery) to kings, princes, ambassadors, and tycoons. One of her eight husbands was hotel magnate Conrad Hilton, though she spent more time in bed with his young son, Nicky, who later married Elizabeth Taylor.

*The caption to this press photo states:* HOLLYWOOD: Actress Zsa Zsa Gabor strikes a series of poses as she talks to reporters after her arrival here with Porfirio Rubirosa in his private plane. Miss Gabor did all the talking for the couple while the Dominican diplomat unloaded their luggage.

As the wife of a Turkish diplomat (Burhan Belge), she became the young mistress of a dictator, Kemal Atatürk, known today as "The Father of Modern Turkey."

"He taught me the sexual secrets of the sultans of the Ottoman Empire," she confessed.

Zsa Zsa was the best known of the fabled Gabor sisters (Magda and Eva), each born in the twilight of the Austro-Hungarian Empire. These *"vonderful vimmen"* transferred their dreams and gaudy flamboyance to the New World, arriving as symbols of an antiquated age of gold-diggers and sugar daddies.

In time, the Gabors were hailed as a modern manifestation of the mythical Helen of Troy, Madame du Barry, and Madame de Pompadour.

In 1960, at the pinnacle of Zsa Zsa's career, Dorothy Parker commented on her celebrity: "To me, the lady is a figment of mythology. She is one with the unicorn, all shining white and gold, forever swift and lovely, immortal and fabulous."

Long before the Kardashians, she was the pioneer of self-promotion, anticipating an array of future celebrities such as Paris Hilton and Ivanka Trump, who are famous for being famous.

The late Debbie Reynolds said, "Zsa Zsa was the first reality TV star, fast with a hilarious quip, while sheathed in chiffon and maribou feathers. She was her own impersonator."

Ironically, she died on the same day as her adopted son, Oliver Prinz von Anhalt, 45, who died from injuries sustained in a motorcycle crash. His father, Frederick, the ersatz German prince, was Zsa Zsa's last husband.

Blood Moon was fortunate to have published the only definitive biography of the three sisters. Called *Those Glamorous Gabors, Bombshells from Budapest,* it came out in 2013. There is now renewed interest in Hollywood in adapting it into either a feature film or a TV series.

It's a saga of shimmering goddesses who collectively snared twenty husbands and some 500 lovers.

One problem has risen: What actresses today could possibly impersonate these larger-than-life Magyar temptresses, who dished out "guts, glamor, and goulash?"

In 1970, long before her death, Zsa Zsa, the author of a self-help book *How to Catch a Man, How to Keep a Man, and How to Get Rid of a Man,* had some final advice: "All women should have at least three husbands, *dahlink.*"

*Left to right and ready to party:* **Eva, Zsa Zsa**, and **Magda Gabor**

**WINNER Best Biography of 2013**
The Hollywood Book Festival

# THOSE GLAMOROUS GABORS
## BOMBSHELLS FROM BUDAPEST

APPLYING THE TABLOID STANDARDS OF TODAY
TO THE COURTESANS OF AMERICA'S IMPERIAL PAST.

*BloodMoonProductions.com*

In America's postmodern landscape, where fame is often associated with profits, Zsa Zsa, Eva, and their less-understood sister, Magda, are instantly recognizable pop icons. Thanks to the release of Blood Moon's newest award-winning biography, America will understand why.

Blood Moon announces the release of a triple-play bonanza whose gossip quotient surpasses that of anything else on the book market this season. It's an overview of THE GABORS, three unlikely but ferociously glamorous siblings who obsessively "boot-strapped" themselves into "television-age" celebrities who became famous merely for being famous. On the surface, at least, their stylish and glittering myths and legends represent the fulfillment of some aspect of every immigrant woman's dream.

The force behind the strip-off of the sisters' diamonds, ermine, and sable is celebrity biographer Darwin Porter, who is already well known for his award-winning overviews of myth vs. reality in the Entertainment Industry. His knowledge base about the glamour queens' lives in Central Europe, prior to their assault on Hollywood, has been described as "encyclopedic."

How were the Gabors trained, who advised them, and what were the social contexts and "glamour quotients" which applied to their conquests of what evolved, collectively into 20 famous, attractive, and/or fabulously rich husbands? And to what degree did they compete for the attention and approval of their charming but shrewd and "tough as nails" matriarch, Jolie?

All of these questions, and more, are richly and abundantly answered in this hot new biography, available wholesale through the National Book Network, this summer.

"We have a tiger by the tail, thanks to the timing of this book," said Danforth Prince, Blood Moon's president.

"Everything previously published about the Gabors has been heavy on the 'camp' factor and superficial about the historical and political contexts in which these charming ladies thrived. The Gabors themselves, through misinformation and 'artfully unspecific' references to the embarrassing aspects of their individual histories, certainly

Among the Gabors, there was always a sense of self-satirizing glamour and playfulness, even when they were applied with deadly earnestness.

In the photo above, four "Damsels from the Danube" pose, on holiday, beside the shores of Hungary's Lake Balaton. Here, *left to right* are pubescent versions of **Eva, Zsa Zsa,** and **Magda,** cavorting under the ambitious supervision of *(far right)* their ferociously entrepreneurial mother, **Jolie,** a friend of the book's author, Darwin Porter.

Against the backdrop of Darwin Porter's home, historic **Magnolia House,** in Saint George, Staten Island, appear insets of *(left inset photo)* **Greta Keller,** the Austrian cabaret singer (who lived there, with Darwin, for two years in the mid-1980s). The *right inset photo* shows Greta's friend from the society circuits of *Old Europa*, **Jolie Gabor,** the formidable mother of the three Bombshells from Budapest.

During Greta's residency within Darwin's home, **Jolie** (by then, a resident of nearby Manhattan) would visit Greta for *Auld Lang Syne*, cooking and gossiping. Roasted goose with chestnuts in the style of the Hussars was a favorite, along with gossip about Jolie's astonishing trio of talented daughters.

Many of the tales the "old acquaintances" would discuss were later replicated in Darwin's biography, *Those Glamourous Gabors.*

**Jolie Gabor,** mother of the notorious Bombshells from Budapest, as she appeared during the era when she regularly visited Greta Keller, then living as an honored guest within Darwin Porter's Magnolia House

contributed to what has become a 'mink-and-diamond curtain.' All of that has changed, thanks to the investigative zeal with which Darwin Porter has pursued his craft."

"This book will intrigue the enquiring mind of anyone who ever saw a late-night episode of Merv Griffin, Johnny Carson, or *Green Acres,* and anyone who ever studied the evolution of Pop Culture in the wake of the devastation of World War II," Prince continued. "It's a true-life tale about LOVE, DECEIT, PASSION, MANIPULATIONS, BETRAYALS, BEAUTY, WIT, GLAMOUR, and (did I say) HOLLYWOOD? We're emphatically committed to publicizing it as broadly and as widely as possible in the months immediately following its availability this summer."

**ABOUT THE AUTHOR: Darwin Porter**, one of the most famous celebrity biographers in the world, has made passing references to the Gabors in earlier biographies of celebrities who befriended and/or romanced one or more of them (**Merv Griffin, Frank Sinatra, Marlon Brando, and The Kennedys**). A one-time entertainment columnist with *The Miami Herald,* and a self-admitted *"Gaboraphile,"* Porter has spent more than a half-century collecting anecdotes and interviews with virtually everyone ever associated with The Gabors, including--within the context of his authorship of Frommer's Guide to Austria and Hungary--a gaggle of Hungarian and Viennese eyewitnesses who remembered the Gabors before their American debuts. Jolie Gabor, the trio's mother, was a frequent guest within Porter's home in NYC, and the Austrian-born cabaret singer **Greta Keller, (Jolie Gabor's best friend and each of the three sisters' godmother)** was a resident within his NYC home. Jolie and Greta, "two shrewd and hard-nosed battleaxes from the mine fields of *Old Europa,*" are included among the many sources which contributed to the hundreds of never-before-published revelations which permeate this astonishing new book.

A hardworking journalist on the make, **Darwin Porter** appears in this photo snapped around the time he was compiling—within Austria and Hungary from frenemies of the Gabors—the interviews which he later wove into the narrative of *Those Glamorous Gabors.*

**ENCHANTRESSES THREE, EXOTIC, CLEVER, GORGEOUS AND GLAM**

Shown here during a break in their legendary feuds are *(left to right),* **Zsa Zsa** (the wittiest, most frequently married, and most trenchant of the sisters), **Eva** (the most dedicated actress, with the most potent Hollywood credentials), and **Magda,** aka "The Countess of Warsaw."

Of the three, Magda ended up richer than either of her sisters, thanks to her long-standing marriage to Tony Galluci, "the plumbing king of Long Island."

# THE GABORS! WE ADORE THEM! AND THEY'RE BACK!

In advance of its publication in 2013, Blood Moon presented this list of its revelations to **THE GLOBE**. We've replicated that list of "talking points," culled from firsthand interviews with her contemporaries, and on reports we gathered during the research of this book, assisted by scholors who spoke Hungarian, Turkish, Albanian, and Arabic. We present them here as a Twenty-One Gun Salute to *THOSE GLAMOROUS GABORS*

HERE'S AN ABBREVIATED LIST OF SCANDALS THAT JUSTIFIES THESE SISTERS' STATUS AS POP-CULTURE ICONS:

DID YOU KNOW? **That Zsa Zsa** had a scandalous and richly sexual life as a courtesan **EVEN BEFORE SHE REACHED AMERICA**. Here are some of the revelations this book reveals about Our Favorite Hungarians:

**ONE:** Details about Zsa Zsa's early romantic liaisons with Kemal Ataturk, the dictator (and father of) modern Turkey; King Farouk, the decadent autocrat of Egypt; and the tragic last monarch of Albania, King Zog.

**Gaboraphilia:**
Here's **Zsa Zsa**

*Left to right,* **Kemal Ataturk,** the founder and father of modern Turkey; **King Zog** of Albania; and **Farouk,** the British-sponsored and very debauched "puppet king" of Egypt

**TWO:** Zsa Zsa also got very in-

249

Zsa Zsa

volved in the uppercrust infidelities of "Embassy Row," thanks to her role as the wife of Turkey's Minister of Propaganda and Ambassador-to-Europe-at-Large (including Nazi Germany), Burhan Beige. One evening in Ankara she taught the art of "French kissing" to a young visiting colonel from Paris, Charles de Gaulle. Zsa Zsa, an avid Anglophile and lifelong connoisseur of English men, also sustained a pre-World War II affair with Sir Anthony Eden (Britain's Foreign Secretary and later, Prime Minister, and a highly vocal early opponent of the Nazis) in London.

***EARLY ADVENTURES OF ZSA ZSA***, *left to right:* **Zsa Zsa** with her first husband, **Burhan Belge**, propaganda minister of Turkey; then-Colonel **Charles de Gaulle**, later, President of France; and **Sir Anthony Eden**, Britain's Foreign Secretary.

***

Eva

**THREE:** Eva's early days in Hollywood during the 1940s as a contract player at Paramount, and her affairs with the leading men of the era--Gary Cooper, David Niven, Errol Flynn, and the "three Roberts": (Taylor, Walker, and Preston). Also, her fling with aviator Howard Hughes and Clark Gable. As a preface to their lovemaking, Gable insisted she wear the negligee of his recently deceased wife, Carole Lombard. Also, the full story of Eva's notorious affair with gangster Bugsy Siegel and her inadvertent involvement in the hushed-up theft of the Hope Diamond.

*Left to right:* **Gary Cooper, David Niven,** and **Errol Flynn**

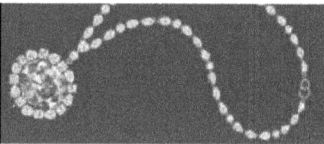

*Left to right,* Mobster **Bugsy Siegel, Clark Gable,** billionaire **Howard Hughes,** and *(right)* **The Hope Diamond.**

*Left to right:* **Robert Taylor, Robert Walker,** and **Robert Preston**

***

Magda

**FOUR:** In war-torn Budapest, Magda was raped by Adolf Eichmann, the mass murderer ordered by Hitler to carry out "The Final Solution" as it applied to eradication of the Hungarian Jews. She managed to escape extermination because of her association with (and protection by) her lover, the Portuguese Ambassador to Hungary.

Later, she became the richest of the Gabor sisters because of her marriage to "the plumbing king," Tony Gallucci.

***

Adolf Eichmann

**FIVE:** A rundown of Zsa Zsa's early affairs in Hollywood-John F. Kennedy (then a fledgling Congressman from Massachusetts); novelist Erich Maria Remarque (Zsa Zsa had to compete for his affections with Marlene Dietrich); Franchot Tone (former husband of Joan Crawford); Douglas Fairbanks, Jr. (Hollywood royalty and also a former husband of Joan Crawford); and the eccentric (some say "demented") billionaire, Howard Hughes.

Zsa Zsa

**SIX:** The two great loves of Eva's life—Tyrone Power and Glenn Ford. Eva's affair with John F. Kennedy was his final fling before he flew to Dallas and his assassination. Also, her surprise seduction of the gay playwright Noël Coward

*Left to right:* **JFK, Erich Maria Remarque,** and **Franchot Tone**

during a road tour of *Present Laughter*.

Frank Sinatra's dynamic with **Zsa Zsa vs. Eva**: Zsa Zsa claimed rape; Eva called it love.

***

Eva

*Left to right:* **Glenn Ford** with **Rita Hayworth**; **Tyrone Power** with **Annabella**; President **John F. Kennedy shortly before his assassination**; and **Frank Sinatra** after a bout with the police.

**SEVEN, EIGHT, NINE, TEN, ETC.** Zsa Zsa's turbulent marriage to hotel magnate Conrad Hilton, Sr., and her simultaneous affair with his young son, Nicky Hilton, who later married Elizabeth Taylor.

Zsa Zsa's tumultuous marriage to the abusive actor, George Sanders. *[Sanders was a serial adulterer, his conquests ranging from super-rich Doris Duke to Marilyn Monroe and "young boys of the Mediterranean," from his villa on the island of Majorca.]*

Zsa Zsa

Zsa Zsa's rule as the queen of international society and her affairs with Prince Aly Khan (when he was not involved with his wife, Rita Hayworth), and with the wealthy Eric de Rothschild.

*Left photo* **Zsa Zsa** with **Conrad Hilton,** and Conrad's son, **Nicky Hilton,** with **ElizabethTaylor**

The lurid details, most of which have never been told, of Zsa Zsa's notorious romance with the Dominican playboy, Porfirio Rubirosa, and his ultimate marriage to Barbara Hutton, the Woolworth heiress that Zsa Zsa succeeded in breaking up.

Greta Garbo's passion for Zsa Zsa, whom the Swedish actress pursued.

Zsa Zsa's romantic links to movie Tarzan, Lex Barker, during the filming of *The Girl from the Kremlin* and her surprise affair with gangster Johnny Stompanato, who went to live in Lana Turner's house, where he was stabbed to death.

*left photo* **George Sanders,** and "dressed for Ascot," **Prince Aly Khan**

The scandal that Zsa Zsa provoked with her notorious affair with Ramfis Trujillo, son of the Dominican dictator. Lots of new material here.

Zsa Zsa's affairs with a host of actors: Richard Burton, Sean Connery, Richard Harris, and Tony Curtis.

Zsa Zsa's final affairs with a string of high-profile men— NYC mayor John Lindsay, A&P heir Huntington Hartford, super-rich H.L. Hunt, and J. Paul Getty (world's richest man).

Zsa Zsa's shocking (and speedy) marriage to Jack Ryan, famous for inventing the Barbie Doll.

Zsa Zsa's dalliance with "a shady person from a sunny place, **Ramfis Trujillo,** son of the dictator of the Dominican Republic

Zsa Zsa's brief fling with two unlikely men: Elvis Presley and President Richard Nixon, whom she defined as "the sexiest man in politics."

Zsa Zsa's appearance with the Beatles in London and the night she spent with George Harrison, "My favorite of the Beatle bugs."

Porter's book even reveals widespread allegations of Zsa Zsa's affair with **Prince Philip,** the philandering consort to **Queen Elizabeth II.**

Zsa Zsa's secret affairs with Prince Philip and Lord Louis Mountbatten.

251

## THOSE GLAMOUROUS GABORS, BOMBSHELLS FROM BUDAPEST,
### As Reviewed for *The New York Review of Books*
on September 20, 2013,
### by Vinton Rafe McCabe

## "YOU WILL NEVER BE GA-BORED. IT GIVES NEW MEANING TO THE TERM 'COMPELLING.'"

**Once upon a time,** in the faraway kingdom of the Magyars, there lived a woman who had three daughters. This woman was very, very wise and knew well the cost of diamonds and the ways of the world. And she looked upon her daughters and her ample bosom swelled with pride.

One daughter, she saw, was a great beauty who was soon named Miss Hungary. And once more her mother was proud. A second daughter married well and became the Countess of Warsaw and told her sisters to refer to her as "Her Excellency," and again the mother was proud. The third, the youngest and blondest of the three girls, seeing that her homeland seethed with turmoil as the world prepared for war, quickly married Garbo's chiropractor and fled to the mythical land called Hollywood. And that made the mother proudest of all.

And as she boarded the Cunard liner *The Queen Mary,* the youngest and blondest of the girls suppressed a chill as she clutched tight to the gift that enveloped her, a castoff mink coat that her mother had given her along with her blessings. And the girl stood on the deck facing westward to the New World.

"I was a pauper in mink," she sighed, years later, as she remembered that day for the nice reporter sitting next to her.

Given the fact that the vast majority of us have never lived in a Gabor-free world, it is hard to image what that joyless place might be like. Because despite what any number of Hiltons or Kardashians or even Real Housewives might tell you, no other family has so contributed to Western pop culture as have the Gabors, with a reach extending from the years preceding World War II to the present day.

And for that reason they are now being rewarded with the longest, most exhaustive, most salacious of family biographies, *Those Glamorous Gabors: Bombshells from Budapest.*

Be warned, *Gabors* is both an epic and a pip. Not since *Gone With the Wind* have so many characters on the printed page been forced to run for their lives for one reason or another. And Scarlett making a dress out of the curtains is nothing compared to what a Gabor will do when she needs to scrap together an outfit for a movie premiere or late-night outing.

*Gabors* is a work festooned with diamonds, rubies, minks, and ermines, champagne, caviar, and talk shows and game shows and B movies like *Arrivederci Baby!* and husbands (their own and other people's) and lovers and sexy sex and sexy lies and sexy secrets galore. The author has a particular penchant for "outing" Hollywood lesbians, of whom there seem to be a great number, from the aforementioned Garbo to Marlene Dietrich to Barbara Stanwyck to Tallulah Bankhead to Agnes Moorehead . . . so much so that a sort of Gabor-fatigue sets in around page 500 (about when a Gabor Sister Act is ready to open in Vegas).

But I promise you this: You will never be Ga-bored.

For those not up to speed, Jolie Tilleman came from a family of jewelers and therefore came by her love for the shiny stones honestly, perhaps genetically. She married Vilmos Gabor somewhere around World War 1 (exact dates, especially birth dates, are always somewhat vague in order establish plausible deniability later on) and they were soon blessed with three daughters: Magda, the oldest, whose hair, sadly, was naturally brown, although it would turn quite red in America; Zsa Zsa (born "Sari") a natural blonde who at a very young age exhibited the desire for fame with none of the talents usually associated with achievement, excepting beauty and a natural wit; and Eva, the youngest and blondest of the girls, who after seeing Grace Moore perform at the National Theater, decided that she wanted to be an actress and that she would one day move to Hollywood to become a star.

Given that the Gabor family at that time lived in Budapest, Hungary, at the period of time between the World Wars, that Hollywood dream seemed a distant one indeed.

The story—the riches to rags to riches to rags to riches again myth of survival against all odds as the four women, because of their Jewish heritage, flee Europe with only the minks on their backs and what jewels they could smuggle along with them in their decolletage, only to have to battle afresh for their places in the vicious Hollywood pecking order—gives new meaning to the term "compelling."

The reader, as if he were witnessing a particularly gore-drenched traffic accident, is incapable of looking away.

Has American fiction ever produced a fictional character equal to the one that Zsa Zsa Gabor created to inhabit her own flesh whenever she was unleashed in front of the populace in seven-minute bits on TV with Merv Griffin?

Has anyone ever lived a life publicly in an arc that carried her from Miss Hungary to the *Queen of Outer Space*?

Magda was the valiant one (the account of her bravery in staying in Europe during the war and rescuing downed pilots as a key member of the resistance impresses). Eva (immortalized finally for her work on the 1960s sitcom *Green Acres*, the theme song for which has remained lodged in the American consciousness for the past five decades) was the talented one.

But the simple truth is that Zsa Zsa was always the one: the Hungarian Bombshell who battled Marilyn Monroe for George Saunders and snared him, who actually managed to hold her own up against Oscar winner Jose Ferrer as Jane Avril to his Toulouse-Lautrec in the original *Moulin Rouge*, and who actually created a new category of achievement in America, one that is cherished today—the celebrity who is famous for being famous.

Thus we owe her big time.

And in writing *Those Glamorous Gabors*, author Darwin Porter attempts to repay the debt.

Potential readers should be aware that, along with many anecdotes that will elicit loud laughter (most often from Zsa Zsa's way with words), there is language that is both graphic and lewd, and sexual acts (dozens and dozens and dozens of them) of every sort and for every reason from passion to gold-digging to rape.

And where there is sex, of course, there are men. Multitudes of them, as Zsa Zsa and Eva (who had sex with Errol Flynn, David Niven, Clark Gable, and Bugsy Siegel, among others) seem to enter into a competition of sorts, with Zsa Zsa the clear winner.

Along the way, she beds so many that a complete list would run nearly as long as the book itself. Suffice this short list and see the volume in question for details.

While older sister Magda tended to marry and stay married, Zsa Zsa romanced actors like Charlie Chaplin (who promised to cast her in a picture as Mary Magdalene); Franchot Tone; the aforementioned George Saunders, who was the love of her life; Saunders' brother, Tom Conway; Richard Burton (before he married Elizabeth Taylor); Richard Harris; Paul Henreid; Sean Conway; and Elvis, with whom she shared a single night of passion in a hotel suite in Vegas.

In addition to this, she enjoyed liaisons with businessmen like Howard Hughes and Conrad Hilton (and his son Nicky, who would also wed Elizabeth Taylor, with whom Ms. Gabor was involved during her marriage to his father); world leaders including Kemal Ataturk, the "Father of Turkey;" Egyptian King Farouk; Prince Ally Kahn; Joseph Kennedy; his son, John F. Kennedy; and, in the most surreal section of the book, Richard Nixon:

"Zsa Zsa later referred to Nixon's seduction of her as 'very professional, very competent, but no one would ever call him a great lover.'

"'He was very stiff around women,' she recalled. 'Forgive the pun dahlink.'

"'Even in bed, he insisted on being called Mr. President, although 'Dick' might have been more appropriate," Zsa Zsa said.

*Those Glamorous Gabors* is a triumph of pop culture over journalism.

And even in a book laden with the rich, the famous, and the lusty, the greedy and the wildly, aggressively self-obsessive all rushing about showing off their jewelry and finding their key lights, Zsa Zsa finds and holds center stage, and as the only surviving Gabor (married now to her much younger husband, ersatz royal Frederic Prinz von Anhalt, she is in ill health as her hundredth birthday nears) stands as the ultimate survivor of a time now passed.

Which makes all the more bittersweet the account of her life's arc that she shared with Merv Griffin:

"I blazed through the century making headline after headline. Not bad for a little girl from Budapest who launched her love life by kissing the coalman and getting soot all over my white dress. Men have been 'blackening' me ever since. I don't regret the men who seduced me, only those who didn't get around to it."

"There's an axiom in Hollywood . . . actors get older, but actresses get old. My life goes on, although I don't know for how long. It's shocking to have been called the most beautiful woman on earth and have to confront my mirror in the morning. Most of my lovers or husbands are long gone, except for my dear Prince. The grim reaper is at my door, but I've lived a great life. I was brought into intimate contact with some of the luminaries of my age. I met everyone from Adolf Hitler to Jack Kennedy. I've loved a few but been loved by countless others."

Did I forget to mention Adolf Hitler?

Believe me, that's a whole other story.

Those Glamorous Gabors, Bombshells from Budapest

| Magda | Zsa Zsa | Eva | Jolie |

253

## Tongues Wagged about Zsa Zsa.
## But some of the SHOCKERS came directly from her:

*"Zsa Zsa Gabor made different claims about how she lost her virginity. It depended on what year it was."*
**—Columnist Mike Connolly**

*"She's unbelievable. You can't believe a damn thing that comes out of that beautiful mouth of hers."*
**—Columnist Earl Wilson**

*"Nicky Hilton, my son-in-law, claimed I was a much better lay than Elizabeth Taylor."*
**—Zsa Zsa Gabor**

*"Zsa Zsa has discovered the secret of perpetual middle age."*
**—Oscar Levant**

*"I believe in large families. Every woman should have at least three husbands. I married eight men. It should have been twelve.'*
**—Zsa Zsa Gabor**

*"Prince Aly Khan was a far better lover than John F. Kennedy."*
**—Zsa Zsa Gabor**

*"Sean Connery was better in bed than Richard Burton."*
**—Zsa Zsa Gabor**

*"Porfirio Rubirosa [the Dominican playboy] was my greatest thrill."*
**—Zsa Zsa Gabor**

*"Frank Sinatra once raped me in Palm Springs."*
**—Zsa Zsa Gabor**

*"When I was married to my first husband, Belge Burhan, a Turkish diplomat, he introduced me to Hitler. I heard later that he thought i was the most beautiful woman he'd ever met. I knew that he wanted to seduce me, but I heard that his genitals were underdeveloped."*
**—Zsa Zsa Gabor**

KEEP CALM AND GO TO HUNGARY

FROMMER'S
COMPREHENSIVE TRAVEL GUIDE
AUSTRIA & HUNGARY

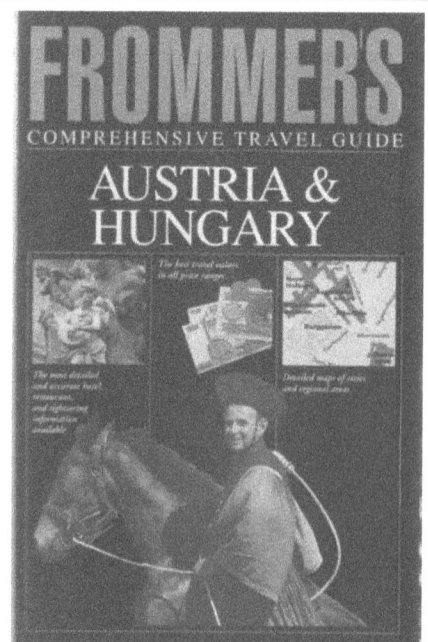

**Did You Know?** That many of Darwin Porter's observations about the fabled Gabors were "unearthed' during his on-site research for Simon & Schuster in Budapest and Vienna?

**And Did You Know?** That another by-product of his research in *Mittel Europa* became a "Jewel in the Crown" of the world's best-sellng travel bibles, **THE FROMMER GUIDES.**

*As a sideshow to the release of Darwin Porter's
award-winning biography of the Florida native,
**Burt Reynolds** (see cover on the next page) Anita Finlay's
**Boomer Times** asked him if he recalled any details about
VIRGINITY IN HOLLYWOOD or the lack thereof.
Here's what he said:*

# MOVIE STARS REVEAL "THEIR FIRST TIME"

*SEX & SCANDAL
DO YOU THINK THAT THE LIFE OF A CELEBRITY IS EASY? THINK AGAIN!*

Hollywood biographers face many challenges when they attempt to describe the lives of celebrities, male or female. Many readers want to know when details about how a star became acquainted with what was once politely described as "the facts of life."

In the biography I'll release in September—it's about Florida's Burt Reynolds—I was lucky to have acquired that tantalizing data when I worked for *The Miami Herald's* branch offices in Fort Lauderdale and Palm Beach.

In Palm Beach, I met this wealthy and sexually aggressive 42-year-old woman who specialized in young teenaged boys. Burt was just 14 when he began a year-long affair with her. After she sent him on his way, she took up with another 14-year-old, George Hamilton, who later evolved into the perpetually suntanned actor. George became a household word when he dated Lynda Bird Johnson, during the presidential tenure of her father, LBJ. Both Burt and George later seduced Elizabeth Taylor.

Just for fun, and because baby boomers have reached the age where we're no longer bashful about these things, here's how some other big stars were introduced to sex.

When his son turned 15, the father of Desi Arnaz took him to the best brothel in Santiago, Cuba. Milton Berle was only 12 when he lost it to a dancer in the Broadway show *Florodora*. Marlon Brando was all of 19 when a married Colombian woman, Rosa Maria Consuelo Cruz, took him into her boudoir.

During Richard Burton's first appearance on the stage, a teenaged usherette, "Lil," came into his dressing room for his introduction to sex.

In Norfolk, Nebraska, Johnny Carson tangled with "Francine, a girl of easy virtue," in the back seat of his father's 1939 green Chrysler Royal. He pronounced the experience "a disaster."

While walking down a London street, Sean Connery, 14, was picked up by a woman in her 50s who was dressed in a military uniform.

Riding a train to London, Noël Coward was seduced by actress Gertrude Lawrence, two years his senior. He was so turned off by the experience, he self-identified as gay for the rest of his life, taking up first with Prince George, the Duke of Kent.

Long before Marilyn Monroe came into his young life, Tony Curtis was eighteen and in the U.S. Navy when he visited a

whorehouse in Panama City.

A teenaged James Dean surrendered it to Dr. James DeWeerd, the pastor of the Wesleyan Church in Fairmont, Indiana. Ironically, this same pastor delivered the eulogy at Dean's funeral in 1955.

Kirk Douglas, the subject of my most recent biography, *More Is Never Enough,* was seduced by his English teacher in high school, a long-term relationship that lasted on and off for years.

Singer Eddie Fisher, 14, was "assaulted" by his voracious next door neighbor, Tootsie Stern.

As a late teenager, Henry Fonda went to a whorehouse in Omaha, Nebraska. Later referring to the experience as "horrible—just a *wham-bam* that turned me off sex for years."

At age 15, Clark Gable lost his in Cadiz, Ohio, to a 58-year-old widow. The Tasmania-born swashbuckler, Errol Flynn, was only 12 when the maid entered to clean up his room and piled into his bed. That was the first of what he recalled as 14,000 seductions to come, both female and male.

Now for the women: Lucille Ball, at 14, surrendered to a local hoodlum, Johnny DeVita, 21, in the back seat of a car in Jamestown, New York. During her early years in Hollywood, she was a "gun moll."

French director Roger Vadim successfully pursued Brigitte Bardot, 15, and later married her.

Joan Blondell, the blonde bombshell of the 1930s who later married Dick Powell and Mike Todd, was 17 when an Oklahoma millionaire raped her.

Cher, 14, blamed her introduction to sex on "the boy next door, a little Italian with his brain in his crotch."

Joan Crawford, 14, was introduced to sex through a gang rape when her brother, Hal Le Sueur, brought home three of his pals from school.

Doris Day was already married when, at age 17, she experienced "the brutality" of her first husband, musician Al Jorden.

Many actresses were raped as their introduction to sex. Hedy Lamarr, 14, was assaulted by her family's laundryman in the basement. Marilyn Monroe, 15, was attacked by a man in his forties who lived in her foster home.

Barbra Streisand was all of 18 when she surrendered to Barry Dennen, a young New York actor.

Natalie Wood was 14 when her mother ordered her fellow actor, Nick Adams, to teach her daughter "the ways of the world." Separately, each of them was later seduced by James Dean when they co-starred with him in *Rebel Without a Cause* (1955)

On a warm and long summer night beside a lake in Sweden, the future Greta Garbo was seduced by her sister, Alva.

Ava Gardner waited until her wedding night, January 10, 1942, to be seduced by Mickey Rooney. She later cracked, "Mickey lost his virginity when he was three."

Rita Hayworth, 13, "surrendered the pink" to her father, Eduardo Cansino. She survived his repeated assaults on her and went on to seduce some of the most legendary men of the 20th Century.

# BURT REYNOLDS

### PUT THE PEDAL TO THE METAL:

#### HOW A NUDE CENTERFOLD SEX SYMBOL

#### SEDUCED HOLLYWOOD

LESBIAN LADIES & BOX OFFICE SMASHES FROM A GOOD OL' BOY

ANOTHER OUTRAGEOUS CELEBRITY EXPOSÉ BY
DARWIN PORTER & DANFORTH PRINCE

She became so famous, her pinup image was plastered onto the *Enola Gay* the plane that carried the atomic bomb that was dropped on Hiroshima, Japan, a strike so effective (and horrible) that it led to the end of World War II a few days later.

A terrible introduction to sex was suffered by Gloria Swanson, the legendary screen vamp of the silent era. She married Wallace Beery, the ungainly, gravel-voiced, rubber-faced movie star. On her wedding night, as she confessed in her memoirs, "I was brutalized in pitch blackness by a man who whispered filth in my ear and ripped me almost in two. I spent the rest of the night huddled on the bathroom floor, swathed in towels to soak up the blood and to ease the pain."

**HAPPY BURT DAY**

# BURT REYNOLDS

## How a Nude Centerfold Seduced Hollywood

During a reign of almost twenty years, a good old Southern boy made hearts throb and audiences laugh. He was Burt Reynolds, former football hero, who died in Jupiter, Florida, at the age of 82 in September of 2018. He predicted his own death: "Soon, I'll be racing a hotrod in Vallhala in my cowboy hat and a pair of aviators."

After he posed nude for *Cosmo*, he became the male sex symbol of the 1970s. Fan mail from horny females poured in from across the nation, with outrageous requests for him to seduce them.

Before Burt agreed to be the nude model, the editors at *Cosmo* made an equivalent offer to Clint Eastwood, Joe Namath, and Steve McQueen. Each of them rejected it.

"When I die," he said, "they're going to write on my tombstone, "Here lies Burt Reynolds, the first movie star to post nude in a magazine."

His first wife, Judy Carne, claimed, "It's true, Burt has the most divine little ass." She failed to answer the question of whether he wore his toupée while making love.

Regarding his long love affair with Dinah Shore, he said, "I went for a long time with her, a fine and remarkable lady. But I ran out of steam. When I think of her, I cherish the memories, the good times, the loving support she gave me. I treasure those memories, and we'll always be friends. I don't think a man is supposed to spend a lifetime with just one woman."

Dolly Parton downplayed rumors of a romance with Reynolds. "Burt and I are too much alike for a serious involvement. We both wear wigs and high heels. We both have a roll around the middle."

As for his troubled marriage (his second) to Loni Anderson, Burt was sarcastic: "I believe in a good marriage. I also believe in the tooth fairy."

He was self-deprecating, combative, sometimes hilarious, a hellraiser. He was also an enigmatic figure of dark moods and sudden violence, a victim of tabloid fodder for his generation.

His exploits and boudoir invasions generated "Second Coming" headlines.

He broke hearts and also had his own heart broken, chasing fading love with a lingering regret. A former football hero and a dare-devil stuntman, he pursued the American Dream to the point where it morphed into a nightmare.

At the end, he became a tortured soul brutalized by the pitfalls of fame and runaway celebrity.

"I became a redneck icon, but really wanted to be Cary Grant," he said.

\*\*\*

**Burt Reynolds** thrived in an era before the term "Redneck charm" became on oxymoron. Men and women seemed to like him equally, in part because he was always ready, willing, and able to self-deprecate and subtly self-satirize—to laugh," his fans and co-workers often said, "at himself."

He appears here in one of his biggest hits, *Deliverance* (1972). a dark, brooding movie about beauty, danger, and existentialist horror.

During his heyday, in an era that was less politicized and less judgmental, fans consistently interpreted **Burt Reynolds** as charming, funny and unpretentious, both onscreen and off.

Here, moving clockwise from the *upper left*, is how he appeared 1) as a motorized prankster in the road-racing masterpiece, **Smokey and the Bandit** (1977); 2) as a happy-go-lucky football star in **Semi-Tough** (1977); *3)* as the South's most corrupt county commissioner in **The Dukes of Hazzard** (2005); and 4) as the porn industry's most jaded director in a film loved by anyone who's ever wondered about the onscreen dynamics of a XXX film, **Boogey Nights** (1997).

*Love in a Whorehouse:* **Burt Reynolds and Dolly Parton** gave the concept humor, wit, and charm through their interactions in *The Best Little Whorehouse in Texas.* (1982)

Dolly took it all in stride, later quipping, "It takes a lot of time and money to look this trashy!"

257

THE YEAR OF ITS PUBLICATION (2019) ANITA FINLEY'S *BOOMER TIMES* INCLUDED **NEWS** ABOUT DARWIN PORTER'S THEN-MOST-TALKED-ABOUT BIOGRAPHY. ITS SUBJECT WAS THE CHARMING, SELF-DEPRECATING FLORIDIAN WHO BECAME THE KING OF HOLLYWOOD'S BOX OFFICE

**BURT REYNOLDS**

PUT THE PEDAL TO THE METAL:

HOW A NUDE CENTERFOLD SEX SYMBOL SEDUCED HOLLYWOOD

ANOTHER OUTRAGEOUS CELEBRITY EXPOSÉ BY DARWIN PORTER & DANFORTH PRINCE

# BURT REYNOLDS

In the 1970s and '80s, Burt Reynolds represented a new breed of movie star: Charming and relentlessly macho, with footprints in country-western, rural America, he was a good old Southern boy who made hearts throb and audiences laugh. He was Burt Reynolds, a former football hero, and a guy you might have shared some jokes with in a redneck bar. After an impressive but tormented career, rivers of negative publicity, a self-admitted history of bad choices, and a spectacular fall from Hollywood grace, he died in Jupiter, Florida, at the age of 82 in September of 2018.

He lives again in the pages of my latest biography, *Burt Reynolds: Put the Pedal to the Metal*, co-authored with Danforth Prince.

During his heyday, when he reigned as the premier American male sex symbol of the 1970s, he posed nude for a woman's magazine. Even though, by his admission, it ultimately hurt his career, fan mail from horny females poured in from across the nation, with outrageous requests for him to seduce them "any time he was passing through."

For five years, both in terms of earnings and popularity, he was the number one box office star in the world, most visibly in *Smokey and the Bandit* (1977), which became the biggest-grossing car-chase film of all time. As he put it, "I was hotter than a firecracker, a hunk of male flesh who likes nothing better than lying on my bearskin rug, making love to some of the most beautiful women in the world." Perhaps he was referring to his romantic and sexual involvements with the French goddess, Catherine Deneuve, or to America's own female sex symbol, Farrah Fawcett.

He might also have been referring to Dolly Parton, Tammy Wynette, Lucie Arnaz, Kim Basinger, Candice Bergen, Lauren Hutton, Lorna Luft, Sarah Miles, Angie Dickinson, or Elizabeth Taylor. Long before he became famous, and shortly after some well-received appearances in a TV Western (*Gunsmoke*), he picked up Marilyn Monroe on his way to the Actors Studio in New York City.

Love with another VIP came in the form of that singing sensation, Dinah Shore, known as the "Sweetheart of the G.I.s" who won World War II. Their May-September affair sparked endless chatter: "I appreciate older women," he said in a moment of self-revelation, "ever since a rich 42-year-old woman in Palm Beach made love to me for one whole year."

He entered another much-publicized romance with actress Sally Field, the "second love of my life" and his co-star in Bandit. After his death, The Flying Nun said, "Burt still lives in my heart," but then expressed relief that, because of his recent death, he'd never read what she'd said about him in her memoir.

Men liked him too: He played poker with Frank Sinatra; shared boozy nights with John Wayne; intercepted a "pass" from closeted Spencer Tracy; talked "penis size" with Mark Wahlberg; went "wench-hunting" with Johnny Carson; and threatened to kill Marlon Brando, to whom his appearance was often compared. He also hung out with Bette Davis ("I always had a thing for her.")

His least happy (some said "most poisonous") marriage—to the blonde bombshell, Loni Anderson—was rife with dramas played out more in the tabloids than in the boudoir. According to Reynolds, "She's vain, she's a rotten mother, she sleeps around, and she spent all my money."

This highly revealing biography—the first comprehensive overview of the "redneck icon" ever published—reveals the joys and sorrows of a movie star who thrived in, but who was then almost buried by the pressures and insecurities of the New Hollywood. A tribute to "truck stop" America and to the courageous spirit of a hometown boy who "made good, bigtime," it's about the accelerated life of a courageous spirit who "Put His Pedal to the Metal" with humor, high jinx, and pizzazz.

He predicted his own death: "Soon, I'll be racing a hotrod in Valhalla in my cowboy hat and a pair of aviators." On his tombstone, he wanted it writ: **"He was not the best actor in the world, but he was the best Burt Reynolds in the world."**

As he aged, **Burt Reynolds,** without apology, morphed into characterizations that matched his own advancing age, and Boomers loved him for it.

Here, in **The Last Movie Star**, he (brilliantly, with searing honesty) portrayed an actor brutalized by life, multiple betrayals, and the rigors of show-biz.

# GOODBYE GARY COOPER, GOODBYE JEAN HARLOW

# MOVIE STARS
## THE EXTINCTION OF A SPECIES

Once upon a time, there existed a magic kingdom called "The Dream Factory." It thrived in a place known as "Tinseltown" (aka Hollywood).

In that land before computer-generated effects, talented men and women put everything on the silver screen that the human mind could conjure.

Perhaps a gigantic ape on top of the Empire State Building, holding a helpless Fay Wray in his mammoth hand. Maybe the Land of Oz on the other side of the Rainbow through which Little Dorothy wandered. Perhaps it was Rhett Butler departing forever, informing Scarlett O'Hara, "Frankly, my dear, I don't give a damn." Or perhaps Bogie telling Ingrid Bergman, "We'll always have Paris."

Our parents, and later the postwar Baby Boomers, created what were called "Gods and Goddesses" of the Golden Years of Cinema. An enchanting creature called "The Movie Star" appeared. Some of them could dance (Gene Kelly); others could sing (Frank Sinatra and Judy Garland).

Soldiers in World War II took pinups of Betty Grable and Rita Hayworth with them into battle. A pinup of Rita was pasted onto a plane carrying the first atomic bomb.

At the rate of 90 million a week, Americans flocked to see movie stars emote on the screen. In countless magazines, we lived through their love affairs, ill-fated marriages, scandals, good films, bad films…whatever. We loved and worshipped them.

Fan clubs rose up across America. At personal appearances, these stars were mobbed; the police had to be called in to save them from being stripped of all their clothing. We wanted a piece of them.

Sadly, with the exception of Kirk Douglas and Olivia de Havilland (each 102 years old), these stars have faded into our history. Some disappeared quietly into the Pacific sunset; others waited for the phone call from a producer that never came again.

But while they lasted, their fans could temporarily abandon their workaday worlds, and with a bag of popcorn, enter a darkened theater and be carried away into fantasy.

The gorgeous women were surrogate mistresses to men in the audience, and those beautiful men like Errol Flynn or Tyrone Power allowed women to dream of what might have been.

Sadly, with the emergence of a new generation and new priorities, the Dream Factory disappeared like a mirage in a mirror. Studio backlots where pirate adventures, wartime battles, Westerns, melodramas, were filmed have been sold to real estate developers who turned the terrain into condos and offices. On the spot where Clark Gable made love to Lana Turner, McDonald's offers empty calories in the form of burgers and fries.

Fortunately, an estimated five to six million Americans, mostly Baby Boomers but an increasing number of young viewers, too, can wander back to Yesterday, thanks to modern, digitalized technology. From the convenience of their den or living room, they savor everything from Edwin S. Porter's *The Great Train Robbery* (1903) to Greta Garbo making love to Robert Taylor in *Camille* (1936). Viewers can hear Marlon Brando screaming "Stella! Stella! Stella!" in *A Streetcar Named Desire* (1951), and Rita Hayworth putting the blame on Mame in *Gilda* (1946 as she reprises what's been called "the sexiest dance ever choreographed."

If you're of a certain age, you've heard of Clark Gable, Gary Cooper, Cary Grant, Barbara Stanwyck, Bette Davis, Joan Crawford, James Cagney, Burt Lancaster, James Stewart, John Wayne, Katharine Hepburn, Spencer Tracy, Claudette Colbert, Lucille Ball, and Hedy Lamarr, who was hailed as "the most beautiful woman in the world."

But times have changed. The 91st Academy Awards presentation is coming up, and after a year of screen rage, silliness, or sublimity, the winners will walk off with gold.

Here is a sample list of actors and actresses who have been cited as worthy of various awards for their performances in the year just passed. The question is, when the winner is announced, will you know who he or she is? They include Steve Buscemi, Daniel Gimenez Casho, Lakeith Stanfield, Yalitz Aparicio, Elsie Fisher, Regina Hall, Simon Russell Beale, Adam Driver, Brian Tyree Henry, Steven Yeun, Sakura Ando, Shayna McHayle, Haley Richardson, Kathryn Hahn, John Cho, and Zain Al Rafeea.

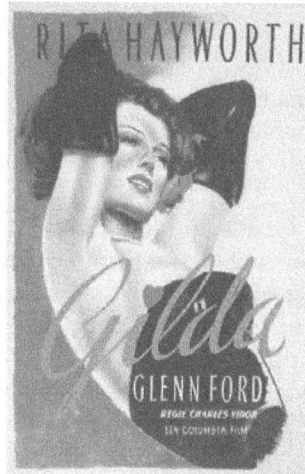

**MOVIE STARS**
**Celebrating an Extinct Species**

*Clockwise from upper left:* **Judy Garland** and **Billie Burke** in *The Wizard of Oz* (1939)**; Clark Gable** and **Lana Turner** in *Honky Tonk (*1941)**; Jean Harlow; Gary Cooper;** and **Kong** with **Fay Wray** in *King Kong* (1933).

260

# A STARMAN WHO FELL TO EARTH
# DAVID BOWIE

In January, Baby Boomers lost one of rock's greatest chameleons, David Bowie, who succumbed to liver cancer after bravely fighting it for eighteen months without the world knowing it. Tributes poured in from fans around the world, even from heads of state. After hearing the news, one man in Tokyo attempted suicide.

Andrea Peyser, a columnist for *The New York Post,* wrote: "He made the world a better place for rebels, oddballs, and misfits like me."

In all his life, nothing he did was more elegant than the way he left it, blossoming out in a burst of creativity during his final months.

His death came after his 69th birthday when he had just released his last and 28th studio album, *Blackstar,* which zoomed to the top of Billboard charts. The music dealt with lust, spirituality, fame, death, and startling transformations—a tribute to his changing *personae* over a career spanning half a century.

His last public appearance was in December at the New York premiere of *Lazarus,* a play he co-authored. Although backstage, he collapsed, the press wrote about how healthy and vibrant he looked. For the continuation of its short run off-Broadway, some tickets are selling for $2,500. Ironically, its theme song (entitled "Lazarus,") begins with the words "Look up here. I'm in heaven."

Tony Visconti, Bowie's longtime manager, said, "David always did what he wanted to do. He wanted to do it his way, and he wanted to do it the best way. His death was no different from his life—a work of art."

Bowie specified that he did not want any fuss made about a funeral. So he was quietly cremated.

His last work of art capped the career of rock's last great polymath, an artist unafraid to expand the boundaries of popular music, blending rock, jazz, cabaret, and what he labeled "plastic soul." Few careers in show business have been as artistically diverse as Bowie's.

With his dyed hair and gender-bending sexuality, this innovative Londoner first appeared on the scene as part of an interview with the BBC. He was sticking up for young men with long hair. "We're tired of hearing, 'Can I carry your purse, dearie?'"

The jukebox musical, **Lazarus**, was inspired by the 1963 novel, *The Man Who Fell to Earth.* It continues the story of Walter Tevis, a humanoid alien who is stuck on earth, unable to die or to return to his home planet.

Multiple, Oft-Changing Looks for the Same, Multi-Faceted Artist. **David Bowie.** A Londoner, Bowie was a singer, songwriter, musician, and actor. He was hailed as one of the most influential musicians of the 20th Century.

In the years that followed, he marched forth to astonish the world with his androgynous *personae* and his outlandish outfits, bouncing out in platform boots and glitter, in skintight, sci-fi inspired outfits or as a sequin-wearing drag queen. He defined the glam-rock era of the turbulent 1970s, influencing fashion throughout the world.

At first, he asserted that he was gay, later amending that to being "a closet heterosexual." The *New York Daily News* wrote: "Lonely people cracked open their closet doors because of him." The staid *Wall Street Journal* claimed, "Bowie's outrageous characters made it acceptable to come out as gay, bisexual, or different."

Albums that included *The Rise and Fall of Ziggy Stardust* (1972) made him world famous, winning millions of fans.

He dressed as an astronaut in the 1976 film, *The Man Who Fell to Earth*. As "Major Tom," he thrilled the world as the lost space alien in his career-making 1968 hit single, "Space Oddity." In the 70s, he was the self-destructive "Thin White Duke," appearing vapid, detached, and drug addicted.

In his 1983 hit, "Let's Dance," he invited us to "Put on our red shoes and dance the blues." The world did just that.

Bowie entered a dark phase in the 1970s, succumbing to drugs. He lived for months on brain-sizzling cocaine, drinking only milk for nourishment, nothing solid.

Recovering after he moved to Switzerland, he appeared in the 1980s looking like the world's most elegantly dressed serial killer.

It was in 1980 that he starred on Broadway in the memorable title role of *The Elephant Man*. An older "cougar," Oona Chaplin (widow of Charlie) came backstage and launched an affair with him.

In the wake of Bowie's death, his ex-paramour, Ava Cherry, for a while his backup singer, came forward to tell the press, "I was the tasty filling in the cookie between Bowie and Mick Jagger." Her phraseology obviously suggested a three-way.

Bowie married twice, his first union an "open marriage" with the American model, Mary Angela Barnett. As Bowie rather inelegantly put it, "We met when we were both f…ing the same bloke."

For the last 24 years of his life, he was married to the Somalia-born supermodel known only as "Iman." Originally, their interracial marriage was viewed as daring. His wife, who speaks five languages, today runs a $25 million-a-year business.

For some 20 years, the happily married couple lived unobtrusively in Manhattan. *The New York Times* called him "The invisible New Yorker who walked the streets with his spiky orange hair and snow-white tan unrecognized."

Bowie's death marks the final nail in the coffin of rock-'n'-roll music.

"Now, we're left with this pop twit, Justin Beiber," moaned a devoted Bowie fan.

**Bowie: A Controversial but Genuine Iconoclast**

*Upper photo*: Poster for *The Man Who Fell to Earth*, and *Lower photo*: front cover of Terry O'Neill's Bowie retrospective, *When Ziggy Played the Marquee: The Last Performance of Ziggie Stardust*.

**Iman:** Married to David Bowie in 1992, this Somali-American model and actress was a muse of such designers as Calvin Kelin and Gianni Versace. In 1994, she started her own cosmetics firm, turning it into a $25-million-a-year enterprise.

**Justin Bieber:** A Canadian, Bieber invaded America and soon became a teen idol. He is one of the best-selling artists of all time, selling more than 150 million records worldwide.

# SHELLEY WINTERS' DEATHBED WEDDING

*"I desperately needed to get fucked."*

—Shelley Winters explaining to a director why she had fled from a Hollywood film set for a weekend in New York.

*"I was drowned by Monty Clift, run over by James Mason, crushed to death by Robert Mitchum—been strangled, raped, and otherwise done away with. I think I am must about due for an incineration."*

—Shelley Winters (again)

We used to hear about "shotgun weddings." But no one has ever heard of a deathbed wedding as it relates to a two-time Oscar winner. Ten hours before her death earlier this year at the age of 85 (possibly 83), Shelley Winters took as her fourth husband, her longtime boyfriend, Gerry DeFord. Fellow actress Sally Kirkland, an ordained minister, performed the ceremony. The 11th hour marriage was vehemently opposed by Winters' daughter, Dr. Vittoria Gassman.

The death of the superstar brought an end to one of Hollywood's most flamboyant careers. Winters won her first Oscar nomination in 1951 for *A Place in the Sun* in which she starred with Montgomery Clift and Elizabeth Taylor.

Then a blonde bombshell, Winters roomed with another blonde at 8573 Holloway Drive in Los Angeles. One lazy Sunday afternoon, that roomie, Marilyn Monroe, sat down with Winters and composed a list of "hunks" they'd like to seduce. Albert Einstein and Arthur Miller topped Monroe's list. It's still debatable if she seduced Einstein, but she married playwright Miller.

Winters managed to seduce the men on her list, too. They included Marlon Brando and Burt Lancaster. In time, Sean Connery, Robert De Niro, and countless others were added to the list. She even bagged the politician whose name appeared near the top of her list, Adlai Stevenson, who unsuccessfully ran against Eisenhower twice for the presidency of the United States in the 1950s. Winters also had a torrid affair with a future president of the United States, Jack Kennedy, then a senator from Massachusetts.

After her arrival in Hollywood, Winters said, "I couldn't decide between Clark Gable and Errol Flynn, so I went for both of them."

Her figure ballooned in later life, as she assumed an aging "kept-woman-of-the-Habsburg-Empire" appearance, as was evident when she played Rosanne's grandmother on the TV sitcom hit. At that time, she denounced nudity both on the stage and on the screen. "It's disgusting, shameful. But if I were 22 with a great body, it would be artistic, tasteful, patriotic, and a progressive religious experience."

Over a decades-long career, Winters made some 150 odd films—she was never certain. One night after returning to Italy, she called Darwin Porter, claiming she'd just filmed an "artistic production." However, she warned that the director had lost the soundtrack, so the movie would never be released.

Seated at a dinner table with Winters one night at Sardi's in New York, Porter spotted actor Anthony Franciosa approaching her table. His fiery marriage to Winters

During her sexual glory in the 1940s and 50s, Shelley Winters was a "hot dame" known for her saucy (some said "degenerate and filthy') tongue and her obsession with catching the spotlight.

**Shelley Winters** *(left)* and **Marilyn Monroe** had a reunion in 1960. In the late 40s, they were men-devouring roomies.

*Question*: In addition to carloads of scandal, what else did they share? *Answer:* Young **John F. Kennedy** *(see photo, below)*.

As **Shelley Winters** morphed from a voluptuous sexpot into a frowsy-looking blimp, casting directors tapped into one of her greatest talents: Her skill at portraying annoying, over-the-hill, cling-ons.

Here, she appears with **Elizabeth Taylor** *(left)* and **Montgomery Clift** *(center)* as the frumpy contender for his love in *A Place in the Sun* (1951). Both Clift and Winters were nominated for Oscars.

Presiding over Shelley Winters' deathbed wedding was retired actress and spiritualist **Sally Kirkland,** known for what she defines as her "blending of sexuality with spirituality."

in the 1950s was the talk of Tinseltown. Assuming that he was a stranger, she brushed him away, warning him that this was a private party.

"But Shelley, don't you know me? Franciosa protested. "You used to be my wife." "My God, it's you, Tony," Winters bellowed to him. "Give me a big wet one and sit down for a night of heavy drinking, just like in the old days."

Ironically, Franciosa passed away from complications following a stroke merely five days after the death of his former wife.

CATCHING, BUT NOT NECESSARILY KEEPING, HER MEN

## SHELLEY WINTERS' HUSBANDS FOUR

*Sometimes, it really is "till death do us part" From left to right, above:*

**Paul Mayer, Vittorio Gassman, Tony Franciosa**, and **Gerry DeFord**

Did **Sexy Shelley** get better with age?

You decide.

**MORE FRUMPY CLING-ON ROLES IN WHICH SHE EXCELLED:**

**LOLITA,** Nabokov's Award-Winner Exploration of a Mature Man's Love for a pubescent adolescent, played in this case by **Sue Lyons** (center).

Dowdy and annoying, **Shelley** played the nymphet's mother until she conveniently died, enabling the teenaged-obsessed **James Mason** (left figure in photo above) to continue his seductive pursuit.

For the affection of presidential candidate **Adlai Stevenson** (left), **Shelley Winters** had to compete with Joan Fontaine.

According to Winters, "On a scale of one to ten, I'd give Adlai 1 1/2"

Frank Sinatra called **Shelley Winters** "A bowlegged bitch of a Brooklyn broad." She retorted, "You are a stupid, skinny, no-talent Hoboken bastard."

Although few Hollywood insiders really believed that **Shelley** had an affair with the (charming and gay) actor, **Farley Granger** (left in photo above), rumors about intimacies with Sean Connery, Marlon Brando, JFK, and William Holden were widely accepted as accurate.

# JUNE ALLYSON

## Goodnight, Sweetheart

She played the perfect wife on screen, but her real life belied the sunshiny image presented to us in films. June Allyson led a roller-coaster life that at times matched the tumultuous adventures of fellow MGM contract player, Lana Turner.

"America's Sweetheart" in the 1940s, June died on July 8, 2006 at her home in Ojai, California, of pulmonary respiratory failure after a long illness. For those of us who grew up in the 1940s and 50s, her husky voice—"like Jimmy Durante's"—enchanted us, as did that pageboy hairdo and Peter Pan collars.

Louis B. Mayer said, "She's not pretty. She certainly isn't sexy. She sings fairly well. She doesn't dance all that well, either. But she's got something. Hire her!"

June never exaggerated her talent. "I have big teeth. I lisp. My eyes disappear when I smile. My voice is funny. I don't sing like Judy Garland or dance like Cyd Charisse. But women identify with me. Our soldiers in World War II desired Betty Grable or Rita Hayworth, but I was the kind of gal they took home to meet Mom."

When I once called upon her long after her film career was over, she was surprisingly candid about her life, even giving a slightly different spin on some aspects of her story that contradicted her autobiography.

In 1985 she'd come back into public awareness by becoming the national spokeswoman for Depend, a diaper for adults with incontinence. With these TV commercials, she aroused national awareness about this once-taboo subject. "I wanted to call attention to this unfortunate condition, but also wanted to let the world know I am still here."

She spoke wistfully of lost loves. "Judy said it all when she sang of the man who got away." Judy Garland was one of June's best friends and her longtime confidante.

June revealed that John F. Kennedy, when just a young man, not only dated her but suggested he might marry her. "It's just as well," she said. "Jackie made a better First Lady than I ever could."

With **Jimmy Durante** in *Music for Millions* (1953)

With **Peter Lawford** in *Good Times* (1947)

Two view of J**une Allyson** with **James Stewart** in *The Glenn Miller Story*

June and her husband, Dick Powell, whom she'd married in 1945, were best friends of Ronald Reagan and his wife, Jane Wyman. June said that she and "Richard" (as she always called Dick Powell) were to be credited with switching Reagan from the Democratic Party to the Republican side. I asked her about rumors of a love affair with Reagan. "A passing fancy—call it a two-week fling," she said. "Nothing very serious. It was the same with Jimmy."

She was referring to her romance with Jimmy Stewart, with whom she appeared as the steadfast wife to his one-legged baseball player in *The Stratton Story* in 1949 and the widow he left behind in *The Glenn Miller Story* in 1953.

She confessed that the greatest love of her life was Alan Ladd, with whom she'd co-starred in *The McConnel Story* in 1955. "We were both married at the time, he to Sue Carol and me to Richard. It was the hardest thing that either of us ever did, going back to our spouses. Even after we parted, Alan and I talked for hours on the phone. I loved him until the day he died."

He sent her a recording of "Autumn Leaves," and she played it for years and wept. Tears welled in her eyes when she recalled that he attempted

Three views of what was promoted as the "most fun" and "most wholesome" couple in postwar Hollywood: **June Allyson** with **Dick Powell** and *(photo right)* their children.

suicide over her on November 1, 1962. He was found in a pool of his own blood, a gun beside him. A .38 caliber bullet had to be removed from his heart. The star survived until January 29, 1964, when he died of an acute overdose of alcohol and sedatives. Dick Powell had died the year before of cancer.

"With Alan and Richard dead, my own life fell apart," June confessed. "I had a series of nervous breakdowns. A disastrous rebound marriage to Richard's hairdresser. I was too much of a coward to commit suicide, so I tried to drink myself to death."

She credited her recovery to Dr. David Ashrow, a dentist she'd married in 1976. He was at her bedside when she died.

During my time with her, June said, "Whenever those autumn leaves start to fall, I think of Alan. Everybody has a 'What If' in their life."

**Allyson** with the self-confessed "love of her life," **Alan Ladd.**

Short, sultry, seductive, and ambitious, young June Allyson never lacked for attention from men, both in and out Hollywood. She even sustained a brief (slam, bang) affair with young **JFK** (*photo above*).

That, however, didn't influence her self-image as a devout Republican who proudly (and publicly) voted for Richard Nixon (JFK's Republican opponent) in the presidential election of 1960.

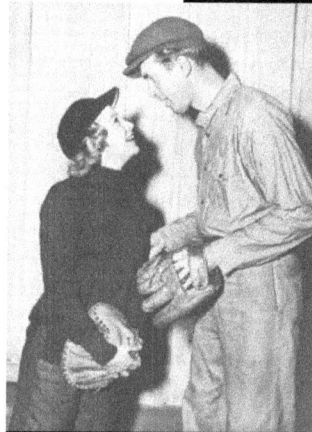

**Then and Later:** Two views of **Allyson** *with* **James Stewart.** *Left photo:* in *The Stratton Story (1949), and (right photo),* during a nostalgia-soaked reunion and photo op with him in Cannes in 1985.

**THERE WAS A LOT TO TALK ABOUT:**

**Allyson** with **Judy Garland** on *The Judy Garland Show,* (Episode 6, broadcast 27 October, 1963)

**The Girl a G.I. could take home to Mom***:* **June Allyson** publicity photo

266

# RAYMOND BURR

## The Secret Life of Perry Mason

Actor Raymond Burr immortalized himself as the truth-seeking lawyer Perry Mason in one of the biggest TV series of all time. In front of millions of TV fans, Raymond solved mysteries, often in court before judge and jury, virtually every week between 1957 and 1966.

The Perry Mason series has been in re-run syndication ever since, appearing on DVD for the first time in 2006. The character actor also starred in another successful TV series, *Ironside,* (1967-1975), in which he portrayed a wheelchair-bound chief of detectives.

Until Perry Mason came along, Raymond had distinguished himself playing heavies in B-movies and *noir* thrillers, most notably as the wife-killer in Alfred Hitchcock's *Rear Window.*

Until he was cast as Perry Mason, his private life had caused little speculation. But with his sudden fame, millions of fans clamored for details about his private life. Faced with this dilemma, he created an absolutely fake biography, which is only now becoming unraveled, despite the fact that his death from cancer occurred nearly fifteen years ago, on September 12, 1993.

Two views of hugely popular TV characters portrayed by **Raymond Burr**: *Left,* as the lawyer we all wish we'd had, *Perry Mason.*

*Right photo:* older, more experienced, and disabled, **Burr** appears in the popular TV series, *Ironside.*

To mask his homosexuality, he invented a fictional life as a heterosexual. As a gay man living in the repressed 1950s, he feared that an "outing" as a homosexual would destroy what would in time become one of the most successful of all TV careers. The mystery he created about himself would rival any of the fiction of the Perry Mason series.

Raymond revealed to reporters that he'd married "Annette Sutherland," an aspiring Scottish actress, in 1942. He even made the outrageous claim that on June 2, 1943, she boarded BOAC flight 777-A in Lisbon on a flight to war-torn London. A fellow passenger on that ill-fated flight was actor Leslie Howard, who'd played Ashley Wilkes in *Gone With the Wind.* The Luftwaffe shot down that plane, killing everyone aboard. But ironically, none of the people aboard that ill-fated flight was named Annette Sutherland Burr.

Conjuring up his fine-tuned sense of drama, Raymond also claimed that his marriage to Annette had produced a son, Michael Evan Burr, who had died of an "incurable disease" 10 years later, after embarking on a year-long "farewell to life" road trip with his (fictional) father, Raymond. There was no such trip, and no such son.

As a spinner of tall tales, Raymond didn't stop there. He falsely but vaguely claimed that he had served in the military during World War II, even citing to reporters that he had won the Purple Heart, an award usually given to soldiers wounded in action. And despite the fact that these claims were fabricated, they were nonetheless widely reported in

**Burr** (as Perry Mason) on the cover, in 1960, of *TV Guide* with **Barbara Hale**, who—in hundreds of episodes of that hit series—played Della Street. To thousands of TV viewers, she morphed into the most effective legal secretary on network TV.

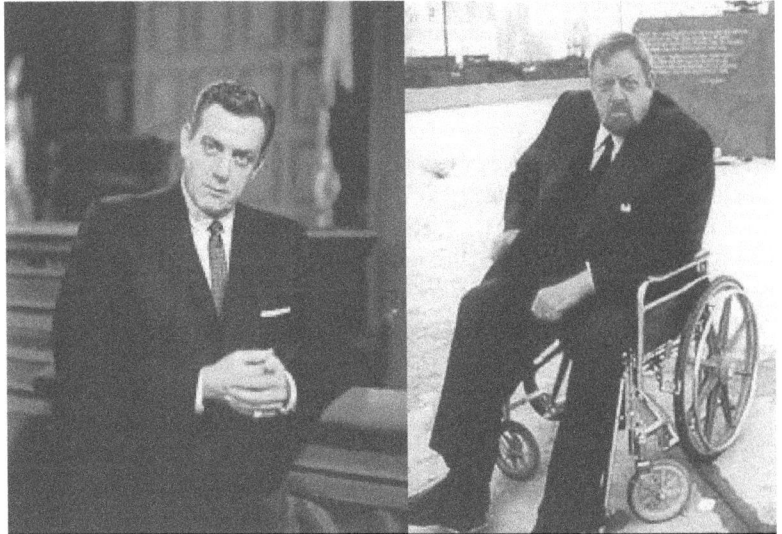

Though capable of producing rivers of facile charm, **Raymond Burr** got a lot of screen mileage from his performances as humorless and very dangerous "heavies." Above, left, he appears as the homicidal neighbor of James Stewart and Grace Kelly in *Rear Window.*

*Above right,* kidnapping a very young Natalie Wood in *A Cry in the Night* (1956)

267

the press.

Ironically, Raymond actually married a real person in 1947, an actress named Isabella ("Bella") Ward. The marriage, such as it was, lasted for about a week before Bella fled back to Delaware, leaving her husband in Los Angeles. She would remain married to him for another four years, although she never saw him again. Neither Bella nor Raymond ever revealed what went wrong in their marriage.

Raymond invented yet another wife, this time claiming her name was "Laura Andrina Morgan," and revealing that they were married in 1955. (Once, to a reporter, he forgot some of the details of his previous life and cited the year of that fictitious marriage as 1953.) He told reporters that that wife had "put up a brave battle against cancer," and died. Laura never existed.

For publicity purposes, the corpulent 38-year-old Raymond suggested that he was having an affair with the seventeen-year-old actress Natalie Wood, who appears to have fallen in love with him. Raymond taught her about literature and good wine, but did little else to her, with the possible exception of delivering a good night peck on the cheek. Natalie later lamented, "Elizabeth Taylor had better luck seducing gay men than I did."

At the time, Raymond was actually living with Frank Vitti, a Korean War veteran, who he passed off as "my nephew." All allegiance to Frank vanished when Raymond met an actor, Robert Benevides, on the set of the Perry Mason series. It was love at first sight. The two men not only bonded that day, but lived together for the rest of Raymond's life.

The 1940s actress, Barbara Hale, who played Perry Mason's leggy secretary, Della Street, called the Burr/Benevides union "the most successful marriage in Hollywood." The two actors owned and operated first an orchid business and later a vineyard in Dry Creek Valley in California. After Raymond's death, despite unsuccessful legal challenges from Raymond's niece, his $32 million estate went entirely to Robert. Today, the award-winning Raymond Burr Vineyards, producing Chardonnay and Cabernets, are run by Robert.

Raymond's faithful companion was at his bedside on the day of his death at the age of 76. Raymond's last morphine-sedated words to Robert were, "Try to live your life the way you wish other people would live theirs."

Old Faithful: **Robert Benevides** with a glass of one of the Raymond Burr Vineyard's, in the Russian River Valley, Cabernets. Barbara Hale described their long-term relationship as "the most successful marriage in Hollywood."

**MARRYING HER SEEMED LIKE A GOOD IDEA AT THE TIME**

**Isabella Ward**—the girl Raymond Burr briefly married in an Eisenhower-era attempt to camouflage his status as a homosexual. appears in this photo snapped when she was in high school.

Although **Raymond Burr** was technically not a lawyer, the TV character he played oozed shrewd intelligence and good legal values and judgment. "Today," one of his fans mourned, "we need him more than ever."

But who was the actor who portrayed Perry Mason's private detective, **Paul Drake**?

It was **William Hopper** (left) the real-life son of columnist Hedda Hopper. A closeted gay, he once developed a crush on a young Ronald Reagan.

# JENNIFER JONES
## THE MERYL STREEP OF HER DAY

The world took little notice of the passing of one of the great movie icons of the 1940s and 50s, Miss Jennifer Jones (1919-2009). She was also one of the world's richest women and a member of the very exclusive club of female Oscar winners who survived to the age of 90 and beyond. Other Oscar winners aged 90 and beyond who are still alive include sisters Olivia de Havilland and Joan Fontaine, plus that ageless wonder, Luise Rainer, who was born in 1910.

Ironically, Jennifer Jones outlived most of her fans, and, unless you're over 50, you're not likely to even know who she is. But she was such a big star that *The New York Times* included her on its short list of all-time greats whose death came during the first decade of the 21st century but whose lives helped define the 20th. In those celestial ranks, she joined such luminaries as Katharine Hepburn, Paul Newman, Marlon Brando, Gregory Peck, and Loretta Young.

Born in Tulsa, Oklahoma, Phyllis Lee Isley (Jennifer's original name) was the daughter of parents who ran a "traveling tent show" theatrical troupe. As a child, Phyllis sold tickets and candy bars, even acting in the company.

In New York in 1939, she met and married a handsome young actor, Robert Walker, who was emotionally unstable. Both decided to take the train to Hollywood, each hoping to become a star. After a long and rocky road, they each achieved that goal.

Their union produced two sons, Robert Walker Jr., born in 1940, and Michael Walker, born in 1941. (He died in 2007.)

By the time Phyllis met David O. Selznick, fresh from his success with *Gone With the Wind*, her marriage to Walker was already doomed. The producer changed her name to Jennifer Jones and signed her to a seven-year contract. He also took her away from Walker and, in 1949, married her himself, the union lasting until his death in 1965.

Long before her first meeting with Selznick, there had been serious trouble in her relationship with Walker, who had become an alcoholic, and who was having affairs of his own, most notably with Peter Lawford, the future brother-in-law of John F. Kennedy. Both Walker and Lawford were also engaged in affairs with Nancy Davis in the years leading up to her marriage to Ronald Reagan. Although their marriage had ended long before, Jennifer finally divorced Walker in 1945.

Walker came to a tragic and early end on August 27, 1951, having succumbed to respiratory failure following a drink-

The object of desire and fantasy throughout movieland, **Jennifer Jones** appears here between **Gregory Peck** and **Joseph Cotten** in *Duel in the Sun* (1946).

With **Montgomery Clift** in *Stazione Termini (aka Indiscretions of an American Wife)*

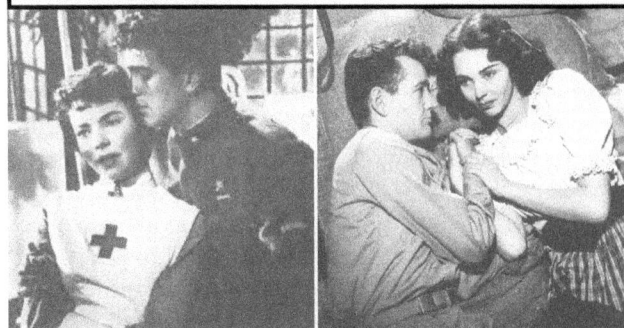

Left, with Rock Hudson in *A Farewell to Arms* (1957), and with her emotionally fragile first husband, **Robert Walker**.

In addition to "JJ," other female winners of Oscars who survived to the age of 90 and beyond include, left to right, **Olivia De Havilland** (depicted as Melanie in 1939's *Gone With the Wind*); Olivia's estranged sister, **Joan Fontaine**, shown with the malevolent Mrs. Danvers (Dame **Judith Anderson**) in *Rebecca* (1940); and **Louise Rainer,** the only star to ever win two Oscars in a row.

ing binge.

Although Selznick may have destroyed her marriage, he carefully guided Jennifer's career. She had shot to stardom and an Oscar in the 1943 *The Song of Bernadette*, in which she played a French peasant girl who claimed to have been visited by the Virgin Mary. Four other Oscar nominations would follow, including one for the 1944 *Since You Went Away* in which she played Claudette Colbert's wishy-washy daughter; the 1945 *Love Letters*, in which she was an amnesiac; the 1946 *Duel in the Sun*, where she was cast as a wicked, half-breed temptress opposite Gregory Peck; and the uninspired romance, the 1955 *Love Is a Many Splendored Thing*, that nonetheless earned her final Oscar nomination. Her co-star was William Holden.

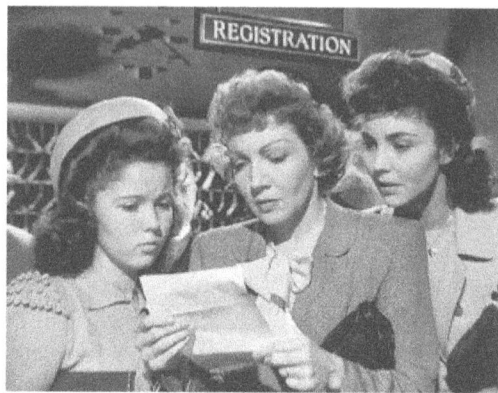

**Jennifer Jones** *(right)* shares wartime neuroses with a grown-up **Shirley Temple** *(left)* and **Claudette Colbert** *(center)* in *Since You Went Away* (1944)

During the course of her marriage to Selznick, Jennifer fell in love twice, each with disastrous results. She became enamored of Montgomery Clift when they starred together in 1954 in *Indiscretion of an American Wife*. That ended when Truman Capote told her that Clift was into guys She also fell for Rock Hudson when they starred in Ernest Hemingway's *A Farewell to Arms* in 1957, but Peter Lawford told her that Hudson, too, was into guys. In the aftermath, she returned home to Selznick.

All good things must end, and so it did for Jennifer. After Selznick died, so went the great roles. In *The Idol* (1966) and in the aptly named *Angel, Down We Go* (1969) she played a woman dallying with younger men. In the latter, she was cast as a former porn star. Her last appearance involved dancing opposite Fred Astaire in the 1974 *The Towering Inferno*, in which her character fell 110 stories from a panoramic elevator outside the building: An inglorious end to a spectacular career.

Selznick and Jennifer give birth to a daughter, Mary Jennifer Selznick, on August 12, 1954. At the age of 21, the heiress jumped to her death from a tall building in West Los Angeles.

Jennifer herself had attempted suicide on November 9, 1967, the result of which left her unconscious on a beach in Malibu. She was rushed to a nearby hospital, where she eventually recovered from an overdose of sleeping pills.

**Jennifer Jones** around the time of her marriage in 1971 to the industrialist, conglomerate developer and world-class art collector **Norton Simon.**

In 1971, she married one of the richest men in America, Norton Simon, the union lasting until his death in 1993. His son, Robert, had committed suicide in 1969. Early in his career, the industrialist and art collector had taken over a bankrupt orange juice bottling plant, quickly transforming it into a conglomerate and personal empire that included such brand names as Hunt Foods and Canada Dry.

He retired at age 62 to concentrate on his art collection, which is now displayed in the Norton Simon Museum in Los Angeles. He spent some $100 million on his art, now almost priceless in value. After his failing health forced him to retire from too active a role in the administration of the world-famous museum, Jennifer took over as chairwoman.

I was fortunate to meet her only once, a rendezvous arranged by my friend, the California industrialist Gordon Howard, who was also a close friend of Simon. During the course of an evening with her, I remember her exact words: "When I was young, I was filled with hope and dreams. But as you age and experience life, you learn that it is filled with nightmares as well. Some of us get through our nightmares and live on. Others do not."

Obviously, Jennifer Jones lived through her triumphs and tragedies, and did so with a certain grace.

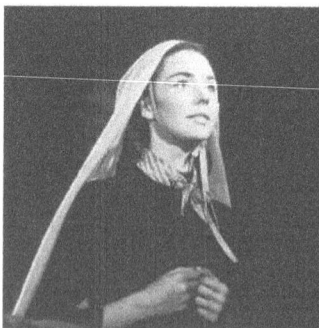

This is the role that launched her career, even if it were hard to imagine her as a nun who channeled ecstatic religious visions.

Here's **Jennifer Jones** in the title role in *The Song of Bernadette (1943)*

**Jennifer Jones** *("the temperamental beauty ")* with her second husband, film producer **David O. Selznik** *("the temperamental beast").*

# PINK TRIANGLE

## THE PRIVATE LIVES OF **TENNESSEE WILLIAMS, GORE VIDAL, TRUMAN CAPOTE**, AND FAMOUS MEMBERS OF THEIR ENTOURAGES

One hot summer night in 1945, three young American writers, each an *enfant terrible*, come together in a stuffy Manhattan apartment for the first time. Each member of this pink triangle was on the dawn of world fame—Tennessee Williams for *A Streetcar Named Desire*; Gore Vidal for his notorious homosexual novel, *The City and the Pillar*; and Truman Capote for *Other Voices, Other Rooms* a book that had been marketed with a photograph depicting Capote as a underaged sex object that caused as much controversy as the prose inside.

Each of the three remained competitively and defiantly provocative throughout the course of his writing career. Initially hailed by critics as "the darlings of the gods," each of them would, in time, be attacked for his contributions to film, the theater, and publishing. Some of their works would be widely reviewed as "obscene rantings from perverted sociopaths."

From that summer night emerged betrayals that eventually evolved into lawsuits, stolen lovers, public insults, and the most flamboyant rivalries in America 's literary history. The opinions of these authors about their celebrity acquaintances usually left scar tissue.

Williams' longtime lover was Frank Merlo, but he was also rumored to have had sexual encounters with aspirant actor Warren Beatty and with Marlon Brando as a prelude to his getting cast in *A Streetcar Named Desire*.

Vidal often hired hustlers, particularly when he lived in Rome and on the Amalfi Coast.

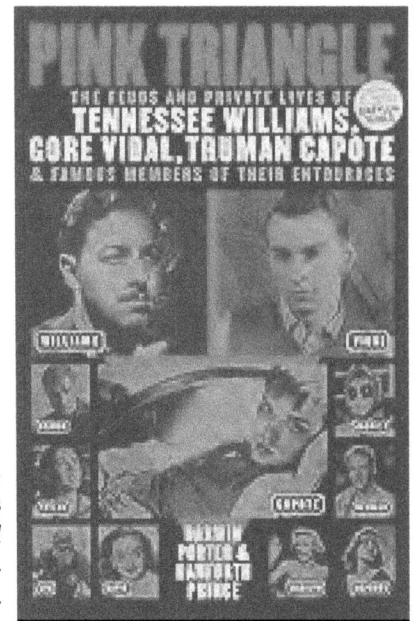

The best overview of a literary bitchfest ever compiled. **Darwin Porter,** its author, was a friend (or tormented acquaintance) of each of its main characters.

This is believed to be the only "group photo" of the "Unholy Trio" ever taken. As they matured, their mutual hatred grew to the point where, as a threesome, they refused to be anywhere near each other.

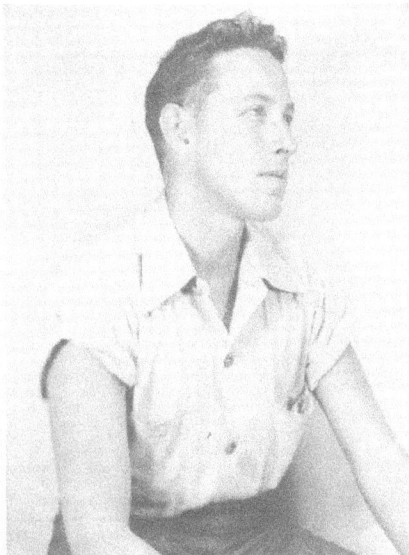

## HELL HATH NO FURY LIKE A DIVA SCORNED

**Portraits of the Artists as Young Men:**  *Left to right:*  **Tennessee Williams, Truman Capote**, and **Gore Vidal**

271

Capote's alltime biggest conquests were Errol Flynn and Marlon Brando. Humphrey Bogart lost a bet with him and had to let the writer fellate him.

Vidal became the most iconoclastic writer since Voltaire, needling and satirizing ·the sacred cows of his era and explosively describing subjects which included America 's gay founding fathers, the lesbian affairs of Eleanor Roosevelt, Henry Miller's "hydraulic" approach to sex; the feminism (or lack thereof) of Norman Mailer; and his own seduction of the Beat Generation's spiritual leader and guru, Jack Kerouac. The book contains an overview of Vidal's hot, then glacial, relationship with the fabled diarist Anaïs Nin—"She came on like a hothouse flower masking cannibalistic vegetation"— and the drawn-out slugfests which followed.   It also includes details about the night Attorney General Robert F. Kennedy kicked Vidal out of the White House for "inappropriate behavior."

Capote became the mascot of the ultra-fashionable jet set, surrounded and showcased by his glamorous "swans." Eventually, Capote feuded not only with Vidal, but with "The Queen of the Best-Sellers," Jacqueline Susann, publicly referring to her as "a truck driver in drag." Capote's own struggles for bestsellerdom are depicted during the research of his all-time hit, *In Cold Blood*, wherein he falls hopelessly in love with one of its killers. The book contains details about his hosting of "The Party of the Century," and his self-destructive descent into isolation, alcohol, and drug abuse.

Tennessee Williams, attacked for his "incurable sense of decadence," became as notorious as his plays. His tumultuous private life is explored as never before in a portrait that's as poignant and flamboyant as any character he created, including that of Blanche DuBois.

Plays which included *Cat on a Hot Tin Roof* and *Suddenly, Last Summer* shocked audiences and catalyzed international celebrity. Williams' wildly promiscuous life as a gay man "depending on the kindness of strangers" found him wandering the globe for sexual satisfaction he never found. Eventually falling from grace with critics, he became trapped in a world dominated by alcohol and pills, culminating, in 1970, with his confinement in a mental hospital.   Did Tennessee really perform fellatio on JFK at his Palm Beach compound? Did Warren Beatty really have sex with him as a means of procuring his role as the gigolo in *The Roman Spring of Mrs. Stone*? What really happened when a then-unknown actor, Marlon Brando, arrived on Tennessee's doorstep in Provincetown during World War II?

The book's cast of supporting characters included the most talked-about *glitterati* of the 20th Century—Paul Newman (all three writers claimed that they seduced him); John and Jackie Kennedy; Marilyn Monroe, Grace Kelly, Anna Magnani, Burt Lancaster, Eleanor Roosevelt, Irene Selznick, Carson McCullers, Vivien Leigh, Lana Turner, Greta Garbo, the Duke of Windsor and his notorious Duchess, Ava Gardner, Leonard Bernstein, Tallulah Bankhead, Monty Clift, Audrey Hepburn, and Richard Burton.

The opinions of these authors about their celebrity acquaintances—which they shared with almost anyone who would listen—were usually highly entertaining but devastating.

***

Bigamist **Anaïs Nin** with one of her two then-husbands, **Rupert Pole,** at a "Come as Your Madness" Party in the mid-1940s.  Her New York husband was **Ian Hugo** (aka Hugh Parker Guiler).

Nin sometimes referred to her simultaneous marriages as her "bicoastal trapeze."

**Anais Nin**—her era's most famous diarist— during a *détente* with her frenemy, **Gore Vidal**.

When their mutual admiration soured, it (publicly) became divisive, trenchant, and toxic.

Passionate and promiscuous, young **Leonard Bernstein** got tugged into the vortex of the trio's feuds.

The **Windsors, Edward and Wallis**—seen here dancing at the Waldorf-Astoria—were frequent visitors to New York City during their notorious heyday.

Even they—abdicated scions of Britain's royal family—got messy in the *brouhahas* associated with the Unholy Trio.

# TENNESSEE, GORE, & TRUMAN

### An Eyewitness, "Up Close and Personal" Account of Literary Ambition and Despair
### by Darwin Porter

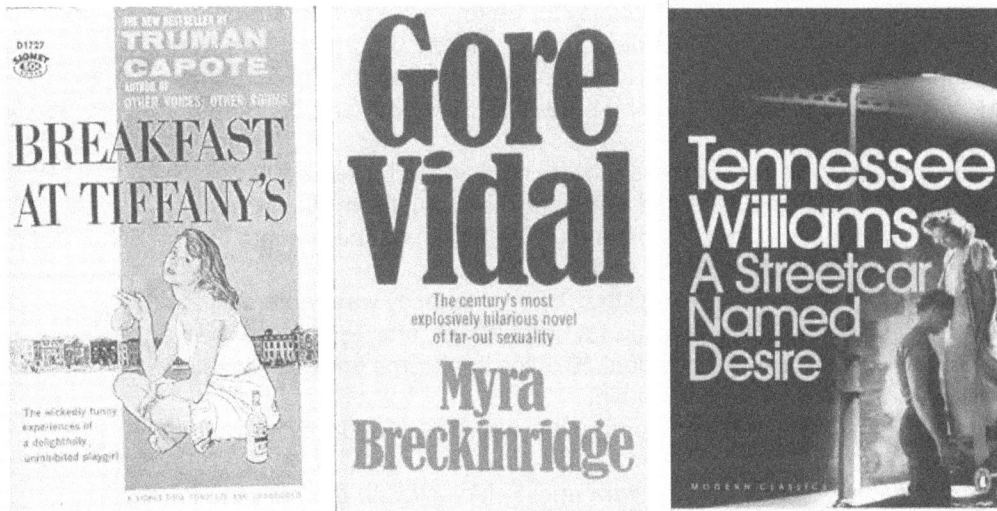

> The war was over, the United States had emerged as the most powerful and richest nation in human history, and its arts scene was flourishing. Into this cauldron of potentiality emerged three provocative and "highly quotable'" writers of merit. Each of them spent the rest of his life in ferocious (some said "bloodthirsty") competition with the others.

## The atomic bomb had fallen on the Japanese city of Nagasaki, ending

World War II, when three gay writers—Tennessee Williams, Gore Vidal, and Truman Capote—arrived in New York to explode shock waves of their own.

In the post-war era, each of them rose to infamy in the plays, novels, and film scripts they'd create—among them Capote's *Breakfast at Tiffany's,* Tennessee's *A Streetcar Named Desire,* and Vidal's notorious gender-bending *Myra Breckinridge.*

It was not their literary works that shocked audiences, but their scandal-plagued private lives. My latest biography, **Pink Triangle**, explores the secret lives of these three writers, whom I knew intimately over the decades, sharing many of their triumphs and tragedies.

It is not just their story, but the saga of celebrated members of their entourages. What a cast! Tallulah Bankhead, Vivien Leigh, Marilyn Monroe, Marlon Brando, Paul Newman, Elizabeth Taylor, Bette Davis, Katharine Hepburn, Anna Magnani, Burt Lancaster—and the list goes on. Drawn from their drama-filled lives, *Pink Triangle* has a revelation on every page.

In the beginning, Tennessee became friends with both Vidal and Capote, although the latter two became each other's worst enemies, even suing one another for libel.

Tennessee told me, "I liked Gore, but only through the strenuous effort to overlook his conceit. He had studied ballet and was constantly doing pirouettes and flexing his legs. The rest of the time, he attacked Capote."

Tennessee had a more colorful description of Capote: "He speaks with a forked tongue. He's a sodomite's delight, a little monster unleashed from vaginal portals—but charming nevertheless."

Each author was sexually voracious, none more so than Vidal. He claimed that in a style equivalent to the legendary Don Juan, he in time seduced 1,003 men.

In their younger days, their conquests were not just associated with hustlers and wannabee actors, but with major stars— Marlon Brando, James Dean, Montgomery Clift, Rock Hudson, Sal Mineo, Peter Lawford—all of them predictable staples on the list of promiscuous gay or bisexual movie stars of that era. It seemed that every male and female star in Hollywood or on Broadway wanted to appear in a play or screen adaptation by Tennessee.

Both Vidal and Capote had promiscuous mothers, each of them named Nina. Vidal caught his mother "winging low" with Charles Lindbergh, when she wasn't otherwise involved with *Time/Life* publisher Henry Luce. Simultaneously, Gore's dear old Dad, Eugene Vidal, was "flying high" with Amelia Earhart. In Hollywood, Nina Vidal launched a torrid affair with Clark Gable, wanting him to become her son's stepfather.

In parallel patterns, Truman's mother, Nina Capote seduced everyone from boxing champ Jack Dempsey to Marlene

Dietrich.

At various times, Vidal and Jacqueline Bouvier shared the same stepfather, Hugh Auchincloss. In Washington, they became confidants of each other. When she worked as an inquiring photographer for a newspaper, she visited the office of a rising young California politician, Richard M. Nixon. She confessed to Gore, "He made a pass at me."

Sometimes, Jackie and Vidal fell for the same man. Both were balletomanes, each becoming entranced with John Kriza when they saw him perform his folkloric ballet, "Billy the Kid" wearing a white jockstrap and chaps. Later, both of them became romantically involved with the Russian ballet dancer, Rudolf Nureyev.

In Hollywood in the 1950s, Vidal wrote a screenplay for Bette Davis (*The Catered Affair*, released in 1956*)*. He moved in with an unmarried couple, Joanne Woodward and Paul Newman. He told them that one day he wanted to run for president of the United States. According to Vidal, "If I become president, Joanne agreed to marry me and become my First Lady."

One morning in Key West, Vidal and Tennessee were mapping out a screenplay, *Suddenly, Last Summer*, to star Elizabeth Taylor and Katharine Hepburn. From Palm Beach a call came in from Jackie, who wanted them to drive to Palm Beach to share a late lunch with her husband, then a senator from Massachusetts.

On the way there, Vidal revealed to Tennessee that John F. Kennedy was contemplating a run for the presidency. During the lunch, the quartet bonded, but later Tennessee made a forecast to Vidal: "Jack will never become president. He's too handsome and sophisticated for the American public. But he has some butt on him."

Vidal scolded him. "Tennessee, you can't cruise the future president of the United States."

Capote became the darling of high society, surrounding himself with the rich, the famous, and the infamous. He sailed the Aegean on the yacht of Gianni Agnelli; he sunbathed in Greece in the nude with Aristotle Onassis, and he visited Charlie Chaplin at his home in French-speaking Switzerland. He also became best friends with Babe Paley (voted best dressed woman in America), and her husband, Bill Paley, the chief honcho at CBS. His 1966 "Black and White Ball" at the Plaza Hotel in Manhattan was hailed as "the party of the century."

But in time, he betrayed his friends, painting cruel caricatures of them in the first chapters of his unfinished novel, *Answered Prayers*, published in *Esquire*. His beautiful swans, as he called his high society ladies, glided away from him, never to return.

Regrettably, Capote and Tennessee fell victims to their own self-destruction, their lives devoured by drugs and alcohol. Tennessee died in 1983, Capote in 1984.

Of the trio, only Vidal lived to a ripe age of 86, dying in 2012, although in his final years, he suffered from dementia.

In Vidal's final assessment, he claimed, "All three of us will resurface even though buried under six feet of earth. We'll be back, perhaps as cannibalistic vegetation sprouting up."

In reference to the trio and the profound influence they exerted on the arts and the American psyche, Orville Prescott, the stodgy critic for *The New York Times,* summed things up differently: "Once you spill mercury from a bottle, you can never brush it all back in."

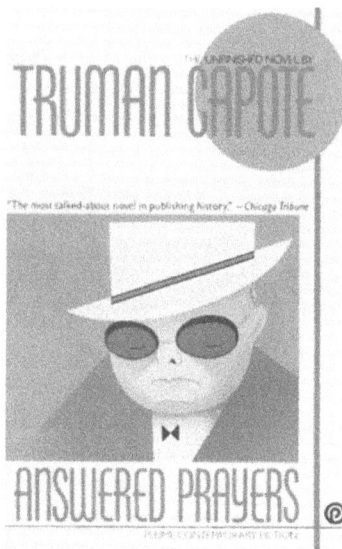

**TRUMAN CAPOTE**

"The most talked-about novel in publishing history." ~ Chicago Tribune

**ANSWERED PRAYERS** ℗

**Answered Prayes,** the book EVERYBODAY waited for (and waited for, and waited for) did not evolve into the literary masterpiece Truman had promised.

**The Paleys, Bill and Babe**, with **Truman Capote**, on holiday together in 1959 at Round Hill, Jamaica.

Each member of the "Unholy Trio" had difficult mothers, but the matriarch of Gore Vidal's family was especially toxic, inspiring rivers of invective from her articulate, sometimes vengeful son.

Here are two views of the promiscuous and sadistic socialite **Nina Vidal,** *left photo*, with her habitual cigarette holder, and *right photo* at the beach with *(left to right)* **Tennessee Williams**, her son, **Gore** (who hated her) and **herself.**

***

**The sagas of the mid-20th century's literary and sexual outlaws—Tennessee Williams, Gore Vidal, and Truman Capote**—are previewed in the latest blockbuster from biographer Darwin Porter, who knew all three writers intimately. His latest work, co-authored with Danforth Prince, is **Pink Triangle**, which not only previews their secret lives but also those of some of the famous members of their entourages: Tallulah Bankhead, Vivien Leigh, Marilyn Monroe, Katharine Hepburn, Anna Magnani, But Lancaster, and many others. There's practically a revelation of a previously unknown celebrity exposé on every page.

Tennessee and Truman were sexually voracious. Actors in search of choice roles—James Dean, Marlon Brando, Montgomery Clift, Paul Newman, and Farley Granger—ended up on Tennessee's casting couch. But Truman outdid either of his cohorts with "odd couple" pairings. His sexual conquests included director John Huston, Errol Flynn, John Garfield, and on one night, Humphrey Bogart, who lost a drunken bet during the filming of Capote's script for *Beat the Devil*, in southern Italy. In sheer volume of celebrity seductions, however, Gore won Lotto.

Perhaps Vidal's adulterous parents set an example for him. His father, Eugene Vidal, was Franklin Roosevelt's aviation czar. Eugene ended up "flying high" (in Gore's words) with the doomed Amelia Earhart. "Meanwhile," Vidal said, "My mother, Nina, was 'winging low' with aviator Charles Lindbergh when not otherwise occupied with *Time/Life* publisher Henry Luce. At least Luce put both Eugene and me later, separately, on the cover of *Time*."

According to Porter, Nina's greatest disappointment involved her failure in persuading Clark Gable to marry her. During his pre-Rhett Butler days, she'd had a torrid affair with "The King of Hollywood"' urging him to "make a man out of my pansy son.'"

Gore and Jacqueline Bouvier had shared the same stepfather (Hugh Auchincloss) during their formative early years. In Washington, the handsome young pair became sexual confidants of each other, sharing details about their early escapades.

"Jackie and I learned about sex by secretly exploring Hugh's vast collection of pornography," Gore claimed.

"He had a huge stash devoted to child porn, which would get him arrested today."

In the meantime, Gore had become friends with a young congressman from Massachusetts, John F. Kennedy. "Jack told me he had to have a different girl every week, or every day as the case may be, or else he got a migraine."

Gore claimed that the greatest triumph that Jackie and he scored was an affair with Rudolf Nureyev. Gore met him first after he'd defected from the Soviet Union. Lee Radziwill soon discovered the charms of Nureyev, as did a host of others, including the Danish ballet star, Erik Bruhn. "What intrigued me the most was not Rudi's numerous affairs, mostly with men, but he seemed to be systematically seducing the Kennedys," Gore said. "He carried on simultaneous affairs with both Jackie and Lee. Once at my home in Ravello, Italy, he told me that he and Bobby Kennedy once shared an American soldier."

Jackie eventually had an argument with Rudi when he was paying too much attention to her son, John, Jr., going away with him and trying to persuade him to become either a ballet dancer or a movie actor.

Gore's heyday of movie star seductions occurred when he became an MGM scriptwriter. Two of his screenplays, *The Catered Affair* and *The Scapegoat*, starred Bette Davis.

He lived in Hollywood at the Château Marmont in quarters next to director Nicholas Ray, who was preparing a script for *Rebel Without a Cause*. "Nick was seducing both James Dean and Natalie Wood, but he lent me the other young members of the cast, Dennis Hopper and Sal Mineo," Gore said.

JFK arranged for Gore to meet his brother-in-law, actor Peter Lawford, who was married at the time to Patricia Kennedy, JFK's sister. "It didn't work out," Gore claimed. "We weren't sexually compatible, but I hit pay dirt when Elizabeth Taylor intro-

Even as a child, **Jacqueline Bouvier Kennedy** (left photo) shared an on-again, off-again friendship with young **Gore Vidal** (middle photo), in part because they shared a stepfather, multi-millionaire **Hugh Auchincloss** (right photo). That gave Vidal a decided advantage in the "high society sweepstakes" of access to the White House after the 1960 election of JFK.

Naturally, Vidal's rivals, Tennessee Williams and Truman Capote, had to "catch up" in various, sometimes underhanded ways.

**Auchincloss**, scion and heir to an Industrial-age fortune, was described by both of his ex-wifes as "dependable, henpecked, and dull." Gore, Auchincloss's ultra-precocious stepson, cited that his first introduction to the implications of sex derived from breaking into Auchincloss's "world-class collection of porn—some of it devoted to children.."

275

duced me to Rock Hudson. The boulder that his gay agent, Henry Willson, named him after must have been a big one!"

Gore also seduced Tony Perkins in his pre-*Psycho* days. "Tony didn't enjoy 1ex unless some bloodletting took place," Gore said.

He also launched an affair with Tom Drake, Judy Garland's "Boy Next Door" in *Meet Me in St. Louis*. "Tom was still depressed from having been dumped by Lawford" 'Gore said.

He also launched an affair with Dick York (the husband of Samantha Stevens in *Bewitched*) when he came to audition for a part in Gore's play *Visit to a Small Planet*, which was later adapted into a movie starring Jerry Lewis.

At one point, Gore flew to Rome to work on the script of MGM's biggest epic, *Ben-Hur*, a remake of its silent screen classic. Gore later said, "I didn't get to seduce *Ben-Hur* (Charlton Heston), but I made it with Stephen Boyd, who had been cast as Messala. Stephen and I had many a gay Roman night." Gore's most abiding crush was on Paul Newman, who became his lifelong friend and sometimes lover. Their friendship, too, began at the Château Marmont. Later, Gore and his longtime companion, Howard Austen, rented a house with Joanne Woodward and Newman while his divorce from his first wife was being finalized. Gore said that, "Joanne and I talked of marriage one day if I ran for President. She could become my First lady and camouflage my homosexuality." The most intense time in the Gore/Newman affair occurred on the Aegean Sea when they went island hopping in a rented yacht. "I taught Paul a lot about Greek history-and a lot of other things, too."

In London, critic Kenneth Tynan arranged an interlude between Gore and Marlon Brando, who had already been seduced by Truman Capote and Tennessee. "Likewise, both Tenn and that Capote creature had already seduced Monty Clift by the time I got around to him when we were filming my script for *Suddenly, Last Summer*, starring Elizabeth Taylor."

In 1958, Gore drove Tennessee to Palm Beach to meet his friend, Jack and Jackie Kennedy. JFK was then a senator from Massachusetts. Surprisingly, the apolitical Tennessee had never heard of him.

"Have you heard of Ike?" Gore asked.

"Only that he's impotent," Tennessee said. "Poor Mamie."

"The guy I'm going to introduce you to is anything but impotent," Gore said. "He's also going to run for President of the United States."

After a lobster lunch, Gore drove Jackie to Worth Avenue to shop for summer dresses. Back at the Kennedy compound, Tennessee and JFK went for a nude swim in the Kennedy pool. Later, according to Tennessee, they got better acquainted in the locker room.

When JFK became president in 1960, Tennessee dined out on his time with him, parroting a line from JFK's inaugural speech, saying, "I didn't ask what my president could do for me, but what I could do for my president."

\*\*\*

JFK told Gore, "I'm not finished with a woman until I've had her three ways."

Was he referring to Marlene Dietrich, Zsa Zsa Gabor, Susan Haywar, Hedy Lamarr, Janet Leigh, Jean Simmons, Gene Tierney, Kim Novak, Lana Turner, or Marilyn Monroe? Or his sister-in-law, Lee Radziwill?

Each member of the "Unholy Trio" made it clear that they'd been saddled with extravagantly vexing mothers. It was a situation they shared with Jackie Kennedy and her sister, Lee.

*Left to right* in the photo above are **Lee Bouvier Radziwell**, looking forlorn; her imperious mother **Janet Auchincloss** (wife of multimillionaire "Hughdie" Auchincloss), and Lee's sister, eventual First Lady **Jacqueline Bouvier Kennedy.**

**Truman Capote,** after it was clear that Jacqueline's attentions had already been absorbed by his rival, **Gore Vidal,** began aiming his gossipy charms at the celebrity he elevated to the rank of his "chief swan," **Lee,** instead.

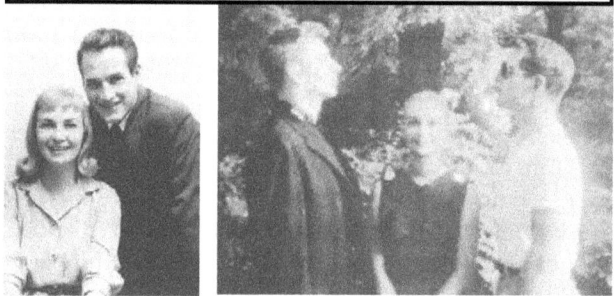

### GORE VIDAL'S LONG-STANDING "AFFAIR OF CONVENIENCE" WITH PAUL NEWMAN

The widely publicized "perfect marriage" of the cinematic stud, **Paul Newman,** with his Oscar-winning wife, **Joanne Woodward,** was less pristine than it appeared in the left-hand photo, above.

It involved aesthetic fascination (on the part of **Gore Vidal**), casting ambitions (from **Paul**), and an indulgent sense of "iaissez-faire" indulgence from the bisexual **Joanne,** who pursued occasional lesbian liaisons of her own "on the side."

The ambiguous-looking photo *above on the right* was snapped during the trio's co-habitation of a rented house on the California coast before each of them became "impossibly famous." In this photo, they're playing charades in a mock ceremony that only they fully understood.

The complicated dynamic of their collective friendship is explored in *Pink Triangle,* and also—in even greater detail—within Darwin Porter's seminal biography of Paul Newman himself. Its cover is displayed here.

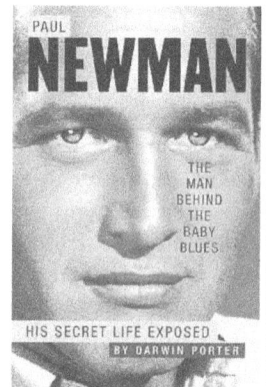

276

# *Pink Triangle*, as Evaluated by the *New York Journal of Books*

## by Vinton Rafe McCabe

"YOU MAY NOT WEEP FOR ANY OF THE THREE—BUT YOU WILL BE ENTHRALLED BY THEM AND BY THE OVER-POPULATION OF WITS, TALENTS, ARTISTS, STALKERS, HANGERS-ON, AND THE TRULY DERANGED WHO POPULATED THEIR WORLD."

**In the banquet that is Pink Triangle,** the first meeting between Gore Vidal and Truman Capote seems too good, too revealing of the natures of both of these men, to be true.

It is said to have taken place in those post-World War II years in which the streets of Manhattan sparkled with possibilities. Vidal was 20 and Capote 21 (although the author tells us that he looked 12 and "spoke like strangled child") when each entered into the Greenwich Village home of author and tireless diarist Anaïs Nin, with whom Vidal, fresh from the military and being stationed in the Aleutian Islands, was having a brief flirtation.

Vidal, we are told by Paul Cadmus, a painter among mostly poets, playwrights and other forms of literary life, "was formal and stiff, with military posture." Capote, for his part, walked up the stairs on West 13th street to tap on the door of Anaïs Nin's skylit apartment and make a late entrance into the party wearing a long black cape and matching black fedora, on the arm of critic and literary lion Leo Lerman.

Said Anaïs Nin of Truman Capote: He was "a small, slender young man, with hair over his eyes, extending the softest and most boneless hand."

Vidal, who had, to that point, been pursuing poet James Merrill, could not have helped but notice Capote's entrance. And the two circled each other for some time. Vidal, who had just recently published the admittedly outright gay novel *The City and the Pillar*, divided his attention between poet Robert Duncan and his lover, painter Robert DeNiro, Sr. Capote flitted and fussed and, finally, just walked right up to Gore Vidal and said, in his characteristic whine: "How does it feel to be an *onn-font-tarribull* [*enfant terrible*]?"

To which Vidal, ignoring the question altogether, replied: "Did you know that in Italian *capote* means 'condom?'"

And in this brief exchange, the two managed to both reveal completely the nature of their ongoing dialogue that would last for decades (ignoring each other) and the central characteristic that each brought to the friendship (the need to outdo each other).

Concerning the Aleutians, Capote would later say that, while serving there, Gore Vidal suffered from frostbite, and that "he's not melted down yet."

Anaïs Nin, who witnessed the historic meeting, summed it up this way:

"Almost from the beginning, Gore and Truman sized each other up as future rivals. After all, there could be only one *enfant terrible*. Gore was almost a historian, dealing in facts, whereas Truman came from the Southern school of raconteur, meaning he never wanted a fact to get in the way of a good story. Gore camouflaged his homosexuality, whereas Truman used it to draw attention to himself. The more flamboyant he was, the more onlookers he attracted."

And so it begins, nearly seven hundred pages of the most entertaining histrionics ever sliced, spiced, heated and serviced up to the reading public—as already noted: a banquet.

And the best part of it is that, good as Vidal and Capote are as a "sister act," it only gets better when Tennessee Williams is added into the mix. The three together in their various flirtations and feuds, their *tableau vivant* postures, their hissy fits on *The Tonight Show* and their courtroom dramas—to say nothing of their literary and theatrical triumphs and their culture-shaping creative output—make for a story, a triplicate biography, that has long needed to be told. Thus, if *Pink Triangle* (a perfect *double entendre* title, by the way, that would have had Williams issuing his honeyed whoop, Capote giggling and Vidal rolling his eyes) had not been written for us, we would have had to research it and type it all up for ourselves.

*Pink Triangle* is the product of **Darwin Porter and Danforth Prince,** the partners behind Blood Moon Productions. Blood Moon has already produced biographies on such folks as Katharine Hepburn (in what turned out to be a highly controversial, highly entertaining tome), J. Edgar Hoover and Clyde Tolson, Elizabeth Taylor, Merv Griffin (*A Life in the Closet*), *Brando Unzipped* and, in one of the most addictively readable biographies of the past few years, the Gabor Sisters.

But as the classicists tell us the past is but preamble, because all that Blood Moon has done before pales in comparison with *Pink Triangle.*

Never before have so many names been dropped—scattered like rose petals at a wedding, actually—as here in these many, many pages. And certainly, never before has Frank Merlo, the most put-upon man who ever lived, had a book dedicated to him (and to actor/writer/taste-setter Stanley Mills Haggart as well.)

Merlo, Tennessee Williams's One Great Love, was deserted by the writer and allowed to shrivel up and die all on his own in an antiseptic hospital room. Which reveals a good bit of what there is to know about Williams. (Along with the fact that he allowed his sister Rose to be first hospitalized and then lobotomized before guiltily writing about her in *The Glass Menagerie* and *Suddenly, Last Summer*.)

The chief weakness of the work is that, in spite of the fact that the book is dedicated to him, Frank Merlo's impact upon Williams's life is reduced to the fact that he accompanied the playwright to most of his triumphant opening nights. The tale of the complex and tormented love between Williams and Merlo is largely left untold. Ditto Gore Vidal's long-time, reportedly chaste bond with Howard Austen and Truman Capote's tortured, alcohol-soaked relationship with Jack Dunphy.

For this is a book of marquee names and not a place in which the deepest emotions are explored.

Such is the fabric of *Pink Triangle:* lovers lost, faces slapped, trysts undertaken and trysts uncovered, and fame and drink and drugs, and New Orleans and Key West and Los Angeles and New York and Rome and Paris and the Amalfi Coast, and the *paparazzi,* the red carpet, and excess—to the point that hundreds of pages into the book it seems as if the dizzying whole of it is an account of the fever dreams of Myra Breckinridge, Holly Golightly, and Blanche DuBois.

Admittedly, the reader suspects that Porter and Prince may err more on Capote's side than on Vidal's in terms of their aforementioned authorial approach to the material—that they may be more *raconteurs* than historians. That they may be unable to bear the idea of not sharing with their reader a particularly juicy anecdote or two just because their sources may a bit more gossip-based than researched fact.

But given the fact that the subjects of the book themselves were nearly delusional on the subject of themselves (to say nothing of each other) it is hard to find fault. Most especially when many the stories contained herein have been oft-repeated (again, often by Williams, Capote, and Vidal, while they were still with us) and are certainly not the creations of the authors.

What we have here in *Pink Triangle* is something over-the-top, compulsively readable, even—to use one of Tennessee Williams's favorite words for those that he hated or loved—deranged. Certainly some of the "tabloid-speak" chapter titles and section headlines bring that particular word to mind: "Marlene Dietrich Lip-Locks Pearl Bailey," "Broadway Falls in Love with a Sweaty Red T-Shirt and Too-Tight Jeans," and perhaps the best when Vidal meets and beds Russian ballet dancer Rudolf Nureyev: "Gore 'Dances' with Rudi in the Nudi."

The tales of old Hollywood, of Elizabeth Taylor calling Tennessee Williams from the set to complain about Paul Newman's behavior ("He's doing everything he can to steal every scene from me, even indulging in male burlesque. He's been stripping down to his underwear and running around, anything to distract from my best dialogue.") of Capote's work on the John Houston/Humphrey Bogart film *Beat the Devil,* of Gore Vidal's insistence on writing a homosexual subtext into *Ben-Hur,* while himself having an affair with one of the film's lead actors, these alone are worth the cost of the book.

To say nothing of Mae West's so disliking Gore Vidal during the making of *Myra Breckinridge* that she firmly instructed him to "Don't come up and see me sometime." Or the truly hilarious ongoing love/hate relationship between Tennessee Williams and actress/gay icon Tallulah Bankhead. Or the Hollywood True Story of the making of *Breakfast at Tiffany's* and of the loving friendship between Truman Capote and Marilyn Monroe, who he had wanted to star in the film.

But add to all this the intertwined jungle that was the relationship among Williams, Capote and Vidal, of the times they vied for things they loved most—especially attention—and the times they enthralled each other and the world, and you have the perfect antidote to the Polar Vortex.

And while, let's face it, the book does in truth have more penis than heart, the authors do show compassion to their subjects, both in times of ill health (brought on variously by overindulgence, alcoholism and old age) and obscurity (Capote was famously "blocked" and unable to complete his final novel *Answered Prayers* after the publication of selected chapters brought about his ruin in Manhattan society; Williams found the title "has been" more and more affixed to his reputation as he turned out vaguer and stranger new works of theater).

Particularly touching is this, Truman Capote's statement of his experience of old age: "My eyes are tired and sad, and I am growing weary day by day. The world has grown stale like a piece of week-old bread left in an abandoned kitchen."

To which Vidal rejoined: "In my fantasy, I dream of going back to Rome in that rented penthouse on top of the decaying 17th century Palacio Origo where Howard Austen and I lived for some thirty years. I had never had a proper human-scale village life anywhere on Earth until I settled there. Literature? Two blocks to our north, back of the Pantheon, Thomas Mann lived and wrote *Buddenbrooks*. Nearby, George Eliot stayed at the Minerva Hotel. Aristo lived in Pantheon Square; Stendhal was also close by. In that apartment, I wrote *Myra Breckinridge* in one month, one spring, from new moon to new moon. But I am too weak to return."

"The question remains. On that upcoming dark and stormy day, as thunder is heard across the skies of Los Angeles, will there be any real sadness at my funeral?"

You may not weep for any of the three—for Tennessee Williams, Truman Capote, or Gore Vidal—but you will, in reading *Pink Triangle*, be enthralled by them and by the over-population of wits, talents, artists, stalkers, hangers-on, and the truly deranged who populated their world.

**Vinton Rafe McCabe** is the author of the novel, *Death in Venice, California*. He's worked as a journalist, and, in turns, a theater, book, and restaurant critic. He is an award-winning poet and a produced playwright, and was the producer/host of the regional PBS TV show "*Artsweek*."

# A VERY SHORT LIST OF WHAT THE DIVAS SAID ABOUT EACH OTHER

Here's **Gore Vidal** (right) with one of his *"passions de passage,"* the ultra-avant-garde modern dancer, **Harold Lang.**

The year was 1947—still early enough to set tongues wagging throughout the "creative community."

Naturally, both Truman and Tennessee took full advantage of Vidal's affair with the flamboyant showman to gossip about it to anyone who was even remotely interested.

Here's **Truman**, as posted on the back cover of his early, seminal, and groundbreaking novel, *Other Voices, Other Rooms*. deliberately posing—with the intention of amplifying both his notoriety and book sales— as underaged but sexually available "jailbait,"

The photo went down in literary history as one of the most provocative and notorious anyone could remember.

**Vidal and Williams** mockingly referred to him, even during the late stages of his physical and emotional decay, as "Little Lolito."

Here's **Frank Merlo** with his long-time companion, **Tennessee Williams**, in the front yard of the house they shared together in Key West.

**Darwin Porter,** their neighbor, and confidant, was fully aware of the degree to which whatever they said and did morphed into hurricane-force gales of gossip, innuendo, and often, ridicule, Every potentially embarrassing nuance was amplified to whomever would listen, by both Truman and Vidal.

*"I have never known anyone to complain as much as The Bird. If he were not dying of some new mysterious illness, he was in mourning for a dead lover, usually discarded long before the cancerous death, or he was suffering from the combinations of various cabals, real and imagined, that were to out to get him"*

—Gore Vidal on Tennessee Williams

*"He was a hell's angel. Having received daily instruction from the Lord of the Flies, he gleefully surfaced to do his dirty work."*

—Gore Vidal on Truman Capote

*"There can be no more painful experience in life than to have to read a novel by Gore Vidal. His talent is as small as his dick. He is Captain Queeg in* The Caine Murtiny. *He's suing me for libel for telling the truth about him. He had to give depositions and had to answer embarrassing questions. I'm releasing his testimony to* New York Magazine. *I will have the greatest single revenge in literary history. The humiliation for him. I live it! I love it! I love it! When he dies, they'll write on his tombstone, 'Here lies Gore Vidal. He messed around with Truman Capote.'"*

—Truman Capote on Gore Vidal

# ZOOMERTIMES TV
## HEALTH • WEALTH • ENTERTAINMENT • LIFESTYLE

**HEEERE'S ANITA!**
As she appeared during a ZoomerTimes
TV interview with Darwin Porter

BLOOD MOON ANNOUNCES THE SELECTION OF ITS NEWEST RELEASE, **PINK TRIANGLE**, AS BOOK OF THE MONTH BY SOUTH FLORIDA'S BEST MAGAZINE FOR SENIORS, *BOOMER TIMES AND SENIOR LIFE MAGAZINE*, AS ANNOUNCED BY THAT MAGAZINE'S PUBLISHER AND FOUNDER,

# ANITA FINLEY

A noted gerontologist whose 23-year publishing history has constantly addressed issues of interest to South Florida's growing population of seniors, Ms. Finley is famous for seminars, workshops, and conventions drawing thousands of consumers interested in lifestyle issues for Boomers. Ms Finley is also famous for her weekly radio programs, scheduled every Saturday from 5am to 8am, Thanks to Ms. Finley's characteristic charm and verve, her blend of consumer issues, arts features, and lifestyle options draws thousands of early-morning listeners for access to experts associated with trends and issues of concern to seniors. *(Tune in to Anita's show every Saturday from 5-BAM through WSBR at 740 on the AM dial; WWNN at 1470 on the AM dial; or at www.wsbrradio.com for live streaming through the internet.)*

According to Ms. Finley, "Blood Moon Productions, particularly in the titles written by Darwin Porter, has consistently published fascinating overviews of Hollywood Remembered, up close and personal, by thousands of Boomers. *Pink Triangle* has captured a behind-the-scenes glimpse of show-biz gaffes, compromises, embarrassments, and ironies never published in any other source. So because so many of our fans are passionately interested in the entertainment industry, and because we adore Darwin's peppery blend of show-biz news and gossip, as featured monthly on our radio show, we're honored to have featured him every month as a columnist in our magazine,"

According to Danforth Prince, Blood Moon's Founder and President, "We're honored with the designation of *Pink Triangle* as book of the month from this prestigious and trendsetting magazine. And we note with special pride the association of *Boomer Times* with the *MIAMI HERALD*, which has included Ms. Finley's magazine as a regular supplement every month to 19,000 subscribers throughout Broward and North Miami-Dade counties."

# BLOOD MOON: THEY BROUGHT YOU LINDA (LOVELACE); THEY BROUGHT YOU ZSA ZSA GABOR AND HER SISTERS; AND THEY BROUGHT YOU HOLLYWOOD BABYLON IN THREE SEPARATE VOLUMES.

## NOW IT'S TIME FOR
# PINK TRIANGLE
The Feuds and Private Lives of Tennessee Williams, Gore Vidal, Truman Capote and Famous Members of Their Entourages, by Darwin Porter. from Blood Moon Productions

**How Myra Breckinridge, IN COLD BLOOD, took a ride on *A Streetcar Named Desire*.**

Softcover, 700 pages, with hundreds of photographs. ISBN 978-1-936003-37-2

## PINK TRIANGLE:
The best compendium of gossip ever published about what was really going on in literary Show-Biz during "the American Century"

## "Hell Hath No Fury Like a Diva Scorned"

\*\*\*

After World War II, three writers, each a homosexual, rose to prominence across the literary landscape of America. *PINK TRIANGLE* documents their ambitions, their slugfests, their roles as media stars, their descents into hell, and their phenomenal success in redefining the scope and texture of entertainment on the Broadway stage, in Hollywood, and in 20th century American literature.

Each of these ferociously competitive writers incited public outrage, defied censorship, and engaged in feuds which were followed, with fascination by the American public, in movies, in TV interviews, and in the tabloids.

In the *Pink Triangle* were **Tennessee Williams** (the lavishly nostalgic survivor of a Gothic Southern upbringing, whose heroines such as the sexually hysterical Blanche DuBois were sometimes accused of being alter egos for his own proclivities); **Truman Capote** (whose wit and bitchery made him the centerpiece of the famously wealthy, until—betrayed and in horror from their depiction in works such as *Answered Prayers*—they flew away), and **Gore Vidal** (the trenchant, imperial, aristocratic classicist whose analyses of The American Empire and the incompetence of its rulers almost propelled him into a successful bid for the U.S. Congress).

Each of these men was a brilliant and frequently vindictive eccentric. Each was intensely competitive, promiscuous, thin-skinned, and sought after by the rich, the famous, and the fabulous. Their interactions, and their outrageous, substance-abusing, profoundly decadent private lives have never before been fully exposed until now.

The story of how this flamboyant and brilliant trio interacted with other celebrities such as **Marilyn Monroe, Elizabeth Taylor, Marlon Brando, Tallulah Bankhead, Sal Mineo, James Dean**, and **Paul Newman**—and with one another—was compiled by **Darwin Porter**, based on secrets he discovered beginning as a young and ambitious bureau chief and entertainment columnist for **THE MIAMI HERALD** in Tennessee Williams' hometown of **Key West, Florida.**

PINK TRIANGLE is an anthology of betrayals and outrage, liberally fueled with sex, drink, and drugs. It illustrates, better and more comprehensively than anything previously published, the behind-the-curtain flamboyance of the literati during the most artistically productive years of "The American Century."

It will change your perceptions of Who Was Who during an era of almost unimaginable change in America's self-definition and its involvement in the arts. **Orville Prescott**, the stodgy critic for *The New York Times*, summed up the legacy of this PINK TRIANGLE: "Once you spill mercury from a bottle, you can never brush it all back in."

![SGN Seattle Gay News]

# PINK TRIANGLE,

## as reviewed by **Maggie Bloodstone** at *the Seattle Gay News*, their edition of June 27, 2014

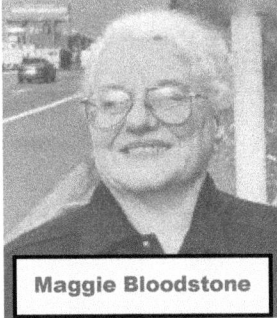

**Maggie Bloodstone**

"This is a book that should be included in the curriculum of Gay 101 for every 20-something Gay man (and an elective for Lesbian women) who have never experienced the trashy catastrophe that was *Boom!* and only knew of *In Cold Blood* from the Phillip Seymour Hoffman flick. It's also primo beach reading for any Gay theatre/gossip queen over the age of 35. And it is definitely one of the top achievements of writer Darwin Porter, co-author/publisher Danforth Prince, and the notorious imprint, **Blood Moon Productions**.

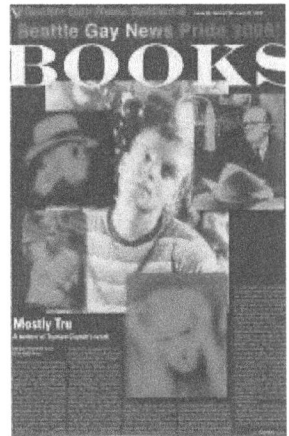

"Imagine Blanche DuBois, Holly Golightly, and Myra Breckenridge attending the Black and White Ball accompanied by Caligula and Stanley Kowalski, sharing their drugs, booze, and carnal charms with anyone who was anyone. That's pretty much the tone and tenor of *The Pink Triangle*... a trifecta of geniuses who turned Broadway, Hollywood, and the literary world on its collective ear in the space of two and a half decades... Three extraordinary men, they partied, feuded, admired, and despised each other for a sizable chunk of late 20th century cultural history... It's depressing to contemplate what America's cultural landscape would look like without the influence of these three men—a lot more dull, a lot less passionate and transgressive, and definitely less trashy and spectacular."

\*\*\*

## PINK TRIANGLE WAS ALSO REVIEWED BY
# DONALD WINDHAM

### WHO WAS DONALD WINDHAM?
HERE IS THE TEXT OF HIS OBITUARY FROM THE NEW YORK TIMES, THEIR EDITION OF JUNE 5, 2010

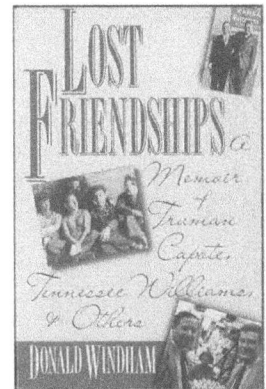

Donald Windham, a novelist and memoirist who left vivid pictures of literary life in New York, both fictional and factual, when he was an intimate of Tennessee Williams, and Truman Capote, died on Monday at his home in Manhattan. He was 89. The death was confirmed by his lawyer, Eugene V. Kokot.

Mr. Windham, who briefly shared a Manhattan apartment with Williams and collaborated with him on the play, plunged into the thick of New York's artistic life after arriving on a Greyhound bus from Atlanta at the age of 19. He formed friendships with Kirstein, George Platt Lynes, Christopher Isherwood, Glenway Wescott and the artists Paul Cadmus and Jared French.

In 1942 he began collaborating with Williams on *You Touched Me!*," based on a story by D. H. Lawrence. It opened on Broadway in 1945, after "The Glass Menagerie" had established Williams as the theater's brightest new star.

Mr. Windham's fiction never reached more than a small audience, but that audience was select. Thomas Mann and Paul Bowles counted themselves as admirers, and E. M. Forster wrote the introduction to his short-story collection "The Warm Country" (1962).

His novels and stories often touched on gay themes, which exposed him to critical contempt, notably with the publication of *Two People* (1965), about a love affair between a New York stockbroker whose wife has left him and a 17-year-old Italian boy in Rome. The novel was savagely reviewed and failed commercially. It was recently republished by Mondial.

His memoirs, however, were warmly received. One of them was *Tennessee Williams's Letters to Donald Windham, 1940-1965* (1977), a book that severely strained the relationship between the two men, and *Lost Friendships* (1987), about his relationships with Williams and Capote. He also published his correspondence with Alice B. Toklas and Forster.

Donald Windham was born on July 2, 1920, in Atlanta, where his mother traded in her grand family house on Peachtree Street as her fortunes declined and went to work as a receptionist at

**Donald Windham** is shown on the left with **Tennessee Williams** during their unhappy collaboration on their play, *You Touched Me*, in 1945.

Decades later, Windham published a memoir, *Lost Friendships*, which infuriated Williams, who never forgave him.

Coca-Cola.

He found his footing quickly. Kirstein, a founder of the New York City Ballet, hired him as an assistant on his magazine, *The Dance Index*, which Mr. Windham edited after Kirstein went into the Army. The collaboration with Williams brought in enough money for him to pursue writing as a career.

In 1943 he met Sandy Campbell, a Princeton undergraduate, who helped publish many of his books through the *Stamperia Valdonega* in Verona, Italy. They were a couple until Mr. Campbell's death in 1988. No immediate family members survive.

In 1950 Mr. Windham published his first novel, *The Dog Star,* about a young Southerner plunged into despair when his best friend from reform school commits suicide.

"I disagree with the advice 'Write about what you know,' " he once wrote. "Write about what you need to know, in an effort to understand."

Although he published abroad in prestigious magazines like *Horizon* and *The Paris Review,* fame eluded him in the United States. He summed up the 1950s succinctly: "Hard work and no success."

His collaboration with Williams on Broadway planted the seeds of future discord. As Williams's reputation ballooned, Mr. Windham found himself nudged to the sidelines. Plans for Williams to direct a play of Mr. Windham's, "The Starless Air," fell apart.

The publication of his correspondence with Williams was intended, in part, to set the record straight, but Williams took offense at the way his character came across.

In a preface, Mr. Windham called his erstwhile partner "the rarest, most intoxicating, the most memorable flower that has blossomed in my garden of good and evil."

Robert Brustein, reviewing the book for *The New York Times,* wrote, "If revenge is a dish that tastes best cold, then Donald Windham has certainly fixed himself a satisfying frozen dinner."

Blood Moon's
## PINK TRIANGLE
### as reviewed by Donald Windham

This is the most turbulent report on this literary trinity ever to hit the public library. Exposed is an unholy trio of celebrity-obsessed hurricanes who terrorized the worlds of film, theater, and publishing. Individually, they were witty, disorderly, scathing, dissipated, licentious, extravagant, and profligate. Collectively, they were time bombs waiting to explode.

In this scandalous memoir, celebrity spinmeister Darwin Porter, after years of intimate familiarity with the three most notorious writers in America, comes clean with the world's first description of their ferocious battles for fame, literary supremacy, and young men. Based on years of dialogue with each of them, this book reveals how Myra Breckinridge, In Cold Blood, took a ride on A Streetcar Named Desire.

"Darwin Porter sent me the rough draft of this bitchfest. It has the fascination of a cobra about to strike. His scattershot profiles of the 20th century's glitterati should lead to his arrest."

**—Donald Windham**

# FROM THE LOS ANGELES BOOK FESTIVAL

## PINK TRIANGLE

Blood Moon proudly announces that *Pink Triangle*, its overview of the Feuds and Private Lives of three of 20th-century America's most influential writers, was designated for an HONORABLE MENTION at the 2014 LOS ANGELES BOOK FESTIVAL. The award, presented at a gala ceremony on March 22 within Hollywood's most historic hotel, the Roosevelt, is one of the approximately two dozen prestigious awards presented to Blood Moon for its output, during the previous decade, of books which challenge many of the prevailing assumptions about celebrity in America.

As stated by **Bruce Haring**, a spokesperson for the Awards, "The Los Angeles Book Festival is an annual competition honoring excellence in books, with particular focus on projects that deserve closer attention from the film-making community. Congratulations to Blood Moon and its authors, especially Darwin Porter, for his methodical research into literary and showbiz history, his storytelling flair, and for his clear delineation of some of the oral histories of show-biz which might otherwise have been lost forever. "

## *Pink Triangle*, as Reviewed by *the Huffington Post*

THE
HUFFINGTON
POST

"I have been a friend and follower of Blood Moon Productions' tomes for years, and always marveled at the amount of information in their books--it's staggering.

The index alone to *Pink Triangle* runs to 21 pages and the scale of names in it runs like a *Who's Who* of American social, cultural and political life through much of the 20th century ... The only remedy is for you to run out this February, in time for Valentine's Day, and buy *Pink Triangle.*"

**--Perry Brass in THE HUFFINGTON POST**

# WHAT READERS CAN EXPECT FROM PINK TRIANGLE

IT'S A CORNUCOPIA OF SCANDAL—A JUICY OVERLOAD—ABOUT THE VANITIES OF AMERICA'S
MOST FAMOUS TRIO OF WRITERS,
AND ATTEMPTS BY OTHER CELEBRITIES TO EITHER INDULGE OR AVOID THEM.

✓ Nina Vidal's affair with Clark Gable and her attempt to marry him and make him the stepfather of her young son, Gore Vidal.

✓ Montgomery Clift and Marlon Brando--Both of them seduced by all three of this book's namesake authors Truman Capote and his mother, Nina Capote, competing for Errol Flynn and John Garfield, *et. al* .

✓ Nina's lesbian involvements with Marlene Dietrich and Tallulah Bankhead, and her affairs with Charles Lindbergh and Henry Luce.

✓ Gore Vidal's seduction of Jack Kerouac.

✓ On the set of *Beat the Devil*, Truman Capote sleeps with director John Huston. Humphrey Bogart "pays the penalty" for losing an arm-wrestling contest to Capote.

✓ When rival teams meet at Andover, Massachusetts, in the shower, a young Gore Vidal "strikes out" with a seventeen-year-old baseball pitcher, and future president, **George Herbert Walker Bush**.

✓ Gore Vidal's movie star seductions in Hollywood of the 1950s: Peter Lawford, Sal Mineo, Dennis Hopper, Dick York, Guy Madison, Anthony Perkins, and Tom Drake, Judy Garland 's "Boy Next Door" in *Meet Me in St. Louis*.

✓ The affair between Gore Vidal and Rudolf Nureyev.

✓ Elvis Presley wanted to appear in dramas on the screen written by "those two queers," a reference to William Inge and Tennessee Williams.

✓ In Havana, Tennessee Williams confronts Ernest Hemingway and ends up nude in the steambath with "my dreamboat," Fidel Castro. The Cuban dictator enlists the playwright's help in winning the approval of two of his supporters in the United States (Marilyn Monroe and Marlon Brando). Castro wanted the pair to appear together in a film about his revolutionary days in the hills, with Brando cast as Fidel, and Marilyn cast as his mistress. Marilyn's secret trip from Mexico City to Havana, specifically organized as part of a rendezvous with Castro.

✓ At last, the true story of why Tennessee Williams appears on all those lists of JFK's seductions. The details of his encounter with JFK (then a Senator) at his Palm Beach compound, as told to three of his female confidante-- Margaret Foresman, Marion Vacarro, and Maria St. Just—in Key West.

✓ How Truman Capote fell in love with, and expressed it sexually, with a cold-blooded killer, Perry Smith, during his research in western Kansas for *In Cold Blood*.

# *Pink Triangle* is a 700-page overview of a toxic saga of literary feuds that rocked the glitterati of the mid-20th century

In the immediate aftermath of World War II, three writers, each a homosexual, rose to prominence across the literary landscape of America. PINK TRIANGLE documents their ambitions, their slugfests, their roles as media stars, their descents into hell, and their phenomenal success in redefining the scope and texture of entertainment on the Broadway stage, in Hollywood, and in 20th century American literature.

Each of these ferociously competitive writers incited public outrage, defied censorship, and engaged in feuds which were followed, with fascination, in literary journals, in TV interviews, and in the tabloids. Collectively, they changed America's cultural landscape forever.

The members of this Pink Triangle were Tennessee Williams, Truman Capote, and Gore Vidal: three brilliant, thin-skinned and strong-willed eccentrics.

The story of how this flamboyant and brilliant trio interacted with other celebrities and with one another was compiled by Darwin Porter, based on information he gathered, beginning as a young and ambitious bureau chief for THE MIAMI HERALD in Tennessee Williams' home town of Key West, Florida.

It's a book unlike anything ever published--an anthology of slugfests and scandal, liberally fueled with sex, drink, and drugs, that illustrates the behind-the-curtain flamboyance of the *literati* during the most artistically productive years of "The American Century."

It contains 46 short but scandalous chapters, each devoted to a separate creative statement in the entwined network of these ferociously competitive writers. Collectively,

Young **Darwin Porter,** photographed during the peak of intensity of his conversations with members of the Pink Triangle

The "not so underground' omnisexual playgrounds of urban American life in the 1930s and 40s were brilliantly depicted by the queer artist **Paul Cadmus** (1904-1999), whose gritty works are revered in major museums worldwide, today.

Above, in *The Fleet Is In* (1934), sailors carouse with women and other men in a raunchy, alcohol-soaked preface to intimacies to come  Truman Capote, Tennessee Williams, and Gore Vidal's sex lives thrived in the illegal sexual underground of the war years and the decades that followed. Darwin Porter did his best to describe the contexts of the underground postwar era within the pages of **Pink Triangle.**

they illuminate the inner yearnings and presuppositions of the *avant garde* during what critics now define as "The Golden Age of American letters."

The friendships of these authors ranged from street hustlers to A-list celebrities from the Entertainment Industry and from High Society, all of whom seemed desperate for a role in one of their plays, an invitation to one of their parties, or access to their ravenous network of press agents and publicists.

Unlike Gore and Truman, Tennessee Williams was a late bloomer to the world of sex, delaying entry until he reached his late twenties. After his move to New Orleans, he became sucked into the world of the *demi-monde,* peopled with prostitutes, overt homosexuals, drug addicts, alcoholics, gamblers, and thieves, many of whom would later appear as characters in his plays.

In time, Tennessee would seduce, or be seduced by, a vast array of street hustlers and paid companions, as well as illustrious screen icons such as James Dean, Marlon Brando, Paul Newman, Warren Beatty, and Montgomery Clift. At one point late in 1959, Tennessee shared a steambath in Havana with his alltime macho fantasy, Fidel Castro, described in a chapter of *Pink Triangle.* That chapter includes astonishing appearances from Hemingway, Jean-Paul Sartre, Simone de Beauvoir, and the very bitchy, flamboyantly bisexual English critic, Kenneth Tynan.

As Tennessee's fame grew, it seemed that every major female star in America wanted to star in one of his movies, plays, or teleplays. Many of them did, but others, such as Gloria Swanson and Marilyn Monroe, failed. Elizabeth Taylor starred in three of his films, the most memorable of which was as Maggie the Cat in *Cat on a Hot Tin Roof.* She also played Catherine Holly in *Suddenly, Last Summer.* With Richard Burton, she also starred in *Boom!* as Flora Goforth, a fabulously wealthy aging actress facing death.

Other career milestones were achieved through Tennessee's dramas by Bette Davis as the horny innkeeper, Maxine Faulk, and later by Ava Gardner in *Night of the Iguana*; Tallulah Bankhead, whose interpretations of at least two of Tennessee's heroines led to cascades of laughter and her indelible reputation as the feminine aspect (or was it the masculine aspect) of Tennessee's alter ego; Vivien Leigh, whose day in and day out channeling of the sexually hysterical Blanche DuBois led her to the brink of madness and also to a hot affair with Marlon Brando; Katharine Hepburn (no actress could have played a psychotically protective matriarch better than she did); Anna Magnani, whose feud with Burt Lancaster on the set of *The Rose Tattoo* made headlines throughout Europe; Jane Fonda, Natalie Wood, and Helen Hayes, among many others. This book reveals intimate details about all of them.

**Gore Vidal** with his boyhood best friend, **Jimmie Trimble.**

Decades after Trimble's death, Gore continued, publicly describing Trimble as "the love of my life."

"A part of me died with this brave Marine on the sands of Iwo Jima on February 2, 1945."

**Truman Capote** with his longtime companion, **Jack Dunphy**—"the only person who stayed with me after everyone else rejected me."

**Bette Davis,** "a hellion on wheels," as she appeared in the NYC stage production of Tennessee Williams' *The Night of the Iguana.*

EVERYBODY —including Tennessee and his companion, Frankie Merlo—had a lot to say about it. Porter describes it fully in *Pink Triangle.*

It was inevitable that Tennessee would eventually meet Gore Vidal. "In the beginning, Gore and I became great friends, in spite of his many faults. Once, we briefly shared an apartment together. I got to see him in the nude. The less said about that, the better. That treacherous soul wanted to become known as the American Balzac."

When Tennessee later met Truman Capote, he found him filled with fantasies and mischief. "Truman speaks with a forked tongue," Tennessee claimed. "He's a sodomite's delight--a monster unleashed from vaginal portals."

Actually, about half of everything Truman claimed was true; with the rest, he took

Notoriously indiscreet, **Truman Capote** bragged about sexual conquests which involved many of the household names of the 20th-century elite: *Left to right, above,* they included **Albert Camus, André Gide, Errol Flynn** (depicted above as he appeared in *The Adventures of Robin Hood;* 1938)**,** and Lana Turner's well-hung co-star, **John Garfield.**

his own kind of poetic license. Back when he defined himself as young and pretty, he is said to have seduced both John Garfield and Errol Flynn. That may indeed have happened, But he invented a sexual union, for press and publicity purposes, and for the gratification of his ego, with both André Gide and Albert Camus, and bragged about it widely to other writers.

There is no doubt that Truman moved into the world of the very rich and the discreetly famous, and that he learned, after years in their gossipy midst, many of their secrets. Among his closest friends was Babe Paley, once the best-dressed woman in the world, and the wife of Bill Paley, the head honcho at CBS.

Referring to them as "my beautiful swans," Truman's friends included Gloria Guinness, Princess Lee Radziwill (sister of Jackie Kennedy), and Katharine Graham, owner of *The Washington Post* and *Newsweek*, and the most influential woman in America.

Author Katharine Anne Porter called Capote "the pimp on the face of American literature." Actress Estelle Winwood claimed, "He had the warmth of an alligator." He defined himself as "an alcoholic, a drug addict, a homosexual, and a genius."

In 1948, Gore Vidal had shocked America with his publication of *The City and the Pillar*, the story of a doomed homosexual love affair during an era when the subject was "the Love that Dared Not Speak Its Name." Its publication outraged his sexually voraciouos mother, contributing to one of the most poisonous matriarchal conflicts in the history of American literature. Even the usually liberal *New York Times* announced that it would no longer review any of Gore's novels. Time, and *The Times* itself, changed over the years. Gore went on to write a series of highly successful novels, many of them political, such as *Burr, Lincoln*, or *Washington, D.C.*

It was the tale of an outrageous transsexual, *Myra Breckinridge*, that elevated Gore Vidal into a household name. Even Mae West came out of retirement to star in the movie version, playing the role of a horny talent scout who, instead of a casting couch, uses a four-poster bed in her office to audition new male talent.

Gore, like Tennessee, also wrote plays, including *The Best Man*. President Kennedy and Jackie flew to New York from Washington to attend a performance. Reportedly, JFK recognized a portrait of himself in one of the characters, an adulterous politician.

Gore's later involvement with, and feud with, elements associated with the founder of *Penthouse* magazine, Bob Guccione, later made headlines with the release of a film he at first scripted, and then denounced, *Caligula*, one of the most maligned and viciously condemned cult films in history.

Before Gore, Truman, and Tennessee, America, of course, fostered many great gay writers, including Henry James, Gertrude Stein, Willa Cather, Hart Crane, Thornton Wilder, and Walt Whitman, among so many others. But none had been so openly homosexual as Tennessee, Gore, and Truman.

In time, all three writers turned on each other over various betrayals. Gore even sued Truman for claiming in print that Bobby Kennedy had forcibly evicted him from a party at the White House.

In one of the completed (and published) segments of his otherwise unfinished novel, *Answered Prayers*, Truman crafted a hideous caricature of Tennessee, identifying him as "Mr. Wallace." Tennessee was described as a "chunky, paunchy, booze-puffed runt with a play mustache glued above laconic lips." His hotel suite was littered with dog feces, and he spoke in "a way down yonder voice as mushy as sweet potato pie," Truman's description of Tennessee continued, mercilessly, in ways described in *Pink Triangle*.

But in a nutshell, Truman's satirical darts—most of them aimed directly at the heart of his friends, competitors, and detractors-- exiled him forever from the social world.

Vidal lost his virginity to his boyhood lover, Jimmy Trimble. At the age of twelve, Capote was raped at St. John's Military Academy in Ossining, New York. Tennessee lost his virginity to Bette Reitz, a fellow student at the University of Iowa. He was 26 years old.

Of the three writers, only Gore lived to the ripe old age of 86, dying in 2013. He said, "Truman and Tennessee were like delicate moths, a Blanche DuBois in *A Streetcar Named Desire*. I was the strongwilled *Myra Breckinridge*, who could be possessed by no man. I outlived my worst nemeses."

"I hope," Gore continued, "that some of my political works will be read in the 22nd Century when only three or four literary scholars will have heard of Truman and Tennessee."

# TONY MARTIN & CYD CHARISSE

## HOWARD HUGHES OFFERED HER MINK COATS AND DIAMONDS, BUT MARTIN OFFERED LOVE

Three views of **Tony Martin:** *Middle photo* with his wife, **Cyd Charisse.**

*Right photo:* **The Martin-Charisse family** with their Baby Boomer son, **Tony Jr.**, in 1950.

To loosely paraphrase a line from a Beatles' song, "Will you still love me when I'm 95?" If the man is Tony Martin and the woman is Cyd Charisse, the answer is a resounding "yes."

The slick-haired vocalist, Alvin Morris (later Tony Martin), was born in San Francisco in 1912, four years before America entered World War I. In March of 2008, he was the oldest living performer in show business.

A few Saturdays ago, I caught his act, a five-night engagement at Feinstein's, within the Loews Regency Hotel, on Park Avenue in New York City. His voice, of course, is not what it was when he made *Ziegfeld Girl* in 1941 and sang "You Stepped Out of a Dream." In that star-studded musical, he serenaded three of the most glamourous women who ever lived--Lana Turner, Judy Garland, and Hedy Lamarr.

Lovely **Lana Turner** serenaded by **Tony Martin** singing "You Stepped Out of a Dream" in *Ziegfeld Girls* (1941).

**Mirror Mirror on the Wall, Who's the Campiest of Them All?**

Three "Über-Glams" factoring into the "eye candy' accessorized by Martin's gallantry in *Ziegfeld Girls* included (left to right) Eurovixen **Hedy Lamarr, Judy Garland,** and "The Sweater Girl, aka the already-noted **lovely Lana Turner.**

At the beginning of that New York event, Tony needed a little help in ascending the steps to the stage. But once he was there, the audience returned to the 1940s and 50s when he launched into sixteen numbers, beginning with "Almost Like Being in Love." His fans loved him, especially because of his nostalgic anecdotes. He had known virtually everybody in show business, including Frank Sinatra and Marilyn Monroe. Tony was slated to be in her last film, *Something's Got to Give* (1962). But MM was fired and the film was never made. She died shortly thereafter.

That night, onstage in 2008, Tony sang some of his biggest numbers, including Cole Porter's "Begin the Beguine." Fortunately, when it was new, Bing Crosby turned down that song. Tony's other big hit, "There's No Tomorrow" (1950), was adapted from the Neapolitan ballad, "O Sole Mio." Elvis Presley later turned it into another hit, "It's Now or Never."

For a performer of his years, Martin claims, "I'm still in pretty good shape. I'll go on as long as I can. It makes me feel younger. Dear, sweet ladies still swoon over me."

As a performer who had been singing since the 1930s, Tony still looked like ... well, Tony Martin. Not so Cyd Charisse. The years had taken a toll, and she no longer resembled the bright, bubbling star of *Singin' in the Rain* (1952). That same year, she insured her long legs for $1 million, topping the alltime record set by Betty Grable.

Swathed in ermine and diamonds, **Cyd Charisse** appears in this 1957 promotional photo for MGM's *Silk Stockings*, a dance-a-thon film that showed off her legs and made her famous.

Born in Amarillo, Texas, in 1921, Cyd was, for a while, the dancing partner of Fred Astaire and Gene Kelly. In *Silk Stockings* (1957), the remake of *Ninotchka*, her "Red Blues" number is one of the most enthralling ever recorded on film, but her performances as the icy Russian gave the original star of the 1939 version, Greta Garbo, no competition. Ironically, Cyd, too, had been set to star in MM's last film, cast as "the other woman."

In 1937, Tony Martin married the glamourous blonde star and singer, Alice Faye, one of the biggest entertainers in Hollywood musicals. A whole new generation became familiar with her, thanks to the wildly successful sitcom, *All in the Family*. She was Archie Bunker's dream girl.

Martin's marriage to Faye lasted until 1940, when the couple divorced.

During the late 1940s, Tony was in love with Rita Hayworth, successfully maintaining a torrid affair until the Titian-haired goddess called him and announced. "It's all over, Tony, but it was fun while it lasted. I'm going back to my husband. Goodbye." Rita, of course, was referring to Orson Welles.

One night in 1947, Tony met the glamourous, seductive Cyd.

"She stepped out of a dream," he later recalled.

In wooing her, Tony faced some stiff competition in the form of reclusive billionaire Howard Hughes. "He could give her everything," Tony said. "Jewelry, furs, a movie studio, an airline. I could give her love and Cyd went for my love instead of Howard's billions. A gold digger she was not."

There was one problem, however. "It was obvious that I couldn't have her unless I could get her to marry me. So I proposed." Their 1948 marriage became one of the most successful and long-lasting in show business history, resulting in the birth of Tony Martin Jr. in 1950.

I'm a one-woman man," he once said, "the most faithful husband in show business. When I'm captured, I'm nailed."

Borrowing a title from his 1953 film, Tony claimed that Cyd was "Easy to Love."

The love of Tony Martin and Cyd may continue forever, but not on this planet. After suffering a heart attack on June 16, 2008, Cyd was rushed to a hospital, where she died the following day at the age of 86.

After a seven-decade career, Tony Martin, born Alvin Morris, died on July 27, 2012, at the age of 98 in Los Angeles.

*Silk Stocking's* (Cyd Charisse's "masterpiece") was a musical remake of MGM's *Ninotchka* (1939), a tongue-in-cheek satire of Josef Stalin's Soviet Union. In it, **Greta Garbo** *(left)*, cast as a humorless communist bureaucrat, resists the gallant and very capitalist overtures of **Melvyn Douglas**.

Here's **Cyd Charisse,** near the peak of her energy, talent, and beauty, in a still shot from *Easy to Love.*

Before marrying Cyd, Tony Martin married **Alice Faye** *(left)* and fell madly in love with **Rita Hayworth** *(right)*

The demented bisexual billionaire, **Howard Hughes** tried to marry Cyd too, but based on her love for Tony Martin, Cyd said NO.

**HEEEERE'S MARILYN!** as she appeared off the set during rehearsals in 1962 for *Something's Got to Give.*

Tony Martin got a part in it too, but the film was never made. Marilyn was fired before it was completed, and shortly thereafter, she died.

# HOWARD HUGHES
## HELL'S ANGEL

### THIS IS WHAT HAPPENS WHEN A DEMENTED BILLIONAIRE HITS HOLLYWOOD

### HOWARD HUGHES, HELL'S ANGEL
**(from Boomer Time's edition of March 2005)**

Thanks in part to THE AVIATOR, the world already knows about Howard Hughes' filming of *Hell's Angels,* his links to blonde goddess Jean Harlow, his transglobal flight, his obsessive tinkering with *The Outlaw,* the bra he designed for Jane Russell, and the Senate investigations associated with his Spruce Goose. Many readers know about his long hair and fingernails, his drug addictions, his obsessive-compulsive disorder, and his role as America's first billionaire.

This, however, is a journey into the private and shadowy world of Howard Hughes, revealing for the first time the inside details about destructive and usually scandalous associations with other Hollywood players.

It's an astonishing tale of outrageous fortune, unbounded ambition, and tragic greed, the signs of which were already visible during Hughes's years as a teenager. It's the story of a man whom most of America celebrated, at least briefly, as a genuine hero, and a man whom many of his former associated loved to vilify.

Hughes led a life of almost unprecedented debauchery, at least for his era. This biography documents the corruption and the A-list legends who collaborated. Hughes's sexual and emotional odyssey is described frankly and even graphically, without apologies to the faint of heart. Throughout the unimaginable changes that affected America between Hughes's birth in 1905 and the sinister circumstances of his death in 1976, this biography gives an insider's perspective about what money can buy--and what it can't.

Hughes emerges as the century's greatest Lothario, with origins that included a devouring and incestuous mother, an indulgent but absent father, and seductions of the greatest all-star cast of lovers--male and female—ever assembled in a single lifetime.

Hughes feverishly seduced some of the world's greatest women, but in this epic biography, he is also dragged kicking and screaming out of the closet. As his pimp, Johnny Meyer, once said: "Bossman was an equal opportunity seducer. The gender of his victim didn't matter. He had just one requirement: Beauty."

Howard was involved, some-times pivotally, in Hollywood murders whose victims included Paul Bern (Jean Harlow's tragic husband); Thelma Todd ("Hot Toddy"); and David Bacon, publicized as "the handsomest man in Hollywood."

There were peripheral involvements with the mysterious deaths of as many as four or five lesser luminaries as well.

Thanks in part to these revelations, the canon of Hollywood legend will

He was impossibly rich, impossibly demanding, and impossibly influential in industries that were vital to the American War Effort. They included the manufacture of aviation supplies and sexually suggestive Entertainment that kept work forces motivated.

He was **Howard Hughes**, an eventually demented obsessive-compulsive who even made a (failed) bid for the U.S. presidency.

As he aged, he maneuvered his way into the beds of every Hollywood celebrity who mattered, and eventually shunned contact with everyone except his closest "handlers," some of whom manipulated and abused him. Darwin Porter's biography of the "Angel from Hell" is widely acknowledged as the best ever published.

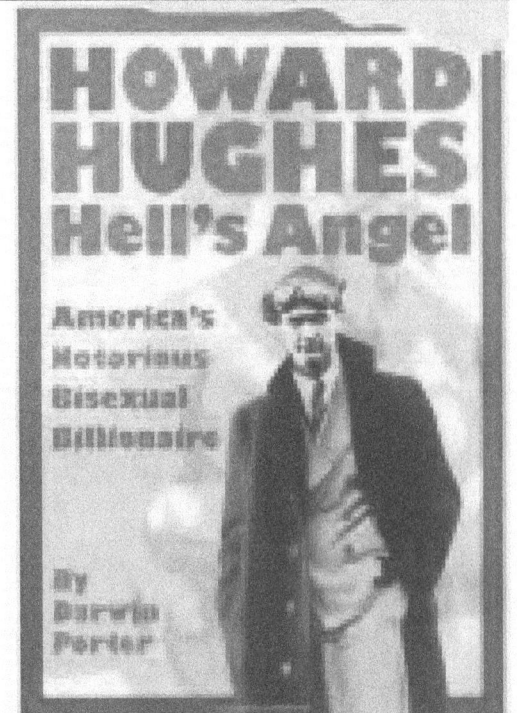

*Widely reviewed in the mainstream press, this one-of-a-kind insight into the American Experience was the WINNER of a respected literary award from the Los Angeles Book Festival.*

844 pages, with photos. Available everywhere now, online and in bookstores

ISBN 978-1-936003-13-6

293

never be the same. The author's rundown on the relationship of Hughes with Cary Grant, Tyrone Power, Ava Gardner, Bette Davis, and Katharine Hepburn challenges virtually everything that has ever been filmed or written about those famous figures.

This is an intimate, carefully authenticated account of a great but bizarre American life, often drawn from courtiers who factored in some way into Hughes's empire.

From his reckless pursuit of love as a rich teenager to his final days as a demented and decaying fossil, he tasted the best and worst of the century he occupied. Along the way, he changed the world of aviation and entertainment forever.

Porter's biography is a tribute to a flawed but majestic American icon. As one critic said, "If Howard Hughes did not exist, no one would dare invent him. His life would defy a novelist!"

This biography reveals inside details about his destructive and usually scandalous associations with other Hollywood players.

*** 

*"The Aviator flew both ways. Porter's biography presents new allegations about Hughes' shady dealings with some of the biggest names of the 20th century."*

—New York Daily News

*"Darwin Porter's access to film industry insiders and other Hughes confidants supplied him with the resources he needed to create a portrait of Hughes that both corroborates what other Hughes biographies have divulged, and go them one better."*

—Foreword Magazine

"Thanks to this bio of Howard Hughes, we'll never be able to look at the old pinups in quite the same way again."

—The Times (London)

Winner of a respected literary award from the Los Angeles Book Festival, this book gives an insider's perspective about debauchery.

*** 

**Actor, Stabbed in Back, Dies in Mystery Here**
Victim Succumbs Pleading for Help After His Car Leaps Curb and Stops in Field

## MYSTERIOUS HOLLYWOOD DEATHS

Was Howard involved in the sudden unexpected deaths of *photos top to bottom*

1) Jean Harlow's husband, **Paul Bern**? or

2) Greta Keller's husband, **David Bacon**?, and,

3) through (Pat DiCiccio lover and short term husband of, among others, Gloria Vanderbilt) **Thelma Todd**

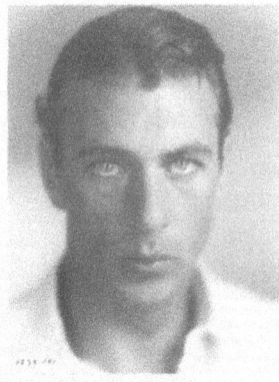

**REVELATIONS** that hit many Classic Hollywood fans by surprise involved the **PREDATORY BISEXUALITY of Howard Hughes**, as revealed in Porter's book through eyewitness accounts of **THE AVIATOR's FLINGS** with (*left photo*) **Ava Gardner,** (*middle photo*) **Gary Cooper**, and (*right photo*) both **Katharine Hepburn** and **Cary Grant.**

# SECRETS OF THE DEMENTED BILLIONAIRE
# HOWARD HUGHES
# EXPOSED

In his new tell-all biography, *HOWARD HUGHES: HELL'S ANGEL*, Darwin Porter, one of America's leading celebrity expose journalists, reveals the pansexual life and intrigues of one of the 20th Century's most enigmatic figures. The publication of this bio is timed to coincide with the worldwide release in mid-December of Martin Scorsese's big-budget film *The Aviator*, starring Leonardo DiCaprio as Howard Hughes.

It's unlike anything ever published previously about Hughes, who was a character who inspired endless gossip, and dozens of books and magazine articles both during his lifetime and after his death.

Porter's book, more than any biography of Hughes that's preceded it, is a tale of debauchery, corruption, and what money can buy ... or what it can't buy. Other bios have documented broad but relatively 'safe' (i.e., uncontroversial) aspects of Hughes' life--his career in aviation, his investments in Las Vegas, his paranoic health concerns, and the long-lasting coma that punctuated the final days of his life.

But in vivid contrast, Porter's book takes readers on an inspection of the Hughes boudoirs of yesterday, in and out of which moved a mind-boggling cast, only some of whom were female. It also looks at some of the dirtier deals that inspired oral speculation but not, until now, a detailed and carefully researched analysis in published form.

In *Hell's Angel,* the dashing, handsome, hyper-wealthy movie mogul, aviator, playboy, and the century's greatest Lothario emerges in all his flesh and blood--a true "warts-and-all" portrait—with more than a bit of attention to the traumas of his spectacularly dysfunctional family.

## THE NEAR-EXTINCTION
### OF A HOLLYWOOD LEGEND

Cynics told **Darwin Porter** that the story of **Howard Hughes** was on the verge of extinction until director/producer **Martin Scorsese a**dapted his story for the movies.

Here's a poster for **THE AVIATOR** (2004) a movie that touched on (but never even tried to comprehensively cover) the convoluted life of its subject, Howard Hughes. It starred **Leonardo DiCaprio** as the alienated (some said "insane') genius.

A few of the objects of Howard's desire managed to elude him, but not many. The list of those who fled from his seduction sofas included Joan Crawford; Joan Fontaine; Sophia Loren; Jane Russell; Elizabeth Taylor (he wanted to pay a million dollars for her); Robert Mitchum; the heavily endowed Dominican playboy Porfirio Rubirosa; a young John F. Kennedy; and, years later, his widow, Jacqueline Kennedy.

Insights into each of the behind-the-scenes, headline-grabbing events of Hughes' life are outlined within *Howard Hughes: Hell's Angel*. They include, but go far beyond, such episodes as Jane Russell's legendary bra and the ill-fated flight of the Spruce Goose.

In 1976, *Time* was one of the first publications to break the story that Hughes had died, his skeletal frame shrunken beyond recognition, as he was being flown from his hideaway in Mexico to his hometown of Houston. After the news of his death broke, a reporter, challenging the Duchess of Windsor's famous slogan, wrote that the aviator's life "disproves that you can never be too rich or too thin."

***

*Note to Editors: Blood Moon Productions and its administration wants to clearly state that, as of mid-November, 2004, there are no publishing or business-related links of any kind between Martin Scorsese's film The Aviator and Darwin Porter's biography, Howard Hughes: Hell's Angel.*

*The production of the book and the production of the film have occurred as completely independent events, and each will almost certainly present radically different interpretations of Howard Hughes, his accomplishments, and key events in his personal life and career. To date, there has been absolutely no communication of any kind between the two organizations, and to date, neither organization has either refuted or supported the merits of the other's artistic product. But there is certainly room for controversy.*

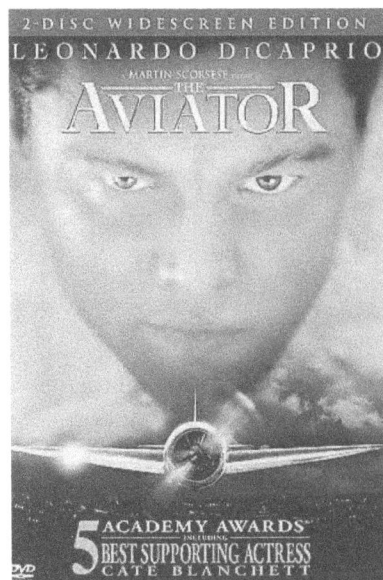

# DID HOWARD HUGHES REALLY LIVE TO THE AGE OF 96?

### And
## DESPERATELY TRYING TO ESCAPE FROM BOXES

*BOXES, The Secret Life of Howard Hughes*, by Douglas Wellman
as reviewed by Darwin Porter

When a great or infamous man dies under mysterious circumstances, there is often bizarre speculation about his demise that can last for decades. "Elvis" was recently seen in a Sioux City shopping mart buying peanut butter and bananas for white bread sandwiches. "Hitler" is still alive and was just spotted in Argentina the other day, although getting rather old at this point.

The mysterious death of a woman can also lead to unfounded speculation. While working as bureau chief for *The Miami Herald* in Key West in 1959, I was sent to Big Pine Key to interview "Amelia Earhart," the doomed aviator missing since July 2, 1937, and the subject of a recent movie.

The real Earhart disappeared on July 2, 1937 on a circumnavigational flight of the globe. She was last heard from somewhere near tiny Howland Island in the Pacific.

The woman I interviewed had some convincing proof that she was actually Amelia. But she flunked three questions I'd carefully constructed, the answers of which would be known to the real Amelia Earhart.

The latest mystery man to return from the dead is Howard Hughes, the famed aviator and mogul who once owned RKO Studios. In the 2004 biopic, Leonardo DiCaprio played Hughes in *The Aviator*, a film that had almost nothing to do with the subject himself.

Generating a lot of tabloid exposure is a book, *Boxes: The Secret Life of Howard Hughes*, authored by Douglas Wellman. If you like to believe in the tooth fairy, Hughes lived to the age of 96, faking his own death. He was said to have married Eva McLelland (now deceased) in the Panama Canal Zone in 1970, a union lasting to his death in 2001.

Eva called herself an Elizabeth Taylor look-alike. Having seen her picture in 1970, I determined she looked as much like Dame Elizabeth as Carol Burnett.

According to *Boxes*, the tycoon assumed the identity of one Verner (Nik) Nicely, who spent a lot of time wandering in the Alabama woods without any clothes on.

Howard Hughes was not the only person of his era with an abiding fascination for airplanes. Depicted above is **Amelia Earhart,** the aviatrix who disappeared over the Pacific in 1937, the year Darwin Porter was born.

More than 20 years after her unexplained disappearance, an imposter defined herself as the mysterious flyer "suddenly returned from exile." After interviewing her, young Darwin, then a news reporter with the **Miami Herald**, re-affirmed the stranger's status as an imposter, and wrote a story about it.

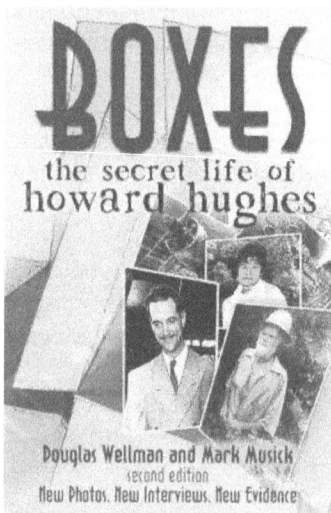

Decades of my own life were spent researching a biography called *Howard Hughes: Hell's Angel*. It was just reprinted in 2010, since interest in the billionaire aviator and movie mogul never dies.

In 1976 the body of the feeble man, former Playboy of the Western World, was lying in a $2,000-a-night penthouse in the Acapulco Princess Hotel in Mexico. Right before his death, the frail body, riddled with needles, was fading fast, suffering from dehydration and malnutrition. While he was still breathing, Hughes was examined by Dr. Lawrence Chaffin, who had helped him survive his almost-fatal plane crash over Beverly Hills in 1946, and who had administered to him ever since. He was also examined by his chief physician, Dr. Wilbur Thain. Both doctors who knew Hughes intimately said their patient was the real Howard Hughes.

Hughes died at 10 o'clock on the morning of April 5, 1976 and was placed on a private plane flying to his native Houston. Rumors surfaced even at the time that the actual Hughes had been murdered in 1968 in Las Vegas and that the corpse flown into Texas was an impostor.

Hughes' ailing aunt, Annette Lummis, got the rumor mill spinning again when she claimed that the cadaver was not her nephew. She'd last seen him in 1938.

As for Nik Nicely we'd call him a nutbag. If he were running naked through the Alabama woods, it was probably to escape a butterfly net.

We will believe the claims of the book "Boxes," when pigs learn to fly, as the saying goes.

**BOXES**
**the secret life of**
**howard hughes**

Douglas Wellman and Mark Musick
second edition
new Photos. new Interviews. new Evidence

There was a lot wrong with this recent biography of Howard Hughes , **Boxes,** spearheaded by Douglas Wellman. A review by Darwin Porter, positioned on this page, describes what sounded screwy

\*\*\*

# AH-NOLD & RAMBO

## AGING ACTION HEROES RETURN TO KILL AGAIN

Call it a blast from the past. The big box office names in action hero movies today carry their AARP cards and are virtually the same as they were back in the Reagan 1980s or early 90s.

The butt-kicking heroes of yesterday, including Arnold Schwarzenegger or Sylvester Stallone, are appearing on the screens of 2014, alongside a number of so-called "badass women." These men are no longer viewed as an endangered species.

Foreigners, especially, flock to see these aging Hollywood stars of our immediate past far more than they go to watch such younger action heroes as Chris Hemsworth, 30. Worldwide, producers know that the old guys usually attract bigger box office than the younger challengers to the throne.

"Age is no longer a disease in movies," claimed film student Norma Jones. Another critic said, "Let's face it: It's no fun watching some buffed 23-year-old mow down a room of bad guys. It's more thrilling to see some grandfather type cracking wise and laying waste a pack of terrorists."

Of course, there are physical risks for older stars. As Schwarzenegger admits, "At night, you've got to put a lot of ice on your knees and hips. You need daily cortisone shots."

Even Stallone confesses that he no longer is either Rocky or Rambo. "We move a little slower," he said. "Your body is like a machine. The parts wear out."

In contrast to what is happening today, with older heroes on screen, in the 1980s *Cocoon* was one of the few films that dealt with age. And in that movie, a coven of Florida senior citizens have to use "alien pods" for rejuvenation.

Foreign sales now account for a staggering 70 percent of box office grosses for American films, as opposed to 20 percent only a few years ago. Stateside movie audience demographics are also changing. Young people seem to be staying home by the millions, surfing the web.

After a long absence, Baby Boomers are once again flocking to movie houses, as they did when they were young. In recent years, Baby Boomer attendance went from an annual 11 million to more than 14 million.

Once on the screen, Schwarzenegger, 66 today, vowed, "I'll be back." He's keeping his promise. His cheesy Hercules and Conan the Destroyer are back bigtime. The seven-time Mr. Olympia bodybuilder went from being a monosyllabic movie star to a not very successful governor of California to coming back once again as a monosyllabic star.

He stunned the world of the 80s with his skimpy outfits, powerful muscles, and on-screen killing sprees. His popularity dipped when it was revealed that he had cheated on his wife, Maria, and that he had sired a love child with the family housekeeper.

But his fans seemed to have forgiven him, especially overseas. At home, critics attacked his latest movie, the gritty, grueling *Sabotage*, released in March of 2014. But his fans don't necessarily read movie reviews.

His *Escape Plan*, in which he co-starred with Stallone, brought in a puny $25 million Stateside, but $110 million in foreign revenues. *A Good Day to Die Hard* performed poorly

Aging Ah-nold **Schwarzenegger**, still a box-office champ, and now a leader of a (younger) pack of action-adventure cohorts, as he appeared iin *Sabotage* (2014), not necessary as buff as he'd been, but firmly established as a patriarchal (and avenging) authority figure.

**Chris Hemsworth**, the easy-on-the-eyes star of *Thor* (2011). As a younger player, he's bigger and more photogenically muscled than the (older) Ah-nold, but doesn't draw the box-office numbers of the "Oldie and goodie."

**Ah-nold** in the early 1980s as a very buff **Conan the Barbarian** (left) and Arnold (right) after his stint as governor of California.

in the United States, taking in $67 million, though raking up $237 million in foreign box offices.

In August, *AH-nold* will link up once again with Stallone, 67, for *The Expendables 3*. They'll battle Mel Gibson, 58, an evil arms dealer. Also appearing in the movie is grandfather Harrison Ford, 71. Also among the motley crew is Wesley Snipes, a mere 51. In the past, only the IRS has defeated him.

Cast as a sheriff in that shoot 'em up film, *The Last Stand*, Schwarzenegger said, "Retirement is for sissies."

Once thought washed up in Hollywood, Kevin Costner, 59, is the comeback kid. It's been a long time since the hit he scored in 1990 with *Dances with Wolves*. He was headed for the "Forest Lawn of Stars" until he was cast in a hit TV miniseries *The Hatfields and McCoys in 2012*.

Call his latest film, *3 Days to Kill*, a case of "cardiac arrest." Costner is blackmailed into participating in one last dangerous spy mission in exchange for life-saving medical treatment. As one critic satirically suggested, "He probably doesn't mind working around so much gunfire. His hearing probably went years ago."

Coming up for Costner is the NFL Drama, *Draft Day*, and the track-and-field themed *McFarland*, though he's beyond the point of playing an athlete himself. "Being a tough guy in movies is much easier than bringing up seven kids at home," he claimed.

Another fading star, "wee pup" Bruce Willis, only 58, has made an amazing comeback since the days of his heady marriage to fading screen goddess Demi Moore. This summer, he'll star is *A Dame to Kill For*, reprising his detective role in *Sin City* (2005). To follow, he's slated to make three more action movies in 2014.

Just as he was starting to get a little long in the tooth, Liam Neeson, 61, is back with a vengeance. He played a violent air marshal in *Non-Stop*, which opened in March. Another violent flick, *Taken 3*, will open this summer. "As long as producers keep giving me a paycheck, I'll kill people indiscriminately on the screen."

Like they did 20 or 30 years ago, these senior citizens of the screen do a lot of jumping, climbing, and shooting before the camera. Trainer Harvey Pasternak said, "As the body ages, hormone levels, including testosterone, drop. I doubt if a lot of these guys would look the way they do without a pharmaceutical assist."

As Neeson puts it, "We older guys have got to keep that popcorn flick tension tense."

John Wayne set the stage for veteran actors to keep punching, fighting, shooting, and kicking their way through films such as *Brannigan* or *Rooster Cogburn* deep into their 60s. The action heroes mentioned play their age on screen. No more torrid *High Noon* love scenes between Gary Cooper (born 1901) and Grace Kelly (born 1929). The older male stars today let their time-weathered faces re-

Two views of **Sylvester Stallone,** as Rocky Balboa. *Left photo*, in *Rocky I*; *right photo*, facing off with Swedish heartthrob **Dolph Lundgren** in *Rocky IV* (1985).

**Older, more grizzled, and a bit more arthritic, but still bankable: Kevin Costner** in *(left photo)* a poster for *Hatfields & McCoys*; and *right photo*, for *3 Days to Kill*.

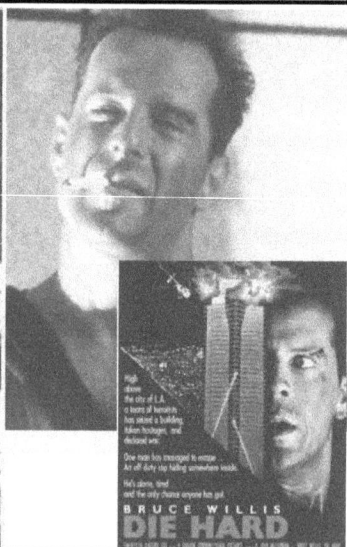

Fans of the Northern Ireland-born stage actor, **Liam Neeson,** would flock to see him in almost anything.

Since 2009, despite his advancing middle age, he accepted strenuous roles in action-adventure movies.

Known for portrayals of tough guys who are hard to kill, **Bruce Willis** will forever be I.D.'d as the guy who—in the movies at least—saved the tallest building (and its occupants) in Los Angeles in the first (in 1988) of the *Die Hard* series.

flect the wisdom they've learned over the decades.

It comes as a surprise that few younger actors are waiting in the wings to fill the big shoes of yesterday's action heroes. Take Channing Tatum, 33, a former male stripper in Florida, as an example. He could become the screen's next Tom Cruise, though he's not as weird as that actor.

Tatum doesn't want to be trapped in action movies the way Schwarzenegger or Stallone were. He wants to be versatile, making only an occasional action movie such as *White House Down*. Otherwise, he can be seen dancing around without his clothes in *Magic Mike* or even in a cop spoof, perhaps cast as G.I. Joe. "I don't want to be pigeonholed," he said. "I'm an actor, not a robot."

\*\*\*

# THE ODD COUPLE
## (SCHWARZENEGGER & SHRIVER)
# PLAN THEIR DIVORCE

Unless Michelle Obama decides to divorce Barack in 2011, the breakup of Arnold Schwarzenegger and Maria Shriver is likely to be the major split of the year.

Arnold—who was originally billed as "Arnold Strong" when he arrived in America in the 1970s—was a 30-year old bodybuilder when he met Maria Shriver, a 21-year old *ingénue*. "It was instant chemistry" Arnold said when he spotted Maria at a 1977 charity tennis event in New York. They wouldn't marry until April 25, 1986. Politically, they were worlds apart: He was a staunch Republican and she was a Kennedy Democrat, a member of a political dynasty.

Jackie Kennedy Onassis was at the wedding to congratulate them. Privately she told author Truman Capote: "Arnold will fit right into the Kennedy family, whose men have always sought their sexual pleasures outside the beds of their wives."

As Arnold became the biggest movie star in the world, revelations about his past were exposed in the tabloids. It was learned that the Austrian-born Gustav Schwarzenegger, Arnold's father, with his "Hitler-style mustache," had been a member of the Nazi Party. Arnold himself was a great friend of the disgraced Kurt Waldheim, former UN chief who participated in Nazi atrocities during WWII.

*Spy* Magazine in 1992 reported that in the 70s Arnold "enjoyed playing and giving away records of Hitler's speeches." During the filming of his 1977 *Pumping Iron*, he said on camera that he "admired" Hitler, although the director cut that controversial footage.

He was also seen smoking pot in the movie. "Marijuana is not a drug," he said. "It is a leaf." In the film, he confessed to using steroids.

In 1978 Arnold posed nude for the talented homosexual photographer Robert Mapplethorpe, the pictures becoming a hot seller in the gay porn world. "I have absolutely no hangups about the fag business," Arnold said.

As a body builder, he became notorious for chasing after women, an activity that would haunt him when he announced his run for the governorship of California in 2003 on *The Tonight Show with Jay Leno*. On the same show, he also discussed how painful a bikini wax was.

A potential First Lady of California, Maria only learned of his decision by watching the show.

In his race for the governor, he was accused of sexual harassment and was labeled "Governor Groper" in the press. At least 16 women came forward describing his sexual misconduct while making movies.

On the set of *Terminator 2*, one female crew member claimed he walked over to her and pulled out her breasts, exposing them. Another said when she went to his trailer to summon him to the set, she discovered him performing oral sex on a woman. He looked up at the script girl, telling her, "Eating is not cheating."

He told *Esquire* Magazine, "When you see a blonde with great tits and a great ass, you say to yourself, 'Hey, she must be stupid or must have nothing else to offer,' which is the case many times."

Finally, Arnold called a press conference, admitting "I behaved badly sometimes."

After he was elected governor, Maria and the children continued to live in the Los Angeles area. In Sacramento, Arnold refused to live in the Governor's Mansion, but rented a hotel suite, flying back to Beverly Hills on weekends.

**CALIFORNIA DREAMING**

A Republican **(AH-nold)** married a famous Democrat **(Maria Shriver,** niece of the the late president, JFK) in 1986. Did he profit from her reflected fame and glory in his bid for the governorship of California?

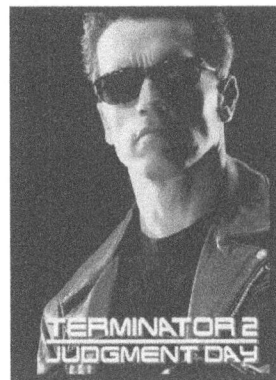

As governor, Arnold's muscles turned to flab. He got very poor marks, which was painful to him. He said, "I'm a winner. I always win." Not this time.

Maria admitted that she never wanted to be First Lady of California. When she married Arnold, she gave up her job as a reporter for TV's *Dateline*, and she may want to go back into journalism.

Arnold has announced that he wants to resume his movie career, although a lot of young men with better, more virile bodies dominate the scene today.

Maria wanted to divorce Arnold in 2009, but held back because of the death of her parents and of her uncle, Teddy Kennedy. She has told friends that she finds Arnold "impossible to live with," because of his ego and womanizing. On a recent tour of Brazil, France, and Nigeria, the "Governator" did not lack companionship.

**MEMORIES (AND REFERENCES) TO JFK, JACKIE, and CAMELOT**

Promotional photo with **Schwarzenegger and his then-wife, Maria Shriver,** celebrating his win as governor of the Golden State.

**Ah-nold** wasn't the first entertainer to win—usually against superhuman odds—a coveted position in California politics. Photo above shows Ronald Reagan, another eventual governor of California, getting lynched in *The Bad Man* (1941)

One of Maria's closest friends said, "She's been a lost soul for a very long time."

The couple have four children-Katherine, 21; Christina, 19; Patrick, 17; and Christopher, 13. Usually children don't want to see their parents' divorce. In this case, the siblings have reportedly urged Maria to divorce their father. Patrick said, "Small speed bump in life; luckily we own Hummers and will cruise right over it."

There are reports that Arnold is trying to win Maria back. But we'll let the lady speak for herself. "I don't know where I will end up, but I will definitely be in a different place next year than I am today.

Ten years ago when Schwarzenegger was dreaming of becoming Governor of California, he proposed himself as the family values candidate. He attacked single mothers for bearing children out of wedlock, and claimed that it was a special problem for minorities. At that same time, he was conducting an adulterous affair with a household employee, which led to the birth of a love child. On May 17, 2011 he admitted his guilt and apologized to Maria and his children, and to his fans and supporters. He offered no apology to those single moms he had attacked.

# AH-NOLD: "I'LL BE BACK"

The novelist, F. Scott Fitzgerald, wrote, "There are no second acts in America." Ronald Reagan proved how wrong that was. Now, Arnold Schwarzenegger is showing the world there's such a thing as a third act—1980s action hero, governor of California in 2003, and now, once again, cinematic action hero at the age of sixty-five when he's eligible for Medicare.

After all, he promised us that in his most famous movie line—"I'll be back"—and he's keeping his word.

Movie critics are calling the all-star crew Sylvester Stallone assembled for his sequel *The Expendables 2*, as *"The Return of the Old Geezers."*

"We guys do it the old-fashioned way—real fight scenes instead of all those special effects in such films as *Iron Man* and *Spider Man,"* said Jean-Claude Van Damm, one of the film's co-stars, who is still "a baby" at 51.

Two summers ago, the first *Expendables* was a big hit with Reagan-era action hero fans, and now Bruce Willis, 57, and Dolph Lundgren, 54, are killing again. Even Chuck Norris, the granddaddy of them all at 72, is returning. "Once again, we're doing what we do best—take a knife, cut a head off, kill a guy," Schwarzenegger said. "Obviously, we're not trying to win an Oscar."

Schwarzenegger's publicists are trying to put his notorious past behind him. He's faced years of bad press, based on allegations of sexual harassment when he ran for governor in 2003, and a 2011 separation from Maria Shriver, his wife of 25 years, when he admitted to fathering a secret child with his housekeeper.

**TIME MARCHES ON**

Even if he does make a radical comeback, it's doubtful that **AH-nold** will ever replicate the staggering bodybuilding triumphs he enjoyed in his 20s.

STALLONE STATHAM LI LUNDGREN NORRIS CREWS COUTURE HEMSWORTH ALSO VAN DAMME WITH WILLIS AND SCHWARZENEGGER

# THE EXPENDABLES 2

**The Expendables 2** (2012) combined every badass action hero alive at the time into a "code of honor" fight film about buddies who avenge the murder of one of their comrades-in-arms.

A hard-to-swallow but bang-em-hard action-adventure film with guns and explosives, its headlines breathlessly announced the joint appearances of (as listed in the credits) **STALLONE, STATHAM, LI, LUNDGREN, NORRIS, CREWS, COUTURE, HEMSWORTH, VAN DAMME, WILLIS,** and (guess who?) **AH-NOLD!**

Their collective reincarnations were celebrated in this poster, which clustered their images into a dinner-table scenario inspired by Leonardo da Vinci's Renaissance depiction of Jesus and his disciples at *The Last Supper*, a mural within the Church of Santa Maria delle Grazie in Milan. A gun-toting **Sylvester Stallone** is positioned in the spot Da Vinci famously assigned to Jesus.

The former governor is set to tell his own story in a massive 656-page autobiography entitled *Total Recall: My Unbelievably True Life Story,* scheduled to appear in bookstores in October. His life in the 1970s was particularly scandalous, and just how much he plans to reveal about those swinging days remains to be seen…or read.

Other movie stars have been older than Schwarzenegger when they appeared as action heroes. Charles Bronson filmed *Death Wish V: The Face of Death* at age 73, and Clint Eastwood had a big hit in the 2008 *Gran Torino,* when at the age of 78 he took on a belligerent Asian gang.

Schwarzenegger says it "feels great to be back jumping off buildings, seeing huge explosions, getting in car chases, and throwing punches."

After *Expendables 2*, his followup film, due in January, called *The Last Stand,* is a story about an aged sheriff confronting border violence. Yet another movie, *The Tomb,* is scheduled for release in the fall of 2013.

On the drawing board now is a remake of his hit 1988 movie, *Twins,* in which audiences were asked to believe that Danny DeVito could be Arnold's brother. In the projected new film, *Triplets,* Schwarzenegger wants Eddie Murphy to be his third "bro."

To skeptics who doubt the validity of his comeback, Schwarzenegger has an answer: "Who would believe that a young weightlifter growing up in Austria would become governor of California? I might even have become President of the United States except that I was told I had to be born here to do that."

"I'm doing what is called 'rebooting' myself, which is not a bad thing for men in their 60s and 70s to do. I may never have learned to pronounce 'California' correctly, but on screen at least, I know how to rip off a car door, smoke out the bad guys with a machine gun, and wag a fat cigar."

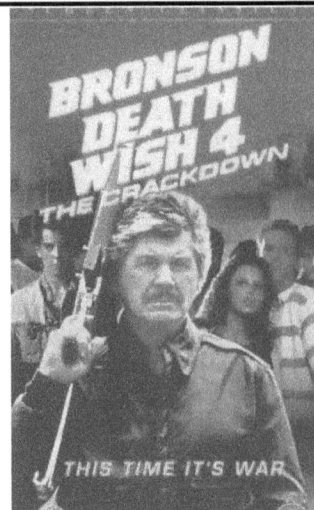

***MORE GUNFIRE!***
***LOUDER EXPLOSIONS!***

Enemies of **Charles Bronson** (depicted above at the age of 74 in *Death Wish 4)*, quipped that the film's title was a reference to suicidal thoughts inspired by geriatric depression.

301

# "AH-NOLD," SON OF A NAZI, CHAMPIONS ISRAEL AND ITS PEOPLE

Born in 1947 in Austria, Arnold Schwarzenegger turned 76 in 2023 and is still going strong. "I want to live forever, and I'm pissed off that people have to die."

He has led an almost unbelievable life. His alcoholic father, Gustav, was one of the Nazi soldiers who laid siege to Leningrad during World War II. A brutal man, he frequently beat his wife and kids.

At the age of 21, Arnold fled to America, where his life took an amazing turn. He began a strenuous exercise regime of "pumping iron" and dramatically transformed his body. He was named Mr. Universe four times and Mr. Olympia seven times.

His documentary, *Pumping Iron* (1977) inspired thousands of young men to create muscular physiques in gyms across America. Movie stardom followed, based on leading roles in *Conan the Barbarian* (1982) and *The Terminator* (1984). By 1993, he was named "International Star of the Decade."

A Republican, he married Maria Shriver, a niece of President Kennedy, in 1986. She urged him to run for Governor of California, and he won the seat, becoming that state's 38th governor, serving two four-year terms from 2003 to 2011.

During his political campaigns, he frequently faced charges of sexual misconduct from his past, admitting, "I was a very bad boy."

His wife divorced him in 2011, after he admitted to having fathered a child with their housemaid in 1997.

When Donald Trump left his TV series, *The Apprentice,* Arnold replaced him in September of 2015. Instead of yelling, "You're fired!" like Trump, he shouted "You're terminated!"

Trump mocked his low ratings on TV. Arnold shot back, "Let's switch jobs. You take over TV since you're an expert in ratings. I'll take over your job so people can finally sleep peacefully at night."

Throughout his political life, Arnold has been a strong supporter of Israel. As governor, he joined in pro-Israel rallies, and in 2004, he visited that country to break ground at the Simon Wiesenthal Center's Museum of Tolerance in Jerusalem. "I love Israel and its people," he said. "They have suffered so much and so bravely."

By 2022, the aging leviathan, who has gone through three heart valve replacement surgeries, paid a highly publicized visit to southern Poland a few days after Rosh Hashanah, the Jewish New Year.

He arrived at the former death camp of Auschwitz, a 500-acre compound where 1.3 million people (1.1 million of whom were Jewish) were brutally exterminated during World War II. Upon their arrival in overpacked cattle cars, victims were yanked into lines to confront SS "exterminators." The ill and elderly were immediately executed, the rest used as slave labor or for medical experiments by sadistic doctors. Most of those who weren't immediately "snuffed" died after brutal torture, forced labor, freezing temperatures, and starvation.

After leaving the camp, a teary-eyed Arnold told the press, "Never again must we let this atrocity happen. I wish I could 'terminate' hatred and prejudice."

**TAKING IT SLOW:** During the pandemic, on his YouTube channel, **AH-nold** famously issued advice that included taking a daily Jacuzzi as an aid to relaxation, and avoiding restaurants, cafes, and public places.

**Arnold** blamed the end of his gig as a replacement for Donald Trump in *The Apprentice* squarely on interference from The Donald himself. "The fart wanted me to fail. What a jealous badass!"

During his 2022 visit to the only remaining synagogue near the site of a 1940s-era Nazi death camp, California's former Governor **Arnold Schwarzenegger** embraces Auschwitz survivor **Lidia Maksymowicz** at the Auschwitz Jewish Center Foundation's synagogue in Oświęcim, the town next to Auschwitz.

IN ITS EDITIONS OF DECEMBER 2014 AND JANUARY 2015, ANITA FINLEY'S BOOMER TIMES PROMINENTLY INCLUDED MEDIA BUZZ ABOUT BLOOD MOON'S THEN-NEWEST PRESIDENTIAL BIOGRAPHY:

# LOVE TRIANGLE

## RONALD REAGAN, JANE WYMAN, & NANCY DAVIS: ALL THE GOSSIP UNFIT TO PRINT

Paperback, Biography/Entertainment, by Darwin Porter and Danforth Prince   6" x 9"   800 pages, with hundreds of photos.  ISBN 978-1-936003-41-9 .   Available everywhere now

*RONALD REAGAN WITH JANE WYMAN*

\*\*\*

**CELEBRITY NEWS FROM BLOOD MOON PRODUCTIONS**: **Nancy Davis** was a debutante, an on-the-make starlette in 1940s Hollywood, an astrology aficionado, and the most influential First Lady since Eleanor Roosevelt.

Despite **Ronald Reagan's** fame as the two-term 40th President of the United States, very few of his ardent political fans ever knew a lot about his famous first wife, the Oscar-winning actress, **Jane Wyman**. In the photos above, they appear together in *Brother Rat*, a fluffy B-list movie about hazing at a college fraternity.

Their coupling was scrutinized in dozens of tabloids and movie magazines—until Nancy Davis, Reagan's second and much more politicized wife, did everything she could to eradicate that union's memory.

**REST IN PEACE**: As cited on the front page of the March 7, 2016 edition of *The New York Times:*

"**NANCY REAGAN**, the influential and stylish wife of the 40th president of the United States, who unabashedly put Ronald Reagan at the center of her life, but became a political figure in her own right, died on Sunday at her home in Los Angeles. She was 94. Mrs. Reagan was a fierce guardian of her husband's image, sometimes at the expense of her own, and during Mr. Reagan's improbable climb from a Hollywood acting career to the governorship of California, and ultimately, the White House, she was a trusted advisor. According to Michael Deaver, a longtime aide to Reagan, 'Without Nancy, there would have been no Governor Reagan and no President Reagan, either.'"

According to Blood Moon's president, **Danforth Prince**, "In the Republican's rush to deify the memory of Ronald and Nancy Reagan, there's a prevailing embarrassment about their convoluted and frequently compromised careers as Hollywood actors and entertainers. In the wake of Nancy Reagan's death, as mainstream media rushes to eulogize her dubious role, first in Hollywood and later, in politics, we want to remind everyone that Nancy had a distinctly scandalous life before Ronnie, and that Blood Moon Productions is the only publishing entity in the world that ever fully explored its implications."

*Two right photos:* From shortly after their first date, **Ronald Reagan's** associates and cohorts were surprised by the grip the minor starlet **Nancy Davis** exerted on her new beau, informally known at the time as "Ronnie."  But for years after his divorce from the increasingly famous **Jane Wyman** *(far right)*, she continued to cast what many insiders called a "dark shadow" over Reagan's marriage to the (ferociously possessive) Nancy.

"*Love Triangle* is an award-winning, lavishly reviewed biography exposing the ambitions and pretentions of three celebrity wannabees scrambling for fame, fortune, respect, and better roles in B-list Hollywood," Prince continued. "One of them (Jane Wyman) became an A-list movie star. The other two ended up ruling the Free World."

**"So enough with the breathless testimonials, already!" Prince continued.**

"With respect to Mrs. Reagan for her long and convoluted life, but as an antidote to the collective amnesia and the sometimes nauseating eulogies sweeping across the media this morning, Blood Moon reminds readers of the availability on line and in bookstores everywhere of the most comprehensive biography ever published about the early days of the Reagan's tempestuous and scandal-soaked marriage: LOVE TRIANGLE."

**"A scandalous new book about Reagan and his two wives claims to fill in the blanks, providing a drastically different portrait of The Gipper."**

*The Daily Mail, Feb 7, 2015*

\*\*\*

# RONALD REAGAN AND HIS LOVE TRIANGLE

### BEFORE TWO OF THEM MORPHED INTO THE MOST POWERFUL COUPLE IN THE FREE WORLD, EVERYONE IN HOLLYWOOD KNEW THEM AS "RONNIE, JANE, AND NANCY"

**GOODBYE FOREVER:** In this press photo snapped from the gangway of Air Force One at Andrews Air Force Base during the final moments of their administration, **Nancy Davis Reagan** and **Ronald Reagan** wave to the assembled crowds before their return to civilian life back in California.

Blood Moon's latest *exposé* differs from everything Darwin Porter has previously written. It focuses on former U.S. President Ronald Reagan and the two beautiful movie stars he married, Jane Wyman (their marriage lasted from 1940-48) and Nancy Davis (1952 to 2004).

This is not a book about politics. (Other tomes have already discussed Reagan's politics, *ad nauseum*.) It's about three movie star wannabees, their young hopes, dreams ambitions, compromises, failures, triumphs, and heartbreaks; their Hollywood movies, good to awful, and their affairs.

Each member of this triangle has gone to considerable trouble to conceal their record in Golden Age Hollywood—and perhaps with good reason.

As Hollywood stars, Ronald, Jane, and Nancy were a libidinous triad before two of them took over the free world in the 1980s, and Jane went on to become the highest paid entertainer on television.

Today, "Ronnie and Nancy" are remembered chiefly as geriatric figures in the White House, with "The Iron Lady," (Nancy) maneuvering as the power behind the throne.

But when each of them was young and beautiful, they led "tabloid lives," falling in love again…and again…and again.

A later generation remembers Wyman as the ferocious "Empress of the Vineyards," Angela Channing, in the hit TV series of the '80s, *Falcon Crest*. Movie fans of Hollywood's Golden Age remember her as the Oscar-winning star of such hit movies as *Johnny Belinda* (1948), in which she played a deaf mute; *The Yearling* (1946), where she portrayed the matriarch of a pioneering family in the swamps of inland Florida; and *The Blue Veil* (1941), a "four-hankie" tear-jerking melodrama in which she played

In marked contrast to the political neutrality ("*I have no comment*") of Reagan's first wife, Jane Wyman, **Nancy** evolved into his most tireless and sometimes intrusive promoter, even during his awkward transition into electoral politics.

*In the upper photo*, **the Reagans** turn a day at the beach into a political statement and slogan.

*In the lower photo*, at a White House gala, **the then-President** interrupts **Frank Sinatra** in a "too close for comfort" moment with **Nancy.**

a self-sacrificing nanny for the children of other people.

Wyman got her start in the 1930s as a wisecracking blonde chorus girl cutie. Many of the matinee idols of the day "conquered" her, notably Clark Gable, Errol Flynn, Bing Crosby, George Raft, Jimmy Stewart, and his friend, Henry Fonda.

***

Born Sarah Jane Mayfield in 1917 in Saint Joseph, Missouri, the future Jane Wyman began her professional career at the age of sixteen in 1933, when she signed a contract with Warner's.

She soon shocked Hollywood when she was photographed in a two-piece bathing suit, the precursor of the bikini.

She started out in bit parts such as Gold Diggers of 1933.

At Warners, she got her first big role in a Dick Foran Western, The Sunday Round-Up (1936).

By the time she made Public Wedding (1937), she had divorced her first husband, Ernest Wyman, although she kept his name for the rest of her career.

She remarried in 1937 to Myron Martin Futterman, a dress manufacturer from New Orleans. She wanted kids: he did not. Their union lasted less than three months.

Their divorce came through in 1938 when she met and was starring with Ronald Reagan in Brother Rat, which was almost immediately followed by its sequel, Brother Rat and a Baby (1940).

"This was the man I'd been looking for," she later claimed. "But he was so damn shy. He didn't ask for my phone number. I had to give it to him. He called three days later."

On the third date, she invited him back to her apartment, which led to a seduction. "I started stripping off his clothes, so he got the idea."

He told a friend, "I was afraid I wouldn't measure up to her previous two husbands. So over breakfast, I had to ask what was on my mind. I put it to her straight."

He asked, "Did I sexually satisfy you?"

"And how!" she said. "In fact, I'm going to need it every night for the next eight days. Then I'll give you a night off, except for heavy petting."

They were married on January 26, 1940 at the Wee Kirk o' the Heather in Glendale, California.

Politically, they did not agree, as she was a Republican, and because at the time, he was an ardent Democrat.

***

Jane was not faithful to him. During World War II, while he was away making war propaganda films for the Army/Air Force, she conducted passionate, long-lived affairs with actor/singer Dennis Morgan and with John Payne, both of whom co-

One of Ronald and Nancy's outspoken children later commented on how his parents (especially Nancy) might have acted differently if they'd known that one day they'd rule the Free World.

Here are two views of **Ronald Reagan** midway through his career as an actor. On the *left*, he's cheerfully promoting Chesterfield cigarettes. On the *right* he appears as part of a publicity campaign for **Louella Parsons,** Hollywood's then-most-powerful gossip columnist.

Louella always liked Reagan, widely promoting his All-American wholesomeness as a refreshing change from more obviously debauched actors like Errol Flynn, whom she despised.

*Left photo:* In this publicity photo for *Pin-Up Girl* (1944), **Betty Grable** struts her stuff as World War II's most popular "girl inside a sailor's locker."

*Middle photo:* a "new in Hollywood" **Susan Hayward** learns how to swim, as coached by former lifeguard **Ronald Reagan** on the set of the frothy, pulpy *Girls on Probation* (1938). Its not-particularly-presidential plot? "A dizzy young girl falls into crime but wins her lawyer's heart," and

*Right photo:* MORE CHEESECAKE, this time a poolside photo-op with **Ronald Reagan** and the actress/dancer he later married**, Jane Wyman,**

Many of the future president's films were silly, shallow, and fluffy.

Here, **Ronald Reagan** appears on the far left with *(left to right)* **Virginia Mayo, Eddie Bracken,** and **Dona Drake** in the prequel to all those "Fun in the Sand" films of Annette Funicello, *The Girl from Jones Beach* (1949).

starred with her in releases for Warner Brothers.

During the filming of *Johnny Belinda* (1948), for which she won an Oscar, Jane fell in love with her co-star, Lew Ayres, the ex-husband of Ginger Rogers. She abandoned Reagan with the understanding that Ayres was desperately urging her to marry him, but after her divorce was finalized, he dumped her.

In 1948, from the rubble of his ruined marriage, Reagan entered the second "horndog" period of his life. He even dipped into the teenage market, seducing Elizabeth Taylor, called "San Quentin Jailbait" at the time, along with the teenaged newcomer, Piper Laurie, who played his daughter in *Louisa* (1950).

Another of his *ingénue* co-stars was the teenaged Shirley Temple in *That Hagen Girl* (1947). Struggling to evolve from a chubby-cheeked child star into a sultry adult actress, she coyly defined him to the press as "a great kisser." *[Note: Upon the release of their sexually ambiguous movie, the public was not amused.]*

Still mourning the loss of Wyman, Reagan proposed marriage to Adele Jergens, a particularly lovely blonde bombshell of the 1940s. At the time, despite an alluring performance in *Ladies of the Chorus* (1948) as a young and comely burlesque queen, she'd been cast as Marilyn Monroe's mother, even though she was only eight years older than Marilyn herself.

Soon, it was "Goodbye, Adele, Hello Marilyn." To complicate matters, and with touches of irony, Marilyn was also competing *(with GUESS WHO? — Wyman!)* for the love of bandleader Fred Karger. Wyman emerged as the winner, marrying Karger, then divorcing him after about three years of marriage, remarrying him, and then re-divorcing him. Jane would never wed again.

After some heavy dates, when Clark Gable didn't deliver a marriage proposal, Nancy pursued Reagan, then president of the Screen Actors Guild. She had to fend off a lot of competition, the most formidable of which came from Doris Day, co-star with Reagan in *Storm Warning* (1951) and *The Winning Team* (also 1951).

Reagan was about to propose marriage to Day until he learned that his future daughter (Patti Davis) "was already in the oven," (his words). In reaction, he and Nancy married hastily and without a lot of fanfare in 1952.

As a wannabee starlet at MGM before her marriage, young Nancy had posed for cheesecake photos and had a liaisons with producers, directors, assistant directors, minor actors, stars, supporting players, and studio executives who included Benny Thau, head of casting at MGM. Her associations with marquee names included Robert Walker and Peter Lawford when these two bisexuals weren't otherwise involved with each other. Marlon Brando and Milton Berle also managed to insert themselves into Nancy's date book.

After Nancy finally coaxed Reagan to the altar after a 2½ year chase, she said, "My life didn't begin until I met Ronnie."

That was hardly the case. Her adventures before Reagan could fill an 800-page tell-all. But it was nonetheless a lovely sentiment to express.

Reagan told the press, "I've found my soulmate."

## And so he had.

To everyone involved, it appeared that Reagan was desperately in love with his increasingly estranged ("I hate politics and Ronnie is boring") wife, **Jane Wyman.**

Here, she appears in a scene from *Johnny Belinda* (1948) with the "love of her life" (for a while at least), **Lew Ayres**, who eventually dumped her.

Depicted above as *Ladies of the Chorus* (1948), are **Adele Jurgens** *(left)* and a then-relatively-unknown **Marilyn Monroe**. Each of them was miscast as part of a mother-daughter dance team.

**Ronald Reagan**, the then-horny "man about town from the wheatfields of the Middle West" got "down and dirty' first with "the mother" (Jurgens) and then, less discreetly, with the daughter (Monroe).

***

# LOVE TRIANGLE,

## RONALD REAGAN, JANE WYMAN, AND NANCY DAVIS
## ALL THE GOSSIP UNFIT TO PRINT

**Darwin Porter and Danforth Prince**
Paperback, Biography/Entertainment
ISBN 978-1-936003-41-9
6" x 9"  800 pages, with hundreds of photos
Available everywhere, as a paperback or electronically, in January, 2015

NANCY DAVIS REAGAN ("QUEEN NANCY") WAS ONE OF THE MOST PUSHY, CONTROVERSIAL, DISLIKED, AND NOTORIOUS FIRST LADIES IN THE HISTORY OF THE AMERICAN REPUBLIC. LEARN MORE ABOUT IT IN THE BOOK THE REPUBLICAN HIERARCHIES REALLY DON'T WANT YOU TO READ: *LOVE TRIANGLE*

*If Ronnie had married Nancy Davis in the '40s instead of Jane Wyman, he'd have won at least two Oscars"*
-Reagan's friend, William Holden, in reference to Nancy's ferocious promotional skills.

*"My first duty as First Lady will be to get rid of that fried catfish stench lingering from the Carters. "*
-Nancy Reagan, after her husband's electoral victory of 1980

*"Clark Gable turned her down, but Ronnie said yes when he learned there was a baby in the oven. His first choice had been Doris Day."*
-Jane Wyman

*"Nancy Davis posed for cheesecake at MGM in a night gown. You could see all the way to Honolulu."*
-Zsa Zsa Gabor

*"First, there were such lovers as Yul Brynner, Alfred Drake, Peter Lawford, Robert Walker, Frank Sinatra, Spencer Tracy, Marlon Brando, and Milton Berle. For Nancy, Ronald Reagan was a late comer."*
—Barbara Stanwyck

*If I had a nickel for every Jew Nancy was under, I'd be rich."*
—George Cukor

*"Nancy got around …. Ask Robert Walker or Benjamin Thau, head of casting at MGM."*
Peter Lawford

*THAT WOMAN! Who on earth does she think she is?"*
Queen Elizabeth II

*"Nancy was one of those girls whose phone number got handed around a lot."*
—Nancy's biographer, Anne Edwards

*"If Nancy ever knew she'd become First Lady one day, she'd have cleaned up her act as a starlet in the '40s."*
—Michael Reagan

Despite her status as a ferociously ambitious B-list actress who was widely disliked and gossiped-about, **Nancy Reagan** in many ways "got the last laugh."

Here is a replica, courtesy of the White House Historical Association, of her official portrait, as painted in 1987 by Aaron Shikler.

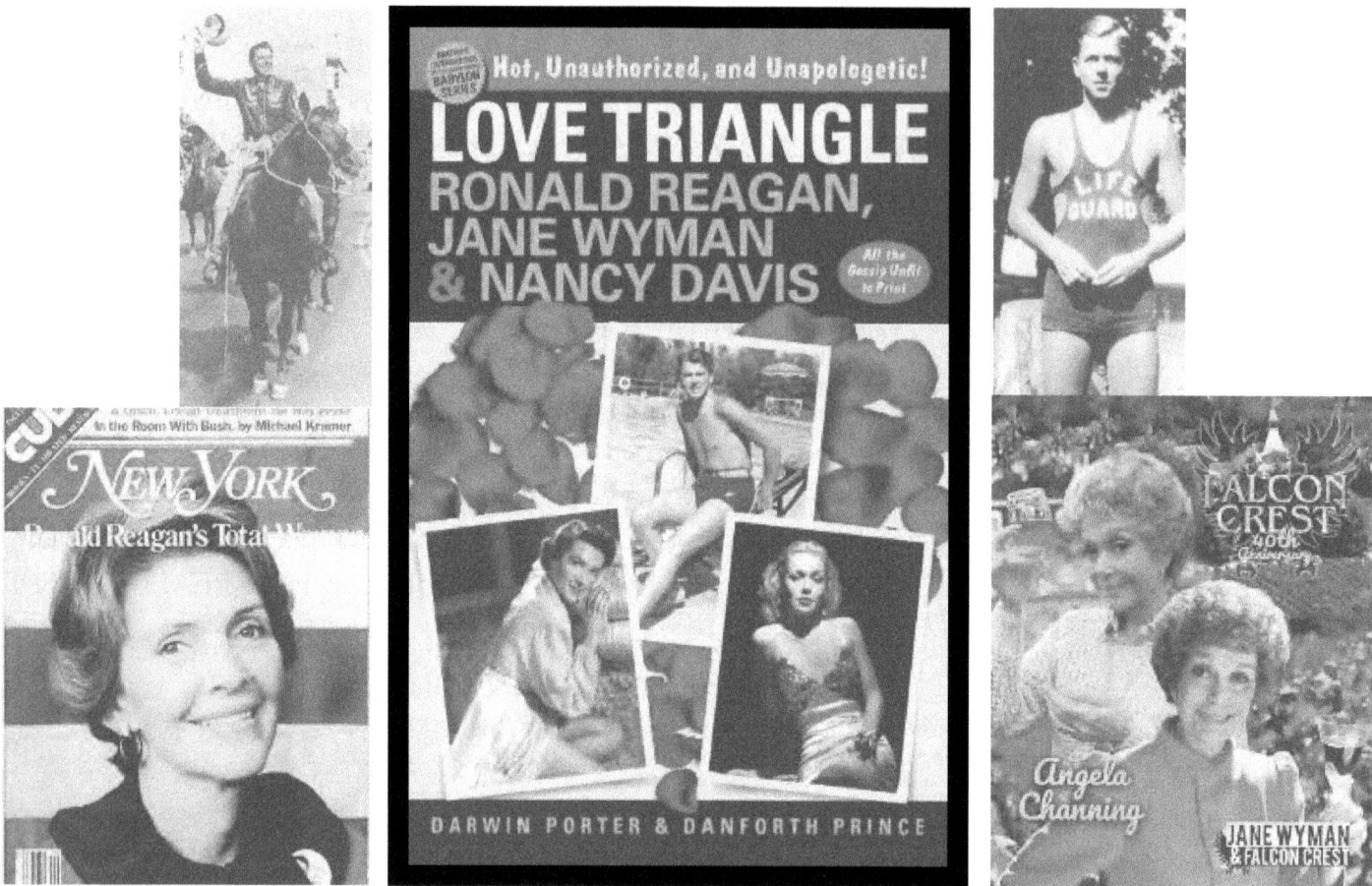

**Hot, Unauthorized, and Unapologetic!**

# LOVE TRIANGLE
## RONALD REAGAN, JANE WYMAN & NANCY DAVIS

*All the Gossip Unfit to Print*

**DARWIN PORTER & DANFORTH PRINCE**

Desite the respective fame of each member of Ronald Reagan's love triangle, very few consumers ever interconnected the dots of each player's ferocious, ongoing rivalry...until now.

**Darwin Porter's book** illustrates the Cold War that raged between **"Jane and Nancy'** that endured until the deaths of all three parties involved. Whereas **Jane Wyman** morphed into an A-list actress and eventually, the instantly recognizable Queen of Daytime Soap Operas (through *Falcon Crest),* **Nancy** developed a formidable bag of tricks (including her sense of fashion and style) to remind the world that indeed, Ronnie was hers.

**Jane Wyman,** as illustrated above on the *left and right*, played an enormous role in the development (and concretization) of Reagan's public image as an affable guy you'd appreciate as a suburban next-door neighbor.

Yet after **Nancy Davis** began her watch, media coverage of anything associated with Wyman seemed to shrivel and die. Even the Reagan Library—the official repository of everything to do with the former President—barely mentions anything to do with Jane Wyman. Historians credit that, in part, to Nancy's intervention,

# LOVE TRIANGLE

## Ronald Reagan, Jane Wyman, & Nancy Davis: All the Scandal Unfit to Print:
### The Ultimate Guide to a Romantic Shuffle that Eventually Affected The Free World & Everyone in Politics

**Here's What They Said About LOVE TRIANGLE
on Australia's version of *The TODAY Show*:**
http://video.news.ninemsn.eom.au/?uuid=4038239202001

**Here's What The Brits Said About it in *The Daily Mail*:**
http:/iW'ww.dailymail.co.uk/news/article-2943309/Rampant-Ronald-Reagan-Former-president-ladies-man-Hollywood-days-new-book-lays-save-affairs-stars-Doris-Day-Lana-Turner-Mon-roe.html

**Here's What They Said About This Book at Southern California's *KNEWS RADIO***
http://youtu.be/yBih8tGYxkU

**And Here's How It Was Reviewed by Diane Donovan,
a Senior Reviewer at the California Bookwatch Subsection
of the May, 2015 edition of *The Midwest Book Review*:**

"*Love Triangle: Ronald Reagan, Jane Wyman & Nancy Davis* may find its way onto many a Republican Reagan fan's reading shelf, but those who expect another Reagan celebration will be surprised: this is lurid Hollywood exposé writing at its best, and outlines the truths surrounding one of the most provocative industry scandals in the world.

"There are already so many biographies of the Reagans on the market that one might expect similar mile-markers from this: be prepared for shock and awe; because *Love Triangle* doesn't take your ordinary approach to biography and describes a love triangle that eventually bumped a major Hollywood movie star (Jane Wyman) from the possibility of being First Lady and replaced her with a lesser-known Grade B actress (Nancy Davis).

From politics and betrayal to romance, infidelity, and sordid affairs, *Love Triangle* is a steamy, eye-opening story that blows the lid off of the Reagan illusion to raise eyebrows on both sides of the big screen.

"Black and white photos liberally pepper an account of the careers of all three and the lasting shock of their stormy relationships in a delightful pursuit especially recommended for any who relish Hollywood gossip."

Winner: Runner up to BEST BIOGRAPHY OF THE YEAR from the Beach Book Festival, 2015

Winner: Honorable Mention for BIOGRAPHY from the Los Angeles Book Festival, 2015, and winner of equivalent awards from the San Francisco and Amsterdam Book Festivals.

# LOVE TRIANGLE
# A U.S. President and His Wives

Ronald Reagan is the first divorced person, and the first former actor, to ever be elected President of the United States. Darwin Porter's *Love Triangle* is the story of a young Ronald Reagan and the two movie stars he married, Oscar-winning JANE WYMAN and MGM starlet NANCY DAVIS.

Today, "Ronnie and Nancy" are remembered chiefly as geriatric figures who ran the Free World in the 1980s, with Iron Lady Nancy as the power behind the throne.

A later generation also remembers Jane Wyman as the fierce empress, Angela Channing, in the decade's hit TV series, *Falcon Crest*. Movie fans of Hollywood's Golden Age recall her as the star of such hit movies as *Johnny Belinda*, in which she played a deaf mute; *The Yearling*, where she portrayed the matriarch of a pioneering family in the swamps of inland Florida: and in *The Blue Veil*, a melodrama in which she played a self-sacrificing nanny for other people's children.

Two of her greatest hits were made in the 1950s, *Magnificent Obsession* and *All That Heaven Allows*, each designated by critics at the time as "women's weepers." In each film, her co-star was the very dashing Rock Hudson.

*Love Triangle* is a three-in-one biography exploring the private, carefully camouflaged lives of this trio during what was once called "their salad days."

But the bio goes behind the scenes as each of them climbed the Hollywood ladder that eventually made them players on the world stage.

Of the three, Wyman was the only one who achieved super stardom. At Warners, Reagan was called "The King of the Bs," and Nancy never went beyond being an MGM starlet, initially posing for cheesecake in a failed attempt by the studio to turn her into a sex symbol.

When Wyman was asked by her adopted son, Michael Reagan, about her background, she grew cold, brusquely instructing him, in his own words, to "Look it up in the Encyclopedia."

Both Nancy and Reagan wrote two memoirs each—first Nancy in 1980, in which she presented a fantasy version of her life.

Her second memoir, *My Turn*, published in 1989, mostly contained "payback," a means of finally expressing her positions against all the enemies she'd made during her tenure as First Lady.

Reagan's first memoir, published in 1965, was *Where's the Rest of Me?*. Despite the title's implication that it would address his career as a Hollywood actor, it actually told fans and readers very little. Its title was borrowed from a line he'd delivered in *Kings Row* (1942), after waking up in a hospital to discover that a sadistic doctor had amputated his legs.

Reagan's second autobiography, published in 1990, was *An American Life*. Most of it was devoted to his presidency. Missing from both were any details about his life with Wyman, whom he married in 1940 and with whom he fathered a daughter, Maureen, and adopted a son, Michael.

When they were young, wannabe actors in Hollywood, all three of our subjects led fascinating lives. *Love Triangle* **is devoted to telling you what these world class icons never wanted you to know.**

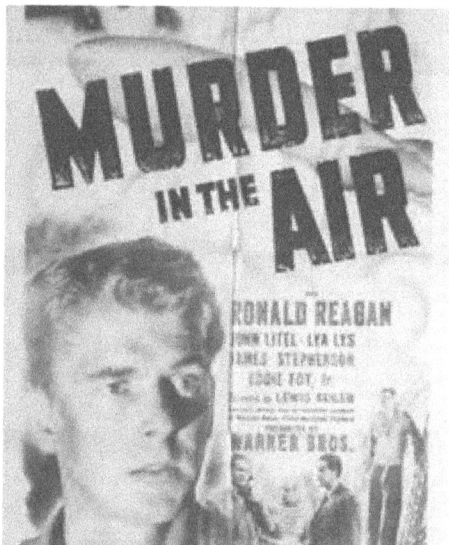

*Murder in the Air (aka The Enemy Within; 1940)* was a sci-fi propaganda film in which **Ronald Reagan**, as a U.S. government agent, heroically battles a network of spies committed to destroying America. In the scene above, he unravels the treachery of his co-star, **Eddie Foy**, an "enemy within."

Like her future husband, **Nancy Davis,** too, made a roster of forgettable films—none of them approaching the critical acclaim of movies that starred her rival, Jane Wyman. One of them was *Shadow in the Sky* (1952), a sappy melodrama famous for losing money. In the photos above, Nancy emotes with her character's onscreen husband, **James Whitmore.**

During the course of her career, in vivid Technicolor contrast, **Jane Wyman** starred in 83 movies and two successful TV series, and was nominated for an Academy Award four times, winning once, for portraying a sexually molested deaf-mute in *Johnny Belinda* (1948).

# RONALD REAGAN

Arriving in Hollywood in 1937 when he was twenty-six, Ronald Reagan was handsome, muscular, and ingratiating, a legendary lifeguard who'd saved 77 lives during his stint in a bathing suit. Women and girls from Illinois, where he was from, lined up for his charms and attention.

After experience as a sports announcer, he made it to Hollywood, where, through a connection. He got scheduled for a screen test, whose success eventually led to a seven-year contract with Warner Brothers.

After two years, his boss, Jack Warner, said, "My God, our boy Reagan is going to seduce every starlet on the lot. He's a greater swordsman than our resident Don Juan, Errol Flynn!"

At Warners, Reagan told a reporter, "I'm too shy to even ask for a gal's phone number." What he didn't say was that he didn't have to. The beautiful starlets called him. And there were many, indeed.

The first to contact Reagan was a luscious blonde starlet, Betty Grable, who at the time was on the verge of world recognition. During World War II, she became the biggest box office attraction in America, and the most visible pinup girl of her era.

Soon, Susan Hayward, that fiery redhead from Brooklyn, came knocking. She'd come to Hollywood with the hopes of playing Scarlett O'Hara in *Gone With the Wind*. She lost the part but won Reagan instead. Within months, however, she launched a feud with Jane Wyman, who had appeared in a film with Reagan entitled *Brother Rat*. Wyman decided that she wanted him, too. Their grappling for his affections led to an epic catfight.

Jane emerged as the victor, marrying Reagan in 1940.

Our young horndog didn't settle just for Hayward, Grable, and Wyman. Another goddess got included in the mix, Carole Landis, Grable's chief rival at 20th Century Fox. Reagan frequently admitted to his vulnerability to something he later defined almost as a chronic disease: LEADING LADY-IT IS, that is, a tendency to fall in love with each of his leading ladies-at least until the end of filming.

Our Lothario launched a long-enduring affair with Ann Sheridan, the officially designated Oomph Girl, followed with romantic encounters with Joan Blondell and her movie starlet sister, Gloria. Added to his list were such players as June Travis, Penny Singleton, Mary Maguire, and Gale Page.

It was Gale who persuaded Reagan to strip down and pose as an artists' model for her sculpture class at USC, where her fellow students voted his as Hollywood's most beautiful male body.

Reagan didn't always collaborate in sex with a star. During the shooting of *Dark Victory*, Bette Davis tried to seduce him, but he rejected her. "But Bette," he said. "In the movie, I play this repressed homosexual. It would be stepping out of character if I tried to seduce you."

Reagan was not faithful to Wyman during the course of their eight years of marriage. As he later told his pal, Dick Powell, "What red blooded American male could reject an offer from Lana Turner? She asked me to go riding and I turned out to be her stallion."

After Reagan's divorce from Wyman in 1948, he entered the second major horndog period of his life. On the doorstep of middle age, and as president of the Screen Actors Guild, he found himself pursued by both A-List Stars and by B and C-list wannabes.

He even got down and dirty with a far too young Elizabeth Taylor, a secret he shared with his best friend, Robert Taylor, who had also become sexually intimate with the then-sixteen-year-old. Robert Taylor's affair with her was conducted in London during the filming of the movie they'd made together, *Conspirator*. Robert subsequently de-

Every diva needs an uncomplicated straight guy as a foil for her flamboyance. That was the case in *Dark Victory* (1939), where **Bette Davis** *(left)* interacted with **Ronnie Reagan.**

Years later, every movie fan who saw it remembers Bette. Very few of them remember Ronnie.

**Hellcats of the Navy** (1957) was the only film **Ronald Reagan** and **Nancy Davis** ever made together. As his political career expanded, so did the fulsomeness of how newspapers like the *Los Angeles Times* described it to their readers: "It previewed the lifelong devotion that its stars displayed for one another."

Other reviewers weren't as kind: Derek Winnert appraised it as "Entertaining in an enjoyably mediocre sort of way, with rather feeble acting from the stars who, interestingly, are at their worst in the love scenes. Clichéd and ordinary, it doesn't really deliver the promised excitement and drama, or act as the fine tribute to bravery that it was meant to be. Nevertheless, it is worth a look for its unique glimpse of the stars on screen together."

fined young Elizabeth as "San Quentin jail bait."

Reagan continued his sexual interest in precocious teenagers. Shirley Temple co-starred with him in *That Hagen Girl*, when, as a middle aged man, he makes off with her in the final reel. The juvenile star of films that included *Rebecca of Sunnybrook Farm* later told the press, "Ronnie is a great kisser."

When he made *Louisa*, the beautiful teenage starlet, Piper Laurie, played Reagan's daughter. He ended up seducing her, too, as she confessed in her memoirs. She nicknamed him "the 40-minute man," a reference to the sexual encounter in which he took her virginity.

Still in mourning the loss of Jane, Reagan proposed marriage to Adele Jergens, a particularly lovely blonde bombshell of the 1940s. At the time, despite an alluring appearance in *Ladies of the Chorus* as a young and comely burlesque queen, she'd been cast as Marilyn Monroe's mother, even though she was only eight years older than Marilyn herself. When Reagan arrived one day to retrieve Adele, he was introduced to Marilyn, who at the time was living with Fred Karger, a young musician and bandleader.

**That Hagen Girl** (1947) was released by MGM in a desperate attempt to steer their immensely profitable child star, **Shirley Temple** *(center figure in photo above left)* into viable adult roles.

It bombed. One reviewer defined it as "One of the 50 Worst Movies of All Time." Others likened scenes such as the one above to an attempt by **Ronald Reagan** to pick up a teenager before she could finish her homework. It also effectively ended the hopes and "adult movie star dreams" of "Little Miss Lollipop," Shirley Temple.

In her autobiography, Temple stated that Reagan hated both the script and his role in the movie.

Almost all prints of the film mysteriously disappeared from various film storage facilities after Reagan morphed into a major political symbol, but resurfaced in the 1990s through Turner Classic Movies. *The New York Times* reviewed the script as amateurish and of Reagan and Temple wrote, "Ronald Reagan keeps as straight a face as he can while doing what must have struck him as the silliest job of his career ... but it is poor, little put-upon Shirley who looks most ridiculous through it all. She acts with the mopish dejection of a school-child who has just been robbed of a two-scoop ice cream cone."

As the plot unfolds, the then-17-year-old Temple attempts suicide. A critic quipped that it was unfortunate that the attempt failed.

A few weeks later, Reagan was injured during a "fundraising for charity" baseball game and broke his upper leg in seven places. To his surprise, while he was recuperating, in traction, in a hospital bed, Marilyn showed up wearing a mink coat, a recent gift from another admirer. During her preparations for her visit, she'd conveniently forgotten to wear any clothes underneath.

She later told Shelley Winters, her roommate, "I come two or three days a week to pay lip service to Ronnie while he's flat on his back. I think I'm helping his broken leg to heal."

Getting down and dirty with a pre-Governorship of California, pre-Presidential Ronald Reagan
## LADIES BEFORE NANCY

*LEFT TO RIGHT* **Selene Walters, Ruth Roman, Christine Larson, Jacqueline Parks, Peggy Knudsen** and (*far right, embracing* **Roy Rogers**), **Penny Edwards**

When he could walk again, Reagan was seen going out with two or three different women every week-some of them as part of serious affairs, others just passing fancies. There was the blonde columnist, Doris Lilly. He wanted to marry her, but she didn't want to marry him.

Then he spent time escorting movie cowgirl Penny Edwards when Roy Rogers didn't have her otherwise occupied.

There was a dalliance with Dorothy Shay, billed as "the Park Avenue Hillbillie," and with the singer, Ruth Roman, promoted as Warner's answer to MGM'S Ava Gardner.

The list was long, and included serious liaisons with Monica Lewis; and with Christine Larson.

Sultry Jacqueline Park, later the mistress of Jack Warner, claimed that Reagan made her pregnant and then encouraged her to get an abortion before he abandoned her.

Actress Selene Walters charged that Reagan raped her, as part of allegations that were widely reported by mainstream news outlets during his presidency.

He had an affair with his attractive co-star, Patricia Neal, when they made *The Hasty Heart* in London.

A PICTURE TO THRILL EVERY WOMAN'S HEART –*because it's all about Men!*

RONALD REAGAN · PATRICIA NEAL · RICHARD TODD
THE *HASTY* HEART

**Ronald Reagan** spent his immediate postwar years making war movies whose plots tried to "explain" to the survivors "what had really happened."

One of them was **The Hasty Heart** (1949). During its filming, and still in "mourning" for the recent failure of his marriage to Jane Wyman, he sustained an affair with his empathetic co-star, **Patricia Neal,** depicted on the left in this movie poster.

At the time, she, too, was healing from the torments of an unhappy affair—in her case with a "married and therefore inaccessible actor," Gary Cooper.

**Richard Todd,** *The Hasty Heart's* third co-star, appears in this poster in the middle.

Before his *schtick* as an actor shriveled and died, **Ronald Reagan** maintained a "last hurrah" with a series of action-adventure movies, many of them Westerns.

Here, he appears with **Rhonda Fleming (aka "The Queen of Technicolor)** in *The Last Outpost* (1951) developing a reputation for military prowess that , years later, in his bid for the governorship of California, played well among voters.

He also made two movies with the endlessly charming Doris Day. They included *Storm Warning*, a tale about the Ku Klux Klan in a small southern town; and a baseball epic, *The Winning Team*, about how to make it in the big leagues. Reagan fell in love with Doris, and was about to propose marriage.

But he'd also been dating Nancy Davis. His hopes of marrying Doris were dashed when Nancy announced that she was pregnant with a child the world later knew, infamously, as Patti. Reagan married Nancy in 1952. After that, with an exception or two, his days as a Hollywood, horndog abruptly ended. To the press, he announced, "I have found my soulmate."

# JANE

Co-starring in Darwin Porter's *Love Triangle* is Miss Jane Wyman, Reagan's first wife, who spent a lot of time and energy deliberately obscuring her origins. After her birth as Sarah Jane Mayfield in St. Joseph, Missouri, in 1917, her parents deserted her, thereby causing to her adopt the name of her elderly, unrelated-by-birth guardians. Subsequently, she became known as Sarah Jane Fulks.

In Hollywood, she went to see Charlie Chaplin at his studio when she heard that his staff was searching for a little girl to cast in one of his upcoming movies. She didn't get the role, but he did proposition her sexually, thereby designating her as one in a long line of sexual indiscretions associated with The Little Tramp.

At the age of sixteen, Jane impetuously married Eugene Wyman, who was called "a walking streak of sex." The marriage lasted less than a month. Although she spent the rest of her life concealing the fact that she had ever been married to him, she nonetheless retained his name as the professional name she used throughout the rest of her life. Ironically, she never actually finalized any divorce proceedings from Eugene, an embarrassing error which technically defined her as a bigamist in each of her subsequent marriages, including the one she shared with Reagan.

For Wyman, the climb up the Hollywood ladder was arduous and long. For years, and in movie after movie, she remained firmly entrenched as either a chorus girl cutie or as a fast-talking, wise-cracking blonde. She became known as "Pug Nose," and attracted the attention of many of her male co-stars, especially those with roving eyes.

She preferred to date, whenever possible, from Hollywood's A-list. Her two most enduring af-

**Jane Wyman,** a model for *haute mode*, photographed in 1940, a year into her nine-year marriage to Ronald Reagan.

fairs, each of which continued throughout the course of her marriage to Reagan, included John Payne, with whom she'd appeared in *Kid Nightingale*. Her longest-running affair was with singer/actor Dennis Morgan, a featured actor at Warner Brothers' from 1943 to 1949.

Her second husband was Myron Futterman, a dress salesman with roots in New Orleans. During the course of her marriage, she discovered that although he sold gowns and dresses and ladies' undergarments during the day, he liked to wear some of his inventories at night.

Jane was finally cast in *Brother Rat*, alongside the blonde Adonis, Wayne Morris, with whom she had an affair. But Reagan, cast into the same movie, eventually won out over Morris.

She later said, sarcastically, about Reagan during the course of their rocky marriage, "He's about as good in bed as he is on screen."

When Wyman made *Johnny Belinda*, released in 1948, rumors spread that she was conducting a torrid affair with her co-star, Lew Ayres, the former husband of Ginger Rogers. When Reagan was pressed by a journalist about his reaction to her affair, he made an astonishing statement,

"Jane very much needs to have a fling, and I intend to let her have it."

Wyman was later deceived by Ayres, who had promised to marry her after her divorce from Reagan became final. But when Jane was finally single again, Ayres backed out of the relationship, leaving her stranded.

Wyman, in the aftermath of "love gone wrong," became a cougar on the prowl, dating handsome young men in their twenties. She fell in love with sportsman, Travis Kleefeld, aged 26. But when her fans found out about it, they bombarded Warners with letters protesting her affair. And threatening to boycott her movies. Consequently, she broke off with Travis.

She then launched an affair with Fred Karger, the band leader, who at the time, was romantically and sexually involved with Marilyn Monroe. Marilyn later said, "Freddie was the only man I ever loved-and that includes Joe DiMaggio."

Karger finally dumped Marilyn, telling her that he didn't think she would be a proper stepmother for his daughter, Terry.

He thought, however, that Jane Wyman would, and soon proposed marriage to her. They wed in 1952, but the marriage lasted only until she began filming *Magnificent Obsession* with Rock Hudson. But one night, she returned to her suite at the Waldorf Astoria in Manhattan and caught Rock and her husband making love. Her divorce from Karger was finalized in 1955.

She remarried the bisexual musician in 1961, but the second time around, it didn't work out either. She divorced him for a second time in 1965, and never remarried again.

Her final comment? "I obviously have no talent for marriage. The one man I really wanted was Gregory Peck, my co-star in *The Yearling*. But he was taken."

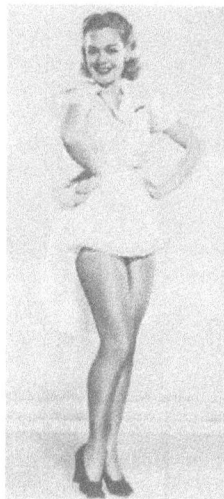

Legs and cheesecake from a (perhaps underaged) *ingénue*, Hollywood newcomer **Jane Wyman.**

**Jane Wyman** *(right)* in the family-friendly equine drama, *The Yearling* (1946) portraying a frontierswoman and overburdened young mother, co-starring with **Gregory Peck.**

*Left to right:* Broadway superstar **Ethel Merman,** known for a voice that could reach the rafters of any musical theater, with **Jane Wyman** and the bisexual bandleader, **Fred Karger,** whom Jane married and divorced twice and fought for with Marilyn Monroe.

The Reagan marriage lasted until 1948 – the same year **Jane Wyman** won an Oscar for her portrayal of a sexually abused deaf-mute in *Johnny Belinda.* Her acceptance speech is sometimes cited as the best in the history of the Academy: "I won this by keeping my mouth shut, and that's what I'm going to do now."

For the remainder of her long career, she remained mute (or at least non-committal) about almost everything associated with her spectacularly famous ex-husband. Cynics later cited that (wise) decision as the primary reason she continued her own spectacular rise through the employment ranks of the television industry, eventually collecting one of the highest paychecks in the history of the medium. Her final gig was on *Falcon Crest*, where she played Angela Channing, the ferocious matriarch of a ferocious clan of California wine producers.

# NANCY

Nancy Davis sometimes told both the press and her friends, "My life began the day I met Ronald Reagan."

That was a romantic thing to say, having little bearing on reality. She had such a full life before Reagan that she could have filled a memoir with information about it.

Through *Love Triangle,* Blood Moon filled in those missing chapters in her life.

First, she was born in 1921, not 1923. Her real name was not Nancy Davis, but Anne Robbins. She changed her name to reflect her gratitude to her stepfather, Dr. Loyal Davis, a well-known neurosurgeon in Chicago.

Her mother was a colorful, tough-talking comedienne who billed herself as "The Scarlett O'Hara of Virginia," Edith Luckett, sometimes known on the stage as "Lucky Luckett."

Lucky was charming, attracting friends from the world of show-biz. When Nancy was growing up, her so-called "uncles and aunts" included Spencer Tracy, Walter Huston, ZaSu Pitts, Lillian Gish, Katharine Hepburn, Helen Hayes, and Mary Martin.

For the role of Nancy's Godmother, Lucky designated Nazimova, the notoriously lesbian star of the Silent Screen. Flamboyantly theatrical, she had been the Queen of Metro in 1920. Nazimova succeeded in doing something her co-star in *Camille.* Rudolf Valentino, could not—She seduced both of Valentino's wives, Jean Acker and Natasha Rambova.

It was Spencer Tracy who arranged a date for Nancy with his best friend, Clark Gable. He took her out every night during the week he was in New York. Wistfully, she later lamented, "If we had gotten to know each other better, I might have fallen in love with him. Gable sort of hinted at a proposal of marriage, but never actually made it."

Tracy also arranged a screen test for Nancy with his friend, the director George Cukor, known for his skill at making women look good through the lens of a movie camera. Howard Keel, star of such MGM movies as *Annie Get Your Gun* and *Showboat,* was her co-star in the test.

In Hollywood, as biographer Anne Edwards noted, "Nancy's phone number was passed around a lot." Her chief sponsor was Benny Thau, head of casting at MGM.

Her boyfriends included Peter Lawford and Robert Walker, when they weren't making love to each other.

Previous affairs had transpired with Yul Brynner (back when he had hair), and Alfred Drake, then the leading musical star of Broadway. Other suitors included Marlon Brando, and Milton Berle, although his mother did not approve.

Nancy's alltime crush was said to have been on Frank Sinatra, her passion for him continuing even after she became First Lady. She frequently invited him to the White House.

Never a great beauty, **young Nancy** was the by-product of a ferociously ambitious mother who was well-versed in show-biz, social skills, and match-making. The stepdaughter of a respected cardiac surgeon, Nancy was respectably reared in the Chicago suburbs....until she left home and headed for adventures, first on Broadway, and then in Hollywood.

**DID YOU KNOW?** That Nancy Davis Reagan's mother (**Edith Luckett,** *depicted above, left*) was a vaudevillian "good time girl" who hoofed her way across many a gaslit stage before she "settled down" with a prosperous doctor, who adopted young, fatherless Nancy, as his own?

And **DID YOU KNOW?** That Nancy Davis Reagan's godmother was the notorious and impossibly famous **NAZIMOVA** (depicted above, right), As one of the first of the Silent Era's "Ultimate Movie Stars," she was, quite simply, the most outrageous, probably depraved, and ultimately tragic eccentrics in the history of Hollywood.

Perhaps recognizing Ronald Reagan as a vessel into which she could pour her magic, the goddaughter of Nazimova, **Nancy Davis** (*seated left on the banquette*) is seen here as victorous in the games of a courtesan: She's fulfilling the erotic dream of the female century: Dinner with the king!"continued scheming:

But as Nancy later confessed frequently, The object of Nancy's affection had been The King of Hollywood, but when **Clark Gable** (*right*) rejected her, she continued "shopping' and turned her gaze toward Ronnie.

One can only wonder what her godmother, Nazimova, would have said.

# RONALD REAGAN & DORIS DAY
## A LOVE AFFAIR

Ronald Reagan's love affair with Doris Day began on the set of *It's a Great Feeling*, a romantic comedy starring (left to right) **Doris Day, Dennis Morgan,** and **Jack Carson.**

Everyone involved in the film seemed to be in a romantic muddle at the time. Doris had abruptly ended an affair with Carson, Ronnie was in mourning because of his separation from Jane Wyman.

Their romantic dramas progressed as filming continued.

As the world knows, that singing sensation, Doris Day, the top female movie star of the 1950s, died recently at the age of 97. What most of her fans don't know is that she came close to becoming First Lady of the United States.

Doris' affair with Ronald Reagan began in 1948 when both of them were under contract at Warner Brothers. His movie career was winding down as hers was blossoming.

Both of them were cast in that feel-good musical, *It's a Great Feeling* (1949). Jane Wyman, who was divorcing Reagan, also was appearing in a cameo. Months before, she'd given birth to their second child, a baby girl who had lived for only a few hours.

Around the time that Wyman delivered her Oscar-winning performance in *Johnny Belinda* (1948), playing a deaf mute who is raped, she'd fallen for her co-star, Lew Ayres. He proposed that she divorce Reagan and marry him, but he changed his mind months later, and left her.

The male lead of *It's a Great Feeling* was Jack Carson, who had been dumped by Doris after a months-long affair. He confessed to Reagan, "She tried to talk me out of drinking two quarts of liquor a day, and I tried to wean her from smoking three packages of Camels a day."

**Doris Mary Anne Kappelhoff** (aka **Doris Day)** was born in Cincinnati, Ohio in 1922, and learned to sing while recuperating from a car accident, listening to the radio.

She morphed into one of the most profit-generating singers, and most popular actresses in cinematic history thanks in part to her humor and wholesome good cheer.

She appears below with Ronald Reagan when they co-starred in a baseball-themed crowd-pleaser, *The Winning Team (1952)*. During its filming, they fell in love.

Their vague and nascent plans to marry were thwarted when Nancy announced to Ronnie that she was pregnant.

One can only wonder about the consequences of a **Reagan-DD marriage** might have been. Would Ronald Reagan and Doris Day morped into a Winning Team on the road to the White House? Many of her move fans believed that she'd have been fabulous as First Lady.

Doris met Reagan one afternoon when both of them arrived, alone, for lunch at the Warners commissary. They shared a table. Reagan later told a jealous Carson, "I thought Doris was a freckle-faced little darling."

Their first date didn't go well. Reagan spent a good part of the meal lamenting his failed marriage to Wyman and Doris discussed her own marital problems with husband #1 (Al Jordan, 1941-43) and #2 (George Weidler, 1946-49).

Their subsequent dates became far more romantic, and they were often seen dancing the night away at their favorite little club on the Sunset Strip with its all-black band.

"We often closed down the club," Doris said. "But I knew Ronnie wanted to do more than dance. He held me so close I could feel his pressing need. When he invited me back to his bachelor pad in the Hollywood Hills, I said, 'Let's go for it.'"

As she later confessed to Ginger Rogers, "Ronnie is a far better lover than my two husbands, with a lot more stamina that either Jack Carson or Tyrone Power."

"I dig Ronnie and think he's really cute," she said. "When I'm in love, I want to make love with that man of mine all the time."

Producer Ross Hunter claimed, "No one knows that under those dirndls Doris wears lurks on of the hottest asses in Tinseltown."

After his first seduction of her, Reagan asked Doris to come and live with him, and she accepted, moving in the next day.

He told his close friend, George Murphy, that he'd fallen in love with her. [*A former song-and-dance man, Murphy became the U.S. senator from California. He was instrumental in urging Reagan to run for governor one day.*]

"Doris would be an ideal first lady, and at your campaign rallies, she could warm up the crowd singing 'Sentimental Journey.'"

Shortly after that, Reagan placed a diamond ring on Doris' finger, and she accepted his proposal. She didn't know at the time that he'd positioned that same ring on the finger of Adele Jergens, the "champagne blonde" of the 1940s and star

316

of *Ladies of the Chorus* (1948) alongside a newcomer, Marilyn Monroe. When Monroe met Reagan, she lured him away from Jergens, who broke off the engagement and returned the diamond.

After his proposal to Doris, Reagan flew to London to make *The Hasty Heart* (1949) with Patricia Neal. Neal had been dumped by Gary Cooper, who had returned to his faithful wife, Rocky. *[Emotionally vulnerable in the wake of her breakup with Cooper, Neal briefly succumbed to Reagan's pre-presidential charms. Word reached Doris of Reagan's intimacies with Neal, but she never confronted him with a direct accusation.]*

Then, by coincidence, both Reagan and Doris were cast together in an upcoming movie, *Storm Warning* (1951), each of them co-starring alongside Ginger Rogers. "Me and Ginger in the same movie?" Doris said. "Our fans will think it's a musical. Actually, it's a tragic story about the KKK, and I'm killed at the end of it."

"During filming, Doris and Ronnie were so very much in love," Ginger said. "I knew they'd have a happy marriage."

The Miami premiere of *Storm Warning* was presented in a movie theater on Flagler Street, and both Doris and Reagan were corralled into attending. But Doris came down with the flu and couldn't accompany him from Hollywood. So instead of Doris, Reagan invited Marilyn Monroe. (He had been dating her on and off.) She accepted, hoping for publicity with a splashy appearance with him at the premiere.

But to her chagrin, Reagan secretly stashed her at the Helen Mar Hotel (he stayed at more expensive lodgings at another hotel) and wouldn't let her attend the premiere. She become so angry at him that she flew back to Los Angeles and ended their affair.

Back in Hollywood, Doris made plans for their wedding. Reagan had also been secretly dating then-starlet Nancy Davis. She was on the road to thirty and still unmarried. Her heart had been broken when her lover, Clark Gable, refused to marry her.

She wanted a husband and none of her previous lovers had agreed to walk down the aisle. They had included Spencer Tracy, Peter Lawford, Robert Walker, Yul Brynner, and Frank Sinatra.

As Reagan confessed to one of his best friends, William Holden, "Unlike my feelings for Doris, when I met Nancy, no bells rang, no fireworks exploded."

One night, Nancy told him she was pregnant with his child and that he had to marry her. Very reluctantly, he agreed. They were married before the birth of their daughter, Patti, whom they claimed had been born prematurely.

"Ronnie broke my heart when he told me about Nancy," Doris said. "I was madly in love with him, and I think we would have had a great marriage. But he had a cheating heart."

It was around that time that Marty Melcher entered Doris' life. She was on the rebound from Reagan, and she married him (1951-68). It ended disastrously. He squandered the $20 million she'd saved during the course of her career, and after his death, he left her with $500,000 in debt.

DORIS DAY · RONALD REAGAN
...in.. and as
*The Winning Team*

*The Winning Team* even included a wedding scene. In the upper photo, **Doris Day**, as bride to the baseball hero played by **Ronald Reagan**, nonchalantly consumes part of her wedding breakfast.

Overall, *Storm Warning* (1950) was a dark and brooding film that contained absolutely none of the winning formulas (charm and humor) which had, till then, been hallmakrs of each of its Hollywood stars.Doris (Day), Ronald (Reagan) and Ginger (Rogers)

It was based on a fearsome and controversial subject, the KKK and its growing influence. *In the left photo*, an unhappily married **Doris Day** gets slapped around by her abusive husband **Steve Cochran** who potrays a local Klansman with ambitons of advancement within its ranks. In the *center photo*, **Ginger Rogers**, restrained during her "mock trial," gets terrorized by Klansmen clad in full "shroud and bonnet' drag."

*In the right photo*, **Ronald Reagan** comforts a grieving Ginger as they jointly mourn the death of a brutalized Doris Day.

In 1952 *[the same year that Reagan married Nancy in a real-life ceremony]*, he also married Doris as part of the plot of a movie. Set in the depths of the Depression, it was *The Winning Team* (1952), a baseball flick.

Sometimes, during reflections on her life, Doris—by now, an animal rights activist, summed up her philosophy of life with this refrain: *QUE SERA, SERA.*

\*\*\*

**EDITOR'S NOTE:** *In its November 2011 edition, Boomer Times ran this feature article, by Darwin Porter, about the ongoing drama of Doris Day. We've replicated it here as a tribute to her great and glorious career.*

## "ENCHANTING," EVERYONE SAID ABOUT MARY ANNE KAPPELHOFF

Despite five or six cinematic triumphs that entrenched her as one of America's most enhanting women, **Doris Day** remained "obstinately unlucky" in her choice of husbands.

She's shown here in 1960 with her cheating husband and larcenous agent, **Marty Melcher,** who embezzled her money, and squandered her considerable earnings, leaving her broke and humiliated before his own unmourned (early) death in 1968. Doris spent the next thirty years working her way out of debt.

In retrospect, Doris probably should have married Reagan, even if it had involved a life on the campaign trail immersed in Republican politics.

In 1959, Doris Day was the most popular film actress in the world. In 2011, she's making a comeback...of sorts.

Living today in Carmel-by-the-Sea in California, Day has just released her first album in two decades. Called *My Heart*, the music is not new but unreleased until now. The album was produced by her son, Terry Melcher, a musician himself, who died of cancer at the age of 62 in 2004. He'd been targeted to be the next victim on the hit list of the psychotic killer, Charles Manson.

Doris Mary Ann Kappelhoff, her real name, burst onto the scene in 1945 singing "Sentimental Journey" for soldiers returning from the war-weary Pacific. American GIs made it their anthem. The hit launched her into a wildly successful film and recording career, which peaked in the late 1950s and early 60s, when she made those romantic comedies with Rock Hudson.

But along came the Baby Boomers of the 1960s, with their different attitudes about sex. "The world's oldest virgin," as she was (bitchily) renamed by frenemies, faded away, a victim of changing tastes.
She could have greatly extended her career if she'd played Mrs. Robinson in Ihe Graduate, the role eventually awarded to Anne Bancroft. Day objected to the part on moral grounds. After her refusal, she remained a relic of the uptight Eisenhower era.

Day was married four times, most notoriously to Martin Melcher for 17 years. When he died in 1968, she discovered to her horror that he had squandered all her money ($20 million, worth about $120 million today). She was $500,000 in debt. She sued his business partner, Jerome B. Rosenthal, and was eventually awarded $22,835,000, the largest civil judgment in California up to that time. She finally settled for $6 million.

The remainder of her life has been spent as an animal rights activist, and the tabloids are reporting that she's going broke. With all those adopted cats and dogs, there are many hungry mouths to feed. Her money doesn't seem to be lasting as long as she is.

Her last album will be a swan song to her thousands of fans, and perhaps will generate some much-needed revenue.

Day's former romantic life also is making tabloid fodder today. It has only recently been revealed that she once had a torrid affair with Paul McCartney.

\*\*\*

*Darwin Porter, formerty a bureau chief for* The Miami Herald, *is an acclaimed entertainment writer. For more information on the literary output of Darwin Porter, click on www.BloodMoonProductions.com*

# NEW, SCANDALOUS, & HOT, FOR MOTHER'S DAY

# HOLLYWOOD NEWS

## ABOUT A CELEBRITY EXPOSÉ THAT UNPACKS THE MOST FAMOUS* MOTHER-DAUGHTER SHOWBIZ TEAM IN AMERICA.

(*or second-most-famous if you voted for Judy Garland & Liza Minnelli)

Blood Moon Productions, in an unauthorized biography, takes us on a wild roller-coaster ride with Debbie Reynolds ("hard as nails and with more balls than any five guys I've ever known") and her talented, often traumatized daughter, Carrie Fisher ("one of the smartest, hippest chicks in Hollywood").

Evolving for decades under the unrelenting glare of public scrutiny, each became a world-class symbol of the social and cinematic tastes that prevailed during their heydays as celebrity icons in Hollywood.

Now, for the first time, their thousands of fans can read about the combative but ferociously loyal relationship of the "boop-boop-a-doop" girl with her intergalactic STAR WARS daughter, Princess Leia, and their iron-willed strength during their "true grit" battles to outrace changing tastes in Hollywood.

According to its co-author and publisher, **Danforth Prince,** "We've defined this as the ultimate conversation-starter for savvy matriarchs transmitting lifestyle advice to their daughters or granddaughters. It's a Mother's Day celebration of the ties that bind (and sometimes torment) different generations of inter-related women, each navigating their way through the shifting currents of pop culture."

Loaded with never-before published revelations about "who was doing what to whom" during the final gasps of Golden Age Hollywood, it's a one-of-a-kind, All-American saga about the price of glamour, career-related pain, family anguish, romantic betrayals, lingering guilt, and the volcanic shifts that affected a scrappy, wryly funny mother-daughter team—and everyone else who ever loved the movies.

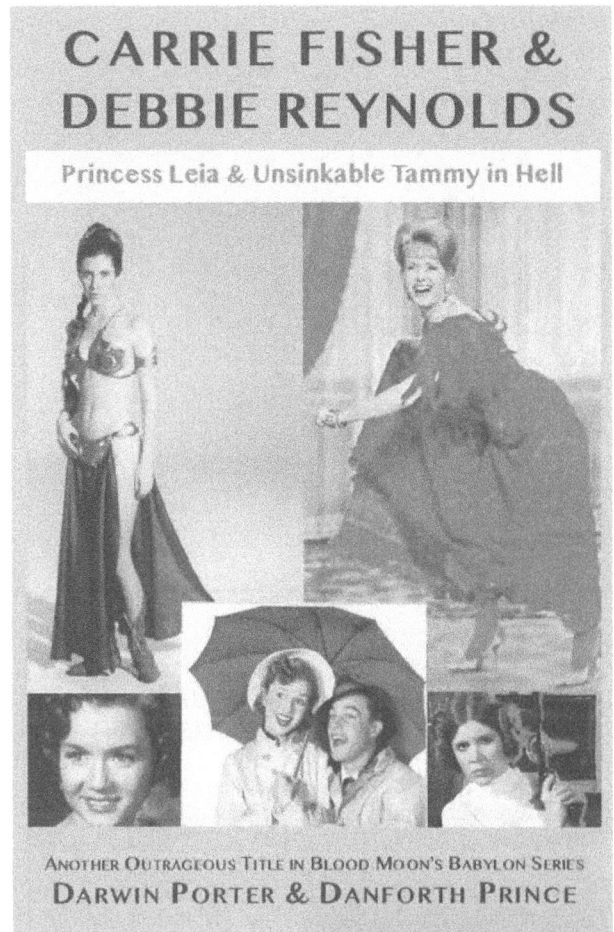

CARRIE FISHER &
DEBBIE REYNOLDS

Princess Leia & Unsinkable Tammy in Hell

ANOTHER OUTRAGEOUS TITLE IN BLOOD MOON'S BABYLON SERIES
DARWIN PORTER & DANFORTH PRINCE

*"Feeling misunderstood by the younger (female) members of your gene pool? This is the Hollywood exposé every grandmother should give to her granddaughter, a roadmap like Debbie Reynolds might have offered to Billie Lourd."*

—Marnie O'Toole

*"How is a 1950s-era movie star, (TAMMY) supposed to cope with her postmodern, substance-abusing daughter (PRINCESS LEIA), the rebellious, high-octane byproduct of Rock 'n Roll, Free Love, and postwar Hollywood's most scandal-soaked marriage? Read about it here, in Blood Moon's unauthorized double exposé about how Hollywood's toughest (and savviest) mother-daughter team maneuvered their way through shifting definitions of fame, reconciliation, and fortune."*

—Donna McSorley

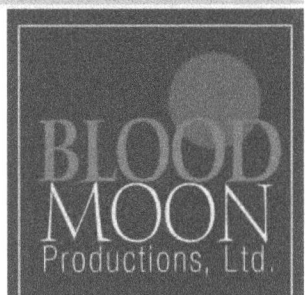

BLOOD
MOON
Productions, Ltd.

**Entertainment
About How
America
Interprets Its
Celebrities**
BloodMoonProductions.com

319

# DEBBIE REYNOLDS & CARRIE FISHER

## PRIVATELY, PRINCESS LEIA & THE UNSINKABLE TAMMY LED LIVES OF TRIUMPH & TRAGEDY

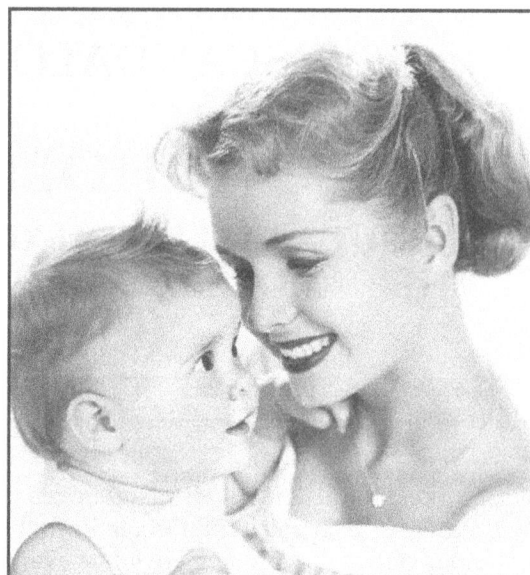

Debbie Reynolds and her daughter, Carrie Fisher, co-starred in some of the greatest off-screen dramas in show-biz history.

Born in a shanty in El Paso, Texas, Debbie, a Texas tomboy, endured a life of poverty--jackrabbit every night for dinner--until she moved to California.

Blossoming into a young beauty, she won the title of Miss Burbank, which led to a movie contract. Stardom came relatively quickly when she was cast as the minty fresh ingenue in *Singin' in the Rain* (1952), hailed as the greatest Hollywood musical of all time.

Frank Sinatra stole her virginity, but she married pop singer Eddie Fisher for the "official deflowering" (her words). "Debbie and Eddie," the darling of fan magazines, reigned as" America's Sweethearts."

The fairytale ended when his best friend, producer Mike Todd, died in a plane crash. Fisher rushed to the side of his widow, the violet-eyed screen vamp, Elizabeth Taylor. He descended from Maggie the Cat's *Hot Tin Roof* into her boudoir. His divorce from Debbie and his subsequent marriage to her best friend provided fodder for the scandal magazines until the day Elizabeth provoked another scandal, divorcing him to marry Richard Burton.

Through storm and rain, Debbie battled on, hitting a high

As millions of mothers and daughters have done for centuries, **Debbie** *(right)* **and Carrie** argued, often ferociously, throughout the course of their early lives. But as they mellowed (and perhaps as their options grew more limited) movie fans realized that they genuinely loved each other.

Here, they appear within a photo that helped cement Debbie's image as the kind of girl G.I.s can fight for and marry.

In the early 1950s, teen idol **Eddie Fisher** (1928 –2010), shown here with his then-wife **Debbie Reynolds** and their children, **Carrie and Todd Fisher,** sold millions of records and hosted his own TV show.

His messy, widely publicized abandonment of Debbie for Elizabeth Taylor scandalized television audiences to the point that he famously "fell from grace," lost his fan base and TV show, and became a parable for a B-list artist who was whiplashed and then crushed by a judgmental American public.

Although the career of Elizabeth Taylor was (temporarily) damaged, too, only **Debbie Reynolds** emerged, triumphant and unscathed, from the ensuing fallout.

## AMERICA'S MOST WIDELY PUBLICIZED "LOVE RECTANGLE" OF THE 1950s

(*Left to right*, above, **Mike Todd,** with his then-wife **Elizabeth Taylor**, and **Eddie Fisher** with his then-wife, **Debbie Reynolds**)

Taylor and Todd ("the love of my life") were bosom buddies with Fisher and Reynolds. The two men were best friends, and Taylor and Reynolds tagged along on many of their outings, including at the race track depicted above.

Two years after this photo was snapped, Fisher starred with Taylor in her to-date "sluttiest' film role in *BUtterfield 8*, and began what the tabloids described as "a torrid affair." When Reynolds found out, she very publicly divorced Fisher, a scandal that caused serious damage to his career.

Taylor and Fisher themselves divorced four years later after she fell in love with the not-particularly well-known Welsh film star Richard Burton, whom she married twice.

Years later, Elizabeth Taylor and Debbie Reynolds, each of them sadder, older, wiser, and more difficult to market, buried the hatchet. The resulting film, *These Old Broads* (2001), co-starring Shirley MacLaine and Joan Collins, re-endeared them to Baby Boomers and Hollywood oldsters everywhere.

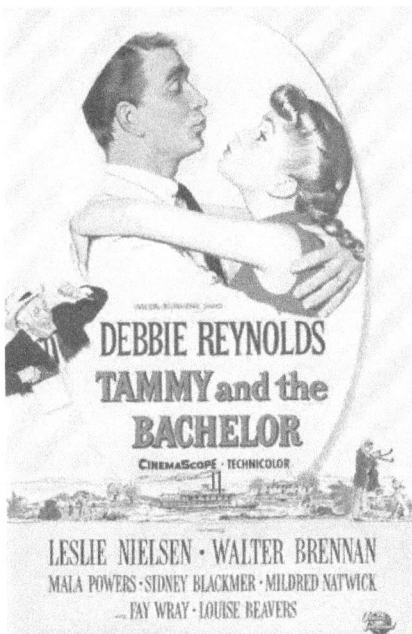

**Debbie Reynold's** appearance in the first of MGM's *Tammy* series (Tammy and the Bachelor; 1957) marked the beginnings of her nationwide fame as a personality of note. In it, cast opposite **Leslie Nielsen** as scion and heir to a plantation in the Mississippi delta, Debbie personified the kind of small-town virgin whom American G.I.s wanted to marry and mate with.

Advertising agencies hyped her "cheerleader next door' image fast and hard...and couples in love (or singles who wanted to be), lapped it up with something approaching frenzy. As the film swept through movie houses nationwide, Debbie became the newest in the long and sometimes tragic line of "America's Sweethearts."

point when she starred as Tammy in 1957, cast as the granddaughter of a Louisiana moonshiner, spouting pithy wisdom. "I'll be singing my hit song on stage for the rest of my years."

Her most memorable role was in 1964, when she was cast in the rags-to-riches saga of *The Unsinkable Molly Brown*. (The character she portrayed even survived the sinking of the *Titanic*.) The role brought her an Oscar nomination.

Each of her three marriages was a disaster, the second one to a millionaire shoe manufacturing mogul who bankrupted both of them. Impoverished after the divorce, she ended up sleeping in her car.

Debbie mingled with the elite of Hollywood in the dying days of its Golden Age. Luminaries included Clark Gable ("if I were only twenty years younger...."); Judy Garland (who propositioned her); Lana Turner; Bette Davis ("she was my daughter"); Katharine Hepburn; Spencer Tracy; Lucille Ball; and Glenn Ford, who fell in love with her.

Mass murderer Charles Manson sent her love letters; Liberace wanted her to enter into a "lavender marriage" with him, and James Dean "forced himself onto me" when she was up for the role of his girlfriend in *Rebel Without a Cause*.

"I turned down Warren Beatty," Debbie claimed, "and didn't even go for the handsome Gary Cooper, although he told me women called him 'The Montana Mule.' Bob Hope, a compulsive womanizer, also had to look elsewhere."

A rebellious daughter, Carrie grew up to endure a life of living hell-pill popping, drug abuse, chronic anxiety, failed love affairs, bipolar disorder, and electroshock therapy.

Carrie sometimes protested: "I don't want to be the daughter of Debbie Reynolds. I battled demons that set my brain on fire."

International celebrity came in 1977, when she played Princess Leia in *Star Wars* as an elaborately coiffed intergalactic princess, spearheading "The Force," and strong enough to oppose the villainy of Darth Vader. She became the fantasy of teenage boys and sci-fi freaks.

---

**IN THE MOVIES AND IN REAL LIFE, DEBBIE WAS UNSINKABLE**

*The Unsinkable Molly Brown* (1964) was based on the life of Margaret (aka Molly) Brown, an adventuress and "scandaleuse" who stumbled into unexpected wealth during the Gilded Age.

In it, Debbie played a hillybilly hick from the Colorado gold mines. She marries for love, then hubby gets rich, and **Debbie Goes to Europe**. During her perky adventures there, she charms, befriends, and enchants the (very indulgent) crowned heads of Europe.

Not since the choreographic gymnastics of *Singin' In the Rain* had **Debbie Reynolds** been forced into such "athleticism' in front of a camera. With spunk, true grit, and style THE DEBBIE WE LOVED rose to the challenge, later citing it and its dance routines as grueling.

Before the end of the film, like the historic figure (Margaret Brown) on which the film was based, Debbie survived the sinking of the *Titanic*, and became an ongoing symbol (to movie audiences, at least) of homespun survival.

MGM's *Singin' in the Rain* (1952), starring **Gene Kelly, Debbie Reynolds** *(each depicted in both photos, above)*, and Donald O'Connor, is still hailed as Hollywood's greatest musical. In it, Debbie popped out of a cake *(right photo)* in more ways than one.

"Louis B. Mayer forced me onto Kelly. He wanted a real dancer—not me. Damn it, I showed the fucker, although he rehearsed me until my feet bled. That dancing role was more painful than childbirth."

An affair with the married Harrison Ford faded into a marriage to singer Paul Simon as they crossed a Bridge Over Troubled Waters. A final marriage to a Hollywood agent ended when he decided he needed not a wife, but a husband for himself.

The princess turned writer in a series of autobiographical books praised for their lacerating insights into human frailty and awash with bubble and bounce, sprinkled with *bons mots*, an adroit verbal acrobat with words. *The New York Times* defined her as "one of the rare inhabitants of La-La Land who can actually write."

In Carrie's writings, Debbie often didn't come out too well, depicted as a "casually narcissistic gorgon ill-suited for the real world." As her star dimmed, cooled, and faded, mother took to the bottle.

Until the end, Debbie was resilient, a singing, dancing, sensation of massive talent, a button-nosed, *boop-boopie-doo* girl for six decades. She never lost her "Debbie-ness," strutting her stuff, emoting like a storm—everything sprinkled with the stardust of yesterday.

What was her secret of perpetual youth? Carrie knew: "She drank bat's blood for breakfast and smeared bug brains on her skin."

After years of separation, Carrie and Debbie came together at the end, not able to live apart. They couldn't even die without each other.

\*\*\*

# DEBBIE (*Unsinkable Tammy*) and CARRIE
## (*Princess Leia from Outer Space*)

### United, in Death, At Last

The most ardent fans of Debbie Reynolds and Carrie Fisher, two movie legends, like to think they are united in a galaxy far, far away. Both of them died within hours of each other in December of 2016.

Debbie still holds the record as the singing and dancing sensation of *Singin' in the Rain* (1952), hailed today as the greatest Hollywood musical ever made. Carrie earned her own kind of immortality when she starred in "my lifetime career" of playing Princess Leia with that "cinnamon bun hairdo" beginning with the first installment of *Star Wars* (1977).

Their tragic lives and loves live again in Blood Moon's latest Hollywood biography, *Carrie Fisher & Debbie Reynolds: Princess Leia and Unsinkable Tammy in Hell*. For the first time, their remarkable lives are revealed in detail with many hidden revelations. They were survivors whose struggles evoke those of heroines by Shakespeare. They faced a total of five failed marriages (three for Debbie, two for Carrie), bankruptcies, bipolar disorders, electroshock treatments, endless lawsuits, hopelessly doomed love affairs, and dreams that never came true. Through it all, both of them endured and kept their careers going at full blast.

Carrie was born to Debbie and Eddie Fisher, the pop crooner of the 1950s. Both "Debbie & Eddie" were hailed as "America's Sweethearts." A forest of trees in Canada were needed for the newsprint that described their glorious love affair that was all a sham.

Away on singing engagements, Eddie was almost never at home, indulging in a series of affairs.

His best friend, producer Mike Todd, the husband of Elizabeth Taylor, died in a plane crash in New Mexico in 1958. Fisher rushed to the side of his widow and never left. As he later told Debbie, "I love Elizabeth. I never loved you. I only married you because my fans would desert me if I walked out on America's Sweetheart."

Through it all, Debbie bounced back as the button-nosed, *boop-boopie-doo* girl, strutting her stuff and emoting as an unpretentious girl next door. She had found her lifetime *schtick*—that of a relentlessly upbeat show-stopper with plenty of spunk, humor, and razzmatazz. America gobbled it up.

That bouncy image was cemented in 1957 when she appeared as the country girl in *Tammy and the Bachelor*. Her recording of "Tammy" went gold, playing on jukeboxes across the land. For the rest of her life, wherever she appeared on stage, Debbie had to sing this song of a virginal innocent.

She was more in tune with her role in the 1964 *The Unsinkable Molly Brown*, which brought her an Oscar nod. It was the tale of the actual Molly Brown, heiress to a Colorado gold mining fortune who survived the sinking of the *Titanic*.

Along the way, Debbie fell in love with a number of men who didn't want to marry her or were already married: Glenn Ford, Robert Wagner (her first love), James Dean, Frank Sinatra, James Garner, and Gower Champion, among others.

She also married two more times, a show manufacturer and a real estate developer, both of whom went through their fortunes and hers as well. Debbie ended up getting booted out of her palatial home by the bank which held hefty mortgages.

"You've heard of Queen for a Day?" Debbie asked. "Well, I was Queen for a long weekend on two different occasions." She was referring to her affairs with the handsome young King Baudouin of Belgium and King Hussein of Jordan during their visits to Hollywood.

Baudouin told his handlers that Debbie Reynolds was his favorite movie star, and they arranged a visit for him to meet her on the set of *It Started With a Kiss* in 1959. The title of the film was apt. Evading his security forces, she ran away with him for a long weekend spent at Rock Hudson's villa in Malibu.

Their disappearance, although hidden from the press, caused much speculation among insiders. She later followed Baudouin to New York, where he bid her farewell and never returned. "There went my chance to become Queen of Belgium and First Lady of the Congo." (At the time, the Congo was a colony of Belgium.)

Back in Hollywood, she entertained another royal visitor, King Hussein of Jordan. She later claimed that her brief fling with him "was straight out of *Arabian Nights*." When he flew out of Hollywood, he too, would never return "There went my chance to become queen of the oldest dynasty in the Muslim world."

Carrie made her first screen appearance as a teenager in *Shampoo* (1975) opposite Warren Beatty. Her opening line on the screen was to ask him if he wanted to seduce her, although she used the "F" word. Apparently, he accepted her invitation off screen. She claimed he took her virginity, whether he did or not.

Debbie sent her daughter to London to study drama for a

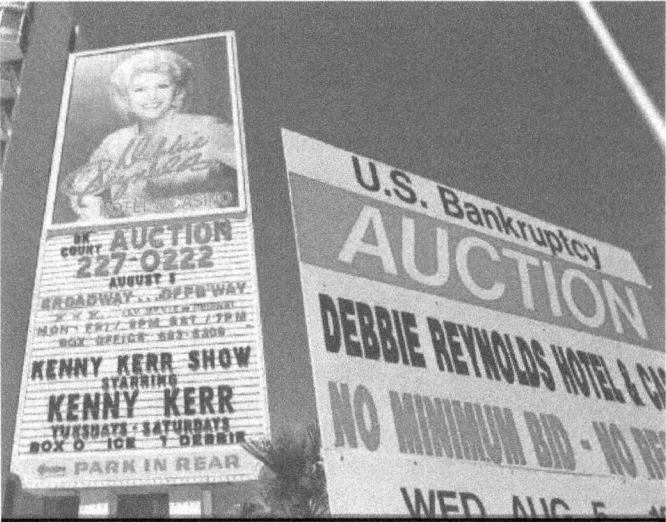

As she aged and evolved into one of Hollywood's feistiest "over the hill' former ingenues, **Unsinkable Debbie** threw herself, wholesale, into the cutthroat world of the entertainment and gambling circuits of Las Vegas.

From the hotel/theater/casino complex she spearheaded **The Debbie Reynolds Hotel**, and hoofed her way through song-and-dance routines culled from the forty-something years of her film career. She attracted middle-American fans from long ago, selling them nostalgia, good cheer, and tickets to her *"Hollywood the Way it Was"* revues.

Accessorized with a mini-museum stuffed with costumes and memorabilia from MGM's golden age, iher hotel opened in 1993 and filed for bankruptcy in 1997, closing a year later.

It all collapsed before her death in 2016. Her hotel was sold and demolished to make room for a more modern replacement (whcih also folded). Her cherished collection of costumes and props from MGM's golden age was sold—rather callously, everyone said—at auction.

In her campaigns to "stay relevant' as she aged, Debbie didn't limit her talents to high-profile venues like Vegas. With grit and tenacity, she brought her nostalgia-soaked-with-perky cheer *schtick* to the boonies, too.

The marquee in the photo, above, promotes her three-day gig at a theater in a small, rust-belt community north of Pittsburgh, Pennsylvania.

Her always-ardent to-the-grave fans continued thinking of her as "unsinkable" through and until the bitter end.

year, and it was here that she became enveloped in Mick Jagger's drugged-out world of the *glitterati*. She also entered into romances with two dazzling bisexual stars, Freddie Mercury and David Bowie.

Back in Hollywood, she made *Star Wars* in 1977 as Princess Leia. In New York, she was lured into the heavily drugged world of John Belushi, her doomed co-star in *The Blues Brothers*.

She would go on to have two husbands of her own. The first was the singer and composer Paul Simon, and together, they crossed a "Bridge Over Troubled Water." Although the marriage ended, their affair continued for years.

When she married for the final time, it was to a top Hollywood talent agent, Bryan Lourd, which led to the birth of a daughter, actress Billie Lourd. One night, he informed her he was leaving her since he wanted "a husband of my own."

After that, all of Carrie's affairs were doomed to fail. Her two most big-name seductions began when she was filming *Liberty* (1985) on the East Coast. There, she was introduced to Senator Chris Dodd of Connecticut, and they began a fling. After he introduced her to one of his best friends, Senator Teddy Kennedy of Boston, a brief romance followed. She said "Both of these men, at different times, ran for President of the United States. Each of them failed in that pursuit, and I failed, too, in not becoming First Lady of the United States."

Lost in a world of drugs and enduring electroshock therapies, Carrie broke with her mother and didn't speak to her for a decade. They finally reunited, living in separate but nearby homes within their enclosed compound in Los Angeles.

While she was in London to promote her latest book, *Princess Diarist*, Carrie made world headlines when she revealed her love affair with Harrison Ford, who had played Han Solo in *Star Wars*. Regrettably, the affair didn't last, as he was already married.

She flew back to Los Angeles but lapsed into a coma during the flight, dying on December 27, 2016. She was only sixty years old, and an autopsy revealed that she had traces of at least five recreational drugs in her system at the time of her death.

During her planning for her daughter's funeral, Debbie said, "My heart is broken."

In less than two days, Debbie herself was dead at the age of 84. Her career had spanned six and a half decades. "The shock of Carrie's death was more than my mother could take," said her son, Todd.

Many medical authorities proclaimed that it is entirely possible to die of a broken heart.

Raised in a shanty without a working bathroom in El Paso, Texas, **Debbie Reynolds** often ate fresh-killed jackrabbit or rattlesnack for supper.

But after moving to California, she entered (and won) the Miss Burbank beauty pageant of 1948. She had borrowed the bathing suit from a friend—and also the high heels, which were two sizes too big.

"I strutted my stuff, as horny men gaped at me. I felt naked."

Whenever public figures (especially royalty) visited Hollywood, MGM "put on a show" and newsreels rolled their cameras. *Photo left, above,* shows a carefully rehearsed Debbie Reynolds chatted with the heir to the Belgian throne, the then-unmarried **King Badouin II**. *Right photo* shows **King Hussein of Jordan** on the MGM lot chitchatting with **Debbie** and **Glenn Ford**. Both photos were snapped in 1958 or 1959, at receptions associated with the imminent release of MGM's frothy romance, *It Started with a Kiss,* co-starring Reynolds and Ford.

According to Debbie, "Neither of them proposed marriage. There went my chance to become queen of Belgium and First Lady of the Congo." *[What was at the time known as "The Belgian Congo," and administered from Brussels* now self-identifies *as the Democratic Republic of the Congo]*

"Likewise, I lost my chance to become Queen of Jordan," Debbie continued, "following a lineup of queens that dated back to ancient history."

Like millions of other mother/daughter teams, during long stretches of the swinging Sixties and sexual Seventies, **Carrie Fisher and Debbie Reynolds** feuded and fought. But as they approached the end of their "joined at the hip" and drama-soaked lives, they demonstrated, frequently, that they really loved each other.

*Photos, left to right, above,* **Carrie with her mother** in a Las Vegas revue; **Carrie as Princess Leia** (aka "the girl with the cinnamon bun hairdo") with a robotic aide in one of the *Star Wars* movies; and **a public display of mother-daughter affection** during one of their frequent photo-ops.

Todd Fisher is famously quoted as telling reporters that after his sister died, his mother had said, "I want to be with Carrie." Debbie died a day later of a stroke.

The HBO documentary *Bright Lights* (2016) is a documentary about the relationship between Debbie and her daughter, Carrie. Debbie Reynold's star on Hollywood's Walk of Fame is at 6654 Hollywood Blvd.

This mother-daughter photo was snapped when **Carrie Fisher** (right) was a precocious and very hip 15-year-old,

The character she developed, Princess Leia Organa. for the Star Wars franchise, was defined by its publicists as "one of the Rebel Alliances' greatest leaders, fearless on the battlefield and dedicated to ending the tyranny of the Empire."

But the road that Carrie traveled for identification with the brand reads like a case study in the Agony and Ecstasy of movie development and marketing during the latter decades of the 20th Century.

Alert to her eclipse by starlettes who by then included her daughter (i.e., Carrie) **Debbie**—with humor— began to self-identify in public as: **"Hello everyone. Let me introduce myself. I am Princess Leia's mother."**

An aging **Elizabeth Taylor** *(left)* was once one of the best friends of **Debbie Reynolds**...that is, untill she ran off with Debbie's then-husband, Eddie Fisher.

Years later, they reunited after feeling bitterness for years. "Both of us decided that Eddie was not worth the fuss."

They were **The Rat Pack**, and in the Madison Avenue heyday of Don Draper, its members were the coolest and edgiest guys in Hollywood. Debbie was an on-again, off-again "honorary member."

With Las Vegas "involvements' that spanned more than 50 years, Debbie Reynolds had a long and rich history there. Her repository of "only in Vegas" stories could have landed a lot of people in jail.

As stated after her death by her son, Todd Fisher, "She played the Tropicana, the Sands, the Desert Inn, the Riviera. She has as many performances in this town as anybody, At one time she once held the record for the most consecutive performances by any performer, including Wayne Newton. She's definitely connected to the original Rat Pack and the roots of Las Vegas."

In the photo above, f**ive of the Rat Pack's most durable members** pose, during their heyday, near the entrance to the **Cal-Neva Hotel and Casino** near Lake Tahoe.

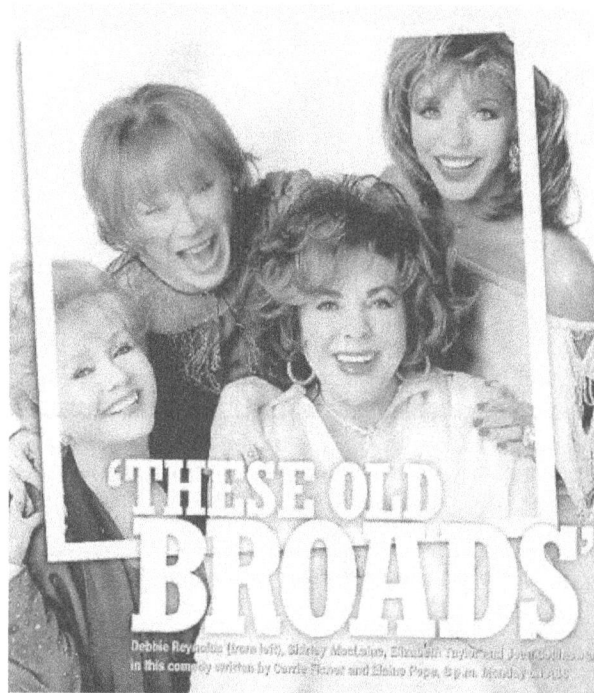

*Left to right in upper photo,* **Debbie Reynolds, Shirley MacLaine, Elizabeth Taylor,** and **Joan Collins**, co-starring in that bitchfest known as *These Old Broads* (2001). These former "hoofers and heifers," satirizing their fading allure, strutted their stuff once again, except for Elizabeth, who was wheelchair bound. Collectively, they represented 269 years of age, and 16 ex-husbands.

*Left to right in lower photo.* In this publicity shot from *These Old Broads,* **Collins, Reynolds**, and **MacLaine,** interacted and self-spoofed like the 'Golden Girls" they'd become. In the process, they "re-endeared" themselves to millions of their Baby Booming fans

## DEBBIE REYNOLDS

1932-2016

**We Love You Debbie!  Rest in Peace**

326

# STEVE McQUEEN
## KING OF COOL

*TALES OF A LURID LIFE*, BY DARWIN PORTER, DESCRIBES
HOW AN ABUSED CHILD AND SEXUAL OUTLAW MORPHED INTO A
### CELLULOID HERO

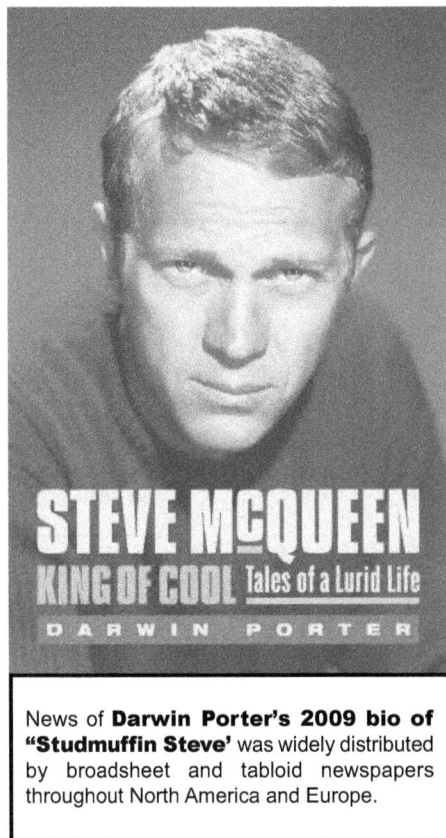

News of **Darwin Porter's 2009 bio of "Studmuffin Steve'** was widely distributed by broadsheet and tabloid newspapers throughout North America and Europe.

When he appeared on Broadway as entertainer Peter Allen, Hugh Jackman delivered a brilliant insight into Hollywood biographies. He asserted that he preferred to skip a book's first two chapters, turning immediately to Chapter 3 where the subject "meets Elizabeth Taylor."

In my Hollywood biography, *Steve McQueen, King of Cool, Tales of a Lurid Life*, Steve indeed meets Taylor in Chapter 3, during his temporary gig as a bartender at the home of Montgomery Clift. She pointedly ignored him.

But it would be a mistake for any reader to skip the beginning chapters of Steve's early life. His drama as a young boy and teenager surpassed any role he eventually played on the screen. Abandoned by his father (a stunt pilot), he followed in the footsteps of his beautiful mother, Jullian Crawford, a prostitute. This sordid drama séguéd into an Oedipal fling.

As a young boy, Steve was brutally molested by one of his "stepfathers," who forced him into work as a child prostitute along Santa Monica Boulevard in Los Angeles. That scenario led to a gang rape that scarred him for life. On his own as a teenager, he got a job on a freighter taking him from New York to Havana. There, he found work in one of the bordellos that flourished during the pre-Castro days. He also made extra bucks by acting in porn and appearing onstage in an erotic revue called "The Cream in Her Coffee."

Steve continued his work as a bordello towel boy when he took a freighter to Santo Domingo (then known as Ciudad Trujillo). Long before he was the top box office star in the world, Steve in the D.R. became involved with the legendary, larger-than-life Porfirio Rubirosa, the "Playboy of the Western World." Steve also inaugurated a torrid affair with Rubirosa's former wife, Flor de Oro, the nymphomaniacal daughter of Rafael Trujillo, the murderous dictator of the Dominican Republic.

After boarding yet another freighter, this one bound for Port Arthur, Texas, Steve found work in yet another bordello, this one patronized by, among others, a rising politician named Lyndon B. Johnson.

After stints as a carnival barker and a tree-topping lumberjack in Oregon, Steve drifted from job to job until, at the age of 17, he joined the U.S. Marine Corps. During his service, the rebellious youth spent a lot of time in the brig for going A.W.O.L. In Labrador, during maneuvers in Arctic waters, he became a hero long before he ever portrayed one on the screen. During a wreck at sea, he rescued several crew members from drowning. For his efforts, he became a member of the honor guard aboard the U.S. presidential yacht, USS *Sequoia*. While aboard, these "two men from Missouri," President Harry S Truman and Steve, played serious poker.

Returning to New York after his tour of duty, Steve had little education and few skills. But his body was in great shape, and he hustled homosexuals in Greenwich Village, clients he secretly despised. One night he encountered his mother in a Village tavern, where she, like him, was trying to ensnare a "john" for a paid sexual encounter.

When Rubirosa arrived in New York, Steve contacted him, a meeting that led to him becoming an employee of a company called "Gentlemen for Rent." Wearing a tux borrowed from Rubi, Steve became the toy boy/escort of visiting Hollywood royalty, a roster of glamourous women who included Lana Turner, Joan

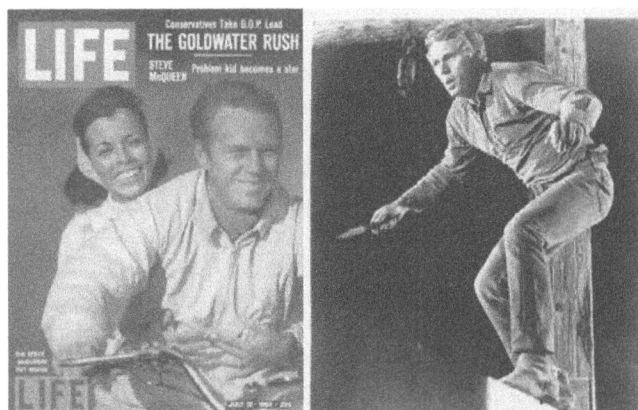

News of **McQueen's** personal life were as widely broadcast as information about his movies. *Left photo* above shows him on the cover of LIFE with then-wife **Neile Adams**. In the *right photo*, in a balancing act, he wields a knife in this movie still from *Nevada Smith (1966)*.

As a working prostitute in a borrowed tuxedo, Steve provided sexual relief to Hollywood dames who included (*left photo, above*) **Lana Turner** and (*right photo*) **Joan Crawford**

**Flor de Oro Trujillo** *(left)*, daughter of the notorious Dominican dictator, appears in fur with her then-husband, the sexually voracious adventurer, **Porfirio Rubirosa,** one of Steve's early friends, mentors, and role models.

**UNPROMISING BE-GINNINGS:** *Upper photo*, **Steve McQueen** as an abused child on a Missouri hog farm run by his grandparents, and *(lower photo)* as a sullen-looking U.S. Marine.

Crawford, and Marlene Dietrich. Truman Capote, who had a crush on Steve, introduced him to Christine Jorgensen, America's most famous transsexual at the time, who wanted to marry him. Following a fling, he turned her down.

After several near misses, both on the stage and in films, Hollywood stardom finally hit him. When it did, the abused became the abuser. "I live for myself," Steve said, "and I answer to nobody. And the last thing I ever want is to fall in love with a broad." Despite that proclamation, he fell for "a broad," the beautiful dancer/actress, Neile Adams, who was on her way to stardom until her philandering husband derailed her career.

Marriage did not stop Steve's string of seductions that earned him an almost mythical status as a pansexual Love Machine. Meeting President JFK, these two Lotharios compared notes, each of them claiming to have had two or three women a day. Surely this was just macho posturing.

Steve began a long-term affair with Frank Sinatra's former wife, Ava Gardner, and one by one knocked off many of his leading ladies and a carload of other actresses as well. They included Barbra Streisand, Judy Garland, Natalie Wood, Mary Wilson of *The Supremes*, the blonde bombshell Mamie Van Doren, and beautiful Tuesday Weld. Along the way he found time for a tryst with Marilyn Monroe, a liaison arranged by the blonde star's former roommate, Shelley Winters.

Publicly, Steve insisted that he loathed homosexuals and bisexuals, yet he sometimes went to bed with them, especially if they were bikers or race car drivers. He maintained a sexual relationship with James Dean and an even longer love/hate affair with closeted Paul Newman. Other trysts developed with Marlon Brando, Sal Mineo, Peter Lawford, and Rock Hudson.

I've detailed for the first time Steve's involvement in a three-way relationship with the doomed hairdresser Jay Sebring and the lovely Sharon Tate, wife of director Roman Polanski. Both Tate (who was pregnant at the time) and Sebring would be murdered by the sociopaths who were choreographed by Charles Manson. Steve was number one on Manson's death list, but Steve escaped mutilation when he didn't show up at that fateful party on the night his friends were murdered.

The compilation of the material that went into this biography involved decades of research. I drew upon hundreds of encounters with Steve's friends, co-stars, bed partners, and, yes, enemies.

Death came to Steve in 1980 in a hospital in Mexico where Steve was undergoing radical treatments to cure his cancer. Even today, his death remains a source of lurid speculation.

In unmasking Steve, I discovered a lonely, terrified man racing toward an untimely death.

Then-president **Harry Truman** took a shine to young Steve, playing extended bouts of poker with him aboard the Presidential yacht *(the Sequoia)* during Steve's military stint as a member of its honor guard.

**McQueen** eventually morphed into his era's most recognizable phallic symbol and studmuffin. **Darwin Porter's biography** reviewed his extraordinary (and tragic) life better than anything else on the literary marketplace.

328

# CAROL CHANNING

## THE SUNFLOWER GIRL

It's never too late for love. As proof of that, show biz legend and octogenarian Carol Channing continues to entertain audiences while launching herself into a fourth marriage to her junior high school sweetheart.

Carol's 2002 memoir was entitled *Just Lucky I Guess*. There was no guessing about my own good luck in catching her latest performance at a night club in New York's Greenwich Village. I can happily report that Carol, born on January 31, 1921, in Seattle, can still do a high kick as well as any Rockette at Radio City Music Hall. In a slit dress, Carol let it rip, and I got to see "all the way to Honolulu," as Zsa Zsa Gabor might so eloquently put it.

Onto that night club staged bounced another octogenarian, Carol's fourth husband, an Armenian-American named Henry Kullijian, with whom she'd fallen in love in junior high school back in Washington State. In her autobiography, she'd written of her lingering love for her long-lost sweetheart.

"I was so in love with Harry I couldn't stop hugging him," Carol wrote. The same year the book was published, Harry's wife of 60 years, Geraldine, had died, and he was ready to move on. His first reaction when he received a copy of Carol's book, was, "I thought she was dead." When he called her, he found her very much alive. Within weeks, he'd proposed marriage. He was 83 at the time, Carol only 82.

Walking down the aisle as a bride, Carol finally made an honest man of Harry on May 10, 2003, seven decades after they broke up. The presiding pastor informed the press, "Carol told me this is her dream of a lifetime. I'd call it a storybook affair."

To judge by how they danced across the stage together that night in Greenwich Village, Carol has at long last found the happiness that has eluded her in her other three marriages.

Her other husbands included writer Theodore Naidish and football player Alexander Caron. With Caron, she had a son, Channing Lowe, a Pulitzer Prize winning cartoonist for the *South Florida Sun-Sentinel* in Fort Lauderdale. He took his stepfather's surname from Carol's third husband, Charles Lowe, her manager and publicist. Their marriage lasted from 1956 until 1998, when Carol abruptly filed for divorce. She charged that Lowe was gay and that they had had marital relations only twice during their 42-year marriage. On nationwide TV, the outspoken Joan Rivers called the head bartender at Splash (NYC's leading gay bar) and asked him if "Mr. Carol Channing" were a frequent visitor. Lowe denied the homosexual allegations, but died before the divorce could become final.

Moving into the "December of my years," as Carol puts it, the entertainer still has that distinctive voice—a cross between a baby squeak and a raspy, baritone growl—and the same unusual mannerisms and bubbling personality that has made her a favorite target of both male and female impersonators. She's allergic to bleach, so her trademark poofy blonde hairdo has always been a wig. "She was Ethel Merman—only more so," wrote one critic.

Carol's career was built largely on two roles—that of the leggy blonde gold-digger, Lorelei Lee, in *Gentlemen Prefer Blondes*, which opened on Broadway in 1949. Carol sang what even today is still her signature song, "Diamonds Are a Girl's Best Friend." Her other celebrated role was of Dolly Gallagher, a combination of Jewish yenta and Mae West, in the 1964,

Two views of one of Broadway's most instantly recognizable stars, **Carol Channing**. *lower photo*, as Dolly Gallagher Levi , a role she made "hers," in the blockbuster hit, *Hello Dolly!*

Two views of **Carol Channing** with her fourth and final husband ("the love of her life,") **Harry Kullijian**: *Left photo*, from 70 years before they eventually tied the knot, and *right photo*, post-nuptials.

**Carol** with her third husband, **Charles Lowe.** During their 40-year marriage where he "doubled" as her manager and publicist, her career thrived, despite her personal unhappiness within the marriage.

*Hello, Dolly!*

Sadly, Carol lost out on both screen roles, with Marilyn Monroe cast as Lorelei in a different, but equally brilliant performance, and a young Barbra Streisand horribly miscast as Dolly.

In her autobiography, Carol revealed for the first time that she was descended from a father of both German and African-American roots. She didn't know her racial origins until her first marriage when her father warned her that "you might have a black baby." For decades, she kept her origins a secret because "I didn't want to be typecast on Broadway or in Hollywood."

Carol has remained one of America's most beloved and uncontroversial figures in show business, yet for enigmatic reasons she ended up on Richard Nixon's "Enemies List," as reported in *The New York Times* on June 27, 1973. "Getting onto that list was the highest honor of my career," Carol once said. Perhaps Nixon was peeved at her singing, "Hello, Lyndon!" based on her hit record, "Hello, Dolly!" which matched the sales of Louis Armstrong's recording of the same song.

At a now defunct theatrical restaurant in New York, called Backstage, I once asked Carol why she decided to embark upon a career "on the wicked stage."

"I owe it all to dear ol' mum," Carol said. "When I was a girl, she told me that I was revolting—not feminine at all. I decided at that point to go on the stage, knowing it was a very tolerant and accepting place."

That same night she also revealed the secret of her longevity. "Eat only cold lobster but it must be served from a silver vacuum bottle. I've survived on just that food for years—and I'm still here!"

Should Carol not live forever, and if I'm still around, I plan to bring a bouquet of sunflowers—her alltime favorite—to her gravesite. Once there, I fully expect "the first lady of musical comedy" to rise from the grave, singing, "we all lose our charms in the end," but reminding us that those rocks—diamonds, of course—don't lost their shape.

Despite her advancing years, **Channing** remained a powerful draw on the cabaret circuit. In 2005, she continued sustaining her image as "the brilliant bimbo" onstage at Feinstein's Cafe in the NYC Regency Hotel. The name of her show? ***The First 80 Years Are the Hardest.***

*Left photo:* **Yvonne Adair** and **Carol Channing** onstage in the 1949 Broadway production of *Gentlemen Prefer Blondes*, To their chagrin, they were not cast in those defining roles in the 1953 film version. Their "blonde and brunette' roles were, instead, famously awarded to **Jane Russell** and **Marilyn Monroe.**

Critics sometimes defined even her early hits as a variation of the same theme. Here **Channing** appears as Molly Wade in the 1956 Broadway production of *The First Traveling Saleslady.*

**DO BLONDES REALLY HAVE MORE FUN?**

**Channing** spent many of her later years humping and pumping revivals of her previous hits. Here, she appears with **Tamara Long** *(left)* and **Dody Goodman** *(right)* in *Lorelei*, a stage and road show revival and adaptation of *Gentlemen Prefer Blondes.*

**OTHERS, SOME OF THEM "IMPOSSIBLY GIFTED" TRIED AND FAILED**

Here, **Barbra Streisand** appears—some said "unsuccessfully" in a film version of the play that Channing virtually defined: **Dolly Levi** in *Hello, Dolly!* (1969).

She even ended up on Richard Nixon's "Enemies List."

# MONTGOMERY CLIFT

## CONSISTENTLY, HE REJECTED SOME OF THE GREATEST ROLES OF CLASSIC CINEMA

Actors, even the most successful and best-known, often make disastrous choices when accepting or turning down roles. If certain benchmark films, each of them a classic, had been cast with different actors, instead of with the lineup that eventually emerged, much of the history of Hollywood would have to be rewritten. Olivia de Havilland, for example, turned down the starring role in the film version of Tennessee Williams's *A Streetcar Named Desire*, which ultimately earned an Oscar (her second) for Vivien Leigh. (Ironically, Vivien's first Academy Award had been earned for her appearance opposite-guess who?—Olivia in *Gone With the Wind*.)

Flushed with success from his starring film role in *A Streetcar Named Desire*, Marlon Brando turned down the lead in *A Rebel Without a Cause* in 1949. Six years later, with his rival, James Dean, in the part, the movie defined the hopes and aspirations of an entire generation, thereby making a legend of its star.

Which actor consistently made the worst career decisions in the history of Hollywood? It was Montgomery Clift, the broodingly sensitive and classically handsome actor who died at the age of forty-five, a haunted, broken man.

His bad decisions began early in his career, in 1942, when he turned down the role of Greer Garson's son in *Mrs. Miniver*, that WWII tearjerker. Richard Ney landed the part instead. Later, in real life, he married his co-star, becoming "Mr. Greer Garson," proving that, indeed, life sometimes imitates art.

In 1949, when Billy Wilder was casting *Sunset Blvd.* he wanted Mae West (that's not a typo) and Monty to co-star in it. West refused to play a has-been ("My fans would never believe me as a has-been.") Perhaps listening to Mae too closely, Monty felt that the role of Sunset Blvd's Joe Gillis was "too close" to his own real life drama as the "kept boy" of the multimillionaire chanteuse (the notorious heiress to part of the Reynolds tobacco fortune) Libby Holman. William Holden and Gloria Swanson were waiting in the wings.

In 1951, when director John Huston offered Monty the lead to the film version of the Stephen Crane novel *The Red Badge of Courage*, Monty once again said "no.". The role went to much-decorated war hero Audie Murphy.

At this point, in most decisions related to film scripts, Monty should have learned enough to let wiser minds prevail. Fred Zinnemann unsuccessfully approached him in 1952, offering him the role of the marshal who faced a deadly enemy in *High Noon*. The director felt that Monty, playing opposite the cool and endlessly blonde Grace Kelly, would "eat up the screen." Into the vacuum stepped Gary Cooper, who ended up playing Grace Kelly's lover. At the time he was old enough to be her father.

In 1953, the lead in another great western, *Shane*, was offered to Monty by director George Stevens. As he was wont to do, Monty said no, but Alan Ladd said yes, thereby winning the role of the weary gunfighter.

In 1954 Monty made two of the worst career decisions of his life. Director George Cukor asked him to appear as the drunken

"It was the biggest mistake of my career," claimed **Olivia de Havilland** *(left)*. She turned down the role of Blanche DuBois in *Streetcar Named Desire* that went to **Vivien Leigh** *(right)*.

At least **Monty Clift** did not reject his most memorable role, playing opposite **Elizabeth Taylor** in *A Place in the Sun* (1951), based on Theodore Dreiser's *An American Tragedy*.

In the late 1940s, a young **Marlon Brando** was offered the lead in *Rebel Without a Cause*, but rejected it. Shot in 1955, it became the picture that immortalized **James Dean**

*Left photo:* The World War II drama, *Mrs. Miniver*, became **Greer Garson**'s greatest role. In it, **Richard Ney** played her son. After the shoot, she married him.

**Mae West** *(right)* was origianlly offered the role of the fading silent screen star, Norma Desmond, in the 1950 *Sunset Blvd.* "No way," she told Billy Wilder.

331

and washed-up movie star, Norman Maine, opposite Judy Garland in *A Star is Born*. Monty fled. That same year director Elia Kazan approached him to star as ex-prize fighter turned longshoreman, Terry Malloy, in *On the Waterfront*. Monty hated the role. Marlon Brando felt differently, embracing a role that eventually led to his first Oscar.

In 1955, Kazan approached Monty once again, this time with the lead role in the film version of John Steinbeck's novel *East of Eden* With characteristic bad judgment, he even turned down this meaty and juicy role. Wisely, James Dean did not.

The following year, Monty refused to play Captain Ahab in *Moby Dick*, a role proposed by the film's director, John Huston. Gregory Peck stepped in to hunt the white whale. Also in 1956, Joshua Logan approached Monty, offering the role of the huckster rodeo cowboy, Bo Decker, in *Bus Stop* opposite Marilyn Monroe. Instead, the male lead in this Marilyn Monroe classic went to the second-rate Don Murray.

A year before Monty died, George Stevens knocked on his door once again, offering the role of Jesus in *The Greatest Story Ever Told*. In this case, even Jesus got a no vote.

Weeks later, just days before he died, a reporter asked Monty why he repeatedly rejected many of the greatest film roles of all time. "Clouds got in my way," he said.

**Gregory Peck** stars as Captain Ahab in Herman Melville's classic sea drama, *Moby Dick*. Monty Clift rejected the role. "I thought the plot—chasing after a big whale—was silly."

**Gloria Swanson**, as Norma Desmond in *Sunset Blvd.* (1950), was forever grateful to Mae West, Pola Negri, and Mary Pickford for rejecting the role.

**Montgomery Clift** with **Libby Holman.** He rejected the role of Joe Gillis in *Sunset Blvd.* "because it came too close to paralleling my own relationship with Libby."

**Bill Maudlin** *(left)* co-stars with **Audie Murphy** in Stephen Crane's *Red Badge of Courage* (1951). Murphy was the most decorated American hero of World War II.

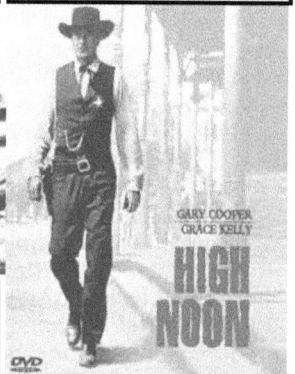

**Gary Cooper** won his second Oscar as the threatened sheriff in the classic western, *High Noon*. His character had married Grace Kelly, his co-star in the movie. Monty Clift would have been more age-appropriate.

**Alan Ladd**'s most memorable file role was in the 1951 western, *Shane* with Jean Arthur, her final film. He played a former gunfighter who defends homesteaders. Once again, Monty Clift bowed out.

In 1954, *On the Waterfront* won a Best Picture Oscar. **Marlon Brando** beat out stiff competition for the Best Actor Oscar. "I was wrong for the role," Monty Clift had said.

**Marilyn Monroe** was cast as a saloon singer opposite a crazed cowboy, **Don Murray**, in *Bus Stop* (1956). Elvis Presley wanted the role, but Col. Tom Parker said No. Monty Clift rejected it.

The same year as *On the Waterfront*, **James Mason** was also up for an Oscar for his performance in *A Star Is Born* with **Judy Garland** in her second most memorable role.

In turning it down, Monty Clift said, "like the character in the movie, I was a fading star in real life."

# The "Inventor" of Women's Lib

# LIZ RENAY

*For the World to See*
**LIZ RENAY**

A call came in to me in New York around 3:30 in the morning. It was from the widow (name withheld by request) of one of the best-selling novelists of the 20th century. "I've just heard the news," she said. "Liz Renay is dead."

I was unexpectedly shocked, having believed that this glamorous blonde bombshell would live forever. "Who is this Liz Renay?" you might ask. The love goddess and cult film star used to be written up in the press as "the most beautiful woman on the planet." She had another reputation as well: she was the most notorious actress ever to step off the train in Los Angeles.

Escaping her parents, both religious fanatics, in the little town of Mesa, Arizona, Liz fled to New York where she found work as a stripper on 52nd Street when she wasn't modeling high-fashion clothes. As a WWII "V Girl," she became a one-woman USO, entertaining love-starved military men returning victoriously on battleships from Europe.

From New York, Liz traveled to Hollywood, winning a Marilyn Monroe look-alike contest, which made her a national celebrity. In 1950, *Life* magazine did a five-page spread on her.

In Hollywood, she took up with the mobster Mickey Cohen, who used his influence to land her bit parts in movies. As a confidante and gun moll to Cohen, she was eventually indicted and later sentenced to three years probation for her unwillingness to testify against the mob boss, for whom she'd laundered money. A violation of that probation landed her in a Los Angeles prison for three years.

In jail she wrote her first memoir, *My Face for the World to See* (1971), which was in time followed by a second tell-all, modestly entitled *My First 2,000 Men* (1992). Both confessionals hit certain bestseller lists.

These memoirs were more curious than revelatory. She wrote, "I've never been known around Hollywood's inner circles as a star-chaser." **Hold on here a minute, Liz.** You were infamous in Hollywood for being the ultimate star-chaser. In fact, she once confided to me that her goal from the day she first set foot in Hollywood was to seduce 200 male movie stars. Liz preferred to date from the A-list, and did so many times. **Frank Sinatra, George Raft,** and **Marlon Brando** come to mind. But not all these actors had to have their names above the title. If a man ranked third or even fourth in the supporting cast, he could qualify as a movie star in Liz's book. It took years but Liz apparently

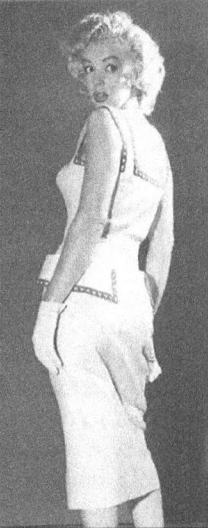

As she aged, the similarities of **Liz Renay** *(left photo)* to **Marilyn Monroe** *(right photo)* grew less distinct. But MM—for Liz, at least—provided the physical inspiration for her first big break.

YA GOTTA GET A GIMMICK

Gypsy Rose Lee—probably the most famous and best-marketed stripper in history—advised exhibitionistic showgirls to pour some imagination into their stage acts.

**Liz Renay,** shown here with the upswept hairdo that became her trademark, appears onstage, in dominatrix drag—a departure from her usual preference for lace and feather boas.

Before he starred her in some of his movies, filmmaker John Waters cited **Liz Renay** as "my idea of total glamour."

In the mid-1950s photos above, when the world was younger and before her acting ambitions were shattered by the notoriety of her mobster connections, she's ready for her closeup.

After refusing to testify against him in court when he was arrested (and later imprisoned) for tax evasion, **Liz Renay** spent three years in the Terminal Island Federal prison in Los Angeles Harbor. There, she wrote her first memoir, made 150 paintings, and taught an art class.

In the photo above, she appears in a Hollywood ice cream parlor with her manfriend, mobster **Mickey Cohen.** Not all of their spooning occurred in public.

achieved her goal. In her secret diary, she rated her conquests on a scale of one to ten. I noticed that **Burt Lancaster** got an impressive 10, **Jerry Lewis** a meager one.

At the back of her diary, she kept a small list of names labeled "the men who got away." I noticed the names of **Ronald Reagan** and **Paul Newman** on that list. She claimed that out of every 10 stars she pursued, 8 of them would succumb to her impressive measurements of 40-26-36. As for the 20% who rejected her "come hithers," Liz dismissed them as gay, although that wouldn't explain her strike-out with Reagan.

"Some of my lovers couldn't get Marilyn, so they settled for me," she said. "In almost every case they were glad they did. I dressed like Marilyn and made my face up like her. I did my hair like Marilyn. And when the lights were low, I even imitated her voice."

Liz may have remained a lady by not mentioning all of her conquests in her memoirs. At the time of publication, many of her lovers were "happy married" men – and still very much alive.

The names of her lovers, many of whom died as recently as 2002, read like a "Who's Who at Forest Lawn." Let's take a brief stroll down memory lane. If you recognize all of these stars of yesterday, you'd deserve some sort of prize. Part of the Liz's Hollywood 200 included **Desi Arnaz, John Agar** (married to Shirley Temple), **Dana Andrews, Scott Brady, Lawrence Tierney** (Scott's older brother), **Yul Brynner, Richard Burton, Bruce Cabot, Errol Flynn, Rory Calhoun, Rod Cameron, Jack Carson, Dane Clark, John Garfield, Steve Cochran, Chuck Connors, Richard Conte, Broderick Crawford, John Ireland, Sammy Davis Jr., John Derek, Howard Duff, Dan Duryea, Jose Ferrer, Clark Gable, Sterling Hayden, William Holden, Bob Hope, Alan Ladd, Fernando Lamas, Dean Martin, Lee Marvin, Victor Mature, Stephen McNally, Steve McQueen, Ralph Meeker, Gary Merrill, Robert Mitchum, Wayne Morris, Forrest Tucker, Donald O'Connor, Johnny Weissmuller** (Tarzan), **Lex Barker** (another Tarzan and the husband of Lana Turner), **Cornel Wilde, Dennis O'Keefe, John Payne, Aldo Ray, Sonny Tufts, Steve Reeves, Franchot Tone, Robert Ryan, Zachory Scott, Robert Stack, Barry Sullivan**, and the whip-tossing cowboy star, **Lash La Rue.**

Before he started making all those millions from *Hairspray*, director **John Waters** cast Liz as Muffy St. Jacques in the cult classic, *Dangerous Living* (1977). Her claim to fame came in a notorious scene from that movie in which she kills her drug-tripping babysitter by smothering her in a bowl of dog food.

At the height of the streaking craze in 1974, Liz stripped off her clothes and ran buck naked down Hollywood Boulevard in full-frontal view of 5,000 male paparazzi. A jury later found her not guilty. After the trial, some male jurors asked her to autograph nude pictures of herself.

As a stripper, Liz was known for a unique act where she appeared with her daughter, Brenda. This mother-daughter act was wildly popular, even though Liz later claimed that "most of the Peeping Toms thought we were sisters."

Through all those lovers – the famous, the infamous, and the unknown – Liz managed to marry eight husbands. Upon her death in Las Vegas at the age of 80, on January 22, 2007, she left behind a son, Johnny McLain. Her daughter, Brenda, had died in 1987. She is also survived by five grandchildren, 12 great-grandchildren, and two great-great grandchildren.

Her last appearance was in Las Vegas in June of 2006 at the 49th annual Striptease Reunion sponsored by the **Exotic World Burlesque Museum**. She was held aloft by four scantily clad Adonis-like young men, who carried her out on a royal pillow – "just like Cleopatra." Although surrounded by some of the world's most beautiful showgals, Liz stole the show from them. Regardless of what you think of her morality (or lack thereof), you have to hand it to an octogenarian granny who could pull off a stunt like that only months before the grave.

\*\*\*

Liz may have remained a lady by not mentioning all of her conquests in her memoirs. At the time of publication, many of her lovers were "happy married" men—and still very much alive.

Before he started making all those millions from *Hairspray*, director **John Waters** cast Liz as Muffy St. Jacques in the cult classic, *Desperate Living* (1977). Her claim to fame came in a notorious scene from that movie in which she kills her drug-tripping babysitter by smothering her in a bowl of dog food.

At the height of the streaking craze in 1974, Liz stripped off her clothes and ran buck naked down Hollywood Boulevard in full frontal view of 5,000 male paparazzi. A jury later found her not guilty. After the trial, some male jurors asked her to autograph nude pictures of herself.

As a stripper, Liz was known for a unique act where she appeared with her daughter,

**Liz Renay** (*née* **Pearl Elizabeth Dobbins**) became famous as a B-movie actress, a burlesque queen, a convicted felon, and as gangster Mickey Cohen's moll. She was also famous as America's first (known) "Streaking Grandmother" for her role in an event in 1974 on Hollywood Boulevard that attracted thousands of cheering onlookers.

During the trial, "La Liz" openly flirted with members of the jury, smiling and suggesting she might be available later. The judge grew furious, pounding his gavel.

The stunt led to her arrest for indecent exposure, but she was later acquitted by a jury, which determined that she'd been "nude, but not lewd."

Obsessively self-promotional, **Liz Renay** (*left*) marketed girlie shows that featured spike heels, big boobs, big hair, and co-starring appearances with her daughter, **Brenda** (*right*).

The act ended when Brenda committed suicide on her 39th birthday in 1982.

Brenda. This mother-daughter act was wildly popular, even though Liz later claimed that "most of the Peeping Toms thought we were sisters."

Through all those lovers—the famous, the infamous, and the unknown—Liz claimed that all eight of her husbands were "unsatisfactory." Upon her death in Las Vegas at the age of 80, on January 22, 2007, she left behind a son, **Johnny McLain.** Her daughter, **Brenda,** had died in 1987. She is also survived by five grandchildren, 12 great-grandchildren, and two great-great grandchildren.

Publisher Lyle Stuart wrote: "Liz Renay is that rarity—an attractive, liberated, independent, yet dynamic woman who believes in the right of very woman to love as she chooses. A poet and a painter, an actress and an author who writes as candidly as she speaks, a former striptease artist who spent three years in prison because she was loyal to gangster Mickey Cohen who'd loved and protected her, Liz Renay wins admiration and respect as a woman who does things her own way."

"Baby," Liz once told **Darwin Porter** in Los Angeles, "I discovered women's lib before the term was invented."

## THE PUBLISHING AND FILM CAREER OF A D-LIST MOVIE STAR

Displayed above are promotional materials for one of the "self-help" memoirs *(left photo)* and some of the films that featured **Liz Renay**. They say as much about "The American Experience that Spawned Her" as they do about Ms Renay herself. It is believed that although she received top billing for her involvements in them, she didn`t participate in the actual sex acts or appear fully nude. During the course of her film career, Renay's greatest lines derived from her portrayal of **Muffy St Jacques** in John Waters' camp classic *Desperate Living* (1977): Two of them include "I was *having* an erotic dream!" and "I sleep in the room next door—naked!"

**Did You Know?** That in 1949, Liz Renay was named **Miss Stardust of Arizona,** winning "$500 cash, a trip to New York, and a modeling contract. At the time, Renay, then 24 years old and known as Pearl McLain, was a twice-divorced, unemployed waitress raising two young children.

## HOW DID DARWIN PORTER MEET LIZ RENAY?

This book's co-author, **Darwin Porter,** met **Liz Renay** in 1977 during a research trip for **The Frommer Guides**, the bestselling *Frommer's Guide to Los Angeles*. He was introduced by their mutual friend, **Gordon R. Howard,** a flamboyant millionaire whose fortune derived from the acquisition of U.S. air bases deemed as "surplus" after World War I by the U.S. Armed Forces. As a real estate developer, Howard bought many of them "on spec," later selling them back to the U.S. government at inflated prices after the Japanese bombing of Pearl Harbor.

A fan of fast women (including **Liz Renay**) and fast cars, Howard, near the end of his life, donated the land and many of the vintage automobiles to what morphed into one of southern California's premier museums. *See photo, right.*

As a friend who genuinely liked and "enabled" Darwin, Gordon housed him for two or three weeks in one of his many investment houses—a sprawling villa near Burbank, which Darwin co-occupied with Gordon's "lady friend," **Liz Renay.**

According to Darwin, "Liz, at the time, was a wounded soul going through a "period of adjustment." During vodka-soaked dialogues beside Gordon Howard's pool, she revealed—with candor and self-deprecating humor—her points of view about various aspects (and the men) of her traumatized past."

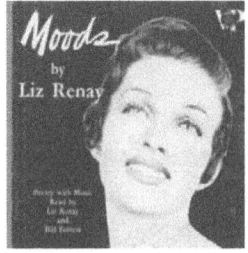

After **Liz Renay's** release from prison in 1963 she became a writer, painter, sex industry player, and professional celebrity, more famous for her associations and striking appearance than any individual film, painting, or book she completed  Many who met her found her charming kind, and fun. .

### Here are some of men she "artfully," described, sometimes with explicitly indiscreet details, during her conversations at Gordon Howard's house with Darwin Porter

**Marlon Brando**

**Burt Lancaster**

**Glenn Ford**

**Frank Sinatra**

**George Raft**

**Desi Arnaz**

**Dana Andrews**

**Errol Flynn**

**Rory Calhoun**

**John Garfield**

**Dean Martin**

**John Payne**

**William Holden**

**Forrest Tucker**

**Clark Gable**

*Left photo:* **Liz Renay** in 1961, entering the Los Angeles courthouse where her refusal to implicate Mickey Cohen led to a 3-year prison sentence

*Right photo:* **Liz Renay** 45 years later, a year before her death, cogent and spunky, at a tribute in her honor at the **Exotic World Burlesque Musem in Las Vegas**

## REST IN PEACE—LIZ RENAY
(1926-2007)

# MOB BOSSES & MOVIE STARS

## AN ACTOR FROM *THE GODFATHER* WRITES A TELL-ALL *EXPOSÉ*

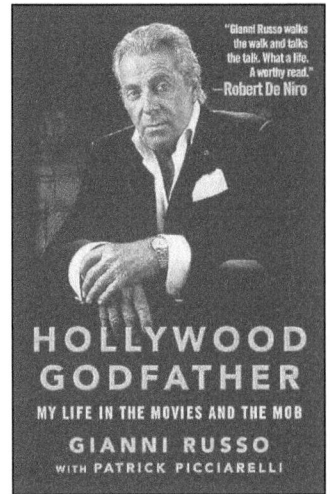

"Gianni Russo walks the walk and talks the talk. What a life. A worthy read."
—Robert De Niro

**HOLLYWOOD GODFATHER**
MY LIFE IN THE MOVIES AND THE MOB
GIANNI RUSSO
WITH PATRICK PICCIARELLI

**Mafia Memoir**

Gianni Russo's early mentor: Crime King **Frank Costello**

Power, Politics, Show-biz, and Sex: **The Kennedys** *Left to right*, **John, Robert,** and **Teddy**

**Juliet Prowse**

Gianni Russo, an actor and singer best known for his role as Carlo Rizzi in *The Godfather* (1972), has written a tell-all exposé called *Hollywood Godfather.*

In this over-the-top memoir, he spares no one, with tantalizing behind-the-scene stories ranging from Marilyn Monroe to JFK.

At the age of seven in Manhattan's "Little Italy," Russo contracted polio and spent the next five years in a state ward. After his release, he sold pencils in front of the Waldorf-Astoria.

There, he met mob boss Frank Costello, known as "The Prime Minister of the Underworld."

"Mr. Costello always gave me a fiver," Russo said.

The gangster admired the boy's spunk, and, as he grew older, hired him to deliver packets of cash for pay-offs in New Orleans, Las Vegas, and Los Angeles. That led to Russo's introduction to some of America's most notorious gangsters and a coven of stars, even political figures.

A handsome man, with startling white teeth and a perma-tan, he appeared in Brioni suits. For a decade, he had an affair with Dionne Warwick and flings with such stars as Zsa Zsa Gabor and Liza Minnelli. With Judy's daughter, he indulged in a "three-way" with a beautiful Las Vegas showgirl.

His special goddess was Marilyn Monroe, whom he met when he was only sixteen, and she was thirty-three. "She was the best lover," he claimed. "She wanted to please you." His on-and-off affair with her continued for the next four years.

Russo was assigned to look after Senator John F. Kennedy during one of his trips to Las Vegas. JFK was the guest of Jack Entratter. Known as "Mr. Entertainment," he ran the iconic Sands Hotel with its Copacabana night club, where Frank Sinatra often was the star attraction.

On the grounds was a luxurious villa where JFK stayed.

Juliet Prowse, a singer and dancer from South Africa, would in time be known for her affairs with both Sinatra and Elvis Presley.

A liaison was arranged between her and JFK. "The Senator wore a thirty-pound metal back brace, and at one point I saw him doing a line of coke off Prowse's stomach," Russo said. "The Senator told me it eased his back pain."

In August of 1962, Russo was a guest of the CalNeva Lodge and Casino on the border of California and Nevada, opening onto Lake Tahoe. Sinatra became one of the owners, and mob boss Sam Giancana was a silent partner.

Right before her death, Marilyn spent her last weekend there. Giancana had learned that both brothers, JFK and RFK, were flying in for a secret weekend, ostensibly for a "three-way" with Marilyn.

Giancana had arranged for hidden cameras to be installed in the suite to capture the action. With the porno film, he was hoping to blackmail RFK who, as attorney general, was pursuing the mob.

Something came up, and the brothers had to cancel.

Coming unhinged, Marilyn threatened to

**Damsels Four, Kiss and Tell**:
*Left to right*, **Marilyn, Zsa Zsa, Liza,** and **Dionne** (Warwick).

call a press conference, exposing both the Kennedy brothers and Sam Giancana. She died unexpectedly on August 5, 1962. Murder or suicide? The debate continues...

Russo held RFK responsible for arranging her murder, but more reliable sources claimed that Giancana arranged her death for her having threatened to expose him.

In 1971, Russo mediated a dispute between the producers of *The Godfather* (1972) and mob boss Joe Colombo, who was threatening to shut down production, claiming that the film slandered Italian-Americans.

As a reward, he was cast in the movie as Carlo Rizzi, who marries Don Corleone's daughter.

Russo is a back-stabbing wife-beating thug, and is beaten up by Corleone's son, Sonny, as portrayed by James Caan. Russo ends up with a piano wire for a necklace, coming to a grisly end.

"The star of the movie, Marlon Brando, didn't want me in the picture. I got in his face and threatened him."

Russo said, "I'll cut your f—-ing heart out, you mother-f—-er. I'm part of this picture, whether you like it or not, c——sucker!"

"I won Brando over by fixing him up with a girl who, on a scale of one to ten, was a twelve," Russo said.

From such an unlikely beginning, he and Brando became friends.

His role in *The Godfather* led to Russo appearing in some thirty-five more movies.

"Perhaps my most exciting job was delivering bundles of cash to the bank of Vatican City," Russo said. "I met Pope John Paul II."

Russo owned a Las Vegas restaurant that was popular with Sinatra and the mob. Over the course of his life, he successfully defeated 23 Federal criminal indictments on charges stemming from his alleged organized crime associations.

In 1968, he killed a member of the Medellin drug cartel, who was harassing a female patron. The drug dealer lunged toward him with a broken wine bottle, and Russo fatally shot him. The case was ruled a justifiable homicide.

Today, Russo still likes to belt out a Sinatra song, especially with the words "I did it my way."

He says, "I've known five U.S. Presidents, every Mafia boss like John Gotti, and three Popes. I'm like a cockroach. You can't kill me."

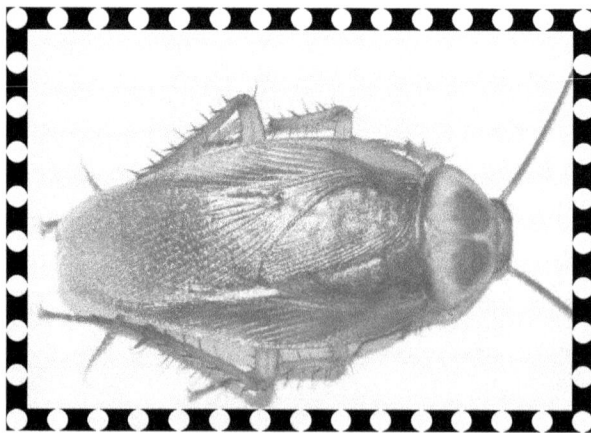

**Marlon Brando**, focal point of the mega-hit crime movie of 1972

In 1972 **Gianni Russo** was approaching 30, and had zero acting experience, when he literally got the job of a lifetime. Here, he appears in a still shot with **Brando** in the iconic film.

**Sinatra**: Flawed and fascinating

In his memoir, Russo cited years of successfully evading prosecution from federal law enforcement, and compared his longevity and durability to that of a cockroach.

When **Gianni Russo's** memoir asserted that during the course of his crime career, he met three separate popes, many clerics were not amused.

338

# THE DIRECTOR WHO SYSTEMATICALLY SEDUCED HIS STARS
# VINCENT SHERMAN

The world took little note of the passing of Vincent Sherman in June, 2006, one of the last survivors of Hollywood's studio era directors. He passed on only days before reaching his 100th birthday.

The ruggedly handsome, squarely built son of Georgia was once a household name, especially in the 1940s and 50s. He directed some of the greatest of all of Hollywood's leading ladies—Bette Davis, Joan Crawford, and Rita Hayworth.

Although Southern gentlemen by tradition aren't supposed to kiss and tell—think Rhett Butler—Sherman did just that in both interviews and his memoirs, appropriately called *Studio Affairs*.

He hated to be labeled a "woman's director," pointing out that he'd guided such stars as Errol Flynn in *Adventures of Don Juan* in 1948, Ronald Reagan in *The Hasty Heart* in 1949, and Clark Gable in *Lone Star* in 1952. But it was with glamorous female stars that Sherman would make his name, both as a director and a Hollywood Lothario.

Surprisingly, he also claimed to be happily married to his wife, Hedda, during all his extramarital adventures. She tolerated his dalliances, sticking with her errant spouse for 53 years until her death in 1984.

Sherman's affair with Bette Davis, his first ever with a film star, began on the set of the 1943 *Old Acquaintance* and continued through *Mr. Skeffington*, released in 1944. He vividly recounted his first experience with the reigning queen of Warner Brothers. "As she walked away from me, nude, the cigarette in her hand, her two well-rounded buttocks moving in tandem with the Bette Davis hip swivel, I could not help but be amused."

Ultimately, Davis failed to get Sherman to leave his wife and marry her. After the affair was over, he vowed never to get involved with any actress he was directing, but he didn't keep that promise to himself.

Along came Joan Crawford in the early 1950s, and he launched into another affair while directing her in three pictures: *Harriet Craig*, *The Damned Don't Cry*, and *Goodbye, My Fancy*. His affair with her, he claimed, began in a projection booth on the Warner lot when she was showing him her film, *Humoresque*. "She took my hand, held it against her breast, and soon followed it by placing her other hand on my knee and moving it up to my leg. I was stunned but aroused. I had never encountered such female aggressiveness."

Rita Hayworth, whom Sherman directed in the 1952 spy melodrama, *An Affair in Trinidad*,

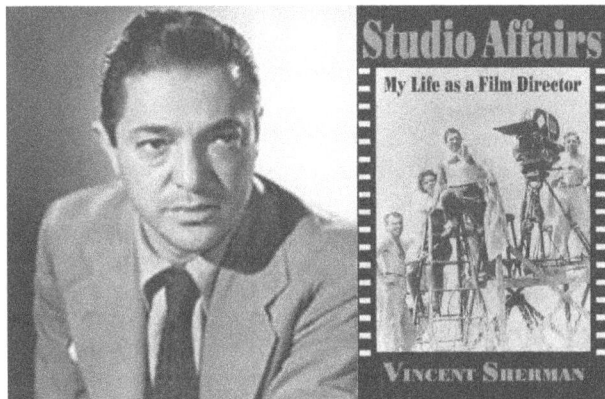

Kiss and Tell Pro **Vincent Sherman** (*left*) in the 1940s, with the cover of his autobiography (*right*), *Studio Affairs*.

Talented and tragic, **Rita Hayworth**, in a poster (*left*) for the film Sherman directed, the spicy *Affair in Trinidad* (1952) and (*right photo*), engaging with Hayworth off set, when the cameras weren't rolling.

Male stars Sherman directed included **Errol Flynn** (*above left*, brandishing a rapier) as he appeared in *The Adventures of Don Juan* (1948); and a future U.S. President, **Ronald Reagan**, as he appeared with his love interest at the time, **Patricia Neal**, in *The Hasty Heart* (1949).

was a more demure seductress than Crawford. Following her breakup from Prince Aly Kahn, Hayworth invited Sherman to her house where she slipped into something more comfortable. As the night progressed, she invited him upstairs to her bathroom. "I bathed her as I would a child. My heart went out to her." But, alas, he would not leave his wife to run off with this Hollywood goddess.

When I visited Sherman at his home in Los Angeles in the 1970s, I asked him about regrets in his career. "Just two," he shot back. "I didn't get to direct Bogie in *Casablanca*, and I didn't seduce Ava Gardner when she asked me to on the set of *Lone Star*."

Two views of the brouhaha whirling around the Sherman-directed melodrama, *Harriet Craig* (1950), starring **Joan Crawford.**

In the photo above, Sherman bonds (conversationally) with his imperial (and very promiscuous) leading lady.

In the photo on the right, **Crawford** adds zing to a teaser involving one of the film's sub-plots.

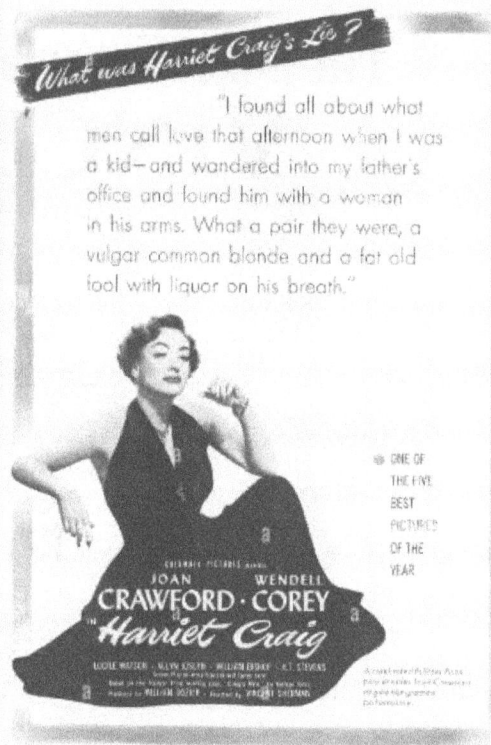

*What was Harriet Craig's Lie?*

"I found all about what men call love that afternoon when I was a kid—and wandered into my father's office and found him with a woman in his arms. What a pair they were, a vulgar common blonde and a fat old fool with liquor on his breath."

ONE OF THE FIVE BEST PICTURES OF THE YEAR

JOAN CRAWFORD · WENDELL COREY *"Harriet Craig"*

**Clark Gable** had first seduced the beautiful and sultry **Ava Gardner** when they co-starred in *The Hucksters* (1947). In the Western movie, *Lone Star (above)* in 1952, they were reunited on the screen once again. At this time, she was in the second year of her turbulent marriage to Frank Sinatra.

"When I first met Ava, I just had to have her," Gable told friends. "She reminded me of my previous seductions of Jean Harlow and Lana Turner, except Ava was not a blonde. There was talk at MGM that in this and future pictures, we might be a co-starring team to equal Warner's Bogie and Bacall."

"I had been in love with Clark Gable since me and my mother attended movies back in North Carolina in the 1930s. And now, if only for one brief shing moment, Clark and I were lovers."

In *Lone Star,* directed by Vincent Sherman, Gable played a Texas adventurer and cattle baron, with Gardner cast as the editor of the local *Austin Gazette.*

Another WARNER Triumph

**BETTE DAVIS** *at her very greatest* in *Mr. Skeffington*

**Vincent Sherman's** affair with **Bette Davis** continued during the filming of *Mr. Skeffington* (1944). Thus, the director's name was added to her list of major-league playmates: Howard Hughes, George Brent, Henry Fonda, Barry Sullivan, Gig Young, Franchot Tone, and Director William Wyler.

As Sherman later recalled, "The only way I could get through the picrture was to visit her dressing room for an hour or so every day. When the picture was wrapped, so was my affair with the insatiable Bette Davis. She was a greedy little bitch, fond of seducing married men."

Originating as a novel published in 1940, *Mr. Skeffington* is the story of Fannie Trellis, who marries a wealthy man (played by Claude Rains) for his money. She puts him through hell.

Under heavy makeup, Davis had to tranform herself from a youthful beauty into a pathetic old woman who cannot deal with her physical decline.

According to Sherman, "At the end of her final days of filming, Davis would retreat to her dressing room, where she would hysterically tear the heavy makeup from her face."

340

# PATTI DAVIS

## DARWIN PORTER'S FEUD WITH RONALD REAGAN'S RENEGADE, X-RATED DAUGHTER

The first call came in at 5AM. That morning's edition of *The New York Post* had hit the streets at 4AM, and Sirius Radio was calling to book me on their show to answer charges leveled against me by Patti Davis, the daughter of former U.S. President, Ronald Reagan.

For anyone out there who's forgotten, Patti Davis shot to fame in the 1980s as the living impersonation of dysfunction and revenge in famous boomer families. As a protest against her father's politics (and to some degree as a vengeful "payback"), she rejected Reagan's name and adopted the maiden name of her mother, the former film actress Nancy Davis.

I quickly realized why Ms. Davis was attacking me: The previous year, I'd written *Hollywood Babylon—It's Back*. In it, I'd included a photo feature on the Reagan family's family dramas. I had included an overview of Ms. Davis' rebellious acts and tasteless public statements during her father's tenure as Governor of California and later, as President of the United States.

My book had included a replica the infamous cover of the July, 1994 edition of *Playboy* in which Davis, at the age of 41, five years after her still-very-visible father had left the presidency, had been photo-featured in coyly (some said blatantly) sexual contexts. The inside pages of that edition of *Playboy* promoted a video in which she had cavorted sexually in two different contexts: One with another woman in a lesbian sex scene; another in a "solo masturbation" scene.

During that early-morning call, the producer at Sirius "corrected" me, explaining that Davis wasn't attacking me for what I'd printed about her in *Hollywood Babylon*, but because Davis had read an even earlier biography I'd written—*Merv Griffin, A Life in the Closet*—and she'd relaunched (perhaps as a publicity stunt) that creaky old *brouhaha* about her father and his belief in flying saucers.

In that biography, I had written about two old friends (**Ronald Reagan** and singer/talk show host **Merv Griffin**) meeting for lunch, near the end of their respective lives, in Los Angeles. During that lunch, Reagan, then in the early stages of his Alzheimer's disease, asserted once again, this time in front of Merv, his belief in flying saucers.

What prompted that 5AM call was that Davis—years after the publication of that

**So what ignited Darwin's feud with the former First Daughter?** Their argument involved her published denial of her father's deep-seated interest in UFOs. a fascination corroborated by many government witnesses. *(For more on this, keep reading).*

Author **Patti Davis**, the former First Daughter, depicted above as she appeared in 1983, wrote a scathing book, *The Way I See It*, that was published in 1992. In it, she flung open the gates to her troubled family life. She later apologized to her father, (the by-then former) President Reagan, for writing such a vengeful and profoundly embarrassing book.

Did she change her point of view? Years later, in an interview, she warned the U.K.'s Prince Harry to tread lightly in exposing the embarrassing dynamics of his own dysfunctional family.

According to a sadder, perhaps wiser Patti, "My justification in writing a book I wish I hadn't written was very similar to what I understand to be Prince Harry's reasoning. I wanted to tell the truth. I wanted to set the record straight. Naïvely, I thought that if I put my own feelings and my own truth out there for the world to read, my family might also come to understand me better."

"In the ensuing years, I've learned something about truth. There isn't just one truth, our truth—other people who inhabit our story have their truths as well."

In this "Sputnik era" family portrait of **Ronald Reagan** and his wife **Nancy**, young **Patti Davis** looks alienated. She later wrote, "He was cold, distant, and aloof to everyone except Nancy. I also suffered physical abuse from my mother."

**HEEERE'S PATTI!** Never shy about promoting the link between herself and her famous parents, here's **Patti** behind a lecturn emblazoned with the presidential seal and the logo of R.R.'s Presidential Foundation.

THE REBEL REAGAN — People Weekly

book— publicly stated that she doubted that a "Ronnie and Merv" lunch had ever taken place (not that she'd really know) and then went on to assert that if such a lunch had indeed occurred at all, her father was probably joking. *[Contradicting her later statements to* The New York Post, *Patti Davis once went on record as describing her father's "fascination with stories about unidentified flying objects and the possibility of life in other worlds."]*

What led her to the conclusion that no such lunch had ever happened? According to Davis, it was **"because my father did not 'do lunch.'"**

*[That statement, of course, is ridiculous. Reagan probably attended more lunches than any man ever occupying the Oval Office. Hundreds of pictures exist of his consuming lunch, beginning with his frequent presence inside the Warner Brothers commissary and continuing through all those General Electric theater days in the 1950s, followed by endless lunches on the way to the Governor's office in California, and trailed by his decades-long quest for the presidency. I once covered a speech for The Miami Herald that Reagan delivered to a luncheon meeting of Republican women. Reagan later quipped to reporters, "I've eaten so many chicken à la King lunches across the country that I've begun to cackle."*

*What did I conclude? That Davis is probably still mad that her father never invited her to lunch. And it should be noted that Davis had begun defending—way too little and much too late— the father she had vengefully shunned, ridiculed, and embarrassed.]*

Davis herself, who turned 71 in 2023, admitted to *USA Today* that, "I was such a punk," during those White House years when her embarrassing acts were played out publicly, worldwide. And although she dropped the Reagan name, she has spent her entire life capitalizing off the "15 minutes of fame" it provided for her. She has written both memoirs and thinly disguised novels about her dysfunctional family.

They caused enormous pain to both of her parents. Responding to Davis' first book (released in 1986, during her father's presidency), Nancy said, "I read it with sorrow and anger. It was a thinly disguised, self-pitying autobiographical novel about a young woman with left-wing politics whose conservative father becomes the president. It was deeply hurtful to both of us."

In later years, from all reports, Patti reconciled with her father during his agonizing battle with Alzheimer's and has since made up with her mother. As described by Janet Kornblum, "Davis once symbolized the rebellious phase in a boomer's life. But perhaps she now stands for a different stage—that of reconciliation, coming home, and taking care of her parents."

That is all well and good, but what Patti Davis can't do—or shouldn't do—is rewrite the history of the Reagan years—particularly in light of her own shameful comportment during their peak.

**PLAYBOY**

ENTERTAINMENT FOR MEN

RONALD REAGAN'S RENEGADE DAUGHTER PATTI DAVIS

MICHAEL MORIARTY TAKES ON JANET RENO

A MAN'S GUIDE TO THE WOMEN WHO RUN WITH WOLVES

PLAYBOY INTERVIEWS THE SUPERMAN OF SOFTWARE BILL GATES

**Patti Davis** shocked America when the July 1994 issue of Hugh Hefner's *Playboy* appeared on newsstands and in mailboxes everywhere. It depicted an African American man covering most of her breasts with his hands.

A pot-smoking liberal who was radically opposed to many of the political views of her parents, Patti was 41 when she posed for it, although she looked much younger.

She also made a direct-to-video, *Playboy Celebrity Centerfold*, the tape showing her cavorting in lesbian contexts outdoors, and in a solo masturbation scene.

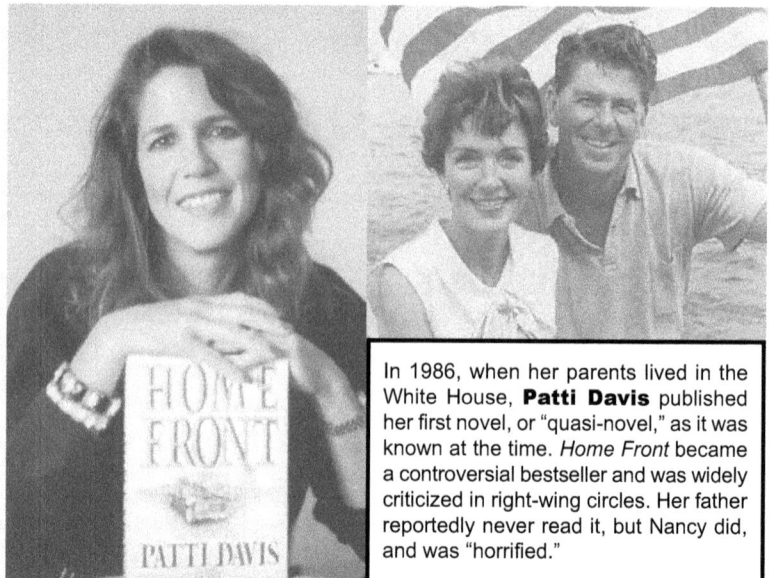

Very long ago, before it went sour: **Baby Patti** with her father.

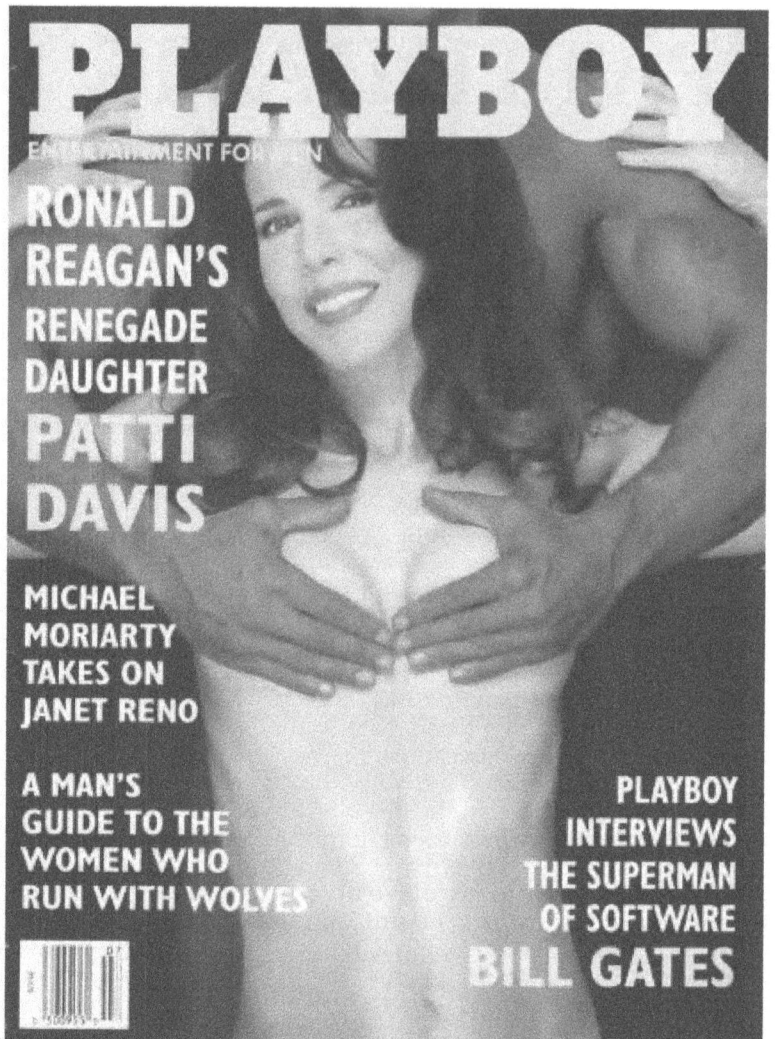

In 1986, when her parents lived in the White House, **Patti Davis** published her first novel, or "quasi-novel," as it was known at the time. *Home Front* became a controversial bestseller and was widely criticized in right-wing circles. Her father reportedly never read it, but Nancy did, and was "horrified."

342

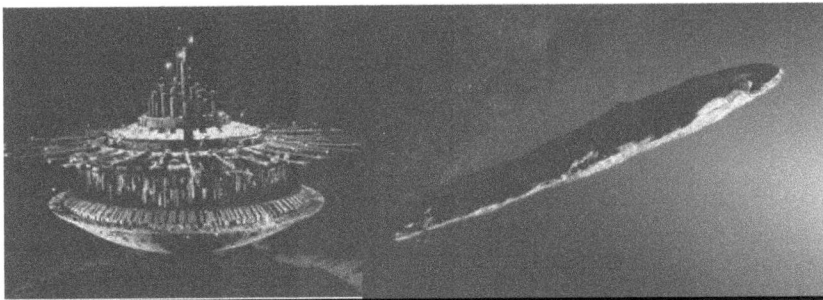

Based on observations and allegations from witnesses, there seem to be two broadly defined categories of **flying saucers**: Bright and shiny as in the simulated prototype on the left; and shrouded and dark, as in the photo on the right, where casings for the machinery (and occupants) inside are shielded from recognition and disguised to look like asteroids.

*WHO SAID RONALD REAGAN BELIEVED IN UNIDENTIFIED FLYING OBJECTS? HERE'S HOW WITNESSES DESCRIBED*

# AMERICA'S FIRST UFO PRESIDENT

By most accounts, Reagan stubbornly insisted on discussing his beliefs, in public, about UFOs. Here's a recap of his points of view about them. *[DISCLAIMER: I don't think Reagan's belief in UFOs means that he was wacko. Far from it. It shows he was open-minded and even optimistic about the unlimited possibilities of what might exist in Outer Space.]*

Dixon Davis, one of two CIA agents charged with briefing Reagan during his transition to the White House, claimed that the president "knew flying saucers existed and there was no need to look further." Feature writer Billy Cox, writing for *Florida Today,* noted an astonishing number of alien invasion remarks that appeared in the president's speeches over the years. He cited Reagan's "abiding fascination with extra-terrestrials."

Kitty Kelley, in her unauthorized and best-selling biography of Nancy Reagan, quoted persons who stated that Reagan admitted to aides that he believed in flying saucers—"and even swore that he had seen a few unidentified flying objects."

Reagan's first sighting of a UFO (year unknown) was made public by Steve Allen on his WNEW-AM radio show in New York. Allen claimed that the story had been told to him personally by Reagan.

Even Lucille Ball, in her memoir *Lucy in the Afternoon,* claimed she was at a dinner party where the honored guests, "Ron and Nancy," were late. "When the Reagans finally arrived, both of them claimed they had seen

**Patti Davis,** born October 21, 1952, was the rebellious daughter of **President Ronald Reagan**, who's looking elsewhere instead of at his oft-alienated daughter.

Unlike her father, Patti refused to link herself with the Republican Party and was never affiliated with it. To distance herself even more from his politics, she officially rejected his name, opting instead to use the last name of her mother, Nancy Davis, a former B-list starlet at MGM.

California's most dysfunctional political dynasty, **the Reagan family**, poses for a family portrait. On the left, the governor himself, **Ronald Reagan Sr,** stands protectively next to **Ron Jr.**

The figures on the right include **Nancy** and **Patti Davis.** In a rare show of affection, Patti places her hand on her mother's knee.

Nancy ruled her family based on the advice of an astrologer. For example, she insisted that her husband be sworn in as Governor of California in the middle of the night, when stars were in favorable alignments.

a UFO as they drove down the coast." Lucille wondered if Reagan would ever have been elected president if he told everyone he'd seen a flying saucer.

In 1974, when he was governor of California, Reagan related the story of his second UFO sighting to Norman C. Millar, then Washington Bureau Chief for *The Wall Street Journal* (and later editor of *The Los Angeles Times)*. Reagan claimed that once, while aboard a private plane, he spotted a white light zigzagging around his aircraft. He went into the cockpit and ordered his pilot to follow it for several minutes. "We followed it to Bakersfield, and all of a sudden, to our utter amazement, it went straight into the heavens. When we got off the plane, I told Nancy all about it." Bill Paynter, the pilot of then-Governor Reagan's plane, backed up the account.

In their book, *Landslide*, Doyle McManus and Jane Mayer relate that Reagan handlers in the White House went to great lengths to "conceal" the president's assertion that he had seen flying saucers.

Despite rigorous pressure from his handlers, who urged him not to, Reagan slipped mention of UFOs into many of his speeches. One of Reagan's reasons for promoting the "Star Wars" defense system was that it could be of possible use against UFOs. *[Incidentally, Reagan wasn't the first authority figure to assert that. General Douglas MacArthur, arguably the most important U.S. military leader in the nation's history, once spoke of "an ultimate conflict between a united human race and the sinister forces of some other planetary galaxy."]*

After mega-producer Steven Spielberg screened a copy of his blockbuster hit film, *E.T. The Extraterrestrial* (1982) for the Reagans at The White House, he said, "Nancy Reagan was crying toward the end, and the President looked like a ten-year-old kid."

Reagan once showed up in Roswell, New Mexico, to deliver a speech urging the re-election of Harrison (Jack) Schmitt, a Republican senator from that state who, as an Apollo 17 astronaut, had been the last man to walk on the moon. Like Reagan, Schmitt was fascinated by UFOs. In his speech that day, Reagan made several references to extra-terrestrials. *[Roswell, of course, was the site where, in 1947, the wreckage of the so-called Roswell flying saucer was sequestered by the US government and kept strictly off-limits.]*

In November of 1985, at the Geneva Summit between Reagan and Mikhail Gorbachev, Reagan said, "If the people of the world were to find out that there was some alien life form that was going to attack the Earth, approaching on Halley's Comet, then that knowledge would unite all the peoples of the world."

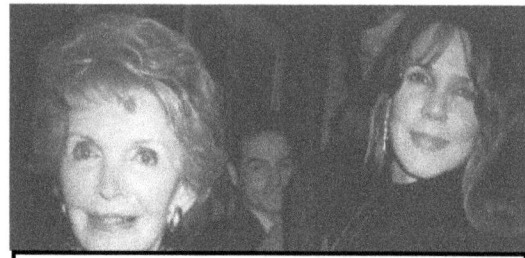

This photo shows an aging **Nancy Davis Reagan** *(left)* with her daughter, **Patti** years after their storms had (perhaps) calmed.

Nancy was horrified when Kitty Kelley alleged in her biography that during Nancy's failed gig as a B-list starlet in Hollywood, she was widely known as "the Fellatio Queen of Hollywood."

## RON JR'S RISKY BUSINESS ON *SATURDAY NIGHT LIVE*

**Tom Cruise** *(right photos)* did it first, and did it better. But **Ron Reagan Jr.s** emulation of the underwear-clad boy dance in *Risky Business* was indeed, risky, too. *(See the trio of photos below.)* Even his detractors, however, conceded that ALL of the Reagans had been influenced by show-biz and reared within California's movie industry. Even Republicans appreciated Ron, Jr.'s abilty to self-satirize through rock and roll moves that were inspired by his training in classical ballet.

In the forty years since the presidency of his father, Ron Jr. has morphed into a respected advocate of social issues that promote a rigorous separation of church and state and an endorsement of agnosticism as a viable foundation for humanistic values.

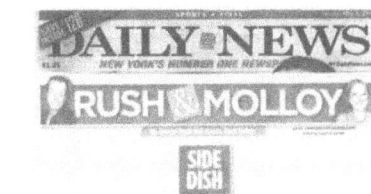

345

**An Irish-American from California**, **Merv Griffin** (1925-2007) evolved into TVs most powerful and richest mogul, earning 17 Emmy Awards for his *Merv Griffin Show*, a durable daytime staple which attracted 20 million viewers daily. He developed a reputation for interviewing "everybody who mattered" in contemporary American life, breaking social barriers and airing interviews with everyone from **Martin Luther King, Jr** (his first major TV appearance) to **Joan Crawford** (one of her last). He also brought on drag queens, revolutionaries, gay activists, and "fringe elements" of the society in ways which at the time were considered radical. Referring to whom he had interviewed during his long career, Merv, with his trademark merriness said, "The only person who ever eluded me was The Pope."

Behind the scenes, Merv became quietly known for his Midas touch, developing two of Hollywood's most popular game shows, *Jeopardy!* and *Wheel of Fortune*. In one now-legendary 15-minutes, he wrote "Think," a melody which played while the contestants were puzzling the questions. He earned $85 million in royalties from that song alone, plus countless additional millions for other television innovations.

A boy singer with Freddy Martin's band in the 40s, Merv failed at a movie career in Hollywood during the 50s, and bombed in the development of many other TV shows until he got it right. When he did, he justifiably earned a reputation as one of the most loved, most reliable, and most consistent of TV personalities. Flush with millions, Merv later became a major player in the resort and gambling business, locking horns with, among others, **Donald Trump**.

Behind the scenes, a radically different man emerged. He married only once in his life, producing a son, but with the notable exception of sexual encounters with **Judy Garland** and **Marilyn Monroe**, he had almost no affairs with women, His romantic interests lay elsewhere, as he learned one night as a teenager when he seduced his uncle's best friend and Merv's swashbuckling screen hero, **Errol Flynn**. From that lofty introduction to the world of intra-male sex, a young, thin, and handsome Merv went on to involvements with heartthrobs **Guy Madison, Montgomery Clift, Rock Hudson, Marlon Brando**, and **Roddy McDowall**.

As he matured, put on weight, and accumulated more extensive assets to protect, he often appeared in public with his friend and "arm candy," the glamorous **Eva Gabor**. But in private, Merv and his best friend, **Liberace**, systematically seduced, usually for pay, some of the most famous and alluring men in America—models, porno stars, bodybuilders, swimmers, surfers, and, of course, actors. Often, Liberace "traded" boyfriends, as well as career advice, with Merv.

Despite, or perhaps because of, Merv's secret life, Merv regularly hung out with the very rich and the very famous. He knew them all: **Mae West, Bette Davis, Tallulah Bankhead, John and Jackie Kennedy, Ronald and Nancy Reagan, Arnold Schwarzenegger, Rita Hayworth, Marlene Dietrich, Greta Garbo, Bob Hope, Dwight Eisenhower, Truman Capote, Gary Cooper,** and **Richard Nixon**. And with the notable exception of lke, who didn't gossip, he swapped stories, advice, and gossip with each of them. Merv "dated" **Elizabeth Taylor** and became the best friend of **Nancy Reagan**. "He was my rock during Ronnie's last years," Nancy told the press after Merv's death (from prostate cancer) in August of 2007. "I can 't stand the thought of losing him." Insights into Merv's encounters with these personalities, both onscreen and off, are scattered throughout this biography, which took decades to compile.

*Merv Griffin, A Life in the Closet* goes backstage, behind the curtains, to explore the private life of this fascinating personality who was adored by millions of fans. Most of them knew nothing about the private life of the man who became one of the most electrifying personalities on TV, largely because of his laidback sincerity and in some cases, "Aw, shucks" folksiness. And whereas he grew adept at getting the world 's most famous people to spill their secrets on TV, he managed to keep the door of his own closet of secrets tightly locked. ***Until now!***

# NATIONAL
# ENQUIRER

**Rock Hudson, Liberace,** and **Marlon Brando** were just a few of Merv Griffin's gay lovers, accorindg to a shocking new biography of the King of Television.

The just-released book **"Merv Griffin: A Life in the Closet"** details the incredibly active—but very secret—love life of the multi-talented entertainment mogul who was determined to stay in the closet to preserve his clean-cut image.

"Merv didn't want the disgrace that Liberace and Rock Hudson suffered through when they got AIDS," a publishing source told The ENQUIRER.

"He worked too hard to create 'Merv Griffin the Star' to let the reality of his personal life interfere with the Hollywood image he desperately tried to sustain until his dying day."

**A FORMER BIG BAND** singer and actor, Merv launched his talk show in 1962 and later parlayed his game shows "Jeopardy!" and "Wheel of Fortune" into a billion-dollar TV empire.

While Merv had the reputation of being "every mother's favorite son-in-law," and may have appeared uncontroversial to some 20 million viewers per day, it was an open secret in Hollywood that he was gay.

When he moved to Hollywood, he set his sights on the big screen's leading men,

> **" What we did in private was our own business "**

**MERV GRIFFIN**
**A Life in the Closet**

*Darwin Porter*

## NEW BOOK BLOCKBUSTER

# Merv Griffin's
# LIFE IN THE
# CLOSET!

## TV legend's gay lovers were
## A WHO'S WHO IN HOLLYWOOD
— Book review

LIBERACE    ROCK HUDSON    JAMES DEAN    MARLON BRANDO    MONTGOMERY CLIFT

Merv's sexual partners were said to include Rock Hudson, Roddy McDowall, and Gordon Scott, who played Tarzan at the time

The book claims that Merv was a regular at the all-male orgies staged by his best friend and lover, **Liberace,** in Palm Springs.

The book also reveals that Merv slept with *Rebel Without a Cause* heartthrob **James Dean**, film legend **Montgomery Clift**, and Kenndy-in-law **Peter Lawford.**

In yet another stunner, the book claims that Griffin—who died in 2007 at age 82—carried on a longtime affair with Hollywood heavyweight **Marlon Brando**.

**THEIR PROLONGED SEXUAL AFFAIR** began when Merv encountered Brando in an alley in New York's theatre district, where he was polishing his motorcycle while acting in *A Streetcar Named Desire* on Broadway, the source said.

In the '70s, a gay male porn star named **Cal Culver**, who died of AIDS in 1987, fed Merv's sexual appetite, according to the book, written by celeb biography **Darwin Porter.**

"After sleeping with Merv, Cal became his 'pimp,' supplying him with a virtual male harem of aspiring actors, models, and porn stars," the publishing sourced divulged.

According to the book, Merv once told Liberace, "You and I have tasted the best that life has to offer, even if we had to spend our lives in the closet. And what we did in private was our own *(expletive deleted)* business."

*Merv Griffin, A Life in the Closet*
## As Reviewed in the *New York Post* by Cindy Adams
in May of 2009

# HE HOSTED MORE THAN TV SHOWS

ONE-TIME TV talk-show host, casino operator, game-show creator **Merv Griffin** would twitch in his grave if he knew this week *Merv Griffin: A Life in the Closet* would hit book stores. **Darwin Porter** told me why he tore the door off Merv's closet.

"I've done biographies of Brando, Hepburn, Bogart, Howard Hughes. It's what I do. And other than his own two books, he's never been done. Also, I'm fascinated with this man. We met in '59 when he sang for my senior prom and the student committee paid him $500. What he made then was a far cry from the billionaire he was at the end."

So let's get right to it. The foibles, indiscretions and mattress romps of Merv Griffin:

"He lost his virginity, to a female, that is, when Judy Garland seduced him. His first crush was Errol Flynn, whom he saw passed out naked on a couch. His roommate a year and a half was Montgomery Clift. He lived with Roddy McDowall here at the Dakota, where he introduced Eddie Fisher to Elizabeth Taylor. He maintained a virtual male harem and a pimp who supplied porn stars, but I don't go into his pay-for-gay guys. I keep it to his A-list dates like Rock Hudson, whom he met through Henry Willson, Rock's agent, and who advised him to keep his sexuality quiet.

"And there was a young James Dean selling his sex for cash. Plus Judy Garland's 'Meet Me in St. Louis' boy next door, Tom Drake, who, by the way, ended up a used car salesman. There was Peter Lawford, Robert Walker, Gordon Scott the then-Tarzan. And lots about Merv's prolonged sexual tryst with Marlon Brando. There are his experiences at Liberace's all-male orgies. His first encounter, a boyhood friend he grew up with, later tried writing a book about Merv. This being an era when male actors felt homosexuality was a danger to their career, lawyers shot down that book fast.

"I write that friends who went to school with him in San Mateo say, when he was a young homosexual growing up, he was sexually molested" by a priest.

When she wrote this review, **Miss Cindy Adams** (*photo above*) was the then-dreaded queen of NYC gossip columnists.

What about his marriage? "Dangerous territory. I don't touch that. I was threatened by his estate. My book ranges from the '30s to the '60s but, being under threat, my legal counsel advised me to stick only to what I myself actually absolutely knew." Another thing he sticks to is people who are gone.

Only in New York, kids, only in New York.

Heeeere's Merv!!

Pre-Release Tips and Titillation
From The National Book Network and Blood Moon Productions

MERV GRIFFIN
A Life in the Closet
By Darwin Porter

Hardcover; approx 550 pages
with photos. SRP $26.95

ISBN 0-9786465-0-9
Available in March 2009
from www.NBNbooks.com

NBN

and Blood Moon Productions

BLOOD MOON

## 20 million viewers a day and almost as many secrets never before revealed—until now.

This is the first post-mortem, unauthorized insight into Merv Griffin, a failed singer and unsuccessful actor who unexpectedly rewrote the rules of America's broadcasting industry. He became the richest man in TV, befriended everyone in media who mattered, bought a casino, and maintained a secret life as America's most famously closeted homosexual. From a controversial writer whose previous work has virtually re-defined the art of the celebrity biography, HERE'S MERV.

Darwin Porter's contacts with Merv began in college, when Darwin (then head of the student press at the University of Miami) hired Merv as the featured entertainer for the graduating class's senior prom. From there, a friendship continued, as well as the systematic compilation of the information which made its way into this book.

Darwin is a well-known biographer of show-biz celebrities. His interpretation of the life of Marlon Brando (Brando Unzipped) was defined by London's Sunday Times as "Luird, raunchy, perceptive, certainly worth reading, and one of the best show-biz biographies of the year." Darwin is also the author of many past and present editions of the world's best-selling travel series, *The Frommer Guides.*

348

In the 1970s, America's leading gay porno star was **Cal Culver**, a.k.a. **Casey Donovan**. After several direct sexual encounters with Merv, he became his number one pimp, supplying him with a virtual male harem of aspiring actors, models, and porn stars.

Merv was the honored guest at the notorious all-male orgies staged by his best friend, the very flamboyant **Liberace**, in Palm Springs.

Merv is the only male who appears on all those lists of **Frank Sinatra**'s love affairs and one-night stands. This biography reveals why Merv's name is on the list, and what role the sultry blonde goddess, **Lana Turner**, played during the development of what emerged as one of Hollywood's most-gossiped about scandals.

Merv once "dated" **Elizabeth Taylor**. He, too, had close and in-your-face encounters with "the beer can" of her errant and abusive first husband, **Nicky Hilton**.

It was known as "America's most notorious striptease." Peeling off clothes was not a curvaceous woman, but **Elvis Presley**. His audience consisted solely of Merv Griffin and his best pal, **Liberace.**

"The Lawsuit that shook Hollywood!" This biography reveals for the first time the complete story of the how Merv's secret life was exposed when *Dance Fever* host **Denny Terrio** claimed, in court, that Merv constantly harassed him sexually, and at one point even tried to rip off his clothes. Even more explosive is the courtroom testimony of Merv's lover of four years, **Brent Plott**, who filed a $200 million palimony suit against Merv.

Darwin Porter's new biography also provides the first-ever published account of what really went on behind the scenes of Merv's highly publicized "romance" with the glamorous Hungarian star **Eva Gabor**, and what led to their split just before her death.

Upper left and immediate left: Merv's pimp and porn superstar **Casey Donovan (Cal Culver)**

Above: **Liberace** as empress, in ermine.
Below: **Elvis Presley** with **Liberace**.

Above: Wedding photo of **Elizabeth Taylor** with hotel heir **Nicky Hilton** Immediate right: **Frank Sinatra**. Far right: movie goddess **Lana Turner**

Before their bitter breakup: **Merv** with **Eva Gabor**

Palimony dramas: Above, left, *Dance Fever* host Denny Terrio. Above, right, **Brent Plott**.

Most of his viewers (they numbered 20 million per day) thought that **Merv Griffin**'s life was an ongoing series of chatty segués--amiable, seamless, uncontroversial.

But things were far more complicated than viewers at the time ever thought.

Here, from the writer who unzipped **Marlon Brando**, is the first post-mortem, unauthorized overview of the mysterious life of **the richest and most notorious man in television**

Shortly after Darwin Porter's newest title was announced, there were attempts to suppress it.

# HERE'S WHY

Merv, as a teenager, was sexually molested while growing up in San Mateo, California. Who did it? One of the most famous ecclesiastics in America, **Bishop Fulton J. Sheen**, "America's bishop," a noted author, TV star, and moral authority.

As a young homosexual, Merv developed an almost obsessive crush on the swashbuckling film star, **Errol Flynn.** Imagine the young boy's surprise when, as part of a visit to his celebrity uncle's home in Los Angeles, he discovered the man of his dreams lying hung over and nude on his uncle's sofa. Here's how he got acquainted with his idol's famous sword.

As a wannabe movie star at Warner Brothers, a young, trimmed-down, and very handsome Merv dated only from the A-list: His "dating" partners included rising stars **Rock Hudson, Guy Madison, Roddy McDowall, Tom Drake** (Judy Garland's "Boy Next Door" from *Meet Me in St. Louis,* and the film actor playing Tarzan at the time, **Gordon Scott.**

One of Merv's most visible and oft-publicized friendships was with B-list Hollywood actress Nancy Davis, whose name changed to "**Nancy Reagan**" after her marriage to California's most famous Republican. In addition to gossip, their "sharing" including the sexual favors of both **Peter Lawford** and the doomed alcoholic, **Robert Walker.**

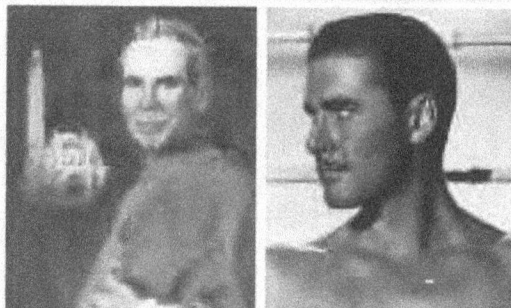

Above, left: celebrity bishop **Fulton J. Sheen;** Above, right: **Errol Flynn**

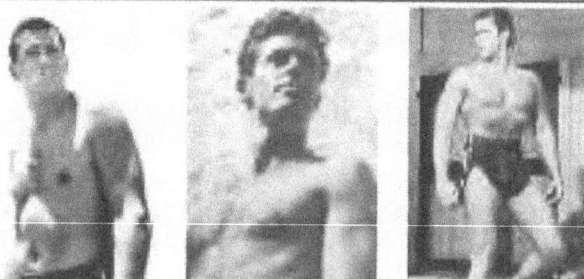

Beefcake, left to right: **Rock Hudson, Guy Madison, Gordon Scott.**

Left to right, above, **Peter Lawford, Nancy Davis Reagan, Robert Walker**

350

Merv's first meeting with **Nancy Davis Reagan** occurred when she suddenly appeared nude from **Robert Walker's bedroom**, searching for a fresh towel and not realizing that Merv was seated in Robert's living room. From that unpromising beginning, Nancy, in time, became Merv's best friend. During the presidency of her husband, she shared with Merv the nation's darkest secret: Her beloved Ronnie was suffering from advanced Alzheimer's disease during his final year in the White House. Merv, in his capacity as a sensitive, devoted friend, heard all about it long before other members of the media.

Merv lost his virginity (to a female, that is), at the Palm Springs retreat of **Peter Lawford** and his then-lover, **Sammy Davis Jr.**, a charter member of Frank Sinatra's Rat Pack. His seducer was **Judy Garland.**

From that platform of intimacy, Merv went on to seduce Judy Garland's fourth husband, **Mark Herron**, before she did. Years later, Merv was dating "one hot stud," **Mickey Deans,** even though Judy, shortly before her death in 1968, stole him away and married him.

Despite his best efforts, Merv failed to seduce **Charlton Heston**, his handsome neighbor at a seedy Hollywood apartment hotel. Merv succeeded, however, with another neighbor from the same building: A young **James Dean** was selling his sexual favors for hard cash.

Merv sustained a long and tortuous relationship with his roommate and sometimes lover, **Montgomery Clift.** They spent many strange and bizarre evenings together, at least one of which included **Greta Garbo.**

While singing onstage at a Broadway theater, Merv ventured into an alley in New York's theater district. There, the young man polishing his motorcycle introduced himself as the lead actor in *A Streetcar Named Desire*, which at the time was being performed next door. It was the beginning of Merv's prolonged sexual tryst with **Marlon Brando**

While occupying Brando's NYC apartment, Merv responded to a knock on the door to reveal a disheveled **Marilyn Monroe**. It was the beginning of another of Merv's few sexual encounters with women.

The Reagans: Two views of Ronnie, one view of Nancy

Sammy Davis Jr., Judy Garland

Left, **Judy Garland** with husband #4 (**Mark Herron**), and center, with husband #5 (**Mickey Deans**). Right: **Charlton Heston**, pre-NRA.

Left, **James Dean**, exhibitionist. Center, **Greta Garbo**, Right, **Montgomery Clift.**.

Marilyn Monroe, Marlon Brando

# THE SWORD: GAY. SEX. LIFE

THEIR EDITION OF MAY 11, 2009

## MOM THOUGHT HE WAS STRAIGHT REDUX: MERV GRIFFIN, MAN WHORE

A new tell-all biography is hitting shelves that focusses on the late TV personality and game show creator Merv Griffin's life in the (very sex-filled) closet. The Sword. of course, has optioned it for a porno.

According to **Darwin Porter's new biography**, *Merv Griffin: A Life in the Closet*, Merv-The-Perv was a total whore! Just from reading through the tips given to Cindy Adams at the *New York Post*, we can hardly wait:

He lost his virginity, to a female, that is, when **Judy Garland** seduced him. His first crush was **Errol Flynn**, whom he saw passed out naked on a couch. His roommate for a year and a half was **Montgomery Clift** . He lived with **Roddy McDowall** here at the Dakota, where he introduced **Eddie Fisher** to **Elizabeth Taylor**. He maintained a virtual male harem and a pimp who supplied porn stars, but I don't go into his pay-for-gay guys. I keep it to his A-list dates like **Rock Hudson**, whom he met through **Henry Willson**, Rock's agent, who advised him to keep his sexuality quiet. And there was a young **James Dean** selling his sex for cash. There was **Peter Lawford, Robert Wa!ker . Gordon Scott**, the then-Tarzan. And lots about Merv's prolonged sexual tryst with **Marlon Brando**. There are his experiences at **Liberace's** all-male orgies.

**Way to fuck the A-list. Merv!** And if anyone in the universe has Super-8 footage of an orgy at Liberace's house {or at Merv's for that matter) stuffed in their attic somewhere, call us.

---

## MERV GRIFFIN'S BODYGUARD OF LIES

BY LARRY GROSS, AS PUBLISHED IN TRUTHDIG, OCTOBER 2, 2007

*"I am a quatre-sexual"*
—Merv Griffin

When Hollywood mogul Merv Griffin died on Aug. 12, queer-savvy media watchers wondered whether notices of his passing would maintain his preference for passing as straight. In recent years, celebrity obituaries have continued the long tradition of burying the departed closet cases in journalistically closed coffins, taking the not-so-secret truth with them to the grave.

In Griffin's case, though, I was somewhat pleasantly surprised, as *The New York Times, the Los Angeles Times* and *The Washington Post* all noted in their obituaries that Griffin had been the target in the early 1990s of unsuccessful palimony and sexual harassment suits, both brought by men who claimed that he had done them wrong, though in different ways, and both dismissed in court.

Still, these lawsuits brought out into the open, if briefly, what had long been known in Hollywood: namely, that the divorced father of one, and highly visible public escort of Eva Gabor, was also gay.

In the years since his legal outing, Griffin was sometimes questioned about his sexuality and always deflected the question with a joke: "You're asking an 80-year-old man about his sexuality right now! Get a life!"

 In 2005 he told The New York Times with a sly grin: "I tell everybody that I'm a quatre-sexual: I will do anything with anybody for a quarter."

# PART THREE

BLOOD MOON'S TRINITY OF TABLOID TRIUMPH

# HUMPHREY BOGART
# KATHARINE HEPBURN
# MARLON BRANDO

# BOGART, HEPBURN, & BRANDO

Since antiquity, religions and cults have tended to cluster objects of devotion into trios. Displayed *left to right*, above, are symbolic representations of important trinities deriving from Christian, ancient Egyptian, and Hindu traditions.

At Blood Moon, we've devoted lots of attention to a trio of blockbusting American movie stars: **Humphrey Bogart, Katharine Hepburn,** and **Marlon Brando**. Each of them exerted enormous influence on the values and belief systems of their respective cinematic heydays. And when we released their unauthorized biographies to the world at large, the tabloids went wild.

**The moviegoing public** refers to them as America's most famous classic movie stars, but because of the fame generated by the release of biographies devoted to their ferociously guarded private lives, their authors call them "Blood Moon's Unholy Trinity."

**Humphrey Bogart, Katharine Hepburn,** and **Marlon Brando,** each evolved into household names during their scandal-soaked careers. But after their respective deaths, they became NOTORIOUSLY famous, thanks in part to their treatment "between the covers" of books crafted by **Darwin Porter** & **Danforth Prince** under the "umbrella" of Blood Moon Productions.

Perhaps it was Fate, or perhaps it was Blood Moon's "beginner's luck" that extensive media coverage of these titles made them immediately known to tens of thousands of readers. Or perhaps it was because very few "movie consumers" ever knew very much about Bogart, Hepburn, and Brando until Blood Moon Productions began showcasing their salacious private histories. Since then, in the words of a writer from the NEW YORK DAILY NEWS, "The authors spare no one—especially not the dead...and this, by the way, is only the tip of the iceberg."

We want to thank the writers who reported the assertions we made during our many publicity campaigns. Indeed, they knew how to broadcast, and did, the many scandals we unearthed and articulated during the course of our work.

As such, on the pages that follow, we proudly present overviews of some of the coverage we received for our research into the lives of these three great movie stars.

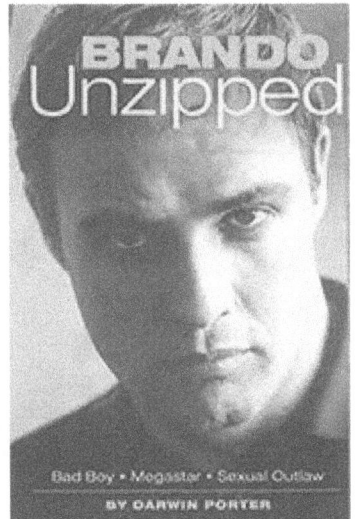

It's difficult to overstate the surge of coverage that mainstream tabloids devoted to what was revealed in the books whose covers are displayed above. Debates raged, both pro and con, about what was referred to as the "salacious de-mystification" of **Humphrey Bogart, Katharine Hepburn,** and **Marlon Brando.**

# HOW THE TABLOIDS HUMPED FOR HUMPHREY

In the early stages of its publishing life, Blood Moon's frenemies sometimes rebuked us for "Courting and Romancing the Tabloids." But our humping paid off.

The Daily Mail and its weekend counterpart, The Mail on Sunday; along with the National Enquirer; The Globe, The Examiner, The New York Daily News, and publications across Europe and what used to be known as The British Commonwealth all delivered SCADS of early publicity —the kind of boost rarely enjoyed by publishing-industry newbies—

The following pages replicate some of the astonishing (and much-appreciated) coverage they lavished on us after the publication of our double-whammied release of revelations about "Humpy & Hunky" Humphrey Bogart

---

SHOCKING JonBenet MURDER VIDEO

1925-2010 TONY CURTIS HEARTBREAK HE TOOK TO HIS GRAV

SPECIAL REPORT

**GLOBE**

Michael Douglas
**NO HOPE!**
● Dying star's secret COLLAPSE
● His LAST Thanksgiving

Blond bombshell claims: 'I HAVE TIGER SEX TAPE!'

MARTHA STEWART BOOZE CRISIS

## REAL REASON BOGIE BEDDED 1,000 DAMES!

### Scandalous torment bared in new book

SCREEN legend Humphrey Bogart secretly feared he was a homosexual – and it drove him to bed his Casablanca leading lady Ingrid Bergman and 999 other beauties, sources reveal in a shocking new book.

According to author Darwin Porter in his book Humphrey Bogart, The Making of a Legend (Blue Moon Productions), set to be released Nov. 16, many of Bogart's conquests came when he was a struggling Broadway actor in the 1920s.

Porter says the Bogie bombshell was contained in

and quotes in his own work. "He was good looking and popular and when Broadway had around 120 theaters, there were four actresses for every available actor," Porter quotes McKenna as revealing. "It's likely Bogart slept with 1,000 women, mostly at this time."

But Porter notes Bogart was sexually insecure and suffered from impotence – linking his problems to his surgeon father who once beat him so brutally he split his lip. The future star's dad then stitched it up – leaving Humphrey with a lisp.

Mary Philips, says the book. McKenna claimed Menken spent the night before marrying Bogart having sex with HIM - and also had "many lesbian affairs during the marriage."

And Philips cheated on the African Queen heartthrob while taunting him about his poor performance in the bedroom. Her scorn of his manhood drove him to suicidal thoughts, the book says.

jazz baby Louise Brooks, says the book.

And after a stormy-violent third marriage to jealous Mayo Methot, who once stabbed him with a butcher's knife, he settled

**GLOBE**

---

THE HUMPHREY BOGART GAY SCANDAL

'FRIENDS' STAR WEDS
15 EXCLUSIVE PHOTOS!

THE NATIONAL **ENQUIRER**

## SECRET WITNESS SAW SCOTT WITH LACI'S BODY

CAUGHT ON TAPE: SCOTT's COVER-UP

ROSIE & KELLI: The truth about their love

PAULA ABDUL NEW ROMANCE

---

BLOCKBUSTER NEW BOOK REVEALS ...

## BOGART PIMPED YOUNG MEN FOR HOWARD HUGHES

EXCLUSIVE ENQUIRER INTERVIEW

PLUS BOGIE'S SEX SECRETS

---

OUR MISSION — to help you be a better writer

**Writers' FORUM**

Sarah's Internet sample leads to book contract

Creative writing courses that week

One man's PhD experiences

---

**BLOOD MOON**

MOVIE STAR BIOGRAPHIES

Katharine The Great

Humphrey Bogart
The Early Years
(1899 - 1931)
Darwin Porter

You've read what "Kate Remembered." Here's what KATHARINE HEPBURN wanted to forget.

---

Blockbuster new book on Bogie

## THE DAY CLARK GABLE PUNCHED OUT BOGART
...and why he did it

---

NATIONAL **Examiner**

---

54 Review

## His father beat him after he kissed a girl and his mother made him strip in public... is this why Bogie loved sex but hated women?

By Darwin Porter

Our final part of an exclusive new biography tells how film legend Humphrey Bogart was scarred by childhood abuse

**Daily Mail**

---

**BLOOD MOON**

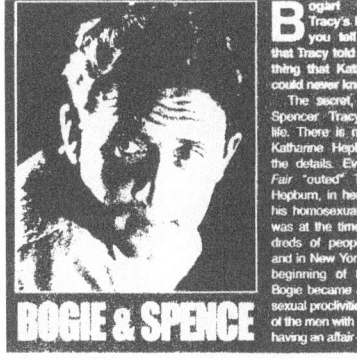

The Secret Life Of Humphrey Bogart

New Bogart Book Shatters Myths About Him

**THE SUNDAY TIMES**

**NATIONAL Examiner**

☆☆ Hollywood Remembered ☆☆
What Really Lay Under That Trench Coat?
Bogie Is Dead, but He Won't Lie Down

Shattering the myth of the strong and silent trenchcoat
The Secret Life of **Humphrey Bogart**

**MANDATE**
12 Hot Hunks! 4 Horny Duos!
Max Orloff— **Portrait of a Super-Stud**

**BOGIE & SPENCE**

# A life of blackmail, lesbians and drugs

**The Mail ON SUNDAY**

# In bed with a married couple

THE GEORGIA LITERARY ASSOCIATION

Humphrey **Bogart** by Darwin Porter

Drag queen Hughes paid Bogart for young men

**BLOOD MOON**

357

*Blood Moon proudly presents the tabloid coverage which accompanied the release, in mid-October of 2010, of Darwin Porter's newest and hottest biography:*

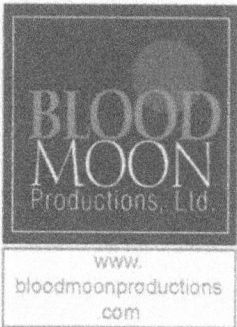

## *Humphrey Bogart: The Making of a Legend:*

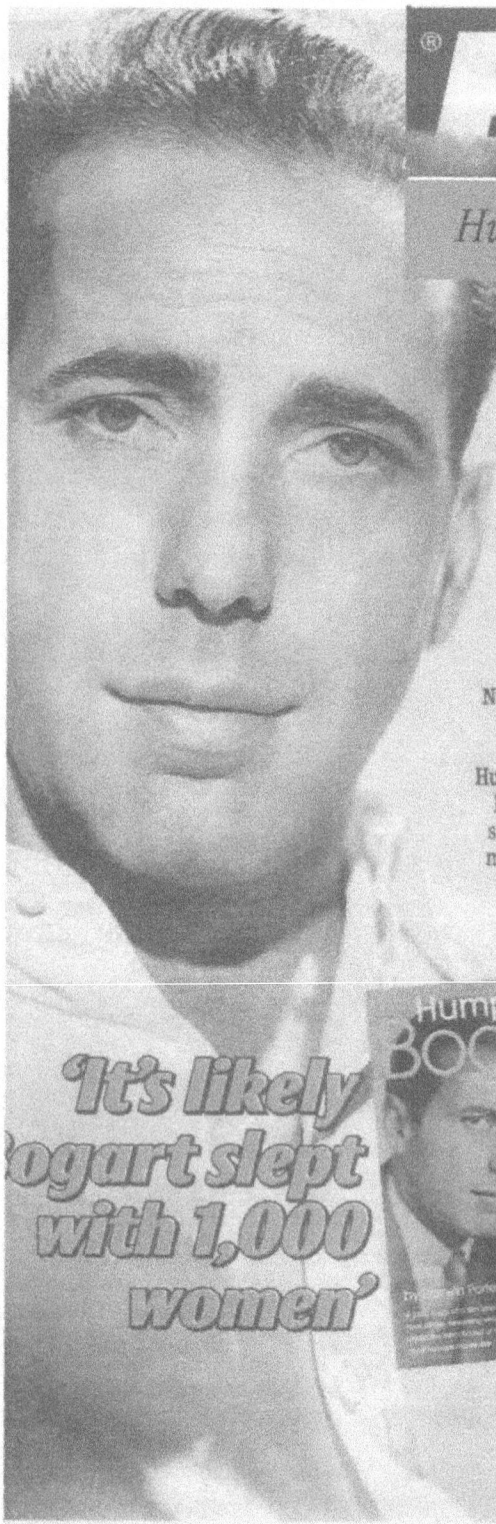

BLOOD MOON
Productions, Ltd.

www.
bloodmoonproductions
com

# NATIONAL Examiner

October 25, 2010

## *Humphrey Bogart's Wild and Wacky Marriages*

### By Nancy Scott

THANK goodness Lauren Bacall came along for Humphrey Bogart, because the screen icon's first three marriages were to wacky, wild women and filled with cheating, lesbian sexcapades and questions about his manhood!

Those are some of the shocking bombshells dropped in the sizzling new bio, Humphrey Bogart, The Making Of A Legend by Darwin Porter.

The author says he read an unpublished memoir by the actor's close pal Kenneth MacKenna that ripped the lid off the tough guy's marriage secrets.

### Lesbian affairs

Bogie first wed stage beauty Helen Menken in 1926, but the union lasted barely a year.

During their time together, she plunged into lesbian affairs, the author writes, adding that they were "both chased by the same women, including Jazz Age star Louise Brooks and Tallulah Bankhead."

His second marriage to Mary Philips was also a disaster.

MacKenna says Mary had a fling with him the night before her wedding to Bogart. And she insisted on continuing her affairs during the marriage.

She would also belittle the movie tough guy over his failures in the bedroom.

"If only Mary didn't make it worse," Bogie confessed to one pal. "When I can't perform, she mocks and ridicules me."

New book rips the lid off Humphrey Bogart's shocking marriage secrets

'It's likely Bogart slept with 1,000 women'

Humphrey Bogart
Making Legend

Bogie's first wife Helen Menken had lesbian affairs

Her taunts nearly drove him to suicide, he said, "but I never get beyond the thinking stage. I just can't see myself taking a razor to my throat."

Despite Mary's cheating and ridicule of his manhood, the marriage lasted nine years until they divorced in 1937.

A year later, he wed actress-singer Mayo Methot. A jealous boozer with a violent temper, she once stabbed Bogart with a butcher knife during a fight, says the book. In Hollywood, they were known as the Battling Bogarts.

The star finally found lasting

® **NATIONAL**
# Examiner
*October 25, 2010*

Another hot, meticulously researched show-stopper from Blood Moon

**BLOOD MOON**
Productions, Ltd.

## *Then Lauren Bacall--The Love of His Life--Came Along*

Bogart and wife Mary in a Broadway play

Bogart and third wife Mayo Methot were dubbed the Battling Bogarts

Fourth wife Lauren Bacall feeds cake to Bogie at their 1945 wedding

Humphrey Bogart starred with Bette Davis in Marked Woman (left) and Ingrid Bergman in Casablanca, and bedded both

Peterson during the marriage.

Porter also claims the silver screen hunk was secretly filled with insecurities about his sexuality and even feared he was gay. But he still managed to bed countless beauties besides his wives.

His Hollywood conquests included his Casablanca co-star Ingrid Bergman, Marlene Dietrich and Bette Davis, says the book.

And MacKenna says the Maltese Falcon star was also a notorious skirt-chaser as a struggling actor on Broadway in the 1920s, where there were plenty of willing actresses.

"There were four actresses for every available actor," MacKenna says. "It's likely Bogart slept with 1,000 women."

And when a new invention, the "zipper," came out, Bogart had them sewn into all his pants because "sex was a lot faster that way," the book says.

Former galpal and actress Joan Blondell was very aware of Bogie's sexcapades.

"He was a busy boy back then," she says, "and rather handsome before he lost his hair and his looks."

happiness with Bacall, a former model who was less than half his age. They wed when he was 45 and she was 21.

Their 12-year marriage, during which they had two sons, ended in 1957 when Bogart died of cancer at age 57.

Even though Bogie considered Bacall the love of his life, Porter writes he continued his longtime affair with his hairdresser Verita

**The National Examiner** and its sister, **The Globe**, are supermarket tabloids which each published sensationalist overviews of **Darwin Porter's HUMPHREY BOGART biographies**. In 2010, when these overviews were published, each belonged to **David Pecker's American Media Group**.

In 2024, **David Pecker** was enrolled as a witness in **Donald Trump**'s notorious "hush money" suit involving porn star **Stormy Daniels**.

# NATIONAL Examiner

# GLOBE

The Secret Life of
**Humphrey Bogart**
The Early Years
(1899 - 1931)
**Darwin Porter**

This myth-shattering biography gives a controversial CLOSEUP of a young, hot and Humpy Bogart pre-Casablanca, pre-Bacall, pre-African Queen. Revealing for the first time what was under the trench coat of history's most famous movie star.

*Shattering the myth of the strong and silent trenchcoat*
The Secret Life of
**Humphrey Bogart**
The Early Years (1899 - 1931)

*A new, controversial and groundbreaking biography from one of Hollywood's most provocative writers*
**Darwin Porter**

**Humphrey Bogart**
The Making of a Legend

by Darwin Porter

What Really Lay Under that Trench Coat?
The Secret of Bogie's Appeal to Each New Generation
He's Dead, but He Won't Lie Down!

BOGART · BERGMAN · HENREID
*Casablanca*

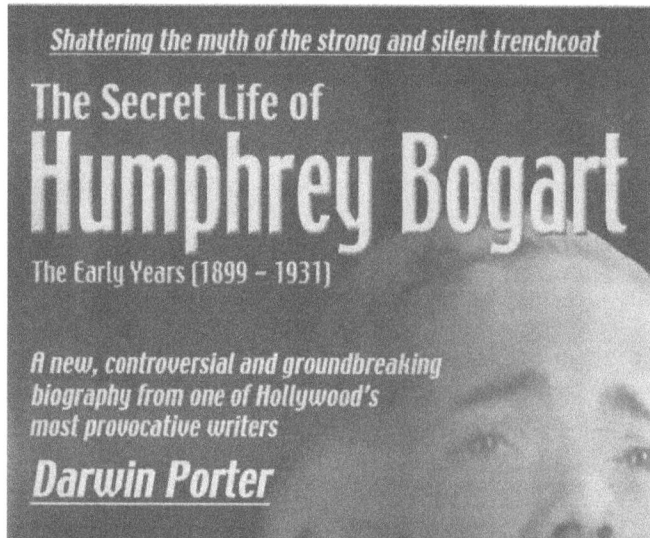

**During its conception and filming,** no one involved ever believed that CASABLANCA (1942), one of the greatest and most poignant love stories of World War II, would even make a profit, much less "become immortal."

In fact, other contenders were considered by the Warner brothers in lieu of **Humphrey Bogart** and **Ingrid Bergman.**

Famously defined as one of the great "screen teams" in entertainment history, **Bogar**t *(left)* and **Bergman** appear with Austria-born **Paul Henreid** *(right)* in this publicity photo.

**The plot involved a love triangle where more was at stake than just hurt feelings. The world was poised for disaster, and political resistance to the Nazis eventually played a role greater than the individual love interests of everyone involved.**

**Bogart** played **Rick Blaine** an American expatriate with a drinking problem. Sweden-born **Ingrid Bergman** played "the girl who walked into my gin joint," **Ilsa Lund Laszlo.** Austria-born **Paul Henreid** played **Victor Laszlo,** Ilsa's husband, a guerilla resistance fighter.

The losers (we call them **"Casablanca Casting Might-Have-Beens")** are noted below. Some never fully recovered from having lost.

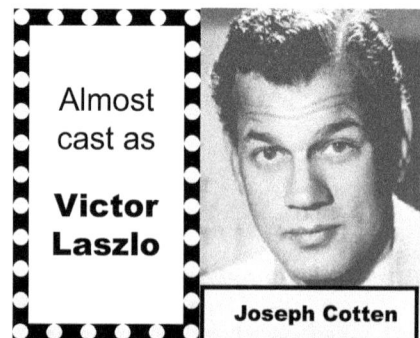

Almost cast as
**Rick Blaine**

**George Raft**

**James Cagney**

**Ronald Reagan**

Almost cast as
**Ilsa Lund Laszlo**

**Ann Sheridan**

**Hedy Lamarr**

**Michelle Morgan**

Almost cast as
**Victor Laszlo**

**Joseph Cotten**

**Herbert Marshall**

**Jean-Pierre Aumont**

# HUMPHREY BOGART

## BOGIE IS DEAD
### BUT HE WON'T LIE DOWN

### HERE'S LOOKING AT YOU KID.
### BUT WHAT REALLY LAY UNDER THAT TRENCH COAT?

Each of its two leading stars, **Humphrey Bogart** and **Ingrid Begman**, are best remembered today for the love story they crafted, **Casablanca,** during the darkest days of World War II. Rushed through production and underestimated at the time by virtually everyone in it, it's sometimes assessed as one of the three or four best movies of all time.

**Humphrey Bogart died of cancer** on January 14, 1957, but he lives on as one of the few Golden Age movie stars who is continually rediscovered by each new generation.

Although the American Film Institute recently voted him as the number one male movie star of the 20th century, it is amazing that so little is known about the private life of such a high-profile public figure. When queried, most people, especially members of the younger generation, connect him with his star role as Rick in *Casablanca* (1943), and to his marriage to screen legend Lauren Bacall when she was young enough to be his daughter.

I wrote my first Hollywood biography of Bogie in 2003. Entitled *The Secret Life of Humphrey Bogart*, it's a controversial book about to run out of its third printing. In that bio, I explored his life as a young man, covering the years between his birth in 1899 up to 1931. But readers wanted more, and so my latest bio, based on years of research, is entitled *Humphrey Bogart, The Making of a Legend*, a cradle-to-grave overview of the star's life that was published by Blood Moon Productions in 2010.

One of the big questions is "How did a functioning middle-aged alcoholic, prematurely wrinkled, and hiding his baldness, become a major-league romantic hero after a string of such horrible movies in the 1930s that he almost got kicked off the lot at Warner Brothers? In one cinematic horror, he wrestles with a giant octopus.

It was a neat trick, but Bogie pulled it off, thanks to George Raft's stupidity in turning down the role of the career-making Rick.

Each chapter of Bogie's life could be configured into a movie unto itself. He married not just one actress (Bacall),

**Bogie** with his **wife #4, Lauren Bacall,** known at the time as "the toughest, coolest chick in Hollywood." Here, as a just-married couple with 21 years difference in their respective ages, they appear together in *To Have and Have Not* (1944).

Perhaps as a means of understanding his craft, Humphrey Bogart always married actresses. Here, in this "lineup' of Bogart's ex-wifes appear **"The Mrs. Humphrey Bogarts" Nos. 1, 2, and 3.**

*Left photo:* Broadway star **Helen Menken** (married 1926-1927) was a famous and well-rehearsed stage actress back when Bogart was a neophyte who stuttered and had trouble getting parts. Some said that he married her for entree into *Haute* Theatrical circles. Their marriage was avant-garde and "modern," meaning that each was free to pursue his or her respective sexual adventures. Many of hers were lesbian.

*Middle photo:* **Mary Philips** (married 1928-1937) Brunette and convent-educated, she could hold her liquor better than most men, and flamboyantly toured many of Manhattan's speakeasies with her new beau. Bogart later credited her with intensifying his commitment to his acting craftsmanship.

*Right photo:* **Mayo Methot** (married 1938-1945), appears here in a scene with Bette Davis in *Marked Woman* (1937). Nicknamed "Sluggy" for her arguentative aggression, she and Bogart were wonderful together...until they weren't. Collectively, they became known at watering holes in Hollywood as "The Battling Bogarts."

but three other actresses before her: Helen Menken (a lesbian); Mary Philips (an adulteress), and Mayo Methot (an argumentative, usually enraged psychotic who once stabbed him with a butcher knife).

Simultaneous with his marriages, he seized opportunities to seduce some 1,000 women (his own estimate). For a movie star, that's not a shocking figure. Warren Beatty, for example, estimates his grand total of seductions at 12,000.

Bogie had affairs with bit players, but also with screen goddesses who included Barbara Stanwyck, Marlene Dietrich, Bette Davis, Joan Crawford, Ann Sheridan, and Tallulah Bankhead.

During the filming of *Casablanca*, his beautiful co-star, Ingrid Bergman, famously said, "I kissed him, but l didn't know him."

Late in her life, I interviewed Bergman at her summer home on an island off the western coast of Sweden, where she served me one gigantic buttered beet (that was it) for lunch. "What else could I say at the time? Bogie and I were both married. He fell madly in love with me, and wanted to divorce that battle axe, Methot, and marry me. I turned him down. I'd fallen madly in love with Gary Cooper, my co-star in *For Whom the Bell Tolls* (1943). But that didn't last very long."

The myth of Bogie's great love affair with Bacall has been the subject of numerous books and even a hit song, "Key Largo." But as a biographer, I have to throw some gin (Bogie's favorite drink) onto the fire of that myth.

There is no doubt that Bogie had a great love for his fourth wife, but he also loved his longtime mistress, Verita Peterson (who because of a subsequent marriage, changed her last name to Thompson). He met this cute, pert hairdresser at the "wrap" party following the end of the shooting of *Casablanca*. They began a torrid affair that lasted until 1954.

Bogie spent weekdays with Bacall, sailing on weekends with Verita on his beloved yacht, *Santana*. During my research for this book, I met Verita in New Orleans, where she ran a successful, nostalgia-drenched bar; "Bogie and Me." She told me the full story.

Another screen legend, Louise Brooks, summed up Bogie's life as a lady-killer. "You've heard of serial killers. Bogie was a serial seducer. He just stood there, waiting for women who swarmed around him like moths to a flame. Once they appeared, he showed them a real good time. That included *moi*."

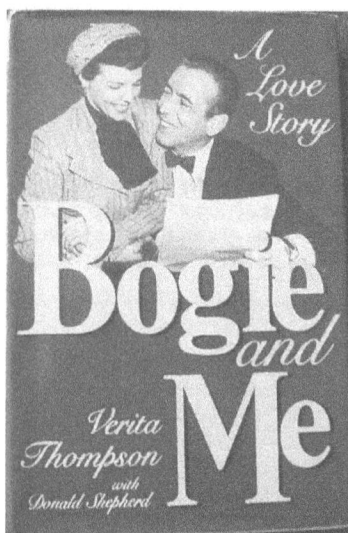

In *The African Queen* (1951), the most ferociously incongruous actors in Hollywood **(Katharine Hepburn** and **Humphrey Bogart)** portrayed—brilliantly—a moralizing teetotaler (Hepburn) and a dissipated drunk (Bogart) better than anyone could ever have imagined.

Considered among the "creamiest" of Hollywood's Classics, it won Oscars for Best Actor (Bogart); Best Actress (Hepburn); Best Director (John Huston) and Best Screenplay.

Some of Bogie's extramarital affairs were widely whispered about within Hollywood, even at his peak. Displayed above is the cover art of the "tell all" memoir by **Verita Thompson,** Bogart's wigmaster, hairdresser, and long-time lover.

During the course of their affair, she morphed into the custodian of two of Bogart's biggest secrets: his marital infidelity and his baldness. During the latter months of his fatal illness, she is believed to have slept with one of his toupées under her pillow.

After Bogart's death, Thompson opened a piano bar (she named it "Bogie and Me") in New Orleans. Before the devastation of coastal Louisiana by Hurricane Katrina in August of 2005, she refused to evacuate her home, commenting, "Lauren Bacall failed to chase me out of Hollywood; Katrina won't force me out of New Orleans."

Bogie's death from lung cancer in January of 1957 was "sudden," but not unexpected. His funeral at Los Angeles' All Saints Episcopal Church was attended by virtually every celebrity who mattered in the Hollywood firmament.

The photo above shows **Mrs. Billy Wilder** *(left)* with **Marlene Dietrich,** both of them dressed "to the nines" in funereal black, entering the church.

Bogart's eulogy was delivered by one of his directors, John Huston.

It's almost impossible to convey how *avant-garde* and sexually rebellious **Louise Brooks** was during her peak in the Jazz Age.

Here, as a bob-haired flapper, she's mauled simultaneously by two lecherous beaux.

Bogie managed to seduce her and was graded A-plus.

# GLAMOUR & GRIT
## HUMPHREY BOGART'S FOURTH AND FINAL WIFE

# LAUREN BACALL

Lauren Bacall, one of the last of the great screen goddesses of Hollywood's Golden Age, is dead at the age of 89. She accurately predicted that obit writers would inevitably link her to her former husband, Humphrey Bogart, whom she'd married in 1945 when she was 21 and he was 45.

"I think I've damn well earned the right to be judged by my own achievements—and not just the wife of a legend. Hell, I'm a legend myself. But I'm sure some tabloid hack will write—'BOGIE'S BABY DIES.'" She was prophetic.

In 1942, Bacall had gone with a girlfriend to see Bogie in *Casablanca*. The role of Rick elevated him from gangster roles to a romantic figure in films. Leaving the theater, Bacall said, "Who could get excited over an ugly, balding old man like that?"

Cast in the role of Slim, Bacall played a thief, and possibly a prostitute, when she burst onto the screen in 1944 in *To Have and Have Not*, opposite Bogie, in an adaptation of an Ernest Hemingway novel of the same name. She stunned audiences with her sultry image, her insinuating pose, her broad shoulders, and her throaty voice. Critics such as Parker Tyler immediately recognized her androgynous quality, writing of "the mild Mephistophelian peaks of her eyebrows, her Hepburnesque Garbotoon qualities that equal Dietrich travestied by a boyish voice."

In the film, Bogie played Steve, a salty, shady, cynical fishing boat captain. In what became her most memorable scene, she delivered two immortal sentences: "You know how to whistle, don't you, Steve? You just put your lips together…and blow."

She took sexual innuendo to a breaking point of Joseph Breen's dreaded Production Code. After playwright Moss Hart saw the film, he told Bacall, "You have nowhere to go but down from here."

As Steve, Bogie fell in love with Slim. Offscreen, he fell in love with this teenager, although he was married at the time. By 1945, he'd divorced his (third) wife, the hot-tempered Mayo Methot, and married Bacall, a union that would last until his death.

My favorite Bogie-Bacall line appeared in *The Big Sleep* (1946):
BOGART:   "You've got a touch of class, but I don't know how far you can go."
BACALL:   "A lot depends on who's in the saddle."
After filming four movies with Bogie, including *Dark Passage* (1947) and *Key Largo* (1948), Hollywood sometimes didn't know what to do with Bacall, particularly after the pneumatic blondes of the 1940s went out of style. Her film career became a roller coaster ride—up and down, and for long periods, without work of any kind. She never won a Best Actress Oscar, but did get an honorary one in 2009.

She did better on Broadway, garnering two Tonys for her starring roles in two musicals adapted from screen classics—*Applause* (1970), based on *All About Eve*, and *Woman of the Year (1981),* based on the movie of the same name, starring Katharine Hepburn and Spencer Tracy.

There is a dispute over which man was the first to "deflower" Bacall. Some have discreetly suggested that it was Bogie himself; others claim it was Kirk Douglas. Douglas admitted in a memoir that he escorted  the sixteen-year-old model up to a rooftop in Greenwich Village and tried to seduce her. He claimed he failed. But his best friend, Burt Lancaster, later said, "Don't believe Kirk. He scored a home run."

Bogie died in 1957 at the age of 57, suffering from cancer of the esophagus. In the final months of his life, Bacall launched an affair with her husband's close friend, Frank Sinatra, who became the leader of the Rat Pack, a group of heavy drinkers whose name Bacall had in-

Famously flat-chested, and sometimes assigned screen names like "Slim" to reflect it, **Lauren Bacall** (aka Betty Joan Perske, a former fashion model), appears here when she was 26 as the *inamorata* of the character played by **Kirk Douglas** in *Young Man With a Horn* (1950).

Many relatively innocent fans of that day did not know that she was actually playing a lesbian.

As has been widely documented in the press, and gossiped about by her frenemies, **Ms. Bacall** conducted several key affairs during the course of her marriage to Bogart. They included an intense liaison with then-Ratpacker **Frank Sinatra** during the final cancer-plagued months of Bogart's life.

Unintentionally, its fallout contributed to a steep diminishment in her approval rating among movie fans.  After he brusquely dumped her, Bacall publicly (and vengefully) refered to Sinatra as "a shit."

The photo above shows **Sinatra** holding his Oscar for Best Supporting Actor for his performance in *From Here to Eternity* at the 26th Academy Awards in March 1954.

vented.

She became more or less "engaged" to Sinatra. But when word leaked out, "Ole Blue Eyes" rather ungallantly dropped her. Her analysis? "Sinatra behaved like a complete shit!"

She moved to New York and married another actor, a Bogie look-alike, Jason Robards, Jr. She is survived by two sons and a daughter from those marriages—Stephen Bogart, Leslie Bogart, and the youngest, Sam Robards, plus six grandchildren.

After Robards, Bacall never married again, taking a string of lovers, including a number of actors: Len Cariou, Harry Guardino, and Basil Hoskins, plus others, including couturier Emmanuel Ungaro, businessman Henry Stewart, and playwright Peter Stone. She also had a torrid affair with James Garner, who recently died.

One journalist noted "The saddest aspect of Bacall's longevity is her haughtiness, a rather hollow grandeur—just the kind of pomp that her character of Slim would have deflated. She was vastly talented, but hardly beloved, particularly among dozens of her co-workers, who found her temperamental, judgmental, explosive, and difficult."

She was also known for her sarcastic remarks. On the eve of the inauguration of President Ronald Reagan, she quipped: "This atrocity would not have happened if Jack Warner had given him better roles."

A DISCLOSURE: (It's time for some truth in advertising here). As readers of *Vanity Fair* and other publications know, Bacall disliked me. In spite of her distaste, I delighted in her screen roles, especially in *How to Marry a Millionaire* (1953) with Betty Grable and Marilyn Monroe.

She had good reason not to like me. I wrote two books about her husband, beginning with *The Secret Life of Humphrey Bogart* (© The Georgia Literary Association, 2003), which documented his life from 1899 to 1931. Later, I wrote *Humphrey Bogart, The Making of a Legend* ©Blood Moon Productions, 2010), covering his entire life. Those books contained extensive, and occasionally unflattering, documentation of his marriage to three actresses (Helen Menken, Mary Philips, and Mayo Methot). He and Methot were known as "The Battling Bogarts," and she physically assaulted him several times, including stabbing him with a butcher knife one drunken, tear-soaked evening in their kitchen. Bacall also objected to my writing of his many affairs, including liaisons with Jean Harlow and Barbara Stanwyck.

Perhaps most painful of all to Ms. Bacall was my exposé of Bogie's long-enduring affair with his hairdresser, Verita Thompson, a short, shapely brunette from New Orleans. He met her before he met Bacall and continued their affair until his death. Often, he'd spend weeknights with Bacall and their children, and then go sailing with Verita on weekends. Bacall tolerated this relationship.

"I was Bogie's other baby," Verita told me, "but most biographies of Bogie—yours is an exception—leave me out. Yet I played a major role in his life."

In a final interview, a few months before her death, Bacall claimed, "I haven't been happy in years. Contented, yes. Pleased and proud, yes. But happy, no. I'm a New Yorker, a tough old broad. I know one thing: The world doesn't owe you a damn thing."

*How to Marry a Millionaire* (1953) is about three seductive and beautiful young women who plot to marry rich husbands. Schatze Paige (**Lauren Bacall** *the middle figure in the photo above*) is the most cynical of the trio and the brains behind the operation. She won't make the mistake of marrying a poor man for love again. Flanking her on the left is **Betty Grable**, the pinup queen of World War II. On the right is Bacall's other co-star, **Marilyn Monroe.**

As the film progresses, Schatze (Bacall) sells off the rented apartment's furniture, including a piano, to continue funding their lifestyle. Meanwhile her roommate Pola (Monroe) is blind as a bat and not too bright, although charming. All three of the ladies eventually marry, but of them all, only Bacall "hits the jackpot."

*How to Marry a Millionaire* was a great success, one of the highest-grossing films of 1953, higher than Marilyn Monroe's other hit that year, *Gentlemen Prefer Blondes.*

On March 30, 1970, on Broadway, **Lauren Bacall** starred as Margo Channing in *Applause*. She dared inviting comparisons to Bette Davis as she'd appeared in the 1950 movie version called *All About Eve.*

Bacall was an instant success, the play running for 896 performances, bringing her a Tony for Best Actress in a Musical. The play itself won a Tony for Best Musical.

Bacall told the press, "The Margo Channing of *Applause* and myself are ideally suited. She is approaching middle age. So am I. She's being forced to face the fact that her career would have to move into another phase. as younger women came along to compete for younger roles. So am I. And she constantly felt that the man she is in love with was going to go off with someone else. someone younger ,of course."

"I, too, have those feelings."

Humphrey Bogart's stern father, **Dr. Belmont DeForest Bogart** *(right)*, and his successful artist wife, **Maud**, *(left)* with her frizzy red hair and strong jaw, sat for these Victorian portraits at their summer home on Lake Canandaigua in New York State's Finger Lakes.

That was the summer that young Bogie discovered that his parents had become morphine addicts. Several years later, in a drunken rage, Belmont slugged his son in the mouth during an argument, partially paralyzing his lip. Latter-day rewrites of the Bogart myth by Hollywood publicists told the American public that the injury occurred during Bogart's (virtually non-existent) wartime action.

**Humphrey DeForest Bogart** at the age of two, "a sissy name if I ever heard one," or so his father claimed.

Already there is a gleam in his baby eyes, no doubt contemplating the legendary ladies he'd eventually seduce: Louise Brooks, Marlene Dietrich, Tallulah Bankhead, Jean Harlow, Barbara Stanwyck, Joan Crawford, Bette Davis, and the beat goes on.

Kicked out of Phillips Academy in Andover, Massachusetts., **Bogie** joined the Navy during the final months of World War I, too late to witness any fighting. His military career--or lack thereof--has been the subject of much speculation and, at least on the part of his Hollywood publicists, many deliberate lies.

---

# THE PAGES THAT FOLLOW ARE DEDICATED TO
# HUMPHREY BOGART'S MOVIE-MAKING COLLEAGUES

## THE ONES FROM HIS EARLY, PRE-CODE ERA WHEN EVERYBODY, IN EVERY CONCEIVABLE COMBINATION, WAS "MAKING WHOOPEE!"

---

Seven years older than Bogie, the beautiful and talented Broadway actress, **Alice Brady**, was one of his earliest conquests. At first, she spurned his advances "until the Navy made a man out of him."

Wearing a slave bracelet, **Bogie** impersonates his version of a fey dillettante as he clowns with **Marie Wilson**, vamping as a *femme fatale*.

Jack Warner, President of Warner Brothers, was convinced that Bogie wasn't merely pretending to be a faggot, but that he actually was one.

It's not Pocohontas, but a young **Tallulah Bankhead**. With her pan-sexual tastes, she went after both Bogie and his first wife, Helen Menken.

As Tallu said to Bogie, "Darling, I've had your wife. Now it's your turn."

A young and beautiful **Tallulah Bankhead** before booze and drugs took their aging toll.

Bogie confided to friends that Tallu was his wife's "other boy friend." The Alabama belle vastly expanded Bogie's sexual experiences.

Here are two views of the toast of Broadway in the 1920s, **Helen Menken**. A Titian-haired beauty, she became Bogie's first wife and was the major bread-winner during their ill-fated marriage. Helen marked the beginning of Bogie's infatuation with lesbians. She didn't always look this good after Bogie blackened her eyes.

When not involved with "my lady loves," such as Greta Garbo and Tallulah Bankhead, she came home to her husband.

Arrested by the New York police during a performance with Basil Rathbone in the lesbian-themed play, The Captive, **Helen Menken** is hauled off to jail, supposedly for violating codes of public decency.

On her way to jail, she shared the same paddy-wagon with Mae West, who was on her way to the same jail for her appearance in *Sex*.

Their unexpected rendezvous in the paddy-wagon led to the most famous and well-publicized catfight in the history of Broadway.

Brooklyn-born **Mae West** as she looked during her appearance in the raunchy but always-sold-out Broadway play *Sex* in 1926, which led to her arrest.

Helen Menken, who was appearing in the lesbian-themed play, *The Captive*, was arrested on the same night after police officers stormed directly onto the stage during one of her performances.

West was accused of writing a "profane" drama and giving a "suggestive" performance. At Texas Guinan's speakeasy, Bogie watched as she swaggered across the floor to his table. The face that launched ten thousand female impersonators greeted him in her adenoidal contralto. Regrettably, or so it seemed to Bogart at the time, only prizefighters had a chance to sample what she referred to as "the honeypot."

When Bogie first saw the three stars (**Mary Boland**, *left*, **Edna May Oliver**, *center*, and **Margaret Dale**) of the 1925 Broadway farce, *Cradle Snatchers*, he wisely chose to ignore them. "For once," he told a friend, "I'm not going to fuck the leading lady."

Once, during a pivotal scene when Bogart forgot his lines, Boland had to frantically ad-lib. When the curtain was pulled, Boland slapped his face and threatened to destroy his career on Broadway.

Boland went on to Hollywood fame playing stately scatter-brains and madcap mothers.

Oliver, thanks partly to her owlish eyes and aristocratic rasp, went on to movie glory as a horse-faced character actress.

366

**Mary Philips**, Bogie's second wife, couldn't make up her mind as to which man to marry: Humphrey Bogart or his friend and confidant, Kenneth MacKenna.

She solved her dilemma by marrying both of them--at different times, of course. Even though married to Bogie at the time, she insisted that she be allowed to service Kenneth and others, too. Theirs was a truly open marriage, conducted for the most part from opposite ends of the country

At the dawn of the Roaring 20s, America was ready for a fiery sex god, and **Rudolph Valentino** was "it."

In *The Sheik* (1921), his imagined prowess as a lover sent tremors through audiences, and inspired sermons denouncing the new morality from church pulpits everywhere.

When Bogie met the real Sheik in New York, and witnessed his off-screen behavior, he knew he'd never be "the next Valentino," despite the press speculation.

Bogie, at Texas Guinan's nightclub, encountered **Rudolph Valentino** shortly before the silent screen star's death.

Bogie's pal, George Raft, and Valentino had been gigolos on upper Broadway, sometimes simultaneously servicing the same clients, until the future "Sheik of Araby" fell in love with Raft. Theater critics often wrote that Bogie was "as handsome as Valentino."

**Here's what Bogie looked like** long before his trenchcoat became a workaday uniform. In 1930, he emoted both on and off-camera with star **Ruth Etting**, "America's sweetheart of song."

When Helen Menken left New York, she gave her husband the telephone number of her girl friend, **Louise Brooks**.

When Bogie eventually got around to opening "Pandora's Box," he was in for surprise after surprise. Her forward-gazing black eyes, her frank, direct look, her carved features, and her trademark, helmet-inspired hairdo captivated him.

Revealing a rare gay sensitivity that could have gotten him cast in *Boys in the Band*, **Spencer Tracy** suffered excessive guilt over his homosexual tendencies that often led to long alchoholic binges, sometimes when he was locked away in obscure hotel rooms in Manhattan and Los Angeles.

Self-destructive, he would sometimes go on rampages, destroying film sets.

Bogie made his second picture at Fox, Up the River, with Spencer Tracy in 1930. Tracy became his lifelong friend. Stocky, round-faced, and not particularly attractive, Tracy nonetheless radiated charisma. Bogie stood by him as Tracy fell hopelessly in and out of love with one beautiful man after another.

Although he had a hard time recalling their first sexual adventure in New York during The Jazz Age, Bogie knew the tough little Brooklyn showgirl Ruby Stevens long before he seduced her again after she had been re-invented as the reigning screen diva, Barbara Stanwyck.

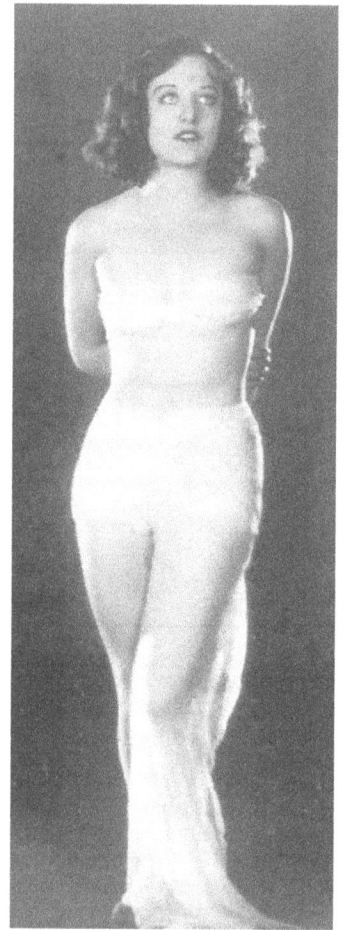

Joan Crawford appears sweet, virginal, innocent, and stunning in her white lingerie.

Before he got to sample Crawford's charms in the flesh, Bogie had seen what a sexual athlete she was, thanks to her appearance in porno flicks screened at Texas Guinan's saloon in New York.

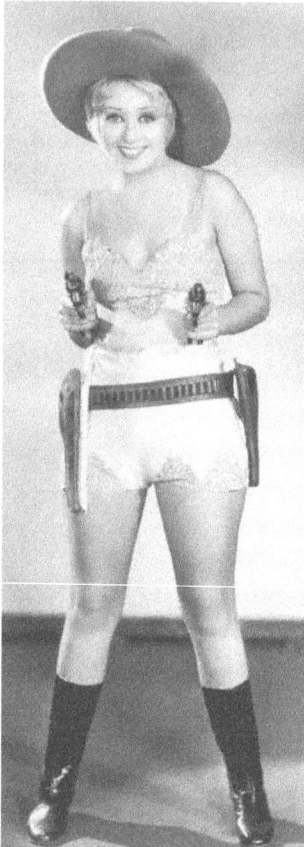

Cowgirl Joan Blondell always liked "to mow down men in my underwear," as this campy studio pose reveals.

One of Bogie's most faithful and longest-enduring mistresses, Blondell was later described by Hollywood agent John Springer as "having the face of a corrupt Kewpie doll and the personality of a hip Orphan Annie."

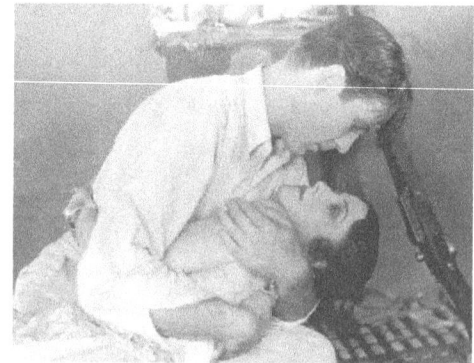

Alhough her hairstyle in this photo is cloned directly from Jean Harlow, those "Bette Davis eyes" still shine through.

During her tumultuous but long-running relationship with Bogie, she seriously, although briefly, considered becoming the third Mrs. Humphrey Bogart.

A studly Humphrey Bogart takes Mona Maris in his arms in the 1931 film, A Devil with Women.

Before she lost the title to Nancy Davis, Mona was known as the leading fellator of Hollywood. Her sensual, perfect lips "serviced the best of crotches," in the words of her co-star, Victor McLaglen.

368

**Sidney Fox** looks relatively demure in the 1931 film *Bad Sisters,* in which she co-starred with both **Bogie** and her nemesis, Bette Davis.

Davis, who had been cast as the drab and mousy sister, coveted Sidney Fox's meaty part, calling her "a whoring bitch" since she was sleeping with Fox producer Carl Laemmle, Jr.

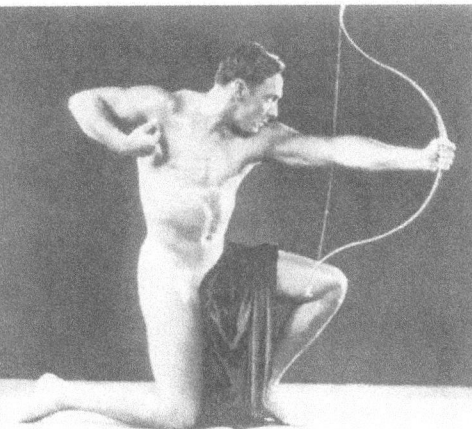

Cupid with an arrow! **George O'Brien** was called "The Chest." But he might as well have been called "The Body."

If the photographer requested it, he would toss that fabric aside for an intimate closeup with the camera focusing on his legendary endowment. He starred with Bogie in the 1931 Fox film, *A Holy Terror.*

**Love in bloom!** A rare picture of **Spencer Tracy** *(right)* gazing into the eyes of the sexy **George O'Brien**, with whom Tracy had temporarily fallen in love.

Notoriously promiscuous during his pre-Katharine Hepburn days, Tracy went from bed to bed, not always confining his charms to women.

When **Bogie** saw this publicity still of himself, he said, "I look like I was auditioning for the role of a Presbyterian minister."

**Donald Dilliway** *(on the left),* **Charles Farrell** (the movie's star) and **Bogie** appeared together in the 1931 Fox film *Body and Soul.*

Farrell, the future mayor of Palm Springs, was one of the screen's great lovers, most often romantically teamed with perky and petite Janet Gaynor. The ironic joke on the American movie-going public was that both Farrell and Gaynor were gay. Farrell definitely wanted to see what lay beneath Bogie's uniform.

Looking rather butch in her silk pajamas and close-cropped hair, screen goddess **Kay Francis** had a lisp like Bogie's. She competed aggressively with Lilyan Tashman for the title of Hollywood's best-dressed woman.

Tall and brunette, and oh, so chic, Kay eventually married Bogie's best friend, Kenneth MacKenna. But guess who enjoyed her sexual charms on the day of her wedding?

Good-looking confidant of Bogie during the early 1930s, **Kenneth MacKenna** went on to glory as the on-again, off-again husband of Kay Francis. MacKenna and Bogie share the honor of having married the same woman, Mary Philips, in 1928 and 1938, respectively.

Early in his career, MacKenna was typecast as "a second-rate Douglas Fairbanks Jr." And because he was so often compared to that charming Prince of Hollywood royalty, MacKenna seduced him to see what all the excitement was about.

Later, after he married Kay Francis, Kay and Kenneth looked to Joan Crawford and Fairbanks, Jr.—Hollywood's most swinging couple—as their role model for marriage.

369

**Kay Francis** consistently appeared as one of the most lavishly dressed women in the world. Facing pressure from her studio and her public to tie the knot, she orchestrated a "lavender marriage" to Bogie's best friend, Kenneth MacKenna.

Both "Kay and Kenneth" were notorious for devouring men and women with equal fervor, often sharing the same conquests. Of her husband, Kay often said, "If a man or woman is good enough for me, then they're good enough for Kenneth."

Never noted as a fashion plate, **Jean Arthur**, with her cracked but distinctive and childlike voice, fell hopelessly in love with Kay Francis

She enlisted Bogie's help in a futile effort to prevent Kay from marrying his friend, Kenneth MacKenna.

By 1931, both Arthur and Bogart considered themselves as Hollywood failures. Completely dejected, they traveled on the same train together back to New York, hoping to revive their careers on Broadway.

**Gary Cooper** was Hollywood's most beautiful male animal. Known as "The Montana Mule" because of his sexual endowment, he gave pleasure to everybody from Lupe Velez to Howard Hughes, from Joel McCrea to Clara Bow.

Bogie met "Coop" quite by chance one night in Myrna Loy's garden. It turned into an evening of sexual intrigue and revelations, ending with a stabbing that was never known to the hungry press of the time.

**Mae Clarke** achieved screen immortality when James Cagney crushed a grapefruit in her face in *The Public Enemy.*

The writer, Anita Loos, met Clarke when she was a dancer in Broadway cabarets. Loos used Clarke as her role model for the creation of her most famous character, Lorelei Lee, the sexy, gold-digging cutie in *Gentlemen Prefer Blondes*. The character eventually brought glory to Carol Channing on the stage and to Marilyn Monroe in the movies.

**Elissa Landi** starred with Bogie in the 1931 Fox film *Body and Soul,* which also featured Charles Farrell and Myrna Loy.

Although Elissa was momentarily infatuated with Bogie, she found the charms of Myrna more alluring.

Because she was rumored to be a direct descendant of the Empress Elizabeth ("Sissi"), wife of Franz-Josef, ruler of the Austro-Hungarian Empire, Bogie teasingly referred to her as "The Empress of Austria."

A Montana-born belle who was known as "Miss Gillette Blade" because she "shaved" on both sides, the great bisexual actress **Myrna Loy** went on to reign as the Queen of Hollywood. She was hip before hip even became a word.

She was still being miscast in roles as an Oriental siren when Bogie became smitten with her. He referred to her tip-tilted nose as "one of the world's greatest treasures."

Looking like she stepped out of a convent, **Glenda Farrell**, the Warner Brother's star, met Bogie during her early days in Hollywood when she was moonlighting in a whore-house.

As an actress, Glenda specialized in playing gangland blondes in such pictures as *Little Caesar* with Edward G. Robinson.

Of Bogart's many mistresses, she enjoyed one of the longest runs.

Like a handsome matinee idol, **Bogie** looks deeply into the eyes of **Claire Luce** in *Up the River*, the film that starred Spencer Tracy.

Tracy saw Luce first, telling Bogie that the "Ziegfeld Cutie is one mighty fine piece of tail."

Although he remained a serial seducer throughout most of his adult life, Bogie--at least this time--gracefully bowed out of the romantic competition.

**Lilyan Tashman** strikes a vampira pose in this rare photograph where, as usual, she's overdressed.

Bogie's love for her turned to hatred when she betrayed him, exposing his most private and primal acts to *le tout* Hollywood for their voyeuristic pleasure.

Matinee idol **Edmund Lowe** *(left foreground)*, **Bogie**, and **Victor McLaglen** starred together in the 1931 Fox film *Women of All Nations*.

During the film, McLaglen was planning future seductions of Hollywood blondes Marlene Dietrich and Mae West, with whom he would later co-star.

In distinct contrast, Lowe, who was married to Lilyan Tashman, was completely turned off by women. When he first spotted Bogie on the set looking dashing in a military uniform, Lowe set out to lure the young recruit into his bed.

Blonde beauty **Sally Eilers** *(upper photo)* was married to fabled western star **Hoot Gibson**. Gibson appears in the lower photo on the cover of *Universal Weekly* promoting his 1922 silent film *The Loaded Door*.

Eilers co-starred with Bogart in *A Holy Terror*, the 1931 Fox film that had also featured George O'Brien. Eilers often sought out Hollywood's handsomest hunks to bring home to share with her cowboy husband.

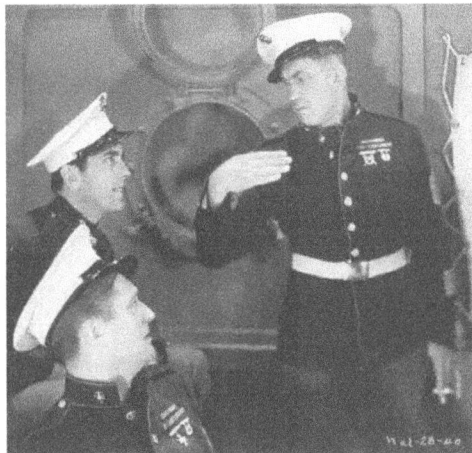

**Bogie** rather awkwardly appeared with **Sally Eilers** as a cowboy in the 1931 film, *A Holy Terror*.

Wearing high heeled boots and padding in his shoulders, Bogie later said, "The only thing wardrobe didn't pad was my crotch."

Soon after they met, Eilers invited him home, not telling him that hubbie Hoot Gibson was part of the sexual package.

Screen tough guy **George Raft** in an uncharacteristic pose as Little Lord Fauntleroy.

This candid shot lends credence to Betty Grable's later remark, "George Raft is the biggest faggot in Hollywood, only he doesn't know it yet."

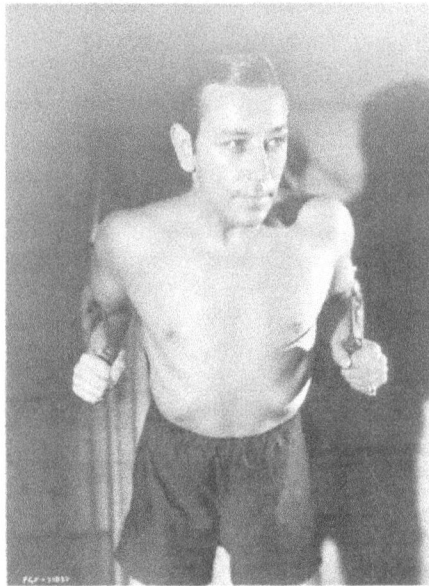

A photo of **George Raft** working out. His upper torso wouldn't be considered buffed by today's standards. But Raft always claimed that his best physical assets weren't exposed until his trunks came off. His lovers nicknamed his endowment "Blacksnake."

He turned down the role of Rick in *Casablanca,* and the rest is film history.

This candid picture hardly reveals why, but screen vamp **Lilyan Tashman** was considered the best-dressed woman in Hollywood.

Today a dim—though legendary—memory, this tough, worldly actress died young, the victim of a brain tumor that might have contributed to her erratic behavior in the months before her death.

With her deep, insinuating voice, she lured Bogie into her bed, although she would probably have preferred an array of Hollywood female flesh instead.

As beautiful as any male movie star, tall and handsome **Howard Hughes** was desired with equal fervor by Hollywood's gays and Tinseltown's most gorgeous women.

After Hughes caught Bogie fooling around with his mistress, Billie Dove, Hughes threatened to ruin Bogie if the actor didn't do his bidding. Later, he used Bogie as his pimp for some male beauties.

*"The weirdest, most God-awful creature ever to set foot in Hollywood,"* was how Bogie later described Howard Hughes. To punish Bogie for moving in on his mistress, Billie Dove, the aviator/movie producer forcibly coerced Bogie on a barnstorming airplane ride that was specifically designed to terrify him. "I literally pissed in my pants," Bogie later said.

Blonde bathing beauties **Joan Blondell** *(left)* and **Bette Davis** strike a pose for the cameras.

Usually it was the other way around: Blondell was the unclothed one. If nothing else, this snapshot puts an end to the rumor that Bette Davis was well-hung.

At the Fat Black Pussycat in Hollywood, Bogie stood at the urinal with heartthrob **Clark Gable**, each of them doing the obligatory pecker checking.

What Bogie then suggested as a helpful surgical alteration for the King of Hollywood caused Clark to knock Bogie out on the cold tiled floor.

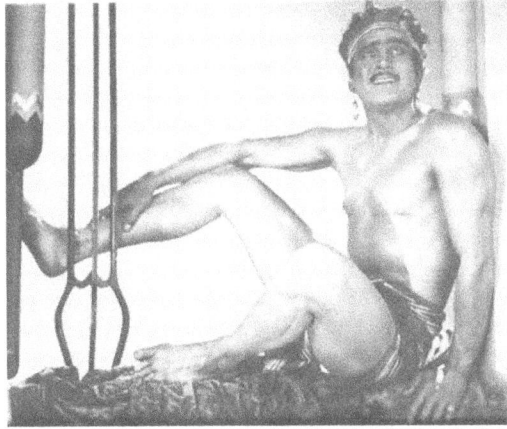

In *Thief of Bagdad (sic)*, **Douglas Fairbanks Sr.**, always had a gleaming smile of chicklet teeth underneath a black mustache.

Escorted by the police, the swashbuckler once invited Bogie out for one of his wildest nights in Los Angeles. Pathologically jealous of the rising star of his son, Douglas Jr., within Hollywood, Douglas Sr., made it a point to seduce his daughter-in-law, Joan Crawford, within the safe haven of Bogie's apartment.

*En route* to Tijuana to get an abortion, **Jean Harlow** briefly considered Bogie's offer to marry her and become the father of her baby.

She eventually opted to marry the impotent and maladjusted Paul Bern, an MGM executive, instead.

Just before the ceremony, in a dark garden, Bern made Bogie a very strange offer.

Known as "the most beautiful woman in the world," screen goddess **Billie Dove** was the captive mistress of tycoon Howard Hughes.

Bogart's rather crude attempt to seduce her led to his being kidnapped and then blackmailed by Hughes.

Bogie later said, "When Billie wanted you, you said yes--and to hell with the risks!"

That loving couple, **Lilyan Tashman** and **Edmund Lowe**, were Hollywood's most typical lavender marriage.

Both had designs on Bogie and both of them got their man. Some of their more notorious parties featured an orgy room with a one-way mirror, through which the shenanigans could be witnessed by other party-goers, with or without the knowledge of the primary players.

Lilyan Tashman's funeral, conducted in Brooklyn, was one of the most widely-attended last rites in the history of entertainment, with a mob so unruly that one of the attendees suffered a broken leg after being pushed into Tashman's open gravesite.

Cast in little-girl roles even after she had matured into an adult woman, "America's Little Sweetheart" (**Mary Pickford**, the wife of Douglas Fairbanks Sr.) was anything but. She liked alcohol and men in that order.

Bogie's short-term role as her chauffeur gave him a rare glimpse into the bizarre private lives of Hollywood's "royalty."

In his two-piece bathing suit, smoking a cigarette, **Douglas Fairbanks Jr.** poses with his bride, **Joan Crawford**, who's wearing high heels on a diving board.

Temporarily impersonating Jean Harlow as a platinum blonde, Crawford and her hubbie Fairbanks, Jr. were called "the Prince and Princess of Hollywood," and "Hollywood's Royal Sweethearts."

For the most part, their marriage was a sham, as each of them took different men and women to bed, sometimes sharing the same lovers.

The Blue Angel of alluring bisexual sensuality, **Marlene Dietrich** was a sultry German-born *Fräulein*, systematically seducing the men and women who moved in and out of Bogie's life.

Bogart was mesmerized by her blonde hair which she wore like a golden halo, cheekbones that were matchless works of art, and eyebrows that arched provocatively above her blue eyes. Dietrich and Bogie often seduced the same women.

**Speedtrap!** A lavishly dressed **Bebe Daniels** was the third actress with the initials BD that Bogie succumbed to. Daniels followed in the wake of Billie Dove and Bette Davis.

Bebe and her hubbie, Ben Lyons, were known as "Hollywood's Happiest Couple" despite Lyon's homosexual liaisons with Howard Hughes and other men.

Hughes sent Bogie to spring Bebe from jail, where she'd been locked up after her arrest for speeding.

Born into an impoverished Swedish family, the heavily endowed **Eric Linden** specialized in playing sensitive youths on the screen.

Off-screen, after a momentary affair with Kenneth MacKenna, Linden fell hopelessly in love with Bogie and actually stalked him.

Bogie wanted no part of the sex thing, but promised Linden that it would be the beginning of a beautiful friendship.

With a pair of six-shooters holding up her titties, a beaming, bright-faced **Joan Crawford** was one of Bogie's early Hollywood seductions when he was traveling from the bed of one gorgeous diva to the next.

He later told Kenneth MacKenna, "A man doesn't fuck Joan Crawford. Crawford fucks the man."

# DID YOU KNOW?

That over the course of many years, **Blood Moon's Darwin Porter** rolled around in the hay with the legacy of Humphrey Bogart not once, but TWICE.

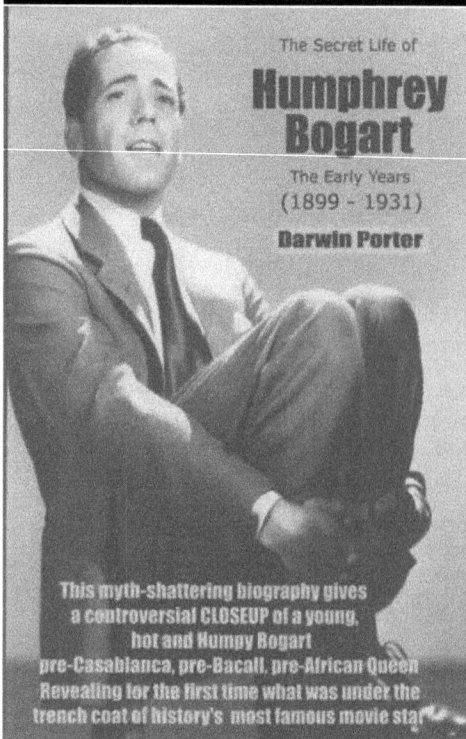

Both of the **"BOGART BIOPSIES'** he produced generated massive tabloid publicity, in part because their revelations at the time were SCANDAL-SOAKED, NEW and UNDERGROUND and appeared in print FOR THE FIRST TIME.

*Left photo:*
**Humphrey Bogart,**
**The Early Years (1899-1931),**
back when his films were Pre-Code and *risqué*
ISBN 0-9668030-5-1

*Right photo:*
**Humphrey Bogart,**
**the Making of a Legend.**

What was the secret of his spectacular popularity? and what REALLY lay beneath his trenchcoat?
ALL of that's here, as aggressively promoted the week of its publication by some of the biggest newspapers and tabloids in the world.
ISBN 978-1-936003-14-3

by
John Austin

*June 11, 2003*

HUMPHREY BOGART'S EARLY YEARS. . . Until recently, at least to our knowledge, very little was known, at least publicly, about the (very) early life of one of Hollywood's most famous stars. But the new biography *The Secret Life Of Humphrey Bogart* – The Early Years (1899-1931) which we received about a month ago has had us pondering as to how to handle it in print of in a town so protective of its own; at least until the Florida tabloids starting picking everyone apart. This biography of Bogart's early years, is exceptionally well written.

We will be as objective as possible while reviewing this 600 page trade paperback by Darwin Porter who devotes a great deal of space to the young Bogart's association with Howard Hughes. Bogart was so afraid that Hughes would tell his then wife, Mary Phillips, about his philandering he agreed to do all sorts of jobs for the reclusive industrialist-cum-film producer. Knowing Hughes' penchant for young ladies, etc., we need not go into detail here. However, he did escort Jean Harlow to Tijuana for a clandestine termination said to have originated with Hughes.

One cannot read a book such as this without a sense of irony of how American myths are created and sustained and a sense of admiration for the biographers who unblock the doors and the windows. Illusions about the chain smoking anti-hero with the trench coat might suffer in the process, but readers emerge with an understanding of who Bogart, the man really was. It also reveals the daunting odds and the exotic temptations he faced during his struggle for survival in early Hollywood. While the book also details Bogart's own healthy sex life, including affairs with Barbara Stanwyck and Bette Davis, Tallulah Bankhead and a one night stand with Hearst movie columnist and Hollywood's resident ogre, Louella Parsons. This was in exchange for a good press which he received from "Lolly" throughout most of his career.

Porter based the book on a "dishy" mss written by Bogey's "friend", actor Kenneth MacKenna who died in 1962. The author fleshed out the stories through his own acquaintance with actresses such as Joan Crawford and Bette Davis. Porter admits that the material might still be sensitive for Bogart's surviving family but he promised MacKenna he would, one day, fulfill the dream of two men, MacKenna and his close friend, Stanley Mills Haggart of having the Bogart story published. It is based on material available to no other author. In Books of the Month for J we will have more of this amazing, well-written tales of the early Hollywood. It is publish the Georgia Literary Association, ISBN #0-9668030-5-1, Trade Paperback 6x9", 64 photos/illustrations and a complete index. $16.95. Tel: 718 556-9410.

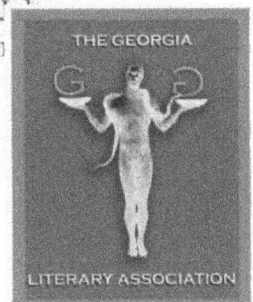

# STONEWALL
## News Northwest

Vol. XII. No.5     Serving the Gay and Lesbian Community of the Inland NW     June 2003

# Bogie bio: Tells tales, names names

### The Secret Life of Humphrey Bogart

*The Early Years (1899-1931)*

Darwin Porter

*Georgia Literary Association, 528 pages, illustrated, paperback, $16.95*

Call if juicy, but if you're interested in a see-all, tell-all book that divulges secrets of Hollywood's most famous movie queens from the Golden Age, pick up a copy of *The Secret Life of Humphrey Bogart*, to be released this month. This biography uncovers "the good stuff" you want to know about the show-biz biggies and wannabes from Bogie's early years, including those trumpeted

Randolph Scott, left, with Cary Grant

as queens and queens who could blow a trumpet themselves.

In this new and untold-until-now biography, author Darwin Porter (*Hollywood's Silent Closet, Rhinestone Country* and others) delves deep into Bogart's salacious, formative years on Broadway and in early Hollywood when "talkies" were the rage.

Compiled after extensive eyewitness interviews, some conducted by friends and companions as early as the 1930s, Porter reveals what movie studio publicists deliberately and studiously suppressed: the intimate details that fans really want to know about.

*Secret Life* exposes the true and tantalizing details of Bogie's big game seductions, including the likes of Joan Crawford, Tallulah Bankhead, Barbara Stanwyck and Bette Davis. Not sparing any of the steamy and sometimes seamy details of Bogart's well-noted life, this book shatters the myth of the

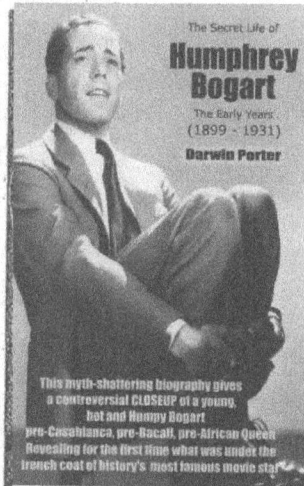

*This myth-shattering biography gives a controversial CLOSEUP of a young, hot and Humpy Bogart pre-Casablanca, pre-Bacall, pre-African Queen. Revealing for the first time what was under the trench coat of history's most famous movie star.*

strong and silent trenchcoat and sheds light on the exotic temptations Bogart faced during his struggle for survival in early Hollywood.

Porter exposes Bogart's thankless role as errand boy, courier and procurer of male escorts for millionaire Howard Hughes. What you read about Spencer Tracy will startle you. And Cary Grant. And Randolph Scott. And ... a long, long list of others.

For those of us who want the dirt and want it quick, the book features a wonderful and handy index.

---

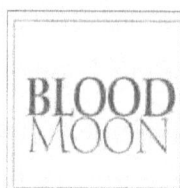

BLOOD
MOON

# KATHARINE HEPBURN

BECAME FAMOUS FOR HER LOVE-HATE RELATIONSHIP WITH THE TABLOIDS.
AND WHEREAS IN THE PREVIOUS SECTION WE DEMONSTRATED HOW
## THE TABLOIDS HUMPED FOR HUMPHREY,
THEY WENT ABSOLUTELY BERSERK FOR BLOOD MOON'S OVERVIEW OF

# KATHARINE THE GREAT

# HOW,

## IN THE WEEKS THAT FOLLOWED THE PUBLICATION OF
## DARWIN PORTER'S THEN-RADICAL BIOGRAPHY,
## THE TABLOIDS SPUN KATHARINE HEPBURN'S LEGACY.

**Katharine Hepburn** appears above *(center photo)* within a rococo oval whose style was favored by the 18th century Empress of Russia.

Her crown derives from the queen she played—**Eleanor of Aquitaine**, the richest and most famous woman of medieval Europe—for which Hepburn won an Oscar. The film—one of many for which her fans virtually swooned—was *A Lion in Winter* (1968). Her co-star? **Peter O'Toole** as her husband, Henry II of England. The setting?: A fortified château in English-occupied France over the Christmas holidays of 1183. The theme?: Family dysfunction, thwarted love, dynastic ambition, and hatred. **Nobody did it better than Hepburn.**

A NEW BIOGRAPHY REVEALS KATHARINE HEPBURN AS A VORACIOUS BISEXUAL, DRIVEN BY HER INSATIABLE LUST.

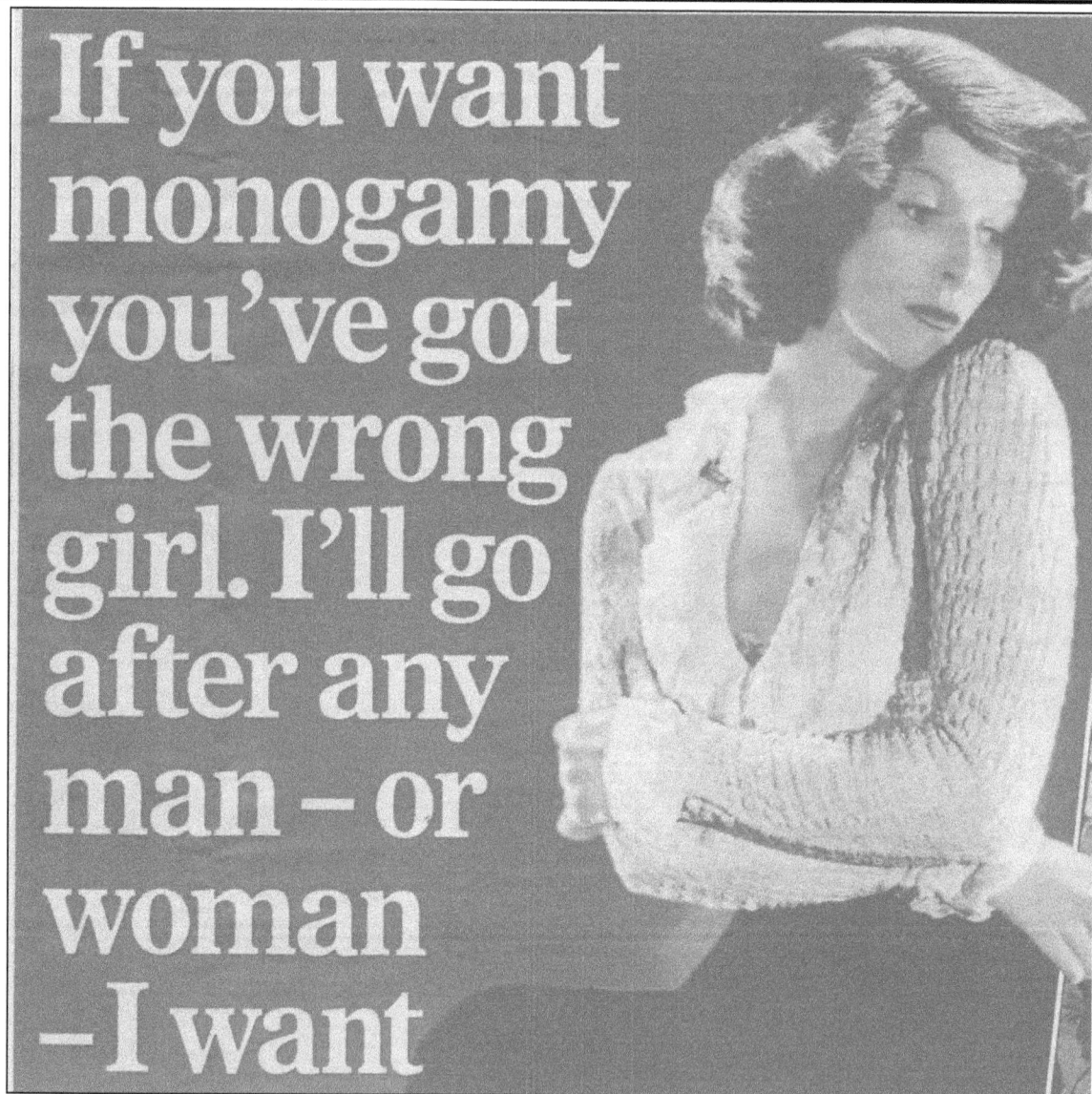

If you want monogamy you've got the wrong girl. I'll go after any man – or woman – I want

**Katharine Hepburn** was the world's greatest screen diva--the most famous actress in American history. But until the appearance of Darwin Porter's new biography, no one had ever published the intimate details of her complicated and ferociously secretive private life.

Thanks to the deferential and obsequious whitewashes which followed in the immediate wake of her death, readers probably know WHAT KATE REMEMBERED.

**HERE, HOWEVER, IS AN UNVARNISHED ACCOUNT OF WHAT KATHARINE HEPBURN DESPERATELY WANTED TO FORGET.**

WWW.GAYCITYNEWS.COM

# 38/Books

Gay City NEWS

# This Time Unauthorized

## New book completes the Hepburn portrait A. Scott Berg left sketchy

BY WINNIE MCCROY

Thirteen days after the death of Katharine Hepburn last year, celebrity biographer A. Scott Berg published "Kate Remembered," reflecting 20 years of interviews with the legendary screen luminary. Almost immediately, The Advocate labeled the tome, "a mixture of cautious disclosure and obsequious deference" and threw down the gauntlet for someone willing to go behind the carefully constructed public persona Hepburn protected throughout her eight decades in film.

Celebrity exposé author Darwin Porter accepted the challenge, and this Valentine's Day, released "Katharine the Great: A Lifetime of Secrets Revealed," a mammoth volume presenting a wealth of evidence that the late, great Kate was not necessarily straight.

In this 570-page unauthorized biography, Porter delves into the spicy sexual conquests of the Connecticut born and bred actress and her cadre of high-profile companions.

Although Porter looks at Hepburn's early childhood, the suicide of her brother Tom, her marriage to "Luddy," Ludlow Ogden Smith, and her career, he focuses largely on the relationship between Hepburn and American Express heiress Laura Harding. The wealth of evidence he provides indicates Hepburn was indeed bisexual, or a "double-gater" as it was

**KATHARINE THE GREAT**
By Darwin Porter
Blood Moon Productions
$17, 570 pages

**KATE REMEMBERED**
By A. Scott Berg
G.P. Putnam
$26, 370 pages

called then, and that she and Harding conducted a closeted, long-term relationship from 1928 until Harding's death in 1994, a relationship that overlapped with her seven-year "lavender marriage" to Luddy that began the same year.

It is difficult to imagine that, even in the 1930s, it was customary for a new bride and groom to bring companions on their honeymoon, as did Hepburn with Harding, and Luddy with his longtime companion Jack Clark.

Even Berg's more discrete bio mentions Harding, noting that, after her marriage to Luddy, Hepburn moved to Hollywood and "continued to live quietly in the hills with Laura Harding (furthering speculation of a lesbian relationship)."

Hepburn's longtime relationship with Spencer Tracy seems to have found her in more of a caretaker role than that of a lover. Berg notes that, "As she told me that first night in Fenwick [where her Connecticut home was located], 'I never wanted to marry Spencer Tracy.'"

The American Express heiress, **Laura Harding** *(right figure in photo above)*, began her romance with **Kate** *(left)* in 1928. Their love affair, even after passion's fires had died, lasted until Harding's death in 1994.

Kate took Harding with her on her honeymoon with her husband, Ludlow Ogden Smith, as well as his male lover. Kate told friends that Laura might as well go along on her divorce trip, too. They're pictured above at the New York airport awaiting their flight to Miami, where they would sail to Mexico for Hepburn's divorce from her husband, Ludlow Ogden Smith.

Hepburn's long-term relationship with Miss Harding is only one of the romantic liaisons exposed, based on eye-witness accounts, within Darwin Porter's new biography.

Hepburn, unapologetically butch.

379

# GOLDEN TIMES
## MAGAZINE

• June 2004

### Glamour, Sex, Scandals
## OUT OF HOLLYWOOD'S CLOSETS

Katharine
The Great

KATHARINE OF ARROGANCE
(above),
playing Mary of Scotland. Regal and patrician both on and off the screen, KATHARINE HEPBURN maintained a blessing distance for the press and its invasions of her privacy, sometimes physically assaulting journalists she considered impertinent.

"Write anything about me you like" [Her own words, repeated often to journalists.] "Just don't ever tell the truth."

That is a directive that Darwin Porter, in his newest biography, pointedly chose to ignore.

a lifetime
of secrets...
revealed by Darwin Porter

JOHN STICKLER BOOK REVIEW, PG. 10

SPENCER TRACY
Katharine
HEPBURN

WOMAN OF THE YEAR

George STEVENS

SPENCER TRACY
KATHARINE HEPBURN
Keeper
of the
Flame

**Woman of the Year** (1942) brought together one of the greatest screen pairings in the history of Hollywood, **Katharine Hepburn** and **Spencer Tracy**. It marked the first teaming of these two friends in what led to nine motion pictures over a quarter-century, ending with **Guess Who's Coming to Dinner?** (1967).

**Time** magazine wrote, "For once, strident Katharine Hepburn is properly subdued. She was cast as a columnist, Tess Harding."

**Katharine Hepburn** and **Spencer Tracy** followed their first pairing on the screen with another hit, **Keeper of the Flame** (also released in 1942). What made it unusual was that it included no romantic interest between the two superstars. Tracy was cast as a reporter seeking an exposé involving a rich woman trying to keep a secret.

At its first screening, **Louis B. Mayer** of MGM found the teaming of Tracy with Hepburn inspired. He told his associates, "These two make the sparks fly off the screen. This time, her exaggerated theatricality is perfect."

# Katharine the Great (1907-1950)
## A lifetime of secrets revealed

**By Darwin Porter** Blood Moon Productions, Ltd., Feb. 2004
Trade paperback, ISBN 0-9748118-0-7, 569 pages, 58 photos, $16.95

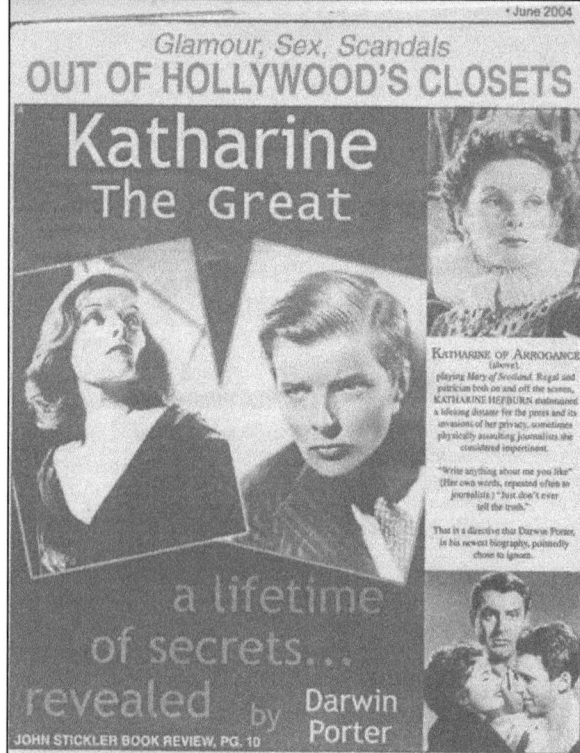

In the spring of 1958 I was driving north with some college buddies from New Haven to Hartford, Connecticut. We caught up with a classic 1948 Lincoln Continental bearing the custom license plate KATE. It had to be someone special and we were not disappointed. As we cruised past we immediately recognized the unmistakable patrician profile of Katharine Hepburn, driving herself, alone in the camel-colored convertible.

Her mouth held the hint of a smile; an aura of superiority and mystery surrounded her. We tried not to stare. (OK, we were gawking.) She wore that mantle of mystery all her life, thanks to her skill in keeping the press at bay, until her passing in 2003 at age 96.

Author Darwin Porter, following his remarkable 2003 book on the private life of Humphrey Bogart, has surpassed himself with this incredibly detailed biography of one of the 20th century's premier stage and movie stars. "Write anything about me you like," she told Porter, "just don't ever tell the truth."

Sorry, Kate. Here comes the truth.

Even as a child Katharine Hepburn was a self-centered, headstrong, tomboy. After graduating from Bryn Mawr she launched her acting career on the East Coast, just as Humphrey Bogart did, with the help of friends in the theater business. Her agent (and later, lover) Leland Hayward, encouraged her to head to Hollywood, where the big money was. The studios didn't know what to make of her, demanding (and receiving!) ten times what first-time movie actresses were being paid. When her train pulled into Los Angeles' Union Station in July 1932, she had a $6,000 RKO one-picture contract under her arm and an attitude that preceded her like a snowplow. She never looked back.

Although Katharine the Great catalogs her work on 25 films up until 1950, including how close she came to landing the role of Scarlett O'Hara (opposite Errol Flynn?) in Gone With the Wind, the author focuses on what happened behind the movie camera—on the set and off. There is not room here to discuss her hapless husband or list the 30-year diary of Hepburn's intimacies, from Jimmy Stewart, Howard Hughes and Spencer Tracy to Greta Garbo, Claudette Colbert and Judy Garland, meticulously chronicled by Porter. The key question is how did he do it? Half a century and more after the fact?

The answer lies in the unlikely confluence of three facts: A) Porter's mother began a scrapbook on Hepburn back in the 1920s, and Porter kept it up; B) Katharine couldn't keep from gossiping about herself to close friends who later recalled all too well the private life she revealed, and C) Porter became an entertainment journalist, interviewing literally hundreds of people over a period of decades who knew and worked with Hepburn during her long career. Every source is annotated in a 21-page afterword, name by name.

He also met Miss Hepburn through his employer, Tennessee Williams, and had the opportunity to interview her.

If you are curious about the four-time Oscar winner once dubbed "Katharine of Arrogance," and would like to peek under her covers and into her closets, this thorough volume will more than satisfy your curiosity. Be warned, Porter's research is not for prudes. If this book were a movie it would carry an R rating, for grownups only.

Stay tuned. Darwin Potter isn't done yet; he promises more on Katharine Hepburn in Volume II.

*Reviewed by John Stickler, Mature Market Editorial Services.*

# Katharine Hepburn

There's a carload of other biographies about Hepburn that either got the facts wrong or whitewashed them to the point where there's almost been a consistent act of academic sabotage. But here at last is a biography that isn't afraid to wrestle with the outrageous ego and ferociously guarded privacy of Hollywood's most mysterious *Über-diva*, **Katharine the Great.**

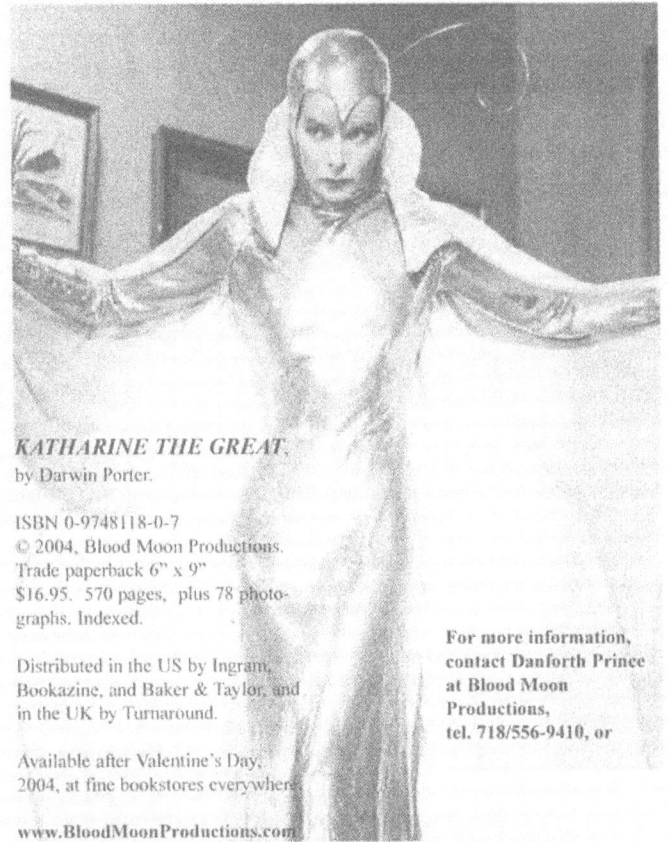

# DAILY ☉ NEWS

www.nydailynews.com    **NEW YORK'S HOMETOWN NEWSPAPER**    Monday, February 2, 20

## RUSH & MOLLOY

BY GEORGE RUSH AND JOANNA MOLLOY    WITH BEN WIDDICOMBE AND SUZANNE ROZDEBA

# KATE'S 'L' WORLD

## *New bio says Hepburn was busily bisexual*

A new biography of Katharine Hepburn claims to rip open the star's little black book of A-list lesbian lovers. "Katharine the Great" alleges the lipstick thespian romanced many of Golden Age Hollywood's hottest stars, including Claudette Colbert, Greta Garbo, Judy Holliday and Judy Garland. ....and actors John Barrymore

Excerpt from **Rush & Molloy**'s syndicated column of Feb. 2, 2004, quoting Darwin Porter's text:

"First Lady **Eleanor Roosevelt** was said to have had an "infatuation with Hepburn during the darkest days of World War II, which led to a series of 'Oh, my darling Katharine' love letters."

381

PARIS
MATCH

# THE SEXUAL INDISCRETIONS OF
# KATHARINE HEPBURN

By **Danforth Prince**, a former staff member at the Paris office of **The New York Times**. This material was submitted to *Paris-Match* before the publication of Blood Moon's *Katharine the Great*.

**The indiscretions of Katharine Hepburn,** the indomitable *grande dame* of American actresses will be revealed for the first time in Darwin Porter's ground-breaking biography *Katharine the Great*, after its release in February of 2004.

At long last, the secretive, closeted world of the 20th-century's most acclaimed female film star will be exposed. The New Englander screen legend died in June of 2003 at the age of 96 in her home in Old Saybrook, Connecticut.

Shortly after her death, G.P. Putnam's Sons published *Kate Remembered* by A. Scott Berg, a 500,000 copy first printing of this biography-cum-memoir. In this much ballyhooed release, Berg drew upon conversations he'd had with Hepburn but claimed the book could not be published until after her death.

Fans eager for "close encounters" with Hepburn made the book an international bestseller, as they rushed to read the "from-the-grave" revelations of the screen icon and four-time Academy Award winner. Surprisingly, the book offered no major revelations at all, and was denounced by critics for its "vanilla" or "white bread" portrait of Hepburn, which had already been done countless times.

Amazingly, Hepburn guarded her secrets all her life, even though living in an international spotlight. Of all the screen icons of the golden age, she kept the door to her closet locked and padded, rivaled only by another closet lesbian, Barbara Stanwyck. Even the most private details of Hollywood's other secretive and mysterious actress, Greta Garbo, have been exposed in one rich biography after another.

Biographer **Darwin Porter** began gathering material for his book on Hepburn in 1960 when he first became a Hollywood reporter. He knew that it could never be published in Hepburn's lifetime. "At one point I was afraid she might outlive me," Porter said.

The author was first introduced to Hepburn at her Manhattan Turtle Bay residence by **Tennessee Williams.** The playwright was trying to persuade Hepburn to appear on the stage opposite Bette Davis in *The Night of the Iguana*. She turned him down.

"Although Miss Hepburn gave me insights into many subjects, including what she thought about depicting 'perversion' on the screen, she provided not one clue about her own life," Porter said. "When she learned from friends that Porter was compiling extensive documentation on her, she said, "Write whatever you want about me--but never the truth. No, not that!"

**Porter has chosen not to obey Hepburn's demand**. Throughout the summer and autumn of 2003 the American press has been clamoring for some author to "out" the great screen diva. With the imminent publication of *Katharine the Great*, the door to Hepburn's closet is about to be thrown wide open.

Filled with information never published in book form before, *Katharine the Great* is top heavy with stunning revelations, the most sensational of which is that both **Katharine Hepburn and Spencer Tracy** were bisexuals, effectively serving as each other's "beards" during their notorious but at-the-time unpublicized love affair.

Porter maintains that theirs began as a great love affair in the early 1940s but quickly became platonic as "caretaker" Hepburn struggled with the verbally abusive and alcoholic actor.

Hepburn publicly said she considered Tracy "the ideal American man--sports loving, a man's man, strong looking, big sort of head, boar neck and so forth. And I think I represent a woman. I needle him, I irritate him, and I try to get around him, and if he put a big paw out and put it on my head, he could squash me. And I think that is the romantic ideal picture of male and female in this country."

Porter dismissed this statement as one of Hepburn's many attempts to conceal from the public the real character of Tracy, "who was a Dr. Jekyll and Mr. Hyde, like one of his film roles in the 1940s."

The author claims that there was no one in American film history as different in person from his screen image as Tracy. "On screen he was the most brilliant of American actors," Porter claims. "Off-screen, he was a disaster, often a violent disaster. Only Kate Hepburn knows for sure why she endured this relationship. But in spite of the success of the Tracy and Hepburn pictures, he also did much to retard her career."

The biography reveals that Hepburn endured Tracy's affairs with such legends as **Ingrid Bergman, Nancy Davis (who later married the man who would become the American president, Ronald Reagan), Paulette Goddard, Gene Tierney**, and even **Grace Kelly.** Tracy had previously enjoyed romances with such stars as **Joan Crawford, Loretta Young,** and **Joan Bennett.** Throughout these liaisons, Tracy, a guilt-ridden Catholic, was still married to former actress, **Louise Treadwell,** with whom he had two children.

In the book Porter quotes various stars, citing their opinions of Tracy. Crawford found him a "very disturbed man and a mean drunk and bastard." Loretta Young claimed "he made women feel warm and wanted, but there was no flattery about him." When asked about her relationship with Tracy, Hepburn would reveal only that "He made the best cup of coffee in the world."

When not chasing half the attractive women in Hollywood, Tracy exhibited a dark side, Porter reveals. He was a "binge" alcoholic, and would disappear for weeks at a time, often with a suitcase loaded with liquor bottles.

He'd check into a hotel, settle into the bathtub, where he would drink, sleep "and do everything else" for days at a time. Sometimes after he sobered up, he would hire young male prostitutes. Porter claims that Tracy preferred "rather macho men, not pretty boys, and he would indulge in his passion far from the preying eyes of Hollywood."

Sobered up, Tracy would then return to life with Hepburn who might or might not be there. Often she deserted him for long periods, pursuing her own film and stage career and her own sexual affairs.

**Laura Harding** (1902-1994) and Tracy, Hepburn's two greatest loves, could hardly abide each other, Porter says. "But they maintained an uneasy truce with each other for the sake of their mutual love, Hepburn."

*Katharine the Great* reveals that Hepburn married a homosexual (**Ludlow Ogden Smith** on December 12, 1928) and took her new husband and his lover, **Jack Clarke**, on their honeymoon to Bermuda. And accompanying Hepburn was her long-time companion, Laura Harding, the banking heiress whose father founded American Express.

Porter maintains that in some respects Ms. Harding was even more vital in her role as Hepburn's lover than Tracy. The Hepburn/Harding romance began in 1928, and their affair continued throughout both of their lives. Hepburn visited Harding at her death bed.

"I maintain the greatest respect for Katharine Hepburn," Porter said, "but she was never truthful about her own life. Of course, given the homophobia that still exists in Hollywood today, that's completely understandable. Even in her later years when her career was out of harm's way, this great screen diva never made even a small gesture of support to the struggling gay and lesbian movement in America."

Page by page, chapter by chapter, the carefully researched and documented *Katharine the Great* sheds light on America's icon of feminist strength, with her chiseled beauty and patrician bearing. The lights of Broadway dimmed to honor Hepburn's death but the bulbs are turned on again in this startling book.

In explicit detail, the book documents not only the two great loves of Hepburn's life, Laura Harding and Spencer Tracy, but her minor affairs off-camera.

Her lesbian lovers included the beautiful and once famous but now largely forgotten film star, **Elissa Landi.** Landi was alleged to have been the direct descendant of Empress Elizabeth (Sissi) of Austria.

Some of Hepburn's other romantic trysts with women featured an all-star cast that included **Claudette Colbert, Greta Garbo, Judy Holliday,** and **Judy Garland**. But there were lesser lights as well, including film editor **Jane Loring**, concert singer **Suzanne Steele**, and songwriter **Nancy Hamilton.**

Among men, the biography explores in detail Hepburn's affairs with directors **John Ford** and **George Stevens,** as well as such co-stars as **John Barrymore, Douglas Fairbanks, Jr.,** and **Charles Boyer. Dr. Thomas Hepburn**, Katharine's father, called his daughter "a charging bull," in describing her sexual exploits. He witnessed her very brief but tantalizing involvements with such Hollywood hunks as **Franchot Tone, Robert Ryan, Robert Mitchum,** and **Burt Lancaster.**

Hepburn also shared her charms with actors **Paul Henreid, Robert Walker,** and **Leslie Howard**, who fired her after bedding her.

Hepburn also had an affair with another actor, **Van Heflin,** when they were appearing on stage together in her hit play, *The Philadelphia Story*. But he broke off their romance when he didn't get his coveted role in the film version. That went to **Jimmy Stewart,** another leading man that Hepburn temporarily became involved with romantically.

Porter's book dispels the rumor that Hepburn was ever sexually involved with another one of her leading men in *The Philadelphia Story*, **Cary Grant**. At a party hosted by director **George Cukor,** both Hepburn and **Marlene Dietrich** agreed that Grant was "too homosexual" for their tastes.

One of the most shocking chapters explodes the myth of Hepburn's largely romanticized and fictionalized affair with the dashing and handsome young billionaire, **Howard Hughes.** Like Hepburn, Hughes was a bisexual and seemed more interested in Cary Grant than Hepburn during his troubled relationship with the actress.

Porter claims that the relationship between Hughes and Hepburn being depicted in *The Aviator*, a film now being shot, will largely be a Hollywood fantasy, with **Leonardo DiCaprio** playing Hughes and **Cate Blanchett** appearing as Hepburn.

In direct contrast to Berg's *Kate Remembered*, Porter's *Katharine the Great* documents what the reclusive star wanted to forget--or never wanted her fans to know in the first place.

Revelations include:

* **Hepburn's brief affair** with author **Ernest Hemingway**, who brutally rejected her when she fell in love with him.
* **Richard Nixon's surprise intervention** with FBI director **J. Edgar Hoover** to save the careers of "those two pinkos" Tracy and Hepburn.
* **Eleanor Roosevelt's infatuation with Hepburn** during the darkest days of World War II, which led to a series of "Oh, my darling Katharine" love letters.
* **The behind-the-scenes story of the suicide by hanging of Hepburn's beloved older brother, Tom**, and why she deliberately suppressed the details of her sibling's death, including distortions in her notoriously unrevealing autobiography,

entitled, *Me.*

    *    **Hepburn's early "career" as a nude model** posing for the celebrated sculptor, **Robert J. McKnight.** No stranger to nudity, the actress grew up in a household of casual nudity, her doctor father often having her girl friends brought in for long conversations with him as he bathed. Hepburn also posed for countless nude pictures taken by her husband, who sometimes photographed his wife and his lover together. In later life, Hepburn paid "a handsome dividend" to a blackmailer who had obtained some of these pictures which she had lost in a wicker basket at a picnic.

***

    The full story is explored of Hepburn's disastrous involvement in the British play, *The Lake*, which created material for countless female impersonators over the decades. The play prompted critic and writer **Dorothy Parker** to utter her famous line: "Katharine Hepburn ran the gamut of emotions from A to B." The biography reveals the behind-the-scenes jealousy of Hepburn that might have provoked Parker's catty remark.

    Another surprising story is unraveled about Hepburn's romantic involvement with the director and producer of *The Lake*, **Jed Harris.** He was called the "Vampire of Broadway." When he made an agreement with Hepburn to let her play the role, he received her in his Broadway offices stark naked. She later became involved with him in her only real S&M relationship, much to the shock of the cast. Years later, she confided to friends that she still didn't understand why she had become so obsessed with Harris. The producer admitted that he deliberately set out--for reasons known only to himself--to wreck Hepburn's still fledging career.

    Hepburn's remarkable love affair with **Irene Mayer Selznick** is explored. She was the daughter of **Louis B. Mayer** and the wife of producer **David O. Selznick.** Hepburn had such power over Selznick that she could persuade her friend and lover to indulge in Hepburn's favorite pastime: Breaking into elegant Beverly Hills homes when the rich owners were away. Hepburn boasted that she did not steal--after all, she and Selznick were two of the richest women in Hollywood--but gained illegal entry "for the thrill of the adventure." Once she was caught when the fading silent-screen star, **Ramon Novarro,** famous for the MGM film, *Ben-Hur*, arrived back at his house unexpectedly.

    Porter tackles the single most gossiped about and scandalous involvement in Hepburn's life in the 1950s. Rat Packers **Frank Sinatra** and **Peter Lawford** spread the word that Hepburn was having a "gay-for-pay" affair with **Bettie Page.** Enjoying a massive revival in the 21st century, Bettie Page was the most famous "cheesecake-and-glamour" model of the Fifties, and eventually became the first big name in soft porn. Hepburn is alleged to have used her services for $1,000 (U.S.) dollars a night, even though Page claimed that **Bette Davis** was actually her favorite actress on the screen.

"In my search I talked to any and everyone I could meet about Katharine Hepburn--both those who loved her and those who hated her," Porter said, "including the screen star, **Margaret Sullavan**, Hepburn's nemesis, who called her a dykey bitch," Porter said.

    At one point both Hepburn and Sullavan were in love with their mutual agent, **Leland Hayward.** Sullavan eventually married him. Hayward in time would marry **Pamela Harriman**, Winston Churchill's former daughter-in-law, who became Bill Clinton's ambassador to France, dying in a swimming pool at the Ritz Hotel in Paris.

    "Everybody, it seemed, had a story (or stories) to tell about Hepburn," Porter said. "Sources ranged from **Tennessee Williams** to **Bette Davis**, from **Gregory Hemingway** (son of Ernest) to **Marlene Dietrich**, from director **George Cukor** to actress **Ruth Gordon** and **Garson Kanin**, who wrote *Adam's Rib* and other screenplays for Spencer Tracy and Hepburn.

    Porter also had access to the journals of **Anderson Lawler,** a minor actor known mainly in Hollywood history for his love affair with **Gary Cooper.** Lawler's manuscript was deemed unpublishable in his day because of its libelous tell-all contents. Porter also drew extensively on the journals of actor **Kenneth MacKenna**, whom Hepburn always referred to as "my original deflowerer." MacKenna was the longtime pal of **Humphrey Bogart**, and he married Bogart's second wife, actress **Mary Philips**.

    Poignant moments are revealed in the biography, as when former lovers Hepburn and MacKenna came together on the set of *Judgment at Nurnberg* in 1961 shortly before his death. Hepburn had a nostalgic reunion with MacKenna who played an Allied judge sitting on the bench with Spencer Tracy. During the filming, Tracy renewed his friendship with his former lover, **Marlene Dietrich**, and Hepburn helped her former *inamorata*, **Judy Garland,** struggle through the script. She also helped her friend, **Montgomery Clift,** with whom she'd appeared in **Tennessee Williams's** controversial homosexual drama, *Suddenly, Last Summer*, a role Hepburn detested even though it brought her an Academy Award nomination.

    Porter also used the extensive Hollywood journals of his former writing partner, **Stanley Haggart**, who knew Hepburn intimately in the 1930s and 1940s and was a close friend of Hepburn's only husband, "Luddy."

    Both Haggart and Porter knew **George Cukor**, who provided valuable insights and stories but with the stipulation that nothing was to be published during his lifetime or Hepburn's lifetime..

    Porter is also the author of the previous bestseller, *The Secret Life of Humphrey Bogart*, published worldwide in 2003.

    **Danforth Prince**, president of Blood Moon Productions, publishers of *Katharine the Great*, said, "We think we're about to issue what has every chance of being the most talked about, even the most notorious, Hollywood biography of 2004. Maybe even the decade's hottest."

# WHEN, FOR A CHANGE, KATE DECIDED TO SEDUCE A MAN, HERE ARE SOME OF THOSE WHO SAID YES.

Howard Hughes

James Stewart

Kate, Artfully androgynous in the 30s

Charles Boyer

Robert Mitchum

George Stevens

John Ford

Van Heflin

Leland Hayward with Margaret Sullavan

Kate, Artfully macho in the 50s

Douglas Fairbanks Jr.

Franchot Tone

John Barrymore

Fred MacMurray

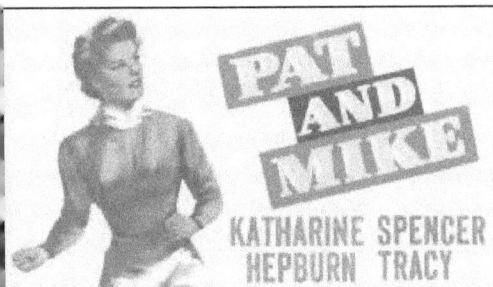

**QUESTION:** In which of her movies was "**Incorrigible Kate**" the most unapologetically butch?

**ANSWER:** *PAT and MIKE* (1952). In ways that surpassed even the macho posturings of *Sylvia Scarlett* (1935, see *photo right*), she played her scenes in ways that were SO macho that urban hipsters REALLY began to doubt the heterosexual illusions *(KATE! MADLY IN LOVE WITH SPENCER!)* on which it was based

PAT AND MIKE

KATHARINE SPENCER
HEPBURN TRACY

# THE NUANCED ART OF HOLLYWOOD GOSSIP
## WHAT KATE'S FRENEMIES SAID, AND WHAT SHE SAID ABOUT HERSELF

*"If you survive, you become a legend. I'm a legend because I have survived over a long period of time. You might as well call me timeless."*

—**Katharine Hepburn**

*"I just adore her, even when she slaps the hell out of me. I nicknamed her 'Old Hag.' Her nickname for me was 'Pig.'"*

—**Peter O'Toole**

*"I married Leland Hayward, the famous talent agent. He told me that he had once bedded Katharine Hepburn. He claimed that it was about as much fun as an imagined seduction of Marjorie Main."*

—**Margaret Sullavan**

*"On a dare, and just wanting to be provocative, I once asked John Ford who was a better lovr—a young John Wayne or yours truly. He did not answer."*

—**Katharine Hepburn**

*"John Barrymore lost his virginity to his stepmother when he was fifteen. He seduced Carole Lombard before Clark Gable got into her honeypot. Kate Hepburn put up a fight in the beginning but finally succumbed to my brother's manly charms."*

—**Lionel Barrymore**

*"There is talk that Katharine Hepburn is going to star opposite me as Scarlett O'Hara in* Gone With the Wind. *I'm not good enough an actor to convince the audience that I would lust after her for years. I hear she likes pussy as much as I do."*

—**Clark Gable**

*"I don't know why, but I often ended up with lesbians in my salad years. Take Kate Hepburn for example. Better yet, Tallulah Bankhead and Marlene Dietrich. I even married a bisexual: Miss Joan Crawford. She had sex without gender preference."*

—**Douglas Fairbanks, Jr.**

*"Katharine Hepburn immortalized herself on Broadway by becoming the first actress to utter the word 'shit' on stage. The sludge came out of her mouth when she starred in the musical Coco. She uttered the word in a song."*

—**Walter Winchell**

*"I'm often asked to name some of the famous actresses I have seduced. You're my best friend, and the only person to whom I would reveal such secrets. To name only a few, I would put Hollywood's royalty at the top of the list. Miss Katharine Hepburn, when we co-starred in* The Philadelphia Story. *Throw in Jean Harlow, June Allyson, Diana Barrymore, Rita Hayworth, Marlene Dietrich (I made her pregnant), Grace Kelly, Margaret Sullavan (your former wife), Jeanette MacDonald, Lana Turner, Loretta Young, Norma Shearer, Ginger Rogers. I'll stop here. If memory serves me right, I plowed you, too, on many a night when we were roomies in the 1930s sharing a single cot."*

—**James Stewart to Henry Fonda**

*"I heard Charles Boyer seduced Katharine Hepburn when they co-starred in* Break of Hearts *in 1935. I'm told that when he removes his wig, his corset, and the lifts in his shoes, he looks like the Pillsbury doughboy."*

—**Bette Davis**

*"Katharine Hepburn and Spencer Tracy were my best friends. They had a platonic relationship. For sex, he turned to young actors, with an occasional movie star like Loretta Young, Myrna Loy, Joan Crawford, and Grace Kelly. Mostly, he preferred men. Her lifetime love was Laura Harding, the American Express heiress."*

—**George Cukor**

*"Gertrude Stein had her lover and lifetime companion, Alice B. Toklas. Kate had her own Toklas, too. It was Phyllis Wilbourn, who remained at her beck and call for forty years."*

—**George Cukor**

# SPENCER TRACY
## HAD A CRUSH ON "PRETTY BOY"
# JOHN DEREK

**"Who was John Derek?"** a Generation Z movie fan might ask today.

In the 1950s (Derek's heyday) he received tons of fan mail from both teenaged girls and loads of homosexuals aged 13 to 83.

In the early 1950s, he was voted the handsomest male actor in Hollywood.

Before "anti-hero uglies" like Dustin Hoffman came along, the 1950s witnessed "the Golden Age of the Pretty Boy."

In the flesh markets of that era, Derek reigned supreme, although an array of other actors had fan bases too: Rock Hudson, Tab Hunter, Troy Donahue, Rory Calhoun, Tony Curtis, James Dean, John Saxon, and Robert Wagner, to name a few. Many of them were represented by the notorious gay agent, Henry Willson, who, in most cases, "sampled the merchandise of the young studs he was representing."

Beginning the first day he met John Derek, Spencer Tracy considered him his favorite.

\*\*\*

Just who was this charismatic young man who cast such a spell?

A son of Los Angeles, he was born Derek Delevan Harris on August 12, 1928. His parents were actor/director Lawson Harris and actress Dolores Johnson.

Even as a teenager, Derek decided he wanted to be a movie star. He was the most popular boy in his high school.

"After gym class, when I stripped down to take a shower, I attracted many admirers," he confessed.

Somewhere, somehow, Henry Willson first laid eyes on Derek, whom he renamed Dare Harris. Willson worked for David O. Selznick at the time and managed to get this hot new personality very minor roles in two film classics, *Since You Went Away*, and *I'll Be Seeing You*, both released in 1944. Although these two classics were loaded with stars, most of the fan mail they generated (from all regions of the "sexual preference" map) focused on Dare.

Derek's career was derailed by Uncle Sam in 1944 after he was drafted into the U.S. Army and sent to the Phillipines. That was before the *Enola Gay* was loaded with "Little Boy" and aimed at the coast of Japan as part of a strategy that would launch the Atomic Age.

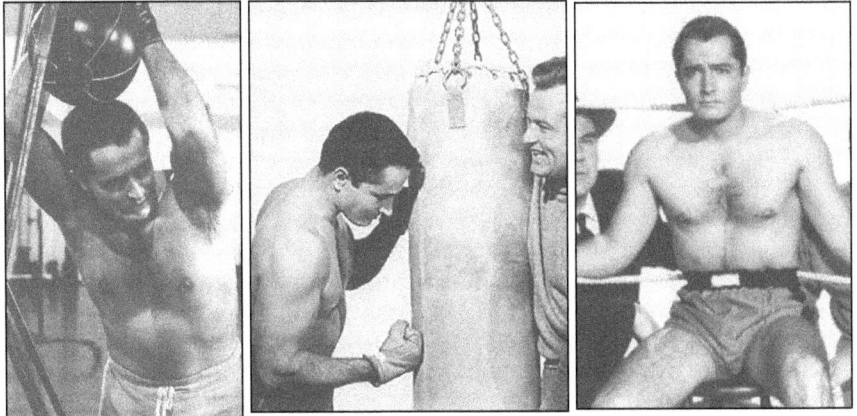

Three views of **John Derek** as a prizefighing priest in *The Leather Saint* (1956).

Two views of **John Derek** in *Rogues of Sherwood Forest* (1950; *Left photo* with **Diana Lynn**)

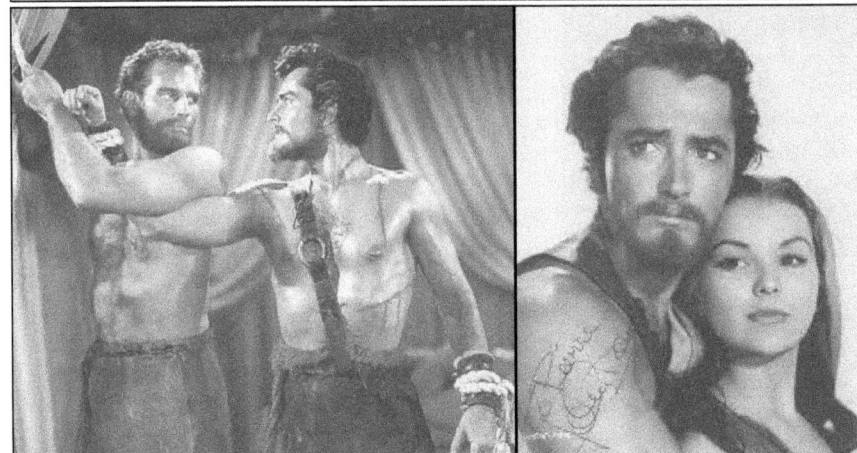

Two views of **John Derek** in *The Ten Commandments* (1956; *Left photo* with **Charlton Heston**, *right photo* with **Debra Paget**)

387

Back from the war, Dare continued his quest to break into the movies. By chance, he was randomly discovered by Humphrey Bogart.

Bogie persuaded him to change his name to John Derek and got him cast in his latest picture, *Knock on Any Door* (1949) as Nick ("Pretty Boy") Romano, an unrepentant killer. Nicholas Ray was the director. By the third day of filming, he maneuvered Derek onto his casting couch.

A very young Elizabeth Taylor had been among Derek's first admirers. She proclaimed, "There is this most beautiful boy—to me, he's like a God. One day, when we're older, we should co-star in a romantic story."

Roddy McDowall also spotted him, later telling friends, "Every homo in Hollywood wants to de-pants this walking streak of sex."

During the filming of *Knock on Any Door,* Spencer Tracy visited the set with the understanding that his friend, Humphrey Bogart, thought Derek might be ideal as Tracy's son in the upcoming movie, *All the King's Men.*

*[In 1947, Robert Penn Warren had sold the screen rights to this saga loosely based on the notorious political career of Louisiana governor Huey ("Kingfish") Long. At the time, Harry Cohn, the mogul at Columbia, wanted Tracy to play the role of Willie Stark, who has a son named Tom in the picture.]*

**John Derek** *(left)* with **Humphrey Bogart** in the *noir* crime thriller *(Derek: "I couldn't go straight if I wanted to.")* **Knock on Any Door** (1949)

On the set, Tracy met Derek and seemed enchanted by him, thinking he would be perfect for the role. With that in mind, he invited him for a long weekend of sailing to Catalina Island. Derek eagerly accepted. As a coincidence, Tracy was the young man's alltime movie idol.

No one knows for sure, but it was rumored that Tracy seduced the young man during the course of that waterborne weekend, and that it evolved into a one-way sexual encounter. A heterosexual, Derek may have had to close his eyes and dream that the mouth of the person "doing the deed down below" belonged to a young Elizabeth Taylor.

As it turned out, Tracy never got the role he'd wanted in *All the President's Men,* the part going instead to Broderick Crawford. For his efforts Crawford won that year's Best Actor Oscar, beating out Kirk Douglas, Gregory Peck, and John Wayne.

Thus (albeit dysfunctionally) began a long-term relationship between Derek and Tracy, who rendezvoused from time to time. Occasionally, the young actor allowed Tracy to fellate him while he perhaps looked at nude centerfolds in a then-new magazine, Hugh Hefner's *Playboy.*

At the time, Derek's movie career was just getting started, and he didn't have a lot of money.

So taken was Tracy with Derek that he bought him a new car and expensive gifts that included a Rolex. He also gave him a small piece of undeveloped real estate on the outskirts of Palm Springs.

Discreetly, Tracy lobbied for Derek behind the scenes, using his influence to get him launched into the movies, first at Columbia and later at Paramount. In some of them, he played a swashbuckler, evoking something akin to what Errol Flynn had been in the 1930s.

It wasn't until the 21st Century that the Derek/Tracy alliance became public. Now, they are intimately linked in several "tell all" YouTube documentaries. The word is out.

"They seemed like such an unlikely pair," wrote the entertainment columnist Mike Connolly, years later. *[Connally, it should be noted, never published any items about their pairing during the peak of its heat. Derek had once threatened Connolly that if he ever exposed anything about his very private life, he would come over to his house "and pound lumps into me."*

*Connelly, who was gay, responded, "That sounds exciting. After the beating, you can violently rape me—not once, at least twice. Maybe more."]*

\* \* \*

In time, Derek abandoned acting, preferring the role of director instead. Never at any time, according to rumor, did he ever carry his relationship with Tracy beyond the limits of just submitting to fellatio.

Derek became famous for his pursuit of beautiful women. His first wife was Turkish-born Pati Behrs, a *prima donna* ballerina. They married in 1948 and had a son and daughter. Their son, Russell, became paralyzed from the waist down in the wake of a 1969 motorcycle accident.

In the summer of 1953, Derek met and fell in love with a Swiss teenager, the future actress, Ursula Andress. She spoke almost no English, and he began to improve both her vocabulary and her understanding of "the language of love."

He and Behrs divorced in 1956. The following year, he married Andress in a quick ceremony in Las Vegas.

By 1964, he learned that she was having an affair with the sexy actor, Ron Ely, who was—for a while—the screen Tarzan.

**John Derek** with the first of his four wives, **Pati Behrs.** Born to Russian *emigré* parents in Turkey, and raised in Paris, she was a grandniece of Leo Tolstoy.

Derek ejected her from their home, and she returned to Europe, taking up with Marcello Mastroianni. That was followed by an affair with Jean-Paul Belmondo.

Derek and Andress finally divorced in 1966.

In 1965, Derek began dating the fast-rising TV star, Linda Evans. Their widely publicized affair morphed into a marriage that lasted from 1968 to 1973. In 1971, at the behest of her then-husband, she appeared as a "tastefully undraped," widely publicized centerfold in *Playboy*.

Blonde and personable, Evans eventually became best known for her portrayal of Krystal Carrington on TV's evening soap opera *Dynasty* (1981-1989).

Evans' marriage fell apart in 1973, when Derek met and fell in love with a 16-year-old high school dropout, Mary Cathleen Collins (later known as Bo Derek), 30 years younger than him. Their love affair began on the Greek Island of Mykonos. At the time, he was directing the low-budget, West German-produced *Once Upon a Time*. Filmed in less than ten days, it wasn't released until 1981, when it was "re-worked" with the hope of profiting from the fame derived from Bo Derek's success in *10*. *Once Upon a Time*'s revised title was *Fantasies*.

Evans filed for divorce in 1974. Derek remained in Europe with Collins until she turned 18 as a means of avoiding charges of statutory rape.

She became known as "Bo Derek" following her marriage to him on June 10, 1976.

As an actress, she would achieve international fame when she, in 1979, starred in the Blake Edwards movie, *10*.

\*\*\*

In 1981, Bo and actor Miles O'Keeffe co-starred in *Tarzan, the Ape Man*. Together, they heated up the jungle in what was called "the sexiest Tarzan film ever made." In almost every scene, he wore only the skimpiest loincloth as a means of concealing his oversized genitals. In contrast, Bo wasn't afraid to show everything.

"Bo and John" remained a loving couple until his death at the age of 71 in 1998.

**Ursula Andress,** John Derek's second wife (married 1957-1966), appears above in a press photo from 1963.

During the course of her marriage to Derek, she nabbed her "breakthrough role" as Honey Ryder in the James Bond superhit, *Dr. No* (1962), co-starring with **Sean Connery** as 007.

Beginning as an *ingénue* in the 1960s, **Linda Evans** auditioned tirelessly for film and TV roles until her breakthrough appearance alongside **Barbara Stanwyck** in on-and-off episodes of the soapy western, *The Big Valley* (1965-69). *En route*, she scored a role in the frothy-cutsie *Beach Blanket Bingo* (1965; *see photo above*) before maturing into the role of Krystal Carrington—a virtuous "good girl" foil for the conniving Alexis Colby, played by **Joan Collins.** As a ferociously catty team, **Evans vs. Collins** helped propel the nighttime soap series, *Dynasty* in the mid-1980s into the number one show on American television, even outranking *Dallas*

Evans' marriage to **John Derek** (1968-74) ended before the major career surge she enjoyed during the 1980s.

Just when he thought it was safe to go back in the water

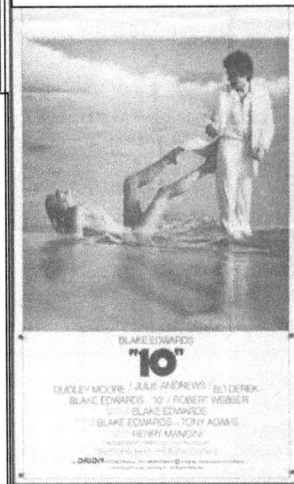

Two views of **Bo Derek,** *upper photo* in a publicity shot for her all-time most famous movie *(10)*.

*Lower photo* shows a poster with **Bo** cavorting and awash with sand and saltwater, with an awkward-looking **Dudley Moore** as a geeky British foil to her widely touted all-American beauty.

As reviewed in the U.K. by *The Telegraph*, "A run across the beach made **Bo Derek** a star. Her husband turned her into a softcore sensation. What happened next?"

\*\*\*

And then there was that OTHER famous "Ode to Beauty" film from the Derek *ménage*, this time a 1981 remake of the Tarzan legend. Enrolled to amplify the pulchritude quotient was **Miles O'Keeffe,** in a non-speaking portayal of the Ape Man *(see photos above.*

389

# THE SORDID SAGA OF SCOTTY BOWERS
## How, Over the Course of Many Decades, a Hollywood Pimp Supplied 150 Sex-for-Pay Women to Katharine Hepburn

Director Matt Tyrnauer said, "It's fascinating to me how enduring the myths of the so-called Golden Age of Hollywood are. The publicity departments of the studios really did their job. For the better part of 100 years, a lot of people are still clinging to these myths, including the 'passionate' love affair between Katharine Hepburn and Spencer Tracy."

"It was all a sham," Tyrnauer claimed. "They were, however, good friends, but he turned to young men—plus an occasional actress—to satisfy his libido."

Mike Connolly claimed, "Hepburn and Tracy were good friends of a platonic nature. In the 1930s, perhaps for career advancement, Hepburn had a number of affairs with directors like John Ford. But over the decades, she turned to an array of young women for sex. This posse of beauties was supplied by Hollywood's leading pimp, a handsome, heavily endowed young man named Scotty Bowers."

It wasn't until 2012 that Grove Press dared publish his startling memoir of the secret sex lives of Hollywood stars, *Full Service.*

Author Gore Vidal wrote, "I have known Scotty Bowers for the better part of a century. I'm so pleased that he has finally decided to tell his story to the world. His startling memoirs include great figures like Spencer Tracy and Katharine Hepburn. Scotty doesn't lie—the stars sometimes do—and he knows everybody."

Just who was this sex trafficker? Active from 1945 at the end of World War II until 1980, Bowers procured prostitutes for Hollywood insiders for straight, gay, or bisexual liaisons. Before revealing the sex lives of his clients, he waited until all the celebrities he serviced had died. "That way, the truth can't hurt them anymore."

That may be true, but it sure hurt their reputations.

Scotty himself bedded such stars as Vivien Leigh and was Spencer Tracy's "trick" over the course of many years. But even for a Hollywood insider, the most shocking revelation concerned not movie stars, but members of the British royal family, namely the Duke of Windsor.

*[The Duke of Windsor was the title bestowed on the former British monarch King Edward VIII following his abdication from the throne in December of 1936 so that he could marry the scandal-soaked, twice-divorced American socialite, Wallis Warfield Simpson. After a frenzy of public speculation, Parliament ruled that such a proposal would be impossible for the then Head of the Church of England. Suppressed at the time, but spectacularly compelling, were espionage reports that pinpointed the Duke's support for (and collusion with) the Nazi regime then dominating much of central Europe.*

Sexually available: Two views of **Scotty Bowers**, both in and out of uniform.

*Following his abdication, the Duke, with Wallis Simpson— by then elevated to the British peerage as the Duchess of Windsor—led lives of cosseted but perennially bored members of café society. Although associated with residences in, among others, Paris and The Bahamas, the Windsors traveled frequently and in splendor, always with flashbulbs popping, to posh watering holes that included New York, Palm Beach (Florida) and Los Angeles. Overall, the Duke and his American-born Duchess evolved into two of the most controversial, embarrassing, and ultimately tragic figures of the 20th Century.]*

Whenever they visited the West Coast, Scotty catered to the needs and whims of the Duke and his Duchess. But whereas the Duke preferred handsome young men who would sodomize him, his wife wanted young and beautiful women. Some of them, mostly aspirant actresses who had come to Hollywood with dreams of stardom, were supplied to her by Scotty.

\*\*\*

Scotty was born on July 1, 1923 in Ottawa, Illinois, a small town about 80 miles southwest of Chicago. He matured early, and word soon spread about his heavy endowment.

He was first "discovered" by a Catholic

Three views of the **Duke of Windsor and his unpopular American Duchess:** *Left,* after their wedding in France in 1937; *center,* on the cover of the May 22, 1950 edition of **Life** magazine ("Re-assessing the Romance of the Century")"; and *right,* at an ill-advised audience with **Adolf Hitler** the year they were married.

priest at his church, who paid for his service from funds pilfered from the Sunday collection plate. He spread the word of his "discovery" to other priests. Scotty later admitted, "That helped me get through the Great Depression."

In 1942, Bowers joined the U.S. Marine Corps and fought as a paramarine in the Pacific theater, with active involvement in the Battle of Iwo Jima (later depicted in a famous John Wayne movie).

After the war, he opted to settle in Hollywood, where his masculine charms were soon discovered by none other than Walter Pidgeon.

Scotty worked as a "gas jockey" at the Richfield Oil Station (now gone), that stood at 5777 Hollywood Boulevard, at the corner of Van Ness Avenue.

Pidgeon invited him to his home, which he shared with his male lover. The actor invited Scotty into their swimming pool, suggesting that he did not need swimming trunks. Within two hours, he was upstairs in their bedroom for a three-way.

Pidgeon spread the word. Soon, director George Cukor arrived at the gas station, inviting Scotty to one of his weekend parties. There, he was introduced to Hollywood's gay elite, including lovers Cary Grant and Randolph Scott, who wanted him for a *ménage á trois*.

Thus, Bowers' career as a Hollywood pimp was launched. From his perch within the gas station, he provided customers with a supply of young men. A trailer was moved to, and parked, in back of the station, for private assignations. The "filling station's" handsome crew of staffers never knew who would be waiting inside that trailer—perhaps composer Cole Porter.

It's been said that Scotty never accepted cash for his services, but his customers often rewarded him with gifts. At first he catered exclusively to gay men, but it time, he began to arrange female partners for such performers as Desi Arnaz. Scotty also rounded up a bevy of young women who could (and would) bring sexual pleasure to lesbians.

In time, Scotty became a "celebrity bartender" at parties of the Hollywood elite. From within that venue, he navigated sexual rendezvous for himself and/or members of his entourage with many a famous actor or actress.

He maintained these venues and these activities throughout many years of his life. By the mid-1970s, when *Deep Throat* was popular to the point of becoming a national obsession, Scotty worked to pimp and promote Linda Lovelace.

At some of Hollywood's wilder parties, she and Scotty performed before select crowds, giving instructions in deep-throating.

Of course, all this came tumbling down during the AIDS epidemic that swept through California (and the rest of the world, too) in the 1980s.

According to Cecil Beaton, "Scotty showed what a handsome, studly man can do with a charming personality and a big penis."

In nearly all cases, his arrangements with stars came off smoothly. Hollywood was filled with handsome young men and beautiful young women, many of whom had arrived with hopes of becoming movie stars. Facing disappointments, many were desperately in need of money for food and rent.

"I pleased all of my clients with one exception: Montgomery Clift. He was Princess Tiny Meat himself, but he was very critical of the penis of very man I sent over. It turns out that their dicks were always either too small or too large for his taste."

Katharine Hepburn entered Scotty's life when George Cukor invited him to his house for lunch one Saturday afternoon. Scotty walked in on an argument: Sydney Guilaroff—MGM's 40-year veteran hairstylist, one of the most sought-after in the history of Hollywood's Golden Age—and Cukor were having an argument over how Hepburn's hair would be styled in an upcoming film.

*[The film was* Adam's Rib *(1949), which Hepburn would make with Spencer Tracy and Judy Holliday, with whom Hepburn would have a lesbian encounter.]*

When Cukor was out of the room and as Hepburn was getting ready to leave, Guilaroff made a date with Scotty for a rendezvous the next day.

***

Even back then, Scotty didn't believe all those myths about the enduring romance between Hepburn and Tracy. According to Scotty, "She was far, far too butch to make me believe she would surrender the pink to any man."

Although Cukor and Hepburn remained friends for life, that afternoon ended badly. As she was leaving with Scotty, he called her "a real spoiled bitch." They made up later.

Scotty walked Hepburn to her car. She stopped him at one point and looked into his eyes. "Cukor told me all about you. I want you to supply me with a steady stream of young women—I rarely do repeats. I don't go in for blondes except Judy Holliday. Also, the gal must not have any blemishes. I can't stand even one pimple."

Thus began their decades-long association. "I liked her," Scotty said. "However, without makeup, she was a fright. She had awful skin, and it took clever lighting to

**Walter Pidgeon** with **Greer Garson** in one of the greatest romantic dramas (and morale-builders) of World War II, **Mrs. Miniver** (1942).

**FILL IT UP, HANDSOME**:

News of the venue for Scotty's pimp ring spurred a raft of jokes on late-night TV.

**Cary Grant** and **Randolph Scott** during a fan magazine interview whose writer asked a lot of questions about their status as long-term housemates. **Darwin Porter's** former partner, **Stanley Haggart,** worked for them as their personal assistant and house manager.

391

conceal it."

In *Full Service,* he made a shocking revelation: "Over the next few decades, I would fix her up with some 150 women. She rarely wanted repeats."

"Her alltime favorite was a girl named Barbara. She had just gotten over being 'Sweet Sixteen' when I sent her into Hepburn's lair."

Barbara became Hepburn's on-and-off "trick" for almost half a century. Sometime, weeks would go by before she sent for Barbara again.

In the meantime, Barbara met and married three husbands.

When Hepburn passed on in June of 2003, she made a provision in her will to have a $100,000 check sent to Barbara.

After she received it, Barbara phoned Scotty and told him about Hepburn's parting gift. "I don't really need it," she said. "My third husband has died and left me a vast fortune."

*\*\*\**

Later in life, Scotty defined that tired legend about a romance between Tracy and Hepburn as "a nonexistent fairytale of romance, the creation of studio publicists to conceal her lesbianism and his bisexuality. I should know what I'm talking about."

"Soon after we became friends, Hepburn called me: 'I want you to set up a date with Spencer. You're his type.'"

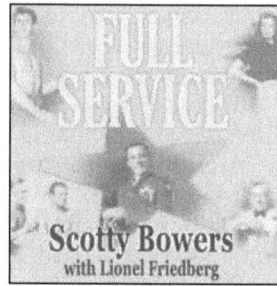

Even though hipster insiders had been gossiping about "insider secrets of the entertainment industry's sexually promiscuous for years, here's an up-close-and personal view of the tell-all that busted Scotty's pimp ring open: *Full Service*

# HOW, OVER THE YEARS, SCOTTY BOWERS BECAME SPENCER TRACY'S MOST RELIABLE TRICK

Katharine Hepburn met Spencer Tracy long before Scotty Bowers did. Although she had seen most of his films, he had never seen one of her pictures. "Too butch for me," he had proclaimed to director George Stevens. "Wears pants."

Nonetheless, Stevens thought they would morph into a compelling duo in the upcoming film *Woman of the Year* (1942).

She was not so sure, preferring that she be cast opposite Cary Grant, her former co-star.

She had heard that Tracy "played the field" in spite of his 1923 marriage to Louise Treadwell. Together, they had produced both a daughter and a son, John, who had been born deaf.

Stevens insisted on pairing them, and finally, they were introduced. Hepburn, at the time, was living with Laura Harding, the American Express heiress. Tracy was involved in other film endeavors as well as a series of adulterous flings, so at first they had little time for each other.

However, she was impressed with his bull neck. "It takes a real man to have a bull neck," she told Stevens.

Left photo: **Scotty Bowers**, a congenial hustler, in uniform, sits astride a vintage car from his heyday as a pimp, and *right photo*, his "regular trick," **Spencer Tracy.** On his last legs, and in his final days, the veteran superstar is seen here looking skeptically at **Katharine Hepburn**. No stranger to "pay for play," she knew a lot more about carnality and the flesh than she ever admitted.

When he met Hepburn, Tracy was turned off by her dirty fingernails. Later, he asked Stevens, "You expect me to make love to a woman with dirty fingernails?"

Tracy and Hepburn took quite a while to become friends. It wasn't until George Cukor cast them in *Keeper of the Flame* (1943), that the duo connected.

"Somehow, they seemed to fulfill some emotional—not sexual—need in each other," Cukor said. "I never figured out what it was. They certainly proved that *cliché* that opposites attract. In fact, even though they were among my closest friends, I never asked if they ever bumped pussies during all the time I knew them."

When Hepburn was asked about their budding friendship, she answered, "We can talk and talk until the sun comes up. It's man-to-man talk."

Garson Kanin, one of their closest mutual friends, admitted, "Spencer and Kate never mentioned any sexual attraction. In spite of what I've written or talked about, I doubt if they ever shared a bedroom. Kate demanded eight hours of uninterrupted sleep. Spencer was an insomniac, wandering drunk around his bedroom for most of the night."

Irene Mayer Selznick, a close friend of Hepburn, also talked about Tracy and Hepburn. "She was very concerned about his heavy drinking," she said. "He'd sometimes disappear for more than a week. He'd retreat to a remote hotel room with a suitcase filled with liquor. He would drink himself into a stupor."

George Cukor was privy to Tracy's homosexual life, and often arranged "tricks" for him. At the time, Tracy lived in a cottage on Cukor's property.

It was Cukor who arranged the first rendezvous between Tracy and Scotty Bowers.

"I arrived at Cukor's home at five in the afternoon," Scotty recalled. "I thought it was to service Cukor, but it seemed he had arranged this thing with me and Tracy. He insisted I call him Spence. At that time, I didn't know he had a gay side. He seemed to me to be the most masculine of men, like Anthony Quinn or John Wayne."

After dinner at Cukor's, Tracy invited Scotty down to his cottage, where he continued to drink. In his memoir, Scotty recalled that he was furious at Hepburn. "He was an angry, bruised, and bitter man. He had been hurt by her. He told me she was always rude to him and treated him like dirt. He felt that she was always contemptuous of him. Nothing that I had read about their tabloid romance matched up with what Spencer was telling me as the night drummed on."

For years to come, Scotty would accept invitations from Tracy. "It was always the same beginning, with heavy drinking in the afternoon. It was two in the morning before we undressed and got into bed together. In spite of his drunken state, he could always manage to have sex with me."

"He was a foreskin queen, nibbling away at my uncut dick. Finally, after an hour of nibbling, ball sucking, and rimming, he would suck me dry."

"The next morning, no mention was ever made of what had happened the night before. He would cook me a big breakfast and then I was shown to the door. Most often, I was expected to climb the hill and have a session with Cukor before going on my way."

"It was always the same over the next few years whenever I would answer his summons," Scotty said. "He'd always have to get drunk before beginning his nibbling. He told me that mothers were cruel in circumcising their baby boys."

"It's a deliberate attempt to cut down on their later sexual enjoyment," Tracy claimed.

Virtually unchallenged in her status as "Hollywood Super-Royalty," **Irene Mayer Selznick** appears here with her then-husband, **David O. Selznick**, producer of *Gone With The Wind* (1939).

**"Selznick** was very sexually oriented. My God, he would try to tear your clothes off," claimed **Joan Fontaine.**

\*\*\*

# A PHOTO ALBUM

## FROM THE SECRETIVE LIFE OF A HOLLYWOOD SUPERSTAR

### A SCANDALOUS FAMILY

Kate at age four was born to maverick New England parents, Dr. and Mrs. Thomas Hepburn. "Neighbors considered my mother, Kit, a dangerous and wicked woman because of her unpopular political stands such as birth control," Kate said. Her doctor father could talk for hours about venereal disease, even when the ladies at tea called for their smelling salts.

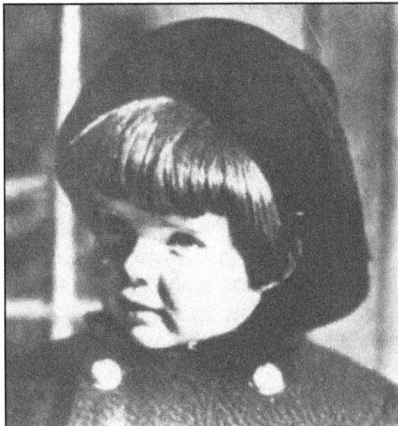

### THE TRAGEDY OF HER LIFE

In their fetching antiseptic bonnets, Kate at age two is escorted through the Connecticut woods by her loving brother, Tom (left). He was her greatest friend and confidant, and grew into a handsome, athletic, and intelligent boy. His suicide by hanging during the Easter season of 1920 cast a long, dark shadow over her young life.

## AT 18, A LION IN ANY SEASON

An intrepid tomboy who demanded to be called "Jimmy," **Kate** became withdrawn and morose after Tom's death. She developed and relished her eccentricities such as a lifelong passion of breaking into other people's homes to invade their privacy. Yet, if someone, especially the press, invaded her own privacy, she would often assault them.

## SIBLINGS

**Marion** *(center)* and **Peggy** *(right)*—Kate's virtual double—were captured on film on the grounds of the Hepburn family home in 1940 as **Kate** *(left)* was making a comeback with *The Philadelphia Story*. Kate always overshadowed her sisters and got them to wear pants when "respectable" young ladies did not. Rumors that the sisters were "insanely jealous" of their fabled sibling were just that—rumors.

## "MY DEFLOWERER"

That was Kate's pet name for the handsome young actor, **Kenneth MacKenna**, who took her virginity in 1928.

Years later, Kate said, "Someone had to do the dirty deed. Why not Kenneth?" They became lifelong confidants, each sharing the secrets of their bisexual lives with each other. On one occasion they ended up seducing the same man—Douglas Fairbanks Jr.

## A RELUCTANT CELEBRITY

Snapped on the streets of New York near her townhouse in 1934, **Kate** hated having her picture taken at random. Often she'd grab the camera of the photographer and smash it. Here, her determined face endures what she viewed as an assault on her privacy. At this point in her life she was living with her homosexual husband and his lover

## A CRUSADER FROM THE FEMINIST TRENCHES

**Kit Hepburn**, Kate's mother, was one of America's leading advocates of women's suffrage. Waving a placard, young Kate often paraded in protest marches with her mother, including one to shut down the brothels of Hartford—not for moral reasons but to prevent the spread of venereal disease.

Kit was also a disciple of Margaret Sanger in the advocacy of birth control.

## ONSTAGE, A FEROCIOUS WARRIOR WHO SHIELDED HER BREASTS WITH ARMOR

Projecting athletic prowess and a sense of macho fury, Kate defined her sex-role reversal comedy on Broadway, *The Warrior's Husband* (1932), as "putting on a leg show." Portraying an Amazon who keeps her husband in place.

She brought down the house in one scene where, to show her physical agility and strength, she lifted one actor over her head.

## INSPIRATION & COMPETITION

"My role model," was the way Kate later described lesbian actress **Hope Williams** when she appeared in the leading role of *Holiday,* the comedy by Philip Barry that opened in 1929 at Brodway's Plymouth Theatre.

As Williams' understudy for the role of Linda Seton, Kate waited in the wings every night, studying Williams' every move, hoping for the actress to break a leg or at least an ankle. To defy Kate, Williams went on even when she was sick.

## ONE NIGHT STAND

After her aborted romp in the hay with actor **Leslie Howard**, Kate could never understand why Scarlett O'Hara in *Gone With the Wind (1939)* pined for his character of Ashley Wilkes.

After seeing it, Kate told George Cukor, "Thank God that Miss Scarlett never actually went to bed with Ashley. She would have been so disappointed."

After an unsuccessful sexual interlude with her, the London-born actor was so disappointed with her that he fired her from the 1931 play, *The Animal Kingdom*.

## "I NEVER GOT INTO HIS BATHING TRUNKS"

That was Kate's irony-soaked quip after she arrived in Hollywood and briefly dated handsome leading man **Joel McCrea.**

They were to have co-starred in a film together, *Three Came Unarmed*, but script problems arose and the movie was never made. Kate later recalled, "I think Joel was in love with Gary Cooper at the time—who wasn't?—but Frances Dee was waiting in the wings."

*Editor's Note: Before the end of their time together,* **Frances Dee** *and* **Joel McCrea** *co-starred in three films together, produced three sons, and stayed togehther for almost 57 years.*

## THE ULTIMATE "CHICK FLICK' OF THE EARLY 1930s:

### LITTLE WOMEN

One of Kate's alltime most successful films, *Little Women* (1933), teamed her with **Joan Bennett** (*on the left*) whom she hated; **Jean Parker** (whom she ignored, *second from left*), and **Frances Dee** *(far right)*, who fought with Kate, accusing her of sleeping with her man, Joel McCrea.

That's **Kate**, of course, with the enigmatic grin (*second from the right*). Playing the hoydenish Jo March, Kate won favorable reviews—except one. Critic Philip Barnes claimed that "Louisa May Alcott is turning over in her grave."

## THE TOSCANINI OF THE TELEPHONE

Deal Maker, super agent, and super stud, **Leland Hayward**, was Hollywood's hot shot agent in the Thirties.

His clients included **Ernest Hemingway, Judy Garland**, and **Kate** herself.

When Hayward wasn't seducing **Garbo**, (or whenever Kate wasn't seducing Garbo), Hayward became Kate's magnetic lover—at least until "that dreaded fiend" [Kate's words] **Margaret Sullavan**, stole him away from her.

## "THAT GOD DAMN MOTH COSTUME"

Although Kate's assessment of her alltime most famous costume, worn in RKO's *Christopher Strong* (1933), was negative, it turned out to be the best thing in the picture.

Around the RKO lot, the movie about a female aviatrix, as played by Kate, was nicknamed *Sapphos on Parade*. The reference was to the lesbianism of Kate herself, her director (**Dorothy Arzner**), her co-star (**Billie Burke**) and the scenarist, the notorious **Zöe Akins.**

## THE BEAST AND VAMPIRE OF BROADWAY

Broadway producer **Jed Harris** liked to receive business clients—male or female—in his offices stark naked. He often seduced his leading ladies, including **Ruth Gordon** (with whom he had a son), and he sometimes forced actors to perform fellatio on him, especially if they were straight.

Kate's best friends claimed that Jed Harris was Kate's only S&M love affair—"that is, if you could call anything with Harris love," in the words of **Helen Hayes.**

## CALL IT INCEST

**Kate** made her film debut in *A Bill of Divorcement* (1932), with **John Barrymore** playing her mentally unbalanced father.

According to Hollywood legend, *The Great Profile* invited **Kate** to his dressing room, pulled off his clothes, and suggested that the two of them "get on with it."

Legend has it that Kate ran shrieking into the afternoon, claiming that her father didn't want her to have any babies.

The truth? Both Barrymore and Kate later admitted that he succeeded with his seduction skirmish, "but only on the second attempt."

## TO SHOW OR NOT TO SHOW BASKET

That was the question for **Douglas Fairbanks Jr.** when he appeared in the balcony scene of *Romeo and Juliet* with **Kate** in *Morning Glory (1933)*.

Fairbanks told Kate that John Barrymore, his pal, always claimed that when he stuffed a sock in his green tights, theater attendance rose.

Kate advised the young actor to conceal "your goodies with a carefully arranged jock strap so as not to distract from my performance as Juliet."

Ironically, even after all that drama, the scene ended up on the cutting room floor.

## THE TRUE LOVE OF KATE'S LIFE

American Express heiress, **Laura Harding**, began her romance with **Kate** in 1928 and their affair, even after passion's fire died, lasted until Harding's death in 1994.

Kate took Harding with her on her honeymoon with her husband, **Ludlow Ogden Smith**, as well as his male lover.

Kate told friends that Laura might as well go along on her divorce trip, too. They are pictured at the New York airport waiting for their flight to Miami where they would sail to Mexico for the divorce.

## "DON'T BE A MUG"

That was the advice from **Ernest Hemingway** when he heard that **Kate** planned to elude the press as the ocean liner, *Paris,* sailed into New York harbor. Fresh from her ocean-going affair with him, she agreed to put on a "crimson slash of lipstick" and to "face those beastly cameramen." For Don Ernesto, it was only a shipboard romance that Kate took too seriously.

When he dumped her, Kate told friends, "At least he went for me—and not Marlene." The woman Hemingway called "The Kraut" (**Marlene Dietrich**) also sailed on the homebound journey.

That's **Katharine Hepburn** staring back at the photographer from her position on deck, near the top of the snapshot.

## HORRIBLE CASTING IN A BAD PICTURE: SPITFIRE

After seeing the final cut of the 1934 box office bomb, *Spitfire,* its associate producer **Pandro S. Berman** asked its director **John Cromwell,** "What idiot thought to cast **Hepburn** with her Bryn Mawr accent as Trigger Hicks?" A good question.

Pictured above with **Sara Haden** (*left*), **Kate** played a hot-tempered, hopelessly ignorant hillbilly yokel—a warmhearted hoyden.

Making things worse, she was assigned such cornporn lines as "consarned Son of Satan."

## FRENCH CHARM, *EEW-LA-LA*

*Break of Hearts* (1935) an RKO release, evolved into another embarrassing disaster for **Kate,** although it launched her into a brief affair with her co-star, **Charles Boyer.**

Kate was momentarily intrigued with the seductive sound of this Frenchman's Gallic voice, that and his penetrating heavy-lidded eyes.

Today, he's mimicked and ridiculed for a line he never said in *Algiers* (*"Come wiz me to ze Cashbah"*).

Kate didn't find him a joke at all, but the audience didn't buy the script's romantic piffle.

## SHARING GOSSIP FROM THE TRENCHES OF HOLLYWOOD

Tossed aside after his long affair with Gary Cooper, actor **Anderson Lawler** (*left figure, above*) met **Kate** (*reclining, above*) around George Cukor's pool. They became "confidants for life." If Kate needed to know something, Lawler was the first man she called. (Usually he'd already called her first.)

Kate once expressed a desire to find a person to whom she could speak frankly about her sexual affairs. In Lawler, she found one.

**Tallulah Bankhead** also used Lawler—"and everybody else"—as a confidant, too.

## "THAT DYKEY BITCH"

Those were the words of rival **Margaret Sullavan** when she saw this RKO-released photograph of **Katharine Hepburn.**

When **Pandro S. Berman** spotted it, he asked that it be recalled.

"We're not filming *The Well of Loneliness*," (a reference to that era's best-known lesbian-themed novel) he told his publicity department,

Berman ordered the department to take some "cheesecake pictures" of Kate to counter what seemed to be developing into a hard-bitten Sapphic *cliché.*

## SEX KITTEN

RKO at first didn't know what to make of its new $1,500-a-week contract player.

So, as cameras clicked, they posed her like a sultry siren with plunging *décolletage.*

On viewing these glossies, Kate said, "There's nowhere to plunge."

## "ONE OF THE BEST MALE BODIES"

That was Kate's assessment of **Fred Mac-Murray**, the first day she encountered her co-star resting in the sun without his shirt on the set of *Alice Adams* (1935). Of course, she was speaking of the physique standards of her era. MacMurray filled out and developed his chest even more in the years ahead. Kate found him a "real catch," but they soon drifted apart.

## SEXUAL AMBIGUITY

Thinking **Kate** is a boy, actor **Brian Aherne** *(right)*, in the gender-bending film, *Sylvia Scarlett* (1935), seems enchanted. The picture bombed but Kate was hailed as the handsomest boy of the year. The homosexual overtones of George Cukor's direction was largely lost on the Thirties audience. **Cary Grant**, a study in sexual ambiguity himself, stole the picture with his bitingly humorous performance of a Cockney ne'er-do-well.

## ARTIFICE (Hepburn)
## vs. THE ROCK (MacMURRAY)

In her famous front-porch scene with **Fred MacMurray**, Kate gave one of her most memorable performances playing *Alice Adams*, a young, ambitious woman striving for social recognition. Her interpretation of the Booth Tarkington heroine, who was actually a klutz, won Kate her second Academy Award nomination.

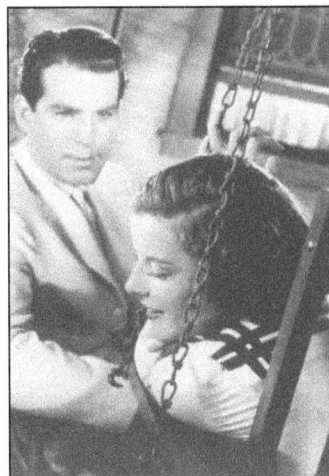

Even though she was initially attracted to MacMurray, Kate eventually gravitated to her director, **George Stevens**, finding that in spite of his rather bland façade "he was all fire and brimstone when you peeled off his layers."

## THE NYMPHOMANIACAL (and eventually, suicidal) SOUTHERN MAGNOLIA

Kate's nemesis, **Margaret Sullavan**, was called a "rude, contrary, spiteful bitch" by columnist **Louella Parsons**. She stole **Leland Hayward** from Kate.

He later confided in Kate that he regretted the marriage. "She castrates a guy," Hayward said. "Makes him feel like two cents—and two inches." Maggie was said to have invented highway pickups before they became fashionable. She waited in her car and blinked her lights whenever she saw a virile, handsome guy walking by.

**Sullavan** appears alone in the photo (left) and with **Leland Hayward** (in the *photo right*).

## "ALL ACTORS ARE CRAP"

Director **John Ford** had harsh words for his performers, but fell big for Kate in spite of his initial judgement. A heavy-drinking Irishman of few words and a political reactionary, John Ford became the "third most important love" of young Kate's life, after Laura Harding and ultimately Spencer Tracy.

Kate failed in her attempts to pay off **Mary Ford,** offering her $150,000 if she'd give John his freedom. Mary booted Kate out the door.

## "A DRIED UP BOOT"

Acid-tongued **Cecil Beaton**, known for his glamorous portraits, had nothing but praise for Kate's beauty when he photographed her in the mid-Thirties.

Seeing her in later years, he changed his opinion. "Her appearance is appalling, a raddled, rash-ridden, freckled, burnt, mottled, bleached and wizened piece of decaying matter. It is unbelievable, incredible that she can still be exhibited in public."

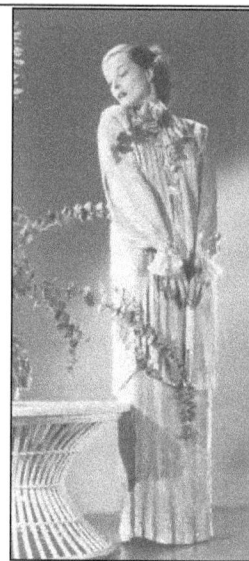

## THE RUDE SURPRISE UP KATE'S DRESS

Handsome **Fredric March**, was cast by **John Ford** as Kate's co-star in the badly received 1936 film, *Mary of Scotland*, a scene from which appears on the left.

March viewed it as "obligatory" to make passes at his leading ladies. His reputation had preceded him when he entered Kate's dressing room to seduce her.

As he later told producer Pandro S. Berman, "My God, I reached up her dress and felt nine hard inches—maybe ten. **Kate Hepburn** is a man after all."

What March felt was actually an unripened banana Kate had placed there waiting for his roving hand.

## MARY, MARY, SO CONTRARY

Trying on her *Mary of Scotland* bonnet, **Kate** sits as her lover, the film's pipe-smoking director **John Ford**, stands.

He had discovered **Spencer Tracy** on Broadway in the early Thirties, and thought Tracy could make it as a film star, even though he wasn't particularly good looking. But after he tested Kate, then appearing in *The Warrior's Husband,* he concluded that she had no sex appeal at all.

By the time he'd cast her in *Mary of Scotland*, Ford had changed his mind about Kate. Whereas she found him "wayward and odd," he told John Wayne that "Kate Hepburn is the kind of woman a man could almost leave his wife for."

## CHEEK-TO-CHEEK

**Ginger Rogers** and **Kate Hepburn** hardly managed to conceal their loathing for each other when they made *Stage Door* in 1937.

Kate had utter contempt for "Miss Ginger Snap," and often told friends, "If you have anything good to say about Ginger Rogers, don't say it in my presence."

Kate found herself competing with Rogers for some of the same men —**Howard Hughes, George Stevens, Jimmy Stewart**. Kate went after Ginger's husband **Lew Ayres**, but **Howard Hughes** got to him first.

## "SEEMINGLY SLEEPY BUT INTENSELY WATCHFUL"

That's how Kate defined her director **George Stevens** when they teamed together to make an ill-fated costume drama, *Quality Street,* in 1937.

Kate later told her *confidantes* that "George is a perfect example of the adage that 'still waters run deep.'" She never quite explained exactly what she meant by that. The director not only propelled her through the picture but skillfully lured her to his bed where she would remain—on and off—for years until she met **Spencer Tracy**. Of course, there was the matter of "the invading praying mantis," as Kate said of her rival, **Ginger Rogers.**

## JAWBREAKER

**Kate's** male co-star in *Quality Street* was the suave, sophisticated **Franchot Tone**, married at the time to **Joan Crawford.** Thanks in part to his looks, education, and breeding, Kate found Tone appealing, but she didn't fall in love with him as **Bette Davis** did when they filmed *Dangerous* together in 1935.

After a one-night stand with this super-endowed Hollywood stud, Kate pronounced him "too much man for me," sending him back home to Crawford.

## IS IT GARBO? NO! IT'S HEPBURN!

Shielding her face from photographers (they weren't called *paparazzi* back then), **Kate** was consistently voted the most uncooperative actress in Hollywood by the members of the women's press corps.

**Hedda Hopper** once said, "The damn dyke always claimed that she wanted nothing more than to be famous. Once famous, she went psychotic when someone tried to take her photograph. You figure! Dames. I'm glad I'm not one!"

**Hopper.** an implacably vindictive entertainment columnist, appears below *(left photo)* in 1945 at her office in the Guaranty Building on Hollywood Boulevard, and *(right photo)* in Milwaukee as a self-promoting participant in the American Legion's convention parade of 1941.

A ferociously outspoken conservative and a relentless critic of "liberal" lifestyle options, she and **Katharine Hepburn** absolutely, totally and positively loathed each other.

## DON'T ASK, DON'T TELL

**Kate and Cary Grant,** the two most closeted bisexuals in the history of Hollywood, appeared together again in the 1938 Columbia film, *Holiday,* for which Kate had once understudied **Hope Williams** on Broadway. When Kate was living at the Muirfield estate of **Howard Hughes**, Cary was his bedtime partner—**not Kate.**

## "HOLLYWOOD'S MOST HAPPILY MARRIED COUPLE"

This was **Joan Crawford's** assessment of **Cary Grant** and **Randolph Scott**. They appear below, photographed in a cozy scene when they lived together.

Crawford had also made the same assessment of the "marriage" of actor **William Haines** and his lover, **Jimmie Shields**. Kate and Laura Harding were often guests of Grant and Scott when they were live-in lovers, until studio pressure forced them to live separately and even get married to women.

It was suggested that Kate, Laura, Randy, and Cary go out on double dates to confuse snoopy columnists, who'd accurately hinted at the time that all four of them might be homosexuals, or at least bisexuals.

## THE SON-OF-A-BITCH & THE ÜBER BITCH

Fans loved **Ginger Rogers**, who toppled Kate as Queen of RKO, and who appears here wearing the ultimate "*grand chic*" accessories of the 1940s.

Although they were completely different types, **Ginger & Kate** often competed to see which would become the bigger moneymaker at RKO. Rogers' career soared when Hepburn, at the end of the 1930s, was defined as "box office poison."

The dancer/actress was always stealing Kate's men—including deal broker **Leland Heyward** (*pictured with Rogers here*) who proposed marriage to both women on the same day.

## PSYCHOTIC OBSESSIONS WITH PRIVACY

Clad in a bathing suit white emerging from George Cukor's swimming pool, the elusive Swede, **Greta Garbo**, preferred swimming in the nude, "in the Swedish style." When Kate first met Garbo, it was Kate who was nude emerging from the same pool. **George Cukor** provided the introductions. Garbo and Kate became sometime lovers and forever friends. "Both women carried their privacy to psychotic limits," said Anderson Lawler.

## "THE GRANDE DAME OF ALL WESTERN DYKES"

When he described her like that, **Noël Coward** was talking about veteran actress, **Constance Collier** *(right)*, more than he was referring to **Kate.**

When the two actresses came together to make *Stage Door* in 1937, they embarked on a lifelong love affair. Nonsexual, that is. Kate was constantly attacked for her voice and her Bryn Mawr diction, and Constance struggled valiantly to help her overcome some of her worst problems. The skilled thespian even taught Kate how to play Rosalind in Shakespeare's *As You Like It.*

## WISE ADVICE FROM MARLENE DIETRICH

Although it eventually built up a cult audience of devoted fans, *Bringing Up Baby*, which co-starred **Kate** once again with **Cary Grant**, flopped after its release in 1938. They're depicted here, pretending that everything is normal, with a leopard in a baby carriage

Before Kate ever appeared in a film with Cary Grant—much less in one with a leopard—one of the most sophisticated women in the world, **Marlene Dietrich,** warned her about how foolish it was to fall in love with a homosexual.

Kate became Cary's friend instead, although George Cukor felt the relationship was more "like two sisters."

## "A MARRIED MAN WHO IMPREGNATES HER"

**Van Heflin** did not have the kind of good looks usually associated with a leading man, but he captured Kate's fancy when she saw him in a play on Broadway. She recommended that RKO cast him as the married man who impregnates her in her 1936 film, *A Woman Rebels*. During its production, she launched an affair with Heflin that did not survive for long.

She later lobbied to get him cast into the role of the reporter in the stage version of *The Philadelphia Story*. When she did not insist that he be hired for the screen version too, Heflin broke off relations with her.

## SEXY, SHOCKING, ROMANTIC, AND SCANDALOUS

Both **Howard Hughes** and **Katharine Hepburn** led complex, mysterious, action-packed lives. But, contrary to thousands of published reports, their so-called love affair was one of the most misunderstood of the century, ranking right up there with the Duke and Duchess of Windsor.

Hughes did ask Kate to marry him, although at the same time he had proposals out to **Joan Fontaine**, her sister **Olivia de Havilland**, and **Ginger Rogers**.

Kate told her friends that she thought **Cary Grant** would be a more suitable bride for Hughes. Pulp fan magazines, such as *Modern Screen*, gushed over their non-romance

## EMPTY WITHOUT YOU

In later years, the notorious lesbian letters between **Eleanor Roosevelt** and Associate Press reporter **Lorena Hickok** have been published. Although many of those letters were destroyed, enough have remained to reveal the passion between these two remarkable women.

Beginning in the early 1940s, the First Lady also wrote equally passionate letters to **Katharine Hepburn**. It was an unrequited love affair, the outpouring of affection coming mainly from the White House. When there was talk of Mrs. Roosevelt seeking the presidential nomination in 1948, Kate burned the letters "lest they fall into the wrong hands."

Eleanor Roosevelt

## THE AVIATOR: AN ENIGMA WITH MANY FACES

Kate's "romance of the century," as hailed in the press, with **Howard Hughes** (*six photos above*) was a sham. The bizarre aviator and tycoon had far more emotionally incestuous ties to his once beautiful but dead mother than he ever did with Kate.

Hughes hated to pose for pictures unless he was standing in front of an airplane. *The middle picture in the lower row of the six photos, above,* is one of the few ever taken of Hughes with a smile on his face.

"Stinking like rotting horseshit," **Hughes** is seen (*left photo, below*) in the back seat of a limousine with New York's Mayor **Fiorella LaGuardia** after the Aviator's record-breaking flight around the world.

Claudette Colbert

**LOVE AT FIRST SIGHT** One of Kate's longest and most enduring lesbian affairs was with Cecil B. DeMille's "alluring siren," the chic and totally feminine French actress, **Claudette Colbert**. Kate found her "incandescent." Colbert, winner of the 1934 Oscar for *It Happened One Night* opposite **Clark Gable**, is pictured *on the far right* in costume for the film, *Zaza*, that big flop in which George Cukor directed her. Even famed **Fanny Brice** couldn't help Colbert in her performance a music hall trouper.

Kate's affair with Colbert, with lots of other men and women in between, lasted for eight years. Then in 1948 Kate made a discovery that elevated Colbert to the top of what she called "my shit list."

## A CURE FOR IMPOTENCE

In spite of what the fan magazines proclaimed, the romance of **Howard Hughes** and Kate was going nowhere. **Bette Davis**, meeting the lanky, uncommunicative filmmaker and aviator at the Tailwaggers Ball in Beverly Hills in 1938, felt that she knew a secret way to get a rise out of this reluctant swain.

## BOYISHLY HANDSOME AND ON THE MAKE

**James Stewart** (photo right) managed to elude the clutches of **Marlene Dietrich**, only to fall into Kate's arms where he "polluted myself" [his words]. Kate wasn't his only love. Jimmy believed in sharing the wealth with her two most dreaded female enemies— **Ginger Rogers** and **Margaret Sullavan**. Actor **Wendell Corey** once said of Jimmy: "There was a whopping, big ego underneath that allegedly shy, stuttering, bumbling persona." Kate set out to discover what made him tick when the lights went out.

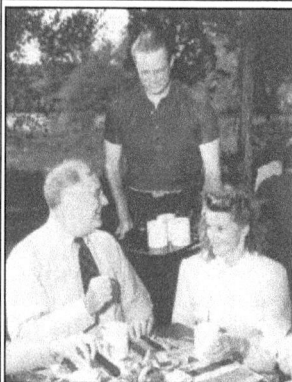

## PRESIDENTIAL INTRIGUE

**Elliott Roosevelt** (center), son of then-president **Franklin D. Roosevelt**, served cups of seafood chowder when the President invited Kate and other stars to his home at Hyde Park, New York in 1940.

Freckles showing, and with just a slash of lipstick, Kate arrived in a seaplane. Elliott discovered her splattered with mud and gave her a lift in his limousine.

Hepburn became the Hollywood actress whom the First Lady (**Eleanor Roosevelt**) most admired. Through her assistant, she always had the latest Hepburn film screened at a private showing at the White House.

## AN ODD COUPLE

**Spencer Tracy**, who demanded top billing, was teamed for the first time with **Katharine Hepburn** in the highly successful *Woman of the Year* (1942). It would mark a string of Tracy/Hepburn movies [he always demanded top billing]—some good, some bad.

It would also mark the beginning of Hollywood's most mythologized screen pairing. Highly touted as one of the 20th Century's great romances, it was marked by turbulence, infidelities, heavy boozing (on his part), and many violent arguments.

## TRACY & HEPBURN WEREN'T THE ONLY ODD COUPLE IN HOLLYWOOD

**Irene Mayer** was the daughter of **Louis B. Mayer**, when she wed **David O. Selznick**, who is today primarily remembered as the producer of *Gone With the Wind* (1939). In the photo (left), they're snapped during a (probably business-soaked) "night on the town."

Although she pretended to, Kate never forgave Selznick for his failure to cast her as Scarlett O'Hara. The producer had been responsible for bringing Kate to Hollywood in 1932 to appear opposite **John Barrymore** in *A Bill of Divorcement*.

Years from the date this picture was taken, Kate would begin an affair with **Selznick's wife, Irene**, her only known lesbian relationship.

## BOX OFFICE POISON

"If I can act, I want the world to know it. If I can't *I* want to know it." After a series of failures at the box office in the mid- to late 1930s, the Independent Theatre Owners Association published a list of actors they considered "box office poison."

Hepburn's name led the list. She was in distinguished company. **Greta Garbo, Marlene Dietrick,** and **Joan Crawford** were on it too. In this photo, **Kate** parodies herself for having been tossed away and into the garbage.

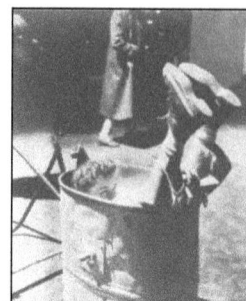

## A LOVE TRIANGLE

In the 1940 *The Philadelphia Story*, **Cary Grant** , playing Kate's former husband, was supposed to be jealous of her new romantic fixation on handsome **Jimmy Stewart.**

In real life, the scenario was different. The picture's director, **George Cukor,** desired Jimmy but knew he didn't have a chance. **Cary Grant** made his romantic intentions very clear to Jimmy but was rebuffed. **Kate**, like the "charging bull" her father claimed that she was, went after Jimmy and got her man. There were competitors, of course, for Kate. Even **Nöel Cowar**d came onto the set and volunteered to help Jimmy get into his bathing trunks.

## THOSE SMILES ARE MISLEADING

**Spencer Tracy's** long-suffering wife was **Louise Treadwell**, an actress who met and married Tracy when they were both struggling in the theater. Whenever a drunken **Tracy** was being particularly cruel to **Kate,** he claimed that **Louise** had been a much "better actress than you'll ever be."

Louise and Tracy had two children, **John and Susie**. John was born deaf, and Tracy used his son's affliction to justify his heavy boozing on many an occasion. Contrary to hundreds of published reports, Louise knew of the Hepburn/Tracy affair from the beginning. Her reaction? ***"I'm going to be Mrs. Spencer Tracy until the day I die."*** And so she was

## A-ACTORS IN SEARCH OF A DIRECTOR

**George Stevens** (center), directed **Spencer Tracy** and **Katharine Hepburn** (each with their backs to the camera) in their first picture together, the 1942 *Woman of the Year* for Metro-Goldwin-Mayer.

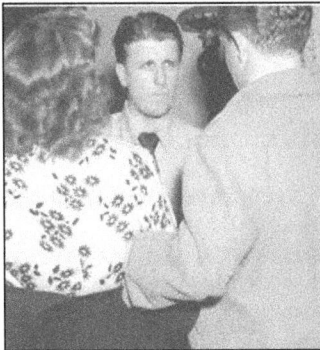

Stevens seems to be carefully eyeing his male competition, Tracy. At some point, Stevens decided that Kate was falling in love with him and bowed out. Up to then, he'd been dating her on and off. But before kissing her goodbye, he warned her that life with Tracy would be "living hell."

She responded, "no more so than coming in unexpectedly and catching you buck naked in a bathtub with **Ginger Rogers**."

## THE CANDLE DIDN'T BURN TOO BRIGHTLY

In *Keeper of the Flame,* the second pairing of **Spencer Tracy** and **Katharine Hepburn** for Metro-Goldwyn-Mayer in 1942, the odd couple fizzled in this unlikely casting.

Both Kate and Tracy, inspired by **George Cukor**, had set out to make another *Citizen Kane*, but Cukor was no Orson Welles. Cukor also lacked Alfred Hitchcock's talent for making a psychological thriller. The film was shot at the height of Kate's love affair with Tracy, before the onset of "the bad years."

## WITHOUT LOVE

**Spencer Tracy** and **Katharine Hepburn** must have desperately needed a film vehicle when they agreed to make *Without Love* in 1945. Kate knew Philip Barry's play well, having flopped with it on the stage. Nonetheless, her friend, writer **Donald Ogden Stewart** convinced both Tracy and Kate that he could rewrite the script and make a hit out of it.

It was a promise made in vain. At the end of the war, the flower was off the bloom of the Tracy/Hepburn romance. They had begun to redefine their romance as something akin to an obsessive co-dependency.

The studio marketed it as "The amusing story of two young moderns who hate romance but who are simply crazy about each other." But whereas in their real lives, that might have been true for a while, the flame, by now, was sputtering low.

## MISCASTING KATE AS A DEFIANT COOLIE

In the decade's biggest case of miscasting, the exotic **Turhan Bey**—known among ladies as "**The Turkish Delight**"—appeared with **Kate** in the film adaptation of Pearl S. Buck's ***Dragon Seed***. Released in 1944, it focused on Japan's aggression in China during World War II. It was made in an era when white actors frequently appeared in "yellowface" for portrayals of Asian characters.

Bey once admitted to having what he called "the kind of crush on Katherine Hepburn that only a teenage boy can have for a movie star." But when they met, no sparks were ever generated, either on or off camera. In contrast, Bey's opionion of Lana Turner was wildly different: "Ecstacy, my dear! But not for every day."

403

# KATE'S ADVENTURE WITH ROBERT MITCHUM
## (WAS IT "DATE RAPE?")

When **Kate** met **Robert Mitchum** on the set of *Undercurrent* (1946) she began by claiming she hated him and accused him of getting by on his good looks—not talent. The more she attacked him verbally, the more Hollywood's "most outrageous maverick" began to view her assault as a disguised physical attraction for him.

One day in his dressing room, he proved to her how right he was. Morphing himself from a hobo into a star, **Mitchum** emerged as "a devil with women." His (brief) dalliance with **Katharine Hepburn** marked the beginning of his seductions of movie queens.

## BEHIND THE MOON AND OVER THE RAINBOW

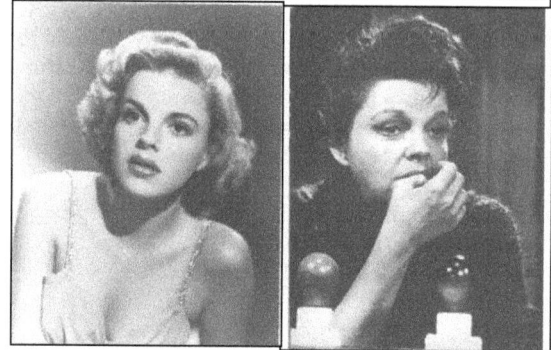

When **Judy Garland** made a major revelation to **Kate** about what was really going on in her marriage to **Vincente Minnelli,** Kate befriended her and was touched by her beauty, poignancy, and pain.

Kate fell in love with "Dorothy," and it became an enduring affair. The first person by Garland's side after her suicide attempt in 1950 was caretaker Kate herself. Kate's relationship with Garland went from the white heat passion of 1946 to loving support by 1961 when an ailing **Garland** appeared with **Spencer Tracy** in **Judgment at Nuremburg** (*photo right*).

## THE LAWN NEEDED MOWING

Directed by young **Elia Kazan**, *The Sea of Grass* (1947) was the fourth Tracy/Hepburn film, this one also released by Metro-Goldwyn-Mayer. Kazan faced a lame script; footage of the grass already shot in Nebraska; a male star "with a ton of lard around his waist," and a female star who more or less directed herself. **Kate** overacted, and **Tracy's** underacting resembled boredom. He was also increasingly bored with their own relationship, and was patronizing male hustlers and seen dating an occasional woman on the side during the filming.

## STATE OF THE DISUNION

During the filming of the 1948 MGM film, Frank Capra's *State of the Union*, **Tracy** told his friend, George Cukor, that he'd rather be spending nights with his co-star, handsome **Van Johnson** (*right figure in photo, standing next to* **Angela Lansbury**), than with **Kate** herself.

Right-wing critics found the movie "part of the Communist conspiracy." But when **President Harry Truman**, victim of several jabs in the film, claimed he liked it, the movie sailed by without any more protests. **Claudette Colbert** was slated to play Kate's role, Mary Matthews, until *"It" Happened One Night*, and the two actresses never spoke again

## THE OBJECT OF THEIR AFFECTION

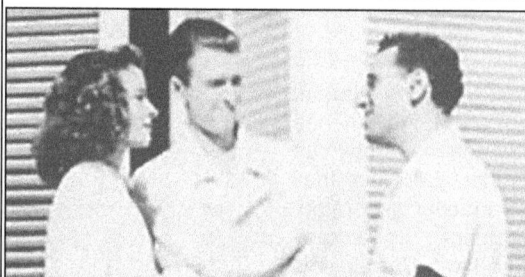

On the set of *The Philadelphia Story* (1940), both **Kate** and **George Cukor** (*right*) wanted to "de-pants" **Jimmy Stewart** to learn what all the excitement was about. With her beauty and charm, Kate beat out the ugly homosexual director. But Kate's nemesis, **Ginger Rogers**, made off with the prize. The shy, lanky actor's reaction to both Kate and Ginger: *"I polluted myself with both of them."*

404

## THE "MEN" OF ADAM'S RIB

A brief courtroom scene in *Adam's Rib* called for **Judy Holliday** to wear drag.

**Kate**, playing an attorney, had asked the jury how they would judge Holliday's character of Doris Attinger, accused of shooting her husband, if she were a man.

This photograph was taken off the set during the filming of this courtroom scene. **Tracy** suspected at the time that Kate's interest in Holliday was more than professional and had "metastacized" into something personal. But considering that he was secretly having an affair with **Nancy Davis** (*aka* **Nancy Reagan**), and buying male hustlers on the side, he could hardly protest.

Before the eyes of the jury, Holliday's character—onscreen, at least—becomes a man.

## ENTRY OF THE GODS INTO VALHALLA

In the only known photograph ever taken of **Katharine Hepburn** dining at a public restaurant, **Kate** (*far right*) was snapped, against her wishes, talking to **Tracy** (*left*), and her friend, the author and actress, **Ruth Gordon** (*second from left*), and her much younger husband, the acclaimed playwright **Garson Kanin**.

Their subject of conversation was the upcoming screenplay of *Adam's Rib*, co-authored by Gordon and Kanin. Kanin has eyes only for Kate.

He once confided to friends that his original intent was to marry Kate instead of his much older wife, Ruth Gordon. The Tracy/Hepburn menage and the Gordon/Kanin household often clashed. Insiders assessed the dynamic as "a great but troubled friendship" where the various pairings would go for months without speaking.

## TWO KINGS AND A PRINCESS

*Left photo:* With their jowls drooping, their drinking heavy, and their midriffs expanding, **Spencer Tracy** (*left*) and **Clark Gable** were by the late Forties, no longer box office champions at MGM.

In this candid photograph, Tracy is telling Clark Gable that he is turning down the role of a mayor in *A Key to the City* (1950). Gable accepted the role instead. The female star of the picture was to be **Loretta Young**.

*Right photo:* During the filming in 1935 of **The Call of the Wild**, Gable had impregnated **Loretta Young,** who is displayed here in all her pre-Code glory. She gave birth to a daughter out of wedlock and pretended that she was adopted.

Tracy had had an even more intense affair with her and briefly considered divorcing Louise to marry her. He once told Gable, "I love Loretta more than I've ever loved Kate."

## LOVE TRIANGLE: JOHANNES BRAHMS VS. ROBERT SCHUMANN
### (Hepburn Played Clara, the Concert Pianist Caught in the Middle)

In one of the worst career decisions of her turbulent career, **Kate** in 1947 signed to make the box office failure, *Song of Love*, co-starring two handsome leading men, **Robert Walker** *(left)* and **Paul Henreid** *(center)*. Kate was cast as the pianist, **Clara Wieck Schumann**, married to **Robert Schumann** (Paul Henreid) but "worshipped from afar" by Robert Walker, miscast as the spectacularly brilliant 19th-century composer, **Johannes Brahms**.

In what might be interpreted as a feminist's nightmare, **Clara (Kate)** abandons her thriving career as an acclaimed pianist to care for her emotionally fragile (aka suicidal) husband and their seven children. Walker (aka Johannes Brahms), bears the brunt of his unrequited love for her.

Although sparks dazzled off screen, Kate, Henreid, and Walker didn't even light a match on celluloid.

## "THE DUMB BLONDE" WITH THE IQ OF 172

Kate saw **Judy Holliday's** performance as Billie Dawn on stage in Garson Kanin's play, *Born Yesterday,* and predicted to **Spencer Tracy** that she'd be a big star.

Tirelessly, Kate also lobbied to get Holliday cast in the 1949 film, *Adam's Rib*, with Spencer Tracy and herself. Kate cajoled director **George Cukor** into "throwing the picture" to Holliday, which became film history's "most elaborate screen test." The way Holliday played it eventually won her the Oscar-winning female lead in *Born Yesterday*'s 1950 film adaptation.

Off-screen, Kate found the bisexual actress "mesmerizing" and invited the doomed *comedienne* for several "sleepovers" at her Turtle Bay townhouse in Manhattan.

## GENDER WARS

By the time *Adam's Rib* was released in 1949, the movie-going public had thoroughly confused the illusion of what they saw on screen with **Tracy and Hepburn** in real life. But when the cameras weren't rolling, their long-term relationship was suffering through some of its greatest pain. His excessive drinking and violence made her want to flee, and each of them was dating other partners—male and female.

## THE GIRL WHO GOT AWAY

After the filming of *Adam's Rib*, **Judy Holliday** virtually dumped Kate as a lover but wanted—even demanded—her lifetime friendship. At first, Kate was bitter, confiding to trusted friend **Patricia Peardon** that she'd been used by Holliday. Later, Kate forgave Holliday for her desertion and did indeed form a to-the-grave-friendship, Kate offering support and professional advice.

Holliday often didn't listen to Kate and turned down her professional opinion that she should accept the dumb blonde role in *Gentlemen Prefer Blondes* (1953), which went to **Marilyn Monroe** instead.

## NEVER TRUST AN ACTOR

On screen, as battling attorneys in *Adams's Rib*, this appeared as a loving reconciliation for **Spencer Tracy** and **Katharine Hepburn**.

It was directed by their friend **George Cukor**. Their co-stars, configured as a separate and even more contentious husband-and-wife team, were stage actors **Judy Holliday** and **Tom Ewell**.

Their off-screen antics were the stuff of high drama. **Kate** was falling madly in love with the bright, witty, and charming **Judy Holliday**. Meanwhile, **George Cukor, Tracy**, and **Tom Ewell** were devoting time off-screen to the patronage of some of the highest-priced male hustlers in Hollywood.

The life of the indomitable *grande dame* of American actresses, **Katharine Hepburn**, covering the years between her birth in 1907 and the debut of her role in *The African Queen* in 1950 is extensively revealed for the first time in Darwin Porter's ground-breaking biography **Katharine the Great**, appearing throughout the world for the first time in February of 2004.

At long last, the secretive, closeted world of the 20th-century's most acclaimed female film star is exposed. The New Englander screen legend died in June 2003 at the age of 96 in her home in Old Saybrook, Connecticut.

Biographer Darwin Porter began gathering material for his book on Hepburn in 1960 when he first became a Hollywood reporter. He knew that it could never be published during Hepburn's lifetime. "At one point I was afraid she might outlive me," Porter said.

The author was first introduced to Hepburn at her Manhattan Turtle Bay residence by Tennessee Williams. The playwright was trying to persuade Hepburn to appear on the stage opposite Bette Davis in *The Night of the Iguana*. She turned him down.

"Although Miss Hepburn gave me insights into many subjects, including what she thought about depicting 'perversion' on the screen, she provided not one clue about her own life," Porter said. When she learned from friends that Porter was compiling extensive documentation on her, she said, "Write whatever you want about me--but never the truth. No, not that!"

Porter has chosen not to obey Hepburn's demand. With the imminent publication of *Katharine the Great*, the door to Hepburn's closet is about to be thrown wide open.

Laura Harding (1902-1994) and Spencer Tracy, Hepburn's two greatest loves, could hardly abide each other, Porter says. "But they maintained an uneasy truce with each other for the sake of their mutual love, Hepburn."

Porter maintains that in some respects Ms. Harding was even more vital in her role as Hepburn's lover than Tracy. The Hepburn/Harding romance began in 1928, and their affair continued throughout both of their lives. Hepburn visited Harding often during her years of infirm health, and at her death bed.

"I maintain the greatest respect for Katharine Hepburn," Porter said, "but she was never truthful about her own life. Of course, given the homophobia that still exists in Hollywood today, that's completely understandable. Even in her later years when her career was out of harm's way, this great screen diva never made even a small gesture of support to the struggling gay and lesbian movement in America."

Page by page, chapter by chapter, the carefully researched and documented *Katharine the Great* sheds light on America's icon of feminist strength, with her chiseled beauty and patrician bearing. The lights of Broadway dimmed to honor Hepburn's death but the bulbs are turned on again in this startling book.

"Everybody, it seemed, had a story (or stories) to tell about Hepburn," Porter said. "Sources included Tennessee Williams, Bette Davis, Gregory Hemingway (son of Ernest), Marlene Dietrich, director George Cukor, actress Ruth Gordon, and Garson Kanin, who wrote *Adam's Rib* and other screenplays specifically for Spencer Tracy and Hepburn."

Porter also had access to the journals of Anderson Lawler, a minor actor known mainly in Hollywood history for his love affair with Gary Cooper. Lawler's manuscript was deemed unpublishable in his day because of its libelous tell-all contents. Porter also drew extensively on the journals of actor Kenneth MacKenna, whom Hepburn always referred to as "my original deflowerer." MacKenna was the long-time pal of Humphrey Bogart, and he eventually married Bogart's second wife, actress Mary Philips.

Porter also used the extensive Hollywood journals of his former writing partner, Stanley Haggart, who knew Hepburn intimately during the 1930s and 1940s and was a close and personal friend of Hepburn's only husband, "Luddy."

Both Haggart and Porter knew George Cukor, who provided valuable insights and stories but with the stipulation that nothing was to be published during his lifetime or during Hepburn's lifetime.

This vivid account of the life of this controversial star contains 78 revealing photographs. For additional information about the sources used in compiling this biography, please refer to "A Cast of Thousands," beginning on page 537 of *Katharine the Great*. It's also available at www.BloodMoonProductions.com

Porter is also the author of the previous bestseller, *The Secret Life of Humphrey Bogart (ISBN 09668030-5-1)*, which was published worldwide in June, 2003.

---

# StarNews

You Read It Here First! The Breaking News Of The Week

# HEPBURN'S Starlet Sex Scandal

### Were female pals more than friends?

THE doors to Katharine Hepburn's closet have been thrown open, revealing a pile of sexual skeletons----both male and female.

In the new book, *Katharine the Great* (Blood Moon Productions, $16.95), author Darwin Porter writes that Hepburn — known for her very public 25-year love affair with actor Spencer Tracy — also romanced several Hollywood starlets, including Judy Garland, Greta Garbo, Claudette Colbert and Judy Holliday. "The relationship with Garland is a big surprise,

because [Judy] was basically a very heterosexual woman," Porter tells *Star*. "But that was more of a caretaker relationship; she was assigned by [movie mogul] Louis B. Mayer to take Judy off drugs and straighten her out."

Porter says Hepburn's tryst with Garbo was the steamiest — and the smoothest. "There were no fights," he says. After 40-plus years researching Hepburn, Porter adds that the star "never identified herself as bisexual. She thought, 'If I want to do it, I'll do it.' She had a very sexual life." — **DAVID CAPLAN** ★

Left to right: **Greta Garbo, Claudette Colbert, & Judy Garland**

**Laura Harding** (left) with **Hepburn** in the mid-1930s. Though they remained friends, when lesbian rumors grew too loud, Hepburn sent her packing "back East."

**GLBT hipsters** who viewed this still shot from Hepburn's "transgendered classic," *Sylvia Scarlett* (1935) fully understood the roleplaying ironies of its script. *"I won't be a girl, I won't be weak and silly. I'll be a boy, rough and hard!,"* Hepburn's character *(right figure in photo)* shouts as she chops off her braids and morphs into something more butch. "Sylvia" becomes "Sylvester" before deporting for exotic climes with her ne'er-do-well father. Hepburn's frenemies said she was born to play the role.

# PULP
MAGAZINE

# The BottomLine
magazine

BOOK REVIEW

## Katharine The Great

### a lifetime of secrets... revealed by Darwin Porter

# A Rounded Portrait

By Conrad J. Doerr

Last year, Darwin Porter dumped *The Secret Life Of Humphrey Bogart* on us, and we lapped up every sentence of it, despite some doubt about its veracity. We wanted to believe what we were reading even while questioning the sources noted. His avowed sources were there, reliable and substantiated, amassed over several years and guarded until such time that the subjects had shed these mortal coils. The quoted conversations were a tad unsettling — was everything recorded?

The author again draws upon his vast storehouse of notes and quotes regarding the movie stars of an earlier period — notes and quotes that could never be published in the time of the good old, bad old days of studio fiefdom, when damage control was the name of the game.

This time out, Katharine Hepburn is the subject, covering her from birth until 1950, and the advent of *The African Queen*. The Hepburn Basics have always been available. Her tomboy childhood (she liked to be called Tommy) in Connecticut, her close ties to her brother who committed suicide, the Bryn Mawr education, her choosing the theater over a "legitimate profession," much to the disdain of her parents (her father a doctor, her mother a women's rights advocate). Cutting less than a swathe through the theater in the early '30s, she had a hit play in *The Warrior's Husband*, which resulted in being signed by RKO. Not too many years on the screen (with an early Oscar) in a series of bad script choices rated her the "Box Office Poison" appellation (great company, though — Garbo, Dietrich, Crawford, West). Returning to the Broadway theater between movies flops, she starred in *The Lake* (prompting Dorothy Parker's famous quip, "She ran the gamut of emotions from A to B"). Hepburn was one of many actresses who vied for the role of Scarlett O'Hara. She saw

Errol Flynn as Rhett, and the two of them went to great lengths to be photographed in costume for the roles. Losing the role left a dent. It wasn't until another return to Broadway in 1939 and *The Philadelphia Story* that she crested. She returned to Hollywood (and MGM) to star in the film version that finally established her film credentials for the decades ahead.

The inner workings of a studio (RKO in the early '30s) in that period are relished. Hepburn co-reigned as queen of the lot with Ginger Rogers. Hepburn and Rogers hated each other, though co-starring in *Stage Door*. She never had a kind word to say about Rogers,

that tramp.' Hepburn would later turn down the lead in *Kitty Foyle*, which garnered Rogers her Oscar. (Note: I attended a Ginger Rogers book signing at Temple Isaiah in Palm Springs in 1991. The assemblage was cautioned before the question-and-answer period that we could ask Miss Rogers anything about her career, but nothing about her personal life).

Hepburn's private life was just that. She shunned publicity as much as Garbo. There was speculation about Hepburn's sexual persuasion. She is right up there with the Sewing Circle Ladies — those female stars who swung both ways. We knew that she had a lady friend, Laura Harding, the American Express heiress, from 1929 until Laura's death in 1994. We knew that she had been married. What we didn't know was that Laura and Luddy's lover, Jack, accompanied Kate and her new husband, Luddy. The marriage was never consummated. What we also didn't know was that Kate had a propensity for getting involved with her leading men and film directors. She bedded many, loved some. In those early years they encompassed such notables as George Stevens, John Ford, Tone, Heflin, Cotton, Henreid. Then there was Hemingway, Garbo, the Judys (Garland and Holliday), as well as a long-term affair with Claudette Colbert — among others. Kate and Laura broke up several times due to Kate's peccadilloes.

Hepburn's only public romance was with Howard Hughes, then considered the playboy of Hollywood, and fresh from his around the world triumph. Hughes proposed. The headline romance finally fizzled — unconsummated. Hughes proposed to many leading ladies of the era—and kept his stable of boys on the side. (There is some insight into Hughes' phobias — Oh, boy, do I remember Mama!)

408

**Humphrey Bogart** and **Katharine Hepburn** are often cited as the most notable actors of Golden Age Hollywood. Director John Huston came up with the idea of co-starring them in *The African Queen* (1953). Bogie was cast as a drunken, creatively inventive American, Charlie Allnut.

Set in German East Africa in 1914, during World War I, he navigates his battered steamboat up an African river. His passenger, **Sister Rose Sayer (Hepburn)** is a British missionary and spinster. At first, she can barely tolerate his coarse behavior, but as their voyage continues, she begins to fall in love. Together, they face natural beauty, discomforts, and perils.

Almost everyone on the cast and crew got sick from drinking infected water, but not **Bogie and Huston**, as their hydration came almost exclusively from liquor. Bogie had previously been nominated for an Oscar for his performance as Rick in *Casablanca* (1943). For his performance in *The African Queen*, he won his one and only Best Actor Academy Award. For her performance as the judgmental spinster, **Hepburn** was nominated for Best Actress, losing to **Vivien Leigh** for her portrayal of Blanche DuBois in Tennessee Williams' *A Streetcar Named Desire.*

Directed by **Anthony Hervey** and set in the 12th Century, *The Lion in Winter* (1968) brought together **Peter O'Toole** as Henry II of England and **Katharine Hepburn** as his ferocious wife and rival, Eleanor of Aquitaine, the most famous woman of the Middle Ages. As a pawn of her era's complicated politics, Eleanor has spent many years of their marriage in prison, although for dynastic reasons, she's been released in time for a family get-together at Christmas.

**Anthony Hopkins** was cast as Richard the Lionheart, the royal couple's eldest son, and **Timothy Dalton** played King Philip II of France. Transcending the bizarre historical circumstances on which it was based, the film became an enormous and very fascinating, rather "high-brow" hit.

At Oscar time, **O'Toole** was nominated for Best Actor, losing to **Cliff Robertson** for *Charly.* **Hepburn** became the Academy's first triple Oscar-winner. She faced a tie vote with **Barbra Streisand**, who also won a Best Actress Oscar for her memorable performand in *Funny Girl*.

Theater producer **Frederick Brisson** wanted his wife, **Rosalind Russell** to star in a Broadway musical inspired by the life of Coco Chanel, the fabled French designer. Russell developed acute arthritis and could not accept the role. In a daring move, Brisson cast **Katharine Hepburn** instead. It would be her first musical, and it opened in 1969. She began voice lessons immediately, studying the lyrics and book by **Alan Jay Lerner.** During rehearsals, imperiously, she demanded that the thermostat be set at 60 degrees during a freakishly chilly New York autumn. Other members of the cast and crew came down with colds and/or the flu.

Some sequences recalled Coco's romantic flings of yesteryear. It also featured a fashion *défilé* of Chanel confections crafted between 1918 and 1959. Paramount financed the stage production, shelling out $900,000, making it the most expensive Broadway show at that time. Yet for some reason, the fabled studio opted not to spin it off as a film adaptation.

Hepburn was in Cleveland, starring in a road show version of *Coco* when news broke that Coco Chanel had died in Paris. On January 11, 1971, Hepburn announced, from the stage, during a curtain call, with poignancy, the death of the legendary Empress of Fashion.

A family-themed drama, *On Golden Pond* (1981), adapted from a successful play by **Ernest Thompson**, brought together **Henry Fonda** and his often estranged daughter, **Jane**. Henry played a curmudgeonly retired professor grappling with the effects of aging. He is alienated from his daughter, Chelsea (Jane).

At their summer home beside Golden Pond in New England, Norman and his wife **Ethel (Katharine Hepburn)** agree to care for Billy, the 13-year-old son of Chelsea's new boyfriend, for a month so that the young couple can spend some time alone. Jane bought the screen rights with the specific hope that it would be configured as a vehicle for herself and her father. Before that, **James Stewart** had been offered the role, but he rejected it.

*On Golden Pond* morphed into both a critical and commercial success. At the 54th Academy Awards, it was nominated for Best Picture. **Henry Fonda** won the Best Actor Oscar. Because he was ill, and couldn't attend, his daughter gracefully accepted it in his place. As for **Hepburn**, once again, she carried home the gold, winning the Best Actress Award—her fourth.

NEWS from

# DAVID HARTNELL'S CELEBRITY GOSSIP
## by David Hartnell

*David Hartnell, New Zealand's resident expert on Hollywood lore,*
*was the recipient, in 2012, of New Zealand's Order of Merit (MNZM)*
*for services to the entertainment industry,*
*as defined by Her Majesty, Queen Elizabeth II.*

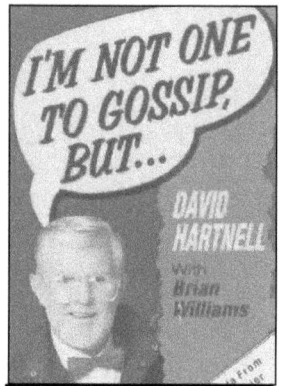

*His review of KATHARINE THE GREAT (it's replicated below) appeared in newspapers*
*throughout the Southern Hemisphere, a few days after it was released.*

Famously associated with New Zealand, where he works tirelessly as a fundraiser for the performing arts, **David Hartnell** is the most widely read and most influential entertainment journalist in the Southern Hemisphere.

**Blood Moon Productions** of New York have published o book about **Katharine Hepburn** called *"Katharine The Great, A Lifetime of Secrets ... Revealed"* by Darwin Porter. The back cover of the book boasts, "You've read what "Kate Remembered...now read what Katharine Hepburn wanted to forget."

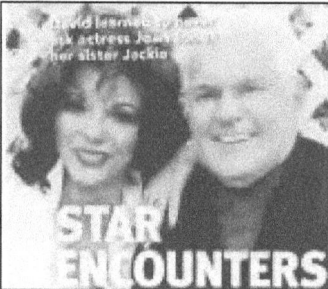

This book goes way beyond the roles we thought we knew. Ohmigod are they right! There are lo's of extraordinary gay twists and turns in this book It's been compiled over many years, from many eyewitnesses. Trust me this book is like no other on Katharine. It's a multi billion-dollar treasure trove of stories compiled into this one blockbuster of a read about her life. It covers love, sexuality, pain, joy, lesbianism, regrets, money, power, pornography, sorrow and evangelical Christianity in America today. It's an explosive exposé read from page l to page 558, with never before published material about her.

"Now that the child (i.e., this book) has been birthed, I freely admit that we nearly drowned in the deep and murky lake associated with the life and psyche of Katharine Hepburn. EVERY-ONE who ever met her seemed to have o strong, and sometimes violent, opinion or anecdote about her. So, in sync with our role as social historians, we're honored to have been the first to publish the revelations contained within this book," said Danforth Prince the President of Blood Moon Productions who published the book.

**David Harnell** appears with two of the dozens of celebrity co-horts he cultivated as a friend and mouthpiece over the course of a long and distinguished media career. He appears above with **Joan Collins** (upper photo) and **Phyllis Diller.**

Over the course of Blood Moon's existence, he consistently defined himself as a friend, ally, and supporter of its many insights into the once-repressed underground of Golden Age Hollywood.

One reader said: "My favorite movie actress, Katharine Hepburn, is a lot less mysterious after reading this enthralling book, The amazing thing about Miss Hepburn's life is that no one has, until now, published anything with any meat in it." The book is so hot and controversial that no book shop here in little old New Zealand will stock it ... but wait there's more: It can be purchased through Amazon.com or Bulldog in Melbourne.

Or check out their website **www. bloodmoon-productions.com.**

**David Hartnell** appears here with the Australian comedian **Barry Humphries**, aka **Dame Edna Everage**, the most famous drag entertainer in the Southern Hemisphere. During a theatrical career that spanned almost 68 years, **Dame Edna** satirized everything from the Australian suburbs to the cult of celebrity for which she became famous.

In 1982, her "alter ego" (Barry Humphries) was made a Commander of the Order of the British Empire for services to entertainment. In 2007, a city street (Dame Edna Place) was officially opened by the Lord Mayor of Melbourne. In 2009, a bronze statue was unveiled in her honor at Melbourne Docklands.

Her death in 2023 was mourned within cabaret circles worldwide..

THE WEEKEND AUSTRALIAN FEBRUARY 18-19 2006
**INQUIRER 19**

## Brando: all sex

Marlon Brando smouldered in real life as well as on the screen. Darwin Porter reveals the extraordinary life

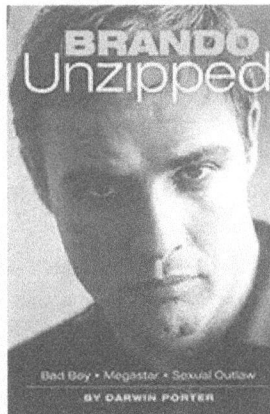

Darwin Porter reveals the extraordinary story that lay behind Marlon Brando's smouldering image

**BRANDO Unzipped**

Bad Boy • Megastar • Sexual Outlaw
BY DARWIN PORTER

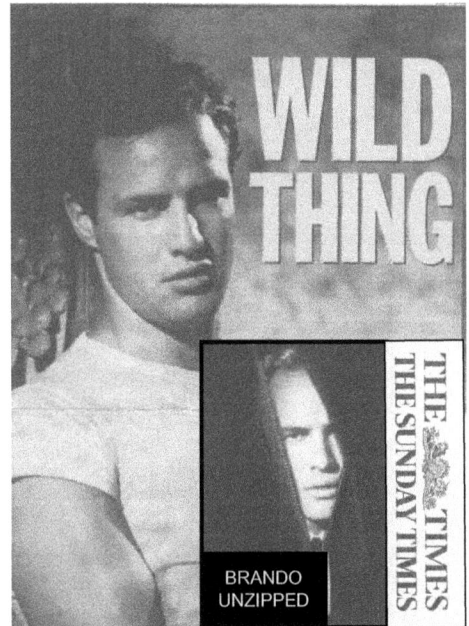

WILD THING

THE SUNDAY TIMES

BRANDO UNZIPPED

The **Courier Mail**

## Brando the sex machine

Alexander McRobbie
March 25, 2006

# DAILY EXPRESS

THE WORLD'S GREATEST NEWSPAPER — AND PROUD OF IT — THURSDAY JANUARY 26, 2006 30p

# THE Godfather

of lust

by Peter Sheridan

FAME

**How to dress like Marlon Brando**

# BRANDO UNZIPPED

*The New York Daily News:*
*"Brando Unzipped* is the definitive gossip guide to the late, great actor's life."

*The Sunday Times (London):*
"The contents of this biography are for the most part compelling, reflecting the underground quality of much of the information, and there is an astounding revelation on almost every page. If you enjoy gossip and are not too precious about presentation, this book is certainly worth reading. Of course, if you enjoy salacious gossip and tales of sexual abandon, you will find yourself in hog heaven."

*Bookmarks/Books to Watch Out For:*
*"YUMMY!* That sums up Porter's titillatingly tabloidish account of Marlon Brando's eccentric, sex-centric years. The author barely pauses to take a deep breath as he dishes, drawing on 50 years of conversations with dozens of Brando's intimates-about the late, great actor's personal life. But there's way more to this biography than sex: Porter writes with an insider's astuteness about the actor's movie career, critical passages that provide welcome depth. But it's no exaggeration to report that practically every page discloses a fascinating tidbit about Liberace successfully seducing Dean, for example, but failing to seduce Brando. This is an irresistibly flamboyant romp of a read."

*Le Journal du Dimanche (Paris):*
*Brando Unzipped,* from Blood Moon, contains major revelations about the tumultuous love affairs of the American actor who died in July of 2004. Its author, Darwin Porter, spent 50 years assembling meticulously documented source material. Amazingly, revealed for the first time are details about the involvement of Brando with Edith Piaf in the early 1950s. Three days of lovemaking and carnal excess began with a misunderstanding ....

*Daily Express (London):*
"The tempestuous affair with James Dean is just one of dozens of homosexual relationships, flings, and one-night stands in which Brando indulged during a lifetime of sexual voraciousness, according to a shocking new book that is sparking a major reassessment of Brando's legacy as one of Hollywood's most macho lotharios."

*Women's Weekly (Australia):*
"Astonishing ... Veteran reporter Darwin Porter paints a portrait of Brando that's as blunt, uncompromising, and X-rated as the man himself."

*Frontiers Magazine* (Southern California's Oldest and Largest LGBTQ magazine):
"Entertainingly Outrageous."

*Gay Times (London):*
He was considered one of the most dynamic and imposing actors of his generation, but as author Darwin Porter finds, it was just the acting world that Marlon Brando conquered. It was the actors, too.

*The Georgia Literary Association:*
"Original and at times amazing, BRANDO UNZIPPED documents a life of gargantuan excess that only Hollywood could have produced."

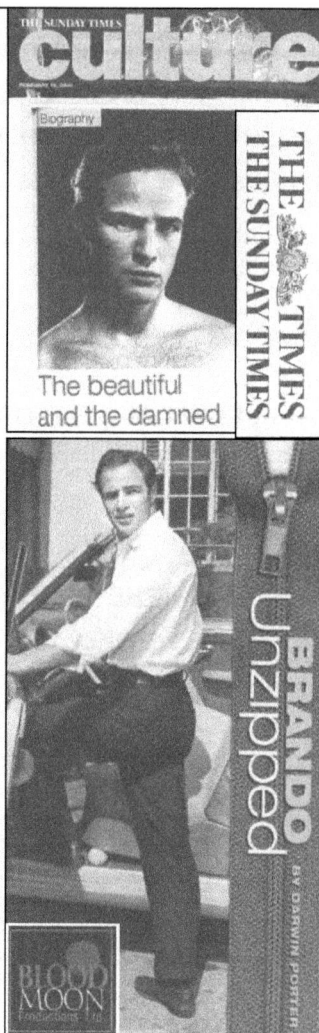

THE SUNDAY TIMES

3WC

# The first images of Brando, as the rebel who stole the show

**Unseen footage shows the actor trying out for the role that would make James Dean a star, reports Dalya Alberge**

PHOTOGRAPHS: WARNER BROS

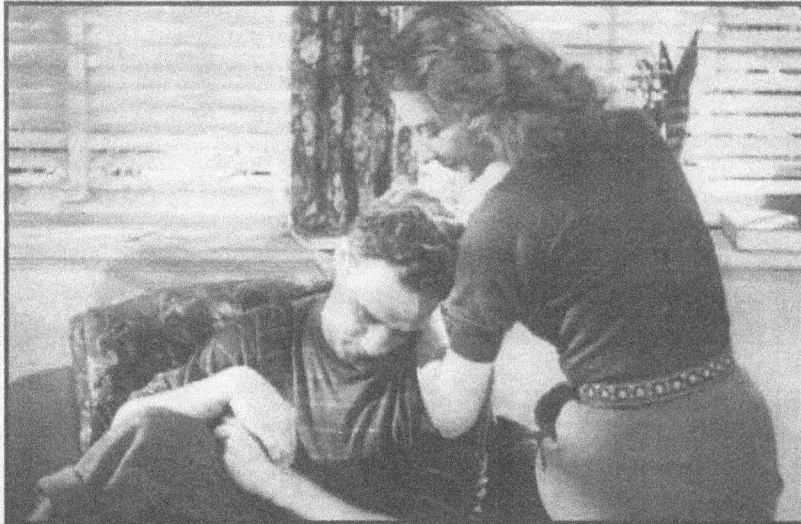

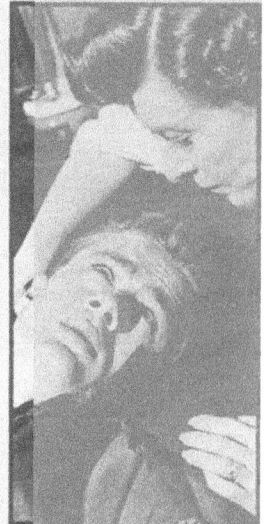

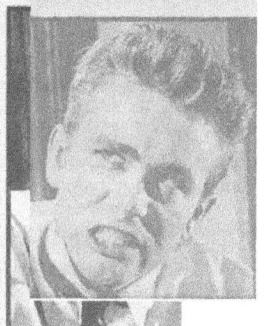

HE WAS the most influential film actor of the 20th century, electrifying audiences with his charisma and brooding menace in classics such as *A Streetcar Named Desire*, *On the Waterfront* and *The Godfather*.

Now Marlon Brando's first-screen test — shot more than half a century ago and three years before he had made a single film — has been discovered.

Stills from the five-minute footage are published in *The Times* today. What makes it all the more fascinating is that it was a screen test for *Rebel Without a Cause* — a film that he never made, but which was to make the name of another star, James Dean.

The footage shows how, even in his earliest years, Brandon exuded a mesmerising quality that was to inspire generations of actors. He is seen crying, slamming his fist on a table, vulnerable and kissing the girl. He was 23 and, already, he sizzled on screen.

The test, dating from 1947, convinced the producers that he was the man for the rebel role, but Brando turned them down. After a long delay — including at least 40 revisions of the script — the role was taken by Dean in 1955.

Darwin Porter, author of *Brando Unzipped*, a biography of the actor, said that he was "gasping for breath" with excitement after being shown the "important" screen test footage.

He said: "Screen tests preserved of the great stars are usually pretty awful … This one had me mesmerised. I would have done everything to hire him … From the moment Brando enters the room in the test, he is lightning on legs. There is a magnetic appeal to him, as he is at the peak of his physical beauty and virile power — both as a man and an actor."

413

# Meet Me at the Fair!

## A News Alert from

Foreword

### REVIEWS OF INDIE BOOKS, SINCE 1998

**Meet Me at the Fair** was an American musical film. Like Danforth, it was made in 1953.

their Newsletter of Feb 22, 2006

"Earlier this month, **Darwin Porter's** biography *Brando Unzipped* (09748118-2-3, **Blood Moon Productions**) was serialized in *The London Times*. The 3,000-word serialization appeared in *The London Times'* Sunday edition of February 12. The newspaper also ran a full-length book review much to the delight of Blood Moon's president **Danforth Prince**: "We're honored and delighted that *The London Times* understands the merit of our new breed of celebrity biography," he said. Blood Moon will be exhibiting at the London Book Fair in March at Booth G-840."

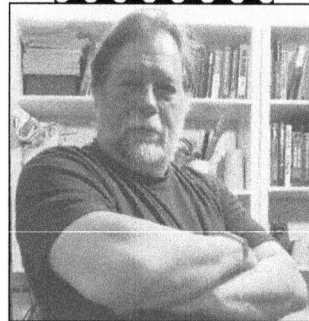

THE ROAD TO PUBLISHING SUCCESS

**LONDON BOOK FAIR**
EXCEL LONDON 5-7 MARCH 2006

**Danforth**: Marketing across cultural chasms, and soldiering on.

Frommer's England 2007

Frommer's London 2007

**DID YOU KNOW?** That long ago and far away, as BRANDO UNZIPPED was being conceived, written, and edited, both **Darwin Porter** and **Danforth Prince** were co-authors and directors of research for many of the (*remember them?*) **Frommer Guides**?

Some critics have surmised that Porter's familiarilty with the British press derived from his years of on-site research in the U.K., sussing out the hidden gems of **Merry Olde England** and gathering interview notes from some of Marlon Brando's many (sometimes scorned, often abandoned) British lovers.

In reference to his deep dive with "the ghost of Marlon" into that year's **London Book Fair** (where the British media was cranking out publicity like fish 'n chips on the boardwalks of Blackpool), **Danforth said**, "Humping Brando's legacies among the Brits that year was loaded with adventures and MORE than a lot of fun. It was the best book fair I've ever been involved with—*and, with a nod to Sinatra, 'I've had a few.'*)"

"I'll remain forever grateful for London, its intellectual life, and its legions of readers," Prince continued. "Adding clotted cream to my afternoon teas involved re-confirming the status of Frommer stalwarts such as THE BERKELEY, THE STAFFORD, THE RITZ, THE DORCHESTER, and a raft of other British staples that help make London great. Overall, my time at the Fair, touting the legacy of Marvelous Marlon, made that particular trip to the U.K. *An Affair to Remember.*"

# The Courier Mail

## Brando the sex machine

*Alexander McRobbie*
*March 25, 2006*

### Alexander McRobbie reviews a book that details the lurid life of surely Hollywood's busiest satyr

WITHOUT doubt this has to be the most lurid, eye-popping and often unsettling film-star biography ever

The bisexual Marlon Brando was a satyr extraordinaire whose male and female lovers were a roll call of Hollywood's greats from its Golden Age.

His female lovers included Ursula Andress, Pier Angeli, Tallulah Bankhead, Rita Hayworth, Anne Baxter, Ingrid Bergman, Bette Davis, Marlene Dietrich, Ava Gardner, Greer Garson, Grace Kelly, Veronica Lake, Hedy Lamarr, Vivien Leigh, Marilyn Monroe, Merle Oberon, Jean Simmons and Shelley Winters.

Most threw themselves at the charismatic and insatiable young Brando. So did many of his male lovers who included Richard Burton, Montgomery Clift, Noel Coward, James Dean, John Gielgud, Stewart Granger, Cary Grant, Rock Hudson, Burt Lancaster, Laurence Olivier, Tyrone Power and Michael Wilding.

The biography stands or falls on its believability — and the sources of the author's facts.

Veteran *Miami Herald* journalist Darwin Porter, now 68, relies mainly on primary sources — people who knew Brando, many still living.

His anecdotes have an authentic ring, although Porter says direct quotations have been rendered "as they were remembered" by the people who originally heard the remarks.

This works well and usually sounds factual, although it falls down in a few places, such as in the episodes dealing with Hedy Lamarr and Anne Baxter. They seem too-pat and manufactured, unlike the rest of the narrative.

Many film star biographies give the impression that the author is throwing in everything he can find about the subject to reach book length, and some of the material is often very thin.

With *Brando Unzipped*, one feels Porter has a large reserve of material he didn't use, despite the book's massive 625 pages plus index.

It is perhaps a mercy that the author didn't use all he knew about the often disgusting Brando. Some parts will test the strongest stomach, like the squalid grottiness of his living arrangements and his habit of urinating in public. But it is compulsive reading.

The book's first half covers Brando's successful career on the New York stage before he appeared in a film. This would be unknown to most people, even present-day New Yorkers. But it was during his career on stage that Brando was at his most active sexually.

The story moves from one jaw-dropper to another.

Examples: Brando and the super-macho Burt Lancaster in bed. A naked Brando and Laurence Olivier kissing in a pool while Vivien Leigh waits tolerantly in the house. She told director Elia Kazan: "I must say this for Marlon, when it comes to couples he is an equal oppor-

tunity seducer. On many an occasion he rose from Larry's bed and joined me in mine."

Another source for this episode is David Niven, who walked into the Oliviers' garden to discover Brando and Larry naked in the pool. "Larry was kissing Brando, or maybe it was the other way around."

Niven felt that both Olivier and Vivien were hopelessly in love with Brando.

*Brando Unzipped* is almost Dickensian in its relentless piling of detail upon detail. I doubt if there has ever been such a comprehensive study of satyriasis — defined as "a morbid and uncontrollable sexual desire in men".

When noted journalist and movie writer Joe Hyams tried to compile a list of all the women Brando had seduced he gave up,

claiming: "It takes a statistician rather than a reporter."

One would have expected his promiscuity to result in venereal disease, and transmitting it to others (there is no mention of him ever wearing a condom). But in the decades-long period covered in the narrative he only gets gonorrhea once, while filming *Mutiny on the Bounty*.

Tallulah Bankhead complains that Brando gave her the crabs — a minor affliction compared with syphilis or genital herpes. Of course none of these diseases compared with the scourge of AIDS which caused the promiscuity of the Swinging Sixties to be considerably curtailed.

Pregnancy among his women was relatively rare. One of his lovers, Marilyn Monroe, was one of the few to tell him she was pregnant. She said this

wasn't unusual for her because she "preferred natural sex". She had several abortions.

Actress Geraldine Page said one night Brando boasted to her that he had "at least six women pregnant". He said he was going to raise money to pay for them to have illegal abortions.

There seems no doubt that future film star biographies will be heavily influenced by the frankness of *Brando Unzipped*.

A major casualty in the book is old-fashioned boy-meets-girl romance. But then, that kind of stuff is long gone from the movies, so maybe it's time to grow up.

When Brando was asked about his love life he snapped: "I can't talk about something that doesn't exist."

*Brando Unzipped by Darwin Porter (Bloodmoon, $49.95)*

The Courier Mail

415

The Sunday Times - Books; February 19, 2006
Biography

Brando Unzipped by Darwin Porter
REVIEWED BY CHRISTOPHER SILVESTER

**Sunday Times**
# BOOKS

British historian
**Christopher Sylvester**

"Pride of Britain"
**Vivien Leigh** with **Marlon Brando**

# BRANDO UNZIPPED by Darwin Porter
*Blood Moon £17.99 pp621.*

*Satyriasis* is defined in the dictionary as an uncontrollable desire in and behaviour by a man. This seems an apt description of **Marlon Brando**, based on the evidence of this lurid, raunchy though perceptive biography. Various individuals attest to his fleeting passions, his lack of emotional commitment and cruel treatment of lovers, both male and female. When asked by an impertinent interviewer, "What about your love life, Brando?", he gave the flippant but true response: "I can't talk about something that doesn't exist."

Brando was an earthy individual who delighted in shocking with his carefree and liberated manners. His first Hollywood screen tests were a disaster because he appeared with a runny nose; he would scratch his genitals during interviews; he liked to intersperse high-flown conversation with profanities and dirty talk; he referred to his manhood as "my noble tool"; he was preternaturally given to public urination; and he acquired the ability to fart on cue. At the same time, he was the "ultimate wet-dream fantasy" of gay intellectuals such as **Tennessee Williams** and **Truman Capote**, and in his classic performances his raw, animal magnetism was tempered by a poetic vulnerability.

When he starred in Ben Hecht's pep-Zionist Broadway play *A Flag is Born*, in 1946, he "must have f***ed half the Jewish gals in New York," said the actress **Stella Adler**. "They flocked backstage to meet him, and he took his pick". The effect was similar, though amplified by celebrity, when he played the brutish Stanley Kowalski in *A Streetcar Named Desire*.

With an oedipal complex as big as his monstrous ego (indeed, Brando claimed to one lover that his alcoholic mother had molested him as a child), he was a sexual outlaw who used sex as a means of control as much as a means of self-expression. Directed at some male and female actors, it was his way of slaying, or at the very least taming, the professional competition. This was his approach with **Montgomery Clift, James Dean** and even **Burt Lancaster**. At the same time, he had to indulge his appetite. One girlfriend, the actress **Geraldine Page**, compared him to a dog in a park: "He pisses on the elm tree. He pisses on the birch. Then, for a change of pace, he pisses on a fire hydrant or a patch of grass. His actual address shifted from day to day, depending on who—in his case, what—he was seducing. His ass *du jour,* so to speak."

Apart from his relationships with high-profile men and women, from **Marilyn, Rita and Ava to Montgomery, Rock** and **James Dean**, relationships that are studiously catalogued here by Darwin Porter, Brando also engaged in liaisons with minor male actors. According to **Elia Kazan**, the director, Brando was briefly "smitten" in 1947 by Sandy Campbell, the young actor he stole from the playwright **Donald Wyndham**. On the set of *The Wild One*, it was a 23-year-old Latino biker. In the summer of 1953, it was William Redfield, a young stage actor, who took his fancy. And there was always **Wally Cox**, Brando's childhood friend, who played the TV sitcom character Mr Peepers. Cox was Brando's soulmate and lover. In 1965, Brando used his influence to have Cox and Redfield cast in *The Saboteur: Code Named Morituri.* "Marlon shared a two-bedroom villa with both Wally Cox and Redfield," recalled **Sam Gilman**, Brando's Boy Friday, a dialogue coach on the film. "One night he'd share Wally's bed. On another night he'd sleep with Redfield. Personally, I think Wally was his favourite."

In Fred Zinnemann's 1949 film *The Men*, in which Brando played a wheelchair-bound veteran, he prepared for the role by spending time with paraplegics. He befriended one homosexual quadriplegic vet ("not even able to light a cigarette"), who harboured suicidal thoughts, and allowed him to perform fellatio on his "noble tool". When they were caught by an attendant, Zinnemann excused Brando's behaviour as charitable.

What makes Brando even more of a puzzle is that he enjoyed being, in gay parlance, both pitcher and catcher. He would sometimes be a classic "top"; on other occasions he was happy to submit. He was a narcissist one minute, a tender lover the next. Not so much sexual outlaw, perhaps, as existential hero of the bedroom.

Porter is not big on analysis or evaluation, preferring to let the witnesses speak, nor is he much interested in the second half of his subject's life. He deals with it in a final chapter that takes up about 40 pages consisting of picture captions and gobbets. After 1961, Brando's career slowed down (with the exception of his role in *The Godfather*), while his private life became increasingly bizarre.

*Brando Unzipped* deserves to stand alongside Peter Manso's 1993 doorstopper of a biography, because it explores a dimension of Brando's personality that Manso felt constrained to underplay, either through lack of access to certain sources or through undue delicacy. The occasional misspelling and flaws in page design can be forgiven because the contents are for the most part compelling. Indeed, the samizdat quality of the text reflects the underground flavour of much of the information, and there is an astounding revelation on almost every page. **If you enjoy gossip and are not too precious about**

416

presentation, this book is certainly worth reading. Of course, if you enjoy salacious gossip and tales of sexual abanqon, you will find yourself in hog heaven.

## MARLON'S DEEPWATER DIVE WITH THE OLIVIERS

During the filming of *A Streetcar Named Desire*, Brando had affairs with both his co-star, **Vivien Leigh**, and her husband, **Laurence Olivier**. One witness was **David Niven,** who remembered walking into the garden of the house where the Oliviers were staying: "Brando and Larry swimming naked in the pool. Larry was kissing Brando. Or maybe it was the other way around. I turned my back on them and went back inside to join Vivien. I'm sure she knew what was going on, but she made no mention of it. Nor did I. One must be sophisticated about such matters in life."

Brando Unzipped is *available at the Books First price of £16.19 on 0870 165 8585*

**Casual Debauchery and Remembered Pain**. Photos, *left to right*: **Laurence Olivier** with **Vivien Leigh**; **David Niven**; **Stella Adler**; and **Truman Capote**.

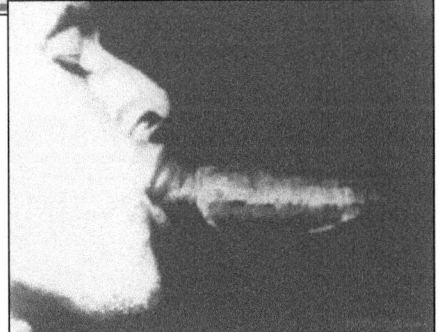

Weather: Breezy & showers, 59/33    RACING ★ FINAL    Saturday, January 21, 2006

# DAILY NEWS

NEW YORK'S HOMETOWN NEWSPAPER    www.nydailynews.com
50¢

Ben Widdicombe
## GATECRASHER
gatecrasher@nydailynews.com

# Brando: Truly the wild one

A thick new biography of Marlon Brando promises to be the definitive gossip guide to the great actor's life.
"Brando Unzipped," by **Darwin Porter**, claims he covered as much ground on the Kinsey Scale as the bathroom scales.
The book says: "From Rock Hudson to Vivien Leigh, from Bette Davis to Cary Grant, Brando [l.] slept around, even managing to seduce two of America's First Ladies." The plausibility of that is debatable, but there's a (literally) jaw-dropping scene on page 320, involving Peter Lawford, another actor and "a motor trip to Palm Springs" which you can bet they didn't run by Nancy Reagan's lawyers before publication.

Collectors of Brando ephemera might appreciate the inclusion of a certain infamous photograph. (Confidential to **Hazel Gutberlet** of Palisades Park, N.J. — who finds me a tad vulgar, according to the mail — this is your cue to turn away.) The image depicts a **Monica Lewinsky** moment between Brando and another man.
"We ran it at a tasteful 2 inches by 1¼ inches on page 404," says Blood Moon publisher **Danforth Prince**.
In journalism, we call that "burying the lead."

### SOMETIMES "BURYING THE LEAD" IS A GOOD IDEA

According to **Darwin Porter**, "Contrary to burying the story broadcast by **Ben Widdicombe** in the *Daily News*, we opted to 'tastefully downplay" a graphic photo that has circulated through the underground since the mid-1950s. *(Text continues on right.)*

According to **Brando Unzipped**, the penis being serviced by Marlon Brando in the photo above belonged to **Wally Cox**. Brando posed for it in 1952, when they attended one of Phil Black's legendary M4M parties in Harlem. WAY off the radar (yet still "accessorized with a hidden camera, much to Marlon's regret) *invitees* paid $10 for all the food, booze, and sex they could handle.

Days after the photograph was taken, it was on sale on the East and West Coasts. Soon it was being sold openly on the streets of Paris. Gay men around the world had copies pinned to their bedroom walls. It remains to this day the only photograph of a major Hollywood star engaging in the "delivery" side of fellatio.

417

# Brando: all sex

Marlon Brando smouldered in real life as well as on the screen. **Darwin Porter** reveals the extraordinary life of one of history's greatest actors

A COUPLE of years ago, many newspapers printed a report from the Associated Press news agency that the family of the recently deceased Marlon Brando had scattered his ashes in Tahiti and in Death Valley, California. The report continued, intriguingly: "The ashes of Brando's late friend Wally Cox, who died in 1973, were also poured onto the desert landscape as part of the same ceremony; how Cox's ashes were in the possession of Brando's family was unknown."

It is hard to credit that neither the agency nor the papers knew that Cox, a comedian, had been Brando's long-term lover. But such was the strength of the macho heterosexual myth surrounding the actor that he had to be protected even after his death.

What the media may be excused for not knowing is that Brando not only kept his friend's ashes for more than 30 years but, when lonely, would sometimes dine *a deux* with the urn, holding conversations in which he would perfectly imitate Cox's voice. He left instructions that after his own death their ashes should be mingled and scattered together.

The media may also be excused for not knowing that Cox was only one of many men with whom Brando had liaisons. Brando was bisexual and voracious. The roles he lived off screen were even more provocative than those he created in films.

At his peak, his list of lovers read like a Who's Who of Hollywood and beyond, including Burt Lancaster, Laurence Olivier, John Gielgud, Marilyn Monroe, Marlene Dietrich, Grace Kelly, Rita Hayworth, Leonard Bernstein, Noel Coward, Shelley Winters, Ava Gardner, Gloria Vanderbilt, Tyrone Power, Hedy Lamarr, Anna Magnani, Montgomery Clift (they once ran naked on Wall St together for a dare), James Dean, Tallulah Bankhead, Ingrid Bergman, Edith Piaf and Doris Duke (at the time the world's richest woman).

Yet just as the film studio publicity machines covered up the proclivities of closet gays such as Rock Hudson — another Brando lover — so they hid the extent of Brando's excesses.

The world knew of his predilection for "dark-skinned women", particularly Tahitian and American-Indian beauties. That he had a skinny, bespectacled male lover called Wally just didn't fit the image. Yet he once admitted he had never been happy with a woman, adding: "If Wally had been a woman, I would have married him and we would have lived happily ever after."

Is this the reason for Brando's self-destructive behaviour, the boorishness and the obesity that blighted the career of a man who was hailed 50 years ago as an electrifyingly handsome and talented new star?

Exuding a sense of brooding power and bottled-up anger, the iconoclastic Brando was arguably the greatest film star of all time. He changed the way stars, both male and female, acted and even the way young men dressed. His "uniform" of blue jeans and white T-shirts became standard issue, he reigned as the male sex symbol of the 1950s.

Yet he never found a movie role he really liked, not even his two Oscar-winning perfomrances in *On the Waterfront* and *The Godfather*. He was even disdainful of his memorable role as Stanley Kowalski, which made him famous both on Broadway and on the screen in Tennessee Williams's *A Streetcar Named Desire*.

During his twilight, he admitted, "I searched for but never found what I was looking for either on screen or off. Mine was a glamorous, turbulent life but completely unfulling."

*(Continued on next page)*

418

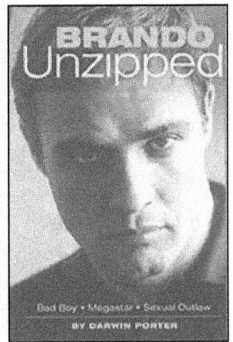

# and sadness

*(Continued from previous page)*

How do I know so much about Brando? I began meeting movie stars as a young boy when my mother was girl Friday to Sophie Tucker, the "last of the red hot mommas". But I started hearing Brando's dark secrets in my 20s when I was a neighbour and friend of Williams, the playwright and one of Brando's early seducers.

In the four decades since, I have been hearing further secrets from the actor's former lovers, friends, rivals and colleagues, and I have built up a body of notes that would fill several books. This is sourced material and a rare insight behind the screen that separates the real life of an idol from the fantasy that the world is forced to feed on.

To explain where all this began, I have to go back to the American Midwest in the '20s. Brando might never have become a screen legend were it not for a willowy, ash-blonde beauty called Dorothy Pennebaker Myers. Nicknamed Dodie, the daughter of a gold prospector who died when she was two, she experienced a chaotic childhood before entering into an even more chaotic marriage to an insecticide salesman called Marlon Brando Sr in Omaha, Nebraska.

From the beginning of her marriage and even after the birth of her three children, Dodie disdained child-rearing and housekeeping. She did not believe in heavy discipline for her children but preferred that they "discover their own true natures".

For young Brando, born in 1924, that often meant "running wild through the town, raising hell and causing trouble", in the words of a former Omaha neighbour, Casey Culler, who added: "The kid was a menace. The father was always on the road with one of his whores, the mother out drunk in some cheap motor court with someone's husband."

Once, to shame his parents about their excessive beer drinking, Brando placed all the empty bottles prominently in front of their Omaha home to shock the prohibition-supporting churchgoing neighbours.

Even so, he was very supportive of his mother throughout her alcoholic binges. After she broke her leg while driving drunk to a secret rendezvous with a lover, eight-year-old Brando told his older sister Jocelyn, "Dad drives her to drink."

When sober, Dodie was usually involved in a production at the semi-professional Omaha Community Playhouse, where she was both a producer and often the lead actress. Henry Fonda always thanked Dodie for launching him into acting. He remembered lying around his home one summer in Omaha, having dropped out of university. A call came in from Dodie offering him a juvenile lead. Although the play didn't run long, Hank stayed around.

Dodie fell in love with this shy young actor and seduced him. She promised to divorce Marlon Sr and marry Fonda right away. He turned her down but they maintained their liaison for years.

Brando's sisters left for New York and he followed them, aged 19, to study acting while supporting himself through odd jobs such as a lift operator. After discovering "too many lipstick collars" on her husband's white shirts, Dodie headed east, too. She rented a 10-room apartment on Manhattan's West Side and invited her children to move in with her. It quickly became an "open house" to many struggling actors of that day.

Bobby Lewis, a founder of the avant-garde Actors Studio, remembered: "People dropped in at all times of the day and night to the Brandos. Often they slept on her living-room floor. And yes, fornicated there as well."

Lewis heard a rumour that a drunken Dodie was picked up one night by two sailors and taken to a flophouse where she was repeatedly raped until Brando found out and went to rescue her.

"Through all the crap she put him through," close friend Ann Hastings said. "Marlon continued to worship his mother. He forgave her for everything. She worshipped him as well. She called him 'that acting genius that popped out of my womb'."

Hastings also reported that one afternoon when she dropped in on the Brandos, "I saw the strangest sight. Marlon was sitting in the sparsely furnished living room. He had on one of Dodie's street dresses and a pair of those Joan Crawford f----me shoes, as ankle-strap high heels were called in those days. He was fully made up, lipstick and all. He didn't seem at all embarrassed for me to see him dressed like that."

Hastings went on to claim that Dodie was indulging in sexual intercourse with her own son. This could be dismissed as nonsense were it not for some supporting testimony from Lewis, who said Dodie often slept in the same bed with her son.

He added: "One night while I was alone with Marlon and Dodie in their living room, listening to classical music, they seemed to have forgotten that I was there. Although she was wearing a housecoat, fully dressed, he snuggled into her breasts as part of a nursing ritual learnt long ago. In spite of her heavy drinking, Dodie always kept that special bond with her son. It was very Oedipal. A little too Oedipal for my tastes."

Also in those early times in New York there was Wally Cox, whom Brando had befriended in boyhood — when, with his horn-rimmed glasses and frail body, Cox was the type of little guy bigger boys "liked to beat the shit out of", in the words of a former classmate.

"Sometimes Marlon would protectively put his arm around Wally on the school grounds as if to signal to the bullies that he'd beat them up if they so much as laid a hand on Wally," recalled former classmate Eric Panken.

**Best actors:** Grace Kelly and Brando after they won the best-actor Oscars in 1955

*(Continued on next page)*

They were separated when Brando was sent away to military school but were reunited by chance years later in New York. Brando was trying in vain to persuade his sister Fran to get into a pushcart so he could race her through the traffic for fun. As if by magic, Cox suddenly appeared and got into the cart without protest. They disappeared into the traffic.

By the time Brando reappeared three days later, he had become "bonded at the hip for life," with his long-lost boyhood friend. He made skinny Cox copy the tight jeans and T-shirt that were already part of the Brando image.

Lewis recalled seeing a lot of Brando and Cox in those days. "those two attended parties together and everybody just assumed they were a couple." But Brando had also discovered his magnetism for women and took them to Cox's flat. "It was a hellhole," said Lewis.

"There was a nasty little bedroom to the side, a kitchen where no dish was ever washed, a living room with a battered sofa with the springs broken, and the most disgusting urine-stained mattress I'd ever seen in my life with nothing to cover it."

"Wally was obviously playing the role of the dutiful wife. But Marlon ould never commit to anyone, much less a man. He loved his women too much."

"As if to humiliate his friend, Marlon often brought his girlfriends over to Wally's apartment to screw them. He'd take over the bedroom, and make Wally sleep on that filthy mattress in the living room. Wally had to listen to the sounds of Marlon's love-making all night. It was sadistic, really."

Cox reacted to Brando's new set of rules by becoming a bit of a womaniser himself, and he married, twice. "But if Marlon called, Wally dropped whatever he was doing and came running, like a faithful puppy dog to his master," said Lewis. "I think that Wally continued to love Marlon until he drew his last breath."

The other significant person to enter Brando's life during his early years in New York was **Marilyn Monroe**. He mentioned fleetingly in his own memoirs that he "first met her briefly shortly after the war," but in all of the many exhaustive reports on their lives, virtually no light has been shed on this historic first encounter between the future god and goddess. The only insider to offer a clue is **Carlo Fiore**, a Brooklyn Sicilian who became Brando's close friend at drama school Brando told

**(This text continues below, beneath the photo of Wally Cox.)**

Long-time lover: TV personality Wally Cox

## BRANDO'S LOVES

■ Wally Cox, Burt Lancaster, Laurence Olivier, John Gielgud, Marilyn Monroe, Marlene Dietrich, Grace Kelly, Rita Hayworth, Leonard Bernstein, Noel Coward, Shelley Winters, Ava Gardner, Gloria Vanderbilt, Tyrone Power, Hedy Lamarr, Anna Magnani, Montgomery Clift, James Dean, Tallulah Bankhead, Ingrid Bergman, Edith Piaf, Doris Duke, Rock Hudson and Tennessee Williams, among others

**Brando** first met Monroe at a bar in New York city in 1946. According to Fiore, he offered her $US15 to go back to his rented room, where he claimed they made love all night. In the morning Monroe was gone.

Was Marilyn Monroe, for a brief period in 1946, hustling in New York City? It appears entirely possible.

"With me, Marlon didn't have to fantasise about encounters with broads," Fiore said. "I could see it taking place right in front of my eyes. Often it was my broad he was scoring with. Long before he became famous he was ploughing such big names as Marlene Dietrich. Why not Marilyn? When he told me he'd screwed Marilyn in 1946, I found him completely believable. Still do."

Lena Pepitone, Monroe's maid in later life, also revealed that the star had admitted to turning tricks for $US15 "pocket money" in the '40s. Monroe herself said she had worked as a hooker on the back streets of Hollywood but "I never took money. I only did it for food. Once I connected with a man, I'd negotiate for breakfast, lunch or dinner, depending on the time of day".

Brando next met her some years later when both were rising stars. Details are sketchy but afterwards Brando told both Fiore and film director Fred Zinnemann the same story.

Brando said he was waiting in his car outside a Los Angeles apartment building when a beautiful woman came out and apparently mistook him for her date for the evening. She peered inside the car.

"You're not Sammy," she said, stepping back. "But you look familiar. You're Marlon Brando!"

"And who might you be?" Brando asked. "Do I know you?"

"You don't recognise me with my new hair colour," she said. "I'm Norma Jean, but now I'm known as Marilyn Monroe. You don't remember the time we got together in New York and you invited me back to your place?"

"That could fit a thousand encounters," he said. "Get in the car. Perhaps you can do something to me to joggle my memory."

She wiggled into the passenger's seat and reached over to him as he drove off to his apartment. "I practically had three accidents before we got there," Brando told Zinnemann. "Since that night in New York someone had been teaching Marilyn new tricks. Maybe a lot of someones."

The next morning, Monroe lingered over breakfast and stayed with Brando "for a matinee performance". Brando kept Zinnemann up to date about the affair. He once told his director: "Marilyn's studio is claiming her bust measurement is 37. However, Marilyn herself disputes that. She says her bust measurement is 38. As for me, I have a built-in tape measure in my brain. I'm never wrong about these things. I'd put her bust at 35, and I should know!"

The affair would stop and start again, heating up in the mid-1950s but never completely disappearing until her mysterious death in 1962.

"He was privy to her secrets and often gave her very good advice," Fiore said. "She never seemed to heed Marlon's words but continued to call him for guidance she rarely followed."

Perhaps the most surprising discovery about Brando's early relationships comes from Paris. He and the teenage Brigitte Bardot spurned each other when introduced by her lover, Roger Vadim.

"Brigitte was not at all dazzled by Marlon's physique and he found her charming but no more than that," said Vadim. Yet Brando found Coco Chanel, the ageing couturier, "the single most fascinating woman I've ever met", and he seduced the tiny middle-aged singer Edith Piaf.

Not that the conquest of Piaf was easy, as Brando later told Jacques Viale, a young actor whom he also seduced. When she took him back to her apartment after lunch he made the mistake of assuming she had seduction on her mind, slipped off all his clothes and crawled into her bed.

She chased him naked from the apartment and slammed the door — opening it to throw out his blue jeans but not his T-shirt or shoes.

"I felt she definitely wanted to sample my noble tool," he told Viale. "But she must have some mating ritual, the niceties with which I'm not familiar. I didn't play it right."

The next day, however, she sang *La Vie En Rose* down the telephone to him as an apology. And that night she dressed in rags and took him to Pigalle to sing incognito on the streets, as she had done before becoming famous. Brando held the cap to collect coins. They arrived home drunk at 6am and Brando put her chastely to bed.

The following night she invited him and seven nightclub dancers from the Lido to her apartment. Brando hoped for an orgy; he told Viale. But before dawn Piaf ushered the girls out of the door and invited Brando to share her bed and her small, frail body.

"She was still asleep when I left her bed in the late morning. She looked deathly pale. In fact, she didn't even seem to be breathing."

Friends say women gradually became more important to Brando than men. "As he grew older, it appears that he led more or less a straight life ... but with Marlon, you could never be sure," said Lewis.

Copyright Darwin Porter 2006. Adapted from *Brando Unzipped* by Darwin Porter, published by Blood Moon.

Burt Lancaster

Ava Gardner

Montgomery Clift

Ingrid Bergman

James Dean

Hedy Lamarr

Rock Hudson

Marilyn Monroe

Marlene Dietrich

> **Wally was obviously playing the role of the dutiful wife. But Marlon could never commit to anyone, much less a man. He loved his women too much**
>
> Bobby Lewis, Actors Studio Founder

420

Published in Sydney, **The Australian Women's Weekly** (aka "*The Weekly*"), rivaled only by *Better Homes and Gardens*, is Australia's most read magazine.

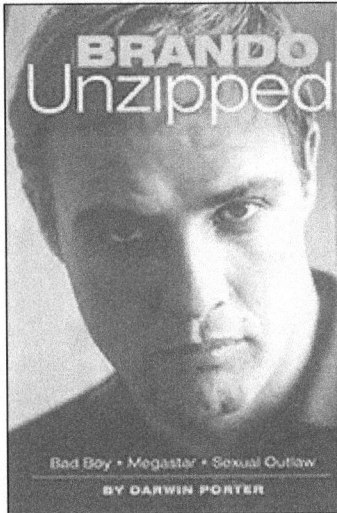

# brando's little **black** book

IN THE '50S, MARLON BRANDO BECAME THE PERSONIFICATION OF MALE SEX APPEAL-AN ATTRACTION THE YOUNG ACTOR EXPLOITED TO THE FULL. NOW A SHOCKING NEW BIOGRAPHY, **BRANDO UNZIPPED,** REVEALS WHICH CELEBRITIES OF THE DAY—WOMEN AND MEN—THE CHARISMATIC PHILANDERER BEDDED.

**KAREN MOLINE REPORTS.**

"The charismatic, talented, and very beautiful young Brando at the height of his career. He attracted—and was attracted to—both men and women "

THERE HAS NEVER BEEN AN ACTOR like Marlon Brando. Impassioned, iconoclastic, imaginative, impulsive, indomitable and, most of all, impossibly attractive. How well he knew it!

In an astonishing new biography, *Marlon Brando Unzipped*, veteran Hollywood reporter Darwin Porter paints an extraordinarily detailed portrait of Brando, particularly about his early years, that is as blunt, uncompromising and X-rated as the man himself.

"I don't think I was constructed to be monogamous," Brando once declared. "I don't think it's in the nature of *any* man to be monogamous. Sex is the primal force of our and every other species."

From a starving young "wannabe" who jumped off a train from Nebraska headlong into New York's theatre scene, the sexually charged Brando became, within a few scant years, one of the greatest performers ever - "lightning on legs," he was called by critics in 1947 as he strode

onto the stage as Stanley Kowalski in *A Streetcar Named Desire*, and changed acting forever.

For many, it is nearly impossible to remember the man decades before the tragedies of Brando's personal life overshadowed his early accomplishments. After three tempestuous marriages and countless other relationships that produced 11 children (five from his wives; three from his former maid; one adopted; two from affairs), the fiercely private Brando was shocked and grief-stricken after his son Christian killed the fiancé of his troubled daughter, Cheyenne, in 1990. He blamed himself for Cheyenne's lifelong unhappiness and never recovered from her suicide by hanging in 1995.

It is nearly impossible to explain to those who have only seen Brando as *The Godfather* in 1972, or as a bloated behemoth in his last films, how his uninhibited carnality and skin-tight jeans shocked and astonished audiences in  »»

421

the late '40s and early '50s. He was the living, breathing embodiment of sexual desire in an era when movie censors even forbade the word "virgin" on-screen.

No one who swooned for Brando in his early years would have dreamed that he would end his days as an obese recluse in his home in the Hollywood Hills, before dying at age 80 of congestive heart and lung failure on July 1, 2004.

While in his final years, Brando replaced his voracious appetite for sex with food, in his heyday, he wielded what he happily called his "noble tool" with deliberate impunity. Women (and a fair share of men) literally fell at his feet.

The list of his lovers was a who's who of Hollywood and society: one-night stands and brief relationships with Marlene Dietrich, Grace Kelly, Jacqueline Kennedy (who claimed, "Marlon is one of the most interesting men I've ever met"), Ingrid Bergman, Gore Vidal, Leonard Bernstein, Ursula Andress, Edith Piaf, Joan Collins, Faye Dunaway, Bianca Jagger, Kim Stanley, Veronica Lake, Hedy Lamarr, Joan Crawford, Bette Davis (Her first words to him were, "I've done everything a woman can do in life, but meet Mr Marlon Brando"), Jean Peters, Gloria Vanderbilt, Doris Duke (then the richest woman in the world), John Gielgud, Burt Lancaster (originally intended to play Stanley in Streetcar), even (allegedly) Princess Margaret, and hundreds if not thousands of other players.

Perhaps Brando's "noble tool" provided some measure of oblivion; perhaps he was merely a sex addict. After all, he did say, "All my life I've never been interested in someone else's sex life — only my own. My noble tool has performed its duties through thick and thin without fail!"

He was only half-joking, as ever hiding his true feelings behind bluster and a blunt façade. "I put on an act sometimes, and people think I'm insensitive," he admitted. "Really, it's like a kind of armour because I'm too sensitive. If there are 200 people in a room and one of them doesn't like me, I've got to get out."

The great tragedy of his life was that Brando did doubt himself, and he never seemed to have been able to come to terms with his unparalleled gift for acting, often belittling himself and suffering debilitating depression.

He was, according to Darwin Porter, suicidal after his mother, Dorothy, died of acute alcoholism in 1954. His grief was so deep that he didn't bathe or eat for weeks, veering wildly between praising his mother and blaming her for what he considered to be the "mess" of his life.

"It's because of her that I have never been able to commit to another woman," he bitterly claimed.

"Marlon has a very, very dark side," his best friend and confidant, actor Wally Cox, once said. "Sometimes he can go for months and repress that side of him. But sometimes it comes out."

Raised by a cruel bully of a father and an alcoholic passive/aggressive mother, who doted on him and shared his bed — whether sexually or not is a matter of conjecture — it's hardly surprising that Brando was a mass of contradictions.

He was nakedly (in every sense of the word) ambitious while intensely ambivalent about his profession; determined to fully reap the benefits of stardom while craving privacy; staggeringly promiscuous, yet willing to marry several of his girlfriends when they became pregnant; hostile to the press, yet deeply hurt by cutting reviews; profoundly egomaniacal, yet generous and steadfast in his willingness to help the underdog in a wide variety of charities and causes; a loyal friend to his inner circle, yet stunningly disdainful, if not cruel, to those who fell out of favour.

B rando was at ease in his own skin long before even partial nudity was fashionable, and he was often quite the exhibitionist. Early in his career, he was appearing in the Jean Cocteau play, The Eagle Has Two Heads, opposite the theatre's grande dame and great eccentric, the alcoholic and equally sexually ravenous Tallulah Bankhead. By the time the play was about to preview in Boston, Tallulah and Marlon knew the play was going to be a flop, calling it The Turkey with Two Heads. On opening night, Brando showed his disdain for the production during one of Tallulah's long, dramatic monologues. He turned his back to the audience, unbuttoned his fly, and proceeded to urinate against the scenery. The audience could clearly see what he was doing. When she found out what Brando had done, Tallulah had him fired.

After that, Brando was lucky his talent was so immense producers took a chance on him anyway. But he was too much the prankster to care. When his first film, The Men was trounced by critics, Brando took the train back from Hollywood to New York, displaying his buttocks through the window at railway stops all the way across America. "I made an arse of myself in The Men, so before America sees it, I wanted them to look up close and personal at the real thing," he said. >>>

"I've never been interested in someone else's sex life — only my own."

From top: Brando, Julie Harris and James Dean on the set of East of Eden; Marilyn Monroe and Brando enjoyed a sexual friendship; Brando with Vivien Leigh in a scene from A Streetcar Named Desire, where they met. Later, they became lovers.

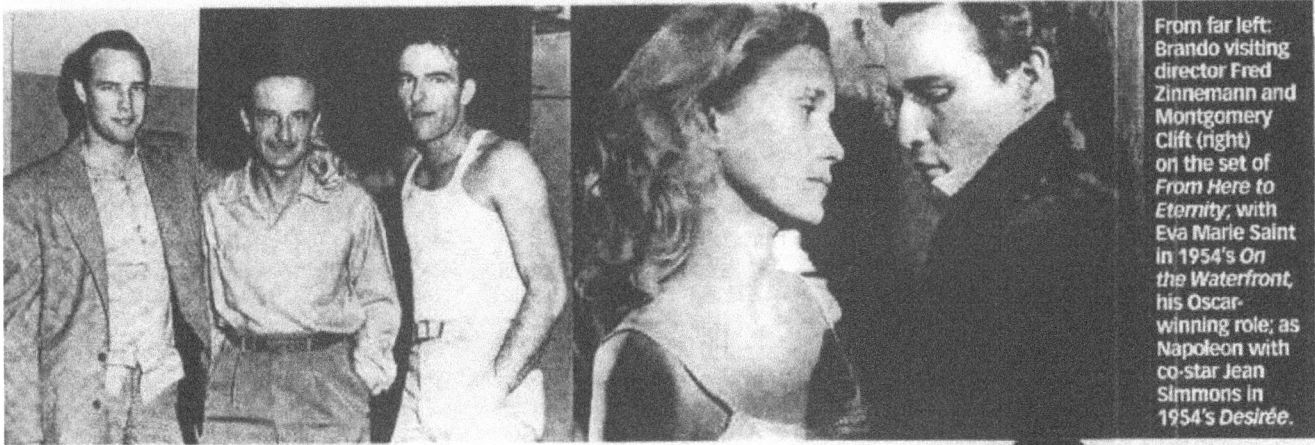

From far left: Brando visiting director Fred Zinnemann and Montgomery Clift (right) on the set of *From Here to Eternity*; with Eva Marie Saint in 1954's *On the Waterfront*, his Oscar-winning role; as Napoleon with co-star Jean Simmons in 1954's *Desirée*.

Several years later, he took a girlfriend to a screening of *The Wild One*. Ever his own worst critic, he couldn't bear to watch himself. Before running out, he shouted at the audience, "Look at Marlon Brando's fat arse!"

Brando was also an equal opportunity lover. Perhaps most surprising is his casual bisexuality, switching easily as he did between male and female lovers with equal ardour. *Streetcar* co-star and lifelong friend Kim Hunter said, "Marlon told me some of his deepest, darkest secrets, including his fear of being forever a mama's boy." Marlon also told her that after a particularly intense affair with a man, he'd go crazily promiscuous: "screwing every girl who will go to bed with me — and very few of them say no."

His agent, Edith Van Cleve, explained Brando's penchant for going after men: "Instead of being hostile to actors with whom he was competing, Marlon tried to seduce them," she said. "It was as if the act of seduction gave him the edge. Take poor Monty [Montgomery] Clift, for instance. Instead of being leery of Monty, Brando overpowered him sexually. At any rate, when I combed all of New York for Brando to tell him he was on again for the part of Stanley, he was screwing Burt Lancaster. If I had been a man, I too would have wanted to screw Burt Lancaster."

"I have guilt about sleeping with men, and, almost to atone for it, I go in the opposite direction," Brando claimed. "The more the merrier. That way, I manage to convince myself I'm a bona fide heterosexual, until the queer side of me comes out again."

As well as countless casual encounters, Brando had much more complicated relationships with Rita Moreno (whom many said was the one woman he should have married and didn't); Tyrone Power; Burt Lancaster's lover Shelley Winters; playwright Tennessee Williams and actor

Montgomery Clift, his great rival. Privately, he called Clift "Princess Tiny Meat."

"Their friendship — dare I call it an affair? — was brief and intense," his acting teacher Stella Adler said. "So intense that it was destined to burn out quickly. It was rivalry that tore them apart. They were both the two young geniuses of 1940s Broadway and later the two young geniuses of Hollywood."

Years later, Brando told Clift's dearest friend, Elizabeth Taylor, "Your friend Monty and I were alike in only one regard. Both of us had desperate hopes and nursed unspeakable desires."

Brando's heart often seemed to beat in many places at once. Elia Kazan was blunt: "During the months he appeared under my direction as Stanley Kowalski, Marlon was a sex machine. He became a phallic dream for both gay men and thousands of female theater-goers. Later he would become the wet dream for millions of film fans around the world. He was, in essence, the male sex symbol of the '50s, with Marilyn Monroe wearing the crown for women."

Kazan ought to know. According to Darwin Porter, Brando had first met Marilyn Monroe at a bar in New York in 1946, when she was so strapped for cash that she was turning tricks in-between modeling gigs.

"I wouldn't call her a rising starlet," Brando said, when she came to "entertain" him several years later in Hollywood. "Seems to me she spends more time on her back."

Yet they became great friends, more than occasional lovers, and confidantes, sharing the same intense drive. "I know a lot of gals arrive in Hollywood dreaming of becoming a movie star," Marilyn told him. "But I have one up on them. I can dream harder than they can."

They were also sexual kindred spirits, for Marilyn was a lot more complicated and pragmatic than the vulnerable girly-girl of legend.

"A girl should use sex like a weapon,"

"He was, in essence, the male sex symbol of the '50s ..."

she told Brando with characteristic candour. "I think this is the only way a girl can get ahead in a town ruled by men."

Over the years, she and Brando stayed in touch, often falling into bed when the urge struck. When he was filming *Viva Zapata* in Mexico, Monroe showed up to visit director Elia Kazan, with whom she was having an affair. When Kazan's wife unexpectedly arrived, Monroe happily took to Brando's bed, which made his own affairs with co-stars Rita Moreno and Mexican actress Movita (who later became his second wife) a tad complicated.

Kazan later told Tennessee Williams that, on a lark, Brando and Monroe slipped away and got married under assumed names.

Brando obviously had no problem with adultery. He flatly denied having an affair with *Streetcar* co-star Vivien Leigh in >>>

423

his autobiography, *Songs My Mother Taught Me*, claiming that her husband, Sir Laurence Olivier, was such a "nice guy". In truth, however, he had already spent some time under the covers with the bisexual Olivier.

Like Monroe, Vivien Leigh was sexually uninhibited. She surprised Brando when she introduced herself by saying, "Her Ladyship is bored with formality."

Then she went on: "As you'll get to know me, and I hope you will, there is nothing respectable about me. In London, I pick up taxi drivers and have sex with them. Don't be surprised – I'm just as whorish as Blanche DuBois."

Director Kazan referred to the couple as the pairing of "a gazelle with a wild boar". The jungle did become a bit overcrowded during the filming of *Streetcar*, when Brando was invited to stay with the Oliviers in their Hollywood home. He spent nights playing musical beds, even though Olivier was then having a well-known affair with the actor/comedian Danny Kaye.

At one party, when Brando showed up on the arms of both Leigh and Olivier, Kaye, whose hair had been dyed a bright red for a film role, saw them and flipped. He slapped Brando full in the face.

Brando, who'd had no idea about Kaye's relationship with Olivier, merely said, "Like your hair colour."

Then he went back to the house and packed his bags, leaving a note for his hosts: "Dear Vivien and Larry," it read. "Thank you for your hospitality. You were both wonderful to me. But it is time to move on now and I'm heading back to New York to resume my life. My regret is never having gotten to know either of you. But, then, I have always depended upon the kindness of strangers."

One famous stranger he soon met was Cary Grant, with whom he had a brief relationship. "Spending some time with Cary Grant has convinced me of one thing," Brando said. "Of all the possibilities for me in all the world, I don't want to be a movie star."

Another was the young James Dean, who approached his idol after Brando gave a talk at the Actors Studio. The two spent quite a lot of time together in the winter of 1951.

"He was completely in charge of our lovemaking," Dean reportedly said. "He told me what he wanted and I went along for the ride."

Yet Dean quickly became obsessed, showing up unannounced at Brando's apartment, often spending the night outside in the cold, hoping to be let in.

Brando sometimes took pity on Dean – and sometimes ignored him completely.

Later, after he learned that James Dean had died, he commented: "The trouble with Jimmy is that he wanted to be me. I don't know why. Even I, myself, don't want to be me."

Finally, Brando got an Oscar for Best Actor in 1954 for his role in *On the Waterfront*. Later that night, he left a star-studded party. "I've got a date with a blonde," he said.

The blonde was Grace Kelly, that year's Best Actress Oscar winner for *The Country Girl*, who couldn't resist Brando's charms, even though she'd been having an affair with her co-star, Bing Crosby.

"What happened in Grace's suite around three o'clock that morning is still not known in exact detail, but Bing Crosby arrived for a showdown with Grace. Instead of that, he found a nude Marlon in her bed," Darwin Porter relates.

The affair was short-lived. Kelly went on to marry Prince Rainier, and Brando went on to make a string of less than stellar films. Although vowing never to wed, he nonetheless fell for Indian-born actress Anna Kashfi (her real name Joan O'Callaghan), marrying her in 1957 when she was pregnant with Christian.

"She was probably the most beautiful woman I've ever known, but she came close to being as negative a person as I have met in my life," Brando said.

*Viva Zapata* co-star, Movita (born Marie Casenada) became his second wife in 1960. "I think Movita is funny – she makes me laugh. She's also beautiful in her own kind of way, smart and very sympathetic to my problems, when I lay my head on her breast at night."

That union barely lasted two years. While filming *Mutiny on the Bounty* in Tahiti, Brando fell in love with the young and lovely Tarita Teriipaia, married her in 1962, and bought a private Tahitian island, which became his retreat from the pressures of Hollywood and his own tormented, contradictory nature.

Although Brando again astonished filmgoers when *The Godfather* and *Last Tango in Paris* became blockbuster hits in 1972 and 1973 respectively, his passion for acting gradually dissipated and his eccentricities became more pronounced.

After he died, his ashes were to be mixed with those of his best friend, Wally Cox, then scattered to the winds of the California desert. "Now we'll be united for eternity," Brando said.

Even in death, he had not wanted to be by himself. Still, the glory that was Brando in his prime will live on forever. ∎

## "The trouble with Jimmy is that he wanted to be me. I don't know why."

Top: Brando starred with his close friend Elizabeth Taylor in the 1967 film *Reflections in a Golden Eye*; (above) He met Tahitian actress Tarita Teriipaia when filming *Mutiny on the Bounty* in 1962. They fell in love and later married, living on a Tahitian island that Brando bought.

# An American Dionysus

## Brando's insatiable appetites unmasked

By Jack V. Booch

Darwin Porter's salacious *Brando Unzipped* is a book that delivers exactly what its title suggests: an intricately detailed description of stage and screen star Marlon Brando's sexual profligacy.

Page after page of documentation reveals Brando's propensity to engage anything with a pulse in sexual congress, and were it not for personal acquaintances in the theatrical world that have personally confirmed many of these astonishing accounts of sexual depravity for me, I could scarcely believe they were true.

But they are true. Brando apparently seduced just about everyone who ever got him a job on the stage or on film, co-starred with him, directed him, or wrote him a part.

Given the number of sexual encounters listed in *Brando Unzipped*, the real shocker is the number of exploits necessarily omitted for fear of litigation from those former partners who remain with the living.

Unfortunately, Porter is ultimately disinterested in exploding the myth of Brando's great acting skills, even as he conveys Brando's contempt for the craft of acting, his lack of discipline, and his disregard for artistic aims and ambitions in general.

Countless reports of Brando's uniformly awful auditions complement firsthand confessions from writers, directors, and producers who admit their sexual obsession with the actor. Nonetheless, Porter neglects to draw the obvious conclusion that Brando's true talents rested in his pants.

It comes as no surprise to me that the same actor who perpetrated the offenses against cinema that are *Teahouse of the August Moon* (1956), *One-Eyed Jacks* (1961),

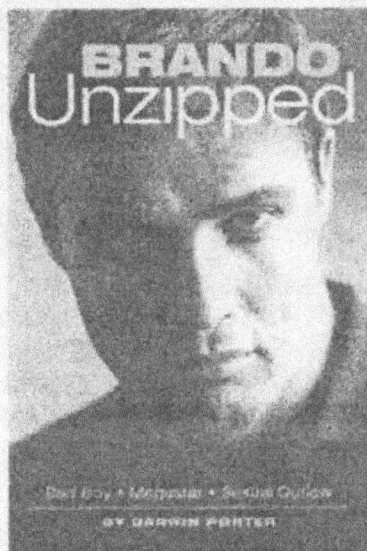

**BRANDO UNZIPPED**
Bad Boy, Megastar, Sexual Outlaw. *By Darwin Porter.*
*550 pp. Blood Moon Productions, Ltd*

*The Ugly American* (1963), etc., was totally undisciplined, totally dissipated, probably the victim of incest (according to one account in *Unzipped*), and just generally an indescribable mess.

Brando is remembered fondly—even by me—for what I would argue were his four best performances: *The Men* (1950), *A Streetcar Named Desire* (1951), *The Wild One* (1953), and *On the Waterfront* (1954). In *The Men*, Brando spent time in a paraplegic ward to get a firm grasp of his character—and his performance showed it. The other films in which he succeeded featured opportunities for him to explore aggrandized versions of who he was personally and what he wanted to become. In *The Wild Ones*, he was a rebel. In *On the Waterfront*, he played the part of populist hero. In *Streetcar*, he inhabited the persona—so familiar to him in life—of an animalistic brute.

But four good films out of an entire career don't make an actor legendary. Porter makes a case—whether inadvertently or on purpose—that Brando's legend is mainly derived from what the actor himself often referred to as his "noble member."

*Unzipped* is worth a look if you are interested in a cautionary tale about the many myths surrounding celebrity and the obfuscation of real talent in the entertainment industry. But what little evidence there is in the book of Brando's supposed great acting gifts indicates to me that he ultimately had none—outside the bedroom, that is. ▨

*Jack Booch is the former Executive Producer for the Theatre Guild, Inc., in Manhattan, and was the director of the Portland Civic Theatre from 1966 to 1969.*

# MARLON'S MEN

He was considered one of the most dynamic and imposing actors of his generation, but as author Darwin Porter finds, it wasn't just the acting world Marlon Brando conquered – it was the actors, too

Combative, moody, iconoclastic, polarising, impulsive, enigmatic – and a lot more – Marlon Brando died of lung failure in July, 2004, in LA. He was 80 years old. Throughout his long life, he was an equal-opportunity seducer, once claiming that he was "75% straight, 25% gay".

"I've had sex with men", Brando once confessed, "and I'm not ashamed. In fact, sexually, I'm willing to try anything twice". Brando's openness stood in contrast to the more closeted Cary Grant, with whom Marlon had a brief fling during his early days in Hollywood.

In skin-tight jeans, Brando was called "lightning on legs" when he walked onto a Broadway stage in New York in 1947 to electrify the world with his uninhibited carnality in the steamy Tennessee Williams play *A Streetcar Named Desire*. In the closing months of World War II, the playwright had seduced Brando on a moonlit beach in Provincetown, a gay resort at the tip of Cape Cod.

In the 40s and 50s, instead of feuding with rival actors, Brando often seduced them. Such was the case when handsome hunk Burt Lancaster flew to New York to audition for the role of Stanley. Burt didn't get the role, but spent the weekend in bed with Brando in a hotel suite.

Brando's years on Broadway were also the time of his greatest number of homosexual affairs. To the sound of the bongo drums, Brando, a Katherine Dunham "tribal dancer", often performed in the nude at private parties.

His longest-running affair was with the television actor Wally Cox, who starred in the 1950s' hit sitcom, *Mr Peepers*. These two roomies were known as "the odd couple".

Brando never pretended to be faithful to any one lover, male or female. Among countless others, he seduced some of the stellar lights of the British Empire; Laurence Olivier, Noël Coward, and Cecil Beaton. For Beaton, Brando posed for a series of classic nude studies.

It wasn't the classic Beaton photographs but a candid snapshot that would bring notoriety to Brando. On a dare, a drunken Brando, at a Greenwich Village party in 1952, allowed himself to be photographed while performing fellatio on Cox. The snapshot was reprinted and widely distributed throughout the gay underworld.

In Hollywood, where young Brando quickly became the male sex symbol of the 1950s, he continued his seductions, including Marilyn Monroe, Ava Gardner, Rita Hayworth, Grace Kelly and even starlet Nancy Davis (later Reagan). Among men, he seduced "the usual suspects", as Bogie might say. These included gay actor Rock Hudson and such bisexuals as Tyrone Power and Stewart Granger.

More enduring were his relationships with Montgomery Clift and James Dean, the other two "bad boys of Hollywood". Ironically, Clift and Dean were Brando's two chief rivals, often up for the same roles. "Marlon always did want to check on what the competition had hanging", said his best pal, Carlo Fiore.

Brando and Clift had become lovers when the "two male beauties", as they were called, were the most sought-after actors on Broadway. But in Hollywood, Brando grew disillusioned with Clift, as he plunged deeper into booze and pills. In later life, Brando contemptuously referred to Clift as "Princess Tiny Meat".

Meeting Dean at the Actors' Studio in New York, Brando found not only someone who worshipped him, but a virtual masochistic sex slave. Dean fell madly in love with Brando. "Marlon offered Jimmy sex, never love", Fiore claimed.

Like Clift, Dean, too, was on the road to self-destruction. Brando told Fiore that in the twilight of his life, Dean descended to cruising the gay meat racks of Hollywood Boulevard at night, patronising the shadowy world of leather-and-chain clubs. "He's an instant hit with the fist-fuck set", Brando told Fiore. "Jimmy will do stuff no other guy will". Like a promise unfulfilled, "The Rebel Without a Cause" (Brando turned down the classic role) died in a car crash on September 30th, 1955.

Beginning in the late 1940s, Brando made frequent trips to Paris, where he launched two of his most enduring love affairs with men, both handsome French matinee idols, Christian Marquand and Daniel Gélin. In French cinema, they were the Brad Pitt and Tom Cruise of their day, but Brando called them "my French froggies".

On his return to Hollywood, Brando continued a string of seductions, which included "half the chorus boys on the set of *Guys & Dolls*", according to Fiore. When making *Julius Caesar*, a film that starred Sir John Gielgud, among others, Brando took lessons in Shakespeare. He later told movie director Joseph Mankiewicz, that "to pay Sir John back for his lessons, I threw off my toga for him".

In perhaps the longest and most active love life of any other Hollywood actor, Brando once looked back on his successes in the boudoir with men and women: "I've never been circumcised, and my noble tool has performed its duties through thick and thin, without fail", he said.

Upon his cremation in 2004, Brando's ashes were mixed with those of Wally Cox's that he'd kept in an urn since his friend's death in 1973. The combined ashes were taken to California's Death Valley, where they were thrown to the winds. It had been Brando's wish to have his ashes "united for eternity" with those of his long-departed lover. ■

*Brando Unzipped by Darwin Porter, published by Blood Moon Productions, £17.99*

426

De Morgen

ONAFHANKELIJK DAGBLAD

WOENSDAG 12 APRIL 2006 · 28STE JAARGANG NR. 87 / 50 PAGINA'S

WEKELIJKSE LITERAIRE BIJLAGE VAN DE MORGEN                    WOENSDAG 12 APRIL 2006

DMBOEKEN

## Marlon Brando met de billen bloot

Marlon Brando, voor velen de grootste filmacteur van de twintigste eeuw,
is weer helemaal terug. De jongere generatie kan hem leren kennen via
een nieuwe game gebaseerd op *The Godfather* en een nieuwe biografie
verzamelde (vooral smeuige) getuigenissen over de legende.

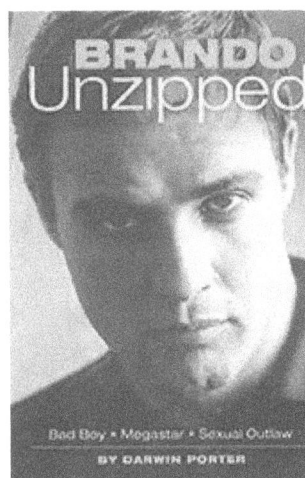

Darwin Porter
## De weg naar de top

Een filmcarrière
van Nazi-Berlijn tot Hollywood

MARLON BRANDO

MET DE BILLEN BLOOT

BRANDO Unzipped

Bad Boy · Megastar · Sexual Outlaw

BY DARWIN PORTER

---

De Morgen (aka *The Morning*) is a Flemish-language newspaper published in Antwerp, Belgium. The publication of their article (its banner headline is replicated above) coincided with the sale to **Houtekiet** (with offices in Antwerp and Amsterdam), by Blood Moon, of the Dutch-language publication rights.

The title they assigned their Dutch translation? "*Marlon Brando met de billen bloot*" (aka *Brando with his Buttocks Exposed.*) De Morgan's reviewer (**Hans Muys**) evaluated it as *"Lovers of the genre and admirers of Marlon Brando are well served by Darwin Porter."*

It was the second Dutch-language rights deal that Darwin had arranged in Holland. The first, *Marika (aka Der Weg Naar De Top)*, was a critically acclaimed *roman-à-clef* based on the life of Marlene Dietrich.

Blood Moon also sold *Brando Unzipped's* reprint rights to a publisher in France. T*heir cover design is replicated on the lower right, above)*. Also sold were the Portuguese-language reprint rights for distribution of the book in Portugal and Brazil.

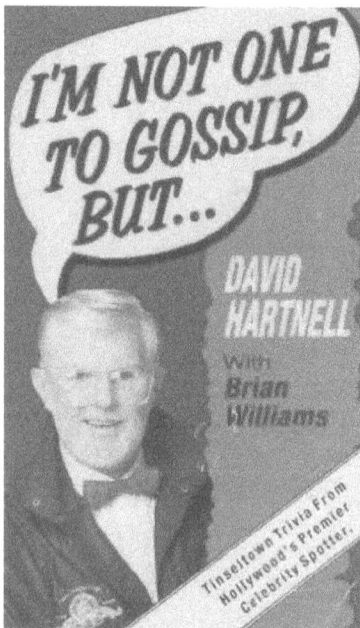
The book **Brando Unzipped** by Darwin Porter is a staggeringly good read—the definitive gossip guide to the Hollywood icon. At Brando's peak, his list of lovers included members of the world's pop and cultural elite: **Bob Dylan, Gore Vidal, Leonard Bernstein, Joan Collins, Faye Dunaway, Bianca Jagger, Kim Stanley** (then queen of Broadway), **Rita Moreno, Shelley Winters, Tyrone Power, Gloria Vanderbilt,** and **Jean Peters** (his co-star in *Viva Zapata!* and the unhappy mistress of **Howard Hughes**).

This book is entertainingly outrageous at every page turn. I can't recommend this **Brando Unzipped** enough. That's if you're even brave enough to read the intro. It's published by **Blood Moon Productions Ltd** in New York, and run by the delightful and wickedly witty **Danforth Prince**, who, along with **Darwin Porter**, is the co-author of *Hollywood Babylon, It's Back.* **This book is an absolute "Must Read"** for anyone interested in celebrity gossip.

—**David Hartnell,** www.grownups.co.nz

## THE SUNDAY TIMES

# NEWS REVIEW 5

TimesOnline.co.uk/newsreview

FEBRUARY 12, 2006

Hulton Getty

John Gielgud, right, and, Stewart Granger, left, were his lovers, but not Granger's wife Jean Simmons, centre

Brando claimed to have slept with Monroe when she was a hooker

Brando turns his charms on Carmen Miranda. Laurence Olivier, inset, was also his lover

428

1/30/2006: A new biography of **MARLON BRANDO** claims the actor slept his way through Hollywood with many of his leading male contemporaries. In **BRANDO UNZIPPED**, author **Darwin Porter** claims the bisexual *The Godfather* star had sexual liaisons with **James Dean, Cary Grant, Montgomery Clift**, and **Sir John Gielgud**, among others.

Porter writes, "**James Dean** was one of Brando's most lasting yet troubled gay relationships. They had a relationship for a number of yers, but it was always turbulent

"At one point, they had a big stand-up fight at a party in Santa Monica, California, witnessed by dozens of people.

"His affair with **Montgomery Clift** was a long and enduring relationship."

"Marlon had a bit of a fling with **Cary Grant**, spending a weekend with him in San Francisco. Cary was also pursuing the British actor **Stewart Granger**, who became another of Marlon's conquests.

"Marlon admired **John Gielgud**, but they didn't have a relationship. Rather, Brando performed favours for Gielgud and told friends, 'I owed it to him because he really helped me with lines in *Julius Caesar.*'

In his 1979 biography, *The Only Contender,* Brando, who was married three times, admitted his homosexuality.

He was quoted as saying, "Like a large number of men, I, too, have had homosexual experiences and I am not ashamed."

Brando was 80 when he died of lung disease in July, 2004.

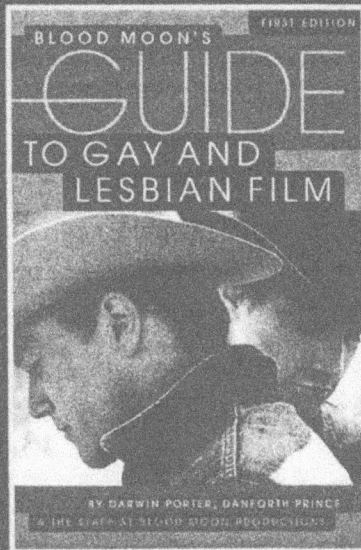

# MARLON BRANDO'S
# ROMANTIC ADVENTURES IN FRANCE

### By Danforth Prince for *Paris-Match*.
He formerly worked for the Paris Bureau of
*The New York Times*. Here is an English translation of his article.

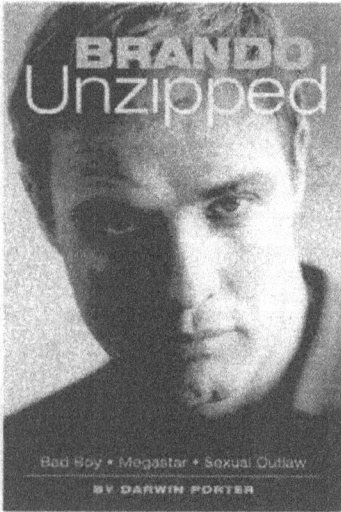

The late Marlon Brando, hailed as the greatest screen actor of the 20th century, spoke French and claimed France as "my second home." With the recent release of Darwin Porter's biography, BRANDO UNZIPPED, the actor's heretofore unknown life in Paris and on the Riviera is revealed for the first time.

In 1947, after the phenomenal success of his appearances on the New York stage as Stanley Kowalski in Tennessee Williams' *A Streetcar Named Desire*, Brando fled to Paris.

But despite his fame in New York, Brando, when he first arrived in Paris, was virtually unknown by the French, even within the top echelons of the theater world.

Brando as Fletcher Christian in *Mutiny on the Bounty,* with Tarita Teriipaia

Brando's passage to Paris was paid for by the French film director, Claude Autant-Lara, who wanted the new star to appear as the lead in his production of Stendahl's *Le rouge et le noir*. Sailing to France, Brando read the classic for the first time, planning to star in the role of its hero, Julien Sorel.

As Brando would later reveal, "In Paris, I embarked on the grandest sexual adventure of my life. I became one of the wild boys—I did everything, anything that was imaginable. I slept with a lot of women." What he didn't say, but which he might have said, "I also slept with a lot of French men."

The very liberal Brando later defined his benefactor, Autant-Lara, as a neo-Nazi. Their artistic union ended bitterly.

Brando moved briefly into the circles of expatriate Americans in Paris, and had encounters with his former lover, the black American novelist, James Baldwin, whom he had known back in New York during his debut as a actor.

*A Streetcar Named Desire*

Young Brando

But Brando soon tired of Paris' expatriate American community, and moved into "that fleabag," the Hotel d'Alsace, on Paris's Left Bank. Several decades previously, Oscar Wilde had died penniless and in disgrace at this seedy hotel.

On a chance encounter, while sitting on the terrace of La Coupole, Brando encountered that "wolf from the steppes," Roger Vadim, and his roommate, the handsome actor, Christian Marquand. On that very day, Brando moved in with them, sharing their cramped apartment. Brando and Marquand, both bisexual, would become "lovers for life." Eventually, Brando would even name his troubled son, Christian (later convicted of murder), in honor of Marquand. Marquand, a French matinee star, would eventually star in *And God Created Woman* with Brigitte Bardot.

Christian Marquand

When he met Brando, Vadim had just spent several days at the Hotel du Cap in Antibes, rooming with a young American from Massachussetts, John F. Kennedy.

Brando was soon seen wandering through Paris with his recently acquired friends, Marquand and Vadim. Soonafter, Vadim's new girlfriend, the very young and very beautiful Brigitte Bardot. joined them. The actress remembered one early dawn along the Champs Elysées when Brando acted out the entire script of *A Streetcar Named Desire* for them and for startled passersby on their way to the Metro.

BRANDO UNZIPPED is the first biography to offer details about the relationship between Brando and the elusive Ms. Bardot. For years, they were rumored to be lovers.

Roger Vadim at home with Brigitte Bardot

For several months, Brando shared a large apartment along quai d'Orléans with Marquand and Vadim. Soon. the three men acquired yet another roommate, the handsome French actor, Daniel Gélin, who was at the time separated from his wife, the French actress, Danièle Delorme. As with Christian Marquand, Brando would form a romantic involvement with Gélin that would last a lifetime. Like Marquand, Gélin was also a bisexual, and his friendship with Brando quickly blossomed into an affair.

Ironically, Brando would later star in his most controversial, and most pornographic publicly distributed film, *Last Tango in Paris*, with Gélin's illegitimate daughter, Maria Schneider.

Christian Brando (left) with his father, Marlon.

Accompanied by Vadim, Marquand, and Gélin, Brando was soon introduced to the most prestigious intellectual circles in France, socializing with Simone de Beauvoir, Jean-Paul Sartre, Boris Vian, and Juliette Gréco. Of that group, only Sartre was contemptuous of the rising young star, claiming, "I have no interest in American actors."

Not all of Brando's escapades in Paris were sexual. "He was a wild man," according to Vadim. "Completely out of control." He cited "egg fights" that Brando and Vian would stage with each other at the Café de Flor. One night, when an egg hit

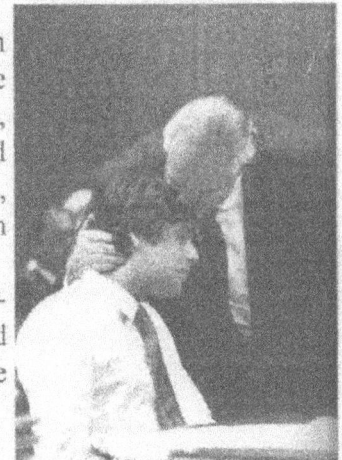
Daniel Gélin

431

Sartre in the head, the writer had both Brando and Vian barred from his favorite literary hangout.

Even so, Brando retained fond memories of The Flor, claiming that it "was the best place in Paris to take advantage of the first rays of the sun after a night of hell-raising on the town."

Juliette Gréco

"Marlon had Christian for love in the afternoon and Daniel at night, with lots of beautiful women on the side, each of them picked up and randomly discarded, whereas both Christian and Daniel stayed around almost until the end." These were the words of Jacques Viale, a close friend of Brando's in Paris.

Daniel referred to the chanteuse, Juliette Gréco, as "my cellar friend," a reference to the fact that they often met in Left Bank nightclubs or boîtes. Brando was immediately entranced by the beautiful brunette, and ardently pursued her. Night after night he showed up at the jazz club, Le Tabou, to hear Juliette, the darling of Left Bank café society, sing. Brando, according to some of his friends, finally won Juliette one night when he climbed over the wall of her apartment building. Back in Hollywood, Juliette's recording of *Je suis comme je suis* was played over and over by Brando, who reveled in its haunting, evocative sound.

BRANDO UNZIPPED relates how both Daniel Gélin, who had played the tom-toms in the film, *Rendez-vous de juillet*, and Brando, who played the drums, entertained audiences in Left Bank boîtes late at night. Brando would later recall that these appearances as an entertainer in Paris were "the most exciting moment of my life," far more so than appearing in *A Streetcar Named Desire* on Broadway.

Night after night, Brando was seen smoking marijuana with the American jazz trumpet player, Miles Davis, and he always stayed up to watch dawn break over the Paris skyline before heading back to Vadim's apartment to sleep the day away.

While in Paris, Brando became involved with Hervé Mille, the editorial director of *Paris-Match*. To Brando, Mille and his brother, Gérard, one of the leading interior decorators of Europe, were the epitome of French taste, charm, and style. Hervé, in fact, was called "the Richelieu of Jean Prouvost," a reference to the French press lord and wool magnate who owned *Paris-Match*.

The Mille brothers, both of whom were intrigued with the handsome, sexy young American actor, introduced Brando to their collection of friends, members of le tout Paris, including Charles Aznavour, Edith Piaf, and Coco Chanel.

Coco Chanel

Marquand, referred to as "the sexiest man in France," and Brando, hailed as "the sexiest man in America," enjoyed free run of the elegant Mille family townhouse on rue de Varenne, which soon became the setting for many of their sexual and emotional adventures. It was here that the Mille brothers had lunches or dinner parties, as he proudly presented Brando to some of the leading French artists and designers of the late 1940s. Bardot and Vadim were often in attendance.

For her luncheon with Brando, Madame Chanel showed up in a pair of blue jeans, in honor of the trademark wardrobe of the fast-rising star from America. They formed a flirtatious bond, even though they were the most unlikely of couples. He admired her independence and her sharp tongue. She referred to him as, "mon petit indien," a reference to his origins on the Great Plains of America's Middle West (i.e., Nebraska). She promised to design men's clothing especially for him, and attacked her rival male designers in Paris, referring to them as "pederasts."

432

She delivered to Brando her candid assessment of the wardrobes worn by the wives of American presidents, speaking disparagingly of the outfits selected by Eleanor Roosevelt and Bess Truman. Year later, she amplified her negative assessment of the wardrobes worn by America's First Ladies, with a critical assessment of Jacqueline Kennedy: "She wears her daughter's clothes."

Edith Piaf

During their meeting, an invitation arrived for Chanel for a luncheon with Charles de Gaulle. She instructed de Gaulle's messenger to tell the President of the French Republic, "The only invitation I'll accept is to your funeral."

Brando later told friends that *La Grande Mademoiselle* was the most fascinating woman he'd ever met.

His relationship with Chanel remained flirtatious but distant. With Edith Piaf, however, it turned into a brief but turbulent affair. He was mesmerized by Piaf, even though "the little sparrow" feared that her "pale face and mousy hair" were no match for the glamorous women Brando was accompanying around Paris— women who included Chanel, Bardot, and Juliette Gréco.

Long before Brando played Napoléon in the 1954 film *Désirée*, Piaf became convinced that he had been Napoléon in a former lifetime. His first attempt to seduce Piaf failed, but he eventually succeeded. He loved hearing her sing *La Vie en rose* only to him. On one occasion, she dressed herself in rags and took him with her to the streets around Pigalle, where she sang on the sidewalk, accepting donations, as she had during her early days. One French woman, thinking she was a Piaf impersonator, gave her a franc, but warned her that, "You don't have the voice of the real Piaf."

Brando accompanied Piaf on many of her nocturnal adventures, including a visit to The Lido, where they invited the long-legged and sexy showgirls back to her apartment to—of all things—"cook pommes frites."

Before going to bed with Brando, Piaf issued a warning to him. She had the impression that all American men thought that all French women are prostitutes, expecting them to do "all those nasty things their wives back home won't do for them." She told him, "I'm not a pervert. I believe in hygienic love. If you want dirty love, get yourself a whore."

Early in the 1950s, Hervé Mille acquired the rights to produce a French-language version of *A Streetcar Named Desire*, hiring Jean Cocteau to stage the production. Brando had already appeared in a play by Cocteau presented in the United States. *The Eagle Has Two Heads* starred the legendary but notorious American actress, Tallulah Bankhead. Brando had been fired from the play because he'd urinated against the stage scenery during a performance, as Bankhead delivered a 20-minute monologue written by Cocteau.

Tallulah Bankhead

The Mille brothers were urging Brando to repeat his Broadway role as Stanley Kowalski in the Paris production. Although not entirely proficient in French, he spoke, in the words of his friends, with a perfect French accent. "You speak as if you're a Parisian," Piaf told him.

For the co-starring role of Blanche DuBois, Hervé Mille had hired the notorious French actress, Arletty.

Jean Cocteau

When the Mille brothers arranged a first meeting between Brando and Cocteau, Cocteau was mesmerized by the handsome young star. He invited Brando to his country home at Milly in the Île de France, a place where, reputedly, Joan of Arc had once spent the night. Brando was intrigued by Cocteau's mind, not his fakir-thin body. Cocteau, however, was definitely intrigued by Brando's body, even though at the time he was living with a handsome Italian/Yugoslav, Edouard Dermithe, whom he affectionately referred to as "Doudou."

Doudou later painted Brando's portrait, for which Brando posed nude in Cocteau's garden, and the three men temporarily bonded into a dysfunctional ménage à trios. Cocteau promised to choreograph a ballet for Brando, to be presented in Paris, and he warned Brando that he'd have to dance nude in the final scene.

Ever since 1945, Brando had been intrigued by Marcel Carné's film, *Les Enfants du paradis*, which had starred the beautiful but controversial film star Arletty. Cocteau told Brando that Arletty was "the most beautiful woman ever captured on film." Brando was eager to meet her. At the time, Arletty was struggling to regain her reputation after having been charged with Nazi collaboration during the occupation, several years previously, of France. Despite her many comedic victories on stage, the most memorable line she ever uttered was in front of a French judge. When questioned in court about her widely publicized association with the Nazis, she said, publicly, "My heart is French, but my arse is international."

Brando rejected the opportunity to repeat his role of Stanley, in French, on the Paris stage, but he attended the production's first performance, and later stated that Arletty gave a "more authentic performance than that of Jessica Tandy" in the American original.

Backstage, at the time of their first meeting, Arletty was horrified by Brando's "dirty, smelly" appearance, and dismissed him. Diplomatically, Cocteau intervened and arranged a second meeting. Brando "cleaned himself up" for this second meeting, wearing a jacket and necktie. Arletty, relenting, became mesmerized by this handsome, virile American, and invited him to spend a night in her boudoir. Soon, she was introducing him as "my new protégé," and having French tailors design suits for him. Temporarily, at least, he became her "kept boy," but her emotional demands, coupled with Brando's legendary sense of independence, sometimes clashed, publicly.

One morning, Arletty awoke to find that her young lover had disappeared. Abandoning Paris, Brando, along with Christian Marquand, headed for a series of new and different adventures in Rome, many of which are described in BRANDO UNZIPPED.

\*\*\*

After his Italian sojourn, Brando arrived back in Paris with only ten francs in his pocket. In a move that surprised many, he did not call upon his prosperous, well-connected new friends, many of whom would have gladly housed him. Instead, he impulsively decided to live under bridges

Arletty

and on the streets with the *clochards* of Paris. At night, he ventured out with this motley crew onto the streets, searching for scraps of food in the alleyways behind restaurants.

It was during one such nightly jaunt, in one of the surprise coincidences of his life, that Brando spotted his agent, Maynard Morris, who had been sent from Hollywood specifically to find and retrieve him. Unable to find him, despite having scoured Paris for many days previously, Maynard had planned to sail to America the following day. Maynard's itinerary changed soon after he accidentally ran into Brando during Maynard's final nighttime walk along the Seine.

Maynard immediately installed Brando in a Left Bank hotel, fed him in a bistro, lent him money, and provided a one-way ticket back to America. Director Fred Zinneman wanted Brando to star in *The Men*, to be shot within a few weeks in Hollywood. Thus, from an unlikely setting among the beggars of Paris, Brando was launched into one of the most spectacular screen careers of all time.

Brando with Josanne Mariana-Berenger

In the years that followed, interspersed with his many successes in Hollywood, Brando returned to Paris again and again. One of his visits became the subject of international headlines. He'd met and had fallen in love with a French actress, Josanne Mariana-Berenger, whose mother and stepfather (a fisherman) lived in the hamlet of Bandol, along the French Riviera. Members of the French paparazzi followed the romantic couple to Paris, and French newspapers blared headlines announcing their impending marriage. "Half of the press of the world" descended on Bandol, hoping to report stories about the romance. The intensity increased after Josanne's parents announced the news of their engagement.

Then, French reporters discovered that the bride-to-be had posed nude for a Polish artist at the age of seventeen. Soonafter, a major department store in Paris devoted one of its display windows to replicas of these nudes, causing a near-riot among Parisian shoppers.

During the most intense of the publicity generated by these developments, Brando sent Josanne to Paris, while he remained on the Riviera. Friends later confirmed that the American actor "got to know a few olive-skinned provençal boys" before his return to Hollywood.

His romance with Josanne eventually flickered out, although he remained friends with her for several years after, even returning to Bandol on occasion to visit with her and her parents.

BRNDO UNZIPPED reveals the heretofore brief affair between Brando and the woman who would soon become Princess Grace of Monaco, Grace Kelly. They had originally met on the night of the Oscars in Hollywood, when she'd won for her role in *The Country Girl* and he'd walked off with the Best Actor award for his role in *On the Waterfront*.

Even when the regal blonde reigned with her husband, Prince Rainier, over her little kingdom in southeastern France, Brando visited the princess on at least two occasions for "secret weekends" at secluded hideaways on the Côte d'Azur.

BRANDO UNZIPPED also contains revelations about Brando's escapades during his enactment of Napoléon in *Désirée*. Years later, he asserted that his casting as Napoléon was "a sick joke on me."

Grace Kelly

Brando, in *Desiree*,
playing Napoleon.

Even his director, Henry Koster, agreed. "Brando simply didn't have it in him to play Napoléon. Stanley Kowalski was no Bonaparte, not even a distant cousin."

As related in Porter's book, a real emperor, Haile Selassie of Ethiopia, showed up on the set of *Désirée* to meet the *faux* emperor of France, Brando. The meeting between the two men was a disaster. Brando's single chest medal, part of his costume, contrasted markedly with Selassie's "chest of medals." On that day, Brando grabbed a fire hose and shot streams of water over the sets and the hundreds of extras, each expensively outfitted in silk and brocaded costumes that evoked the fashions of France in the early 1800s. The loss to the studio was astronomical.

After filming, Koster told reporters, "It's too bad that Désirée wasn't shot back in the 1930s. Then I could have cast Charles Boyer, and he would have pulled off the role."

Brando (left) as a Nazi in
*The Young Lions*

After another stint in Hollywood, Brando returned to Paris to shoot *The Young Lions*, directed by Edward Dmytryk and released in 1958. His costar was Montgomery Clift, Brando's one-time lover from his Broadway years in the 1940s. The many disasters that evolved behind the scenes are detailed in *Brando Unzipped*. One of them involved the nearly complete emotional breakdown of the mentally troubled Montgomery Clift. During one particularly disastrous moment of that filming, Brando had to rescue a deeply drugged Clift, who was being repeatedly sodomized in the back of a gay bar in Paris.

Tennessee Williams

Back in Paris, Brando resumed his relationships with Christian Marquand and Daniel Gélin. But he caused a near-riot when, dressed in the Nazi uniform he was assigned for his role in *The Young Lions*, he marched imperially down the Champs-Elysées. Horrified, an elderly French woman spat on him.

During the course of the filming, Brando became involved with Liliane Montevecchi, a prima donna from Roland Petit's ballet company. She had been cast as a French prostitute in the film. Regrettably, she accidentally scalded Brando's genitals with a pot of hot water during teatime at the Hotel Prince de Galles. Brando was hospitalized for a time during his recovery from that accident.

Bernardo Bertolucci

When *The Young Lions* eventually opened in Paris, French critics denounced it as "an on-screen boxing match" between Brando and Clift.

Brando returned once again to Paris to shoot his most controversial film, *Last Tango in Paris*, released in 1972 and directed by Bernardo Bertolucci. Brando appeared opposite the outspoken Maria Schneider, who claimed that she got along with the American actor "because we are both bisexual."

Brando, with Maria Schneider, performing their *Tango*

At one point, Brando agreed to appear frontally nude in *Tango*, but the scene was cut from the final print. The news that Brando was appearing in a porno film was broadcast first by the French press, and later made headlines around the world.

Bertolucci told Brando that the film was "about the reincarnation of your prick." The relationship between Brando and Schneider was described as "a flying fuck on a rolling doughnut." All of Paris buzzed with the "news" that Brando and Schneider were engaged in a torrid romance, in spite of the fact that she was Daniel Gélin's daughter. When Tennessee Williams saw the film at its premiere in Paris, he told reporters, "I thought I was watching a film scripted by Jean Genet." At one point, Bertolucci had insisted that Brando and Schneider engage in actual sex on camera.

It is said that an aging Brando cried on the day he bid adieu to his French friends, just before heading back to California and what he feared was, "my upcoming death."

"My only regret in life," he told his intimates, "was that I was not born a Frenchman."

\*\*\*\*

*Editor's note:*

*Brando Unzipped*, by Darwin Porter (ISBN 0-9748118-2-3), has received more press and publicity, on both sides of the Atlantic, during the first four weeks of its life than most other books generate during an entire lifetime. For more about this fine title from Blood Moon Productions, click on **www.BloodMoonProductions.com**

# Le Journal du Dimanche

## Brando-Piaf, premier tango à Paris

### Carlos Gomez

LE PARRAIN était un séducteur. L'histoire est bien connue. Mais il manquait quelques épisodes. Publiée jeudi en Grande-Bretagne, une biographie de Marlon Brando (*Brando Unzipped*, chez Blood Moon) apporte des révélations majeures sur les amours tumultueuses de l'acteur américain disparu en juillet 2004. Son auteur, le journaliste Darwin Porter, a rassemblé cinquante ans de souvenirs, tous soigneusement sourcés. Brando a aimé hommes et femmes avec le même naturel, comme il le révéla en partie lui-même dans ses Mémoires en 1976. On savait pour James Dean et Marlene Dietrich, on

ne savait pas pour Marilyn Monroe. C'était en 1946 et pour 15 dollars, Brando convia dans son lit celle qui gagnait encore sa vie dans les petites rues de Hollywood, a révélé le *Times* de Londres dimanche, en offrant une tribune à l'auteur du livre. Encore plus surprenante, l'idylle, pour la première fois révélée, entre Marlon et Edith Piaf, à Paris, au début des années 1950. Trois jours d'amour et d'excès commencés dans un malentendu. « Quand elle l'emmena chez lui après déjeuner, il fit l'erreur de croire que c'était fait, se déshabilla et courut se mettre sous les draps. "Pour qui tu me prends, petit bâtard ! Une de ces filles faciles ? Tire-toi !" hurla Piaf. » Le biographe est

documenté au point de pouvoir nous dire que Brando se retrouva en jean sur le palier, sa conquête ayant gardé son tee-shirt et ses chaussures… Le jour suivant, leurs affaires s'arrangeaient. Dans la soirée, Piaf emmenait son ami américain à travers Pigalle, chantant dans la rue comme elle le faisait à ses débuts, Brando s'amusant à tendre son chapeau aux badauds médusés. « Ils rentrèrent à 6 h du matin, saouls, et Brando mit chastement Piaf au lit. » Leur relation trouvera une conclusion charnelle le lendemain, chez la chanteuse, avec des danseurs du Lido pour témoins. « Elle dormait encore quand je suis parti le lendemain. Elle était si pâle… »

# STALKING BRANDO

## (AKA, SEXUAL OBSESSION WITH MURDEROUS INTENT)
### Marlon's Intimacies With a Homicidal Cannibal Who Interpreted Him as Jesus

No other actor on Broadway in the late 1940s had as much male flash as **Marlon Brando,** who appears in four of the six photos, above, as the intensely sexual (and brutish) Stanley Kowalski in various productions of Tennessee Williams ode to repressed sexuality and loss, *A Streetcar Named Desire.*

His charms made strong impressions on many members of the audience, perhaps especially on gay men and straight women. One of them, a psychopath who identified herself to him only as "Maria," came very close to murdering him before being swept away with religious visions that likened him to Jesus.

Here follows the bizarre tale of a deranged—and probably dangerous—stalker who, except for his quick thinking and courage, might have killed Marlon Brando during the peak of his fame, glory, and male beauty.

**A concept that's increasingly in the news involves "celebrity stalking."** It's increasingly recognized as the price that many actors and actresses pay for their fame. And although it's an oft-repeated and sinister issue today, it was rarely heard of in the early 1950s.

An exception to that rule during that era revolved around Marlon Brando after his success at portraying Stanley Kowalski in the film *A Streetcar Named Desire.* Based on the smashing Broadway success, it was released in 1951.

At the time, he had rented a small apartment in New York City on 6th Avenue at 57th Street, where he was constantly pestered by anonymous phone calls. The person on the other end would hang up without saying a word. This continued for three months. Finally, one night, he heard the delicate voice of a woman.

For three full hours, he kept her on the phone, learning that her profession was that of a "stick-up artist." She robbed liquor stores in New Jersey at night, fleeing on a motorcycle piloted by another woman friend who was "deaf and dumb," to quote her words.

She told Brando that for months, she'd had a fixation on him, and that she'd plastered the walls of her bedroom with billboards from *Streetcar*. She kept his picture under her pillow every night, and talked to it. During their marathon first dialogue, she revealed that—with the help of her motorcyclist friend—she planned to kidnap him. They planned to take him to a remote boathouse she'd rented on Long Island, where they'd imprison him and gradually cannibalize him in a scene evocative of the modern-day film *Hannibal*.

At that point, most sane people might have put down the phone and called the police. But not Brando. Years later, he recalled the event in interviews, claiming that he knew at the time that the woman was "deadly serious."

In spite of that, he invited her to his apartment. He took the precaution of opening the door with the chain attached. After he'd frisked her, he let her inside, despite the danger to himself.

She identified herself only as "Maria," and begged him to let her wash his feet. As she slowly and sensuously immersed his feet in warm water, he came to realize that in her fantasy, he'd become Jesus to her Mary Magdalene.

Brando later admitted that as she was drying his feet with her long hair, he became sexually aroused. That led to her seduction in his bedroom. In some bizarre (and supremely decadent) kind of reasoning, it became thrilling for him to seduce a woman who thought that he was Jesus, and who wanted, literally, to devour his flesh.

After the sex act, he managed to get her out of his apartment, suggesting that she seek psychiatric help. He never let her inside his apartment ever again, although he often encountered her at two or three o'clock in the morning, waiting for him in his hallway. At their last meeting, Brando, "as Jesus," commanded her to go away and leave him alone. She did.

When he moved to Hollywood, firmly entrenched in his status as a movie star, he tracked her down to see what had become of her. He finally reached her brother in New Jersey, who informed him that Maria had come home one night covered in blood as if she'd tried to lacerate herself with shards of broken glass. In this condition, she entered her bedroom, gathered up all the *Streetcar* and Brando memorabilia, and outside, in their back yard, ignited them into flames.

Back inside the house, she announced to her family. "Jesus is dead. He will never rise again."

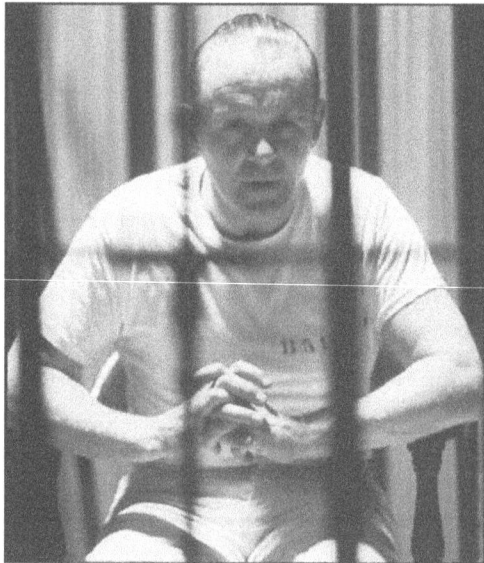

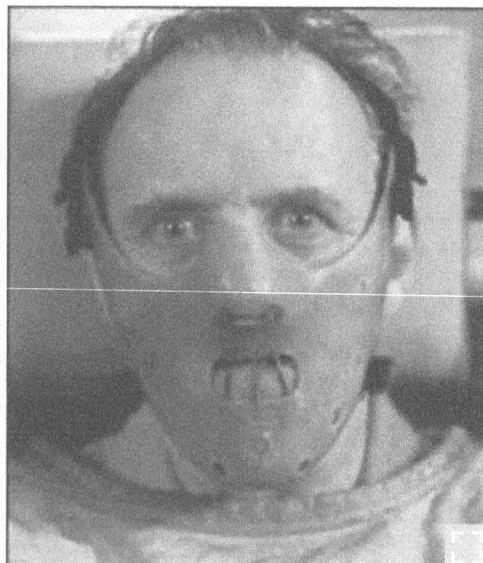

Artists have, since the millennia, attempted to depict psychotic evil. Here's how the costume and casting department at MGM did it, in this case with **Anthony Hopkins** in his portrayal of **"Hannibal the Cannibal" Lecter**, a stalking and murderous psycho, in the taut psychological thriller, *Silence of the Lambs* (1991).

# THE SAD AND TRAGIC DEMISE OF MARLON BRANDO'S KILLER SON

He lived hard and died young. He was Christian Brando, the bad boy son of the late acting icon Marlon Brando and the fiery Welsh actress, Anna Kashfi, Brando's first wife, who had claimed throughout most of her adult life that she was from India.

Marlon met Anna in 1955, telling friends he'd found "the most beautiful woman in the world." He would later say, "in the worst decision of my life, I married the bitch." One outcome of that union was the birth of Christian in Los Angeles on May 11, 1958. He entered the world as the couple was divorcing, launching the most violent and hostile 16-year custody battle in the history of Hollywood.

Spending the last two weeks of his life in a Los Angeles city hospital on a ventilator, Christian died on January 26, 2008 of complications from pneumonia. He was living on welfare, as his father's executors battled each other over how to divide up an estate worth more than $20 million. Christian left behind six half-brothers and half-sisters.

Children of famous movie stars sometimes end up tragically. The charismatic quality it takes to achieve stardom is not what is required to make a good parent. Take Joan Crawford, Bette Davis, or Bing Crosby, for example. In a court appearance, Marlon delivered an incredible understatement: "I think that perhaps I failed as a father."

He failed not only with Christian but with his daughter, the incredibly beautiful Cheyenne, born to Marlon's third wife, a Polynesian lovely named Tarita Tariipaia, whom he'd met while filming *Mutiny on the Bounty* in 1962.

Throughout their short lives, Christian and Cheyenne were extremely affectionate with each other. When Cheyenne went to live in Tahiti with her mother (who had separated from Marlon), Christian was furious. He became extremely jealous when he learned that she'd found a boyfriend, a handsome Polynesian in his mid-20s, Dag Drollet. Christian was hostile to Dag when Cheyenne brought him to Los Angeles to stay at Marlon's home, where Christian was also living.

Inviting Cheyenne out for dinner, Christian did not ask Dag to accompany them. Over spaghetti at Frank and Musso's restaurant, Cheyenne broke down in tears, falsely claiming that Dag was beating her even though she was pregnant. Unknown to Christian, she'd only an hour previously, just before she left for the restaurant, told Dag that she was carrying Christian's baby—not Dag's child.

Drugged, and fueled by alcohol, Christian exploded in a rage. He drove to his girlfriend's house where he retrieved an assault weapon— "the Porsche of handguns."

After the birth of their son, Anna Kashfi and Marlon Brando engaged in a battle over their son's little penis. She wanted him to be circumsized, and Marlon was violently opposed. "My uncut noble tool has given me the greatest pleasure of my life."

Toxic even by Hollywood standards, the Brando-Kashfi *ménage* was among the worst environments possible for child-rearing. *Photo above* shows baby Christian with his violent and abusively alcoholic mother, **Anna Kashfi.**

Scene in a Santa Monica courthouse after a child custody hearing in 1961. **Anna Kashfi** (*left*), Christian's mother, has just assaulted **Marlon Brando** (*right*) over resentments associated with their then 3-year-old son, Christian

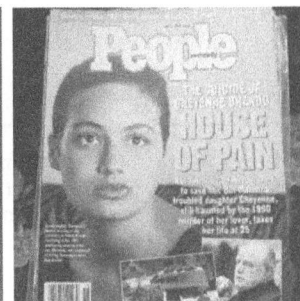

*Left photo*: A modeling shot of Brando's deeply disturbed, drug abusing and suicidal daughter, **Cheyenne,** snapped "on one of her very rare "good days"; *middle photo*: Head shot of Cheyenne's boyfriend, **Dag Drollet,** murdered by Christian and son of a prominent French Polynesian politician; and *right photo*, Cheyenne is—this time unwillingly—configured as the cover girl on a *People* magazine *exposé* aply entitled *House of Pain*, dated May 1, 1995.

Returning in fury to his father's home, Christian stormed into the living room and fatally shot the 26-year-old Dag as he was watching TV. When the police arrived, Christian claimed it was an accident, but it was later defined by the district attorney, and a jury, as coldblooded murder

The killing made headlines around the world. Yet at the time, the press did not learn the true motive for the murder: *Christian was in love with Cheyenne*.

Sentenced to ten years at the California Men's Colony at San Luis Obispo, Christian served half that time before he was released on probation.

In Tahiti on June 26, 1990, Cheyenne gave birth to a baby boy named Tuki. The infant was born drug addicted. At that point, Cheyenne was so demented that she tried to drown her newborn son under a cold-water faucet in the bathroom of her hospital room. A nurse rescued the infant, and Cheyenne was committed to a psychiatric ward.

Upon her release, she made two suicide attempts, the first with sleeping pills. Later, she tried to hang herself. In 1995, she finally succeeded in hanging herself in her bedroom by tying her neck to a rope attached to a ceiling beam. Standing on a chair, she kicked it away and fell to her death at the age of 25.

Weeks before, during sessions with her psychiatrists, she had made explosive charges against Marlon, claiming that he'd molested her since she'd been eight years old. She testified that when she was 16, he'd tried to entice her to a seaside motel in Santa Monica so "I can spend hours making love to you." She also claimed that after the birth of her child, Marlon flew to Tahiti and once again tried to seduce her, claiming "I want to be the father of your next baby."

In 2004 Christian married Deborah Presley, who claims to be the illegitimate daughter of Elvis Presley. A year later, she sued Christian for domestic violence, claiming that he'd repeatedly beaten her and threatened to kill her in the presence of her teenaged daughter. He countersued, alleging that she broke into his house and beat him after his announcement that he wanted to have their marriage annulled after their first ten weeks together. Both lawsuits were settled in 2006, with undisclosed terms.

Christian's death has led to an array of charges, including accusations of fraud or possibly murder. In the wake of threatened lawsuits, one Los Angeles attorney predicted that the estate of Marlon Brando, now complicated by Christian's death, probably won't be settled until 2050—"and I'm being optimistic."

Marlon himself died at the age of 80 on July 1, 2004. He could win Oscars, but no "Parent of the Year" awards.

An expression of tenderness between **Father and Son Brandos** before sentencing in a California court.

Noted for a half-century of bisexual stud-dom in venues throughout the world, **Brando** *père* appears above in *left photo* with co-star **Mary Murphy** in the blockbuster anti-hero movie, *The Wild Ones*, and with Polynesian actress **Tarita Teriipaia**, later his wife (from 1962-1972) and Cheyenne's mother, in *Mutiny on the Bounty* (1962).

Marlon Brando was not the only "unsuccessful" parent in Hollywood. Infamous competitors for that title included *(left to right)* **Joan Crawford** (aka "Mommie Dearest"): **Adda-badda Bing (Crosby)**, whose feuds with his suicide-prone sons was the stuff of legend; and *(right photo)* **Bad-ass Bette (Davis)**, whose own daughter wrote a blistering "anti-Bette" memoir of her own.

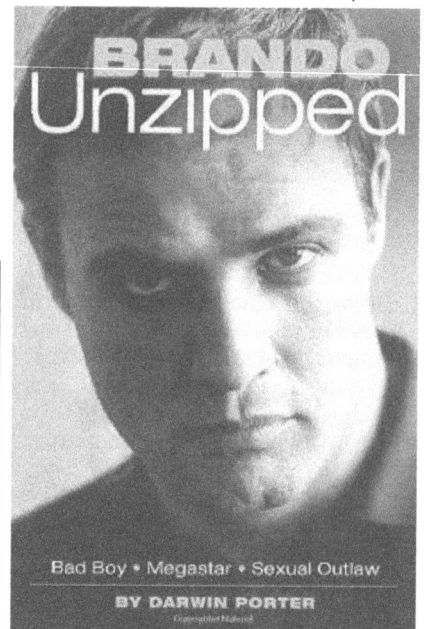

BRANDO
Unzipped

Bad Boy • Megastar • Sexual Outlaw
**BY DARWIN PORTER**

# PART FOUR

## IN THE AGE OF SELFIES AND SOCIAL MEDIA

# EVERYONE IS A STAR

# IN THE ERA OF THE "SELFIE,"
# EVERYONE IS A STAR

Producers back in Hollywood's Golden Age, including Darryl F. Zanuck and Louis B. Mayer, could never have imagined the direction film would take in the 21st Century. Today, thanks to modern technology, everyone can be a star in his or her own drama.

Around the world, attention-seeking hipsters are posting "selfies" (portraits of themselves) on Instagram, Facebook, and Twitter. Selfies are snapped on a smartphone. Many of them are subsequently posted on social media, with or without a caption, inane or otherwise.

In 2013, "selfie" became the most popular new word in the English language, rivaled only by the word "twerking," a reference to the kind of dirty dancing that Miley Cyrus made notorious during her appearance at the MTV Video Music Awards in Brooklyn late in 2013.

So far, the most infamous selfie ever shot was snapped on December 10, 2013. It starred Barack Obama during his presence at the funeral rites for Nelson Mandela in South Africa. In it, a sexy blonde, the Danish Prime Minister Helle Schmidt, posed flirtatiously with the U.S. president. Also in the photo, on her left, and hovering a bit apart from the other two, was David Cameron, the British prime minister, famous for absent-mindedly leaving his 8-year-old daughter alone in a pub in London's Mayfair district, much to the horror of his wife.

As Helle's selfie was being set up with Obama and Cameron in the frame, a regular (i.e., "conventional") photographer snapped an overview of the trio within a bigger context. The wide-angle shot included First Lady Michelle Obama glaring at her husband, who seemingly was putting the moves on the blonde bombshell. Helle had flirtatiously hiked up her skirt to reveal Betty Grable legs encased in (funeral appropriate) black hosiery.

Where was Helle's husband? Whereas she rules her country from Copenhagen, he lives in Davos, Switzerland. According to the Danish press, he's "either gay or bisexual."

In South Africa, the selfie of Obama and Helle was widely distributed in the media with the caption, "Today Obama is in Heaven, but at least we still have 'Helle' on Earth!"

The speculation in the press was that when Obama returned to the White House, he'd be sleeping on the sofa. From her stance as an onlooker to the "having a good time threesome," in the selfie, Michelle looked genuinely enraged. Evidence of the U.S. president's "horn-dog behavior" at Mandela's funeral was blasted in editorials around the globe.

Obama is not the only politician to achieve notoriety with a selfie. New York Congressman, Anthony Weiner, a failed

Star-makers **Darryl F. Zanuck** (left photo) and (right photo) **Louis B. Mayer** with **Joan Crawford** in 1953.

**BUT AS HEADS OF STATE, THEY WERE STARS EVEN BEFORE THE SELFIE! (Weren't they?)**

British Prime Minister **David Cameron** poses with Danish Prime Minister **Helle Schmidt** and U.S. President **Barack Obama** collectively pose for a selfie at the funeral rites for Nelson Mandela in 2013

What do **Pope Francis** (left) and **Kim Kardashian** REALLY share in common? Each has gracefully acquiesced to being the subject of an "almost infinite" number of selfie portraits from adoring fans.

mayoral candidate, took pictures of his erect penis in see-through bikini underwear and shared them with the world, especially young women. In the aftermath of their public exposure, he was forced to resign.

You might ask what exhibitionistic Kim Kardashian and Pope Francis have in common: Both are the subjects of endless selfies. Incidentally, in case you missed the revelation, the Pope, during his long uphill road to the Vatican, used to work as a bouncer at a notorious night club in Buenos Aires.

Movie stars who spend their lives in front of the lens take selfies of themselves when the day's work is done. Sometimes, their selfies give them more exposure than their movies. Orlando Bloom takes his son, Flynn, for a piggyback ride in the park—instant selfie. The actor, John Leguizamo, self-poses in front of an open-mouthed, teeth-baring, flesh-eating facsimile of a dinosaur. Hollywood legends Tom Hanks and Steve Martin ham it up for their selfies. Attention-hog Kris Jenner tries to be hip by wrangling super-hot "Extra" host, Maria Menounos, into posing with her for a selfie.

Selfies have been around long enough to have both designated and crowned "The King of the Selfies." He is the handsome, very talented actor, James Franco, who is one of the most selfie-indulgent personalities in the entertainment industry. He's a star of TV, film, and "performance-art spoof fame." If you want to know what Franco looks like when he wakes up in the morning, when he has lunch, eats dinner, heads for the shower, or whatever, check the internet. On Instagram, from Canada, recently, the 35-year-old actor posted a half nude portrait of himself that subsequently appeared in tabloids around the world.

It carried this message to his fans: "#Almostnude—YOU ASKED FOR IT, YOU GOT IT. Tryna work that body, tryin', tryin'." Since the picture exposed only four inches of skin below his navel, thousands of his followers immediately demanded that he go much farther and reveal what the English call "the Full Monty." Go figure.

Two views of NYC Mayoral candidate **Anthony Weiner**:

*Left photo:* Campaigning with his then-wife, **Huma Abedin**, a ferociously loyal aide to Hillary Clinton.

*Right photo:* Weiner appears partially undressed as Carlos Danger, his sexting *nom de plume,* on the cover of the *NY Post,* which excoriated him for posting indiscreet selfies on the web.

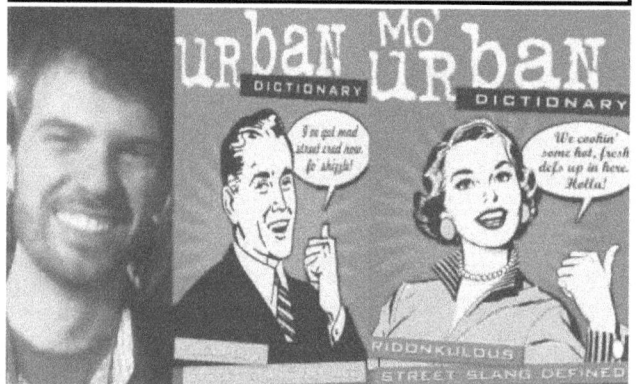

Then college freshman **Aaron Peckham,** creator of two editions of the new go-to source for fast-emerging new words, *The Urban Dictionary*

Selfies can pop up anywhere. During the dead of winter, one gorgeous Manhattan blonde spotted a man about to commit suicide by jumping off the Brooklyn Bridge. She photographed herself in the foreground, with the suicidal man appearing over her left shoulder. In Florida, a high school student took a selfie of himself with his teacher as she was going into premature labor.

Basid McLean, a 25-year-old Bronx man, shot a selfie posing with the severed head of a man who had just had his head chopped off. The troubled actress Amanda Bynes chronicles her ongoing emotional breakdown by posting topless selfies.

Sometimes, the publication of a selfie can lead to professional embarrassment, or even a person getting fired. A New York fireman, Trilain Smith, was heavily disciplined for posing in his fireman's uniform exposing too much of his muscled body, as his right hand traveled south into his unzipped fireman pants.

As we move deeper into 2014, "selfie" has been proclaimed as "word of the year" by the Oxford University Press.

Regardless of its subject or context, a selfie usually carries a lot of connotations (or "heavy baggage"). It often suggests the subject's familiarity with advanced technology, social media, instantaneous global transmission. It can also suggest carelessness, frivolity, callow youth, inappropriateness, and ironic juxtapositions.

Of course, word usage frequently changes. When North America was discovered by Europeans, a whole new vocabulary had to be invented to describe what the settlers found here. Centuries later, World War II introduced additions to the American-language vocabulary too. But back then, years would pass before those new words were formally defined in dictionaries.

Today, if someone invents a new word on Twitter, it can go viral within 24 hours.

Only today, I learned what the word "Directioner" means. It refers to a superfan of the boy band *One Direction*, in case you care.

Because of the growth of the Internet and the hundreds of new words being added to the English language, that old Webster's dictionary in your library is hopelessly out of date. In 1999, a college freshman, Aaron Peckham, set out to change that. He created *Urban Dictionary*, a crowd-sourced online dictionary that lets anyone contribute words and their definitions to a fast-expanding, publicly accessible database.

More than seven million definitions of words, acronyms, and phrases have been published there so far, with additional entries added daily. A word can be added no matter how vulgar and controversial. Because of that, much of the Urban Dictionary is X-rated, or at least R-rated.

# REVENGE PORN

## WHERE LOVE HAS GONE

Thomas Edison could hardly have foreseen how his newly invented medium of film had evolved by the dawn of the 21st Century. The rise of "revenge porn" has emerged as a dark shadow across the American landscape.

What is it exactly? Revenge porn is one of those things that sounds illegal, but actually isn't, although there are laws pending in state legislatures, mostly in California and New York. Efforts to have a law passed in the Florida legislature failed in 2013. Only New Jersey has a law to protect victims.

Revenge porn is defined as the term for disseminating sexual photos of someone without his or her (usually her) permission. Child pornography remains illegal, but present laws are inadequate to stem the flow of jilted partners seeking revenge through non-consensual pornography posted on the web.

Critics of proposed legislation charge that it infringes on the First Amendment. But in response, Sheila Ferguson, of Naples, Florida, said, "Breaking up with someone you loved is hard enough. But to discover your ex-boyfriend is a horrible person filled with vengeance is even worse."

It's estimated that 80 percent of the images posted on the Internet were recorded by the victim, then handed over to a person he or she trusted. It is usually a young woman (or girl) giving the sexually explicit photos to a boyfriend, who later posts them online after they separate.

Women have been fired from their jobs, and weddings have been cancelled. Such was a recent case in Atlanta when the intended best man showed the prospective bridegroom pictures, downloaded without charge from the Internet, of his naked bride-to-be posing obscenely for sex venues with her former boyfriend.

Once an image is posted, it's often picked up by hundreds of other web sites. Even if the original site is shut down, the pictures are still out there—in many cases re-posted in myriad other electronic venues.

Danielle Citron, a law professor at the University of Maryland, is writing a book about on-line sexual harassment. She defines revenge porn as a growing menace of immense proportions, "making people, both men and women, unemployable, undateable, and potentially at physical risk."

On CNN in an interview with Anderson Cooper, Hunter Moore, the creator of *IsAnyoneUp.com*, claimed he had no qualms about profiting from public revenge. "I not only get to look at pictures of naked girls, but I make $10,000 a month in ad revenue."

Even though they allegedly try to prevent the posting of one of their sex tapes on the Internet, some victims are richly rewarded anyway. The most famous of these cases involved Paris Hilton, who had a torrid affair with Rick Salomon, the son of a former executive at Warner Brothers.

After he and Paris broke up, he posted a sex tape of the two of them on the web, with copies for sale. It was entitled *A Night in Paris*.

The sex tape which Paris defined as "the most embarrassing, humiliating episode of my life," sold briskly, worldwide.

*Upper photo*, **Paris Hilton** on cover of the sex video she insists she did not want. *Lower photo:* **Paris Hilton** with her director, **Rick Salomon**

**Kim Kardashian** and **Ray J**

Even so, she eventually received profits of $13 million (with more to come) from the intimate video and received priceless publicity for her TV show, *The Simple Life,* which debuted just as the tape was released.

Solomon today is worth $40 million, with his fortune growing daily. He invested his profits into becoming "The King of Poker" in America through the purchase of an online gambling web site.

Even without the formal protection of either State or Federal laws, revenge cases are filling court dockets across the country, with no clear guidelines for judges to follow.

Within the same week, three such cases achieved national prominence. In Manhattan, Alec Katsnelson, a former student at St. John's University, testified that his girlfriend, Yekaterina Pusepa, stabbed him with a 12-inch steak knife when he received a nude picture from a young woman on his cellphone. He survived, and she must now face a charge of attempted murder.

A day after news broke across the country that Snapchat, a photo sharing "app," had rejected a $3 billion purchase offer from Facebook, its backers landed in legal trouble. In Montréal, police arrested ten teenage boys on charges of child porn. They'd coaxed their girlfriends, ages 13 and 15, to pose while performing sexual acts, then posted the footage online. Snapchat had been in the news because of its developers claims that users can send photos, explicit or not, that electronically disintegrate (usually after about ten seconds) after being viewed. The computer-savvy boys from Montréal, however, found a way to get around the time limit.

Another bizarre case emerged in New York. Louise Silberling, a scorned Ivy League philosophy editor who became way too articulate in the aftermath of her breakup, was sued by her ex-boyfriend, John Wender, the CEO of a prestigious architectural firm. He's seeking $1.25 million in damages, claiming he was "irreparably harmed" by Silberling's slanderous and far-reaching postings on the web. Silberling claimed that Wender "is a sex-obsessed sicko with a micro-penis who engages in animal role playing with his tiny, STD-infested wiener, taking sick pleasure in degrading women with bondage, rape play, auto-erotic asphyxia, and strangulation."

Paris Hilton is not the only public figure who has made millions off revenge porn. Of course, to profit, you've got to be a celebrity. Kim Kardashian, the so-called "selfie queen," appeared outraged when her sex tapes with singer Ray J went public. But after settling for a $5 million payout, she became a household name overnight.

Tori Spelling, once one of the richest movie stars in Hollywood, is now strapped for cash. She and her husband, Dean McDermott, co-starred together in a sex tape à la Kim Kardashian, on Valentine's Day in 2009. She writes about it in her newly published memoir, *Spelling It Like It Is.* An insider claims, "Tori really needs the money, as she's deeply in debt after blowing a multi-million dollar fortune. She's considering cashing in on those who want to watch her husband and herself make love on camera."

But these are special cases. Thousands upon thousands of women, and more and more young men, are victims, not cash cows collecting porno millions. Mary Anne Franklin, a professor of law at the University of Miami, said, "Opposition to revenge porn legislation often stems from a blame-the-victim attitude that holds women responsible for allowing photos to be taken in the first place. That attitude is similar to blaming rape victims for what they wear, or where they walk. The moment a potential victim is shown to have given explicit photographs of herself to her boyfriend, all sympathy disappears."

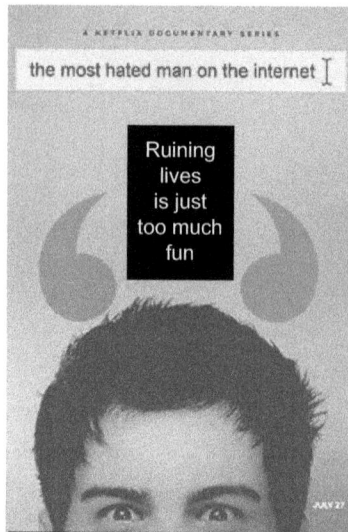
the most hated man on the internet

Ruining lives is just too much fun

Cover art for the 2022 Netflix documentary that exposed **Hunter Moore,** the "Revenge Porn Maestro." Moore was the sociopathic kingpin (and convicted felon) behind **IsAnyoneUp.com**.

**LONG AGO & FAR AWAY**

**Thomas Edison,** the inventor of film, circa 1900.

PORN! THE INTERNET IS FOR IT!

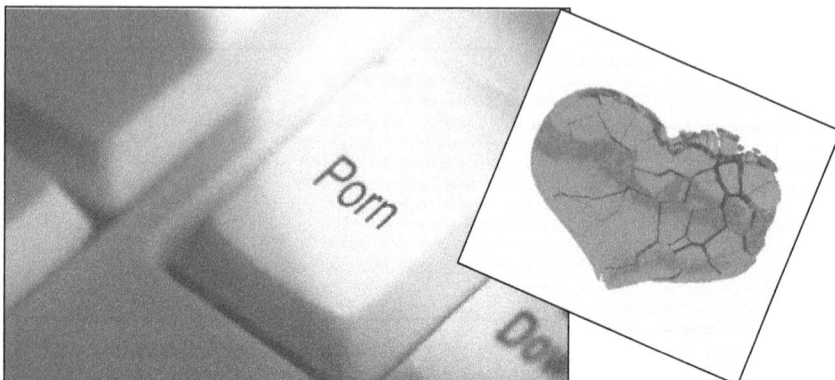

**Tori Spelling** and **Dean McDermott**.

448

# CELEBRITY FRAUDS & SOCIAL MEDIA

## *Is That Really You, Beyoncé?*

From athletes to movie stars, celebrities in all fields are plagued with thousands of fans or charlatans who are impersonating them on social media. Sometimes these phony celebrity social media accounts are just for fun, but often, they are frauds to cheat fans out of money.

Bogus profiles litter the landscape, a major headache to Facebook' Twitter, and Instagram, among others. Facebook alone reported that it has removed 583 million accounts: Even its executive, Mark Zuckerberg, has had fake accounts established in his name.

Fans might ask the question, "Is that really you, Oprah, Justin, or Beyonce, or are you an impersonator? It's roughly estimated that a fake account posts something online every four seconds.

Some fraudulent accounts are so crudely conceived that only the most gullible are sucked in; others are incredibly professional and authentic-looking. Such was the case with Empire actor Derek Luke. Every photo on his fake account was captioned and personalized with heartfelt messages from the star.

Dr. Elle Boag, a lecturer in social psychology, claims, "People often imitate a celebrity if they feel alone or bored. They may not have friends, and they like to attract people pretending to be someone they are not. It's a form of escapism, an extension of fan fiction."

"Some people like to lie and manipulate others," Boag said. "It entertains them and makes them feel powerful. You can be anybody you want to be. Why not a celebrity? Perhaps you're a 45-year-old bored housewife who gets a kick out of impersonating Justin Bieber in your spare time?"

Sometimes, crimes are committed. While on vacation, Bieber was snapped in the nude on a beach. One middle-aged man posted the nude photo of the star on a fake account and solicited some of his young fans, girls ages 13 to 14, to send him nudes of themselves. He received hundreds of responses before he was arrested.

When there was speculation that Oprah Winfrey might run for president, fake accounts were set up in her name, urging supporters to send campaign contributions to clearly designated post office boxes, each of them false. Thousands upon thousands of dollars were fraudulently collected in her name.

An account was fraudulently established under the name of Chris Pratt, whose authentic social media sites correctly define him as one of the stars of the mega-hit Jurassic World. It had him soliciting sex from some of his young fans. As a countermove, he had to issue warnings on his own (authentic) Facebook account that the the sexual solicitations were bogus and unauthorized.

Beyoncé

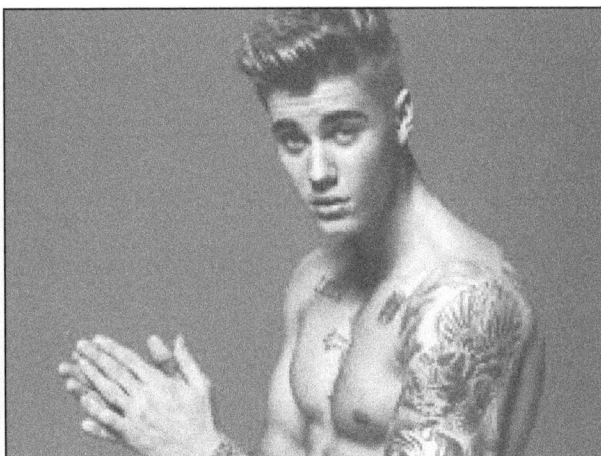

Justin Bieber

Oprah Winfrey

Another fake account offered to sell a sex tape of Beyonce and her rapper husband, Jay-Z, for fifty dollars. Hundreds e-transmitted payment, but no such tape existed.

Based on fake social media postings, country singer Kip Moore has had some awkward moments, too. Women have materialized from the audience at his concerts, informing him that they've left their husbands because Moore had posted that he loved them. But despite Moore's innocence, many women turned on him, calling him a "scumbag."

A watchdog company that protects celebrities from exploitation took a survey, finding that the greatest number of fake accounts (almost 2,000), had been inspired by the Brazilian heartthrob known simply as Neymar, a player for that nation's soccer team. SportsPro named him "the most marketable athlete in the world."

Second runner-up for the number of fake social media accounts established with various derivations of his or her name was a Texan, Selena Gomez, who shot to fame through the Disney Channel's hit TV series, Wizards of Waverly Place.

Mega-star Jennifer Lawrence is very outspoken about not having (or wanting) an Instagram account, yet at least twenty fake Instagram accounts exist with confusing derivations of her name.

Some "real" negative postings from "real" celebrities can be lethal to a social media venues resale value. When Kylie Jenner, a player in the Kardashian-Jenner empire, announced that she was angry with and would no longer post on Snapchat after a re-design of its platform, the value of its stock dropped by one billion dollars.

It's easy to believe that because of all this upset and confusion, there might be a "rethinking" of social media and its usefulness. Perhaps the headaches, damage, and danger involved aren't worth maintaining such accounts any more.

Derek Luke

Kip Moore

Neymar

Jennifer Lawrence

Selina Gomez

Kylie Jenner

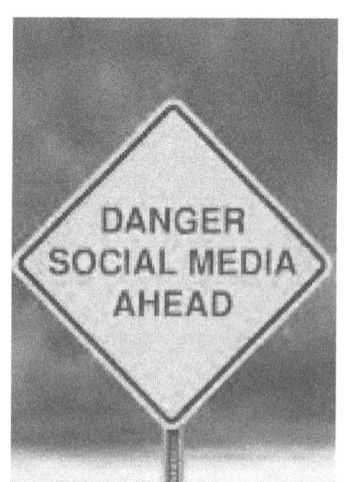

DANGER SOCIAL MEDIA AHEAD

# ANTHONY PELLICANO

## "HOLLYWOOD'S DIRTIEST PRIVATE INVESTIGATOR,"

*Tout* Hollywood is having that extra martini every night this month, quaking in its boots, waiting for what may become Tinseltown's trial of the decade. Hollywood's celebrity sleuth, Anthony Pellicano, has been hit with 110 Federal indictments, each of them stemming from charges of illegal practices he either committed or sanctioned during his self-anointed role as a Sunset Boulevard "gumshoe to the stars." Indictments charge that the detective destroyed evidence, tampered with witnesses, perpetrated identity theft, and organized illegal wiretaps.

It's not the first time Pellicano has raised eyebrows. In 2002, during a police raid on his offices, officers discovered enough C-4 plastic explosives to bring down a jetliner. Pellicano pleaded guilty and was consequently sentenced to 30 months in prison.

His current legal woes are even more serious. They began early in 2006, when Anita Busch, a reporter for the *Los Angeles Times*, began investigating claims that action star Steven Seagal had ties to the Mafia. The journalist charged that during her probe, she'd been the victim of a "campaign of terror" from Pellicano's goons. If Pellicano is convicted of those charges, penalties could be devastating.

The son of Sicilian immigrants, Pellicano grew up in Chicago's Mafia-dominated suburb of Cicero. The life he led before his downfall reads like a *noir* detective novel from the 1940s.

But how did Pellicano become Hollywood's celebrity sleuth, a man frequently cited as the nation's foremost forensic expert on illegal tape recordings? Blame it on a dame—Dame Elizabeth in this case. In 1977, nineteen years after his original burial, grave robbers dug up the remains of Mike Todd, the Broadway producer and third husband of Elizabeth Taylor. He had been interred in a cemetery at Forest Park, Illinois, after his death in a plane crash in 1958. Apparently, the grave robbers were looking for a 12-karat diamond ring, which, according to rumor, had been placed on the corpse's finger by Ms. Taylor shortly before burial. Allegedly, such a ring never existed.

Local police were baffled and after an intense and widely publicized search, never succeeded in finding the stolen body. With gusto, our "hero," Pellicano, rushed to the rescue, arriving unexpectedly at the graveyard with a TV crew. Miraculously, he directed cameramen to a pile of leaves 200 feet from Todd's violated grave. Beneath a protective covering of leaves, Todd's decayed remains were found inside a plastic bag.

Pellicano's rivals were suspicious. It was all too pat, leading to charges that he'd pulled off this stunt for publicity purposes, and might even have orchestrated the grave-robbing incident himself.

Back in Hollywood, although deeply immersed in newer romantic preoccupations, Ms. Taylor was most grateful, and began to recommend Pellicano to her friends in trouble. One of them was Michael Jackson, who would later pay the detective $2 million when the pop star was charged with molesting a 13-year-old boy.

The word soon spread through Tinseltown: If you were in trouble, get a checkbook, practice writing extra zeros, and call "The Pelican." The private dick's phone line was busy. Rosanne Barr wanted to find the daughter she'd put up for adoption 18 years previously. The CEO of one of Hollywood's biggest studios was about to be exposed for cavorting with hookers. A woman claimed that Kevin Costner had been a longtime "friend" and wanted a payoff. Farrah Fawcett's current boyfriend had been "roughing me up." Enemies of Arnold Schwarzenegger wanted the dirt on his involvements with women since his marriage to Maria Shriver. Another caller wanted "All the dirt on Stallone!"

It's rumored that even the current New York senator, Hillary Clinton, had previously hired Pellicano to discredit two women alleging affairs with her husband, Gennifer Flowers (who claimed a 12-year involvement) and later, Monica Lewin-

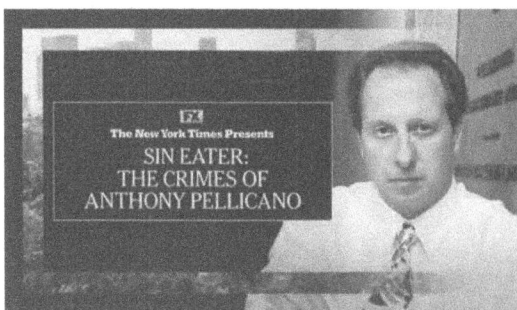

In October of 2006, Anita Finley's **Boomer Times** reported the shadowy misdeeds of Hollywood "fixer," **Anthony Pellicano**. The text of that report by Darwin Porter is replicated on this and the following page.

The details from those reports from 2006—amplified and enlarged with eyewitness testimonials from some of the New Hollywood's major stars—were reformatted and amplified by the documentarians at FX Streaming Video (in collaboration with *The New York Times*) in March of 2023. The mobster's story, in other words, continues to attract interest today, decades after his imprisonment.

A photo of **Pellicano**, set against the backdrop of one of the new documentary's banner headlines, is replicated above. The moral? Hollywood is still a ruthless, larceny soaked, and very scary place.

His nicknames included **The Celebrities' Thug, Tony Fortune,** and **The Big Sleazy.** His real name was **Anthony Pellicano**, the "Godfather" of Hollywood private investigators. His clients included Michael Jackson, Tom Cruise, Chris Rock, super agent Michael Ovitz, and dozens of others.

In 2008, he was sentenced to 15 years in prison for , among others, running a wiretapping operation and a criminal enterprise.

That information was often used in court to undermine the cases of famous Hollywood defendants or plaintiffs. One witness testified that Pellicano's longstanding intimidations were like "death by a thousand cuts."

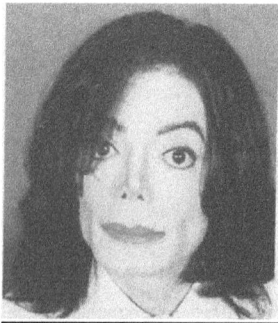
Michael Jackson

Tom Cruise & Nicole Kidman

sky.

Priscilla Presley had private business to discuss with Pellicano, as did actor Robert Blake, who had been charged with murdering his wife. Even the famous "bloody glove" cop of the O.J. Simpson trial, Mark Fuhram, called for a secret chat. And even before Fuhram's outreach to him, Pellicano was already involved in the O.J. case when police investigated reports that he had been shadowing Nicole Simpson (the athlete's former wife) on the night she and Ronald Goldman were brutally murdered. Does Pellicano know who the real killer is?

But why, as suggested by accusations that will probably be aired at his upcoming trial, was Pellicano gathering evidence on the very clients who hired him to dig up dirt on others making trouble for them? Was he planning on betraying his famous clients, plotting to blackmail Michael Jackson, Ms. Taylor, and perhaps even Tom Cruise?

Allegedly Pellicano has (illegal) wiretaps of Cruise and Nicole Kidman discussing the hush-hush reasons for their divorce and some of their financial agreements, among other juicy Hollywood scandals.

The fear among stars is that some judge will allow the illegal tapes to be introduced as evidence in court. If that occurs, in addition to establishing dangerous legal precedents, they will become fodder for the tabloids.

During his time in prison, Pellicano wrote his memoirs, but they'll probably never be published. Too many superstars are likely to buy them and suppress publication. The ex-detective also wrote a screenplay based on his life. He wants Johnny Depp to star as himself in *The Celebrities' Thug*.

Elizabeth Taylor
with her husband #3,
Mike Todd

Priscilla Presley

# FIXERS

Bette Davis feigning horror in What Ever Happened to Baby Jane? (1962)

MGM Fixer **Eddie Mannix** (left) with "The King of Hollywood," **Clark Gable**

**Although he became notorious, Anthony Pellicano** was only one of many dozens of Hollywood "fixers." The most successful of the lot—depending on your interpretation of the term successful—was **Eddie Mannix**, depicted on the left in the *photo left*. Born in New Jersey, in 1891, he was recognized by studio chiefs at MGM as a man with the kind of contacts and talents that could calm a crisis.

One actor who tested his skill was **Clark Gable** (right figure in the photo, left). Allegedly, The King of Hollywood accidentally killed an actress when he ran her over. Eddie cleaned things up and made sure the story stayed out of the media. Later, when Gable impregnated **Loretta Young**. Mannix smoothed things over, maneuvering her into "enforced seclusion," after which she appeared with a child she had "adopted."

**Joan Crawford,** before she became famous, had starred in a porn movie. Eddie was tasked with finding and destroying every copy, allegedly paying $100,000 for the master copy.

In 1935, the nightlife queen of Hollywood, **Thelma Todd,** was found dead in her car, the victim of a mob slaying. Once again, Eddie cleaned things up, encouraging the police to rule the death as accidental—which they did.

Horrible stories persist to this day about **Eddie Mannix**. After beating her severely and frequently (once reportedly breaking her back), his estranged wife died in the mangled wreck of a car crash. Was Eddie involved?

He got involved in the suspicious death of Superman (**George Reeves**), who threatened to blackmail the studio. Reeves brakes were disabled, and his car crashed, throwing him through the windscreen. He barely survived. A mechanic said, "Somebody wanted him dead" after discovering that the car had no brake fluid.' A few weeks later Reeves was found dead with a bullet lodged in his head. It was classified as a suicide but rumors persist to this day.

The reign of Eddie Mannix came to an end with the breakup of the studios. For the last few years of his life he was confined to a wheelchair. He died in 1963 of a heart attack at the age of 72.

# THE EXHIBITIONISTIC STUPIDITY OF
# ANTHONY WIENER

## (AKA CARLOS DANGER)

## DID IT COST HILLARY CLINTON THE PRESIDENCY?

Released a few months before the 2016 presidential elections, **13 Hours** emerged as a "playing card" in the electoral politics of THE DONALD and his Republicans vs HILLARY and the Democrats.

It, along with **Weiner,** each emerged as one of two films that, prior to the elections, poured cold water and hot condemnations onto Hillary and/or her advisors.

In both cases, tragic-comic (or stupid, depending on your point of view) events spiraled out of control through absolutely no fault of Hillary herself.

In any event, both of the films were based on events that later returned to haunt her.

Two films—one in current release, another due in May—are guaranteed to cause Hillary Clinton's campaign workers acute embarrassment.

Paramount Pictures has released director Michael Bay's *13 Hours: The Secret Soldiers of Benghazi.* Hillary has faced seemingly endless probes about the implications of her association, as U.S. Secretary of State, with the attack on an American embassy outpost in Libya in September of 2012, during which four Americans were killed.

Fox News, in an unprecedented move, has given the film nearly three hours (millions of dollars of free publicity) in broadcasting promotional segments of the film. One commentator, Andrea Tantaros, claimed that anyone who watched the movie and then voted for Hillary "is a criminal."

Commercially, so far, the movie has performed well in Red States, but it's drawing half-empty houses in Blue State movie theaters.

As if that weren't enough damage, another film, *Weiner,* was previewed at the Sundance Film Festival in Park City, Utah, to tidal waves of derisive laughter. It will be reaching theaters during the upcoming presidential primaries, and will be released on Showtime in October, perhaps with the intention of influencing the November elections.

The film focuses on the doomed 2013 New York mayoral run of Anthony Weiner, the disgraced former Brooklyn-Queens congressman who was forced to resign for sexting X-rated pictures of himself, revealing his erection through a pair of thin briefs. He sent these pictures of his privates to young women, using the *nom de plume* (or *nom de porn)* of "Carlos Danger."

Right in the middle of the brutal campaign, he was caught sexting again. This time, the press nicknamed him "Seven Inches." Of course, he lost the mayor's race, garnering only five percent of the vote. Donald Trump appears in the film. At the time, he said, "We don't want perverts elected in New York City. No perverts."

Weiner has asserted that he will not go to see the film. ("After all, I know the ending.")

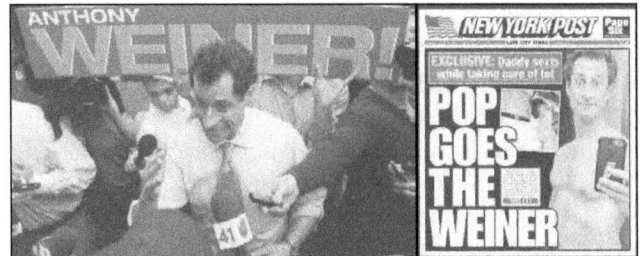

The double-barreled release of two otherwise unrelated films was calibrated to embarrass **Hillary Clinton** in advance of the presidential elections of November, 2016.

Each of them trumpeted the unhappy aftermath of events beyond her control. "Reviews' and ongoing news about the events that had inspired them was endlessly publicized by Fox News and other right-wing media outlets. Years later, it's widely conceded that they eventually influenced the 2016 preisidential election in favor of Trump.

Of the two, the one associated with **Anthony Weiner** husband of Hillary's most trusted personal assistant and "fixer," **Huma Abaden**, was the more devastating.

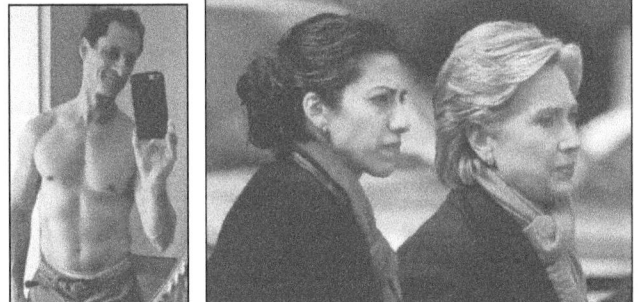

Some liberal Democrats viewed **Anthony Weiner** *(left photo above)* as one of the most effective (albeit eccentric) social progressives of his age. A ferocious infighter and candidate for NYC's mayor, he was also a gym rat *(i.e., proud of his worked-out body)* and an (anonymous) player on the social media sites. His *nom de plume* on those underground "dating games" was **Carlos Danger.**

When it was revealed that he'd texted (or "sexted") indiscreet photos through social media to women online, his opponents from the Right responded publicly with legal and moral venom. Salacious rehashings were replayed endlessly on Fox.

Weiner was married at the time to **Huma Abedin** *(left figure in photo, right),* a peronal friend, trusted advisor, and "gatekeeper" to **Hillary Clinton** *(right figure in photo, right).*

The ensuing scandal **("Weinergate')** washed, like a *tsunami,* over Huma, Hillary Clinton—and, some say, every Democrat on that year's electoral ticket. Even after the shattering of his campaign for mayor of New York, Weiner continued his recreational "sexting." That was the straw that persuaded Abedin to separate from her husband. .

453

He has accused its filmmakers, Josh Kriegman (Weiner's former chief of staff) and Elyse Steinberg, of exploiting the fact that his wife, Huma Abedin, 39, is one of Hillary's closest aides. One segment in the film (it may not make the final cut) depicts Hillary's campaign workers urging Huma to split from her "deviant husband."

One headline read: "WEINER SHOWS HIS JUNK IN HIS SKIVVIES."

Columnist Andrew Peyser wrote, "He got a sleazy thrill sexting pictures of his engorged manhood to random babes."

During the peak of the controversies that raged, in a dig at Bill Clinton, Weiner said: "I didn't rape anyone, didn't sexually assault anyone, and didn't commit adultery."

The mere news of the Wiener film's upcoming release has sparked numerous articles in newspapers across the country. Both "Hillary and Huma," based on unfounded but lurid accusations and insinuations, have faced endless rumors about their own "special friendship."

Both of them have also been hailed (even celebrated) for standing by their men. And in Hillary's case, she's been noted for working to destroy her husband's attackers, while simultaneously championing women's rights.

The right-wing *New York Post* summed it up: "Hill & Bill, Huma & Carlos—are two political couples mired in sex, lies, and enabling. Not what any presidential campaign wants displayed on the big screen."

Perhaps in response to the unrelenting attacks, Hillary was overheard telling her staffers: "Contrary to popular belief in some quarters, I am not the Bride of Frankenstein. Nor do I make lampshades out of human skin. I just want to be a Baby Boomer grandmother lifting Americans out of their current malaise."

If **Hillary Clinton** had been elected 45th President of the United States in 2016, her closest aide, **Huma Abedin**, of Indian and Pakistani extraction but born in Kalamazoo, Michigan, would probably have become her White House Chief of Staff—and one of the most powerful women in the world .

At ease behind the scenes, and notoriously private, Abedin had began working for Mrs. Clinton in 1996 as a young intern from George Washington University. "I have one daughter," Hillary said. "But if I had a second daughter, it would be Huma." Some of Hillary's enemies asserted that their relationship might have been more than platonic.

At first **Weiner and Abedin** appeared as a flawless "power couple". Weiner was a legislative showman, a gifted and audacious "tribune of the people." He was Jewish, she was Muslim. They complemented one another perfectly. Bill Clinton himself presided at their wedding. Six years later, it all went horribly wrong

Despite its flaws, the long-ago presidential regime of **Bill and Hillary Clinton**—in comparison to that of Donald Trump—now seems dignified, benign, and stately.

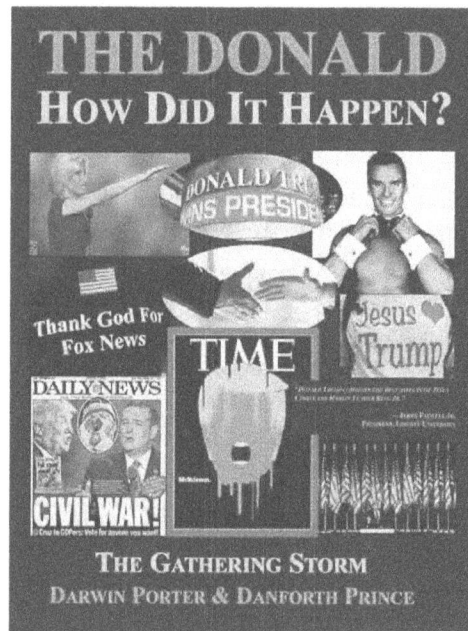

in reference to **Weinergate, Trump** said, "No perverts. We don't want any perverts as Mayor of NYC."

# THE DEMOCRATS' SAVVIEST GUTSY WOMEN,
# HILLARY AND CHELSEA CLINTON

This September (2022), the streaming *Apple TV+* will launch a new series devoted to "trail-blazing women." With each passing year, industrious women are excelling in all fields of endeavor; one is even Vice-President of the United States.

Political forecasters predict that America may have at least two, maybe three, women presidents in this century. Other nations such as Germany and Britain have already had female prime ministers.

The gutsy TV series is hosted by Hillary and Chelsea Clinton, a mother-daughter team. Hillary is admired by millions, and perhaps disliked by an equal number of people. However, those on both sides of the political fence can watch the series, because the focus is on women who have not only forged ahead in various fields but are using their positions to help others less fortunate. The Clintons are not the focus of the series. They are the interviewers.

The complete guest list has not been announced, but here's a preview:

Goldie Hawn is an actress, producer, and singer, a bankable star for three decades, noted for such films as *Private Benjamin* (1980), which won her an Oscar nomination. Before that, she won a Best Supporting Actress Academy Award for her role in *Cactus Flower (1969).* Today, her Hawn Foundation helps educate underprivileged children.

Kim Kardashian is a socialite, businesswoman, and a media personality with millions of followers on Twitter and Instagram. She rose to prominence in the reality TV series *Keeping Up with the Kardashians* (2007-2021). Today, she runs a beauty products empire and is a political activist, lobbying for such causes as prison reform.

An African American entertainer, Wanda Sykes, is a stand-up comedian, actress, and writer. She has been hailed by *Entertainment Weekly* as "one of the 25 funniest people in America." Born in Virginia, she came up the hard way and never allowed rejections to stop her. Today, she is a proud advocate of LGBTQ+ rights.

Born in 1934 and still going strong, Gloria Steinem is a journalist and political activist nationally recognized as a leader of the feminist movement in the late 1960s and early 1970s. Her motto is, "After Black Power, Women's Liberation." In 2005, working with Jane Fonda, she founded Women's Media Center, an organization that works to make women more visible and powerful in the media.

Megan Thee Stallion, born in Texas, overcame great odds to become the most noted female rapper in America. She tops *Billboard* charts and is showered with awards. *Time* magazine has hailed her as "one of the 100 most influential people in America."

Today, she also runs a non-profit group helping underprivileged black communities in Texas and elsewhere gain access to education, housing and health care.

The new TV series stemmed from *The New York Times* bestseller, *The Book of Gutsy Women,* written by Hillary and Chelsea. They profiled every woman from Eleanor Roosevelt to Anne Frank, from Florence Nightingale to Coretta Scott King.

**Two spectacularly gutsy and influential women:**

**Chelsea Clinton** *(left)* and her mother, former U.S. Secretary of State and Presidential candidate **Hillary Rodham Clinton**, are a force behind (and inspiration for) other gutsy women.

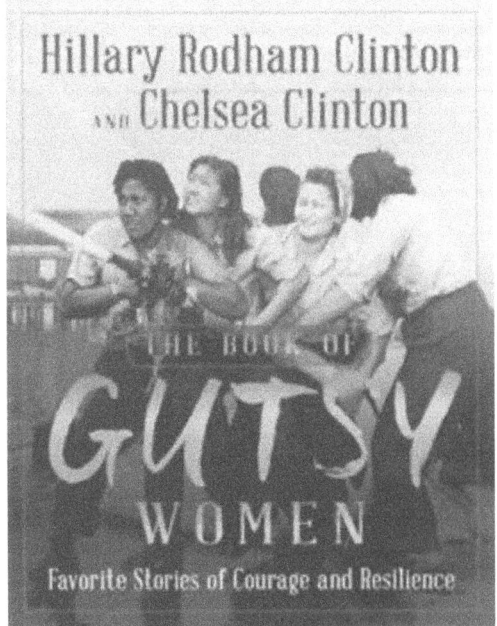

**WOMEN WHO MAKE THE WORLD A BETTER PLACE:**
*Stories of Courage and Resilience*

In the book that inspired a recent series on Apple TV, **Hillary Rodham Clinton** and her daughter, **Chelsea**, share the stories of gutsy women who have inspired them—women with the courage to stand up to the status quo, ask hard questions, and, as promoted by the authors, get the job done.

A book reviewer, George Slater, wrote: "The book suggests that women may one day rule the world. Let's face it: We men haven't done such a great job, especially when millions of lives were sacrificed in needless wars, and we've heated up the planet so much that the Arctic is melting seven times faster than predicted."

**Eleanor Roosevelt** with young **FDR**

**Activist feminist Gloria Steinem**

Aviation pioneer **Amelia Earhart**

Nigerian activist and environmentalist **Wangari Maathai**

Singer & rap activist **Megan Thee Stallion**

Diarist **Anne Frank**

Former Chancellor of Germany **Angela Merkel**

Environmentalist & activist **Rachel Carson**

LGBTQ+ Activist **Edie Windsor**

**Lottie Shackelford,** first female mayor of Little Rock, Arkansas

# THE BITCH GODDESS
# THEY CALL FAME

## THE ULTIMATE DREAM?
## OR A NIGHTMARE?

The mother of Hollywood gossip columnists, Louella Parsons, once remarked, "Fame is a destructive goddess. I've seen not only starlets destroyed in pursuit of it, but the lives of bigtime stars also wrecked. When sudden fame comes to some young stars, they are not prepared to cope with the pressures."

A poll once taken at Hollywood High School asked both boys and girls their wish in life. Eight out of ten listed "fame and fortune," preferably in the movie business.

Parson's dire assessment still rings true today, as these recent cases of those who fell from grace reveal:

Canadian pop singer Justin Bieber has gone from adorable teenager to arrogant, self-destructive "wild child." His fresh-faced youth and charm brought him millions of fans from around the world, but the overnight sensation couldn't handle it, at one point admitting that his behavior was "reckless and immature."

Caught on tape delivering racist remarks, he has gone from one mishap to another, including battles with paparazzi resulting in a death; expulsion from deluxe hotels; curses at President Clinton; photographs showing him urinating in a mop bucket; damaging his neighbors' property; reckless driving; and the list goes on. In some circles, there have been calls for his deportation from the United States. Since he's still so young, there is hope that he will pull back from the brink.

The most recent and tragic example of an actress who squandered her stardom is "tabloid queen" Lindsay Lohan. As she admitted, "It is clear to me that my life has become completely unmanageable because I am addicted to alcohol and drugs."

A star at the age of ten, based partly on pictures she starred in for Disney, she won America's hearts. Since then, millions of her fans have turned away. She lost the chance to play porn queen Linda Lovelace, and her starring role as Elizabeth Taylor in the film, *Liz and*

A recent and more tortured depiction of **Daniel Radcliffe**, formerly known as the wholesome and bespectacled apprentice sorcerer, *Harry Potter* before he morphed into an occasionally exhibitionistic adult.

**Lindsay Lohan**, grown up and a lot more tormented and self-destructive than when she thrived as the poster girl for Sweet Sixteen-ers everywhere.

Two views of **Justin Bieber**: *Left,* during his teeny-bopper, boy band period and *right* from his Instagram page, depicting him as ultra-urban, alienated, weirdly non-conformist, and, according to some, "artfully hostile."

REST IN PEACE & THANK GOD FOR LITTLE BOYS: **Whitney Houston** (left) and "The King of Pop," **Michael Jackson**.

*Dick* was ridiculed by critics.

Today, she is almost unrecognizable, fast-aging, with lips and face botched by Botox and failed attempts at plastic surgery.

At her peak, she was paid $7 million for the film, *Just My Luck,* but everything went downhill after that: DUI arrests, jail time, unsuccessful rehab at the Betty Ford Clinic, probation violations, arrest for stealing a diamond necklace. Her future is uncertain. But despite it all, she still wants to party.

The two most notorious examples of super stars who descended the road to ruin and ultimately, death, were singers Michael Jackson and Whitney Houston.

*Seguéing* from the cuddly kid star of the Jackson 5 to the king of Pop, Jackson morphed into a bizarre legend who, at the peak of his career faced charges of drug abuse and homosexual child molestation.

There was a "laughable" marriage to Elvis Presley's daughter, Lisa Marie, plus another "marriage" to Debbie Rowe that produced three beautiful white children with unknown fathers.

Jackson's bizarre behavior earned him the title of "Wacko Jacko." On June 25, 2009, while trying to stage a comeback, he suffered a fatal heart attack after taking large doses of sedatives and anesthetics. In the aftermath of it all, his doctor was jailed for involuntary manslaughter.

Now, six years later, additional lawsuits are pending for child molestation, and the IRS is knocking on the door, demanding $702 million in back taxes, plus interest.

The list of stars who collided with fame and suffered the consequences include Britney Spears, Zac Ephron, Gary Coleman, *Home Alone's* Macaulay Culkin, *Harry Potter* star Daniel Radcliffe, *Transformers* actor Shia LaBeouf, and too-hot-to-be-handled Miley Cyrus, who's always lasciviously sticking out her tongue. (She's the singer who introduced the word "twerking" into our vocabulary.)

Let's end on an upbeat note: The best role model for an actor who ended his cycle of arrests and rehab is Robert Downey, Jr. His out-of-control drug habit, arrests, and jail time are now subcomponents in a tale of resurrection.

Sobering up, Downey re-entered films with one mega-hit after another, his *Iron Man* grossing more than $600 million. It was followed by box office sequels, each a hit, and other big successes which included *The Avengers* and yet another big success, *Sherlock Holmes* and its sequels. Downey's latest film, *The Judge,* wherein Robert Duvall plays his cantankerous father, is arguably his greatest performance to date.

According to Downey, as noted in a recent interview, "I'm the poster boy for hitting rock bottom and then making one of the biggest comebacks in Hollywood history. My bank account went from overdraft to millions I haven't had time to count yet."

Arbiter of fame during Classic Hollywood: **Louella Parsons.**

## GRACELAND, IT'S NOT

Here's **Lisa Marie Presley,** ex-wife of Michael, daughter of Elvis, shortly before her death.

Landing on his feet: **Robert Downing, Jr.**

**Shia LaBoeuf.** His road ahead was rocky, filled with dangerous curves.

**Macaulay Culkin:** "What do you do when your best work was as a child?"

Looking unhinged, here's **Britney Spears,** as posted on her Instagram account, dancing, waving a weapon, and evoking panic in some of her fans.

# TURNING FIFTY

## An Ode to Actors Who've Said "Goodbye Forever" to the Big 5-0

Filmmakers at long last are beginning to pay attention to a powerful, fast-rising demographic in American life: Some forty million women who've kissed 50 goodbye are now the richest, healthiest, and most active in world history. They earn yearly salaries of more than $100,000 and control $15 trillion in disposable income.

To an increasing degree, savvy Hollywood producers of feature films and television shows are realizing that this powerful group of women want to see their chronological equivalents on the screen—and certainly not "Miss Teen of 2022."

*left photo* **Julia Roberts** who recently (and brilliantly) portrayed; *Right photo:* **Martha Mitchell,** who appears with her husband, **John Mitchell.** Attorney General of the United States during the presidential administration of Richard Nixon,

*The Golden Girls* are back *en masse,* asserting themselves as never before. Joan Collins, the former "sex kitten" imported long ago from England, is now 88, still generating rave reviews and living with a much younger man.

After a long absence from the screen, Julia Roberts is back, too. Her films have brought in more than $4 billion globally, prompting *People* magazine to cite her as the most beautiful woman in the world a record five times.

She has stunned TV audiences in her series *Gaslit,* in which she plays the outspoken Martha Mitchell, the hard-to-forget wife of Richard Nixon's Attorney General, John Mitchell, whose character was portrayed by Sean Penn. "Had it not been for 'Martha the Mouth,' Nixon claimed, ruefully, "There'd have been no Watergate."

In Roberts' upcoming "rom-com," *Ticket to Paradise,* set for an October 2022 release, she co-stars with age-appropriate George Clooney (born in 1961).

Sandra Bullock, born in 1964, the last year of the Baby Boomers' demographic, was the world's highest-paid actress in 2010 and again in 2014. *Time* Magazine named her as one of the one hundred most influential people in the world.

*Left photo*: Golden Girls (*clockwise from left*), **Rue McClanahan, Betty White, Estelle Getty,** and **Bea Arthur.**

*Right photo:* **Joan Collins,** still sexy in her 80s.

At age 57, she's in *The Lost City* co-starring with still-studly Channing Tatum, 42, no longer a male stripper in a Florida night club, as he was in *Magic Mike.* Brad Pitt also stars. (Would you believe this actor, once voted "sexiest man in the world," is almost 60?)

The beat goes on, even for Jane Fonda, who will turn 85 in December. She recently completed the final episode for the TV series *Grace and Frankie,* with Lily Tomlin, 82. It ran for seven seasons on Netflix, its longest-running show. Early in the

series, their characters' respective husbands divorced them to wed each other.

The sexually alluring Jennifer Lopez, 52, starred in the "rom-com" *Marry Me* (2022) which brought in $52 million. It later became the most-streamed title on *Peacock.* Prime Video is set to release her latest vehicle, *Shotgun Wedding.*

To make two "rom-coms" with actresses over 50, director Nancy Meyers struggled with negativity from male producers who asked her "Who wants to see movies with old broads?"

Meyers, who will be 73 this year, made her mark with *Something's Got to Give* (2003) with Diane Keaton, which brought in $270 million.

That was followed by *It's Complicated,* starring Meryl Streep, whose character re-launches an affair with her ex-husband, played by Alex Baldwin. That movie generated $225 million.

Facing financial woes, Netflix wants to rehire Meyers, this time giving her *carte blanche.*

The moral to all this? Let's face it: Love is not just for the young.

*Left photo:* **Meryl Streep;** *Right photo:* **Sandra Bullock.** How to rake in millions.

**Jane Fonda:** "I went wild at Vassar."

**Barbra Streisand:** "I appeal to everyone."

**Jennifer Lopez:** The multi-million "Rom-Com Girl."

**Lily Tomlin:** A comeback with Jane Fonda.

**Tom Cruise,** whose talent for money-making movies justifies his title, "The Last Movie Star."

**Bianca Jagger** *(right)* shown here as she appeared in 1971 during her chaotic wedding to **Mick Jagger.**

# GREY-HAIRED BOOMERS
## How to Shift the Bottom Lines of New-Age Marketers From Red to Black

---

# SALES & MARKETING 101
### How to "Sell" a Consumer Product, Successfully, to Baby Boomers

1. Pick a role model that all of them know and understand. **Lucille Ball** *(center photo, top)*, **Marlene Dietrich** *(left photo, top)*, and **Elizabeth Taylor** *(right photo, top)* are excellent examples.
2. Emphasize the role model's credibility and durability. The "LUCY WE LOVED" entertained Boomers for longer than virtually any of them can remember. Her reruns are still being screened, frequently and worldwide.
3. If you can, and if the product you're marketing is upscale enough, emphasize the role model's "**Glam Quotient**." Even on her last legs, Lucille, a former fashion model for Hattie Carnegie—*remember her?*—could always, if enough stylists and makeup pros were there to prep her, look fabulous. *Ditto for Marlene. Ditto for "La Liz."*

### Black What??

In 1968, before (fully justified) protests from Animal Rights activists made fur unfashionable, **The Great Lakes Mink Association (aka Blackglama)** inaugurated an ad campaign to sell more mink. Aimed at Baby Boomers, their campaign focused more on WHO was wearing it than it did on the garment itself.

In 1979, **Lucille Ball**, with the help of some WAY overworked stylists, pulled herself together and joined the ranks of equivalent celebrities who plugged Blackglama with the slogan, "**What Becomes a Legend Most?**" She wasn't the first: **Taylor** and **Crawford**, with equivalent brouhahas, preceded her by a decade.

As payment, many received a furpiece of their choice and the satisfaction of knowing that they were "instantly recognizable," even without spelling out their names, to millions of Baby Booming consumers.

Since then, **Blackglama** has been cited in marketing manuals as the sponsors of one of the 20th Century's most BOOMER-CENTRIC (and spectacularly successful) ad campaigns.

461

**Advertisers and marketers** should take note of the profit potential of an aging population. At present, the 60-plus generation (i.e., "Late in Life Baby Boomers") control 80 percent of the American economy. It's not going to stop there.

By the end of the decade, seniors will far outnumber millennials and members of Generation Z, and will control even more of the wealth. Every day, 12,000 American men and women celebrate their 60th birthday. In China, the older population increases by 54,000 every day.

Senior incomes in America tend to be higher (and more resilient and durable) than that of younger generation because many older people collect pensions or have investment incomes. Of course, others are heavily in debt and not prepared. Studies have shown that American women outnumber American men by more than 25%, and that women tend to be better at managing their incomes.

Surveys have also shown that a 70-year-old today lives better than a 50-year-old in the 1980s, during which Ronald Reagan was president for eight years.

In a recent article, AARP claimed, "Baby Boomers have the bucks, but advertisers often don't seem to care."

In this election year, more than any other in political history, politicians seem to have gotten hip to the message that as a demographic, Boomers can mean the difference between their party's victory and its defeat. Of course, aging is not what it used to be: In 1900, men faced a life expectancy of 42.

According to estimates, Boomers control $60 trillion of the nation's assets, maybe a lot more.

Of course, they had a lot of breaks when they entered life. After World War II, Americans experienced the greatest economic growth in the history of the world. For example, on my street in Staten Island, houses that sold for $28,000 in 1970 now pull in $1.3 million, even $2 million.

As one economist put it, "Whereas the Boomer generations enjoyed enormous prosperity, they seem to have made a collective decision to pull the ladder up behind them."

In distinctive contrast, millennials faced a different world: Housing costs rose 300% to 700% above what their parents paid, and college tuition soared 1,100% Expenses in virtually every other field also went skyward.

Of course, there are downsides to the senior economy: After retirement, many Boomers find it difficult to maintain their former lifestyle. And instead of an early retirement, many are staying on the job market longer than ever instead of retiring at age 62 or 65.

And to an increasing degree, Boomers seem to be clear that they must use their voting power to overcome major legal and institutional barriers.

Marketing expert G. Richard Ambrosius suggested that "advertising should focus on lifelong health and well-being, productivity, later life autonomy and empowerment, and connectedness to family, friends, and community. By doing so, perhaps the general public will come to view later life as something to look forward to and enjoy, defining 'old age' as a time to celebrate the uniqueness and worth of each individual regardless of their age or infirmity."

Perhaps, indeed, marketers and advertisers will look upon seniors as a potentially profitable consumer demographic. One can only hope that they'll directly address and appeal to them, bypassing Generations X and Z in favor of their (wealthier) elders.

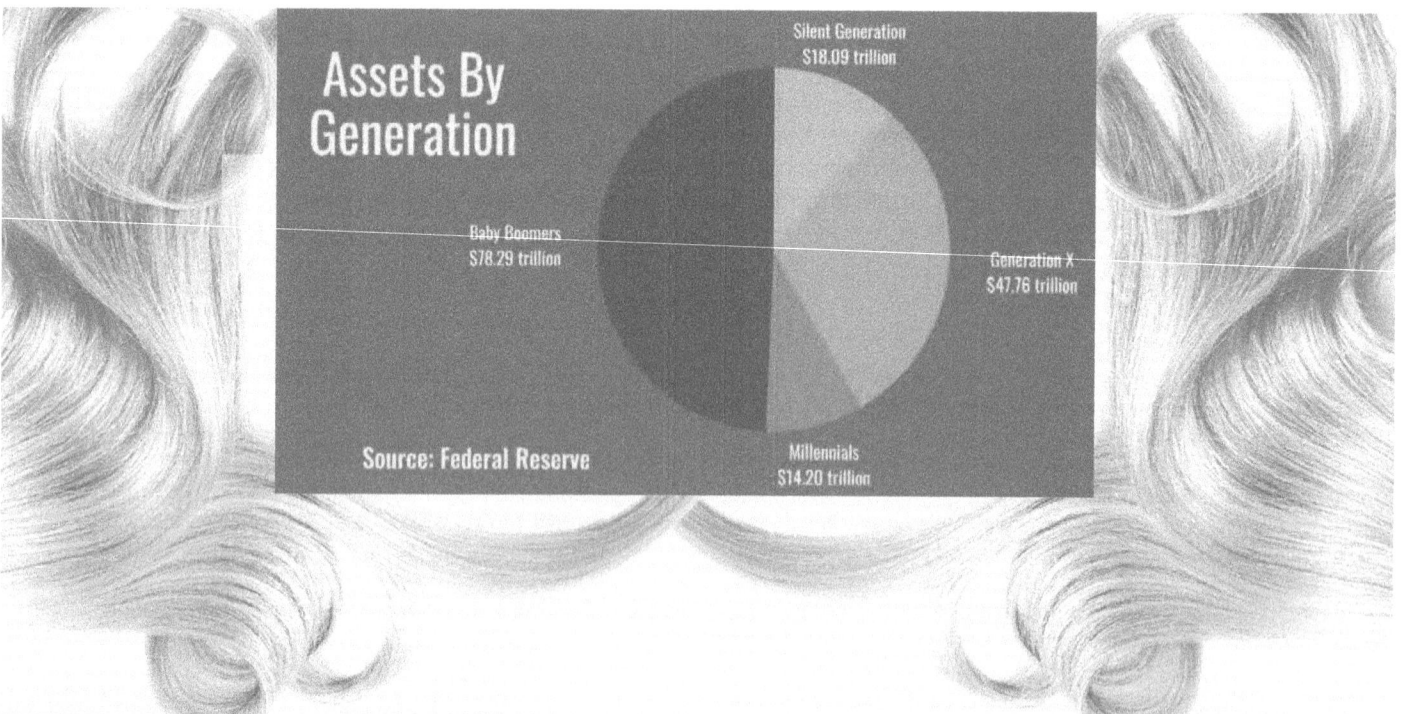

Assets By Generation

Silent Generation
$18.09 trillion

Baby Boomers
$78.29 trillion

Generation X
$47.76 trillion

Millennials
$14.20 trillion

Source: Federal Reserve

**This chart from the Federal Reserve** says a lot about who really holds most of the wealth in the USA. *And who really wants to argue with the Federal Reserve?*

# GRAY
## IS THE NEW BLACK

The last of the Baby Boomers have crossed the half-century mark, and they have never lived their lives without TV. The average TV viewer in America today is 54 years old, and Boomers watch their sets at the rate of 6 to 12 hours a day.

At long last, TV bigwigs and advertisers are paying attention to this "booming" market. Boomers between 50 and 68 shell out $2.3 trillion a year in consumer spending, as opposed to the Millennials (ages 14 to 32) who part with $1 trillion.

Show after show on TV is now being specifically targeted to senior citizens. So many gray-haired stars are being hired, it's called "The Gray Revolution."

CBS executive David Potrack told the press: "An affluent 58-year-old is more valuable than a 22-year-old, who is often struggling to make ends meet with student loans. Perhaps they are still living with their parents. If TV executives try to 'young-down' their viewing audience, they are defying gravity."

Boomers buy vacation homes. They redecorate existing houses. They purchase cars. They organize luxurious vacations. They are the chief clients of investment firms. And they buy presents for their grandchildren.

Before the dawn of the Gray Revolution, two hit shows featuring veteran actresses, each a senior citizen, were canceled even though they were hits. These included *Murder, She Wrote,* starring Angela Lansbury, 89, as a crime-solving mystery book writer. Still going strong in 1996, it was axed even though drawing an audience of 23 million. Oscar-winner and cancer survivor Kathy Bates won two Emmys with her hit TV show, *Harry's Law,* but it bit the dirt in 2012 in spite of its wide following. TV executives wanted to replace these shows with programs aimed at younger audiences.

In opposition to the earlier trends as noted above, here is a sample of the post-millennial "graying" of TV. Some time-tested stars are being summoned out of retirement.

As he nears his 70th birthday, TV veteran Tom Selleck stars in the popular series, *Blue Bloods,* a police drama that entered its fifth year on CBS in 2014. Selleck is cast as a police commissioner.

Ted Danson, 66, played bartender Sam Malone in the hit TV series, *Cheers,* when he was younger. Now older and grayer, he's back, starring in *CSI: Crime Scene Investigation*, a drama that premiered on CBS in 2000. In 2012, the series was named the most watched TV show in the world for the fifth year, and in 2014, it was renewed for its 15th season.

In 1986, *People* magazine designated Mark Harmon as "the Sexiest Man Alive." At 62, he's now starring in the hit CBS series, *NCIS*, where he has interpreted the role of Leroy Jethro Gibbs since 2003 when the show premiered.

James Spader, 54, stars in the crime drama *The Blacklist,* a hit since it premiered on NBC in 2013. The Boston-born actor, who was once a stable boy and later a truck driver, was previously known for his interpretation of eccentric characters in such films as *Sex, Lies, and Videotape.*

Another "oldster," Robin Williams, 62, headlines *The Crazy Ones,* a sitcom which first aired on CBS in 2013. He plays an eccentric Chicago advertising executive who can sell anything, "even clouds to God."

Another sitcom, *The Millers,* premiered on CBS in 2013. It follows the zany exploits of a family living in Leesburg, Virginia. In the series is

New television dramas reflect the understated **"Gray Revolution"** that has permeated some aspects of American entertainment.

Generating impressive ad revenues, they're cast with proud, sometimes eccentric but dignified older characters who are wiser, smarter, and less self-indulgent than the 20-something "teeney-boppers" who preceded them.

Many of them are "Boomies" who came of age in the 1950s and 1960s. They clearly remember the assassinations of JFK and Martin Luther King; Beatlemania and the Vietnam War: and some of them remember transistor radios, the first color TV sets, and jitterbugging jive.

In quiet recognition of their impressive spending power, TV networks like CBS are quietly cashing in, showcasing actors who appear, at least, to have benefitted from the battles they've waged and their hard-won survival skills.

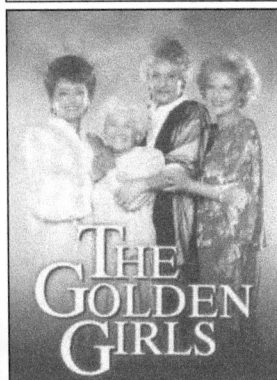

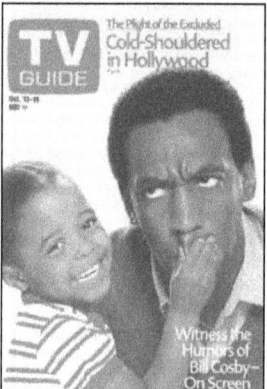

Beau Bridges, 72, the son of movie star, Lloyd Bridges. In his private life, he is a vegan and a devout Christian who will not utter a line of dialogue that "takes the Lord's name in vain." A Texan, Margo Martindale, 62, also stars in *The Millers*. When she won the Critics' Choice TV award for her role as a charmingly villainous and occasionally brutal matriarch in *Justified* in 2012, she asked, "Who said turning 60 was a bad thing?"

The grandfather of them all, Bill Cosby, 76, despite his widely publicized disgrace for sexual aggression with many of his television co-stars, is attempting a comeback, as of this writing, as a sitcom hero. Prospects for this aren't lookng good for him, for any involvement in other TV series. But for the reord, for five years in a row (1985-89), *The Cosby Show,* which aired from 1984 to 1992, was the number-one most watched TV show in America. The series highlighted the experiences and interactions of an affluent African-American family.

As regards the growing "Gray Revolution" appeal of older actors in sitcoms and TV dramas, media consultant William Davenport said, "It isn't an ocean wave, it's a tsunami."

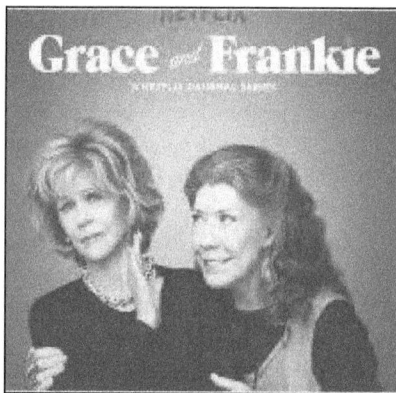

Jane Fonda and Lily Tomlin discussing the ironies of their failed marriages, with humor, in *Grace & Frankie*, a hip, "postmodern" sitcom series.

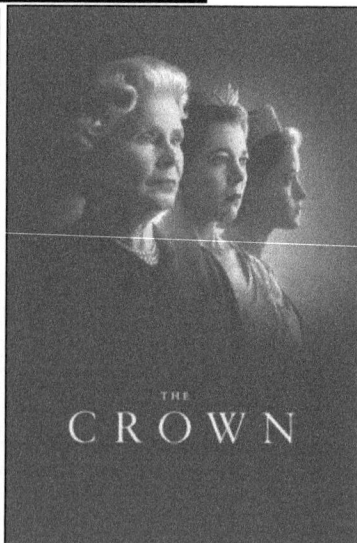

---

## WHAT MIGHT BE THE "MOTHER LODE" OF TELEVISION DRAMAS AIMED AT OLDER AUDIENCES?

Older viewers fascinated by updated views of characters they might have revered in earlier years might become binge-addicted to any of the historical dramas pumped out by the BBC as broadcast on PBS: Examples include **Downton Abbey** and **The Crown**: "Who?" a sophisticated, well-seasoned viewer might ask, "could resist gossip, pith-packed overviews of archtypes from the deeply flawed but "stately" old days of the British Empire?

**Warning**: Watch them at your own peril, because—if you're anything like us—they can quickly become addictive.

# 2017: One of the Greatest Years Ever for
# SOPHISTICATED FILMS

**Recognition of films** and the actors who help create them come and go, but at least some of the great movies released during the closing months of 2017 may stick around for the century.

At least 25 of them deserve honors for acting, writing, and directing.

Is there a residue of sorrow associated with these awards? Perhaps it derives from the unhappy truth that good roles in the film industry are rare, and many of the actors who competed and lost might never again be rewarded with such pithy parts.

Here in a nutshell is a short list of recent films not to be missed:

***

Widely heralded from the New York islands to the California coast, *The Post,* a Steven Spielberg drama, stars Meryl Streep as the publisher of *The Washington Post.* With the kind of white knuckles that might evoke some of the current stress associated with the White House's present occupant, she makes the controversial decision to publish "The Pentagon Papers" about the Vietnam War. She is backed up by Tom Hanks as her crusading editor, Ben Bradley.

In this era of allegations about sexual harassment, *Three Billboards Outside Ebbing, Missouri* explores a timely theme. Frances McDormand delivers a brilliant performance as the avenging mom of a rape-murder victim. The film has been hailed as a gut-twisting renegade masterpiece.

Attracting millions of straight people, *Call Me By Your Name* is the greatest gay-themed film in history. The plot is miles beyond the relatively morbid *Brokeback Mountain.* With tender, loving care, the story follows a 17-year old, living with his parents in Italy, who falls in love with a 24-year-old American graduate student, played by Armie Hammer, who comes to live with them. It's one of the screen's greatest explorations of male adolescence. Its protagonist, the much-lauded Timothée Chalamet did the unthinkable: He not only starred in *Call Me By Your Name,* but also appeared in two of 2017's most lauded films, *Lady Bird* and *Hostiles.*

Laden with honors, *The Shape of Water* opened the year by winning a dozen Bafta (the British equivalent of the Oscars) nominations. In the role of a lifetime, Sally Hawkins played a mute custodian at a high-security government lab. During the course of the film, she falls in love with an amphibian creature. Not all of its reviews were raves. The acerbic critic of yesterday, Rex Reed, defined it as "a loopy, lunkheaded load of drivel." His voice was in the minority, almost lost within an ocean of approval.

Like Hawkins, Gary Oldman also played the role of a lifetime—in his case, that of Winston Churchill—in *The Darkest Hour.* The British Prime Minister led Britain in the 1940s when it stood virtually alone facing the Nazi menace on the verge of overthrowing the Western democracies.

Another World War II drama, *Dunkirk,* has been hailed as one of the greatest films ever made about World War II. It depicts the frantic evacuation from a beach in northern France of some 300,000 British soldiers who would otherwise have been annihilated. Virtually every boat or ship on the southern coast of England sailed across the storm-tossed English Channel to rescue the men.

In another era in England—in this case at the turn of the 20th Century—Judi Dench virtually inhabits the soul of the aging Queen Victoria in *Victoria & Abdul.* Based on a true story, it depicts the controversial *amitié-amoureuse* between Victoria (aka the Empress of India, as played by Dench), and her Indian Muslim servant, Abdul.

In *Phantom Thread,* Daniel Day-Lewis reaches the pinnacle of his career as a couturier who designs clothes and sews secrets into them. Set in the 1950s, he turns

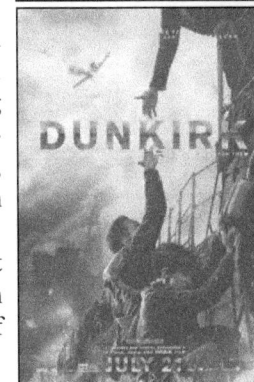

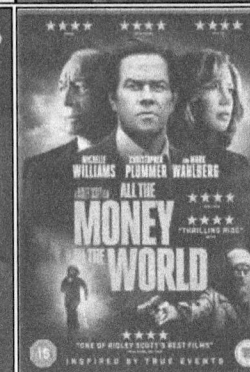

drawings into dreams.

In what may be his swan song to movies, Christopher Plummer returns to the screen in *All the Money in the World.* Cast as billionaire J. Paul Getty, he refuses to pay a ransom for his kidnapped grandson, John Paul Getty III.

*Hostiles,* a period drama set in 1892, is the most acclaimed Western since Gary Cooper's *High Noon.* Christian Bale, in his greatest role, stars as an army captain escorting a dying Cheyenne chief on a treacherous journey back to his birthplace.

America's two leading film critics, A.O. Scott and Manohla Dargis of *The New York Times,* each selected *The Florida Project* as Best Picture of the Year. Brooklyn Price plays an impoverished six-year-old urchin living in a shabby motel near Disney World. Her depressive, uncouth world is turned into a masterpiece of remorse.

An ensemble cast has scored a hit with the much-publicized *Mudbound,* an epic drama tracing the intersecting lives of two families—one black, one white—living on the same piece of Mississippi farmland in 1940.

*Lady Bird* (no, it's not about the former First Lady) is a coming-of-age drama hailed as "a stray emerald in a discarded pile of rhinestones." Saoirse Ronan evoked Meryl Streep in the delivery of her character with an unshowy honesty, like an artichoke thistle, spiky and layered.

In his greatest role, *Stronger,* Jake Gyllenhaal portrays a survivor of the Boston Marathon massacre, who has his lower legs amputated and must adjust to his diminished body.

Cynthia Nixon in *A Quiet Passion* becomes the poet Emily Dickinson, "The Belle of Amherst," who wrote with mercurial and almost terrifying perception.

So, which film did our president order to be shown at the White House? He selected Hugh Jackman cast as P.T. Barnum in *The Greatest Showman.* The creator of the Barnum & Bailey Circus is still famous for saying, "There's a sucker born every minute."

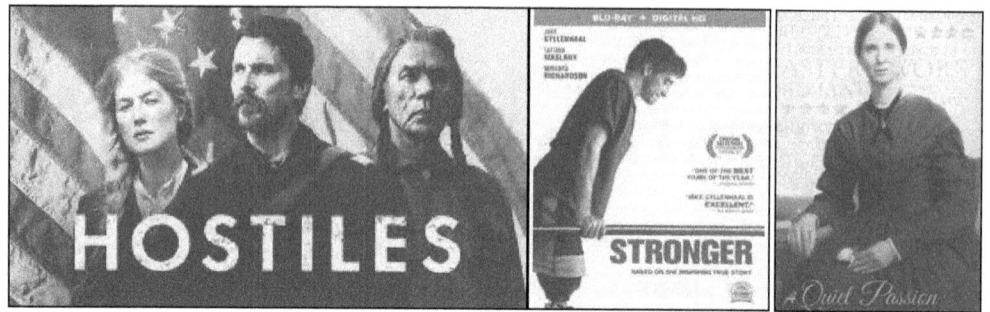

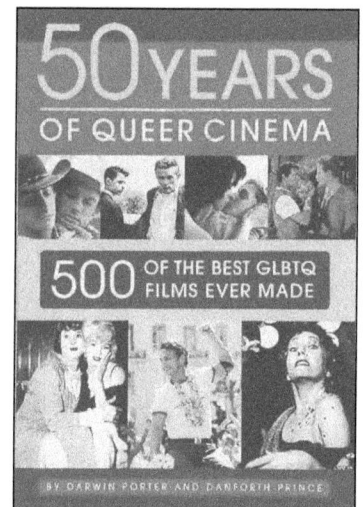

---

**Did you Know?** *That Darwin Porter and Danforth Prince (the authors, as you probably guessed, of the three volutmes displayed above) have been very visibly fascinated by filmmaking and the style in which they're reviewed? .*

*After their releases, each them won some widely publicized literary awards and respectable numbers of positive (sometimes rave) reviews, too. Here are just a few of them:*

*** 

*"Authoritative, exhaustive, and essential, Blood Moon's Guide to Gay and Lesbian Film is the queer girl's and queer boy's one-stop resource for what to add to their feature-film queue. The film synopses and snippets of critic's reviews are reason enough to keep these compendiums of cinematic information close to the DVD player. But the extras—including the Blood Moon Awards and commentary on queer short films—are butter on the popcorn."*

**—Books to Watch Out For**

*"This 400-page first edition of everything fabu in movies is an essential guide for both the casual viewer and the hard-core movie-watching homo."*

**—Bay Windows (Boston)**

*"Something new that's a lot of fun is* Blood Moon's Guide to Gay and Lesbian Film. *It's like having access to a feverishly compiled queer film fan's private scrapbook. It's valuable and a lot of fun and, like screen representations of us, it verges wildly between tribute and titillation. Now, I'm ready for my closeup."*

**—Gay Times (London)**

# 2019's OSCAR RACE FOR BEST PICTURE OF THE YEAR

(THIS ARTICLE APPEARED IN THE DECEMBER 2019 EDITION OF *BOOMER TIMES*)

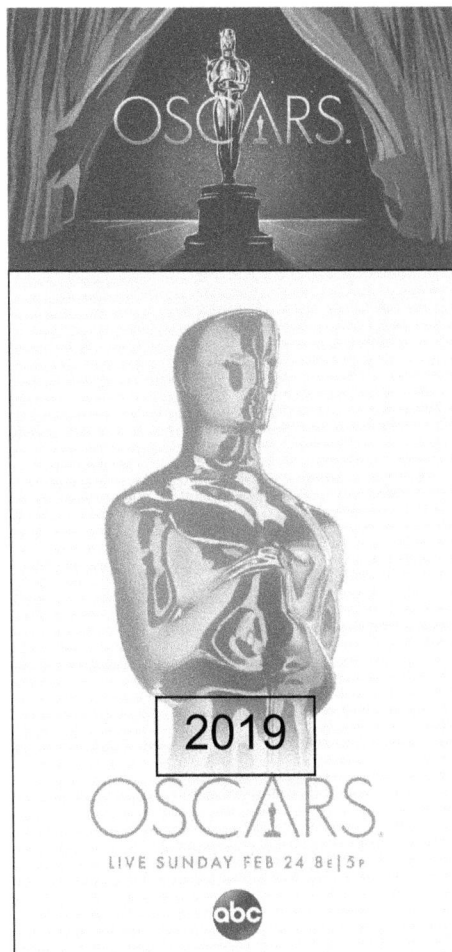

At the end of every year, Hollywood producers unleash upon us what they hope will be the Oscar-nominated Best Picture of the Year. The field was particularly overheated for 2019.

Critics who saw the films listed below began extolling their virtues at festivals in Cannes, Sundance, or Toronto. The race is so close that a photo finish is predicted.

Here in a nutshell is a preview of some of the movies that generated the most buzz, even controversy.

Helen Mirren and Ian McKellen, a Dame and a Knight of the British Empire, are paired as a dynamic duo in *The Good Liar*, a crime thriller of fake identities and deception. A clever, dangerous con man moves in on a rich widow, hoping to make off with her fortune.

Some critics have attacked director Bill Condon for not being Alfred Hitchcock, but the film is worth the cost of a ticket just to see these two veteran stars face off against each other. Each seems incapable of delivering a bad performance.

A trio of America's most talented veteran actors teamed to make *The Irishman*, an epic crime drama. Directed by Martin Scorsese, Al Pacino is cast as Jimmy Hoffa, the powerful boss of the Teamsters Union. The film follows Frank Sherman (Robert De Niro), a truck driver who becomes a hitman for mobster Russell Bufalino (Joe Pesci).

Scorsese has already been nominated for seven Best Picture Oscars, and he has a good chance again in the most expensive film he ever made, and one of his most compelling.

If you want a chilling panoramic movie adventure for the entire family, check out *The Aeronauts*, a biographical adventure based on the 1862 flight of British aeronauts who reached a death-defying altitude of 39,000 feet in their hot air balloon. Felicity Jones is cast as a daredevil pilot, with Eddie Redmayne playing a weather scientist on their epic flight up into the heavens. The film is enhanced greatly by its special effects, a real visual treat.

If you thought that all the heroic real-life stories of World War II had already been filmed, guess again and arrange a screening of *A Hidden Life.* Director and screenwriter Terrance Malick dramatized the emotional story of a peasant Austrian, a devout Catholic named Franz Jägerstätter who refuses to join the Nazi Army. His heartbreaking story is replicated by actor August Biehl. The historical figure of Jägerstätter was imprisoned and later executed by the Third Reich in August of 1943.

Scarlett Johansson returns to the screen in one of her best roles in years, the thought-provoking comedy-drama, *Marriage Story*. In it, she plays actress Nicole Barber, who is divorcing her stage director husband, Charlie (Adam Driver), and engaged

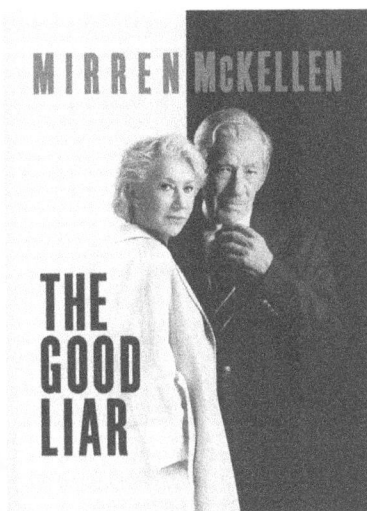

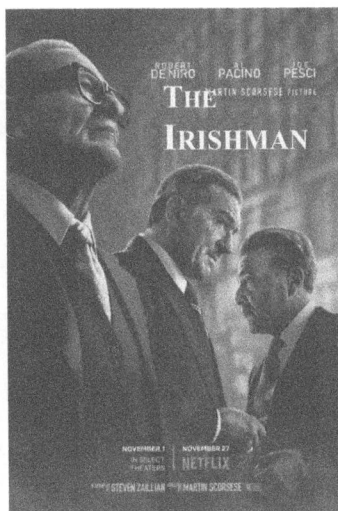

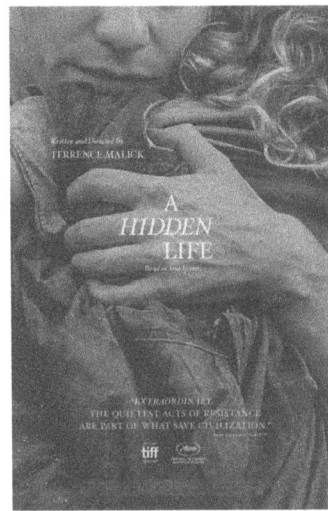

From the entertainment industry, 2019 was studded with sophisticated and nuanced films specifically aimed at Boomers, *Left to right* in the lineup above, Oscar contenders included **The Good Liar, The Irishman, The Aeronauts,** and **A Hidden Life.**

Other films timed for release in 2019—a year studded with contenders aimed at Boomers, included, *left to right*, **Marriage Story, Honey Boy, The Two Popes,** and **Dark Waters.**

in a grueling coast-to-coast battle of wills. The film was no doubt inspired by the real divorce of its director, Noah Baumbach from his ex-wife, actress Jennifer Jason Leigh.

Another personal saga, the autobiographical *Honey Boy,* was ripped from the childhood of Shia LaBeouf, dramatizing his relationship with his father. Bad Boy LaBeouf wrote the screenplay while in rehab.

Not for the faint of heart, it has been hailed as a cinematic act of courage and self-revelation. For it, LaBeouf has been cited as a possible double Oscar contender as Best Actor and Best Screenplay.

This year's coven of Oscar hopefuls is characterized by its use of senior citizen stars. Such is the case in the casting of Jonathan Pryce as Cardinal Bergoglio and Anthony Hopkins as Pope Benedict XVI. Many scenes of their movie, *The Two Popes*, were shot in Argentina. The dialogue between these two veteran actors is brilliant. If each were nominated for an Oscar, it might be a tie vote. Interest in the movie is not confined just to Catholics—for its articulate presentation of dilemmas, it has universal appeal.

A legal thriller, *Dark Waters*, is not necessarily a cheery flick that evokes good cheer at Christmas. A grim, tight-fisted drama, it was based on an article in *The New York Times* entitled "The Lawyer Who Became DuPont's Worst Nightmare."

It depicts the story of a brave environmentally sensitive attorney, Mark Ruffalo (Robert Blott), who explores a number of unexplained deaths downstream from a chemical manufacturer. During his eventual prosecution of one of the world's largest corporations, DuPont, he risks everything—his future, his family, and even his own life— to expose the truth.

Foreign films don't win Best Picture Oscars. If they did, this year's entry, *Parasite*, might have a fighting chance. At its world premiere in Cannes, it won the Palme d'Or as Best Picture, the first Korean film ever to do so.

It was written, produced, and directed by the multi-talented Bong Joonho. It relays the tale of a poor young man who's hired as the tutor of a daughter born into a rich family. With unexpected results, he slowly infiltrates their most private lives. In a nutshell, "It's like a tick that's swollen with bitter blood and class rage."

*The Wall Street Journal* compared it to "a high wire act where the acrobat suddenly reaches up to a higher wire, then to another even higher wire."

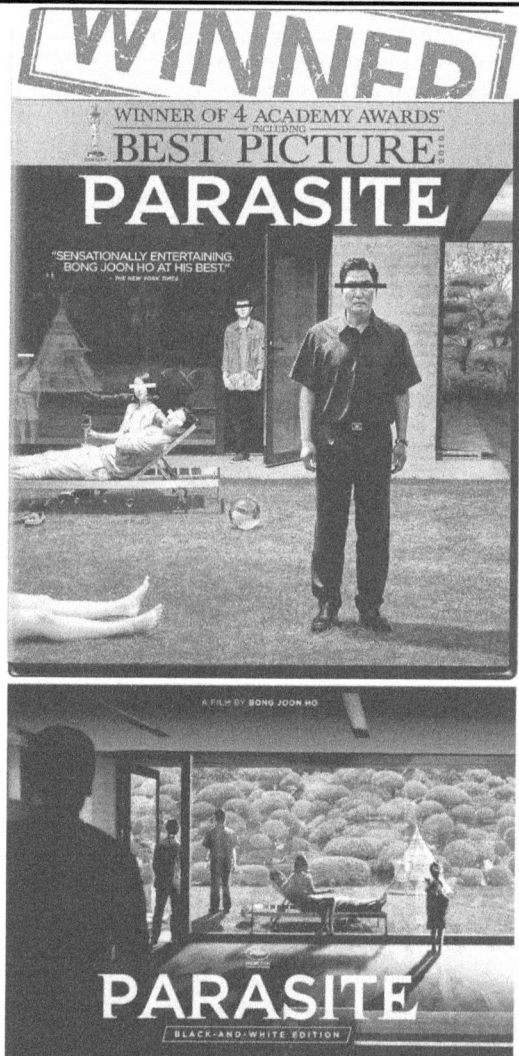

**FASCINATING:** It's historically rare for a foreign (*i.e., "not made in the U.S."*) film to be designated as the Academy Awards' Best Picture of the Year.

But in 2019, **Parasite**, a film written, produced, and filmed in South Korea, won BEST PICTURE within a landscape where the competition was ferocious.

# POLYAMORY

## *What's Love Got to Do With It?*

Promotional photos for Showtime's *Polyamory, Married & Dating.(left)* and for TLC's *Sister Wives (right)*

You won't find the word "polyamory" in all dictionaries, yet tens of thousands of Americans practice it as a lifestyle. Polyamory is the practice, desire, or acceptance of having more than one intimate relationship at a time with the knowledge and consent of everyone involved. It is often described as "consensual, ethical, and responsible non-monogamy."

Although several film scripts devoted to "sex triangles" are being shopped around to various studios in Hollywood, television (in the form of recent reality series) has done more than any other media in showcasing this emerging lifestyle. "Polyamorists" have been extensively interviewed about their shared lovers on news and feature programs.

The most high-profile TV series is Showtime's *Polyamory: Married & Dating,* which has been called "trashy and profound, hilarious, shocking, titillating, cringe-inducing, and the best reality show on TV."

Another TV reality show, *Sister Wives,* entered its fourth season in July of 2013, attracting millions of viewers. Patriarch Kody Brown is legally married to only one of his four wives; together, the family has 17 children. He refers to his relationships with his other wives as "spiritual unions." Before *Sister Wives, Big Love*—a series about multiple partners—was a big hit for HBO, running for several years. The Fox Channel entered the game with its own drama series, *Lone Star,* launched in 2010.

The distinguished junior senator from Utah, **Mitt Romney,** a politician and businessman with deep ancestral roots to polyamory.

The "High Priestess' of Polyamory: **Tristan Taormino**

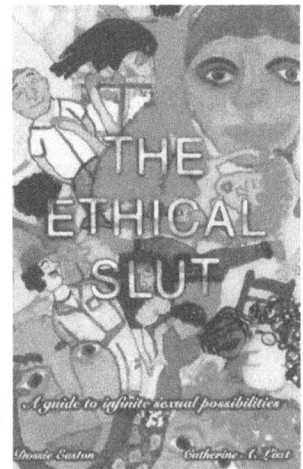

For the bisexual, polyamory is ideal, but it's estimated that followers of this lifestyle are mostly straight—that is, two men sharing one woman or two women sharing one man. Polygamy, of course, is illegal. That's why Mitt Romney's ancestors fled from Utah to Mexico. But within most polyamory relationships today, a participating (often married) couple, brings in another partner, in the form of either a woman or another man. Trios of gay men often form loving relationships, with or without marriage in states where gay marriage is legal.

Because of the potential for cultural diversity of these relationships, scriptwriters of the future will have endless possibilities for drama. Scenarios involving "boy-meets-girl" will be amplified into setups where a girl meets boys, or a boy meets girls, as part of whatever sex triad warms their hearts.

The high priestess of polyamory is award-winning author, Tristan Taormino, whose articles appear in media outlets that range from *The New York Times* to *Playboy.* She wrote "the Bible of Polyamory"—*Opening Up: A Guide to Creating and Sustaining Open Relationships,* a bestseller.

*The Ethical Slut: A Practical Guide to Polyamory,* by Dossie Easton.

She asks, "Is monogamy realistic? In polyamory, you get to do different things with different partners, both emotionally and physically. Monogamy sets us up to fail, or be deceitful. It assumes that one person is going to meet all of our needs—emotional, physical, sexual, spiritual, financial—and that is impossible."

Dr. Jack Morin, author of *The Erotic Mind,* has hailed Taormino's work as "a luscious *smörgåsbord* of non-monogamy as an opportunity for breaking free of one-way models of sex and love."

Since 2000, there have been a load of other books exploring non-monogamy and polyamory, including a hot seller called *The Ethical Slut: A Practical Guide to Polyamory* by Dossie Easton.

Local support groups—some clandestine, some open—are forming in every state in the union. Gette Levy, President of

**Carl Dean** (left) with his wife, **Dolly Parton.**

**Vivien Leigh** as Scarlett with **Hattie McDaniel** as Mammy in *Gone With the Wind* (1939).

| | |
|---|---|
| **Mo'nique** | **Tilda Swinton** |

**TESTING LIMITS: Robin Thicke** with **Miley Cyrus** at the Video Music Awards Ceremony in August of 2013.

Open Love in New York, claims "Monogamy is no longer a fiscal and social requirement. The Eisenhower '50s are dead and gone."

A recent survey by the University of Wisconsin revealed that women, almost as much as men, inaugurate polyamorous relationships. "It's so convenient," said Linda (*last name withheld*) a free-lance magazine writer. "I have two men I call my husbands. Both of them work for the same company, and often travel. When one husband is away, I have a spare. When both of them go on the road together, they can make love to each other and keep it all in the family. On our king-size bed at night, we are one happy, loving family, each devoted to the other. We contribute equal expenses to the household and divide the chores. Fortunately, we like the same food, movies, and TV shows."

The celebrity-crazed tabloids have been busy searching for famous married couples suspected of having an open relationship. The most visible speculation centers around country singer Dolly Parton and her longtime husband Carl Dean. Forests in Canada have been felled to make newsprint to write about their mutual "Don't Ask, Don't Tell" policy, although she denies it.

Mo'Nique, the funny, edgy comedian and actress, is married to Sidney Hicks. She told *The New York Times*, "If sex happens with another person, that's not a deal breaker or reason to rush to the divorce court."

Mo'Nique won an Oscar as Best Supporting Actress for her role in *Precious* (2009). She is currently in pre-production on a film devoted to Hattie McDaniel, the first black actress to win an Oscar for her role as Mammy in *Gone With the Wind* (1939). Hattie once said, "I'd rather play a maid on screen than be one."

The brilliant actress, Tilda Swinton, constantly faces rumors that she's involved in simultaneous relationships with her boyfriend, Sandro Kopp, and with John Byrne, the father of her twins.

Jada Pinkett Smith is an American actress, singer-songwriter, and businesswoman (music and fashion companies). She is married to Will Smith. On her Facebook pages, she claims, "Will and I both can do whatever we want. We have a relationship that is 'grown.'"

Finally, Hollywood's (arguably) hottest couple is singer Robin Thicke and Paula Patton. "Paula and I have done just about everything," Thicke told shock jock Howard Stern in July.

Thicke outraged millions of Americans with his notorious performance with Miley Cyrus and her twerking, tongue-lolling VMA performance this past August. Paula seems to have no trouble with her husband's indiscretions, claiming "a little bit of jealousy makes marriage fun."

What's the ultimate conclusion? *In any form, shape, gender, or numbers, love is here to stay.*

**Jada Pinkett Smith** with her husband, **Will Smith**

**LOVE:** Regardless of the configurations involved, it's here to stay.

# Latino Actors: "WHAT ABOUT US?"

Who Will Replace Rita Hayworth or Anthony Quinn?

In 2015 and 2016, the all-white Oscar nominations provoked an uproar at the Academy of Motion Picture Arts & Sciences, which is 72 percent male and 87 percent white, roughly reflecting the demographics of the movie industry itself.

These protests led to the creation of the "Oscars So White" movement. By the very next year (2017), the color filters had changed. *Moonlight,* with its African American cast, won as Best Picture of the Year, beating out *La La Land.* And as U.S. society becomes more nominally all-inclusive, additional changes seem inevitable.

Oscar host Chris Rock said, "Forget whether Hollywood is black enough. A better question is, 'Is Hollywood Mexican enough?'"

In January of this year, when the Oscar nominees were announced for films released in 2017, African Americans were amply represented and several new milestones had been established. For example, for the first time in the Academy's history, two black men were nominated for the Best Actor award: Denzel Washington for his performance in *Roman J. Israel, Esq.* and Daniel Kaluuya for his role in *Get Out.*

Jordan Peele is the African American screenwriter and director of *Get Out,* a film that made history when it received a trifecta of Oscar nominations (Best Picture, Best Director, and Best Original Screenplay) for a film defined as "an assault on the smugness of white liberalism."

Another group under-represented as players in the movie industry (older actresses) staged a kind of comeback, too: Eight of the ten Oscar-nominated actresses for 2017 were over 40, and all of them played characters you wouldn't want to cross. More and more women are demanding better and pithier roles in the film industry, and more and more of them refuse to tolerate even a hint of sexual harassment. Also, to an increasing degree, women behind the camera are being recognized as well: Greta

**BRILLIANT, PASSIONATE, TALENTED, AND ALLURING: LATINO STARS WE LOVED**

Counterclockwise from upper left: **Ramon Novarro** in the 1925 version of *Ben-Hur,* **Anthony Quinn; Rita Hayworth** as *Gilda;* and **Jose Ferrer** as Cyrano de Bergerac.

Gerwig became the fifth woman in film history to receive a Best Director nod for her brilliant work on *Lady Bird.*

Although more diversified than Oscar nominees in years past, one major segment of the population, the Latino community, is still relatively under-represented. The Mexican director, Guillermo Del Toro, carried a lone Latino banner into battle for his direction of the widely celebrated *The Shape of Water,* the story of a mute cleaning woman who falls in love with a Merman.

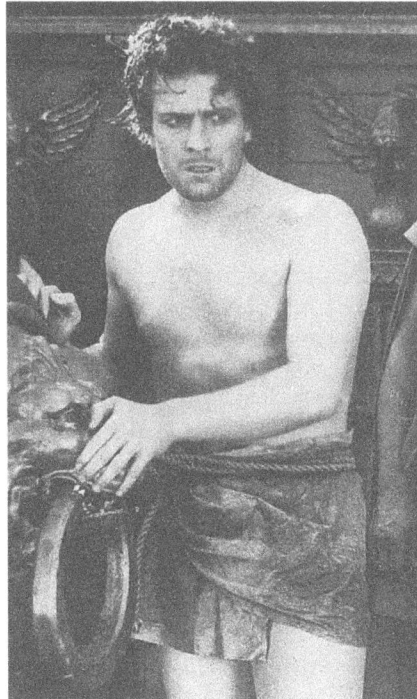

One out of every four people who attend a movie theater in the U.S. is Latino, a group that comprises 18 percent of the population. *[In contrast, 13.3 percent of the population defines itself as African American.]*

In the long and tormented history of Hollywood, only a few Latinos have emerged into super stardom, beginning with Ramon Novarro in his breakthrough performance as *Ben-Hur* in that film's 1925 silent version.

The biggest Latina star in U.S. entertainment history was the love goddess, Rita Hayworth. Born in Brooklyn, she was of Mexican ancestry. Anthony Quinn, who some fans incorrectly remember as Greek because of his brilliant performance as *Zorba*, emerged from South of the Border.

Only one Hispanic actor, José Ferrer, ever won an Oscar, taking the gold for *Cyrano de Bergerac* (1950). *[Despite many brilliant performances, no Latina has ever won a Best Actress Oscar.]*

**Leonardo DiCaprio** (left) with his Oscar-winning director, Mexico-born **Alejandro Iñárritu.**

Latinos can be equally talented behind the camera too, but they're rarely honored. A notable exception is Alejandro G. Iñárritu, who won the Best Director gold for his memorable insight into the anguish of show-biz with *Birdman* (2014), starring Michael Keaton, and for that grim evocation of vengeance on the American frontier, *The Revenant* (2015), starring Leonard DiCaprio.

Dream Works and Creative Artists are helping aspirants get a leg up on a Hollywood career by offering internships to women and people of color. Creative also manages careers for at least 100 Latino clients. One of them is Penelope Cruz, who won a Best Supporting Actress Oscar for her role in *Vicky Cristina Barcelona* (2009).

During the next two years, new high-profile films will visibly feature Latino stars. Sony is prepping the release of a remake of the 2011 Mexican crime thriller *Miss Bala*, which includes a teeth-grinding role for a sensitive and empowered Latina. And insiders tell us that other Hollywood projects with strong Latino casts will soon be announced.

Alex Nogales, president of the National Hispanic Media Coalition, picked up the bullhorn. "Enough is enough," he said. "We Latinos are going to start protesting left and right. If that doesn't work, we'll pick one of the studios and launch a boycott. We will not be denied any longer."

April Reign, creator of the *Oscars So White* movement, asserted that her goal "is to promote a media culture where everyone can visit a theater and see themselves on the screen. America is becoming a more inclusive society and definitely browner. People who pay $15 to sit in a movie theater deserve to see their stories being told."

Talented, proud, & Latina: Mexico-born **Salma Hayek** *(left)* and Spain-born **Penelope Cruz,** co-starring in a mass-market "beautified" spin on the Wild West, *Banditas*

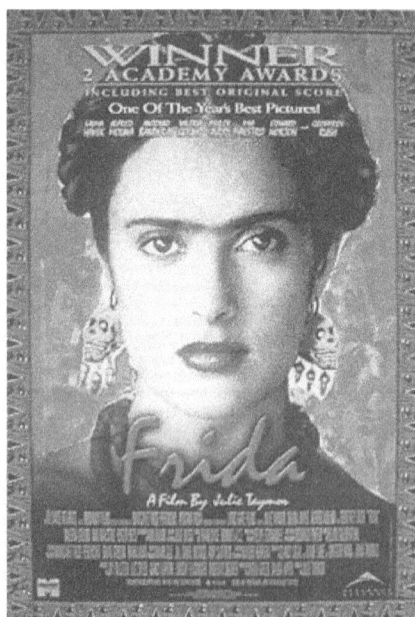

**Salma Hayek's** most celebrated performance involved her 2002 onscreen portrayal of the Mexican painter **Frida Kahlo,** viewed, postmortem, as an icon of female creativity.

Up Close and Personal with the Mexican Cartels: **Stephanie Sigman** in *Miss Bala (2011).*

**Javier Bardem,** an Oscar-winner, born in Spain and married (since 2010) to Penelope Cruz.

Mexican director **Guillermo Del Toro,** winner of three Oscars for his celebration of "anti-fascism and imperfection."

472

# WOMEN DEMAND EQUAL EYE CANDY RIGHTS

Women movie-goers are now demanding the same amount of "eye candy" and soft-core porn that men have enjoyed for decades in movie theaters and on television.

In the past decade, women are happily receiving equal opportunity in sexploitations. Why not? Women control 60% of the private wealth in the United States and make 85% of all customer purchases. Certain Republicans may debate a woman's access to birth control and abortion, but Duane Reade stocks vibrators in its aisles.

Women's interest in erotica is hardly confined to the movies, as the tremendous popularity of E.L. James' trilogy, *Fifty Shades of Grey*, demonstrates, with sales figures so far topping 16 million readers. James earns one million dollars a week in royalties for this primer to the ins and outs of (heterosexual) S&M bondage rituals aimed at twenty-and thirty-something, mostly female readers. A film studio has just acquired the rights to dramatize *50 Shades* after a spirited bidding war.

The famous author, Anne Rice, who wrote the best-selling *Interview With a Vampire,* also penned an erotic *Sleeping Beauty* trilogy in the 1980s (published under a pseudonym). Her trilogy has just been re-released. "As a feminist," said Rice, "I'm very supportive of equal rights for women in all walks of life. And that includes for me the right of every woman to write out her sexual fantasies and to read books filled with sexual fantasies she enjoys."

For the first time in cinema history, Oscar winner Steven Soderberg has released a box office bonanza, *Magic Mike,* targeted specifically at straight women and gay men.

Audiences buy tickets to enjoy the abs, but stay for the spectacular dance moves, the guy-bonding humor, the dark side of debauchery, and the struggle of men who want to be more than a piece of meat.

The star of the film is Channing Tatum, who began his show business career in Florida as a Chippendale-style dancer/stripper. His experience inspired *Magic Mike.*

"It took a lot of courage to go out there in a thong every night and get attacked by 100 love-starved women," Tatum said.

His co-star in *Magic Mike* is Matthew McConaughey who, it seems, rips off his shirt in real life every time he spots a photographer. He's perfectly cast as an aging beefcake dancer at a sleazy Tampa strip club. In his latest movie, *The Paperboy,* the talk of the Cannes Film Festival, he turns gay with a taste for rough sex.

There is one essential difference in male and female tastes

Male erotica, and plenty of it, in E.L. James' S&M trilogy, **Fifty Shades of Grey.**

Exhibitionistic, sometimes "omnisexual" male vampires strutting their stuff in **True Blood** (left photo) and in Season One of Anne Rice's **Interview with a Vampire** *(upper photo).*

Scenes of **Emma Stone** and and "artfully undraped" **Ryan Gosling** in *Crazy, Stupid Love.*

in their choice of eye candy. "Fifty Shades of Grey" claims Jenny Hutt, the SiriusXM host, "is about women wanting to be adored and ravaged, but respected. The book serves as a reminder to women that it's OK to like sex, to want it. But at its base, it's romantic." Even in *Magic Mike*, the protagonist may be an unabashed libertine, but he's really looking for love.

Anthony Cantranzaro, a 41-year-old New York stripper known as "The Italian Stallion," confirmed that a male stripper can find love while performing. He's posed frontally nude for *Playgirl* and some 1,500 covers of romance novels. "One night at a strip club, I pulled down my pants to reveal my G-string. Then I turned around and locked eyes with my future wife. It was love at first sight. She's been married to this hot, hot body for 18 years."

In movie after movie today, shirtless or even bare-butt men are depicted. In *Crazy, Stupid Love*, Ryan Gosling, with his six-pack abs, strips down but his love interest keeps her clothes on. Jake Gyllenhaal has been known to run around in front of the camera with only one hand covering his privates. Tom Cruise, 50, in *Rock of Ages*, appears only in a thong.

*True Blood*, the wildly popular American TV series about vampires, is also about shirtless men. Chris Pine, best known for his role as James T. Kirk in the 2009 *Star Trek*, strips for his fans, as do those two Australian actors, Liam Hemsworth, and his older brother Chris Hemsworth who appeared stripped down as the mighty *Thor*. The brothers are hired for their pounds of muscle more than for any acting talent.

*Trivia question*: Who was the first major Hollywood star to appear frontally nude in a general release film?

*Answer*: Tom Cruise in a high school football movie, *All the Right Moves*, released way back during the Reagan era in 1983.

The best advice for a young actor going into films today? Get yourself a gym membership.

**Matthew McConaughey** emulating a Chippendale stripper in *Magic Mike*.

**Tom Cruise**, portraying a (very fit, very high) rock star in *Rock of Ages*.

**Jake Gyllenhaal** celebrating Christmas, in his "Marines among Marines" movie, *Jarhead*.

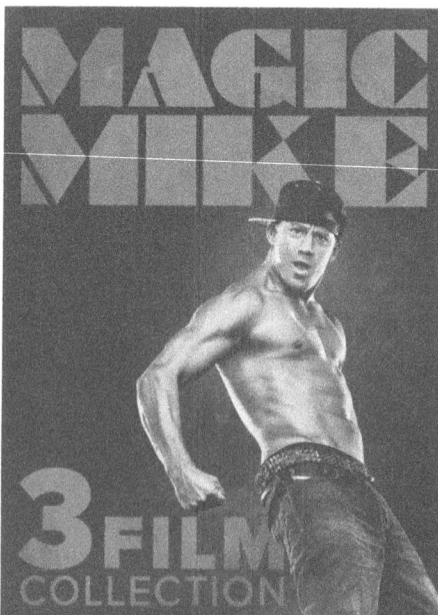

**Tatum Channing:** His casting challenge in his *Magic Mike* series involved "Hiring male strippers that anyone's Mom would like."

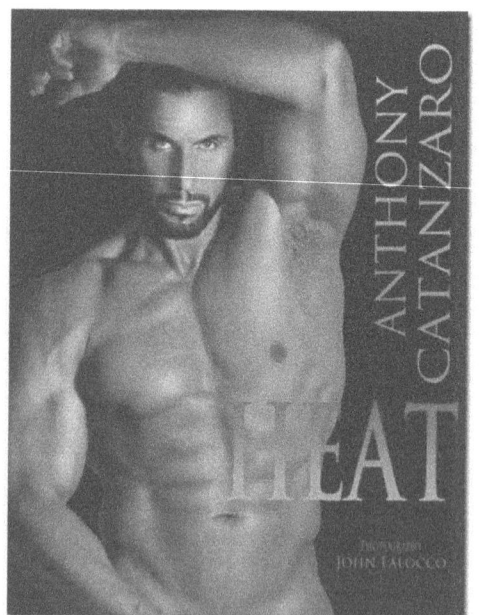

**Anthony Catanzaro,** most of whose male erotica is aimed at women.

474

# DEFYING REALITY

## TECHNOLOGIES THAT INCLUDE VFX CREATE THE ILLUSION THAT FILM STARS OF YESTERDAY HAVE, LIKE LAZARUS, RISEN FROM THEIR TOMBS, AND THAT CITIES LIKE LONDON HAVE BEEN BOMBED AND ENGULFED IN FLAMES

Elvis Presley and Marilyn Monroe always wanted to co-star in a movie, especially William Inge's *Bus Stop* (1956). Regrettably, Elvis' agent, Col. Tom Parker, objected, and consequently Marilyn shot the film with Don Murray as the lovesick rodeo cowboy instead.

However, within five years, it is highly likely that Marilyn and Elvis will finally get to team up and make a movie together, and Clark Gable and Vivien Leigh might bring back Rhett Butler and Scarlett O'Hara in a sequel to *Gone With the Wind.* And perhaps those ill-fated lovers of *Casablanca*, Humphrey Bogart and Ingrid Bergman, whose onscreen images parted from one another in 1942, will reunite in a sequel that brings them together at war's end in 1945.

"Impossible!" you say. "These stars have either been cremated or are in the ground!" But they (or at least their moving images) can live again as a new frontier of movie magic has already begun.

This new technology is best seen in *Rogue One: A Star Wars Story*, that 2016 space opera epic that has already grossed more than $1 billion. Peter Cushing, the English horror actor who died in 1994, is back on the screen again as General Moff Tarkin, one of Darth Vader's top officers.

Carrie Fisher died in December of 2016, but she reappears as a young Princess Leia in this latest release of the *Star Wars* franchise.

Although other attempts have been made to bring back the dead, *Rogue One* succeeds as no movie before. It's a product of technical wizards who have conquered one of the final visual effects frontier: The Human Face.

This miracle is possible as a result of "visual effects" (a term sometimes abbreviated by techies as "VFX"), a process where imagery is created and/or manipulated outside the live

**Oliver Reed's** final role was that of an elderly slave dealer, Proximo, in Ridley Scott's *Gladiator* (2000), It was released after Reed's "inconveniently timed" death, when a few scenes essential to the plot remained unfilmed.

Its final cut included digitally enhanced footage filmed with a stand-in which was then mixed with outtake footage from earlier clips.

The *upper photo* shows Reed alive and spunky in 1968. The *lower photo* is a movie still culled from the footage of his post-mortem digital "elevation" from the grave.

### DIGITAL TRICKS USING "GREENBOARD"

The photos above demonstrate a gamekeeper keeping Raptors at bay in *Jurassic World* (2015) before and after the scenes were digitalized and "enhanced" with technologies that included VXF. In the upper photo, note how the actors (or stuntmen) have been fitted into their terrifying costumes.

### "LIGHTING UP LONDON"
#### IN WAYS NEVER IMAGED BY THE LUFTWAFFE:

#### WHAT WOULD SIR WINSTON HAVE SAID?

The Nazis never had access to today's grab-bag of digitalized tricks, as demonstrated in the still shot above, a terrifying triumph of the cinematographer's art.

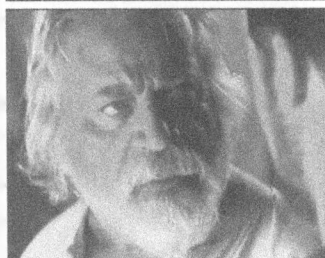

action shot. This technique involves the integration of live action footage and generated imagery to create an environment that looks realistic.

Cushing looks as he did in the first *Star Wars* in 1977. Critics found that his reappearance dazzles because it is seamless—not cheesy, pasted-in, or wooden—but a living, breathing, resurrected star. As one critic noted, "We always knew that movie stars were gods. Now they've become immortal, too."

During the next five years, VFX wizards will be hell-bent on perfecting this technology, which already is stunning. The prospects are endless. James Dean and Audrey Hepburn interacting in a love story; Ava Gardner and John Wayne emoting together in a western.

Of course, the estates of these dead actors will have to approve, and they've proven themselves a greedy bunch. Many of today's heirs have never even met the stars generating millions for them. James Dean died with $3,000 in the bank and left no will, but his heirs are raking in millions by leasing his image for the manufacture of everything from T-shirts to coffee mugs.

VFX has already been employed when an actor died before completing his final scenes. Such was the case when the English actor, Oliver Reed, died in 1999 during the filming of *Gladiator* in Malta. His scenes had to be completed through the use of computer-generated imagery (CGI) and, in one instance, a studly-looking mannequin. A more advanced application of these techniques were used for the completion of the 2015 film, *Furious 7,* when actor Paul Walker died.

Technicians were able to shave 25 years off Brad Pitt's face for a brief sequence in *The Curious Case of Benjamin Button* (2008). It was the story of a man who ages in reverse, dying as an infant despite his chronological age of 84.

The possibilities associated with the upcoming decade are endless: Kirk Douglas, age 100 today, might play the son of his own son, Michael Douglas. What about Greta Garbo *("I want to be alone")* in a space adventure? Emma Stone dancing with Gene Kelly? Even Paul Newman teaming up for a bromance movie with Cary Grant?

The morality of bringing back the dead for mass entertainment has been questioned. A lot of Baby Boomers fear that their memories of these stars will be spoiled. *The Huffington Post* called it "a giant breech of respect for the dead." *The Guardian* admitted that although the technology works incredibly well, even now in its infancy, "It's still a digital indignity."

Many of today's actors don't like either the technology or its associations. "It's hard enough getting an acting job today, with all the competition," complained an actress. "Now, I'll have to compete with Bette Davis and Joan Crawford."

There is, however, a brighter side. Off-screen lovers Tyrone Power and Lana Turner, at the height of their beauty and wrapped up in the intensity of their passion in the 1940s, wanted to co-star in a romance entitled *Forever.* Although their involvement in that wannabe deal fell apart during their heydays, it seems appropriate (and poignant) that the technology might be available to pull it off, post-mortem.

As they themselves might have defined it, it's an ethereal story about an eternal love longer than life and stronger than death.

## REPLICATING CARRIE FISHER
### (AKA PRINCESS LEIA) POST-MORTEM

**Carrie Fisher** died, inconveniently and unexpectedly in December of 2016, before producers of the *Star Wars* franchise had finished filming her scenes from their then-most-recent installment.

A day after Fisher's death (it happened aboard a London-to-Los Angeles airplane flight), her mother, the legendary Debbie Reynolds, died of a stroke at age 84.

"We weren't going to recast Carrie's character (it would have been too expensive to reshoot all of her previous scenes), and we couldn't replicate her through computer graphics alone," one of *Star Wars* tech experts said. "So we looked at the footage we had not used from *The Force Awakens* (2015), and we realized we had a number of shots that we could actually use. It was a bit like having a dozen pieces of a jigsaw puzzle and then having to make other pieces around it and paint a cohesive image from these separate pieces."

In *The Curious Case of Benjamin Button* (2018), **Brad Pitt** played a man who ages backward. Born as an 80-year-old baby the film depicts that he gets younger as he ages, a plot loosely based on a short story by F. Scott Fitzgerald.

Although Brad's character goes through an entire lifetime, different actors were not used for different stages of his lifespan. Thanks to high tech," experts said, "it's all Brad."

To that, Pitt responded, "It's kind of Brad, but with a lot of help from CG [Computer Graphics]."

476

# THE PANDEMIC

## CORONAVIRUS ATTACKS THE ENTERTAINMENT INDUSTRY

**THE MOVIE INDUSTRY WAS ALREADY ON A PRECIPICE. DID THE PANDEMIC JUST GIVE IT A PUSH?**

*"With theaters shuttered all over the world and hundreds of millions of people ordered to stay at home, it's unclear when the movie industry can resume business as normal, or even whether that "normal" will look anything like Hollywood wants it to. Pivotal pieces of the film calendar - including the summer blockbuster season and the year-end awards gantlet — have been thrown into disarray, and in their absence the gulf between streaming media and the theatrical experience may only widen further."*

*"How will the movie industry cope with these disruptions, and what will happen to the rest of 2020 if fearful audiences can't be coaxed back to the theater? Season by season, the outlook is bleak."*

According to surveys, more Americans are watching movies at a greater rate than ever before in the history of Hollywood. But there's a catch. They're screening them cheaply at home instead of schlepping off to see them in a movie theater. As such, Tinseltown's reputation as the Boulevard of Broken Dreams has devolved into a new kind of pain.

Hundreds of films that are either midway through being shot or in pre-production have been abruptly canceled. Many hopefuls—directors, producers, scriptwriters, or actors, after years of toil—have been told that their projected projects may never be revived. Of particular interest to Baby Boomers was a movie to have starred Meryl Streep and Nicole Kidman.

Before the virus, Hollywood was anticipating a blockbuster summer that focused on the gala release of movies made for multi-millions of dollars. Thanks to the pandemic, most have been postponed. They include two of Disney's lavishly (and expensively) promoted hopefuls *Antlers* and *Mulan, the New Mutants.* Even the latest member of the James Bond franchise, *Time to Die,* has been postponed until November. (*Considering the terrifying mortality rates of the Covid pandemic, its title should probably be reconsidered.*)

In reaction to the crisis, Disney announced that it will start streaming the film version of *Hamilton* (one of the biggest hits in the history of Broadway) on July 3 on its TV channel—fifteen months prior to its original plan of a blockbusting in-theater release.

Film festivals across the globe have been canceled. They include the Festival at Cannes, normally a durable staple, conducted with fanfare every May, for the *glitterati* of the international movie industry.

On Broadway, lights have been extinguished in every theater along Great White Way. Even the toughest analysts don't know when it will reopen. (Some producers have suggested "possibly next year.") At the time of its shutdown, eight shows were in previews and eight in rehearsal. Businesses deriving income from the shows—restaurants, bars, and in some cases, the theaters themselves—face bankruptcy.

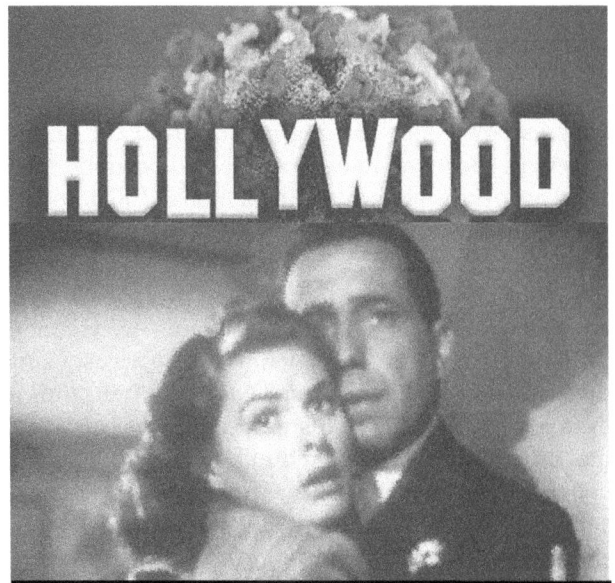

**Ingrid Bergman** and **Humphrey Bogart** seem to be huddled together awaiting the oncoming virus. Actually, they are co-starring in that wartime hit, *Casablanca* (1942). The film is now hailed by dozens of critics as the greatest movie ever made, beating out Orson Welles' *Citizen Kane.*

During the pandemic, it was one of the most requested films on television, reaching new generations of younger viewers.

Hollywood was turned upside down (*upper left*) during the pandemic. Many stores, dependent on the film industry, went out of business (*upper right*).

*Hamilton,* one of the biggest hits on Broadway, was suddenly made available to television watchers (*lower left*) . Even a James Bond movie, (*lower right*) was shut down.

Before the virus attacked, Netflix (the most watched movie channel), Amazon Prime, and Hulu, among many others, were already threatening the movie industry. Many have canceled all their TV and feature film productions. A monthly subscription to Netflix costs from $8.99 to $15.90. A whole family can see a lot of movies for that low price, as opposed to the price of just a single ticket at a movie theater.

Some producers of less costly movies are pivoting to digital debuts, including the recently crafted *Lovebirds,* which has been sold to Netflix.

Oscar contenders are also in disarray. The Academy must answer a big question: Will films be eligible for an Oscar nomination if they do not go through a theatrical release, which had been the rule before the C-Wars.

The virus is already taking a human toll on people in the movie industry. Tom Hanks became the first big name to succumb to the virus. He and his wife, Rita Wilson, both contracted it in Australia. Now in quarantine back in California, "we're taking it day by day," he told his fans. (Ironically, Hanks won an Oscar in 1993 for his portrayal of an AIDS victim in the movie *Philadelphia*.)

Films aren't the only victims of the virus. Gambling casinos, including those in Nevada, have become empty as thousands of workers lost their jobs. Concerts such as that of Justin Bieber, have been postponed indefinitely, with the music industry predicted to lose billions. Likewise for professional sports like baseball, whose profit margins survive because of overcrowded stadiums and live events.

William Schaffner, one of the leading specialists in infectious diseases, has advice for Baby Boomers: "If you are 60 or over, especially if you have some medical condition like a heart condition, diabetes, or lung disease, stay home and rent a movie."

Kwiakowsky, the Trupa Trupa singer, suggests we should be brave: "We should remember that from tragic moments great things are born. I hope the pandemic will improve relations between America, Europe and the whole world community. It's important that we save as many people as we can, because this is all in our clean hands now. We are responsible for others."

\*\*\*

# "Binge Watching" of Pandemic Movies

*"The single biggest threat to man's continued dominance of the planet is the virus."*

So said Dr. Joshua Lederberg, Nobel Laureate, in the introduction to the film, *Outbreak* (1995). When that movie opened 25 years ago, it became the top-grossing film in the United States.

Here's its 2020 update: *Outbreak* is now one of the most requested films in America for quarantined viewing. In every state, including Florida, housebound audiences have recently screened it, via Netflix, in their living rooms. Millions are tuning in to dystopian films about pandemics and the battered realities that emerge in their wakes.

An apocalyptic medical disaster film, *Outbreak* starred Dustin Hoffman, Cuba Gooding, Jr., and Kevin Spacey. Its plot centers on a (fictitious) Ebola-type virus from Zaire that erupts in (and decimates) a small town in America. *[Ironically, at the time of the movie's real-life release in 1995, a virus epidemic was already wreaking havoc across Zaire.]*

Challenging *Outbreak* in home viewing is *Contagion* (2011). Available on Hulu, it stars Marion Cotillard and Matt Damon and was directed by Steven Soderbergh. Its plot deals with frantic efforts to contain a virus and the social

**Tom Hanks** with his wife, **Rita**. Both contracted the Corona virus. .

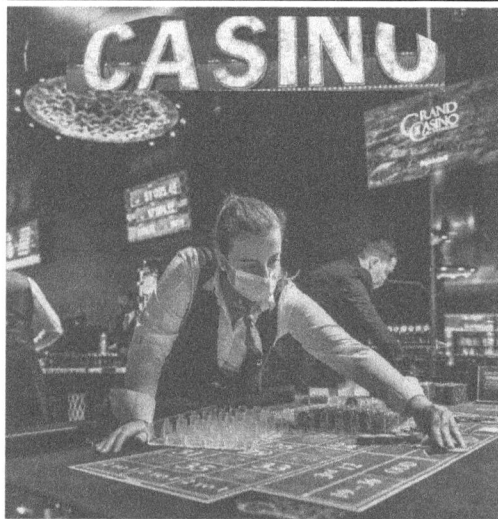

**Casinos** have also been hit hard by the pandemic. In the photo above a casino croupier, despite being "protected" with a mask, plays to a reduced number of patrons.

**Dr. Joshua Lederberg** was featured in the 1995 dystopian film, *Outbreak*. When the pandemic swept America, millions of newer viewers watched the movie on television.

chaos it causes. Its screenwriter, Scott Z. Burns, conferred with medical experts, some from the World Health Organization, for his script. Unlike most pandemic movies (and there are dozens of them), *Contagion* was well received by scientists.

Of course, many viewers—especially those who can't abide the 24-hour news cycle about the Coronavirus—are accessing fantasy or absurdist reality TV instead.

Others are wandering back to the Golden Age of Hollywood for access to pandemic films and watching *Jezebel* (1938), starring Bette Davis and Henry Fonda, an antebellum drama set in 1852 New Orleans, when a yellow fever epidemic sweeps like an out-of-control fire through the city.

Yet another movie set being resurrected is set within a vintage "Age of Sputnik" venue that's already seventy years old. *Panic in the Streets* (1950) depicts Richard Widmark as a heroic doctor who's trying to outmaneuver a deadly outbreak of "pneumonic plague." Occasionally campy yet oddly relevant to modern times, it's available through iTunes, Amazon Prime, and YouTube.

The current pandemic and its disruptive fallout will be the subject of future, roughly equivalent plots about heartburn, heartbreak, despair, fear, loathing, and death, and perhaps eventually, hope and redemption.

Actually, the first film about Covid-19 has already been released: Aptly entitled *Corona* (2020), it was written and produced by the Canadian director Mostafa Keshvari. It centers on a group of people trapped inside a (closed) elevator with an infectious and symptomatic Chinese woman, who's coughing, again and again, on everyone around her. In a recent interview Keshvari said that he hoped that it would "combat Covid-related xenophobia." There's even controversy about what to call the current virus. To the horror of the Center for Disease Control, the President of the United States has publicly identified it as "The Chinese Virus," instigating a backlash in the press. Hundreds of Chinese Americans have already endured hate crimes sparked by the fast-rising tensions.

*Corona* was conceived, crafted, and filmed in Vancouver (aka "Hollywood North"), Canada's gateway to Asia and the epicenter of that country's Covid-19 virus.

"At the time I shot my movie, there was a belief in Vancouver that white people were immune from the virus," Keshvari said. "How wrong they were. The Coronavirus does not discriminate."

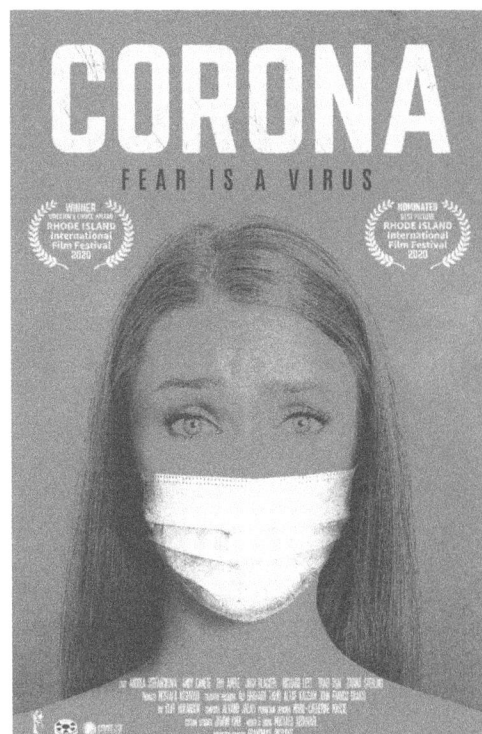

**Corona** was a film about people trapped inside a stalled elevator with a Chinese woman who is coughing and spreading the infection.

During the pandemic, then-President Donald Trump ignorantly called the disease "The Chinese Virus." That led to attacks on Asian Americans across the country.

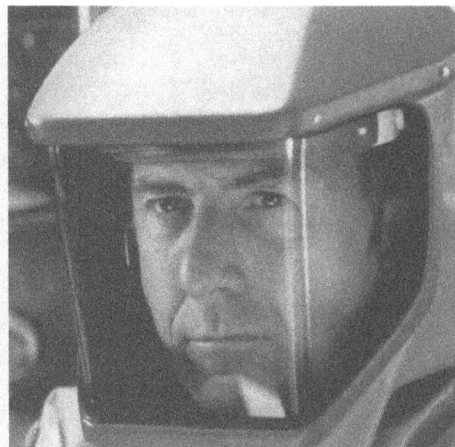

Real-life contagions have inspired dozens of neuroses-inducing films, some of them evolving into blockbuster hits They include, *left to right, above,* **Contagion** (2011), **Panic in the Streets** (1950), and **Jezebel** (1938). **In it,** motivated by love, **Bette Davis,** as *Jezebel,* braves New Orleans' outbreak of yellow fever to save the man (Henry Fonda) she loves.

In the *right-hand photo,* **Dustin Hoffman** stays negative, builds antibodies, and saves humanity in *Outbreak* (1995).

479

# THE PANDEMIC BRINGS BLOCKBUSTERS
# DIRECTLY TO YOUR COUCH

Warner Brothers has announced that all of its 2021 movies will be released on HBO Max, an "on demand" subscription service launched in May of 2020 as a showcase for entertainment products associated with AT&T's WarnerMedia. Ann Sarnoff, WarnerMedia's CEO, cited their reasoning as: "In these unprecedented times, the reality is that movie houses are likely to be closed for most of 2021."

As a sign of changing times, *Wonder Woman 1984*, (The newest sequel to the version of *Wonder Woman* released in 2017) appeared—on Christmas Day, 2020, with lots of publicity for its star, Gal Godot— on the HBO Max streaming service, too.

Many other studios, after deliberately delaying the release of blockbusters, may follow Warners' example and pivot their newest big-ticket releases to video-on-demand streaming services, too.

Some producers still believe in the viability of conventional movie theaters. One of them is Christopher Nolan, who insisted that his latest film, *Tenet*, (reviewed as a "time-bending tent pole") be released in movie houses this past summer. Despite his midsummer optimism, ticket sales were disappointing.

In spite of that setback, Nolan still remains one of the leading advocates of a return to the way we were: "When the theaters come back, and when the vaccine has been fully rolled out, I'm bullish on the long-term future of movie theaters. People love to go out to the movies, and they're going to get to go again."

In contrast, because of Covid, armies of producers are now forced to face the realities of 2021. "That vaccine is going to hang around longer than we want," one executive said.

That means that in the months to come, you may be able to see such super-charged mega-buck biggies as *Dune* and *The Matrix 4* from the comfort and safety of your living room couch.

Actually, movie houses were already suffering even before the pandemic. For years, cable TV networks like HBO and Netflix have presented formidable competition through the "streaming" at-home release of such superhits as *Game of Thrones,* "a couch era blockbuster." Hundreds of small theaters had shut down even before the pandemic in favor of multiplexes that could screen five or six movies simultaneously under one roof. Now, since Covid, even some of these giant houses have

**PANDEMIC-PROOF**

Netflix, Prime Video, and MAX.

*Upper photo:* **Gal Godot:** Gorgeous and "mythical" in *Wonder Woman*

*Middle photo:* **Tenet** Engaging for more than just its special effects.

*Lower photo:* PLAYING WITH NUMBERS: Publicity photo for **The Matrix**

480

closed down, sometimes because of sanctions from local governments.

Peter Suderman, Features Editor of *Reason*, said, "The theatrical experience of yesterday is threatened. Perhaps it will be gone in the near future. I don't think theaters will completely disappear, but it's likely that they'll become venues for major first-class events."

Ironically, some producers have responded to the coronavirus by making the pandemic the theme of their new products. A bright spot is a recent four-episode TV series, *Love in the Time of Corona, a* quarantine-themed rom-com that explores how we've been spending our homebound months and whether we're truly "more connected than ever," as its trailer suggests.

With so many people confined to their homes, more viewers watched TV than ever before in history. Some early films were released with the actors wearing masks, but the policy was quickly abandoned. "The public wants to see the faces of our actors," one director said.

Movie theaters aren't the only enterprises devastated by the virus. In Manhattan, Broadway (formerly "The Great White Way") is dark, some say, black. On stage after stage, rats scurry across where Hamlet or Dolly Levi (Carol Channing) once trod. Frigid January winds whistle through mostly deserted streets and through cracks in otherwise locked doors. Some 100,000 workers, formerly employed in such side industries as bars and restaurants, are out of jobs, and the theater crowds of yesterday have disappeared.

Broadway stars and workers aren't the only ones hit. An estimated $30 billion was lost to the bug through the cancellation of live events. "No show, no dough." Stars like Elton John and Celine Dion could have made millions.

The revenue spigot was also turned off for everyone from truck drivers to ticket agents. Some artists have taken to performing online.

From Hollywood to Broadway, most experts agree that the entertainment industry (and ways to monetize it) will undergo major changes in the years to come.

Surely times will get better, perhaps after widespread distribution of a vaccine. We can hope, at least.

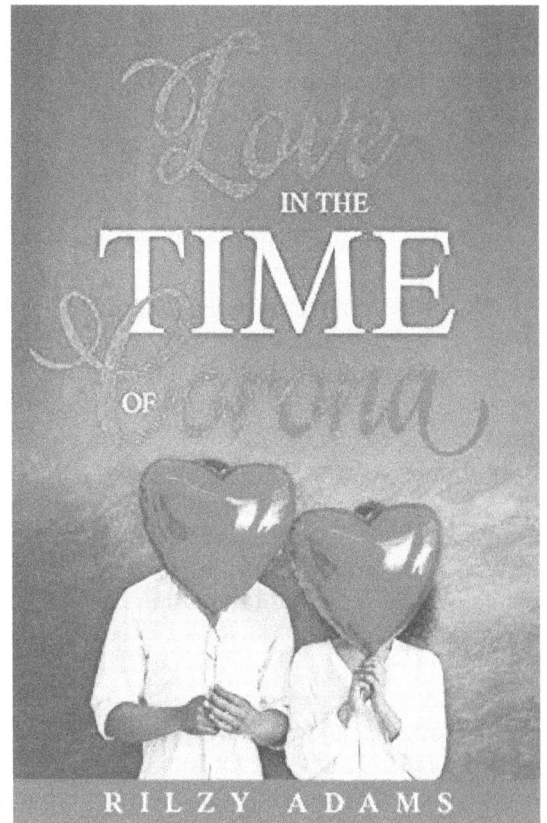

**Love in the Time of Corona**: Something "amusing and cozy" to watch during pandemic shutdowns

\*\*\*

# PANDEMIC PROFITEERS ADD BILLIONS TO THEIR FORTUNES

You hardly need to be told that the virus crisis has devastated millions of households and forced small businesses to close, paralyzing such industries as tourism and the airlines.

In contrast, since its outbreak, dozens of American billionaires, some of them labeled in the press as the "Pandemic Profiteers," grew richer.

JEFF BEZOS:  Founder of Amazon in 1994, he's now the richest man in the world, with a fortune that, since Covid, grew from $48 billion to $200 billion. It's now the world's largest online sales company, forcing the closure of shopping malls across the country. Incidentally, Bezos spent his teenaged years in Miami.  His newest dream involves the "suborbital" (non-orbiting) launch of commercial human spaceflight.

MARK ZUCKERBERG:  Enough gold bars have almost buried him under their avalanche. In recent years, his fortune rose from $55 billion to $100 billion, making him the fourth richest person on earth. Born only in 1984, the media magnate and co-founder of Facebook launched his social networking service from his dormitory room at Harvard in 2004. By 2012, it had a billion users, and by then he had become the youngest self-made billionaire.

Even the theaters of Broadway went dark during the Pandemic

481

ELON MUSK: A native of South Africa, the Tesla and SpaceX czar witnessed his bank account rise in recent years from $25 billion to $92 billion. An industrial designer and engineer, he's now the fifth richest person in the world. On November 14, he revealed that he probably has COVID-19. "Two tests came back negative, two tests came back positive, so I probably have it."

BILL GATES: He recently retained his position as the second richest person on earth thanks to a net worth of $112 billion.

WARREN BUFFET: He remains in fourth place among rich Americans with a nest egg of $74 billion.

Very few women are on the list of *über*-rich Americans. JULIA KOCH of Koch Industries appears as number sixteen among the wealthy, with a war chest of $45 billion. At the age of 58, her goal is to have a billion for every year of her life.

An oddball appears conspicuously on the list of Americans with enormous inherited wealth. He's CHUCK COLLINS, the great-grandson of Hot Dog King Oscar Mayer. When he was 26, he gave away his fortune, and has spent the rest of his life urging rich people to take up liberal causes. He is a senior scholar at the Institute for Policy Studies, a Washington-based think tank.

He often speaks of income inequalities, citing the "racial wealth divide" as dangerous. If the status quo remains, he predicts that the rich will get richer, the poor poorer. He anticipates breathtaking future profits for members of "the Billionaires' Club," new developments in video conferencing, prescription drugs, online retail sales, and "Cloud-based technologies."

As brick-and-mortar stores continue their decline and bankruptcies, Collins also foresees vast new profits for the ultra-wealthy from electric cars, sustainable power, and space travel. He also predicts a dim future for the former fossil fuel barons.

Indeed, Petroleum King PHILIP AN-SCHUTZ, who is heavily invested in fossil fuels,

## LOSERS IN THE PANDEMIC WARS

**Celine Dion** (left) and **Elton John** (right)
Attendance at their concerts was either way down or cancelled altogether.

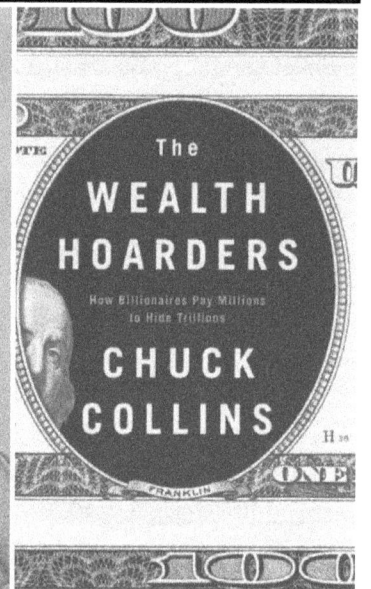

**Chuck Collins**, self-sacrificing heir to the Oscar-Mayer fortune. and his book about how the rich will generate vast new amounts of wealth, in part, because of the pandemic.

recently saw his fortunes decline. Even worse (for him, at least) many of his vast holdings are in movie theaters and music and sports arenas, whose revenues suffered devastating declines since the onslaught of Covid.

Ironically (and ominously) as high-tech billionaires added to their vast empires, the U.S. government recorded a record-breaking deficit of $3.1 trillion for the fiscal year that ended in September.

Robert Reich, who served in the governments of Gerald Ford, Jimmy Carter, and Bill Clinton (he was U.S. Labor Secretary from 1993 to 1997), loudly agrees that Donald Trump's tax cuts of 2017 massively benefitted billionaires and "mere" millionaires. Reich has publicly exposed fifteen Republicans in the Senate and House who served on the committees that revised the tax laws. Each of them benefitted from tax cuts that averaged $314,000 annually.

The previously mentioned Chuck Collins, the philanthropist, claimed that rich people frequently hire "wealth defense lawyers," who conceal vast reservoirs of cash in dynasty trusts, tax havens such as those in the Cayman Islands, and in anonymous shell companies.

According to Collins, "When the day dawns that the government will have to deal with deficit spending, I suspect that these super-rich fellows will become freeloaders, skipping out the back door of the restaurant without paying their tabs."

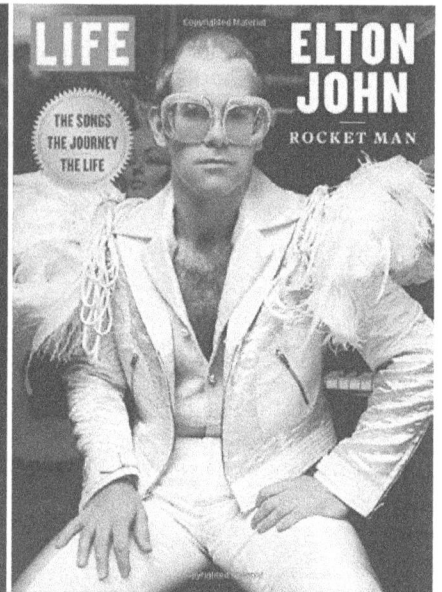

# MOVIE STARS EARN MILLIONS DURING PANDEMIC

You might have been only six years old when your grandmother uttered the *cliché* to you: "It's an ill wind that doesn't blow somebody some good."

As Corona virus decimates business after business, Granny's words are truer than ever. By the millions, families are staying home watching films on television. That has brought record-breaking millions of dollars to some (very lucky) actors.

Standing on top of the gold pile is Dwayne ("The Rock") Johnson, 48, who in the past twelve months has hauled in an eye-popping $90 million, unheard of in the history of Hollywood.

In 1991, Johnson was a national football champ at the University of Miami, and he later became one of the greatest and most visible professional wrestlers of all time. He starred in *The Scorpion King* (2002), which he followed with a series of movies that broke records at the box office.

He also hauls in big bucks with his clothing line, "Project Rock," which focuses on sportswear such as his "Zero Gravity" training shoes. His entire worldwide inventory sold out in 30 minutes after their online debut in 2018.

Johnson's latest movie, *Red Notice*, is set for release in November of 2021. It's the saga of a global pursuit of the world's most wanted art thief.

Co-starring in it with him is Ryan Reynolds, 43, a native of British Columbia. Among the highest-paid actors, he is No. 2 worldwide, netting $72 million this past year. In *Red Notice*, he'll be cast as the world's greatest con artist. Reynolds became a living, breathing version of Fort Knox after the worldwide grosses came in on *Deadpool* (2016), in which he played a superhero based on the Marvel Comics franchise.

To make room for the newcomers, a number of famous actors had to fall off the list, notably Robert Downey, Chris Evans, Chris Hemsworth, and Paul Rudd.

Their "demise" paved the way for the ascension of Mark Wahlberg, 42, the former rapper known as "Marky Mark," who became famous for singing in his Calvin Klein underwear.

Wahlberg made nearly $60 million this past year, hauling in most of the loot through his Netflix hit *Spenser Confidential*, the third most-watched film to date on the streaming service.

After a hiatus, Ben Affleck, 47, came back like a tidal wave, depositing $55 million in his bank(s). His hits included *The Way Back* about a recovering alcoholic, and *The Last Thing He Wanted*, a British/American political thriller.

Vin Diesel, No. 4 at the box office, joined the bigtime with the release of his blockbuster franchise, *Fast & Furious*, making him one of the highest-grossing actors of all time. He made $55 million this past year and would have made many more millions had not his latest installment been delayed, because of the pandemic, until 2021.

A surprise newcomer on the list of spectacularly wealthy actors is Akshay Kumar, a Bollywood star born in the Punjab region of India. He weighs in with $50 million for his TV series, *The End.* An action thriller, it's scheduled for release several months from now.

Lin-Manuel Miranda, 40, made the list of hyper-rich actors for the first time with a $46 million war chest—his take-home cut from the record-breaking sale of the hit Broadway musical, *Hamilton*. Disney paid $75 million for its film rights.

Trailing these colossal millionaires is Will Smith,

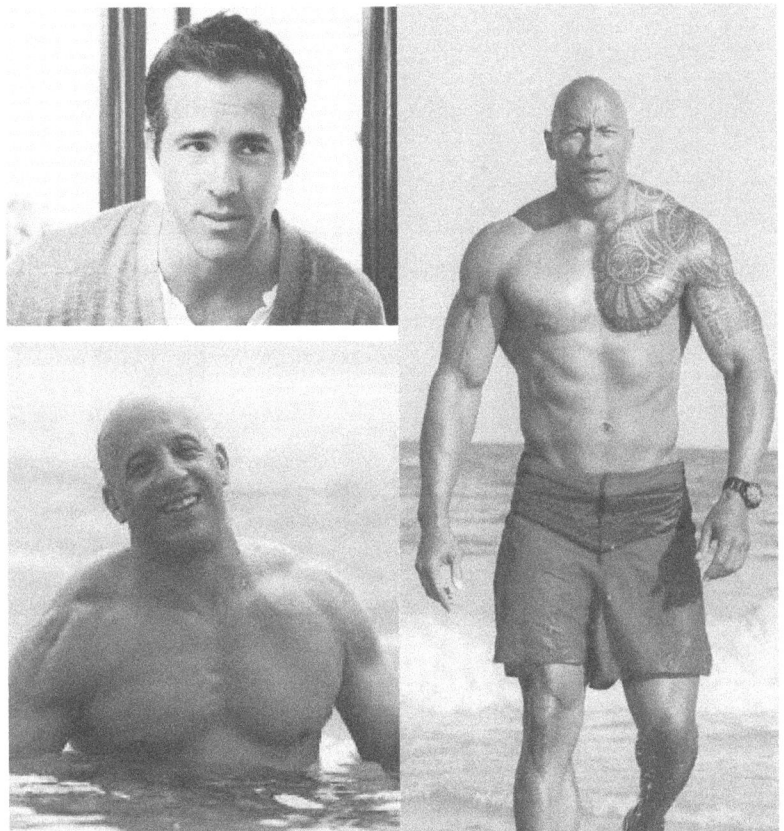

## WINNERS IN THE PANDEMIC WARS

*Clockwise from upper left:* **Ryan Reynolds, Dwayn ("the Rock") Johnson, and Vin Diesel.**

who took home only $45 million this past year. He'll be a lot richer after the November release of *King Richard,* the story of the father and trainer of tennis greats Venus and Serena Williams.

All right, so Adam Sandler and Jackie Chan fell off the list this year. But "Don't Cry for Them, Argentina." Each of these stars loaded up wheelbarrows, each filled with $40 million, and headed for the bank.

NEWS FOR SENIORS: Whereas in years past, younger actors headed the list of box office champs, this year, each of the mega-million dollar stars is over forty, with many of them moving deep into middle age.

**Spectacularly profitable: Lin-Manuel Miranda** in *Hamilton.*

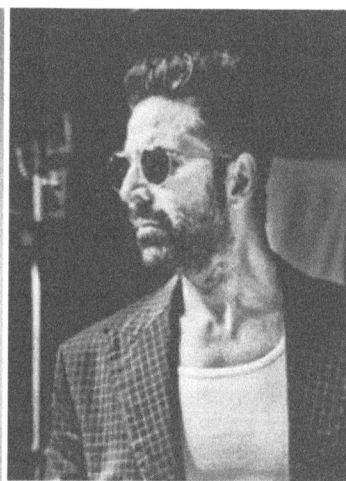

**WINNERS** *Left to right:* **Ben Affleck, Meryl Streep, Mark Wahlberg,** and the fast-rising Bollywood star, **Ackshay Kumar.**

Feeling alienated during the lockdown? Consider renting an at-home screening of **Dune,** noted for its brooding vision of power-mongering in a strange new world.

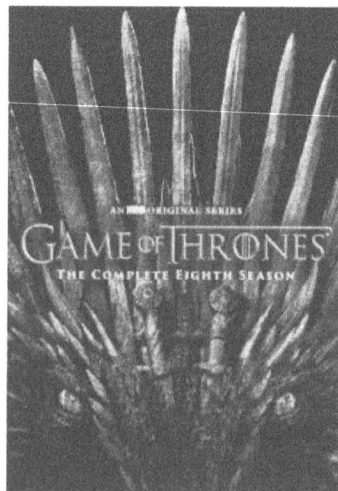

The ever-intriguing **Game of Thrones**—always ready-and-waiting with swords and reliably cathartic bloodbaths**.**

Opinionated and insanely wealthy: **Julia Flesher Koch,** Iowa-born widow, since 2019, of David Koch, conservative mega-donor.

# WILLIAM RANDOLPH HEARST

The poster girl of all love children ever associated with Hollywood was Patricia Van Cleve (1919-1993). She was the daughter of press baron William Randolph Hearst and his mistress, Marion Davies, an actress who eventually became known as "the last great courtesan of the 20th century."

The 52-year-old Hearst picked the 19-year-old blonde chorine out of a lineup at the Ziegfeld Follies. With his wife stashed back East, he journeyed with her to California. There he built for her a multi-million-dollar pleasure palace, San Simeon. With his mistress at his side, Hearst entertained everybody from Albert Einstein and Sir Winston Churchill to all the big-time movie stars of Hollywood's Golden Age, including Gloria Swanson and Clark Gable.

Orson Welles used Hearst and Marion as inspirations for his characters in *Citizen Kane* (1941), still hailed by film critics as the greatest film ever made. Along the way, Hearst and Marion found time to have a daughter, but could not admit to that publicly, fearing a scandalous backlash. News of the girl's birth was suppressed, and it remained one of the great mysteries of Hollywood.

Secret love child **Patricia Douras Van Cleve (aka Patricia Lake)**, unpublicized daughter of jazz-age billionaire William Randolph Hearst and screen vamp Marion Davies.

Silent screen actor **Arthur Lake**, the loyal, discreet, and collaborative husband of Patricia Van Cleve. Marion Davies paid many of their expenses throughout the course of their long marriage.

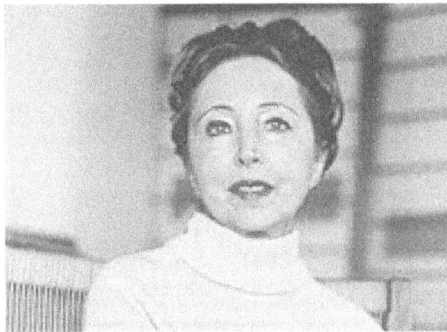

The Hearst biographer, David Nasaw, author of *The Chief*, wrote that there is no evidence to support the rumors that the infamous couple ever had a child.

*We disagree.*

In 1966, I drove with the author, Anaïs Nin, to Louveciennes, a small town in the Île de France outside Paris. This is where Anaïs wrote many of the diaries that would make her a feminist icon during the 1970s. She wanted me to see her former home.

While there and knowing of my interest in Hollywood, she took me to visit a 95-year-old former nurse, Agnes Monosiet. Frail but articulate, she related how she had once worked as a nurse in a nearby hospital. She claimed that Hearst had hired her as a nanny for Marion, who came to stay for six weeks in a cottage on the hospital grounds. There, on June 18, 1923, she gave birth to a baby girl.

According to the nurse, Marion stayed on for two weeks after the birth of her daughter before returning alone to Hol-

Who inaugurated Darwin Porter's exposure to the brouhaha surrounding the love-child of William Randolph Hearst and Marion Davies?

It was the notorious diarist, feminist, pornographer, and *zeitgeist* queen, **Anaïs Nin,** whom Darwin interviewed extensively for his roman-a-clef, *VENUS.*

Many of the then-most famous people in the world came to visit William Randolph Hearst and Marion Davies at San Simeon. They included:

| Albert Einstein | Sir Winston Churchill | Gloria Swanson |

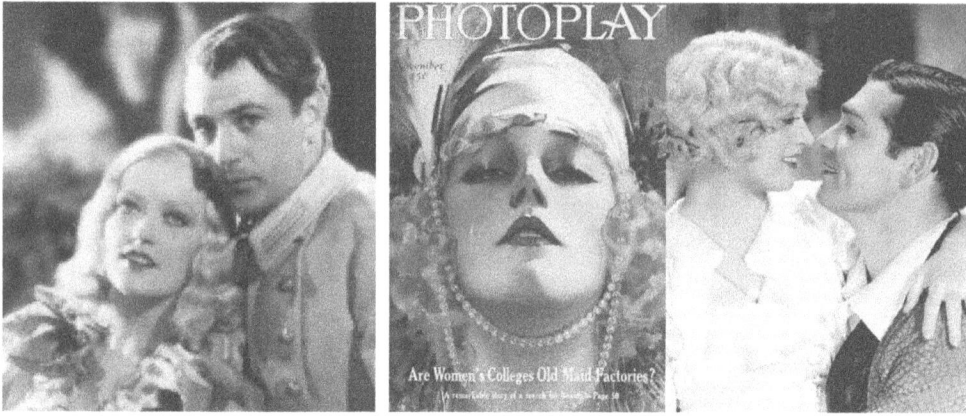

Views of **Marion Davies** as a player in a career for the most part funded by Hearst: *Left photo* showcases her in the early 1930s with **Gary Cooper**; *Center photo* features her as a cover girl for *Photoplay*; *right photo* displays her legendary humor and charm during a moment of lighthearted intimacy with **Clark Gable**.

lywood. Within two weeks after that, Hearst sent both a doctor and a nurse to sail with the child to America. The trio then crossed the country by rail, delivering the baby to the home of Rose Davies Van Cleve, Marion's sister.

Rose and her husband, George Van Cleve, passed the daughter off as their own, nicknaming her "Pat." The baby girl often spent time with her real mother, whom she called "Aunt Marion." Reportedly, Hearst doted on the girl, lavishing presents on her and paying all her expenses and seeing to her education.

Rose was not a good mother. She was an alcoholic and had numerous affairs. Fed up with her, George quit his job with Hearst Pictures and kidnapped seven-year-old Pat and fled East. Not wanting to alert the police, Hearst hired private detectives, but George and Pat eluded them for five years.

Pat was eventually "captured" and returned to Rose in California but ended up spending more time with her "Aunt Marion" than she did with Rose.

In years to come, Pat married actor Arthur Lake, who is known for bringing the comic strip character, Dagwood Bumstead—the bumbling husband of Blondie—to life in film, radio, and television.

When "Aunt Marion" died on September 22, 1961, her daughter was at her bedside.

Pat would live until 1993, never revealing her true identity until she was on her own deathbed. She summoned her son, Arthur Lake Jr. to her bedside where she confessed that all the rumors about her were true. She was indeed the daughter of William Randolph Hearst. Marion was not her aunt, but her biological mother.

Young Arthur kept this secret to himself for years, but finally admitted the truth about his mother. "She lived her life on a satin pillow," he said. "They took away her name, but gave her everything else."

EVERYONE knew about **William Randolph Hearst**, his staggering wealth and power, and his movie star partner, Marion. Many critics define *Citizen Kane*, the rogue bio-pic inspired by Hearst's life and rapacious greed, as the best film ever made. **Orson Welles**, its producer and star, appears in both of the photos, above.

Three views of **the Hearsts**. *Upper photo*: Very formally in the early 1920s; *Middle photo*: During the darkest year of World War II (1942) at a costume party (**Marion** is dressed as a G.I.); and in the late 1950s, as their relationship endured through sickness and ill health "untill the end."

SO MANY FILMS, SO MANY SECRETS

# WIKILEAKS

## ASSANGE AND MANNING
## STIR UP A HORNET'S NEST

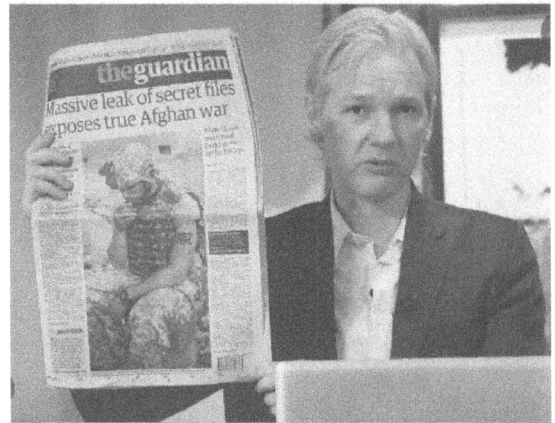

Biopics were all the rage in 2012, with Daniel Day-Lewis' portrait of *Lincoln* winning top awards. The genre will continue for the 2013 and 2014 seasons, but with a bizarre twist: Many will focus on the massive leak of classified documents owned by the U.S. Military.

Never in the history of Hollywood have so many films been made, or are being made, or in pre-production which focus on just two men—one an Aussie, Julian Assange, the other an American soldier, Pfc Bradley Manning.

The decade's most awesome and controversial whistleblower, the Australian activist, Assange, is the founder of WikiLeaks, which in 2010 began to publish secret U.S. military and diplomat documents whose revelations were embarrassing as regards State Department appraisals of various world leaders, some of them U.S. Allies. Of the thousands of government files leaked and subsequently published on the Internet, none deemed as immediately compromising of National Security, but many tended to enrage government officials within the Pentagon and on location in Iraq, Afghanistan, and other hot spots around the globe.

Manning was later arrested on suspicion of supplying the cables to WikiLeaks. Currently in jail, where he's cited various prison abuses, he is charged, among other indictments, with passing top military secrets to the "aid of the enemy," a capital offense. Many right-wing figures such as Mike Huckabee, former presidential candidate (and now TV host) has called for Manning's execution.

While he's behind bars, Assange is camped out in London at the Ecuadorian Embassy, where he has been granted diplomatic asylum. He fled there when he learned that the British planned to extradite him to Sweden, where he is wanted on a charge of sexual assault. Assange fears that if he's forced to go to Sweden, he will be extradited to the United States to face charges over the diplomatic cable cases.

*We Steal Secrets* is one of the first of the Hollywood films devoted to Assange and Manning to be released. It premiered at the Sundance Film Festival in January of 2013, the creation of Alex Gibney, who had previously (in 2007) won an Oscar for his direction of the documentary, set in Afghanistan, *Taxi to the Dark Side*.

Gibney has just finished *The Rise and Fall of Eliot Spitzer*, the saga of the former governor of New York State who resigned in the wake of a prostitution scandal.

At the Toronto Film Festival last autumn, *Underground: The Julian Assange Story* was premiered. In February of this

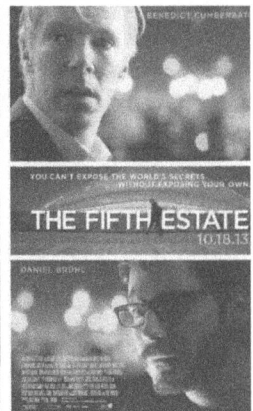

WikiLeaker and rogue activist **Julian Assange** holding a copy of one of the newspapers that broke news of a series of "betrayals" that enraged the U.S. Military, the FBI, the CIA, and thousands of law enforcement officials.

Army Pfc **Bradley Manning**, an intelligence analyst in Iraq, was court-martialed in 2013 on charges of espionage, and convicted for passing classified secrets (an estimated 750,000 documents) on to Assange for publication as part of the WikiLeaks scandal. He later spent seven years in prison for role in this "activist indiscretion."

A transgendered male-to-female who now identifies as "**Chelsea Manning**" is shown in both manifestations of his (now her) personality in the *two photos, above*.

Since the debut of WikiLeaks and their national implications, **a rush of books and docu-dramas have been, with controversy, birthed,** sometimes to the rage of sensitive-to-security-issues patriots who resent what they interpret as the "glorification" of treason.

year, DreamWorks will begin shooting *Inside WikiLeaks: My Time with Julian Assange at the World's Most Dangerous Websites.*

Mark Boal, the writer of the highly acclaimed *Zero Dark Thirty,* is also at work on an Assange drama: *The Boy Who Kicked the Hornet's Nest.* And HBO is in pre-production on an untitled Assange drama as well. At least thirteen other scripts are being written by other players within the entertainment industry.

Assange wanted a $1 million fee for his contribution (and endorsement) of *We Steal Secrets,* but was turned down. However, he signed a deal of $1.5 million with a publisher for a tell-all biography.

Although Manning is a key figure in each of the films which focus on Assange, the private also has films devoted to his own story. Of the films in pre-production about him, the one likely to attract the most attention is *Private Bradley Manning, WikiLeaks, and the Biggest Exposure of Official Secrets in American History.*

The rather meek private was deeply disturbed at what he read in secret documents and decided to share them with the world.

As a character worth dramatizing, he has been called a young man of great loneliness and sexual confusion. At the age of thirteen, he was judged effeminate and was bullied at school. Before joining the Army, he had various boyfriends. A fellow soldier referred to him as "a real runt, only barely five feet tall. Some soldiers yelled faggot at him and beat him up."

At one point, Manning wrote to a gender counselor in Boston to discuss sex reassignment surgery. During a two-week holiday in Boston, he dressed in women's clothes, with a wig, all the time, and even sent a picture of himself to his master sergeant, Paul Adkins.

Back on duty in Iraq, Manning appeared increasingly disturbed, and sometimes spiraled out of control, attacking fellow soldiers, male and female, and destroying computers. Amazingly, his security clearance was not taken away from him. He grew increasingly agitated about the secrets he was learning about the wars in Afghanistan and Iraq.

At one point, he began sending documents to Assange at WikiLeaks. In the wake of that decision, he is widely seen as a catalyst for the Arab Spring launched in December of 2010. Sarah Palin thinks of him as a "21st Century Tianamen Square Tank Man and an embittered traitor."

Finally, Manning posted one too many secrets, often to acquaintances. This led to his arrest in February of 2012, where he is now detained under harsh conditions at Fort Meade, Maryland. He has declined to enter a plea, and his upcoming military trial is expected to begin in June of 2013.

That comes none too soon to all those scriptwriters who are forced to write "TK" at the head of their unfinished scripts. TK is journalistic shorthand for "facts yet to come."

Various actors have been suggested for the roles of Assange and Manning, ranging from Brad Pitt to Tom Cruise, from Ben Affleck to Matt Damon.

## JULIAN ASSANGE

Born in 1971 in Queensland, Australia, Julian Assange founded WikiLeaks in 2006. He became notorious on the international front in 2010 when he posted a series of leaks from Charles Manning, including war logs from both Iraq and Afghanistan.

To prevent his extradition to Sweden to face sexual misconduct charges, he took refuge in the Embassy of Ecuador in London. But after a dispute with Embassy personnel, his asylum was withdrawn. The police were invited into the embassy and Assange was arrested.

He was found guilty of breaching the Bail Act and sentenced to 50 weeks in prison.

The United States has been unsuccessful in getting Assange extradited. Since April of 2019, he has been confined to Belmarsh, a prison in London.

In 2015, Assange began a romantic relationship with Stalla Moris, his South African lawyer. Apparently, during visits to him in prison, they obviously had sex because she later gave b irth to two sons, one in 2017, another in 2019.

On March 23, 2022, the couple finally got married—in Belmarsh Prison.

Vladimir Putin has weighed in, supporting "the Leaker."

At a press conference, the Soviet dictator asked, "Why is Mr. Assange in prison? They call that democracy?"

## CHELSEA MANNING

Born Bradley Edward Manning in 1987, a trans woman, Chelsea Manning, was a former U.S. Army soldier. She was convicted by court martial in July of 2013 for violating the Espionage Act and other offenses. She had disclosed to WikiLeaks some 750,000 sensitive military or diplomatic documents. She was confined to prison from 2010 until 2017, when her sentence was commuted *[i.e., reduced, but without forgiveness of the person convicted.]* After her release and having no money, Manning made her living from speaking engagements.

In 2016, she ran against Senator Ben Cardin for the Democratic nomination for the U.S. Senate from Maryland and received about six percent of the vote.

She was later jailed for contempt and fined $250,000 for refusing to testify before a grand jury investigating WikiLeaks founder Julian Assange.

# LIFE: REAL TO REEL

## THE NEW BIOPICS

FDR, ELIZABETH TAYLOR, PRINCESS DIANA, JOHN BARRYMORE, ABRAHAM LINCOLN, LIBERACE, & LINDA LOVELACE

*Left to right,* **Lindsay Lohan** as Elizabeth Taylor, **Naomi Watts** as Diana Spencer, and **Christopher Plummer** as John Barrymore

In an almost unprecedented development within the entertainment industry, famous Hollywood stars are now impersonating famous American icons onscreen, everybody from Franklin D. Roosevelt to screen goddess Elizabeth Taylor, who died in 2011. Some of these biopics have already been released and others are coming out in early 2013. But because of advance previews, the critics are already screaming.

The most "subversive" casting of the year focuses on Jane Fonda's impersonation of Nancy Reagan in the movie *The Butler*. Film critic Sara Stewart stated, "A pinko liberal feminist plays arch-conservative First Lady Nancy—and does so brilliantly." Another critic, Kyle Smith, became catty: "At least, Jane knows as much as Nancy about having your face tightened so many times that you start to look like a Halloween mask of yourself."

One of the most controversial casting choices involved hiring "train wreck" Lindsay Lohan to impersonate Elizabeth Taylor, Dame Commander of the British Empire, in *Liz and Dick*. But whereas Elizabeth racked up husbands, "LiLo" is known to some degree for her extended police blotter. Lindsay is hoping this movie will be interpreted as a major comeback for her, but early reviews lash her. Grant Bowler was cast as Richard Burton, and although his performance isn't inspired, he pulls off the role creditably. More to the point, however, these two young actors succeed in making us miss the originals.

*Left to right:* **Laura Linney** as FDR's lover and cousin, Margaret "Daisy" Suckley; **Bill Murray** as Franklin Delano Roosevelt, and **Samuel West** as King George VI in *Hyde Park on Hudson*

Incidentally, Lohan—because she's being to an increasing degree interpreted as "unreliable"—was fired from the cast of the film entitled *Lovelace*. Eventually, the role of the skilled fellatio artist, Linda Lovelace, star of *Deep Throat*, the highest-grossing porno movie of all time, went to Amanda Seyfried. Simultaneous with the release of Lovelace's film version with Seyfried, Blood Moon Productions will release my upcoming book-version of the Linda Lovelace saga, *Inside Linda Lovelace's Deep Throat*, passages from which will certainly invite comparisons of Miss Seyfried's performance with that of Lovelace herself, a New York-born, Florida-residing original.

*Left to right,* **Sir Anthony Hopkins** emulating Alfred Hitchcock; the real **Alfred Hitchcock**, and **Olivia Williams** portraying First Lady Eleanor Roosevelt.

489

Many actors were considered for the role of America's most patrician president, Franklin D. Roosevelt. But in a shocking casting decision, comedian Bill Murray was selected as the male lead in *Hyde Park on Hudson,* with Laura Linney cast as the president's distant cousin and mistress, Margaret Suckley. Olivia Williams struggles valiantly in this upcoming film to re-create a striking American original, Eleanor Roosevelt.

As one critic stated, "This earthy Midwesterner (Murray) we all know as Carl the Gardener is a terrible choice to play FDR." One thing Murray got right, and that involved the way FDR maneuvered his cigarette holder.

Another icon, Princess Diana, will live again onscreen in the upcoming film *Diana.* The talented British/Australian actress, Naomi Watts, is already drawing daggers from critics. Lou Lumenick wrote: "This second-string Nicole Kidman is perhaps a bit long in the tooth for the role." Despite her icy blonde elegance and her perfect British accent, Watts may not be the ideal reincarnation of Princess Di.

All wrong for the part, Scarlett Johansson was cast as Janet Leigh in the film *Hitchcock,* a story set in 1959 during the making of the Alfred Hitchcock classic, *Psycho.* One of the ten most famous movie scenes of all time, that of Tony Perkins wearing drag while slashing poor Janet in the shower, will be re-created. Sir Anthony Hopkins will play the pear-shaped Hitchcock, with Dame Helen Mirren cast as his archly indulgent and ever-forgiving wife, Alma.

"ScarJo," as Johansson is nicknamed in the tabloids, would have been more creditable interpreting Marilyn Monroe than in trying to create the vacuous primness of Janet Leigh. Scarlett's smoky voice has nothing to do with Janet's flat intonations. Miscast or not, Scarlett looks fabulous, judging from those illegally hacked nude photographs that went out on the Internet. Originally, they were intended for viewing by her then-husband, Hollywood hunk, Ryan Reynolds, but he dumped her anyway.

The most Method-y of Method actors, Daniel Day-Lewis is generating mostly rave reviews playing the Great Emancipator, Abraham Lincoln, our most iconic president. Steven Spielberg's ambitious, often ponderous, and "Oscar-mongering" *Lincoln* is the saga of the President pushing the 13th Amendment through the House of Representatives. As good as Day-Lewis is, Tommy Lee Jones, as an abolitionist congressman, practically steals the picture.

The list of impersonators goes on and on, with the supremely talented Christopher Plummer taking on the role of legendary actor John Barrymore, known during his heyday as "The Great Profile." The film is entitled *Barrymore.*

But are you really ready to see Michael Douglas play Liberace, the Prince of the Piano, in *Behind the Candelabra?* Produced by Steven Soderbergh, Michael is all here in a riot of color, pomade, mincing steps, and mascara. His sequined jackets could be spotted from Outer Space. Under a sandy thatch of 1970s hair, Matt Damon is improbably cast as Liberace's hustler lover, chauffeur, bodyguard, and boy toy, who later sued him for "palimony."

First Lady Michelle Obama has already announced her choice of an actor to play her husband on the screen. She cast her vote for Denzel Washington. But the wishes of First Ladies don't always come true. Jackie Kennedy fought to have Warren Beatty play JFK in *PT 109,* a film released shortly before JFK's assassination in 1963, but the role went instead to Cliff Robertson. Jackie, however, got Beatty after all: For a brief time, he became her lover in real—not reel—life.

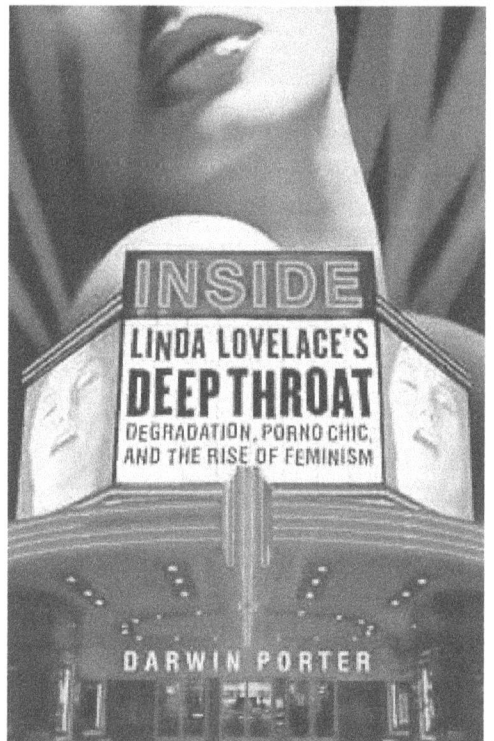

*Upper photo*: **Amanda Seyfried** emulating porn star **Linda Lovelace** in the shallow and utterly failed biopic of the woman who changed the face of American entertainment..

*Lower photo*, cover art for **Darwin Porter**'s widely reviewed biography of what REALLY lay between the intrigue-soaked sheets during the steamy, tragic, and horrible life of the REAL Linda Lovelace.

**Michael Douglas,** thanks to his flashy, flamboyant, and brilliant film portrayal of Liberace in *Behind the Candelabra*, got his dragged-out image positioned on the covers of magazines like this.

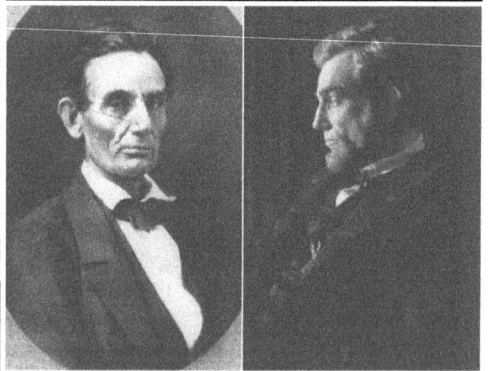

A Great President **(Abraham Lincoln)** and a great actor **(Daniel Day-Lewis)** who replicated him on film.

# BABY BOOMING TEEN IDOLS

FABIAN, DAVY JONES, BOBBY RYDEL, PAUL ANKA, BOBBY VINTON, AND BOBBY VEE

## WHERE ARE THEY TODAY?

In the 1950s and early 60s, we danced to their music, we listened to it on the car radios of our pink Cadillacs, we made love to it, and we found solace in their sad songs after enduring one more heartbreak.

But where are those teen music idols today?

Overcome with a feeling of nostalgia, a few months ago, I walked ten blocks from my home on Staten Island to the St. George Theater, one of the last of the great old vaudeville palaces that once welcomed the likes of Fanny Brice, Sophie Tucker, Milton Berle, and Al Jolson.

Two views of Baby Boomer, teen idol and icon, **Fabian**. *Left* with **Ed Sullivan** in 1959; *above* a detail of one of his "artfully nude" shots from *Playgirl*.

On the night in question, the show featured those "Daydream Believers" of yesterday, idols such as Fabian. Their great hits went out with Eisenhower, but many of these music makers are still rock 'n' rolling around the stage despite their status as grandparents. For the most part, they have tragically learned that "getting old is not for sissies," to quote Bette Davis, who knew what she was talking about.

The good news is that all of these idols, who had stood on top of the world when they were young, are still alive, with one notable exception.

Davy Jones, of Manchester, England, died February 29, 2012. The 66-year-old singer, the best known member of the pop rock group, the Monkees, had been given a clean bill of health right before he suffered a fatal heart attack. He had been told that he had the heart of a 25-year-old, but he died unexpectedly on his ranch in Indiantown, Florida, where he raised race horses. At his peak, Davy was known as the No. 1 teen idol of all time.

**THE MONKEES**, *Left to right*, **Mike Nesmith, Davy Jones, Peter Tork,** and **Mickey Dolenz.**

Born in 1942, Fabian Forte, billed professionally as Fabian, was discovered in his native Philadelphia and almost overnight became America's dreamboat. In his pompadour and white bucks, he shot to the top, following appearances on Dick Clark's *American Bandstand*. His songs, "Turn Me Loose," and his biggest hit, "Tiger," attracted millions of fans. The wavy-haired pop singer of the late 1950s took to the screen, mostly as a supporting actor to bigger names like James Stewart and John Wayne, but his fame was short lived.

Desperate to reactivate his career, he posed nude for *Playgirl*, showing what the British call "the Full Monty" to his fans. Today he regrets that. "I looked fat and stupid in those pictures," he said. As his career faded, he drowned his sorrows in booze.

He eventually cured himself of his alcoholism but suffered heart problems. Surgeons replaced an aortic valve and unblocked an artery. Over the years, he's made a living appearing at Golden Oldie concerts.

Another teen idol, Bobby Rydell, also born in Philadelphia in 1942, is alive today because of modern medicine. He starred in the movie *Bye Bye Birdie* in 1963, and young fans screamed when he performed his songs, "Wild One" or "Volaré." Long after his major fame faded, Rydell toured as a solo act and sometimes as one

**Bobby Rydell:** Consistently charming, consistently popular, despite chronically horrible health.

491

of "The Golden Boys," performing with Frankie Avalon and Fabian.

But none of his rival singers ever suffered as many medical problems as Rydell did. For him, it has been one health crisis after another. Like Fabian, he has also battled the bottle. In 2009, he underwent hip surgery and faced a DUI bust. The following year, he slipped on ice and broke his right shoulder in three places. The joint was repaired with a plate and screws.

Late in 2012, the diabetic star received liver and kidney transplants at the Thomas Jefferson Hospital in Philadelphia. In March of 2013, his doctors wondered why he wasn't dead. A stress test revealed he had a 95 per cent blockage in one major artery and a 75 percent blockage in another. He had to endure a double bypass surgery to prevent a fatal heart attack.

Today, he's smiling again, claiming, "I've been reborn. I have all new parts."

Emerging in 1941 in Ontario, Paul Anka popped onto the music scene with such hits as "Diana" and "Put Your Head On My Shoulder." He's also a songwriter, having written "My Way," Frank Sinatra's signature song. He also composed songs with Michael Jackson, including such hits as "This Is It."

Unlike some of the other teen idols, Anka escaped most medical crises, but if anything, he's still nursing a broken heart. The twice divorced star admits in his 2013 autobiography, *My Way,* that the love of his life was Annette Funicello, who died at the age of 70 in the spring of 2013 from complications associated with multiple sclerosis. The couple never married, but he wrote of his hot steamy liaisons with the Mouseketeer cutie pie—"and I've always loved her."

"Bobby" was the favorite first name of three dreamboats of yesteryear. We listened not only to Bobby Vinton and Bobby Rydell, but also to Bobby Vee, who was born in 1943 in Fargo, North Dakota. Those of us who were around during the summer of 1961 could not turn on our car radios without hearing his hit, "Take Good Care of My Baby."

After a successful career that endured for decades, the 70-year-old singer released his final album in 2011. It's called "The Adobe Sessions," and was recorded in Tucson, Arizona, his home. He made these farewell songs to the world when his doctors told him he had Alzheimer's disease. Before his voice was silenced, he wanted to revisit his hits such as "The Night Has a Thousand Eyes."

Then he was socked with additional tragic news: In 1963, he'd married Karen Bergen of Minnesota. But she, too, had had medical problems, undergoing a lung transplant because she suffered from hypersensitivity pneumonitis and pulmonary hypertension.

That brings us to 79-year-old Bobby Vinton, from Pennsylvania. He was hailed as "The Polish Prince" after the release of his most popular song, "Blue Velvet."

From a reject pile of discarded songs by other writers, Vinton picked up "Roses Are Red (My Love)," which, after he recorded it, became number one on the Billboard Hot 100 chart. He broke our hearts in 1964 when he sang "Mr. Lonely."

*Billboard* has hailed Vinton as "the all-time most successful love singer of the rock era," having more number one hits than any other male vocalist, including Elvis Presley and Frank Sinatra.

Don't believe all those reports that spread like wildfire on the Web in 2014. Millions of fans posted their condolences, based on a fake "R.I.P. Bobby Vinton" Facebook page. Vinton told the press, "reports of my death are greatly exaggerated. I'm alive and well and enjoying the sunshine at my home in Florida."

Paul Anka's Early Years

**Paul Anka**, an early album cover that still evokes his "on the downlow" love affair with Disney's "Chief Mouseketeer," Annette Funicello. Remember her?

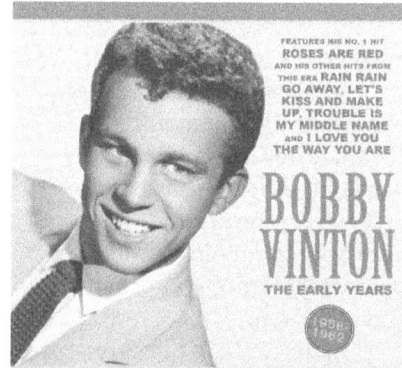

**Bobby Vinton,** after his long and formidably successful gig as "the all-time most successful love singer of the rock era," became a long time resident of *Boomer Times'* home state of Florida.

**Bobby Vee.** *Take Good Care of My Baby.*

# THE ENTERTAINMENT INDUSTRY'S SCANDAL METER

*MEASURING WHO'S IN AND WHO'S OUT, WHO'S UP AND WHO'S DOWN*

How **BILL COSBY** MORPHED FROM AN OBJECT OF PUBLIC ADORATION TO AN OBJECT OF PUBLIC HATRED

Since 1964, a company named Q Scores has measured the "popularity quotient" of celebrities, whether they're currently beloved, or whether they've fallen from grace.

Among males, no one has taken a plunge like Bill Cosby, who was known as "America's Father," when he starred as Dr. Huxtable, an obstetrician on *The Cosby Show,* the most popular TV series from 1985 to 1990.

Today, Cosby is vilified as a serial rapist who drugged women before raping them. Dozens of women have already come forth with roughly equivalent allegations, some of them dating from the early 1980s. Defamation suits (a response to Cosby's charges that they're liars) have been filed by some of the victims in states ranging from Pennsylvania to California.

Cosby himself has denied all wrongdoing and, as of this writing, no criminal charges have been filed against him because of the statute of limitations. But nonetheless, Cosby wins the dubious distinction of being the most despised celebrity in America.

Among female entertainers, pop singer Ariana Grande, 26, tumbled from her perch because of just one secret video footage taken of her in July. It depicts her visit to a local donut shop, where she licked one of the pastries before returning it for someone else to eat. Within the video, she also declared, "I hate America!"

Since the dawn of Hollywood, movie stars have landed in the crosshairs of the celebrity news media, especially the scoop-hungry *paparazzi* of today who supply shocking pictures for the tabloids. Among so many others, two London-born actors, Hugh Grant and Jude Law, have seen their private lives turned into tabloid fodder.

Police arrested Grant in the Red Light district of Sunset Strip, Los Angeles, with an African American hooker, "Divine Brown." Splashed across the front pages, his good boy image was shattered as well as his affair with the beautiful Liz Hurley.

Divine has defined her $50 "trick" as "the divine intervention of God." She went on to earn upward of $2 million in media interviews and guest show appearances on TV. She claimed that "Grant, in his Prince Charles voice, nicknamed me 'Cherry Red' because of my succulent red lips and scarlet-painted toenails. He definitely has a foot fetish."

Today, she enters posh restaurants in Prada heels and *haute couture* dress designs, carrying a Chanel handbag.

Jude Law also lost the love of a beautiful actress, Sienna Miller. Their affair began during their remake of the movie *Alfie* (2004), with Law redoing the famous Michael Caine performance.

Law's affair with the couple's young nanny, Daisy Wright, was later labeled "Nannygate" by the press. Regrettably, one of Law's kids caught the couple in the act. Wright told the world that "Jude is a great lover and knows how to satisfy a woman. We couldn't get enough of each other."

Grant and Law have long since been replaced in the

**Then** vs. **Now** on the Scandal Meter
**The Rise and Embarassing Collapse of Bill Cosby**

## IN FLAGRANTE DELICTO
aka **After-effects of a Blow Job**

**Mug Shots of Hugh Grant** with **Divine Brown**
*(aka Estelle Marie Thompson)*

*BUT JUDE, IT'S REALLY NOT A GOOD IDEA
TO SLEEP WITH MEMBERS OF YOUR STAFF*

## NANNYGATE

*(Left to right)*, **Siena Miller, Jude Law, Daisy Wright**

493

tabloid headlines by Ben Affleck, 43.

First, Affleck was caught pressuring the administrators of the PBS TV series, *Finding Your Roots,* hoping to suppress data that he was descended from slave owners. Today, headline after headline exposes his crumbling ten-year marriage to actress Jennifer Garner, in the aftermath of which he stands to lose a vast fortune. The couple have three children.

He's stuck with a reputation of having a cheating heart. In one such case, he was caught with stripper Tammy Morris in Vancouver, who gushed to the press about their love-making, giving him "high marks as a cavalier in the bedroom." He'd previously been linked, like Law himself, with the couple's young nanny.

Affleck's latest scandal arose from his reunion with his former lover, Jennifer Lopez, whose affair began when they co-starred in *Gigli* (2003), now known as one of the most disastrous films ever made.

Collectively, the press nicknamed them "Bennifer." The tabloids have recently obtained steamy home videos showing the red-hot lovers locking lips, embracing passionately, and sharing a lusty romp in a hot tub.

Affleck's career rose from the depths of one bad movie after another before his filming of the political thriller, *Argo,* voted Best Picture of the Year in 2013. That led to Warner Brothers investing millions upon millions of dollars in production and marketing costs for a series of upcoming pictures in which Affleck will star.

Set for release in March of 2016 is the first teaming of *Batman vs. Superman: Dawn of Justice.* Affleck portrays Batman, and Henry Cavill was cast as Clark Kent (alias Superman).

Designed for more mature audiences is *Live by Night,* based on the award-winning novel by Dennis Lehane. It takes us back to the Prohibition Days of 1926, an era rife with corrupt cops, underground distilleries, speakeasies, and murderous gangsters.

Affleck is also the star of *The Accountant,* which is slated for release in October of 2016. Some insiders have predicted that it might win an Oscar.

Based on its massive investment in Affleck, Warners is justifiably worried that his many scandals will diminish his popularity at the box office. Q Scores found that men are relatively forgiving of the star's philanderings. Surveys have also shown a generational shift between Baby Boomers and Millennials. Women, age 50 and over—a key market for a movie like *Live by Night*—have soured on Affleck, their opinions for the most part shifting to the negative.

In contrast, women under 50, who comprise approximately 75% of movie audiences, have shown absolutely no shift in their high opinion of the actor.

"Ben has become a polarizing figure among Baby Boomer women," claimed Henry Schafer, executive VP of Q Scores. "But Millennial women are a forgiving lot. There's been a generational shift in morality. Just ask Bill Clinton, America's first Baby Boomer president."

Although the ups and downs of the Scandal Meter were usually "predictable"—at least as they applied to Baby Boomers, its conclusions get murky whenever they're applied to Generation X- and Z-ers and the love antics of **Ben Affleck.**, who appears as the centerpiece of a beautiful trio of wives, lovers, and playmates.

To his left is is ex-wife **Jennifer Garner** (married 2005-2018), to his right is his present wife, **Jennifer Lopez** (married 2022), and (lower photo) **Tammy Morris**, an outspiken and very "in-shape" pole dancer.

**Henry Cavill**. One Hollywood insider told us that even if he evolves into a "serial cheater' on the Scandal Meter, his fans are likely to forgive him.

**Bill Clinton** and **Monica Lewinski** never really recovered from their involvement in one of the most cringe-worthy affairs in presidential history.

# PART FIVE

## IN THE ENTERTAINMENT INDUSTRY, YESTERDAY IS GONE, AND MANY OF ITS PLAYERS ARE DEAD

# CREATIVE MALADY

*From Florence Nightingale to Marcel Proust,*
*The Anguish of Great Artists Who Suffer*

**Sigmund Freud**, the father of psychoanalysis, suffered from sometimes crippling anxiety throughout his life, particularly in his later years. As a Jew living in Vienna, and deeply traumatized by the contempt with which many of his then-radical ideas were received, his fears grew (justifiably) more intense after the Nazis annexed Austria in 1938.

**Paul Gauguin**, a pioneer of post-Impressionistic painting, brawled and feuded with his companions, He abandoned his family for more exotic climates (and sexual scenes) in Tahiti, and was addicted to both morphine and his own self-aggrandisement. But he remains a giant in the history of 19th-century French art. According to one critic, "He made a good story out of a life that was, in many respects, terrible."

Provocative issues are being raised about the private lives of painters, actors, musicians, dancers, directors, authors and composers. Should we judge them strictly on their artistic creations, regardless of their morals?

Reputations are being destroyed by revelations about the private lives of certain artists and other creators. Morality tests are being applied to artists of yesterday who are being subjected to a 21$^{st}$ Century perspective of their politics and sexual improprieties.

A study of the private lives of some of the leading figures in world culture would reveal dozens of maladjusted personalities, even demented ones. Examples come to mind: Sigmund Freud, Florence Nightingale, Charles Darwin, Marcel Proust.

Should we no longer read the groundbreaking modernist novels of Louis-Ferdinand Céline because he was an anti-Semite? Let's not look too closely into the secret beliefs, recreations, and politics of Cervantes, Richard Wagner, or even Shakespeare.

There is a condition called "Creative Malady," which suggests that great art is often produced by the psychologically damaged. It is said that mental illness, often in the form of a psychoneurosis, can sometimes lead to major success in the production of artwork.

Sir George Pickering, a brilliant septuagenarian physician and author of a book about it (*Creative Malady*, first published in 1974 and today a widely recommended academic text), claimed that "great work would not have been done, or done in such splendid style, by relatively sober people leading ordinary lives."

Years ago in Key West, Tennessee Williams told me that his plays "stem from my tormented soul, my shattered dreams. I was Blanche DuBois in *A Streetcar Named Desire*—demented,

**Marcel Proust** was sometimes called a martyr to his art, Modern-day psychologists believe that he suffered from obsessive-compulsive disorders, an inability to make decisions, and psychological frenzies which manifested themselves in ways that were detrimental to his health, including asthma and chronic insomnia.

He remains a luminary in the world of French letters. As defined by Jean Cocteau, "Just as the voice of a ventriloquist comes out of his chest, so Proust's emerged from his soul."

**Florence Nightingale** (aka "The Lady with the Lamp,") was born of English parents in Florence, Italy, in 1820. She's remembered today as the founder of modern nursing and for her social advocacy of better hygiene as it applied to wartime treatment of the wounded. One of the most admired women of the Victorian Age, she became a heroine of the Crimean War (1853-1856), addressing typhus and cholera among British troops on duty there at the time.

She suffered from what would probably be defined as a bipolar disorder. In her diary, she wrote, "Why, oh my God, can I not be satisfied with the life that satisfies so many people?" She heard mysterious voices calling out to her, and suffered through bouts of extreme depression while saving the lives of others.

497

delusional, self-destructive."

In the past two years, artist Paul Gauguin (1848-1903), that self-professed "savage, exploiter, chauvinist, colonialist," has come under fire for his private life.

Moving to Tahiti in 1891, he became a notorious pedophile, fathering countless children born to girls aged twelve to thirteen. He painted them as dusky, bare-breasted, almond-eyed, mysterious, and dark-skinned beauties. He has also been criticized for promoting racial stereotypes.

Gauguin did not confine his painting to nubile Polynesian maidens. He also painted self-portraits, one of himself as Jesus Christ, another of himself as a decapitated John the Baptist, with a ruby-red glaze of blood on his neck.

Some of his sharpest critics have even demanded that museums and galleries displaying his works cease to do so. Exhibitions of his masterpieces have also been condemned. Yet reproductions of his works decorate thousands of bedrooms. His last painting, "Will You Marry?" sold for $210 million in 2014, the third-highest price ever paid for a painting.

When London's Tate Gallery presented an exhibition of Gauguin's works, many writers were highly critical of its curators for "displaying the art of a child molester." The director at the time, Vicente Todoli, said, "As a person, I might have loathed Gauguin, but as an artist, he is a genius, inspiring future painters such as Picasso and Matisse. When an artist creates something, it no longer belongs to him, but to the world."

As his legacy, Gauguin has inspired novels, operas, even movies such as *Lust for Life* (1956). It starred Kirk Douglas as Vincent Van Gogh, who cut off his ear before being incarcerated in a mental asylum. Anthony Quinn's portrayal of Van Gogh's rough-edged frenemy (Paul Gauguin) brought him an Oscar.

In 1903, the year of Gauguin's death at the age of 54, he said, "No one is good, no one is evil, everybody is both, in the same way and in different ways. It is so small a thing, the life of a man, and yet there is time to do great things."

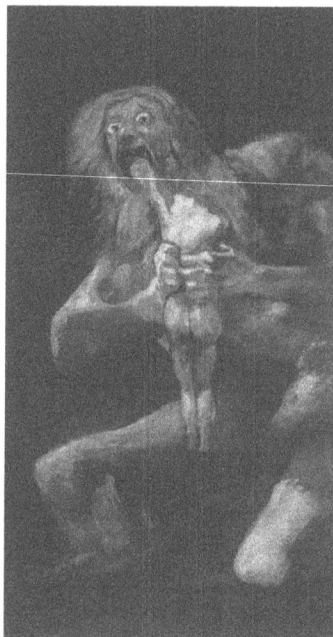

**Miguel de Cervantes Saavedra**

**Tennessee Williams**

**J. Robert Oppenheimer,** was the American physicist who led the team that developed the atomic bomb that ended World War II. In his early life, he suffered from chronic depression and emotional breakdowns. In 1925, as a student at the University of Cambridge (UK), he became so angry with his tutor that he left a poisoned apple on his desk.

As he aged, his mental health improved, although he was plagued with the fear that he had helped create a weapon that might one day destroy the world.

**William Shakespeare**

**Charles Darwin**

**Alan Turing** cracked the Nazi's "unbreakable" Enigma Code, thereby shortening World War II by two years and saving an estimated 14 million lives.

How did the British government reward him? After being arrested on a charge of homosexuality and chemically castrated, he committed suicide in 1954 at the age of 41. Queen Elizabeth II pardoned him in 2013—a bit late, many of his supporters said. He is heralded today as the Godfather of Modern Computers, and as one of the most important technical geniuses of the 20th Century. Psychologists today believe that he had autism.

*Saturn Devouring His Son,* by **Francisco Goya** (1746-1828), probably the most important Spanish artist of his era. Some art historians interpret this gruesome painting as a representation of the artist's psychological demons—the kind that many creative people struggle to keep tightly leashed.

# BABY BOOMERS AS HISTORY'S GREATEST MOVIE FANS

Throughout the pandemic, many Baby Boomers, cut off from their grandchildren, binged on classic films and movie star biographies.

Fourteen of my best-selling titles disappeared from warehouses, books devoted to the lives of such stars as Marilyn Monroe, Elizabeth Taylor, and Frank Sinatra, and a "celebutante" star who lived in an even larger sphere, Jaqueline Kennedy Onassis.

Distributors want new editions, sometimes with additions and amplifications, reprinted at once.

Surveys have shown that Baby Boomers and their parents, in the years between 1930 and 1959, created the greatest movie stars in film history. To name a few from that staggering list (each covered extensively in one or several of my biographies): Humphrey Bogart, Bette Davis, Joan Crawford, Greta Garbo, Clark Gable, James Cagney, Rock Hudson, Judy Garland, Frank Sinatra, Cary Grant, and Katharine Hepburn.

Surveys also revealed that hordes of Baby Boomers often selected films based on their association with a particular star—and not just for the picture itself.

In the past 18 months, wonderful letters have poured into Blood Moon Productions—the entity that publishes my books—from readers across the country. Some of them were critical, not because of what I'd written, but because of what I hadn't.

Typical of the mail coming in are these comments. Names are withheld.

From Bangor, Maine, a reader wants to know, "When are you going to publish a book on Errol Flynn, that swashbuckler on the screen and in the boudoir? Was he really a Nazi spy? Did he promote the Slave Trade as a young man in New Guinea? Did he seduce underage boys and girls?"

A woman living in Lake Placid, New York, wrote in with: "I read that you're planning a book on Rita Hayworth, who was known to my generation as 'the Love Goddess of the World.'

Depicted above is the facade of a once-prosperous theater in downtown Brimingham, Alabama. Its marquee announces **Kirk Douglas** as Vincent Van Gogh in *Lust for Life*. The **inset photo** shows Douglas in one of the best roles he ever played—the manic-depressive genius who during his lifetime never sold a painting

The Cold War confronted by Baby Boomers was either very cold or very hot, depending on when and where they looked. But the nuanced complexities of **Grace Kelly** and **Cary Grant,** shown here in the jewel-theft caper, *To Catch a Thief (1955)* kept Boomers alert and intrigued for months.

Many questions have been asked about her life, and most of them remain unexplored—including the incestuous nature of her relationship with her father. Did her first husband, Edward Judson, really pimp her out to promote her career? What scandals and humiliations did she endure during her ill-fated marriage to Prince Aly Khan?"

From Toledo, Ohio, came this challenge: "Don't you think it's about time you relayed the complete story of Marlene Dietrich minus all those stylish but untrue fabrications published to date? Tell us of her early life growing up in the decadent Weimar Republic, where anything and everything went on. Why don't you document her many love affairs, including those with Greta Garbo and John F. Kennedy."

A reader from Tulsa, Oklahoma wrote me with this: "Like Dietrich, Gary Cooper in his youth had sex without preference for any particular gender. Beginning tomorrow, Mr. Porter, why don't you sit down and document the incredible life of this great American icon, who blazed a trail across Tinseltown. For the first time ever, give us the whole story."

"One of the greatest stars in the history of cinema was William Holden," claims a reader from Baltimore. "Right now, there are only two slim paperbacks written about him. He deserves one of those complete biographies of the kind you write. His love affairs with just four of the many women he was involved with would fill a book: Jacqueline Kennedy, Barbara Stanwyck, Audrey Hepburn, and Grace Kelly. What about his hell-raising drunken days with Ronald Reagan after Jane Wyman divorced him? Did they really have a three-way with Marilyn Monroe in 1949?"

"Would you please write the tell-all book on Joan Crawford, as there is so much contradictory data out there?" says a reader from Omaha, Nebraska. "Also include data on her pre-Hollywood days when it's alleged that she was repeatedly raped by her brother and his gang, and that she was once a prostitute. Let us know about *that*. Her long-enduring "Golden Age" affair with Clark Gable would in itself merit a book."

"Based on your previous writings, you could devote an entire volume to the secret lives of Peter Lawford and Patricia Kennedy," suggests a reader from Philadelphia. "The scandals that emerged from their house in Santa Monica would make a tantalizing read, plus all the other shocking details, some involving Marilyn Monroe."

***

My conclusion? These Baby Boomers are "right on" in their suggestions. Alas, all it takes is time, that most precious of gifts. As the clock ticks away, and as the need to archive these histories grows more persistent and intense, I vow to do all in my power to see that many of the untold sagas of these Hollywood legends end up on the printed page.

**Marilyn** (Monroe) and **Jane** (Russell), anyone?

In the years before DVRs and streaming video services, Baby Boomers flocked to theaters to see them. Here they are, together, in **Gentlemen Prefer Blondes.**

Later in the lifespan of Boomers, as Europeans like Roberto Rossellini and his New Wave counterparts threw *avant-garde* newcomers onto America's cinematic landscapes, we continued heading to theaters for access to films like **Stromboli**, starring **Ingrid Bergman.** That film's marquee and Bergman's photo are displayed above.

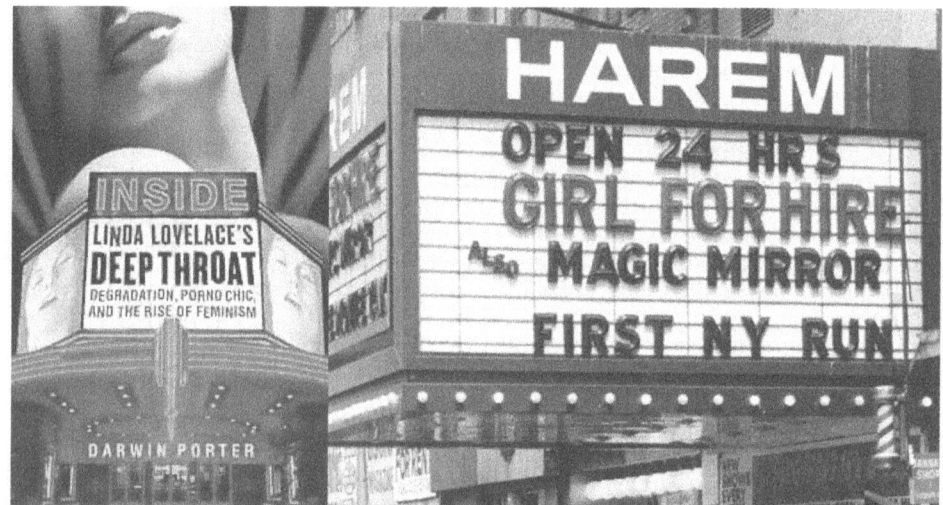

Boomers, during their sexual awakenings, even headed to brick-and-morter movie theaters for porn, as shown outside this 1970s-era NYC theater where members of the Salvation Army demonstrate against what they considered lewd films within.

The inset photo shows the front cover of Darwin Porter's exploration of the "beloved by Boomers" fellatio-centric movie that starred **Linda Lovelace.**, *Deep Throat.* After its release in 1972, it became a movie that defied everything everyone had ever believed about the film industry

Unwittingly, Linda became a lightning rod for censorships issues that "rocked the Baby Booming boat" at levels that reached high into the U.S. Supreme Court.

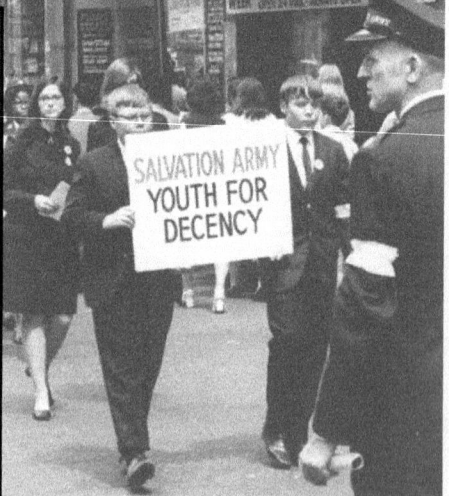

# THE DEATH OF BABY PEGGY
## THE SILENT SCREEN'S LAST SUPERSTAR,
## "THE MILLION DOLLAR BABY"

### (LATER KNOWN AS DIANA SERRA CARY, SHE LIVED TILL THE AGE OF 101)

In the 1930s, before Shirley Temple became box office champion of the world, "Baby Peggy" captured the hearts and box office receipts of the moviegoing public. Born in San Diego in 1918, she had, by the age of five, starred in more than 150 films—most of them shorts—often co-starring with Brownie, the Wonder Dog.

Her death was announced on February 24, when she died at the age of 101, having outlasted all the legendary figures of the silent film era.

Discovered at the age of nineteen months, she went to work for the Century Film Corporation in 1921. Dubbed "The Million Dollar Baby," she was soon earning $1.5 million a year, the equivalent of $24 million a year in 2020 currency. At her peak, she received two million fan letters a year.

Here's **Baby Peggy** experimenting with one of those newfangled radios. Everyone in the early 1920s related...

America fell in love with this apple-cheeked little darling. On celluloid, she escaped from a burning building; held ruthless gangsters at bay with a pistol; and clung to the underside of a fast-moving train. She performed her own stunts, even being held so long underwater that she fainted and nearly drowned.

"The Baby Peggy Doll" became the national bestseller, as did many other products marketed in her name. One couldn't pass a newsstand without seeing her on the cover of fan magazines. In 1924, at the Democratic National Convention, she was on the stage holding the hand of Franklin D. Roosevelt.

Her father, Jack Montgomery, a former stand-in for Tom Mix, the era's reigning cowboy star, put his daughter through a grueling schedule—"no time for lollipops." She worked six long days a week, turning out potboilers and tear jerkers.

Both parents spent lavishly, living in a mansion "stuffed with servants" near Mary Pickford and Douglas Fairbanks, Sr. Recklessly, they squandered her money on wardrobes, jewelry, bad investments, custom-made cars, and spectacularly expensive vacations.

"And then one day the sky fell on me," she said. Her money-grubbing father got into a salary dispute with her producer, Sol Lesser, who fired Peggy. At the age of eight she found herself blacklisted at the other movie studios.

Since she was still a famous name, Peggy's father booked her as part of a taxing cross-country vaudeville tour, which damaged her health. She recalled that for many performances, she was "yellow dog sick. He waited in the wings with a pail for me to vomit between acts." He gave her a nickel for every performance, keeping the rest of the money for himself.

Even before the Wall Street Crash of October, 1929, her finances were almost depleted. What was left was confiscated by her step-grandfather, who fled with the money and was never heard from again.

Peggy and her parents ended up in dire poverty as the Depression descended upon the land. She found

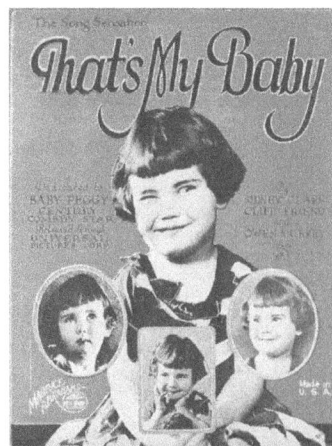

**Baby Peggy** was satirically precocious, too. In addition to what critics defined as "nursery fare," she spoofed the adult heartthrob and star Rudolph Valentino as a bullfighter in **Carmen, Jr** (1923). Audiences roared their approval, nationwide.

Years after her fall from grace, **Diana Cary** wrote that her spectacular fame as a child actress encouraged the mothers of both Shirley Temple and Judy Garland to push their emotionally fragile daughters into showbiz.

A still from one of her first big pictures: *The Darling of New York* (1923) appears above. Working long hours, she often had to do her own stunts, which terrified her. One of them involved escaping from a room set on fire.

501

As a remarkably gifted childhood actress, **Baby Peggy** was noted for following the instructions and demands of both her (larcenous) father and whomever was directing her at the time.

Both the monocle and the mustache were early satirizations of The Little Tramp.

herself competing with hordes of other out-of-work people trying to find work as extras on movie sets for $3 a day.

After two marriages, she changed her name to Diana Serra Cary, and made a living as a switchboard operator, gift shop manager, bookstore clerk, and, in time, a freelance writer. She even penned her autobiography, *What Ever Happened to Baby Peggy?*.

During one of my annual updates to the *Frommer Travel Guide to California* that I co-authored for many years, I learned of Baby Peggy's circumstances and whereabouts in Gustine, in Central California. I phoned her, telling her that as a sideline, I was a film historian of silent pictures.

When I pulled into the driveway of her modest suburban home, she received me warmly. I asked if her neighbors knew that she was one of the alltime biggest movie stars of the silent era.

"I did tell a neighbor, and she responded, 'Yeah, and I was the Queen of Sheba.'"

She revealed that there was very little left of her screen legacy, and that most of celluloid for her body of work burned to ashes in a fire that swept through the warehouses of Century Studios in 1926. The Museum of Modern Art in New York rescued *Little Red Riding Hood* (1922) and *The Darling of New York* (1923), and in 2016, it was announced that a copy of (previously lost) short film *Our Pet* had been re-discovered in Japan.

"It's been a life of triumphs and tragedies," she said. "But I'm a survivor. If you live long enough, most people will have to go through the bad years waiting for the good. Many of the child actors of the 1920s and '30s, except for Shirley Temple, ended up impoverished, emotionally scarred, and, worse that that, forgotten. I've spent many years working for the protection of the rights of child actors."

"All in all, it's been a hell of a ride. If I have any advice at all to give to my fellow senior citizens, it's to learn to make peace with your past."

Inspired by either Gloria Swanson or Pola Negri, a relentlessly overworked **Baby Peggy** appears above, vamping it up with **Jackie Morgan.**

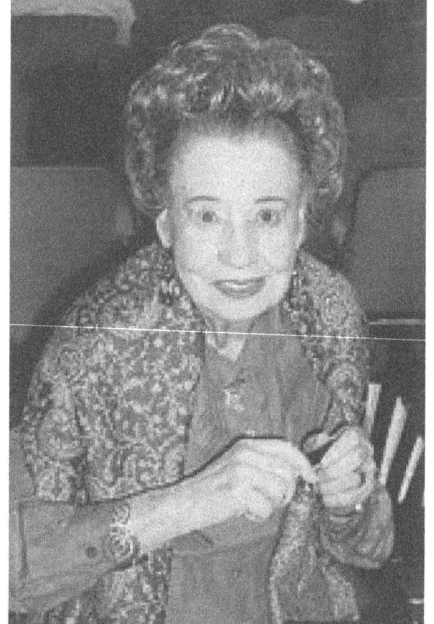

In *Peg o' the Movies* (1923), audiences of her era instantly recognized the salaciously sexual Pola Negri in **Baby Peggy**'s pre-Code cigarette-smoking spoof.

Although demure and lovely in her late teens, the actress formerly known as **Baby Peggy** painfully learned that the movies (and their casting rituals) had moved on without her.

Shortly before she died, in an interview with a silent film blog, *Silence is Platinum*, **Diana Serra Cary** analysed her career like this: "I knew from the age of four that I was a separate person in a way. I never brought that person on the screen. I knew that she was projected by me, but I didn't occupy her. It never occurred to me that she was working for me and she remembered all these little things… it was she who was providing me with all the stories, the things nobody keeps a record of."

## AMERICA'S GESTAPO CHIEF
# J. EDGAR HOOVER

## CLINT EASTWOOD'S BIOPIC SHOVES HOOVER'S PRIVATE LIFE BACK INTO THE CLOSET

Countless movies have been made about the FBI and its director, J. Edgar Hoover, including the latest failed attempt, *J. Edgar*, a Clint Eastwood film starring Leonardo DiCaprio in an unlikely role with bizarre makeup. Regrettably, no director and no script ever written has managed to penetrate the "iron curtain" around J. Edgar himself.

Let's go back to 1928: Into Director Hoover's office at the Bureau of Investigation (it wasn't called the FBI back then) walked a job applicant. Clyde Tolson, fresh from America's Corn Belt, was handsome, macho, well-built, and soft-spoken. Later, as associate director of the FBI, he'd be called "the Gary Cooper of G-Men."

Hoover sat up and took notice of Tolson's commanding presence, especially his piercing black eyes. After an hour's chat, Hoover proclaimed, "Our bureau needs men like you. Why not have dinner with me tonight?"

Tolson became "The Man Who Came to Dinner"—and never left. Before the rooster crowed after their first night together, Hoover was nicknamed "Speed" and Tolson was called "Junior." Their breakfasts, lunches, dinners, and "sleepovers" lasted 44 years. In fact, Tolson cooked Hoover's last meal just three hours before he died in 1972.

Hoover's first instruction to "Junior" involved telling him that "blackmail is the road to power." And so it was. Eight presidents would come and go, and none of them ever managed to get rid of Hoover. With Tolson at his side, he pursued gangsters, Nazis, spies, and his two favorite targets, communists and homosexuals. Enemies were made, of course, including the woman he called "horse face," Eleanor Roosevelt, and that feisty Harry Truman. Both of them accused Hoover of running an American Gestapo.

When not pursuing public enemies (including John Dillinger) in the 1930s, Hoover and Tolson investigated presidents, senators, scientists, congressmen, and movie stars. "Everybody's got something to hide," Hoover told Tolson. "Let's find out what they don't want us to know."

They discovered FDR's mistresses and Eleanor's "squaws," a reference to her lesbian girlfriends. Their largest and most incriminating files were compiled on Presidents Kennedy and Nixon. At least for appearance's sake, Lyndon B. Johnson was their friend. But, as LBJ told Senator George Smathers of Florida, "What else? He's got me by the *cojones.*"

My latest biography, *J. Edgar Hoover and Clyde Tolson: Investigating the Sexual Secrets of America's Most Famous Men and Women,* took decades to complete. Anyone today who knows anything about Hoover immediately labels him a homosexual and a cross dresser. Amazingly, loyalists still dispute both of those charges, but the evidence is overwhelming.

Fortunately, I knew many people who were close to Hoover and Tolson. (Yes, they actually had friends.) Some of them were willing to talk about both men, but only after they'd died.

Two views of America's scariest lawman, **J. Edgar Hoover.** Upper photo, with an "alter ego" and pet; *Lower photo,* on the right with his work cohort and long-time companion, **Clyde Tolson,** in the early 1930s.

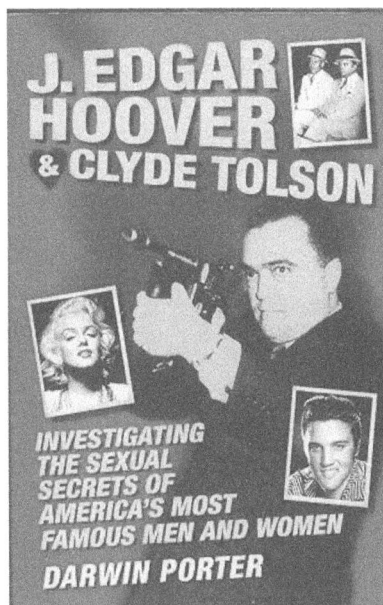

**Darwin Porter's** biography of the FBI chief *(cover art above)* ripped the lavender veil of secrecy off the coffin of the late J.Edgar Hoover's vile and destructive obsession with celebrity and the sexual preferences of those who pursued it during his long-lived administration.

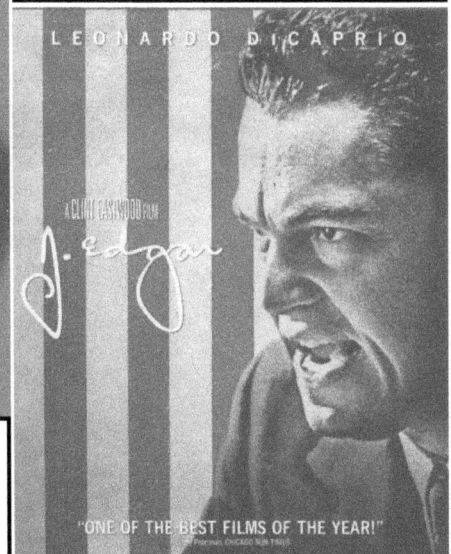

Hollywood kingpin **Leonardo DiCaprio,** in the movie poster above, emulates the FBI chief in the widely contested film version of the lawman's life, *J. Edgar*

Objects of J. Edgar's obsessive voyeurism included, *left to right, above,* the far-sighted U.S. diplomat and statesman **Sumner Welles**; **Albert Einstein;** the mega-corrupt superlawyer **Roy Cohn** (*right figure in the photo,* shown colluding during the McCarthy trials with commie-hating **Joseph McCarthy** himself; and a portrait, at a podium of "that rabble-rouser," **Dr. Martin Luther King, Jr.**

These included what Hoover affectionately referred to as "my favorite gun molls," Ethel Merman and Dorothy Lamour, who aided Hoover with his wardrobe. The notorious Roy Cohn, Joseph McCarthy's chief aide, knew all about Hoover. But the best source was Guy Hotell, an FBI agent and their longtime friend who vacationed with them and often dined with them. Officially, he was Tolson's roommate, although "Junior" spent his nights with "Speed."

Amazingly, Hoover and Tolson exposed everybody else, but kept a tight lock on their own closet. Of course, there were many attempts to disgrace them, but they managed to squelch any outburst, threatening to expose their fiercest enemies, some of whom ended up in jail.

For their amusement, they vacationed together in Florida and California and were always seen at horse races. At night, they voyeuristically viewed pornography seized during FBI raids.

Their hobby revolved around the investigation of the sexual secrets of famous Americans. They opened a Pandora's box of secrets associated with Errol Flynn *(was he a secret Nazi?)*; Marilyn Monroe *("did she sleep with all four of the Kennedy men?")*; Elvis Presley *("did he have an incestuous relationship with his own mother?")*; Albert Einstein *("was he a communist spy?")*; and Martin Luther King, Jr. *("was he a notorious womanizer and a closeted homosexual?").*

In writing about Hoover, I managed to uncover some real shockers. For example, Hoover might have prevented the surprise Japanese attack on Pearl Harbor if he'd shared his secret data with other government agencies, including the occupant of the Oval Office (FDR).

There is, however, a disappointment that accompanies the completion of what is likely to be the major journalistic assignment of my life: Chances are high that I will never again find such a powerful subject to write about. U. S. presidents couldn't fire him or control him because he knew too much. The Mafia used his own most powerful weapon, blackmail, and secretly gathered evidence on the private lives of Hoover and Tolson. That is why Hoover for years denied the very existence of the Mafia to the rest of America.

In 1940, FDR told his trusted homosexual aide, Sumner Welles (the subject of another Hoover investigation): "The director has caught all of us with our trousers down, but some day, someone is going to catch him jaybird naked and involved in the most lustful, perverted behavior."

It is my fervent hope that I have fulfilled FDR's prophecy.

*Left to right in the photos above:* **Lorena Hickok**, activist journalist and lesbian cohort of First Lady **Eleanor Roosevelt**; "The Sarong Queen," **Dorothy Lamour**; **Elvis Presley,** and an uncharacteristic view, in his wheelchair, of polio victim and four-term U.S. President, **Franklin D. Roosevelt,** with a relative.

# AGING WITH RAZZMATAZZ

## HOLLYWOOD'S TRANSFORMATION OF AN "OVER THE HILL" SILENT SCREEN VAMP INTO A MODERN-DAY HORROR ICON

# CARLA LAEMMLE

WILL YOU STILL LOVE ME WHEN I'M 104?

Born in 1909, the silent screen vamp, Carla Laemmle [pronounced **LAM**-lee] retired from motion pictures in 1939, just as Europe went to war.

But in an amazing feat, unmatched in film history, she made a comeback in the 21st Century. In fact, her last picture, *Mansion of Blood,* was released in 2014, making her the oldest living star still working in Hollywood.

Looking thirty years younger than her actual age of 104, Carla doesn't mind being called "a bona fide horror icon."

As she puts it, "I didn't just witness the birth of the horror movie, I helped create it."

Arriving in Hollywood at the age of eleven, she lived with her parents in a bungalow on the lot of Universal Pictures. The studio had been founded by her uncle, movie pioneer Carl Laemmle, or "Uncle Carl" to her. Her pet was the studio camel, used in Sahara desert pictures. "I fed him oatmeal," she said.

Film historian Scott Essman defined Carla as "almost the last tie to an era that is largely gone," referring to the Silent Screen heyday of such legendary stars as Mary Pickford, Rudolph Valentino, Gloria Swanson, and Charlie Chaplin.

Day by day, Carla watched Lon Chaney perform in monster makeup or sat on the lap of the great director, Erich von Stroheim.

Long before Marilyn Monroe posed for her nude calendar, Carla shocked Uncle Carl when she posed for a series of nudes. "I was just a teenager, but everybody said I had a beautiful body. So I decided to show it off."

"I still have those nude pictures," she says, "but I don't display them on my wall of memories."

Her lovely curves were on view in her first movie, the classic 1925 *The Phantom of the Opera,* starring Chaney and based on Gaston Leroux's 1910 novel. The story is about a deformed phantom who haunts the Paris Opera, causing mayhem and murder. Carlo was only 15 when she appeared as a beautiful dancer in a very revealing costume, playing the role of the film's Prima Ballerina.

She would continue making movies through the Silent era, including *The Hollywood Revue of 1929* in which she played a sexy chorus girl against a set designed by Erté. She seductively danced out of of a clamshell.

With the advent of Talkies, Carla made film history, speaking the first lines of dialogue ever heard in a horror thriller. Depicted in a coach, reading from a guidebook to fellow passengers, she said, "Among the rugged peaks that frown down upon the Borgo Pass are found crumbling castles from a bygone era."

In fact, those words became so immortal that author Rick Atkins named his 2009 bio of Carla *Among the Rugged Peaks.* She worked with him on that book, providing details of her 42-year-old love affair with Raymond Cannon, the late actor, director, and screenwriter.

He once wrote a play for her, *His Majesty the Prince,* in which she starred at the Hollywood Music Box in 1936.

"Ray lived with my mother and me until his death in 1977," Carla said. "It was a beautiful experience to be with him, and I miss him still."

Before her comeback, Carla's last picture was the 1939 musical, *On Your Toes,* in which she co-starred with Eddie Albert and Donald O'Connor.

In an unprecedented move, this centenarian was summoned out of retirement to face the

From cheesecake to vaudevillian belles, **Carla Laemmle** (*four photos above*) did it all...cheerfully, eventually evolving into an icon of the film industry.

cameras. Cast as an aging vampire, she starred in the thriller, *The Vampire Hunters Club* (2001). She appeared opposite John Agar, famous for having married Shirley Temple in the late 1940s when she was still a teenager.

After that, Carla took a nine-year break from films until she was cast in the 2010 *Pooltime,* playing a character called Zelda. It was her first gay movie. "In my day, the bathing beauties were always women. But I learned that in today's movies, male actors seem to disrobe as frequently as females."

*Pooltime* was followed by the 2011 movie, *The Extra,* which was followed by the 2012 *A Sad State of Affairs,* where she played Connie at the age of 102. This was her first musical comedy since she'd appeared in 1930 in the original *King of Jazz,* one of Hollywood's first singing-talking musicals. Carla danced in that picture's "Rhapsody in Blue" sequence. The director of *A Sad State of Affairs* claimed that it seemed only fitting to bring Carla back in a musical.

Her latest screen appearance came in the 2014 release of yet another horror movie, *Mansion of Blood,* the plot spinning around a haunted house, with Carla cast as the aging Maribelle.

Time has not aged nor dulled the wit and charm of Carla who, when not making films, maintains a series of personal appearances and speaking engagements. "I still get fan mail from all over the world, including from countries I've never heard of."

Unlike many of her contemporaries, who fell on bad days with the advent of the Talkies, Carla invested her money wisely and still lives well. She resides at her home on Melrose Avenue in Los Angeles, where she's lived for sixty years.

She welcomes visitors and usually appears wearing colorful Chinese silk robes. She is quite articulate about her illustrious past.

"I'm always asked one question: 'What is the secret of my longevity?' I never think about age. I always feel I'm in my 20s. I think I still have a lot to offer the world."

Her formula for a life beyond the century mark might be "Beware of vampires and hearses!"

**Carla herself** insisted that she appeared within this lineup of bathing beauties, circa 1929, although we, at least, can't ascertain which of them was actually her. It shows, at least, the spirit of bemused fun that permeated many of the Pre-Code films she "accessorized."

The Ironies of Age: Two views of **Carla Laemmle,** a survivor from the entertainment industry of the Jazz Age: *Upper photo,* as a ballerina, cheerfully posing in something akin to a contortion.

In her portrayal of the faded screen star, Norma Desmond, in *Sunset Blvd,* Gloria Swanson said, **"I'm still big. The pictures got small."**

Whether her late-in-life films involved *blood and horror* or *sand, sun, and sex,* Carla—as an actress-for-hire—marched bravely onward.

**REST IN PEACE**

**CARLA LAEMMLE**

1909-2014

506

# AMERICA'S BLUEBEARD

## A SOCIOPATHIC and HOMICIDAL BIGAMIST,
### HE HAD A ONE-INCH PENIS AND AN UNDEVELOPED VAGINA

American
Bluebeard
Lies and Dead Wives

Alene Burnett-Reaugh

Everyone's heard of Bluebeard. The lusty old psycho even made it into Webster's dictionary, which defines it as a man who kills one wife after another. He's making a Hollywood-style comeback.

The first known literary manifestation of this archetypal serial killer appeared in 1697, in a French literary folktale penned by Charles Perrault. The same author later crafted, or at least recorded, early versions of characters which included both *Cinderella* and *Sleeping Beauty*. Disney should pay the author's heirs royalties for their rip-off of those characters.

Perrault may have based his freakily morbid fairytale on a real person, Gilles de Rais (1404-1440), a Breton knight, leader in the French army, and a companion-in-arms to Joan of Arc. Baron de Rais killed not wives, but children, numbering in the hundreds. In his Bluebeard saga, Perrault took poetic license, changing the children victims to wives.

This lusty tale has returned to the screen and is playing in cinemas across the country. The controversial filmmaker Catherine Breillat has released her film, simply called *Bluebeard*, giving it her own unique interpretation. The new Bluebeard is as erotic as anything she's ever released. In her earlier film *Romance* the sex was real. In *Anatomy of Hell* it *might* have been real.

Whereas the archetype of Bluebeard has captured the world's imagination for centuries, what is not well known is that America had its own "Bluebeard," and two filmmakers are working on a script to bring it to the screen for the first time. It's the grisly but fascinating story of "Walter Andrews," whose real name was James P. Watson. In 1939, when he was 61, he died in prison after a bout of pneumonia.

Watson was a plain dull man—his looks were described as "gnomelike." Nonetheless, he managed to persuade at least 22 women to marry him, maybe a lot more.

He hooked up with them through ads in the "lonely hearts" columns of newspapers and periodicals. Literally hundreds of women around the country responded to his ads. Fortunately for them, he couldn't get around to all of them.

The problem these brides faced turned out to be much bigger than the wholesale bigamy of their husband. The women often disappeared on their honeymoon. Watson would announce a honeymoon for his bride of the moment in some faraway destination, like Chile. She never returned.

In time, "Bluebeard" married the wrong woman, Kathryn Wombacher. In 1919 he wed this dressmaker from Spokane, Washington. Their honeymoon was short, and he soon left, claiming he was a Federal agent on a secret mission for the government. She didn't believe him and hired a private eye, Detective J.B. Armstrong, who tracked Watson down and found him in Los Angeles living with another woman he'd married two weeks earlier. Armstrong also found a trunk owned by Watson within a private locker. It was filled with marriage licenses, wedding rings, photographs, and bankbooks. It turned out that Watson had been married to as many as 22

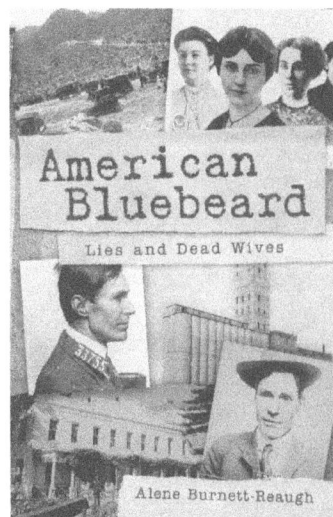

Frontispiece to a 19th-century English-language translation of a folk tale that was set into print in 1697 by **Charles Perrault**. When he wasn't recording sophisticated bedtime stories for the *literati*, he worked as an aide to the Finance Minister (**Colbert**) of **King Louis XIV**. An engraving of Perrault's image fills the illustration's central oval.

*La Barbe Bleue* goes like this: "There once lived a scary-looking blue-bearded man who slit the throats of his many wives, stashing their corpses in the basement of his castle."

Engraved illustration in an English-language translation of Perrault's *Blue Beard*. Published in London in 1895, its stately and voluptuous style is known as "Pre-Raphaelite."

One of its author's female ancestors (**Beatrice Maud Roscorla Andrewartha**). a recent immigrant to the Pacific Northwest from Cornwall (UK), disappeared in 1919 shortly after marrying a stranger she met on a train. At the time, there was nothing anyone could do. "The scandal of murder was a smudge on the respectfulness of our family, so it became a family secret."

After years of research, its author wrote and published this book with the intent of exposing the danger of "sudden seductions."

It's one of the most complete overviews of the serial murders of "The American Bluebeard" ever published.

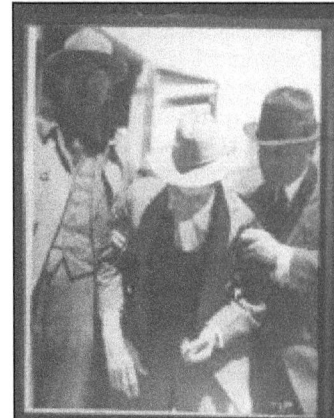

**James P. Watson's** (one of his many aliases) arrest by Los Angeles sheriffs in 1920.

women over the previous decade. When the LAPD caught up with this psychopath in a local café, he was romancing yet another in his string of women.

Thrown into a high security cell, he was severely beaten until he agreed to lead police to a grave site in a shallow marsh. There they found the acid-burned remains of a dozen women, each of whom had been beaten, knifed, drowned, or chopped to death during the previous three years. The bodies of the other brides were never found.

It was never determined just how many other women he'd killed, maybe more than a hundred to whom he was not married.

A question was raised but never answered. How did this deadly Romeo, this murderous Casanova attract so many women into his viperfish nest? When the police arrested Watson, and he was strip searched at the jail, a tantalizing fact was discovered: According to the police report, Watson possessed a "one-inch penis *and* an undeveloped vagina."

This illustration, in water-color pigments (aka *gouache*), depicts "La Barbe Bleue" attacking one of his wives.

It appeared within one of the original circa 1695 editions of **Charles Per-**

Scene from (and poster for) French filmmaker **Catherine Breillat's** 2009 release, *Bluebeard*, a critically acclaimed nod to feminism *(or the utter lack thereof)* during the French Middle Ages.

20th-Century rendering of **Gilles de Rais**, the blood-soaked 15th century inspiration for Charles Perrault's literary folk tale, *La Barbe Bleue*.

Academic debates about his role in the pseudo-science of alchemy and the "wars of unification" between Brittany and France have raged since **Voltaire,** during the Age of Enlightenment, resurrected the possibility that he was innocent.

Despite his many perplexing acts of defiance of the feudal codes that dominated France at the time, De Rais was accused by an ecclesiastic court, based on "public rumour" of raping and murdering numerous children, as well as of demonic invocations and pacts. An occultist and mysterious ally of **Joan of Arc**, he remains a subject of vivid debate within 21st-Century France.

**James P. Watson's** favorite method of procuring a wife was through the classifieds. Entire sections of regional newspapers were dedicated at the time to "matrimonials."

"Would be pleased to correspond with refined young lady or widow," read one he'd placed in a newspaper in Washington State: "Object, matrimony. This advertisement is in good faith."

Even after it was all discovered — the multiple bigamies, the brutal murders —many of his surviving wives spoke breathlessly, sometimes reverentially, about him: "The man," they said, "was a real romantic."

**James P. Watson** was born Charles Gillam in 1871. As he told it, his childhood was a nightmare from hell, soaked with physical and mental abuse. His father was absent, and his mother was psychotic. After she remarried, she changed young Charles' name to Joseph Holden. His stepfather tormented and abused him, and he left home at age 12.

In 1918, he took at least three wives, two in Canada and one in Seattle. He murdered all three of them, either by bludgeoning or pushing them to their deaths off panoramic ledges.

In 1919, he added more wives: **Maude Goldsmithy** in January; **Beatrice Andrewartha** (whose ancestor later recorded his saga in a book), and two women from Sacramento and Vancouver, respectively in February. He married **Elizabeth Prior** in March, **Bertha Goodrich** in June, and **Alice Ludvigson** in July. Beatrice he drowned in Lake Washington. Elizabeth he beat to death with a hammer. Bertha and Alice were held underwater until they died.

When police asked Watson how he'd kept so many women simultaneously, he told them that money was never a problem: He always demanded (successfully) that his new wife sign over her assets and change her will. Having asserted that he was a government agent, "work" took him away frequently. He'd use his "business trips" to see his other wives, sometimes as many as four in the same town

No one, including Watson, knew how many women he'd married. He guessed it was about 19 in three years. Some have estimated it was closer to 40.

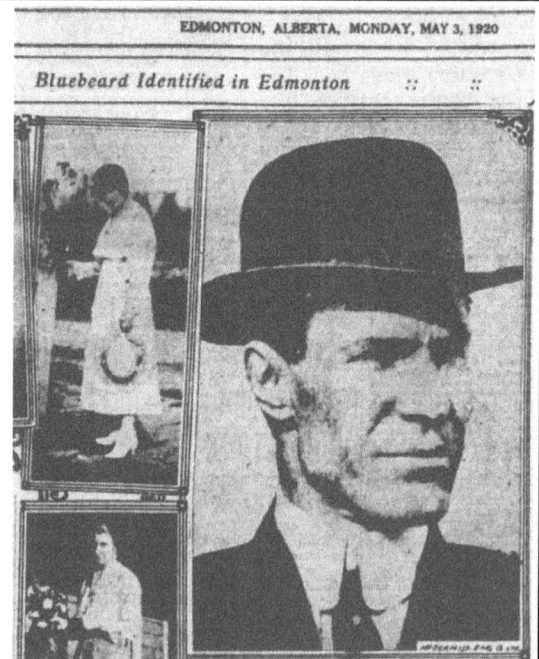

EDMONTON, ALBERTA, MONDAY, MAY 3, 1920

*Bluebeard Identified in Edmonton*

# BEAUTY IS A BEAST

## CAN A WOMAN BE AWARDED (OR PUNISHED) FOR HAVING (OR NOT HAVING) IT? ASK GWYNETH PALTROW, ANNE HATHAWAY, OR JULIA PASTRANA

*Left photo:* The embalmed bodies of **Julia Pastrana and her newborn child,** as exhibited for years as part of a traveling, Victorian-era burlesque show.

*Right Photo:* **Press photo of a Catholic memorial service** acknowledging the burial of the mother and child's remains.

Born in 1834, Julia Pastrana, once hailed as "the ugliest woman in the world," has at long last been buried near her birthplace in Sinaloa, Mexico. For decades, her mummified corpse was shamelessly exhibited around the world.

She was born with a genetic condition whereby her face and body were covered with black hair; her ears and nose unusually large; her double row of teeth irregular; her lips and gums extraordinarily thick—in all, a gorilla-like appearance. She was called "the missing link between mankind and an ourangoutang. Her tragic life was depicted in the 1964 film, *The Ape Woman*, an Italian-French drama.

Although slavery had been abolished in Mexico decades earlier, Julie was purchased by a circus, which exhibited her in freak shows. In New York, she fell in love with Theodore Lent, an impresario who married her only as a means of exploiting her ugliness in various traveling exhibits across the country.

He was a scoundrel, but Julia had a kind heart, even giving money to charities. She possessed a sweet singing voice and had great taste in music, speaking three languages.

While touring in 1859, she became pregnant. Born with her same genetic condition, her infant died within two days. She, too, developed postpartum complications and died five days later.

Her husband embalmed the bodies of his wife and son and continued to exhibit them in a glass coffin.

In 1884, Lent was committed to a mental asylum in Moscow, where he died. The mummies of his wife and son disappeared until 1921, when they resurfaced on a fairground in Oslo, Norway. They were displayed until the 1970s when they were put into storage. However, vandals broke into the facility and mutilated the baby's corpse. In the aftermath, its remains were consumed by mice. Left intact, Julia's mummy was stolen in 1979 but later resurfaced.

After a series of legal battles, her mummy was finally returned to her native Mexico in February of 2013, where it was given a proper

Ironically, it was Pastrana's LACK of conventional beauty that placed her squarely on the vaudeville freak show circuits of Europe. Here's a scene from the very avant-garde Franco-Italian film *La Donna Scimmia (aka The Ape Woman;* 1964*).*

In the *lower photo*, the respected French actress, **Annie Girardot**, as Pastrana, reacts to the shrewd "appraisals" of her impresario (later, husband) Theodore Lent, as portrayed by the Italian veteran actor, **Ugo Tognazzi.**

509

Catholic burial attended by hundreds. She had become a virtual *cause célèbre* in Mexico.

\*\*\*

In total contrast to Julia, *People* magazine designated Gwyneth Paltrow as "The world's most beautiful woman," which sparked outrage among her critics, who didn't think the 40-year-old actress deserved the title. Two weeks later, *Star* magazine named Paltrow as "The Most Hated Celebrity."

Paltrow is lovely, articulate, rich, an Oscar winner, married to a rock star, and is the mother of two adorable children. As one woman wrote online: "What's not to hate?"

She is seen as "an insufferable elitist," even telling people what to eat. Vegetarian chili is her favorite dish. Paltrow advised women that $450,000 is needed just for the "essentials" of a spring wardrobe. She also suggests that every woman should have a personal trainer, a cook, and frequent $500 colon cleanses.

Paltrow admits she is not perfect and claims that, "I wear more makeup than a transvestite, especially *Terry Or de Rose Baume Précieux* lip balm, which is "enriched" with 24-carat pink gold. "I've also got crow's feet and one boob sags more than the other."

\*\*\*

Runner-up for the title of "World's Most Hated Celebrity" was Anne Hathaway, who won a Best Supporting Oscar for her appearance in the recent film version of *Les Misérables*. On Google, she's been attacked 31 million times as opposed to Osama bin Laden, who racked up only 21 million hits.

What's wrong with Hathaway? Critics cite her "saccharine smugness, her transparent self-congratulations." She's also been called "carefully rehearsed, pretentious, and irritating," among other charges, which include "fawning and gushing."

"She's totally manufactured and desperate to be liked," wrote one critic.

Originally, fans interpreted her as a goofy but lovable star in such films as *The Princess Diaries*. Hathaway has begun consultations with PR image control experts to win back her fans.

Personally, I admire the talents of Paltrow and especially, of Hathaway. Maybe they are too good, too beautiful. There is, as virtually anyone can attest, such a thing as jealousy.

*My Takeaway?* That Beauty (or the lack of it) and "Likeability" (or the lack thereof) are fleeting and tragicomic, the subject of passionate, even furious, debate in the new, internet-crazed America.

Illustration within a circa 1865 German-language circus handout associated with the marriage of the sadistically unstable **Theodore Lent** *(left)* and his unconventional wife, **Julia Pastrana**

JULIA PASTRANA
THE TRAGIC STORY OF THE
VICTORIAN APE WOMAN

**Pastrana** "resurrected" in a biography by Gylseth & Toverud.

Beautiful by conventional standards, but frankly, with life stories considerably less interesting than Julia Pastrana's: **Gwyneth Paltrow** *(left)* and **Anne Hathaway.**

# MITT ROMNEY'S MOTHER

## WAS A *FEMME FATALE* IN CLASSIC HOLLYWOOD AND A FORCE OF NATURE IN MICHIGAN POLITICS?

In this press photo from 1962, young **Mitt Romney** joins his mother, the former Hollywood ingenue **Lenore LaFount Romney** and his father, **George Romney**, after their declaration that George would run on the Republican ticket as a candidate for the governorship of Michigan.

Although at one time known to thousands and thousands of Americans, Lenore LaFount is hardly a household name. But if her youngest child, Williard Mitt Romney, born in 1947, becomes president next month, she no doubt will become better known.

She married American businessman and politician George W. Romney in 1931, and presided as the very active—and most popular—First Lady of Michigan from 1963 to 1969. George fell in love with her in high school in Utah, but it took him seven years to lure her to the altar.

She wasn't at all certain that she wanted to get married. George had been born in Mexico, where, in 1886, the forebears of today's Romney clan had fled when Utah cracked down on polygamists. (They returned to the U.S. in 1912, after Mexico erupted in revolution.)

Lenore was a Mormon, too, but with less of the religious zeal of her boyfriend and future husband. He announced that he was leaving for Great Britain to convert Anglicans to the tenets of the Mormon church, and he made her promise never to kiss another boy during his long absence. She later said, "When I made that promise, I had my fingers crossed."

Transatlantic aviator and national hero **Charles Lindbergh**, one of Lenore's early celebrity crushes.

DEVOUT MORMON SEEDS OF A REPUBLICAN FAMILY DYNASTY:

Teen-aged **Mitt Romney** with his father, **George Romney.**

Although no one knows for sure, her first lover appears not to have been George, but the fabled aviation hero, Charles Lindbergh. After his historic *Spirit of St. Louis* flight to Paris, he flew into Salt Lake City to be welcomed by thousands of cheering fans. The slender 5-foot, 6-inch Lenore, with her porcelain skin and curly chestnut-colored hair, was one of six local girls selected to welcome the aviator. He was immediately attracted to her, and she seemed thrilled to meet the handsome and dashing world hero. She was seen leaving his hotel suite at 6am on the morning after his arrival.

Her mother, Alma Luella, born in 1882, urged her beautiful daughter to forget about George and go to Hollywood to become a movie star. In school, Lenore had won acclaim in student theatrical productions, mastering Shakespearean roles which included Ophelia, but also characters in plays by Ibsen and Chekhov. In Hollywood, a talent scout from MGM was immediately taken by her talent and natural beauty and signed her right away.

Almost overnight, she found herself appearing in bit parts, playing a fashionable young Frenchwoman in a Greta Garbo film. The bisexual Swede became enchanted with Lenore.

She also appeared as an *ingénue* in the William Haines film, *A Tailor Made Man,* and soon was in scenes opposite Jean Harlow and Ramon Novarro. Her body resembled that of the sultry Lili Damita, the former mistress of the King of Spain and the future wife of Errol Flynn. Lenore signed on as Damita's stand-in.

She became one of the most sought-after party guests in Hollywood. Soon, she was seen around town with Damita and her lover *du*

Before she married and "settled " into a life as the wife as a politician, **Lenore LaFount**, mother of Mitt Romney, either dated or appeared in brief *ingénue* roles as an attractive "accessory" to entertainers who included (*upper row, left to right*) **Greta Garbo, Jean Harlow, Gary Cooper** (*shown making love to* **Tallulah Bankhead**) and (*lower row, left to right*) **Robert Montgomery, Ramon Novarro, William Haines** (*shown in a scene from* Tailor-Made Man *with* **Dorothy Jordan**), and **Clark Gable.**

*jour,* Marlene Dietrich. When Lenore appeared in a film with Gary Cooper, he fell in love with her and pursued her, although Tallulah Bankhead, trying to become "the next Garbo," was also chasing after Cooper.

When Harlow introduced Lenore to Clark Gable, with whom she was having an affair, Gable dropped the platinum blonde and went for Lenore. At the time, Gable was in the process of getting a divorce from his older wife, a lesbian, Josephine Dillon, who was more his business manager than his spouse. When Gable started dating Lenore, she infuriated another of his lovers, Joan Crawford, who was married at the time to Douglas Fairbanks, Jr. Joan came over to Lenore's apartment at 3am and beat her up.

Dropping Gable, Lenore fled into the arms of another handsome actor, New York born Robert Montgomery. After a few dates, she learned he'd been married since 1928 and involved in only a temporary separation from his wife. He eventually went back to her and broke Lenore's heart.

Before George Romney returned from his missionary work to reclaim Lenore, she ran around with what was known in those days as "a fast crowd." Novarro, along with Haines and his lover, Jimmy Shields, took her to many of Hollywood's wild gay parties, where Lenore danced a wild Charleston and was the life of the party, flirting with the straight men.

Louis B. Mayer at MGM became so impressed with her beauty and talent that he offered her a three-year contract and a promise to transform her into "one of the biggest stars in my galaxy."

Then something happened: George Romney returned from his missionary work in Europe at around the same time Lenore had reached a crossroads in her life—marriage or career? She opted for marriage, and the rest is dynastic history.

But Lenore wasn't satisfied with the role of just a homemaker. Although a traditionalist, she advocated a greater involvement of women in business and politics. She was an early civil rights advocate, appearing on stage with Martin Luther King, Jr. Over the years, even though married, she attracted the amorous attentions of both Bob Hope and Art Linkletter. She was even accused of having a brief fling with Gerald Ford.

Although hailed as an early feminist, she always maintained that she was not interested in burning bras and denouncing men as male chauvinistic pigs. However, when she ran for Senator from the State of Michigan in 1970, male chauvinistic pigs did attack her, flashing signs at her rallies—GO BACK TO RATTLING THOSE POTS AND PANS, LENORE. She lost the race.

At the age of 85, Lenore emerged from seclusion to back Mitt in his race for the U.S. Senate seat from Massachusetts. She drew contrasts between her son and his opponent, the hell-raising, hard-drinking Teddy Kennedy.

Mitt eventually lost that race, of course, even though Lenore told the press that, unlike Teddy, Mitt and his wife, Ann, had waited until their honeymoon night to have sex. But she didn't want him to sound too square in liberal Massachusetts. She admitted that, unlike her husband, George, and unlike her other children, "Mitt goes to bed wearing as little as possible." That was her polite way of saying that, like Marilyn Monroe, he slept in the nude.

Blessed with a lithe body and classic features, Lenore LaFount, during her (brief) Hollywood heyday, worked as **Lili Damita's** *(left photo)* standin during distant shots and scene setups.

The *über*-fabulous **Marlene Dietrich**, Lili's on-again, off-again lesbian companion, appears on the right.

**Joan Crawford** in *Dancing Lady* (1933) lights Clark Gable's cigarette.

Cast as a showgirl, she did more than that. At this point in their careers, their off-screen romance was ablaze.

There were rumors of a deep-seated affection between Lenore Romney and former U.S. President **Gerald Ford,** who appears in the photo above with his well-intentioned wife, **Betty Ford**, co-founder of the substance- abuse clinic that bears her name.

Like the Romney's, Gerald and Betty Ford had been active in Michigan politics, Ford having served from 1949 to 1973 as a Congressional representative from Michigan.

**Mitt Romney** greets **Ted Kennedy** during their 1994 race for Senator from Massachusetts

**Lenore Romney** *(who dropped widespread use of her maiden name early in her marriage to George Romney)* appears above beside a highway in Michigan's sparsely populated Upper Peninsula during her losing campaign for senator in 1970. In the distance appears a billboard with her effigy.

On the left is one of her campaign buttons. At the time, a Republican nomination of a woman as a gubernatorial candidate was so unusual that everyone in politics recognized its slogan ("That's My Girl!") as associated with Lenore.

# DEATH: IT'S A GRAVE MATTER
## EXHUMING CHAPLIN'S CORPSE

The French actress, Claudette Colbert (1903-1996), who won the Oscar for *It Happened One Night*, claimed, "I must never think about death. People who think about death are mentally sick." She might be completely alone in her opinion.

The former gossip columnist, Rona Barrett, disagreed, claiming that people are fascinated with the subject of death, "especially when you get older."

Playing on that fascination is Alan W. Petrucelli, who has penned a book called *Morbid Curiosity: The Disturbing Demises of the Famous and Infamous.*

Of course, some deaths are announced prematurely. A Florida radio station broadcast the news that, "Death came suddenly today to Elizabeth Taylor, who gained national prominence as the star of *National Velvet*." The station later retracted the bulletin.

Just as the *CBS Evening News* was going on the air one night, an anchor received a bulletin that President George H.W. Bush had died in Tokyo. After vomiting on the Japanese prime minister, he'd collapsed in full view of squadron of photographers. News of his "death" was flashed immediately to the United States. Two seconds before air time, the CBS broadcaster was told to axe the story. Bush was alive but unwell.

Some tombstones say REST IN PEACE. But bodies often aren't allowed to do that. On March 1, 1978, the corpse of Charles Chaplin (1889-1977) was dug up and held for ransom. The thieves were caught and The Little Tramp's body was recovered. To prevent this from happening to her corpse as well, the heirs of Greta Garbo (1905-1990) arranged for the ashes of the fabled star to be buried in her native Sweden, two meters deep in an urn built of reinforced concrete.

Sometimes the executor of an estate has even exhumed the body. Sammy Davis Jr. (1925-90) was buried wearing $70,000 of his beloved jewelry. But when his wife discovered that he'd left her owing millions in back taxes, she had the body dug up and the jewelry reclaimed.

Some celebrities make their own funeral arrangements, but often their desires aren't carried out. The playwright Tennessee Williams (1911-1983) choked to death on February 24 on a medicine bottle's cap. He requested that he wanted to be buried at sea "12 hours north of Havana." Instead, his heirs sent his ashes to the Calvary Cemetery in St. Louis, Missouri.

The last words of a dying celebrity often become fodder for legend-making. "Codeine, bourbon!" were the final words ordered by that Alabama belle, Tallulah Bankhead (1902-1968). Joan Crawford (1904-77), who could never be mistaken for Mother Theresa, spoke to her maid only moments before death struck. "Damn it! Don't you dare ask God to help me!"

It is said that you can't take it with you, but in some cases, that's not true. Take the case of a heavy boozer like Errol Flynn (1900-1959). He was buried at Forest Lawn with six bottles of whiskey, a farewell gif from his drinking buddies.

Frank Sinatra (1915-1998) was sent with a small bottle of Jack Daniels, a pack of Camels, a Zippo lighter, a roll of cherry-flavored Life Savers, three Tootsie Rolls, and an envelope containing ten dimes. Tina, his daughter, knew that he always needed change to make a phone call.

Princess Di (1961-1997) went to her grave with photographs of her beloved sons William and Harry and her father.

**Claudette Colbert**

**Charles Chaplin**

**Frank Sinatra**

Columnist **Rona Barrett** in 1975

Cover art of **Alan Petrucelli's** *Morbid Curiosity.*

**Greta Garbo**

Funeral cortège of **Princess Diana**

A "late in life' view of **Elizabeth Taylor**

**Judy Garland** *(right)* with **Mickey Rooney**

**Billie Holiday**

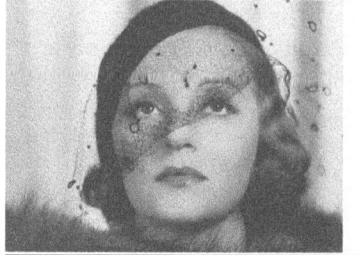

**Tallulah Bankhead**

Some 2.5 billion people watched her funeral, the largest audience in the history of television.

Some stars die in virtual poverty.  Judy Garland (1922-1969) made millions of dollars for studios, especially MGM.  But she died owing millions.

Upon her death, she was placed in a makeshift vault until her heirs could come up with the money to bury her.  Finally, Liza Minnelli, more than a year after Judy went over the rainbow, paid for an undertaker to place her in a marble crypt.

Judy admired Billie Holiday (1915-59), who also died in dire circumstances.  As she lay dying in New York's Metropolitan Hospital, armed police officers were stationed at her door.  She'd been arrested for heroin possession and ran the immediate risk of doing time in jail.

Lady Day had just 70 cents in the bank when she expired on July 17.  But the staff discovered $750 in $50 bills strapped to her leg.  She'd been given that advance from a publisher as a down-payment on her autobiography, tentatively entitled *Songs That Will Never Be Sung.*

Many living celebrities are already planning their final resting place, including Hugh Hefner (born 1926).  He bought the crypt next to Marilyn Monroe (1926-62), who posed as the first-ever *Playboy* Playmate.

Michael Jackson did not succeed in buying the bones of Marilyn, so her remains are still there, perhaps not looking as good as she did in 1953, when, in *Gentlemen Prefer Blondes,* she uttered the famous refrain, "And we all lose our charms in the end."

**Hugh Hefner** with his third and final wife, **Crystal**

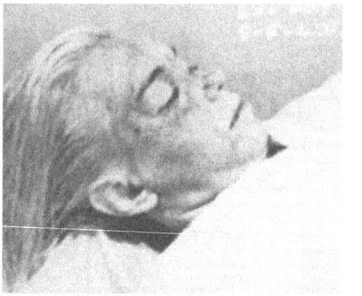

Coroner's photo from **Marilyn Monroe's** autopsy

**Tennessee Williams**

**Joan Crawford**

**Errol Flynn** in *Charge of the Light Brigade.*

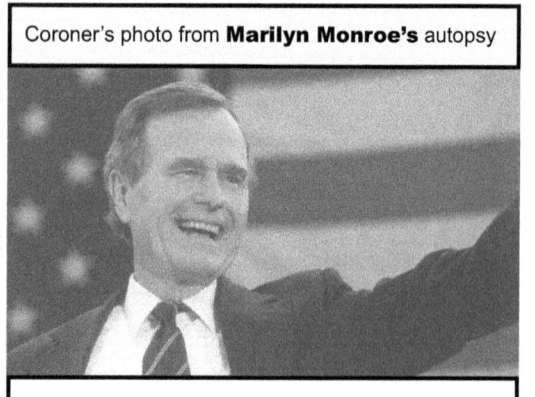

**George H.W. Bush:** News of his death after a state dinner with the prime minister of Japan were greatly exaggerated.

**DID YOU KNOW?** That books about Presidential (or pre-Presidential) scandals are as much a part of Blood Moon's repertoire as the ones we've associated with movie stars?

If you're in the mood for salacious (and accurate) overviews of what really went on in POTUS rumpus rooms, or if you're interested in embarassments that show Presidents (or pre-Presidents, before they were elected) and their Ladies as less than Saintly, check out Blood Moon's quintet of Presidential *exposés* on the pages that follow.

# THE KENNEDYS

### ALL THE GOSSIP UNFIT TO PRINT

A Staggering Compendium of Indiscretions Associated With Seven Key Players in the Kennedy Clan; A Cornucopia of Relatively Unknown but Carefully Documented Scandals from the Golden Age of Camelot. Jaw-dropping, a myth-shattering overview of a family consumed by its own passions.

Darwin Porter & Danforth Prince

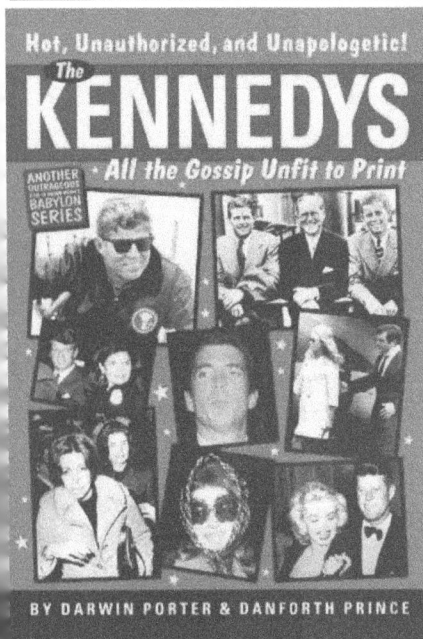

The great enemy of truth is very often not the lie—deliberate, contrived, and dishonest, but the myth—persistent, persuasive, and unrealistic."
    —John F. Kennedy

"God, I hate Camelot. I've begged Jackie to tell them to play something else, but it's like talking to a goddamn brick wall."
    —JFK, on the Marine String Orchestra playing at the White House.

"A vulgar slut, a publicity seeker, an egomaniac, a self-promoter, a vicious bitch, an unbalanced drug addict, an alcoholic whore, a dime-a-dance floosie"
    —Jacqueline Kennedy on Marilyn Monroe

"Listen, honey, if it wasn't for me, your boyfriend wouldn't even be in the White House."
    —Sam Giancana to Judith Campbell Exner

"The greatest twenty seconds of my life."
    —Angie Dickenson, describing JFK

"JFK was a man thoroughly out of control, thoroughly out of his depth, and maybe thoroughly out of his mind.. He was just a hoodlum Prince of Camelot. He was the incarnation of Sodom and Gomorrah."
    —Seymour Hirsch, *The Dark Side of Camelot*

**The Kennedys were the first true movie stars to occupy the White House.** They were also Washington's horniest political tribe, and although America loved their humor, their style, and their panache, we took delight in this tabloid-style documentation of their hundreds of staggering indiscretions.

Keepers of the dying embers of Camelot won't like it, but Kennedy historians and aficionados will interpret it as required reading.

Hardcover, with hundreds of photos and 450 meticulously researched, highly detailed, and very gossipy pages with more outrageous scandal than 90% of American voters during the heyday of Camelot could possibly have imagined.

ISBN 978-1-936003-17-4.
Temporarily sold out of hard copies, but available for e-readers.

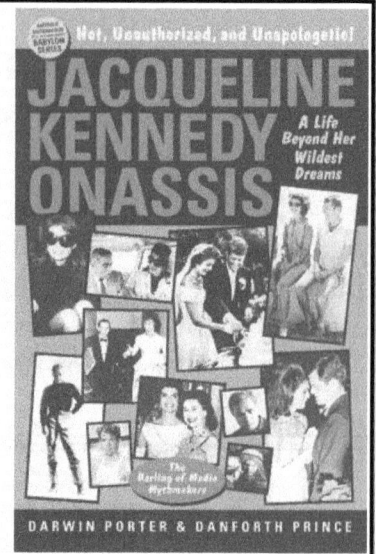

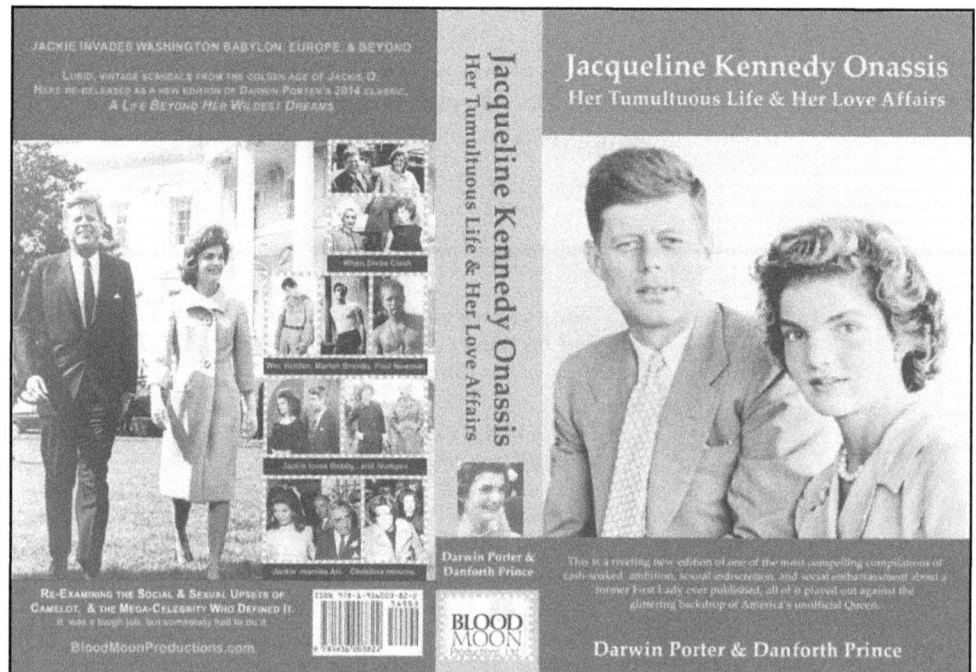

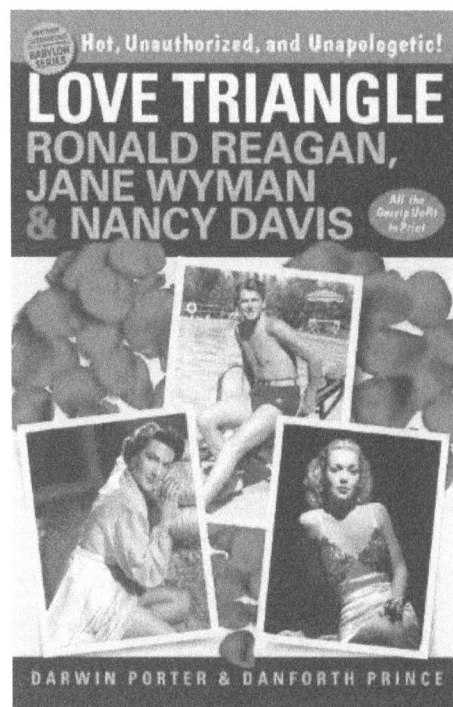

# BILL & HILLARY

## *SO THIS IS THAT THING CALLED LOVE*

### CONFUSED ABOUT HOW TO INTERPRET THEIR RAUCOUS PASTS?

THIS UNCENSORED TALE ABOUT A LOVE AFFAIR THAT CHANGED THE COURSE OF POLITICS AND THE PLANET IS OF COMPELLING INTEREST TO ANYONE INVOLVED IN THE SLUGFESTS AND INCENDIARY WARS OF THE CLINTONS.

"This is both a biographical coverage of the Clintons and a political *exposé;* a detailed, weighty exploration that traces the couple's social and political evolution, from how each entered the political arena to their White House years under Bill Clinton's presidency.

"Containing gossip, scandal, and biographical sketches, it delves deeply into the news and politics of its times, presenting enough historical background to fully explore the underlying controversies affecting the Clinton family and their choices.

"Sidebars of information and black and white photos liberally peppered throughout the account offer visual reinforcement to the exploration, lending it the feel and tone of both a gossip column and political piece—something that probes not just Clinton interactions but the D.C. political milieu as a whole.

"The result may appear weighty, sporting over five hundred pages, but is an absorbing, top recommendation for readers of both biographical and political pieces who will thoroughly enjoy this spirited, lively, and thought-provoking analysis."

— THE MIDWEST BOOK REVIEW

\*\*\*

Shortly after its release in December of 2015, this book received a literary award *(Runner-up to Best Biography of the Year)* from **the New England Book Festival.** As stated by a spokesperson for the Awards, "The New England Book Festival is an annual competition honoring excellence in books, with particular focus on projects that deserve closer attention from the academic community. Congratulations to Blood Moon and its authors, especially Darwin Porter, for his highly entertaining analysis of Clinton's double-barreled presidential regime, and the sometimes hysterical over-reaction of their enemies."

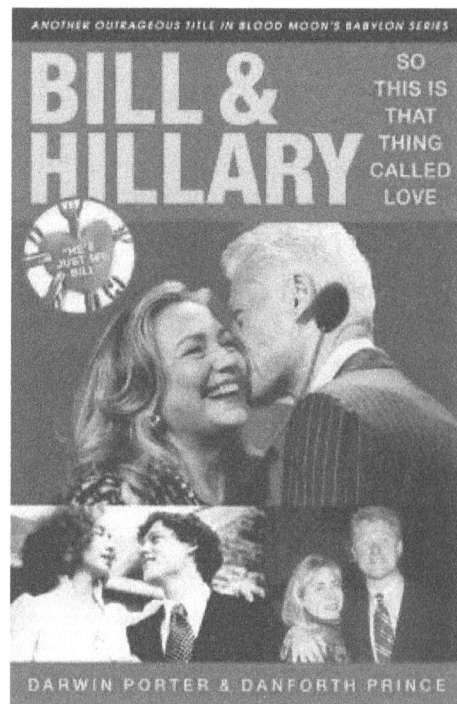

## BILL & HILLARY—SO THIS IS THAT THING CALLED LOVE
### Softcover, with photos.   ISBN 978-1-936003-47-1

# DONALD TRUMP

## *WAS THE MAN WHO WOULD BE KING.   HOW DID IT HAPPEN?*

These are the most famous books about our incendiary ex-President you've probably never heard of.

Winner of three respected literary awards, and released three months before the Presidential elections of 2016, it's an entertainingly packaged, artfully salacious bombshell, a scathingly historic overview of America during its 2016 election cycle, a portrait unlike anything ever published on **CANDIDATE DONALD** and the climate in which he thrived and massacred his political rivals.

Its volcanic, much-suppressed release during the heat and venom of the 2016 Presidential campaign has already been heralded by the *Midwestern Book Review, California Book Watch, the Seattle Gay News,* the staunchly right-wing *WILS-AM radio,* and also by the editors at the most popular Seniors' magazine in Florida, *BOOMER TIMES,* which designated it as one of their **BOOKS OF THE MONTH.**

**TRUMPOCALYPSE:** *"Donald Trump: The Man Who Would Be King* is recommended reading for all sides, no matter what political stance is being adopted: Republican, Democrat, or other.

"One of its driving forces is its ability to synthesize an unbelievable amount of information into a format and presentation which blends lively irony with outrageous observations, entertaining even as it presents eye-opening information in a format accessible to all.

"Politics dovetail with American obsessions and fascinations with trends, figureheads, drama, and sizzling news stories, but blend well with the observations of sociologists, psychologists, politicians, and others in a wide range of fields who lend their expertise and insights to create a much broader review of the Trump phenomena than a more casual book could provide.

"The result is a 'must read' for any American interested in issues of race, freedom, equality, and justice—and for any non-American who wonders just what is going on behind the scenes in this country's latest election debacle."

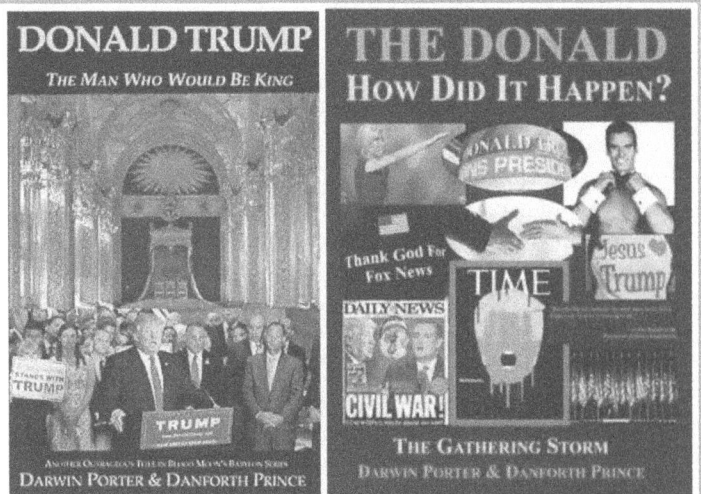

In 2023, six years after its original publication in September of 2016, we reformatted *THE MAN WHO WOULD BE KING* to reflect circumstances associated with Trump's repetitive cycle of "dumpster fires." Then we renamed it: *THE DONALD: HOW DID IT HAPPEN?* (ISBN 978-1-936003-90-7)

**—Diane Donovan,** Senior Editor, California Bookwatch

## DONALD TRUMP, THE MAN WHO WOULD BE KING
### WINNER OF "BEST BIOGRAPHY" AWARDS FROM BOOK FESTIVALS IN NEW YORK, CALIFORNIA, AND FLORIDA

by Darwin Porter and Danforth Prince
Softcover, with 822 pages and hundreds of photos. ISBN 978-1-936003-51-8.
Available now from Ingram, Amazon.com and other purveyors, worldwide.

**Hugh Hefner**, the most iconic Playboy in human history, was a visionary, an empire-builder, and a pajama-clad pipe-smoker with a pre-coital grin.

In 1953, he published his first edition of *Playboy* with money borrowed from his puritanical, Nebraska-born mother. Marilyn Monroe appeared on the cover, with her nude calendar inside.

Rebelling against his strict upbringing, he lost his virginity at the age of 22.

His magazine, punctuated with nudes and studded with articles by major literary figures, reached its zenith at eight million readers. As a "tasteful pornographer," Hef became a cultural warrior, fighting government censorship all the way to the U.S. Supreme Court. As the years and his notoriety progressed, he became an advocate of abortion, LGBT equality, and the legalization of marijuana. Eventually, he engaged in "pubic wars" with Bob Guccione, the flamboyant founder of *Penthouse*, which cut into Hef's sales.

Lauded by millions of avid readers, he was denounced as "the father of sex addiction," "a huckster," "a lecherous low-brow feeder of our vices," "a misogynist," and, near the end of his life, "a symbol of priapic senility."

During his heyday, some of the biggest male stars in Hollywood, including Warren Beatty, Sammy Davis, Jr., Mick Jagger, and Jack Nicholson, came to frolic behind Hef's guarded walls, stripping nude in the hot tub grotto before sampling the rotating beds upstairs. Even a future U.S. president came to call. "Donald Trump had an appreciation of Bunny tail," Hef said.

Hefner's last Viagra-fueled marriage was to a beautiful blonde, Crystal Harris, 60 years his junior. "There's nothing wrong in a man marrying a girl who could be his great-granddaughter," he was famously quoted as saying.

This ground-breaking biography, the latest in Blood Moon's string of outrageously unvarnished myth-busters, was the first published since Hefner's death at the age of 91 in 2017. It's a provocative saga, rich in tantalizing, often shocking detail. Not recommended for the sanctimonious or the faint of heart, and loaded with ironic, little-known details about the trendsetter's epic challenges and the solutions he devised.

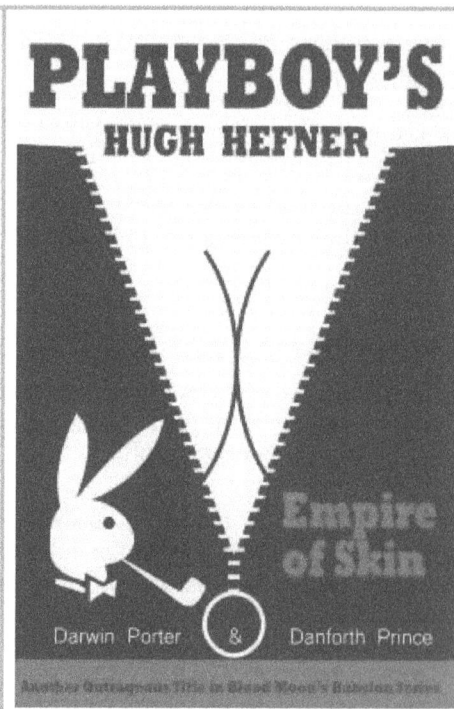

*PLAYBOY'S HUGH HEFNER*
# EMPIRE OF SKIN

by Darwin Porter and Danforth Prince
978-1-936003-59-4

Milton Keynes UK
Ingram Content Group UK Ltd.
UKHW021057140724
445228UK00026B/449